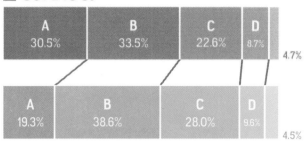
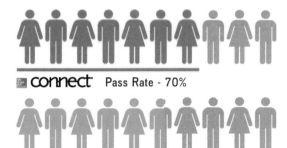
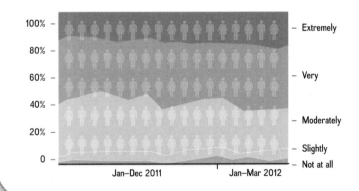

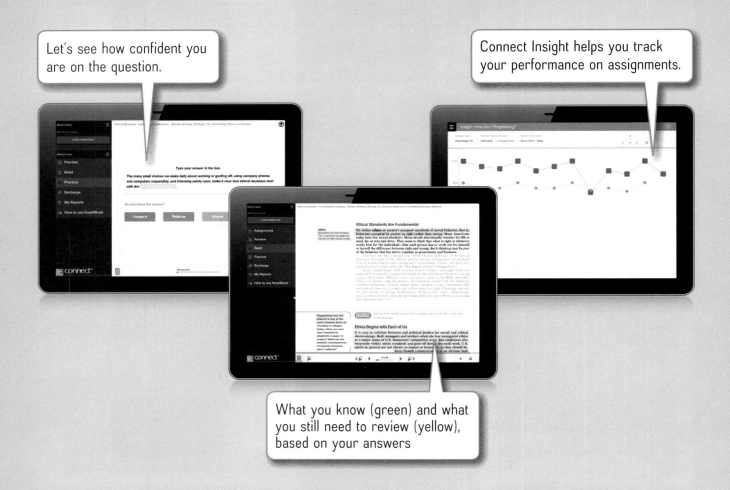

Let's see how confident you are on the question.

Connect Insight helps you track your performance on assignments.

What you know (green) and what you still need to review (yellow), based on your answers

COMPARE AND CHOOSE WHAT'S RIGHT FOR YOU

	PRINT BOOK	SMARTBOOK	ASSIGNMENTS	
Mc Graw Hill Education **connect**		✓	✓	SmartBook—all in one digital product for maximum savings!
Mc Graw Hill Education **connect** Looseleaf	✓	✓	✓	Pop the pages into your own binder or carry just the pages you need.
Mc Graw Hill Education **connect** Bound Book	✓	✓	✓	The #1 Student Choice!
Mc Graw Hill Education **SMARTBOOK®** Access Code	✓	✓		The first and only book that adapts to you!
Mc Graw Hill Education **create™**	✓	✓	✓	The smartest way to get from a B to an A.

> Buy directly from the source at http://shop.mheducation.com.

McGraw-Hill Education Operations and Decision Sciences

Operations Management

Operations Management

Gérard Cachon
The Wharton School, University of Pennsylvania

Christian Terwiesch
The Wharton School, University of Pennsylvania

Mc
Graw
Hill
Education

OPERATIONS MANAGEMENT

Published by McGraw-Hill Education, 2 Penn Plaza, New York, NY 10121. Copyright © 2017 by McGraw-Hill Education. All rights reserved. Printed in the United States of America. No part of this publication may be reproduced or distributed in any form or by any means, or stored in a database or retrieval system, without the prior written consent of McGraw-Hill Education, including, but not limited to, in any network or other electronic storage or transmission, or broadcast for distance learning.

Some ancillaries, including electronic and print components, may not be available to customers outside the United States.

This book is printed on acid-free paper.

1 2 3 4 5 6 7 8 9 0 DOR/DOR 1 0 9 8 7 6

ISBN 978-1-259-14220-8
MHID 1-259-14220-5

Senior Vice President, Products & Markets: *Kurt L. Strand*
Vice President, General Manager, Products & Markets: *Marty Lange*
Vice President, Content Design & Delivery: *Kimberly Meriwether David*
Managing Director: *James Heine*
Brand Manager: *Dolly Womack*
Director, Product Development: *Rose Koos*
Lead Product Developer: *Michele Janicek*
Product Developer: *Christina Holt*
Marketing Manager: *Britney Hermsen*
Director of Digital Content Development: *Douglas Ruby*
Digital Product Analyst: *Kevin Shanahan*
Director, Content Design & Delivery: *Linda Avenarius*
Program Manager: *Mark Christianson*
Content Project Managers: *Kathryn D. Wright, Bruce Gin, and Karen Jozefowicz*
Buyer: *Jennifer Pickel*
Design: *Debra Kubiak*
Content Licensing Specialists: *Shawntel Schmitt and Shannon Manderscheid*
Cover Images: Cropped shot of young male skateboarder photographing feet on smartphone: © *Cultura/Chad Springer/Getty Images; (bottom row)* Vertu manufacturing/work stations and device assembly: *Courtesy of Vertu;* McDonnell Douglas DC-10-30F cargo aircraft taking on load: © *Charles Thatcher/Getty Images;* Store Manager assisting customer in phone store: © *Echo/Getty Images*
Compositor: *SPi Global*
Printer: *R. R. Donnelley*

All credits appearing on page or at the end of the book are considered to be an extension of the copyright page.

Library of Congress Cataloging-in-Publication Data

Names: Cachon, Gérard, author. | Terwiesch, Christian, author.
Title: Operations management/Gerard Cachon, Christian Terwiesch.
Description: New York, NY : McGraw-Hill Education, [2017]
Identifiers: LCCN 2015042363 | ISBN 9781259142208 (alk. paper)
Subjects: LCSH: Production management. | Industrial management.
Classification: LCC TS155 .C134 2017 | DDC 658.5—dc23 LC record available at
http://lccn.loc.gov/2015042363

The Internet addresses listed in the text were accurate at the time of publication. The inclusion of a website does not indicate an endorsement by the authors or McGraw-Hill Education, and McGraw-Hill Education does not guarantee the accuracy of the information presented at these sites.

DEDICATION

To my core: Beth, Xavier, Quentin, Annick, and Isaac.

—Gérard

To the Terwiesch family—in Germany, Switzerland, and the United States.

—Christian

About the Authors

Gérard Cachon

Gérard Cachon is the Fred R. Sullivan Professor of Operations, Information, and Decisions and a professor of marketing at The Wharton School at the University of Pennsylvania.

Professor Cachon studies operations strategy with a focus on how new technologies transform competitive dynamics through novel business models.

He is the chair of the Operations, Information, and Decisions department; an INFORMS Fellow; a Fellow of the Manufacturing and Service Operations Management (MSOM) Society; a former president of MSOM; and a former editor-in-chief of *Management Science* and *Manufacturing & Service Operations Management*.

His articles have appeared in *Harvard Business Review, Management Science, Manufacturing & Service Operations Management, Operations Research, Marketing Science,* and the *Quarterly Journal of Economics,* among others.

At Wharton, he teaches the undergraduate course in operations management, and an MBA and executive MBA elective on operations strategy.

Before joining the Wharton School in July 2000, Professor Cachon was on the faculty at the Fuqua School of Business, Duke University. He received a Ph.D. from The Wharton School in 1995.

He is a bike commuter (often alongside Christian) and enjoys photography, hiking, and scuba diving.

Christian Terwiesch

Christian Terwiesch is the Andrew M. Heller Professor at The Wharton School of the University of Pennsylvania. He is a professor in Wharton's Operations, Information, and Decisions department; is co-director of Penn's Mack Institute for Innovation Management; and also holds a faculty appointment in Penn's Perelman School of Medicine.

His research appears in many of the leading academic journals ranging from operations management journals such as *Management Science, Production and Operations Management, Operations Research,* and *The Journal of Operations Management* to medical journals such as *The Journal of General Internal Medicine, Medical Care, Annals of Emergency Medicine,* and *The New England Journal of Medicine.*

Most of Christian's current work relates to using operations management principles to improve health care. This includes the design of patient-centered care processes in the VA hospital system, studying the effects of emergency room crowding at Penn Medicine, and quantifying the benefits of patient portals and remote patient monitoring.

Beyond operations management, Christian is passionate about helping individuals and organizations to become more innovative. Christian's book *Innovation Tournaments* (Harvard Business School Press) proposes a novel, process-based approach to innovation that has led to innovation tournaments in organizations around the world.

Christian teaches MBA and executive classes at Wharton. In 2012, he launched the first massive open online course (MOOC) in business on Coursera. He also has been the host of a national radio show on Sirius XM's Business Radio channel.

Christian holds a doctoral degree from INSEAD (Fontainebleau, France) and a diploma from the University of Mannheim (Germany). He is a cyclist and bike commuter and so, because his commute significantly overlaps the commute of Gérard, many of the topics in this book grew out of discussions that started on the bike. After 15 years of Ironman racing, Christian is in the midst of a transition to the sport of rowing. Unfortunately, this transition is much harder than predicted.

This introductory-level operations management title provides the foundations of operations management. The book is inspired by our combined 30 years teaching undergraduate and MBA courses and our recent experience teaching thousands of students online via Coursera.

Seeing the need for a title different from our (highly successful) MBA textbook, we developed this new book for undergraduate students and the general public interested in operations. To engage this audience, we have focused our material on modern operations and big-picture operations.

Modern operations means teaching students the content they need in today's world, not the world of 30 or 40 years ago. As a result, "services" and "global" are incorporated throughout, rather than confined to dedicated chapters. Manufacturing, of course, cannot be ignored, but again, the emphasis is on contemporary issues that are relevant and accessible to students. For example, a Materials Requirement Planning (MRP) system is important for the functioning of a factory, but students no longer need to be able to replicate those calculations. Instead, students should learn how to identify the bottleneck in a process and use the ideas from the Toyota Production System to improve performance. And students should understand what contract manufacturing is and why it has grown so rapidly. In sum, we want students to see how operations influence and explain their own experiences, such as the security queue at an airport, the quality of their custom sandwich, or the delay they experience to receive a medical test at a hospital.

Big-picture operations mean teaching students much more than how to do math problems. Instead, the emphasis is on the explicit linkages between operations analytics and the strategies organizations use for success. For example, we want students to understand how to manage inventory, but, more importantly, they should understand why Amazon.com is able to provide an enormously broad assortment of products. Students should be able to evaluate the waiting time in a doctor's office, but also understand how assigning patients to specific physicians is likely to influence the service customers receive. In other words, big-picture operations provide students with a new, broader perspective into the organizations and markets they interact with every day.

We firmly believe that operations management is as relevant for a student's future career as any other topic taught in a business school. New companies and business models are created around concepts from operations management. Established organizations live or die based on their ability to manage their resources to match their supply to their demand. One cannot truly understand how business works today without understanding operations management. To be a bit colloquial, this is "neat stuff," and because students will immediately see the importance of operations management, we hope and expect they will be engaged and excited to learn. We have seen this happen with our own students and believe it can happen with any student.

Acknowledgments

This project is the culmination of our many years of learning and teaching operations management. As such, we are grateful for the many, many individuals who have contributed directly and indirectly, in small and large ways, to our exploration and discovery of this wonderful field.

We begin with the thousands of students who we have taught in person and online. It is through them that we see what inspires. Along with our students, we thank our co-teachers who have test piloted our material and provided valuable feedback: Morris Cohen, Marshall Fisher, Ruben Lobel, Simone Marinesi, Nicolas Reinecke, Sergei Savin, Bradley Staats, Xuanming Su, and Senthil Veeraraghavan.

We have benefited substantially from the following careful reviewers: Bernd Terwiesch took on the tedious job of proofreading early drafts of many chapters. Danielle Graham carefully read through all page proofs, still finding more mistakes than we would like to admit. We also thank Kohei Nakazato for double checking hundreds of test bank questions.

"Real operations" can only happen with "real" people. We thank the following who matched supply with demand in practice and were willing to share their experiences with us: Jeff Salomon and his team (Interventional Radiology unit of the Pennsylvania Hospital System), Karl Ulrich (Novacruz), Allan Fromm (Anser), Cherry Chu and John Pope (O'Neill), Frederic Marie and John Grossman (Medtronic), Michael Mayer (Johnson&Johnson), and Brennan Mulligan (Timbuk2).

From McGraw-Hill we thank our long-term friend Colin Kelley, who started us on this path and kept us motivated throughout, and the team of dedicated people who transformed our thoughts into something real: Christina Holt, Dolly Womack, Britney Hermsen, Doug Ruby, Kathryn Wright, Bruce Gin, and Debra Kubiak.

Finally, we thank our family members. Their contributions cannot be measured, but are deeply felt.

Gérard Cachon
Christian Terwiesch

We are grateful to the following professors for their insightful feedback, helpful suggestions, and constructive reviews of this text.

Stuart Abraham, New Jersey City University
Khurrum Bhutta, Ohio University—Athens
Greg Bier, University of Missouri—Columbia
Rebecca Bryant, Texas Woman's University
Satya Chakravorty, Kennesaw State University
Frank Chelko, Pennsylvania State University
Tej Dhakar, Southern Hampshire University
Michael Doto, University of Massachusetts—Boston
Wedad Elmaghraby, University of Maryland
Kamvar Farahbod, California State University—San Bernardino
Gene Fliedner, Oakland University
James Freeland, University of Virginia
Phillip Fry, Boise State University
Brian Gregory, Franklin University
Roger Grinde, University of New Hampshire
Haresh Gurnani, Wake Forest University
Gajanan Hegde, University of Pittsburgh
Michael Hewitt, Loyola University—Chicago
Stephen Hill, University of North Carolina—Wilmington
Zhimin Huang, Hofstra University
Faizul Huq, Ohio University—Athens
Doug Isanhart, University of Central Arkansas
Thawatchai Jitpaiboon, Ball State University
Peter Kelle, Louisiana State University—Baton Rouge
Ron Klimberg, St. Joseph's University
Mark Kosfeld., University of Wisconsin—Milwaukee
John Kros, East Carolina University
Matthew Lindsey, Stephen F. Austin State University
David Little, High Point University
Alan Mackelprang, Georgia Southern University
Douglas L. Micklich, Illinois State University
William Millhiser, Baruch College
Ram Misra, Montclair State University

Adam Munson, University of Florida
Steven Nadler, University of Central Arkansas
John Nicholas, Loyola University—Chicago
Debra Petrizzo, Franklin University
William Petty, University of Alabama—Tuscaloosa
Rajeev Sawhney, Western Illinois University
Ruth Seiple, University of Cincinnati
Don Sheldon, Binghamton University
Eugene Simko, Monmouth University
James E. Skibo, Texas Woman's University
Randal Smith, Oregon State University
James Stewart, University of Maryland University College

Yang Sun, California State University—Sacramento
Sue Sundar, University of Utah—Salt Lake City
Lee Tangedahl, University of Montana
Jeffrey Teich, New Mexico State University—Las Cruces
Ahmad Vessal, California State University—Northridge
Jerry Wei, University of Notre Dame
Marilyn Whitney, University of California—Davis
Marty Wilson, California State University—Sacramento
Peter Zhang, Georgia State University
Faye Zhu, Rowan University
Zhiwei Zhu, University of Louisiana—Lafayette

Guided Tour

Key Features

Structured with Learning Objectives

Great content is useless unless students are able to learn it. To make it **accessible** to students, it must be highly organized. So, all of the material is tagged by **learning objectives**. Each section has a learning objective, and all practice material is linked to a learning objective.

Process Analysis

3

LEARNING OBJECTIVES

LO3-1 Draw a process flow diagram
LO3-2 Determine the capacity for a one-step process
LO3-3 Determine the flow rate, the utilization, and the cycle time of a process
LO3-4 Find the bottleneck of a multistep process and determine its capacity
LO3-5 Determine how long it takes to produce a certain order quantity

---

Check Your Understanding 3.2

Question: It takes a color printer 10 seconds to print a large poster. What is the capacity of the printer expressed in posters per hour?

Answer: The capacity of the printer is $\frac{1}{10}$ poster/second, which is 360 posters per hour.

Question: A call center has one operator who answers incoming calls. It takes the operator 6 minutes to answer one call. What is the capacity of the call center expressed in calls per hour?

Answer: The capacity of the call center is $\frac{1}{6}$ calls/minute = 10 calls/hour.

© Digital Stock/Royalty-Free/Corbis/RF

Check Your Understanding

Given the learning objective structure, it is possible to present the material in **small chunks** that logically follow from each other. And each chunk ends with several straightforward **Check Your Understanding** questions so that students can feel confident that they have absorbed the content.

CONNECTIONS: Amazon

© Gregor Schuster/Photographer's Choice RF/Getty Images/RF

When Jeff Bezos started his company in 1994, he wanted to create the world's largest bookstore in terms of selection. So he named it Amazon.com after the world's largest river system. His initial business model was simple. He would have a single warehouse in Seattle, near a large book distributor. The tech climate of Seattle allowed him to hire the coders

---

CASE TESLA

The Tesla Model S, one of the most sought-after luxury cars, is produced in Tesla's Fremont factory in California. The production process can be broken up into the following subprocesses.

Stamping: In the stamping process, coils of aluminum are unwound, cut into level pieces of sheet metal, and then inserted into stamping presses that shape the metal according to the geometry of the Model S. The presses can shape a sheet of metal in roughly 6 seconds.

Subassembly: The various pieces of metal are put together using a combination of joining techniques, including welding and adhesion. This creates the body of the vehicle.

Paint: The body of the vehicle is then moved to the paint shop. After painting is completed, the body moves through a 350° oven to cure the paint, followed by a sanding operation that ensures a clean surface.

General assembly: After painting, the vehicle body is moved to the final assembly area. Here, assembly workers and assembly robots insert the various subassemblies, such as the wiring, the dash board, the power train and the motor, the battery pack, and the seats.

Quality testing: Before being shipped to the customer, the now-assembled car is tested for its quality. It is driven on a rolling road, a test station that is basically a treadmill for cars that mimics driving on real streets.

Overall, the process is equipped with 160 robots and 3000 employees. The process produces some 500 vehicles each week. It takes a car about 3–5 days to move from the beginning of the process to the end.

© Paul Sakuma/AP Images

QUESTIONS

Imagine you could take a tour of the Tesla plant. To prepare for this tour, draw a simple process flow diagram of the operation.

1. What is the cycle time of the process (assume two shifts of eight hours each and five days a week of operation)?
2. What is the flow time?
3. Where in the process do you expect to encounter inventory?
4. How many cars are you likely to encounter as work in progress inventory?

SOURCES

http://www.wired.com/2013/07/tesla-plant-video/
http://www.forbes.com/sites/greatspeculations/2014/09/26/fremont-factory-delays-shouldnt-affect-teslas-sales-this-quarter/

Big-Picture Connections

Each chapter includes several Connections that don't teach new concepts; rather, their role is to intrigue students, to raise their curiosity, and to give a broader understanding of the world around them. For example, we talk about policy issues (emergency room overcrowding), the people who have influenced operations (Agner Erlang), and the companies that have transformed industries (Walmart).

Exercises and Cases

We have an extensive portfolio of exercises and cases. These exercises are entertaining but also illustrate key concepts from the text. Cases bring the "real world" into the classroom so that students appreciate that operations management is much more than just theory.

End-of-Chapter Content

The end of chapter provides students with the resources to reinforce their learning. Conceptual Questions explore their understanding of big-picture operations. Solved Example Problems give step-by-step illustrations into the chapter's analytical tools and Problems and Applications allow students to practice.

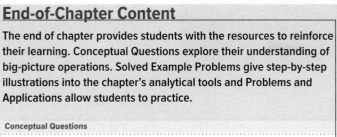

Conceptual Questions

LO6-1

1. A bank is underwriting loans for small businesses. Currently, about 5 percent of the underwriting decisions are found to be incorrect when audited by the bank's quality assurance department. The bank has a goal of reducing this number to 1 percent. What form of an improvement trajectory is most likely to occur?
   a. Exponential growth
   b. Exponential decay
   c. Diminishing return growth

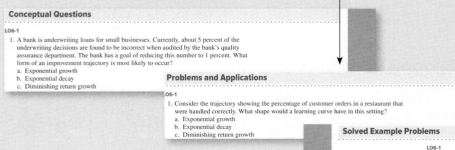

Problems and Applications

LO6-1

1. Consider the trajectory showing the percentage of customer orders in a restaurant that were handled correctly. What shape would a learning curve have in this setting?
   a. Exponential growth
   b. Exponential decay
   c. Diminishing return growth

Solved Example Problems

LO6-1

1. Consider the trajectory showing the percentage of patients with depression that were not appropriately screened for suicide risk. A doctor's practice aims to reduce this percentage over time. What shape would a learning curve have in this setting?
   a. Exponential growth
   b. Exponential decay
   c. Diminishing return growth
   Answer: B.

Interactive Learning Resources

Students today don't learn by just reading. They expect to learn via multiple modalities. In particular, they like to learn (and in fact do learn) via video tutorials. Each tutorial is targeted to a single learning objective and provides a focused lesson in 1 to 5 minutes. These tutorials provide students with a "safety net" to ensure that they can master even the most challenging material.

Real Operations, Real Solutions, Real Simple

Our chapters are motivated by a diverse set of *real operations*—of companies that students can relate to. They include Subway, Capital One, Medtronic, O'Neill, LVMH, and many more. They are central to the core content of the chapters: We show students how to analyze and improve the operations of these actual companies, in many cases with actual data from the companies, that is, *real solutions*.

Next, *real simple* means that the material is written so that students can actually learn how to implement the techniques of operations management in practice. In particular, we write in a logical, step-by-step manner and include plenty of intuition. We want students to be able to replicate the details of a calculation and also understand how those calculations fit into the overall objectives of what an organization is trying to achieve.

Focus on Process Analysis

All operations management books talk a little bit about process analysis; we believe that not only is process analysis the starting

point for operations management, it also is the heart of operations management. Process analysis is at the core of how an organization delivers supply. Hence, students need to understand the key metrics of process analysis (inventory, flow rate, flow time, utilization, labor content, etc.), how they are related, and, most importantly, what the organization can do to improve its processes. Most students will not work in a factory or be in charge of a global supply chain. But all students, no matter where they work or in what industry they work, will be involved in some organizational process. This is why process analysis deserves the prominence it is given in our product.

Written for the Connect Platform

Operations Management has been written specifically for the McGraw-Hill Connect platform. Rather than fitting a learning management system to a book, we designed the product and the learning management system jointly. This co-development has the advantage that the test questions map perfectly to the learning objectives. The questions are also concise and can be assessed objectively. It is our experience that open-ended discussion questions ("What are the strengths and weaknesses of the Toyota Production System?") are important in a course. But they make for great discussion questions in the classroom (and we mention such questions in the instructor support material). However, they are frustrating for students as homework assignments, they are difficult to grade, and it is hard to provide the student with feedback on mastery of the topic.

Brief Contents

Contents

Introduction to Operations Management

1

LEARNING OBJECTIVES

LO1-1 Identify the drivers of customer utility

LO1-2 Explain inefficiencies and determine if a firm is on the efficient frontier

LO1-3 Explain the three system inhibitors

LO1-4 Explain what work in operations management looks like

LO1-5 Articulate the key operational decisions a firm needs to make to match supply with demand

CHAPTER OUTLINE

Introduction

As a business (or nonprofit organization), we offer products or services to our customers. These products or services are called our **supply**. We provide rental cars, we sell clothes, or we perform medical procedures. Demand is created by our customers—**demand** is simply the set of products and services our customers want. Our customers may want a rental car to travel from A to B, or a black suit in size 34, or to get rid of an annoying cough.

To be successful in business, we have to offer our customers what they want. If Mr. Jamison wants a midsize sedan from Tuesday to Friday to be picked up at Chicago O'Hare International Airport (demand), our job is to supply Mr. Jamison exactly that—we need to make sure we have a midsize sedan (not a minivan) ready on Tuesday (not on Wednesday) at O'Hare (not in New York) and we need to hand it over to Mr. Jamison (not another traveler).

If on Saturday Sandy wants a green dress in size M in our retail outlet in Los Angeles, our job is to get her exactly that—we need to make sure we have a green dress in size M (not in red or in size L) in the Los Angeles store (not in San Francisco) on Saturday (not on Friday of last week).

And if Terrance injures his left knee in a soccer game and now needs to have a 45-minute meniscus surgery in Philadelphia tomorrow, our job is to supply Terrance exactly that—we need to make sure we reserve 45 minutes in the operating room (not 30 minutes), we need to have an orthopedic surgeon and an anesthesiologist (not a dentist and a cardiologist) ready tomorrow (not in six weeks), and the surgeon definitely must operate on the left knee (not the right one).

Another way of saying "we offer customers what they want" is to say, "we match supply with demand"! Matching supply with demand means providing customers what they want, while also making a profit. Matching supply with demand is the goal of operations management.

© Photodisc/Getty Images/RF

Supply Products or services a business offers to its customers.

Demand Simply, the set of products and services our customers want.

This book is about how to design operations to better match supply with demand. It thus is a book about getting customers what they want. Our motivation is simply stated: By better matching supply with demand, a firm is able to gain a significant competitive advantage over its rivals. A firm can achieve this better match through the implementation of the rigorous models and the operational strategies we outline in this book.

In this introductory chapter, we outline the basic challenges of matching supply with demand. This first requires us to think about demand—what do customers want? Once we understand demand, we then take the perspective of a firm attempting to serve the demand—we look at the supply process. We then discuss the operational decisions a firm has to make to provide customers with what they want at a low cost. Now, typically, customers want better products for lower prices. But, in reality, this might not always be simple to achieve. So, a subsequent section in this chapter talks about overcoming three inhibitors that keep the operation from delivering great products at low prices. Beyond overcoming these inhibitors, the operation also needs to make trade-offs and balance multiple, potentially conflicting objectives. We conclude this chapter by explaining what jobs related to operations management look like and by providing a brief overview of operations management in the remainder of the book.

1.1 The Customer's View of the World

You are hungry. You have nothing left in the fridge and so you decide to go out and grab a bite to eat. Where will you go? The McDonald's down the street from you is cheap and you know you can be in and out within a matter of minutes. There is a Subway restaurant at the other end of town as well—they make an array of sandwiches and they make them to your order—they even let you have an Italian sausage on a vegetarian sandwich. And then there is a new organic restaurant with great food, though somewhat expensive, and the last time you ate there you had to wait 15 minutes before being served your food. So where would you go?

© John Flournoy/The McGraw-Hill Education/RF

Economic theory suggests that you make this choice based on where you expect to obtain the highest **utility**. Your utility associated with each of the eating options measures the strength of your preferences for the restaurant choices available. The utility measures your desire for a product or service.

Now, why would your utility associated with the various restaurant options vary across restaurants? We can think about your utility being composed of three components: consumption utility, price, and inconvenience.

Consider each of these three components in further detail. Let us start with **consumption utility**. Your consumption utility measures how much you like a product or service, ignoring the effects of price (imagine somebody would invite you to the restaurant) and ignoring the inconvenience of obtaining the product or service (imagine you would get the food right away and the restaurant would be just across the street from you). Consumption utility comes from various attributes of a product or service; for example, "saltiness" (for food), "funniness" (for movies), "weight" (for bicycles), "pixel count" (for cameras), "softness" (for clothing), and "empathy" (for physicians). There are clearly many attributes and the relevant attributes depend on the particular product or service we consider. However, we can take the set of all possible attributes and divide them into two sets: performance and fit. These sets allow us to divide consumption utility into two subcomponents:

- **Performance**. Performance attributes are features of the product or service that most (if not all) people agree are more desirable. For example, consumers prefer roasted salmon cooked to perfection by a world-class chef over a previously frozen salmon steak cooked in a microwave. In the same way, consumers tend to prefer the latest iPhone over an old iPod, and they are likely to prefer a flight in first class over a flight in economy class. In other words, in terms of performance, consumers have the same ranking of products—we all prefer "cleaner," "more durable," "friendlier," "more memory," "roomier," and "more efficient."

- **Fit**. With some attributes, customers do not all agree on what is best. Roasted salmon sounds good to us, but that is because we are not vegetarian. Customers vary widely in the utility derived from products and services (we say that they have **heterogeneous preferences**), which is the reason why you see 20 different flavors of cereals in the supermarket aisles, hundreds of ties in apparel stores, and millions of songs on iTunes. Typically, heterogeneous preferences come from differences across customers in taste, color, or size, though there are many other sources for them.

The second component of the customer's utility is **price**. Price is meant to include the total cost of owning the product or receiving the service. Thus, price has to include expenses such as shipping or financing and other price-related variables such as discounts. To state the obvious, holding everything else constant, customers prefer to pay less rather than paying more.

The third and final component of the customer's utility function is the **inconvenience** of obtaining the product or receiving the service. Economists often refer to this component as **transaction costs**. Everything else being equal, you prefer your food here (as opposed to three miles away) and now (as opposed to enduring a 30-minute wait). The following are the two major subcomponents of inconvenience:

- **Location**. There are 12,800 McDonald's restaurants in the United States (but only 326 in China), so no matter where you live in the United States, chances are that there is one near you. McDonald's (and many other restaurants for that matter) wants to be near you to make it easy for you to get its food. The further you have to drive, bike, or walk, the more inconvenient it is for you.

- **Timing**. Once you are at the restaurant, you have to wait for your food. And even if you want fast-food, you still have to wait for it. A recent study of drive-through restaurants in the United States found that the average customer waits for 2 minutes and 9 seconds at Wendy's, 3 minutes and 8 seconds at McDonald's, and 3 minutes and 20 seconds at Burger King. All three of those restaurants are much faster than the 20 minutes you have to wait for the previously mentioned roasted salmon (though the authors think that this is well worth the wait).

LO1-1 Identify the drivers of customer utility.

Utility A measure of the strength of customer preferences for a given product or service. Customers buy the product or service that maximizes their utility.

Consumption utility A measure of how much you like a product or service, ignoring the effects of price and of the inconvenience of obtaining the product or service.

Performance A subcomponent of the consumption utility that captures how much an average consumer desires a product or service.

Fit A subcomponent of the consumption utility that captures how well the product or service matches with the unique characteristics of a given consumer.

Heterogeneous preferences The fact that not all consumers have the same utility function.

Price The total cost of owning the product or receiving the service.

Inconvenience The reduction in utility that results from the effort of obtaining the product or service.

Transaction costs Another term for the inconvenience of obtaining a product or service.

Location The place where a consumer can obtain a product or service.

Timing The amount of time that passes between the consumer ordering a product or service and the consumer obtaining the product or service.

Figure 1.1
Consumer utility and its components and subcomponents

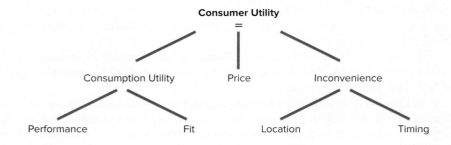

Figure 1.1 summarizes the three components of a consumer's utility for a product or service along with their subcomponents.

Customers buy the products or services that maximize their utility. They look at the set of options available to them, including the option of doing nothing (make their own lunch or stay hungry). We can define the demand of a business as the products or services that customers want; that is, those products that are maximizing their utility. So, our demand is driven by the consumption utility of our product or service, its price, and the associated inconvenience for our customers. In the case of a McDonald's restaurant, on any given day the demand for that restaurant corresponds to those customers who, after considering their consumption utility, the price, and the inconvenience, find that McDonald's restaurant is their best choice. Because we most likely have multiple customers, our demand corresponds to a total quantity: 190 cheeseburgers are demanded in Miami on Tuesday at lunch.

Marketing The academic discipline that is about understanding and influencing how customers derive utility from products or services.

Understanding how customers derive utility from products or services is at the heart of **marketing**. Marketers typically think of products or services similar to our previous discussion in conjunction with Figure 1.1. As a business, however, it is not enough to just understand our customers; we also have to provide them the goods and services they want.

© Rob Melnychuk/Digital Vision/
Exactostock/SuperStock/RF

Check Your Understanding 1.1

Question: What drives your utility in terms of choosing a hotel room in San Francisco?

Answer: Consider each of these items:

- Performance attributes of consumption include the number of amenities and the size of the room (think two-star versus five-star hotel). Fit attributes are driven by personal preferences. For example, some like classic décor, while others like modern styling, and some like a noisy, busy atmosphere, while others prefer a subdued, quiet ambience.
- Price is simply the price you have to pay to the hotel.
- Inconvenience is driven by the availability of the hotel relative to your travel plans. You might be off from work or study in July, but the hotel might only have rooms available in March. This is the timing piece of inconvenience. Inconvenience can also relate to location. If you want to go sightseeing, chances are you would prefer a hotel in the Fisherman's Wharf area of San Francisco over one next to the airport.

Therefore, the utility is driven by the utility of consumption, price, and inconvenience.

1.2 A Firm's Strategic Trade-Offs

In a perfect world, we would provide outstanding products and services to all our customers, we would tailor them to the heterogeneous needs of every single one of our customers, we would deliver them consistently where and when the customer wants, and we would offer all of that at very little cost.

Unfortunately, this rarely works in practice. In sports, it is unlikely that you will excel in swimming, gymnastics, running, fencing, golf, and horse jumping. The same applies to companies—they cannot be good at everything. Companies have **capabilities** that allow them to do well on some but not all of the subcomponents making up the customer utility function. We define a firm's capabilities as the dimensions of the customer's utility function it is able to satisfy.

Consider the following examples from the food and hospitality industry:

- McDonald's is able to serve customers in a matter of three minutes (see the previous section). One reason for this is that they make the burgers before customers ask for them. This keeps costs low (you can make many burgers at once) and waiting times short. But because McDonald's makes the burger before you ask for it, you cannot have the food your way.

- Subway, in contrast, is able to charge a small premium and has customers willing to wait a little longer because they appreciate having sandwiches made to their order. This approach works well with ingredients that can be prepared ahead of time (precut vegetables, cheeses, meats, etc.) but would not work as well for grilled meat such as a hamburger.

- Starbucks provides a fancy ambiance in its outlets, making it a preferred place for many students to study. It also provides a wide array of coffee-related choices that can be further customized to individual preferences. It does, however, charge a very substantial price premium compared to a coffee at McDonald's.

So companies cannot be good at everything; they face **trade-offs** in their business. For example, they trade off consumption utility and the costs of providing the products or services. Similarly, they trade off the inconvenience of obtaining their products or services with the costs of providing them; and, as the McDonald's versus Subway example illustrated, they even face trade-offs among non-cost-related subcomponents of the utility function (fit—the sandwich made for you—versus wait times).

Such trade-offs can be illustrated graphically, as shown in Figure 1.2. Figure 1.2 shows two fast-food restaurants and compares them along two dimensions that are important to us as potential customers hunting for food. The y-axis shows how responsive the restaurant is to our food order—high responsiveness (short wait time) is at the top, while low responsiveness (long wait time) is at the bottom. Another dimension that customers care about is the price of the food. High prices are, of course, undesirable for customers. We assume for now that the restaurants have the same profit per unit. For the sake of argument, assume they charge customers a price of $2 above costs, leaving them with $2 of profit per customer. So, instead of showing price, the x-axis in Figure 1.2 shows cost efficiency—how much it costs a restaurant to serve one customer. Cost performance increases along the x-axis.

Consider restaurant A first. It costs the restaurant an average of $4 for a meal. Customers have to wait for 10 minutes to get their food at restaurant A, and restaurant A charges $6 to its customers for an average meal ($4 cost plus $2 profit).

Restaurant B, in contrast, is able to serve customers during a 5-minute wait time. To be able to respond to customers that quickly, the restaurant has invested in additional resources—they always have extra staff in case things get busy and they have very powerful cooking equipment. Because staffing the kitchen with extra workers and obtaining the expensive equipment creates extra expenses, restaurant B has higher average costs per customer (a lower cost performance). Say their average costs are $5 per customer. Because they have the same $2 profit as restaurant A, they would charge their customers $7.

Capabilities The dimensions of the customer's utility function a firm is able to satisfy.

Trade-offs The need to sacrifice one capability in order to increase another one.

Figure 1.2
The strategic trade-off between responsiveness and productivity

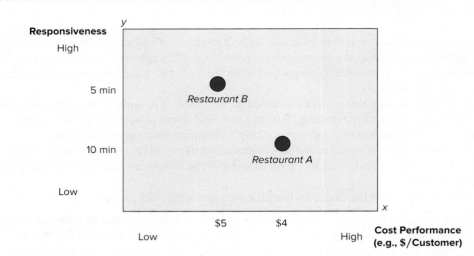

Assuming the restaurants are identical on all other dimensions of your utility function (e.g., cooking skills, food selection, location, ambience of the restaurant, etc.), which restaurant would you prefer as a customer? This clearly depends on how much money you have available and how desperate you are for food at the moment. The important thing is that both restaurants will attract some customers.

Figure 1.2 illustrates a key trade-off that our two restaurants face. Better responsiveness to the needs of hungry customers requires more resources (extra staff and special equipment), which is associated with higher costs. Most likely, restaurant B is occasionally considering cutting costs by reducing the number of staff in the kitchen, but this would make them less responsive. Similarly, restaurant A is likely to also investigate if it should staff extra workers in the kitchen and invest in better equipment, because that would allow it to charge higher prices. We refer to trade-offs such as the one between responsiveness and costs as a **strategic trade-off**—when selecting inputs and resources, the firm must choose between a set that excels in one dimension of customer utility or another, but no single set of inputs and resources can excel in all dimensions.

Considering restaurants A and B, which one will be more successful? Low cost (and low price) with poor responsiveness or higher costs (higher prices) with good responsiveness? Again, assuming the two restaurants are identical in all other aspects of their business, we first observe that neither restaurant is better on both dimensions of performance. From the customer's perspective, there exists no dominant choice. As discussed earlier, some customers prefer the fast service and are willing to pay a premium for that. Other customers cannot afford or do not want to pay that premium and so they wait. As a result of this, we have two different **market segments** of consumers in the industry. Which restaurant does better financially? The answer to that question strongly depends on the size and dynamics of these market segments. In some areas, the segment served by restaurant A is very attractive (maybe in an area with many budget-conscious students). In other regions (maybe in an office building with highly paid bankers or lawyers), the segment served by restaurant B is more attractive.

Now, consider restaurant C, shown in Figure 1.3. Restaurant C has its customers wait for 15 minutes for a meal and its costs are $6 for the average customer (so the meals are priced at $8). The restaurant seems to be slower (lower responsiveness; i.e., longer waits) and have higher costs. We don't know why restaurant C performs as it does, but (again, assuming everything else is held constant) most of us would refer to the restaurant as underperforming and go to either restaurant A or B when we are hungry.

As we look at restaurant C, we don't see a rosy future simply because restaurants A and B can provide a better customer experience (faster responsiveness) for a lower price. Why would any customer want to go to restaurant C? We say that both restaurant A and restaurant B

Market segment A set of customers who have similar utility functions.

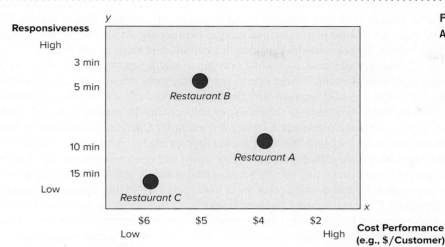

Figure 1.3

An underperforming operation (restaurant C)

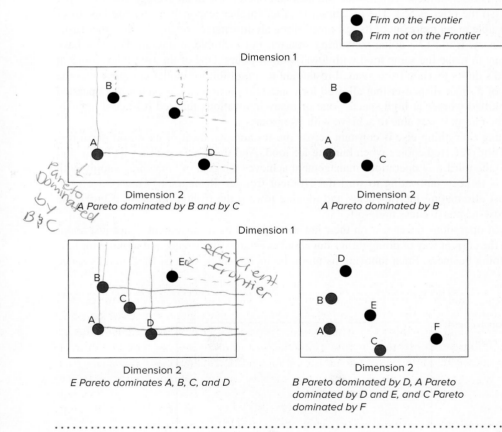

Figure 1.4

The definition of the efficient frontier

Restaurant C is **Pareto dominated** by restaurants A and B. They perform equally or better on all attributes of the customer's utility function. Or, put casually, they are simply *better*.

We define the **efficient frontier** in an industry as the set of firms in the industry that are not Pareto dominated. In other words, firms that are on the efficient frontier have no firms in the industry to their upper right (i.e., are better on all dimensions). In Figure 1.3, the efficient frontier consists of restaurants A and B. Restaurants on the frontier have made different strategic trade-offs and thus focus on different market segments, but no single firm on the frontier Pareto dominates another.

Pareto dominated Pareto dominated means that a firm's product or service is inferior to one or multiple competitors on all dimensions of the customer utility function.

Efficient frontier The set of firms that are not Pareto dominated.

LO1-2 Explain inefficiencies and determine if a firm is on the efficient frontier.

Some firms, in our case restaurant C, are not on the frontier. The fact that others can provide better (equal) customer utility at equal (lower) costs suggests that restaurant C is **inefficient**. We can visualize inefficiency as the gap between the firm's current position and the efficient frontier. Figure 1.4 helps illustrate this definition of the efficient frontier.

Figures 1.2 and 1.3 illustrate two ways operations management achieves the goal of "matching supply with demand." First, operations management designs the operations that match the demand of a market segment with the supply of products and services appropriate for that segment. The management of the restaurant achieves this by making a strategic trade-off—does it want to be like restaurant A or like restaurant B? Operations management helps to execute on that strategy by building an operation appropriate for that market segment.

Second, operations management seeks to utilize inputs and resources to their fullest potential. Restaurant C is not doing this simply because restaurants A and B can provide a better customer experience (fast responsiveness) for a lower price. Applying operations management to restaurant C means figuring out how to eliminate inefficiencies (and thereby move the firm to the efficient frontier). This might mean changing the inputs and resources it currently has, or it might mean managing those inputs and resources more effectively.

But there is a third, and very crucial, way that operations management achieves the goal of "matching supply with demand." To explain, consider restaurant D, as shown in Figure 1.5. Restaurant D offers a meal within three minutes and operates with an average cost of $3 per customer (so the price is $5). The restaurant is faster (higher responsiveness) and has lower costs! It is able to get more out of its resources along all dimensions relative to the other firms in the industry. It must be doing something smarter. For example, restaurant D might have found a way to make the same food with fewer worker hours. One of the first innovations at McDonald's on its journey from a small restaurant to a multibillion-dollar company was the invention of a sauce dispenser that allowed for consistent portion sizing even when operated by an unskilled worker at high speed—one of many innovations that led it to continuously increase the output it was able to achieve with its resources.

Assuming everything else is constant across the restaurants, most of us would make restaurant D our preferred choice when hunting for food. And that bodes well for its future and profits. So the third way operations management achieves the goal of "matching supply with demand" is to keep innovating to shift the efficient frontier. Restaurant D must have gone beyond just eliminating inefficiencies and moving toward the frontier. Instead, it broke the existing cost–responsiveness trade-off.

So, great operations never rest on their laurels. Operations management is not just about executing the current way of doing things but about constantly improving and looking for new ways of doing business. Such innovations might be incremental, such as McDonald's sauce

inefficient The gap between a firm and the efficient frontier.

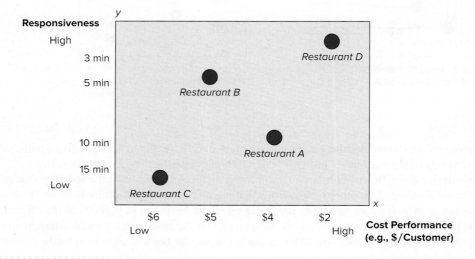

Figure 1.5

A high-performing operation (restaurant D) enters the market

Check Your Understanding 1.2

Question: There are four automotive companies competing with otherwise very similar products on the dimensions of fuel economy (measured in miles per gallon, mpg) and price.

- Company A: price = $40,000; mpg = 50
- Company B: price = $50,000; mpg = 60
- Company C: price = $30,000; mpg = 40
- Company D: price = $45,000; mpg = 45

Which of these companies are on the efficient frontier?

Answer: The only company that is Pareto dominated is company D; all others are on the efficient frontier. Company D is Pareto dominated by company A, because A is both cheaper ($40,000 instead of $45,000) and more fuel efficient (50 instead of 45 mpg).

© Blend Images/JGI/Getty Images/RF

. . . .

CONNECTIONS: Airlines

© Kevin Clark/Alamy/RF

The airline industry is a difficult industry to succeed in. Many companies have gone bankrupt. Some (Delta and United) have reemerged from bankruptcy; others have disappeared forever even though they were once big players in the industry (TWA and PanAm). Consider the data shown in Figure 1.6(a). The figure shows how much U.S. air carriers can charge for each mile they transport a passenger (*y*-axis) as a function of what costs they incur to provide that mile (*x*-axis).

For example, we see that **American Airlines** is able to charge a little less than 20 cents ($0.20) per passenger mile. We also see that American Airlines is able to fly a little more than 5 miles (5.1 miles to be exact) for every dollar of expense. The figure illustrates the concept of the efficient frontier. In the year 2012, no carrier Pareto dominated another carrier. Firms faced the trade-off between customer service, which arguably leads to higher prices, and efficiency (which allows you to get more miles per dollar of expense).

Continued

This was not always this way. For many years, **Southwest Airlines** was the most efficient airline. For example, Southwest Pareto dominated America West Airlines. This is shown in Figure 1.6(b). America West subsequently was acquired by US Airways.

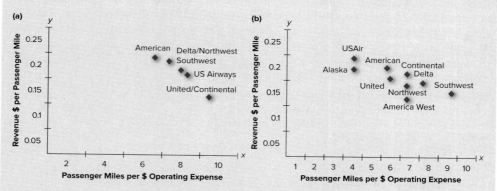

Figure 1.6   The x-axis shows the miles obtained per dollar of expense, while the y-axis shows the revenue dollars per mile. Figure 1.6(a) (on the left) was the situation in 2012. Figure 1.6(b) (on the right) was the situation in 2000.

dispenser, or they might be more radical. Either way, such innovations make a firm more competitive in the marketplace.

In sum, you can think about three ways in which operations management can improve a business as it seeks to match supply with demand:

- Make trade-offs among the dimensions of performance.
- Reduce inefficiencies so that the business does not have to sacrifice one performance dimension versus another, thereby moving toward the efficient frontier.
- Innovate and improve the operations, corresponding to a shift in the efficient frontier.

1.3 Overcoming Inefficiencies: The Three System Inhibitors

LO1-3 Explain the three system inhibitors.

A company can only be successful if its customers are willing to pay a sufficiently high price to cover the cost of the product or service it offers. The difference between the revenue it earns and the costs it incurs is its **profit.** There are two types of costs:

- **Costs for inputs:** Inputs are the things that a business purchases. A fast-food restaurant has to purchase meat, salad, buns, soda, etc. Car manufacturers have to buy steel, seats, and tires; computer makers have to buy displays, chips, and power supplies. And hospitals have to purchase medications, bandages, and food.
- **Costs for resources:** Resources are the things in a business that help transform input into output and thereby help provide supply for what customers demand. In a fast-food restaurant, the resources are the cooking equipment, the real estate of the restaurants, and the employees, among others. Car manufacturers and computer makers have plants, warehouses, and employees. And hospitals have to pay for doctors, nurses, and their building.

As a firm reduces inefficiencies (moves toward the efficient frontier), it increases the customer's utility (and thus is able to charge a higher price) or it decreases the cost of serving the customer. Sometimes, reducing inefficiencies allows a firm to simultaneously increase price and decrease costs. Either way, reducing inefficiencies will increase the firm's profitability.

But why aren't all firms in the upper right corner? Why would a company ever carry out its operations inefficiently and be Pareto dominated? And, from a practical perspective, what do such inefficiencies look like?

Let's tackle the last question first. Imagine you spent a day at Subway or McDonald's in order to identify inefficiencies. We have to confess that our previous definition of inefficiency being the gap between the firm's current position and the efficient frontier is rather abstract.

We find it helpful to think of inefficiencies as a combination of three forces: *waste, variability,* and *inflexibility.* We refer to these three forces as the **three system inhibitors**. Let's define the three system inhibitors one by one.

Waste corresponds to all the consumption of inputs and resources that do not add value to the customers. Because waste consumes inputs and resources, waste is costly. But because it does not add value to the customer, the customer is not willing to pay for this. We have extensive discussions of waste in subsequent chapters of this book. But, for now, look at the following examples from the restaurant industry:

- Restaurants have to dispose of food that has been purchased but has not been used before its expiration date. Even worse, oftentimes, food is prepared but then not sold (think of leftover beef patties), costing the restaurant inputs (the beef) and resources (the time and energy to cook).

- Just as they waste food, restaurants also can waste the time of their employees. We already mentioned the sauce dispenser at McDonald's. If you would measure the time it takes a McDonald's employee to prepare a burger and you compared it with the preparation of a burger at a small local diner, you would see a significant difference in speed. Similarly, restaurants vary in their layout. In some restaurants, employees need to run around from one corner to the other, which again constitutes mere waste.

- Another form of waste is giving customers something they don't value. What is the point of having a long menu of side dishes if almost all of your customers want fries? And why pay a waiter for bringing food to the customer if the customer is perfectly willing to pick up the food herself. Take the case of Chipotle, a restaurant chain that recently has been very successful. Chipotle customers pay around $10 for a burrito and a drink, but they are perfectly happy having few choices and picking up the food themselves.

We will see various other sources of waste throughout the subsequent chapters. In particular, we have an entire chapter on lean operations, which is all about waste reduction.

The second system inhibitor is variability. **Variability** corresponds to changes in either demand or supply over time. Consider the variability associated with customer demand first. We can distinguish between the following forms of demand variability:

- *Customer arrivals:* Customers come at very different times of the day. Some of this variability is predictable. A restaurant has more demand at noon than at 3 p.m. However, every day is somewhat different and we can never perfectly plan in advance.

- *Customer requests:* Not only is the number of customers requiring food on a given day unknown to us, we also don't know what particular menu item a customer wants to order.

- *Customer behavior:* Imagine two customers coming at the same time and both ordering a chicken salad sandwich. Same time, same order—both customers will cost us the same to serve, right? But what if one customer spends one minute at the checkout looking for his credit card? What if one customer has a ton of questions about other menu items before placing the order? And what if one customer expects a culinary delight from the fast-food restaurant and now decides to complain to the manager?

Companies also face variability in their supply. This is variability internal to their operation and could take the following forms:

- *Time to serve a customer:* Just like how customers differ from one another (see earlier), so do employees. Some employees are faster; others are slower. Even our fast employees will have times when they slow down a bit, be it because of fatigue or distraction.

Waste The consumption of inputs and resources that do not add value to the customer.

Variability Predictable or unpredictable changes in the demand or the supply process.

Human beings are not robots and so we always will have some variation coming from our workforce.

- *Disruptions:* Sometimes a worker is faster; sometimes he is slower. And sometimes he does not show up. Sickness, bad weather, poor motivation—there are many reasons why workers might be absent. Similarly, equipment can break and computer systems might run slowly or require a reboot.

- *Defects:* Things go wrong in a business. Waiters enter the wrong order, food gets over-cooked, and bills can get messed up. Again, all of this leads to more variability in the process.

Given the variability that exists in an operation, it would be wonderful if we would be able to react to it. It would be nice if we could double the size of the restaurant at noon so that we can serve more customers, only to then have it contract to its usual size in the afternoon so we don't have to pay too much rent. It would also be great if our waiter could cook, too, especially on days when our cook is sick. And, even better still, it would be great if our beef patty could become a salmon—say, if we have extra beef but a customer wants a fish dish. We define **flexibility** as an operation's ability to react to variability. **Inflexibility**, which is our third process inhibitor, is thus the inability of an operation to quickly and cheaply change in response to new information.

So, inefficiencies result from the three system inhibitors: waste, variability, and inflexibility. Fighting these three system inhibitors is an ongoing process. Just as a one-time visit to the gym will not turn you into an amazing athlete, reducing the negative impacts of waste, variability, and inflexibility is an ongoing process. And just as some athletes outperform their peers, some operations are better in their battle against the three system inhibitors than others. Table 1.1 shows examples for the three system inhibitors.

Inflexibility The inability to adjust to either changes in the supply process or changes in customer demand.

TABLE 1.1   Examples of Demand–Supply Mismatches

	Fast-Food Restaurant	Rental Cars	Fashion Retailer	Emergency Room
Waste	Leftover food	Cars sitting in the parking lot	Items that stay in the store all season	Time spent on patients who could have been seen in primary care
Variability	Swings in customer demand	Bad weather conditions delaying the arrival of cars	Consumer demand driven by fashion	Sudden increases in patient volume due to the flu season
Inflexibility	Rigid staffing levels	Inability to move vehicles across rental centers	Long times to replenish items from overseas	Inability to admit patients due to a lack of inpatient beds

Check Your Understanding 1.3

Rubberball/Getty Images/RF

Question: Recall the last time you were standing in line at the checkout of the grocery store. Where did you see signs of the system inhibitors?

Answer: The following provide some examples for the three system inhibitors.

- **Waste:** employees being idle; fresh food needing to be trashed because of reaching its expiration date; employees moving back and forth to replenish items in the shelves from the back of the store.
- **Variability:** long lines form before the holidays.
- **Inflexibility:** inability to move employees from being cashiers to replenishing shelves.

1.4 Operations Management at Work

© Irene Alastruey/Author's Image/Punchstock/RF

You are reading an operations management book. Why? Why learn something about operations management? What does a (paid) job in operations look like? And where are these jobs?

Before we answer these questions, let us make a rather broad statement. Every work requires operations. The word *operations* comes from the Latin word *opus,* and *opus* means "work." So, by definition, operations is about work.

If "operations" is about work, "operations management" is about improving the way we and/or others do their work. At Toyota, a company that is often associated with great operations (and a company we will study in greater detail throughout the book), it is often said that "Everybody has two jobs: (1) do their work and (2) improve their work."

So, if we think about the importance of operations management for your future professional career, we have to distinguish between two cases. First (and, empirically, most likely), you will not work in operations management. You might become a software developer, a doctor, a lawyer, an accountant, a technician—your job description does not mention the word *operations.* In this case, you will need other academic and nonacademic training to *do* your work (go to medical school, do an internship, learn a programming language). However, this does not mean that operations management is not important for your work. After all, you will have two jobs: *do* your work and *improve* your work. We argue that the tools you will learn in this book will help you improve your work.

Second, some jobs are all about operations management. Broadly speaking, these jobs can be divided up into two groups:

LO1-4 Explain what work in operations management looks like.

- Companies have employee and management positions that are in charge of acquiring the inputs and managing the resources they need to serve their customers. This includes managing a fleet of rental cars, determining the right staffing level in a call center, ensuring the quality of a manufacturing process, or designing new products and services.

- Oftentimes, companies seek external help when it comes to improving the way they work. This help is offered by consulting companies. There exist hundreds of consulting companies that work in operations management, ranging from one-person boutique consulting companies to global service providers such as Deloitte and McKinsey & Co.

Thus, outside of you being a doctor or a management consultant, you get paid to improve the way you or somebody else works. How do you do this? You do this by overcoming the three system inhibitors we described earlier: You eliminate waste, reduce variability, and try to overcome inflexibility. You are permanently on the lookout for operations that could benefit from further improvement. Poor quality, customers waiting in line, idle resources, or piles of inventory are for you what an open wound is for a doctor—the opportunity to make something better. That is why the largest professional organization of operations management defines *operations management* simply as "The Science for the Better."

1.5 Operations Management: An Overview of the Book

LO1-5 Articulate the key operational decisions a firm needs to make to match supply with demand.

So, at the 30,000 foot level, operations management is about matching supply with demand— providing the goods and services that customers want while making a profit. Matching supply with demand while making a profit is complicated by the fact that we face the three system inhibitors. We waste our inputs and resources (our supply). Variability in supply and demand makes matching supply with demand difficult. And, while demand is variable, supply often-times is inflexible, which again prevents us from matching supply with demand.

There does not exist a single magic formula we could teach you that you could apply to solve all operations problems you might encounter. Instead, matching supply with demand needs to happen at many levels and in many areas of a business. We will have to confront the three system inhibitors in any one of these areas, but waste, variability, and inflexibility will take different forms depending on the type of problem you face. Consequently, operations management requires knowing how to use an entire assortment of tools, rather than just one. For this book, we have broken up the set of operational problems you might encounter into four modules:

- Process Analysis and Improvement
- Process Productivity and Quality
- Anticipate Customer Demand
- Respond to Customer Demand

Each of these modules supports you in answering a set of managerial questions that help you match supply with demand and thus overcome its own sort of inefficiencies. The modules are relatively independent of each other. With few exceptions, this is also true for the chapters within a module; that is, most chapters stand on their own as opposed to requiring you to have read the previous chapters.

Consider each of these modules in turn. The first module is entitled "Process Analysis and Improvement." In the module, you will learn to address the following questions:

- How should we produce the products or services we provide to our customers? You probably know how to cook and you might have made sandwiches for you, your family, and your friends. But a McDonald's restaurant oftentimes serves over 1,000 burgers per day, and all McDonald's restaurants combined make dozens of burgers every second. Moving from the craftsmanship associated with making a handful of products to creating operations based on processes is at the heart of this module.

- How can we improve our processes? Having a process is one thing; having a *good* process is another. Because customers don't like to pay high prices and because at least some of our competitors will try to undercut our prices, we have to be able to improve our processes.

The second module in this book is entitled "Process Productivity and Quality." Lean operations is a central theme of this module. Lean, as we will see, is the response to the three system inhibitors we introduced earlier. We have a dedicated "lean chapter" in this module, but the concept of "lean" is really central to this entire module and, in fact, to the entire book. Specifically, the second module will help you answer questions such as these:

- *How do we improve the productivity of the process?* Some companies are able to provide the same utility to the customer at lower costs. Other companies are held back by their inefficiencies. The difference between these companies is their ability to make productive use of their resources.

- *How do we respond to the heterogeneous preferences of our customers without sacrificing too much productivity?* Once you start making something in large quantities, you will find it easier to keep everything the same. McDonald's does not ask their customers if they want their burger to be grilled "medium rare" or "well done." Why not? Because it is a lot easier to make one type of Big Mac rather than making 10 types. Accommodating a variety of options to respond to the fit subcomponent in the customer utility function (Figure 1.1) often causes an increase in variability.

- *How can we consistently deliver the products and services?* Car companies like Volkswagen, GM, and Toyota produce many millions of vehicles per year and fast-food restaurants service millions of customers per day. To provide high-quality products to the customer, it is thus critical that a company performs its operations as consistently as possible.

McDonald's has to prepare food and make some purchasing decisions before the customer even places an order. Each McDonald's restaurant must purchase ingredients, and its employees must prepare some food—all without knowing how many burgers it will exactly sell. If too much food is prepared, McDonald's risks spoilage; if too little food is prepared, McDonald's faces hungry customers who might take their business elsewhere. Central to this decision is the management of inventory. Thus, we start the third module, "Anticipate Customer Demand," by talking about inventory management. We then address questions such as these:

- *How much of the products should we produce and how many customers should we serve?* Producing without having a customer order in your hand is risky; after all, you might prepare a burger that never sells. Vice versa, you might not have enough food prepared, leading to lost sales and unhappy customers.

- *How do we design a supply chain and distribution system?* Modern operations are complex, involving entire networks of operations, potentially including warehouses, suppliers, and sub-suppliers.

- *How can we predict demand?* Perfectly knowing demand ahead of time is rare in a world of variability. But we can try to predict it, which is the topic of a chapter on forecasting.

The management of inventory is at the heart of the third module. You forecast demand, you produce some inventory, and then you sell it. However, this approach to producing before having the actual demand does not work in many settings, including most of the service sector. After all, you cannot operate on a patient's broken leg before the patient has had the corresponding accident leading to the broken leg. So, the fourth and final module is about responding to customer demand. This includes the following questions:

- *How can we quickly respond to the customer demand of one customer?* Imagine the president of the United States (or the queen of England) walks into a Subway store (admittedly, a somewhat odd example). It seems like a safe assumption that the employees there would be willing to do everything possible to give him/her a customized sandwich as soon as possible. How long would it take? Even with just one single customer, the supply process is not instantaneous. Even if your customer is the president or the queen, you still need to cut the bread, put it in the toaster, and put on the ingredients. Project management is about planning the work for a single, unique job.

- *How can we quickly respond to the customer demand of many customers?* Subway takes about 2.5 minutes to take an order, make a sandwich, and ring up the customer. However, unless you are the president or the queen, you most likely will spend a longer time in the restaurant; you wait until it is your turn. We discuss models that explain how long customers have to wait (and how they react to that waiting).

- *What products and services best meet the needs of our customers?* Be it the recipe for a hamburger at McDonald's, the specifications of a BMW sports car, or the service standards in a call center or hospital, a firm needs to decide how it will address the needs of the customer.

Matching supply with demand is the theme that is common across all chapters. And this requires overcoming the three system inhibitors of waste, variability, and inflexibility. Throughout the book, we use examples from many different industries, ranging from hospitals to scooter plants, from banks to automotive companies, and from fast-food to fashion apparel. All examples are based on real operations.

While we cannot possibly cover all industries, companies, and examples, the operational questions, techniques, and strategies covered in this book are applicable broadly. At the risk of offending doctors and nurses in the readership, the challenges of managing an emergency room in a hospital have a lot in common with managing a fast-food restaurant. Recall from earlier: The tools and training for "doing the work" will certainly differ between cook and doctor, but the tools for improving the operations are remarkably similar. Patients want the care that is right for them, they want it delivered nearby, they don't want to wait in the waiting room, and they or their insurance company do not want to pay too much, just as hungry students want food that is right for them, delivered or served nearby, without too much of a wait at an affordable price.

Table 1.2 summarizes the operational decisions of a firm and groups them by the components of the customer utility function discussed at the beginning of the chapter. The first two rows correspond to the consumption utility, the next two rows to price (and cost), and the last two rows to convenience. The table illustrates the decisions for a restaurant chain, a rental car agency, a fashion retailer, and an emergency room.

© Dougal Waters/Photodisc/Getty
Images/RF

Check Your Understanding 1.4

Question: You and a group of fellow students are starting a new venture providing tutoring services for high school kids in your neighborhood preparing them for the SAT and ACT. What type of operational decisions do you have to make?

Answer:

- **What** is the product or service? Do we offer SAT and ACT? Do we help with subject SATs?
- **Who** are the customers and what are their heterogeneous needs? Do we cater to all students or only students who are aiming for very high scores? How do we deal with customers who are struggling?
- **How much** do we charge? What is the price for our preparation?
- **How efficiently** are the products or services delivered? How many tutors do we hire? Do we operate our own building? What are class sizes? Is there any online work that is automated?
- **Where** will the demand be fulfilled? Are students coming to us or are we coming to the students?
- **When** will the demand be fulfilled? Are we operating on a fixed schedule or whenever a customer needs our service?

TABLE 1.2 Key questions in operations management

	Fast-Food Restaurant	Rental Cars	Fashion Retailer	Emergency Room
What is the product or service?	Define the recipes and the cooking instructions	Pick vehicles for the fleet	Choose an assortment of attractive apparel	Create a care path for a specific procedure
Who are the customers and what are their heterogeneous needs?	Let customers choose from a menu; potentially allow for special requests	Choose different car types	Determine sizes and colors	Diagnose the unique medical needs of each patient and deliver the appropriate care
How much do we charge?	Pricing for the various items on the menu	Pricing for the vehicles; potentially advance booking discount	Pricing; potentially discounts at the end of season	Reimbursement rates
How efficiently are the products or services delivered?	Decide on how much equipment to buy, how much staff to hire, and how to organize cooking and the cash register	Make sure to not have too many or too few vehicles in the parking lot	Make sure to not have too many or too few items of a particular piece of clothing	Determine staffing plans for doctors and nurses and organize the flow of patients through the ER
Where will the demand be fulfilled?	Location of restaurants; potentially take-out or home delivery services	Location of rental stations; potentially pick up customer from home	Store locations	Location of hospitals; potentially provide some care in out-patient clinics
When will the demand be fulfilled?	Decide if you prepare the food ahead of the customer order; ensure fast service	Right level of staff enabling fast service	Avoid long lines at checkout	Ensure short wait times, especially for high acuity patients; decide on triage process

Conclusion

Operations management is about giving customers what they want while making good use of inputs and resources so that costs are low enough to yield a profit. Matching supply with demand while making a profit is complicated by the fact that we face the three system inhibitors. As you read through other chapters in this book, keep this basic framework in mind. Always ask yourself what the customer really wants and what keeps us from matching this demand with a supply that we can provide at sufficiently low cost to still make a profit.

Summary of Learning Objectives

LO1-1 Identify the drivers of customer utility

Customer utility is driven by the consumption utility, the price, and the inconvenience. The consumption utility depends on the absolute performance and the fit to a given customer. The price includes all costs associated with the product or service. Inconvenience, also called transaction cost, is driven by time and location.

LO1-2 Explain inefficiencies and determine if a firm is on the efficient frontier

The efficient frontier consists of all firms that are not Pareto dominated. *Pareto dominated* means that a firm's product or service is inferior to that of one or multiple competitors on all dimensions of the customer utility function.

LO1-3   Explain the three system inhibitors

The gap between our current performance and the efficient frontier is our inefficiency. This inefficiency results from a combination of the three system inhibitors: waste, variability, and inflexibility.

LO1-4   Explain what work in operations management looks like

Operations comes from the Latin word *opus,* which means "work." Operations management is about helping people do their work. But it is also about helping people to improve the way that they work by overcoming the inefficiencies that they face.

LO1-5   Articulate the key operational decisions a firm needs to make to match supply with demand

A firm or company needs to make a number of operational decisions. This includes answering the following questions: (a) **What** is the product or service? (b) **Who** are the customers? (c) **How much** do we charge? (d) **How efficiently** are the products or services delivered? (e) **Where** will the demand be fulfilled? (f) **When** will the demand be fulfilled?

Key Terms

1.1   The Customer's View of the World

Supply Products or services a business offers to its customers.

Demand Simply, the set of products and services our customers want.

Utility A measure of the strength of customer preferences for a given product or service. Customers buy the product or service that maximizes their utility.

Consumption utility A measure of how much you like a product or service, ignoring the effects of price and of the inconvenience of obtaining the product or service.

Performance A subcomponent of the consumption utility that captures how much an average consumer desires a product or service.

Fit A subcomponent of the consumption utility that captures how well the product or service matches with the unique characteristics of a given consumer.

Heterogeneous preferences The fact that not all consumers have the same utility function.

Price The total cost of owning the product or receiving the service.

Inconvenience The reduction in utility that results from the effort of obtaining the product or service.

Transaction costs Another term for the inconvenience of obtaining a product or service.

Location The place where a consumer can obtain a product or service

Timing The amount of time that passes between the consumer ordering a product or service and the consumer obtaining the product or service.

Demand The set of customers for whom a specific product or service is the best choice (also called the utility maximizing choice).

Marketing The academic discipline that is about understanding and influencing how customers derive utility from products or services.

1.2   A Firm's Strategic Trade-Offs

Capabilities The dimensions of the customer's utility function a firm is able to satisfy.

Trade-offs The need to sacrifice one capability in order to increase another one.

Market segments A set of customers who have similar utility functions.

Pareto dominated Pareto dominated means that a firm's product or service is inferior to one or multiple competitors on all dimensions of the customer utility function.

Efficient frontier The set of firms that are not Pareto dominated.

Inefficiency The gap between a firm and the efficient frontier.

1.3 Overcoming Inefficiencies: The Three System Inhibitors

Waste The consumption of inputs and resources that do not add value to the customer.

Variability Predictable or unpredictable changes in the demand or the supply process.

Inflexibility The inability to adjust to either changes in the supply process or changes in customer demand.

Conceptual Questions

LO 1-1

1. Below are a number of slogans used for advertisement. Which dimensions of customer utility do the slogans emphasize?
   a. We build lenses uniquely to the needs of your eyes.
   b. Get your burger in 1 minute or less—otherwise, you eat free.
   c. We match any price in town.
   d. Our dealership network provides service, wherever in the country you may be.
   e. The fastest Internet in the nation.

2. Which of the following is not a dimension or subdimension in a customer's utility function?
   a. Convenience
   b. Price
   c. Location
   d. Customer satisfaction
   e. Performance

LO 1-2

3. The efficient frontier is given by the cheapest company in the industry. True or false?

4. There can be no more than two firms on the efficient frontier. True or false?

5. Two retailers compete on costs and the ambience of their retail stores. They are identical in all other dimensions of customer utility. Retailer A is cheaper than retailer B. Retailer A also has the better ambience. Does this mean that retailer A is on the efficient frontier? Yes or no?

LO 1-3

6. Which of the following is NOT one of the three system inhibitors?
   a. Waste
   b. Variability
   c. Fatigue
   d. Inflexibility

LO 1-5

7. Which of the following questions is NOT related to operations management?
   a. **When** will the demand be fulfilled?
   b. **How much** will the CEO be paid?
   c. **Who** are the customers?
   d. **How efficiently** are the products or services delivered?
   e. **Where** will the demand be fulfilled?
   f. **What** is the product or service?

Solved Example Problems

LO 1-1

1. The following is a list of customer complaints. To which dimension of customer utility do the complaints relate?
   a. I had to spend 27 minutes on hold before talking to an agent.
   b. This car is not fuel-efficient at all.
   c. When I needed a restroom in the amusement park, I had to walk almost a mile.
   d. I had this suit tailored for me, but now I realize that the shoulders are too wide.

   Answer: The complaints relate to

   a. Timing
   b. Performance
   c. Location
   d. Fit

LO 1-2

2. There are four cab companies in a large urban area. Prices are identical across the four companies, and so the companies compete on (a) the response time it takes between receiving a call requesting a cab and the arrival of the cab, and (b) the cleanliness of the cab and the courtesy of the driver. The following table lists past performance data.

Cab Company	Response Time	Courtesy (1: very low ... 5: very high)
1	6 min	3
2	9 min	5
3	3 min	2
4	11 min	2

   Which of these companies are NOT on the efficient frontier?

   Answer: We observe that company 4 is Pareto dominated by companies 1 and 2; none of the other companies are Pareto dominated.

3. You have a choice between five restaurants that differ from each other with respect to their food quality [as measured by the number of stars (*) the restaurant received in customer reviews; this ranges from one to five stars, with five being the best] as well as their price.

Restaurant	Quality	Price
1	***	$30
2	**	$25
3	*****	$50
4	***	$20
5	*	$5

   Which of these restaurants are on the efficient frontier?

   Answer: Restaurants 3, 4, and 5 are on the efficient frontier. Restaurant 4 pareto dominates both 1 and 2.

LO 1-3

4. You are organizing a pizza night with your friends. You expect somewhere between 10 and 20 guests, so you decide to order food for 15. What mismatches between supply and demand can you envision? What would be costs related to these mismatches?

Answer: Depending on how many guests show up and how much they want to eat, we can end up in one of two cases:

- *Too much demand:* This corresponds to more guests than you have expected showing up; in this case, some guests will not get to eat. They might be mad at you as the host. Or you might have to run and order more food, leading to waiting time and probably also worse food.
- *Too much supply:* This corresponds to you ordering more food than your guests want to eat. In this case, you will have leftover food—food that you paid for but really don't need.

5. What are supply–demand mismatches for the operator of a fleet of ambulances? What economic and social costs could you envision?

   Answer: At any given time, there are either too many ambulances (with the associated costs of resources) or too few ambulances (with the tragic costs of patients having to wait for an ambulance, putting them at an increased medical risk).

LO 1-2

6. Lunch@Work is a student-initiated venture that provides office workers with lunch brought right to their desks. What operational decisions will the venture have to make?

   Answer: The questions include the following:

- *What is the service?* Determine what food you provide.
- *Who are the customers?* Determine if there are any dietary restrictions and how you deal with those.
- *How much do we charge?* Determine the price.
- *How efficiently is the service delivered?* Decide how many people make the food, how to run the kitchen operations, and how to distribute the food to the offices.
- *Where will the demand be fulfilled?* Determine where you would ship to (which zip codes, where in the building).
- *When will demand be fulfilled?* Ensure that waiting times are not too long.

Problems and Applications

LO 1-1

1. What are the subcomponents of inconvenience in a customer utility function?
   a. Location and price
   b. Price and volume
   c. Location and time
   d. Time and performance

2. Custom-built windows are designed and produced for the unique needs of a particular building. Which dimension of the customer utility function is particularly emphasized with the concept of "custom built"?
   a. Performance
   b. Fit
   c. Price
   d. Location

3. Which of the following characteristics is a subcomponent of the consumption utility in a customer utility function?
   a. Performance
   b. Location
   c. Timing
   d. Price

4. A national restaurant chain has just opened a sit-down location at Chicago's O'Hare International Airport. Next to the sit-down location, it has also established a "to-go" section where travelers can purchase pre-made sandwiches and salads, as well as drinks and snacks. Which dimension of the customer utility function is particularly emphasized with the "to-go" section?
   a. Performance
   b. Fit
   c. Price
   d. Timing

5. A car manufacturer has designed a "special edition" version of its popular two-door coupe. This special edition has increased horsepower compared to the standard model and a sports suspension. Which dimension of the customer utility function is particularly emphasized with the special edition coupe?
   a. Performance
   b. Fit
   c. Price
   d. Timing

6. There are four hotels competing with otherwise very similar products on the dimensions of price ($ per night) and amenities (measured by the number of *s awarded by customer reviews).

   Hotel A: price = $200 per night; rating: ***

   Hotel B: price = $150 per night; rating: ****

   Hotel C: price = $300 per night; rating *****

   Hotel D: price = $80 per night; rating **

   Which of these hotels are on the efficient frontier? You may select more than one answer.

LO 1-2

7. Four regional less-than-truckload (LTL) carriers handle shipments traveling from Lexington, Kentucky, to Springfield, Illinois. All four companies say that their normal service time to deliver these shipments is two business days. The four carriers compete with each other on the basis of price and service quality rating, as shown in the following table. The price reported in the table is the (nondiscounted) cost per hundredweight (cwt) of sending a 600-pound shipment from Lexington to Springfield at freight class 70. The service quality rating measures a carrier's loss and damage record and goes from 0 (poor quality) to 100 (high quality).

Carrier	Price	Service Quality Rating
A	$103.90	95
B	$98.50	91
C	$127.20	98
D	$111.40	94

   Which of these LTL carriers are on the efficient frontier?

8. A suburb of Dayton, Ohio, has four local dry cleaners that compete with each other on the basis of price and service speed. Each of them can perform the same basic services at the same level of quality. The following table provides the price that each dry cleaner charges to clean a two-piece suit, as well as the quoted number of days that the service will take.

Dry Cleaner	Price	Number of Days
A	$8.00	3
B	$9.50	3
C	$9.00	2
D	$7.50	4

Which of these dry cleaners are NOT on the efficient frontier?

LO 1-3

9. Which of the following items would be considered an input in the operations of a soft drink manufacturer?
   a. Brand image
   b. Bottling machines
   c. Empty bottles
   d. Workers

10. Which of the following items would be considered a resource in the operations of a soft drink manufacturer?
    a. Water
    b. Bottling machines
    c. Empty bottles
    d. Sugar and/or concentrate

11. Which of the following items would be considered an input in the operations of a doctor's office?
    a. Examination table
    b. Nurse
    c. Needle
    d. Stethoscope

12. Which of the following items would be considered a resource in the operations of a movie theater?
    a. Popcorn
    b. Projector
    c. Printer ink
    d. Soda

13. Which of the following inefficiencies in a grocery store's operations results from inflexibility?
    a. Leftover fruits and vegetables
    b. Delivery delays from the warehouse
    c. A surge in customer arrivals at one time
    d. Employee work schedules set a week in advance

14. Which of the following inefficiencies in a bank's operations results from variability?
    a. Employees entering the same information twice
    b. Associates reading the terms and conditions of each account to the customer
    c. Customers incorrectly listing information on forms
    d. Employee work schedules set a week in advance

LO 1-5

15. Which of the following operational decisions correspond(s) to the convenience component of the consumer utility function?

    Instructions: You may select more than one answer.
    a. When will the demand be fulfilled?
    b. How efficiently will the products or the services be delivered?

    c. What is the product or service to be delivered?

    d. Where will the demand be fulfilled?

16. Which of the following operational decisions correspond(s) to the price component of the consumer utility function?

    Instructions: You may select more than one answer.

    a. When will the demand be fulfilled?

    b. What are the shipping charges to the customer?

    c. What is the product or service to be delivered?

    d. Where will the demand be fulfilled?

17. Which of the following operational decisions correspond(s) to the consumption utility component of the consumer utility function?

    Instructions: You may select more than one answer.

    a. When will the demand be fulfilled?

    b. How efficiently will the products or the services be delivered?

    c. What is the product or service to be delivered?

    d. Where will the demand be fulfilled?

References

http://www.nationmaster.com/graph/foo_mcd_res-food-mcdonalds-restaurants

http://wzozfm.com/average-wait-time-at-popular-drive-thrus/

Introduction to Processes

2

Introduction

We live our lives from one process to another—there is a process for getting a driver's license, a process for completing a college degree, a process for talking to a doctor, and on and on. In those cases, and in many others, we take the perspective of a customer— we participate in the process to receive a good or service. But there is another perspective, the view of a process observer—not the view of somebody in the process or receiving the process, but rather the view of somebody watching or managing the process. That is the view we take in this chapter and throughout this book.

© Corbis Super RF/Alamy/RF

There are two key questions the manager of a process should ask: (i) Is the process performing well? and (ii) How can we make the process better? In some sense, the operations manager is very much like the coach on a sports team. The coach must first decide how to measure the performance of the players. For example, a basketball coach might want to track the number of shots attempted, the number of assists, and the number of points scored per game. Next, the coach needs to figure out how to make each player better and especially how to make the team better. The first step (measure the process) is critical for the second (improve the process)—if you do not know how to measure a process, then it is difficult to know how to improve it (or even to know if you have improved it).

In this chapter, we focus on the manager's first question—what should the operations manager measure to determine if the process is performing well? The second question (How to improve the process?) is discussed extensively in the subsequent chapters. Through an example from our health care system, we show that there are three key measures of a process. We identify these measures and show how they are linked together through Little's Law. Finally, we explain why these measures are important to an organization.

2.1 Process Definition, Scope, and Flow Units

A **process** is a set of activities that takes a collection of inputs, performs some work or activities with those inputs, and then yields a set of outputs. For example, interventional radiology at Presbyterian Hospital in Philadelphia accepts patients (inputs); performs minimally invasive advanced imaging techniques like real-time X-ray, ultrasound, computer tomography, and magnetic resonance imaging; and then sends patients home (output), hopefully with better health or at least with the information needed to improve their care. This can seem like a very complex process. There are many people involved, such as patients, receptionists, nurses, physicians, and lab technicians. There are numerous pieces of complicated equipment and there are multiple rooms, including a waiting area and procedure rooms. Despite the complexity of an interventional radiology unit, if we step back a bit, the complexity can be boiled down to the simple picture shown in Figure 2.1.

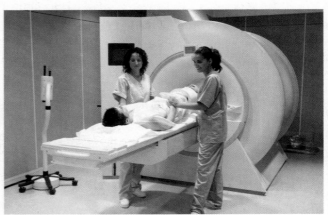

© Javier Larrea/ Pixtal/AGE Fotostock/RF

Figure 2.1 is called a **process flow diagram** because it provides a graphical representation of the process. It has several components. The inputs to the process are indicated with arrows flowing into the process and outputs are indicated with arrows flowing out of the process. Boxes within the process flow diagram represent **resources**—a resource is a group of people and/or equipment that transforms inputs into outputs. In Figure 2.1, there is a single resource, the radiology unit, but as we later see, process flow diagrams can have multiple resources with the output of some resources used as the inputs to other resources.

So at a basic level, the interventional radiology unit takes in patients as inputs, the unit then performs some tasks on them when they are in the unit, and then treated patients leave as the

Process A set of activities that take a collection of inputs, perform some work or activities with those inputs, and then yield a set of outputs.

Process flow diagram A graphical way to describe the process. It uses boxes to depict resources, arrows to depict flows, and triangles to depict inventory location.

Resource A group of people and/or equipment that transforms inputs into outputs.

Figure 2.1

A simple process flow diagram of the radiology unit at Presbyterian Hospital

Figure 2.2

A process flow diagram for just real-time X-rays within the radiology unit

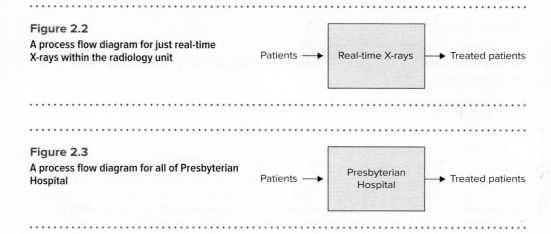

Patients ⟶ Real-time X-rays ⟶ Treated patients

Figure 2.3

A process flow diagram for all of Presbyterian Hospital

Patients ⟶ Presbyterian Hospital ⟶ Treated patients

outputs. This describes the radiology unit's **process scope**—the set of activities included in the process.

We have defined the scope of this process to include the entire interventional radiology unit. This is appropriate if we are responsible for the entire unit and we want to keep track of how the entire unit is doing. But other scopes are certainly reasonable, depending on your perspective. For example, if you are a technician who assists with real-time X-rays, you might only be interested in the portion of the unit that performs real-time X-rays. In that case, your process flow diagram might look like Figure 2.2.

We have retained the same inputs and outputs, but our scope has narrowed to just a single type of procedure.

If our scope can narrow, it can also expand. For instance, say you are the CEO of Presbyterian Hospital. Then your process could be described with the "high level" picture displayed in Figure 2.3.

In addition to the process scope, to begin to understand and analyze a process, we must define a flow unit. The **flow unit** is the basic unit that moves through a process. It is generally associated with the outputs of a process. In the case of the interventional radiology unit, a natural flow unit is a "patient" because the purpose of the interventional radiology unit is to provide care to patients.

Figure 2.4 illustrates three other processes and possible flow units. In each case, it is not hard to imagine that the flow unit could be something different than what is listed. For example,

Process scope The set of activities and processes included in the process.

Flow unit The unit of analysis that we consider in a process analysis; for example, patients in a hospital, scooters in a kick-scooter plant, and calls in a call center.

LO2-1 Identify an appropriate flow unit for a process.

Processes **Flow unit**

Figure 2.4

An illustration of three other processes and possible flow units

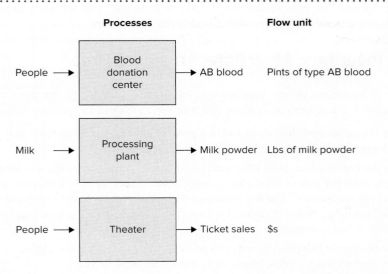

People ⟶ Blood donation center ⟶ AB blood   Pints of type AB blood

Milk ⟶ Processing plant ⟶ Milk powder   Lbs of milk powder

People ⟶ Theater ⟶ Ticket sales $s

Check Your Understanding 2.1

Question: Which of the following is an appropriate flow unit for a roller coaster at an amusement park?

a. Seats on the roller coaster
b. Riders
c. Employees
d. Miles per hour (as in the speed of the roller coaster)
e. Operating time (as in the number of hours operated per day)

Answer: The roller coaster is a process that takes in riders and provides them with an exciting ride. The riders are the ones who receive this service, not the seats or the employees. While speed (miles per hour) and operating time are relevant to understanding how the process works, they are neither the input nor the output of the process per se. The correct answer is b.

the flow unit in a blood donation center could be a "blood donor," but "pints of AB blood" is better if your interest is specifically on the output of AB blood. The processing plant could use "gallon of milk" as the flow unit, but generally it makes more sense to define the flow unit in terms of output rather than input. And while entertained "people" certainly flow through a theater, the theater may more directly be concerned with the output of revenue in terms of "$s."

To summarize, there are several important rules with respect to defining the flow unit:

1. Choose a flow unit that corresponds to what you want to track and measure with respect to the process.

2. Stick with the flow unit you defined. Don't measure some aspects of the dairy process using a "gallon of milk" as the flow unit and then switch to "lbs of milk powder." It makes no sense to combine things in different units.

3. Choose a flow unit that can be used to measure and describe all of the activities within the process. To use an exercise example, "distance traveled" might not be the best measure of all activities for a triathlete who must swim, bike, and run because people generally bike much further than they swim. A more unifying flow unit could be "minutes of workout" or, to be even more sophisticated, "calories burned" (or some other measure of power). In business, a currency (such as a euro, dollar, or yen) is a common flow unit that can be used to span all of the things and activities in a process.

Once you have defined the scope of the process and its flow unit, you are ready to start analyzing and measuring some key performance variables for the process.

2.2 Three Key Process Metrics: Inventory, Flow Rate, and Flow Time

Process metric A scale or measure of process performance and capability.

Inventory The number of flow units within the process.

Flow rate The rate at which flow units travel through a process.

Flow time The time a flow unit spends in a process, from start to finish.

A **process metric** is something we can measure that informs us about the performance and capability of a process. For a process observer or designer, there are three key process metrics:

- **Inventory** is the number of flow units within a process. For example, "dollars" in process, "kilograms" in process, or "people" in process.

- **Flow rate** is the rate at which flow units travel through a process. As a rate, it is measured in "flow units per unit of time"; for example, "dollars per week," "kilograms per hour," or "people per month." The key feature of a rate is that it is always expressed in terms of some unit (e.g., boxes or dollars) *per unit of time.* If the "per unit of time" is missing, then it is just inventory.

- **Flow time** is the time a flow unit spends in a process, from start to finish. Typical units for this measure are minutes, hours, days, weeks, months, or years.

Inventory tells us how much "stuff" is in the process. This is useful to know because inventory generally takes up space and may cost money. For example, if the average inventory of people in the radiology unit increases, then the radiology unit might eventually need a bigger building, which comes with a cost. If a retailer needs to increase the number of items in the store, then it might need a bigger store (which means higher rent) and it needs to have more cash to buy that inventory.

Flow rate tells us how much stuff moves through the process per unit of time. More units flowing through a process is generally desirable because the point of the process is to produce output.

Flow time tells us how much time stuff spends in the process. If you are a patient in the radiology unit, then you surely care about your flow time. The manager of the radiology unit is therefore interested in flow time because it influences the satisfaction of its patients.

To see how these process metrics can be evaluated for the interventional radiology unit, we can collect data on when patients arrive and depart our process, like those reported in Table 2.1. Over the course of the day, the table reports that there were 11 patients. Using these data, among our three process metrics, it is probably easiest to evaluate the flow time for each patient. To do so, we simply subtract the patient's departure time from his or her arrival time. According to the table, the flow times varied from a short 15 minutes to a maximum of 220 minutes. The average of the patients' flow times is 125 minutes, which is 2.08 hours.

The next easiest process metric to evaluate is flow rate. The first patient arrives at 7:35 a.m. and the last patient leaves at 18:10, or 6:10 p.m. The interval of time between those two events is 635 minutes, or 10.58 hours. During the day there are 11 patients. So the average flow rate is 11 patients/10.58 hours = 1.04 patients per hour. This flow rate applies throughout the process. For example, patients enter the process at the rate of 1.04 patients per hour and patients exit the process at the rate of 1.04 patients per hour. The entry rate and the exit rate do not have to match at every moment (e.g., in the morning more patients are entering than exiting), but they do have to match on average over the long run. This is simply a reflection of the fact that "what goes in must come out."

Finally, using the data from Table 2.1, we can also evaluate the inventory of patients at any time in the radiology unit. For example, there is one patient from 7:35 to 7:45, then two patients from 7:45 to 8:10. The third patient arrives at 8:10, but our inventory of patients drops back down to two at 8:50 because that is when the first patient departs. Figure 2.5 plots

LO2-2 Distinguish among the three key process metrics (flow rate, flow time, and inventory) and evaluate average flow rate and flow time from departure and arrival data.

TABLE 2.1 Arrivals and Departures to the Interventional Radiology Unit over the Course of a Day

Patient	Arrival	Departure	Flow Time (min)
1	7:35	8:50	75
2	7:45	10:05	140
3	8:10	10:10	120
4	9:30	11:15	105
5	10:15	10:30	15
6	10:30	13:35	185
7	11:05	13:15	130
8	12:35	15:05	150
9	14:30	18:10	220
10	14:35	15:45	70
11	14:40	17:20	160
Average			125

© Heath Korvola/Digital Vision/Getty Images/RF

Check Your Understanding 2.2

Question: Over the course of an eight-hour day, a dentist's office treats 24 patients. What is the flow rate of patients in this dentist's office per hour?

Answer: Flow rate = 24 patients/8 hours = 3 patients per hour

Question: From 5 a.m. to 6 a.m., four callers contact a help desk. The callers spend 2, 5, 3, and 10 minutes on their calls. What is the average flow time of a caller at this help desk?

Answer: The average time for these callers is (2 + 5 + 3 + 10)/4 = 5 minutes.

Figure 2.5

Inventory of patients in the interventional radiology unit throughout the day

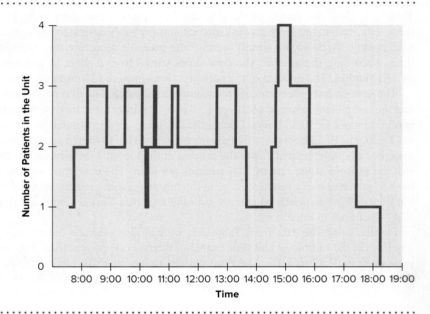

these ups and downs in our inventory. While it is relatively straightforward to calculate the average flow time and average flow rate, the calculation of the average inventory is clearly more involved. Although it is apparent from Figure 2.5 that on average there are about 2 patients in the unit at any given time, it is not obvious how to evaluate the exact average inventory of patients. Fortunately, there indeed exists a very simple method, as we are about to describe.

2.3 Little's Law—Linking Process Metrics Together

LO2-3 Use Little's Law to evaluate the three key process metrics.

Little's Law The law that describes the relationship between three key process metrics: inventory, flow rate, and flow time.

Within any process, the three key process metrics are related to each other in the following way, known as **Little's Law**:

$$\text{Inventory} = \text{Flow rate} \times \text{Flow time}$$

(See Connections: Little's Law for why this is called Little's Law.) This relationship is so central to process analysis that it is often described in its shorthand version:

$$I = R \times T$$

Little's Law is deceptively simple, but at the same time it is also remarkably powerful. It tells us that if we know any two of the process metrics, we can know, or derive, the third. In addition, it means that if by changing our process we modify one of the metrics while holding a second one constant, then we can determine how the third one changes.

Let's apply Little's Law to the radiology unit. Based on the data in Table 2.1, the flow time is $T = 2.08$ hours and the flow rate is $R = 1.04$ patients/hour. Thus, according to Little's Law, the average inventory of patients throughout the day is

$$I = 1.04 \frac{\text{patients}}{\text{hr}} \times 2.08 \text{ hrs} = 2.16 \text{ patients}$$

The beauty of Little's Law is that it works for any process. For example, suppose we watch people (our flow unit) loading onto the escalator in the Vastraskogen subway station in Stockholm, which is 220 feet (67 meters) long. It is a busy time of the day and we observe that the flow rate of people onto the escalator is 2.5 people per second, $R = 2.5$ people per second. We then hop on the escalator ourselves and record that the flow time from bottom to top is 88 seconds, $T = 88$ seconds. While riding on the escalator, we try to count the number of people riding with us, which is the inventory metric for this process, but it is hard to see everyone. Besides, there seem to be too many people to count. No worries; we can use Little's Law to determine the average inventory of people on the escalator:

$$\text{Inventory} = R \times T$$
$$= 2.5 \text{ people per sec} \times 88 \text{ seconds}$$
$$= 220 \text{ people}$$

To emphasize a point again, if you are told (or can observe) any two of the key process metrics, you can use Little's Law to derive the third. To give another (odd) example, suppose we define the U.S. House of Representatives as a process, as shown in Figure 2.6.

Politicians enter the House and eventually they leave the House as retired representatives. We know there is an inventory of 435 members in the House; that is, $I = 435$ people. Looking at past data, we see that, on average, there are 52 new members of the House in an election year and 0 new members of the House in nonelection years. (Every seat in the House is up for election every two years.) So, on average, there are $\frac{52}{2} = 26$ new members of the House per year. This is the flow rate; that is, $R = 26$ people per year. So how much time does the average representative remain in the House? Use Little's Law:

$$I = R \times T$$
$$435 \text{ people} = 26 \text{ people per year} \times T$$
$$T = \frac{435}{26}$$
$$= 16.73 \text{ years}$$

If you are a politico, you might respond to our answer with "But John Dingell served in Congress much longer than 16.73 years. In fact, he served more than 55 years!" And you are correct! Little's Law does not tell us the time a particular flow unit spends in the process. Rather, it tells us the average time a flow unit spends in the process. Some, like John Dingell,

Figure 2.6

A process flow diagram for the U.S. House of Representatives

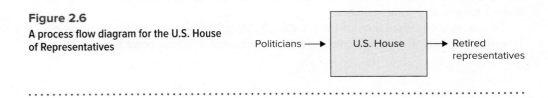

© FoodCollection/StockFood/RF

Check Your Understanding 2.3

Question: During a typical Friday, the West End Donut Shop serves 2400 customers during the 10 hours it is open. A customer spends, on average, 5 minutes in the shop. On average, how many customers are in the shop simultaneously?

Answer: Flow rate is

$$\frac{2400 \text{ customers}}{10 \text{ hours}} = 240 \frac{\text{customers}}{\text{hour}} = 4 \frac{\text{customers}}{\text{min}}. \text{ Flow time} = 5 \text{ min}.$$

$$I = R \times T = 4 \frac{\text{customers}}{\text{min}} \times 5 \text{ min} = 20 \text{ customers}.$$

Question: During the course of an 8-hour day, there are, on average, 5 students in an undergraduate advising office, and each student spends, on average, 10 minutes with an advisor. At what rate do students go to the advising office (in students per hour)?

Answer: Average inventory, I, equals 5 and average flow time, T, equals 10 min $= \frac{1}{6}$ hour. From Little's Law, $R = \frac{I}{T}$. Thus, $R = 5$ students $\frac{1}{6}$ hour $= 30$ students per hour.

TABLE 2.2   Examples of Flow Rates, Flow Times, and Inventory

	U.S. Immigration	Champagne Industry	Undergraduate Program	Tablet Manufacturer
Flow unit	Visa application	Bottle of champagne	Student	Tablet
Flow rate	6 million apps per year	250 million bottles per year	5000 students per year	20,000 tablets per day
Flow time	9 months	3.5 years	4 years	10 days
Inventory	4.5 million applications	875 million bottles	20,000 students	200,000 tablets

may spend more than 55 years in the House, whereas others spend less than 16.73 years. But if there are 435 representatives (which there are) and there are 26 new names per year (which we learn from the historical data), then when we average the tenures of all representatives, we get 16.73 years. In fact, all three of the performance metrics in Little's Law are averages and only averages. For example, the radiology unit can have 2 or 3 patients at a given moment, but it never has exactly 2.16 patients even though, on average, it does have 2.16 patients. (It is OK to be the first or second patient, but who would want to be the 0.16th patient?) Similarly, the average patient's flow time in the radiology unit is 2.08 hours, but some spend less time and others more. On a related point, your next comment might be: "With elections every two years, the tenure of a representative must be a multiple of two. Nobody has spent exactly 16.73 years in the House." Right again. Even though everyone's tenure is a multiple of two (ignoring resignations and other reasons for not completing a term), the average across the tenures of all representatives can be something other than a multiple of two, as in 16.73 years. In other words, the average of a bunch of whole numbers doesn't have to be a whole number.

To conclude our discussion of Little's Law, Table 2.2 gives more examples of processes in which the three key process metrics can be evaluated and connected to each other via Little's Law.

CONNECTIONS: Little's Law

Little's Law

Given its importance to operations management, why not call it "Big Law" or "Grand Law"? Because it was first proved in a paper published in 1961 by a professor at the Massachusetts Institute of Technology named John Little.* As we will see in this book, there are numerous applications of Little's Law to operations manage-ment, but applications of this principle have extended to many environments, including health care and computer science. The law is remarkable in its simplicity—the average number of units in a process depends only on the average flow rate and the average time a unit spends in the process. The law excludes a number of factors that you might think are relevant, such as whether arrival and processing times are random or not (e.g., does the rate of arrivals to the ski lift change over time or does the lift operate at different speeds) or the sequence in which units are processed (e.g., does a doctor's office take patients on a first-come, first-served basis or does it operate with a priority scheme such that the sickest patients get treated first). All of those details don't matter for the aver-age number of units in the process, the average flow rate, and the average flow time a unit spends in the process.

© John D C Little
John Little, who first discovered Little's Law.

*Little, J.D.C. 1961. A proof for the queuing formula: $L = \lambda W$. Operations Research. **9**(3): 383–387.

Conclusion

A process is a set of activities performed on a collection of inputs to yield useful outputs. As a manager of a process, we want to first measure its performance and then improve its per-formance. Improvement cannot happen without tracking performance. For any process, there are three fundamental metrics to evaluate performance: inventory, flow rate, and flow time. These measures are linked via Little's Law: Inventory = Flow rate × Flow time. Hence, if you know any two of these measures, you can evaluate the third.

Summary of Learning Objectives

LO2-1 Identify an appropriate flow unit for a process

Define the flow unit to be what you are interested in tracking, usually the output of the process. In choosing a flow unit, be sure to stick with that flow unit throughout the process and choose a flow unit that applies to all of the activities in a process.

LO2-2 Distinguish among the three key process metrics (flow rate, flow time, and inventory) and evaluate average flow rate and flow time from departure and arrival data

The three key process metrics are inventory, flow rate, and flow time. Inventory is the average number of flow units in the process. Flow rate is the rate at which flow units are moving through the process. As a rate, it must be expressed in "flow units per unit of time"; for example, "gallons of milk per day." Flow time is the average amount of time a flow unit spends in the process. This time should be the same as the time period used to describe the flow rate. For example, if the rate is "gallons of milk per day," then the flow time should be expressed in "days."

LO2-3   Use Little's Law to evaluate the three key process metrics

Little's Law relates the three key process metrics: Inventory = Flow rate × Flow time, or $I = R \times T$. If you know any two of the three, you can use Little's Law to evaluate the third. In all cases, each metric is an average and only an average. For example, while on average a service station might have 10,601 gallons of gasoline in a storage tank, this does not mean it always has that amount.

Key Terms

2.1   Process Definition, Scope, and Flow Units

Process A set of activities that take a collection of inputs, perform some work or activities with those inputs, and then yield a set of outputs.

Resource A group of people and/or equipment that transforms inputs into outputs.

Process scope The set of activities and processes included in the process.

Flow unit The unit of analysis that we consider in a process analysis; for example, patients in a hospital, scooters in a kick-scooter plant, and calls in a call center.

2.2   Three Key Process Metrics: Inventory, Flow Rate, and Flow Time

Process metric A scale or measure of process performance and capability.

Inventory The number of flow units within the process.

Flow rate The rate at which flow units travel through a process.

Flow time The time a flow unit spends in a process, from start to finish.

2.3   Little's Law—Linking Process Metrics Together

Little's Law The law that describes the relationship between three key process metrics: inventory, flow rate, and flow time.

Key Formulas

LO2-3   Use Little's Law to evaluate the three key process metrics

Inventory = Flow rate × Flow time

Conceptual Questions

LO2-1

1. From the perspective of process analysis, which of the following could be appropriate flow units for a hardware store?
   a. Number of workers
   b. Number of cash registers
   c. Number of customers
   d. Number of suppliers

2. Over the course of a month, which of the following is most likely to describe an appropriate flow unit for a process analysis of a hospital?
   a. The number of physicians
   b. The number of beds
   c. The square footage of the building
   d. The number of patients

LO2-2

3. At a cruise ship terminal, each day on average 1000 passengers embark on ships. On average, passengers spend 5 days on their cruise before returning to this terminal. If the flow unit is a passenger, then what are the flow rate and flow time of this process?

4. It is election day and 1800 voters vote in their precinct's library during the 10 hours the polls are open. On average, there are 15 voters in the library and they spend on average 5 minutes in the library to complete their voting. What is the inventory of voters, the flow rate, and the flow time for each voter?

5. Over the course of a day, fans pour into a NASCAR venue at the rate of 8000 people per hour. The average rate at which fans leave the venue _____.
   a. must be less than 8000 people per hour
   b. must be exactly 8000 people per hour
   c. must be more than 8000 people per hour
   d. could be more or less than 8000 people per hour

LO2-3

6. A computer server experiences large fluctuations in the amount of data requests it receives throughout the day. Because of this variation, Little's Law does not apply. True or false?

Solved Example Problems

LO2-2

TABLE 2.3   Arrival and Departure Times from a State Park

8.5 hrs

Car	Arrival	Departure
1	7:00	15:00
2	7:30	10:30
3	8:00	12:00
4	8:00	17:00
5	8:30	10:30
6	9:30	15:30
7	11:00	16:00
8	11:30	18:30
9	13:30	18:30
10	15:30	18:30

1. A state park is open from 7 a.m. to 6:30 p.m. Table 2.3 displays data regarding arrivals and departures of cars during the day from the park. What is the average flow time of cars in this park?

   Answer: Evaluate the flow time of each car and then take the average across all cars. For example, car 1 spends $15 - 7 = 8$ hours in the park. The flow times for the 10 cars are 8, 3, 4, 9, 2, 6, 5, 7, 5, and 3 hours. The average flow time is 5.2 hours.

2. A state park is open from 7 a.m. to 6:30 p.m. Table 2.3 displays data regarding arrivals and departures of cars during the day from the park. What is the average flow rate of cars in this park?

   Answer: The park is open for $18:30 - 7:00 = 11.5$ hours. During that time, 10 cars arrive. So the flow rate is 10 cars/11.5 hr = 0.87 car/hr.

LO2-3

3. At rush hour, two people per second step onto an escalator. The escalator takes 30 seconds to bring a person from the bottom to the top. How many people are on the escalator during rush hour?

   Answer: Use Little's Law. We are looking for the inventory of people on the escalator. (The flow unit is a person.) We are given that the flow time on the escalator is

$T = 30$ seconds and the flow rate is $R = 2$ people per second. Thus, $I = R \times T = 2$ people per second $\times$ 30 seconds $= 60$ people.

4. A call center receives 25 callers per minute on average. On average, a caller spends 1 minute on hold and 3.5 minutes talking to a service representative. On average, how many callers are "in" the call center (meaning that they are either on hold or talking to a service representative)?

     Answer: Use Little's Law. The flow unit is a caller. The flow rate is $R = 25$ callers per minute. The flow time is $T = 1 + 3.5 = 4.5$ minutes. The average number of callers in the call center is then $I = R \times T = 25 \times 4.5 = 112.5$ callers.

5. A shipping company operates 10 container ships that can each carry 5000 containers on each journey between ports. They want to be able to load and unload 20,000 containers each week. Assume their ships always travel fully loaded. What is the longest average travel time between ports that allows them to meet their goal of 20,000 containers per week?

     Answer: Use Little's Law. The flow unit is a container. On average, there are $10 \times 5000 = 50,000$ containers on ships traveling between ports. The desired flow rate is $R = 20,000$ containers per week. Rearrange $I = R \times T$ to get $T = I / R$. Thus, the longest average flow time that will accommodate that flow rate is $T = 50,000$ containers/20,000 containers per week $= 2.5$ weeks.

6. A furniture maker purchases 1200 kgs of wood per week to make Adirondack chairs. Each chair uses 25 kgs of wood. At any one time, on average, there are 300 chairs being made at various stages of production. On average, how much time elapses between when the wood arrives for a chair and when the chair is shipped to a customer (i.e., until when production is completed)?

     Answer: Use Little's Law. The flow unit is a chair. The flow rate is $R = 1200$ kgs per week/25 kgs of wood per chair $= 48$ chairs per week. Inventory is $I = 300$ chairs. So flow time is $T = I / R = 300$ chairs/48 chairs per week $= 6.25$ weeks.

Problems and Applications

LO2-1

1. For the purpose of process analysis, which of the following measures would be considered an appropriate flow unit for analyzing the operation of a coffee shop? **Instructions:** You may select more than one answer.
 a. Square footage of the store
 b. Number of employees working each week
 c. Number of hours the store is open each week
 d. Number of customers served each week

2. For the purpose of process analysis, which of the following measures would be considered an appropriate flow unit for analyzing the main operation of a local accounting firm? **Instructions:** You may select more than one answer.
 a. Number of accountants working each week
 b. Number of tax returns completed each week
 c. Number of customers with past-due invoices
 d. Number of reams of paper received from suppliers

3. For the purpose of process analysis, which of the following measures would be considered an appropriate flow unit for analyzing the main operation of a gas station? **Instructions:** You may select more than one answer.
 a. Sales dollars
 b. Number of gasoline pumps
 c. Number of employees working per day
 d. Number of customers served per day

LO2-2

TABLE 2.4 Time Stamps of the 8 Callers Who Called from 8:00 a.m. to 8:20 a.m. to the Reservation Desk of a Ferry Service

Caller	Time in	Time Out
1	8:01	8:05
2	8:02	8:07
3	8:06	8:08
4	8:09	8:12
5	8:10	8:15
6	8:12	8:20
7	8:16	8:19
8	8:17	8:19

4. Based on the data provided in Table 2.4, what is the flow rate of callers from 8:00 a.m. to 8:20 a.m.?

5. Based on the data provided in Table 2.4, what is the flow time of callers from 8:00 a.m. to 8:20 a.m.?

TABLE 2.5 Time Stamps of 10 Customers Who Visited a Local Bank Branch from 9:00 a.m. to 10:00 a.m.

Customer	Time In	Time Out
1	9:01	9:07
2	9:06	9:21
3	9:08	9:20
4	9:14	9:19
5	9:20	9:28
6	9:26	9:33
7	9:31	9:39
8	9:40	9:46
9	9:44	9:59
10	9:53	9:57

6. Based on the data provided in Table 2.5, what is the flow rate of customers from 9:00 a.m. to 10:00 a.m.?

7. Based on the data provided in Table 2.5, what is the flow time of customers from 9:00 a.m. to 10:00 a.m.?

LO2-3

8. A campus deli serves 300 customers over its busy lunch period from 11:30 a.m. to 1:30 p.m. A quick count of the number of customers waiting in line and being served by the sandwich makers shows that an average of 10 customers are in process at any point in time. What is the average amount of time that a customer spends in process?

9. A Rhode Island company produces communion wafers for churches around the country and the world. The little company produces a lot of wafers, several hundred million per year. When in production, the process produces wafers at the rate of 100 per second. During this production process, the wafers must spend 15 minutes passing through a cooling tube. How many wafers does the cooling tube hold, on average, when in production (in other words, don't count the time they are not in production)?

10. One of the chair lifts at a ski resort unloads 1800 skiers per hour at the top of the slope. The ride from the bottom to the top takes 12 minutes. How many skiers are riding on the lift at any given time?

11. Last year, there were 3,400,000 visitors to a national park and, on average, each visitor spent 22 hours in the park. Last year, on average, how many visitors were in the park simultaneously?

12. Patients take a drug for severe acne for 6 months and there are 150,000 new patients each month. How many patients are taking this drug on average at any given time?

13. CodeDeskInc matches programmers with freelance jobs. It has 30 employees who staff its online chat room. It receives, on average, 240 chat requests per hour, and the average chat session takes 5 minutes to complete (i.e., from start to finish). On average, how many chat sessions are active (i.e., started but not completed)?

14. A large-scale bakery is laying out a new production process for its packaged bread, which it sells to several grocery chains. It takes 12 minutes to bake the bread. How large of an oven is required so that the company is able to produce 4200 units of bread per hour (measured in the number of units that can be baked simultaneously)?

15. LaVilla is a village in the Italian Alps. Given its enormous popularity among Swiss, German, Austrian, and Italian skiers, all of its beds are always booked in the winter season and there are, on average, 1200 skiers in the village. On average, skiers stay in LaVilla for 10 days. How many new skiers are arriving, on average, in LaVilla every day?

16. Consider the baggage check-in process of a small airline. Check-in data indicate that from 9 a.m. to 10 a.m., 240 passengers checked in. Moreover, based on counting the number of passengers waiting in line, airport management found that the average number of passengers waiting for check-in was 30. How long did the average passenger have to wait in line?

17. A consulting company must hire 15 new associates per year to replace those who have left the company for other positions or have retired. The company employs 120 associates overall. How long is the average associate employed at the consulting company?

CASE COUGAR MOUNTAIN

Those of you who are skiers or snowboarders know that some resorts have "high-speed" chair lifts. These lifts are called "detachable" because the chair detaches from the main cable just before loading people. Once the passengers are "on board," the chair reattaches to the main cable and "rockets" to the top at a much faster speed than the traditional "fixed-grip" counterparts that remain firmly attached to the main cable.

Cougar Mountain, a medium-sized and profitable ski resort, currently has a traditional fixed-grip quad lift that takes guests from the main lodge at the bottom of the mountain up to the peak. While it prides itself on the quality of its terrain and friendly service, Cougar Mountain's owner, Jessica Powder, is concerned that the traditional (a.k.a., slow) lift will start to deter its established guests from returning year after year. It is time for it to consider replacing the traditional lift with a high-speed quad.

Jessica asked her chief operating officer, Doug Bowl, to collect some data on the current lift and the proposed new one. Once he had the data, listed in Table 2.6, he met with Jessica and Mark Ketting, who is responsible for Cougar's sales and advertising.

Mark immediately started the conversation by saying, "Customers are going to love that their ride time will be cut in half by the new lift. But there must be a mistake in Doug's data. If the new lift doubles the speed at which skiers travel up the mountain, then it must be that it can unload more skiers at the top at a faster rate! Shouldn't the unloading capacity double?" Doug responded, "I think the table is correct because from what I have observed, people are not able to load onto a detachable lift any faster than on a fixed-grip lift." Jessica jumped in, "Doug, assuming you are right, and I am not sure you are, does that mean the only difference between a fixed-grip and a detachable lift is that one moves faster than the other?"

© Glowimages/Getty Images/RF

1. Who do you think is correct, Mark (the unload capacity should be twice as high) or Doug (the two lifts have the same capacity)?

2. Can you give a response to Jessica—is there any other difference between the two lifts?

TABLE 2.6 Performance Data for the Current Fixed-Grip Quad Lift and a Proposed Detachable Quad Lift at Cougar Mountain

	Fixed-Grip	Detachable
Length of lift (meters)	700	700
Passengers per chair	4	4
Time from bottom to top (sec)	250	125
Unloading capacity (skiers per hour)	2400	2400

Process Analysis

3

Introduction

Imagine you owned a restaurant and would be in charge of its daily operations. How would you know, on any given day, that your restaurant operates well? If you were an accountant, you probably would track the revenues and the costs of the restaurant. As long as revenues exceed costs, you might be content and leave the operations of the restaurant to the people working therein. As an operations expert, however, we want you to take a different perspective. Yes, money clearly matters and we want you to make a nice profit. But to make a profit day in and day out, to please your customers, and to secure your success in an environment where you compete with other restaurants, we argue that this requires looking inside the "black box" of the restaurant. Beyond keeping track of revenues and costs, what are some questions you would ask about the restaurant's operation? They might include the following:

- How many customers does the restaurant serve each day? And what keeps the restaurant from serving more customers?

© Andersen Ross/Digital Vision/Getty Images/RF

- How busy are those working in the restaurant?
- How long does it take the restaurant to serve a given number of customers?

Knowing the answers to these questions will help you better manage the restaurant. If you can serve more customers, you can make more revenue. If your staff is busy all day, you might need to hire a new employee, but if your staff spend half of their day playing Angry Birds, chances are you might be able to reduce your expenses on labor. And if it takes you three hours to serve a group of 10 customers, you might be at risk of losing these customers to the restaurant next door.

3.1 How to Draw a Process Flow Diagram

Process analysis, the topic of this chapter, provides a rigorous framework for understanding the detailed operations of a business, including the answers to the questions raised in the previous section. Process analysis opens the black box of the operations and peeks inside by identifying and analyzing all the activities involved in serving one unit of demand, or, put differently, in providing one unit of supply. In this chapter, you will learn how to perform a process analysis. Once you have analyzed the process, you can improve it: You can serve more customers, you can find the right number of employees to work for you, and you can get your customers what they want in less time. In short, you can make your process better.

© Andrew Resek/The McGraw-Hill Education/RF

Process analysis is a framework that can be used for everyone running a business. It can be used by the one who owns the restaurant, by those managing the restaurant, by those working in the restaurant, or by those consulting to the restaurant. In smaller restaurants, this is the responsibility of the owner. In bigger restaurants or restaurant chains, many job positions exist that include the term "operations" in it (such as Vice President of Operations, Chief Operating Officer, Director of Operations, Operations Expert, etc.). But understanding the operations of a business, we argue, is important to everybody. After all, wouldn't everybody in the business have an interest in making it better?

To state the obvious, this book and this chapter are not just about restaurants. At the risk of offending the (future) doctors and nurses in our readership, we propose that the framework of process analysis is just as valuable in a hospital as it is in a restaurant. Serving more patients, making sure that we have the right number of doctors and nurses available, and avoiding long patient wait times—in other words, to improve health care operations requires process analysis. So, for restaurants, hospitals, or any other business, the purpose of process analysis is to make the business better.

The best way to begin any analysis of an operation is by drawing a **process flow diagram**. A process flow diagram is a graphical way to describe the process. It will help us structure the information we collect as we try to improve our understanding of the process.

We will illustrate this new material using the case of a Subway restaurant. We feel that a restaurant provides a good example, because we assume that most of you have been in restaurants, maybe even a Subway restaurant. This way, you can connect the academic content with the reality of daily life.

At the aggregate level, the restaurant consists of a number of customers, a set of employees (at Subway, oftentimes called "sandwich artists," though we will label them as employees), some work stations, and a cash register.

LO3-1 Draw a process flow diagram.

Process analysis A rigorous framework for understanding the detailed operations of a business. Among other things, the process analysis determines how many flow units can be processed per unit of time (the process capacity) and how busy the resources of the process are (utilization).

Process flow diagram A graphical way to describe the process. It uses boxes to depict resources, arrows to depict flows, and triangles to depict inventory location.

TABLE 3.1   Recipe for a Sandwich (Including Handling of a Customer)

Activity
Greet customer
Take order
Get bread
Cut bread
Add meat
Add cheese
Add onions
Add lettuce
Add tomatoes
Add cucumbers
Add pickles
Add green peppers
Add black olives
Add hot peppers
Place condiments
Wrap and bag
Offer fresh value meal
Offer cookies
Ring up bill on register

Just as you have a recipe when you prepare a meal, Subway has a recipe for its sandwiches. The recipe for a sandwich provides you with detailed instructions on how to make the sandwich. Table 3.1 provides you with instructions on how to prepare a sandwich. We refer to the steps shown in the table as **activities.** Some of the activities in Table 3.1 directly relate to making a sandwich (e.g., cutting the bread). But Table 3.1 also includes activities that need to happen when interacting with customers in a restaurant, from greeting the customer to ringing up the customer at the cash register.

As useful as a recipe is for the purpose of cooking, it does not offer you any information about the operations of the restaurant. Will customers have to wait? Will the restaurant serve enough customers to pay the rent and wages? The only way we can find out is to look at the process of serving the customer. Our customer is the unit of analysis—we refer to her or him as our flow unit. We also label the number of customers in the process as inventory.

If we arrive at a busy time, say during lunch hour, the first thing we notice is a line of waiting customers. When we draw a process flow diagram, we depict flow units waiting in the process without being worked on as a triangle. It is common to refer to these waiting flow units as a **buffer inventory.**

Once a customer reaches the front of the line, he or she is greeted by the first employee. That employee is in charge of taking the customer's order and starting the preparation of the sandwich. We refer to the employee as a resource. **Resources** help the flow units move from being a unit of input to becoming a unit of output.

We use directional arrows in a process flow diagram to capture the **flow unit's** journey from input to output. In our case, the flow unit has just moved from the waiting line (inventory) to the first resource. Resources are shown as rectangular boxes in the process flow

Resource A group of people and/or equipment that transforms inputs into outputs.

Flow unit The unit of analysis that we consider in a process analysis; for example, patients in a hospital, scooters in a kick-scooter plant, and calls in a call center.

Figure 3.1

Arrows for flow, triangles for inventory, and boxes for activities

diagram. So, by now, our process flow diagram consists of a triangle, an arrow, and a box (see Figure 3.1).

After the first employee has completed her work, the second employee takes over to now put the vegetables onto the sandwich (onions, lettuce, tomatoes, etc.) and then finishes the sandwich. She then puts it into a bag. The second employee is in charge of a different set of activities for the flow unit, which is why we create a second box for her with an arrow going from the first box to the second box. Depending on how fast employee 1 works relative to employee 2, we might see a line forming between the two stations, which is, you guessed correctly, inventory. So, we put a triangle between employee 1 and employee 2 to capture this in the process flow diagram.

Following employee 2, employee 3 is in charge of offering the customers a dessert and ringing up the customer. Once again, we add a box to the process flow diagram, along with two more arrows and a triangle between employee 2 and 3. Now the customer has a sandwich and so we finish the process flow diagram. Figure 3.2 shows the complete diagram.

The process flow diagram outlines a directional flow in the process. With this in mind, we refer to the beginning of the flow as the **upstream** of the process and the end of the process as the **downstream**. We further observe that a resource upstream from another resource serves half-finished sandwiches to the resource downstream. In other words, we can think about station 2 being the customer of station 1.

The process flow diagram alone does not tell you anything about the flow rate in the process (the number of customers that go through the restaurant); however, it captures some useful information and will be the starting point for our more quantitative analysis in a moment. But before we get to the numbers, consider three alternative process flow diagrams, all summarized in Figure 3.3(a)–(d):

- Figure 3.3(a) shows three parallel processes, each with its own dedicated waiting line. This is somewhat similar to a supermarket checkout as far as the waiting line is concerned (three separate triangles). Note that a flow unit will only visit one single box in this process flow diagram. This suggests that that resource will be in charge of ALL the activities provided to the customers, going all the way from taking the order to ringing up the customer. In other words, rather than dividing up the work and each resource specializing in a subset of the activities, this process flow diagram suggests that each customer is served by only one employee.

- Figure 3.3(b) shows three parallel resources but a common waiting line. This is somewhat similar to how most airlines have you check in your luggage (ignoring priority lines and curbside check-in). Whoever is at the front of the line will be served by the next available resource.

- Finally, Figure 3.3(c) shows a three-step process similar to our first process flow diagram (Figure 3.2), except that there is no triangle at the beginning of the flow.

Upstream The parts of the process that are at the beginning of the process flow.

Downstream The parts of the process that are at the end of the process flow.

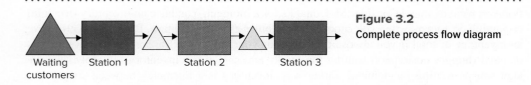

Figure 3.2

Complete process flow diagram

Figure 3.3
Alternative process flow diagrams

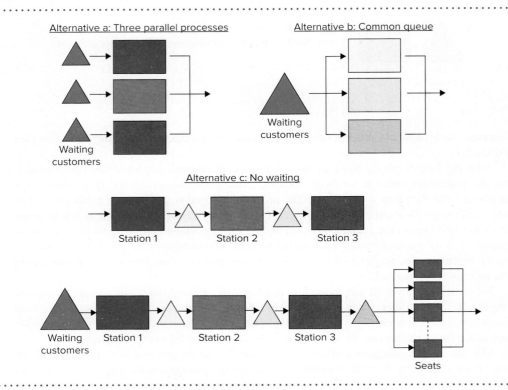

This means that there never is any inventory (waiting line) in this process. For example, such a situation might represent a drive-through restaurant where there is no place for waiting cars. Either a customer gets lucky and there is room at the first station or there is not (in which case the customer has to continue her journey on the road and the flow unit gets lost).

- If we also want to capture what happens to the customer after she has paid, we need to add the seats in the restaurant as an additional resource. We would extend the process flow diagram to what is shown in Figure 3.3(d). One might argue that the customers eating their sandwich in the restaurant are just another form of inventory and hence choose a triangle over a box in the process flow diagram. We chose a box here because we feel that providing eating space is part of the Subway service. One should use triangles only for those parts of the customer journey that, had the customer missed these parts, he or she would still be an equally happy customer flowing out of the process.

Before we can do a process analysis, we must first make sure we fully understand the process flow. This is why drawing a process flow diagram should always be the first thing you do in a process analysis. It is worth emphasizing that there are many process flows happening in a Subway restaurant and we could have picked a different flow unit than the customer. For example, we could analyze the flow of loaves of bread or the flow of cheese through the restaurant. We could even model the flow of employees and capture the process from recruitment to hiring to working. With different flow units, we would have obtained different process flow diagrams.

Process flow diagrams are thus very flexible and it is up to you which aspects of the operation you want to study. Consider McDonald's for a moment. You have an inventory (triangle) of waiting customers when you choose the customer as your flow unit. But you can also have an inventory of food if you choose the burger as your flow unit. So, sometimes inventory is demand (hungry customers) waiting for supply and sometimes inventory is supply (burgers kept warm) waiting for demand. Either way, inventory is a mismatch between supply and demand, and so we want to make sure we understand why it exists.

Check Your Understanding 3.1

© David R. Frazier/David R. Frazier
Photolibrary/RF

Question: Airport security consists of the steps (1) verifying ID and boarding pass, (2) searching the passenger for metal objects using some form of a scanner or metal detector, and (3) running the carry-on luggage through an X-ray machine. There is a long line of passengers before the first step, but sometimes lines also build up at steps 2 and 3. Steps 2 and 3 are carried out in parallel; that is, customers go through the metal detector while their luggage is in the X-ray machine. Draw a process flow diagram of this process.

Answer: See Figure 3.4.

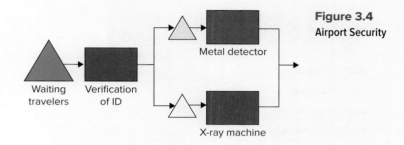

Figure 3.4
Airport Security

In the remainder of this chapter, we focus on the flow unit being the customer and analyze three alternative process flow diagrams. The first is a single employee serving the customer. Second, we will look at three employees working in parallel, as was shown in Figure 3.3(a). And third, we will look at the process flow of three (specialized) employees making sandwiches, as was shown in Figure 3.2.

3.2 Capacity for a One-Step Process

How do you make a sandwich? You follow the process recipe as was previously shown in Figure 3.3. How do you make 100 sandwiches? You move from focusing on the product (the sandwich) to focusing on the process. Part of this process focus is that you now want to figure out how you can organize your process flow—you have to choose between the various process flow diagrams discussed in the previous section. For now, assume that we follow a one-step process where one employee is in charge of completing the entire customer order.

There are many activities involved in completing one customer order, starting with "Greet the customer" and ending with "Ring on register." Table 3.2 shows these activities along with how long each activity takes per customer. Across all activities, it takes our employee 120 seconds per customer. We refer to this time as the **processing time**. The processing time of a resource is how long that particular resource takes to complete one flow unit. Table 3.3 shows examples of processing times from a range of operational settings.

For now, we will be very careful with the units, which in this case are [seconds/customer]. We encourage you to be equally concise—somewhat similar to what you most likely did in physics during high school. In physics, meters are different from meters per second. In the same way, in operations management, seconds are different from seconds per customer.

In the following calculations, we will assume that the processing times are exactly as shown in Table 3.2. This is a strong assumption. Not everybody wants hot peppers on his or her sandwich and so, sometimes, some of the activities might not be applicable. One way of interpreting the data in Table 3.2 is that it captures the average across many customers. For example, imagine it takes 10 seconds per customer to place the hot peppers on the sandwich, but only 2 out of 10 customers request hot peppers. This way, you get 2 seconds per customer, on average. You can also imagine that employees are sometimes faster and sometimes slower—they

LO3-2 Determine the capacity for a one-step process.

Processing time The time it takes a resource to complete one flow unit.

TABLE 3.2 Activity Times of a Sandwich, Leading to a 120-Second-per-Customer Processing Time

Activity	Activity Time [sec/customer]
Greet customer	4
Take order	5
Get bread	4
Cut bread	3
Add meat	12
Add cheese	9
Add onions	3
Add lettuce	3
Add tomatoes	4
Add cucumbers	5
Add pickles	4
Add green peppers	4
Add black olives	3
Add hot peppers	2
Place condiments	5
Wrap and bag	13
Offer fresh value meal	3
Offer cookies	14
Ring up bill on register	20
Total	**120**

TABLE 3.3 Typical Processing Times

Activity	Processing Time
Cardiac surgery (double-bypass procedure)	4 hours/patient
Installation of a rearview mirror in automotive assembly	50 seconds/vehicle
Underwriting a simple small business loan	40 minutes/loan
Simple transaction call in a bank's call center	5 minutes/transaction
Primary care encounter	15 minutes/patient

are human beings, not robots. Again, thinking in terms of averages will help. We will spend a great amount of time later in the book relaxing this assumption and capturing models of flow with variability. But, for now, this assumption will make our lives a little easier.

Next, we define the **capacity** of our single resource (the employee) as:

$$\text{Capacity} = \frac{1}{\text{Processing time}}$$

$$= \frac{1}{120} \text{ customer/second}$$

$$= 0.008333 \text{ customer/second}$$

Capacity The maximum number of flow units that can flow through that resource per unit of time.

Check Your Understanding 3.2

Question: It takes a color printer 10 seconds to print a large poster. What is the capacity of the printer expressed in posters per hour?

Answer: The capacity of the printer is $\frac{1}{10}$ poster/second, which is 360 posters per hour.

Question: A call center has one operator who answers incoming calls. It takes the operator 6 minutes to answer one call. What is the capacity of the call center expressed in calls per hour?

Answer: The capacity of the call center is $\frac{1}{6}$ calls/minute = 10 calls/hour.

© Digital Stock/Royalty-Free/Corbis/RF

It is arguably somewhat difficult to imagine what 0.008333 of a customer looks like—but keep in mind that one second is also a very short moment of time. We can change units:

$$\text{Capacity} = 0.008333 \, \frac{\text{customer}}{\text{second}} \times 60 \, \frac{\text{seconds}}{\text{minute}}$$

$$= 0.5 \, \frac{\text{customer}}{\text{minute}} \times 60 \, \frac{\text{minutes}}{\text{hour}} = 30 \, \frac{\text{customers}}{\text{hour}}$$

So we get a capacity of 0.008333 customer/second, or 0.5 customer/minute, or 30 customers/hour—all three mean exactly the same thing. The capacity of a resource determines the maximum number of flow units that can flow through that resource per unit of time.

Because our one lone employee is the only resource in the process, we say that the capacity of the process—that is, the **process capacity**—is also 30 customers/hour. The process capacity determines the maximum flow rate a process can provide per unit of time. It thus determines the maximum supply of the process.

Process capacity The maximum flow rate a process can provide per unit of time. This determines the maximum supply of the process. The process capacity is the smallest capacity of all resources in the process.

3.3 How to Compute Flow Rate, Utilization, and Cycle Time

Now, assume we have a **demand rate** of

$$\text{Demand} = 40 \, \frac{\text{units}}{\text{hour}}$$

The demand rate is the number of flow units that customers want per unit of time. So 40 customers want a sandwich each hour, but we only have capacity to make 30. We next define the flow rate as:

$$\text{Flow rate} = \text{Minimum \{Demand, Process capacity\}}$$

$$= \text{Minimum} \left\{ 40 \, \frac{\text{customers}}{\text{hour}}, 30 \, \frac{\text{customers}}{\text{hour}} \right\} = 30 \, \frac{\text{customers}}{\text{hour}}$$

In this case, the factor limiting the flow rate is the process capacity. For that reason, we call such a situation in which demand exceeds supply and the flow rate is equal to process capacity as **capacity-constrained**. If the process capacity exceeds demand, the flow rate will be equal to the demand rate and so we refer to the process as **demand-constrained**. Note that, instead of flow rate, you often will hear the term **throughput**. From our perspective, the terms *flow rate* and *throughput* are identical.

Demand rate The number of flow units that customers want per unit of time.

Capacity-constrained The case in which demand exceeds supply and the flow rate is equal to process capacity.

Demand-constrained The case in which process capacity exceeds demand and thus the flow rate is equal to the demand rate.

Throughput A synonym for flow rate, the number of flow units flowing through the process per unit of time.

LO3-3 Determine the flow rate,
the utilization, and the cycle time
of a process.

Next, we define the **utilization** of a process as the ratio between the flow rate (how fast the process is currently operating) and the process capacity (capturing how fast the process could be operating if there was sufficient demand). So,

$$\text{Utilization} = \frac{\text{Flow rate}}{\text{Capacity}} = \frac{30}{30} = 1$$

We can define the utilization at the level of an individual resource or at the level of the entire process. In this case, it does not make a difference because the only resource in this process is our one employee.

Finally, we define the **cycle time** in a process as

$$\text{Cycle time} = \frac{1}{\text{Flow rate}} = 0.0333\,\frac{\text{hour}}{\text{customer}} = 120\,\frac{\text{seconds}}{\text{customer}}$$

The cycle time measures the time between ringing up two consecutive customers. Imagine this store using a nice, old cash register that makes a loud "Riiinnnggg" every time the cash register is opened. So, cycle time measures the time between two such sounds—music to our ears because we only make money when the register rings.

Now, assume demand would be 20 units/hour. In this case, the flow rate (the minimum between demand and capacity) would be 20 units/hour and the process is now demand-constrained. Also, the utilization of the process goes down to

$$\text{Utilization} = \frac{\text{Flow rate}}{\text{Capacity}} = \frac{20}{30} = 0.6667$$

In contrast, the cycle time goes up to

$$\text{Cycle time} = \frac{1}{\text{Flow rate}} = 0.05\,\frac{\text{hour}}{\text{customer}} = 180\,\frac{\text{seconds}}{\text{customer}}$$

That nice sound of the cash register that indicates we just got money from another customer now does not appear every 120 seconds, but every 180 seconds. So the cycle time has increased, indicating that the flow moves more slowly.

Now, imagine demand goes up to 100 customers per hour. If we continue to rely on our one-employee process with a process capacity of 30 customers per hour, we would be 70 customers per hour short. So, instead of working with one employee, assume we would now work with three. Moreover, for now, assume that these three employees operate three parallel work stations such as that depicted in Figure 3.5. Note that the figure shows two process flow diagrams. To the left, we show three parallel resources fed from a common inventory of waiting customers. To the right, we show one resource that is staffed with three employees (let m denote the number of multiple, parallel workers or machines in a resource). These process flow diagrams are equivalent; the right one is simply an abbreviation of the left one. All our calculations will be the same for these two process flow diagrams.

Utilization The ratio between the
flow rate (how fast the process
is currently operating) and the
process capacity (capturing
how fast the process could be
operating if there was sufficient
demand). Note that utilization
can be defined at the level of an
individual resource or at the level
of the entire process.

Cycle time The time between
completing two consecutive flow
units.

Figure 3.5
Three parallel resources

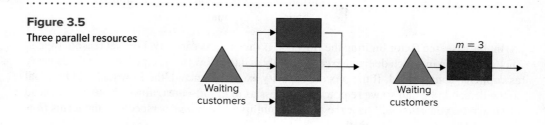

Now that we have three employees, it is intuitive that we have (three times) more capacity than with one employee. More formally, define the capacity of a resource with m (for multiple) employees staffing that resource as

$$\text{Capacity} = \frac{m}{\text{Processing time}} = \frac{3}{120 \text{ seconds/customer}}$$

$$= 0.025 \text{ customer per second}$$

$$= 90 \text{ customers per hour}$$

With more demand and more capacity, our flow rate would increase to

$$\text{Flow rate} = \text{Minimum \{Demand, Process capacity\}}$$

$$= \text{Minimum \{100, 90\}}$$

$$= 90 \text{ customers/hour}$$

We can also compute our utilization as

$$\text{Utilization} = \frac{\text{Flow rate}}{\text{Capacity}} = \frac{90}{90} = 1$$

Our cycle time thus goes down to

$$\text{Cycle time} = \frac{1}{\text{Flow rate}} = 0.0111 \frac{\text{hour}}{\text{customer}} = 40 \frac{\text{seconds}}{\text{customer}}$$

Check Your Understanding 3.3

Question: A primary care doctor has the capacity to see 16 patients per day. The demand rate is, however, only 12 patients per day. (a) What is the flow rate? (b) What is the utilization of the doctor? (c) What is the cycle time, assuming a 10-hour workday?

Answer: We compute the flow rate as the minimum of demand and process capacity:

$$\text{Flow rate} = \text{Minimum \{Demand, Process capacity\}}$$
$$= \text{Minimum \{12, 16\}}$$
$$= 12 \frac{\text{patients}}{\text{day}}$$

The utilization is the ratio between flow rate and capacity:

$$\text{Utilization} = \frac{\text{Flow rate}}{\text{Capacity}} = \frac{12}{16} = 75\%$$

The cycle time is 1/Flow rate. Over the course of the 10-hour workday, we serve 12 patients. So the cycle time is

$$\text{Cycle time} = \frac{1}{\text{Flow rate}} = \frac{1}{12} \text{ day/patient}$$

This can be expressed as:

$$\text{Cycle time} = \frac{1}{12} \text{ day/patient} \times 10 \frac{\text{hours}}{\text{day}} = \frac{10}{12} \text{ hour/patient}$$

Many people, even those experienced in operations, confuse the terms *cycle time* and *lead time*. We define the **cycle time** as 1/Flow rate. Consequently, cycle time is expressed in units of time per unit.

Lead time, in contrast, is the time between a customer placing his or her order and that order being filled. Lead time is thus what we previously defined as flow time, the time a flow unit (a customer order) takes to get through the process. Lead time (and flow time) are expressed in units of time.

Because cycle time is driven by flow rate and lead time is the same as flow time, you may notice that cycle time and lead time are related by Little's Law. Because $I = R \times T$, and Cycle time $= 1/R$ (thus $R = 1/$Cycle time), we get $I \times$ Cycle time $=$ Flow time.

Think about the following example. You come to a walk-in clinic and there are 10 patients (including you) in the clinic to see the doctor. After some observation, you notice that the doctor works on a 15-minute cycle (i.e., calls in and sends out one patient every 15 minutes). How long will you be in the clinic? The answer is simply Flow time = Inventory × Cycle time = 10 patients × 15 minutes/patient = 150 minutes.

Be aware of these differences in terminology and don't be afraid to ask. Operations vocabulary is used very differently across industries and what might be called lead time in one industry is cycle time in the other. Just clarifying the measurement units (customers versus customers per hour; minutes versus minutes per unit) typically is enough to avoid misunderstandings. Thus, always be careful with the units that you use.

Lead time The time between when an order is placed and when it is filled. Process lead time is frequently used as an alternative term for flow time.

3.4 How to Analyze a Multistep Process and Locate the Bottleneck

Instead of having our three employees each serve a customer from beginning to end (i.e., carry out all the activities from greeting the customer to ringing out the customer at the cash register), we can also imagine the alternative process flow pattern that we discussed at the beginning of this chapter: three employees serving the customer, with the first employee being in charge of all activities up to (and including) putting the cheese on the sandwich, the second employee doing all activities from putting the onions onto the sandwich to bagging the sandwich, and the third employee offering cookies and the value meal as well as ringing up the customer. Assume, for the sake of argument, that the demand rate would remain constant at 100 customers per hour.

What will be the flow rate of this process? Three employees, with the same demand—one might argue that the flow rate will remain unchanged. However, things are slightly more complicated than this now that we have moved from one resource staffed by three employees to three resources staffed with one employee each. Rather than having one processing time of 120 seconds/customer, we now have three processing times. More specifically, the processing times are

$$\text{Processing time}(1) = 37 \frac{\text{seconds}}{\text{customer}}$$

$$\text{Processing time}(2) = 46 \frac{\text{seconds}}{\text{customer}}$$

$$\text{Processing time}(3) = 37 \frac{\text{seconds}}{\text{customer}}$$

Just as before, we can compute the capacity for each of the three resources as

$$\text{Capacity} = \frac{1}{\text{Processing time}}$$

Given that we now have one employee again for each of the three resources, we get:

$$\text{Capacity}(1) = \frac{1}{\text{Processing time}(1)} = \frac{1}{37} = 0.027 \text{ customer per second}$$

$$= 97.3 \text{ customers per hour}$$

$$\text{Capacity(2)} = \frac{1}{\text{Processing time(2)}} = \frac{1}{46} = 0.022 \text{ customer per second}$$

$$= 78.3 \text{ customers per hour}$$

$$\text{Capacity(3)} = \frac{1}{\text{Processing time(3)}} = \frac{1}{37} = 0.027 \text{ customer per second}$$

$$= 97.3 \text{ customers per hour}$$

Note that in a process with multiple resources (a process flow with multiple boxes that are not in parallel), each resource has its own capacity. To get from the resource's capacity to the overall capacity of the process—that is, to compute the process capacity—we define

$$\text{Process capacity} = \text{Min}\{\text{Capacity}(i)\} = 78.3 \text{ customers per hour}$$

So we find the process capacity by looking for the smallest capacity in the process. After all, a chain is only as strong as its weakest link. We define this weakest link, the resource with the lowest capacity, as the **bottleneck** of the process. It is not possible to get more customers through the process than what we have capacity for at the bottleneck.

Understanding the location of the bottleneck is critical for improving a process. Take the example of airport security. Typically, airport security consists of the steps (1) verifying ID and boarding pass, (2) searching the passenger for metal objects using some form of a scanner or metal detector, and (3) running the carry-on luggage through an X-ray machine. Most of us associate airport security with long waiting times and, all too often, a long queue greets us when we arrive at the airport—a line of passengers who wait before the first step.

So is the first step (verifying ID) the bottleneck? It certainly looks like it. But recall our definition of the bottleneck. It does not matter if a resource comes first or last; what matters is the capacity of the resource. In most airports we have visited, it is step 3 (X-raying the luggage) that slows down the process, even though the inventory (waiting passengers) are further upstream. The airport security example also helps to illustrate another point. Oftentimes, steps 2 and 3 are carried out in parallel. Does this increase the capacity of the process? The answer is a clear NO. The capacity of the security checkpoint is determined by the bottleneck and that is the smallest capacity of the three resources. Working in parallel might reduce the flow time, but it does not increase capacity.

Figure 3.6 compares the processing times visually. It is clear from the comparison that employee 2 is the bottleneck—she has the most work to do. In general, however, we caution you to jump from the processing times to identifying the bottleneck. We could have a process in which two employees would be staffing the second resource. In this case, the capacity of the second resource would be 2/46 customers/second, which is more than the capacity of either resource 1 or 3, even though resource 2 has the longest processing time.

But what is flow rate? As before, when finding the flow rate, we need to look at the minimum of demand and capacity and so

$$\text{Flow rate} = \text{Minimum }\{\text{Demand, Process capacity}\}$$

$$= \text{Minimum }\{100, 78.3\} = 78.3 \frac{\text{customers}}{\text{hour}}$$

In this case, we are constrained by the (bottleneck) capacity, not by demand. So it is intuitive that the bottleneck will be working "all out," which is confirmed by the following computations of utilization:

$$\text{Utilization(1)} = \frac{\text{Flow rate}}{\text{Capacity(1)}} = \frac{78.3}{97.3} = 0.804$$

$$\text{Utilization(2)} = \frac{\text{Flow rate}}{\text{Capacity(2)}} = \frac{78.3}{78.3} = 1$$

$$\text{Utilization(3)} = \frac{\text{Flow rate}}{\text{Capacity(3)}} = \frac{78.3}{97.3} = 0.804$$

LO3-4 Find the bottleneck of a multistep process and determine its capacity.

Bottleneck Resource with the lowest capacity in a process.

Figure 3.6
Comparison of processing times

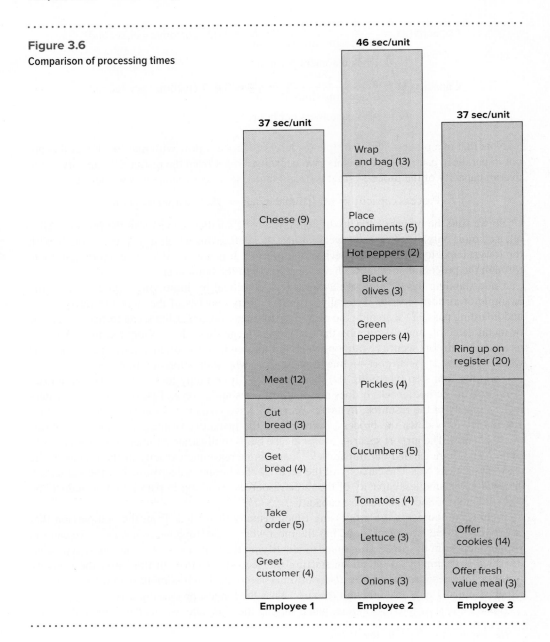

Note that the nonbottleneck resources have slack capacity—that is, they have utilization levels that are strictly less than 100 percent—while the bottleneck has a utilization of 100 percent. In general, a resource might have a utilization of less than 100 percent for one of two reasons:

- A nonbottleneck resource has, by definition, some extra capacity relative to the bottleneck.

- In the case of a demand-constrained process, even the bottleneck would not be working at 100 percent.

If a process is constrained by demand, we might think of demand being the bottleneck. In that case, one might argue that no single resource in the process should be called the bottleneck. However, we find it easier to always refer to the resource with the lowest capacity as the bottleneck, even in a process that is demand-constrained. So every process has a bottleneck, even if the capacity constraint created by the bottleneck might not be binding.

The calculations for the cycle time of the process also remain unchanged. So we get:

$$\text{Cycle time} = \frac{1}{\text{Flow rate}} = 0.012778\,\frac{\text{hour}}{\text{customer}} = 46\,\frac{\text{seconds}}{\text{customer}}$$

Congratulations, this completes your first process analysis. Figure 3.7 summarizes these calculations.

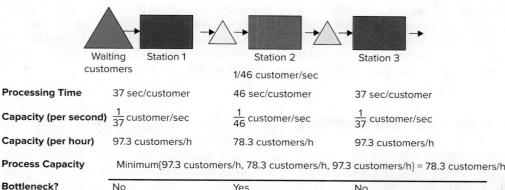

	Station 1	Station 2	Station 3
	Waiting customers	1/46 customer/sec	
Processing Time	37 sec/customer	46 sec/customer	37 sec/customer
Capacity (per second)	$\frac{1}{37}$ customer/sec	$\frac{1}{46}$ customer/sec	$\frac{1}{37}$ customer/sec
Capacity (per hour)	97.3 customers/h	78.3 customers/h	97.3 customers/h
Process Capacity	Minimum{97.3 customers/h, 78.3 customers/h, 97.3 customers/h} = 78.3 customers/h		
Bottleneck?	No	Yes	No
Flow Rate	Minimum{78.3 customers/h, Demand} = 78.3 customers/h		
Utilization	78.3/97.3 = 80.4%	78.3/97.3 = 100%	78.3/97.3 = 80.4%
Cycle Time	$\frac{1}{1/46\ \text{customer/sec}} = 46$ sec/customer		

Figure 3.7
Summary of key calculations

Check Your Understanding 3.4

Question: Consider again the example of the three-step airport security. The first step, verifying ID and boarding pass, takes 30 seconds per passenger. The second step, searching the passenger for metal objects using a metal detector, takes 10 seconds per passenger. The third step, running the carry-on luggage through an X-ray machine, takes 60 seconds per passenger. Assume that there are many customers waiting in the process.

(a) Which resource is the bottleneck? **(b)** What is the capacity of the process? **(c)** What is the flow rate? **(d)** What is the utilization of the metal detector? **(e)** What is the cycle time?

Answer: Note, first of all, that none of the calculations is affected by the fact that the metal detector works in parallel with the X-ray machine for the luggage.

© Ryan McVay/Photodisc/Getty Images/RF

We first find the capacity levels as:

$\text{Capacity(ID)} = \frac{1}{30}$ passenger/second; $\text{Capacity(Metal detector)} = \frac{1}{10}$ passenger/second; $\text{Capacity(X-ray)} = \frac{1}{60}$ passenger/second. The lowest capacity is thus at the X-ray machine, which makes the X-ray machine the bottleneck and $\frac{1}{60}$ passenger/second the process capacity.

The flow rate is the minimum of demand and capacity; because many customers are waiting, the process is capacity-constrained and the flow rate is given by the process capacity—that is, $\frac{1}{60}$ passenger/second or 1 passenger per minute.

The utilization of the metal detector is

$$\text{Utilization} = \frac{\text{Flow rate}}{\text{Capacity}} = \frac{1/60}{1/10} = \frac{10}{60} = 0.1666$$

The cycle time of the process is $\frac{1}{\text{Flow rate}} = 60\,\frac{\text{seconds}}{\text{customer}}$.

Note that the process flow with three workers only handling a part of the customer order is slower than the previously analyzed process of three parallel employees. We see this in the lower process capacity (78.3 customers/hour now versus previously 90 customers/hour). But why is this the case? Wouldn't we expect this process, in which each worker specializes on only a few activities, to have a *higher* capacity?

The key advantage of the parallel stations in which each employee would carry out all activities was one of utilization. Assuming sufficient demand, we had all three employees utilized 100 percent. In contrast, we saw that in the specialized process flow, only one out of three employees (employee 2, the bottleneck) was fully utilized. The other employees had capacity that was left unutilized. However, we had made the assumption that the time to carry out a particular activity (say, "greet the customer") would be the same in both the case of one employee doing all the work and the case in which workers specialize.

3.5 The Time to Produce a Certain Quantity

© Comstock/PictureQuest/RF

LO3-5 Determine how long it takes to produce a certain order quantity.

Imagine our Subway restaurant received a sudden surge in demand. A school bus would stop and 20 hungry students would rush into the restaurant, each demanding a sandwich. How long would it take to complete that demand? There are two cases that our bus of hungry students might face: They arrive at a restaurant that currently is empty or they arrive at a restaurant that is currently serving other customers (with potentially an inventory of waiting customers). For this section, assume that the restaurant is empty when the 20 students arrive.

First, let's consider a Subway restaurant that is staffed by one single employee. As discussed before, the processing time in the single-employee case would be 120 seconds/customer and we would have a capacity of 0.5 customer per minute.

Given the sudden surge in demand, the restaurant is going to be supply constrained and the flow rate is dictated by the process capacity:

$$\text{Flow rate} = \text{Min}\{\text{Demand, Capacity}\} = \frac{1}{120}\text{customer/second} = 0.5\frac{\text{customer}}{\text{minute}}$$

We can also calculate the process's cycle time for the single-employee case:

$$\text{Cycle time} = \frac{1}{\text{Flow rate}} = 120\frac{\text{seconds}}{\text{customer}}$$

We then define the time to produce 20 sandwiches as simply

$$\text{Time to make 20 units} = \text{Cycle time} \times 20 \text{ customers}$$

$$= 120\frac{\text{seconds}}{\text{customer}} \times 20 \text{ customers}$$

$$= 2,400 \text{ seconds}$$

Or, more generally, we write the **time to make Q units** as:

$$\text{Time to make } Q \text{ units} = \text{Cycle time} \times Q$$

Next, consider the case in which we have three employees available to make sandwiches and we want to use the three-step process we had analyzed previously (see Figure 3.7).

Recall that we determined that station 2 was the bottleneck, with a capacity of $\frac{1}{46}$ customer/second, or 78.3 customers/hour, as the process capacity and 46 seconds/customer as the cycle time.

Again, we will attempt to move as many sandwiches through the system as possible. Therefore, we are capacity-constrained and the flow rate of the process is determined by the capacity of the bottleneck. We will operate on the 46 second/customer cycle time derived earlier. A naïve analysis suggests that

$$\text{Time to make 20 units} = \text{Cycle time} \times 20 \text{ customers}$$

$$= 46 \frac{\text{seconds}}{\text{customer}} \times 20 \text{ customers}$$

$$= 920 \text{ seconds}$$

However, this analysis is not 100 percent accurate. The reason for this is that these calculations implicitly assume that each of the workers would be able to start working immediately. In a process flow with one step, nothing holds the associated employee back from starting work. However, in the case of three employees, the third employee will remain unutilized until the sandwich finally arrives at her station. We therefore need to adjust our calculations for the time it takes the first unit to flow through the empty process.

The current system is called a **worker-paced** line because each worker is free to work at his or her own pace: if the first worker finishes before the next worker is ready to accept the sandwich (the customer), then the first worker puts the completed work in the inventory between them. This is why we included the triangles between process steps in the process flow diagram.

The first customer order will be served once all three employees have done their work, which will take 37 seconds + 46 seconds + 37 seconds. The calculations would change if steps in the process are carried out in parallel; for example, if all three steps could be carried out in parallel, the time it would take to serve the first customer would be driven by the longest processing time. So, working in parallel helps with getting the first customer through the process, but, as we discussed before, it does not alter the capacity and flow calculations.

An alternative to the worker-paced process is a **machine-paced** process, as depicted in Figure 3.8. In a machine-paced process, all steps are connected through a conveyor belt and all of the steps must work at the same rate even if some of them have more capacity than others. Except for sushi bars, we have not seen restaurants use a machine-paced line. However, they are common in assembly operations, such as the production of electronic devices or automotive vehicles.

Imagine, for example, an automotive plant with 300 assembly stations. In such settings, the process flow diagram corresponds to a set of 300 boxes in a row, with no triangles in between (though, as we will discuss in later chapters, in practice, automotive assembly lines do have some buffer inventory between a select few assembly stations). But, for now, what matters is that every resource has to work in perfect synchronization. The flow unit stays with each resource for exactly the duration of one cycle time (46 seconds in our process), irrespective of whether the processing time at that resource is 20 seconds per unit or 46 seconds per unit.

In these settings, we determine the **time through the empty system**:

Time through an empty machine-paced process = # of stations × cycle time

Worker-paced A process line in which each resource is free to work at its own pace: if the first resource finishes before the next one is ready to accept the flow unit, then the first resource puts the completed flow unit in the inventory between the two resources.

Machine-paced A process in which all steps are connected through a conveyor belt and all of the steps must work at the same rate even if some of them have more capacity than others.

Time through the empty system The time it takes the first flow unit to flow through an empty process; that is, a process that has no inventory.

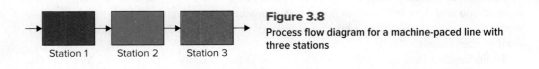

Figure 3.8
Process flow diagram for a machine-paced line with three stations

Check Your Understanding 3.5

Question: Recall the example of the three-step airport security from Check Your Understanding 3.1 (refer to Figure 3.4). The first step, verifying ID and boarding pass, takes 30 seconds per passenger. The second step, searching the passenger for metal objects using a metal detector, takes 10 seconds per passenger. The third step, running the carry-on luggage through an X-ray machine, takes 60 seconds per passenger.

The process is empty at 7 a.m in the morning when a group of 30 passengers arrives. How long will it take to serve all 30 passengers?

Answer: The process is empty and so we first have to compute the time until the first customer is served. The first customer will take 30 seconds at the verification of her ID and then 60 seconds at the X-ray machine. Note that the time at the metal detector does not matter because it happens in parallel with the X-ray machine. Thus, it takes 90 seconds = 1.5 minutes until the first customer is served.

From then onward, we are serving a customer every minute. Because we have 29 customers to serve, this will take 29 minutes, for a total time of 1.5 + 29 = 30.5 minutes.

We can also use the previously introduced formula:

$$\frac{\text{Time to finish } X \text{ units}}{\text{starting with an empty system}} = \frac{\text{Time through}}{\text{an empty process}} + [(X-1) \times \text{Cycle time}]$$

$$\frac{\text{Time to finish 30 units}}{\text{starting with an empty system}} = 1.5 \text{ minutes} + [29 \times 1 \text{ minute}] = 30.5 \text{ minutes}$$

Now return to our worker-paced process. Ignoring any parallel work, we saw that the time through the empty process was given by:

Time through empty worker-paced process = Sum of all processing times

In our case, this was given by 37 seconds + 46 seconds + 37 seconds = 120 seconds.

After waiting for 120 seconds, we have completed our first order; that is, we have fed the first of the 20 hungry customers. Now we have 19 more to go. How long will it take us? Customer 2 will be served after 120 + 46 = 166 seconds. Customer 3 after 120 + 46 + 46, and so on. From now on, we are completing a new customer order every 46 seconds. So we need 19 customers × 46 seconds/customers more time to finish the job.

In general, we can compute the **time that is required to produce a given quantity X starting with an empty system** as

$$\frac{\text{Time to finish } X \text{ units}}{\text{starting with an empty system}} = \frac{\text{Time through}}{\text{an empty process}} + [(X-1) \times \text{Cycle time}]$$

Conclusion

In this chapter, we introduced the framework of process analysis. Instead of looking at the process as a black box, merely tracking inventory, flow rate, and flow time, we want to understand how the process works. We saw that the process flow diagram is a useful tool to visually describe the flow. The process flow diagram is like a map of the process, using triangles for inventory locations, arrows for the movement of flow units, and boxes for resources. We also saw how the same work (making one sandwich) can be organized in very different ways. Even when the activities were the same, we could organize the process flow in different ways.

But the process flow diagram only tells parts of the story. Just like a street map will not provide you with any information about how many cars are actually traveling on the road or where to expect a traffic jam, a process flow diagram will not tell you how many units flow through the process.

To understand flow rate, you first have to look at the capacity of the process. You find the capacity of the process by looking for the resource with the smallest capacity, the resource that

Time required to produce a given quantity X starting with an empty system The time it takes a process with no inventory to produce a given quantity.

we labeled the bottleneck. The bottleneck will determine the process capacity. Flow rate, then, is found by looking at the minimum between demand and capacity. The flow rate determines how many flow units are flowing through the process per unit of time, while the capacity measures how much could be flowing through the process if there were no demand constraints. The ratio between flow rate and capacity captures the utilization of the process; we can also define utilization at the level of individual resources by taking the ratio between flow rate and the capacity at that resource. Resources might not be fully utilized, either because they are nonbottleneck resources or because the process is currently constrained by demand.

Finally, with flow rate you can compute the cycle time of a process. The cycle time of the process captures the "rhythm" of the operation. If your cycle time is 46 seconds/customer, that means every 46 seconds your cash register rings and you are bringing in money. Cycle time will also be an important starting point for several calculations in the next chapter on process improvement.

Exhibit 3.1 shows the calculations from the process flow diagram.

Summary Calculations—HOW TO Exhibit

EXHIBIT 3.1

Processing time	Time to carry out all activities for a flow unit at one resource
Capacity of a resource	Number of workers at resource/processing time
Process capacity	Minimum of the capacity of all resources
Bottleneck	Resource with the smallest capacity
Flow rate	Minimum{Demand, Process capacity}
Utilization of a resource	Flow rate/Capacity of the resource
Utilization of a process	Flow rate/Process capacity
Cycle time	1/Flow rate
Time to produce X units (with a "full" system)	$X \times$ Cycle time
Time to produce X units starting with an empty process	Time through empty system $+ \left[(X - 1) \times \text{Cycle time} \right]$

Summary of Learning Objectives

LO3-1 Draw a process flow diagram

A process flow diagram is a graphical way to describe the process. When drawing a process flow diagram, map the flow of a flow unit from input to output. Use boxes to depict the resources, arrows to depict flows, and triangles to depict inventory location. The process flow diagram alone provides no quantitative information—it is like a map of the process.

LO3-2 Determine the capacity for a one-step process

The capacity of a process is the maximum number of flow units that can flow through that resource per unit of time. If there is only one step in the process, the capacity of the process is equal to the capacity of the resource that carries out this one step. To find this capacity, simply divide the number of machines or workers by the processing time.

LO3-3 Determine the flow rate, the utilization, and the cycle time of a process

The flow rate of a process is given by the minimum of the capacity of the process and the demand for the process. For the process as a whole, we can then compute the utilization as the ratio between the flow rate (how fast the process is currently operating) and the process capacity (capturing how fast the process could be operating if there was sufficient demand). We can also define utilization at the level of an individual resource. To find the cycle time, we take the reciprocal of the flow rate. Instead of saying that a process makes 4 units per hour, we can say it makes a unit every ¼ of an hour. So the cycle time measures how much time goes by between completing two consecutive units.

LO3-4   **Find the bottleneck of a multistep process and determine its capacity**

A chain is only as strong as its weakest link. One of the resources in the process has the lowest capacity. We refer to that one resource as the bottleneck. By definition, the capacity of the bottleneck determines the capacity of the entire process.

LO3-5   **Determine how long it takes to produce a certain order quantity**

When computing the time it takes to produce a certain order quantity, we have to first ask ourselves if we face a situation in which the process starts empty or a situation in which the process already includes some inventory (customers). If the process is already running, we find the time it takes to produce a certain quantity by simply multiplying that quantity by the cycle time of the process. If the process starts empty, we have to add the time it takes the process to produce the first unit.

Key Terms

3.1 How to Draw a Process Flow Diagram

Process analysis A rigorous framework for understanding the detailed operations of a business. Among other things, the process analysis determines how many flow units can be processed per unit of time (the process capacity) and how busy the resources of the process are (utilization).

Process flow diagram A graphical way to describe the process. It uses boxes to depict resources, arrows to depict flows, and triangles to depict inventory location.

Resource A group of people and/or equipment that transforms inputs into outputs.

Flow unit The unit of analysis that we consider in a process analysis; for example, patients in a hospital, scooters in a kick-scooter plant, and calls in a call center.

Upstream The parts of the process that are at the beginning of the process flow.

Downstream The parts of the process that are at the end of the process flow.

3.2 Capacity for a One-Step Process

Processing times The time it takes a resource to complete one flow unit.

Capacity The maximum number of flow units that can flow through that resource per unit of time.

Process capacity The maximum flow rate a process can provide per unit of time. This determines the maximum supply of the process. The process capacity is the smallest capacity of all resources in the process.

3.3 How to Compute Flow Rate, Utilization, and Cycle Time

Demand rate The number of flow units that customers want per unit of time.

Capacity-constrained The case in which demand exceeds supply and the flow rate is equal to process capacity.

Demand-constrained The case in which process capacity exceeds demand and thus the flow rate is equal to the demand rate.

Throughput A synonym for flow rate, the number of flow units flowing through the process per unit of time.

Utilization The ratio between the flow rate (how fast the process is currently operating) and the process capacity (capturing how fast the process could be operating if there was sufficient demand). Note that utilization can be defined at the level of an individual resource or at the level of the entire process.

Cycle time The time between completing two consecutive flow units.

Lead time The time between when an order is placed and when it is filled. Process lead time is frequently used as an alternative term for flow time.

3.4 How to Analyze a Multistep Process and to Locate the Bottleneck

Bottleneck Resource with the lowest capacity in a process.

3.5 The Time to Produce a Certain Quantity

Worker-paced A process line in which each resource is free to work at its own pace: if the first resource finishes before the next one is ready to accept the flow unit, then the first resource puts the completed flow unit in the inventory between the two resources.

Machine-paced A process in which all steps are connected through a conveyor belt and all of the steps must work at the same rate even if some of them have more capacity than others.

Time through the empty system The time it takes the first flow unit to flow through an empty process; that is, a process that has no inventory.

Time required to produce a given quantity X starting with an empty system The time it takes a process with no inventory to produce a given quantity.

Conceptual Questions

LO3-1

1. Which of the following questions would be asked in a process analysis of a college admissions office?
   a. When was the college founded?
   b. How long does it take the office to process an application?
   c. How much is the yearly tuition at the college?
   d. How long does it take the average student to complete a degree program at the college?

2. Which of the following items would be considered resources in a restaurant?
   a. Recipes
   b. Food
   c. Brand image
   d. Chefs

3. You are sitting in a restaurant and the waiter brings you the food you ordered a while ago. If you think about you being the flow unit in the process of the restaurant, which step of this process will be downstream relative to your current position in the process?
   a. Waiting to order
   b. Being seated at a table
   c. Paying the bill
   d. Reviewing the menu

LO3-2

4. What is the relationship between the processing time at a resource and its capacity?
   a. They are the same.
   b. They are reciprocals of each other.
   c. They are multiples of each other.
   d. They are not related.

5. You observe a long line at the airport security. The process currently is:
   a. capacity-constrained.
   b. demand-constrained.
   c. unconstrained.
   d. linearly constrained.

LO3-3

6. You observe a bank and notice that a customer leaves the bank about every five minutes. These five minutes between customers are:
   a. the capacity of the process.
   b. the processing time of the last resource.
   c. the cycle time.
   d. the lead time.

7. What is the maximum utilization a resource can achieve?
   a. A value equal to the demand
   b. A value equal to the capacity
   c. There is no maximum utilization.
   d. 1.00

LO3-4

8. Is the capacity of the bottleneck larger than, equal to, or smaller than the capacity of the process?
   a. Larger than
   b. Equal to
   c. Smaller than
   d. The answer depends on the specific process under consideration.

LO3-5

9. Smartphones are made on a 40-step assembly process. All 40 steps are connected through a conveyor belt and all of the 40 steps must work at the same rate even if some of them have more capacity than others. Is this process a machine-paced process or a worker-paced process?
   a. Machine-paced
   b. Worker-paced

10. You observe a vehicle registration department at your local township. Assume that all employees are ready to work at 9 a.m. You arrive at 9 a.m. sharp and are the first customer. Is your time through the empty process longer or shorter than the flow time averaged across all customers that arrive over the course of the day?
    a. Longer than the average flow time
    b. Shorter than the average flow time

Solved Example Problems

LO3-1

1. The School of Dentistry at Penn provides general dental care to residents of Philadelphia on a walk-in basis. Upon arrival, customers first provide health-relevant information such as personal health records and insurance provider to a receptionist who enters the information into the computer system for the dentist to see. A dental assistant then takes an X-ray of the patient. A dentist then performs the checkup and discusses any issues with the patient. Depending on the day, patients might have to wait at any of these resources. This concludes the process. Draw a process flow diagram of this process.

   Answer: There are three resources in the process, corresponding to three boxes: the receptionist, the dental assistant, and the dentist.

   Because patients might have to wait in the process, we draw a triangle in front of every box in Figure 3.9.

Figure 3.9

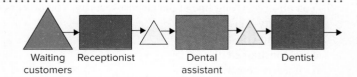

Waiting customers   Receptionist   Dental assistant   Dentist

LO3-2

2. It takes a dentist 20 minutes to see one patient. What is the capacity of the dentist expressed in patients per hour?

   Answer: The dentist has a capacity of $\frac{1}{20}$ patient per minute, which is 3 patients per hour.

3. A plumbing company has 8 crews fielding repair calls. It takes a crew 2 hours to complete one repair call (including travel time and breaks). What is the capacity of the plumbing company over the course of a 10-hour workday?

   Answer: Each crew has a capacity of $\frac{1}{2}$ call per hour. The 8 crews together have a capacity of $8 \times \frac{1}{2} = 4$ calls per hour. Over a 10-hour workday, this equates to 40 calls per workday.

LO3-3

4. A food-truck can produce 20 meals per hour. The demand rate is, however, only 15 meals per hour. (a) What is the flow rate? (b) What is the utilization of the food-truck? (c) What is the cycle time?

   Answer: (a) Flow rate = Min{Demand, Capacity} = Min{15, 20} = 15 meals per hour

   (b) Utilization $= \dfrac{\text{Flow rate}}{\text{Capacity}} = \dfrac{15}{20} = 0.75$

   (c) Cycle time $= \dfrac{1}{\text{Flow rate}} = \dfrac{1}{15}$ hour/meal $= 4\ \dfrac{\text{min}}{\text{meal}}$

LO3-4

5. Mr. K's is a very popular hair salon. It offers high-quality hairstyling and physical relaxation services at a reasonable price, so it always has unlimited demand. The service process includes five activities that are conducted in the sequence described below (the time required for each activity is shown in parentheses): activity 1: Welcome a guest and offer homemade herb tea (10 minutes); activity 2: Wash and condition hair (10 minutes); activity 3: Neck, shoulder, and back stress release massage (10 minutes); activity 4: Design the hairstyle and do the hair (25 minutes); activity 5: Ring up the guest's bill (5 minutes).

   Each activity has one employee dedicated to it. For the following questions, assume unlimited demand. Also assume that the employee at activity 1 only admits new guests at the rate of the bottleneck.

   (a) Which resource is the bottleneck? (b) What is the capacity of the process? (c) What is the flow rate? (d) What is the utilization of the employee at activity 3? (e) What is the cycle time?

   Answer: (a) The capacity of each employee is given by $\dfrac{1}{\text{Processing time}}$. The lowest capacity is at activity 4 with $\frac{1}{25}$ guest/minute.

   (b) The capacity is $\frac{1}{25}$ guest/minute $= \dfrac{60}{25}$ guests/hour $= 2.4\ \dfrac{\text{guests}}{\text{hour}}$.

   (c) There is unlimited demand; thus, the flow rate is equal to the capacity at 2.4 guests per hour.

   (d) The capacity at employee 3 is $\frac{1}{10}$ guest/minute, which is 6 guests/hour.

   Utilization $= \dfrac{\text{Flow rate}}{\text{Capacity}} = \dfrac{2.4}{6} = 0.4$

   (e) Cycle time $= \dfrac{1}{\text{Flow rate}} = 2.4\ \dfrac{\text{hours}}{\text{guest}} = 25\ \dfrac{\text{min}}{\text{guest}}$

LO3-5

6. Consider the process described in question 5. How long would it take to serve five guests, starting with an empty system?

> **Answer:** We first have to think about how long it will take to serve 1 guest. This is a worker-paced process, so the first guest will be served after $10 + 10 + 10 + 25 + 5 = 60$ minutes.
>
> From then, we will have to serve 4 more guests:
>
> Time to serve 5 guests starting with empty system = 60 minutes + [4 × 25 min/guest] = (60 + 100) minutes = 160 minutes

Problems and Applications

LO3-2, 3-3

1. It takes a barber 15 minutes to serve one customer.
   a. What is the capacity of the barber expressed in customers per hour?
   b. Assuming the demand for the barber is 2 customers per hour, what is the flow rate?
   c. Assuming the demand for the barber is 2 customers per hour, what is the utilization?
   d. Assuming the demand for the barber is 2 customers per hour, what is the cycle time?

2. A community health system's nurse team consists of 12 nurses working in the local community. It takes a nurse 1.5 hours to complete one patient visit (including travel time and breaks).
   a. What is the capacity of the nurse team over the course of a 9-hour workday?
   b. Assuming the demand for the nurses is 60 patients per day, what is the utilization of the nurse team?
   c. Assuming the demand for the nurses is 60 patients per day, what is the cycle time?

LO3-1, 3-2, 3-4, 3-5

3. Consider a process consisting of three resources. Assume there exists unlimited demand for the product.
   - Resource 1 has a processing time of 6 minutes per unit.
   - Resource 2 has a processing time of 3 minutes per unit.
   - Resource 3 has a processing time of 5 minutes per unit.

   All three resources are staffed by one worker.
   a. Draw a process flow diagram of this process.
   b. What is the capacity of resource 2?
   c. What is the bottleneck in the process?
   d. What is the utilization of resource 2?
   e. How long does it take the process to produce 200 units starting with an empty system, assuming this is a worker-paced process?

4. A small, privately owned Asian company is producing a private-label soft drink called Yoggo. A bottling line puts the soft drinks into plastic bottles and then packages the bottles into boxes holding 10 bottles each. The bottling line is comprised of the following four steps: (1) the **bottling machine** takes 1 second to fill a bottle, (2) the **lid machine** takes 3 seconds to cover the bottle with a lid, (3) a **labeling machine** takes 3 seconds per bottle, and (4) the **packaging machine** takes 4 seconds to place a bottle into a box. When a box has been filled with 10 bottles, a worker tending the packaging machine removes the filled box and replaces it with an empty box. Assume that the time for the worker to remove a filled box and replace it with an empty box is negligible and hence does not affect the capacity of the line. Problem data are summarized in the following table.

Process Step	Number of Machines	Seconds per Bottle
Bottling	1	1
Apply a lid	1	3
Labeling	1	3
Packaging	1	4

    a. Draw a process flow diagram of this process.

    b. What is the capacity (bottles/hour) at the resource "Apply a lid"?

    c. What is the bottleneck in the process?

    d. Assuming unlimited demand, what would be the flow rate?

    e. Assuming unlimited demand, what would be the utilization at resource "Apply a lid"?

    f. Assume the process started empty and that this is a machine-paced process. How long would it take to produce 500 bottles?

5. Glenn Dental Clinic provides general dental care to residents of Philadelphia on a walk-in basis. The clinic has started receiving complaints from patients that the waiting time is too long and has asked you to investigate whether this problem can be solved.

Upon arrival, customers first receive a series of paperwork from the receptionist and fill out relevant information such as personal health records and insurance provider. The form is then handed back to the receptionist who enters the information into the computer system for the dentist to see. A dental assistant then takes an X-ray from the patient. A dentist then performs the checkup and discusses any issues with the patient.

Based on conversations with staff members at the clinic, you have obtained the following information on the process:

- It takes about 5 minutes for a customer to fill out the paperwork.
- Entry of information on the paperwork into the system and verification with past records takes another 5 minutes for a receptionist. There are two receptionists.
- It takes 15 minutes, on average, for the dental assistant to take an X-ray. There are three dental assistants on shift at any moment.
- There are 10 dentists working at the clinic. Each checkup takes 30 minutes, on average.

The following table summarizes the process data collected above.

Resource	Process	Staffing (Number of Workers)	Activity Time (Minutes per Patient)
Self-serve	Paperwork	–	5
Receptionists	Data entry	2	5
Dental assistant	X-ray	3	15
Dentist	Checkup	10	30

Assume that there exists unlimited demand, unless otherwise stated.

    a. Draw a process flow diagram of this process.

    b. What is the capacity (patients/hour) at the resource "Dentist"?

    c. What is the bottleneck in the process?

    d. Assuming unlimited demand, what would be the flow rate?

    e. Assuming unlimited demand, what would be the utilization at resource "Receptionists"?

    f. Assume the process started empty. How long would it take to serve 20 patients?

LO3-2, 3-4, 3-5

6. Consider the following production process for manufacturing biscuits. The first step of the process is mixing, where all of the ingredients are combined in the correct proportion to form dough. In the next step of the process, the dough is formed into sheets and cut into pieces in preparation for baking. The cut dough is then baked into biscuits and subsequently must be cooled. The final step of the process is packaging the biscuits for the consumer.

The following table summarizes the production process along with the processing times at each step of the process. The process is highly automated, so assume that this is a machine-paced process with one machine available at each step.

Process Step	Activity Time (Minutes per Batch)
Mixing	15
Forming	10
Baking	12
Cooling	18
Packing	10

a. What is the capacity of the baking process step (in batches per hour)?
b. What is the bottleneck of the manufacturing process?
c. Assuming unlimited demand, what is the process flow rate (in batches per hour)?
d. Assuming unlimited demand, what is the utilization of the mixing process step?
e. If the manufacturing process is currently full of work-in-process inventory, how long would it take to complete 50 batches of biscuits?

LO3-4, 3-5

7. A small mortgage lender has one receptionist, four loan officers, and two office managers. When applicants apply for a new loan in person, they first fill out paperwork with the receptionist. Then the applicants meet with one of the loan officers to discuss their needs. The loan officer spends additional time processing the application after the applicants leave the office. Finally, the application must be reviewed by an office manager before it can be approved. The following table lists the processing times at each stage. The office is open for eight hours per day, five days per week.

Resource	Staffing (Number of Employees)	Activity Time (Hours per Loan)
Receptionist	1	1
Loan officers	4	7
Office managers	2	4

a. What is the bottleneck of the process?
b. Assuming unlimited demand, what is the process flow rate (in loans per week)?
c. If the customer demand is 18 loans per week, what is the utilization of the office managers resource?
d. Assuming that the office currently has no backlog of loans that it is processing, how long will it take to complete 10 loans?

LO 3-5

8. Consider a four-step serial process with processing times given in the following list. There is one machine at each step of the process, and this is a machine-paced process.
   - Step 1: 25 minutes per unit
   - Step 2: 15 minutes per unit
   - Step 3: 30 minutes per unit
   - Step 4: 20 minutes per unit

   Assuming that the process starts out empty, how long will it take (in hours) to complete a batch of 105 units?

9. Consider a four-step serial process with the number of workers at each step and processing times given in the following table.

Process Step	Number of Workers	Time per Customer (in Minutes)
1	1	5
2	5	15
3	3	10
4	1	3

   Assuming that the process starts out empty and is worker-paced, how long will it take (in minutes) to serve 20 customers?

LO 3-4

10. An automated car wash serves customers with the following serial process: pre-treat, wash, rinse, wax, hand dry. Each of these steps is performed by a dedicated machine except for the hand-dry step, which is performed manually on each car by one of three workers. The steps of the process have the following processing times:
    - Pre-treat: 1 minute per car
    - Wash: 5 minutes per car
    - Rinse: 2 minutes per car
    - Wax: 3 minutes per car
    - Hand dry: 8 minutes per car
    a. If the car wash has a demand of 15 cars per hour, what is the flow rate of the process?
    b. If the car wash has a demand of 15 cars per hour, what is the utilization of the machine that performs the wax process?

11. The local driver's license center processes applications for driver's license renewals through the following three steps. First, the customer registers with the receptionist, who updates the customer's information in the database. This first step takes 2 minutes per customer. Then, the customer visits one of two cashiers to pay the associated fees for the license renewal. This takes 8 minutes per customer because several forms must be printed from the computer and signed by the customer. Finally, the customer visits one of three license processing stations where the customer's picture is taken and the license is printed. This final step takes 15 minutes per customer.
    a. Assuming unlimited demand, what is the flow rate of the process in customers per hour?
    b. Assuming unlimited demand, what would the new flow rate be if the center added one server to the bottleneck resource?

CASE TESLA

The Tesla Model S, one of the most sought-after luxury cars, is produced in Tesla's Freemont factory in California. The production process can be broken up into the following subprocesses.

Stamping: In the stamping process, coils of aluminum are unwound, cut into level pieces of sheet metal, and then inserted into stamping presses that shape the metal according to the geometry of the Model S. The presses can shape a sheet of metal in roughly 6 seconds.

Subassembly: The various pieces of metal are put together using a combination of joining techniques, including welding and adhesion. This creates the body of the vehicle.

Paint: The body of the vehicle is then moved to the paint shop. After painting is completed, the body moves through a 350° oven to cure the paint, followed by a sanding operation that ensures a clean surface.

General assembly: After painting, the vehicle body is moved to the final assembly area. Here, assembly workers and assembly robots insert the various subassemblies, such as the wiring, the dash board, the power train and the motor, the battery pack, and the seats.

Quality testing: Before being shipped to the customer, the now-assembled car is tested for its quality. It is driven on a rolling road, a test station that is basically a treadmill for cars that mimics driving on real streets.

Overall, the process is equipped with 160 robots and 3000 employees. The process produces some 500 vehicles each week. It takes a car about 3–5 days to move from the beginning of the process to the end.

© Paul Sakuma/AP Images

QUESTIONS

Imagine you could take a tour of the Tesla plant. To prepare for this tour, draw a simple process flow diagram of the operation.

1. What is the cycle time of the process (assume two shifts of eight hours each and five days a week of operation)?

2. What is the flow time?

3. Where in the process do you expect to encounter inventory?

4. How many cars are you likely to encounter as work in progress inventory?

SOURCES

http://www.wired.com/2013/07/tesla-plant-video/
http://www.forbes.com/sites/greatspeculations/2014/09/26/fremont-factory-delays-shouldnt-affect-teslas-sales-this-quarter/

References

Activities and processing time data are taken from Subway training materials.

Process Improvement

4

LEARNING OBJECTIVES

LO4-1 Compute the costs of direct labor, labor content, idle time, and average labor utilization

LO4-2 Compute the takt time of a process and translate this to a target manpower

LO4-3 Find ways to improve the process efficiency by off-loading the bottleneck

LO4-4 Balance a process by reallocating work from one step to another

LO4-5 Explain the benefits and limitations of specialization

LO4-6 Evaluate the financial benefits of process improvements

CHAPTER OUTLINE

Introduction

4.1 Measures of Process Efficiency

4.2 How to Choose a Staffing Level to Meet Demand

4.3 Off-Loading the Bottleneck

4.4 How to Balance a Process

4.5 The Pros and Cons of Specialization

4.6 Understanding the Financial Impact of Process Improvements

Conclusion

Introduction

When Carl Benz built the first car with a combustion engine in 1886, he most likely did not care about the production process. His focus was on the vehicle he produced. His wife, Bertha Benz, was the key investor in this venture. She was the first person to drive a car for a meaningful distance when she drove her husband's invention from Mannheim, Germany, to the city of Pforzheim, which is roughly a 100 km drive. This story would not be complete without mentioning that en route Bertha Benz ran out of fuel. For obvious reasons, no gas stations existed along the way, so she purchased her fuel at a local pharmacy, which enabled her to successfully complete her journey back to Mannheim and secured her and her husband a place in automotive history.

Thirty years later, Henry Ford created the assembly line. But Ford did not employ thousands of automotive experts akin to Carl Benz. He hired unskilled labor off the street. Each worker would only have to master a couple of seconds of work, so labor was cheap and plentiful. Carl Benz spent months making one vehicle; Henry Ford built hundreds of vehicles in one day. More vehicles at lower costs—that accomplishment secured Henry Ford a place in business history.

Henry Ford understood how it is possible to create operations that increased output in a given time period while also using relatively unskilled labor. Obtaining high output at low costs is the key idea behind efficiency, the focus of the present chapter. Here, we will start out by introducing a set of measures for efficiency. Before diving into the details of efficiency, however,

Courtesy of Library of Congress Prints and Photographs Division [LC-USZ62-50219]

it is important to remind ourselves that efficiency is only one of multiple dimensions of operational performance and that businesses should not set efficiency as their only goal. In fact, setting ethical considerations aside (and somewhat simplifying the world of finance), we can think of **profit maximization** as the primary goal for most corporations, where

$$\text{Profit} = \text{Flow rate} \times (\text{Average price} - \text{Average cost})$$

In the next sections, we discuss various forms of improving the efficiency of a process. We then discuss how these improvement opportunities impact the profits derived from the operation. We will do this in the following steps:

1. We start by developing a set of measures of efficiency. After all, what you cannot measure, you cannot manage.
2. We then turn to finding the right number of employees for a given level of customer demand. Having more process capacity than demand does not increase flow rate, yet it is expensive because we have to pay our employees. This creates extra costs. Having less process capacity than demand reduces flow rate, and thus reduces revenue.
3. We then will try to help the bottleneck resource to increase its capacity. Because the process capacity is dictated by the resource with the smallest capacity, this will help us increase capacity and potentially the flow rate.
4. We then will attempt to divide up the work equally across the employees working in the process. This avoids paying wages to labor that is underutilized, which, again, will help keep costs low and might lead to a higher flow rate.
5. The next level in improving efficiency is specialization. To the extent that we can design the process flow in a way that our employees specialize in one or two activities, it is possible that we can reduce the time they take to carry out the activities, which would lead to more capacity. Specialization is also often related to lower wages, which would lower our costs.
6. Finally, we will evaluate the impact of improvement opportunities on the profits of the operation. Most importantly, we will see that even small efficiency improvements can have large financial benefits, especially when the process is presently capacity-constrained.

Given that efficiency drives the profits of an operation, managing an operation efficiently is a very valuable skill. It does not matter if you work in a five-person startup or in a multibillion-dollar enterprise, efficiency (and, of course, profits) matters everywhere in business. It is also misleading to believe that efficiency is limited to manufacturing workers. Hospitals aim to use their doctors and nurses efficiently. Energy companies want to efficiently use their power plants. Marketing executives want to efficiently utilize their salesforce. And, as a society, we ought to make efficient use of our resources, be they water, land, or energy. So, efficiency is key to many parts of our lives.

To illustrate the concepts of efficiency, we perform an analysis of a Subway restaurant. And, in the spirit of Henry Ford's auto plant, we will focus on the process flow that employs specialization. Instead of one person taking care of all the activities, from greeting the customer to running the cash register, we consider a process where multiple employees serve the customer, each worker specializing in a different set of activities.

Profit maximization The objective of an enterprise—to maximize the difference between revenue and costs.

4.1 Measures of Process Efficiency

Subway provides custom-made sandwiches to its customers. Consider the three-step process of serving a customer depicted in Figure 4.1. It takes the first employee ("station") 37 seconds to greet the customer and perform all activities up to adding the cheese onto the sandwich. From there, employee 2 takes over and performs all activities from placing the onions to wrapping and bagging, which, taken together, takes 46 seconds per customer. Finally, station 3 offers a fresh value meal and a cookie and then rings up the purchase on the register, which takes together 37 seconds per customer. In the following calculations, we assume that these times are exact; that is, that it will take an employee exactly that amount of time to carry out an activity. Moreover, we assume that every customer wants all the ingredients. Arguably, these are strong assumptions, but they make for a good starting point in our analysis.

Depending on what dictionary you consult, you will find the word "efficiency" defined as "acting directly to produce an effect," "acting or producing effectively with a minimum of waste, expense, or unnecessary effort," and "obtaining a high ratio of output to input." Whatever definition you want to pick, all of them share what in business is often referred to as a "big bang for the buck." So, in the context of process analysis, we define a process as **efficient** if it is able to achieve a high flow rate with few resources. In the case of our Subway analysis, our focus is primarily on the employees (the labor) as the key resource (as opposed to the oven or the real estate). And so rather than talking about efficiency in general, we will focus on labor efficiency.

A first measure of labor efficiency is the labor cost associated with serving one customer. We call this measure the **costs of direct labor**. We compute the costs of direct labor as

$$\text{Costs of direct labor} = \frac{\text{Wages per unit of time}}{\text{Flow rate}}$$

Efficiency A process is efficient if it is able to achieve a high flow rate with few resources.

Costs of direct labor The labor cost associated with serving one customer, which is the total wages paid per unit of time divided by the flow rate.

LO4-1 Compute the costs of direct labor, labor content, idle time, and average labor utilization.

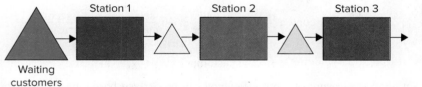

Waiting customers

Station 1	Station 2	Station 3

Processing time   37 sec/customer   46 sec/customer   37 sec/customer

Figure 4.1

Process flow for serving one customer, assuming three employees

	Activity	Activity Time [sec/customer]
Station 1	Greet customer	4
	Take order	5
	Get bread	4
	Cut bread	3
	Meat	12
	Cheese	9
Station 2	Onions	3
	Lettuce	3
	Tomatoes	4
	Cucumbers	5
	Pickles	4
	Green peppers	4
	Black olives	3
	Hot peppers	2
	Place condiments	5
	Wrap and bag	13
Station 3	Offer fresh value meal	3
	Offer cookies	14
	Ring up Register	20
	Total	**120**

How many customers will the process shown in Figure 4.1 serve? The first station has a capacity of $\frac{1}{37}$ customer/second, the second one of $\frac{1}{46}$, and the third one of $\frac{1}{37}$. Hence, the second station has the lowest capacity and is the bottleneck. Assuming sufficient demand, we are thus making a sandwich at a rate of $\frac{1}{46}$ customer/second $\times$ 3600 seconds/hour = 78.3 customers/hour. Given that we presently have three employees in our process and assuming that we pay them $12 per hour, we get

$$\text{Costs of direct labor} = \frac{3 \times 12 \text{ \$/h}}{78.3 \text{ customers/h}} = 0.46 \text{ \$/customer}$$

If we think about output and input (or the bang and the buck, if you prefer), we could casually say that the wages we pay our employees are an input into the operation and the number of sandwiches that the labor produces constitutes an output. Thus, the definition of the costs of direct labor looks at the ratio of inputs to outputs. Note that this is slightly different from the dictionary definition that called for computing the ratio of output to input. To state the obvious, high costs of direct labor are associated with a low labor efficiency and our measure is just the reciprocal of the dictionary definition.

But the ratio of wages and flow rate are not the only output-to-input calculations we can perform. For example, we might think about the amount of work that goes into serving one customer as the input into the process and turning that customer into a served customer as the output. With this in mind, we define a second efficiency measure as the **labor content**:

Labor content = Sum of the processing times involving labor

The labor content measures how much work is required in serving one flow unit. As with the costs of direct labor, holding everything else constant, a high number is arguably less desirable than a low number and so we are again looking at a ratio of input to output.

In our Subway example, we get

$$\text{Labor content} = 37 \frac{\text{seconds}}{\text{customer}} + 46 \frac{\text{seconds}}{\text{customer}} + 37 \frac{\text{seconds}}{\text{customer}}$$

$$= 120 \frac{\text{seconds}}{\text{customer}}$$

Yet another measure of labor efficiency can be derived based on the utilization levels of the employees in the process. Assuming sufficient demand, we determined a flow rate of 78.3 customers/hour. The three stations have a capacity of $\frac{1}{37}$ customer/second, $\frac{1}{46}$ customer/second, and $\frac{1}{37}$ customer/second, which can be translated to hourly capacity levels of 97.3, 78.3, and 97.3, respectively. Because the utilization of a resource is the ratio between its flow rate and its capacity, we obtain utilization levels of 80.4 percent, 100 percent, and 80.4 percent. So we can compute the **average labor utilization** in a process as

$$\text{Average labor utilization} = \text{Average utilization across employees}$$
$$= \text{Average}(80.4\%, 100\%, 80.4\%)$$
$$= 87.0\%$$

Labor content The amount of work that goes into serving one customer (or, more generally, one flow unit), which is the sum of the processing times involving labor.

Average labor utilization The average utilization across resources.

Idle time The amount of time per flow unit for which a resource is paid but is not actually working.

The average labor utilization is a measure of efficiency—we have to pay our employees whether they are working or not. Thus, an unutilized worker creates an unnecessary expense and so an efficient process is one in which the average labor utilization is as high as possible. We refer to the time we pay a resource even though the resource is not working as **idle time**.

We can compute the idle time for each resource as

Idle time(Resource i) = Cycle time $-$ Processing time(Resource i)

The idle time measures how long the resource is idle for each flow unit it serves, which is why the idle time is expressed in seconds/customer (or, more generally, in units of time per flow unit). The cycle time tells us how long we have to wait between completing the order of two consecutive customers. The cycle time is 1/Flow rate, in this case 46 seconds/customer. So, we get

$$\text{Idle time(Station 1)} = 46 - 37 = 9 \frac{\text{seconds}}{\text{customer}}$$

$$\text{Idle time(Station 2)} = 46 - 46 = 0 \frac{\text{seconds}}{\text{customer}}$$

$$\text{Idle time(Station 3)} = 46 - 37 = 9 \frac{\text{seconds}}{\text{customer}}$$

We can also add up the idle time across the employees, which gives us the **total idle time** in the process:

$$\text{Total idle time} = \text{Sum of idle time across resources}$$

$$= 9 + 0 + 9 = 18 \frac{\text{seconds}}{\text{customer}}$$

So, for every customer that we serve, we incur (and pay for) 18 seconds of idle time. Is this a lot? This question is difficult to answer. Eighteen seconds of idle time per unit seems like a small number in the assembly of a car, in which hundreds of people and multiple hours of labor content per vehicle are involved. But for a sandwich? To evaluate the magnitude of the idle time, it is useful to compare the idle time with the labor content. Recall that we had defined the labor content as the sum of the processing times in the process—in our case, 120 seconds/customer.

Now, compare the labor content (which we can think of as the productive time of our resources) relative to the labor content plus the idle time (which we can think of as the total time that we have to pay our employees for each unit because we pay them if they are working or if they are idle). We get

$$\frac{\text{Labor content}}{\text{Labor content} + \text{Idle time}} = \frac{120 \text{ seconds/customer}}{120 \text{ seconds/customer} + 18 \text{ seconds/customer}} = 87.0\%$$

Note that this is exactly the same value as the average labor utilization. This is not a coincidence. In both calculations, we compare the idle time to the time that the employees actually work. When we computed the average across the utilizations, we took the perspective of the employees. When we looked at the labor content relative to the labor content + idle time, we took the perspective of the flow unit. Either way, we can generalize and write

$$\text{Average labor utilization} = \frac{\text{Labor content}}{\text{Labor content} + \text{Idle time}}$$

There exists a third way to obtain the average labor utilization, which is based on the cycle time:

$$\text{Average labor utilization} = \frac{\text{Labor content/Number of employees}}{\text{Cycle time}}$$

Let's just try it out:

$$\frac{\text{Labor content/number of employees}}{\text{Cycle time}} = \frac{120/3}{46} = \frac{40}{46} = 87.0 \text{ percent}$$

The intuition behind this third way of computing the average labor utilization is as follows. In a perfectly balanced process (a process that has an average labor utilization of 100 percent), the labor content is divided up equally across the number of employees. In the case of three

Total idle time The amount of idle time per flow unit added up across all resources.

employees, each employee gets a third of the labor content as his or her processing time. This allows them to produce at a cycle time that equals their (common) processing time. So, three different ways of computing the average labor utilization all get the same result: which one should you pick? Pick whichever is easiest for you. The benefit of the last measure is that it also works in processes where you have different staffing levels across resources (for example, three employees at station 7, but only one employee at station 2).

Check Your Understanding 4.1

Question: Consider the example of the three-step process. The first step takes 20 minutes/unit, the second step takes 10 minutes/unit, and the third step takes 15 minutes/unit. Each step is staffed by one worker. What is the labor content of the process?

Answer: The labor content is 20 + 10 + 15 = 45 minutes/unit.

Question: What is the total idle time of the process assuming unlimited demand?

Answer: We first have to establish that the first step is the bottleneck. It has the lowest capacity (1/20 unit/minute). This gives us a process capacity of 1/20 unit/minute. Given that we have unlimited demand, we also get a flow rate of 1/20 unit/minute and a cycle time of 1/Flow rate = 20 minutes/unit. With this, we can compute the idle times for the three steps as

$$\text{Idle time(Step 1)} = 20 - 20 = 0 \; \frac{\text{minutes}}{\text{unit}}$$

$$\text{Idle time(Step 2)} = 20 - 10 = 10 \; \frac{\text{minutes}}{\text{unit}}$$

$$\text{Idle time(Step 3)} = 20 - 15 = 5 \; \frac{\text{minutes}}{\text{unit}}$$

So, the total idle time is $0 + 10 + 5 = 15 \; \frac{\text{minutes}}{\text{unit}}$

Question: What is the average labor utilization?

Answer: We compute the average labor utilization as

$$\text{Average labor utilization} = \frac{\text{Labor content}}{(\text{Labor content} + \text{Idle time})}$$

$$= \frac{45}{(45 + 15)} = 0.75$$

Note that this is the same as

$$\text{Average labor utilization} = \frac{\text{Labor content/Number of employees}}{\text{Cycle time}}$$

$$= \frac{45/3}{20} = \frac{15}{20} = 0.75$$

Question: What is the cost of direct labor, assuming that each of the three employees gets paid $15 per hour.

Answer: We already computed that the flow rate is $\frac{1}{20}$ unit/minute = $3 \frac{\text{units}}{\text{hour}}$. Given that we have three employees, we have to pay

$3 \times \$15$ per hour = $45 per hour, giving us

$$\text{Cost of direct labor} = \frac{\$45 \text{ per hour}}{3 \text{ units per hour}} = \$15 \text{ per unit}$$

4.2 How to Choose a Staffing Level to Meet Demand

Matching supply with demand almost always starts with taking the demand rate as given and attempting to staff a sufficient number of resources in order to meet that demand. So, let us assume that our current demand in the Subway restaurant is given and it is 100 customers per hour.

To serve 100 customers per hour, we have to produce at one customer every 36 seconds. This is called the **takt time** of the process.

$$\text{Takt time} = \frac{1}{\text{Demand rate}} = \frac{1}{(100 \text{ customers/hour})}$$

$$= \frac{0.01 \text{ hour}}{\text{customer}} \times 3600 \frac{\text{seconds}}{\text{hour}} = 36 \frac{\text{seconds}}{\text{customer}}$$

Note that takt time is a measure that is entirely driven by demand; it is our goal to design a process flow that meets exactly this demand rate. *Takt* is a German word—the takt of the music tells the musician at which tempo (speed) to play a particular piece. The tempo of a musical piece is typically expressed in beats per minute—or, to be more exact, the number of quarter notes to be played per minute (just for completeness, in music, tempos lower than 100 beats per minute are typically considered slow, while tempos above 100 beats are considered fast).

The fact that takt is a musical term is appropriate. Just as how the musician should not play the notes in a musical piece at her own discretion, a process should not be operating at the discretionary flow of the resources. Instead, the flow should be happening at the rate of demand.

In the previous calculations of takt time, we assumed that demand was expressed in the form of a demand rate—that is, a required *quantity* per *unit of time*. Sometimes, however, demand might be expressed as a quantity, say of 100 units. In that case, we find the takt time as follows:

$$\text{Takt time} = \frac{\text{Available time}}{\text{Required quantity}}$$

where Available time measures the amount of time we have available in the process to produce the quantity. For example, if we work 8-hour work shifts and we want to produce 120 widgets, we have to produce at a takt time of

$$\text{Takt time} = \frac{\text{Available time}}{\text{Required quantity}} = \frac{8 \times 60 \text{ minutes}}{120 \text{ widgets}}$$

$$= 4 \frac{\text{minutes}}{\text{widget}}$$

Note that this definition of takt time is a generalization of the previous definition of takt time = 1/Demand rate in which we set the Available time equal to one unit of time.

It is important to understand the difference between takt time and cycle time. Recall that cycle time is 1/Flow rate (and that the flow rate is the minimum of demand and process capacity). So, cycle time depends on process capacity; takt time does not. The only thing that drives takt time is the demand rate. Cycle time, as 1/Flow rate, measures the current reality of the process flow. In the spirit of matching supply with demand, our goal is to have a cycle time that is as close to the takt time as possible. If customers order a sandwich every 36 seconds, our goal ought to be to produce a sandwich every 36 seconds.

Instead of matching our cycle time to our takt time, we can also think about matching our capacity to the demand rate. These two approaches are entirely equivalent. In both cases, we will adjust the staffing levels. If we are currently capacity-constrained, we will add more employees. More employees mean a higher capacity. More capacity in turn will lead to a higher flow rate (because we are capacity-constrained) and that translates to a shorter cycle time. If we are currently demand-constrained, we will aim to reduce the number of employees.

Fewer employees mean a lower capacity and thus a capacity that is closer to the demand rate. Fewer employees will not hurt our cycle time, because our flow rate is currently driven by the demand rate.

In our Subway example, facing a demand rate of 100 customers per hour, our three-step process (with processing times of 37, 46, and 37 seconds/unit, respectively) is capacity-constrained and the flow rate is 78.3 customers per hour. Thus, we leave 21.7 customers per hour not served (they go home hungry). But how many employees do we need to add? Assume for the moment that every employee would be fully utilized (that is a big IF, but more on this later). We can compute the required staffing level using the **target manpower** formula:

$$\text{Target Manpower} = \frac{\text{Labor Content}}{\text{Takt Time}}$$

As computed above, we have

$$\text{Takt time} = \frac{1}{\text{Demand rate}} = \frac{1}{100 \text{ customers/hour}}$$

$$= 0.01 \frac{\text{hour}}{\text{customer}} \times 3600 \frac{\text{sec}}{\text{hour}} = 36 \frac{\text{seconds}}{\text{customer}}$$

So, our target manpower is

$$\text{Target Manpower} = \frac{\text{Labor Content}}{\text{Takt Time}}$$

$$= \frac{120 \text{ seconds/customer}}{36 \text{ seconds/customer}} = 3.333$$

Assuming that all our employees are fully utilized, we need 3.33 employees. Because it is hard to hire a fraction of an employee, we have to round this up to four employees. For ease of notation, we refer to the target manpower as 3.333 and the staffing level as 4. In other words, the target manpower can be a decimal; the staffing level, however, can only be an integer.

Should you always round up to get the staffing level? What about the case in which the target manpower is 3.0001? The answers to these questions depend on your goal. If your goal is to definitely meet demand in its entirety (i.e., do not turn a single customer away), you should round up. If your goal is to maximize profits, it is a little more complicated. In this case, you should do the calculations with a staffing level obtained from rounding down, and then with a staffing level obtained from rounding up; you then compare the profits (as we do at the end of the chapter) and determine which of these two options yields more profits.

Now, assume that demand goes up to 160 sandwiches per hour. This is a very high demand rate, even for large Subway restaurants. A higher demand rate means that we have a lower takt time. The tempo of the music has picked up—we need to operate at a faster cycle time to keep up with the takt of demand. How many employees do we need now? Again, we start by computing the takt time:

$$\text{Takt time} = \frac{1}{\text{Demand rate}} = \frac{1}{160 \text{ customers / hour}}$$

$$= 0.00625 \frac{\text{hour}}{\text{customer}} \times 3600 \frac{\text{sec}}{\text{hour}} = 22.5 \frac{\text{seconds}}{\text{customer}}$$

Target manpower The ratio between the labor content and the takt time determines the minimum number of resources required to meet demand. Note that this minimum does not have to be an integer number and that it assumes all resources are perfectly utilized.

We can then use the target manpower formula to find the required staffing level:

$$\text{Target manpower} = \frac{\text{Labor content}}{\text{Takt time}}$$

$$= \frac{120 \text{ seconds/customer}}{22.5 \text{ seconds/customer}} = 5.333$$

So, more demand means a shorter takt time, and a shorter takt time requires more employees to handle the same amount of labor content. As explained earlier, instead of deriving the staffing level based on takt time, we might also ask ourselves: How many employees would it take to obtain a capacity of 160 customers per hour (which is the demand rate)? Given an unknown number of employees, m, we know that the capacity of a resource with m employees is

$$\text{Capacity} = \frac{m}{\text{Processing time}} = \frac{m}{120 \text{ seconds/customer}} = \frac{3600 \times m}{120 \text{ customers/hour}}$$

If we substitute Capacity = 160 units/hour, we get the equation

$$160 \frac{\text{customers}}{\text{hour}} = \frac{3600 \times m}{120 \text{ customers/hour}}$$

$$\Leftrightarrow 160 = 30 \times m \Leftrightarrow m = 5.333$$

So, the solution comes out exactly the same and we leave it to you if you want to find the target manpower level by matching capacity to flow rate or by matching cycle time to takt time. The following calculations, as you will see, are easier to follow when working with takt time, and so we keep our focus on takt time.

In most businesses, demand varies, be it by the hour of the day, the day of the week, or the time of the year. We typically cannot adjust our staffing level for every little change in demand and so the first thing that operations managers in practice do for planning purposes is to **level the demand**; that is, set an expected demand rate for a given period of time (say one hour at a Subway restaurant). Then, we turn that leveled demand into a takt time (remember: high demand means a short takt time) and then translate the takt time into a staffing level. That way, we always staff to demand. Figure 4.2 captures how an operation can translate a time-varying demand and adjust the staffing over time.

Leveling the demand Setting an expected demand rate for a given period of time so that one can look for an appropriate staffing plan for that time period.

Check Your Understanding 4.2

Question: A large manufacturer of laptop computers operates two eight-hour shifts; thus, it has 16 hours available for production. The goal of the manufacturer is to produce 480 computers a day.

What takt time does the manufacturer have to set?

Answer: We know that

$$\begin{aligned}
\text{Takt time} &= \frac{\text{Available time}}{\text{Required quantity/hour}} \\
&= \frac{16 \text{ hours/day}}{480 \text{ computers/day}} \\
&= 0.0333 \frac{\text{hour}}{\text{computer}} \\
&= 2 \frac{\text{minutes}}{\text{computer}}
\end{aligned}$$

© Sot/Digital Vision /Getty Images/RF

Question: Now assume it takes 20 minutes of labor to assemble a computer. What would be the target manpower?

Answer: The target manpower would be

$$\text{Target Manpower} = \frac{\text{Labor Content}}{\text{Takt Time}} = \frac{20 \text{ minutes/computer}}{2 \text{ minutes/computer}} = 10$$

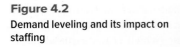

Figure 4.2

Demand leveling and its impact on staffing

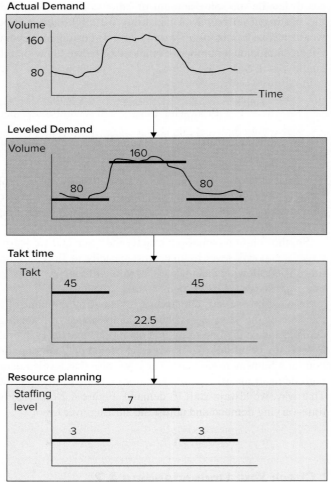

Given our takt time of 22.5 seconds per customer, let us now try to create a process that is able to work according to that beat of demand. If we assume for now that each activity is only carried out by one and only one worker, then we have to keep all processing times at 22.5 seconds/customer or below. In other words, the activities carried out by one employee can together not take longer than 22.5 seconds/customer. This simply reflects that to achieve a flow rate of the process of 160 customers per hour ($\frac{1}{22.5}$ customer per second), each resource in the process must have a capacity of at least 160 customers per hour ($\frac{1}{22.5}$ customer per second).

Further, assume that the activities in the process recipe have to be carried out in the sequence in which they appear in Figure 4.1. Thus, as we are now deciding which employee will carry out which activity, we can simply start with the first employee (resource) and keep on adding activities to the resource as long as her processing time remains at or under 22.5 seconds/unit. Or, put differently, we continue to load activities to the resource until the resulting processing time of the resource exceeds 22.5 seconds/customer and then take the last activity added and move it to the next resource. That sounds complicated, but really is not.

Let's just do the calculations:

- The first employee in the process can greet the customer (4 seconds/customer). Because that still is well below the takt time, we give the employee additional work and have her take the order (5 seconds/customer). The resulting processing time would now be 4 + 5 = 9 seconds/customer, still well below the 22.5 target. So, we keep on adding work, including getting the bread (4 seconds/customer) and cutting the bread (3 seconds/customer). That now gets us to $4 + 5 + 4 + 3 = 16$ seconds/customer. The next activity is dealing with the meat, which takes 12 seconds/customer of work. Because $16 + 12 = 28 > 22.5$, this is too much work for the employee to operate on a 22.5-seconds-per-customer cycle. So we leave the first employee in charge of greeting, taking the order, getting the bread, and cutting the bread and get a resulting processing time of 16 seconds/customer.

- The second employee gets to deal with the meat, the activity that would have moved the processing time above 22.5 seconds per customer for the first employee. We can also put employee 2 in charge of the cheese (9 seconds/customer) because $12 + 9 = 21 < 22.5$. But that's it—the next activity (the onions, 3 seconds/customer) needs to be carried out by employee 3.

- For employee 3, we start with the onions (3 seconds/customer) and can add lettuce (3 seconds/customer), tomatoes (4 seconds/customer), cucumbers (5 seconds/customer), and pickles (4 seconds/customer), yielding a processing time of $3 + 3 + 4 + 5 + 4 = 19$ seconds/customer.

- Employee 4 then can deal with the green peppers, black olives, and hot peppers, with activity times of 4, 3, and 2 seconds per customer, respectively. Because the resulting processing time of $4 + 3 + 2 = 9$ seconds/customer is still below our 22.5 seconds/customer target, we can also have her add the condiments (5 seconds/customer), getting the processing time to 14 seconds/customer.

- Employee 5 then can wrap and bag and offer the fresh value meal, getting a processing time of $13 + 3 = 16$ seconds/customer.

- Employee 6 can offer cookies but will not be able to ring up the sale on the register, leaving her with 14 seconds/customer.

- And, finally, employee 7 will be in charge of the cash register, yielding a 20-second-per-customer processing time.

The resulting allocation of activities to the seven employees is shown in Figure 4.3. Each box in the figure corresponds to one activity, with the height of the boxes capturing the duration of the activity. So, the cumulative height across boxes that are stacked on each other corresponds to the processing time. In addition to the seven processing times, the figure also

Figure 4.3

A Subway sandwich line with seven employees

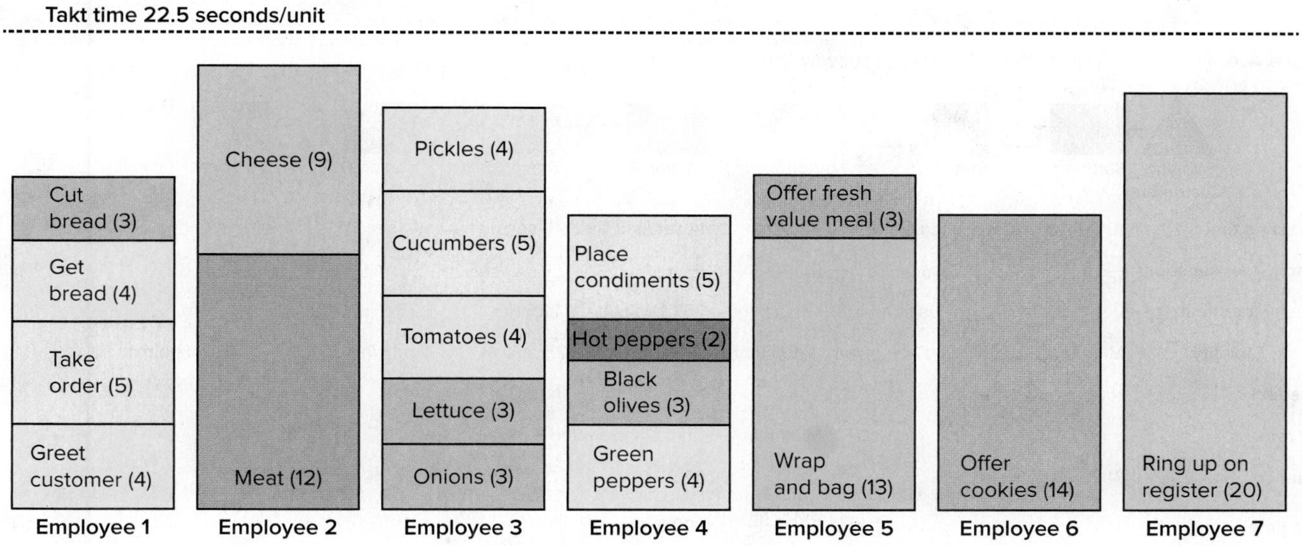

Takt time 22.5 seconds/unit

| Employee 1 | Employee 2 | Employee 3 | Employee 4 | Employee 5 | Employee 6 | Employee 7 |

shows our takt time. We observe that all resources have processing times below the takt time, indicating that the process will be able to operate at the rate of demand.

But wait a minute! Why are we talking about seven employees? Didn't we just compute that it would take 5.333 employees to achieve the takt time of 22.5 seconds/customer? Weren't we "generous" by rounding up to a staffing level of six employees? And now we find that we need seven employees. That does not look like efficiency at all. But where is the inefficiency here?

The answer is quite simply the idle time. The target manpower calculation implicitly assumes that all resources are utilized at 100 percent—that is, there is no idle time in the process. However, this is typically not the case. And, as we will see in a moment, we have more idle time in the process compared to when we had three employees make the sandwich. To see this, let us perform a careful process analysis of our seven-step process. We compute the capacity levels of each resource, which will get us the bottleneck. We then can compute flow rate as the minimum between demand and process capacity. From there, we can get the utilization levels and the cycle time. The resulting analysis is shown in Figure 4.4.

We see that with a processing time of 21 seconds/customer and hence a capacity of $\frac{1}{21}$ customer/second, station 2 is the bottleneck. Further, we observe that the process is presently demand-constrained, given that it has a process capacity of 171.4 customers/hour and a demand rate of 160 customers/hour. This results in a flow rate of 160 customers/hour and a cycle time of one customer every 22.5 seconds.

As was done earlier in this chapter, we can compute the idle time for each resource as

$$\text{Idle time(Resource } i) = \text{Cycle time} - \text{Processing time(Resource } i)$$

So, we get

$$\text{Idle time(Station 1)} = 22.5 - 16 = 6.5 \frac{\text{seconds}}{\text{customer}}$$

$$\text{Idle time(Station 2)} = 22.5 - 21 = 1.5 \frac{\text{seconds}}{\text{customer}}$$

$$\text{Idle time(Station 3)} = 22.5 - 19 = 3.5 \frac{\text{seconds}}{\text{customer}}$$

$$\text{Idle time(Station 4)} = 22.5 - 14 = 8.5 \frac{\text{seconds}}{\text{customer}}$$

$$\text{Idle time(Station 5)} = 22.5 - 16 = 6.5 \frac{\text{seconds}}{\text{customer}}$$

Figure 4.4 Process analysis of the seven-station subway line

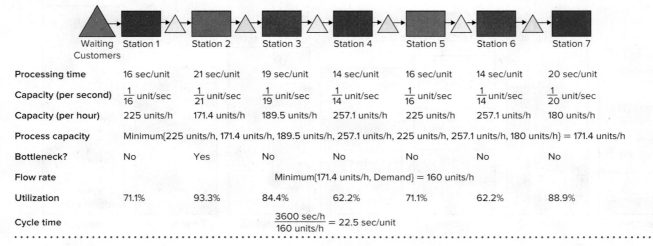

	Station 1	Station 2	Station 3	Station 4	Station 5	Station 6	Station 7
Processing time	16 sec/unit	21 sec/unit	19 sec/unit	14 sec/unit	16 sec/unit	14 sec/unit	20 sec/unit
Capacity (per second)	$\frac{1}{16}$ unit/sec	$\frac{1}{21}$ unit/sec	$\frac{1}{19}$ unit/sec	$\frac{1}{14}$ unit/sec	$\frac{1}{16}$ unit/sec	$\frac{1}{14}$ unit/sec	$\frac{1}{20}$ unit/sec
Capacity (per hour)	225 units/h	171.4 units/h	189.5 units/h	257.1 units/h	225 units/h	257.1 units/h	180 units/h
Process capacity	Minimum{225 units/h, 171.4 units/h, 189.5 units/h, 257.1 units/h, 225 units/h, 257.1 units/h, 180 units/h} = 171.4 units/h						
Bottleneck?	No	Yes	No	No	No	No	No
Flow rate	Minimum{171.4 units/h, Demand} = 160 units/h						
Utilization	71.1%	93.3%	84.4%	62.2%	71.1%	62.2%	88.9%
Cycle time	$\frac{3600 \text{ sec/h}}{160 \text{ units/h}} = 22.5$ sec/unit						

$$\text{Idle time(Station 6)} = 22.5 - 14 = 8.5 \frac{\text{seconds}}{\text{customer}}$$

$$\text{Idle time(Station 7)} = 22.5 - 20 = 2.5 \frac{\text{seconds}}{\text{customer}}$$

We add up the idle time across the employees, which gives us the total idle time in the process:

$$\text{Total idle time} = \text{Sum of Idle time across resources}$$

$$= 6.5 + 1.5 + 3.5 + 8.5 + 6.5 + 8.5 + 2.5 = 37.5 \frac{\text{seconds}}{\text{customer}}$$

So, for every customer that we serve, we incur (and pay for) 37.5 seconds of idle time. Is this a lot? As done before, we compare the idle time with the labor content, a measure that we previously introduced as the average labor utilization:

$$\text{Average labor utilization} = \frac{\text{Labor content}}{(\text{Labor content} + \text{Idle time})}$$

$$= \frac{120 \text{ seconds/customer}}{(120 + 37.5) \text{ seconds/customer}}$$

$$= 76.2 \text{ percent}$$

Note that this number is lower than the process with three employees, where we obtained an average labor utilization of 87.0 percent. This decrease in efficiency is also reflected in the costs of direct labor:

$$\text{Costs of direct labor} = \frac{\text{Wages per unit of time}}{\text{Flow rate}}$$

With our three-person process, our costs of direct labor were $0.46 per customer. With the seven employees, we now get

$$\text{Costs of direct labor} = \frac{7 \times 12 \text{ \$/h}}{160 \text{ customers/ah}}$$

$$= 0.525 \frac{\$}{\text{customer}}$$

So, by running the process faster, we have actually increased our costs. But why is this? To identify the source of the cost increase, consider again the average labor utilization. With the three-employee process, that measure was 87.0 percent; now, with seven employees, it is down to 76.2 percent. There are two reasons for this:

- First, with a demand of 100 customers/hour and a process capacity of 78 customers/ hour, we were capacity-constrained. That is, our bottleneck resource (employee 2) was operating at 100 percent utilization. Now, in contrast, even our bottleneck resource (again, employee 2, though now with a different set of activities and a shorter process-ing time) is only running at a 93.3 percent utilization. Thus, we have slack capacity relative to demand.

- Second, balancing the process becomes harder as we spread out the activities over more resources. Consider the extreme case of having one worker being in charge of all activities. Assuming sufficient demand, that resource would have an average labor utilization of 100 percent. No surprise, a process with one employee is perfectly bal-anced. But balancing the process becomes harder as we add more employees to the process and we spread out the activities over more and more resources.

But, again, the goal of an operation is not to maximize the labor utilization. By adding more employees, we have suffered some efficiency loss (a couple of percentage points of labor utilization, a couple of pennies of costs of direct labor), but, in contrast, our flow rate has gone up by a lot. Because a Subway sandwich sells for around $6 per customer and the material costs of a sandwich are substantially smaller than that, we most likely have increased our profits.

4.3 Off-Loading the Bottleneck

© Mario De Biaso/Digital Stock/Royalty-Free/Corbis/RF

In the previous section, we saw how to choose an appropriate staffing level given a certain amount of demand. Choosing the right staffing level makes sure that we don't have too much capacity (leading to idle time and high costs of direct labor) but still serve demand (leading to no lost revenues from turning customers away). We now consider other forms in which we can improve the process to make it more efficient.

In 1984, Eli Goldratt wrote a highly successful book entitled *The Goal.* It's hard to believe, but the book is an operations management textbook written as a novel and has sold millions of copies. The hero of the book is a fictional plant manager by the name of Alex who discovers the principles of process analysis. Alex experiences his epiphany when he takes a group of Boy Scouts for a hike in the forest. The group takes a single-file path and starts out close to each other. But the longer they march, the more the group spreads out. The boys in the front tend to be the fast ones and so they walk at their own rate, leaving the others behind. One chubby Scout by the name of **Herbie** is holding the group back. He has hundreds of meters of empty trail in front of him and a group of impatient Boy Scouts behind him (Scouts who, due to the narrowness of the trail, cannot overtake Herbie). Alex realizes that this hike has a lot in common with his production process. He associates the speed with which the entire group is moving with the flow rate in the plant. Just as the plant cannot produce faster than the bottleneck, the group of Boy Scouts cannot walk faster than Herbie. The amount of empty hiking path between the kids, Alex recognized, is similar to inventory in a plant where the inventory piles up in front of the bottleneck.

Herbie A fictitious character in Eli Goldratt's book *The Goal.* Herbie is the slowest hiker in a troop of Boy Scouts. He thus holds up the troop in the same way a bottleneck holds up a process.

Since the publication of the book, many operations experts have referred to the bottleneck as Herbie. The example of the Boy Scouts reminds us that whatever process improvement we might consider, we have to start with the bottleneck. It might be possible to reduce the time required to put the meat on the sandwich (12 seconds/customer). For example, we could already organize the meat on a little plastic foil, ready to be put on the sandwich, which might reduce the time of this activity to 5 seconds/customer. However, this improvement in and by itself will be of no value. Employee 1 is not the bottleneck, and so all that will be accomplished with this "improvement" is to increase the amount of idle time for the employee. Such an improvement would be similar to making one of the fast Boy Scouts walk even faster and then having to wait for Herbie at the next campsite.

So, any process improvement starts by looking at the bottleneck. In the case of Herbie, Alex soon found out that his ability to walk as fast as the others was not just constrained by his physiological limitations, but also by Herbie carrying a rather large and heavy backpack with plenty of snacks inside. To improve the hiking speed of his group, Alex then takes Herbie's backpack and spreads the content among the faster Scouts. Yes, those are now slowed down, but Herbie is able to walk faster and that is all that counts.

In general, we refer to the improvement strategy of moving work away from the bottleneck step as **off-loading the bottleneck.** Off-loading the bottleneck can take multiple forms:

- Reassign activities to other resources with more capacity, an improvement strategy that we refer to as line balancing and discuss in the next section.

- Automating some of the activities consuming time at the bottleneck by using technology; for example, we might be able to automate the dispensing of the wrapping paper, which has the potential of reducing the processing time for employee 2.

- Outsourcing some of the activities consuming time at the bottleneck. Imagine it would be possible to put the condiments in the bag at the beginning of the shift or to even purchase bags that are already "loaded" with condiments. This would reduce the time for employee 2, which, given that employee 2 is the bottleneck, would increase the capacity of the process.

In addition to off-loading the bottleneck, we can increase the process capacity by adding more employees. If you add just one employee (or, in general, one unit of capacity), where would you put him or her? The answer is "to the bottleneck" because that is what constrains the process—the chain is only as strong as its weakest link. Adding an employee to the bottleneck is like boosting the fitness of Herbie. . . . In addition to adding more employees, we can also boost the bottleneck capacity by either having the bottleneck resource work longer hours (overtime) or assigning a more skilled employee to the bottleneck resource, assuming that this employee would have a shorter processing time.

> **LO4-3** Find ways to improve the process efficiency by off-loading the bottleneck.

4.4 How to Balance a Process

In general, we balance a process by allocating the activities that need to be carried out in the process across the process resources as evenly as possible. Because most of these tools have their roots in the management of assembly lines, we speak of **line balancing** rather than process balancing. In practice, two cases of such balancing have to be distinguished:

- **Balancing for a fixed sequence of activities:** In this case, we have to carry out the activities in a given order, one activity is the first, one the second, and so on. This corresponds to what we did as we moved from the three-employee line to the seven-employee line. We first compute takt time and then keep on adding activities to a resource just so long as the resulting processing time of that resource stays under the takt time. We then proceed to the next resource, until all activities are assigned.

- **Balancing for activities with no fixed sequence:** It is hard to wrap a sandwich before it is made. But could you put hot peppers on a sandwich before dealing with the pickles? Probably you could. In some cases, you can reshuffle the activities in your process. This gives you an extra bit of flexibility, which makes assigning activities to resources in a balanced way easier, and thus should lead to a higher average labor utilization and lower costs of direct labor.

> **LO4-4** Balance a process by reallocating work from one step to another.

> **Line balancing** The act of allocating the activities that need to be carried out in the process across the process resources as evenly as possible so that all resources have a comparable utilization level.

Figure 4.5 By moving an activity away from the bottleneck, we can increase capacity

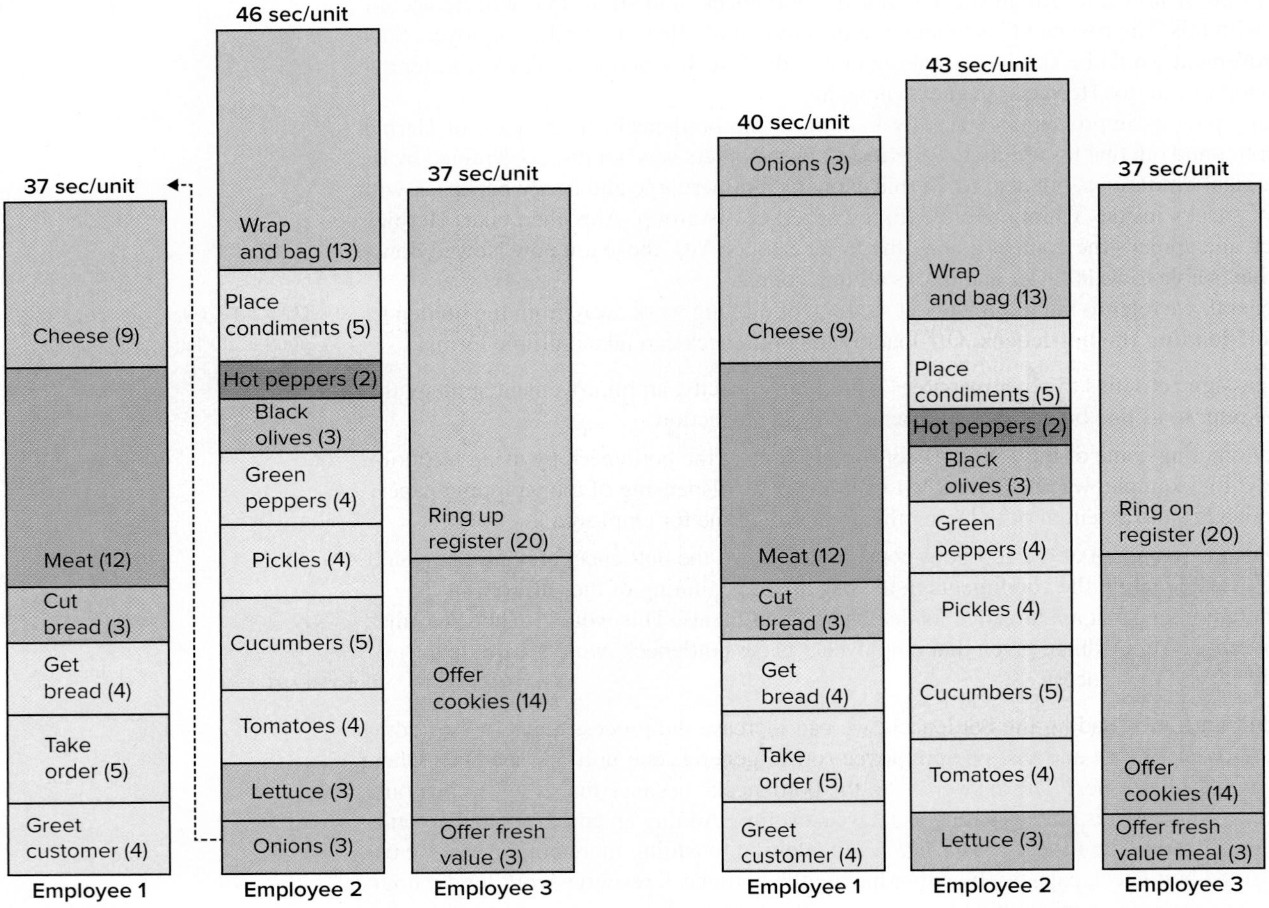

To see the idea of line balancing in action, consider Figure 4.5. Figure 4.5 goes back to our base case of a three-employee process. Moreover, assume for now a demand of 80 customers per hour. With 80 customers per hour, we have a takt time of 3600/80 = 45 seconds/customer. As we look through the activities required for making a sandwich, we can put employee 1 in charge of everything from greeting the customer to putting the onions on the sandwich. This corresponds to a processing time of 4 + 5 + 4 + 3 + 12 + 9 + 3 = 40 seconds/customer. This is different from the previous assignment of activities, as we now have moved the onion task from employee 2 to employee 1. This leaves employee 2 in charge of everything from the lettuce to wrapping, with a new (lower) processing time of 43 seconds/customer. Employee 3's responsibilities remain unchanged. With processing times of 40, 43, and 37 seconds/customer, we can meet our takt time of 45 seconds/customer. In fact, our average labor utilization has gone up and we can even fulfill all 80 units of customer demand per hour.

Note that the process on the right of **Figure 4.5** is able to achieve a higher labor utilization. With a demand rate of 80 customers per hour (takt time of 45 seconds/customer), we have idle times of 4, 2, and 8 seconds per customer, respectively, yielding a total idle time of 14 seconds/customer. Given that the bottleneck on the left side of **Figure 4.5** was employee 2 with a processing time of 46 seconds/customer, the process on the left was capacity-constrained and the cycle time would have been 46 seconds/customer, yielding idle times of 9 + 0 + 9 = 18 seconds/customer. Thus, by rebalancing the process, we have improved labor utilization, but we also increased the process capacity and the flow rate.

Check Your Understanding 4.3

Question: An assembly process requires the completion of six activities, labeled A1 to A6, that have to be carried out in exactly this sequence. A1 takes 3 minutes/unit; A2, 2 minutes/unit; A3, 6 minutes/unit; A4, 1 minute/unit; A5, 2 minutes/unit; and A6, 1 minute/unit. Right now, the six tasks are assigned to three workers as follows. The first worker takes activities A1 and A2, the second worker takes activities A3 and A4, and the third worker takes activities A5 to A6. How can you improve the process by balancing the line?

Answer: We first determine the bottleneck. Worker 1 has a processing time of $3 + 2 = 5$ minutes/unit and hence a capacity of $\frac{1}{5}$ unit/minute. Worker 2 has a processing time of $6 + 1 = 7$ minutes/unit and hence a capacity of $\frac{1}{7}$ unit/minute. And worker 3 has a processing time of $2 + 1 = 3$ minutes/unit and hence a capacity of $\frac{1}{3}$ unit/minute. So, clearly step 2 is the bottleneck.

We can off-load the bottleneck by reassigning activity A4 to worker 3. In both scenarios, the labor utilization and the costs of direct labor would be the same.

© *Digital Vision/Getty Images/RF*

4.5 The Pros and Cons of Specialization

Contrast the following ways of assigning employees to activities:

- Option 1: Each employee takes care of all activities required to serve a customer. In this situation, each employee would do all the work, from greeting the customer to using the cash register. We can replicate this process up to the point when capacity matches demand.

- Option 2: We do what we did in the previous section—each employee specializes in one or several activities. We can increase the level of specialization leading to shorter and shorter processing times for each employee and thus more capacity.

LO4-5 Explain the benefits and limitations of specialization.

As we saw in the calculations with the seven-employee process (Figure 4.3), option 2 is associated with extra idle time and thus a lower labor utilization. In contrast, option 1 leads to a more balanced process and thus a higher labor utilization. In a one-employee process, that one employee is going to be the bottleneck. The one-employee process is, by definition, perfectly balanced and so we would keep our idle time low (at zero) and our labor utilization high (at 100 percent).

But the problem is that not everything else remains constant as we compare six one-employee operations with one six- (or, to be accurate, seven-) employee operation. There are benefits of specialization that we so far have left ignored. This makes option 2 look worse than it is. The benefits of specialization are the reason why Adam Smith observed the rapid flow in the pin factory (mentioned in the Connections section further down):

- **Reduction in processing times due to elimination of setups**: The times for the various activities might be reduced (and thus the capacity levels increased) as workers specialize in fewer activities. For example, an employee who is doing all activities might have to take his gloves off when he switches between touching the sandwich and operating the cash register, which will increase processing times. A person who does nothing but operate the cash register would not face such an inconvenience. We will refer to such disruptions as **setup times,** a topic we will discuss further in a later chapter.

- **Reduction in processing times due to learning**: If you cut 1000 tomatoes per day, chances are you will get very good at this. Simply put, practice makes perfect and this perfection also manifests itself in shorter processing times. This will be the topic of the chapter on learning curves.

Reduction in processing times due to elimination of setups The fact that specialization increases efficiency by eliminating setups.

Reduction in processing times due to learning The fact that specialization increases efficiency by providing more practice to the operator in the execution of a particular activity.

- **Lower-skilled labor**: More specialized labor tends to require a shorter training period and oftentimes receives lower wage rates. It takes less time to teach an employee how to assemble a rearview mirror compared to teaching her how to assemble an entire car. So even if specialization does not decrease the processing times, it has the potential to decrease the nominator in the costs of direct labor (i.e., wages).

- **Equipment replication**: Another benefit of the specialized process flow relates to the amount of equipment that is required to operate the process. Six parallel stations in which each employee carries out all activities either would require that each employee get her own equipment (including a cash register, which is rather expensive) or would likely lead to interferences among the six employees if more than one employee would attempt to use similar ingredients at the same time (too many cooks in the kitchen).

These benefits of specialization have to be compared with the costs of specialization in the form of increased idle time. We also want to point out that there are other benefits of having a worker develop the skills to master a broad set of activities. In a classic study of worker motivation, Hackman and Oldham describe the characteristics of a job that keeps the workforce engaged and motivated. Variety in the activities carried out by the employee was one of the key characteristics of a motivating work environment. Many companies have responded to these findings by organizing their work in **work cells** where small teams of employees perform a job (complete a flow unit) from beginning to end. Organizing the work in work cells is the exact opposite of specialization.

Lower-skilled labor Labor that is not able to master multiple activities and thus can only work as a resource with very short processing times.

Equipment replication The need to provide extra equipment to nonspecialized labor at resources often leads to a low level of equipment utilization.

Work cells An organization of work where small teams of employees perform a job (complete a flow unit) from beginning to end.

CONNECTIONS: The History of Specialization

Adam Smith, Scottish philosopher and economist, 1723–1790.

....

Courtesy of Library of Congress Prints and Photographs Division [LC-USZ62-17407]

In 1776, the Scottish economist Adam Smith authored a rather voluminous book entitled *The Wealth of Nations*. Though most of the book was dedicated to economics, Smith must also have had a deep interest in the operations of business. Writing at a time when the field of operations management had not even been invented, Smith reported his observation on a pin factory.

One man draws out the wire, another straights it, a third cuts it, a fourth points it, a fifth grinds it at the top for receiving the head; to make the head requires two or three distinct operations; to put it on, is a peculiar business, to whiten the pins is another; [. . .] I have seen a small manufactory of this kind where ten men only were employed, [. . .] they could, when they exerted themselves, make among them about twelve pounds of pins in a day. There are in a pound upwards of four thousand pins of a middling size. Those ten persons, therefore, could make among them upwards of forty-eight thousand pins in a day. [. . .] But if they had all wrought separately and independently, and without any of them having been educated to this peculiar business, they certainly could not each of them have made twenty, perhaps not one pin in a day [. . .].*

Notice how Adam Smith basically does what we now would consider a process analysis. And he proposes that the process can be improved if workers specialize in the tasks they work on.

....

*Adam Smith, *An Inquiry into the Nature and Causes of the Wealth of Nations,* ed. Edwin Cannan, 5th ed. (London: Methuen & Co., 1904), http://www.econlib.org/library/Smith/smWN1.html

© Inti St Clair/Blend Images LLC/RF

Check Your Understanding 4.4

Question: Two students, Bill and Mary, are selling pancakes for a fund-raiser at school. It takes about 1 minute to take an order and collect the payment. It takes 1.5 minutes per order to make the pancakes. The two students debate which of the approaches would lead to a higher capacity. Bill argues that having each of them specialize in an activity would increase their labor utilization. Is he right?

Answer: No, specialization typically reduces the labor utilization as it becomes harder to balance the line.

Question: Mary nevertheless also favors specialization. However, she argues that this will benefit them because it will reduce processing time. Why might this be the case?

Answer: Specialization can reduce processing times because

- It reduces setups.
- It will facilitate learning.

4.6 Understanding the Financial Impact of Process Improvements

Staffing to demand, balancing a line, off-loading the bottleneck, or specializing employees—all of these improvements have in common that they can improve efficiency. A second saved per customer, an extra percentage point of utilization, or an extra penny saved in the costs of direct labor are certainly welcome, but do such variables really matter? Improving processes is hard work and so before we continue we will have to tackle the question: "Is the juice worth the squeeze?" Or, put differently: "Is this book worth the read?"

As we discussed earlier, the goal of most operations is to help generate profits. We observed that

$$\text{Profits} = \text{Flow rate} \times (\text{Average price} - \text{Average costs})$$

For now, let's leave the price constant across all customers—say everybody ordered food for $6 per customer. We have two types of costs, in a restaurant and in most other operations as well: fixed and variable costs.

Fixed costs are those costs that we have to pay anyway, pretty much independent of how much we produce and sell. The rent for the restaurant, the marketing campaigns, the insurance, the utility bills—all of those are fixed costs. **Variable costs**, in contrast, increase with the number of units we sell. The material costs for sourcing the food, as well as the packaging for the food, are examples of variable costs.

This allows us to rewrite profits to

$$\text{Profits} = \text{Flow rate} \times (\text{Average price} - \text{Variable costs}) - \text{Fixed costs}$$

Typically, the line between fixed costs and variable costs is not clearly defined. It oftentimes will depend on the time frame within which decisions are made. When it is noon and you have six employees in the restaurant ready to work, we can think of the employees as fixed costs. If you can make them more productive (e.g., by balancing the line) and sell an extra sandwich, you will not increase the labor costs at all. On the other hand, when you decide how many employees you should staff for next Tuesday, labor cost is much more of a variable cost, because you will attempt to staff to demand.

For the following calculations, assume the labor costs are fixed at 4 workers $\times$ 12 $/worker hour = 48 $/hour. Moreover, assume we face fixed costs of 250 $/h as far as various

LO4-6 Evaluate the financial benefits of process improvements.

Fixed costs Those costs that a firm has to pay anyway, independent of how much it produces and sells.

Variable costs Those costs that grow in proportion to the amount a firm produces and sells.

TABLE 4.1   **Profit Implications of Various Process Improvements in a High-Demand Setting**

	Base Case	10% Lower Material Costs	10% Lower Fixed Cost	10% Faster at BN	Units
Processing time for employee 2	47	47	47	42.3	sec/customer
Demand rate	100	100	100	100	customers/hour
Average revenue per customer	6	6	6	6	$/customer
Average food cost per customer	1.5	1.35	1.5	1.5	$/customer
Staff	4	4	4	4	
Wage	12	12	12	12	$/hour
Fixed cost	250	250	225	250	$/hour
Process capacity	76.6	76.6	76.6	85.1	customers/hour
Flow rate	76.6	76.6	76.6	85.1	customers/hour
Revenue	459.6	459.6	459.6	510.6	$/hour
Material costs	114.9	103.4	114.9	127.7	$/hour
Staffing	48	48	48	48	$/hour
Fixed cost	250	250	225	250	$/hour
Profit	46.68	58.17	71.68	84.98	$/hour
Increase to base case		25%	54%	82%	

overhead-related costs are concerned. We will leave it somewhat vague how these costs are calculated. In most operations, you can have long discussions about fixed costs, because typically these fixed costs get allocated following some accounting rules. For example, one might argue that the monthly rent for the restaurant should be evenly allocated over the 30 days/ month × 24 hours/day. However, chances are that we do very little business at 3 a.m. and so allocating the rent evenly across all hours of the month is not necessarily the right thing to do. More realistically, one might allocate the rent in proportion to the amount of sandwiches sold in each hour. The point is, for now, that there are many ways in which the $250 per hour might have been derived, and we will simply take this number as given.

As far as material costs are concerned, say it takes us $1.50 to pay for the ingredients of the average customer order and that we are selling the average customer order at $6. Table 4.1 shows the profit calculations for a process with three workers operating the line (with processing times of 37, 46, and 37 seconds/customer, respectively) and one worker acting as indirect labor in charge of refilling the bins, making bread, handling the phone, and cleaning the restaurant, assuming a demand rate of 100 customers per hour. The process (the base case) is currently capacity-constrained (with a process capacity of 76.6 customers per hour, driven by the processing time at station 2) and so revenues are 76.6 customers/h × 6 $/customer = 459.6 $/h. Costs for the materials (the ingredients for the food) are also proportional to the flow rate, while the fixed costs include labor and the previously mentioned $250 per hour. This leaves a profit contribution of 46.68 $/hour.

The next three columns of Table 4.1 show the financial implications of three operational improvements. First, consider the effect of 10 percent lower material costs. Revenue and other costs remain constant and the material cost reduction of 10 percent of $114.9 per hour

= $11.49 improves profits, which corresponds to a profit increase of 25 percent. Second, consider the benefit of reducing the overhead expenses by 10 percent of $250 per hour = $25, which corresponds to an increase in profit of 54 percent. Because overhead costs make up a large chunk of the overall costs compared to material costs, a 10 percent improvement has a higher financial impact. Finally, consider the effect of reducing the processing time of employee 2 by 10 percent (from 47 seconds/customer to 42.3 seconds/customer). By cutting the processing time by 4.7 seconds/customer, we improve profits by 80 percent! How can that be? How can a few seconds have such a big impact?

The improvement in profits is so large because of a combination of three effects coming together. Employee 2 is the bottleneck, so every improvement we make at the bottleneck is an improvement to the entire process. After all, it is the capacity of the bottleneck that determines the process capacity. Saving 4.7 seconds/customer at employee 1 would have had absolutely no effect on profits.

The process is currently capacity-constrained. Thus, by increasing capacity, we increase flow rate. If we had been constrained by demand, the situation would have been very different. Table 4.2 evaluates the same operational improvements but for a lower-demand environment. Notice that the profits are much lower in the base case—we have held fixed costs constant but now have less revenue. Notice further that the cost reductions of materials costs and fixed costs have (in percentage points) a larger effect than before. The reason for this is that they are applied to a smaller base: 10 percent less fixed costs still translates to $25 saved per hour and 10 percent of material costs is only slightly less than in Table 4.1 as we are now serving fewer customers. But the effect of a shorter processing time is zero—the process is constrained by demand, and so more capacity (even at the bottleneck) simply does not make a difference.

TABLE 4.2 Profit Implications of Various Process Improvements in a Low-Demand Setting

	Base Case	10% Lower Material Costs	10% Lower Fixed Costs	10% Faster at BN	Units
Processing time employee 2	47	47	47	42.3	sec/customer
Demand rate	70	70	70	70	customers/hour
Average revenue per customer	6	6	6	6	$/customer
Average food cost per customer	1.5	1.35	1.5	1.5	$/customer
Staff	4	4	4	4	
Wage	12	12	12	12	$/h
Fixed cost	250	250	225	250	$/h
Process capacity	76.6	76.6	76.6	85.1	customers/hour
Flow rate	70.0	70.0	70.0	70.0	customers/hour
Revenue	420.0	420.0	420.0	420.0	$/hour
Material costs	105.0	94.5	105.0	105.0	$/hour
Staffing	48	48	48	48	$/hour
Fixed cost	250	250	225	250	$/hour
Profit	17.00	27.50	42.00	17.00	$/hour
Increase to base case		62%	147%	0%	

© Monty Rakusen/Cultura RF/Getty
Images/RF

Check Your Understanding 4.5

Question: A process consisting of 10 assembly-line workers is currently demand-constrained. The product is brand new and has a very high margin. Management is evaluating the acquisition of a new tool that would reduce labor content by 10 percent. What would be the implications on revenues and profits?

Answer: Because the process is demand-constrained, shorter processing times or a lower labor content has no impact on revenues. A lower labor content would impact the target man-power and potentially reduce labor costs. This depends on whether this reduction is large enough to carry out the process with nine workers.

Question: Consider again our two students, Bill and Mary, selling pancakes for a fund-raiser at school. Recall that it takes about 1 minute to take an order and collect the payment. It takes 1.5 minutes per order to make the pancakes. Bill and Mary are selling the pancakes at $1 per unit and they have material costs of $0.25 per unit and no fixed costs. They have one hour in which they can make and sell pancakes. Bill's cousin has a pancake maker that reduces the time to make a pancake from 1.5 minutes/unit = 90 seconds/unit to 80 seconds/unit. However, his cousin demands a $5 payment for his pancake maker. From a purely financial perspective, should Bill and Mary take him up on this offer?

Answer: In the present process, the two students are producing at a flow rate of one unit every 1.5 minutes (constrained by making the pancakes). This gives them 40 units per hour (and, because they only have one hour, this is also their total revenue). Their profit would be

$$\text{Profit} = \text{Flow rate} \times (\text{Average price} - \text{Variable cost}) - \text{Fixed costs}$$
$$= 40 \text{ units/h} \times (1 \text{ \$/unit} - 0.25 \text{ \$/unit}) - 0 = 30 \text{ \$/h}$$

If they used Bill's cousin's pancake maker, they could make a pancake every 80 seconds. This corresponds to a capacity of $\frac{1}{80}$ unit/sec = 45 units/h. Now, however, they would have fixed costs of 5 $/hour, yielding profits of

$$\text{Profits} = 45 \text{ units/h} \times (1 \text{ \$/unit} - 0.25 \text{ \$/unit}) - 5 \text{ \$/h} = 33.75 \text{ \$/h} - 5 \text{ \$/h} = 28.75 \text{ \$/h}$$

Thus, at least from a financial approach, they should not use the pancake maker. They would, however, feed five more students.

· ·

The third effect that makes the profit increase so large in Table 4.1 relates to the restaurant's cost structure. The restaurant has a relatively high **gross margin**; that is, the ratio between price and variable costs is large ($6 in revenue per order to $1.50 in material costs per order, giving a ratio of 4:1 and margins of 75 percent). So every additional customer we serve will give us $4.50 in extra profits. Such situations are common in service industries, most of which have high fixed costs and relatively low variable costs. The situation is different in most manufacturing settings, where margins can be 20 percent or less. So getting an extra order through in these cases simply has a lower impact on profits.

So, every second counts. In operations, even seemingly small improvements in process variables can have a big financial effect. Moreover, this effect varies dramatically across operations and industries. Demand-constrained versus capacity-constrained, high margin versus low margin, bottleneck or not—all these variables matter. And this is why we cannot leave the financials of a company to accountants or financial managers. What we need is an understanding of how the operations of the business drive financial results.

Gross margin The ratio between profits and revenues.

Conclusion

Improving efficiency is an important topic for almost any organization. If we can get more output with an equal or lower amount of input, we will profit financially. This can take the form of lower costs or, if we are presently constrained by capacity, can also translate into higher revenues.

In this chapter, we saw a number of ways we can define efficiency. We defined the costs of direct labor as the ratio between the total wages paid per unit of time and the flow rate. We also defined the labor content as the sum of the processing times involving labor and the labor utilization as the percentage of time that our workforce is working as opposed to being idle. All calculations are summarized in Exhibit 4.1.

Key Calculations for Efficiency and Process Improvement Strategies

EXHIBIT 4.1

Efficiency Measure	Calculation
Costs of direct labor	(Number of employees × Wage rate)/Flow rate
Labor content	Sum of the processing times
Average labor utilization	Average utilization across resources or Labor content/(Labor content + Total idle time) or (Labor content/Number of employees)/Cycle time
Process improvement strategies	Staff to demand Off-load the bottleneck Balance the line Determine specialization level

To improve the efficiency of an operation, management can adjust the process flow in a number of ways:

- **Matching supply with demand based on takt time.** Having too little capacity is costly because it leaves demand unfilled. Having too much capacity is costly because the underutilized resources will cost us, yet their idle time will not contribute to our profits. So making sure that we adjust the capacity of the process to demand is critical. We saw that we could compute the staffing level that would be required in a perfectly balanced line based on the target manpower formula. We also saw that the target manpower is an absolute minimum staffing level required to serve demand. The actual staffing level needs to be higher than the target manpower because of the integer constraint associated with hiring employees. Moreover, we will typically not be able to utilize all resources at 100 percent and so, depending on imbalances in utilization, the actual staffing level might have to be even higher.

- **Capacity increase at the bottleneck.** A chain is only as strong as its weakest link. As far as capacity is concerned, the weakest link in a process is the bottleneck and so we will never be able to move more units through the process than we have capacity at the bottleneck. So whenever we are capacity-constrained, we ought to look at the bottleneck and consider capacity increases. Because the capacity of a resource is given by the number of employees divided by the processing time, we have two options to increase capacity: either we have to increase the staffing level at the bottleneck (or, if the resource consists of equipment, install more equipment) or we have to decrease the processing time (off-load the bottleneck).

- **Matching the internal supply with the internal demand through line balancing.** Just like the overall process serves the demand coming from the end customer, we can think of each individual resource in the process serving the demand of its preceeding resources. Employee 3 can be thought of as an internal customer of employee 2. Just as we aimed to match supply with demand at the process level, we have to match supply with demand within the process. Mismatches between internal supply and demand cause the process flow to be imbalanced, leading to idle time and poor utilization. By improving line balance, we can increase capacity or decrease the staffing level without having to pay for more employees. As a result, efficiency goes up.

- **Finding the right level of specialization.** Finally, processes can be improved by finding an appropriate level of specialization. Specialization typically allows us to employ workers with lower skill levels, it avoids replicating expensive equipment, and it has the potential to decrease the labor content. In contrast, specialization comes at the expense of line balance. Balancing a one-person line is trivial (it is, by definition, already balanced), yet the longer the line, the harder it will be to achieve a high labor utilization. Specialization can also have a negative effect on employee motivation, which also has the potential to hurt our efficiency.

Which process improvement approach is right? There exists no silver bullet and no universal strategy to improve a process. Every process has its own challenges and a good process analysis will position you well to come up with the right process improvement strategy. When evaluating process improvement, it is important that we do this in the context of the operation's profitability. Increasing efficiency is not a goal in and of itself; increasing profits is. We saw that even small improvements in process performance can have a large financial impact. We also saw that efficiency is not just about reducing costs. If the operation is currently constrained by capacity, efficiency improvements in the form of shorter processing times at the bottleneck or a better line balance also will increase the flow rate and thus revenues.

Summary of Learning Objectives

LO4-1   **Compute the costs of direct labor, labor content, idle time, and average labor utilization**

We start out by computing the flow rate of the process. If we divide the wages by the flow rate, we get the costs of direct labor. We then add up all processing time involving labor to get to the labor content. In addition to the labor content, we have to pay for the time a worker is idle. Per flow unit, this is simply the difference between the processing time and the cycle time of the process (where the cycle time is 1/Flow rate). The average labor utilization can be found by taking the average across all resources involving labor. It also can be found by taking the ratio between the labor content and the sum of labor content and the idle time added up across all resources.

LO4-2   **Compute the takt time of a process and translate this to a target manpower**

We find the takt time of a process by dividing the available time by the required output quantity. That tells us how much time should elapse between completing two consecutive units. If we divide the labor content by the takt time, we find how many workers we need to produce to this takt time, assuming we have a perfectly balanced process.

LO4-3   **Find ways to improve the process efficiency by off-loading the bottleneck**

By definition, the bottleneck has the highest utilization among all resources in the process. The idea of off-loading the bottleneck is to reduce the processing time at the bottleneck, thus increasing its capacity. We can do this by moving work to other resources, by automating some of the work, or by shifting some of the work to a supplier.

LO4-4 Balance a process by reallocating work from one step to another

Because a process can never operate faster than for what we have capacity at the bottleneck, any excessive capacity at nonbottleneck steps is wasteful. Balancing a process means moving some work away from the bottleneck (thus increasing process capacity) and moving this work to unused capacity elsewhere in the process. As a result, the average labor utilization in the process will increase.

LO4-5 Explain the benefits and limitations of specialization

Specialization reduces setups and allows a worker to increase the number of repetitions, which leads to learning. Specialized work also requires shorter training periods and hence allows a firm to work with lower-skilled labor. Another benefit of specialization is that it typically avoids excessive equipment replication. The downside of specialization is that it can make work very repetitive, which has the potential to be demotivating.

LO4-6 Evaluate the financial benefits of process improvements

Operations typically are there to make a profit. Process improvements should thus be evaluated on their ability to increase profits. Improvements can help increase revenues if the process is currently constrained by its capacity. Such improvements are especially valuable if the process has high gross margins. Otherwise, process improvements help reduce the costs per unit.

Key Terms

Introduction

Profit maximization The objective of an enterprise—to maximize the difference between revenue and costs.

4.1 Measures of Process Efficiency

Efficiency A process is efficient if it is able to achieve a high flow rate with few resources.

Costs of direct labor The labor cost associated with serving one customer, which is the total wages paid per unit of time divided by the flow rate.

Labor content The amount of work that goes into serving one customer (or, more generally, one flow unit), which is the sum of the processing times involving labor.

Average labor utilization The average utilization across resources.

Idle time The amount of time per flow unit for which a resource is paid but is not actually working.

Total idle time The amount of idle time per flow unit added up across all resources.

4.2 How to Choose a Staffing Level to Meet Demand

Takt time The ratio between the time available and the quantity that has to be produced to serve demand.

Target manpower The ratio between the labor content and the takt time determines the minimum number of resources required to meet demand. Note that this minimum does not have to be an integer number and that it assumes all resources are perfectly utilized.

Leveling demand Setting an expected demand rate for a given period of time so that one can look for an appropriate staffing plan for that time period.

4.3 Off-Loading the Bottleneck

Herbie A fictitious character in Eli Goldratt's book *The Goal*. Herbie is the slowest hiker in a troop of Boy Scouts. He thus holds up the troop in the same way a bottleneck holds up a process.

4.4 How to Balance a Process

Line balancing The act of allocating the activities that need to be carried out in the process across the process resources as evenly as possible so that all resources have a comparable utilization level.

Balancing for a fixed sequence of activities Balancing a line in which the activities have to be completed in a predefined order.

Balancing for activities with no fixed sequence Balancing a line in which the activities do not have to be completed in a predefined order, which typically leads to higher utilization levels.

4.5 The Pros and Cons of Specialization

Reduction in processing times due to elimination of setups The fact that specialization increases efficiency by eliminating setups.

Reduction in processing times due to learning The fact that specialization increases efficiency by providing more practice to the operator in the execution of a particular activity.

Lower-skilled labor Labor that is not able to master multiple activities and thus can only work as a resource with very short processing times.

Equipment replication The need to provide extra equipment to nonspecialized labor at resources often leads to a low level of equipment utilization.

Work cells An organization of work where small teams of employees perform a job (complete a flow unit) from beginning to end.

4.6 Understanding the Financial Impacts of Process Improvements

Fixed costs Those costs that a firm has to pay anyway, independent of how much it produces and sells.

Variable costs Those costs that grow in proportion to the amount a firm produces and sells.

Gross margin The ratio between profits and revenues.

Key Formulas

Introduction

1. $\text{Profits} = \text{Flow rate} \times (\text{Average price} - \text{Average cost})$

LO4-1   Compute the costs of direct labor, labor content, idle time, and average labor utilization

1. $\text{Costs of direct labor} = \dfrac{\text{Wages per unit of time}}{\text{Flow rate}}$

2. $\text{Labor content} = \text{Sum of the processing times involving labor}$

LO4-2   Compute the takt time of a process and translate this to a target manpower

1. $\text{Takt time} = \dfrac{\text{Available time}}{\text{Required quantity}}$

LO4-3   Find ways to improve the process efficiency by off-loading the bottleneck

1. $\text{Average labor utilization} = \dfrac{\text{Labor content}}{\text{Labor content} + \text{Idle time}}$

2. $\text{Idle time(Resource } i) = \text{Cycle time} - \text{Processing time(Resource } i)$

Conceptual Questions

LO4-1

1. A process is replicated in another country where wages are 50 percent lower. Staffing and processing times are identical. What would be the effect on the costs of direct labor?
   a. Costs of direct labor would be 50 percent lower.
   b. Costs of direct labor would be the same.
   c. Costs of direct labor would be 50 percent higher.
   d. Cannot determine from the given information.

2. You and three of your friends run a car wash for a fund-raiser. Between interior and exterior cleaning, you spend about 40 minutes per vehicle. You are so successful that the next day you invite four more friends to help. How does this impact the labor content?
   a. The labor content goes up.
   b. The labor content stays the same.
   c. The labor content goes down.
   d. Cannot determine from the given information.

3. A nonbottleneck worker currently has an idle time of 20 seconds per unit. Because of the large demand, the company improves the process by adding more capacity to the bottleneck. How does this impact the idle time of the worker?
   a. The idle time would decrease.
   b. The idle time would stay the same.
   c. The idle time would increase.
   d. Cannot determine from the given information.

4. A group of workers works really hard. In fact, they work so hard that one of them claims to have an average labor utilization of 120 percent. Is that possible?
   a. Yes
   b. No

5. The bottleneck resource in a process has the least idle time. True or false?
   a. True
   b. False

LO4-2

6. Which of the following statements about takt time and cycle time is true?
   a. Takt time only depends on demand, not capacity. Cycle time does depend on capacity.
   b. Takt time only depends on capacity, not demand. Cycle time depends on demand.
   c. Takt time and cycle time only depend on capacity.
   d. Takt time and cycle time only depend on demand.

7. If the takt time is shorter than the cycle time, the process needs to run faster. True or false?
   a. True
   b. False

8. How does the takt time change as the demand rate increases?
   a. The takt time increases.
   b. The takt time stays the same.
   c. The takt time decreases.
   d. Cannot determine from the given information.

9. How does the target manpower change as the demand rate increases?
   a. The target manpower increases.
   b. The target manpower stays the same.
   c. The target manpower decreases.
   d. Cannot determine from the given information.

10. What happens to the target manpower if the labor content is doubled?
    a. The target manpower increases by 50 percent.
    b. The target manpower doubles.
    c. The target manpower decreases by 50 percent.
    d. The target manpower decreases by a factor of 2.

LO4-3

11. Which of the following actions does not relate to off-loading the bottleneck?
    a. Reassigning activities to other, nonbottleneck resources
    b. Automating some of the activities at the bottleneck
    c. Increasing wages for production workers
    d. Outsourcing some of the bottleneck activities

LO4-4

12. It is possible to increase process capacity by balancing a process. True or false?
    a. True
    b. False

13. Balancing a process with a fixed sequence of activities will achieve a higher average labor utilization than balancing a process with no fixed sequence of activities. True or false?
    a. True
    b. False

LO4-5

14. Specialization increases the costs of labor because specialists will command a higher wage rate. True or false?
    a. True
    b. False

15. Specialization typically lead to a higher average labor utilization. True or false?
    a. True
    b. False

LO4-6

16. A process has high fixed costs and low variable costs. It is currently capacity-constrained. Will the impact of an efficiency improvement be small or large?
    a. Small
    b. Large

17. A process has low fixed costs and high variable costs. It is currently capacity-constrained. Will the impact of an efficiency improvement be small or large?
    a. Small
    b. Large

18. When an operation improves its efficiency, its revenue will always stay constant, while its costs will go down. True or false?
    a. True
    b. False

Solved Example Problems

LO 4-1

1. Consider the example of the three-step airport security. The first step, verifying ID and boarding pass, takes 30 seconds per passenger. The second step, searching the passenger for metal objects using a metal detector, takes 10 seconds per passenger. The third step, running the carry-on luggage through an X-ray machine, takes 60 seconds per passenger. Assume that there are many customers waiting in the process and that each of the three employees gets paid $15 per hour.

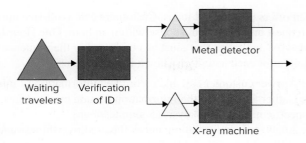

(a) What is the cost of direct labor?

(b) What is the labor content?

(c) What is the average labor utilization?

Answer:

(a) We compute the capacity levels as

Capacity(Luggage) = $\frac{1}{30}$ passenger/second; Capacity(Metal detector) = $\frac{1}{10}$ passenger/second; Capacity(X-ray) = $\frac{1}{60}$ passenger/second. The lowest capacity is thus at the X-ray machine, which makes the X-ray machine the bottleneck and $\frac{1}{60}$ passenger/second the process capacity.

The flow rate is the minimum of demand and capacity. Because many customers are waiting, the process is capacity-constrained and the flow rate is given by the process capacity; that is, $\frac{1}{60}$ passenger/second or 1 passenger per minute or 60 customers per hour. Given that we have three employees, we have to pay 3 × $15 per hour = $45 per hour, getting us

$$\text{Cost of direct labor} = \frac{\$45 \text{ per hour}}{60 \text{ customers per hour}} = \$0.75 \text{ per customer}$$

(b) The labor content is simply the sum of the activity times:

Labor content = 30 seconds + 10 seconds + 60 seconds = 100 seconds

(c) To get the average labor utilization, we first find the utilization of the three resources as 0.5, 0.1666, and 1, respectively. Taking the average, we get 0.5556.

2. A machine-paced line has six stations with processing times of 30, 20, 25, 28, 22, and 24 seconds per unit, respectively. The process is capacity-constrained and runs on a 30 second/unit cycle time.

(a) What is the total idle time across all six stations?

(b) What is the average labor utilization?

Answer:

(a) We know the cycle time is given as 30 seconds/unit. We now need to compute the difference between each processing time and the cycle time to get the idle time for each station. For example:

Idle time for station 2 = Cycle time − processing time = 30 − 20 = 10 seconds per units.

In the same way, we get all six idle times as 0, 10, 5, 2, 8, and 6 seconds, respectively. The total idle time thus is 31 seconds.

(b) To get to the average labor utilization, we first compute the labor content as the sum of the processing times, which gives us 149 seconds/unit. We then compute the average labor utilization as

$$\text{Average labor utilization} = \frac{\text{Labor content}}{\text{Labor content} + \text{Idle time}} = \frac{149}{149 + 31} = 0.82778$$

3. One Hour Loan offers customized loans. Customers call a toll-free number with a specific loan request and obtain a response within an hour. One Hour Loan's business process includes five activities that must be conducted in the sequence described below. (The time required for each activity is shown in parentheses.)

- **Activity 1:** Answer customer call and record key information (4 minutes/loan).
- **Activity 2:** Gather and format the information (obtain credit scores, organize customer-specific needs) for analysis (5 minutes/loan).
- **Activity 3:** Analyze the information: check the creditworthiness and decide the loan amount and APR to offer (7 minutes/loan).
- **Activity 4:** Perform final checks on the loan offer (2 minutes/loan).
- **Activity 5:** Call customer back with the new loan offer and close (4 minutes/loan).

The whole process is conducted by three workers in a worker-paced line. The assignment of tasks to workers is the following: W1 does activity 1, W2 does activities 2 and 3, and W3 does activities 4 and 5. Each worker is paid $20 per hour. You can assume that there exists unlimited demand and that loans are only entering the process at the rate of the bottleneck.

(a) What is the bottleneck in the process?

(b) What are the costs of direct labor?

(c) What is the labor content?

(d) Across all three workers, what is the average labor utilization?

Answer:

(a) We first compare the capacity levels across the three workers; they are $\frac{1}{4}$ loan per minute, $\frac{1}{12}$ loan per minute, and $\frac{1}{6}$ loan per minute, respectively; so, worker 2, with a processing time of 12 minutes per loan (5 + 7), is the bottleneck.

(b) Given unlimited demand, we get a flow rate determined by the capacity of the process, which is $\frac{1}{12}$ loan per minute or 5 loans per hour. The costs of direct labor are then given by

$$\text{Cost of director labor} = \frac{\text{Wages}}{\text{Flow rate}} = \frac{\$60 \text{ per hour}}{5 \text{ loans per hour}} = \$12 \text{ per loan}$$

(c) The labor content is the sum of the processing times, which gives us

$$4 + 5 + 7 + 2 + 4 = 22 \frac{\text{minutes}}{\text{loan}}$$

(d) The utilization of worker 1 is:

$$\frac{\text{Flow rate}}{\text{Capacity}} = \frac{\frac{1}{12}}{\frac{1}{4}} = 0.3333$$

The utilization of worker 2 is 1, as she is the bottleneck (and we have unlimited demand).

The utilization of worker 3 is $\frac{\frac{1}{12}}{\frac{1}{6}} = 0.5$.

So, the average across the three workers is Average(0.3333, 1, 0.5) = 0.6111.

LO 4-2

4. Consider again the case of One Hour Loan. Assume that the demand rate would be 20 loans per hour.

(a) What would be the takt time of the process?

(b) What would be the target manpower?

Answer:

(a) The takt time is given by:

$$\text{Takt time } \frac{1}{\text{Demand rate}} = \frac{1}{20} \text{ hours per loan} = 3 \text{ minutes per loan}$$

(b) The target manpower is then computed as

$$\text{Target Manpower } \frac{\text{Labor Content}}{\text{Takt Time}} = \frac{22 \text{ minutes per loan}}{3 \text{ minutes per loan}} = 7.333$$

LO 4-3

5. Consider again the case of One Hour Loan and assume there exists unlimited demand. If you had one additional worker available to help another worker, to which worker would you assign her?

    Answer: You would deploy the worker at the bottleneck, which means helping worker 2.

LO 4-4

6. Consider again the case of One Hour Loan. Recall that activity 1 takes 4 minutes/loan, activity 2 takes 5 minutes/loan, activity 3 takes 7 minutes/loan, activity 4 takes 2 minutes/loan, and activity 5 takes 4 minutes/loan. Recall further that currently the assignment of tasks to workers is as follows: W1 does activity 1, W2 does activities 2 and 3, and W3 does activities 4 and 5.

    How would you rebalance the process to maximize process capacity, assuming that the five activities have to be carried out in the given order?

    Answer: The current processing time at the bottleneck is 12 minutes and makes worker 2 the bottleneck. So we have to see if we can move some of worker 2's work to somebody else:

    • We could move the 5 minutes/loan of activity 2 to worker 1. In this case, worker 1 has 9 minutes/loan as a processing time, worker 2 is left with 7 minutes/loan, and worker 3 remains at 6 minutes per loan. The new capacity of the process would be $\frac{1}{9}$ loan per minute.

    • We could also try to move the 7 minutes/loan of activity 2 to worker 3. However, worker 3 already has 6 minutes/loan of processing time, so her new processing time would now be 13 minutes/loan. This would decrease the process capacity.

    Hence, the best we can do is move activity 2 to worker 1.

LO 4-5

7. A cabinetmaker producing custom-built kitchen cabinets contemplates how to organize his workforce. One way he can envision his production process is that each of his craftsmen would take ownership of an entire order, including all the woodworking such as cutting, sanding, staining, all the way to assembly and installation. The alternative he considers is to have workers specialize in specific activities. One worker would be in charge of cutting the wood, a second worker would be in charge of sanding, a third in charge of staining, and a whole separate team would take care of assembly and installation. What pros and cons do you see with respect to these two ways of organizing the work?

    Answer: The main benefits of specialization here are

    + Reduction in processing times due to elimination of set-ups: A worker could operate the sanding machine all day long as opposed to rotating between equipment.

    + Reduction in processing times due to learning: The volume of a particular activity a worker would carry out would accumulate faster, which will lead to shorter processing times.

+ Lower-skilled labor: The wages of somebody who could just cut would be lower than those for somebody who could take on the entire commission.

+ Equipment replication: If each worker would operate as a work cell, more equipment would be needed.

The main disadvantages are:

− Line balancing: It is harder to balance the process if workers specialize. If each worker carries out all activities, balancing is easy.

− Repetitive work, which might be less stimulating or motivating.

LO 4-6

8. Consider again the case of One Hour Loan and the initial process design in which activity 1 takes 4 minutes/loan, activity 2 takes 5 minutes/loan, activity 3 takes 7 minutes/loan, activity 4 takes 2 minutes/loan, and activity 5 takes 4 minutes/loan. Recall further that currently the assignment of tasks to workers is as follows: W1 does activity 1, W2 does activities 2 and 3, and W3 does activities 4 and 5.

Assume that One Hour Loan obtains $50 for each loan it originates. The company faces fixed costs of $1200 per 8-hour work day, which includes the labor costs of $20 per hour for each employee. Variable costs for paper and express mailing are estimated to be $5 per loan. By how much would One Hour Loan's profit increase if it decreased the processing time of activity 3 from 7 to 5 minutes per loan? Note that there exists unlimited demand and the assignment of activities to the workers remains the same.

   Answer: We previously computed a flow rate of 1/12 loan per minute = 5 loans per hour.

   Profits = Flow rate × (Average price − Variable cost) − Fixed Costs

   If we divide the daily fixed costs by 8 to spread them over the workday, we get $150 per hour in fixed costs. This gives us

   Profits = 5 loans per hour × ($50 per loan − $5 per loan) − $150 per hour = $75 per hour

   If we reduce the processing time to five minutes, worker 2 now would have a capacity of $\frac{1}{10}$ loan per minute = 6 loans per hour. In this case, profits would change:

   Profits = 6 loans per hour × ($50 per loan − $5 per loan) − $150 per hour = $120 per hour

   So, the profit increase is $45 per hour or $\frac{120}{75} = 1.6$, which corresponds to a 60 percent increase in profit.

Problems and Applications

LO4–1

1. It takes a lawyer 120 minutes to serve one customer. Demand is 2 customers per eight-hour day. The lawyer has a wage rate of $200 per hour. What is the cost of direct labor for the lawyer expressed in $ per customer?

2. Consider a process consisting of three resources. Assume there exists unlimited demand for the product.
   • Resource 1 has a processing time of 6 minutes per unit.
   • Resource 2 has a processing time of 3 minutes per unit.
   • Resource 3 has a processing time of 5 minutes per unit.

All three resources are staffed by one worker and each worker gets paid $12 per hour.
   a. What is the cost of direct labor?
   b. What is the labor content?
   c. How much idle time does the worker at resource 3 have per unit?
   d. What is the average labor utilization?
   e. Assume the demand rate is 20 units per hour. What is the takt time?
   f. Assume the demand rate is 20 units per hour. What is the target manpower?

3. Glenn Dental Clinic provides general dental care to residents of Philadelphia on a walk-in basis. The clinic has started receiving complaints from patients that the waiting time is too long and has asked you to investigate whether this problem can be solved.

   Upon arrival, customers receive a form from the receptionist and fill out relevant information such as personal health records and insurance provider. The form is then handed back to the receptionist who enters the information into the computer system for the dentist to see. A dental assistant then takes an X-ray from the patient. A dentist then performs the checkup and discusses any issues with the patient.

   Based on conversations with staff members at the clinic, you have obtained the following information on the process:
   - It takes about 5 minutes for a customer to fill out the paperwork.
   - Entry of information on the paperwork into the system and verification with past records takes another 5 minutes for a receptionist. There are two receptionists.
   - It takes 15 minutes, on average, for the dental assistant to take an X-ray. There are three dental assistants on shift at any moment.
   - There are 10 dentists working at the clinic. Each checkup takes 30 minutes, on average.

   The following table summarizes the process data collected above.

Resource	Process	Staffing (Number of Workers)	Processing Time (Minutes per Patient)
A. Self-serve	Paperwork	—	5
B. Receptionists	Data entry	2	5
C. Dental assistant	X-ray	3	15
D. Dentist	Checkup	10	30

   Assume that there exists unlimited demand, unless otherwise stated. Assume further that the dentists get paid $100 per hour while the receptionists and dental assistants get paid $30 per hour.
   a. What is the labor content?
   b. What is the cost of direct labor?

4. Mr. K's is a very popular hair salon. It offers high-quality hairstyling and physical relaxation services at a reasonable price, so it always has unlimited demand. The service process includes five activities that are conducted in the sequence described next (the time required for each activity is shown in parentheses):

   Activity 1: Welcome a guest and offer homemade herb tea (10 minutes).
   Activity 2: Wash and condition hair (10 minutes).
   Activity 3: Neck, shoulder, and back stress-release massage (10 minutes).
   Activity 4: Design the hairstyle and do the hair (25 minutes).
   Activity 5: Check out the guest (5 minutes).

Three servers (S1, S2, and S3) offer the services in a worker-paced line. The assignment of tasks to servers is the following: S1 does activity 1, S2 does activities 2 and 3, and S3 does activities 4 and 5.

a. What is the labor content?

b. What is the average labor utilization?

c. At a wage rate of $20 per hour, what is the cost of direct labor per customer?

d. Mr. K considers hiring a new employee to help any one (and only one) of the servers without changing the tasks performed by each server. How would this change his cost of direct labor?

e. Mr. K also contemplates redesigning the assignment of tasks to servers. For this, Mr. K is evaluating the reassignment of activity 5 from S3 to S1. How would this change his cost of direct labor?

5. The Geneva Watch Corporation manufactures watches on a conveyor belt with six stations. One worker stands at each station and performs the following tasks:

Station	Tasks	Processing Time (seconds)
A	1. Heat-stake lens to bezel	14
Preparation	2. Inspect bezel	26
	3. Clean switch holes	10
	4. Install set switch in bezel	18
	Total time for A	**68**
B	5. Check switch travel	23
Preparation 2	6. Clean inside bezel	12
	7. Install module in bezel	25
	Total time for B	**60**
C	8. Install battery clip on module	20
Battery installation	9. Heat-stake battery clip on module	20
	10. Install two batteries in module	22
	11. Check switch	8
	Total time for C	**70**
D	12. Install band	45
Band installation	13. Inspect band	13
	Total time for D	**58**
E	14. Cosmetic inspection	4
Packaging preparation	15. Final test	71
	Total time for E	**75**
F	16. Place watch and cuff in display box	20
Watch packaging	17. Place cover in display box base	14
	18. Place owner's manual and box into tub	30
	Total time for F	**64**

Workers get paid $10 per hour. You can ignore any idle time of workers resulting from the beginning or the end of the day.

a. What is the labor content?

b. Assume a demand rate of 50 watches per hour. What is the takt time?

c. Assume a demand rate of 50 watches per hour. What is the target manpower?

d. An external supplier suggests shipping the battery module with preinstalled batteries, thereby eliminating the need for step 10. How would that impact process capacity?

e. How could you increase the capacity of the process by rebalancing it?

6. Atlas Inc. is a toy bicycle manufacturing company producing a five-inch small version of the bike that Lance Armstrong rode to win his first Tour de France. The assembly line at Atlas Inc. consists of seven work stations, each performing a single step. Stations and processing times are summarized here:

- Step 1 (30 sec.): The plastic tube for the frame is cut to size.
- Step 2 (20 sec.): The tube is put together.
- Step 3 (35 sec.): The frame is glued together.
- Step 4 (25 sec.): The frame is cleaned.
- Step 5 (30 sec.): Paint is sprayed onto the frame.
- Step 6 (45 sec.): Wheels are assembled.
- Step 7 (40 sec.): All other parts are assembled to the frame.

Under the current process layout, workers are allocated to the stations as shown here:

- Worker 1: Steps 1 and 2
- Worker 2: Steps 3 and 4
- Worker 3: Step 5
- Worker 4: Step 6
- Worker 5: Step 7

Assume the workers are paid $15 per hour. Each bicycle is sold for $6 and includes parts that are sourced for $1. The company has fixed costs of $200 per hour. Despite Lance Armstrong's doping confession, there exists substantially more demand for the bicycle than Atlas can supply.

a. What is the cost of direct labor for the bicycle?

b. How much profit does the company make per hour?

c. What would be the profits per hour if Atlas would be able to source the parts 10 percent cheaper ($0.90 for the parts of one unit)?

d. What would be the profits per hour if Atlas were able to reduce fixed costs by 10 percent (to $180 per hour)?

e. What would be the profits per hour if Atlas were able to reduce the processing time at the bottleneck by 5 seconds per unit (assume unlimited demand)?

Reference

http://www.econlib.org/library/Smith/smWN1.html

CASE XOOTR

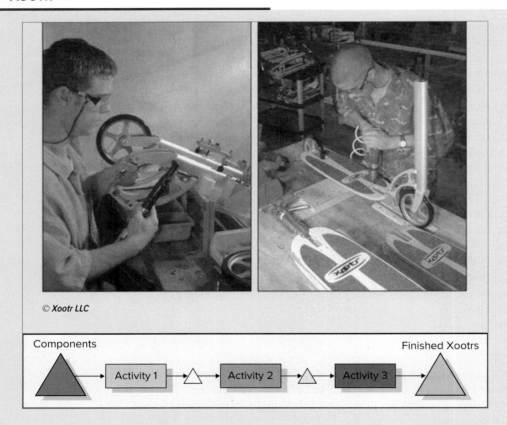

© Xootr LLC

Xootr LLC is the producer of a high-end, award-winning kick scooter, known as the Xootr (pronounced "zooter"). The basic Xootr model (known as the Ultra Cruz) sells for slightly over $200.

The company started production using a three-step assembly process depicted in the preceding figure. Three workers assemble the Xootr. The processing times are 13 minutes/unit for the first worker, 11 minutes/unit for the second worker, and 8 minutes/unit for the third worker. The assembly operation runs for 35 hours per week. The average salary for an assembly worker is $12 per hour.

As demand for the Xootr grows, the company needs to change its assembly operations to increase its process capacity. Two experts are consulted for advice. The first expert comments: "As we grow our business, we really have to benefit from our workers specializing in a small set of activities. Right now, our longest processing time is 13 minutes per unit. If Xootr wants to double its process capacity, it should simply take each of the three activities and break them up into two subactivities. That way, six workers can produce a unit every 6.5 minutes."

Another expert, however, disagrees. She observes: "Division of labor leads to frustrating, monotone work for the workers. Instead of having workers specialize in small subactivities, Xootr should do the opposite. Imagine one worker would perform all activities from beginning to end. This would avoid the problem of line balancing and increase the labor utilization. And the workers would see how all pieces come together, providing a more meaningful production experience. If we have six workers operating this way, we can have even more capacity."

What do you think of the comments of these two experts? Draw a process flow diagram for each of the two expert proposals. For each proposal, compute process capacity, labor utilization, and costs of direct labor, assuming that the processing times in the proposal of the first expert would be cut in half (i.e., it would take 6.5 minutes per unit to do the first set of tasks currently included in activity 1 and another 6.5 minutes per unit to do the second set of tasks). Then, ask yourself what other variables might differ across these two proposals.

Process Analysis with Multiple Flow Units

5

Introduction

Choosing an appropriate flow unit is an essential step when preparing a process flow diagram. Yet what happens if a process does not have one type of flow unit, but multiple types? And what happens if these different types of flow units don't always follow the same path through the process flow diagram? Before we consider the answers to these questions, let's make sure such situations in which we face multiple types of flow units really exist in practice. The following examples help illustrate that processes can have multiple flows going through them and that we thus face multiple types of flow units:

© Ariel Skelley/Blend Images LLC/RF

1. In the development of new pharmaceutical products, chemical compounds have to complete multiple rounds of testing. This typically includes preclinical studies, followed by Phase 1, Phase 2, and Phase 3 clinical trials. What complicates the flow is that compounds that fail in a phase are basically eliminated from further consideration. This, in turn, creates a process flow with multiple outflows, as opposed to a single point of exit as we had considered before.

2. In the production and assembly of motor vehicles, vehicles in the process are inspected and checked for their conformance with quality standards. Units that fail to meet these quality criteria are reworked; that is, they have to visit an extra set of resources so that their defects can be fixed. In contrast, vehicles that meet the quality standards are allowed to continue toward the outflow of the process.

3. In an emergency department, patients arrive via multiple entry points, including walk-in patients, ambulance arrivals, and helicopter arrivals. The flow pattern then gets further complicated by the fact that the different patients will be in very different medical conditions, which in turn require different diagnostic services and different courses of treatment. For example, a patient with a gunshot wound needs to quickly be routed toward a trauma surgeon, a patient with a twisted ankle might have to be directed toward an X-ray machine first, while a patient with the flu might receive some fluids but oftentimes does not even require the help of a medical doctor.

These three examples show that process flows can be sufficiently more complicated than the process flow diagrams we have encountered so far. In this chapter, we teach you how to perform a process analysis for more complicated flow patterns such as these. We start this chapter with the development of more sophisticated process flow diagrams. We then discuss how you can find the bottleneck for process flows that have multiple types of flow units and how to compute the flow rate. Knowing the bottleneck lets us consider adding capacity to the resource where it matters the most. Next, we discuss a set of common forms of such complicated flow patterns. We conclude this chapter by articulating some common ways of improving these processes.

5.1 Generalized Process Flow Patterns

As we saw in the introduction to this chapter, not all process flow diagrams consist of a linear flow in which each flow unit visits every resource. Consider the following example from the world of financial services. Capital One is one of the largest financial services companies in the United States.[1] In its division in charge of consumer and small business loans, the marketing department solicits potential customers through direct mail and/or e-mail campaigns that highlight the loan product features and specials of various products that are offered by Capital One. These campaigns have an information card that can be returned by the customer. Customers use this card to provide information concerning their name, the type of loan they are interested in, and the phone number/time range that is best to reach them. Customers who respond by sending this information back enter the loan approval process and are referred to as an "app." Each app flows through a process that consists of the following five steps:

- At interviewing, an employee interviews the customer about his or her financial needs.
- Underwriting is the most complex activity in the loan approval process. This is the step where the decision of awarding the loan is made.
- Quality assurance is in charge of reviewing all documents prepared by the underwriter.
- Closing is in charge of printing all relevant documents, of preparing them for submission to the customer, and of calling the customer to inform him or her that the loan is approved.
- The manager signs the final paperwork and releases a check for payment.

Not every customer who applies for a loan will receive a loan. In fact, one might argue that this is the entire point of an underwriting process—figuring out who deserves a loan and who

---

[1] The following analysis is based on the case study written by Aravind Immaneni and Christian Terwiesch.

does not. About 52 percent of all loan applications are rejected following the underwriting step. In other words, these flow units are processed by interviewing and by underwriting, but they do not move on beyond this point; they leave the process after underwriting.

In addition to the loan applications that are rejected, there exists a second reason why not every app processed at interviewing and underwriting will lead to a closed loan. Customers withdraw their applications, oftentimes because they have received a loan from one of Capital One's competitors. Out of 100 apps handled at interviewing, 52 are declined by underwriting. Of the remaining 48, 14.6 are withdrawn by the customers before the app reaches quality assurance. So out of the initial 100, only 33.4 reach quality assurance. From these 33.4, an additional 7 are withdrawn by the customer after closing has prepared all documents and called the customer, which leaves only 26.4 of the initial 100 apps turning into loans signed off by the manager. This is shown in Figure 5.1. Whether they are rejections or withdrawals, we refer to flow units that exit the process before completing it as **attrition losses.**

Depending on where the loan application exits the process, we can distinguish between four types of loan applications:

- Type 1 (funded loans) visits all resources in the process.
- Type 2 (withdrawn after closing) visits all resources in the process except for the manager.
- Type 3 (withdrawn after underwriting) only requires work at interviewing and at underwriting as the customer withdraws the loan application.
- Type 4 (rejected by underwriting) only requires work at interviewing and at underwriting as the loan application is rejected.

We refer to a combination of different flow unit types moving through a process as a **product mix**.

Now, assume that Capital One faces a demand rate in the form of a daily inflow of loan applications of 110 applications per day. This means that interviewing needs to handle 110 applications each day and so does underwriting. However, because of the attrition losses (rejections and withdrawals), that number is lower for quality assurance and closing, and lower yet for the manager.

Table 5.1 shows how the 110 loan applications per day are distributed across these four types. For example, we find the number of loans withdrawn after closing by multiplying the 110 loans/day by the probability of a loan being withdrawn after closing, obtained from Figure 5.1.

Note the difference between this process flow and the process flows analyzed in the previous chapters. Loan applications take different paths through the process flow diagram and

LO5-1 Compute the demand for a resource in the presence of a product mix.

Product mix A combination of different flow unit types moving through a process.

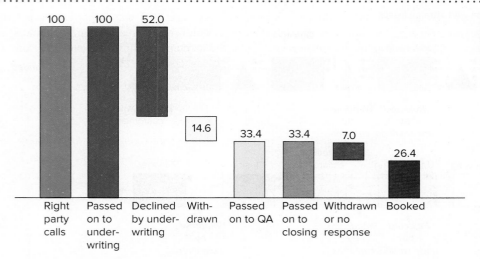

Figure 5.1
Attrition losses in the loan processing operation

| 100 | 100 | 52.0 | 14.6 | 33.4 | 33.4 | 7.0 | 26.4 |

Right party calls | Passed on to underwriting | Declined by underwriting | Withdrawn | Passed on to QA | Passed on to closing | Withdrawn or no response | Booked

TABLE 5.1   Number of Applications of the Four Types

Type	Description	Demand rate
1	Funded	29.04
2	Withdrawn after closing	7.7
3	Withdrawn after underwriting	16.06
4	Rejected	57.2
	Total	**110**

not every loan application will be handled by every resource. This has strong implications for our flow calculations, including the location of the bottleneck. So a careful description of the process flow pattern is critical, which brings us to the process flow diagram.

The main difference between a process flow diagram with one type of flow unit and a process flow diagram with multiple types of flow units is that we now use different arrows to capture the different types of flow units. These arrows could be depicted using different colors or by adding a little label identifying the flow unit next to the arrow, as is done in Figure 5.2 (top). Note that though we are dealing with a service operation here and no customers are standing in line, we do have inventories between resources, which we again depict as triangles. These inventories simply correspond to "piles" of applications that are in process; they might take the form of physical paper or electronic entries in a database. For our purposes, this does not matter; flow units in the process that are not currently handled by a resource are depicted as triangles.

Notice that the process flow diagram depicted at the top of Figure 5.2 is rather complex, which is largely a result of the many places where inventory could pile up in the process. We can simplify the process flow diagram by simply dropping all triangles. This is shown in the bottom part of Figure 5.2.

We now need to take this demand (loan applications) of the overall process and translate it to a demand for each individual resource. Remember that some resources (e.g., the employees at interviewing) are requested by all types of loan applications, whereas others (e.g., the manager) are requested by only one type. This is (hopefully) clear by looking at the process flow diagram.

Figure 5.2 Process flow diagram with attrition losses

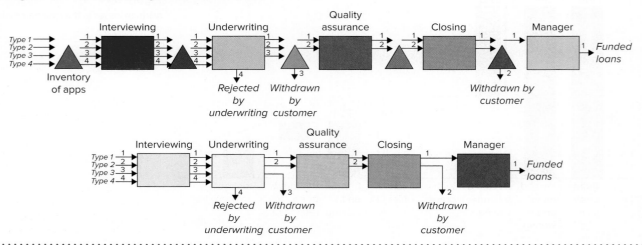

For example, we see that 29.04 type 1 flow units will have to go through interviewing each day. Since type 1 flow units make it "all the way" through the process, they also create 29.04 units to be processed per day by the manager. In contrast, 57.2 type 4 flow units will have to go through interviewing each day. But none of them will reach the manager because—by definition—type 4 flow units are rejected by the underwriter.

This information—how many flow units of each type are flowing through each resource—is summarized by the **demand matrix**. We define the demand matrix as follows. For each resource i and for each flow unit of type j, the demand matrix is

$$D(i, j) = \text{Number of flow units of type } j \text{ that need to be processed at resource } i$$

That is, each row in the demand matrix corresponds to a resource and each column in the demand matrix corresponds to a flow unit type. The demand matrix can be created by combining the demand rate information with the process flow diagram. The demand matrix has a zero for resource i and customer type j if customer type j does not require any attention from resource i.

For our Capital One example, our demand matrix has five rows, corresponding to the five resources, and four columns, corresponding to the four types of loan applications. By combining the information of the process flow diagram with the aggregate demand information in Table 5.1, we obtain the following demand matrix:

	Type 1	Type 2	Type 3	Type 4
Interviewing	29.04	7.7	16.06	57.2
Underwriting	29.04	7.7	16.06	57.2
$D =$ Quality assurance	29.04	7.7	0	0
Closing	29.04	7.7	0	0
Manager	29.04	0	0	0

When constructing the demand matrix, it is helpful to first create a table with the number of rows corresponding to the number of resources, and the number of columns corresponding to the number of flow unit types. We also encourage you to write the different flow unit types in an extra row above the table (as column headers) and the different resources in front of each row (as a row header).

The demand matrix shows us that

- All four loan types visit the first two resources in the process, interviewing and underwriting, which is why there are no zeroes in these rows.

- Only type 1 loans require attention from the manager, which is why the 29.04 loans per day of type 1 are the only nonzero entry in the fifth row.

Once we have created the demand matrix, we can then find the **total demand rate** for each resource as

$$\text{Total demand rate for resource } i = \Sigma_j\, D(i, j)$$

The total demand rate for resource i tells us how many flow units need to be processed at resource i across all different flow units. In our case, we get

Demand(Interviewing)	$= 29.04 + 7.7 + 16.06 + 57.2 = 110$	applications per day
Demand(Underwriting)	$= 29.04 + 7.7 + 16.06 + 57.2 = 110$	applications per day
Demand(Quality assurance)	$= 29.04 + 7.7 + \quad 0 \quad + \quad 0 \quad = 36.74$	applications per day
Demand(Closing)	$= 29.04 + 7.7 + \quad 0 \quad + \quad 0 \quad = 36.74$	applications per day
Demand(Manager)	$= 29.04 + \quad 0 \quad + \quad 0 \quad + \quad 0 \quad = 29.04$	applications per day

Demand matrix Determines how many flow units of each type are flowing through each resource. For resource i, $D(i, j)$ is the number of flow units of type j that need to be processed.

Total demand rate The total demand rate for resource i tells us how many flow units need to be processed at resource i across all different flow units.

Check Your Understanding 5.1

Question: A process has three resources and two types of flow units. The first flow unit has a demand of 10 units per day, and the second flow unit has a demand of 30 units per day. The first flow unit type visits all three resources, while the second flow unit type only visits the first and the third resources. What does the demand matrix for this process look like?

Answer:
$$D = \begin{bmatrix} 10 & 30 \\ 10 & 0 \\ 10 & 30 \end{bmatrix}$$

Question: What does the total demand rate look like for the three resources?

Answer:

Demand(1st resource) $= 10 + 30 = 40$

Demand(2nd resource) $= 10$

Demand(3rd resource) $= 10 + 30 = 40$

5.2 How to Find the Bottleneck in a General Process Flow

After understanding the demand side of the process—that is, how much work is requested from each resource—we can switch over to looking at the supply side; in other words, how much work each resource is capable of doing. Our goal is to find the bottleneck and determine how many loans per day the process can fund. Once we have the bottleneck, we have found the resource that is the best candidate to add on further capacity.

In the case of our Capital One operation, here is how many employees work at each resource and how long it takes them to process one app:

- At interviewing, there are seven employees and it takes, on average, 23 minutes per app to interview a customer.
- At underwriting, there are eight employees and it takes, on average, 40 minutes per app.
- At quality assurance, there are two employees and it takes, on average, 25 minutes per app.
- At closing, there are six employees and it takes 70 minutes per app.
- There is one manager who takes about 5 minutes per app.

Let us begin by computing the capacity levels for the five resources. Just as before, we compute the capacity of a resource staffed by multiple workers as

$$\text{Capacity} = \frac{\text{number of employees}}{\text{processing time}}$$

which gives us:

$$\text{Capacity(Interviewing)} = \frac{7}{23} = 0.304 \ \frac{\text{app}}{\text{min}}$$

$$\text{Capacity(Underwriting)} = \frac{8}{40} = 0.2 \ \frac{\text{app}}{\text{min}}$$

$$\text{Capacity(Quality assurance)} = \frac{2}{25} = 0.08 \ \frac{\text{app}}{\text{min}}$$

$$\text{Capacity(Closing)} = \frac{6}{70} = 0.086 \ \frac{\text{app}}{\text{min}}$$

$$\text{Capacity(Manager)} = \frac{1}{5} = 0.2 \ \frac{\text{app}}{\text{min}}$$

TABLE 5.2 Capacity Levels at Capital One

Resource	Capacity (per min)	Capacity (per day)
Interviewing	0.30	121.74
Underwriting	0.20	80.00
Quality assurance	0.08	32.00
Closing	0.09	34.29
Manager	0.20	80.00

These capacity calculations are summarized in Table 5.2. Assuming that all employees work 400 minutes per day on the described activities (employees also need time for meetings, training, breaks, and other things), we can compute the daily capacity by simply multiplying the per minute capacity by 400, as shown in the last column of Table 5.2.

Based on these capacity levels, we find that the capacity at quality assurance is the smallest from among the five resources. So, we conclude that quality assurance is the bottleneck. Right? No.

The problem with this approach is that it does not factor in that not every flow unit is going to every resource. For example, the demand matrix shows that type 3 and type 4 loans do not require any attention from quality assurance because they will already be either rejected by underwriting or withdrawn after underwriting. So, things are different now. Yes, the capacity level at quality assurance might be the lowest, but this does not necessarily constrain the flow, because not every unit has to be processed at this resource. In the extreme case, a process in which all apps are rejected at underwriting would leave no work for quality assurance and it would make no sense to call this resource the bottleneck.

So a refined definition of our bottleneck concept is needed. Instead of looking at capacity levels in absolute terms, we need to look at the capacity levels available relative to the capacity levels requested by the demand rate. We do this by defining the **implied utilization** of a resource as

$$\text{Implied utilization} = \frac{\text{Total demand at the resource}}{\text{Capacity at the resource}}$$

The implied utilization captures the mismatch between what could flow through the resource (demand) and what the resource can provide (capacity).

Note the difference between utilization and implied utilization. Given the way we defined utilization (the ratio between flow rate and capacity, where flow rate is defined as the minimum of demand and capacity), utilization can never exceed 100 percent. Thus, utilization only carries information about excess capacity, in which case utilization is strictly less than 100 percent. In contrast, we cannot infer from utilization how much demand exceeds the capacity of the process. This is why we need to introduce an additional measure, namely the implied utilization.

Table 5.3 combines the capacity calculations from Table 5.2 with the demand calculations from the demand matrix computed in the previous section. This gives us, for each resource, the demand as well as the capacity. The last column of Table 5.3 shows the levels of implied utilization for the process. We observe that underwriting has the highest implied utilization and so we label it the bottleneck.

Several points in the table deserve further discussion:

- Unlike utilization, implied utilization can exceed 100 percent. Any excess over 100 percent reflects that a resource does not have the capacity available to meet demand.

- The fact that a resource has an implied utilization above 100 percent does not make it the bottleneck. As we see in Table 5.3, it is possible to have several resources with an implied utilization above 100 percent. However, there is only one bottleneck in the process! This is the resource where the implied utilization is the highest. Why isn't

Implied utilization The ratio of demand to capacity: Implied utilization = Demand at the resource/Capacity at the resource. The implied utilization captures the mismatch between demand and capacity.

TABLE 5.3   Deriving the Implied Utilization Levels for the Loan Approval Process

Resource	Capacity (per min)	Capacity (per day)	Demand (per day)				Total	Implied Utilization
			1	2	3	4		
Interviewing	0.30	121.74	29.04	7.70	16.06	57.20	110.00	0.90
Underwriting	0.20	80.00	29.04	7.70	16.06	57.20	110.00	1.38
Quality assurance	0.08	32.00	29.04	7.70	0.00	0.00	36.74	1.15
Closing	0.09	34.29	29.04	7.70	0.00	0.00	36.74	1.07
Manager	0.20	80.00	29.04	0.00	0.00	0.00	29.04	0.36

quality assurance a "second bottleneck"? Observe that there are only 80 apps per day flowing out of underwriting. That is the maximum this resource can handle (it is the capacity of underwriting). Of these 80, only 80 × 0.335 = 26.72 apps/day will arrive at quality assurance (because the others are either declined or withdrawn), which is significantly less than the capacity at quality assurance (32 apps/day).

- Having said this, it is important to keep in mind that in the case of a capacity expansion at underwriting, it might be worthwhile to add capacity to quality assurance as well. In fact, depending on the margins we make and the cost of installing capacity, we could make a case to install additional capacity for all resources with an implied utilization above 100 percent. In other words, once we add capacity to the current bottleneck, our new process (with a new bottleneck) could still be capacity-constrained, justifying additional capacity to other resources.

LO5-2 Find the bottleneck in a general process flow by computing implied utilization levels.

So, we have found that underwriting is the bottleneck with an implied utilization of 137.5 percent. Or, put differently, we have demand exceeding capacity by 37.5 percent.

Finally, we want to compute the flow rate. In fact, it is more accurate to speak about the flow rates because there are multiple flows going through the process, one for each flow unit. To compute the flow rates of the process, we have to first ask ourselves if we are capacity-constrained or demand-constrained. If any one of the implied utilization levels is above 100 percent, we are capacity-constrained, otherwise we are demand-constrained. If we are demand-constrained, we know that the flow rates are given by the demand rates for each flow unit. Our calculation of the flow rates thus is simple.

If we are capacity-constrained, things are somewhat more complicated. In this chapter, we assume that the product mix is given; thus, the relative magnitude between the different flow units is fixed. In our case, that means that for 29.04 funded loans, we have 7.7 loans withdrawn after closing, 16.06 loans withdrawn after underwriting, and 57.2 loans rejected (see Table 5.1).

For the sake of illustration, assume we have an implied utilization of 200 percent at the bottleneck. What would this mean for our mix of 29.04, 7.7, 16.06, and 57.2? We could only process half of it, meaning we could process 14.52, 3.85, 8.03, and 28.6 loans per day of the four different types.

Now, the implied utilization for our scenario is not 200 percent, but 138 percent. All we need to do is divide the demand rates for the flow units by the highest implied utilization. In our case, we get:

$$\text{Flow rate(Funded)} = \frac{29.04}{1.38} = 21.12 \text{ loans per day}$$

$$\text{Flow rate(Withdrawn after closing)} = \frac{7.7}{1.38} = 5.6 \text{ loans per day}$$

$$\text{Flow rate(Withdrawn after underwriting)} = \frac{16.06}{1.38} = 11.68 \text{ loans per day}$$

$$\text{Flow rate(Rejected)} = \frac{29.04}{1.38} = 41.6 \text{ loans per day}$$

Because in the case of the implied utilization exceeding 100 percent we are capacity-constrained, the flow rates computed this way are the maximum possible flow rates. They thus correspond to our process capacity.

We can add this up to a total flow rate across all units:

Flow rate(all units) = 21.12 + 5.6 + 11.68 + 41.6 loans per day = 80 loans per day

Exhibit 5.1 summarizes the steps you need to take when doing a process analysis with multiple flow units.

EXHIBIT 5.1

How to Find the Bottleneck and the Flow Rates in a Process with Multiple Flow Units

Step 1: Compute the demand matrix.

For each resource i, $D(i, j)$ is the number of flow units of type j that need to be processed.

Step 2: Compute the total demand rate for each resource by summing up the demand rates across all flow unit types that visit the resource.

$$\text{Total demand rate for resource } i = \Sigma_j D(i, j)$$

Step 3: Compute the capacity level for each resource.

Step 4: Compute the implied utilization for each resource:

$$\text{Implied utilization} = \frac{\text{Total demand at the resource}}{\text{Capacity at the resource}}$$

The resource with the highest implied utilization is the bottleneck.

Step 5: Compute the flow rate for each flow unit type.

- If the highest implied utilization is less than or equal to 100 percent, the demand rates are the flow rates.

- If the highest implied utilization exceeds 100 percent, divide the demand rate for each flow unit type by the highest implied utilization.

Either way, the process capacity for each type of flow unit assuming a constant mix is the demand rate for that flow unit divided by the highest implied utilization.

Check Your Understanding 5.2

Question: A process has three resources and two types of flow units. The first flow unit has a demand of 10 units per day, and the second flow unit has a demand of 30 units per day. The first flow unit type visits all three resources, while the second flow unit type only visits the first and the third resources. The capacity is 30 units per day at the first resource, 20 units per day at the second resource, and 40 units per day at the third resource. Which resource is the bottleneck? What would be the flow rates for the two flow unit types assuming that the relative proportion between the two remains constant?

Answer: We follow the five steps outlined in Exhibit 5.1.

Step 1: We compute the demand matrix as

$$D = \begin{bmatrix} 10 & 30 \\ 10 & 0 \\ 10 & 30 \end{bmatrix}$$

Continued

Step 2: We compute the total demand rates for the three resources. 40 units will come to the first resource per day, 10 to the second, and 40 to the third.

Step 3: We compute the capacity for each resource. In this case, the information is directly given in the question: 30 units per day for the first resource, 20 units per day for the second, and 40 units per day for the third.

Step 4: We compute the levels of implied utilization as the total demand rate of a resource divided by its capacity.

$$IU\ 1 = \frac{40}{30} = 1.33$$

$$IU\ 2 = \frac{10}{20} = 0.5$$

$$IU\ 3 = \frac{40}{40} = 1$$

So, resource 1 has the highest implied utilization and thus is the bottleneck.

Step 5: Since we have an implied utilization that exceeds 100 percent, we are capacity-constrained. To find the flow rates, we divide each demand rate by the implied utilization of the bottleneck; that is, by 1.33:

$$Flow\ rate\ 1 = \frac{10}{1.33} = 7.5\ units\ per\ day$$

$$Flow\ rate\ 2 = \frac{30}{1.33} = 22.5\ units\ per\ day$$

With these two flow rates, the process operates at capacity; thus, these are also the capacities.

· ·

5.3 Attrition Losses, Yields, and Scrap Rates

In a process with **attrition losses**, all flow units start at the same resource but then drop out of the process (or are actively removed from the process) at different points. Attrition losses are common in business going well beyond the pharmaceutical development example mentioned at the beginning of this chapter:

- In recruiting processes/job applications, hundreds of CVs get reduced to tens of interviews, which get reduced to one job offer.
- In sales processes, hundreds of leads get reduced to tens of customer visits, which get reduced to one closed sale.
- Attrition losses also happen in many educational processes (many more students start a course than get credits for the course).
- Many production processes suffer from defects, and defective units are removed from the process.

While the vocabulary that we now introduce is more commonly used in manufacturing, the flow calculations can be used in any process. All that matters is that we have good units that journey through the process and defective units that are removed from the process, a practice also known as **scrapping**. In this section, we assume that a flow unit, once it is defective, is eliminated from the process. Later on in this chapter, we discuss the case in which defective flow units are "fixed," a practice known as **rework.**

We define the **yield** of a resource as

$$Yield\ of\ resource = \frac{Flow\ rate\ of\ good\ output\ at\ the\ resource}{Flow\ rate\ of\ input}$$

$$= 1 - \frac{Flow\ rate\ of\ defects\ at\ the\ resource}{Flow\ rate\ of\ input}$$

Attrition loss In a process with attrition losses, all flow units start at the same resource but then drop out of the process (or are actively removed from the process) at different points.

Scrap Defective flow units that are eliminated from the process.

Yield The yield of a resource measures the percentage of good units that are processed at this resource.

LO5-3 Compute the yield of a process and be able to analyze a process flow with yield loss

Thus, the yield of a resource measures the percentage of good units that are processed at this resource. Similarly, we can define the yield at the level of the overall process:

$$\text{Process yield} = \frac{\text{Flow rate of good output at the process}}{\text{Flow rate of input to the process}}$$

$$= 1 - \frac{\text{Flow rate of defects at the process}}{\text{Flow rate of input to the process}}$$

In a process in which defective units are eliminated and each good unit has to visit all resources, we can write the process yield as

$$\text{Process yield} = y_1 \times y_2 \times y_3 \times \ldots \times y_m$$

where m is the number of resources in the sequence and y_i is the yield of the ith resource.

Consider the example of Capital One discussed earlier in this chapter. We found that the yield of interviewing was 100 percent, the yield of underwriting was 33.4 percent (we are scrapping both withdrawals and rejects), the yield of quality assurance was 100 percent, and the yield of closing was 79.04 percent (26.4 out of 33.4 loans were not withdrawn).

So, the overall process yield was

$$\text{Process yield} = 1 \times 0.334 \times 1 \times 0.7904 \times 1 = 0.264$$

If we now want to compute the **number of flow units that have to be processed to get a certain output Q**, we can write:

$$\text{Number of units started to get } Q \text{ good units} = \frac{Q}{\text{Process yield}}$$

Say we wanted to have an output of 100 funded loans; that is, loans that are neither withdrawn nor rejected. How many interviews would we have to conduct?

$$\text{Number of loans required at interviewing to get 100 funded loans} = \frac{100}{0.264}$$
$$= 378.79 \text{ loans}$$

Processes with scrap resemble a big funnel—they have a wide mouth at the upstream of the process and, because of the scrap losses, a narrower opening at the end of the process. Note though that the metaphor of a funnel is not entirely appropriate. After all, in a funnel, everything that you push into one end comes out the other end. Thus, from a mechanical perspective, processes with scrap are really like a sequence of filters that get tighter and tighter as you move from the upstream to the downstream.

Number of units started to get Q good units Number of units started to get Q good units = Q/Process yield.

Check Your Understanding 5.3

Question: Consider the following two-step process. Step 1 has an 80 percent yield. Step 2 has a 60 percent yield. What is the yield of the overall process?

Answer: The overall process yield is

$$\text{Process yield} = 0.8 \times 0.6 = 0.48$$

Question: How many units would the process have to process to get 50 units of good output?

Answer: We compute

$$\text{Number of units started to get } Q \text{ good units} = \frac{Q}{\text{Process yield}}$$
$$= \frac{50}{0.48} = 104.166$$

Figure 5.3

Process flow diagram with attrition loss using just one flow unit type

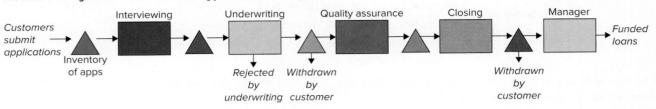

In our search for the bottleneck at Capital One, we created a number of flow unit types, depending on where the flow unit exits the process. In the Capital One case, there were four such flow units. However, as we now show, these calculations can be simplified by using our yield-based calculations. Toward that goal, we first compute the number of units that have to be processed at each resource to produce one *good* unit at the end of the process, in our case an approved loan. So, instead of working with four flow unit types, we are down to one. An updated process flow diagram is shown in Figure 5.3.

We start our computations at the end and then work backward toward the upstream of the process. At each resource, we compute

$$\text{Number of units started to get } Q \text{ good units out of the resource} = \frac{Q}{\text{Yield at the resource}}$$

At Capital One, to obtain one good unit of output (a funded loan), the manager has to process

$$\text{Quantity to be processed at manager} = \frac{1}{\text{Yield(Manager)}} = \frac{1}{1} = 1 \text{ loan}$$

At closing, in contrast, the yield is less than 100 percent and so we have to produce some extra loans to compensate for the yield losses. We compute

$$\text{Quantity to be processed at closing} = \frac{1}{\text{Yield(Closing)}}$$
$$= \frac{1}{0.7904} = 1.265 \text{ loans}$$

The yield at quality assurance is 100 percent and so we also have to process 1.26 loans for each funded loan. Underwriting has a yield of only 33.4 percent and so underwriting has to handle

$$\text{Quantity to be processed at underwriting} = \frac{1.265}{\text{Yield(Underwriting)}}$$
$$= \frac{1.265}{0.334} = 3.788 \text{ loans}$$

Because the yield of interviewing is 100 percent, we also have to process 3.788 loans at interviewing to get one funded loan at the end of the process. These yield calculations allow us to determine the demand matrix for the flow unit "one approved loan" in the hypothetical scenario where we create one unit of output (i.e., we fund one loan) every minute. Specifically, we get

$$
D =
\begin{array}{ll}
\text{Interview} \\
\text{Underwrite} \\
\text{Quality Assurance} \\
\text{Closing} \\
\text{Manager}
\end{array}
\begin{bmatrix}
3.788 \\
3.788 \\
1.265 \\
1.265 \\
1
\end{bmatrix}
$$

TABLE 5.4 Calculation of Implied Utilization

Resource	Yield	Demand	Capacity	Implied Utilization
Interviewing	1.000	3.788	0.304	12.446
Underwriting	0.334	3.788	0.200	18.939
Quality assurance	1.000	1.265	0.080	15.814
Closing	0.7904	1.265	0.086	14.760
Manager	1.000	1.000	0.200	5.000

Recall from our earlier calculations that the capacity levels were as follows: 0.304 app/min at interviewing, 0.2 app/min at underwriting, 0.08 app/min at quality assurance, 0.09 app/min at closing, and 0.2 app/min at the manager.

This gives us the levels of implied utilization for the hypothetical case in which one unit is funded every minute. As we can see, the level of implied utilization is the highest at underwriting, which confirms our earlier calculation that this is the bottleneck (Table 5.4).

We start the calculation with one unit funded by the manager and then adjust for the yield loss in each stage. As in our earlier calculations, the implied utilization levels guide us to the bottleneck. But how do you interpret an implied utilization of 18.939 (that is, 1893.9 percent)? The implied utilization level obtained this way is the answer to the following question: If we wanted to create one unit of good output for every unit of time, what would be the associated implied utilization of the bottleneck?

For the sake of illustration, assume we have an implied utilization computed this way of 200 percent. What does this mean? This means we can make a good unit every 2 units of time. If our implied utilization is 400 percent, this means we can make a good unit every 4 units of time. In general, we write:

$$\text{Capacity in good units per unit of time} = \frac{1 \text{ good unit per unit of time}}{\text{Implied utilization}}$$

How to Find the Bottleneck and the Capacity in a Process with Attrition Loss

EXHIBIT 5.2

Step 1: Compute the demand matrix, which only has a single column.

For each resource i, $D(i, 1)$ is the number of flow units that need to be processed for one good unit of output. For that, start with the last resource and then work from the downstream to the upstream of the process.

Step 2: Compute the capacity level for each resource.

Step 3: Compute the implied utilization for each resource:

$$\text{Implied utilization} = \frac{\text{Total demand at the resource}}{\text{Capacity at the resource}}$$

The resource with the highest implied utilization is the bottleneck.

Step 4: To find the capacity of the process in good units per unit of time, divide one good unit per unit of time by the highest implied utilization:

$$\text{Capacity in good units per unit of time} = \frac{1 \text{ good unit per unit of time}}{\text{Implied utilization}}$$

CONNECTIONS: TV Shows

Have you ever wondered how somebody comes up with the idea of a new TV show such as *Game of Thrones* or *Survivor*? What seems to be the result of a moment of genius by a creative producer is actually the output of a carefully planned process—a process with substantial attrition losses. The process leading to new shows starts with writers making pitches in early summer. A pitch is a short textual description of the key idea behind the show. For example, the pitch "Dark but fantastical cop drama about a world in which characters inspired by fairy tales exist" was the idea leading to the NBC show *Grimm*. Pitching is relatively cheap and so a big network each year receives some 500 pitches. Of these, about 70 will receive further attention and are turned into scripts. The best 20 of these scripts are then piloted, including a full casting operation, but only four–eight new series will make it to us as consumers. Only the best one or two shows are sufficiently successful to last for multiple seasons. So, the artistic process goes from 500 pitches to ultimately one or two shows that are shown again year after year. See Figure 5.4.

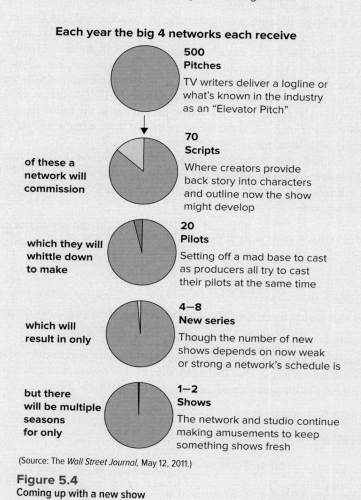

(Source: The *Wall Street Journal*, May 12, 2011.)

Figure 5.4
Coming up with a new show

So, in the case of Capital One, the current capacity of the process is 1/18.939 of producing one good loan per minute. Recall that there are 400 minutes the employees work per day. So we see that the capacity of the loan approval process can be computed as

$$400 \text{ minutes per day} \times \frac{1}{18.939} \text{ loan per minute} = \frac{400}{18.939}$$

$$= 21.12 \text{ loans per day}$$

This is exactly the daily capacity (expressed in approved loans per day) that we had obtained previously using the calculations with the four different flow units. The corresponding calculations for a process analysis with yield loss are summarized by Exhibit 5.2.

Check Your Understanding 5.4

Question: Consider the following two-step process. Step 1 takes 10 minutes per unit and has an 80 percent yield. Step 2 takes 15 minutes per unit and has a 60 percent yield. Where in the process is the bottleneck? How many good units can the process produce?

Answer: We follow the four-step approach outlined in Exhibit 5.2.

Step 1: We compute the demand matrix for one good unit of output coming out of step 2.
For one good unit of output, we have to produce

$$\text{Quantity to produce at step 2} = \frac{1}{0.6} = 1.666$$

We also adjust for the 80 percent yield at step 1 and get

$$\text{Quantity to produce at step 1} = \frac{1.666}{0.8} = 2.08333$$

So our demand matrix is

$$D = \begin{bmatrix} 2.0833 \\ 1.666 \end{bmatrix}$$

Step 2: Our capacity levels are 1/10 unit per minute at step 1 and 1/15 unit per minute at step 2.

Step 3: We compute the implied utilization as

$$\text{Implied utilization} = \frac{\text{Demand}}{\text{Capacity}}$$

$$\text{Implied utilization(step 1)} = \frac{2.08333}{\left(\frac{1}{10}\right)} = 20.8333$$

$$\text{Implied utilization(step 2)} = \frac{1.666}{\left(\frac{1}{15}\right)} = 25$$

So the implied utilization is higher at step 2, which makes step 2 the bottleneck.

Step 4: To find the capacity of the process in good units per unit of time, we divide one good unit per minute by the highest implied utilization, which is 25:

$$\text{Capacity in good units per minute} = \frac{1 \text{ good unit per minute}}{25}$$

$$= 2.4 \text{ good units per hour}$$

5.4 Flow Unit–Dependent Processing Times

© Slobodan Vasic/E-plus/Getty Images/RF

Consider the following example involving multiple product or customer types. An urgent care clinic provides health care services to patients who feel sick but cannot get a timely appointment. The center does not deal with very complicated cases because patients with severe conditions go to the emergency room of the local hospital. However, the center is able to provide basic imaging diagnostics (X-ray) and also do some simple lab analysis. It is staffed by one nurse greeting the patient and making an initial diagnostic (triage), two nurse practitioners, a doctor, a lab technician, a technician for the X-ray machine, and an administrative clerk.

An analysis of past patient flow patterns reveals that patients can be grouped into five types:

- Type 1 patients have only minor ailments and are seen by the nurse practitioner only.
- Type 2 patients are seen by the nurse practitioner, but the nurse practitioner also wants the doctor to look at the patient.
- Type 3 patients are seen by the doctor only.
- Type 4 patients are seen by the doctor, who then requests labs.
- Type 5 patients are seen by the doctor, who then requests X-rays.

All patients first see the triage nurse and all patients finish the process by seeing the clerk to deal with billing. This flow is captured in Figure 5.5.

As long as we know the demand rate of the five patient types, we can determine the demand matrix. However, in the case of our urgent care center, one complication arises when trying to formulate the capacity levels. The processing times that the doctor and the nurse practitioners spend on a patient differ by patient type. Specifically:

- Type 1 patients take 20 minutes with the nurse practitioner. However, for type 2 patients (the ones in which the nurse consults with the doctor), this processing time is 30 minutes per patient.
- From the doctor's perspective, type 2 patients are easy and it only takes the doctor 5 minutes per patient to collaborate with the nurse practitioner. Doctors take

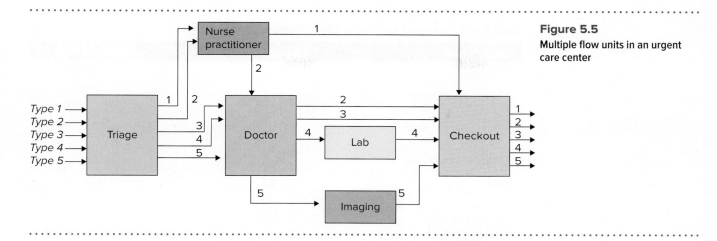

Figure 5.5
Multiple flow units in an urgent care center

15 minutes for each type 3 patient, but they take 20 minutes for patients of types 4 and 5, because these patients require some extra coordination with the lab and the imaging, respectively.

- In all other cases, the processing time is identical across patient types. It takes 6 minutes per patient at triage and 4 minutes per patient at checkout regardless of patient types. Labs take 5 minutes per patient and imaging takes 20 minutes per patient.

So, we are facing a case with **flow unit dependent processing time**. The fact that the processing times now can vary across flow unit types has implications for our process analysis, in particular our calculation of capacity (the meaning of "one patient" is no longer clear in the case of doctor and nurse practitioner, because we have to ask ourselves "What type of patient?").

The flow unit "one patient" allows us to evaluate the demand at each resource in this process, as well as its capacity expressed in patients per unit of time. But now that the different patient types require different processing times at one and the same resource, this approach reaches its limitations. In order to appropriately handle this case of flow unit–dependent processing times, we have to change our flow unit.

Instead of using the patient as our flow unit, we now define the flow unit as "one minute of work." That seems confusing at first, so let us elaborate. Consider the perspective of a doctor:

- Whenever a type 2 patient arrives, the doctor receives 5 minutes of work.
- Whenever a type 3 patient arrives, the doctor receives 15 minutes of work.
- Whenever a type 4 or 5 patient arrives, the doctor receives 20 minutes of work.

Given that these patient types are very different from each other, they make for bad flow units. What is the point of the triage nurse shouting, "Hey, doc, you have another patient," if each patient requires a different amount of work. It makes more sense for the nurse to shout, "Hey, doc, you have a type 4 patient." And what does the doctor think when she hears of another type 4 patient? She most likely thinks, "Yikes, that means another 20 minutes of work for me." So, every flow unit comes with some amount of work for a resource. To make things comparable, we thus change the flow unit from a patient type to the minutes of work that are caused by that patient to a given resource.

As before, we need to define our demands and our capacities in terms of our flow unit. In the case of capacity, each worker has "60 minutes of work" available per hour. (By definition, we all do!) So the capacity of each resource is

Capacity expressed in available time per hour at resource i

$$= \text{Number of workers}(i) \times 60 \left[\frac{\text{minutes}}{\text{hour}} \right]$$

LO5-4 Analyze a process flow with flow unit–dependent processing times

Flow unit dependent processing times The fact that the processing times can vary across flow unit types.

....

TABLE 5.5 Demand for Care (a day consists of 10 hours)

Patient Types	Cases per Day	Cases per Hour
1: Nurse only	20	2
2: Nurse and doctor	5	0.5
3: Doctor only	15	1.5
4: Doctor with labs	15	1.5
5: Doctor with images	8	0.8
Total	**63**	**6.3**

....

For example, we have two nurse practitioners. So, their combined capacity is $2 \times 60 = 120$ minutes of work per hour. Each worker has 60 "minutes of work" available per hour, so two of them can deliver 120 minutes of work. We do this for all six resources in the process and get capacities of 120 minutes of work per hour for the nurse practitioners and 60 minutes of work per hour for everybody else.

Now turn to the demand for work; that is, the workload. Based on past data, the center finds that there are typically 20 type 1 patients per day shift, 5 type 2 patients, 15 type 3 patients, 15 type 4 patients, and 8 type 5 patients. The day shift is 10 hours long and the arrivals are relatively uniform across the day. Table 5.5 shows this daily demand and also translates it into hourly demand by dividing the demand for the day shift by the duration of the day shift (10 hours).

We now need to take this demand (arriving patients) of the overall process and translate this to how much work is required from each individual resource. Remember that some resources (e.g., the triage nurse) are requested by all patients, whereas others (e.g., labs) are requested by only one type of patient. This is (hopefully) clear by looking at the process flow diagram. Moreover, the processing times at a given resource might differ across the patient types.

Consider the triage nurse. There are 6.3 patients to be handled by the triage nurse in each hour and each patient takes 6 minutes. So the workload created for the triage nurse is $6.3 \times 6 = 37.8$ minutes per hour. We can split these minutes up by patient type. We know that there are 2×6 minutes/hour caused by type 1 patients, 0.5×6 minutes/hour caused by type 2 patients, 1.5×6 minutes/hour caused by type 3 patients, 1.5×6 minutes/hour caused by type 4 patients, and 0.8×6 minutes/hour caused by type 5 patients.

Next, consider the nurse practitioner. There are 2 patients/hour of type 1. Each of them requires 20 minutes/patient of work. In addition to this, there is 0.5 patient/hour of type 2. Each type 2 patient requires 30 minutes/patient of work. So the total amount of work required from the nurse practitioners is

$$2 \frac{\text{patients}}{\text{hour}} \times 20 \frac{\text{minutes}}{\text{patient}} + 0.5 \frac{\text{patient}}{\text{hour}} \times 30 \frac{\text{minutes}}{\text{patient}} = 55 \frac{\text{minutes}}{\text{hour}}$$

For each resource and for each flow unit type, we define the **workload matrix** as

$$\text{WL}(i, j) = \text{Number of flow units of type } j \text{ that need to be processed by resource } i \times \text{Processing time that resource } i \text{ takes for customer type } j$$

Workload matrix For each resource i and for each flow unit type j, WL(i, j) = Number of flow units of type i that need to be processed by resource j × Processing time that resource j takes for customer type i.

Put differently, the workload matrix is just like the demand matrix introduced at the beginning of the chapter in which each cell is multiplied by the appropriate processing time.

In the case of our urgent care center, we get

$$
D = \begin{array}{c} \\ \text{Triage nurse} \\ \\ \text{Nurse practitioner} \\ \\ \text{Doctor} \\ \\ \text{Lab} \\ \\ \text{Images} \\ \\ \text{Checkout} \end{array}
\begin{array}{ccccc}
\text{Type 1} & \text{Type 2} & \text{Type 3} & \text{Type 4} & \text{Type 5} \\
2 \times 6 & 0.5 \times 6 & 1.5 \times 6 & 1.5 \times 6 & 0.8 \times 6 \\
\\
2 \times 20 & 0.5 \times 30 & 0 & 0 & 0 \\
\\
0 & 0.5 \times 5 & 1.5 \times 15 & 1.5 \times 20 & 0.8 \times 20 \\
\\
0 & 0 & 0 & 1.5 \times 5 & 0 \\
\\
0 & 0 & 0 & 0 & 0.8 \times 20 \\
\\
2 \times 4 & 0.5 \times 4 & 1.5 \times 4 & 1.5 \times 4 & 0.8 \times 4
\end{array}
$$

Just like when constructing the demand matrix, it is helpful to first create a table with the number of rows corresponding to the number of resources and the number of columns corresponding to the number of flow unit types. And, again, we encourage you to write the different flow unit types in an extra row above the table (as column headers) and the different resources in front of each row (as row headers).

Based on the workload matrix, we add up the workloads for each resource across all customer types:

$$\text{Demand rate for resource } j \text{ in minutes of work} = \Sigma_j\, D(i, j)$$

This gives us workloads of 37.8, 55, 71, 7.5, 16, and 25.2 minutes per hour for the six resources.

Now that we know how to express the demands and the capacities in terms of the "minutes of work," the implied utilization of each resource is simply one divided by the other:

$$\text{Implied utilization} = \frac{\text{Demand rate in minutes of work}}{\text{Capacity in minutes of work}}$$

Table 5.6 summarizes these calculations. Notice that the demand rate is constant within a column (for example, it is always 2 in the column for type 1 patients). Processing times can differ within a row to the extent that processing times are flow unit–dependent. Note further, that our process is capacity-constrained, because the implied utilization of the doctor is 1.1833 and thus exceeds 100 percent. Some patients will not get treated and will have to look for care elsewhere.

To find the flow rate of the process, we again have to assume that the product mix is given; thus, the relative magnitude between the different flow units is fixed. In our case, that means we get 2 patients of type 1 each hour, 0.5 of type 2, 1.5 of types 3 and 4, and 0.8 of type 5 (see Table 5.5).

TABLE 5.6   Calculating the Implied Utilization Based on the Flow Unit "One Minute of Work"

Resources	m	Available Time	Demand (min of work)					Total	Implied Utilization
			1	2	3	4	5		
Triage nurse	1	60	2 × 6	0.5 × 6	1.5 × 6	1.5 × 6	0.8 × 6	37.8	0.63
Nurse practitioner	2	120	2 × 20	0.5 × 30	0	0	0	55	0.458333
Doctor	1	60	0	0.5 × 5	1.5 × 15	1.5 × 20	0.8 × 20	71	1.183333
Lab	1	60	0	0	0	1.5 × 5	0	7.5	0.125
Images	1	60	0	0	0	0	0.8 × 20	16	0.266667
Checkout clerk	1	60	2 × 4	0.5 × 4	1.5 × 4	1.5 × 4	0.8 × 4	25.2	0.42

Next, we divide the demand rates for the flow units by the highest implied utilization, which is 1.1833. In our case, we get:

Flow rate(Type 1—Nurse only) $\quad = \dfrac{2}{1.1833} = 1.69$ patients per hour

Flow rate(Type 2—Nurse and doctor) $\quad = \dfrac{0.5}{1.1833} = 0.42$ patient per hour

Flow rate(Type 3—Doctor only) $\quad = \dfrac{1.5}{1.1833} = 1.27$ patients per hour

Flow rate(Type 4—Doctor with labs) $\quad = \dfrac{1.5}{1.1833} = 1.27$ patients per hour

Flow rate(Type 5—Doctor with images) $\quad = \dfrac{0.8}{1.1833} = 0.68$ patient per hour

The approach introduced in this section is general. The processing times don't have to be flow unit–dependent. In Table 5.7, we revisit the Capital One analysis discussed at the beginning of the chapter. This time, however, we calculate the implied utilization levels based on the "minutes of work" approach outlined in this section. As you see when you compare these data in Table 5.7 with the data in Table 5.3, all implied utilization levels are identical. To state the obvious, these calculations of using "minutes of work" as a flow unit also work for other units of time, be they seconds, hours, days, etc. Exhibit 5.3 summarizes the steps you need to take when doing a process analysis with multiple flow units.

. . . .

EXHIBIT 5.3

How to Find the Bottleneck and the Flow Rates in a Process with Flow Unit–Dependent Processing Times

Step 1: Compute the workload matrix as

$\text{WL}(i, j)$ = Number of flow units of type j that need to be processed by resource i × Processing time that resource i takes for flow unit type j

Step 2: Based on the workload matrix, add up the workloads for each resource across all customer types:

Demand rate for resource i in minutes of work $= \Sigma_j \, \text{WL}(i, j)$

Step 3: Compute the available time at each resource (this is, the number of workers at the resource times 60 minutes per hour).

Step 4: Compute the implied utilization for each resource:

$$\text{Implied utilization} = \frac{\text{Demand rate in minutes of work}}{\text{Capacity in minutes of work}}$$

The resource with the highest implied utilization is the bottleneck.

Step 5: Compute the flow rate for each flow unit type.

- If the highest implied utilization is less or equal to 100 percent, the demand rates are the flow rates.

- If the highest implied utilization exceeds 100 percent, divide the demand rate for each flow unit type by the highest implied utilization.

. . . .

TABLE 5.7 Recalculating the Implied Utilization at Capital One (Table 5.3) Using "One Minute of Work" as the Flow Unit

Resource	Staff	Available Time	1	2	3	4	Total	Implied Utilization
Interviewing	7	2,800	29.04 × 23	7.7 × 23	16.06 × 23	57.2 × 23	2,530	0.90357143
Underwriting	8	3,200	29.04 × 40	7.7 × 40	16.06 × 40	57.2 × 40	4,400	1.375
Quality assurance	2	800	29.04 × 25	7.7 × 25	0	0	918.5	1.148125
Closing	6	2,400	29.04 × 70	7.7 × 70	0	0	2,571.8	1.07158333
Manager	1	400	29.04 × 5	0	0	0	145.2	0.363

Check Your Understanding 5.5

Question: Consider a two-step process that handles three types of customers. Each resource is staffed by one employee. Type 1 customers spend 5 minutes at resource 1 and 2 minutes at resource 2. Type 2 customers also spend 5 minutes at resource 1, but spend 10 minutes at resource 2. Finally, type 3 customers spend no time at resource 1 and 8 minutes at resource 2. Each hour, the demand is 10 customers of type 1, 4 customers of type 2, and 2 customers of type 3. Where in the process is the bottleneck? What is the flow rate for each customer type?

Answer: We follow the five-step process outlined in Exhibit 5.3.

Step 1: Compute the workload matrix as

$$WL = \begin{bmatrix} 10 \times 5 & 4 \times 5 & 0 \\ 10 \times 2 & 4 \times 10 & 2 \times 8 \end{bmatrix}$$

Step 2: Based on the workload matrix, add up the workloads for each resource across all customer types:

$$\text{Resource 1: } 10\ \frac{\text{customers}}{\text{hour}} \times 5\ \frac{\text{minutes}}{\text{customer}} + 4\ \frac{\text{customers}}{\text{hour}} \times 5\ \frac{\text{minutes}}{\text{customer}} = 70\ \frac{\text{minutes}}{\text{hour}}$$

$$\text{Resource 2: } 10\ \frac{\text{customers}}{\text{hour}} \times 2\ \frac{\text{minutes}}{\text{customer}} + 4\ \frac{\text{customers}}{\text{hour}}$$
$$\times 10\ \frac{\text{minutes}}{\text{customer}} + 2\ \frac{\text{customers}}{\text{hour}} \times 8\ \frac{\text{minutes}}{\text{customer}} = 76\ \frac{\text{minutes}}{\text{hour}}$$

Step 3: Compute the available time at each resource:
   Because each resource has one employee, each has 60 minutes of labor available each hour.

Step 4: Compute the implied utilization for each resource:

$$\text{Implied utilization(Resource 1)} = \frac{\text{Workload resource 1}}{\text{Available time resource}} = \frac{70}{60} = 1.166$$

$$\text{Implied utilization(Resource 2)} = \frac{\text{Workload resource 2}}{\text{Available time resource}} = \frac{76}{60} = 1.266$$

   Resource 2 is the bottleneck because it has the higher implied utilization.

Step 5: Compute the flow rate for each flow unit type.
   Because we have an implied utilization of 1.266, we are capacity-constrained. We divide the three demand rates (10, 4, and 2 customers per hour) by 1.266 and get flow rates of

$$\text{Flow rate(Type 1): } \frac{10}{1.266} = 7.90\ \text{customers/hour}$$

$$\text{Flow rate(Type 2): } \frac{4}{1.266} = 3.16\ \text{customers/hour}$$

$$\text{Flow rate(Type 3): } \frac{2}{1.266} = 1.58\ \text{customers/hour}$$

5.5 Rework

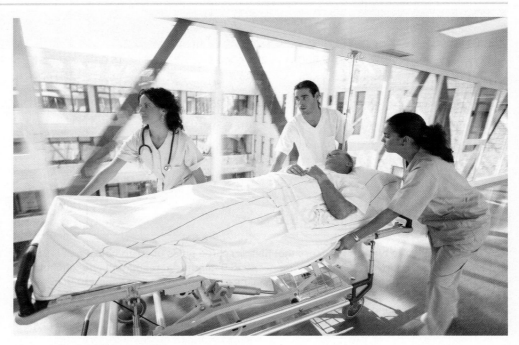

© *Javier Larrea/Pixtal/age fotostock/RF*

LO5-5 Analyze a process flow with rework

Oftentimes, flow units that fail to meet certain quality standards have to repeat activities in the process. When analyzing patient flows in a hospital, one observes that patients who are discharged from the intensive care unit to the medical wards of the hospital often have to be readmitted to the intensive care unit later on because of complications. Similarly, patients who are discharged from the hospital frequently have to be readmitted to the hospital if their health condition is deteriorating. We refer to **rework** as a repetition of activities or an extra set of activities that have to be completed by a defective flow unit in order to be restored to a good flow unit.

Consider the following situation in the cardiac ICU at a large hospital. There are 12 beds in the cardiac ICU and 18 beds in the cardiology ward. Patients admitted to the ICU from the operating room stay in the ICU for five days. This, however, assumes that patients do not develop complications. About 20 percent of the patients develop complications in the ICU. These patients stay in the ICU for 13 days (i.e., they spend an extra eight days in the ICU). They need to be "reworked." Once discharged from the ICU, patients are moved to the cardiology ward. Here, they spend, on average, four days. We also assume that there is no "rework of rework"; that is, the absolute maximum a patient can spend in the ICU is 13 days.

It helps to start with a process flow diagram of this situation, which is shown in Figure 5.6.

Next, we have to think about the potential flows of a patient through the hospital. There are two scenarios, each of them corresponding to different capacity requirements of the patient in the ICU:

- The patient develops no complications in the ICU: This happens with a probability of 0.8 (in 80 percent of the cases). In that case, the patient will spend five days in the ICU and then four days in the ward.

Rework The repetition of activities or an extra set of activities that have to be completed by a defective flow unit in order to be restored to a good flow unit.

Figure 5.6

Patient flow with rework

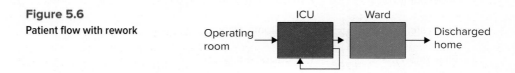

- The patient develops complications in the ICU: This happens with a probability of 0.2. In that case, the patient will spend 13 days in the ICU and then four days in the ward.

We can think of these two scenarios as two different patient types. Assume a demand rate of one patient per day coming out of the operating room. With a demand rate of one patient a day, we get 0.8 patient per day with no complications and 0.2 patient per day with complications. This leads to the following workload matrix (the first row is the workload for the ICU and the second row is the workload for the ward):

$$WL = \begin{array}{c} \\ ICU \\ Ward \end{array} \begin{array}{cc} \text{No Complication} & \text{Readmission} \\ \left[\begin{array}{cc} 0.8 \times 5 & 0.2 \times 13 \\ 0.8 \times 4 & 0.2 \times 4 \end{array} \right] \end{array}$$

If we add up the workload for our two resources, we get

$$\begin{aligned} \text{Workload(ICU)} &= 0.8 \times 5 + 0.2 \times 13 \\ &= 6.6 \text{ days per patient discharged from the OR} \\ \text{Workload(Ward)} &= 0.8 \times 4 + 0.2 \times 4 \\ &= 4 \text{ days per patient discharged from the OR} \end{aligned}$$

Now that we know how to express the demands and the capacities in terms of the "days of work," the implied utilization of each resource is simply one divided by the other:

$$\text{Implied utilization} = \frac{\text{Demand rate in days of work}}{\text{Capacity in days of work}}$$

Consider the ICU first. We have a workload of 6.6 days per patient discharged from the OR. Each ICU bed, by definition, has one day of work available as capacity each day. Because we have 12 ICU beds, that gives us an implied utilization of

$$\text{Implied utilization(ICU)} = \frac{6.6 \text{ days}}{12 \text{ days}} = 0.55$$

In the same way, we can find the implied utilization of the ward. Here, the workload is four days and we have 18 bed-days available, one day for each of the 18 beds. So we get

$$\text{Implied utilization(Ward)} = \frac{4 \text{ days}}{18 \text{ days}} = 0.22$$

Thus, the implied utilization of the ICU is higher—it is the rate-limiting factor and thus the bottleneck.

How many patients can flow through this process each day? To find the capacity of the process, divide one unit per unit of time by the highest implied utilization:

$$\begin{aligned} \text{Capacity per unit of time} &= \frac{1 \text{unit per unit of time}}{\text{Implied utilization}} \\ &= \frac{1}{0.55} = 1.82 \text{ patients per day} \end{aligned}$$

Just as with yields, the term *rework* has its origins in the world of manufacturing. Two examples of process flow diagrams with rework are shown in Figure 5.7 (inventory locations are left out for simplicity). In the upper part of the figure, defective units are taken out of the regular process and moved to a separate rework operation. This is common in many production processes such as automotive assembly lines. In the lower part of the figure, defective units are reworked by the same resource that previously processed the unit, as in the hospital example discussed earlier. If rework is always able to turn a defective unit into a good unit, the process yield returns to 100 percent.

EXHIBIT 5.4

How to Find the Bottleneck and the Capacity in a Process with Rework?

Step 1: Compute the workload matrix as

WL(i, j) = Number of flow units of type j that need to be processed by resource i × Processing time that resource i takes for customer type j

The processing times are longer in the column corresponding to rework.

Step 2: Based on the workload matrix, add up the workloads for each resource across all customer types:

Demand rate for resource i in minutes of work = Σj WL(i, j)

Step 3: Compute the available time at each resource (this is the number of workers at the resource times 60 minutes per hour).

Step 4: Compute the implied utilization for each resource:

$$\text{Implied utilization} = \frac{\text{Demand rate in minutes of work}}{\text{Available time at the resource}}$$

The resource with the highest implied utilization is the bottleneck.

Step 5: To find the capacity of the process, divide one unit per unit of time by the highest implied utilization:

$$\text{Capacity per unit of time} = \frac{1 \text{ unit per unit of time}}{\text{Implied utilization}}$$

Rework means that a resource needs to process more flow units, which means that the demand rate for a particular resource is higher relative to the case of no rework. With a higher demand rate, rework can potentially change the location of the bottleneck. Thus, when analyzing the influence of yields (and rework) on process capacity, we need to distinguish between bottleneck and nonbottleneck resources.

If rework involves only nonbottleneck machines with a large amount of idle time, it has no effect on the overall process capacity. In many cases, however, rework is severe enough to make a resource a bottleneck (or, even worse, rework needs to be carried out on the bottleneck). As the capacity of the bottleneck equals the capacity of the overall process, all capacity invested in rework at the bottleneck is lost from the perspective of the overall process.

Figure 5.7

Example of two processes with rework

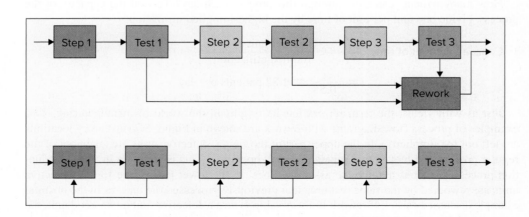

Check Your Understanding 5.6

Question: Consider the following three-step process with rework. The first resource takes 5 minutes per unit, the second 3 minutes per unit, and the third 2 minutes per unit. After the third step, 60 percent of all units have to be reworked. For that, they have to revisit the second and third resources. In that case, the processing times are the same as in the first pass. Moreover, rework also always fixes the problem. Where is the bottleneck and what is the capacity of the process?

Answer: We follow the framework outlined in Exhibit 5.4.

Step 1: Compute the workload matrix as

$$
WL = \begin{matrix} & \overbrace{}^{\text{Good}} & \overbrace{}^{\text{Rework}} \\ \text{Resource 1} \\ \text{Resource 2} \\ \text{Resource 3} \end{matrix} \begin{bmatrix} 0.4 \times 5 & 0.6 \times 5 \\ 0.4 \times 3 & 0.6 \times [3 + 3] \\ 0.4 \times 2 & 0.6 \times [2 + 2] \end{bmatrix}
$$

Step 2: Based on the workload matrix, add up the workloads for each resource across all customer types:

Resource 1: $0.4 \times 5 + 0.6 \times 5 = 5$ minutes per unit

Resource 2: $0.4 \times 3 + 0.6 \times (3 + 3) = 4.8$ minutes per unit

Resource 3: $0.4 \times 2 + 0.6 \times (2 + 2) = 3.2$ minutes per unit

Step 3: Next, we have to look at the capacity levels. Because each resource has one worker, each resource can provide one minute of work each minute.

Step 4: We compute the levels of implied utilization for each resource as the ratio between workload (step 2) and available time (step 3):

$$IU\ 1 = \frac{5}{1}, IU\ 2 = \frac{4.8}{1}, IU\ 3 = \frac{3.2}{1}$$

So, the implied utilization is at the highest (500 percent) at the first resource, making it the bottleneck.

Step 5: To find the capacity of the process, divide one unit per unit of time by the highest implied utilization:

$$\text{Capacity per unit of time} = \frac{1 \text{ unit per unit of time}}{\text{Implied utilization}} = \frac{1}{5} \text{ unit per minute}$$

Conclusion

In this chapter, we have extended our framework of process analysis to deal with more complicated process flow patterns. We have discussed the concept of a product mix and we also saw the flow implications of scrap and rework.

Now that we understand the more general process flows, let us reflect upon how we might be able to improve these flows. In this context, it is important to remember that everything we discussed in the previous chapter about process improvement remains valid. If we are capacity-constrained, we should consider adding capacity to the bottleneck, Thus, we should aim to balance the line and standardize work.

A famous saying in operations management has been "Do it right the first time." As we saw earlier, rework consumes extra capacity from resources. If rework involves the bottleneck, it reduces process capacity. It also can make a nonbottleneck resource the bottleneck. As we will see in later chapters, rework also has other undesirable effects on process flow. Rework can be reduced and sometimes be avoided entirely by implementing appropriate standards and having clear criteria (often in the form of checklists) that need to be checked before a flow unit is passed on to the downstream resource.

Just as we would like to avoid rework, of course, it would also be nice to avoid scrap. But, as we saw with the Capital One case, scrap oftentimes is a result of external factors outside our control. So, in many industries, scrap is part of operations (underwriting tasks, pharmaceutical development, search processes, etc.). Strictly speaking, the scrap process is a special form of rework where all operations between the resource where the defective unit leaves the process and the beginning of the process have to be reworked. Given that all operations up to the point of defect detection must be reworked, the earlier we can detect and eliminate the corresponding flow unit, the less we waste capacity. So, early upstream detection of scrap is critical. In particular, we gain a lot of process capacity if we find the defect before it consumes bottleneck capacity. At Capital One, for example, we would increase the capacity of the loan approval process to the extent that we can reject some apps already at the interviewing step.

Summary of Learning Objectives

LO5-1 **Compute the demand for a resource in the presence of a product mix**

When facing a process with multiple flow units (a product mix), we have to first figure out which flow unit visits which resource. A process flow diagram with multiple types of arrows helps with this. Next, we can find out how much demand is caused by each type of flow unit for each resource, which creates the demand matrix. For each resource, we can then add up the demands of the different flow unit types to get to the total demand rate for that resource.

LO5-2 **Find the bottleneck in a general process flow by computing implied utilization levels**

To find the bottleneck in the presence of a product mix, for each resource we look at the ratio between the demand rate and the available capacity. This determines the implied utilization. The resource with the highest implied utilization is the bottleneck.

LO5-3 **Compute the yield of a process and be able to analyze a process flow with yield loss**

The yield of a process is simply the percentage of units processed correctly. A process with yield loss is analyzed similarly to a process with multiple flow units. To find the bottleneck, we first figure out how much we have to process at each resource for one good unit of output (giving us the demand matrix). We then compute the levels of implied utilization. The resource with the highest implied utilization is the bottleneck.

LO5-4 **Analyze a process flow with flow unit–dependent processing times**

To find the bottleneck in a process where the processing times at a given resource differ across the products/customers in the product mix, we have to change the unit of analysis. Instead of using a unit of demand as a flow unit, we choose a minute of work as the flow unit. Each product/customer is associated with a certain amount of work for each resource, which is captured in the workload matrix. If we add up the rows in the workload matrix, we know how much work needs to be done. To find the levels of implied utilization, we compute the ratios of the work requested at each resource to the time the resource has available. The resource with the highest implied utilization is the bottleneck.

LO5-5 **Analyze a process flow with rework**

Rework means that some flow units have to be processed multiple times by a resource. To analyze the process, we first compute the workload matrix. Reworked units will consume more time at the resource involved with rework than good units. If we add up the workload for each resource for the good units and the units requiring rework, we get a total workload. We divide this by the time available at that resource to get to the implied utilization. The resource with the highest implied utilization is the bottleneck.

Key Terms

5.1 Generalized Process Flow Patterns

Product mix A combination of different flow unit types moving through a process.

Demand matrix Determines how many flow units of each type are flowing through each resource. For resource i, $D(i,j)$ is the number of flow units of type j that need to be processed.

Total demand rate The total demand rate for resource i tells us how many flow units need to be processed at resource i across all different flow units.

5.2 How to Find the Bottleneck in General Process Flows

Implied utilization The ratio of demand to capacity: Implied utilization = Demand at the resource / Capacity at the resource. The implied utilization captures the mismatch between demand and capacity.

5.3 Attrition Losses, Yields, and Scrap Rates

Attrition loss In a process with attrition losses, all flow units start at the same resource but then drop out of the process (or are actively removed from the process) at different points.

Scrap Defective flow units that are eliminated from the process.

Yield The yield of a resource measures the percentage of good units that are processed at this resource.

Number of units started to get Q good units Number of units started to get Q good units = Q/Process yield.

5.4 Flow Unit–Dependent Processing Times

Flow unit–dependent processing times The fact that the processing times now can vary across flow unit types.

Workload matrix For each resource i and for each flow unit type j, $WL(i, j)$ = Number of flow units of type j that need to be processed by resource i × Processing time that resource i takes for customer type j.

5.5 Rework

Rework The repetition of activities or an extra set of activities that have to be completed by a defective flow unit in order to be restored to a good flow unit.

Conceptual Questions

LO5–1

1. A process has six resources and three types of flow units. How many rows will there be in the demand matrix?
   a. 2
   b. 3
   c. 6
   d. 18

2. A process has 10 resources and two types of flow units. How many columns will there be in the demand matrix?
   a. 2
   b. 5
   c. 10
   d. 20

3. The total demand rate for a resource is the sum of the individual demand rates that need to be processed by the resource. True or false?
   a. True
   b. False

4. The resource with the largest total demand rate is the bottleneck. True or false?
   a. True
   b. False

LO5–2

5. The implied utilization can never be bigger than 100 percent. True or false?
   a. True
   b. False

6. A resource has an implied utilization of 150 percent. This is the highest implied utilization in the process. This means that the resource is the bottleneck. True or false?
   a. True
   b. False

LO5–3

7. A process has a yield of 50 percent. How many units are needed as inflow to create an outflow of 40 units per day?
   a. 10
   b. 20
   c. 80
   d. 90

8. What is the highest possible yield a process can obtain?
   a. 95 percent
   b. 100 percent
   c. 200 percent
   d. It depends on the process.

9. To find the bottleneck in a process with attrition loss, all we need to do is find the resource with the lowest capacity. True or false?
   a. True
   b. False

10. As the attrition loss in a process increases, what happens to the yield?
    a. The yield increases.
    b. The yield stays the same.
    c. The yield decreases.
    d. Cannot determine from the given information.

LO5–4

11. What flow unit do you use when dealing with flow unit–dependent processing times?
    a. Revenue dollars
    b. Customers
    c. Each different type of finished goods
    d. Minutes or hours of work

12. The workload matrix has exactly the same number of rows and the same number of columns as the demand matrix. True or false?
    a. True
    b. False

13. If a flow unit type j does not consume any time at a resource i, the corresponding cell in the workload matrix, $WL(i, j)$, is zero. True or false?
    a. True
    b. False

LO5–5

14. Rework can increase the costs of an operation but has no impact on the capacity of the process. True or false?
    a. True
    b. False

15. What is the relationship between a process with rework and a process with scrap?
    a. Scrap and rework are not related.
    b. Scrap and rework are sequential processes. First, items are scrapped and then they are reworked.

c. A process either has scrap or rework. The two are mutually exclusive.

d. Scrap is a special case of rework in which flow units have to repeat all resources in the process up to the defect.

16. In a process with rework, we find the bottleneck as the resource with the highest implied utilization. True or false?

   a. True

   b. False

Solved Example Problems

1. Located along a cobblestone street in Old City, Old City Photographics (OCP) specializes in processing traditional 35mm film negatives, the once-dominant photographic medium that is now in decline due to the popularity of digital photography. OCP offers three packages to its customers. With the standard package, the customer gets a set of 6" × 4" prints. The deluxe package adds to the standard package a CD-ROM of high-resolution scans of the pictures. Finally, the pro package is similar to the deluxe package in that it comes with a CD-ROM, except that the customer gets a contact print rather than a set of prints.

   The workflow for OCP is shown in Figure 5.8 (s = standard, d = deluxe, p = pro; a unit corresponds to an entire roll of film).

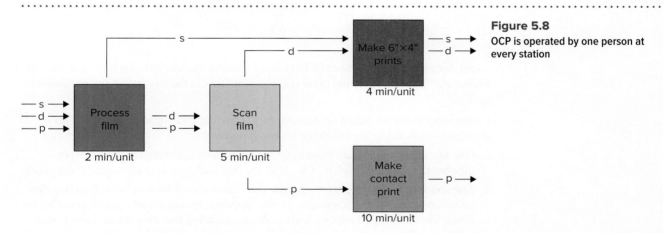

Figure 5.8
OCP is operated by one person at every station

On average, OCP receives 15 jobs per hour consisting of 50 percent standard, 30 percent deluxe, and 20 percent pro.

How many jobs will arrive per hour at each station?

   Answer: We begin by computing the total demand rate for the overall process. Out of the 15 jobs per hour, 50 percent = 7.5 jobs per hour of type s, 30 percent = 4.5 jobs per hour of type d, and 20 percent = 3 jobs per hour of type p.

We can then construct the demand matrix as:

$$
D = \begin{array}{l}
\text{Process film} \\
\\
\text{Scan film} \\
\\
\text{Make } 6 \times 4 \text{ print} \\
\\
\text{Make contact print}
\end{array}
\begin{array}{ccc}
s & d & p \\
\begin{bmatrix} 7.5 & 4.5 & 3 \\ \\ 0 & 4.5 & 3 \\ \\ 7.5 & 4.5 & 0 \\ \\ 0 & 0 & 3 \end{bmatrix}
\end{array}
$$

This creates a total demand rate of 15 jobs per hour processing film, 7.5 jobs per hour scanning film, 12 jobs per hour making 6 × 4 prints, and 3 jobs per hour making contact prints.

LO5-2

2. In the Old City Photography scenario in the preceding problem, where is the bottleneck? What is the flow rate?

> **Answer:** We begin by computing the capacity levels (step 3 in Exhibit 5.1). The capacity levels are 30 jobs per hour processing film, 12 jobs per hour scanning film, 15 jobs per hour making 6 × 4 prints, and 6 jobs per hour making contact prints.
>
> Next, consider step 4. We then compute the levels of implied utilization as 15/30 (process film), 7.5/12 (scan film), 12/15 (6 × 4 prints), and 3/6 (contact prints). The highest of these is 12/15, which makes the 6 × 4 prints the bottleneck.
>
> Finally, step 5 helps us with the flow rate. The highest implied utilization is 12/15 = 0.8 < 1. Because we are demand-constrained, the flow rate is equal to the demand rate.
>
> We find the capacity of the process (assuming a constant mix) by dividing the demand rates by 0.8 (the highest implied utilization):
>
> $$\text{s} : \frac{7.5}{0.8} = 9.375$$
> $$\text{d} : \frac{4.5}{0.8} = 5.625$$
> $$\text{p} : \frac{3}{0.8} = 3.75$$

LO5-3

3. Experience the Tour de France (ETF) allows amateur cyclists to experience the Tour de France cycling race by letting them ride the same course the day before the professional cyclists.

Customers fill out an online application form showing their interest. ETF reaches out to these customers using the following four-step process:

1. One salesperson spends 20 minutes on the phone with a potential customer to put together the customer's full profile. After the call, each profile is forwarded to the coach.
2. The coach looks at the cyclist's profile and organizes a follow-up call. Together, this takes, on average, 40 minutes per profile. Between customers who are rejected by the coach for not being fit enough and customers deciding that they are no longer interested, only 20 percent of the profiles are forwarded to the ETF accountant.
3. ETF's accountant spends 20 minutes per customer discussing financing options.
4. Finally, the coach's assistant contacts the customer to confirm the trip and to complete a travel schedule. This takes, on average, 50 minutes for each contacted customer. Unfortunately, at this point, on average, two-thirds of the cyclists decide that they will not participate in the trip. The other third are booked and confirmed for the trip.

All employees work 8 hours per day.

(a) How many cyclists must ETF contact each day through its call center to obtain, on average, a target of booking and confirming two cyclists per day? (b) Where is the bottleneck? (c) What is the maximum number of target bookings the process can expect per day?

> **Answer:** The yields for the four steps are 1, 0.2, 1, and 0.333, respectively. Now, consider step 1 in Exhibit 5.2. For one target booking, we have to produce
>
> $$\text{Quantity to produce at step 4} = \frac{1}{0.333} = 3$$
> $$\text{Quantity to produce at step 3} = \frac{3}{1} = 3$$
> $$\text{Quantity to produce at step 2} = \frac{3}{0.2} = 15$$
> $$\text{Quantity to produce at step 1} = \frac{15}{1} = 15$$

In other words, for each target booking, we have to process 15 applications. Our demand matrix is:

$$D = \begin{bmatrix} 15 \\ 15 \\ 3 \\ 3 \end{bmatrix}$$

If we wanted to book 2 cyclists per day, we would have to process 30 cyclists at the first step.

For step 2, we have to look at the capacity levels. The capacity levels are 24, 12, 24, and 9.6 applications per day for salesperson, coach, accountant, and assistant, respectively.

Step 3: With that, we can compute the implied utilization levels as 15/24, 15/12, 3/24, and 3/9.6. The highest implied utilization is thus at the coach, which makes the coach the bottleneck.

We know that the coach as the bottleneck will work at capacity. The coach has a capacity of handling 12 applications per day. Of these, $12 \times 0.2 \times 0.333 = 0.8$ will be booked per day. We also get this result from step 4 in Exhibit 5.2.

$$\text{Capacity in good units per unit of time} = \frac{1}{\text{Highest implied utilization}}$$

$$= \frac{1}{\left[\frac{15}{12}\right]} = \frac{12}{15} = 0.8$$

Thus, the process has a capacity of 0.8 booked cyclists per day (which is not enough to meet the target of 2 booked cyclists per day).

LO5-4

4. An employment verification agency receives applications from consulting firms and law firms with the request to validate information provided by their job candidates. Figure 5.9 shows the process flow diagram for this agency. Note that while the three customer types share the first step and the last step in the process (filing and sending a confirmation letter), they differ with respect to other steps:

   • For internship positions, the agency provides information about the law school/business school the candidate is currently enrolled in, as well as previous institutions of higher education and, to the extent possible, provides information about the applicant's course choices and honors.
   • For staff positions, the agency contacts previous employers and analyzes the letters of recommendation from those employers.
   • For consulting/lawyer positions, the agency attempts to call former faculty from the university in addition to contacting the previous employers and analyzes the letters of recommendation from those employers.

   As far as demand, this process receives 3 consulting, 11 staff, and 4 internship applications per hour. It takes 3 minutes per candidate at filing, no matter what job category. Contact faculty takes 20 minutes per application. Contact employer takes 20 minutes for consulting applications and 10 minutes for staff applications. Benchmarking grades takes 8 minutes. Finally, the confirmation letter takes 4 minutes for consulting, 3 minutes for staff, and 2 minutes for internship positions.

   There is one worker at filing, two at contacting faculty, three at contacting former employers, two at benchmarking grades, and one for sending confirmation letters.

   Where in the process is the bottleneck? What would be the flow rate? What is the process capacity?

Figure 5.9
Multiple flow units

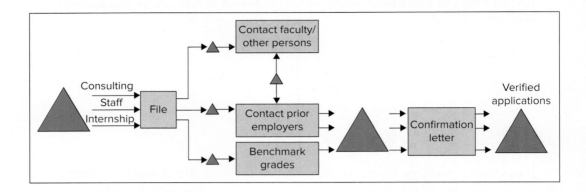

Answer: We start with step 1 in Exhibit 5.3, which is computing the workload matrix. We get

$$
\text{WL} = \begin{array}{c}
\\
\text{File} \\[6pt]
\text{Contact faculty} \\[6pt]
\text{Contact employers} \\[6pt]
\text{Benchmark grades} \\[6pt]
\text{Confirmation letter}
\end{array}
\begin{array}{ccc}
\text{Consulting} & \text{Staff} & \text{Internship} \\
\left[\begin{array}{ccc}
3 \times 3 & 11 \times 3 & 4 \times 3 \\[6pt]
3 \times 20 & 0 & 0 \\[6pt]
3 \times 20 & 11 \times 10 & 0 \\[6pt]
0 & 0 & 4 \times 8 \\[6pt]
3 \times 4 & 11 \times 3 & 4 \times 2
\end{array}\right]
\end{array}
$$

In step 2, we add up the total workload per hour for each of the resources:

$$
\text{WL} = \begin{array}{c}
\\
\text{File} \\[6pt]
\text{Contact faculty} \\[6pt]
\text{Contact employers} \\[6pt]
\text{Benchmark grades} \\[6pt]
\text{Confirmation letter}
\end{array}
\begin{array}{cccc}
\text{Consulting} & \text{Staff} & \text{Internship} & \text{Total} \\
\left[\begin{array}{ccc}
3 \times 3 + & 11 \times 3 & + 4 \times 3 \\[6pt]
3 \times 20 + & 0 & + 0 \\[6pt]
3 \times 20 + & 11 \times 10 & + 0 \\[6pt]
0 + & 0 & + 4 \times 8 \\[6pt]
3 \times 4 + & 11 \times 3 & + 4 \times 2
\end{array}\right] &
\begin{array}{c}
= 54 \\[6pt]
= 60 \\[6pt]
= 170 \\[6pt]
= 32 \\[6pt]
= 53
\end{array}
\end{array}
$$

In step 3, we compute the available time at each of the five resources. The available times are 60, 120, 180, 120, and 60 minutes per hour, respectively. The differences reflect the different staffing levels.

For step 4, we compute the resulting levels of implied utilization. They are 54/60 (at File), 60/120 (for Contact faculty), 170/180 (for Contact employers), 32/120 (for Benchmark grades), and 53/60 (for Confirmation letter). This makes Contact employers the bottleneck with an implied utilization of 170/180 = 94.4%.

For step 5, we first observe that the process is demand-constrained. Thus, the flow rate is equal to the demand rate. To find the process capacity (holding the mix constant), we divide each demand rate by the highest implied utilization; that is, by 0.944. This gives us

$$\text{Consulting}: \quad \frac{3}{0.944} = 3.176 \text{ per hour}$$

$$\text{Staff}: \quad \frac{11}{0.944} = 11.647 \text{ per hour}$$

$$\text{Internship}: \quad \frac{4}{0.944} = 4.235 \text{ per hour}$$

5. Consider the following three-step assembly operation with quality problems. All resources are staffed by one employee.
   - The first resource has a processing time of 7 minutes per unit.
   - The second resource has a processing time of 6 minutes per unit.
   - The third resource has a processing time of 5 minutes per unit. With a 40 percent probability, the flow unit coming out of the third resource has to be reworked. In that case, the operations at the second and third resources are repeated. You can assume that (a) rework always succeeds (i.e., a unit going through the rework loop will always work after the third resource) and (b) the processing times for units in rework are the same as for regular units.

Where in the process is the bottleneck? What is the capacity of the process?

Answer: We can distinguish between two types of units, the ones that work immediately (60 percent) and the ones that have to repeat the second and third steps (40 percent). Use the framework in Exhibit 5.4.

Step 1: We get the following workload matrix:

$$
\text{WL} = \begin{array}{c} \text{Resource 1} \\ \text{Resource 2} \\ \text{Resource 3} \end{array}
\begin{array}{cc}
\text{Good} & \text{Rework} \\
\begin{bmatrix} 0.6 \times 7 & 0.4 \times 7 \\ 0.6 \times 6 & 0.4 \times 12 \\ 0.6 \times 5 & 0.4 \times 10 \end{bmatrix}
\end{array}
$$

Step 2: Add up the workloads for each resource:

$$
\text{WL} = \begin{array}{c} \text{Resource 1} \\ \\ \text{Resource 2} \\ \\ \text{Resource 3} \end{array}
\begin{array}{ccc}
\text{Good} & \text{Rework} & \text{Total} \\
\begin{bmatrix} 0.6 \times 7 & + 0.4 \times 7 \\ \\ 0.6 \times 6 & + 0.4 \times 12 \\ \\ 0.6 \times 5 & + 0.4 \times 10 \end{bmatrix} & \begin{array}{c} = 7 \\ \\ = 8.4 \\ \\ = 7 \end{array}
\end{array}
$$

Thus, for each unit started, we expect 7 minutes per unit at resource 1, 8.4 minutes per unit at resource 2, and 7 minutes per unit at resource 3.

Step 3: Look at the available time for each resource expressed in minutes per hour. This is simply 60 minutes per hour because each resource is staffed by only one employee.

Step 4: Compute the levels of implied utilization:

$$\text{Implied utilization(Resource 1)} = \frac{7}{60}$$

$$\text{Implied utilization(Resource 2)} = \frac{8.4}{60}$$

$$\text{Implied utilization(Resource 3)} = \frac{7}{60}$$

So, resource 2 is the bottleneck with an implied utilization of 8.4/60 = 0.14. This would be the implied utilization if we started one unit every hour.

Step 5: Because the implied utilization is much smaller than 100 percent, we can start more units than just one unit per hour. Specifically, we have a capacity of

$$\text{Capacity per unit of time} = \frac{1 \text{ unit per unit of time}}{\text{Implied utilization at the bottleneck}}$$

$$= \frac{1}{0.14} = 7.14$$

Problems and Applications

LO5-1

1. GV is a small accounting firm supporting wealthy individuals in their preparation of annual income tax statements. Every December, GV sends out a short survey to its customers, asking for the information required for preparing the tax statements. Based on 50 years of experience, GV categorizes its cases into the following two groups:
   - Group 1 (new customers): 20 percent of cases
   - Group 2 (repeat customers): 80 percent of cases

   This year, there are 50 income tax statements arriving each week.

   In order to prepare the income tax statement, GV has three resources.

   The activities are carried out by the following three persons:
   - An administrative support person who processes every tax statement.
   - A senior accountant (who is also the owner) who processes only tax statements for new customers.
   - A junior accountant who only processes tax statements for repeat customers.

   What is the total demand rate for each of the three resources?

LO5-2

2. Consider the case of GV described in the preceding problem and the following processing times and assume that everyone works 40 hours per week.

Group	Administrator [min/unit]	Handling by Senior Accountant [min/unit]	Handling by Junior Accountant [min/unit]
1	20	40	n/a
2	20	n/a	15

   a. Which of the three persons is the bottleneck?
   b. For a mix of 20:80 between new and old cases, what is the flow rate and what is the capacity?

LO5-3

3. To obtain your first driver's license, you must successfully complete several activities. First, you must produce the appropriate identification. Then, you must pass a written exam. Finally, you must pass the road exam. At each of these steps, 10 percent, 15 percent, and 40 percent of driver's license hopefuls fail to fulfill the step's requirements. You are only allowed to take the written exam if your identification is approved, and you are only allowed to take the road test if you have passed the written exam.

   Each step takes 5, 3, and 20 minutes, respectively (staff members administering written exams need only set up the applicant at a computer). Currently, the DMV staffs 4 people to process license applications, 2 to administer written exams, and 15 to judge the road exam. DMV staff work 8 hours per day.
   a. Where is the bottleneck, according to the current staffing plan?
   b. What is the capacity of the process (expressed in approved cases per day)?

LO5-4

4. Consider a process consisting of five resources that are operated 8 hours per day. The process works on three different products, A, B, and C:

Resource	Number of Workers	Processing Time for A (minutes)	Processing Time for B (minutes)	Processing Time for C (minutes)
1	2	5	5	5
2	2	4	4	5
3	1	15	0	0
4	1	0	3	3
5	2	6	6	4

Demand for the three different products is as follows: product A, 40 units per day; product B, 50 units per day; and product C, 60 units per day.
a. What is the bottleneck?
b. What is the flow rate for each flow unit, assuming that demand must be served in the mix described above (i.e., for every four units of A, there are five units of B and six units of C)?

LO5-5

5. Consider the following four-step assembly operation with quality problems. All resources are staffed by one employee.
   - The first resource has a processing time of 5 minutes per unit.
   - The second resource has a processing time of 6 minutes per unit.
   - The third resource has a processing time of 3 minutes per unit. With a 30 percent probability, the flow unit coming out of the third resource has to be reworked. In that case, the operations at the first, second, and third resources are repeated. You can assume that (a) rework always succeeds (i.e., a unit going through the rework loop will always work after the third resource) and (b) the processing times for units in rework are the same as for regular units.
   - The fourth resource has a processing time of 4 minutes per unit.
   a. Where in the process is the bottleneck?
   b. What is the capacity of the process?

CASE AIRPORT SECURITY

On a typical day, more than a quarter of a million passengers and crew members arrive at U.S. airports, requiring the attention of U.S. Customs and Border Protection (CBP). For many years, this process was organized as follows. Passengers would move from their landing gates to the CBP officers. Passengers would then join one of two lines. U.S. citizens and permanent residents would be welcomed by one set of officers. Visitors from other countries would join another line leading to a separate set of officers. Typically, waiting times were longer for visitors than for citizens, though this could change depending on the day, and a substantial waiting time was possible for citizens as well as visitors. Because all visitors are fingerprinted, they take longer to be processed by the CBP.

In the early 2000s, the United States and Canada instituted the NEXUS program (initially known as the Trusted Traveler Program). The program allows eligible travelers who have been prescreened to bypass the lines using self-service technology at a number of kiosks. At the kiosks, the passenger answers a couple of questions, the passport and NEXUS membership card are scanned, fingerprints are scanned and compared to fingerprints on record, and a photo is taken. From there, most travelers can proceed directly to the luggage area. Only a randomly selected sample of passengers must be seen by a CBP officer.

© Photodisc/PhotoLink/Getty Images/RF

(continued)

In 2014, several airports, including Los Angeles (LAX), introduced an additional technology to streamline the process at CBP, creating a third flow of travelers. LAX, together with 20 other U.S. airports, allows eligible travelers to seek out a self-service kiosk. U.S. citizens and permanent residents are eligible, and so are travelers from 38 nations that are part of the U.S. waiver program. Similar to NEXUS, at the kiosks, passengers answer a couple of questions, their passport is scanned, fingerprints are scanned for non-U.S. citizens, and a photo is taken. At the end of their self-check-in, customers receive a printout that they then must personally present to a CBP officer. Passengers who have taken advantage of the kiosks require less time with the CBP officer, creating an overall increase in capacity and hence a reduction in waiting times.

For the following calculations, assume that

- It takes the CBP officer twice as long to process a visitor compared to a U.S. citizen or permanent resident. This is true for the traditional process, the randomly chosen passengers in the NEXUS process, and the new kiosk process.

- Eighty percent of the passengers use the traditional process, 10 percent use the NEXUS process, and 10 percent use the new kiosks. In each of these processes, the share of U.S. citizens and permanent residents is about 50 percent.

- Passengers spend no time with a CBP officer in the Nexus process except when they are randomly sampled for an inspection. In that case, they spend the same amount of time with the CBP officer as in the traditional process. Five percent of passengers are randomly chosen for inspection (independent of being visitors or U.S. residents).

- Compared to the traditional process, passengers spend 50 percent less time when using the new kiosks (though U.S. residents still only spend half the time with the CBP compared to visitors).

Question 1: Evaluate the impact of increasing the usage of the new kiosks. To do this, first draw a process flow diagram that combines the three different flows (traditional process, NEXUS program, new kiosks). Then, compute by what percentage the workload of the CBP officers would decrease if the usage of the new kiosks doubled (from the current 80 percent, 10 percent, and 10 percent for traditional, NEXUS, and new kiosks to 70 percent, 10 percent, and 20 percent).

http://www.latimes.com/local/la-me-passport-readers-20140925-story.html

http://www.cbp.gov/newsroom/local-media-release/2014-09-24-000000/lax-unveils-new-automated-passport-control-kiosks

http://www.cbp.gov/newsroom/stats/on-typical-day-fy2011

References

Immaneni, Aravind, and Christian Terwiesch, "Loan Processing at Capital One," Case at The Wharton School.

Learning Curves

6

Introduction

In his bestselling book *Outliers,* Malcolm Gladwell articulates the "10,000 hour rule."[1] The rule, which goes back to prior studies by Anders Ericsson, stipulates that exceptional success requires substantial amounts of practice. For example, as Gladwell reports, the music group The Beatles allegedly performed live in Hamburg, Germany, 1,200 times between 1960 and 1964, accumulating 10,000 hours of practice before rising to the top of the charts. Similarly, Microsoft founder Bill Gates is reported to have spent 10,000 hours programming the computer in his high school before beginning his well-known career in software development.

While most of us probably have not yet had the time or energy to invest 10,000 hours into a particular area of life, we are well familiar with the idea that we have to invest some time and effort before mastering a particular task. Whether studying for the SAT or ACT test, participating in varsity or intramural sports, or creating pieces of art, practice makes perfect.

The same holds for the world of business. Employees individually, corporations, or even industries as wholes must practice before excelling in what they do. Consider the following examples:

- *Individual level:* Retailing giant Amazon faces a major operational challenge in November each year. The number of shipments from the company's warehouses needs to increase

© Tim Pannell/Corbis/RF

[1]Malcolm Gladwell, *Outliers: The Story of Success* (Back Bay Books, 2008).

dramatically for the holiday season. To respond to this new demand, Amazon recruits thousands of temporary workers. However, these temporary workers are new to the job. Over six to eight weeks, the productivity of these employees increases by over 200 percent. In other words, an employee can handle three times the number of shipments in his or her eighth week of work compared to his or her first week of work. Similarly, research has demonstrated that doctors doing surgery for prostate cancer keep improving their outcomes until they reach an experience level of 250 procedures (CNN).

- *Company level:* Over the course of a production ramp-up in the disk-drive industry, it commonly takes one to two months for defect rates, processing times, and production volumes to hit the target levels that these processes then remain at for the rest of the product life cycle.[2] Improvements of more than 20 percentage points in quality (as measured by the percentage of disk drives processed correctly) and doubling of production output are the norm. Similarly, over the course of a production ramp-up, automotive plants will take two to four months to reduce defect levels by 80 percent and to triple labor productivity.[3]
- *Industries:* In the thin film photovoltaic industry, the costs per watt have been steadily declining. In 2006, the costs were around $2 per watt. With the production of some 5000 megawatts by 2010, this cost was cut to 70 cents per watt.

The phenomenon of improving performance over time is called the **learning curve** or also the **experience curve.** In this chapter, you will learn how operations can benefit from such experience effects and how this drives the productivity of the process.

- We first distinguish between various shapes of learning curves, depending on what performance measure is used.
- The following sections then focus on cost-based learning curves, in which the cost of a unit of output is reduced by a fixed percentage every time the process doubles its cumulative output. We show how one can estimate learning rates and how it is possible to make predictions about future costs.
- We conclude the chapter by discussing the organizational drivers of learning. In particular, we focus on employee retention and standardization as import drivers of learning.

Learning curve A function that captures the relationship between a performance metric of an operation and the experience as measured in the number of repetitions with which the operation has been performed.

Experience curve Synonym for learning curve; the term *experience* emphasizes that learning is driven by experience.

[2]Christian Terwiesch and Roger E. Bohn, "Learning and Process Improvement during Production Ramp-up," *International Journal of Production Economics* 70, no. 1 (2001), pp. 1–19.

[3]Steven D. Levitt, John A. List, and Chad Syverson, "Toward an Understanding of Learning by Doing: Evidence from an Automobile Assembly Plant," *Journal of Political Economy* 121, no. 4 (August 2013), pp. 643–81.

6.1 Various Forms of the Learning Curve

LO6-1 Distinguish between various shapes of learning curves.

A **learning curve**, also called an **experience curve**, captures the relationship between a performance metric of an operation and the experience as measured in the number of repetitions with which the operation has been performed. As the cumulative experience increases, so does performance. The most common forms of learning curves use processing time, labor content, or unit cost as their measure of performance on the *y*-axis, while the *x*-axis plots the experience of the process. Whether processing time, labor content, defect rates, or unit cost, a lower number means a better performance and so the learning curve slopes down.

However, we can also think about other measures of performance such as production yield, flow rate, or customer satisfaction scores. In these cases, the learning curve goes up with experience.

Whether or not the learning curve goes up or down is entirely a matter of deciding how to measure performance. Consider the following example. Assume it takes us one week to produce one unit of output. However, every time we repeat this operation, we reduce this processing time by 5 percent. If we use the processing time as the measure of performance, we will see a downward-sloping learning curve. If however, we plot the capacity over time (recall, Capacity = 1/Processing time), we see an upward-sloping learning curve.

For this example, Figure 6.1 shows how the process improves with experience. One curve plots the processing time; the other curve plots the capacity. Note that although the underlying amount of learning is exactly the same for both curves, it appears that the processing time changes very little with high levels of experience, while the capacity seems to increase forever. Eye-balling data is oftentimes misleading, which is why later on in this chapter we provide a more formal way of estimating a learning curve.

Operations also differ as far as the rate of improvement is concerned. Some improvements in operations and in technology seem to happen exponentially. Probably the most commonly known example of such **exponential growth** is Moore's Law, which states that the number of transistors on an integrated circuit doubles approximately every two years. Though Moore's Law has been true for multiple decades now, it is important to notice that it is not a law of nature but simply an empirical regularity. This is a caveat in all learning curve analysis—learning curves look at improvements in the past and we have no guarantee that the future will be like the past. Having said this, the past is the only place to which we can go to collect data, and so extrapolating past trajectories of improvement is typically the best predictor for the future.

In contrast to improvements with exponential growth, as in the case of Moore's Law, are improvements that happen with diminishing returns. Consider improvements in production yields; that is, the percentage of flow units an operation processes correctly. By definition, a yield cannot increase beyond 100 percent, so an exponential growth process is unlikely to take place; instead, we face an asymptote of 100 percent. Similarly, because the number of defects we make or the number of customer complaints we receive cannot go below zero, it simply levels off slightly above 0. In such cases of **diminishing returns**, improvements do not follow the pattern of exponential growth. Instead, we can think of them as an exponential decay of a **performance gap**. We define a performance gap as the difference between the current performance and an ideal performance level (100 percent quality, 0 customer complaints).

Figure 6.2 shows three examples of learning curves. All three have in common that process performance changes with a certain rate as the process accumulates experience. We see that learning curves can take three distinct forms:

- *Exponential growth:* The graph on the left of Figure 6.2 corresponds to exponential growth. The rate of performance improvement increases over time; this is the case of Moore's Law. Exponential growth models also exist in other branches of business,

Exponential growth An improvement trajectory in which the rate of improvement increases over time or experience.

Diminishing returns A performance trajectory in which the improvement rate decreases over time or experience.

Performance gap The difference between the current process performance and some target or optimal value.

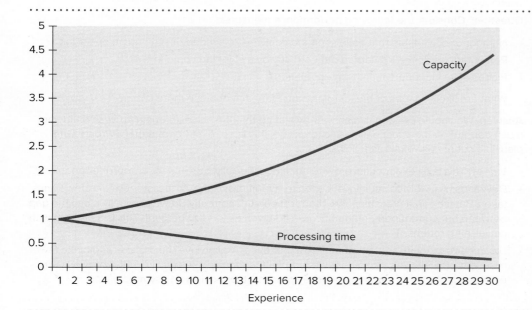

Figure 6.1

Processing time and capacity as a function of experience

Figure 6.2

Three shapes of learning curves

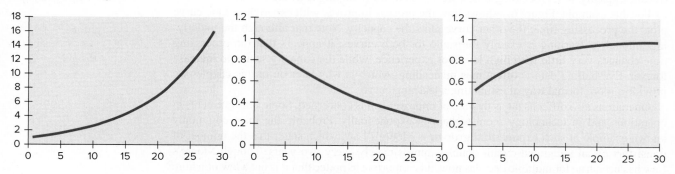

most prominently models of product awareness in marketing. We can describe a learning curve with exponential growth by quantifying by what factor the performance improves every time we double experience. This factor is bigger than one—otherwise, the learning curve would not bend upward.

- *Exponential decay:* The graph in the middle of Figure 6.2 corresponds to exponential decay. The rate of performance improvement decreases over time; this is the case for many cost reductions. Because costs cannot become negative, cost reductions tend to exhibit diminishing returns. Other examples of exponential decay are customer complaints or the number of defects. We can describe a learning curve with exponential decay by quantifying by what factor the performance improves every time we double experience. This factor is less than one. This is the most commonly used form of the learning curve and the one we use throughout the chapter.

- *Diminishing return growth:* The graph on the right of Figure 6.2 flattens out with growing experience and ultimately reaches an asymptote. This is the case for production yields. The same is true for other forms of efficiency improvements where waste is reduced toward an asymptotic performance. For example, a heating system cannot

Check Your Understanding 6.1

Question: Consider the following performance measures:

- Number of consumers that have seen the cool YouTube video describing an operation.
- Percentage of deliveries carried out correctly by a shipping company.
- Pieces of lost luggage at an airline operation.

What are likely shapes of the learning curve for each of these three cases?

Answer: We should preface this answer by stating that the actual learning curves would very much depend on the exact business context; so, this is not a matter of right or wrong. One plausible set of answers is as follows:

- *Videos:* This is an exponential growth process, especially if the video on YouTube "goes viral."
- *Deliveries:* As we accumulate experience, we improve the process and make fewer mistakes. But we can never ship more than 100 percent correctly, so we gradually close the gap between our current percentage of correct deliveries and 100 percent. This is a process with diminishing returns.
- *Lost luggage:* Again, as we accumulate experience, we improve the process and make fewer mistakes. However, because here we are plotting the mistakes (unlike in the previous question), we deal with an exponential decay process; there exists an asymptote at 0.

obtain an energy efficiency of above 100 percent. We can still use an exponential function to describe the learning curve. The gap between the learning curve and the asymptote capturing the ideal process performance is reduced with experience following exponential decay.

CONNECTIONS: Learning Curves in Sports

© Digital Vision/Getty Images/RF

Consider the performance development of Asafa Powell, a Jamaican sprinter and Olympic gold medalist. The data in Figure 6.3 show the development of his personal best in the 100m sprint. The data suggest a smooth learning curve with diminishing returns. The improvements were a result of experience (in the form of training). Unfortunately, they also might have been a result of doping—Powell tested positive on the drug Oxilofrine.

Figure 6.3

Year	Time	Windspeed	City	Date
2000	11.45	−2.3	Kingston	13 March
2001	10.50	0.40	Kingston	22 June
2002	10.12	1.30	Rovereto	28 August
2003	10.02	0.80	Brussels	5 September
2004	9.87	0.20	Brussels	3 September
2005	9.77	1.60	Athens	14 June
2006	9.77	1.00	Zürich	15 August
2007	9.74	1.70	Rieti	9 September
2008	9.72	0.20	Lausanne	2 September
2009	9.82	1.40	Szczecin	15 September
2010	9.82	0.60	Rome	10 June
2011	9.78	1.00	Lausanne	30 June

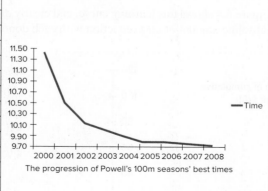

The progression of Powell's 100m seasons' best times

Source: https://en.wikipedia.org/wiki/Asafa_Powell

6.2 The Power Law

LO6-2 Determine the unit cost of a process given a learning rate and an experience level.

The most common form of a learning curve is one that uses unit costs as a dependent variable (y-axis) and cumulative experience as the independent variable (x-axis). The cumulative experience measures the total number of units produced up to a point in time, which we refer to as the cumulative output. Moreover, it assumes that with each doubling of the cumulative experience, the performance improves by a fixed percentage. This constant improvement with each doubling of cumulative experience is referred to as the **power law.**

To capture this effect of doubling cumulative output on improvement in operational performance, let's introduce some notation. Let $c(i)$ be the cost of making the ith unit of the process. Every time we double the cumulative output, $c(i)$ gets multiplied by a positive number less than one, which we call the **learning rate**, or LR for short.

For example, assume that it costs us $100 per unit to make the first unit of a new product.

$$c(1) = 100$$

Assume further that our learning rate LR = 0.8; that is, it takes us 80 percent of the previous unit costs after we have doubled the cumulative output. As we are producing the second unit, we double the cumulative output from one to two and so we get:

$$c(2) = c(1) \times LR = 100 \times LR = 100 \times 0.8 = 80$$

Similarly, we get:

$$c(4) = c(2) \times LR = c(1) \times LR \times LR \qquad\qquad = 100 \times LR^2 = 100 \times 0.8^2 = 64$$

$$c(8) = c(4) \times LR = c(1) \times LR \times LR \times LR \qquad\quad = 100 \times LR^3 = 100 \times 0.8^3 = 51.2$$

$$c(16) = c(8) \times LR = c(1) \times LR \times LR \times LR \times LR \quad\;\; = 100 \times LR^4 = 100 \times 0.8^4 = 40.96$$

$$c(32) = c(16) \times LR = c(1) \times LR \times LR \times LR \times LR \times LR = 100 \times LR^5 = 100 \times 0.8^5 = 32.768$$

In this example, our unit costs decrease by 20 percent each time that we double the cumulative output. In general, the unit costs are decreased by $(1 - LR)$ percent every time we double cumulative output.

The example shows that learning curves with a constant improvement percentage for each doubling of cumulative output exhibit diminishing return. It took us four units to reduce the unit costs from 64 to 51.2 (i.e., by 12.8), but it took us eight units to reduce the unit costs from 51.2 to 40.96 (i.e., by 10.24).

In general, we can express the unit costs as a function of the cumulative output as follows:

$$c(\text{After doubling cumulative output n times}) = c(1) \times LR^n$$

Figure 6.4 shows this learning curve, and clearly displays the effect of diminishing returns: the absolute amount of cost reduction with each doubling of cumulative experience.

Learning rate The amount by which the process performance is multiplied every time the cumulative experience doubles. The learning rate (LR) is a number between 0 and 1. Higher numbers correspond to slower learning. 1-LR is the percent improvement associated with a doubling of cumulative experience.

Figure 6.4

Costs of a component as a function of cumulative experience that has an initial cost of $100

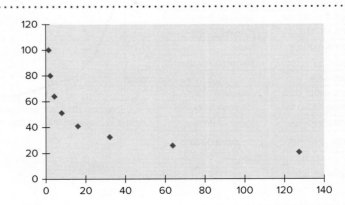

Check Your Understanding 6.2

Question: Consider a process with a unit cost of $40 for the first unit; that is, $c(1) = 40$, and a learning rate of LR = 0.9. What will be the unit costs for the 16th unit?

Answer: To reach the 16th unit, we have to double the cumulative output four times (from 1 to 2, from 2 to 4, from 4 to 8, and from 8 to 16). We can then use the formula:

$$c(\text{After doubling cumulative output 4 times}) = c(1) \times \text{LR}^4 = 40 \times 0.9^4 = 26.244$$

So far, our application of the learning curve for the estimation of the unit cost was limited to the 1st, 2nd, 4th, 8th, 16th, 32nd, and so on units. But what will be the cost for the 29th unit? To reach 29 units of output, we have to double our output more than four times ($2^4 < 29$) but less than 5 times ($2^5 > 29$). In other words, the number of times we have to double cumulative output to get to the 29th unit is not an integer number.

In such cases, we find the noninteger number of times that cumulative output has to be doubled by using logarithms:

$$\text{Number of times to double output to get to 29} = \log_2(29) = \frac{\ln(29)}{\ln(2)} = 4.85799$$

Where $\log_2(x)$ is the logarithm of x to the base 2 and $\ln(x)$ is the natural logarithm of x. You might remember from your algebra course that $\log_a(b) = \ln(b)/\ln(a)$. If you don't remember, don't worry; just take our word for it and use the following formula to compute the cost of the Nth unit as

$$c(N) = c(1) \times \text{LR}^{\log_2 N} = c(1) \times \text{LR}^{\frac{\ln(N)}{\ln(2)}}$$

Given that $\ln(2)$ is equal to 0.6931, we can rewrite this to

$$c(N) = c(1) \times \text{LR}^{\frac{\ln(N)}{0.6931}}$$

Check Your Understanding 6.3

Question: Consider a process with a unit cost of $40 for the first unit; that is, $c(1) = 40$, and a learning rate of LR = 0.9. What will be the unit costs for the 19th unit?

Answer: We can directly use the formula:

$$c(19) = c(1) \times \text{LR}^{\log_2 19} = c(1) \times \text{LR}^{\frac{\ln(19)}{\ln(2)}} = 40 \times 0.9^{4.248} = 25.567$$

Note that the exponent of 4.248 captures the fact that we are doubling production more than 4 times (4 times doubling output got us to 16, see above), but less than 5 times (which would get us to 32).

6.3 Estimating the Learning Curve Using a Linear Log-Log Graph

LO6-3 Estimate the learning rate using past cost data.

In our example, the absolute improvement in unit costs gets smaller from unit to unit. However, the percentage improvement remains constant with each doubling of our cumulative output. This reflects our assumption that the learning curve rate (LR) is constant at 0.8. One way to see that constant improvement with each doubling of cumulative output is to change the format of Figure 6.4.

Instead of plotting the cumulative output on the x-axis and the unit costs on the y-axis, we now plot the logarithm of the cumulative output on the x-axis and the logarithm of the unit costs on the y-axis. Table 6.1 shows the calculations for our example with LR = 0.8 and $100 initial unit costs. Figure 6.5 shows the resulting plot. Such plots are also known as **log-log plots**.

Observe that Figure 6.5 shows the improvement trajectory as a straight line. This reflects the constant learning rate. It is a matter of algebra to find the slope, b, of this straight line. In general, in algebra, to compute the slope, b, of the line of a function $f(x) = bx + c$, we first need to pick two values on the x-axis with $x_1 < x_2$ and then compute

Log-log plot A graphical representation in which we plot the logarithmic value of both the x and y variables.

$$\text{Slope } b = \frac{[f(x_2) - f(x_1)]}{[x_2 - x_1]}$$

TABLE 6.1 Logarithmic Transformation of Experience and Cost Data; ln(x) Stands for the Natural Logarithm of x

Experience	Cost	ln(Cumulative experience)	ln(Unit cost)
1	100	0.000	4.605
2	80	0.693	4.382
4	64	1.386	4.159
8	51.2	2.079	3.936
16	40.96	2.773	3.713
32	32.768	3.466	3.489
64	26.2144	4.159	3.266
128	20.97152	4.852	3.043

Figure 6.5

A log-log graph of a 0.8 learning curve

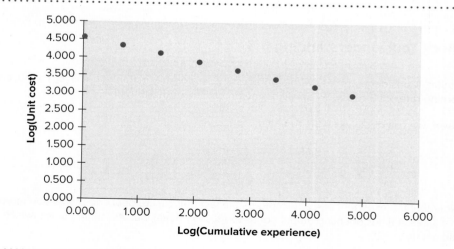

In this equation, the numerator tells us by how much the value of the y-axis moves (by how much costs go down) for every unit change on the x-axis (for every doubling of output). We can pick any two data points along the line—it does not matter because the slope computed this way will always be the same. Let's say we pick the values 16 and 64 for our values of cumulative output. Given that in our case $f(x)$ is $\ln(c(\text{output}))$ and x is $\ln(\text{output})$, we get

$$\text{Slope } b = \frac{[\ln(c(x_2)) - \ln(c(x_1))]}{[\ln(x_2) - \ln(x_1)]} = \frac{[\ln(c(64)) - \ln(c(16))]}{[\ln(64) - \ln(16)]}$$

Using the values we have in Table 6.1, ($\ln(c(16)) = 3.713$, $\ln(c(64)) = 3.266$, $\ln(16) = 2.773$, and $\ln(64) = 4.159$), we get

$$\text{Slope } b = \frac{[3.266 - 3.713]}{[4.159 - 2.773]} = \frac{(-0.446)}{1.386} = -0.3219$$

So, in the log-log graph, the line capturing the learning curve slopes down with a slope of $b = -0.3219$.

The slope of the line in the log-log version of the learning curve was entirely driven by the learning rate, LR, introduced previously. Recall that our example is based on a learning rate LR = 0.8. So, a learning rate LR = 0.8 corresponds to a slope of $b = -0.3219$. If learning happens slower, the learning rate LR is closer to 1 and the downward slope is less steep. If learning happens faster, the learning rate LR is smaller and the downward slope is steeper.

Because the only variable determining the slope of the learning curve in the log-log representation was the learning rate LR, we can form a 1:1 relationship between the learning rate and the slope. Given a learning rate, we can find a slope and given a slope, we can find a learning rate. Table 6.2 shows this 1:1 relationship between the learning rate LR and the slope of the learning curve in the log-log graph. Based on our earlier definitions, we can write that relationship algebraically as

$$\text{LR} = 2^{\text{Slope}}$$

At this point, you might be wondering why we complicated matters by finding a slope of a (linear) learning curve in the log-log graph with a learning rate LR. After all, we knew LR

TABLE 6.2   Relationship between the Learning Rate, LR, and the Slope of the Learning Curve in a Log-Log Graph (computed based on the relationship LR = 2^{Slope})

Learning Rate	Slope	Learning Rate	Slope	Learning Rate	Slope	Learning Rate	Slope	Learning Rate	Slope
0.5	−1	0.6	−0.73697	0.7	−0.51457	0.8	−0.32193	0.9	−0.152
0.51	−0.97143	0.61	−0.71312	0.71	−0.49411	0.81	−0.30401	0.91	−0.13606
0.52	−0.94342	0.62	−0.68966	0.72	−0.47393	0.82	−0.2863	0.92	−0.12029
0.53	−0.91594	0.63	−0.66658	0.73	−0.45403	0.83	−0.26882	0.93	−0.1047
0.54	−0.88897	0.64	−0.64386	0.74	−0.4344	0.84	−0.25154	0.94	−0.08927
0.55	−0.8625	0.65	−0.62149	0.75	−0.41504	0.85	−0.23447	0.95	−0.074
0.56	−0.8365	0.66	−0.59946	0.76	−0.39593	0.86	−0.21759	0.96	−0.074
0.57	−0.81097	0.67	−0.57777	0.77	−0.37707	0.87	−0.20091	0.97	−0.04394
0.58	−0.78588	0.68	−0.55639	0.78	−0.35845	0.88	−0.18442	0.98	−0.02915
0.59	−0.76121	0.69	−0.53533	0.79	−0.34008	0.89	−0.16812	0.99	−0.0145

from the beginning, it was easy to interpret, and the calculations were straightforward. So why now worry about the logarithmic transformation and the slope of the line?

The main reason for working with the log-log version of the learning curve is that, in practice, the learning rate is unknown. But, with the method introduced in this section, we now can estimate the learning rate. The method can be summarized as follows:

1. Plot the learning curve in a log-log representation (and make sure it is indeed linear).

2. Estimate the slope, b, of the curve in the log-log representation using the formula for the slope as $b = [\ln(c(x_2)) - \ln(c(x_1))]/[\ln(x_2) - \ln(x_1)]$, where x_1 and x_2 can be any two points with $x_1 < x_2$.

3. Use Table 6.2 to find the learning rate, LR, given the slope b.

Let's try this method out in the real world. Consider the cost development in the production of photovoltaic panels (data from Paul Maycock, Bloomberg New Energy Finance). Figure 6.6 provides cost data for almost 30 years of production of photovoltaic panels. The first column in the table provides the year. The second column shows the cumulative production as measured in megawatts (you can think of this as how many megawatts all previously produced panels combined have in a given year). The third column shows the cost of producing the panel expressed in dollars per watt.

Clearly, the costs per watt are going down. But at what learning rate? And what cost should we anticipate two years from now? Eye-balling the data, one might wonder if the effects of learning have diminished and little progress has been made since the year 2000.

To answer these questions, we take the following steps. First, we transform both the x-axis and y-axis by taking natural logarithms ($\ln(x)$). We do this for both the cumulative output as well as the cost. The resulting data are shown in Figure 6.7. Notice the relatively linear reduction in the log-log representation of the learning curve. With the exception of one bump around $\ln(\text{output}) = 5.2$, the rate of improvement has remained relatively constant.

Next, we compute the slope of the learning curve in the log-log representation. We do this by finding the slope, b, with the formula

$$\text{Slope } b = \frac{[\ln(c(x_2)) - \ln(c(x_1))]}{[\ln(x_2) - \ln(x_1)]}$$

Figure 6.6

Cost of PV power as a function of cumulative experience; adapted from Paul Maycock, Bloomberg New Energy Finance

Year	Cumulative Output [MW]	Cost [$/W]
1976	1.88	97.28
1977	3.76	78.02
1978	6.10	57.61
1979	8.27	39.16
1980	12.25	29.31
1981	18.98	24.17
1982	26.08	18.34
1983	38.59	16.66
1984	57.12	14.31
1985	82.05	12.47
1986	104.42	11.80
1987	137.03	9.08
1988	169.05	7.00
1989	205.45	6.18
1990	245.97	6.70
1991	285.78	7.37
1992	342.14	7.26
1993	409.62	6.59
1994	461.84	6.59
1995	528.60	5.82
1996	596.00	5.29
1997	713.54	5.58
1998	829.02	5.97
1999	963.19	5.96
2000	1188.28	4.92
2001	1465.97	4.72
2002	1891.79	4.97
2003	2404.96	4.39
2004	3150.44	3.89

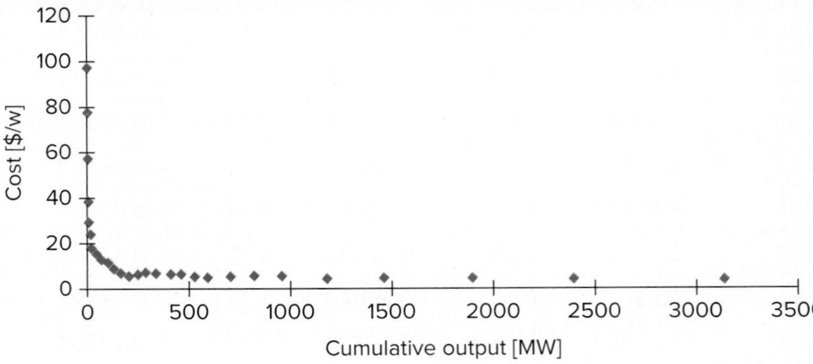

Figure 6.7

Data and log-log representation of the PV learning curve

Year	Cumulative Output [MW]	Cost [$/W]	ln (output)	ln(Cost)
1976	1.88	97.28	0.631	4.578
1977	3.76	78.02	1.325	4.357
1978	6.10	57.61	1.809	4.054
1979	8.27	39.16	2.112	3.668
1980	12.25	29.31	2.505	3.378
1981	18.98	24.17	2.943	3.185
1982	26.08	18.34	3.261	2.909
1983	38.59	16.66	3.653	2.813
1984	57.12	14.31	4.045	2.661
1985	82.05	12.47	4.407	2.523
1986	104.42	11.80	4.648	2.468
1987	137.03	9.08	4.920	2.206
1988	169.05	7.00	5.130	1.945
1989	205.45	6.18	5.325	1.822
1990	245.97	6.70	5.505	1.902
1991	285.78	7.37	5.655	1.997
1992	342.14	7.26	5.835	1.982
1993	409.62	6.59	6.015	1.886
1994	461.84	6.59	6.135	1.885
1995	528.60	5.82	6.270	1.762
1996	596.00	5.29	6.390	1.665
1997	713.54	5.58	6.570	1.719
1998	829.02	5.97	6.720	1.786
1999	963.19	5.96	6.870	1.785
2000	1188.28	4.92	7.080	1.593
2001	1465.97	4.72	7.290	1.551
2002	1891.79	4.97	7.545	1.604
2003	2404.96	4.39	7.785	1.480
2004	3150.44	3.89	8.055	1.356

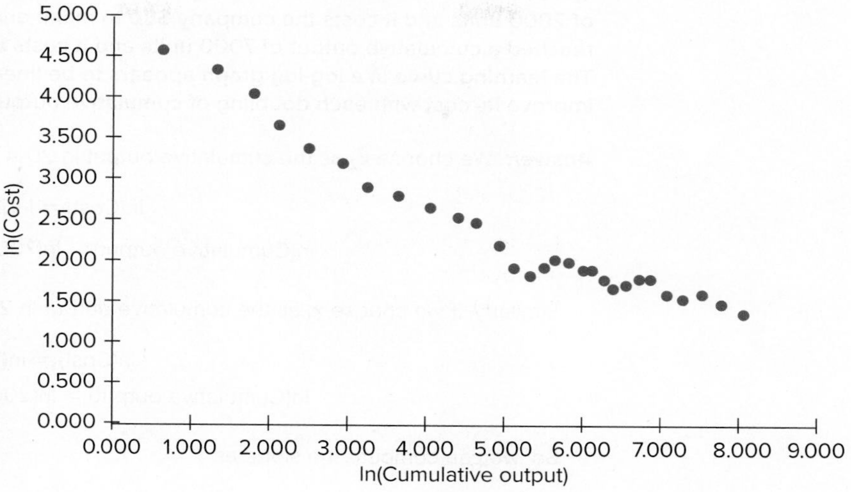

Again, we have to take two values for x_1 and x_2 (with $x_1 < x_2$). Which values should we take? Since the graph is linear, we can simply take the first and last values (i.e., the data corresponding to the years of 1976 and 2004). If we choose x_2 as the cumulative output in 2004, we get

$$\ln(\text{Cost}) = \ln(3.88) = 1.356, \text{ and}$$

$$\ln(\text{Cumulative output}) = \ln(3150.44) = 8.055$$

Similarly, if we choose x_1 as the cumulative output in 1976, we get

$$\ln(\text{Cost}) = \ln(97.28) = 4.578, \text{ and}$$

$$\ln(\text{Cumulative output}) = \ln(1.88) = 0.631$$

So, we can compute the slope as

$$\text{Slope } b = \frac{[\ln(c(x_2)) - \ln(c(x_1))]}{[\ln(x_2) - \ln(x_1)]}$$

$$b = \frac{[1.356 - 4.578]}{[8.055 - 0.631]} = \frac{-3.222}{7.424} = -0.434$$

Thus, we obtain a slope of the learning curve in a log-log graph of $b = -0.434$.

If you have taken advanced statistics classes, you might be familiar with the technique of regression analysis. **Regression analysis** provides a statistically more rigorous approach to estimating the slope of a linear line through the log-log representation of the learning curve. But our approach of just looking at the Δy relative to the Δx works well and is much easier to grasp.

Finally, we can use Table 6.2 to translate the slope of the learning curve in a log-log graph to a learning rate. We see that a slope of -0.434 corresponds to a learning rate of 74 percent. In other words, every time we double the cumulative output, costs come down by 26 percent.

Question: You are given the following data. In 2000, a company has a cumulative output of 2000 units and it costs the company \$30 to make one unit. In 2014, the company has reached a cumulative output of 7000 units and it costs the company \$22 to make one unit. The learning curve in a log-log graph appears to be linear. By how much does the company improve its cost with each doubling of cumulative output?

Answer: We choose x_2 as the cumulative output in 2014 and get

$$\ln(\text{Cost}) = \ln(22) = 3.091, \text{ and}$$

$$\ln(\text{Cumulative output}) = \ln(7000) = 8.854$$

Similarly, if we choose x_1 as the cumulative output in 2000, that yields

$$\ln(\text{Cost}) = \ln(30) = 3.401, \text{ and}$$

$$\ln(\text{Cumulative output}) = \ln(2000) = 7.601$$

So, we can compute the slope as

$$\text{Slope } b = \frac{[\ln(c(x_2)) - \ln(c(x_1))]}{[\ln(x_2) - \ln(x_1)]} = \frac{[3.09 - 3.401]}{[8.853 - 7.601]} = \frac{-0.310}{1.253} = -0.248$$

Thus, we obtain a slope of the learning curve in a log-log graph of $b = -0.248$. We can then use Table 6.2 to find the corresponding learning rate LR, which is between 0.84 and 0.85. So the process reduces its cost by 15 to 16 percent every time it doubles its cumulative output. Instead of using Table 6.2, we can also use the equation $\text{LR} = 2^{\text{Slope}}$, which gives us $\text{LR} = 2^{-0.248} = 0.842$.

6.4 Using Learning Curve Coefficients to Predict Costs

Earlier on in this chapter, we computed the cost of the Nth unit in a process with an initial cost of $c(1)$ and a learning rate of LR as

$$c(N) = c(1) \times \text{LR}^{\log_2 N}$$

We can rewrite this equation as follows:

$$c(N) = c(1) \times \text{LR}^{\log_2 N} = c(1) \times \text{LR}^{\frac{\ln(N)}{\ln(2)}}$$

The equation shows us that, maybe not surprisingly, the costs are expressed as a multiple of the initial cost $c(1)$. Compare the following two processes. Process A has an initial cost of $c(1) = 100$ and process B has an initial cost of $c(1) = 1000$. Both processes have the same learning rate. Thus, process B is 10 times more expensive in the production of the initial unit. As long as the two processes have the same learning rate, process B will be 10 times more expensive for the 2nd unit, the 16th unit, the 29th unit, and the 3943th unit.

With this pattern in mind, we can simplify our cost estimation by considering a generic process that has an initial cost of $c(1) = 1$. We can then compute cost values for different learning rates and different cumulative output levels for this \$1 item and store these cost data in a table. This is shown in Table 6.3. The table uses a range of cumulative output levels (each cumulative output level is one row) and a range of learning rates (each learning rate is one column). For each combination of cumulative output and learning rate, the table then shows the cost of producing one unit in a process with an initial cost of $c(1) = 1$. For example, the table shows that for a process with initial cost $c(1) = 1$, assuming a learning rate of LR = 0.85, the costs of making the 30th unit are equal to 0.450471.

We call the data in Table 6.3 the **learning curve coefficients**, or LCC for short. We define

LCC(x, LR) = the cost of producing one unit in a process that has an
initial cost of $c(1) = 1$, a cumulative output of x, and a learning rate of LR.

If we then want to find out how much it would cost to produce a unit in a process that has a learning rate of LR = 0.85, a cumulative output of 30 units, and an initial cost $c(1) = 7.5$, we first need to look up the learning curve coefficient LCC(30, 0.85) in Table 6.3. This coefficient is LCC(30, 0.85) = 0.450471. To obtain the cost, all that remains to be done is to compute

c (After 30 units of cumulative output, LR = 0.85, $c(1) = 7.5$) = 7.5 × LCC(30, 0.85) = 3.3785

This is the idea behind the learning curve coefficient method, or LCC method for short. So, for a given cumulative experience, the LCC method allows us to quickly compute the costs of a unit as a function of the costs for the first unit and the learning rate.

LO6-4 Predict unit cost by using the LCC method and by using the learning curve directly.

Learning curve coefficient The cost of producing one unit in a process that has an initial cost of $c(1) = 1$, a cumulative output of x, and a learning rate of LR.

TABLE 6.3 Learning Curve Coefficients for Various Learning Rates and Experience Levels

Experience	LR 0.65	0.7	0.75	0.8	0.85	0.9	0.95
1	1	1	1	1	1	1	1
2	0.65	0.7	0.75	0.8	0.85	0.9	0.95
3	0.505213	0.56818	0.633836	0.702104	0.772915	0.846206	0.921919
4	0.4225	0.49	0.5625	0.64	0.7225	0.81	0.9025
5	0.367789	0.436846	0.512745	0.595637	0.685671	0.782987	0.88772
6	0.328389	0.397726	0.475377	0.561683	0.656978	0.761585	0.875823
7	0.298388	0.367397	0.445916	0.5344449	0.633656	0.743948	0.865889
8	0.274625	0.343	0.421875	0.512	0.614125	0.729	0.857375
9	0.25524	0.322829	0.401748	0.49295	0.597397	0.716065	0.849935
10	0.239063	0.305792	0.384559	0.47651	0.58282	0.704688	0.843334
11	0.225313	0.291157	0.369643	0.462111	0.569941	0.694553	0.837407
12	0.213453	0.278408	0.356533	0.449346	0.558431	0.685427	0.832032
13	0.203094	0.267174	0.344883	0.437916	0.548048	0.677138	0.827118
14	0.193952	0.257178	0.334437	0.427592	0.538608	0.669553	0.822595
15	0.185812	0.248208	0.324996	0.418199	0.529965	0.662568	0.818406
20	0.155391	0.214055	0.288419	0.381208	0.495397	0.634219	0.801167
25	0.135268	0.190835	0.262907	0.354784	0.470145	0.613068	0.788046
30	0.120778	0.173745	0.243747	0.334559	0.450471	0.596311	0.777485
50	0.087924	0.133584	0.19718	0.283827	0.399623	0.551761	0.748644
100	0.057151	0.093509	0.147885	0.227062	0.33968	0.496585	0.711212
200	0.037148	0.065456	0.110914	0.181649	0.288728	0.446927	0.675651
500	0.021019	0.040849	0.075827	0.135246	0.232908	0.38882	0.631356
1000	0.013663	0.028594	0.056871	0.108197	0.197972	0.349938	0.599789

Check Your Understanding **6.5**

Question: Consider a process with an initial cost c(1) = 24, a learning rate of LR = 0.8, and a cumulative experience of 200. Using the LCC method, what unit costs do you expect?

Answer: We start by looking up the learning curve coefficient in Table 6.3 for a cumulative output of 200 and a learning rate of LR = 0.8. We get

$$LCC(200, 0.8) = 0.181649$$

We then compute the costs as

$$c(\text{After 200 units of cumulative output, } LR = 0.8, c(1) = 24) = 24 \times LCC(200, 0.8) = 4.3596$$

Thus, we expect a unit cost of $4.3596.

When faced with a learning curve problem, all that needs to be done is to

1. Estimate the slope of the learning curve, b, in the log-log graph, as discussed in the previous section.
2. Translate the slope, b, into a learning rate, LR, using Table 6.2.
3. Based on the cumulative output and the learning rate LR, look up the learning curve coefficient, LCC, in Table 6.3.
4. Multiply the initial cost $c(1)$ by the learning curve coefficient LCC.

As easy as this method is in its application, we should not forget that we can also compute the cost directly by using the previously introduced formula:

$$c(N) = c(1) \times LR^{\log_2 N} = c(1) \times LR^{\frac{\ln(N)}{\ln(2)}}$$

We can rewrite this formula as a function of the slope, b, of the learning curve in the log-log graph, as discussed in the previous section:

$$c(N) = c(1) \times LR^{\log_2 N} = c(1) \times LR^{\frac{\ln(N)}{\ln(2)}} = c(1) \times N^b$$

This computation is somewhat faster because it only requires two steps:

1. Estimate the slope of the learning curve, b, in the log-log graph, as discussed in the previous section.
2. Compute the costs as $c(1) \times N^b$.

Check Your Understanding **6.6**

Question: Consider a process with an initial cost c(1) = 24, a slope of the learning curve in the log-log graph of b = −0.32193, and a cumulative experience of 200. Using the learning curve function directly—that is, without using the LCC method—what costs do you expect?

Answer: We compute costs directly as

$$c(1) \times N^b = 24 \times 200^{-0.32193} = 4.3596$$

Thus, we expect a unit cost of $4.3596.

Computing the costs directly as $c(1) \times N^b$ or using the LCC method—which approach should you use? In general, we prefer to compute the costs directly, especially if you already know the slope of the learning curve, b, in the log-log graph. However, one benefit of the

LCC method is that it can help you in situations in which you don't just predict the cost of making one unit but the costs for making multiple units. This is the topic of the next section.

6.5 Using Learning Curve Coefficients to Predict Cumulative Costs

Imagine that you are sourcing a component from a supplier. For a single unit, the supplier quotes you a price of $19,000. You consider not just buying one unit, but 20 units. Anticipating that the supplier will go down the learning curve, it would be naïve (too generous) to offer the supplier 20 × $19k = $380,000. After all, the supplier would learn as production goes on and, by the time she hits the 20th unit, will have lower unit costs than the initial $19,000.

LO6-5 Predict cumulative cost using the LCC method.

Assume the supplier has a learning rate of 0.85. Using the LCC method, we can estimate that it costs the supplier $c(20) = \$19k \times 0.495397 = \$9,412$ to produce the 20th unit. But, if we offered the supplier 20 × $9,412, this price would be too aggressive (too low). After all, the first 19 units were produced at higher costs.

What we need is a method that computes the sum of the costs for the 20 units, recognizing that the costs for each of the units will differ because of learning effects. This sum would be given as

$$\text{Total cost}(20) = c(1) + c(2) + \ldots + c(20)$$

TABLE 6.4 Learning Curve Coefficients for the Cumulative Costs of Producing a Certain Quantity

	LR						
Experience	0.65	0.7	0.75	0.8	0.85	0.9	0.95
1	1	1	1	1	1	1	1
2	1.65	1.7	1.75	1.8	1.85	1.9	1.95
3	2.155213	2.26818	2.383836	2.502104	2.622915	2.746206	2.871919
4	2.577713	2.751118	2.946336	3.142104	3.345415	3.556206	3.774419
5	2.945502	3.195027	3.459081	3.737741	4.031086	4.339193	4.662139
6	3.27389	3.592753	3.934457	4.299424	4.688064	5.100778	5.537962
7	3.572278	3.96015	4.380373	4.833914	5.32172	5.844726	6.403851
8	3.846903	4.30315	4.802248	5.345914	5.935845	6.573726	7.261226
9	4.102144	4.625979	5.203996	5.838863	6.533242	7.289791	8.11116
10	4.341206	4.931771	5.588554	6.315373	7.116063	7.994479	8.954494
11	4.56652	5.222928	5.958198	6.777484	7.686003	8.689031	9.7919
12	4.779972	5.501336	6.314731	7.226831	8.244434	9.374458	10.62393
13	4.983066	5.768511	6.659614	7.664746	8.792483	10.0516	11.45105
14	5.177018	6.025688	6.99405	8.092338	9.331091	10.72115	12.27364
15	5.36283	6.273896	7.319046	8.510537	9.861056	11.38372	13.09205
20	6.194963	7.406536	8.828351	10.48494	12.40228	14.60776	17.13024
25	6.908642	8.404015	10.19069	12.3086	14.80073	17.71323	21.09545
30	7.539799	9.305035	11.44577	14.019189	17.09066	20.72689	25.00317
40	8.631226	10.90242	13.72316	17.19346	21.42516	26.54271	32.68379
50	9.565429	12.30688	15.77609	20.12171	25.51311	32.14196	40.22385
100	13.03445	17.79071	24.17858	32.65081	43.75387	58.14102	76.58639

Check Your Understanding 6.7

Question: Consider a process with current cost of $c(1) = 24$ and a learning rate of LR = 0.8. How much would it cost to produce 10 units?

Answer: We start by looking up the cumulative learning curve coefficient in Table 6.4 for an output of 10 and a learning rate of LR = 0.8. We get

$$CLCC(10, 0.8) = 6.315373$$

We then compute the costs of making 10 units as

$$CC(\text{Making 10 units, } LR = 0.8, c(1) = 24) = 24 \times CLCC(10, 0.8) = 24 \times 6.315373 = 151.569$$

Thus, we expect a total cost of $151.569.

. . . .

We can compute the coefficients for the cumulative (total) cost of producing N units in a way similar to how we computed the data for Table 6.3. These coefficients are shown in Table 6.4.

Using the information in Table 6.4, we can find the coefficient for the cumulative cost of producing 20 units, an initial cost of $c(1) = 1$, and a learning rate 0.85 as 12.40228. In our example, we can then compute the cumulative cost as

$$\text{Cost of producing 20 with learning} = \$19k \times 12.40228 = \$235,643$$

Observe that this number is much lower than our naïve estimate resulting from multiplying the initial unit cost by 20 and is much higher than our aggressive estimate of multiplying the 20th unit cost by 20.

In general we define **cumulative learning curve coefficient**, CLCC, as

$$CLCC(x, LR) = \text{the cost of producing } x \text{ units in a process that has an}$$

| **Cumulative learning curve coefficient** The cost of producing x units in a process that has an initial cost of $c(1) = 1$ and a learning rate of LR. | initial cost of $c(1) = 1$ and a learning rate of LR. |

We can then write

$$\text{Cumulative cost to produce } x \text{ units with learning} = \text{Cost for first unit} \times CLCC(x, LR)$$

6.6 Employee Turnover and Its Effect on Learning

LO6-6 Determine employee turnover and average tenure.

Employees working in operations accumulate experience and thus have the potential to improve their performance. And, as employees learn, so does the company that employs them. But what happens to experience when employees leave the company? This turns out to be a difficult question.

Consider two companies, A and B, both installing highly efficient energy systems. Assume that both companies have 100 employees and that at both companies it takes an employee with no experience $c(1) = 500$ hours to complete an installation. As the employee accumulates experience, this time gets reduced following a learning rate of 90 percent. Now, company A has a relatively stable workforce, whereas company B suffers from a significant number of its employees leaving every year. Though each company is able to hire new employees, keeping their overall workforce constant at 100, these new employees start their job with no experience with respect to the system installation. For them, their learning curve starts anew.

Employee turnover Employee turnover = (Number of new employees recruited per year)/ (Average number of employees). The higher the employee turnover, the less experience the average employee will have with his or her job.

We define a company's **employee turnover** as

$$\text{Employee turnover} = \frac{\text{Number of new employees recruited per year}}{\text{Average number of employees}}$$

© Elenathewise/iStockphoto/Getty Images/RF

The higher the employee turnover, the less experience the average employee will have with his or her job; that company's employee tenure is, on average, lower compared to a company with less employee turnover. This is a simple application of Little's Law. We now compute the turnover of employees. The key difference is that high inventory turns are typically a good thing, but high employee turnover is a bad thing. However, both turn numbers capture the average time a unit spends in the company. Typically, we like products to spend a short amount of time in our company and like employees to spend a long amount of time at their respective company.

To see the link to Little's Law, recall that

$$\text{Inventory} = \text{Flow rate} \times \text{Flow time}$$

Using the employee as the flow unit here, this translates to

$$\text{Avg employees} = \text{Number of new employees each year} \times \text{Avg time spent in company}$$

Now, we can compute the employee turnover as

$$\text{Employee turnover} = \frac{1}{\text{Average time employees spend in the company}}$$

Company A has a more stable workforce. Assume that it has an employee turnover of 20 percent while the average employee turnover at company B is 50 percent. This means that for company A, the average employee spends:

$$\frac{\text{Average time employees}}{\text{spend in the company}} = \frac{1}{\text{Employee turnover}} = \frac{1}{0.2 \text{ turn per year}} = 5 \text{ years}$$

with the company. Put differently, the average employee leaves the company five years after he or she is recruited. Now, we have to be careful not to confuse this time with the **average tenure** of the employee. At any given moment in time, some employees will be relatively new

Average tenure The average time an employee has spent on his or her job. Average tenure = 1/(2 × Employee turnover).

to the company and others will have a longer tenure. If we took the average over all employees presently employed at company A, we would find they have an average tenure of 2.5 years:

$$\text{Average tenure} = \frac{1}{2} \times \text{Average time employees spend with the company}$$

$$= \frac{1}{(2 \times \text{Employee turnover})}$$

In our example, we obtain for company A:

$$\text{Average tenure} = \frac{1}{(2 \times \text{Employee turnover})} = \frac{1}{(2 \times 0.2)} = 2.5 \text{ years}$$

Using the same equation, we find that the average tenure for an employee at company B is

$$\text{Average tenure} = \frac{1}{(2 \times \text{Employee turnover})} = \frac{1}{(2 \times 0.5)} = 1 \text{ year}$$

How many installations did this employee complete in his career? Assuming sufficient demand (i.e., assuming the employee was not idle for prolonged periods of time and installed systems more or less "back-to-back"), we know that

Cumulative time to produce x units with learning = Time for first unit $\times$ CLCC(x, LR)

where CLCC(x, LR) is the cumulative learning curve coefficient derived in Table 6.4.

For company A, we know that the average employee has had 2.5 years' time to accumulate experience. Assuming 250 workdays in a year and 8 hours of work time each day, this would give us 2000 hours of experience per year, which would suggest that the average employee has a tenure of 5000 hours. Further recall that the first unit takes 500 hours to install and the learning rate is 90 percent. Substituting this in the above equation, we get

Cumulative time to produce x units with learning = Time for first unit $\times$ CLCC(x, LR)

$$5000 \text{ hours} = 500 \text{ hours} \qquad \times \text{CLCC}(x, 0.9)$$

$$\text{CLCC}(x, 0.9) = 10$$

Check Your Understanding **6.8**

Question: It is estimated that Costco has an employee turnover of 17 percent a year and an employee base of 67,600. How many new employees must Costco hire every year and what is the average tenure of an employee?

Answer: We know that the employee turnover is

$$\text{Employee turnover} = \frac{\text{Number of new employees recruited per year}}{\text{Average number of employees}}$$

Substituting in the values, we get

$$0.17 = \frac{\text{Number of new employees recruited per year}}{67,600}$$

which we can easily solve for the Number of new employees recruited per year to be

Number of new employees recruited per year = $0.17 \times 67,600 = 11,492$

Next, we compute the average tenure as

$$\text{Average tenure} = \frac{1}{(2 \times \text{Employee turnover})} = \frac{1}{(2 \times 0.17)} = 2.94 \text{ years}$$

Source for Costco data: http://hbr.org/2006/12/the-high-cost-of-low-wages/ar/1

So, we have to look at the column in Table 6.4 and look for how many units of experience correspond to a CLCC of 10. For that, simply go down the column of the 90 percent learning rate until you come to a number close to 10. In our case, we get:

$$CLCC(12, 0.9) = 9.374459$$

$$CLCC(13, 0.9) = 10.0516$$

$$CLCC(14, 0.9) = 10.72115$$

This suggests that the average employee at company A has had the time to complete 12 installations and is now on the 13th installation. We can then use Table 6.4 to compute how much time it takes the employee to do the 13th installation:

Time to produce with an experience of 13 = Time for first unit × LC(13, 0.9)

$$= 500 × 0.677138 = 338.569 \text{ hours}$$

Now, compare this to the average employee at company B. With an average tenure of one year, this employee will have had 2000 hours on the job. How many installations will that person have completed? Recall that

Cumulative time to produce x units with learning = Time for first unit × CLCC(x, LR)

So, we get

$$2000 \text{ hours} = 500 \text{ hours} × CLCC(x, 0.9)$$

$$CLCC(x, 0.9) = 4$$

Again, we have to check the column in Table 6.4 and look for how many units of experience correspond to a CLCC of 4. For that, simply go down the column of the 90 percent learning rate until you come to a number close to 4. In this case, we get

$$CLCC(4, 0.9) = 3.556206$$

$$CLCC(5, 0.9) = 4.339193$$

Our average employee at company B will thus have completed four jobs and will be working on the fifth job. As with company A, we can use Table 6.4 to compute how much time it takes the employee to do the fifth installation:

Time to produce with an experience of 5 = Time for first unit × LC $C(5, 0.9)$

$$= 500 × 0.782987 = 391 \text{ hours}$$

> **Process standardization** A careful documentation so that the operation does not permanently have to reinvent the wheel. Standardization can take the form of a standard work sheet.

This corresponds to a 14 percent disadvantage compared to company A (338/391 = 0.86). Fast employee turnover is, because of learning curve effects, a significant challenge to the productivity of an operation.

6.7 Standardization as a Way to Avoid "Relearning"

> **LO6-7** Understand the benefits of documentation and standardization.

Instead of having every worker go through the learning curve, it would be helpful if we could codify some of the learning of the workers and build it into the process. This way, when a worker leaves, the new worker would not start his learning from scratch, but instead could benefit from the cumulative experience of those who came before him. This is really the idea of **process standardization**. Unlike in the days of the craftsmen, when knowledge was tacit and rested in the brains of a few individuals, modern operations require careful documentation and standardization (as dull as this might sound) so that the operation does not permanently have to "reinvent the wheel."

Standards should take the form of a standard work sheet. The **standard work sheet** documents the best practice of how to conduct a particular activity in a process. It avoids the recurrence of defects, accidents, or other forms of mistakes that occurred in the past and that have subsequently been eliminated through process improvement. So, the standard work sheet is the knowledge reservoir of the operation.

According to Taichi Ohno, the father of the famous Toyota Production System, which will be discussed in Chapter 8, the standard work sheet should list

1. The processing time for an activity.
2. The work sequence of all steps making up the activity.
3. The standard amount of inventory at the resource.

It is the responsibility of the supervisor to help a new worker become comfortable adhering to the standard work sheet.

You might find Ohno's framework of standardization to be somewhat unique to the world of manufacturing. You might also find that the idea of a standard inventory does not apply to your own work or life experiences. We agree with you. Ohno's criteria for a standard are a high bar to clear, and both the idea of a standard processing time and a standard amount of inventory are somewhat unique to manufacturing. In service settings, in contrast, the inventory consists of human beings, and so setting an inventory standard can be much more complicated. The same holds true for processing times. In service settings, the processing time strongly depends on the customer. Imagine booking a flight through a call center. Even if the customer service representative could be 100 percent consistent in her work from one customer to the next, chances are that the processing times would differ across customers. One customer has special meal requirements, others can't find their customer loyalty card, yet others have questions about connecting flights. So, standards for processing times in service settings need to acknowledge the presence of variability in the processing times.

So, if you take out the standard inventory and the standard processing times, what is left from Ohno's framework? You still have a sequence of tasks. This task sequence gives you all the tasks you need to complete in order to correctly perform an activity. This is what is called a checklist. You can think of a checklist as a "standard light." Checklists are very useful in day-to-day life and in the operations of a business.

In your personal life, a checklist might be a list of things you want to put in your bag when you travel (from passport to toothbrush and from underwear to credit card). Such lists are inexpensive in their creation. They also can be easily shared. In fact, one might argue that many cooking recipes basically are checklists.

Checklists are also powerful beyond your toothbrush. Consider the information shown in Figure 6.8. The figure shows a checklist created by the World Health Organization that hospitals should go through before and after a surgery. Similar checklists (and, often, much longer ones) are used in aviation. Instead of relying on a pilot's experience, the checklist makes sure that the work is performed to the same safety standards, independent of which pilot is on the plane.

Standard work sheet A form of standardization compiling the processing time for an activity, the work sequence of all steps comprising the activity, and the standard amount of inventory at the resource.

Check Your Understanding **6.9**

Question: Which of the following is not part of a standard work sheet?

a. The processing time for an activity
b. The work sequence of all steps
c. The salary of the operator
d. The standard amount of inventory

Answer: C.

Figure 6.8 A surgery checklist provided by the World Health Organization

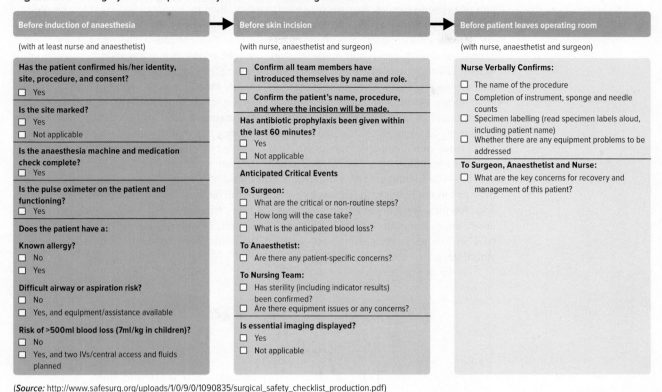

Before induction of anaesthesia	Before skin incision	Before patient leaves operating room
(with at least nurse and anaesthetist)	(with nurse, anaesthetist and surgeon)	(with nurse, anaesthetist and surgeon)

Before induction of anaesthesia

Has the patient confirmed his/her identity, site, procedure, and consent?
☐ Yes

Is the site marked?
☐ Yes
☐ Not applicable

Is the anaesthesia machine and medication check complete?
☐ Yes

Is the pulse oximeter on the patient and functioning?
☐ Yes

Does the patient have a:

Known allergy?
☐ No
☐ Yes

Difficult airway or aspiration risk?
☐ No
☐ Yes, and equipment/assistance available

Risk of >500ml blood loss (7ml/kg in children)?
☐ No
☐ Yes, and two IVs/central access and fluids planned

Before skin incision

☐ Confirm all team members have introduced themselves by name and role.

☐ **Confirm the patient's name, procedure, and where the incision will be made.**

Has antibiotic prophylaxis been given within the last 60 minutes?
☐ Yes
☐ Not applicable

Anticipated Critical Events

To Surgeon:
☐ What are the critical or non-routine steps?
☐ How long will the case take?
☐ What is the anticipated blood loss?

To Anaesthetist:
☐ Are there any patient-specific concerns?

To Nursing Team:
☐ Has sterility (including indicator results) been confirmed?
☐ Are there equipment issues or any concerns?

Is essential imaging displayed?
☐ Yes
☐ Not applicable

Before patient leaves operating room

Nurse Verbally Confirms:

☐ The name of the procedure
☐ Completion of instrument, sponge and needle counts
☐ Specimen labelling (read specimen labels aloud, including patient name)
☐ Whether there are any equipment problems to be addressed

To Surgeon, Anaesthetist and Nurse:
☐ What are the key concerns for recovery and management of this patient?

(*Source:* http://www.safesurg.org/uploads/1/0/9/0/1090835/surgical_safety_checklist_production.pdf)

CONNECTIONS: Process Standardization at Intel

© Digital Stock/Royalty-Free/Corbis/RF

Continued

An example of how standardization can help with process improvement is the production of semiconductors. As new processes launch, they face substantial yield losses. With experience, the production yields improve. Data for this appear in Figure 6.9(a). The figure shows how Intel production facilities (also known as Fabs) improve. Over time, for a given processor design, more and more fabs are brought online. It is interesting how each fab indeed seems to reinvent the wheel. The late-coming fabs might be on a somewhat steeper improvement trajectory, yet all of them require many months before reaching high levels of yield. In the 1990s, Intel created a strategy referred to as CopyExactly! The idea was that rather than having each fab that is added to the resource pool for producing a particular design go through its own learning curve, the process would be standardized across all fabs.[*] Now, semiconductor manufacturing is a highly complex process in which even minor variations in the process can create dramatic differences. In the Intel CopyExactly! method, processes are standardized and fabs are replicated at a very detailed level. This includes the paint in the building (paint leaves particles in the air that could contaminate production) and even the location of bathrooms (water flowing through the pipes could cause vibrations). Intel's attention to details has been rewarded, as we can see in Figure 6.9(b). New fabs are not reinventing the wheel—instead, they learn together and combined form one virtual fab with a common performance.

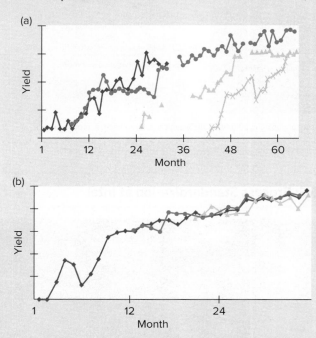

Figure 6.9   Yield trajectories in Intel's production (a) before (left) and (b) after (right) implementing the CopyExactly! Method (Terwiesch and Xu)

Autonomous learning Improvements due to on-the-job learning of employees.

*Christian Terwiesch and Yi Xu, "The Copy-Exactly Ramp-up Strategy: Trading-off Learning with Process Change," *IEEE Transactions on Engineering Management* 51, no. 1 (2004), pp. 70–84.

6.8 **Drivers of Learning**

LO6-8 Understand the key drivers of learning, including autonomous learning, induced learning, and the PDCA cycle.

Imagine your job is to bake cookies. You bake, you bake, and you bake. Your cumulative output increases and chances are that you get better at baking. In general, it is useful to distinguish between two types of learning. We refer to **autonomous learning** as improvements due to on-the-job learning of employees. Autonomous learning simply happens and does not require managerial intervention. As you are baking cookies, you will, tray by tray that you bake, figure out how to avoid having dough stick to the tray, determine how much time it takes to preheat the oven, and learn how to visually inspect the cookies to avoid burning them.

In the same way, autonomous learning happens in larger organizations. Employees work together in a group, and the more often the group carries out an activity, the less time it needs to spend on coordination. Employees learn to fix broken equipment and they get better interacting with customers. Especially in manual tasks such as making a sandwich or assembling a component, the employees build a skill ("muscle memory"), allowing them to reduce their processing times.

In contrast to autonomous learning there is **induced learning**. Induced learning requires a deliberate action and an investment in resources, be it in the form of time or material. At the heart of the concept of induced learning is the question, "Can the learning rate discussed in this chapter be improved?" Imagine that you are not the only one baking cookies; you are doing so in competition with 10 of your classmates. Will all of you learn at exactly the same learning rate? Or is there something one could do to learn faster?

Let's continue with the example of baking. One important driver of learning is your ability to either taste the cookies or get any other feedback from those who are eating your cookies. This allows you to make some connections between your actions—for example, how much chocolate you put into the dough or how long you leave the cookies in the oven—and some performance measures, such as the happiness of those who eat your cookies. Short of such feedback from the customer, your ability to learn and improve will be limited.

Induced learning is a deliberate process. Instead of just optimizing short-term performance, you experiment to learn the underlying science of your operation. You do something, and then you see the results. You try out your new way, and you look at the results. This iteration typically happens in four steps:

- *Plan:* You establish the performance measures most relevant to you in the operation. This might be the processing time, the unit costs, or your customer satisfaction scores. You think about how you might improve this performance by adjusting the process.

- *Do:* You try out the improvement (most likely on a small scale first). As you are doing this, you collect data about the process performance.

- *Check:* You analyze the performance results you collected and compare them against past data to see if you indeed improved the process.

- *Act:* You act on your new knowledge and adjust the process. What used to be an improvement idea now becomes the new work standard.

The iteration between these four steps is often referred to as the **PDCA cycle**, where PDCA stands for plan-do-check-act. The PDCA cycle is also called the **Deming cycle**, honoring the work of **William Edwards Deming**, a pioneer in the quality improvement literature. Deming was instrumental in importing a statistically rigorous approach to learning and experimentation into the field of operations management. Just like any other science based on data analysis, successful operational improvements require empirical validation, not just theories from a book.

In the Quality and Statistical Process Control chapter (Chapter 9), we discuss the idea of input variables and output variables. With the PDCA approach, we aim to fine-tune the operation, adjusting its input variables to achieve a favorable change in the output variables. However, input variables are not the only factors that influence the output variables—the process is also subject to **statistical noise**. How can we find out the effect that baking time has on the chewiness of our cookies if the oven temperature varies from one production run to the next? When we as hobby bakers adjust one input variable for an experiment, we need to be aware that this might not be the only thing that changes. Instead, we are subject to

- *Changes in other input variables:* We might be interested in the effect of baking time and compare two batches of cookies, one that we put in the oven for 12 minutes and one for 13 minutes. But are the cookies identical when we put them into the oven? Are the cookies the exact same size and weight? Was the dough exactly identical when we prepared the cookies? And how about that oven temperature?

- *Changes in environmental variables:* Other variables well outside our control might impact our baking experiment as well. This includes the humidity and temperature of the air as well as the ingredients we procured for the dough.

Induced learning A deliberate action and an investment in resources, be it in the form of time or material.

PDCA cycle Plan-do-check-act cycle; a sequence of steps an organization needs to take to improve the process.

Deming cycle Synonym for PDCA cycle.

William Edwards Deming A 20th-century statistician who pioneered many of the methods of modern quality control.

Statistical noise Variables influencing the outcomes of a process in unpredictable ways.

Check Your Understanding 6.10

Question: John and Mary are both trying to improve their freestyle so that they can compete at a local triathlon. John decides to swim every day for one hour. Mary, in contrast, practices with a coach who has her do a set of technique drills that isolate various parts of the stroke. Which of the two athletes is engaging in autonomous learning and which one is engaging in induced learning?

Answer: John follows the principle of autonomous learning. He just swims and accumulates miles. Mary sets some time aside to make an investment in technique. During that time, she might barely move and is likely to accumulate fewer miles. Despite this, the technique drills teach her about the stroke.

. . . .

Signal-to-noise ratio The relationship between the size of an effect and the statistical noise in the process. A large signal-to-noise ratio is required so that an effect in the process can be identified.

Together, other input variables and environmental variables cause a statistical noise that hinders our experimentation efforts. When we observe a change in customer satisfaction with our cookies, we cannot be certain if this was driven by our experiment (a change in baking time) or by the random fluctuations in other variables. So, in order for learning to happen, we need a strong **signal-to-noise ratio**; that is, we need to come up with good improvement ideas (that really move the needle on our performance measure of interest, leading to a strong signal) and we need to minimize the noise of all other variables influencing the operation.

Conclusion

Practice makes perfect. Whether you study for the final exams of this course, learn how to serve in tennis, or master the art playing the piano, as you accumulate experience, your performance goes up. The same holds for employees, companies, and industries.

In this chapter, you saw how to analyze the longitudinal performance of an operation through the lens of the learning curve framework. We presented a mathematical model of improvement that happens with experience accumulation and we discussed how learning rates can be estimated using log-log representations of the data.

It is important to notice that learning curves are not a law of nature, but simply an empirical regularity. Learning curves look at improvements in the past, but we have no guarantee that the future will be like the past. Having said this, the past is the only place to which we can go to collect data, and so extrapolating past trajectories of improvement is typically the best predictor for the future.

We also saw the managerial implication of the learning curve. In particular, we found a method for estimating performance as a function of cumulative experience using either formulas or the learning coefficients. This method applies to the unit costs (time) of production (the time to produce the 27th unit). But we can also analyze the costs (time) of producing a larger quantity, which is complicated by the fact that unit costs (time) change from the first to the last unit.

Finally, we analyzed the effect of employee turnover. The employee turnover calculations are similar to our calculations of inventory turns in Chapter 2; we can compute how long the average employee stays with the company before he or she leaves. We can also compute the average tenure of an employee, which is important for an employee's cumulative experience.

Learning does not happen by itself. In this chapter, we have been somewhat vague about the exact mechanisms of the underlying learning process. Learning rates vary across companies, reflecting that some companies manage the learning process better than others.

Summary of Learning Objectives

LO6-1 **Distinguish between various shapes of learning curves**

Learning curves show the performance improvement of a process over time. As the process accumulates experience by producing more output (by increasing the cumulative output of the process), one or multiple measures of performance improve—costs go down, defects go down, processing times go down, yields go up, and so on. This improvement can happen with an exponential growth, with an exponential decay, or as a diminishing growth rate. Costs tend to exhibit a pattern of exponential decay; they decrease by a fixed percentage with each doubling of output.

LO6-2 **Determine the unit cost of a process given a learning rate and an experience level**

We assume that costs go down by a constant percentage each time the cumulative output is doubled. This is called the learning rate. If costs go down by 20 percent, we say we have a learning rate $LR = 0.8$. This allows us to compute the cost of the Nth unit, knowing the learning rate and the initial cost $c(1)$.

LO6-3 **Estimate the learning rate using past cost data**

Learning curves in which unit costs decrease by a fixed percentage with each doubling of cumulative output having an exponential decay shape. By taking a log-log transformation (taking logarithms of the cumulative output and of costs), the learning curve becomes a straight line. We can estimate the slope of this straight line using simple algebra. The resulting slope can be translated back to a learning rate.

LO6-4 **Predict unit cost by using the LCC method and by using the learning curve directly**

Because the costs for the Nth unit produced are expressed as a multiple of the cost for the first unit, we can consider a generic process in which it costs $1 to make the first unit. We can then use a table of learning curve coefficients to adjust the initial cost depending on the learning rate and the cumulative output. Alternatively, we can use an exponential expression to evaluate the unit costs directly.

LO6-5 **Predict cumulative cost using the LCC method**

Oftentimes, we don't want to just estimate the cost of one unit, but the costs of an order consisting of multiple units. This can be difficult to the extent that the process continues to improve as it moves from producing the first unit to producing the last unit of the order. We can use cumulative learning curve coefficients to estimate the costs of an order, given the learning rate and the costs of producing the first unit.

LO6-6 **Determine employee turnover and average tenure**

Employee turnover can be disruptive in the learning of an organization. The employee turnover calculations are an example of Little's Law: Employee turnover = Number of new employees recruited/Average number of employees. We can use the employee turnover to predict the average tenure of an employee, which is simply 1/(2 × Employee turnover).

LO6-7 **Understand the benefits of documentation and standardization**

To avoid the situation where knowledge gets lost in an organization as employees leave and to allow for the training of new employees, we attempt to codify the knowledge accumulated. This is done through standard work sheets and checklists.

LO6-8 **Understand the key drivers of learning, including autonomous learning, induced learning, and the PDCA cycle**

Learning can happen for multiple reasons. Autonomous learning refers to the learning that simply happens in a process—it happens even without managerial intervention. Induced learning, in contrast, requires a deliberate learning effort. It might even be detrimental in the short term. Either way, learning follows the pattern of plan-do-check-act, which is also called the Deming cycle.

Key Terms

6.1 Various Forms of the Learning Curve

Learning curve A function that captures the relationship between a performance metric of an operation and the experience as measured in the number of repetitions with which the operation has been performed.

Experience curve Synonym for learning curve; the term *experience* emphasizes that learning is driven by experience.

Exponential growth An improvement trajectory in which the rate of improvement increases over time or experience.

Diminishing returns A performance trajectory in which the improvement rate decreases over time or experience.

Performance gap The difference between the current process performance and some target or optimal value.

6.2 The Power Law

Learning rate The amount by which the process performance is multiplied every time the cumulative experience doubles. The learning rate (LR) is a number between 0 and 1. Higher numbers correspond to slower learning. 1-LR is the percent improvement associated with a doubling of cumulative experience.

6.3 Estimating the Learning Curve Using a Linear Log-Log Graph

Log-log plots A graphical representation in which we plot the logarithmic value of both the x and y variables.

6.4 Using Learning Curve Coefficients to Predict Costs

Learning curve coefficient The cost of producing one unit in a process that has an initial cost of $c(1) = 1$, a cumulative output of x, and a learning rate of LR.

6.5 Using Learning Curve Coefficients to Predict Cumulative Costs

Cumulative learning curve coefficient The cost of producing x units in a process that has an initial cost of $c(1) = 1$ and a learning rate of LR.

6.6 Employee Turnover and Its Effect on Learning

Employee turnover Employee turnover = (Number of new employees recruited per year)/(Average number of employees). The higher the employee turnover, the less experience the average employee will have with his or her job.

Average tenure The average time an employee has spent on his or her job. Average tenure = $1/(2 \times$ Employee turnover).

6.7 Standardization as a Way to Avoid "Relearning"

Process standardization A careful documentation so that the operation does not permanently have to "reinvent the wheel." Standardization can take the form of a standard work sheet.

Standard work sheet A form of standardization compiling the processing time for an activity, the work sequence of all steps comprising the activity, and the standard amount of inventory at the resource.

6.8 Drivers of Learning

Autonomous learning Improvements due to on-the-job learning of employees.

Induced Learning A deliberate action and an investment in resources, be it in the form of time or material.

PDCA cycle Plan-do-check-act cycle; a sequence of steps an organization needs to take to improve the process.

Deming cycle Synonym for PDCA cycle.

William Edwards Deming A 20th-century statistician who pioneered many of the methods of modern quality control.

Statistical noise Variables influencing the outcomes of a process in unpredictable ways.

Signal-to-noise ratio The relationship between the size of an effect and the statistical noise in the process. A large signal-to-noise ratio is required so that an effect in the process can be identified.

Key Formulas

LO6-2 **Determine the unit cost of a process given a learning rate and an experience level**

$$c(\text{After doubling cumulative output n times}) = c(1) \times \text{LR}^n$$

$$c(N) = c(1) \times \text{LR}^{\frac{\ln(N)}{0.6931}}$$

LO6-3 **Estimate the learning rate using past cost data**

$$\text{Slope } b = \frac{[\ln(c(x_2)) - \ln(c(x_1))]}{[\ln(x_2) - \ln(x_1)]}$$

LO6-4 **Predict unit cost by using the LCC method and by using the learning curve directly**

$$c(N) = c(1) \times \text{LR}^{\log_2 N} = c(1) \times \text{LR}^{\frac{\ln(N)}{\ln(2)}} = c(1) \times N^b$$

LO6-5 **Predict cumulative cost using the LCC method**

Cumulative time to produce x units with learning = Time for first unit $\times$ CLCC(x, LR)

LO6-6 **Determine employee turnover and average tenure**

$$\text{Employee turnover} = \frac{\text{Number of new employees recruited per year}}{\text{Average number of employees}}$$

$$\text{Average tenure} = \frac{1}{2} \times \text{Average time employees spend with the company}$$

$$= \frac{1}{(2 \times \text{Employee turnover})}$$

Conceptual Questions

LO6-1

1. A bank is underwriting loans for small businesses. Currently, about 5 percent of the underwriting decisions are found to be incorrect when audited by the bank's quality assurance department. The bank has a goal of reducing this number to 1 percent. What form of an improvement trajectory is most likely to occur?
   a. Exponential growth
   b. Exponential decay
   c. Diminishing return growth

2. A bakery produces cookies; however, it makes some defects, leading to occasionally broken or burnt cookies. Presently, the yield of the process is 90 percent (i.e., 9 out of 10 cookies are good). The bakery has a goal of producing 99 percent good cookies. What form of an improvement trajectory is most likely to occur?
   a. Exponential growth
   b. Exponential decay
   c. Diminishing return growth

3. A regional rail company wants to reduce its delays. Presently, 70 percent of the trains arrive on time. The company's goal is to improve this to 95 percent. What form of improvement trajectory will most likely occur?
   a. Exponential growth
   b. Exponential decay
   c. Diminishing return growth

4. A novice rower is practicing for a 2000-meter test on a rowing machine (an "erg"). He presently takes 7 minutes and 10 seconds to complete the distance. His goal, in order to be recruited by a good college, is 6 minutes and 30 seconds. What form of improvement trajectory will most likely occur?
   a. Exponential growth
   b. Exponential decay
   c. Diminishing return growth

LO6-2

5. The power law describes a learning process with exponential growth in performance. True or false?
   a. True
   b. False

6. Assume a learning curve following the power law. If you double the initial cost $c(1)$ of a product, the cost of the 21st unit, $c(21)$, will:
   a. stay the same.
   b. be reduced by 50 percent.
   c. be doubled.
   d. increase by a factor of $\ln(2)$.

7. Consider two processes, A and B, with an initial cost of $c(1) = 20$. Process A has a learning rate of LR = 0.95 and process B has a learning rate of LR = 0.8. After 20 units:
   a. process A is cheaper.
   b. process B is cheaper.
   c. the two processes will have the same cost.
   d. cannot be determined from the given information.

LO6-3

8. A learning curve following the power law has what shape in the log-log graph?
   a. Exponentially increasing
   b. Exponentially decreasing
   c. Linearly increasing
   d. Linearly decreasing

9. When estimating the slope of the line in a log-log graph, we pick two points with coordinates (x_1, y_1) and (x_2, y_2). Which of the following statements is true?
   a. x_1 has to be exactly one unit bigger than x_2.
   b. x_2 needs to be the value on the x-axis corresponding to the last period for which we have data.
   c. y_1 needs to be the value on the y-axis corresponding to the initial cost, $c(1)$.
   d. The slope of a line can be negative or positive. For a positive rate of learning, however, the slope is always negative.

10. A lower learning rate corresponds to a steeper slope in a log-log graph of the learning curve. True or false?
    a. True
    b. False

11. A firm has a learning rate almost equal to 1 (just slightly less than 1). What does this imply for the slope of the learning curve in a log-log graph?
    a. The slope is close to 0.
    b. The slope is close to -1.
    c. The slope is close to 1.
    d. Cannot be determined from the given information

LO6-4

12. The learning curve coefficient LCC(10, 0.8) captures:
    a. the cost to produce one unit in a process with $c(1) = 1$, a cumulative output of 10, and a learning rate of 0.8.
    b. the cost to produce one unit in a process with $c(1) = 10$, a cumulative output of 1, and a learning rate of 0.8.

   c. the cost to produce 10 units of output in a process with $c(1) = 1$, a cumulative output of 1, and a learning rate of 0.8.

   d. the cost to produce 10 units of output in a process with $c(1) = 1$, a cumulative output of 10, and a learning rate of 0.8.

13. A higher value of the learning rate (LR) leads to a lower value of the learning curve coefficient LCC(x, LR). True or false?
   a. True
   b. False

14. Instead of using the learning curve coefficient method, it is possible to compute the costs of the Nth unit as $c(N) = c(1) \times N^b$, where b is the slope of the learning curve in the log-log graph. True or false?
   a. True
   b. False

LO6-5

15. The cumulative learning curve coefficient CLCC(x, LR) is always bigger than the learning curve coefficient LCC(x, LR) for all $x > 1$. True or false?
   a. True
   b. False

16. The cumulative learning curve coefficient CLCC(20, 0.8) is defined as follows:
   a. the cost to produce 20 units in a process with $c(1) = 1$ and a learning rate of 0.8.
   b. the cost to produce one unit in a process with $c(1) = 20$ and a learning rate of 0.8.
   c. the cost to produce one unit in a process with $c(1) = 1$ and a learning rate of 0.8^{20}.
   d. the cost to produce the 20th unit in a process with $c(1) = 1$ and a learning rate of 0.8.

17. Assume a learning curve following the power law. If you double the initial cost $c(1)$ of a product, the costs of producing an order of 20 units:
   a. stay the same.
   b. are reduced by 50 percent.
   c. are doubled.
   d. cannot be determined from the given information.

LO6-6

18. How does the average tenure of an employee relate to the average time an employee spends with the company?
   a. They are one and the same thing.
   b. The average tenure is twice the average time an employee spends with the company.
   c. The average tenure is half the average time an employee spends with the company.
   d. The average tenure is inversely related to the average time an employee spends with the company.

19. The employee turnover can be computed as:
   a. Number of new employees recruited per year/Average number of employees
   b. Average number of employees/Number of new employees recruited per year
   c. 1/2 × Average time an employee spends with the company
   d. 1/2 × Number of new employees recruited per year

20. If the employee turnover increases, the average tenure of an employee in the company:
   a. increases.
   b. decreases.
   c. stays the same.
   d. cannot be determined from the given information.

LO6-7

21. In an environment with high employee turnover, standards are less important than in environments with low turnover. True or false?
   a. True
   b. False

22. Which of the following is not part of the standard work sheet?
    a. The processing time for an activity
    b. The name of the person in charge of the activity
    c. The work sequence of all steps making up the activity
    d. The standard amount of inventory at the resource

LO6-8

23. John has been fixing bicycles for three years now. He notices that he is getting better with an increase in experience, though he does not necessarily know why. John's learning is most likely a form of autonomous learning. True or false?
    a. True
    b. False

24. Which of the following activities is not part of the Deming cycle?
    a. Plan
    b. Do
    c. Check
    d. Improve
    e. Act

25. A high signal-to-noise ratio makes learning harder. True or false?
    a. True
    b. False

Solved Example Problems

LO6-1

1. Consider the trajectory showing the percentage of patients with depression that were not appropriately screened for suicide risk. A doctor's practice aims to reduce this percentage over time. What shape would a learning curve have in this setting?
    a. Exponential growth
    b. Exponential decay
    c. Diminishing return growth

    Answer: B.

2. Consider the trajectory showing the number of photos that can be stored on a smartphone. What shape would a learning curve have in this setting?
    a. Exponential growth
    b. Exponential decay
    c. Diminishing return growth

    Answer: A.

3. Consider the trajectory showing the percentage of patient records entered correctly into a computer by a typist. What shape would a learning curve have in this setting?
    a. Exponential growth
    b. Exponential decay
    c. Diminishing return growth

    Answer: C.

LO6-2

4. Consider a process that makes LED lamps. The process starts with a unit cost of $30 for the first unit—that is, $c(1) = 30$—and has a learning rate of LR = 0.9. What will be the unit costs for the 64th unit?

    Answer: To reach the 64th unit, we have to double the cumulative output six times (from 1 to 2, from 2 to 4, from 4 to 8, from 8 to 16, from 16 to 32, and from 32 to 64). We can then use the formula:

    $c(\text{After doubling cumulative output 6 times}) = c(1) \times LR^6 = 30 \times 0.9^6 = 15.943$

5. Consider a process assembling shopping carts. The process starts with a unit cost of $20 for the first unit—that is, $c(1) = 20$—and a learning rate of LR = 0.95. What will be the unit costs for the 29th unit?

   Answer: We can directly use the formula:

   $$c(29) = c(1) \times LR^{\log_2 29} = c(1) \times LR^{\frac{\ln(29)}{\ln(2)}} = 20 \times 0.95^{4.858} = 15.589$$

LO6-3

6. A seasoned high school teacher is, once again, writing letters of recommendation for her students as they send in their applications to college. In 2008, the teacher had written 150 letters of recommendation over her career. She estimates that, on average, it took her 45 minutes to write one letter. By 2013, she had written 250 letters of recommendation, and it took her about 33 minutes to write one letter. The learning curve in a log-log graph appears to be linear. By how much does the teacher reduce the processing time of writing one letter with each doubling of the cumulative output?

   Answer: We choose x_2 as the cumulative number of letters written in 2013 and get

   $$\ln(\text{Processing time}) = \ln(33) = 3.497, \text{ and}$$
   $$\ln(\text{Cumulative letters written}) = \ln(250) = 5.521$$

   Similarly, if we choose x_1 as the cumulative number of letters written in 2008, this yields

   $$\ln(\text{Processing time}) = \ln(45) = 3.807, \text{ and}$$
   $$\ln(\text{Cumulative letters written}) = \ln(150) = 5.011$$

   So, we can compute the slope as:

   $$\text{Slope } b = \frac{[\ln(c(x_2)) - \ln(c(x_1))]}{[\ln(x_2) - \ln(x_1)]}$$
   $$= \frac{[3.497 - 3.807]}{[5.521 - 5.011]} = \frac{-0.310}{0.511} = -0.607$$

   Thus, we obtain a slope of the learning curve in a log-log graph of $b = -0.607$. We can then use Table 6.2 to find the corresponding learning rate LR, which is between 0.65 and 0.66. So the teacher reduces the processing time by 34 to 35 percent every time she doubles the cumulative output.

LO6-4

7. Consider the production process of snowblowers. The process starts with an initial cost $c(1) = 104$, a learning rate of LR = 0.9, and by now has reached a cumulative output of 1000. Using the LCC method, what unit costs do you expect?

   Answer: We start by looking up the learning curve coefficient in Table 6.3 for a cumulative output of 1000 and a learning rate of LR = 0.9. We get

   $$LCC(1000, 0.9) = 0.349938$$

   We then compute the costs as

   $$c(\text{After 1000 units of cumulative output, LR} = 0.9, c(1) = 104)$$
   $$= 104 \times LCC(1000, 0.9) = 36.39355$$

   Thus, we expect a unit cost of $36.39355.

8. Consider again the production process of snowblowers. The process starts with an initial cost $c(1) = 104$, a learning rate of LR = 0.9, and by now has reached a cumulative output of 1000. Without using the LCC method, what do you expect production costs to be?

Answer: We first have to look up the slope of the learning curve, b, given the learning rate, LR. In Table 6.2, we see that for LR = 0.9, we get a slope of $b = -0.152$. We then compute costs directly as

$$c(1) \times N^b = 104 \times 1000^{-0.152} = 36.3943$$

Thus, we expect a unit cost of $36.3943. This is within rounding difference of the answer to question 7.

LO6-5

9. Mike and Tom have started a small bike shop where they specialize in assembling high-end race bikes. They just received a large order of 20 bikes from the local university to equip all varsity athletes with a new bike. Mike and Tom expect substantial productivity improvements in their assembly as they move from the first bike in this order to the 20th bike. Their current cost of assembly is $c(1) = 120$ and they expect a learning rate of LR = 0.9. What will be their assembly cost for all 20 bikes combined?

> **Answer:** We start by looking up the cumulative learning curve coefficient in Table 6.4 for an output of 20 and a learning rate of LR = 0.9. We get:

$$\text{CLCC}(20, 0.9) = 14.60776$$

We then compute the costs of making 20 units as

$$\text{CC(Making 20 units, LR} = 0.9, c(1) = 120) = 120 \times \text{CLCC}(20, 0.9)$$

$$= 120 \times 14.60776 = 1752.931$$

Thus, we expect a cumulative cost of $1752.931.

LO6-6

10. A company has 1500 employees, on average, and it recruits, on average, 500 employees per year. What is the employee turnover and what is the average tenure of an employee?

> **Answer:** We first compute the employee turnover as

$$\text{Employee turnover} = \frac{\text{Number of new employees recruited per year}}{\text{Average number of employees}}$$

$$= \frac{500}{1500} = \frac{1}{3}$$

Next, we compute the average tenure as

$$\text{Average tenure} = \frac{1}{(2 \times \text{Employee turnover})} = \frac{1}{(2 \times \frac{1}{3})} = 1.5 \text{ years}$$

LO6-7

11. What are the three elements of a standard work sheet?
   a. They are the processing time for an activity, the work sequence of all steps making up the activity, and the standard amount of inventory at the resource.
   b. They are the processing time for an activity, the responsible operator, and the standard amount of inventory at the resource.
   c. They are the defect rate for an activity, the work sequence of all steps making up the activity, and the standard amount of inventory at the resource.
   d. None of the above

   Answer: A.

LO6-8

12. Which of the following statements is correct?
   a. Autonomous learning happens based on experience alone. In contrast, induced learning requires deliberate effort.

b. Induced learning happens based on experience alone. In contrast, autonomous learning requires deliberate effort.

c. The amount of induced learning is always less than the amount of autonomous learning.

Answer: A.

13. What are the four steps in the Deming cycle?
a. Plan-do-implement-execute
b. Plan-do-check-act
c. Mission-vision-strategy-execution
d. None of the above

Answer: B.

Problems and Applications

LO6-1

1. Consider the trajectory showing the percentage of customer orders in a restaurant that were handled correctly. What shape would a learning curve have in this setting?
a. Exponential growth
b. Exponential decay
c. Diminishing return growth

2. Consider the trajectory showing the number of luggage pieces that an airline loses on a flight. What shape would a learning curve have in this setting?
a. Exponential growth
b. Exponential decay
c. Diminishing return growth

3. Consider the trajectory showing the amount of data storage space that comes with the average PC each year. What shape would a learning curve have in this setting?
a. Exponential growth
b. Exponential decay
c. Diminishing return growth

LO6-2

4. Consider a process that makes high-end boards that get mounted on skateboards. The process starts with a unit cost of $20 for the first unit—that is, $c(1) = 20$—and has a learning rate of LR = 0.95. What will be the unit cost for the 128th unit?

5. Consider a process restringing tennis rackets. The process starts with a unit cost of $10 for the first unit—that is, $c(1) = 10$—and a learning rate of LR = 0.9. What will be the unit cost for the 35th unit?

LO6-3

6. An experienced car mechanic is working on changing the exhaust system. In 2010, the mechanic had performed this operation 100 times over her career. She estimates that, on average, it took her 80 minutes to change one exhaust system. By 2014, she had performed that operation 220 times, and it took her about 55 minutes to change one exhaust system. The learning curve in a log-log graph appears to be linear. By how much does the mechanic reduce the processing time of one operation with each doubling of the cumulative output?

LO6-4

7. Consider the preparation of income tax statements. The process starts with an initial cost $c(1) = 45$ and a learning rate of LR = 0.95, and by now has reached a cumulative output of 100. Using the LCC method, what unit costs do you expect for the 100th unit?

8. Consider again the preparation of income tax statements. The process starts with an initial cost $c(1) = 45$ and a learning rate of LR = 0.95, and by now has reached a

cumulative output of 100. Without using the LCC method, what do you expect production costs to be for the 100th unit?

LO6-5

9. Will has just started a small company making special cakes for retirement parties. He just received a large order of five cakes from a local business. Will expects substantial productivity improvements in his work as he moves from the first cake in this order to the fifth cake. His current cost of making a cake is $c(1) = 40$ and he expects a learning rate of $LR = 0.85$. What will be his cost for all five cakes combined?

LO6-6

10. A company has 2200 employees, on average, and it recruits, on average, 300 employees per year. What is the employee turnover?

11. A company has 2200 employees, on average, and it recruits, on average, 300 employees per year. What is the average tenure of an employee?

LO6-7

12. What are the three elements of a standard work sheet?
    a. They are the processing time for an activity, the work sequence of all steps making up the activity, and the standard amount of inventory at the resource.
    b. They are the processing time for an activity, the most common cause of failure, and the standard amount of inventory at the resource.
    c. They are the defect rate for an activity, the work sequence of all steps making up the activity, and the standard amount of inventory at the resource.
    d. They are the processing time for an activity, the most common cause of failure, and the defect rate for an activity.

LO6-8

13. Consider the navigation skills of two cab drivers (without a GPS). Driver 1 is driving her routes as demanded by the customer and improves her understanding of the region that way. Driver 2 is deliberately taking time off from serving customers to explore new shortcuts. Driver 1 is relying on induced learning and Driver 2 is relying on autonomous learning. True or false?
    a. True
    b. False

14. What is the difference between the PDCA cycle and the Deming cycle?
    a. The PDCA cycle includes four steps (plan, do, check, act), while the Deming cycle includes six steps.
    b. The Deming cycle only applies in manufacturing.
    c. The PDCA cycle is a method for quality improvement, while the Deming cycle applies to the product development process.
    d. There is no difference between the two approaches.

CASE   FORD'S HIGHLAND PLANT

In October 1908, just prior to the launch of his Model T, Henry Ford proclaimed, "I will build a motor car for the great multitude." During the next 19 years, Ford built 15 million vehicles of this model. The success of the Model T was made possible through Ford's development of the moving assembly line, where thousands of workers assembled the cars under harsh conditions. Unskilled labor was cheap. Workers initially received $2.30 for a 9-hour shift.

Given the rough conditions at the factory, absenteeism was a major problem. From the 13,000 workers at the plant, typically 1000 of them did not show up for work. Moreover, the employee turnover was a remarkable 370 percent at Ford's Highland Park plant. Workers were becoming increasingly difficult to hire, and because most workers were immigrants, the plant was plagued by communications problems reflecting poor English language skills.

To respond to this challenge, in January 1914, wages were doubled to $5 per day and shifts were limited to 8-hour durations. In addition to the pay raise, Ford also requested that his workers learn English, take care of their health, and start saving for a home.

Many experts in the industry thought that Ford's move was insane and he would not be able to afford the higher labor costs. But Ford proved them wrong. In the fall of 1908, a new Model T cost $850 (this corresponds to $20,763 in 2013). By 1927, Ford was producing a new Model T every 27 seconds and each cost $260 (this corresponds to $3372 in 2013).

Courtesy of the National Photo Company Collection/Library of Congress Prints and Photographs Division [LC-USZ62-99295]

QUESTIONS

1. In 1913, how long did the average worker stay with the plant?

2. What was the average tenure of a worker?

3. Assume the one-millionth vehicle was produced in 1916 at a cost of $8084 (in 2013 US$). By how much did Ford reduce his cost with each doubling of cumulative output from 1916 to 1927?

SOURCE

Henry Ford Heritage Association, http://hfha.org/the-ford-story/henry-ford-an-impact-felt/

References

Chase, Jenny. *The PV Experience Curve.* Bloomberg | New Energy Finance, February 2011.

Dutton, John M., and Annie Thomas. "Treating Progress Functions as a Managerial Opportunity." *The Academy of Management Review* 9, no. 2 (April 1984), pp. 235–47.

Gladwell, Malcolm. *Outliers: The Story of Success.* Back Bay Books, 2008.

Lapré, Michael A., and Ingrid M. Nembhard. "Inside the Organizational Learning Curve: Understanding the Organizational Learning Process." *Foundations and Trends® in Technology, Information and Operations Management* 4, no. 1 (2010), pp. 1–103.

Levitt, Steven D., John A. List, and Chad Syverson. "Toward an Understanding of Learning by Doing: Evidence from an Automobile Assembly Plant." *Journal of Political Economy* 121, no. 4 (February 2013), pp. 643–81. Accessed September 10, 2013, http://www.jstor.org/stable/10.1086/671137

"Study Tracks 'Learning Curve' in Prostate Surgery." July 24, 2007. http://www.cnn.com/2007/HEALTH/conditions/07/24/cancer.prostate.reut/

Terwiesch, Christian, and Roger E. Bohn. "Learning and Process Improvement during Production Ramp-up." *International Journal of Production Economics* 70, no. 1 (2001), pp. 1–19.

Terwiesch, Christian, and Yi Xu. "The Copy-Exactly Ramp-up Strategy: Trading-off Learning with Process Change." *IEEE Transactions on Engineering Management* 51, no. 1 (2004), pp. 70–84.

Process Interruptions

7

LEARNING OBJECTIVES

CHAPTER OUTLINE

Introduction

Henry Ford founded the Ford Motor Company in the early 1900s, and by the 1920s it was the world's largest auto manufacturer. The growth of the company is largely attributed to the success of one of its vehicles, the Model T. The Model T was rugged, which was needed for the unpaved rough roads of the time. It was also affordable—Ford wanted a car that his assembly-line workers could buy. But the Model T was not flashy—it only came in one color. In fact, it is believed that Ford once said something like, "A customer can have any color he wants, so long as it is black." That business philosophy clearly would not work with today's customers. But why did it work for Ford back then? We'll answer that question in this chapter.

To understand Ford's rationale for his limited color palette, we need to explore a regrettable reality regarding most processes—while an ideal process operates with a smooth flow, in churning out flow units at regular intervals of time (the cycle time), many processes must cope with a jerky flow characterized by bursts of activity separated by complete stops. In other words, instead of consistently operating to a steady beat, like a metronome, processes can look more like the stop-and-go flow of rush-hour traffic.

In this chapter, we focus on one reason for interruptions to the cadence of a process: setups. We begin with the definition of a setup and then introduce the Xootr, a product made with a process that has setups. For the Xootr, we evaluate several key process metrics, such as capacity, utilization, and inventory. Next, we decide how best to manage the production process for the Xootr. We then explore why processes with setups can have a hard time making different types of products (like different color cars). The chapter concludes with a nearly 500-year history of how setups were managed before Ford and how they have been managed after Ford.

7.1 Setup Time

You have decided to open up a bakery and you plan to start simple—you will sell only cupcakes and only two types of cupcakes, chocolate and vanilla. To make cupcakes, you need to mix batter, but because of (very) limited startup funding, you have one mixing bowl. That means that after making a batch of chocolate cupcakes, you need to clean the bowl before you make the next batch of vanilla cupcakes. Whether you make a batch of 5 cupcakes at a time of a particular flavor or a batch of 50 cupcakes, the time needed to clean the bowl is the same, say 2 minutes. The cleaning process is a setup and the 2 minutes is the setup time.

To generalize beyond cupcakes, a **setup** is a set of activities (i) that are required to produce units but (ii) for which the time to complete these activities does not depend directly on the number of units subsequently produced. For example, cleaning the mixing bowl is required between batches of vanilla and chocolate cupcakes, and it takes the same amount of time to clean the bowl no matter if a small amount of batter was used or if the bowl was full. To emphasize a point, the key feature of a setup is that it involves a fixed amount of time that is not directly related to the amount actually produced. This distinguishes a setup from "normal" processing activities. For example, adding frosting to the top of a cupcake is an activity that can be described in terms of "seconds per cupcake"—the processing time of adding frosting is not a setup because that processing time depends on how many cupcakes are topped with frosting. On the other hand, the actual baking of the cupcakes is a setup. Baking a cupcake in an oven may require 40 minutes whether the oven contains 1 cupcake, 24 cupcakes, or 72 cupcakes because cupcakes can be baked together. As the time to bake does not depend on the number of cupcakes baked, the baking step is a setup.

Now let's turn our attention to the Xootr, a rugged, serious kick scooter made by Xootr LLC to provide an alternative form of eco-friendly urban transportation (see Photo 7.1). It will allow the rider to cover 1–2 miles within a city quickly and with relative ease, faster than walking and more convenient than a bicycle.

Two components for the Xootr are made with a computer numerically controlled (CNC) milling machine: (1) the steer support, which is the piece that attaches the steering column to the scooter's deck, and (2) the metal ribs, which run under the length of the deck to provide the deck with structural support to carry the rider. Each Xootr needs one steer support and two ribs. The combination of two ribs is called a "rib pair." The collection of a steer support and a rib pair is called a "component set." Each Xootr requires one component set.

Xootr has a single milling machine because it is an expensive piece of equipment. See Photo 7.2 for a picture of the milling machine and steer support inventory.

The first step to produce a part is to set up the milling machine to make that part. During the 60-minute setup time, an operator needs to (i) install the correct tooling to make a part and (ii) calibrate the equipment to the correct dimensions. As the milling machine cycles between rib production and steer support production, the 60-minute setup time can also be called a **changeover time** or **switchover time**—it is the time needed to change over, or switch, production from one type of part to the other. Once the milling machine is set up to produce one of the parts (either a steer support or a rib), it can make the parts reasonably quickly: the milling machine requires 1 minute to make a steer support and also 1 minute to make a rib pair. Thus, the milling machine requires a total of 2 minutes to produce the components for one Xootr.

LO7-1 Identify the setup time in a process.

Setup A set of activities (i) that are required to produce units but (ii) for which the time to complete these activities does not depend directly on the number of units produced.

Changeover time A setup time to change production from one type of product to another.

Switchover time See changeover time.

PHOTO 7.1 The Xootr

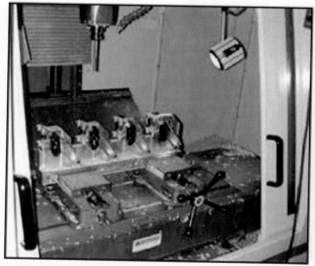

PHOTO 7.2 The milling machine (left) and steer support inventory (right) for the Xootr

Although the milling machine makes critical components for a Xootr, a Xootr isn't a Xootr until it is fully assembled from all of its various components (many of which are purchases from other suppliers). The assembly process is done by three employees who each can assemble a Xootr from its 80 components in 12 minutes. See Photo 7.3. Thus, the combined

TABLE 7.1 Operations Data for the Xootr

Milling—Steer support:	
Setup time (min):	60
Processing time (min)	1
Milling—Rib pair:	
Setup time (min)	60
Processing time (min)	1
Assembly:	
Processing time (min)	12
Number of workers	3
Capacity (Xootrs/min)	0.25

capacity of the three employees is 1/4 Xootr per minute (3 workers/12 minutes per worker per Xootr). With that assembly capacity, one Xootr can be made every 4 minutes. Figure 7.1 displays the relatively simple process flow diagram at Xootr, and Table 7.1 summarizes some of the key operational data for the Xootr.

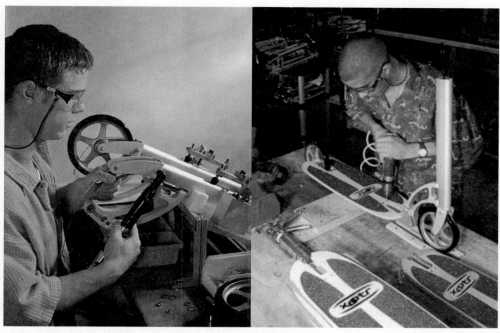

© Xootr LLC

PHOTO 7.3 The assembly process of a Xootr

Figure 7.1
The process flow diagram for making Xootrs

Check Your Understanding 7.1

Question: A blood testing machine at a hospital requires 30 seconds to evaluate each sample, but after testing 50 samples, the machine requires maintenance and recalibration, which requires 5 minutes. What is the setup time of this process?

Answer: The setup time is the time needed to get ready for production while no units are actually tested. The setup time of this process is 5 minutes.

7.2 Capacity of a Process with Setups

What is the capacity of the milling machine? It depends on how the milling machine is operated. Imagine they do something silly like they make one steer support (1 minute), then they switch the milling machine to ribs (60 minutes), then they make one rib pair (1 minute), and then they switch the milling machine to steer supports again (60 minutes). Over the course of 122 minutes, the milling machine produces a grand total of 1 component set. At that pace, the workers in assembly spend a lot of time twiddling their thumbs—they can assemble at the pace of one every four minutes, but milling is giving them the needed parts for a Xootr only after 122 minutes! It is intuitive that this plan makes no sense—if it takes 60 minutes to switch between steer supports and ribs, the smart thing to do is to produce a bunch of the same part so that the milling machine is not wasting too much time in setup mode.

7.2.1 Batches and the Production Cycle

To be more precise about the capacity of the milling machine, let's first define the flow unit. As customers buy Xootrs (as opposed to steer supports or ribs), let's say the flow unit is a Xootr. Thus, we want to evaluate the milling machine's capacity in terms of component sets or, equivalently, Xootrs per minute (because one component set is needed per Xootr). Now let's define a key term. A **production cycle** is a repeating sequence of produced units. For example, say the milling machine is set up to make steer supports, then produces 90 steer supports, then does a setup to make ribs, and then produces 90 rib pairs (i.e., 180 ribs). That would be a production cycle because it is a repeating sequence—at the end of the production cycle it starts all over again. And if this pattern is then followed each cycle, the components needed for 90 Xootrs are made.

Production cycle A repeating sequence of produced units that can include setup time, production time, and idle time.

   The pattern of setups and production is displayed in Figure 7.2. The darker blocks represent a setup time and the lighter blocks represent production of a **batch** of units—a batch is a collection of units. This type of production process is often referred to as a **batch process** because products are made in batches—the milling machine alternates production between a batch of steer supports and a batch of rib pairs. Over the course of a single production cycle, the milling machine makes a batch of 90 Xootrs. (Again, the milling machine actually makes 90 component sets, but we can describe this as if it makes 90 Xootrs.)

Batch A collection of units.

Batch process A type of production in which units are produced in batches.

7.2.2 Capacity of the Setup Resource

Given the production cycle that produces batches of 90 Xootrs, let's again ask the main question we are trying to answer: what is the capacity of the milling machine? In particular, how many Xootrs does the milling machine produce per minute on average?

   Recall, in Chapter 3, Process Analysis, we defined the capacity of a resource with one worker to be

LO7-2 Evaluate the capacity of a resource that has a setup time and is operated with a given batch size.

$$\text{Capacity of a resource with one worker} = \frac{1}{\text{Processing time}}$$

More generally, the capacity of a process equals the following intuitive equation:

$$\text{Capacity} = \frac{\text{Units produced}}{\text{Time to produce the units}}$$

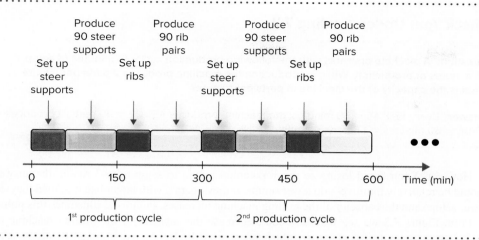

Figure 7.2
A production cycle with 90 component sets

For example, say assembly puts together 90 Xootrs. How long does it take them to assemble 90 Xootrs? They have three workers, so each needs to assemble 90/3 = 30 Xootrs. And each Xootr takes 12 minutes, so each worker requires 12 × 30 = 360 minutes to assemble his or her 30 Xootrs. Thus, based on the data to make 90 Xootrs, the capacity of the assembly process is

$$\text{Capacity} = \frac{\text{Units produced}}{\text{Time to produce the units}}$$
$$= \frac{90 \text{ Xootrs}}{360 \text{ minutes}}$$
$$= \frac{1}{4} \text{Xootr per minute}$$

We can now apply our general equation for capacity in the context of a process with setup times and batches. The "Units produced" is just the batch size or, literally, the number of units produced in the production cycle. The "Time to produce the units" is the total time to complete the production cycle, which includes all of the setup times plus all of the production times in the production cycle. Thus, the equation to evaluate the capacity of a process with batches and setup times is

$$\text{Capacity} = \frac{\text{Batch size}}{\text{Total setup time} + (\text{Processing time} \times \text{Batch size})}$$

To explain the equation, the numerator of the fraction is the batch size, which is the number of units produced in each production cycle. For example, the batch size could be 90 Xootrs. The denominator of the fraction is divided into two parts. The first part is the total setup time in each production cycle. With the milling machine, there are two setups within each production cycle because the milling machine alternates between the production of two different components. So the total setup time is 120 minutes (60 + 60). The second part of the denominator includes the processing time. The processing time for each Xootr is 2 minutes—each Xootr needs one steer support, which requires 1 minute to make, and 1 rib pair, which also requires 1 minute to make. Putting these inputs together, given the production cycle displayed in Figure 7.2, the milling machine's capacity to make component sets is

$$\text{Capacity} = \frac{90 \text{ Xootrs}}{120 \text{ min} + (2 \text{ min per Xootr} \times 90 \text{ Xootrs})} = 0.3 \text{ Xootr per min}$$

Is 0.3 Xootr per minute acceptable? To get a sense of an answer, let's think about what the milling machine could produce if there were no setup times. Without setup times, the milling machine can produce one Xootr every 2 minutes. That translates into a capacity of 0.5 Xootr per minute. Hence, without setup times, the milling machine produces 0.5 Xootr per minute, but with setup times and batches of 90 Xootrs, the milling machine only produces 0.3 Xootr per minute. That means that with batches of 90 Xootrs, setup times cause the milling machine to lose 0.2 Xootr per minute of production capacity (0.5 − 0.3).

Check Your Understanding 7.2

Question: A machine operates with the following production cycle: 15 minutes of setup, 45 minutes of production. While in production the machine produces 2 parts per minute. What is the capacity of the machine in parts per minute?

Answer: Every 15 + 45 = 60 minutes, the machine produces 45 × 2 = 90 parts. It produces 90 parts/60 minutes = 1.5 parts per minute.

How can Xootr avoid losing so much potential output to setup times? Again, the answer should be relatively intuitive—do fewer setups. If they operate with larger batches, then they do fewer setups and the capacity of the milling machine increases. Figure 7.3 illustrates this point.

From Figure 7.3 we see that they could increase the capacity of the milling machine to 0.35 Xootr per minute if they increase the batch size to 140. But even doubling the batch size, to 180 Xootrs, only raises capacity to 0.38 Xootr per minute—a doubling of the batch size resulted only in a 25 percent increase in capacity. In fact, to increase capacity 50 percent, from 0.3 Xootr per minute to 0.45 Xootr per minute, the batch size needs to increase by a whopping 600 percent, to 540 Xootrs. This illustrates a useful observation: increasing the batch size does increase capacity, but capacity increases ever more slowly as the batch size gets large. Put another way, each additional bit of extra capacity requires a larger and larger jump in the batch size.

Figure 7.3 reveals another important observation: operating with a small batch size can destroy a considerable amount of capacity. With a batch size of only 10 Xootrs, the milling machine produces, on average, only 0.071 Xootr per minute, or about one every 14 minutes (1/0.071). That is only about 14 percent of the milling machine's maximum output of 0.5 Xootr per minute! Increasing the batch size might raise capacity by only a minimal amount, but lowering the batch size might decrease capacity considerably.

7.2.3 Capacity and Flow Rate of the Process

The capacity of the milling machine depends on the batch size chosen. In contrast, the capacity of assembly is fixed at 0.25 Xootr per minute, independent of the batch size chosen. So what is the capacity of the process?

In our discussion of process analysis elsewhere, we learned that the capacity of a process equals the capacity of the bottleneck, and the bottleneck is the resource with the smallest capacity. The same concept applies in this situation.

Figure 7.3

The capacity of the milling machine (Xootrs per minute) as a function of the batch size. The arrows indicate that a capacity of 0.25 Xootr per minute is achieved with a batch size of 60.

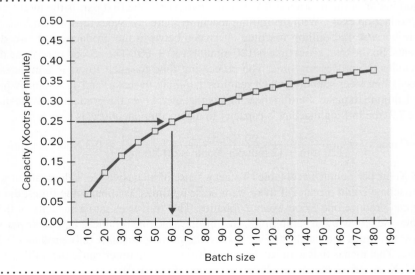

Check Your Understanding 7.3

Question: The setup time for a machine is 30 minutes and the processing time is 5 minutes. The parts produced by this machine are used in an assembly process that has a capacity of 8 units per hour.

a. If the batch size is 6, what is the capacity of the process (in units per hour)?

Answer: The capacity of milling, in units per minute, is 6/(30 + 5 × 6) = 1/10 unit per minute. Converting to units per hour yields 1/10 unit per min × 60 min per hr = 6 units per hr. This is lower than the capacity of assembly, so the machine is the bottleneck and determines the capacity of the process. Therefore, the capacity of the process is 6 units per hr.

b. If the batch size is 30, what is the capacity of the process (in units per hour)?

Answer: The capacity of milling, in units per minute, is 30/(30 + 5 × 30) = 1/6 unit per minute. Converting to units per hour yields 1/6 unit per min × 60 min per hr = 10 units per hr. This is higher than the capacity of assembly, so assembly is the bottleneck and determines the capacity of the process. Therefore, the capacity of the process is 8 units per hour.

· ·

As shown in Figure 7.1, there are only two resources in this process—the milling machine and assembly. Hence, to find the bottleneck, we only need to compare the capacities of these two resources.

Assembly's capacity is always 0.25 Xootr per minute. But as shown in Figure 7.3, the capacity of the milling machine depends on the batch size chosen. In fact, if the batch size is less than 60, then the milling machine's capacity is less than 0.25 Xootr per minute, so then it would be the bottleneck. In contrast, if the batch size is greater than 60 Xootrs, then the milling machine's capacity is greater than 0.25 unit, so assembly would be the bottleneck. In other words, the bottleneck can switch between the milling machine and assembly depending on the size of the batch. This is illustrated in Figure 7.4.

We also learned in Chapter 3, Process Analysis, that the flow rate of the process is the minimum between demand and the process capacity. If demand is less than the process capacity, then the flow rate equals demand and we say the process is demand constrained. On the other hand, if demand is greater than the process capacity, then the flow rate equals the process capacity and we say the process is supply constrained.

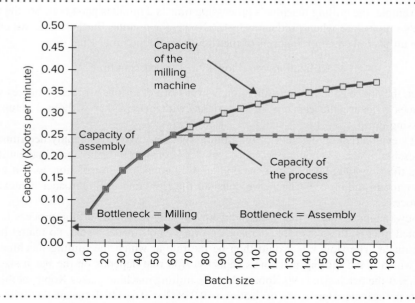

Figure 7.4

Capacity of the milling machine and capacity of the process

7.3 Utilization in a Process with Setups

A process with setup times cannot always be producing—at least every so often the process must do a setup. And, of course, there might also be time in which the process is doing absolutely nothing, neither doing a setup nor producing, which is called **idle time**. This can be frustrating for the process manager, especially because equipment with setup times can be expensive to purchase and maintain. Consequently, managers like to track the utilization of their process—what fraction of time is a piece of equipment in production mode. If utilization drops too low, the manager can intervene to try to determine why the equipment isn't generating output as the manager would like. (See Connections: U.S. Utilization for data on typical utilization levels for the U.S. economy.)

Utilization is the fraction of time a resource is producing output. In Chapter 3, Process Analysis, it is shown that the utilization of a resource without a setup time is

$$\text{Utilization} = \frac{\text{Flow rate}}{\text{Capacity}}$$

That equation for utilization works fine in a process without setups, but we need to generalize it a bit for a process with setups. In particular, with setups, the utilization of a process is

$$\text{Utilization} = \frac{\text{Flow rate}}{\text{Output rate when producing}}$$

The two equations above are not as different as they might seem. They both have the same numerator, the flow rate, which is the rate at which flow units are moving through the process. The denominator of the first is "Capacity," which is the average rate of output for the resource if it is working to produce output all of the time. The denominator of the second is "Output rate when producing," which is also the average rate of output for the resource if it is working to produce output all of the time. However, a resource with a setup time cannot work to produce output all of the time because it must do a setup between batches. Hence, the capacity of a resource with a setup (that accounts for the setup time) is less than its "output rate when producing." In Chapter 3, Process Analysis, we consider only resources that do not have setups. For those resources, the capacity is the same as the output rate when producing.

So what is the "output rate when producing"? It is directly related to the processing time:

$$\text{Output rate when producing} = \frac{1}{\text{Processing time}}$$

For example, the milling machine's processing time is 2 minutes per Xootr. So, the milling machine's output rate when producing is 1/2 Xootr per minute. Furthermore, we can now write the utilization equation in terms of the flow rate and the processing time:

$$\text{Utilization} = \text{Flow rate} \times \text{Processing time}$$

In fact, the above equation for utilization is even correct for one-worker resources without setup times (because the capacity of a resource with one worker without a setup equals 1/Processing time).

So let's evaluate the utilization of the milling machine. We have already determined that the processing time is 2 minutes per Xootr. Now let's consider the other term in the utilization equation, the flow rate. First, let's focus on the milling machine in isolation, as if it were the only resource in the process. Then, we consider the flow rate in the broader context of the entire process.

For now, suppose the milling machine were the only resource and the process is supply constrained; that is, there is ample demand so every Xootr made is sold, no matter how fast they are made. The flow rate would then be the rate at which the milling machine makes Xootrs, which is the milling machine's capacity. And that depends on the batch size. From Figure 7.3, if the batch size is 90 Xootrs, then the milling machine makes Xootrs at the rate of 0.3 Xootr per minute. Hence, the utilization is $0.3 \times 2 = 0.6$, which means that with a batch

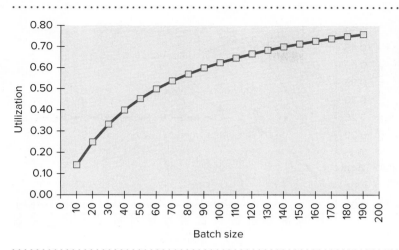

Figure 7.5

The utilization of the milling machine, assuming the milling machine's output is not constrained by demand or other resources (i.e., the flow rate through the milling machine equals the milling machine's capacity)

(Chart: y-axis "Utilization" from 0.00 to 0.80; x-axis "Batch size" from 0 to 200)

size of 90, the milling machine would be producing 60 percent of the time. But if the batch size is 40 Xootrs, then the flow rate is only 0.2 Xootr per minute. In that case, the utilization is 0.2 × 2 = 0.4, or only a 40 percent utilization.

Figure 7.5 displays the utilization of the milling machine for various batch sizes, assuming that we are looking at the milling machine in isolation and there is ample demand. As in Figure 7.3, utilization increases with the batch size. With larger batches, the milling machine spends less time with setups, so it spends a higher fraction of its time actually producing.

Figure 7.5 displays the highest possible utilization for the milling machine for each batch size. This is the utilization of the milling machine if it were the only resource in the process and demand were ample. This is an optimistic situation. To keep the hopeful attitude, let's assume that demand is indeed ample—we can always sell all of the Xootrs we make. But we know for a fact that the milling machine is not the only resource. The other resource is assembly.

As discussed in the previous section, with multiple resources, the flow rate equals the capacity of the bottleneck and the bottleneck is the resource with the lowest capacity. As shown in Figure 7.4, in the Xootr process, the bottleneck is the milling machine when the batch size is fewer than 60 units and it is assembled with batches that are greater than 60 units.

When the batch size is 40 Xootrs, the milling machine is the bottleneck and the flow rate equals the milling machine's capacity of 0.2 Xootr per minute. Thus, as when we viewed the milling machine in isolation, the utilization of the milling machine is 0.20 Xootr/min × 2 min/Xootr = 40 percent. However, things change when the batch size is 90 Xootrs. Now assembly is the bottleneck and the flow rate is 0.25 Xootr per minute. The utilization of the milling machine is then 0.25 Xootr/min × 2 min/Xootr = 50 percent, which is lower than what it would have been if the milling machine operated on its own—from Figure 7.5, on its own, with a batch size of 90 units, the milling machine's utilization is 60 percent. Why the drop in utilization?

When the milling machine's batch size exceeds 60 Xootrs, the milling machine can produce at a faster rate than assembly. For example, with a batch size of 90 Xootrs, the milling machine is producing at the rate of 0.3 Xootr per minute, while assembly is producing only at the rate of 0.25 Xootr per minute. Every minute, if the milling machine were to maintain this rate, 0.30 − 0.25 = 0.05 Xootr per minute would build up in inventory before assembly. This might not seem like much, but eventually even 0.05 Xootr per minute adds up to a decent amount of inventory—this is one Xootr every 20 minutes, 3 per hour, or 24 per 8-hour shift. Eventually somebody in the company would tell the milling machine to take a break—there would be too many components waiting for assembly, taking up too much space. In other words, once the batch size exceeds 60 Xootrs, the milling machine is forced to be idle for some time so that, on average, it doesn't produce any more than 0.25 Xootr per minute in the long run.

Figure 7.6

The flow rate of the Xootr process and the utilization of the milling machine as a function of the batch size

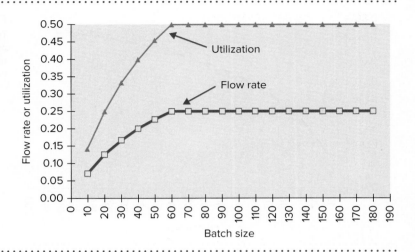

Figure 7.6 plots the flow rate and utilization of the milling machine for various batch sizes when we account for the fact that the flow rate could be constrained by assembly. As we have discussed, when the batch size starts off small, the milling machine is the bottleneck, so it determines the flow rate and thus the milling machine is poorly utilized. As the batch size is increased, the milling machine's capacity increases, increasing the flow rate and its utilization. However, once the batch size reaches a certain threshold (60 Xootrs in this case), further increase in the batch size has no impact on the flow rate because the bottleneck has shifted to another resource (assembly). As the flow rate remains constant for these large batches, so does the utilization.

Check Your Understanding 7.4

Question: Water samples are received to be tested at the rate of 2 per hour. Once set up to conduct tests, the testing equipment can test 3 samples per hour. If the process is demand-constrained, what is the utilization of the testing equipment?

Answer: Because the process is demand-constrained, the flow rate is 2 units per hour. The processing time is 1/3 hr. Utilization = Flow rate × Processing time = 2 units per hr × 1/3 hr = 2/3. Therefore, the utilization of the testing equipment is 2/3.

Question: A lathe requires a 20-minute setup and then requires 3 minutes to produce each unit. The lathe produces in batches of 20 units. The other resource in the process, assembly, can process one unit every 5 minutes. One unit is demanded every 4 minutes.

a. What is the flow rate of this process, in units per hour?

Answer: Demand is 1/4 unit per minute, or 15 units per hour. Assembly's capacity is 1/5 unit per minute, or 12 units per hour. The capacity of the lathe is 20/(20 + 3 × 20) = 1/4 unit per minute, or 15 units per hour. The flow rate is determined by the smallest capacity or demand. In this case, assembly is the bottleneck, so the flow rate is 12 units per hour.

b. What is the utilization of the lathe, expressed as a number between 0 and 1?

Answer: Utilization = Flow rate × Processing time. Flow rate = 12 units per hour and the processing time, which must also be expressed in hours, is 1/20 hour (3 min/60 min per hr). So utilization is 12 units per hour × 1/20 hour = 0.60. Therefore, the utilization of the lathe is 0.60.

CONNECTIONS: U.S. Utilization

What is a typical utilization? This can vary from industry to industry, but Figure 7.7 provides that average utilization across all U.S. industry from 1992 to 2013. As can be seen in the figure, utilizations generally are in the 0.75–0.80 range. When the economy is quickly growing, as in the mid-1990s and 2000s, utilization can rise to over 80 percent. In those situations, demand tends to grow faster than firms can add capacity, allowing (or forcing) the firms to utilize their capacity at a higher level. Historically, utilization has risen to over 90 percent only during wartime periods.

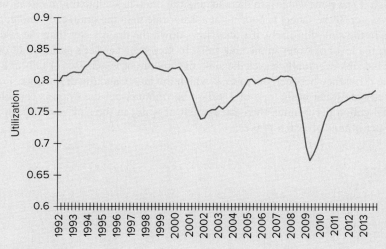

Figure 7.7
Utilization across all industries in the United States (Source: Federal Reserve)

Figure 7.7 also clearly displays the effects of a recession. During the time period displayed in the figure, the United States was in a recession in the early 2000s and utilization dipped below 0.75. As bad as that was, the "great recession" of 2008–2009 caused utilization to drop well below 70 percent. This means that, during that time, only about two-thirds of available capacity was actually utilized, due to the fact that demand dropped very quickly, much faster than firms were able to reduce their capacity. The subsequent uptick in utilization from that recession is due to two factors: demand started to slowly recover and firms reduced their capacity to levels that were commensurate with the new reality. Thus, while utilization fluctuates, it tends to fluctuate in a somewhat narrow band—periods of very high (0.85 or more) or very low (0.70 or less) utilization are not sustainable. But note, this only applies to the economy as a whole. Individual firms may experience very high levels of utilization for long periods of time if they are fortunate enough to grow. On the flip side, even individual firms rarely experience very low levels of utilization for long periods of time, because that situation tends to cause bankruptcy.

7.4 Inventory in a Process with Setups

Both the capacity and the utilization of the milling machine increase as the batch size gets larger. More capacity and higher utilization are both good, so why not operate with really large batches? Yes, we saw that the milling machine's utilization never goes above 50 percent, even for very large batches, but why not choose a big batch size just to be sure that the milling machine does not constrain the flow rate? The reason is simple—inventory.

Let's consider two different cases. Say we watched the Xootr process under two different conditions. In the first, the batch size is 60 Xootrs; in the second, the batch size is 180 Xootrs. Next, we collect data on how many parts are available in the inventory between the milling machine and the assembly process. Finally, we plot out those inventory numbers over time. We get graphs like those in Figure 7.8. Notice the difference? The larger batch size leads to considerably more inventory. So this is why we now evaluate how much inventory there is in the process on average as a function of the chosen batch size.

To help us think about the inventory of Xootr components, let's first consider how the inventory works in a more familiar setting—your sink. A sink can be used for washing hands or dishes, but a sink can do an even more basic task. A sink holds an inventory of water. There is an inflow from your faucet and an outflow through the drain. The faucet has a maximum rate at which it can pour water into the sink and the drain has a maximum rate at which it can suck down water. If the faucet is pouring at a faster rate than the drain can handle, the level of water rises in the sink. Similarly, if water flows down the drain faster than the rate the faucet adds water, the level of water in the sink falls. In fact, because (let's assume) all of the water that enters the sink eventually leaves the sink, the amount of water rises or falls at a rate that is equal to the difference between the rates at which the faucet and the drain work. For instance, if the faucet adds water at the rate of 1 gallon per minute, but the drain is capable of flushing only 0.8 gallon per minute, then the amount of water in the sink increases at the rate of 0.2 gallon per minute ($1 - 0.8 = 0.2$).

LO7-4 Evaluate the average inventory of a product made by a resource that has a setup time.

Figure 7.8

Inventory of steer supports (blue) and rib pairs (green) when the batch size is 60 Xootrs (top graph) or 180 Xootrs (bottom graph)

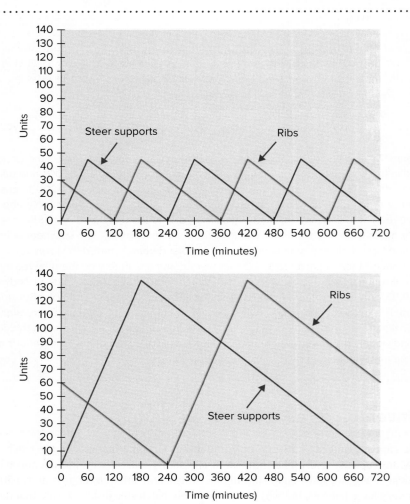

The inventory between the milling machine and assembly behaves just like the water in the sink. The milling machine is the faucet that sometimes adds parts to the inventory and sometimes is turned off. Assembly acts like the drain—it takes the inventory away. Inventory builds when the milling machine adds parts faster than assembly can use them, and inventory falls when assembly uses parts more quickly than the milling machine produces them.

Unlike faucets that tend to operate at different rates, the milling machine has two modes. With one mode, it is producing at its maximum rate of one steer support or one rib pair per minute. With the other mode, it is producing nothing, either because it is being set up or because it is idle (neither in setup nor production). In contrast, because assembly is the bottleneck, it operates only at its maximum rate of 0.25 steering support or 0.25 rib pair every minute.

Look again at Figure 7.8 and let's focus on the case with a batch size of 180 Xootrs. We see that each type of inventory rises and falls over time but their peaks and valleys do not exactly coincide. When the milling machine is making steer supports, the inventory of steer supports increases, while the inventory of rib pairs falls. Similarly, rib pair and steer support inventory move in opposite directions when the milling machine is making ribs. Thus, rather than focusing on total inventory (the sum of steer support and rib pairs), let's focus on the inventory of just steer supports.

At the beginning of the time horizon, Figure 7.8 indicates that there are no steer supports in inventory. At that time, the milling machine must start production of steer supports immediately; otherwise assembly cannot assemble Xootrs due to a lack of steer supports. With the milling machine "faucet" on, steer supports are added to inventory at the rate of 1 per minute. But assembly is "draining" steer supports at the rate of 0.25 per minute. Hence, inventory is building at the rate of 0.75 per minute (1 per minute in, but 0.25 per minute out). Because the milling machine makes 1 steer support every minute, the milling machine produces steering supports for 180 minutes within each production cycle. Hence, for 180 minutes inventory builds at the rate of 0.75 unit per minute. This means that the inventory of steer supports peaks at 135 units = 180 min × 0.75 unit/min.

Inventory of steer supports starts to fall once the milling machine stops producing them. Because assembly is still "draining" steer supports at the rate of 0.25 unit per minute, inventory falls at the rate of 0.25 unit per minute. Given that at the peak there are 135 units in inventory, it takes 135 units/(0.25 units/min) = 540 minutes for the inventory of steer supports to drop down to zero again. During that time, the milling machine does a setup to produce ribs, produces ribs, completes a setup to produce steer supports again, and waits through some idle time (because, with a batch of 180 Xootrs, milling's capacity is greater than the flow rate). If all goes well, the milling machine is again ready to produce steer supports at time 180 + 540 = 720, just as the inventory of steer supports drops to zero. At that point, the pattern of rising and falling inventory begins again. Some refer to this as the "saw-toothed" inventory pattern.

By carefully watching the "faucet" and the "drain" of our inventory process, we are able to calculate the maximum inventory of steer supports in the process. Although that method works, the following equation provides a more direct way to evaluate the maximum inventory:

$$\text{Maximum inventory} = \text{Batch size} \times \text{Processing time} \left(\frac{1}{\text{Processing time}} - \text{Flow rate} \right)$$

The first part, Batch size × Processing time, is the amount of time it takes to make the batch. The second part of the equation is the rate at which inventory builds during production. Note, we can write the equation above in the following simpler form:

$$\text{Maximum inventory} = \text{Batch size} \times [1 - (\text{Flow rate} \times \text{Processing time})]$$

Just to be sure that the equation is correct, let's use it for the steer support inventory with a batch size of 180 Xootrs. The processing time is 1 minute per steer support—we must use the processing time of steer supports (rather than component sets) because we are tracking steer support inventory. The flow rate is 0.25 steer support per minute because assembly is the bottleneck (and it can assemble only 0.25 Xootr per minute). Plugging those values into the equation yields:

Figure 7.9

Maximum inventory of steer supports as a function of the batch size

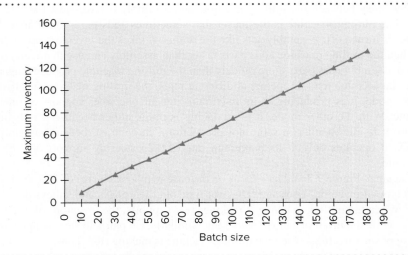

Maximum inventory $= 180$ units $\times [1 - (0.25$ unit per min $\times 1$ min per unit$)]$
$= 135$ units

But why is it useful to evaluate the maximum inventory? Aren't we interested in the average inventory? Shouldn't we record the inventory at various points in time and then take the average of all of those observations to derive the average inventory? We could do that, but it is a lot of work. Just look at Figure 7.8. Inventory varies considerably over time. If we took an observation every 5 minutes, then over the 720 minutes of a single production cycle, we would need 144 observations. What a pain. Fortunately, there is a better approach.

It turns out that when inventory follows a saw-toothed pattern, the average inventory is simply half of the maximum inventory:

$$\text{Average inventory} = \frac{\text{Maximum inventory}}{2}$$
$$= \frac{1}{2} \times \text{Batch} \times [1 - (\text{Flow rate} \times \text{Processing time})]$$

So once we know the maximum inventory, we are only a quick step away from the average inventory—just take the maximum inventory and divide by 2. So the average inventory of steer supports is 67.5 units (135/2), assuming it operates with batches of 180 units.

At this point, we cannot say whether 67.5 units is too much, too little, or just the right amount of inventory. However, if we want less inventory, then we need to reduce the maximum inventory, and to reduce the maximum inventory requires operating with a smaller batch size. By the same logic, if we increase the batch size, then our maximum inventory increases along with the average inventory. Hence, the batch size chosen has a considerable influence on the amount of inventory that is in the process, as is clearly illustrated in Figure 7.9.

Check Your Understanding 7.5

Question: A machine produces two parts. The switchover time between parts is 10 minutes. The process is demand-constrained and demand is received at the rate of 20 per hour. The machine produces 180 units of a part before switching to the other part. The processing time is 1 min per part. What is the average inventory of a part?

Answer: The batch size is 180. The flow rate is 20 per hour or 1/3 per min. The processing time is 1 min per part. Therefore, Maximum inventory = Batch size [1 − (Flow rate × Processing time)] = 180[1 − (1/3 × 1)] = 120. Average inventory = Maximum inventory/2 = 120/2 = 60 units.

7.5 Choose the Batch Size in a Process with Setups

Xootr's choice of batch size influences the capacity of the milling machine (see Figure 7.3), the milling machine's utilization (see Figure 7.6), and the amount of inventory it has in its process (see Figure 7.9). So what batch size should it choose? If the batch size is "too small," then the milling machine's capacity is also small because it spends a considerable amount of time in setup mode. If the milling machine's capacity is small, then it may be the bottleneck of the entire process, thereby constraining the flow rate. This is clearly not desirable, especially if the process is supply-constrained.

To avoid constraining the process, it can choose a "large" batch size. This ensures that the capacity of the milling machine is high, higher than the capacity of assembly. With a large batch size, the milling machine is not the bottleneck of the process and therefore no longer constrains the process's flow rate. However, the larger the batch, the more inventory it has in its process. Inventory is costly to hold and increases the flow time through the process, neither of which is desirable. So a "too large" batch size is also not desirable.

The "just right" batch size makes a smart trade-off between capacity and inventory. We want capacity to be sufficiently large so that the milling machine does not constrain the flow rate of the process. But we do not want the batch size to be larger than that because otherwise there is more inventory than needed in the process. In short, we want the milling machine to achieve the target capacity—the *target capacity* for a resource is the smallest capacity that does not reduce the flow rate of the process. For this process, the target capacity is 0.25 Xootr per minute—if the milling machine has a capacity of 0.25 Xootr per minute, then the milling machine would not constrain the flow rate of the process.

In general, the target capacity should be chosen as follows. If the process is demand-constrained (i.e., the rate of demand is less than the capacity of the bottleneck), then the target capacity is the demand rate—there is no reason to set the process's capacity greater than demand. If the process is supply-constrained (i.e., the rate of demand is greater than the capacity of the bottleneck), then the target capacity is the capacity of the bottleneck.

From Figure 7.3, we can see via the drawn arrows that a target capacity of 0.25 Xootr per minute is achieved with a batch size of 60 units. While we can always use a graph to identify the batch size that achieves a target capacity, this method is cumbersome. Alternatively, we can start with the equation for the capacity of a process with setup times:

$$\text{Target capacity} = \frac{\text{Batch size}}{\text{Total setup time} + (\text{Batch size} \times \text{Processing time})}$$

If we use that equation to solve for the batch size, we arrive at the following (equivalent) equation:

$$\text{Batch size} = \frac{\text{Target capacity} \times \text{Total setup time}}{1 - (\text{Target capacity} \times \text{Processing time})}$$

Let's see if the equation gives us the same answer as our graph. The total setup time with each production cycle is 120 minutes, the target capacity is 0.25 Xootr per minute, and the processing time is 2 minutes per Xootr. Thus,

$$\text{Batch size} = \frac{0.25 \text{ unit/min} \times 120 \text{ min}}{1 - (0.25 \text{ unit/min} \times 2 \text{ min/unit})} = 60 \text{ units}$$

If the milling machine is operated with a batch size of 60, then the company will carry the least amount of inventory while maximizing the flow rate through the process. If it were to carry less inventory, it would have a smaller batch size and then the milling machine would constrain the flow rate. If it were to carry more inventory, it would have a larger batch size but the same flow rate through the process—excessively large batches are pointless because they increase neither the utilization nor the flow rate, but they do increase flow time (because inventory increases), which is clearly undesirable.

Check Your Understanding 7.6

Question: A machine does three setups per production cycle. Each setup requires 15 minutes. The processing time is 0.75 minute. What batch size achieves a capacity of 40 units per hour?

Answer: The target capacity is 40 units per hour, or 40/60 = 2/3 unit per minute. The processing time is 3/4 minute per unit. The total setup time is 3 × 15 = 45 minutes. The desired batch size is then $\frac{2}{3}$ unit/min × 45 min/$\left[1 - \left(\frac{2}{3} \text{ units/min} \times \frac{3}{4} \text{ min/unit}\right)\right]$ = 60 units.

....

7.6 Setup Times and Product Variety

LO7-6 Find the production quantities of each item produced by a resource such that the resource minimizes inventory while satisfying all demand.

As we have seen in the case of the Xootr production process, setup times often occur due to the need to change over production from one type of output to another. In the case of the milling machine, the two types of outputs are combined into a single product (a Xootr). But there are also cases in which the different outputs are sold as separate products. This raises the following question: What is the impact of product variety on a process with setup times? To explore this question, let's consider a simple process that makes two kinds of soup: chicken noodle soup and tomato soup.

Demand for chicken noodle soup is 100 gallons per hour while demand for tomato soup is 75 gallons per hour. Switching from one type of soup to another requires 30 minutes to clean the production equipment so that one flavor does not disrupt the flavor of the next soup—imagine finding something chunky in your tomato soup, not knowing that it is only a piece of chicken. Once production begins, the process can make 300 gallons per hour of either type of soup.

As with the milling machine, the capacity of our soup process depends on how we manage it. Small batches lead to frequent switchovers, which lead to low capacity. Large batches generate greater capacity, but also more inventory. So we want to operate the soup process to achieve a target capacity, a capacity that does not constrain the flow rate and does not result in the company carrying more inventory than is needed to maximize the flow rate.

Xootr is supply constrained, which means that it can sell everything it can make. That also means it cannot sell more than 0.25 Xootr per minute because that is the capacity of assembly. In the case of our soup manufacturer, production is not constrained by another resource, but rather by demand itself. In other words, the soup manufacturer is demand-constrained. So it cannot sell more than 175 gallons of soup per hour (100 chicken noodle and 75 tomato). Thus, the target capacity for the soup manufacturer is 175 gallons per hour—if the soup process yields exactly a capacity of 175 gallons per hour, then it minimizes its inventory while also maximizing its flow rate.

The natural flow unit in this context is a "gallon of soup." Some of the gallons produced during a production cycle are chicken noodle and some are tomato. In fact, for every 100 gallons of chicken noodle produced, it should make 75 gallons of tomato because that is what it can sell in the market.

A production cycle of soup consists of two setups and two production runs. In particular, it must set up to make tomato soup, then make tomato soup, then set up to make chicken noodle soup, and finally make the chicken noodle soup. Each setup time is 0.5 hour, so the total setup time during the production cycle is 1 hour. It can produce 300 gallons per hour, which is equivalent to the processing time of 1/300 hour per gallon.

Recall with the milling machine that the processing time is 2 minutes per Xootr because the machine requires 1 minute to produce one steer support and 1 minute to produce one rib pair. So, with the milling machine, we added the two processing times together, but with the soup manufacturer we don't seem to be doing so. Why? Because the processing time should be the total time to make one flow unit. In the case of the milling machine, the flow unit is a Xootr (or, more precisely, a component set). It takes a total of 2 minutes for the milling machine to make the components for a Xootr. With soup, the flow unit is a gallon of soup—just a single gallon. And it takes only 1/300 of an hour to make a single gallon of soup. In other words, there is no need to combine chicken noodle and tomato soups to construct a flow unit. In contrast, with the milling machine, we do need to combine the two parts to make a flow unit.

We now have the information needed to determine the batch size that achieves our target capacity of 175 gallons per hour:

$$\text{Batch size} = \frac{\text{Target capacity} \times \text{Total setup time}}{1 - (\text{Target capacity} \times \text{Processing time})}$$

$$= \frac{175 \text{ gal/hr} \times 1 \text{ hr}}{1 - \left(175 \text{ gal/hr} \times \frac{1}{300} \text{ hr/gal}\right)}$$

$$= 420 \text{ gallons}$$

Hence, each production cycle should make 420 gallons of soup. So the production of specific flavors matches demand, 100 out of every 175 gallons produced must be chicken noodle and 75 out of every 175 gallons must be tomato. Thus, of the 420 gallons, $420 \times 100/(100 + 75) = 240$ gallons should be chicken soup and the remainder, $420 - 240 = 180$ gallons, should be tomato.

We can also evaluate flow rate, utilization, and inventory. As we have chosen the batch size to match our capacity to demand, the flow rate equals the demand rate, which is 175 gallons per hour. Utilization is therefore

$$\text{Utilization} = \text{Flow rate} \times \text{Processing time}$$

$$= 175 \text{ gal per hr} \times \frac{1}{300} \text{ hr per gal} = 0.58$$

To evaluate the maximum inventory of chicken noodle soup, use 240 gallons as the batch size and 100 gallons per hour as the flow rate:

$$\text{Maximum inventory} = \text{Batch size} [1 - (\text{Flow rate} \times \text{Processing time})]$$

$$= 240 \text{ gal} \left[1 - \left(100 \text{ gal per hr} \times \frac{1}{300} \text{ hr per gal}\right)\right]$$

$$= 160 \text{ gals}$$

Average inventory is then half of the maximum, which is $160/2 = 80$ gallons. These results are summarized in Table 7.2 under the column labeled Scenario I.

TABLE 7.2 Performance Measures for Three Scenarios; Scenarios II and III Expand Variety Relative to Scenario I by Adding Onion Soup

		Scenario I	Scenario II	Scenario III
Demand (gal/hr)	Chicken	100	100	80
	Tomato	75	75	65
	Onion		30	30
	Total	175	205	175
Production cycle batch (gal)	Chicken	240	474	288
	Tomato	180	355	234
	Onion		142	108
	Total	420	971	630
Utilization		58%	68%	58%
Average inventory (gal)	Chicken	80.0	157.9	105.6
	Tomato	67.5	133.2	91.7
	Onion		63.9	48.6
	Total	147.5	355.1	245.9

To understand the impact of variety on this process, suppose we add a third kind of soup to our product offering, onion soup. Fortunately, the marketing department believes that all of the demand for onion soup will be incremental, meaning that adding onion soup to the mix only adds demand. In particular, we can continue to sell 100 gallons per hour of chicken noodle and 75 gallons per hour of tomato. But now we can also sell 30 gallons per hour of onion soup. Thus, with three soups we can sell a total of 205 gallons per hour (100 + 75 + 30). Let's keep "one gallon of soup" as our flow unit. Consequently, the processing time remains 1/300 hour per gallon. However, the total setup time per production cycle is now 1.5 hours (three changeovers due to three types of soup). The batch size that minimizes our inventory while meeting our demand is

$$\text{Batch size} = \frac{\text{Target capacity} \times \text{Total setup time}}{1 - (\text{Target capacity} \times \text{Processing time})}$$

$$= \frac{205 \text{ gal/hr} \times 1.5 \text{ hr}}{1 - \left(205 \text{ gal/hr} \times \frac{1}{300} \text{ hr/gal}\right)} = 971 \text{ gallons}$$

Table 7.2 lists the production quantities for each flavor, the utilization, and the average inventory for this scenario in the second column.

So what happened when we added onion soup to the mix? In short, we have to add a considerable amount of additional inventory—a production cycle of 971 gallons requires more inventory than a production cycle of 420 gallons. To be specific, with just two products, the average total inventory of soup is 147.5 gallons. But with onion soup added to the mix, the average inventory jumps 141 percent to 355.1 gallons.

Why did inventory increase when onion soup was added to the mix? Setup times are to blame. With more varieties, there are more setups within each production cycle. This reduces the capacity of the production cycle (no soup is made during a setup). To increase the capacity back to the desired flow rate (which is even higher), we need to operate with larger batches (longer production cycles), and that leads to more inventory.

One may argue that the previous analysis is too optimistic—adding onion soup to the mix should steal some demand away from the other flavors. However, the spirit of our finding (that inventory increases with variety) does not change. To demonstrate, consider the opposite extreme—adding onion soup does not expand overall demand; it only steals demand from the other flavors. Specifically, the overall flow rate remains 175 gallons per hour, with or without onion soup. With onion soup, the demand rates are 80, 65, and 30 gallons per hour for chicken noodle, tomato, and onion, respectively. Table 7.2 provides the results from this scenario in the third column. Inventory doesn't increase as much as when onion soup expanded total demand, but it still increases considerably, from 147.5 gallons to 245.9 gallons. That is a 67 percent increase!

The conclusion from this investigation is that setup times and product variety do not mix very well. (See Connections: Legos for an example of a company that faces this issue.) If variety is added to a process with setup times, and by doing so the process is forced to make more setups, then the process will have to increase batch sizes. Larger batch sizes lead to more inventory, and from Little's Law we know that more inventory leads to longer flow time.

CONNECTIONS: LEGO

© *Management GmbH & Co. KG/iStock/Getty Images/RF*

LEGO is the well-known toy company that makes those plastic bricks (which the company likes to call "elements") that can be converted into myriad vehicles, animals, buildings, and machines, just to name a few possibilities. In fact, there are 915 million ways to combine just six LEGO® bricks of the same color! Try to get your head around the number of combinations that could be created from the 55 billion elements it manufactured in 2014! And then think about the manufacturing challenge it faces to make the 3000 different types of elements in 50 different colors. Each of those elements is made with a unique mold and there is a setup time for each batch produced of an element. Because it needs to produce 105,000 elements every minute of every hour of every day of the year, it cannot afford to waste too much time in product switchovers.

Offering product variety to consumers is clearly part of LEGO's strategy. One brick in one color will not captivate the imagination of children (or adults) for very long. But that doesn't mean that LEGO should produce whatever its designers can dream up. That is what it did in 2004, and it nearly bankrupted the company—too many different elements contributed to costs that were too high and not sustainable. While 3000 elements might seem like a lot, it is actually a very reasonable number given the variety of different kits that are sold. To put this in perspective, 55 billion elements produced each year among 3000 different types translates into about 18 million units of each type of element, which is indeed a decent volume for each type. And, most importantly, the strategy seems to have worked—in the decade between 2004 and 2013, the company's revenues have quadrupled and it has never been more profitable.

Sources: Hansegard, J. "What It Takes to Build a Lego Hobbit (and Gollum and More)." *The Wall Street Journal,* December 19, 2012. The Lego Group. "A Short Presentation 2014." http://aboutus.lego.com/en-us/lego-group/company-profile.

Check Your Understanding 7.7

Question: Five types of fabric are made on a machine. The machine requires a 2-hour setup time to switch between types of fabric. Once in production, the machine makes 60 meters per hour of fabric. Demands for the 5 types of fabric are 10, 10, 8, 8, and 4 meters per hour, respectively. How many meters of fabric should they produce in each production cycle?

Answer: The total setup time is 5 × 2 = 10 hours. The processing time is 1/60 hr per meter. Total demand is 10 + 10 + 8 + 8 + 4 = 40 meters per hour. The batch size for the production cycle is 40 × 10/(1 − 40/60) = 1200 meters.

Question: How many meters of fabric should they produce of the first type of fabric?

Answer: The first fabric is 10/40 = 1/4 of total demand. So the production of the first fabric should be 1/4 of the batch size for the production cycle, which is 1/4 × 1200 meters = 300 meters.

7.7 Managing Processes with Setup Times

So far, we have not found much to like about setup times. During a setup time, the process does not produce output. As a result of setup times, a process must work in batches, and batches lead to inventory. Even though customers value variety, the amount of inventory needed grows considerably as variety is added to a process with setup times.

7.7.1 Why Have Setup Times: The Printing Press

LO7-7 Explain the different approaches for managing a process with setup times.

Given all of the bad news about setups, why would anyone choose to include a resource with setups in their process? To answer that question, think about the alternative. For example, if Xootr didn't have a milling machine to make steer supports and ribs, how would they make those parts? If this is even possible, they would make each part "by hand." There is very little setup time with a manual process, but good luck finding a worker who can produce a steer support from a rectangular piece of metal in one minute, or even one hour. While setups cause the milling machine to not produce for two hours in every production cycle, as long as the milling machine runs with a sufficiently large batch size, it can pump out, on average, steer supports and rib pairs at a fast enough rate to more than keep up with assembly. And that is the reason why resources with setups are implemented—while there are negative consequences to setups, a resource with a setup generally also has the advantage of a short processing time, much shorter than the next best alternative. The advantage of a fast processing time can outweigh the disadvantage of the setup.

The printing press provides a nice illustration of the trade-off between annoying setups and fast processing times. (See Figure 7.10.) Before Johannes Gutenberg invented the printing press with movable type (around the year 1440), books needed to be written by a time-consuming manual process. A handwritten process has no setup time but a very long processing time for each page. In contrast, with a printing press and movable type, Gutenberg was able to produce books far more efficiently. It did take time to set up the press before it could print a page (metal molds of each letter are manually placed in a tray to form the text of the page), but once set up, the press could print many copies of the page with relative ease. It is hard to overstate the importance of this invention. Due to the dramatic reduction in the cost of printing, books became affordable to a much larger fraction of the population, and the production of books soared. This in turn facilitated the sharing of knowledge and is widely considered to be a crucial catalyst that enabled the Renaissance. All of this from an invention that accepted a setup time to be rewarded with a fast processing time.

While you might be resigned to the fact that setup times are the necessary price to pay for fast processing, there are several solutions to this problem. The first may be obvious: you can avoid setups if you have multiple machines. For example, say Xootr purchased a second

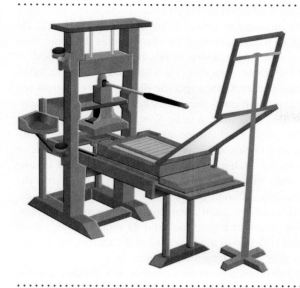

Figure 7.10
A depiction of an early printing press

milling machine. The first milling machine could be set up to produce steer supports and the second machine could be set up to produce rib pairs. With a machine dedicated to each part, there is never a need to do a second setup. If milling machines are cheap, then this is a great solution. Unfortunately, milling machines are not cheap. And this is a common problem with this approach—resources that have setup times tend to be expensive. Furthermore, many resources with setup times are used to produce much more variety than merely two or three products. Try to imagine how difficult it would have been for Gutenberg to build one printing press for each page of every book he wanted to print! So, if it is possible to avoid setup times by purchasing more resources, then by all means do so. Just don't expect this to be a viable option in most cases.

7.7.2 Reduce Variety or Reduce Setups: SMED

About 450 years after Gutenberg, in the early 1900s, Henry Ford had another solution for the problem of setup times. Remember the quote from the beginning of the chapter: "A customer can have any color he wants, so long as it is black." Ford knew that switching between different colors of paint creates a setup time in the process. And Ford recognized that setup times and variety don't mix well, in the sense that if he tried to provide variety in a process with setup times, then he couldn't meet his aggressive goal of a vehicle affordable to the middle class. So Ford's solution to the setup time–variety conundrum was simply to get rid of the variety (Photo 7.4).

PHOTO 7.4 An early Ford automobile from 1908.

Courtesy of Library of Congress, Prints and Photographs Division
[LC-USZ62-21222]

Fast forward about another 50 years and a different approach toward setups emerged on a different continent. Shigeo Shingo was an engineer working for Toyota in the late 1960s. He noticed that it could take hours, if not half of a day, to change the massive dies that were used to stamp metal parts. The operation of a stamping machine is relatively straightforward. A very heavy die is lifted above a piece of flat metal, then dropped with enough force to transform the metal into the desired shape. Each part requires a specific die, so changing between parts requires changing dies. But, as already mentioned, these dies are heavy, big, and cumbersome. So swapping out one die for another took time, a setup time. Shingo's solution was to reengineer the die in such a way as to allow one die to be exchanged for another within nine or fewer minutes. This principle became known as **Single-Minute Exchange of Die**, or **SMED** for short—reengineer the setup process so that the setup time can be achieved in nine (a single digit) or fewer minutes. Once setup times are reduced to such small durations, the process can frequently switch between making different things while maintaining the necessary capacity to not constrain the overall flow. Frequent changeovers mean small batches, which mean that the high costs of carrying inventory are not incurred. In short, Toyota's solution to the tension between setup times and variety was not to get rid of the variety, but to "get rid" of the setup times to the point where they are no longer a nuisance.

It is one thing to know that reducing setup times is good for a process; it is another to know how to do it. To begin, it is useful to divide the various tasks involved with a setup into two types: **internal setups** and **external setups**. Internal tasks can only be done during the actual setup; that is, when the machine is not producing. External tasks can be done while production continues to occur. For example, mounting a jig onto a milling machine probably cannot be done while the machine is running—that is an internal setup activity. Reconfiguring a jig so that it can be ready to make the next part may be feasible when the jig is not attached to the machine—that would be an external setup.

Once the set of internal and external tasks is identified, be sure that all external tasks are indeed done outside of the setup. That reduces the total setup time to just internal activities. But don't stop there. Attempt to change an internal setup into an external setup. For example, if a tool needs a certain pressure to function properly, raise the pressure outside of the setup time (an external task) rather than during the setup time (an internal task). Finally, consider how each remaining internal activity can either be reduced, simplified, or eliminated. Once you have gone through these steps (identify internal versus external activities, convert internal to external activities, and reduce internal activities), you will have reduced the setup time, possibly by a substantial amount. See Connections: Formula 1 for more examples of internal versus external setups.

7.7.3 Smooth the Flow: Heijunka

Toyota didn't only focus on setups associated with die exchanges. They were also concerned with how batching influenced the efficiency of their upstream suppliers. Take a look again at Figure 7.8, especially the lower graph with the large batches. Large batches mean long intervals of time between the production of the same part. The steering support is produced for the first 180 minutes and then production doesn't start again for another 540 minutes. Imagine you were the supplier of aluminum blocks for steering supports. Instead of a nice constant flow of one block every four minutes, for 180 minutes the milling machine requests one block every minute (four times faster than the average rate) and then requests zero blocks per minute for the next 540 minutes. Talk about feast or famine! Toyota realized that if it were to operate with large batches, then the demand it would impose on its suppliers would be very uneven. Such uneven demand would increase the supplier's costs, and because the supplier has to make a profit, this in turn would increase Toyota's costs. The solution is painfully simple but challenging to implement—attempt to make each type of product as close to the rate of demand as possible. For example, suppose every four weeks Toyota needs to make 10,000 midsize cars, 75 percent of which are sedans and 25 percent are wagons. Toyota could spend three weeks making 7500 sedans, then switch to making 2500 wagons for one week, then switch back to 7500 sedans for another three weeks, and so on. The supplier of parts for the

Single-Minute Exchange of Die (SMED) A goal to reduce the setup time to a single-digit number of minutes (i.e., nine or fewer).

Internal setups Activities that can only be done during the actual setup, for example, when the machine is not producing.

External setups Activities that can be done while production continues to occur.

wagon would see demand only one week out of every four. Now contrast this situation with the following plan: every day, 75 percent of the vehicles are sedans and 25 percent are wagons. This is great for the parts suppliers for the wagon because now they receive some demand every day. But why stop there? In fact, for every four cars that roll down the assembly line, three of them could be sedans and one could be a wagon. Now the suppliers for the wagon are likely to have some demand every hour!

This strategy of assembling different products in very small batches one after the other is called **mixed-model assembly**. Toyota calls it **heijunka**—schedule production to resemble as much as possible the true rate of demand. As already mentioned, heijunka is a simple idea but it is challenging to implement. First of all, if there are any substantial setup times when switching between products, then heijunka will lead to an inefficient process—switching back and forth between product types, when there are setup times, will only lead to low utilization and little time actually producing. So, to implement heijunka, it is absolutely necessary to reduce setup times to the point were they are essentially inconsequential.

Figure 7.11 illustrates the trade-offs we just discussed. A process with long setups could still offer considerable variety, but at the cost of very low efficiency. That would place the process in the upper left corner of the trade-off curve. Ford's solution was to dramatically reduce variety to gain much higher efficiency. In effect, Ford moved down the trade-off curve. SMED and heijunka enabled Toyota to push the trade-off curve out and to the right. This allowed Toyota to increase both variety and efficiency. While this was an important innovation, Toyota actually discovered and implemented many more effective ideas to improve manufacturing. In fact, Chapter 8 is dedicated to the various facets of the Toyota Production System.

Mixed-model assembly An assembly process in which production resembles the true rate of demand, even over a short time horizon. Also known as heijunka.

Heijunka Leveling production by reducing variation in the work schedule that arises from either demand variation or the desire to run production or transports in large batches. This is a principle of the Toyota Production System that strives to have production match the true rate of demand.

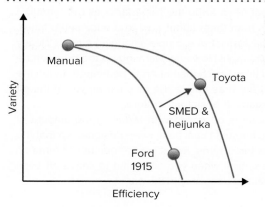

Figure 7.11
The trade-off between variety and efficiency and the use of SMED and heijunka to move the trade-off curve

CONNECTIONS: Formula 1

Formula 1 racing involves superfast cars driving (up to 350 km/hr) around very curvy tracks (reaching lateral acceleration up to five times gravity), sometimes on tracks through city streets (as in the Monaco Grand Prix). Races are won by mere seconds, so to be competitive requires an extreme degree of precision. This is especially true in the pit stop—in all events, the cars must stop one or more times during the race for new tires, additional fuel, and other services.

So how is formula 1 racing related to setup times? Simple—each pit stop is like a setup, a time that is necessary for production (the car cannot continue without the stop), but no production is actually done (the car doesn't make forward progress during the pit stop). And just as in the concept of SMED, whenever there is a setup time, effort should be made

Continued

to reduce the setup time as much as possible. To that end, the formula 1 pit crews are the supreme masters—imagine trying to change all four tires on your car in several seconds!

Although there are few organizations that need to do the same tasks as the formula 1 pit crew, we can all learn several principles from them about how to reduce setup times. First, consider the set of internal and external tasks. For example, changing a tire is clearly an internal task—good luck doing that at 200 mph! However, warming up the tires can be an external task—instead of putting on cold tires, which then need to be heated during the race to reach maximum effectiveness, heat the tires before the race car arrives at the pit stop so that it can leave the pit with tires already at peak temperature.

Next, whenever possible, a formula 1 team is obsessed with reducing the amount of work needed within the setup. For example, formula 1 cars have been designed so that the wheel nuts can be tightened with as few as three turns. Reducing the number of turns on each wheel nut might seem trivial, but it is critical when you are trying to shave off even tenths of a second from the time the race car needs to stay in the pit.

Source: http://www.autosport.com/news/report.php/id/108724

Conclusion

An ideal process operates at a fast and consistent pace. Unfortunately, not all resources can work that way. Some provide fast processing, but at the expense of setup time, which is nonproductive time needed to start production, and independent of the amount subsequently produced.

When a resource has a setup time, then there isn't a simple answer to the question "what is the capacity of the resource?" It depends on how the resource is managed. If the resource produces in small batches and does frequent setups, then its capacity will be low. Alternatively, if the resource produces in large batches and does infrequent setups, then its capacity will be greater. Similarly, small batches yield low utilization while large batches increase utilization. So if the objective were merely to increase capacity or utilization, the manager should choose to operate with large batches. But this does not come for free. As batch sizes increase, so does the average inventory held in the process. Inventory is costly to hold and it lengthens the time units spend in the process, neither of which are desirable. So the manager should choose the "just right" batch size—one large enough to ensure that the process flow is not constrained, but no larger, otherwise inventory increases without any compensating increase in flow rate.

Setup times are not a problem for a resource that needs only one setup. But most resources with setup times are designed to provide fast processing times for different parts or products. However, as variety is added to the mix of products a resource needs to make, inventory can grow considerably—each new variant added to the mix causes the batches for all variants to increase, thereby increasing inventory, often by a considerable amount.

There have been two very different approaches to the tension between setup times and variety. The Henry Ford solution was to eliminate as much variety as possible. With less (or no) variety, setups do not need to be done often and so they are not too problematic. But consumers like variety. So how can a firm offer consumers the variety they desire, at a price they can afford, and also allow the firm to make some profit? The solution from Toyota was to change the setup process so as to drastically reduce the setup time. When the setup time is small, the resource can perform small batches without losing capacity. In the ideal world of small setup times, a firm can offer variety without generating the costs of high inventory.

Maybe more so than any other chapter, this chapter illustrates the three inhibitors of operations management discussed in the introductory chapter: variability, waste, and inflexibility. Component or product variety creates variability that generates the need for setups. As the setup time does not actually produce output, it does not directly generate value for consumers, so it can be considered waste in the process. The same can be said for the inventory in the process—customers don't value the inventory per se, but the inventory does create holding costs. The simple solution for waste is to always work to reduce or eliminate it. Finally, setup times clearly create inflexibility in a process. A process without a setup time has the flexibility to switch quickly and cheaply between different types of output. But an inflexible process with setup times is forced to work in batches, which contribute to inventory and prevent the process from changing its output. As always, an operations manager should be on the lookout to increase the flexibility of his or her process. An obvious strategy is to reduce setup times.

Summary of Learning Objectives

LO7-1 Identify the setup in a process

A setup is a set of activities that are needed to get ready for production but don't actually involve production; the time to complete these activities is independent of the subsequent number of units produced.

LO7-2 Evaluate the capacity of a process that has a setup time and is operated with a given batch size

A production cycle is a repeating sequence of batches. The duration of the production cycle is increased as larger batches are produced. In turn, increasing the size of the production batches increases the capacity of the resource with a setup time. The capacity of the process is determined by the capacity of the bottleneck. When the batch size is small, the bottleneck might be the resource with the setup time. However, as the batch size is increased, so is the capacity of that resource. So the bottleneck may shift to another resource in the process.

LO7-3 Evaluate the utilization of a resource that has a setup time

Utilization is the fraction of time a resource is producing. A resource with a setup time cannot be utilized 100 percent because sometimes it must be doing a setup. However, like capacity, utilization depends critically on the size of the production batch. The larger the batch size, the more utilized the resource will be as long as the resource is the bottleneck (i.e., it determines the flow rate through the process). Once the batch size reaches a certain level, the resource no longer is the bottleneck. After that point, an increase in the batch size raises the capacity of the resource but does not increase the flow rate through the process or the resource's utilization.

LO7-4 **Evaluate the average inventory of a product made by a resource that has a setup time**

The average inventory associated with a resource with a setup depends on the batch size. The larger the batch size, the greater the average inventory.

LO7-5 **Find the batch size that minimizes inventory while not constraining the flow through a process**

There is a trade-off between capacity and inventory—large batches yield greater capacity but also greater inventory. Furthermore, once a batch size reaches a critical level, further increases in the batch size have no impact on capacity but do continue to increase inventory. Thus, an ideal batch size is one that minimizes the average inventory in the system while not constraining the flow rate. That batch size yields a capacity for the resource that matches the bottleneck flow rate of the other resources in the process or demand.

LO7-6 **Find the production quantities of each item produced by a resource such that the resource minimizes inventory while satisfying all demand**

Product variety and setup times do not mix well—as variety is added to a resource that has a setup time, the average inventory of all items produced by that resource increases.

LO7-7 **Explain the different approaches for managing a process with setup times**

Setup times are an undesirable process interruption. Nevertheless, a resource with a setup time can be desirable because it has a lower processing time. The original printing press is a good example: It took a considerable amount of time to set up the printing of a single page, but once set up, subsequent pages could be printed very quickly. One strategy for dealing with setup times is to limit the amount of product variety that is produced, as embodied by Henry Ford's famous declaration to his customers, "You can have any color you want, as long as it is black." Alternatively, the Toyota approach to setup times and variety is to reduce the setup time rather than the variety—processes with short setup times can produce variety without a large incremental expense.

Key Terms

7.1 Setup Time

Setup A set of activities (i) that are required to produce units but (ii) for which the time to complete these activities does not depend directly on the number of units produced.

Changeover time A setup time to change production from one type of product to another.

Switchover time See changeover time.

7.2 Capacity of a Process with Setups

Production cycle A repeating sequence of produced units that can include setup time, production time, and idle time.

Batch A collection of units.

Batch process A type of production in which units are produced in batches.

7.3 Utilization in a Process with Setups

Idle time Time not producing and not performing a setup.

7.7 Managing Processes with Setups

Single-Minute Exchange of Die (SMED) A goal to reduce the setup time to a single-digit number of minutes (i.e., nine or fewer).

Internal setups Activities that can only be done during the actual setup, for example, when the machine is not producing.

External setups Activities that can be done while production continues to occur.

Mixed-model assembly An assembly process in which production resembles the true rate of demand, even over a short time horizon. Also known as heijunka.

Heijunka Leveling production by reducing variation in the work schedule that arises from either demand variation or the desire to run production or transports in large batches. This is a principle of the Toyota Production System that strives to have production match the true rate of demand.

Key Formulas

LO7-2 **Evaluate the capacity of a resource that has a setup time and is operated with a given batch size**

$$\text{Capacity} = \frac{\text{Batch size}}{\text{Total setup time} + (\text{Processing time} \times \text{Batch size})}$$

LO7-3 **Evaluate the utilization of a resource that has a setup time**

$$\text{Utilization} = \text{Flow rate} \times \text{Processing time}$$

LO7-4 **Evaluate the average inventory of a product made by a resource that has a setup time**

$$\text{Maximum inventory} = \text{Batch size} \times [1 - (\text{Flow rate} \times \text{Processing time})]$$

$$\text{Average inventory} = \frac{\text{Maximum inventory}}{2} = \frac{1}{2} \times \frac{\text{Batch}}{\text{size}} \times \left[1 - \left(\frac{\text{Flow}}{\text{rate}} \times \frac{\text{Processing}}{\text{time}}\right)\right]$$

LO7-5 **Find the batch size that minimizes inventory while not constraining the flow through a process**

$$\text{Batch size} = \frac{\text{Target capacity} \times \text{Total setup time}}{1 - (\text{Target capacity} \times \text{Processing time})}$$

Conceptual Questions

LO7-1

1. A chemical process involves adding various agents to a vat and then waiting for the agents to react to make a final compound. The vat holds up to 1000 gallons. Chemical agents are added to the vat at a rate of 4.5 gallons per minute. Once the agents have been added to the vat, the reaction takes 85 minutes no matter the actual number of gallons in the batch. After the batch is complete, the vat must be cleaned. Cleaning always takes 15 minutes. What is the setup time of this process?
   a. 15 minutes
   b. 85 minutes
   c. 100 minutes
   d. 222.22 minutes

LO7-2

2. A machine makes three different components used in a gyroscope. Call these components A, B, and C. The following repeating schedule is used to make components: make 100 units of A, make 50 units of B, and then make 200 units of C. How many components are made in the production cycle?
   a. 50
   b. 100
   c. 200
   d. 350

3. A product requires four parts that are made on the same lathe. Call the parts A, B, C, and D. The product requires 1 unit of A, 2 of B, 4 of C, and 8 of D. Which of the following production cycles is most appropriate?
   a. A: 100, B: 100, C: 100, D: 100
   b. A: 101, B: 102, C: 104, D: 108
   c. A: 100, B: 150, C: 200, D: 400
   d. A: 100, B: 200, C: 400, D: 800

4. Increasing the batch size on a resource with setups always increases the capacity of the resource. True or false?
   a. True
   b. False

5. Increasing the batch size on a resource with setups always increases the capacity of the process. True or false?
   a. True
   b. False

6. The batch size is tripled on a resource that has a setup time. What is the likely impact on the resource's capacity?
   a. Decrease by 1/3
   b. Decrease by less than 1/3
   c. Increase by less than 300 percent
   d. Increase by 300 percent

LO7-3

7. If the flow rate of a process increases, then the utilization of a resource with a setup time must also increase. True or False?
   a. True
   b. False

8. Which of the following is likely to increase the utilization of a resource with a setup time?
   a. Increase the flow rate
   b. Decrease the processing time
   c. Decrease the batch size
   d. Increase the setup time

LO7-4

9. A manager is concerned that there isn't enough time spent on production and too much time spent on setups. The manager decides to double all production batch sizes. This change has no impact on demand. What impact will this likely have on the average inventory in the process?
   a. Average inventory will decrease because the capacity of the resources will increase.
   b. Average inventory will remain the same because demand has not changed.
   c. Average inventory will increase because larger batches require more time to be completed.
   d. Cannot determine from the given information.

LO7-5

10. Which of the following is most likely to be a concern if batches are very large?
    a. The flow rate will be too high.
    b. Utilization will be too high.
    c. Inventory will be too high.
    d. Too much time will be spent on product changeovers.

11. If the batch size is increased, inventory increases, which implies that flow units are likely to spend more time in the process. True or False?
    a. True
    b. False

LO7-6

12. Suppose a resource has setup times and a setup time must be incurred each time the resource switches production to a different product. Requiring the resource to make a new product (that requires its own setup) is likely to have what effect on the process?
    a. Inventory for existing products remains the same, but the process must now carry inventory of the new product.
    b. Inventory of all products is likely to increase.
    c. Inventory of existing products decreases even though the process must now carry inventory of the new product.
    d. Inventory of products with short setup times will decrease, while inventory of products with long setup times will increase.

LO7-7

13. Henry Ford proclaimed about the Model T, "You can have any color you want, as long as it is black." Which of the following best reflects his motivation for this position?
    a. He believed that customers didn't actually like other colors, so why go through the hassle of making different color cars?
    b. With more than one color, the process would have switchover times and that could reduce the overall utilization of the process.

(b) Suppose Cadbury produces 3000 lbs of milk chocolate and 1200 lbs of dark chocolate in each cycle. What would be the utilization of this process (the fraction of time the process is actually producing product)?

> **Answer:** 0.78. The capacity of the process would be $4200/\{1.5 + [(1/800) \times 4200]\}$ = 622 lbs per hour. Demand is 700 lbs per hour, so the process is supply-constrained. Hence, the flow rate is 622 lbs per hour. Utilization = Flow rate × Processing time = 622 lbs per hr × (1/800) hr per lb = 0.78.

(c) Suppose Cadbury produces 8000 lbs of milk chocolate and 3200 lbs of dark chocolate in each cycle. What would be the average inventory (lbs) of milk chocolate?

> **Answer:** 1500. The batch size is 11,200 lbs. The capacity is $11,200/\{1.5 + [(1/800) \times 11,200]\}$ = 723 lbs per hour. Demand is 700 lbs per hour, so the process is demand-constrained. For milk chocolate, the batch size is 8000 lbs and the flow rate is 500 lbs per hr. Hence, Maximum inventory = Batch size × [1 − (Flow rate × Processing time)] = 8000 × [1 − (500 × 1/800)] = 3000 lbs. Average inventory = 1/2 Maximum inventory = 1/2 × 3000 = 1500.

(d) How many lbs of milk and dark chocolate should be produced with each cycle (a batch of milk and a batch of dark) so as to minimize inventory while satisfying demand?

> **Answer:** 8400 lbs. Processing time = 1 hr/800 pounds. The target capacity is demand, which is 500 + 200 = 700 pounds/hr. Batch size = (Capacity × Setup time)/[1 − (Capacity × Processing time) = (700 lbs/hr × 1.5 hr)/[1 − (700 lbs/hr × 1/800 hr/lb)] = 8400 pounds.

Problems and Applications

LO7-2

1. The batch size is cut in half on a resource that has a setup time. What is the likely impact on the resource's capacity?
   a. Decrease by more than 50 percent
   b. Decrease by 50 percent
   c. Decrease by less than 50 percent
   d. No impact

LO7-2, 7-3, 7-4, 7-5

2. A machine makes two components; call them types A and B. It takes 250 seconds to switch production between the component types. During that time, no production occurs. When in production, each unit of A or B requires 0.5 second to be completed. The two components, A and B, are combined in an assembly process to make a final product; call it C. The assembly step can combine the two components into 1 unit every 2 seconds, or 30 units per minute.
   a. Suppose the machine rotates between one batch of 1000 units of A and 1000 units of B. In that case, what is the capacity of the machine in component pairs per minute, where a component pair is one unit of A and one unit of B?
   b. Suppose the machine rotates between one batch of 1000 units of A and 1000 units of B. What is the utilization of the machine?
   c. Suppose the machine rotates between one batch of 1000 units of A and 1000 units of B. What is the average inventory of B components?
   d. If the production schedule could be adjusted with the goal of minimizing inventory in the process, how many units of A should be produced before switching to component B? Assume the same number of units of B would be produced as well.

LO7-1, 7-2, 7-3, 7-5, 7-6

3. The Yum and Yee food truck near the business school serves customers during lunch hour by taking orders and making fresh batches of stir-fry. Customers have only one choice during the lunch hour so that Y&Y can maximize the number of customers served. Assume that each customer places just one lunch order, and all lunch orders are the same size: one unit of stir-fry. The stir-fry cooking works in this manner. First, one person cooks a batch of orders in a wok. The cooking depends upon the number of orders in the batch. The time to cook just one order is 3 minutes. For each additional order in the batch, it takes 0.5 minute more to cook. Thus, cooking two orders in a batch takes 3.5 minutes, cooking three orders takes 4 minutes, and so on. The other process is bagging and accepting payments (done by a separate person), which takes 0.80 minute per order.
   a. What is the setup time of this process?
   b. If Y&Y operates with batch sizes of 6 units, what is their process capacity (in orders per minute)?
   c. If Yum and Yee operates with batch sizes of 10 units, what is the utilization of the wok?
   d. Calculate the batch size (in orders) that maximizes the overall flow rate (assume there is ample demand)? Do NOT round the batch size (i.e., assume for this calculation that a noninteger batch size is possible).

LO7-2, 7-3, 7-5

4. A printed circuit board (PCB) machine installs integrated circuits onto a board. Before starting to produce a board, the PCB machine requires a 20-minute setup. Once in production, the PCB machine requires only 0.15 minute per board.
   a. Currently, the PCB machine produces 500 boards between setups. Given this operating process, what is the capacity of the PCB machine (in boards per minute)?
   b. Currently, the PCB machine produces 500 boards between setups. Given this operating process, what is the utilization of the PCB machine?
   c. Demand for boards occurs at the rate of 2 boards per minute. What is the smallest batch size such that the PCB machine does not constrain the flow rate through the process?

LO7-6

5. Sarah's Organic Soap Company makes four kinds of organic liquid soap: "regular," "lavender," "citrus," and "tea tree." Demands for the four scents are 150, 120, 75, and 50 kgs per hour, respectively. Sarah's production process can produce any soap at the rate of 450 kgs per hour, but 1.5 hours are needed to switch between scents. During those switchover times, the process doesn't produce any soap. Sarah wants to choose a production schedule that (i) cycles repeatedly through the four scents, (ii) meets the required demand, and (iii) minimizes the amount of inventory held.

   How many kgs of "regular" should Sarah produce before switching over to another scent?

LO7-2, 7-3

6. JCL Inc. is a major chip manufacturing firm that sells its products to computer manufacturers like Dell, Gateway, and others. In simplified terms, chip making at JCL Inc. involves three basic operations: depositing, patterning, and etching.
   - *Depositing:* Using chemical vapor deposition (CVD) technology, an insulating material is deposited on the wafer surface, forming a thin layer of solid material on the chip.
   - *Patterning:* Photolithography projects a microscopic circuit pattern on the wafer surface, which has a light-sensitive chemical like the emulsion on photographic film. It is repeated many times as each layer of the chip is built.
   - *Etching:* Etching removes selected material from the chip surface to create the device structures.

   Table 7.4 lists the required processing times and setup times at each of the steps. There is unlimited space for buffer inventory between these steps. Assume that the unit of production is a wafer, from which individual chips are cut at a later stage.

Process Step	Depositing	Patterning	Etching	TABLE 7.4
Setup time (min)	45.00	30.00	20.00	
Processing time (min)	0.15	0.25	0.2	

a. What is the process capacity in units per hour with a batch size of 100 wafers?

b. What is the utilization of depositing if the batch size is 100 wafers?

LO7-2, 7-3, 7-5

7. Kinga Doll Company manufactures eight versions of its popular girl doll, Shari. The company operates on a 40-hour workweek. The eight versions differ in doll skin, hair, and eye color, enabling most children to have a doll with a similar appearance to them. It currently sells an average of 4000 dolls (spread equally among its eight versions) per week to boutique toy retailers. In simplified terms, doll making at Kinga involves three basic operations: molding the body and hair, painting the face, and dressing the doll. Changing over between versions requires setup time at the molding and painting stations due to the different colors of plastic pellets, hair, and eye color paint required. Table 7.5 lists the setup times for a batch and the activity times for each unit at each step.

Process Step	Molding	Painting	Dressing	TABLE 7.5
Setup time (min)	15.00	30.00	No setup	
Processing time (min)	0.25	0.15	0.30	

a. What is the process capacity in dolls per hour with a batch size of 500 dolls?

b. What is the utilization of molding in dolls per hour with a batch size of 800 dolls?

c. Which batch size would minimize inventory without decreasing the process capacity?

d. Which batch size would minimize inventory without decreasing the current flow rate?

LO7-2, 7-3, 7-4, 7-6

8. Bruno Fruscalzo decided to set up a small production facility in Sydney to sell to the local restaurants who want to offer gelato on their dessert menu. To start simple, he would offer only three flavors of gelato: fragola (strawberry), chocolato (chocolate), and bacio (chocolate with hazelnut). After a short time, he determined his demand and setup times, listed in Table 7.6.

	Fragola	Chocolato	Bacio	TABLE 7.6
Demand (kg/hour)	10	15	5	
Setup time (hours)	3/4	1/2	1/6	

Bruno first produces a batch of fragola, then a batch of chocolato, then a batch of bacio, and then he repeats that sequence. For example, after producing bacio and before producing fragola, he needs 45 minutes to set up the ice cream machine, but he needs only 10 minutes to switch from chocolato to bacio. When running, his ice cream machine produces at the rate of 50 kgs per hour no matter which flavor it is producing (and, of course, it can produce only one flavor at a time).

a. Suppose they operate with a production cycle of 150 kgs (50 kg of fragola, 75 kgs of chocolato, and 25 kgs of bacio). What is the capacity of the gelato-making process (in kgs per hr)?

b. Suppose they operate with a production cycle of 150 kgs (50 kg of fragola, 75 kgs of chocolato, and 25 kgs of bacio). What is the utilization of the gelato-making process?

c. Suppose they operate with a production cycle of 150 kgs (50 kg of fragola, 75 kgs of chocolato, and 25 kgs of bacio). What is the average inventory of chocolato?

d. Suppose Bruno wants to minimize the amount of each flavor produced at one time while still satisfying the demand for each of the flavors. (He can choose a different quantity for each flavor.) If we define a batch to be the quantity produced in a single run of each flavor, how many kgs should he produce in each batch?

e. Given your answer to part (d), how many kgs of fragola should he make with each batch?

LO7-2, 7-6

9. In their Portland, Oregon, facility, Wavy Wood Works makes several types of wood bowls from coastal driftwood. To make a bowl, the first step is to clean the driftwood. Each piece of driftwood makes a single bowl. There is one cleaning machine. It takes 40 seconds to load each piece of wood, and the machine can hold up to 35 pieces. Once all of the pieces are loaded into the machine, it takes 45 minutes to clean the set (no matter the number of pieces in the set). Once the wood is cleaned, 15 skilled artisans carve the bowls; each one takes, on average, 100 minutes to produce each bowl. After carving, bowls are finished with a stain. It takes 30 seconds to load each bowl into the stain machine. The staining machine holds up to 35 bowls. Once all of the bowls are loaded, they are soaked for 80 minutes. After staining, bowls are unloaded onto drying racks. There is plenty of space on the drying racks.

a. What is the maximum capacity (bowls per hour) of this process?

b. Suppose Wavy wants to operate with the same number of bowls in each batch that are cleaned or stained. For example, if it cleans in batches of 30, then it stains in batches of 30 as well. What batch size (in bowls) minimizes its inventory while allowing the process to produce at the maximum flow rate?

LO7-2, 7-3, 7-4, 7-6

10. Aquatica makes underwater camera housings for divers. The process begins with a solid rectangular block of aluminum that is used to make a single housing. A computer numerically controlled (CNC) machine drills into the block to make the metal "frame" of the housing. Each block requires 15 minutes of drilling. The frame is then chemically treated in a series of baths. There is ample capacity in the treating stage. Finally, a worker must manually attach the various buttons and components to the metal housing. This assembly takes 120 minutes per housing per worker and Aquatica has 6 workers trained to do this task. The CNC machine requires a 30-minute setup time before the production of a batch can begin.

a. If the CNC machine produces 14 housings between setups, what would be its capacity (in housings per hour)?

b. Assuming the process is supply-constrained, what is the utilization (as a number between 0 and 1) of the CNC machine if it operates in batches of 14 housings?

c. Assuming the process is supply-constrained and operates with batches of 14 housings, what is the average inventory of housings?

d. Aquatica actually makes five different housings. As already mentioned, the CNC machine must be set up whenever production switches from one housing to the other. In each case, the setup time is 30 minutes and it takes 15 minutes to drill the block for each type of housing. Demands for the housings are given in Table 7.7.

TABLE 7.7

Housing Type	Demand Rate (housings per hour)
D7000	0.4
5DS Mark III	0.5
AN-5n	0.6
D300	0.7
T2i	0.8

If it wishes to minimize inventory while satisfying its demand, how many D7000 housings should it produce in each batch?

CASE BONAIRE SALT[1]

Bonaire is a small Dutch island off the coast of Venezuela, best known for its scuba diving and flamingos. Bonaire's only export is salt, produced by solar evaporation in a single facility, called Bonaire Salt (BS), in the southern portion of the island. Bas Tol, a representative from a large international conglomerate, is visiting Bonaire because his company is interested in buying Bonaire Salt. He met with Bart Snelder, the manager of Bonaire Salt, to discuss its operations.

Bart laid out on the table a map of the facility showing 16 different pans. Each pan is a rectangular area about 350 by 300 meters. The pans are filled with sea water, which evaporates over time, leaving a thick layer of sea salt. Half of the pans are dedicated to making "brine"—water with a high salt content (25 percent by weight rather than 3.5 percent, which is typical of sea water). The brine from those pans is pumped into the other eight pans to complete the process. To be specific, each of those eight pans is flooded with brine for 43 weeks. At the end of those 43 weeks, the pans are dry and there is a 30-cm-thick layer of salt covering the entire pan. At that point, the salt is harvested.

Harvesting is done with bulldozers that scrape the layer of salt in the pan. Dump trucks carry the salt to a central area where the salt is stored in large outdoor conical piles. A large conveyor is used to transport the salt from those piles to a pier next to the facility so that the salt can be loaded onto a ship for transportation to markets around the world.

A single bulldozer can complete the harvesting of a pan in 10 weeks. Multiple bulldozers can be used to harvest and the harvesting time is proportional to the number of bulldozers. For example, Bonaire Salt currently has two bulldozers, so on average it takes five weeks to harvest a pan when both bulldozers work continuously on the same pan. They have plenty of dump trucks, so the availability of trucks does not constrain the process.

Each of the eight pans yields about 40,000 tons of salt per harvest. (A ton is 1000 kgs.) The conveyor system can load a ship at the rate of 20,000 tons per week. The storage area can accommodate 15 cones. Each cone can be 18 meters high and 40 meters across, holding about 9600 tons of salt.

© Kbfmedia/iStockphoto/Getty Images/RF

Bas notes that at the current time Bonaire salt sells for about $25 per ton on the market. Before his company can formulate a bid for Bonaire Salt, he needs to do some calculations to better understand both the current output of Bonaire Salt and the potential output from the facility.

1. Given current operations, how much salt can Bonaire Salt produce per week on average (in tons)?

2. Bart suggests that it could increase output if it purchases another bulldozer. If it did, what would be its average weekly output of salt (in tons)?

3. Bas has another idea for increasing output. He suggests that it could divide each of the eight producing pans it has in half, to make 16 producing pans. Bas assumes that this could be done without losing much productive area, meaning that two of the smaller pans can yield as much salt as the combined larger (current) pan. Even under that optimistic assumption, Bart doesn't think it would increase average weekly output because it wouldn't change the amount of area actually producing salt. Who is correct?

4. A third idea for increasing output was also discussed: Add more producing pans. Based on a map of the land around the facility, Bas believes it probably could add three more producing pans of the same size as the eight current ones (and there would be enough capacity in the brine-producing pans to support these three additional producing pans). How much would that increase weekly average output of Bonaire Salt?

[1] This is a fictitious case based on an actual facility and data.

8

Lean Operations and the Toyota Production System

LEARNING OBJECTIVES

LO8-1 Explain the two ways in which an operation can be wasteful

LO8-2 Distinguish between waste, non-value-added work, and value-added work and determine the percentage of value-added work at a resource

LO8-3 Determine the percentage of flow time that is value-added time

LO8-4 Explain the main building blocks of the Toyota Production System

LO8-5 Explain the concepts of single-unit flow, pull, kanban, and just-in-time and be able to compute the appropriate number of kanban cards

LO8-6 Compute takt time and determine a level production schedule

LO8-7 Explain jidoka and be able to compute the information turnaround time

LO8-8 Define the basic vocabulary terms of the Toyota Production System

CHAPTER OUTLINE

© Juice Images/Glow Images/RF

Introduction

Louis Vuitton is one of the most prestigious luxury brands in the world. Products such as their tote bag "Reade" can easily cost over $500 (see Photo 8.1), with products in the four-digit price range being not uncommon at all. It used to take 20 to 30 craftsmen to produce a bag such as the Reade. Craftsmen specialized in the various steps associated with making a bag, such as sewing together the leather panels, gluing in linings, and attaching the handles. This process unfolded over the course of eight days.

Historically, the management of LVMH (the corporate parent of the Louis Vuitton brand) emphasized product design and branding as the main capabilities of the firm. However, pressed by labels such as Zara and H&M that were less expensive and which also responded much faster to customer demand, the company reorganized the way it produces its products.

Inspired by car manufacturer Toyota, and aided by the management consultancy McKinsey, Louis Vuitton totally redesigned their production processes. The results? Now clusters of 6–12 craftsmen work together to produce the bag. Workers are cross-trained and master multiple production steps. The flow of the process is streamlined and all work is carried out in a U-shaped work cell as opposed to being spread out over many departments, which required long (and costly) transportation steps. It now takes less than one single day for a bag to be produced, which keeps inventory low and enables the company to quickly react to fluctuations in market demand.

The story of Louis Vuitton is one of many that broadly fit into the category of **lean operations,** which is the topic of this chapter. In this chapter, you will learn a number of tools that help you identify inefficiencies in a process and generate process improvements that make the process become lean. We do this in the following way.

- In the first section, we first define the term *lean*. The next two sections introduce the concepts of wasting time at a resource and wasting time of a flow unit. We also discuss ways of measuring these two types of waste.
- The next section provides a high-level overview of the Toyota Production System (TPS). Toyota is widely viewed as the birthplace of lean.
- We then introduce the concept of "one-unit flow" and just-in-time (JIT) production, which together constitute the first of the two pillars of TPS. This includes concepts such as demand-pull, takt time, demand leveling, and kanban.
- The second pillar of TPS, discussed in the final section, is built-in quality. This links to the quality chapter in this book and discusses concepts such as detect-stop-alert, root-cause problem solving, and foolproofing.

© *Bloomberg/Getty Images*

PHOTO 8.1   A Louis Vuitton branded handbag sits on display at the LVMH Moet Hennessy Louis Vuitton SA "maison" store in New Bond Street in London, UK.

8.1 What Is Lean Operations?

James Womack An MIT professor who founded the International Motor Vehicle Program and later the Lean Enterprise Institute.

Toyota Production System (TPS) A framework used to run operations with the goal of reducing both the waste of capacity and the waste of flow time, thereby making sure supply and demand are matched just in time.

Waste of time at a resource The waste of time from the perspective of a resource, which reduces the capacity of the resource.

Waste of time of a flow unit The waste of time from the perspective of a flow unit, which makes the flow time of that flow unit longer than what is needed in the eyes of the customer.

Frederick Winslow Taylor An engineer who pioneered the concept of scientific management at the end of the 19th century.

Scientific management A management framework created by Frederick Winslow Taylor that emphasizes efficiency and optimization.

The term "lean" was coined by the management scholar **James Womack** following his study of the global automotive industry in general, and the success behind the **Toyota Production System (TPS)** in particular. The term *lean* reflects the operation's goal to eliminate waste from the system. While there exist many forms of waste, which we will discuss in greater detail throughout this chapter, we find it helpful to distinguish between two forms of waste: the waste of a resource's time and the waste of a flow unit's time:

- **Waste of time at a resource:** One type of waste reflects the perspective of the resource, in this case the workforce or production equipment. Capacity is wasted because of idle time (see earlier chapters). But capacity is also wasted by performing what we will define as waste and non-value-adding work. For example, Louis Vuitton's factory used to have close to 50 percent of their $1000 Tikal bags returned for rework because of frayed inside seams. Also, transporting bags through the factory wastes the time of the worker pushing the cart with half-completed bags on them.

- **Waste of time of a flow unit:** Another type of waste reflects the perspective of the flow unit. In our Louis Vuitton example, this would be the perspective of the handbag. The flow time used to be eight days. Now, the factory can produce the same product within a flow time of one day. This improvement is mostly a result of reducing the flow time. We know from Little's Law that Inventory = Flow rate × Flow time. Because the number of bags produced each unit of time has roughly stayed constant, shorter flow time is directly proportional to less inventory.

So lean operations is about reducing waste, be it in the form of wasted flow time or wasted capacity. Because lean operations has its roots in the automotive industry, in particular in the practice of Toyota and its famous TPS, we will discuss the topics "lean" and TPS together and use the terms *lean* and *TPS* interchangeably. As mentioned above, many of the concepts discussed in this chapter are discussed in greater detail elsewhere in the book. In our view, "lean operations" is really not different from "good operations" and so our ambition is to have the lean ideas "built in" to every one of the chapters in this book. As an alert reader, you will have noticed references to Toyota in other chapters and you will encounter many references in this chapter to the other chapters in the book. This is why we think of this chapter as a capstone chapter, bringing together many distinct elements of operations we already have discussed.

© Picture Partners/Pixtal/Age fotostock/RF

Check Your Understanding 8.1

Question: After just having waited for an hour in the waiting room of your doctor, you complain to the manager of the practice. The manager explains that because of the cost pressure in health care, the practice would now be managed in a lean way. To keep doctors, nurses, and equipment efficient, the practice wants to minimize the idle time of these resources. To do so, the practice always has a number of patients waiting. Which part of lean operations does the practice ignore?

Answer: Lean operations not only looks at the resources of the process (doctors, nurses, equipment), but also at how the flow units spend their time journeying through the process. So lean is as much about using the patient time productively as it is about using the doctor time productively.

8.2 Wasting Time of a Resource

Frederick Winslow Taylor, the father of **scientific management,** wrote in his famous book *The Principles of Scientific Management:* "We can see and feel the waste of material things. Awkward, inefficient, or ill-directed movements of men, however, leave nothing visible or tangible behind them." Taylor in many ways can be seen as the founder of operations management. However, **Taylorism** has (for better or for worse) become the symbol for how NOT to manage a lean operation. The reason for Taylor's plummeting popularity in the lean movement is as follows. Taylor believed in scientific principles of designing work and so organizations following Taylor's work recruited armies of industrial engineers who would carefully study the movements and the work of the workers. Their goal was, simply stated, to squeeze out the last bit of productivity from the workforce. This had substantial organizational consequences. Why would a smart employee honestly share a productivity improvement idea with an industrial engineer if this would ultimately lead to the standard output being raised (the standard processing time being shortened), forcing the worker to work even harder? Similarly, if workers would be rewarded for high output (for example, via piece-rate compensation), why would a worker want to care about quality and defects?

While we believe that Taylor shaped the field of operations management in a profound way, which warrants him a place in the "operations hall of fame," Taylor apparently had a very difficult time relating to the human beings who constituted his workforce. In fact, in his book, Taylor comments on the improvement potential of workers shoveling pig iron (one of the tasks to which he devoted a lot of attention in his studies). He wrote: "This work is so crude and elementary in its nature that the writer firmly believes that it would be possible to train an intelligent gorilla so as to become a more efficient pig-iron handler than any man can be." For Taylor, workers were animals who had to be tamed and taught to operate the way the engineers wanted. Taylor wanted their muscles, not their brains. This, as we will discuss later on in this chapter, was his fundamental flaw—a flaw that unfortunately has left its marks on how management treats factory workers to this day.

Taiichi Ohno, former chief engineer at Toyota and the founder of TPS, also had a deep interest in how members of the workforce spent their time. Ohno commented on worker activity by saying: "Moving is not working"—a statement that we believe F.W. Taylor would have happily agreed with. Ohno distinguished between two types of worker movements:

- **Waste (muda),** which he defined as the needless waste of time and worker movements that ought to be eliminated immediately. This includes, for example, idle time or fixing broken units.

- **Work,** which he further broke up into *non-value-added work* and *value-added work.* **Non-value-added work** he defined as those movements that do not add value in the eyes of the customer but must be done under the current conditions of the process in order to complete a unit. For example, a customer does not value a worker moving from one machine to another, but this work is necessary given the present process. **Value-added work,** in contrast, is those movements valued by the customer as they are absolutely required to transform the flow unit from its inputs to being the output the customer wants.

Figure 8.1 breaks up the total time a worker spends in a day into the components of waste, non-value-added work, and value-added work. We acknowledge that the distinction between waste, non-value-added work, and value-added work can sometimes be a bit fuzzy. Nevertheless, we feel that this framework provides a very useful lens to look at the operations of a business.

Figure 8.1 is also the starting point for a more quantitative analysis, both of the operation's status quo as well as its improvement potential. Specifically, our goal is to measure what percentage of a machine's or a worker's capacity is used productively. This gives us a sense of the improvement potential. If we are currently demand-constrained, this improvement potential can take the form of lower costs because of a redeployment of resources. If we are currently capacity-constrained, this improvement potential can take the form of an increased flow rate.

Consider the following example of a primary care practice. Physicians have 30-minute appointment slots starting at 8 a.m. all the way up to 6 p.m. Physicians spend about 1½ hours each day on electronic medical records and 30 minutes on claims processing/questions related to medical insurance.

The typical physician in the practice has 75 percent of his or her appointments booked. Many appointments are made a long time in advance, which leads to frequent cancellations.

Figure 8.1

Value-added time versus work (adapted from Ohno, 1988)

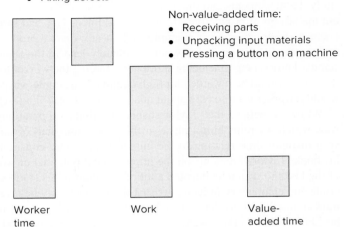

Waste:
- Idle time
- Meaningless transport
- Stockpiling of inventory
- Fixing defects

Non-value-added time:
- Receiving parts
- Unpacking input materials
- Pressing a button on a machine

Worker time

Work

Value-added time

About one out of every six patients does not show up for the appointment. Though the appointment slots are 30 minutes per slot, physicians only spend, on average, 23 minutes with the patient (or doing work related to the patient after the patient has left the office). From those 23 minutes, about 5 minutes could easily be done by one of the nurses working in the practice.

Clearly, there seems to be a lot of improvement potential in the practice. But how much of the physician's work is value-added? Ohno's framework provides us with some guidance. Consider the time a physician is in the practice first. This **total available time** can be computed as

Total available time The amount of time a resource has available to fulfill demand.

$$\text{Total available time} = 60 \, \frac{\text{min}}{\text{h}} \times 10 \, \frac{\text{h}}{\text{day}} = 600 \, \frac{\text{min}}{\text{day}}$$

© Isadora Getty Buyou/Image Source/RF

Check Your Understanding 8.2

Question: An employee in a restaurant spends his time on the following: waiting for a customer order, taking the order, forwarding the order to the kitchen, waiting for the kitchen to confirm the order, bringing the food to the customer, serving the customer, and collecting the payment. Which of these time commitments are waste, which are non-value-added work, and which are value-added work?

Answer:

- *Waiting for a customer order:* This is idle time for the employee and thus waste.
- *Taking the order:* This is value-added time.
- *Forwarding the order to the kitchen:* This is work needed given the current process design (where order taking and cooking are separated); however, this does not add value to the customer.
- *Waiting for the kitchen to confirm the order:* Again, this is idle time and thus waste.
- *Bringing the food to the customer:* This is another form of transport and thus non-value-added work.
- *Serving the customer:* This is value-added work.
- *Collecting the payment:* This is typically perceived as value-added work, though new mobile payment technologies make eating in a restaurant without a formal check-out possible (just like Uber does in the transportation market).

Now, let us consider what actually happens during these 600 minutes. The physician needs to spend 2 hours per day on medical records and insurance issues. This allows the physician to have 8 hours a day (or 480 minutes) for appointments, which translates into 16 appointments per day. Morever:

- Time not booked for appointments = 25 percent of the 480 minutes a doctor is available for appointments; 25% × 480 min/day = 120 minutes are not booked, leading to idle time (4 out of 16 slots).
- Of the 12 appointments per day, one in six patients cancels, which translates to 2 (out of 12) wasted appointments per day due to cancellations (i.e., 2 × 30 = 60 minutes).
- Time is wasted because of early appointment completions. Appointments are 30 minutes long; every time a physician sees a patient (which happens 10 times per day, see earlier), we waste another 7 minutes because of completing the work faster than planned, leaving us with 70 minutes of idle time.

All of these create a form of idle time for the physician; they are purely waste. Beyond this waste, physicians also spend time on activities that are required in the current workflow but are not necessarily adding value from the perspective of the customer (the patient). This includes:

- The 2 hours each day that the physician spends on medical records and insurance.
- Time spent by the physician that could have been done by the nurse. The 5 minutes per appointment that could be carried out by a nurse wastes the time of the higher-paid physician for 10 × 5 = 50 minutes a day.

Altogether, the physician has 10 appointments per day and each appointment is associated with 18 minutes of value-added work. We can thus break up the total available time the physician spends over the course of a day into waste, non-value-added work, and value-added work. This is shown in Figure 8.2.

Figure 8.2, known as the **overall equipment effectiveness** (OEE) framework, is used by McKinsey and other consulting firms. The objective of the framework is to identify what percentage of a resource's time is true, value-added time and what percentage is wasted. This provides a good estimate for the potential for process improvement before engaging in waste reduction.

$$OEE = \frac{\text{Value-added time}}{\text{Total available time}}$$

Of course, an exact analysis would have to carefully consider how the physician would spend his or her day. For example, if the physician would work on administrative work during the time that he or she is not booked, this analysis would overestimate the amount of waste. Finding out how workers (physicians or assembly-line workers) actually do spend their time

Overall equipment effectiveness (OEE) The percentage of total available time that is used in a way that adds value to the customer.

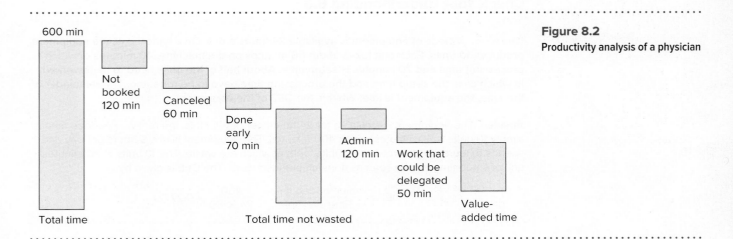

Figure 8.2
Productivity analysis of a physician

is remarkably difficult in practice. As F.W. Taylor already observed: "Employers derive their knowledge of how much of a given class of work can be done in a day from either their own experience, which has frequently grown hazy with age, from casual and unsystematic observation of their men, or at best from records. . . ."

The OEE framework introduced earlier supports a much more systematic observation and analysis. Observation is a key element of good (and lean) operations. To avoid the previously mentioned tension between the observing managers and the hard-working employees, Ohno envisioned an operation in which those performing the work would also be the ones observing and improving this. This is the key idea behind **genchi genbutsu** ("go and see in the real place") and **kaizen** (process improvement). Improvements in operations should come from the front line, rather than being designed by somebody who is not fully familiar with the process and thus has little data about the real operations of the process or opportunities to quickly validate ideas in practice.

Ohno viewed the reduction of waste as the business's first objective. To enable workers and managers to see waste, he distinguished between **seven sources of production waste**:

- *Waiting (time on hand):* If a worker waits for input from the previous step in the process flow, the worker is idle. Idle time and our measures of labor utilization are thus the most obvious form of waste. A particular form of idle time that Ohno observed was operators of machines waiting for the machine to complete its work (just like standing next to a printer and watching the pages come out).

- *Overproduction:* As we will discuss later in this chapter, TPS seeks to only produce in the quantities demanded by the customer. The goal is to produce what the customer wants and when the customer wants it, a principle known as **just-in-time (JIT) production**. Producing too much too soon will waste capacity. Because there exists no demand for the output now (and maybe ever), the capacity should have been used to produce actual demand, or the process should have been slowed down with the goal of saving costs.

- *Inventory:* Inventory is a result of overproduction and, as we have discussed throughout this book, the most visible form of supply–demand mismatch. An accumulation of inventory indicates that the JIT methods have not (yet) been implemented correctly. Inventory is not only a sign of overproduction, it also leads to additional waste in the form of extra demand for material handling, storage, and transportation. Moreover, inventory often hides other problems in the process because it decouples the process steps in the flow and thus leads to workers ignoring the dependencies that exist in the process.

- *Transport:* Internal transport, be it carrying around half-finished computers, wheeling patients through the hospital, or carrying around folders with insurance claims, corresponds to an additional waste of capacity. Processes should be laid out such that the

Seven sources of production waste Seven ways in which, in the eyes of Ohno, a resource can waste its capacity: waiting (idle time), overproduction, inventory, transport, overprocessing, rework, and unnecessary motions.

Just-in-time (JIT) production Supplying a unit of demand when and where it is needed, thus avoiding unnecessary inventory.

Check Your Understanding 8.3

Question: A piece of equipment is available 24 hours a day. On a typical day, the equipment produces 10 units. Each unit takes about 60 minutes on the machine, 40 minutes of which is processing time and 20 minutes is setup time. About half of the units need to be reworked, in which case the setup time and the processing time have to be repeated. The remainder of the time, the equipment is idle. What is the OEE of the equipment?

Answer: The equipment is available for 24 hours per day. Of this, the real value-added time is simply 10 units × 40 minutes/unit = 400 minutes. The equipment is idle 9 hours per day and spends 5 hours per day reworking units, both of which are waste. The 10 units × 20 minutes/unit of setup time can be seen as non-value-added work. The OEE is given by

$$OEE = \frac{\text{Value-added time}}{\text{Time available}} = \frac{400}{24 \times 60} = 0.27777$$

physical layout reflects the process flow to minimize the distances flow units must travel through a process.

- *Overprocessing or incorrect processing:* A close analysis of activity times reveals that workers often spend more time on a flow unit than necessary. A worker might excessively polish the surface of a piece of metal he just processed or a doctor might ask a patient the same questions that a nurse asked 5 minutes earlier.

- *Rework:* A famous saying in the Toyota Production System and the associated quality movement has been "Do it right the first time." As we have discussed in conjunction with the Louis Vuitton handbags, rework requires repeating a particular operation, which takes away time that could be used for regular production.

- *Unnecessary motions and movements:* There are many ways to perform a particular task, such as the tightening of a screw on the assembly line or the movement of a patient from a wheelchair into a hospital bed. But, according to the early pioneers of the industrial revolution, including the previously mentioned F.W. Taylor, there is only one "right way." Every task should be carefully analyzed and should be optimized using a set of tools that today is known as ergonomics. To do otherwise is wasteful.

In addition to these seven sources of waste, scholars of the TPS now commonly refer to an eighth source of waste: the waste of worker intellect. As previously mentioned, Taylorism, as applied throughout the industrial revolution, emphasized the worker as a production resource, not as a source of creativity for process improvement. Leveraging the insights of the frontline employees and allowing them to improve the process (kaizen) is an important element of the TPS. Note that everything we said about waste in production applies in service settings as well. Table 8.1 provides an illustration for a health care setting, as well as for a financial services company.

TABLE 8.1   Examples of Waste in Nonproduction Settings

Waste	Health Care Operation	Financial Services
Time on hand/idle time	Empty operating room Provider waiting for patient	Idle underwriting unit Customer service representatives waiting for inbound calls in a call center
Overproduction	Performing unnecessary procedures Extra visits because of the "fee-for-service" paradigm (providers get paid for work, independent of whether it was needed by the patient)	Preparing loans for customers who have inquired about a loan but will take the loan from another bank
Transport	Patient transporters	Workflow coordinators moving files around (on paper or electronically)
Overprocessing or incorrect processing	Performing additional tests on a patient even though the patient does not need them	Excessive call durations in a call center because of poorly formulated questions
Inventories	Waiting patients in the ER waiting room or before a procedure or operating room	Loan applications that are in process but presently are not worked on
Moving	Looking for syringes or medications Walking through the hospital	Preparing unnecessary paperwork Time to print forms and put them into files
Defects/rework	Readmitting a patient to the intensive care unit because she was discharged too early Readmitting a patient because of complications	Going back to the customer to collect more information on a loan application Revisiting loans that had been processed incorrectly or incompletely
Waste of intellect	Not allowing nurses, patient transporters, and other frontline employees to improve the process	Not allowing call center employees or customer service representatives to improve the process

8.3 Wasting Time of a Flow Unit

So far, our discussion of waste has focused on the resources. But there is another form of waste—not from the perspective of the resources in the process, but from the perspective of flow units going through the process—the waste of time. Instead of asking, "Why does it take so many worker hours to make a bag?" we can ask, "Why are the few hours it takes to make a bag (the labor content) spread out over several weeks (of flow time)?"

Flow units, in the eyes of Ohno, are impatient; they don't like sitting in inventory wasting their flow time without receiving value-added work. Our goal is to turn the incoming raw materials and other process inputs into fulfilled customer demand as quickly as possible. Figure 8.3 shows a three-step process flow diagram of a production process, consisting of casting, machining, and assembly. Note how the process flow diagram itself does not show where and why a flow unit spends time in the process. This is illustrated in the lower part of the figure. We observe that only a small fraction of the flow time is spent productively (the sum of the three processing times corresponding to casting, machining, and assembly). All other time is wasted, including time sitting in inventory, transportation times, or setup times.

Benjamin Franklin, a wise man though certainly not related to the TPS, allegedly said, "Lost time is never found again." Wastes of time do indeed leave no traces behind and so they can easily remain uncovered. However, the waste of flow time becomes visible by taking one of the following two approaches:

- *Taking the perspective of the flow unit:* A good exercise that every process observer at some point in an analysis should take is the perspective of the flow unit. Create a simple time line just like what is shown in Figure 8.3 and document what the flow unit is doing at each moment in time it journeys through the process.

- *Looking at inventory:* Unless one takes the perspective of the flow unit, time itself is hard to observe. But we don't have to observe flow time to know it is there. Instead, we can compute the flow time indirectly. We know from Little's Law that, as long as we hold the flow rate constant, flow time is proportional to the amount of inventory in the process. So instead of looking for flow time, we just have to look for inventory—and that tends to be much easier to observe.

Just as we used the OEE framework to quantify the percentage of a resource's available time that was used for value-added work, we can now follow a flow unit and look at the percentage of flow time used for value-added work.

Figure 8.3 Elements of flow time in a production process

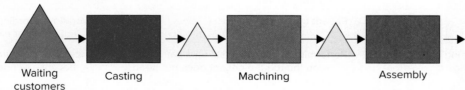

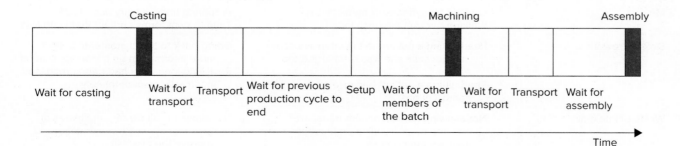

Check Your Understanding 8.4

Question: In the stamping operations of an automotive supplier, a piece of sheet metal has a flow time of a little over 8 hours. The time in the stamping operation is spent as follows: 3 hours waiting in front of the stamping machine for the batch to start, 1 hour waiting for the setup of the machine, 1 hour waiting for the other pieces of the batch to go through stamping, 1 minute at the stamping machine, and 3 hours waiting for shipment. What is the value-added percentage of the flow time?

Answer: The exact flow time is 8:01 hours. Of this, only 1 minute is value-added time. Thus, the percentage of value-added time is

$$\frac{\text{Value-added time of the flow unit}}{\text{Flow time}} = \frac{1 \text{ minute}}{481 \text{ minutes}} = 0.0021 = 0.21\%$$

- -

We define the **value-added percentage** as

$$\text{Value-added percentage} = \frac{\text{Value-added time of a flow unit}}{\text{Flow time}}$$

Note that the value-added time of a flow unit is related to, but not identical to, the definition of labor content (recall that we defined the labor content as the sum of the processing times). The measures are related because they are both flow-unit-centric and both do not count the time the flow unit spends in inventory, which often is the vast majority of the time a flow unit spends in the process. The measures are different because not all processing times necessarily add value.

Holding everything else constant, shortening the flow time improves the extent to which we consider an operation as lean. Because we previously defined 1/(Flow time) as the inventory turns, we can use inventory turns as an additional measure for diagnosing to what extent an operation is lean. A rapid flow with little or no inventory is, as we will discuss in the next section, one of the pillars of TPS. So, in summary, we can define an operation as lean if it simultaneously strives for a reduction of waste in its capacity and in the time a flow unit spends in the system.

LO8-3 Determine the percentage of flow time that is value-added time.

Value-added percentage The percentage of flow time used for value-added work.

8.4 The Architecture of the Toyota Production System

While TPS is frequently associated with certain buzzwords, such as JIT, kanban, and kaizen, one should not assume that simply implementing any of these concepts will lead to the level of operational excellence at Toyota. TPS is not a set of off-the-shelf solutions for various operational problems, but instead a complex configuration of various routines ranging from human resource management to the management of production processes. The books by Liker, *The Toyota Way,* and Fujimoto, *The Evolution of a Manufacturing System at Toyota,* provide excellent overviews of what made Toyota rise from a maker of automated looms to one of the largest auto makers in the world. Liker distinguishes between four principles (**4Ps**) driving the operational excellence at Toyota:

LO8-4 Explain the main building blocks of the Toyota Production System.

- *Philosophy:* A long-term approach that favors quality and capabilities over short-term financial goals.
- *Processes:* Continuous process flows that match supply with demand, aiming to reduce wastage of flow time and capacity.
- *People and partners:* Respectful interactions with employees and partners emphasizing skill development and growth.
- *Problem solving:* Ongoing improvement of the operations leveraging the experience of the front-line employees.

4Ps of Toyota Business principles embraced by Toyota that include philosophy, processes, people, and problem solving.

Figure 8.4
Overview of the Toyota
Production System

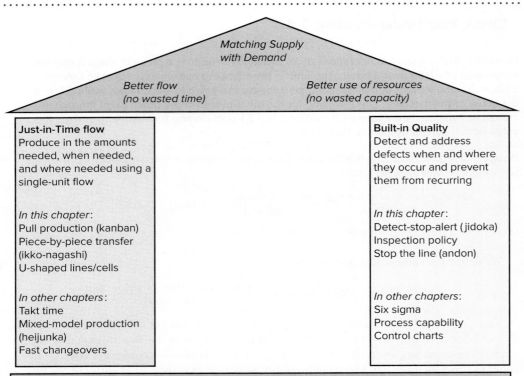

With this book being an operations book, our emphasis in this chapter continues to be on processes. But TPS is more than just operations, and we strongly encourage you to look at the previously mentioned writings.

Figure 8.4 summarizes the architecture of TPS as we discuss it in this chapter. This "house-shaped" representation is widely adopted. At the top (the roof), we have the principle of waste reduction and the goal to match supply with demand. The roof is supported by two pillars: just-in-time production using a single-unit flow and built-in quality. The foundation of the house is a culture of process improvement and a stable environment with limited variability.

As mentioned before, many of these concepts are discussed in other chapters of the book. Figure 8.4 points to these other chapters and previews the new methods we will introduce in this chapter. Because we already have discussed the roof of the **TPS house** (reduction in the waste of flow time and capacity), the coming sections we will discuss the two pillars.

TPS house A representation of the Toyota Production System in the shape of a house with the roof capturing the main goal of the TPS, which is waste reduction; the pillars being just-in-time flow and built-in-quality; and the foundation being process improvement.

8.5 TPS Pillar 1: Single-Unit Flow and Just-in-Time Production

Run like the tortoise, not the hare An ancient fable used by Ohno to illustrate that steady work, even when slow, is better than bursts of speed followed by periods of no movement.

Smooth and continuous flows are at the heart of the Toyota Production System and ensure that the process produces the right materials in the right amounts at the right time; in short, that the process matches supply with demand. Taiichi Ohno used two metaphors to illustrate the benefits of a smooth flow:

- **Run like the tortoise, not the hare**: This is based on an ancient fable that describes the race between a hare (a type of rabbit) and a tortoise (a turtle). The hare ridicules the slow-moving tortoise, who challenges the hare to a race. The hare quickly gains a significant lead and hence feels comfortable taking a little nap in the middle of the race. The tortoise, though tired, keeps on going at a steady pace. When the hare wakes up again, the hare is behind and has to witness the victory of the tortoise.

- *It takes eight men to row a boat:* A crew of eight amateur rowers will get *slower* if one of the rowers is substituted by a *faster,* professional rower. The boat, most likely, will get off course and, paradoxically, it is the fastest rower who does the most damage.

Both stories have the same moral: a steady and even pace wins over a pace that is uneven across time (the hare) or across team members (the amateur boat with a single professional in it). If customers demand 500 units per day, we ought to be producing 500 units per day. If we produce day and night, the day has $24 \times 60 = 1440$ minutes. Thus, ideally, we should be producing a unit every $1440/500 = 2.88$ minutes. In fact, every resource in the process ought to be operating at this pace. This is the pace that will create balance (and thus avoid idle time) and that will match supply with demand.

These calculations should not be new to the reader. In fact, this is the idea of **takt time** that we introduced in Chapter 4. Recall that the takt of the music is telling the musician with which tempo (speed) to play a particular piece. Just like each musician in an orchestra should not play the notes at a pace of her or his own choosing, a process should not be operating at the discretionary flow of the resources. Instead, the flow should be happening at the rate of demand.

Demand for most products, including Louis Vuitton bags and Toyota cars, tends to come in one at a time. Batching, the act of grouping together multiple flow units in one production run, is something we do to make our life in production easier (because of setup times), but this moves supply out of sync with demand.

Moving to a **single-unit flow** (ikko-nagashi) that matches demand is a key flow concept in TPS and helps with the reduction of waste. There are several ways that a one-unit flow exposes and reduces waste. The most important ones are:

- *Less inventory:* By producing to demand, we can reduce the finished goods inventory; also, by balancing the line, we can reduce the amount of work-in-process inventory (WIP), both of which are good for our inventory turns and thus good for working capital requirements.

- *Shorter response times to demand (shorter flow times):* By Little's Law, we know that less inventory also translates into shorter flow times; should we customize what we produce or should we introduce new products, we will be more responsive to the market if we have less inventory.

- *Faster feedback:* If a unit is defective, we want to know sooner rather than later. The problem with WIP, however, is that the pile of inventory that the flow unit will join after being completed at one resource will not provide feedback. But the worker at the next station downstream can, so the sooner we get the unit to the next station, the sooner we will get feedback and thus have the chance to correct our mistakes (this will be discussed further on in the section on built-in quality).

- *Simpler and more flexible staffing:* When we produce at a constant rate throughout the process, every resource gets staffed based on its processing time relative to its takt time. Recall the manpower calculations we did in Chapter 4: If you have a processing time of 50 seconds per unit and you have a takt time of 10 seconds per unit, you need 5 people at that resource. When demand goes up, the takt time goes down and you need to bring in extra workers. When demand slows down, the takt time goes up and we need to staff a resource with fewer operators. No forecasting, no second-guessing demand—just produce to demand.

- *Shorter processing times:* Studies have shown that workers slow down when they have the comfort that there exist big buffers in the process[1]. After all, when they slow down, nothing really happens because the station downstream is protected by a big buffer. In

LO8-6 Compute takt time and determine a level production schedule.

LO8-5 Explain the concepts of single-unit flow, pull, kanban, and just-in-time and be able to compute the appropriate number of kanban cards.

Takt time The ratio between the time available and the quantity that has to be produced to serve demand.

Single-unit flow Operate at a flow of one unit at a time from one resource to the next instead of operating based on transfer batches.

---

[1] Schultz, Kenneth L.; David C. Juran; and John W. Boudreau. "The Effects of Low Inventory on the Development of Productivity Norms." *Management Science* 45, no. 12 (1999), pp. 1664–78.

the absence of such a buffer, a worker slowing down will get immediate feedback from downstream—somebody will run out of work and hence have to stop.

- *More transparency:* As we will discuss further on, inventory helps to "cover up defects and imbalances"; with little or no inventory between stations, imbalances in speed across resources and defects can be easily detected.

So, a smooth single-unit flow has many desirable properties, but it requires some changes in the process. The most significant process changes required are:

- Implementing a pull system.
- Transferring units piece by piece (no transport batching), which typically requires a change in the facility's layout.
- Operating on takt time.
- Leveling the demand rate so that the takt time does not constantly change and providing the flexibility in the process to produce different variants of a product.

The following subsections will look at these four items in greater detail.

8.5.1 Pull Systems

The synchronization with the aggregate level of demand through takt time is an important step toward the implementation of just-in-time (JIT) production with a single-unit flow. However, inventory not only exists at the finished goods level, but also throughout the process (work-in-process inventory). Some parts of the process are likely to be worker paced with some (hopefully modest) amount of inventory between resources. We now have to design a system that coordinates these resources to control the amount of inventory in the process. We do this by implementing a pull system.

In a **pull system**, the resource furthest downstream (i.e., closest to the market) is paced by market demand. In addition to its own production, it also relays the demand information to the next station upstream, thus ensuring that the upstream resource also is paced by demand. If the last resource assembles two electronics components into a computer, it relays the demand for two such components to the next resource upstream. This way, the external demand is transferred step by step through the process, leading to an information flow moving in the opposite direction relative to the physical flow of the flow units.

Such a demand-driven pull system is in contrast to a **push system,** where flow units are allowed to enter the process independent of the current amount of inventory in the process. Especially if the first resources in the process have high capacities, they are likely to flood the downstream with inventory.

Pull system The resource furthest downstream (i.e., closest to the market) is paced by market demand. In addition to its own production, it also relays the demand information to the next station upstream, thus ensuring that the upstream resource also is paced by demand. That is, it is an operating system in which the production or replenishment of a unit is only initiated when a demand occurs.

Check Your Understanding 8.5

Question: A production process has two machines. The first machine has a capacity of 100 units per hour and the second machine has a capacity of 60 units per hour. Demand for the process is 100 units per hour.

1. In a push process, what would be the utilization of the first machine? What would happen to the inventory of the process?

Answer: In a push process, the first machine would simply run at its capacity. This would make it be utilized at 100 percent but lead to a large pileup of inventory in front of the second machine. The exact amount of inventory would change over time. The inventory would grow by 40 units per hour (100 units per hour would flow out of the first machine, but only 60 units would flow into the second machine).

2. How would the situation change with a pull system?

Answer: With a pull system, the first machine would be slowed down to the speed of the second machine. This would lead to a utilization of 60/100 = 60 percent at the first machine.

To implement a pull system, TPS advocates two forms of process control:

- **Kanban**-*based pull:* The upstream resource replenishes what demand has withdrawn from the downstream resource.
- **Make-to-order:** Refers to the release of work into a system only when a customer order has been received for that unit.

Consider the kanban system first. Kanban refers to a production and inventory control system in which production instructions and parts delivery instructions are triggered by the consumption of parts at the downstream step.[2] Ohno and his colleagues had the idea for kanban when visiting U.S. supermarkets. Supermarkets replenish their shelves only when customers take items from the shelf. For each item, there is a designated amount of shelf space and, hence, there can never be more inventory of an item in the store than there is space on the shelf. Kanban relates to the concept of an "order-up-to" policy, which we discuss in a later chapter.

In a kanban system, standardized returnable parts containers circulate between the upstream and the downstream resources. The upstream resource is authorized to produce a unit when it receives an empty container. In other words, the arrival of an empty container triggers a production order. The term *kanban* refers to the card attached to each container. Consequently, kanban cards are frequently called *work authorization forms.*

A simplified description of a kanban system is provided in Figure 8.5. A downstream resource (right) consumes a some input component that it receives from its upstream resource (left). The downstream resource empties containers of these input components—the downstream resource literally takes the part out of the container for its own use, thereby creating an empty container, which in turn, as already mentioned, triggers a production order for the upstream resource. Thus, the use of kanban cards between all resources in the process provides an effective and easy-to-implement mechanism for tying the demand of the process (downstream) with the production of the resources (upstream). They therefore enforce a match between supply and demand.

The main advantage of a kanban system is that there can never be more inventory between two resources than what has been authorized by the kanban cards (just like in a supermarket, where you cannot have more items of a given type than you have shelf space available)—the upstream resource can only produce when it has an empty container, so production stops when all of the containers are full, thereby limiting the inventory to the number of containers. In contrast, with a push system, the upstream resource continues to produce as long as it has work to do. For example, suppose the upstream resource is a lathe that produces the legs for

Kanban Production and inventory control system in which production instructions and parts delivery instructions are triggered by the consumption of parts downstream.

Make-to-order Making the activation of resources in a process contingent on receiving a specific order.

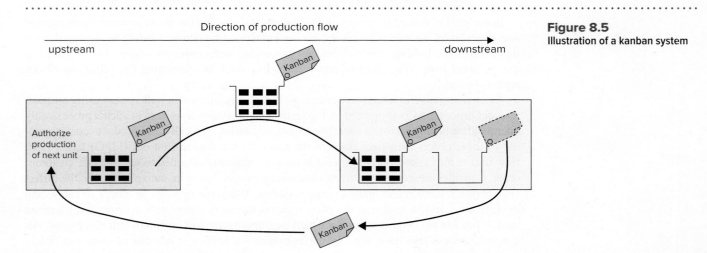

Figure 8.5
Illustration of a kanban system

Direction of production flow

upstream   downstream

Authorize production of next unit

Kanban

[2] Takahiro Fujimoto, *Evolution of Manufacturing Systems at Toyota* (New York: Productivity Press, 1999).

a wood chair. With a push system, the lathe keeps producing legs as long as it has blocks of wood to work on. With a kanban system, the lathe produces a set of chair legs only if it has an empty kanban container. Hence, with a kanban system, the lathe stops working only when it runs out of kanbans, whereas with a push system the lathe only stops working when it runs out of raw materials. The distinction can lead to very different behavior. In a push system, inventory can simply "happen" to management because there is theoretically no limit to the amount of inventory that can pile up after a resource (e.g., think of the plant manager walking through the process and saying, "wow, we have a lot of inventory at this step today"). In contrast, a kanban system inventory becomes a managerial decision variable—the maximum inventory is controlled via the number of kanban cards in the process.

The number of kanban containers—that is, the maximum amount of inventory authorized—is under the control of management. How many kanban containers should management put into the system? This depends on the following factors:

- *The container size:* Each kanban authorizes filling one container with inventory. The bigger the containers, the fewer kanban cards are needed (this is like saying, "if you buy your soda in cases of 24, you will need fewer cases compared to buying cases of 6).

- *The demand rate:* When demand is 1000 units per day, 500 units of inventory is merely half a day of supply. In contrast, when demand is 100 units per day, 500 units of inventory would last five days. A process with a higher demand rate requires more inventory.

- *The replenishment time:* This includes the time to make the units in one container (including any potential setup times) and transport them to the receiver.

- *The safety stock:* To account for breakdowns, defects, or other forms of variation, we allow for a little bit of extra inventory in the system. How much extra inventory is a decision to be made by management in response to the variation in the process. If the process works really well, this safety stock can be small; if things go wrong more frequently, a larger safety stock would be preferable.

These variables influence the number of kanban cards as follows:

$$\text{Number of kanban cards} = \frac{\text{Demand during replenishment time} + \text{Safety stock}}{\text{Container size}}$$

where the demand during the replenishment time is simply computed as

$$\text{Demand during replenishment time} = \text{Replenishment time} \times \text{Demand rate}$$

In our goal to reduce inventory, the kanban containers and the above computations provide useful guidance. To reduce inventory, we need to reduce the demand during the replenishment time, which is—holding demand rate and processing times constant—equivalent to reducing the transport time. We can also reduce the safety stock by improving the reliability of our replenishment.

As an alternative to a kanban system, we can also implement a pull system using a make-to-order process. As is suggested by the term *make-to-order,* resources in such a process only operate after having received an explicit customer order. Typically, the products corresponding to these orders then flow through the process on a first-in-first-out (FIFO) basis. Each flow unit in the make-to-order process is thereby explicitly assigned to one specific customer order. Consider the example of a rearview mirror production in an auto plant to see the difference between kanban and make-to-order systems. When the operator in charge of producing the interior rearview mirror at the plant receives the work authorization through the kanban card, it has not yet been determined which customer order will be filled with this mirror. All that is known is that there are—in the aggregate—a sufficient number of customer orders such that production of this mirror is warranted. Most likely, the final assembly line of the same auto plant (including the mounting of the rearview mirror) will be operated in a make-to-order manner; that is, the operator putting in the mirror can see that it will end up in the car of Mr. Smith.

Check Your Understanding 8.6

Question: The machining department supplies parts to the final assembly line. Management decides to implement a kanban system and has collected the following data:

- The daily demand is 1000 units.
- The replenishment time is driven by the production lead time, which is 3 days (this includes processing time, transport time, and waiting time).
- Management has decided to have a 1-day safety stock.
- One container fits 800 units.

How many kanban containers will be needed to support this system?

Answer: We first determine the amount of demand during the production lead time.

$$\text{Demand during lead time} = \text{Lead time} \times \text{Daily demand} = 3 \text{ days} \times 1000 \frac{\text{units}}{\text{day}} = 3000 \text{ units}$$

We translate the 1-day safety stock into a quantity, which is 1 day × 1000 units/day = 1000 units.

With 4000 units and a container size of 800 units/container, we need

$$\text{Number of kanban containers} = \frac{(\text{Demand during lead time} + \text{Safety stock})}{\text{Container size}}$$

$$= \frac{(3000 + 1000)}{800} = \frac{4000}{800} = 5$$

So, we need 5 containers.

Many organizations use both forms of pull systems. Consider computer maker Dell. Dell's computers are configured in work cells. Processes supplying components are often operated using kanban. Thus, rearview mirrors at Toyota and power supplies at Dell flow through the process in sufficient volume to meet customer demand, yet they are produced in response to a kanban card and have not yet been assigned to a specific order. The actual computers that Dell makes, in contrast, are made to order.

When considering which form of a pull system one wants to implement, the following should be kept in mind:

- Kanban should be used for products or parts (a) that are processed in high volume and limited variety, (b) that are required with a short lead time so that it makes economic sense to have a limited number of them (as many as we have kanban cards) pre-produced, and (c) for which the costs and efforts related to storing the components are low.

- Make to order should be used for products or parts (a) that are processed in low volume and high variety, (b) for which customers are willing to wait for their order, and (c) for which it is expensive or difficult to store the flow units.

8.5.2 Transferring on a Piece-by-Piece Basis

In many production settings, work is organized by department. Recall the LVMH example at the beginning of the chapter. A group of workers together constitute the stitching department. All bags would come to the stitching department. The workers stitching would work on different bags (see Figure 8.6(a)). Some bags would come from one station; other bags would have different sources and different destinations. Note that such functional grouping of work is not unique to manufacturing—just think about the last time you had to visit a hospital! Because the other departments that were doing the work steps before stitching and the work steps after stitching were also organized by department, moving each bag to the next department was uneconomical. Just think about going to the supermarket each time you consume a candy

Figure 8.6 (a) Organization by function (or equipment) versus (b) a flow-based organization; in this case, a U-shaped work cell. The white and black circles correspond to different flow units in the process.

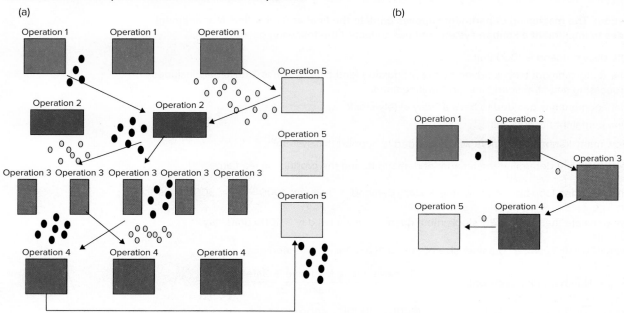

bar. Instead, workers would take advantage of scale economies in transportation. They would load a dozen or more bags on a cart and, once the cart was full, would roll the cart from one department to another. In fact, they might even have calculated an "optimal" transfer batch size based on the balance of inventory costs and transportation costs.

Instead of optimizing transfer batch sizes with a given process layout, TPS takes a different approach. In TPS, the optimal transfer batch size is simple. The optimal transfer batch size is equal to one. If this single-unit batch size is not economical, we have to think about a different **process layout**. And this is a layout in which resources that are close to each other in the process flow diagram should also be co-located in physical space. This avoids unnecessary transports and reduces the need to form transport batches. This way, flow units can flow one unit at a time from one resource to the next (**ikko-nagashi**).

What does a process layout amenable to a single-unit flow look like? The following guidelines are helpful to answer this question:

- *Organize work stations matching the flow of materials:* This has the simple benefit that it reduces transportation needs. If most parts move from machine A to machine B, machines A and B should be close to each other.

- *Create* **baton passing zones***:* Ohno observed that, in swimming relays, the fastest and slowest swimmers must both swim the exact same distance. In track, however, a faster runner can make up for a slower runner in the baton passing zone. Consider the making of a sandwich discussed in Chapter 3. If the second employee (the one who puts the various veggies on the sandwich) falls behind, the first employee can help out and take over some of these tasks. So instead of having fixed allocations of activities to workers, the idea of a baton passing zone is that the process can absorb variations in speed and starting time; this way, a line can be balanced without major reassignments of workers. Of course, such baton passing zones require that stations be next to each other.

- *Use* **U-shaped lines***:* The benefit of organizing the flow not in the shape of an "I" but of a "U" is that it allows for more flexibility and workers helping each other.

Figure 8.6(b) illustrates such a U-shaped flow. Oftentimes, a TPS worker is in charge of multiple machines, especially if some of the work is automated. A worker goes and starts a

Process layout The spatial location of resources in a process that drives the needs for transportation.

Baton passing zone Instead of having fixed allocations of activities to workers, the idea of a baton passing zone is that the process can absorb variations in speed and starting time.

U-shaped line Locating resources in a way that they create a "U," which increases the flexibility of workers to perform multiple tasks.

job on one machine. While that machine is processing, instead of standing idle next to the machine, the worker then goes to another machine "in the U" and completes a task there. This technique of reducing idle time is known as a **multitask job assignment** (think about sending a job to the printer but, instead of standing next to the printer waiting, going back to your computer to answer some e-mails or update your Facebook profile).

The layout that also reflects the process flow, with or without a U-shaped flow, thus provides us with all the benefits from the single-unit flow that we discussed earlier:

- The flow is visual, so idle time and inventory are easily spotted.

- There is a baton passing zone, so idle time can be avoided.

- There is no need for transportation.

- If demand falls, the number of workers can be adjusted; potentially, one worker might take on tasks across multiple machines.

Note that the previously introduced kanban system, though it is a pull system, is NOT a single-unit flow. With a kanban system, units are still batched together. A kanban system is thus a compromise between a traditional push system and the ideal case of a single-unit flow.

8.5.3 Takt Time

Kanban cards ensure that the production of each step is triggered by the next step downstream, and ultimately by final demand. Demand drives the system—demand is the conductor in the orchestra of workers and equipment. Kanban cards will prevent overproduction, and the pileup of unneeded inventory. But we also need to make sure we have neither excessive idle time nor insufficient capacity to respond to demand. Because we know we will be producing to demand, we should also staff the process according to the needs of demand. This was the idea of **takt time** and the associated **manpower** calculations that we introduced in Chapter 4.

Let us review the basic takt time calculations and explain how takt time is an essential element of TPS. To find the takt time of a process, we need two pieces of information:

- How many hours a day we produce (the available time).

- How many units of demand are requested.

We then compute takt time as follows:

$$\text{Takt time} = \frac{\text{Available time}}{\text{Demand rate}}$$

If we work two 8-hour work shifts and we want to produce 960 units, we have to produce at a takt time of

$$\text{Takt time} = \frac{2 \times 8 \times 60 \text{ minutes}}{960 \text{ units}}$$

$$= 1 \frac{\text{minute}}{\text{unit}}$$

Once we have the takt time, we can compute the necessary number of workers using the **target manpower** formula, also discussed in Chapter 4:

$$\text{Target manpower} = \frac{\text{Labor content}}{\text{Takt time}}$$

where labor content is the sum of the processing times across all workers. So, with a 1 minute/unit takt time, and assuming 6 minutes/unit labor content, the target manpower is

$$\text{Target manpower} = \frac{6 \text{ minutes/unit}}{1 \text{ minute/unit}} = 6$$

Multitask job assignment
A technique to reduce idle time by avoiding a worker watching a machine do work.

Target manpower The ratio between the labor content and the takt time determines the minimum number of resources required to meet demand. Note that this minimum does not have to be an integer number and that it assumes all resources are perfectly utilized.

Six workers are needed to serve the demand of 960 units. Note that we can simply substitute the definition of takt time into the target manpower equation and get

$$\begin{aligned}\text{Target manpower} &= \frac{\text{Labor content}}{\text{Takt time}} \\ &= \frac{\text{Labor content}}{\text{Available time/Demand rate}} \\ &= \frac{\text{Labor content} \times \text{Demand rate}}{\text{Available time}} \\ &= \frac{6\text{ min/unit} \times 960\text{ units/day}}{960\text{ minutes/day}} = 6\end{aligned}$$

Consider the six-step operation shown in Figure 8.7. Assume all activities have a processing time of 1 minute/unit, getting us the previously mentioned labor content of 6 minutes/unit. If demand is high (left in the figure), we assign one worker to each one-minute activity. With all the processing times being at 1 minute/unit, each step has the same capacity, and so we have a balanced process that can run at a cycle time of 1 minute/unit. We perfectly match the takt time of 1 minute/unit; that is, we produce exactly at the rate of demand.

When demand goes down, the target manpower goes down. In that case, TPS attempts assigning workers to processes creating other products. Assume the demand rate has gone down to 480 units/day. Holding the available time constant, we get a new target manpower of

$$\text{Target manpower} = \frac{6\text{ minutes/unit} \times 480\text{ units/day}}{960\text{ minutes/day}} = 3$$

So, now we need to assign the 6 minutes of labor content per unit (the six activities) evenly across the three workers, which leaves each worker performing two activities (and thus having a processing time of 2 minutes/unit).

Note how on the right of Figure 8.7 workers need to be capable of handling multiple (two) activities. This requires that the operators are skilled in multiple assembly tasks. Good training, job rotation, skill-based payment, and well-documented standard operating procedures are essential requirements for this. This flexibility also requires that we have a multitiered workforce consisting of highly skilled, full-time employees and a pool of temporary workers (who do not need such a broad skill base) who can be called upon when demand is high.

8.5.4 Demand Leveling

By producing to demand and by utilizing kanban cards, we decrease the amount of inventory in the system. By balancing the line and setting our target manpower based on takt time, we reduce idle time and waste. But what happens if we face a sudden spike in demand? What happens if demand is volatile and is 200 units one day and 500 units the next? Do we have to reshuffle the line every single day?

Recall Taiichi Ohno using the fable adage "Run like the tortoise, not the hare." The Toyota Production System is a system built with the tortoise in mind. Spikes in demand—maybe resulting from new model introductions, marketing campaigns, sudden stoppages of incoming parts (maybe because of a strike in a supplier's organization), and quality problems—are

Demand leveling A way to sequence flow units so that the workflow causes a stable workload for all workers involved in the process.

Figure 8.7 The impact of takt time on staffing requirements (Note: The figure assumes a 1 minute/unit activity time at each station.)

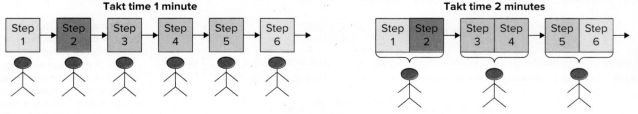

Figure 8.8

Five days of demand data from a firm selling three different models

| Day | Model | | | Total |
---	A	B	C	
1	8	4	3	15
2	4	6	0	10
3	5	3	2	10
4	7	4	3	14
5	6	3	2	11
Total	30	20	10	60

not compatible with TPS. Such external volatilities favor the hare and are detrimental to the tortoise.

Nevertheless, demand is likely to vary over time. Our goal is to match supply with demand, while also trying to avoid unevenness in the flows.

Consider the sales data shown in Figure 8.8. The company sells three different models, A, B, and C. Daily demand varies, at both the product level and in total. The production process requires a setup time to switch from one model to another. In light of these setups, the operation is likely to seek a production batch size $b > 1$ to take advantage of scale economies in production.

One possible production cycle with batches is shown in Figure 8.9. We produce 15 units of A, followed by 10 units of B, and then 5 units of C. Of course, we also spend some production time doing setups. What are the implications of this? Observe that:

- The flow in the process is very uneven. Imagine that model A requires installing a sunroof, while models B and C do not. The operator in charge of sunroof installation is working really hard when producing A and then is either idle or needs to be redeployed when producing B and C. This unevenness is referred to as **mura.** Note that the effects of mura also spill over to the suppliers of the operation. For example, the producer of sun roofs will have to rush 15 units in a row, followed by some long period of idle time. This overburdening of workers or equipment is referred to as **muri.**

- The uneven flow is also associated with waste (muda). While we are producing A, we are "running like the hare," only to then not produce A for a long time. This means that we build up inventory (overproduction) and have periodic idle time.

Ohno observed that an uneven workflow (mura) will lead to an overburdening of workers and equipment (muri) and will drive up waste (muda). These "3M's" are the enemies of the lean operation. Thus, an operation that is trying to be lean in presence of significant variability is likely to fail. A stable flow is at the foundation of TPS. To address variability in demand, TPS attempts to level demand. **Production leveling** (also known as production smoothing or **heijunka**) attempts to lower the peaks of production and raise the valleys in production as much as possible so that the flow at the surface is smooth.

Mura Unevenness in flow.

Muri An unreasonable amount of work, overburdening a machine or operator.

Heijunka Leveling production by reducing variation in the work schedule that arises from either demand variation or the desire to run production or transports in large batches. This is a principle of the Toyota Production System that strives to have production match the true rate of demand.

Slot	1	2	3	4	5	6	7	8	9	10	11	12	13	14	15	16	17	18	19	20	21	22	23	24	25	26	27	28	29	30	31	32	33	34	35	36
Traditional	A	A	A	A	A	A	A	A	A	A	A	A	A	A	A	S	S	S	B	B	B	B	B	B	B	B	B	B	S	S	S	C	C	C	C	C
Toyota	A	B	A	B	A	C	A	B	A	B	A	C	A	B	A	B	A	C	A	B	A	B	A	C	A	B	A	B	A	C						

Figure 8.9

Production sequence in a traditional production process versus TPS

Check Your Understanding 8.7

Question: A process makes two products, A and B, and operates 5 days per week, 8 hours per day. Demand for the two products for the next week is as follows:

Day 1: A: 4; B: 6
Day 2: A: 5; B: 5
Day 3: A: 6; B: 4
Day 4: A: 7; B: 3
Day 5: A: 3; B: 7

What is the takt time of the process? What would a level production schedule look like?

Answer: The total demand across both products is 50 units that we have to process over the course of the 40-hour workweek. So, the takt time would be

$$\text{Takt time} = \frac{\text{Available time}}{\text{Demand}} = \frac{40 \text{ hours}}{50 \text{ units}} = 0.8 \frac{\text{hour}}{\text{unit}}$$

A level production schedule would alternate between product A and product B, as they have the same overall aggregate demand rate. So, the schedule would be ABABABAB. . . .

....

Ideally, leveling should lead to zero fluctuations in the final assembly line. Consider the lower part of Figure 8.9. We are mixing the three models, A, B, and C, in the production flow. No two cars produced back to back are identical. What does this do to the evenness for the worker installing the sunroofs? The work now is leveled, which also simplifies the life of the sunroof supplier.

You notice in Figure 8.9 that we change over from one model to another much more frequently. This is only possible to the extent that we can reduce the duration of the setup times. Elsewhere we have discussed the concept of SMED as an important tool to reduce setups. Shorter setups allow the operation to switch between models more frequently, thereby helping synchronize the process with demand and making the operation lean.

So heijunka mixes models and avoids large production batches—it matches supply with demand and thus reduces the amount of inventory. Heijunka also levels the daily production volume. Observe from Figure 8.8 that daily demand varies from 10 to 15. Ideally, we would match this with our daily production output. But this, again, would lead to muri and "the other two M's." So instead, a leveled production plan would produce 12 units each day and would keep an order queue of a couple of days so that the production sequence can be mixed and the overall output is level. Doesn't this violate the idea of JIT? Yes, it does. TPS simply does not go along with variability. As we discuss in further detail in Chapter 16, an operation facing variability needs to pay a price for that variability, in the form of either a higher inventory or a lower flow rate.

Jidoka Upon detection of a problem, shutting down the machine to force a human intervention, which in turn triggers process improvement.

8.6 TPS Pillar 2: Expose Problems and Solve Them When They Occur: Detect-Stop-Alert (Jidoka)

LO8-7 Explain jidoka and be able to compute the information turnaround time.

Emphasizing the role of quality and addressing quality problems correctly when and where they occur is the second pillar supporting the house of TPS. The basic philosophy is that the production process should halt production when a quality problem is discovered. Lines that do not stop were, according to Ohno, either perfect (which is rare) or facing big problems (that were simply hidden/swept under the rug). Once a quality problem is found, it is addressed locally, hopefully preventing it from recurring.

So the process circles through three steps as illustrated in Figure 8.10:

1. Detecting quality problems, stopping the process, and alerting the operator (**jidoka**).

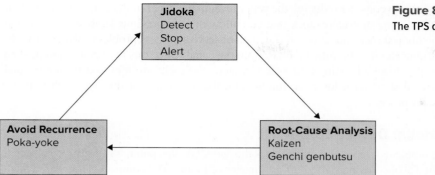

Figure 8.10
The TPS quality improvement framework

2. Thoroughly analyzing the root cause on the shop floor (**kaizen**).

3. Avoiding the recurrence of the problem by implementing improvements (**poka-yoke**).

This loop is similar to the quality improvement framework of Six-Sigma and statistical process control that we discuss in Chapter 9, Quality and Statistical Process Control. The following sections first explain the basic philosophy of exposing problems and then provide more details on the steps jidoka, kaizen, and poka-yoke.

8.6.1 Exposing Problems

In TPS, inventory is seen as the worst form of the previously discussed seven sources of waste. So far, we have emphasized the impact that inventory has on working capital and that inventory has on increasing the flow time as well as decreasing the percentage value-added time (see earlier). But the effects of inventory are worse, much worse.

Ohno observed that inventory helps to "cover up problems." High inventory and poor quality oftentimes go hand in hand. A commonly used metaphor of how inventory hides problems is the following. Consider a boat sailing on a canal that has numerous rocks in it (Figure 8.11). The freight of the boat is very valuable, so the company operating the canal wants to make sure the boat never hits a rock.

One approach to this situation is to increase the water level in the canal. This way, there is plenty of water over the rocks and the likelihood of an accident is low. In a production setting, the rocks correspond to quality problems (defects), setup times, breakdowns, or other problems in the process, and the ship hitting a rock corresponds to lost throughput. The amount of water corresponds to the amount of inventory in the process (i.e., the number of kanban cards).

Poka-yoke Foolproofing an operation to avoid the recurrence of defects.

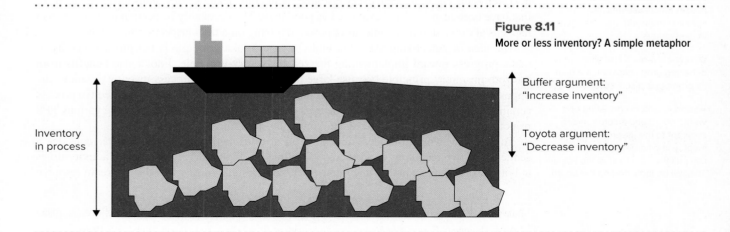

Figure 8.11
More or less inventory? A simple metaphor

Inventory in process

Buffer argument: "Increase inventory"

Toyota argument: "Decrease inventory"

An alternative way of approaching the problem is this: Instead of covering the rocks with water, we could also consider reducing the water level in the canal (reduce the number of kanban cards by reducing the safety stock that you allow in your previous kanban calculations). This way, the highest rocks are exposed (i.e., you observe a process problem), which provides you with the opportunity of removing them from the canal. Once this has been accomplished, the water level is lowered again, until—step by step—all rocks are removed from the canal. Despite potential short-term losses in throughput, the advantage of this approach is that it leads to a better process.

8.6.2 Jidoka: Detect-Stop-Alert

So exposing problems is critical, but how does this work? At this point, it is useful to go back to the history of Toyota. Toyota started off as a maker of looms. The company's founder, Sakichi Toyoda, invented the first fully automated loom well before the company had anything to do with building cars. Automated looms were more efficient with respect to the need for labor—one operator could now oversee multiple pieces of equipment. We already discussed how TPS assigns a worker to multiple tasks so that the operator can work on another task while a piece of equipment is operating (instead of watching that piece of equipment do its work). Things get difficult, however, when a defect occurs. After all, the operator is busy working on something else. Sakichi Toyoda's automated loom was equipped with a device that automatically and immediately stopped the machine if the vertical or lateral threads broke or ran out.[3] This idea of merging the human intelligence required for handling exceptions with the mechanical power of a machine was labeled **autonomation,** which stands for automation with a human touch or **jidoka.**

For autonomation to work, the equipment has to be capable of (1) detecting that a problem exists, (2) stopping production, and (3) alerting the operator. **Detect-stop-alert** is thus at the heart of exposing defects. Shutting down the machine forces a human intervention in the process, which in turn triggers process improvement.[4] The jidoka concept has been generalized to include any mechanism that stops production in response to quality problems, not just for automated machines. The most well-known form of jidoka is the **Andon** cord, a cord running adjacent to assembly lines that enables workers to stop production if they detect a defect. Just like the jidoka automatic shutdown of machines, this procedure dramatizes manufacturing problems and acts as a pressure for process improvements (see Photo 8.2).

The term *Andon* refers to the line-stop indicator board hung above the production line as a visual control. The trouble indicator light works as follows: green refers to normal operations; yellow indicates that a worker wants to adjust something and is calling for help; red indicates that a line stop is needed to rectify a problem and the line should stop.

Stopping a production line in most operations is a "big deal." Historically, in most production environments, the pressure on workers was to keep the line moving. Nobody dared stopping Henry Ford's assembly line. Unfortunately, this created an incentive for the workforce to simply hide problems. Ohno emphasized that workers should not be afraid to stop the line. In TPS, "the next step is the customer" and every resource should only let those flow units move downstream that have been inspected and evaluated as good parts. Hence, quality inspection is "built in" and happens at every step in the line, as opposed to relying on a final inspection step alone.

The idea of detect-stop-alert that underlies the jidoka principle is not just a necessity to make progress toward implementing the zero inventory principle. Jidoka also benefits from the zero inventory principle because large amounts of work-in-process inventory achieve the opposite of jidoka: They delay the detection of a problem, thereby keeping a defective process running and hiding the defect from the eyes of management. This shows how the various TPS principles and methods are interrelated, mutually strengthening each other.

To see how work-in-process inventory is at odds with the idea of jidoka, consider a sequence of two resources in a process as outlined in Figure 8.12. Assume the activity times at both resources are equal to one minute per unit. Assume further that the upstream resource

© Jim West/Alamy

PHOTO 8.2 Example of an Andon cord at an automobile manufacturing factory in Michigan.

Autonomation Automation with a human touch; use machines, but combine them with the intelligence of the workers.

Detect-stop-alert The philosophy of halting production when a quality problem is discovered.

Andon A system consisting of a visible board and a cord running adjacent to the assembly line. An employee who detects a problem can pull the cord to stop the line. This will be indicated on the board.

---

[3] Taiichi Ohno, *Toyota Production System: Beyond Large-Scale Production* (Portland, OR: Productivity Press, 1988).

[4] Takahiro Fujimoto, *Evolution of Manufacturing Systems at Toyota* (New York: Productivity Press, 1999).

(on the left) suffers quality problems and—at some random point in time—starts producing bad output. In Figure 8.12, this is illustrated by the resource producing squares instead of circles. How long will it take until a quality problem is discovered? If there is a large buffer between the two resources (upper part of Figure 8.12), the downstream resource will continue to receive good units from the buffer. In this example, it will take 7 minutes before the downstream resource detects the defective flow unit. This gives the upstream resource 7 minutes to continue producing defective parts that need to be either scrapped or reworked.

Thus, the time between when the problem occurred at the upstream resource and when it is detected at the downstream resource depends on the size of the buffer between the two resources. This is a direct consequence of Little's Law. We refer to the time between creating a defect and receiving the feedback about the defect as the **information turnaround time (ITAT)**. Note that we assume in this example that the defect is detected in the next resource downstream. The impact of inventory on quality is much worse if defects only get detected at the end of the process (e.g., at a final inspection step). In this case, the ITAT is driven by all inventory downstream from the resource producing the defect. This motivates the built-in inspection we mentioned earlier.

Information turnaround time (ITAT) The time between creating a defect and receiving the feedback about the defect.

Check Your Understanding 8.8

Question: Consider the following two production processes making an electronic component for a navigation system. Both processes consist of 20 stations and operate at a cycle time of 1 minute/unit. Their most error-prone operation is step 9:

- Process 1 has a final inspection at the end of the process and has about 300 units of inventory between step 9 and the inspection.
- Process 2 has each worker check the work of the previous steps and about 50 units of inventory between step 9 and the end of the process, roughly equally distributed across the remainder of the process.

What would be the information turnaround time for a defect made at station 9?

Answer: For process 1, the defective flow unit needs to journey through the remaining 11 stations. The flow rate is 1 unit per minute and the inventory is 300 units. So, it will take 300 minutes until the defective unit is detected at inspection.

For process 2, the defective unit will be detected at station 10. There are about 5 units of inventory between steps 9 and 10 (50 units over 11 buffers). So the time to detection is about 5 minutes.

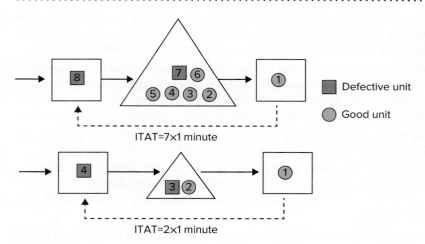

Figure 8.12
Information turnaround time and its relationship with buffer size

8.6.3 Root-Cause Problem Solving and Defect Prevention

Once a problem is detected, we have to understand its root cause. Why did the problem occur in the first place? We have an entire chapter dedicated to quality, so we focus on simply introducing two key concepts that characterize TPS's approach towards root-cause problem solving:

- **Kaizen** stands for continuous improvement, the process of making small changes to the process with the goal of eliminating waste. Kaizen workshops are gatherings of small teams of front-line workers.

- **Genchi genbutsu** is an important philosophy behind kaizen. Problem solving should emphasize going out to the front line and observing the problem yourself, collecting data, and analyzing the data instead of emphasizing personal opinions or management seniority. Everyone dealing with a specific problem should gather firsthand information from the situation. This principle explicitly includes senior management.

While kaizen and genchi genbutsu seem obvious, they are in sharp contrast to the existing culture of most operations. Recall the eighth source of waste and Taylor's animalistic view of the workers. In traditional mass production, process improvement was the domain of engineering and management. Regular workers were to do what they were told—they had no authority to change the process.

The output of a kaizen project is a validated idea for improvement. Oftentimes, such an idea will help prevent the previously detected defect from recurring by foolproofing an activity (**poka-yoke**). These ideas lead to new work standards or new pieces of equipment that prevent defects from recurring. Examples provided by Ohno include:

- When there is a mistake, the material will not fit the tool.
- The machine will not start if there is an irregularity in the material or a mistake in the operation (see Photo 8.3).
- If there are steps left, corrections are made automatically or the machine will not start the next step.

In order to create such poka-yokes, operators need to be empowered to write and rewrite the standards that define how a particular activity is carried out. These standards are displayed visibly at the operation, which also creates a flexibility of the operation when new workers are added to increase capacity.

Conclusion

As we acknowledged earlier on in this chapter, the success of TPS should not be reduced to implementing a set of lean tools, such as JIT, jidoka, or kaizen. TPS is broader and a transition to lean operations certainly requires major organizational changes. The usage of the Andon cord and the frequency and consequences of the associated line stoppages are probably the best litmus test for where an operation stands with respect to its implementation of TPS:

- An Andon cord that is rarely pulled and a workforce that is afraid to stop the line because this might damage the operation's productivity targets are clear indications for an operation that has half-heartedly adapted TPS; the Andon cord is present—but TPS's philosophy of favoring long-term process capability over short-term productivity is not embraced.

- An operation that has embraced TPS is one with a workforce for which stopping the line is a natural instinct. In a Toyota plant, Andon cords are pulled hundreds of times per day—and this includes some of the best production facilities in the world. Instead of complaining about the production loss, local shop-floor leaders are there to support the workers in a matter of minutes (or even seconds) when a yellow or red light shows up on the Andon board.

Scholars of management agree that the various process elements of TPS discussed in this chapter, together with the "other 3Ps"—philosophy, problem solving, and people—reinforce

---

Kaizen The process of making small changes to the process with the goal of eliminating waste.

Genchi genbutsu Gather firsthand information from the situation by going and observing the situation yourself, collecting data, and analyzing the data.

© McGraw-Hill Education, Mark A. Dierker, photographer

PHOTO 8.3 The Ninja professional blender is able to crush frozen fruits or ice. The device will not start until all components are correctly aligned. This protects the operator from harm.

TABLE 8.2 Toyota Vocabulary List (in alphabetical order)

Toyota Term	Definition
Andon	A system consisting of a visible board and a cord running adjacent to the assembly line. An employee who detects a problem can pull the cord to stop the line. This will be indicated on the board.
Autonomation	Automation with a human touch—use machines but combine them with the intelligence of the workers.
Genchi genbutsu	Gather firsthand information from the situation by going and observing the situation yourself, collecting data, and analyzing the data.
Heijunka	Leveling production by reducing variation in the work schedule that arises from either demand variation or the desire to run production or transports in large batches.
Ikko-nagashi	Operate at a flow of one unit at a time from one resource to the next instead of operating based on transfer batches.
Jidoka	Upon detection of a problem, shut down the machine to force a human intervention, which in turn triggers process improvement.
Kaizen	The process of making small changes to the process with the goal of eliminating waste.
Kanban	Production and inventory control system in which production instructions and parts delivery instructions are triggered by the consumption of parts downstream.
Muda	Waste.
Mura	Unevenness in flow.
Muri	An unreasonable amount of work, overburdening a machine or operator.
Poka-yoke	Foolproofing an operation to avoid the recurrence of defects.

each other. To get the full benefits of TPS, the entire organization needs to embrace all dimensions of TPS instead of cherry-picking one. As you will see, after (half-heartedly) adapting some process techniques described in this chapter, many operations claim to "do lean," but actually fail to make use of the full benefits of TPS.

LO8-8 Define the basic vocabulary terms of the Toyota Production System.

Though this book is about operations management and not Japanese vocabulary, we summarize the various elements of TPS together with their Japanese name in Table 8.2. Learning these concepts not only will allow you to appear smart because of your knowledge of Japanese buzzwords, but will serve as a reminder that there are many elements in TPS and it probably won't take long until you start identifying muda in your own life.

Summary of Learning Objectives

LO8-1 Explain the two ways in which an operation can be wasteful

An operation can be wasteful in two ways. It can waste the time of a resource, which causes a reduction in capacity. Or it can waste the time of a flow unit, which causes wait time for the flow unit (and, because of Little's Law, excessive inventory).

LO8-2 Distinguish between waste, non-value-added work, and value-added work and determine the percentage of value-added work at a resource

Waste is the needless waste of time (of workers) that should be eliminated. There exist seven sources of waste. Non-value-added time is the work that needs to happen given the way the process is designed, but it is not valued by the customer. The overall equipment effectiveness measures the percentage of the available time at a resource that is used for value-added work.

LO8-3 Determine the percentage of flow time that is value-added time

Flow units are impatient. If they spend time waiting, they contribute to inventory. So, it is important to keep the flow time short, relative to the value-added time. This is captured in the ratio of value-added time to flow time, which we call the value-added percentage.

LO8-4   Explain the main building blocks of the Toyota Production System

The Toyota Production System can be summarized in the shape of a house with the roof capturing the main goal of the TPS, which is waste reduction: the pillars being just-in-time flow and built-in quality, and the foundation being process improvement.

LO8-5   Explain the concepts of single-unit flow, pull, kanban, and just-in-time and be able to compute the appropriate number of kanban cards

Work should be pulled through the process based on demand, not based on the availability of machine capacity. This can happen via a kanban system or a make-to-order system. As the flow units move through the process, they should be transferred one unit at a time, instead of being batched together. Batching units to economize on transportation costs captures a poor layout of the facility. To avoid this, resources should be located according to the workflow, ideally forming the shape of a U.

LO8-6   Compute takt time and determine a level production schedule

The rate of the process flow ought to be dictated by demand. The demand rate is translated to a takt time, which sets the rhythm for the process. To the extent that demand is variable and that different types of units are demanded, the flow ought to be leveled, which leads to a smooth workflow for all resources, instead of causing ups and downs in workload.

LO8-7   Explain jidoka and be able to compute the information turnaround time

When a problem arises, the problem needs to be detected as early as possible. The process should stop and the operator needs to be alerted. This needs to be followed up with a careful investigation of the root cause for the stoppage. Once the root cause is found, workers look for ways to avoid a recurrence of the problem.

LO8-8   Define the basic vocabulary terms of the Toyota Production System

Toyota Term	Definition
Andon	A system consisting of a visible board and a cord running adjacent to the assembly line. An employee who detects a problem can pull the cord to stop the line. This will be indicated on the board.
Autonomation	Automation with a human touch—use machines, but combine them with the intelligence of the workers.
Genchi genbutsu	Gather firsthand information from the situation by going and observing the situation yourself, collecting data, and analyzing the data.
Heijunka	Leveling production by reducing variation in the work schedule that arises from either demand variation or from the desire to run production or transports in large batches.
Ikko-nagashi	Operate at a flow of one unit at a time from one resource to the next instead of operating based on transfer batches
Jidoka	Upon detection of a problem, shut down the machine to force a human intervention, which in turn triggers process improvement.
Kaizen	The process of making small changes to the process with the goal of eliminating waste.
Kanban	An inventory control system in which production instructions and parts delivery instructions are triggered by the consumption of parts downstream.
Muda	Waste.
Mura	Unevenness in flow.
Muri	An unreasonable amount of work, overburdening a machine or operator.
Poka-yoke	Foolproofing an operation to avoid the recurrence of defects.

Key Terms

8.1   What Is Lean Operations?

James Womack An MIT professor who founded the International Motor Vehicle Program and later the Lean Enterprise Institute.

Toyota Production System (TPS) A framework used to run operations with the goal of reducing both the waste of capacity and the waste of flow time, thereby making sure supply and demand are matched just in time.

Waste of time of a resource The waste of time from the perspective of a resource, which reduces the capacity of the resource.

Waste of time of a flow unit The waste of time from the perspective of a flow unit, which makes the flow time of that flow unit longer than what is needed in the eyes of the customer.

8.2   Wasting Time of a Resource

Frederick Winslow Taylor An engineer who pioneered the concept of scientific management at the end of the 19th century.

Scientific management A management framework created by Frederick Winslow Taylor that emphasizes efficiency and optimization.

Taiichi Ohno An engineer who pioneered the Toyota Production System, built around the principles of waste reduction.

Waste The consumption of inputs and resources that do not add value to the customer.

Muda Waste.

Non-value-added work Those operations that do not add value in the eyes of the customer but must be done under the current conditions of the process in order to complete a unit

Value-added work Those operations valued by the customer because they are absolutely required to transform the flow unit from its inputs to being the output the customer wants.

Total available time The amount of time a resource has available to fulfill demand.

Overall equipment effectiveness (OEE) The percentage of total available time that is used in a way that adds value to the customer.

Kaizen The process of making small changes to the process with the goal of eliminating waste.

Seven sources of production waste Seven ways in which, in the eyes of Ohno, a resource can waste its capacity: waiting (idle time), overproduction, inventory, transport, overprocessing, rework, and unnecessary motions.

Just-in-time (JIT) production Supplying a unit of demand when and where it is needed, thus avoiding unnecessary inventory.

8.3   Wasting Time of a Flow Unit

Value-added percentage The percentage of flow time used for value-added work.

8.4   The Architecture of the Toyota Production System

4Ps of Toyota Business principles embraced by Toyota that include philosophy, processes, people, and problem solving.

Toyota house A representation of the Toyota Production System in the shape of a house with the roof capturing the main goal of the TPS, which is waste reduction; the pillars being just-in-time flow and built-in-quality; and the foundation being process improvement.

8.5   TPS Pillar 1: Single-Unit Flow and Just-in-Time Production

Run like the tortoise, not the hare An ancient fable used by Ohno to illustrate that steady work, even when slow, is better than bursts of speed followed by periods of no movement.

Takt time The ratio between the time available and the quantity that has to be produced to serve demand.

Single-unit flow Operate at a flow of one unit at a time from one resource to the next instead of operating based on transfer batches.

Pull system The resource furthest downstream (i.e., closest to the market) is paced by market demand. In addition to its own production, it also relays the demand information to the next station upstream, thus ensuring that the upstream resource also is paced by demand. That is, it is an operating system in which the production or replenishment of a unit is only initiated when a demand occurs.

Kanban Production and inventory control system in which production instructions and parts delivery instructions are triggered by the consumption of parts downstream.

Make-to-order Making the activation of resources in a process contingent on receiving a specific order.

Process layout The spatial location of resources in a process that drives the needs for transportation.

Baton passing zone Instead of having fixed allocations of activities to workers, the idea of a baton passing zone is that the process can absorb variations in speed and starting time.

U-shaped line Locating resources in a way that they create a "U," which increases the flexibility of workers to perform multiple tasks.

Multitask job assignment A technique to reduce idle time by avoiding a worker watching a machine do work.

Target manpower The ratio between the labor content and the takt time determines the minimum number of resources required to meet demand. Note that this minimum does not have to be an integer number and that it assumes all resources are perfectly utilized.

Demand leveling A way to sequence flow units so that the workflow causes a stable workload for all workers involved in the process.

Mura Unevenness in flow.

Muri An unreasonable amount of work, overburdening a machine or operator.

Heijunka Leveling production by reducing variation in the work schedule that arises from either demand variation or the desire to run production or transports in large batches. This is a principle of the Toyota Production System that strives to have production match the true rate of demand.

8.6 TPS Pillar 2: Expose Problems and Solve Them When They Occur: Detect-Stop-Alert (Jidoka)

Jidoka Upon detection of a problem, shutting down the machine to force a human intervention, which in turn triggers process improvement.

Poka-yoke Foolproofing an operation to avoid the recurrence of defects.

Autonomation Automation with a human touch; use machines, but combine them with the intelligence of the workers.

Detect-stop-alert the philosophy of halting production when a quality problem is discovered.

Andon A system consisting of a visible board and a cord running adjacent to the assembly line. An employee who detects a problem can pull the cord to stop the line. This will be indicated on the board.

Information turnaround time (ITAT) The time between creating a defect and receiving the feedback about the defect.

Genchi genbutsu Gather firsthand information from the situation by going and observing the situation yourself, collecting data, and analyzing the data.

Key Formulas

LO8-2 **Distinguish between waste, non-value add work, and value add work and determine the percentage of value add work at a resource**

$$\text{OEE} = \frac{\text{Value-added time}}{\text{Total available time}}$$

LO8-3   Determine the percentage of flow time that is value add time

$$\text{Value-added percentage} = \frac{\text{Value-added time of a flow unit}}{\text{Flow time}}$$

LO8-5   Explain the concepts of single unit flow, pull, Kanban, and just-in-time and be able to compute the appropriate number of Kanban cards

$$\text{Number of kanban cards} = \frac{\text{Demand during replenishment time} + \text{Safety stock}}{\text{Container size}}$$

$$\text{Demand during replenishment time} = \text{Replenishment time} \times \text{Demand rate}$$

LO8-6   Compute takt time and determine a level production schedule

$$\text{Takt time} = \frac{\text{Available time}}{\text{Demand rate}}$$

$$\text{Target manpower} = \frac{\text{Labor content}}{\text{Takt time}}$$

Conceptual Questions

LO8-1

1. An orthopedic surgeon has read an article about the Toyota Production System and now wants to organize her surgery operation based on lean principles. To eliminate all idle time in the operating room, she decides to call in patients six hours before the scheduled surgery time. Is this a lean process?
   a. Yes
   b. No
   c. Cannot be determined

2. Which car company is most often associated with the term *lean operations*?
   a. General Motors
   b. Ford
   c. Toyota
   d. Honda

LO8-2

3. A worker in charge of assembling a bicycle finds a faster way to mount the pedals. He turns to his supervisor. The supervisor explains that the process had been optimized by the engineering department and so the worker should make sure to stick with the existing procedures. Which management scholar's work does this fit best?
   a. Taylor
   b. Ohno
   c. Womack
   d. Fujimoto

4. Students have to change buildings between classes, which often involves walks of 5 minutes or more. Walking from one building to another is:
   a. waste.
   b. non-value-added time.
   c. value-added time.
   d. Cannot determine from the given infomation

5. An executive declares that his company has achieved an OEE of 115 percent. Is this possible?
   a. Yes
   b. No
   c. Sometimes

6. Which of the following does not belong to the seven sources of waste?
   a. Rework
   b. Overtime
   c. Transportation
   d. Inventory

LO8-3

7. In a service operation, we can compute the value-added time by simply looking at the labor content. True or false?
   a. True
   b. False

8. A company is increasing the percentage value-added time in the operation. Its value-added time and its flow rate remain unchanged. What will happen to its inventory turns? (Recall from Chapter 2 that inventory turns are computed as flow rate divided by inventory.)
   a. Inventory turns will go up.
   b. Inventory turns will stay constant.
   c. Inventory turns will go down.
   d. Cannot determine from the given information

LO8-4

9. What are the two pillars of the Toyota Production System?
   a. Just-in-time and waste reduction
   b. Waste reduction and built-in quality
   c. Built-in quality and just-in-time
   d. Process improvement and waste reduction

10. What is the roof in the "house-shaped" representation of the Toyota Production System?
    a. Just-in-time
    b. Waste reduction
    c. Built-in quality
    d. Process improvement

LO8-5

11. Taichi Ohno built the Toyota Production System with the metaphor of a tiger in mind. Rapid and decisive movements were, in his view, the best way to match supply with demand. True or false?
    a. True
    b. False

LO8-6

12. If customers want to have 1000 units over 10 days, one should aim at producing 100 units per day instead of doing 111 units per day in the beginning and then having a little safety buffer at the end. True or false?
    a. True
    b. False

13. If the demand rate increases, the takt time:
    a. increases.
    b. decreases.

14. If the takt time increases, the operation requires:
    a. more workers.
    b. fewer workers.

LO8-5

15. Which of the following objectives is more important in a pull system?
    a. Producing at the rate of demand
    b. Keeping the equipment utilization

16. What is the relationship between the number of kanban cards in a process and the inventory level?
    a. There is no relationship between the two.
    b. There never can be more inventory in the process than what was authorized via kanban cards.
    c. The inventory of the process grows with the square root of the number of kanban cards.
    d. The inventory of the process can be reduced by adding more kanban cards.

17. Which of the following statements about kanban are accurate?
    a. Deploying the kanban system leads to pulling work through the system instead of pushing work.
    b. Deploying the kanban system leads to pushing work through the system instead of pulling work.
    c. The kanban system controls the work-in-process inventory.
    d. Kanban will always reduce the amount of inventory in the process.
    e. Kanban requires cross-training all workers.
    f. A and B
    g. A and C
    h. A and D

18. What happens to the number of Kanban cards in the process if the replenishment time goes up?
    a. The number of kanban cards increases.
    b. The number of kanban cards stays the same.
    c. The number of kanban cards decreases.
    d. Cannot determine from the given information

LO8-6

19. Because of long setup times, a company chooses to run big production batches. Which of the following actions will level the production schedule?
    a. Using overtime
    b. Mixing the models on the final line
    c. Making sure that rework is kept low
    d. Reducing the waste of the process

20. A company makes two models, A and B. Which of the following production schedules is more level?
    a. ABABABABAB
    b. AAAAABBBBB

LO8-7

21. The information turnaround time is driven primarily by:
    a. the number of workers.
    b. the IT system.
    c. the inventory in the process.
    d. the amount of waste in the process.

22. Pulling the andon cord can cause a loss of output. In TPS, an employee should pull the andon cord:
    a. whenever a problem occurs.
    b. whenever the employee sees the cost of stopping the line as lower than the costs of not stopping it.
    c. whenever he or she needs to go on a break.
    d. at no time.

23. A single inspection system with experts testing the output of the process will help reduce the information turnaround time. True or false?
    a. True
    b. False

24. Kaizen favors automation and investment in technology. True or false?
    a. True
    b. False

LO8-8

25. Which of the following terms is not part of the Toyota Production System (TPS)?
    a. Ikko-nagashi
    b. Kanban
    c. Jidoka
    d. Yakimono
    e. Genchi genbutsu

26. Genchi genbutsu requires the implementation of a pull system. True or false?
    a. True
    b. False

Solved Example Problems

LO 8-2

1. As an equipment provider for several Olympic cyclists, Carbon Bike Frames (CBF) operates a very expensive wind tunnel facility near San Diego, California. The wind tunnel is used to find the best compromise between ergonomics and aerodynamics for the cyclist. Presently, more and more cyclists are interested in CBF's services, and so the company considers building a second facility. However, given the enormous costs of the wind tunnel, it also wants to explore a more effective use of the current facility. An initial data collection reveals that:

   - The standard fitting time for a cyclist is 2 hours. On average, the wind tunnel is used for 7 fitting procedures a day (new customers or customers who want a refit). The wind tunnel is available 24 hours a day.
   - CBF offers a free second session if it turns out that the bike fit was done incorrectly. About 2 out of 7 of the customers come back for such a "refit," which takes the same amount of time as the initial fit.
   - Twenty minutes of each fitting procedure is spent setting up the bike on a stationary trainer and getting the athlete ready. Almost all of this could happen outside the wind tunnel; that is, while another fitting procedure is still going on.
   - About one day out of 10, the wind tunnel is down for maintenance or repair.

   What is the OEE of the wind tunnel? Recall that the wind tunnel can be used 24 hours a day.

   Answer: To find the OEE, we first compute that over a 10-day cycle, the wind tunnel is available 240 hours.

   Given that it is down for maintenance for 1 day, we have 9 days of operations. In 9 days, the wind tunnel does 63 (9×7) fittings. Of those, 2 out of 7 are refits and thus don't count as value-added, leaving 5 out of 7 new fits. Over 9 days, that is 45 new fits. Each fit counts for 100 minutes of value-added work. So we get an OEE of

   $$OEE = \frac{\text{Value-added time (over 10 days)}}{\text{Available time (over 10 days)}}$$

   $$= \frac{45 \times 100 \text{ min}}{10 \times 24 \times 60 \text{ min}} = \frac{4500}{14400} = 0.3125$$

LO 8-3

2. Citizens of a not-to-be-named country are required to renew their passports every 10 years. For passport renewal, they have to collect a set of documents that they then send to the country's capital. The average time in the mail is about 2 days. It takes

4 days before a clerk in the capital looks at the passport renewal. This takes about 10 minutes. The clerk then asks his assistant to prepare a form that is sent to the government's printing office. The assistant completes this task within 3 days and it takes another 2 days in transit to the printing office. There, the dossier waits an average of 10 days before the new passport is printed, an operation that takes about 2 minutes. It is then sent back to the citizen, which typically takes another 2 days. What is the percent value-added time in this flow? Use 24 hours per day as the potential work time.

Answer: We first compute the flow time as

Flow time = 2 days (mail) + 4 days (clerk) + 3 days (assistant)

+ 2 days (mail) + 10 days (printing office) + 2 days (mail) = 23 days

We then compute the value-added time as 10 minutes (clerk) + 2 minutes (printing). This gives us a value-added percentage of

$$\frac{\text{Value-added time of the flow unit}}{\text{Flow time}} = \frac{12 \text{ minutes}}{23 \text{ days}}$$

$$= \frac{12 \text{ minutes}}{33120 \text{ minutes}} = 0.000362$$

LO 8-4

3. What metaphor best summarizes the Toyota Production System?

(a) A house

(b) A circle

(c) A rabbit

(d) A river

Answer: The Toyota Production System's elements take the form of a house.

At the top (the roof), we have the principle of waste reduction and the goal to match supply with demand. Waste reduction includes reducing the waste of the resource's time as well as reducing the waste of a flow unit's time. It thus results in a better match of supply with demand.

The roof is supported by two pillars, just-in-time production and built-in quality. Just-in-time production embraces concepts such as single-unit flow, leveled production, and a pull system. Built-in quality emphasizes the need to stop the process immediately upon creation of defects (jidoka). This leads to short information turnaround time and hence process improvements, potentially in the form of foolproofing.

The foundation of the house is a culture of process improvement and a stable environment with limited variability.

LO 8-5

4. What is the difference between a push system and a pull system?

(a) A push system favors running a machine, even if there exists no demand for it.

(b) In a pull system, the last resource is paced directly by demand.

(c) Generally, there will be less inventory in a pull system.

(d) All of the above.

Answer: d. In a push process, resources operate at a pace that is dictated by their capacity and the available inflows/materials. This can lead to large amounts of inventory in the process, especially if the process is demand-constrained. In a pull process, demand dictates the flow. This can be done with a kanban system or a make-to-order system.

5. In an automotive plant, windshield wipers are replenished using a kanban system. The following data describe the process:

   - The daily demand is 800 units (one unit is a pair of wipers).
   - The production lead time is 2 days (this includes processing time, transport time, and waiting time).
   - Management has decided to have 0.5 day of safety stock.
   - One container fits 200 units.

   How many kanban containers will be needed to support this system?

   Answer: We first determine the amount of demand during the production lead time.

   $$\text{Demand during lead time} = \text{Lead time} \times \text{Daily demand}$$

   $$= 2 \text{ days} \times 800 \frac{\text{units}}{\text{day}} = 1600 \text{ units}$$

   We translate the 0.5 day of safety stock into a quantity, which is 0.5 day $\times$ 800 units/day = 400 units.

   With this and a container size of 200 units/container, we need

   $$\text{Number of kanban containers} = \frac{\text{Demand during lead time} + \text{Safety stock}}{\text{Container size}}$$

   $$= \frac{(1600 + 400)}{200} = \frac{2000}{200} = 10$$

   So, we need 10 containers.

   LO 8-6

6. A process makes two products, A and B, and operates 5 days per week, 7 hours per day. Demand for the two products for the next week is as follows:

   Day 1: A: 3;   B: 5

   Day 2: A: 2;   B: 6

   Day 3: A: 4;   B: 7

   Day 4: A: 2;   B: 5

   Day 5: A: 3;   B: 5

   What is the takt time of the process? What would a level production schedule look like?

   Answer: The total demand across both products is 42 units, which we have to process over the course of the 35-hour workweek. So, the takt time would be

   $$\text{Takt time} = \frac{\text{Available time}}{\text{Demand}} = \frac{35 \text{ hours}}{42 \text{ units}} = 0.83333 \frac{\text{hour}}{\text{unit}}$$

   Over the week, demand is 14 units for A and 28 for B. So, we have to produce in a 1:2 proportion. A level production schedule would thus be ABBABBABBABB. . . .

   LO 8-7

7. In the Toyota Production System, *jidoka* refers to:

   (a) level production, where different models are produced alongside each other on the assembly line.

   (b) continuous improvement, where workers organize meetings to discuss ways of improving the production process.

   (c) the inventory retrieval system, where parts are replenished only when they are needed.

   (d) the aggressive reduction of changeover and setup times.

(e) continuous line-balancing to maximize utilization.

(f) the cross-training of workers for a wide range of skills.

(g) none of the above.

>   **Answer:** None of the above (g) captures jidoka. Jidoka refers to the process improvement triggered by shutting down a machine and physically examining the process whenever a worker detects a problem.

8. Consider a production process making controllers for video game consoles. The process operates on a 30-second/unit cycle time. It has 10 stations, with the most error-prone activity carried out at station 2. Inspection happens at the end of the process and there are about 600 units of inventory between step 2 and the inspection.

>   What would be the information turnaround time for a defect made at station 2?

>   **Answer:** The defective flow unit needs to journey through the remaining 8 stations. The flow rate is 2 units per minute and the inventory is 600 units. So, it will take 300 minutes until the defective unit is detected at inspection. This is a result of Little's Law, with 600 units = 2 units/minute × Flow time.

LO 8-8

9. Which of the following best captures the idea of kaizen?

(a) Examples of this include workers having to make unnecessary movements (i.e., excessive reaching or walking to get tools or parts), working on parts that are defective, and idle time.

(b) A system that enables a line worker to signal that he or she needs assistance from his or her supervisor—for example, in the case of a defect. It is used to implement the jidoka principle.

(c) A brainstorming technique that helps structure the process of identifying underlying causes of a (usually undesirable) outcome.

(d) As an example of this philosophy, workers in the factory have notebooks at their workstations that they use to jot down improvement ideas.

(e) A method that controls the amount of work-in-process inventory.

(f) If an automotive assembly plant used this technique, the adjacent cars on an assembly line would be mixed models (e.g., Model A with sunroof, Model A without sunroof, Model B, Model B with sunroof) in proportions equal to customer demand.

>   **Answer:** d.

10. Which of the following captures the idea of Andon?

(a) Examples of this include workers having to make unnecessary movements (i.e., excessive reaching or walking to get tools or parts), working on parts that are defective, and idle time.

(b) A system that enables a line worker to signal that he or she needs assistance from his or her supervisor, for example, in the case of a defect. It is used to implement the jidoka principle.

(c) A brainstorming technique that helps structure the process of identifying underlying causes of a (usually undesirable) outcome.

(d) As an example of this philosophy, workers in the factory have notebooks at their workstations that they use to jot down improvement ideas.

(e) A method that controls the amount of work-in-process inventory.

(f) If an automotive assembly plant used this technique, the adjacent cars on an assembly line would be mixed models (e.g., Model A with sunroof, Model A without sunroof, Model B, Model B with sunroof) in proportions equal to customer demand.

>   **Answer:** b.

11. Which of the following captures the idea of heijunka?

    (a) Examples of this include workers having to make unnecessary movements (i.e., excessive reaching or walking to get tools or parts), working on parts that are defective, and idle time.

    (b) A system that enables a line worker to signal that he or she needs assistance from his or her supervisor, for example, in the case of a defect. It is used to implement the jidoka principle.

    (c) A brainstorming technique that helps structure the process of identifying underlying causes of a (usually undesirable) outcome.

    (d) As an example of this philosophy, workers in the factory have notebooks at their workstations that they use to jot down improvement ideas.

    (e) A method that controls the amount of work-in-process inventory.

    (f) If an automotive assembly plant used this technique, the adjacent cars on an assembly line would be mixed models (e.g., Model A with sunroof, Model A without sunroof, Model B, Model B with sunroof) in proportions equal to customer demand.

    Answer: f.

Problems and Applications

LO8-1

1. You arrive at the airport and wonder to what extent the security checkpoint is a lean operation. Among other things, you observe that it takes about 30 seconds to check an ID, scan a passenger for weapons, and X-ray their luggage. However, the average customer spends about 20 minutes in the process. This observation is an example of which of the following?
   a. Waste of capacity
   b. Waste of a flow unit's time
   c. Waste of materials
   d. This observation is unrelated to lean.

LO8-2

2. As you think about your experience at the last airport security screening, you wonder which of the tasks that you saw the officers do at the security check were waste, which were non-value-added work, and which were value-added work. The tasks that you observed included officers doing the following: (a) officers checking IDs, (b) officers telling passengers to take off their shoes, (c) officers moving bins back to the beginning of the X-ray machines, (d) officers looking at the screen of the X-ray machine, (e) officers putting bags in the X-ray machine for a second time in case they previously contained fluids, and (f) officers waiting for a passenger to arrive.
   Identify each of the above activities as waste, value-added work, or non-value-added work.

3. A copy machine is available 24 hours a day. On a typical day, the machine produces 100 jobs. Each job takes about 3 minutes on the machine, 2 minutes of which is processing time and 1 minute is setup time (logging in, defining the job). About 20 percent of the jobs need to be reworked, in which case the setup time and the processing time have to be repeated. The remainder of the time, the equipment is idle. What is the OEE of the equipment?

LO8-3

4. In the welding operations of a bicycle manufacturer, a bike frame has a flow time of about 11.5 hours. The time in the welding operation is spent as follows: 2 hours waiting in front of the cutting machine for the batch to start, 2 hours waiting for the setup

of the machine, 1 hour waiting for the other pieces of the batch to go through cutting, 1 minute at the cutting machine, and 3 hours waiting for the transfer to the welding machine. Then, at the welding machine, the unit spends 1 hour waiting in front of the welding machine for the batch to start, 1 hour waiting for the setup of the welding machine, 0.5 hour waiting for the other pieces of the batch to go through welding, 0.5 minute at the welding machine, and 1 hour waiting for the transfer to the next department.

Determine the exact flow time. What is the value-added percentage of the flow time?

LO8-4

5. Which of the following strategies or techniques would reduce inventory in the operation?
   a. Control charts
   b. Jidoka
   c. Poka-yoke
   d. Heijunka

6. Which of the following strategies or techniques would use the principle of jidoka to increase quality?
   a. Reducing changeover time
   b. Ikko-nagashi
   c. Andon
   d. Kanban

LO8-5

7. The welding department supplies parts to the final assembly line. Management decides to implement a kanban system and has collected the following data:
   - The daily demand is 2000 units.
   - The production lead time is 4 days (this includes processing time, transport time, and waiting time).
   - Management has decided to have 1 day of safety stock.
   - One container fits 400 units.

   How many kanban containers will be needed to support this system?

LO8-6

8. A process makes two products, A and B, and operates 5 days per week, 8 hours per day. Demand for the two products for the next week is as follows:

   Day 1: A: 20; B: 26
   Day 2: A: 10; B: 15
   Day 3: A: 20; B: 19
   Day 4: A: 18; B: 20
   Day 5: A: 12; B: 20

   What is the takt time of the process? What would a level production schedule look like?

LO8-7

9. Consider the assembly line of a laptop computer. The line consists of 10 stations and operates at a cycle time of 2 minutes/unit. Their most error-prone operation is step 2. There is no inventory between the stations because this is a machine-paced line. Final inspection happens at station 10. What would be the information turnaround time for a defect made at station 2?

LO8-8

10. Which other Japanese term is most closely related to jidoka?
    a. Andon
    b. Ikko-nagashi
    c. Heijunka
    d. Kanban

CASE NIKE

The sportswear manufacturer Nike has over $25 billion in revenue. Its products are recognized around the world and experts value the Nike brand at some $20 billion alone. But who produces all the shoes and apparel that make up the $25 billion in revenue?

In 2013, Nike roughly produced 900 million units. Given that Nike employs 48,000 people, that corresponds to 18,750 units per employee each year. This would constitute an impossible amount of work to be carried out by a Nike employee. To achieve this production volume, Nike outsources most of its production to 800 contract factories around the world. This increases Nike's workforce to over one million people.

Facing challenges in both workplace conditions and quality, in the late 1990s Nike made a major move in implementing the lean production system. A Toyota consultant was hired to help translate TPS to the needs of Nike's footwear operations, which is where the company had decided to implement lean principles first.

The features of the Nike implementation of the TPS included, among other things:

- Organizing production around the flow of the footwear.

- Balancing the production process using takt time.

- Eliminating waste through the reduction of buffers and work-in-progress inventory.

- Involving the workforce in quality control and process improvement.

- Stabilizing the process by reducing variability and standardizing work.

Nike also developed a Manufacturing Index that the company now uses to evaluate its contract manufacturers on the dimensions of quality, cost, delivery, and sustainability. Factories that meet or exceed the current standards are rewarded. As a result of these efforts, Nike reportedly was able to achieve substantial improvements in productivity, defect rates, and delivery times.

Vietnam is the country that has the most workers involved in Nike contract manufacturing. Though wages

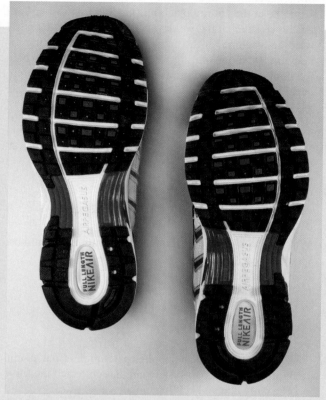

© *Mark Steinmetz/Amanita Pictures/McGraw-Hill Education*

have increased in Vietnam, the country's 2014 minimum wage rate was still under $150 per month. In your view, does Nike's emphasis on lean operations help or hurt its Vietnamese workforce?

SOURCES

Greg Distelhorst, Jens Hainmueller, and Richard M. Locke, "Does Lean Improve Labor Standards? Management and Social Performance in the Nike Supply Chain" (Watson Institute for International Studies Research Paper No. 2013-09; Rotman School of Management Working Paper No. 2337601, September 22, 2014).

http://www.nikeresponsibility.com/how/value/make

http://english.vietnamnet.vn/fms/society/89621/minimum-wage-to-increase-from-2014.html/

References

Fujimoto, Takahiro. *Evolution of Manufacturing Systems at Toyota.* New York: Productivity Press, 1999.

Kc, Diwas S., and Christian Terwiesch. "The Impact of Workload on Service Time and Patient Safety: An Econometric Analysis of Hospital Operations." *Management Science* 55, no. 9 (2009), pp. 1486–98.

Liker, Jeffrey K. *The Toyota Way: 14 Management Principles from the World's Greatest Manufacturer.* New York: McGraw-Hill Professional, 2003.

Marcus, Steve; Christian Terwiesch; and Jennifer Gutierrez. "A Time-and-Motion Study of Primary Care Provider." Working paper.

Ohno, Taiichi. *Toyota Production System: Beyond Large-Scale Production.* Portland, OR: Productivity Press, 1988.

Schultz, Kenneth L.; David C. Juran; and John W. Boudreau. "The Effects of Low Inventory on the Development of Productivity Norms." *Management Science* 45, no. 12 (1999), pp. 1664–78.

Taylor, Frederick Winslow. *The Principles of Scientific Management.* 1911.

Womack, James, and Daniel T. Jones. *Lean Thinking: Banish Waste and Create Wealth in Your Corporation.* 2nd ed. New York: Free Press, 2010.

http://www.post-gazette.com/stories/sectionfront/life/louis-vuitton-tries-modern-methods-on-factory-lines-453911/

9

Quality and Statistical Process Control

© Digital Stock/Corbis/RF

Introduction

Many production and service processes suffer from quality problems. Airlines lose baggage, computer manufacturers ship laptops with defective disk drives, pharmacies distribute the wrong medications to patients, and postal services lose or misdeliver articles by mail. In addition to these quality problems directly visible to us as consumers, many quality problems remain hidden to us, because they are detected and corrected within the boundaries of the process, oftentimes leading to substantially increased production costs. The purpose of this chapter is to better understand what quality problems are, why they occur, and how operations can be improved to reduce the frequency of such problems.

As we will see in this chapter, variation is the root cause of all quality problems. Without variation, a process would either always function as desired, in which case we would not need a chapter on quality, or it would never function as desired, in which case it would be unlikely that the operation would be in business to begin with. Given the importance of variation in influencing quality, this chapter will oftentimes use tools and frameworks taken from the field of statistics.

To see the effect that variation has on quality, consider the following examples:

- European Union commission regulation No 1677/88 states that cucumbers are allowed a bend of 10 millimeters per 10 centimeters of length. Cucumbers that bend more than this do not qualify as Class I or "extra class." Class II cucumbers are allowed to bend twice as much. In other words, the commission acknowledges that cucumbers come in different shapes and sizes, reflecting the variation inherent in an agricultural production process. Moreover, according to the EU bureaucrats, there exists an ideal cucumber shape in the form of a straight line, and the more a cucumber bends, the less desirable it is.

- In the fall of 2013, publicly traded electronics retailer Tweeter saw its (extremely low) share prices rise by 1400 percent in a single day. Why? Some investors apparently confused the shares of Tweeter with the shares of Twitter, which was in the process of launching an initial public offering. While there always existed some variation in the frequency of Tweeter share trades, trades for Tweeter shares increased from a typical volume of 29,000 shares per day to 14.4 million shares per day. Once Twitter changed its ticker symbol from TWTRQ to THEGQ, Tweeter shares dropped to their previous level within a matter of hours.

- In the hospital associated with the medical school of Münster, Germany, an interning medical school student injected the medication prepared in a syringe into a baby's IV instead of delivering the medication orally as intended. The syringe design was the same for medications given orally and for medications to be delivered via an IV. Using one common syringe had previously worked countless times without leading to a mistake. This time, it did not—the baby tragically died the same day.

- Quality problems caused an even bigger loss of lives in the accident of the MS *Estonia.* On September 28, 1994, the MS *Estonia,* a cruise ferry, headed out from Tallin (in Estonia) into the Baltic Sea. That day, the sea was rough and the ship's cargo was distributed with a slight imbalance. However, the MS *Estonia* had mastered rough-weather many times without problems, and it is rare for a ferry to find a perfect load distribution. Yet, this day, the many variables that influenced the safety of the ferry were lined up badly. The MS *Estonia* sank, causing over 800 fatalities in one of the most tragic maritime disasters since the sinking of the *Titanic.*

From the almost comical cucumber regulations of the EU and the funny confusion of Twitter with Tweeter to the tragic loss of lives in the cases of the German hospital and the MS *Estonia,* understanding the roles that variation plays in these settings is critical for analyzing and improving operations.

9.1 The Statistical Process Control Framework

Variation exists everywhere. At the risk of being overly poetic for a business textbook, let us observe that no two snowflakes are identical. The same holds for any two cucumbers. Nature itself creates randomness and so the size and curvature of every cucumber differs. Some of this variation in cucumber shape and size is entirely random. Even if we would grow 50 cucumbers in the same soil, water them with the same frequency, and expose them to the same sunlight, we would still not get 50 identical cucumbers. We refer to this natural form of variation as **natural variation** or **common cause variation**.

Natural variation Variation that occurs in a process as a result of pure randomness (also known as common cause variation).

Common cause variation Variation that occurs in a process as a result of pure randomness (also known as natural variation).

© Ken Welsh/Age fotostock/RF

LO9-1 Distinguish between common cause variation and assignable cause variation, and between input variables, environmental variables, and outcome variables.

Assignable cause variation Variation that occurs because of a specific change in input or in environmental variables.

Input variables The variables in a process that are under the control of management.

Environmental variables Variables in a process that are not under the control of management but nevertheless might impact the outcome of the process.

Outcome variables Measures describing the quality of the output of the process.

Defective Not corresponding to the specifications of the process.

Set of specifications A set of rules that determine if the outcome variable of a unit is defective or not.

Common cause variation also exists in medicine. Two babies are given the same medication under the same medical circumstances. Yet, their reactions might differ. The death of the baby in Münster, however, was not a result of common cause variation. The medical student made a mistake and delivered the medication to the baby by injecting it into the IV, which led to a much faster diffusion of the medication into the baby's body relative to oral delivery. This was not nature's randomness at work. There exists a simple explanation for the variation in how quickly the medication diffused. In this case, we speak of an **assignable cause variation**.

Common cause variation and assignable cause variation impact the performance of a process. At an abstract level, we can think of the outcome associated with a process as depicted in Figure 9.1. The management and the operators of the process influence a number of **input variables**. For trading a share of Twitter (or Tweeter for that matter), these input variables are the choice of which share to buy, how many shares to buy, and what price to pay per share. Few operations, however, are so simple and have so few input variables as electronic trading. Growing cucumbers, while arguably also a rather simple task, already has many more variables, including irrigation settings, fertilizer usage, light exposure, usage of pesticides, and so on. The list of input variables for health care services or the operation of a boat or airplane is much longer.

Input variables are not the only things that affect the outcome of the process. There typically exist a number of **environmental variables** that also matter. For example, in the case of the MS *Estonia,* we can think about the weather and the sea as such environmental variables. In contrast to input variables, environmental variables are not directly under the control of the operation. They simply happen and, in most cases, negatively impact quality. High-tech production processes such as the production of semiconductors are so vulnerable that even minor environmental variables such as small dust particles or miniscule vibrations of the equipment can ruin a large percentage of the production output.

The output of the process can be measured using a number of **outcome variables**. Outcome variables might be the curvature of a cucumber or the degree to which a boat leans over to one side or the other. Whether or not the outcome variables lead to a **defective** unit or not depends on a **set of specifications**. We define the specifications as a set of acceptable values for the outcome variable. In the case of cucumbers, the specifications define the curvature.

Sometimes, as in the case with the cucumber, it is possible to define a defect using a mathematical definition based on the outcome variables ("A cucumber is defective if its curvature exceeds 10mm in 10cm"). At other times, it might be hard to formally define such

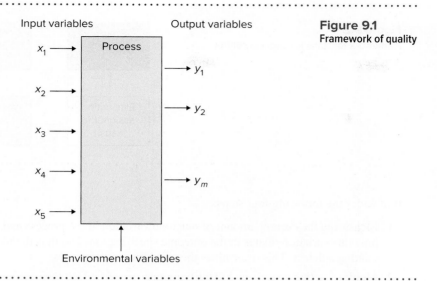

Input variables   Output variables

Figure 9.1
Framework of quality

Environmental variables

mathematical criteria. We know that the medical student delivering the medication via an IV committed a mistake and hence created a defect, but it would not help much to create a mathematical formulation of this situation.

Figure 9.1 illustrates the relationship between input variables, environmental variables, outcomes, and defects. Based on this framework, we make the following comments:

- In order for a defect to happen, we need to have some variation in outcome. But for a variation in outcome to happen, we need to have some variation either in the input variables or in the environmental variables. So when diagnosing a defect, we need to find the input or environmental variable(s) that caused that defect. We refer to that variable or these variables as the **root cause** for the defect.

- Even in a well-managed operation, input variables and environmental variables will always be subject to some common cause variation. The goal of management ought to be to keep that variation small and design the process so that this variation does not translate in large variations in outcome variables and ultimately defects.

- Just as we need to avoid that common cause variation in input and environmental variables leads to a large common cause variation in outcome variables, we need to avoid that an assignable cause variation in an input variable leads to a defect. We define a process as **robust** if it is able to tolerate (common or assignable cause) variation in input or environmental variables without leading to a large amount of variation in outcome variables and ultimately to defects. For example, the process of medication delivery via a common syringe in the German hospital was not robust with respect to inexperienced care providers. A different process design in which syringes used for oral medication delivery would be incompatible with IV delivery would have been a more robust process.

- We also observe in Figure 9.1 that multiple input variables impact the outcome variable. Because of this, it is possible for variability to stack up—sometimes, an unlucky realization of x_1 happens at the same time as an unlucky realization of x_2. A process such as the MS *Estonia* can tolerate bad weather, it can tolerate imbalances in cargo distribution, and it can tolerate operator mistakes. Disasters typically happen when multiple statistically unlikely events coincide.

As managers of operations, our goal is to understand quality problems and reduce their frequency of occurrence by redesigning the process and by addressing the underlying root causes. Figure 9.2 summarizes the approach that we will take in this chapter to achieve this goal. Given the previously mentioned emphasis on variation and statistical analysis, this approach is known as **statistical process control (SPC)**.

Root cause A root cause for a defect is a change in an input or an environmental variable that initiated a defect.

Robust The ability of a process to tolerate changes in input and environmental variables without causing the outcomes to be defective.

Statistical process control (SPC) A framework in operations management built around the empirical measurement and the statistical analysis of input, environmental, and outcome variables.

Figure 9.2
Framework for statistical process control

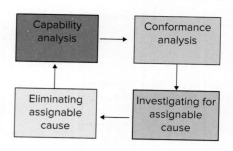

It includes the following four steps:

1. Measuring the current amount of outcome variation in the process and comparing how this variation relates to the outcome specifications and thus the likelihood of making a defect. This determines the capability of the process.

2. Monitoring this process and identifying instances in which the outcome variation is **abnormal**, suggesting the occurrence of some assignable cause variation in input or environmental variables. In other words, we monitor the process and determine if the presently observed variation conforms to the usual patterns of variation (in which case we are dealing with common cause variation). In the cases in which the presently observed variation does not conform to historical data, we expect an assignable cause to have occurred.

3. Investigating the root cause of an assignable cause variation by finding the input or environmental variable(s) that caused the variation.

4. Avoiding the recurrence in the future of similar assignable cause variations and/or changing the process so that it is sufficiently robust to not have its quality be affected by such events in the future.

The following sections will elaborate on these four steps in greater detail.

Abnormal A variation is abnormal if it is not behaving in line with past data; this allows us to conclude that we are dealing with an assignable cause variation and are not just facing randomness in the form of common cause variation.

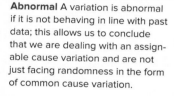

© Michael Lamotte/Cole Group/
Photodisc/Getty Images/RF

Check Your Understanding 9.1

Question: Your cafeteria is serving chicken noodle soup today, which it sources from a distributor and then warms up locally in the kitchen. The soup now sits in a large bowl and a server uses a large ladle to fill the soup into the smaller bowls handed out to the students. Consider the following variables:

- Outside temperature.
- Duration that the soup was heated before being put in the bowl.
- Temperature of the soup in a student's bowl.
- Temperature level to which the soup is warmed up.
- Insulation of the bowl used for storing the soup.
- Duration that the soup bowl is open when the server inserts the ladle to serve a student.

Which of these variables are (a) input variables, (b) output variables, and (c) environmental variables?

Answer: Input variables are "Duration that the soup was heated before being put in the bowl," "Temperature level to which the soup is warmed up," "Insulation of the bowl used for storing the soup," and "Duration that the soup bowl is open when the server inserts the ladle to serve a student." The output variable is "Temperature of the soup in a student's bowl." An environmental variable is "Outside temperature."

Question: Two students compare the amount of chicken meat they have in their chicken noodle soup. Student A has two times more meat than student B. The students debate whether this difference is a result of common cause variation or whether there exist assignable causes. What would be examples for assignable causes?

Answer: The amount of meat will vary from bowl to bowl. There will never be EXACTLY the same amount of soup in two bowls. This, first and foremost, is a result of common cause variation. However, the larger the difference between the two bowls, the more likely we are dealing with an assignable cause. Examples for such assignable causes include (a) the time the student was served (it is possible that the meat falls down to the bottom and so students who were served at the beginning get less meat), (b) any defects/mistakes in the production of the soup, and (c) the person serving was not stirring the soup.

CONNECTIONS: Lost Luggage

Though travelers increasingly rely on carry-on luggage when they travel, larger suitcases still need to be checked in for the flight. Luggage handling is a major operation at a big airport with many opportunities for defects. Depending on the airport and the airline, between 0.1 percent and 1 percent of the luggage gets mishandled. As travelers, we always wonder about the likelihood that the bag will make it to the same destination airport as we do. The most common reasons for lost luggage are:

© Ingram Publishing/SuperStock/RF

- The routing label gets damaged.
- The passenger forgets to pick up the luggage.
- The agent types in the wrong destination code.
- The luggage is picked incorrectly and is put on a wrong flight.

A particularly noteworthy example of luggage-handling defect happened in 2008 when country musician Dave Caroll traveled from Halifax to Omaha. He checked in his concert guitar in Halifax. Upon arriving in Omaha, he noticed that his rather expensive Taylor concert guitar was severely damaged. Caroll requested that the damaged guitar be paid for by United Airlines. The airline, however, was not willing to pay for the damage. After long and unsuccessful negotiation with the airline, Caroll gave up on the idea of receiving compensation. Instead, Caroll created a song, "United Breaks Guitars," that he subsequently posted on YouTube. The video clip with the song (and a rather amusing band posing as United Airlines employees) attracted over 10 million viewers.

Source: http://www.cnn.com/2011/08/26/travel/why-airlines-lose-luggage-bt

---

9.2 Capability Analysis

Achieving consistency by controlling variation is critical for achieving high quality. This is true in operations management, but also applies to other aspects of our lives. Consider the following example from the world of sports. In target shooting, a shooter aims at a target similar to what is shown in Figure 9.3. The figure compares the results of three shooters, each of whom fired six shots at the target. Assume for the moment that each hit in the black area in the center of the target is worth one point. Note that all three shooters hit, on average, the center point (bull's eye). Note further that shooters 2 and 3 both managed to get six points. Who, in your view, is the best target shooter?

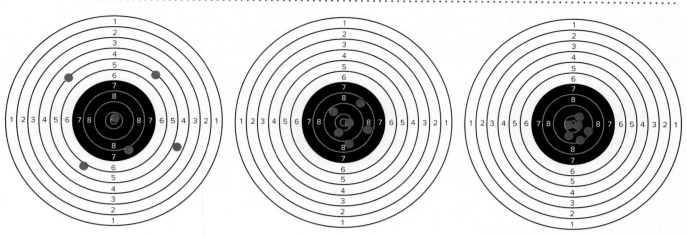

Figure 9.3

Six shots fired at a target by three different shooters (from left to right: shooters 1 to 3)

Let's start looking at the results of shooter 1. A target shooter who misses the target by two feet to the left, only to then "compensate" by shooting the next shot two feet to the right, might be right on average, but nevertheless is a bad target shooter. Next, consider shooters 2 and 3. Both of them managed to get six points (recall that we award one point to every shot in the black area). Yet, intuitively, we would label shooter 3 as being the better shooter.

The example of the target shooters illustrates two important lessons about measuring variation in a process. First, when we measure the capability of the shooter, it is not the average location of the shot that matters (all three, on average, hit a bull's-eye). Instead, it is the spread of shots over the target that makes us call one shooter better than the other. Second, we can infer more from six shots about a shooter's capability than just counting how many shots are "in" versus "out." By carefully measuring the exact position of each shot relative to the ideal point (the bull's-eye), we gain additional information. Imagine we would want to extrapolate and predict how many shots out of 100 shots would be on target. A naïve analysis would argue that shooters 2 and 3 both got 100 percent of their shots on target and so are likely to not make mistakes in the future either. However, knowing that shooter 2 had a number of "near misses" (i.e., shots close to the edge of the black circle) makes us wonder if this shooter really would be able to hit the black area 100 times in a row.

9.2.1 Determining a Capability Index

LO9-2 Compute the process capability index and the defect probability.

From the shooting range, back to the world of operations management. Consider the production of kick scooters at Xootr LLC, a product that has achieved a number of design awards (see Figure 9.4; also see Chapter 7 for details about the Xootr production process). In the production of the steer support for the Xootr, the component is obtained via extrusion from aluminum and subsequent refinement at a computer-controlled machine tool (CNC machine).

Figure 9.5 shows the engineering drawing for the component. Despite the fact that every steer support component is refined by the CNC machine, there still exists some variation with respect to the exact geometry of the output. This variation is the result of many causes, including input variables (such as raw materials, the way the component is placed in the machine, an occasional mistake in programming the CNC machine) and environmental variables (such as the temperature of the room at the time of the processing).

According to the design of the product, the ideal steer support would measure 79.950 mm in height. This is the bull's-eye for Xootr's production process. The engineering drawing specifies that the height must fall between 79.900 mm and 80.000 mm. If the height is less than 79.900 mm, the part may rattle excessively because it fits loosely. If the height is greater than 80.000 mm, then the part may not fit in the available gap in the handle assembly.

Figure 9.4
Rendering of a Xootr scooter, including its steer support component

Height

© Xootr LLC

We refer to 79.900 mm as the **lower specification limit (LSL)** and to 80.000 mm as the **upper specification limit (USL)**. The specification limits determine which units are acceptable and which ones are defective. They correspond to the black circle that determined whether or not a shot was on target in Figure 9.3.

Given that variation of the steer support's height can cause quality problems, the engineers of the company (Xootr LLC) monitor the height very carefully. Every day, a sample of components is taken and measured accurately. This sample allows the engineers to estimate the current amount of variation in the steer support production. It is common in statistics to measure variation using the standard deviation, oftentimes abbreviated by using the Greek letter

Lower specification limit (LSL)
The smallest outcome value that does not trigger a defective unit.

Upper specification limit (USL)
The largest outcome value that does not trigger a defective unit.

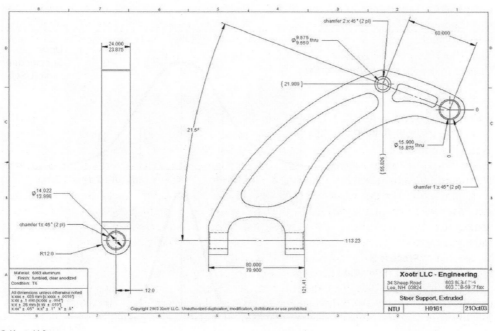

Figure 9.5
Engineering drawing of the steer support unit

© Xootr LLC

sigma (σ). Given that we estimate this standard deviation on a (small) sample, we refer to the estimated variation in the process as sigma-hat ($\hat{\sigma}$).

But given an estimated amount of variation in the process, ($\hat{\sigma}$), what is the likelihood that the process produces a defect? The answers to this questions depend on:

- The tightness of the design specification, which we can quantify as the difference between the upper specification level and lower specification level (USL − LSL).

- The amount of variation in the current process, which is captured by the estimated standard deviation sigma-hat.

Thus, the capability of the process in meeting a given set of design specifications—that is, the likelihood of a defect—depends on the magnitude of variability in the process, sigma-hat, relative to the tolerance levels, USL − LSL. We can combine these two measures into a single score, which is frequently referred to as the **process capability index**:

$$C_p = \frac{\text{USL} - \text{LSL}}{6\hat{\sigma}}$$

The process capability index, C_p, measures the allowable tolerance relative to the actual variation of the process. Both numerator and denominator are expressed in the same units (millimeters in the case of Xootr) and thus C_p itself is unitless. To interpret C_p, consider a $C_p = 1$. For this to happen, the tolerance interval, USL − LSL, has to be six times as large as the estimated standard deviation, sigma-hat. In other words, for a $C_p = 1$, it is possible to fit six times the standard deviation of the variation into the tolerance interval. We know from statistics that the average of a sample tends to be distributed according to a normal distribution. If we assume that the mean (the average) of that normal distribution is in the middle of the tolerance interval (79.5 mm in the case of Xootr), then a C_p value of 1 implies that we can go three standard deviations from that center point to either side before hitting the specification limit. For this reason, we label a process with a $C_p = 1$ as a "three sigma process."

Figure 9.6 compares two different values of C_p for a given set of design specifications.

The upper part of the figure depicts a three-sigma process. We thus know that it's $C_p = 1$. In the lower part of the figure, the specification limits are the same, but the standard deviation, labeled σ_B, of the process is much smaller. We can afford moving six standard deviations to either side of the mean before hitting the specification limit. In other words, in such a

Process capability index The ratio between the width of the specification interval of the outcome variable and the variation in the outcome variable (measured by six times its estimated standard deviation). It tells us how many standard deviations we can move away from the statistical mean before causing a defect.

Figure 9.6

Comparing a three-sigma process with a six-sigma process

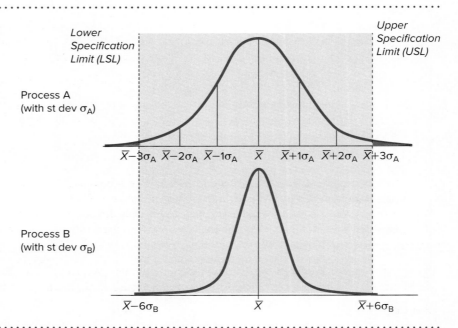

Check Your Understanding 9.2

Question: A bottle-filling process has a lower specification limit of 0.99 liter and an upper specification limit of 1.01 liters. The standard deviation is 0.005 liter and the mean is 1 liter.

What is the process capability index for the bottle-filling process?

Answer: We compute the process capability index as

$$C_p = \frac{\text{USL} - \text{LSL}}{6\hat{\sigma}} = \frac{1.01 - 0.99}{6 \times 0.005} = 0.6667$$

. . . .

six-sigma process, the tolerance interval is 12 standard deviations σ_B wide. The capability index is thus

$$C_p = \frac{\text{USL} - \text{LSL}}{6\hat{\sigma}} = \frac{12\hat{\sigma}}{6\hat{\sigma}} = 2$$

The likelihood of a defect (statistically spoken, this is the probability mass of the bell-shaped density function outside the tolerance interval) is much smaller compared to the upper case.

For the steer support component, Xootr engineers estimated a standard deviation of 0.017291 mm. This lets us compute the process capability measure as follows:

$$C_p = \frac{\text{USL} - \text{LSL}}{6\hat{\sigma}} = \frac{80.000 - 79.900}{6 \times 0.017291} = 0.963889$$

9.2.2 Predicting the Probability of a Defect

Knowing the mean, the standard deviation, and the specification limits of a process, and relying on the fact that the process follows a normal distribution, enables us to predict the probability of future defects. To compute this **defect probability,** we perform the following calculations:

Step 1: Find the probability that a unit falls below the lower specification limit, LSL. This can be achieved by entering NORM.DIST(LSL, Mean, Standard Deviation, 1) into Excel. NORM.DIST returns the value of the cumulative normal distribution. Mathematically, this is the area under the probability density function (the bell-shaped curve associated with the normal distribution) to the left of the LSL. In our Xootr calculations, this gives us

Probability{part too small} = NORM.DIST(79.9, 79.95, 0.017291, 1) = 0.001915954

Step 2: Find the probability that a unit falls above the USL. Do this by entering 1 − NORM.DIST(USL, Mean, Standard Deviation, 1) into Excel. Mathematically, this is the area under the probability density function to the right of the USL.

Probability{part too big} = 1 − NORM.DIST(80, 79.95, 0.017291, 1) = 0.001915954

Note that the results of steps 1 and 2 are identical. This is because, in our case, the mean of the distribution is right in the middle of the tolerance interval. This is not always the case, so we encourage you to do steps 1 and 2 as opposed to simply doing step 1 and then assuming that the probability that the part being too big is the same as the probability of the part being too small.

Step 3: Add the results of step 1 and step 2 to get the defect probability (because a unit is either too big or too small, the probability that it is defective is simply the sum of the two probabilities):

Probability{part defective} = 0.001915954 + 0.001915954 = 0.003831908

Six-sigma process A process that has 6 standard deviations on either side of the mean and the specification limit.

Defect probability The statistical probability with which a randomly chosen flow unit does not meet specifications.

In addition to obtaining the defect probability, it is also common to express the number of units expected to be defective out of one million units (also referred to as **parts per million**, or ppm for short). To obtain the ppm number, simply multiply the defect probability by 1,000,000. In the case of Xootr's steer support part, we get

$$PPM = \text{Probability \{part defective\}} \times 1{,}000{,}000 = 0.003831908 \times 1{,}000{,}000 = 3831.9$$

As we have seen from the preceding calculations, it is possible to translate the number of standard deviations between the mean of the distribution and the specification limit into a defect probability. This is really a matter of applying the statistical calculations of the normal distribution. Table 9.1 shows the defect probabilities and the PPM number for a generic process depending on how many standard deviations fit between the mean and the specification limit.

Parts per million The expected number of defective parts in a random sample of one million.

TABLE 9.1 The Relationship between the Standard Deviations that Fit between Mean and Specification Limit and the Defect Probability

Sigma	Capability Index	Probability Too Small	Probability Too Large	Prob(Defect)	PPM
1	0.333333333	0.1586552539	0.1586552539	0.31731050786	317310.5
1.2	0.4	0.1150696702	0.1150696702	0.23013934044	230139.3
1.4	0.466666667	0.0807566592	0.0807566592	0.16151331847	161513.3
1.6	0.533333333	0.0547992917	0.0547992917	0.10959858340	109598.6
1.8	0.6	0.0359303191	0.0359303191	0.07186063823	71860.64
2	0.666666667	0.0227501319	0.0227501319	0.04550026390	45500.26
2.2	0.733333333	0.0139034475	0.0139034475	0.02780689503	27806.9
2.4	0.8	0.0081975359	0.0081975359	0.01639507185	16395.07
2.6	0.866666667	0.0046611880	0.0046611880	0.00932237605	9322.376
2.8	0.933333333	0.0025551303	0.0025551303	0.00511026066	5110.261
3	1	0.0013498980	0.0013498980	0.00269979606	2699.796
3.2	1.066666667	0.0006871379	0.0006871379	0.00137427588	1374.276
3.4	1.133333333	0.0003369293	0.0003369293	0.00067385853	673.8585
3.6	1.2	0.0001591086	0.0001591086	0.00031821718	318.2172
3.8	1.266666667	0.0000723480	0.0000723480	0.00014469609	144.6961
4	1.333333333	0.0000316712	0.0000316712	0.00006334248	63.34248
4.2	1.4	0.0000133457	0.0000133457	0.00002669150	26.6915
4.4	1.466666667	0.0000054125	0.0000054125	0.00001082509	10.82509
4.6	1.533333333	0.0000021125	0.0000021125	0.00000422491	4.224909
4.8	1.6	0.0000007933	0.0000007933	0.00000158666	1.586656
5	1.666666667	0.0000002867	0.0000002867	0.00000057330	0.573303
5.2	1.733333333	0.0000000996	0.0000000996	0.00000019929	0.199289
5.4	1.8	0.0000000333	0.0000000333	0.00000006664	0.066641
5.6	1.866666667	0.0000000107	0.0000000107	0.00000002144	0.021435
5.8	1.933333333	0.0000000033	0.0000000033	0.00000000663	0.006631
6	2	0.0000000010	0.0000000010	0.00000000197	0.001973

Check Your Understanding **9.3**

Question: Consider again the bottle-filling process that has a lower specification limit of 0.99 liter and an upper specification limit of 1.01 liters. The standard deviation is 0.005 liter and the mean is 1 liter.

What is the probability that a bottle will either have too much or too little fluid in it? How many defects would there be in one million bottles?

Answer: We first compute the probability of the bottle not having enough fluid in it. This is given by:

$$\text{Probability\{not enough\}} = \text{NORM.DIST}(0.99, 1, 0.005, 1) = 0.02275$$

We next find the probability that there is too much fluid:

$$\text{Probability\{too much\}} = 1 - \text{NORM.DIST}(1.01, 1, 0.005, 1) = 0.02275$$

This gives us a defect probability of:

$$\text{Probability\{part defective\}} = 0.02275 + 0.02275 = 0.0455$$

We compute the ppm (parts per million) as $0.0455 \times 1{,}000{,}000 = 45{,}500$.

Note that we had previously found that the capability index of this process is 0.6667. We can also use Table 9.1 and look up the defect probability and the ppm there for $C_p = 0.6667$. This gives us the same result without using Excel.

A capability index of $C_p = 1$ (i.e., a three-sigma process) is defective with a probability of 0.002699796. It thus is not defective with a probability of 0.997300204. Consequently, it would have 2700 defects per 1,000,000 units (2699.796 to be exact).

Traditionally, quality experts have recommended a minimum process capability index of 1.33. However, many organizations, as part of their **six-sigma program,** now postulate that all efforts should be made to obtain a process capability, C_p of 2.0 at every individual step. This is statistically equivalent to requiring that the USL is six standard deviations above the mean and the LSL is six standard deviations below the mean. This explains the name "six-sigma."

A six-sigma process makes a defect with a probability of 0.00000000197, which corresponds to about two defects in a billion units. This number seems almost ridiculously small. Why not settle for less? Why was the previously mentioned quality target of $C_p = 1.33$ corresponding to a defect probability of 0.000063342 not good enough?

This is indeed a tricky question. Let us first point out that the concept of "good enough" is misleading. Every defect is one too many, especially if you recall the third and fourth examples at the beginning of the chapter. Second, one has to understand that processes often consist of many steps, each having the potential of being defective. The Xootr does not only consist of a steer support part, but has many other parts as well. Complex assemblies such as computers, phones, or cars have hundreds of subassemblies and components in them. The final product only functions correctly if all of them work correctly. Consider a product with 200 subassemblies and components, each of them having a probability of 0.01 percent of going defective. Hence, the probability of producing each unit correctly is $1 - 0.0001 = 0.9999$. The probability that the resulting output functions correctly is then given by $0.9999^{200} = 0.980198$, which is a 2 percent defect probability. In other words, in complex systems in which many things have to function correctly, even extremely low defect probabilities at the subassembly or component level can lead to significant amounts of defects.

9.2.3 Setting a Variance Reduction Target

Our previous analysis started out with the empirically observed variation in the process (in the form of the standard deviation estimate, sigma-hat) and we computed the defect probability. We can also do these calculations starting with a desired (targeted) defect probability and then compute the allowable standard deviation in the process. Assume, for example, that Xootr

Check Your Understanding 9.4

Question: Consider again our bottle-filling process, which has a lower specification limit of 0.99 liter and an upper specification limit of 1.01 liters. The standard deviation is 0.005 liter and the mean is 1 liter. The company now wants to reduce its defect probability from the previously computed 0.0455 (ppm of 45,500) to 0.001 (ppm of 1000). To what level would they have to reduce the standard deviation in the process to meet this target?

Answer: We know that the process capability index is

$$C_p = \frac{USL - LSL}{6\hat{\sigma}}$$

Looking at Table 9.1, the capability index for a ppm of 1000 is between 1.0666 and 1.1333. If we set $C_p = 1.0666$, we get

$$1.0666 = \frac{1.01 - 0.99}{6\hat{\sigma}} \Leftrightarrow 1.0666 = \frac{0.02}{6\hat{\sigma}} \Leftrightarrow \hat{\sigma} = \frac{0.02}{6 \times 1.0666} = 0.003125$$

If we use $C_p = 1.1333$, we get $\hat{\sigma} = 0.002941$. So the standard deviation would have to be reduced from its current value of 0.005 to a value between 0.002941 and 0.003125.

. . . .

LLC's management would want to tighten the quality standards. Instead of allowing the present defect frequency of 0.003831908 (i.e., 3831.9 ppm), imagine the new goal would be set to 10 ppm. To what level would Xootr LLC have to reduce the standard deviation in the steer support parts so that this goal is met?

We can see from Table 9.1 that obtaining 10 ppm corresponds to a capability score $C_p = 1.4667$. For this, we simply go down the rightmost column in the table until we find the closest ppm number and then look up the capability index in the second-to-the-left column. Using the definition of the capability score, we thus obtain the following equation:

$$C_p = \frac{USL - LSL}{6\hat{\sigma}} \Leftrightarrow 1.4667 = \frac{80.000 - 79.900}{6 \times \hat{\sigma}}$$

Though the sigma is in the denominator, this equation is a linear equation in sigma. Rearranging terms, we obtain the **target variation** as

$$\hat{\sigma} = \frac{USL - LSL}{6C_p} = \frac{80.000 - 79.900}{6 \times 1.4667} = 0.011364$$

Put differently, if the Xootr engineers are able to reduce the standard deviation they have in the steer support part from its current value of 0.017291 to 0.011364, they will be able to improve their capability score from 0.964 to roughly 1.4667 and reduce their ppm from 3831.9 to 10.

9.2.4 Process Capability Summary and Extensions

In this section on capability analysis, you have learned to use the specification limits of a process alongside its estimated standard deviation and compute the process capability as well as its defect rate. Notice the strong resemblance to the earlier example of the target shooter. You might sample 10 steer support parts and not observe a single defective unit (all measurements fall within the specification limits). Would this make you comfortable in having zero defects in a million parts? To extrapolate to a larger sample, we have to use more information than just the binary classification into defects and good units. Just like we measured the capability of the target shooter by looking at how far his shots are away from the bull's-eye, we look at the variation of the measurements and see how many standard deviations of "wiggle room" we have before we hit the specification limits on either side. We have also seen how one can start with a targeted number of defects and then calculate how much variation is allowed in the process. Clearly, defects and variation go hand-in-hand.

Target variation The largest amount of variation in a process that does not exceed a given defect probability.

CONNECTIONS: Apple iPhone Bending

© luismmolina/iStock/Getty Images

The iPhone 6 is made from a custom grade of anodized aluminum. It also features stainless steel and titanium inserts to reinforce high-stress locations. Apple conducts a battery of intensive testing on each new model. For example, Apple runs a "sit test" that simulates sitting on a hard surface with the phone in the back pocket of a pair of tight jeans. Phones have to withstand thousands of cycles of testing the phone in different positions.

Despite this intensive testing, one week after the launch of the iPhone 6 in the fall of 2014, several pictures and videos of the phone bending made global news. Users complained via social media that when they sat down with the phone in their pocket, the phone would deform. The situation escalated further as a number of customers tried to bend iPhones in Apple retail outlets, putting a rather excessive amount of pressure on the phone.

On the first weekend of sales alone, Apple sold more than 10 million iPhones. Was the company heading into a global quality disaster? Far from it. As Apple responded to the pictures of bending iPhones, it reported that only nine customers had come forward complaining about a bending iPhone—nine complaints out of ten million phones.

Source: http://online.wsj.com/articles/apple-defends-against-complaints-of-bending-iphones-1411668618

In our analysis, we assumed that the process has an upper specification limit and a lower specification limit, with the mean of the collected data being right in the middle. These assumptions might not always be in line with what you observe in practice:

- In some cases, there exists only one specification limit. Imagine you want to track the call waiting time in a call center and measure to what extent customers are served in a given wait time or sooner. In this case, it would not make sense to call a wait time that is exceptionally short a defect. So, we might set our lower specification limit at zero.

- The mean of the distribution is unlikely to always be in the middle of the tolerance interval. We needed to make this midpoint assumption to generate the data in Table 9.1 and when we searched for the allowable level of sigma. All other calculations did not rely on this assumption. You first compute the probability that the unit is below the lower specification limit, then the probability that the unit is above the upper specification limit, and then add up the two.

9.3 Conformance Analysis

Now that we have measured the capability of the process and understand how much variation exists in the process at a given point in time, we are well positioned to monitor the process on an ongoing basis. Specifically, when we observe variation in the process, we want to decide if that variation is normal, in which case it most likely reflects the common cause variation in the process, or if it is abnormal, indicating the presence of an assignable cause.

Control charts plot data over time in a graph similar to what is shown in Figure 9.7. The x-axis of the control chart captures the various time periods at which samples from the process are taken. For the y-axis, we plot the mean of each sample. Such control charts are often called $\overline{X}$ charts (pronounced **X-bar charts**, which captures that **X-bar** typically denotes the mean of a sample). $\overline{X}$ charts can be used to document trends over time and to identify unexpected drifts (e.g., resulting from the wear of a tool) or jumps (e.g., resulting from a new person operating a process step), corresponding to assignable causes of variation.

More formally, we define the mean of a sample consisting of n units, X-bar, as

$$\overline{X} = \frac{x_1 + x_2 + \cdots + x_n}{n}$$

As we are plotting the realizations of $\overline{X}$, we want to know if the sample we obtained was a sample that was in line with past process outcomes. For this, we visually inspect whether the value we enter for a period (say the sample mean for day 11) is above an upper limit, which is also known as the **upper control limit (UCL)** or below a lower limit, which is also known as the **lower control limit (LCL)**.

Consider the data related to the height of the steer support component displayed in Table 9.2 collected by the Xootr engineers in the same way as the data for our capability analysis. The data show five observations for each day over a 25-day period. Based on the preceding definitions of $\overline{X}$, we can compute the mean for each day, which is shown in the last column. For example, for day 14, $\overline{X}$ is computed as

$$\overline{X} = \frac{79.973 + 79.986 + 79.942 + 79.978 + 79.979}{5} = 79.972$$

After computing the mean for every period, we proceed to compute the average across all days. The average $\overline{X}$ across all $\overline{X}$ is called $\overline{\overline{X}}$ (pronounced "**X-double bar**" or "X-bar-bar"), reflecting that it is an average across averages. As we can see at the bottom of Table 9.2, we have

$$\overline{\overline{X}} = 79.951$$

In creating the $\overline{X}$ chart, we use the computed value of $\overline{\overline{X}}$ as a center line and plot the values of $\overline{X}$ for each day in the sample.

Control charts A control chart is a visual representation of variation in the process. It has time on its x-axis and an outcome variable on the y-axis. In each time period, we collect a sample of outcomes, which we plot in the control chart. The control chart also shows a long-run center line (called X-bar-bar), which is the average across all points. It also shows an upper and a lower control limit, which are computed based on past data.

X-bar charts A special control chart in which we track the mean of a sample (also known as X-bar).

X-bar The average of a sample.

Upper control limit (UCL) A line in a control chart that provides the largest value that is still acceptable without being labeled an abnormal variation.

Lower control limit (LCL) A line in a control chart that provides the smallest value that is still acceptable without being labeled an abnormal variation.

X-double-bar The average of a set of sample averages.

Figure 9.7

Example of a generic control chart

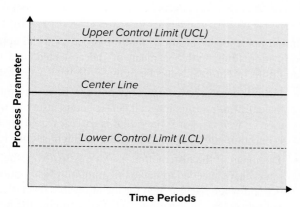

TABLE 9.2 Measurements of the Steer Support Dimension in Groups of Five Observations

Period	x_1	x_2	x_3	x_4	x_5	Mean
1	79.941	79.961	79.987	79.940	79.956	79.957
2	79.953	79.942	79.962	79.956	79.944	79.951
3	79.926	79.986	79.958	79.964	79.950	79.957
4	79.960	79.970	79.945	79.967	79.967	79.962
5	79.947	79.933	79.932	79.963	79.954	79.946
6	79.950	79.955	79.967	79.928	79.963	79.953
7	79.971	79.960	79.941	79.962	79.918	79.950
8	79.970	79.952	79.946	79.928	79.970	79.953
9	79.960	79.957	79.944	79.945	79.948	79.951
10	79.936	79.945	79.961	79.958	79.947	79.949
11	79.911	79.954	79.968	79.947	79.918	79.940
12	79.950	79.955	79.992	79.964	79.940	79.960
13	79.952	79.945	79.955	79.945	79.952	79.950
14	79.973	79.986	79.942	79.978	79.979	79.972
15	79.931	79.962	79.935	79.953	79.937	79.944
16	79.966	79.943	79.919	79.958	79.923	79.942
17	79.960	79.941	80.003	79.951	79.956	79.962
18	79.954	79.958	79.992	79.935	79.953	79.959
19	79.910	79.950	79.947	79.915	79.994	79.943
20	79.948	79.946	79.943	79.935	79.920	79.939
21	79.917	79.949	79.957	79.971	79.968	79.952
22	79.973	79.959	79.971	79.947	79.949	79.960
23	79.920	79.961	79.937	79.935	79.934	79.937
24	79.937	79.934	79.931	79.934	79.964	79.940
25	79.945	79.954	79.957	79.935	79.961	79.950
					Average	79.951

Once we have the x-axis (time periods), the y-axis (the mean), the samples for each period, and the center line, the last information missing is the control limits. Recall the idea behind the control limits. We would like to infer from a sample mean X-bar that lies above the upper control limit or below the lower control limit that the sample was abnormal. Now, any inference that we make with statistical data is subject to noise and so we can only make such a statement with a limited amount of statistical confidence. The data that we sample from the process are noisy and the estimates for X-bar are at best right, on average.

We estimate the standard deviation for the entire sample by using Excel's STDEV.S procedure. So, we compute the **estimated standard deviation of all parts** as

$$\text{Standard deviation for all parts} = \text{STDEV.S}(\text{Day1}_{\text{Part1}}, \ldots, \text{Day1}_{\text{Part}n}, \ldots, \text{Day}m_{\text{Part1}}, \ldots, \text{Day}m_{\text{Part}n})$$

In the above example, the estimated standard deviation for all parts is

$$\text{Standard deviation for all parts} = 0.017846388$$

Each day, we collect a sample and so when we estimate the sample mean, X-bar, we have to acknowledge that it is noisy. Moreover, we know that it gets less noisy the bigger our daily

Estimated standard deviation of all parts The standard deviation that is computed across all parts.

sample size. For a given sample of measurements, we know that the **estimated standard deviation for *X*-bar** (the estimated standard deviation of that sample mean) can be estimated by

$$\text{Estimated standard deviation}(X\text{-bar}) = \frac{\text{Standard deviation of all parts}}{\sqrt{n}}$$

For the Xootr case, we compute the estimated standard deviation (ESD):

$$\text{Estimated standard deviation}(X\text{-bar}) = \frac{\text{Standard deviation of all parts}}{\sqrt{n}}$$

$$= \frac{0.017846388}{\sqrt{5}} = 0.007981147$$

We call the process out of control if the sample is three standard deviations above or below the long-term mean. This leads to the following control limit calculations:

1. Compute the upper control limit for $\bar{X}$ as

$$\text{UCL} = \bar{\bar{X}} + [3 \times \text{ESD}(X\text{-bar})] = 79.951 + (3 \times 0.007981147) = 79.9749$$

2. Compute the lower control limit for $\bar{X}$ as

$$\text{LCL} = \bar{\bar{X}} - [3 \times \text{ESD}(X\text{-bar})] = 79.951 - (3 \times 0.007981147) = 79.9271$$

A process that is behaving in line with historical data will have the estimated sample mean fall between the LCL and the UCL in 99.7 percent of the cases. This is the same logic that was underlying our capability calculations and the derivation of the probability that an outcome would hit the specification limits, which are three standard deviations above the mean.

The control charts obtained this way allow for a visual assessment of the variation of the process. The definition of control limits implies that 99.7 percent of the sample points are expected to fall between the upper and lower control limits. Thus, if any point falls outside the control limits, we can claim with a 99.7 percent confidence level that the process has gone "out of control"—that is, that an assignable cause has occurred.

In addition to inspecting if sample means are outside the three-sigma confidence interval (i.e., below the LCL or above the UCL), we can look for other patterns in the control chart that are statistically unlikely to occur. For example, we can look for a sequence of sample means that are above or below the center line. For example, it is unlikely that we will see a sequence of eight subsequent points above (or below) the center line. Because each point has an equal probability of being above or below the center line, we can compute the likelihood of eight points to the same side simply as $(0.5)^8 = 0.004$, which corresponds to a very unlikely event. Thus, we can also treat such a pattern as a warning sign justifying further investigation.

Figure 9.8 shows the control charts for the Xootr. We observe that the production process for the steer support is well in control. There seems to be an inherent randomness in the exact

Estimated standard deviation for X-bar The standard deviation of a particular sample mean, x-bar.

Figure 9.8

The *X*-bar chart for the steer support part

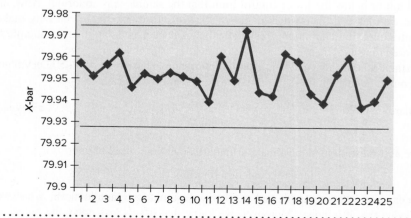

Check Your Understanding 9.5

Question: For 50 consecutive days, a process engineer has measured the weight of a component after it has been coated with a special paint. Each day, she takes a sample of 10 components. The average across all 500 components (50 days, 10 components per day) is 45.343018 grams. The standard deviation across all parts is 0.0076382 gram. When constructing an X-bar chart, what would be the center line and what would be the lines for the upper and lower control limits?

Answer: The center line would be given by the average across all 500 components; that is, it would be 45.343018 grams.

To find the control limits, we first have to estimate the standard deviation for the daily X-bar sample. We use the equation

$$\text{Estimated standard deviation}(X\text{-bar}) = \frac{\text{Standard deviation of all parts}}{\sqrt{n}}$$

$$= \frac{0.0076382}{\sqrt{10}} = 0.002415$$

We then find the upper control limit as

$$\text{UCL} = \overline{\overline{X}} + [3 \times \text{ESD}(X\text{-bar})] = 45.343018 + (3 \times 0.002415) = 45.35026$$

and the lower control limit as

$$\text{LCL} = \overline{\overline{X}} - [3 \times \text{ESD}(X\text{-bar})] = 45.343018 - (3 \times 0.002415) = 45.33577$$

. . . .

size of the component. Yet, there is no systemic pattern, such as a drift or a sudden jump outside the control limits. The process behaves in line with its historical variation—it is in control.

Note that the fact that the process is in control does not rule out that we produce defects. In fact, it is important to not confuse the concepts of control limits and specification limits:

- The control limits measure to what extent the process is behaving the same way it did in the past.

- The specification limits measure to what extent the process meets the specifications of the customer.

So it is possible that the outcome of the process is within the control limits but outside the specification limits. In this case, the process capability is low and defects occur regularly as a result of common cause variation. Vice versa, it is possible that the outcome is outside the control limits but within the specification limits. A very high capability process has very tight control limits. Even a very small assignable cause variation would make the process outcome jump outside the control limits; nevertheless, that corresponding unit does not necessarily have to be a defect, especially not if the specification interval is relatively wide.

9.4 Investigating Assignable Causes

Earlier on in this chapter, we discussed how the outcome of a process and thus its occurrence of defects are driven by a set of input variables and environmental variables (see Figure 9.1). By definition, we know that a defect occurrence reflects some abnormal variation in the outcome variable. And such abnormal variation in the outcome variable must be the result of some abnormal variation in input variables or in environmental variables. So once our control chart has alerted us that some assignable cause variation has occurred in the outcome variable, it is our job to look for what input or environmental variables led to this result. We investigate the root cause for the abnormal variation.

LO9-4 Create a fishbone diagram and a Pareto diagram.

Figure 9.9

Example diagram capturing the root causes of steer support variations

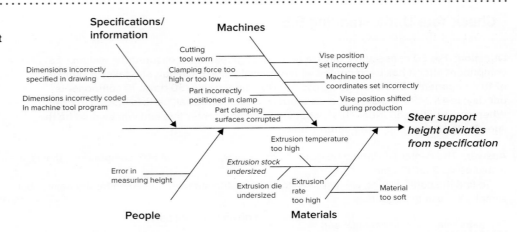

Fishbone diagram A structured way to brainstorm about the potential root causes that have led to a change in an outcome variable. This is done by mapping out all input and environmental variables. Also known as a cause-effect diagram or Ishikawa diagram.

Cause-effect diagram A structured way to brainstorm about the potential root causes that have led to a change in an outcome variable. This is done by mapping out all input and environmental variables. Also known as a fishbone diagram or Ishikawa diagram.

Ishikawa diagram A structured way to brainstorm about the potential root causes that have led to a change in an outcome variable. This is done by mapping out all input and environmental variables. Also known as a fishbone diagram or cause-effect diagram.

Five Whys A brainstorming technique that helps employees to find the root cause of a problem. In order to avoid stopping too early and not having found the real root cause, employees are encouraged to ask, "Why did this happen?" at least five times.

Pareto diagram A graphical way to identify the most important causes of process defects. To create a Pareto diagram, we need to collect data on the number of defect occurrences as well as the associated defect types. We can then plot simple bars with heights indicating the relative occurrences of the defect types. It is also common to plot the cumulative contribution of the defect types.

The first step in our exploration of root causes is to create a more careful diagram illustrating the relationship between the outcome variable and the various input and environmental variables. An example of such a diagram is shown in Figure 9.9. Such diagrams—also known as **fishbone diagrams** (reflecting their resemblance to fish bones), **cause-effect diagrams**, or **Ishikawa diagrams** (in honor of Kaoru Ishikawa, a Japanese quality scholar)—graphically represent the input and environmental variables that are causally related to a specific outcome, such as an increase in variation or a shift in the mean.

When drawing a fishbone diagram, we typically start with a horizontal arrow that points at the name of the outcome variable we want to analyze. Diagonal lines than lead to this arrow representing main causes. Smaller arrows then lead to these causality lines creating a fishbone-like shape. Diagonal lines can capture both input variables and environmental variables. Ishikawa diagrams are simple yet powerful problem-solving tools that can be used to structure brainstorming sessions and to visualize the causal structure of a complex system.

A related tool that also helps in developing causal models is known as the "**Five Whys**." The tool is prominently used in Toyota's organization when workers search for the root cause of a quality problem. The basic idea of the "Five Whys" is to continually question ("Why did this happen?") whether a potential cause is truly the root cause or is merely a symptom of a deeper problem. Consider the example of a student arriving late to class. A quick analysis might ask, "Why did the student come late?" and in response learn that the student wanted to grab a coffee. Argued this way, "grabbing coffee" appears as the root cause for the lateness. However, the "Five Whys" framework digs deeper:

- Why did it take the student so long to grab coffee? Because the coffee shop is far from the classrooms.

- Why does the student go to the coffee shop far away from the classrooms instead of going to the one in the building? Because there the coffee is better and cheaper.

- Why is the coffee shop in the building offering bad coffee at high prices? Because they have a local monopoly and don't really respond to customer needs.

- Why does the coffee shop in the building have a local monopoly? Because the university decided to sell the rights to coffee sales to a third party.

Notice what happened as we asked "Why?" five times. First, we really get to the underlying root causes as opposed to just dealing with the symptoms of the problem. Second, observe how the responsible party for the problem has shifted from the student (who wanted coffee) to the university (that sold the rights to sell coffee to a third party).

Given the multiple potential root causes of a defect, it is frequently desirable to find which of these root causes accounts for the majority of the problems. The **Pareto diagram** is a graphical way to identify the most important causes of process defects. To create a Pareto diagram, we need to collect data on the number of defect occurrences as well as the associated defect types. We can then plot simple bars with heights indicating the relative occurrences of

Cause of Defect	Absolute Number	Percentage	Cumulative
Browser error	43	0.39	0.39
Order number out of sequence	29	0.26	0.65
Products shipped, but credit card not billed	16	0.15	0.80
Order entry mistake	11	0.10	0.90
Products shipped to billing address	8	0.07	0.97
Wrong model shipped	3	0.03	1.00
Total	110		

Figure 9.10
Root causes for various defects in order handling at Xootr

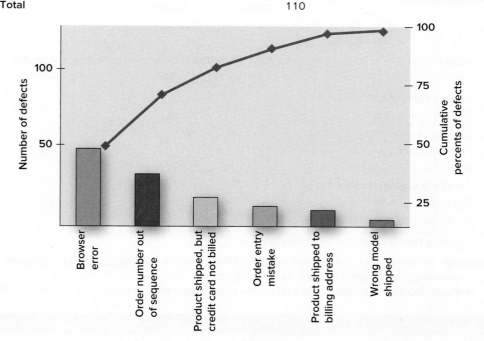

the defect types. It is also common to plot the cumulative contribution of the defect types. An example of a Pareto diagram is shown in Figure 9.10. The figure categorizes defects related to customer orders at Xootr LLC.

The Pareto principle was postulated by J.M. Juran. Juran observed that managers spent too much time trying to fix "small" problems, while not paying enough attention to "big" problems. The Pareto principle, also referred to as the 80-20 rule, postulates that 20 percent of the causes account for 80 percent of the problems. In the context of quality, the Pareto principle implies that a few defect types account for the majority of defects.

Check Your Understanding 9.6

Question: A large express shipping company recently noticed that the fraction of deliveries in which the package was reported broken by the receiver has increased substantially. Create a fishbone diagram, brainstorming why such defects might happen.

Answer: Clearly, there exist many plausible root causes, so there is not just one right answer to this question.

The following fishbone diagram breaks up the root causes into (a) broken during delivery, (b) delivered correctly but then broken by customer/misreported, (c) broken during transport, and (d) broken because of the content. With subcategories, a fishbone diagram would look like Figure 9.11.

(Continued)

Figure 9.11

A fishbone diagram for reported broken packages

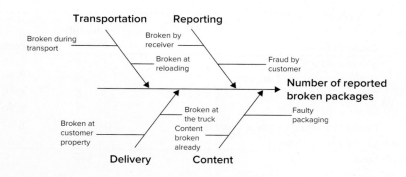

Question: Consider the following data, which report the frequency of broken packages by root cause.

- Broken during transport: 2
- Broken during reloading: 33
- Broken by receiver: 4
- Fraud by the customer: 1
- Broken at the truck: 9
- Broken at customer property: 22
- Content broken already: 7
- Faulty packaging: 9

Create a Pareto chart with this information.

Answer: We first sort this information in order of frequency of occurrence. We then compute the cumulative percentages as shown in Table 9.3.

We can visualize this information in the form of the graph in Figure 9.12.

TABLE 9.3

Root Cause	Frequency	Cumulative %
Broken during reloading	33	38%
Broken at customer property	22	63%
Broken at the truck	9	74%
Faulty packaging	9	84%
Content broken already	7	92%
Broken by receiver	4	97%
Broken during transport	2	99%
Fraud by the customer	1	100%
Total	87	

Figure 9.12

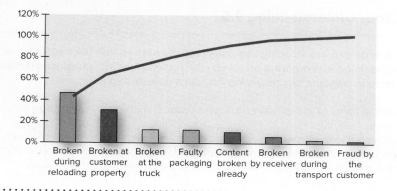

9.5 How to Eliminate Assignable Causes and Make the Process More Robust

As discussed earlier, variation in outcome variables such as the geometry of a part or the duration of a service activity is at the root of all quality problems. So identifying the sources of variation and eliminating them should always be the first priority when aiming for a quality improvement.

However, eliminating variation is not always possible. Especially when dealing with human resources (e.g., assembly-line workers) or human flow units (patients, calls in a call center), we are always exposed to variation that is beyond our control. Moreover, the sources of variation might sometimes be under our control, yet their elimination might be prohibitively expensive.

For these reasons, instead of just fighting variation, we also need to be able to accommodate it. We need to design a process that does not fall apart and produce defects the moment it is exposed to variation. A good tennis player should always aim to hit the ball with the sweet spot of her racket, yet a good tennis racket should also be "forgiving" so that it does not lead to a poor shot the moment the hit is less than perfect. We label a process that can tolerate variation in input variables and environmental variables without an increase in variation in outcome as a **robust process**. Put differently, a robust process is resistant against variation in input and environmental variables.

How can we make a process robust? Here are the most common strategies:

- **Overengineering:** As we saw, defects happen if variation pushes the outcome variable outside the tolerance level. This, in turn, is driven by the variation in input variables and environmental variables. For example, when the MS *Estonia* was designed, the engineers had to decide how much rough water the ferry would be able to handle. They hopefully also considered what handling mistakes the crew might make. Considering even rare variations in input and environmental variables when determining things such as the geometry of the ferry or the maximum allowable load is critical for a robust design. In other words, we make the process so that it can do well, even under very exceptional conditions.

- **Foolproofing:** A large amount of the variation in input variables in a process comes from mistakes committed by the (human) operators in the process. Human actions are prone to variation, be it because of a "trembling hand" or mere forgetfulness. The idea of foolproofing or standards and checklists is to change the work in such a way that the operator attempting to make a mistake cannot complete the task, thereby realizing that he has done something wrong. An example of foolproofing would be to change the syringe design for oral medication delivery so that it does not fit into the IV. Then, a caregiver who mixes up the delivery mechanism (an operator who accidentally attempts to make the mistake) will not be able to do so. The variation in input variable happened (the care provider mixes up the delivery mechanisms), but the outcome remains unaffected by this. This also has the nice side benefit that the operator will get feedback and potentially learn from that mistake, reducing the likelihood of a future recurrence of the defect.

- **Early warning signs on input and environmental variables:** It lies in the nature of a process that there typically exists some time lag between the occurrence of variation in input variables and environmental variables and the occurrence of the variation in the outcome variable and the defect. Sometimes that time lag is very short, as in the case of the confusion in ticker symbols between Twitter and Tweeter. In that case, it was most likely an issue of seconds between making the mistake and submitting the trade. Typically, however, this time lag is much longer. Consider again the mistakes that led to the sinking of the MS *Estonia*. The sea was exceptionally rough many hours ahead of the departure of the ferry. Moreover, the poor balancing of the load occurred also over an hour before the sinking. Most likely, the crew was aware of the weather conditions, but apparently they were not aware of the poor balance. To the extent that the crew could have been alerted to this exceptional variation in the input variable "load balance," the crew might have been able to intervene sooner and have decided either to not leave the harbor or to first rebalance the boat.

LO9-5 Explain how to avoid defects by creating a robust process.

Robust process A process that is robust can tolerate variation in input variables and environmental variables without leading to a defect.

CONNECTIONS: Left and Right on a Boat

© *Gérard Cachon*

Have you ever wondered why the crew of the boat never speak about going left or going right? When you stand on the boat looking toward the front (bow) of the boat, the appropriate term for the left side is the port side and for the right side is the starboard side. The reason for adding these extra terms is not maritime snobbism in language. The benefit of port and starboard is that they are independent of the position of the crew member. Think about a rowing boat. When the coxswain (the person in charge of navigation) tells the rowers to go right, which way to turn? Look at the boat above. The coxswain in this boat faces the bow; the rowers sit the other way around. Things are even more complicated on big ships and ferries that sometimes go forward and sometimes backwards and where crew members are moving around. By using commands such as port and starboard, everybody is in agreement on the direction. The environmental noise of the rowers' position has no impact on the outcome.

9.6 Defects with Binary Outcomes: Event Trees

In the previous sections, we collected data for a specific variable and then compared these data with specification limits in order to classify the associated flow unit as defective or not. However, it is not always possible to come up with a single variable, such as length or duration, that captures the degree of specification conformance. For example, an airline tracking defects corresponding to lost luggage, a pharmacy trying to reduce the number of patients who were provided the wrong drugs, or a data entry operation struggling with handwriting recognition all face discrete outcomes (a unit is either defective or not) rather than a continuous outcome. In such cases, we still want to use the power of statistical analysis to measure and improve the process. However, short of a continuous distribution of outcome variables as we assumed in our previous analysis, we have to now analyze the discrete probabilities of a defect.

9.6.1 Capability Evaluation for Discrete Events

As before, the outcome of the process is influenced by a set of input variables and environmental variables. Under certain conditions, we get a defective outcome. For now, we assume that input variables, environmental variables, and the outcome variable just can have two discrete values—they can either be "good" or "defective." The image we want you to have in your mind for these variables is a simple coin toss, capturing (not necessarily with 50:50 probabilities) the probability of making a defect or not making a defect.

Consider the following two examples. In the assembly of a simple component, there are three steps that potentially can lead to defects. The first step makes defects in 2 percent of the cases, the second step makes defects in 5 percent of the cases, and the third makes defects in 3 percent of the cases. In order for the component to function correctly, all three steps have to be carried out correctly; that is, a defect in any one of the three input variables will lead to a defect in the output.

How do we get from the individual probabilities in the input variables to the defect probability of the outcome variable? We have to think about the likelihoods of the associated events. In this case, in order for the component to function correctly, step 1 has to function correctly AND step 2 has to function correctly AND step 3 has to function correctly. So, the probability of the component functioning correctly is given by

$$\text{Prob}\{\text{Good Unit}\} = \text{Prob}\{\text{Step 1 correct}\} \times \text{Prob}\{\text{Step 2 correct}\} \times \text{Prob}\{\text{Step 3 correct}\}$$
$$= (1 - \text{Prob}\{\text{Step 1 defective}\}) \times (1 - \text{Prob}\{\text{Step 2 defective}\})$$
$$\times (1 - \text{Prob}\{\text{Step 3 defective}\})$$
$$= (1 - 0.02) \times (1 - 0.05) \times (1 - 0.03) = 0.90307$$

And thus the probability of a defect is:

$$\text{Prob}\{\text{Defect}\} = 1 - \text{Prob}\{\text{Good unit}\} = 1 - 0.90307 = 0.09693$$

Now, consider the second example. In the medication delivery of a drug, prescribing doctors sometimes make mistakes overseeing allergies of the patient or interactions of multiple drugs. A three-step medication delivery process is used once the doctor has requested a particular medication. First, the nurse delivering the medication needs to pick it up from the pharmacy. The pharmacy catches 70 percent of the mistakes. Next, the nurse sometimes double-checks the medication with the attending physician, which catches another 80 percent of the mistakes. Finally, sometimes the patient herself alerts the nurse to the medication problem; however, that only happens in 50 percent of the cases.

The medication example is fundamentally different from the first example. In the medication example, the process was more robust because as long as the medication mistake was caught at any one of the three steps, the patient would not receive the incorrect medication. Put differently, in order for a defect to happen, all three steps would have to make a mistake, which would happen with a probability of

$$\text{Prob}\{\text{Defect}\} = \text{Prob}\{\text{Step 1 defect}\} \times \text{Prob}\{\text{Step 2 defect}\} \times \text{Prob}\{\text{Step 3 defect}\}$$
$$= 0.3 \times 0.2 \times 0.5 = 0.03$$

And the probability of providing the right service, given that the doctor has made a wrong prescription, would be

$$\text{Prob}\{\text{Good unit}\} = 1 - \text{Prob}\{\text{Defect}\} = 1 - 0.03 = 0.97$$

In both cases, we had multiple discrete events that together would determine if the overall outcome variable was leading to a defect or not. A nice way to illustrate the different scenarios is shown in Figure 9.13. The representations shown in the figure are also known as **event trees**. On the left, the figure shows the event tree for the assembly process. The event tree captures the three input variables of the process and shows them as discrete branches, each branch either going left with a certain probability or going right. For simplicity, we assume that the left branch corresponds to a defect and the right branch corresponds to a correct processing. Because there are three outcome variables, each of which can have two values, the event tree distinguishes between $2^3 = 8$ different scenarios. For the outcome to be defective, it is sufficient to have one of the three steps go wrong. Any single mistake leads to a defect. Thus, we have only one scenario (all three steps done correctly) that leads to a good unit. The other seven scenarios lead to a defect.

LO9-6 Create an event tree to model defects.

Event tree Visual representation of binary outcome variables. It supports the defect probability calculations by connecting the defects in the process to an overall outcome measure.

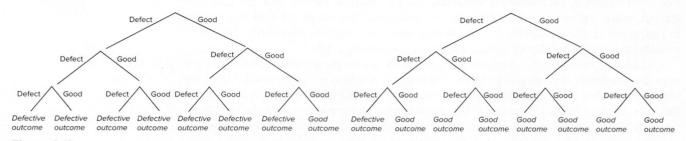

Figure 9.13

Event trees for the assembly operation (left) and medication inspection (right)

On the right, Figure 9.13 shows the event tree for the medication delivery. Again, the event tree captures the three input variables of the process as discrete branches and, given that there are three outcome variables, each of which can have two values, the event tree has $2^3 = 8$ different scenarios. This time, however, for the outcome to be defective, all three steps have to go wrong. As long as anybody catches the mistake, the medication is delivered correctly.

The event trees help us compute the defect probability for a process with binary values for the input, environmental, and outcome variables. We can compute the probability for each combination of outcomes (corresponding to a path in the event tree from the root of the tree to one of its leaves). The leaves correspond either to good outcomes or to defects. When classifying the leaves into good and defective, we have to make sure to understand how the variables are logically connected.

A couple of comments are in order:

- The previously introduced concept of robustness applies also to binary outcomes. The three-step component assembly process was not robust; any one mistake led to a

Check Your Understanding 9.7

Question: An insurance company hands out flyers on which customers leave their contact e-mail so that the insurance company can contact them later. These flyers are transcribed to a computer system. In the data entry operation, a typist reads the handwriting from the flyer. In 95 percent of the cases, the handwriting is read correctly. In 0.5 percent of the cases, the typist makes a mistake and writes something different from what he had read on the flyer. Create an event tree. What is the probability that the data are entered correctly?

Answer: There are two variables with two outcomes each, so we are dealing with $2^2 = 4$ possible scenarios. In order for the data to be entered correctly, we need the data to be both read correctly from the form and entered correctly. The event tree thus looks like Figure 9.14.

We find the probability that the data are entered correctly as

Prob{Data entered correctly} = Prob{Data read correctly} × Prob{Data typed correctly}

= 0.95 × 0.995 = 0.94525

Figure 9.14

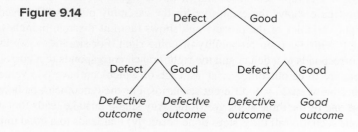

defect. In contrast, the medication process was robust. It had some redundancy (double-checking) built in and so it could tolerate failures in input variables without leading to a defect.

- Just as we looked at variation in the process in our capability analysis for continuous distributions, we should not make the mistake and infer from 100 correctly executed medication delivery processes that the process is operating at a high capability. Near misses, in this case in the form of a medication error made but not caught immediately, are a reason for concern and should be considered when making an assessment of the overall defect probability. Thus, we would grossly underestimate the defect probability in the medication example if we estimated it based on the observed outcome variable alone.

- Tragic outcomes such as the situation in the German hospital and the sinking of the MS *Estonia* are typically a result of a number of input variables. Each individual input variable describes a step that is typically executed correctly. Moreover, the process is robust and so each defect in input variables itself is not causing a bad outcome overall. Unfortunately, this often leads to a false sense of security by the operators of the process ("making a mistake is not a big deal because we have three other people double-checking").

9.7 Defects with Binary Outcomes: *p*-Charts

When constructing an *X*-bar chart, we are able to measure an outcome variable on a single dimension and then use the interval between the lower control limit and the upper control limit to determine if a unit is defective or not. Now that we are dealing with discrete outcomes, this no longer works. All we can do is to distinguish defective and nondefective flow units.

So, when we now take a sample of units from the process, the only information we have on each unit is whether it is classified as a good unit or as a defective unit. We can then compute the percentage of flow units in the sample that are defective. And, similar to what we did with the *X*-bar charts, we can then track this percentage over time. This is the idea behind creating a *p*-chart, also known as an **attribute based control chart**.

Sample sizes for *p*-charts tend to be larger, typically ranging from 50 to 200 for each period. Larger sample sizes are needed in particular if defects are relatively rare events. If

p-chart A special control chart used for dealing with binary outcomes. It has all the features of the *X*-bar chart, yet does not require a continuous outcome variable. However, *p*-charts require larger sample sizes, especially if defects occur rarely. Also known as attribute-based control charts.

Attribute-based control chart A special control chart used for dealing with binary outcomes. It has all the features of the *X*-bar chart, yet does not require a continuous outcome variable. However, attribute-based charts require larger sample sizes, especially if defects occur rarely. Also known as *p*-charts.

Check Your Understanding 9.8

Question: Every day, an online grocery store takes a sample of 200 packages that have been prepared and are now ready to be sent out to customers. Across all days, the average percentage of incorrect shipments is 3 percent. How would you create a *p*-chart based on this information?

Answer: We first create the center line at 3 percent. We then compute the estimated standard deviation as follows:

$$\text{Estimated standard deviation} = \sqrt{\frac{\bar{p}\,(1-\bar{p})}{\text{Sample size}}} = \sqrt{\frac{0.03 \times (1-0.03)}{200}} = 0.012062$$

We then compute the upper and lower control limits:

$$\text{UCL} = \bar{p} + (3 \times \text{Estimated standard deviation}) = 0.03 + (3 \times 0.012062) = 0.066187$$

$$\text{LCL} = \bar{p} - (3 \times \text{Estimated standard deviation}) = 0.03 - (3 \times 0.012062) = -0.00619$$

We then draw the control limits. We use the UCL as 0.066187. Note that the LCL is negative. Because the estimated proportion of defective parts can never become negative, we use the 0 line as the LCL.

CONNECTIONS: Some free cash from Citizens Bank?

© Glow Images/RF

From the perspective of the customer, defects can sometimes be a pleasant surprise (at least initially). Imagine how Steven Fields, an 18-year-old native of Georgia, must have felt. Steven noticed a sudden increase in his bank account. A mistaken transaction at the First Citizens Bank in Hull (Georgia) moved $31,000 to Steven's account. How could this happen? Another customer, also by the name of Steven Fields, made a $31,000 deposit, and, apparently, the teller entering the transaction confused the accounts. Unfortunately (at least from the perspective of the 18-year-old Steven Fields), the joy did not last. Though he was quick to withdraw most of the money, the bank insisted that he pay it back.

Transaction mistakes of that type are an example of a discrete event. Unlike the rattling steer support parts at Xootr with an underlying continuous distribution, a transaction is much more of a black-and-white outcome.

you have a 1 percent defect probability, chances are that you would not find any defects with a sample size as low as 5 or 10. Samples are collected in each period, just as in the case of *X*-bar control charts. Within each sample, we evaluate the percentage of defective items. Let *p* denote this percentage (that's why we call them *p*-charts). We then compute the average percentage of defects over all samples, which we call $\bar{p}$. This "average across averages" is the center line in our attribute control chart, just as we used *X*-double-bar as the center line for variable control charts.

LO9-7 Create a *p*-chart.

To compute the control limits, we first need to obtain an estimate of the standard deviation of defects. This estimate is given by the following equation:

$$\text{Estimated standard deviation} = \sqrt{\frac{\bar{p}\,(1 - \bar{p})}{\text{Sample size}}}$$

We then compute the upper and lower control limits:

$$\text{UCL} = \bar{p} + (3 \times \text{Estimated standard deviation})$$

$$\text{LCL} = \bar{p} - (3 \times \text{Estimated standard deviation})$$

Thus, we again set control limits such that the process is allowed to vary three standard deviations in each direction from the mean. Note that in the case when the lower control limit determined earlier is negative, we use the 0 line as the LCL.

Once we have created the center line and the lower and upper control limits, we use the p-chart in exactly the same way we use the X-bar chart. Every time period, we plot the percentage of defective items in the p-chart. If that percentage goes above the upper control limit, we expect some (negative) assignable cause to be at work. If that percentage goes below the lower control limit, we expect some (positive) assignable cause variation to be at work (after all, the percentage of defects in this case has gone down).

Conclusion

Defects are driven by variability. Due to some variation in input variables or in environmental variables, the process displays a variation in the outcome. And, according to the size of this variation and the tightness of the specifications, this variation in outcome corresponds to a defect.

We have a choice between thinking of defects in a binary way (defect versus no defect) or based on a continuous measure of the outcome variable relative to a tolerance interval (upper and lower specification limits). In the case in which we can classify units only into defective or nondefective, we measure the capability of the process as the percentage of units produced correctly. Alternatively, we can estimate how many defects there will be in a million units (ppm). However, such a binary classification into defective and nondefective wastes a lot of information. As we saw with the example of the target shooter, we can use the information of "near misses" to improve our assessment of the current process capability. In this case, we measure the capability of the process with the capability score C_p, which captures the variation in the process relative to the width of the tolerance interval. The C_p score can then be translated into a defect percentage or a ppm number. When choosing between these two approaches of measuring capability, one should consider the following:

- Can the specifications be mathematically described? We could label a Xootr steer support unit as defective if it was outside the tolerance interval. The variation of the underlying process could be captured in a simple, one-dimensional distribution. This, however, is not the case for the other examples we discussed at the beginning of the chapter. The ticker symbol for a trade in the stock market is either correct or not. We might measure how much of a given medication has been put into a syringe using a tolerance level, but if that medication was given orally or via an IV is again a binary outcome.

- How often do defects occur? If defects are rare and their consequences are substantial, we should try to learn from near misses. Near misses can correspond to variations in the outcome variable that were not quite large enough to make a unit defective. Or they can reflect variation in input variables that are absorbed due to the robustness of the process. Either way, it is important to use this information to measure the capability of the process instead of inferring from the absence of defects that everything functions perfectly.

Binary outcomes or a continuous distribution of outcomes—in either case we can monitor the process and determine to what extent it behaves according to historical data. We can use X-bar charts, which plot the mean of a sample, to track a process with the outcome variable following a continuous distribution. And we can use a p-chart to do the same for binary outcome variables. Either way, the control chart provides us with a simple, graphical way to quickly detect abnormal (assignable cause) variation.

We then either eliminate these root causes or, using the robust process design logic, attempt to minimize their sensitivity to variation in process parameters. The resulting improved process is monitored and analyzed in the same way as previously, which either confirms or disconfirms the usefulness of our action.

TABLE 9.4   Different Methods of Process Control Discussed in This Chapter

	Capability Analysis	Conformance Analysis
Binary	ppm, yield calculations	p-chart
Parametric	Six sigma	X-bar

Statistical process control has a long history that has recently become fashionable again under the buzz word of "six sigma." The strength of the statistical process control techniques discussed in this chapter results from their combination of collecting actual data with using professional analysis techniques.

The importance of data collection cannot be overemphasized. In many industries, collecting data about process performance is the exception rather than the norm. Once you have collected data, process improvement meetings turn fact-based, and objective as opposed to being largely subjective. While most manufacturing facilities by now routinely collect data about their processes, most service processes are lagging behind. Only in the last couple of years have service providers in banking or health care started to systemically track process data. This is somewhat surprising given that services are often blessed with loads of data because of their electronic workflow management systems.

But a successful process improvement project needs more than data. It is important to statistically analyze data. Otherwise, every small, random change in the process (including common cause variation) is interpreted as meaningful and acted upon. The tools outlined earlier help to separate the important from the unimportant.

Summary of Learning Objectives

LO9-1   Distinguish between common cause variation and assignable cause variation, and between input variables, environmental variables, and outcome variables

Outcome variables describe the outcome of the process. Input variables are those that are under the direct control of management. Environmental variables also influence the outcome variables, yet they are not under direct managerial control. As input variables and environmental variables fluctuate over time, so will the outcome variable. To the extent that such a fluctuation is entirely random, we refer to it as a common cause variation. If, however, there exists a specific reason for the variation, we refer to it as an assignable cause variation.

LO9-2   Compute the process capability index and the defect probability

The process capability index, C_p, is the ratio between the width of the specification interval of the outcome variable and the variation in the outcome variable (measured by six times its estimated standard deviation). It tells us how many standard deviations we can move away from the statistical mean before causing a defect. It thus can be translated to a defect probability.

LO9-3   Construct a control chart and use it to determine if abnormal variation exists in a process

A control chart is a visual representation of variation in the process. It has time on its x-axis and an outcome variable on the y-axis. In each time period, we collect a sample of outcomes, which we plot in the control chart. The control chart also shows a long-run center line (called X-bar-bar), which is the average across all points. It also shows upper and lower control limits, which are computed based on past data. If a new sample is outside these control limits, we can infer that some assignable cause variation has impacted the process.

LO9-4 Create a fishbone diagram and a Pareto diagram

A fishbone diagram, also called an Ishikawa diagram, is a structured way to brainstorm about the potential root causes that have led to a change in an outcome variable. Typically, the change in the outcome variable can be explained by a few input or environmental variables. Eighty percent of the problems can be traced back to 20 percent of the root causes. This is shown in the form of a Pareto diagram.

LO9-5 Explain how to avoid defects by creating a robust process

A robust process is one in which we avoid the changes in input or environmental variables that impact the outcome variables. We can do this by overengineering the process, by foolproofing the activities, or by providing checklists. We also should quickly alert operators to abnormal variation.

LO9-6 Create an event tree to model defects

An event tree is a visual representation of binary outcome variables. It supports the defect probability calculations by connecting the defects in the process to an overall outcome measure.

LO9-7 Create a *p*-chart

A *p*-chart is a special control chart used for dealing with binary outcomes. It has all the features of the *X*-bar chart, yet it does not require a continuous outcome variable. However, *p*-charts require larger sample sizes, especially if defects occur rarely.

Key Terms

9.1 The Statistical Process Control Framework

Natural variation Variation that occurs in a process as a result of pure randomness (also known as common cause variation).

Common cause variation Variation that occurs in a process as a result of pure randomness (also known as natural variation).

Assignable cause variation Variation that occurs because of a specific change in input or in environmental variables.

Input variables The variables in a process that are under the control of management.

Environmental variables Variables in a process that are not under the control of management but nevertheless might impact the outcome of the process.

Outcome variables Measures describing the quality of the output of the process.

Defective Not corresponding to the specifications of the process.

Set of specifications A set of rules that determine if the outcome variable of a unit is defective or not.

Root cause A root cause for a defect is a change in an input or an environmental variable that initiated a defect.

Robust The ability of a process to tolerate changes in input and environmental variables without causing the outcomes to be defective.

Statistical process control (SPC) A framework in operations management built around the empirical measurement and the statistical analysis of input, environmental, and outcome variables.

Abnormal A variation is abnormal if it is not behaving in line with past data; this allows us to conclude that we are dealing with an assignable cause variation and are not just facing randomness in the form of common cause variation.

9.2 Capability Analysis

Lower specification limit (LSL) The smallest outcome value that does not trigger a defective unit.

Upper specification limit (USL) The largest outcome value that does not trigger a defective unit.

Process capability index The ratio between the width of the specification interval of the outcome variable and the variation in the outcome variable (measured by six times its estimated standard deviation). It tells us how many standard deviations we can move away from the statistical mean before causing a defect.

Six-sigma program Initiatives within the framework of statistical process control trying to increase the process capability index.

Defect probability The statistical probability with which a randomly chosen flow unit does not meet specifications.

Parts per million The expected number of defective parts in a random sample of one million.

Target variation The largest amount of variation in a process that does not exceed a given defect probability.

9.3 Conformance Analysis

Control charts A control chart is a visual representation of variation in the process. It has time on its x-axis and an outcome variable on the y-axis. In each time period, we collect a sample of outcomes, which we plot in the control chart. The control chart also shows a long-run center line (called X-bar-bar), which is the average across all points. It also shows an upper and a lower control limit, which are computed based on past data.

X-bar charts A special control chart in which we track the mean of a sample (also known as X-bar).

X-bar The average of a sample.

Lower control limit (LCL) A line in a control chart that provides the smallest value that is still acceptable without being labeled an abnormal variation.

Upper control limit (UCL) A line in a control chart that provides the largest value that is still acceptable without being labeled an abnormal variation.

X-double-bar The average of a set of sample averages.

Estimated standard deviation of all parts The standard deviation that is computed across all parts.

Estimated standard deviation for X-bar The standard deviation of a particular sample mean, x-bar.

9.4 Investigating Assignable Causes

Fishbone diagram A structured way to brainstorm about the potential root causes that have led to a change in an outcome variable. This is done by mapping out all input and environmental variables. Also known as a cause-effect diagram or Ishikawa diagram.

Cause-effect diagram A structured way to brainstorm about the potential root causes that have led to a change in an outcome variable. This is done by mapping out all input and environmental variables. Also known as a fishbone diagram or Ishikawa diagram.

Ishikawa diagram A structured way to brainstorm about the potential root causes that have led to a change in an outcome variable. This is done by mapping out all input and environmental variables. Also known as a fishbone diagram or cause-effect diagram.

Five Whys A brainstorming technique that helps employees to find the root cause of a problem. In order to avoid stopping too early and not having found the real root cause, employees are encouraged to ask, "Why did this happen?" at least five times.

Pareto diagram A graphical way to identify the most important causes of process defects. To create a Pareto diagram, we need to collect data on the number of defect occurrences as well as the associated defect types. We can then plot simple bars with heights indicating the relative occurrences of the defect types. It is also common to plot the cumulative contribution of the defect types.

9.5 How to Eliminate Assignable Causes and Make the Process More Robust

Robust process A process that is robust can tolerate variation in input variables and environmental variables without leading to a defect.

9.6 Defects with Binary Outcomes: Event Trees

Event tree Visual representation of binary outcome variables. It supports the defect probability calculations by connecting the defects in the process to an overall outcome measure.

9.7 Defects with Binary Outcomes: p-charts

p-chart A special control chart used for dealing with binary outcomes. It has all the features of the X-bar chart, yet does not require a continuous outcome variable. However, p-charts require larger sample sizes, especially if defects occur rarely. Also known as attribute-based control charts.

Attribute-based control chart A special control chart used for dealing with binary outcomes. It has all the features of the X-bar chart, yet does not require a continuous outcome variable. However, attribute-based charts require larger sample sizes, especially if defects occur rarely. Also known as p-charts.

Key Formulas

LO9-2 Compute the process capability index and the defect probability

$$C_p = \frac{\text{USL} - \text{LSL}}{6\hat{\sigma}}$$

LO9-3 Construct a control chart and use a control chart to determine if there presently exists abnormal variation in the process

$$\bar{X} = \frac{x_1 + x_2 + \ldots + x_n}{n}$$

$$\text{UCL} = \bar{\bar{X}} + [3 \times \text{ESD}(X\text{-bar})], \text{LCL} = \bar{\bar{X}} - [3 \times \text{ESD}(X\text{-bar})]$$

LO9-7 Create a p-chart

$$\text{Estimated standard deviation} = \sqrt{\frac{\bar{p}(1 - \bar{p})}{\text{Sample size}}}$$

$\text{UCL} = \bar{p} + (3 \times \text{Estimated standard deviation}), \text{LCL} = \bar{p} - (3 \times \text{Estimated standard deviation})$

Conceptual Questions

LO9-1

1. In the production of pizza, which of the following four variables is not an input variable?
   a. The amount of dough prepared for the pizza
   b. The temperature of the oven
   c. The type of cheese on the pizza
   d. The time that the customer leaves the pizza in the refrigerator

2. Mary and Tom operate a lemonade stand. They are concerned that the lemonade does not taste fresh at the end of the day. Which of the following variables is an environmental variable in their operation?
   a. The temperature of the lemonade when they take it out of their refrigerator in the morning
   b. The temperature of the air during the day
   c. The temperature of the lemonade
   d. The temperature of the water used to make the lemonade

3. Following the announcement of a major quality problem, the share price of a company falls substantially. This decrease is a result of assignable cause variation. True or false?
   a. True
   b. False

4. You harvest 50 tomatoes. You notice that the tomatoes vary in size and weight. If some of the tomatoes were exposed to extra sunshine or irrigation, this would be a common cause variation. True or false?
   a. True
   b. False

LO9-2

5. You measure the exact size of 100 ping pong balls from manufacturer A and then another 100 balls from manufacturer B. The balls of manufacturer B have a much larger variation. Means and specification limits for the two manufacturers are identical. Which of the two manufacturers has a higher process capability index?
   a. Manufacturer A
   b. Manufacturer B
   c. Cannot be determined from the given information

6. John is a newly minted quality engineer at MakeStuff Inc. His boss tells him to increase the process capability index of their main product. John is somewhat lazy and does not want to tackle the variation in the process, so he decides to simply increase the upper specification limit and reduce the lower specification limit. Does this increase the process capability index?
   a. No, it does not, because the variation in the process stays unchanged.
   b. Yes, it does, though one might question if the underlying process is really better.
   c. That depends on many other variables, including the control limits.
   d. No, the process capability index would only change if the control limits were changed.

7. If a process has a six-sigma capability, what is the process capability index?
   a. 1
   b. 2
   c. 6
   d. 12

8. For one and the same process, what scenario corresponds to a higher variation?
   a. A six-sigma process
   b. A three-sigma process
   c. Cannot be determined from the given information

LO9-3

9. What does X-bar stand for?
   a. The average of a sample
   b. The unknown standard deviation in a process that we have to solve for
   c. A shady bar in West Philadelphia
   d. The maximum observed value in a sample

10. Which of the following elements is not part of an X-bar control chart?
    a. The long-run center line, X-bar-bar
    b. The control limits, LCL and UCL
    c. The specification limits, LSL and USL
    d. X-bar values from each sample

11. How many standard deviations is the upper control limit, UCL, above the long-run center line, X-bar-bar?
    a. 1
    b. 2
    c. 3
    d. 6
    e. 12

LO9-4

12. What is the difference between a fishbone diagram and an Ishikawa diagram?
    a. The Ishikawa diagram has more arrows.
    b. The Ishikawa diagram is based on empirical data; the fishbone diagram is not.
    c. The Ishikawa diagram is an operations management tool; the fishbone diagram is just something made up for this question.
    d. There is no difference.

13. Which of the following statements about Pareto diagrams is correct?
    a. The Pareto diagram shows the possible root causes of a problem along with the number of defect occurrences.
    b. The Pareto diagram shows the process capability index over time.
    c. The Pareto diagram shows the mean of a random sample at various points in time.
    d. The Pareto diagram shows a visual representation of binary outcome variables.

LO9-5

14. Which of the following definitions describes a robust process?
    a. A process is robust if it can tolerate variation in input and environmental variables without producing a defect.
    b. A process is robust if it has a lot of automation built in.
    c. A process is robust if it uses control charts.
    d. A process is robust if its process capability index is greater than 1.

LO9-6

15. In a process for which we have to use discrete probabilities to describe whether an activity was carried out correctly or not, which of the following statements determines the defect probability of the entire process?
    a. The product of the individual defect probabilities
    b. The highest value of the individual defect probabilities
    c. The smallest value of the individual defect probabilities
    d. This really depends on the process, because it is possible that one process is more robust than the other.

16. You look at a process that has three activities; each one can potentially go wrong. How many leaves does the event tree of this process have?
    a. 2
    b. 3
    c. 6
    d. 8
    e. 24

LO9-7

17. What is the difference between p-charts and attribute-based control charts?
    a. p-charts are more quantitative.
    b. Attribute-based control charts really are a marketing tool and have nothing to do with operations.
    c. They are one and the same thing.
    d. p-charts monitor binary outcome variables, and attribute-based control charts monitor continuous outcome variables.

18. In a p-chart, the upper control limit is how many estimated standard deviations above the average p-bar?
    a. 1
    b. 2
    c. 3
    d. 6

Solved Example Problems

LO 9-1

1. A group of students organizes a bake sale in which they sell hundreds of cookies at $1 per piece. They set up a table on campus and wait for students to come and purchase their cookies. Consider the following variables in this bake sale operation:
   1. Size of the cookies
   2. Weather conditions on campus
   3. Organization of the table
   4. Number of cookies sold
   5. Competition from other fund-raisers coinciding on campus
   6. Amount of advertising and shouting of the students at the bake sale table
   7. Number of students on campus that day

   Which of these variables are input variables?
   a. 1 and 2
   b. 1 and 3
   c. 1, 3, and 5
   d. 1, 3, and 6

   > **Answer:** d. Input variables are "Size of the cookies," "Organization of the table," and "Amount of advertising and shouting of the students at the bake sale table."

2. A group of students organizes a bake sale in which they sell hundreds of cookies at $1 per piece. They set up a table on campus and wait for students to come and purchase their cookies. Consider the following variables in this bake sale operation:
   1. Size of the cookies
   2. Weather conditions on campus
   3. Organization of the table
   4. Number of cookies sold
   5. Competition from other fund-raisers coinciding on campus
   6. Amount of advertising and shouting of the students at the bake sale table
   7. Number of students on campus that day

   Which of these variables is an output variable?
   a. 3
   b. 4
   c. 5
   d. None of the above

   > **Answer:** b. The output variable is "Number of cookies sold."

3. A group of students organizes a bake sale in which they sell hundreds of cookies at $1 per piece. They set up a table on campus and wait for students to come and purchase their cookies. Consider the following variables in this bake sale operation:
   1. Size of the cookies
   2. Weather conditions on campus
   3. Organization of the table
   4. Number of cookies sold
   5. Competition from other fund-raisers coinciding on campus
   6. Amount of advertising and shouting of the students at the bake sale table
   7. Number of students on campus that day

   Which of these variables is/are the environmental variable(s)?
   a. 2
   b. 2 and 5
   c. 2, 5, and 7
   d. None of the above

Answer: c. Environmental variables include "Weather conditions on campus," "Competition from other fund-raisers coinciding on campus," and "Number of students on campus that day." All these variables are outside of the control of the bake sale, yet they influence the output variable.

4. John is a varsity runner specializing in the one-mile distance. His coach instructs John on every first Saturday of the month to run one mile at full speed. The coach then uses the times to determine the appropriate training intensity for John. This week, the coach compares the March time with the April time and the times differ by 3 seconds. Which of the following are some common cause variations?
   a. Some inherent variation in the measurement of the time
   b. A strong head wind
   c. The training effect over the last month
   d. None of the above

   Answer: a.

LO 9-2

5. A fast-food company is preparing beef patties for their burgers. The lower specification limit for the burger is 240 grams and the upper specification limit is 260 grams. The standard deviation is 4 grams and the mean is 250 grams.

   What is the process capability index for the beef patty production?

   Answer: We compute the process capability index as

$$C_p = \frac{\text{USL} - \text{LSL}}{6\hat{\sigma}} = \frac{260 - 240}{6 \times 4} = 0.8333$$

6. Consider again the beef patty production process that has a lower specification limit of 240 grams and an upper specification limit of 260 grams. The standard deviation is 4 grams and the mean is 250 grams.

   What is the probability that a beef patty is either too light or too heavy? How many defects would there be in one million beef patties?

   Answer: We first compute the probability of the beef patty being too light.

This is given by

Probability{Too light} = NORM.DIST(240, 250, 4, 1) = 0.00621

We then compute the other probabilities.

Probability{Too heavy} = 1 − NORM.DIST(260, 250, 4, 1) = 0.00621

Probability{Part defective} = 0.00621 + 0.00621 = 0.012419

We compute the ppm (parts per million) as $0.012419 \times 1,000,000 = 12,419$.

Note that we had previously found that the capability index of this process is 0.8333. We can also use Table 9.1 and look up the defect probability and the ppm there for $C_p = 0.8333$. Because $C_p = 0.8333$ itself is not in the table, we have to look at the closest two values, which are $C_p = 0.8$ and $C_p = 0.8666$. For $C_p = 0.8$, we see a defect probability (ppm) of 0.016395 (16,395), and for $C_p = 0.8666$, we see a defect probability (ppm) of 0.009322 (9,322). This is consistent with our earlier result.

7. Consider again our beef patty production process with a lower specification limit of 240 grams and an upper specification limit of 260 grams. The standard deviation is 4 grams and the mean is 250 grams. The company now wants to reduce its defect probability from the previously computed 0.012419 (ppm of 12,419) to 0.0005 (ppm of 500). To what level would they have to reduce the standard deviation in the process to meet this target?

Answer: We know that the process capability index is

$$C_p = \frac{USL - LSL}{6\hat{\sigma}}$$

Looking at Table 9.1, the capability index for a ppm of 500 is between 1.1333 and 1.2. If we set $C_p = 1.1333$, we get

$$1.1333 = \frac{260 - 240}{6\hat{\sigma}} \Leftrightarrow 1.1333 = \frac{20}{6\hat{\sigma}} \Leftrightarrow \hat{\sigma} = \frac{20}{6 \times 1.1333} = 2.941263$$

If we use $C_p = 1.2$, we get $\hat{\sigma} = 2.77778$. So the standard deviation would have to be reduced from its current value of 4 grams to a value between 2.77778 grams and 2.941263 grams.

LO 9-3

8. For 100 consecutive days, a company making nutritional supplements has measured the amount of a protein the company puts into its protein bars. Each day, the company takes a sample of 6 protein bars. The average across all 600 bars was 31.232 grams. The standard deviation was 0.83291 gram. When constructing an X-bar chart, what would be the center line?

   a. The center line would be given by the average across all 600 bars; that is, it would be 31.232 grams.
   b. The center line would be given by the standard deviation; that is, it would be 0.83291 gram.
   c. The center line would be 100.
   d. None of the above

   Answer: a.

9. For 100 consecutive days, a company making nutritional supplements has measured the amount of a protein the company puts into its protein bars. Each day, the company takes a sample of 6 protein bars. The average across all 600 bars was 31.232 grams. The standard deviation was 0.83291 gram. When constructing an X-bar chart, what would the upper control limit be?

   a. 30.2119
   b. 31.232
   c. 32.2521
   d. None of the above

   Answer: c. To find the control limits, we first have to estimate the standard deviation for the daily X-bar sample. We use the equation

   $$\text{Estimated standard deviation}(X\text{-bar}) = \frac{\text{Standard deviation of all parts}}{\sqrt{n}}$$

   $$= \frac{0.83291}{\sqrt{6}} = 0.340034$$

We then find the upper control limit as

$$\text{UCL} = \bar{\bar{X}} + [3 \times \text{ESD}(X\text{-bar})] = 31.232 + (3 \times 0.340034) = 32.2521$$

LO 9-4

10. Consider the following data related to complaints about a restaurant that were made on Yelp. Figure 9.15 lists the causes for the complaints. The frequency counts are shown below the figure.

    - Food was too cold: 2
    - Bad taste: 3
    - Portions too small: 4
    - Grumpy waiters: 1

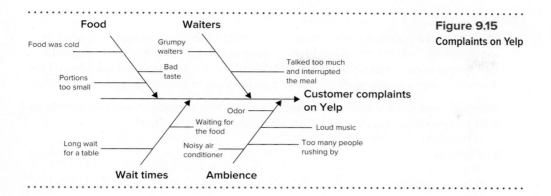

Figure 9.15
Complaints on Yelp

- Waiter talked too much and interrupted the meal: 15
- Long wait for a table: 22
- Waiting for the food: 7
- Noisy air conditioner: 9
- Loud music: 2
- Too many people rushing by: 5
- Odor: 3

Which of the following statements do you agree with?
a. This looks like very noisy data, because some root causes have a high frequency and some a low frequency.
b. This looks like data following the Pareto principle, which states that a few root causes explain the majority of the problems.
c. None of the above

Answer: b.

LO 9-5

11. Which of the following statements best describes the idea of foolproofing?
a. Avoid the recruitment of foolish operators by following best practices in recruiting.
b. Avoid the situation that an operator who made or is about to make a mistake can complete the task.
c. Avoid the situation that an operator who made a mistake is allowed to stay with the company.
d. None of the above

Answer: b.

LO 9-6

12. An airline call center makes travel reservations over the phone. A customer and an agent discuss the travel plans; the agent then books the flight and sends a confirmation e-mail to the customer. In 0.5 percent of the cases, the customer and the agent miscommunicate, confusing the travel destination (one recent flight was booked to Porto instead of Bordeaux). In 99.8 percent of the time, the agent books the way she understood the customer. In the other 0.2 percent of the cases, the agent makes a data entry mistake. What is the probability that the data are entered correctly?

   Answer: There are two variables with two outcomes each, so we are dealing with $2^2 = 4$ possible scenarios. In order for the flight to be booked correctly, we need the agent and the customer to have communicated correctly (happens 99.5 percent of the time) and then the flight must have been booked correctly (happens 99.8 percent of the time).

   We find the probability that the data are entered correctly as

   $$\text{Prob\{Data entered correctly\}} = \text{Prob\{Communicated correctly\}} \times$$
   $$\text{Prob\{Data entered correctly\}} = 0.995 \times 0.998 = 0.99301$$

LO 9-7

13. The health care system wants to encourage a healthy lifestyle. All doctors are asked to speak with all their patients about healthy eating in every visit. Every week, the health care system takes a random sample of 100 patients seen in the week and asks them if the doctor that they saw this week had brought up the topic of healthy eating.

    Across all weeks, the average percentage of visits in which healthy eating was brought up is 91 percent. What would be the center line in the resulting *p*-chart?
    a. 100 percent
    b. 9 percent
    c. 91 percent
    d. None of the above

    Answer: b.

14. The health care system wants to encourage a healthy lifestyle. All doctors are asked to speak with all their patients about healthy eating during every visit. Every week, a health care system takes a random sample of 100 patients seen in the week and asks them if the doctor they saw this week had brought up the topic of healthy eating.

    Across all weeks, the average percentage of visits in which healthy eating was brought up is 91 percent. What would be the upper control limit in the resulting *p*-chart?
    a. 0.0819
    b. 0.004145
    c. 0.175855
    d. 0.9
    e. None of the above

    Answer: c. We first create the center line at 9 percent (this is the 100 percent total minus the 91 percent correct). We then compute the estimated standard deviation as follows:

    $$\text{Estimated standard deviation} = \sqrt{\frac{0.09 \times (1 - 0.09)}{100}} = 0.028618$$

    We then compute the upper control limit based on:

    $$\text{UCL} = \bar{p} + (3 \times \text{Estimated standard deviation}) = 0.09 + (3 \times 0.028618) = 0.175855$$

Problems and Applications

LO9-1

1. Yi is fixing up his road bike to prepare for a triathlon. He looks at his tires and wonders how much he should inflate them. Which of the following variables is an outcome variable?
   a. The outside temperature
   b. The rolling resistance
   c. The number of times he presses the pump
   d. The size of the tire

2. You start a summer job serving ice cream at the shore. The manager notices that since you started the job, the average portion size given to customers has gone up substantially. This is a result of assignable cause variation. True or false?
   a. True
   b. False

LO9-2

3. A company making tires for bikes is concerned about the exact width of its cyclocross tires. The company has a lower specification limit of 22.8 mm and an upper specification limit of 23.2 mm. The standard deviation is 0.15 mm and the mean is 23 mm.

    What is the process capability index for the process?

4. Consider again that the company making tires for bikes is concerned about the exact width of its cyclocross tires. The company has a lower specification limit of 22.8 mm and an upper specification limit of 23.2 mm. The standard deviation is 0.15 mm and the mean is 23 mm.

    What is the probability that a tire will either be too wide or too narrow?

5. Consider again that the company making tires for bikes is concerned about the exact width of its cyclocross tires. The company has a lower specification limit of 22.8 mm and an upper specification limit of 23.2 mm. The standard deviation is 0.15 mm and the mean is 23 mm. The company now wants to reduce its defect probability. To what level would it have to reduce the standard deviation in the process to meet this target?

LO9-3

6. For 120 consecutive days, a process engineer has measured the temperature of champagne bottles as they are made ready for serving. Each day, she took a sample of 8 bottles. The average across all 960 bottles (120 days, 8 bottles per day) was 46 degrees Fahrenheit. The standard deviation across all bottles was 0.8 degree. When constructing an X-bar chart, what would be the center line?

7. For 120 consecutive days, a process engineer has measured the temperature of champagne bottles as they are made ready for serving. Each day, she took a sample of 8 bottles. The average across all 960 bottles (120 days, 8 bottles per day) was 46 degrees Fahrenheit. The standard deviation across all bottles was 0.8 degree. When constructing an X-bar chart, what would be the upper control limit?

LO9-4

8. Which of the following statements about Pareto diagrams is correct?
    a. The Pareto diagram shows the possible root causes of a problem but does not show the frequency of defect occurrences.
    b. The Pareto diagram shows the defects in order from most commonly occurring to least commonly occurring.
    c. The Pareto diagram shows the mean of a random sample at various points in time.
    d. The bars in the Pareto diagram have, on average, roughly the same height.

LO9-5

9. A baking operation reduces the amount of variation in the oven temperature. This is an example of robust process design. True or false?
    A. True
    B. False

LO9-6

10. You are thinking about the things that can go wrong on your trip home over the Thanksgiving break. You have booked a flight with US-Scareways. You know that in 30 percent of the cases the company has canceled the flight you were on. Should such a thing occur, there would be no other air travel option home for you. As a backup, your friend Walter has offered you a ride back. However, you know that Walter only has a seat in his car for you with an 80 percent probability. What is the probability of you making it home for the holidays?

LO9-7

11. For 40 days in the summer, you are working in a small, student-run company that sends out merchandise with university branding to alumni around the world. Every day, you take a sample of 50 shipments that are ready to be shipped to the alumni and inspect

them for correctness. Across all days, the average percentage of incorrect shipments is 5 percent. What would be the center line for a *p*-chart?

a. 40

b. 50

c. 0.05

d. 2.5

e. None of the above

12. You are working in a small, student-run company that sends out merchandise with university branding to alumni around the world. Every day, you take a sample of 50 shipments that are ready to be shipped to the alumni and inspect them for correctness. Across all days, the average percentage of incorrect shipments is 5 percent. What would be the upper control limit for a *p*-chart?

a. 0

b. 0.05

c. 0.03082207

d. 0.142466

CASE   THE PRODUCTION OF M&M'S

The chocolate product M&M's is produced with the following seven-step production process, which can make over one hundred million M&M's per day.

1. Liquid chocolate is poured into molds, creating the chocolate core of the M&M's.

2. The chocolate is tumbled to make the chocolate core smooth and round. The chocolate is then given time to harden.

3. A conveyor belt transports the M&M's to the panning operation.

4. At panning, the chocolate cores are rotated and liquid candy is sprayed onto them. Multiple coatings are applied and each coating is allowed time to dry.

5. Color is added as the final coat. Each batch has a different color and then batches are mixed across colors.

6. The "m" is then stamped onto each M&M by a special machine, avoiding any cracks in the candy shell.

7. A special packaging machine pours the proper amounts of M&M's into the bags and then seals the package. From there, bags are combined into a carton box.

Before packaging (step 7), the quality of the individual M&M's is evaluated. Pieces are sifted to eliminate misshapen pieces. Missing imprints, however, are not considered a reject.

A chocolate-loving operations professor has collected a sample of 120 bags of M&M's. The average weight of the

© Aaron Roeth/Aaron Roeth Photography/RF

bags (chocolate and bag) is 49.9783 grams. The standard deviation across the bags in the sample is 1.037 grams.

1. Assuming a lower specification limit of 47 grams and an upper specification limit of 53 grams, what is the process capability of this process? How many defects would you expect in one million bags?

2. And, finally, which M&M product in your view has the highest standard deviation?

SOURCE

http://www.madehow.com/Volume-3/M-M-Candy.html

References

Citizens Bank: http://abcnews.go.com/Business/ga-teen-spends-31000-mistakenly-deposited-account/story?id523086244

EU cucumbers: http://en.wikipedia.org/wiki/Commission_Regulation_(EC)_No_2257/94

MS *Estonia:* http://en.wikipedia.org/wiki/MS_Estonia

Münster, Germany: http://www.spiegel.de/unispiegel/studium/junger-arzt-wegen-tod-von-baby-verurteilt-a-914839.html

Twitter versus Tweeter: ABC News. Twitter-Tweeter Confusion Forces Stock Symbol Change, Oct. 9, 2013. http://abcnews.go.com/Technology/wireStory/tweeter-stock-symbol-twitter-mix-20506016

10 Introduction to Inventory Management

LEARNING OBJECTIVES

LO10-1 Explain the different types of inventory, the challenges of inventory management, and the reasons for the existence of inventory

LO10-2 Evaluate inventory turns and days-of-supply for different time periods (annual, monthly, weekly, and daily)

LO10-3 Evaluate turns and days-of-supply from financial reports

LO10-4 Evaluate the holding cost of an item held in inventory using an annual holding cost percentage and days-of-supply or turns

CHAPTER OUTLINE

© Andrew Resek/McGraw-Hill Education

Introduction

In 2014, Apple launched its iPhone 6 mobile devices and sold more than 10 million units in the first weekend. Most people hearing that news at the time probably thought something like, "Wow, that must be a popular phone!" But the response from an operations management person probably would be, "Really? They had the inventory to actually make all of those sales?"

As consumers, we generally do not notice inventory unless it isn't available for us. We expect to go to a hardware store like Home Depot and find the latex paint with an Alabaster color that we want for this weekend's fence-painting project—a different color won't do, nor will an oil-based paint. Or we walk into a grocery store to purchase organic strawberries and, of course, the strawberries will be in stock, fresh and in the quantity we want!

So consumers demand perfection. But perfection is not easy for firms to deliver. A hardware store might carry 80,000 different items, from grass seed with starter fertilizer to galvanized ½-inch washers to roofing cement. They might operate hundreds of stores across the country. And as if they need more complexity, the demand for most of what they sell depends heavily upon the randomness of the weather. In short, for the hardware store to achieve perfection, it must have the right product in the right place at the right time! All three are necessary—it isn't enough to have just two of the three. For example, suppose Home Depot has a can of Alabaster latex paint in the store we visit when we visit it. This is great for us because they have the "right product" in the "right place." But what if that can has been sitting in their store for a year or more. From their perspective, they absolutely did not get the "right time"—they incurred the cost to store the can of paint for one year, which they could have avoided if the can was added to their inventory shortly before we arrived!

This chapter begins our exploration of inventory management. In section 10.1, we (i) define inventory management, (ii) list the different types of inventory, (iii) identify the skills needed to be good at inventory management, and (iv) summarize the different reasons for the existence of inventory. Next, in section 10.2 we learn how to measure inventory—as always, you cannot manage what you don't measure. In section 10.3, we see that we can use a company's financial statements to gain some insight into how well it manages its own inventory. Finally, in section 10.4 we identify the costs a firm incurs when it holds inventory and when it does not hold enough inventory. In subsequent chapters, we explore how to make actual inventory decisions to ensure that we have the right product in the right place at the right time.

10.1 Inventory Management

In Chapter 2, Introduction to Processes, **inventory** is defined as the number of flow units within a process. That definition takes a broad interpretation of inventory. For example, it allows us to think of the number of guests waiting for a ride at an amusement park as "inventory." While those people are "inventory" in some sense (they are flow units), they might not appreciate being given the same label as a nondescript brown box in a warehouse. In this chapter, we take a somewhat more narrow or more traditional view of inventory. We still think of inventory as flow units within a process, but here we primarily think of inventory as the physical units within a process that are used for the production of goods or the delivery of services—for example, gallons of milk at a dairy, syringes in a hospital, tons of coal at a steel plant, television sets at a retailer, and, yes, nondescript brown boxes in a warehouse.

Inventory management is the practice of deciding on the quantity, location, and type of inventory in a process. The goal of inventory management, as alluded to in the Introduction, is to have the right product in the right place at the right time so that the firm can maximize its profit. And achieving that goal is important because, for many firms, their success or failure at inventory management has a significant influence on their overall profitability.

> **LO10-1** Explain the different types of inventory, the challenges of inventory management, and the reasons for the existence of inventory.

> **Inventory** The number of flow units within the process.

> **Inventory management** The practice of regulating the quantity, location, and type of inventory in a process.

10.1.1 Types of Inventory

It is customary to divide a firm's inventory into three different categories:

- **Raw material inventory** is used as the inputs to a process and has not undergone any transformation in the process. For example, an auto manufacturer might purchase sheets of metal to stamp into the body parts of the car. Before the stamping occurs, the sheets of metal are part of the company's raw material inventory.

- **Work-in-process inventory (WIP)** is the material and components used within the process to complete a product. For an auto manufacturer, work-in-process inventory includes body frames that will eventually become cars once they are painted, engines are installed, tires are added, and so forth.

- **Finished goods inventory** no longer requires additional processing. Finished goods inventory is ready for sale to the customer, like a completed car that rolls off an assembly line.

> **Raw material inventory** Inventory that is used as the inputs to a process and has not undergone any transformation in the process.

> **Work-in-process inventory (WIP)** The material and components used within the process to complete a product.

> **Finished goods inventory** Flow units that have completed processing.

In some sense, you can think of the three buckets as "inventory before a process," "inventory inside a process," and "inventory after a process." As such, the assignment of an object to one of these three categories depends on which process you are referring to. For example, from the perspective of the auto manufacturer, a piece of sheet metal is raw material inventory because it is "before" the process of assembling cars. However, from the perspective of the steel manufacturer, that same piece of sheet metal is finished goods inventory because it is "after" the process that made it.

Manufacturing firms typically have all three types of inventory (raw material, work-in-process, and finished goods). However, firms lower in the supply chain, such as wholesalers, distributors, and retailers, usually only carry finished goods inventory because they generally do not do additional processing of the inventory they purchase.

10.1.2 Inventory Management Capabilities

For all types of inventory, a firm requires a diverse set of capabilities to be able to manage its inventory effectively: forecasting, product and demand tracking, analytical skills, and product transportation and handling assets.

Forecasting One of the main reasons to hold inventory is to be able to provide immediate service to customers—if you need diapers for your newborn, then you are not going to wait several days for more inventory to arrive at your local store. Hence, forecasting future demand is an essential and critical skill for inventory management. Without a reasonable sense of what demand is about to happen, a firm simply cannot have the right product in the right place at the right time. That said, forecasting is not easy—Niels Bohr, a Nobel laureate in Physics once said, "Prediction is very difficult, especially if it is about the future." Because of its importance and challenge, Chapter 15, Forecasting, is dedicated to the topic.

Product and Demand Tracking The cliché "garbage in, garbage out" applies to inventory management—if a firm does not have good data on its actual demand, then it will not be able to produce accurate forecasts. Similarly, it is hard to have the right quantity of product if you don't know how much product you have at the moment. It may come as a surprise, but most firms find it challenging to maintain accurate inventory and demand data. For example, a hardware store's computer system might think it has three units of a particular faucet. However, one of those faucets broke in the backroom when it was accidentally dropped on the floor, another one was lost to employee theft, and a third is misplaced in the wrong aisle of the store. Because the computer system believes there are three units in the store, it doesn't place additional orders. At the same time, because customers don't find the product (where it should be), there are no sales. Firms that actively engage in lean operations (see Chapter 8, Lean Operations and the Toyota Production System) recognize that these are all sources of process waste and, therefore, the process should be redesigned to avoid them.

One effective solution to deal with data accuracy is to implement technology; for example, bar coding all items, with frequent use of scanners to read those codes, improves data accuracy. A more costly approach is to use **radio-frequency identification (RFID) tags**. An RFID tag is a small electronic device that transmits a unique radio signal to identify the object to which it is attached. If you have used an automatic toll booth on a highway, then you likely have an RFID tag inside your vehicle (that is how the toll booth knows that it is your car driving on the highway). Unlike a bar code, the RFID reader doesn't need to have direct "sight" of the tag, which allows the system to collect data with a minimal amount of product handling. Although technology has been very useful for the problem of data accuracy, even the best firms find that they must continually work toward improvements.

Radio-frequency identification (RFID) tag A small electronic device that transmits a unique radio signal to identify the object to which it is attached.

Analytical Skills Beyond knowing where your inventory is and what your demand is likely to be, you still need to have the skills to use those data to make good decisions regarding inventory quantities and placement. Some firms rely on purchased software to make these decisions for them. But even if a firm uses inventory management software from a vendor, it still needs to understand how to calibrate the software for its particular business (e.g., what are the correct costs to input into the system). And that approach might not be good enough when inventory management is critical for the success of the business. In those cases, firms invest to develop their own in-house talent, solutions, and software.

Product Transportation and Handling Assets In the spirit of "last but not least," a firm cannot be effective at inventory management without the assets needed to physically move inventory quickly, safely, and cost-effectively. These assets could include large automated sorting equipment, robotic forklifts that move inventory in and out of shelves within a distribution facility, or a fleet of dedicated trucks. They also include well-trained and skilled employees who are able to ensure that product is not damaged and the needed data are recorded accurately (back to the point about data quality).

10.1.3 Reasons for Holding Inventory

We can put a man on the moon, but why do we still carry inventory? That is one of those questions with an answer that is both obvious and hard to explain. Of course, it is not possible to make everything precisely where and when needed, so there needs to be some "stuff" lying around in places. But we need to do a better job articulating the set of reasons for why we hold inventory. Depending on the situation, one or more of the following reasons may be relevant to explain the presence of inventory.

Flow Time As our initial intuition suggests, it takes time to create products and to move them from where they are made to where they are needed. In Chapter 2, Introduction to Processes, we labeled the time a flow unit spends in a process as the flow time. Even with unlimited resources, flow units need time to be transformed from input to output. For example, even though Amazon.com can quickly send you a myriad of products—from Camembert cheese to a canoe—they don't deliver instantly. And because flow time in a process cannot be zero (unless we eventually invent the Star Trek transporter), according to Little's Law, $I = R \times T$, there is always inventory in a process.

Seasonality Seasonality is predictable variation in demand. Many (if not most) products exhibit some form of seasonality. For example, pencils and notebooks experience an increase in demand at the end of the summer, just before students return to school. Ties sell well in the fourth quarter before the holiday season and in early June before Father's Day. Demand for lumber in the late spring and summer is always higher than demand during the winter. As these examples suggest, seasonality can be associated with the natural seasons during the year, as well as holidays or events that occur at the same time each year. Seasonality can also occur on a smaller time scale. For example, demand in a grocery store exhibits a regular weekly pattern—sales are usually highest at the end of the week and on the weekend and lowest early in the week.

Seasonality creates inventory when it is combined with rigid capacity. In those situations, capacity is usually less than what is needed to handle peak demand and too much during the time of slow demand. To manage this, a firm can adopt a **production smoothing strategy**—the rate of output remains relatively stable even though demand varies predictably over time.

Monitor Sugar, a large sugar cooperative in the U.S. Midwest, illustrates the use of production smoothing and the seasonality reason for inventory. Due to the nature of the harvesting season, Monitor Sugar collects all raw material for its sugar production over a period of six weeks. At the end of the harvesting season, it accumulates—in the very meaning of the word—a pile of sugar beets, weighing about one million tons, that takes the form of a 67-acre mound of sugar beets.

Given that food processing is a very capital-intensive operation, it would be far too expensive to install enough capacity to process all of the beets during the harvest, only to leave that capacity idle for the rest of the year. Thus, the capacity of the processing facility is chosen such that the 1.325 million tons of beets received, and the almost 1 million tons of inventory that is built, allow for a nonstop operation of the production plant until the beginning of the next harvesting season. As illustrated by Figure 10.1, production is constant, so the total

Seasonality A significant demand change that constitutes a repetitive fluctuation over time.

Production smoothing strategy A strategy for scheduling production such that the rate of output remains relatively stable over time even though demand varies predictably over the same period.

FIGURE 10.1

Sugar beet inventory from the start of one year's harvest to the start of the next year's harvest

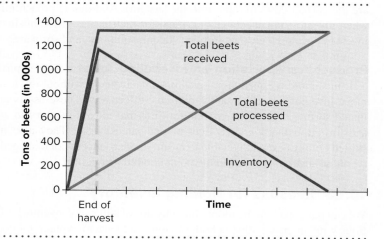

amount of processed beets increases steadily throughout the year. During the harvest, the inflow of beets is much greater than the rate of production, but after the harvest the inflow of beets returns to zero (and, thus, the total amount of beets received levels off). The firm can achieve this smooth level of production because it is able to hold inventory of raw material—which rises during the harvest and then slowly falls during the remainder of the year.

Batching   In Chapter 7, we discuss the impact of setup times on a production process—when a process has a setup time, it makes sense to do production in batches. When a machine is producing a batch, it usually produces at a rate that exceeds the flow rate of the item through the process. For example, the milling machine at Xootr produces steer supports at the rate of one per minute even though it only needs to produce one steer support every three minutes (to match demand). When the milling machine is producing, inventory of steer supports builds. Hence, inventory occurs because of setup time–induced batch production.

Besides setup times, there are other reasons to batch. In particular, there can be fixed costs associated with starting a process, thereby motivating the use of batches. To explain, consider the economics of truck transportation. Whether a truck is dispatched empty or full, the driver is paid a fixed amount, and a sizable portion of the wear and tear on the truck depends on the mileage driven, not on the load carried. In other words, each truck shipment incurs a fixed cost that is independent of the amount shipped. To mitigate the sting of that fixed cost, it is tempting to load the truck completely, thereby dividing the fixed cost across the greatest number of units.

In many cases, this may indeed be a wise decision. But a truck often carries more product than can be immediately sold. Hence, it takes some time to sell off the entire truck delivery. In other words, the fixed cost of shipping by truck creates the need to ship in a large batch (a full truck), which creates inventory in the process. We explore this reason for inventory in Chapter 12.

Buffers Inventory between process steps can serve as buffers, meaning that the process steps can operate independently from each other. For example, consider two workers in a garment factory. Suppose the first worker sews the collar onto a shirt and the second sews the buttons. A buffer between them is a pile of shirts with collars but no buttons. Because of that buffer, the first worker can stop working (e.g., to take a break, repair the sewing machine, or change the thread color) while the second worker keeps working. In other words, buffers can absorb variations in flow rates by acting as a source of supply for a downstream process step, even if the previous operation itself might not be able to create this supply at the given moment in time.

An automotive assembly line is another example of a production process that uses buffers to decouple the various stations involved with producing the vehicle. In the absence of such buffers, a disruption at any one station would lead to a disruption of all other stations, upstream and downstream. Think of a bucket brigade to fight a fire: There are no buffers between fire fighters in a bucket brigade, so nobody can take a break without stopping the entire process. As discussed in Chapter 17, firms either add inventory to a process to create buffers or suffer from a lower flow rate; that is, the concept of "buffer or suffer."

Uncertain Demand Some changes in demand are predictable, like roses before Mother's Day, but other variations in demand are just uncertain, or random, or, to say it in a fancier way, **stochastic**. Predictable variation and stochastic variation usually coexist, but one is often more prevalent than the other. For example, demand for snowblowers is predictably higher in the fall and early winter, but there remains some uncertainty as to how high this peak will be in a particular year. Nevertheless, in that case, predictable variation probably dominates. In other cases, like the number of callers from 11:00 a.m. to 12:00 noon, we can predict the average number of callers, but there remains considerable uncertainty about that average, which is the stochastic part of the demand.

When stochastic demand is present (and it usually is to some extent), a firm may choose (and usually does choose) to carry more inventory than needed to satisfy the predictable demand. The purpose (or reason) for this extra amount of inventory is to protect against unpredictable demand. This is why it is often referred to as **safety inventory** or **safety stock**—inventory needed to buffer against demand uncertainty. For example, if a retailer thinks it can sell 10 gift baskets next week, it might stock 18 gift baskets just in case demand turns out to be high. In all likelihood, some inventory will be left over at the end of the week, leaving the firm with some inventory. Thus, uncertain demand provides one reason for the inventory.

Pricing The reasons for holding inventory, as already mentioned, have to do with either the basic laws of physics (flow time), the nature of the process (e.g., setup times and buffers), or the characteristics of demand (e.g., predictable and unpredictable variation). This last reason is different, however—firms may hold inventory because they are responding to changes in

Stochastic demand Unpredictable variations in demand.

Safety inventory Inventory needed to buffer against demand uncertainty. Also called safety stock.

Safety stock Inventory needed to buffer against demand uncertainty. Also called safety inventory.

Check Your Understanding **10.1**

Question: A Chinese restaurant uses a variety of meat, vegetables, and noodles to produce a large number of dishes. The inventory of stir-fry that is being cooked inside a wok is best described as:

   a. raw material inventory.
   b. work-in-process inventory.
   c. finished goods inventory.
   d. tasty inventory.

Answer: Being cooked in a wok means the food is being processed; hence, it is work-in-process inventory, answer choice B.

Question: Halloween is the big holiday for a candy manufacturer—more than half of its sales occur in the month leading up to Halloween. As a result, the manufacturer produces a large stockpile of inventory before the holiday. Which of the following best explains the reason for this inventory?

   a. Seasonality
   b. Batching
   c. Buffers
   d. Uncertain demand
   e. Pricing

Answer: Halloween is predictable seasonality that requires inventory to be built in advance so that the production facility can spread over time the production needed for the holiday. Therefore, the answer choice is A, seasonality.

© Comstock/PunchStock/RF

the cost or value of inventory. For example, Campbell's Soup offers a discount to retailers every January on chicken noodle soup. The discount motivates retailers to purchase more than they would otherwise because they know that when they run out of inventory purchased during the promotion, they have to purchase more product at the regular, higher price.

Retailers respond to changes in the cost of purchasing inventory, but firms can also respond to changes in the expected future value of their inventory. For example, if a refinery expects the price of gasoline to increase in the future, it might increase production to build up its inventory in anticipation of the higher prices it can obtain in the market. Price fluctuations can be a very powerful reason for holding inventory, as powerful or even more powerful than the other reasons.

10.2 How to Measure Inventory: Days-of-Supply and Turns

It is intuitive to measure inventory in terms of flow units that resemble the physical thing flowing through the system that we are tracking, be it a guitar, a kilogram of milk, or a person. However, some processes handle multiple types of units, so a flow unit tied to a particular type of physical thing does not work well. For example, a manufacturer of musical instruments might make guitars and violins. We need a flow unit that describes both of these objects. A natural solution is to use a currency, such as dollars. Say each guitar costs $200 to make and each violin costs $300. The inventory of the manufacturer can then be expressed in total dollars. If the manufacturer has 100 guitars and 150 violins in inventory, then the manufacturer's total inventory is $(100 \times \$200) + (150 \times \$300) = \$65,000$. We say "the manufacturer has $65,000 in inventory," meaning that the manufacturer spent $65,000 to acquire its inventory—we do not mean that the manufacturer literally has $65,000 in dollar bills sitting in a safe or in the bank.

While measuring inventory in terms of dollars solves one problem (how to aggregate together different types of items), it leaves us with another problem: It is not really possible to know whether a certain amount of inventory is a "small" amount or a "large" amount. Though $65,000 might be a very large amount for a firm that is just starting up, it might be a trivial amount for a well-established manufacturer. A solution to this issue is to measure inventory relative to something else.

10.2.1 Days-of-Supply

Instead of measuring inventory in physical units or in dollars, inventory can actually be measured with time. A common way to do this is with days-of-supply. The **days-of-supply** of a process is the average amount of time (in days) it takes for a unit to flow through the system, which is just the definition of T in the Little's Law equation, $I = R \times T$ where I is inventory, R is the flow rate, and T is the flow time. In other words,

$$\text{Days-of-supply} = T = \text{Flow time}$$

Hence, if an instrument spends 65 days, on average, in the manufacturer's inventory, then the manufacturer has 65 days-of-supply of inventory. Alternatively, and equivalently, if the instrument manufacturer has 65 days-of-supply, then on average an instrument spends 65 days in the manufacturer's inventory.

Although most firms use "days" as their time period, any time period can be used: Months-of-supply is the number of months a flow unit spends, on average, in the process and hours-of-supply is the number of hours in process. Converting between days-of-supply and other time intervals is done as you would expect. For example, if the days-of-supply is 63, then the weeks-of-supply is $63/7 = 9$ (assuming 7 days per week).

In addition to being the average amount of time a flow unit spends in the process, days-of-supply is also the amount of time it takes for the average inventory to flow through the system at the average flow rate. That explanation is a bit cumbersome to parse, so our example might

Days-of-supply The average amount of time (in days) it takes for a unit to flow through the system.

clarify. In the case of the instrument manufacturer, 65 days-of-supply means that at the average flow rate, the $65,000 in inventory would be depleted in 65 days, meaning that the flow rate must be $1,000 per day. We know this because of Little's Law:

$$I = R \times T$$

$$\$65,000 = R \times 65 \text{ days}$$

$$R = \$1,000 \text{ per day}$$

Thus, if the instrument manufacturer has, on average, $65,000 in inventory and this is equivalent to 65 days-of-supply, then it must be that it sells $1,000 of inventory each day.

10.2.2 Inventory Turns

If you don't like to measure inventory in terms of time, there is one more option. The **inventory turns** of a process are the number of times the average inventory flows through a process in a designated interval of time. Again, that is hard to parse, so an example helps to better understand. Using our Little's Law variables,

$$\text{Turns} = \frac{R}{I}$$

For our instrument manufacturer, the annual flow rate is $R = \$1000 \times 365 = \$365,000$ per year and

$$\text{Turns} = \frac{\$365,000 \text{ per year}}{\$65,000} = 5.62 \text{ per year}$$

In words, if we were to watch the instrument manufacturer's inventory, then we would see $65,000 flow through the process once, then twice, then several more times for a total of 5.62 times during the year. The fact that turns is not an even integer is not a problem. It just means that at the end of the year, the last $65,000 hasn't quite completely flowed through the process. (Only $0.62 \times \$65,000 = \$40,300$ has exited the process this year and the remaining $24,700 exits the following year.)

We evaluated annual turns because one year is the most common time interval chosen. It is so common that "annual" is often dropped from the description, as in "Our inventory turns are 5.6" or "We turn over our inventory 11.2 times." Although annual turns are generally assumed, we can choose other time intervals. For example:

$$\text{Daily turns} = \frac{\$1000 \text{ per day}}{\$65,000} = 0.0154 \text{ per day}$$

This example may suggest to you why turns are usually measured in a one-year interval—shorter time intervals usually involve dealing with small numbers that are inconvenient to work with.

Is there a reason to prefer days-of-supply or turns? No, because they are really two sides of the same coin. Notice (using Little's Law again) that

$$\text{Daily turns} = \frac{R}{I} = \frac{1}{T} = \frac{1}{\text{Days-of-supply}}$$

or

$$\text{Daily turns} = \frac{1}{\text{Days-of-supply}}$$

Inventory turns The number of times the average inventory flows through a process in a designated interval of time.

In other words, assuming we use the same time interval, turns is just the inverse of days-of-supply. To emphasize this further, if days-of-supply, 65, is inverted to 1/65, then we get daily turns, $1/65 = 0.0154$. Some people prefer to think in terms of days-of-supply, while others prefer turns. But either way, once you know one of them, you can convert to the other. However, remember that while higher days-of-supply mean *more* inventory (which is intuitive), higher turn means *less* inventory (which is less intuitive). For example, if the instrument manufacturer's annual turns were to increase from 5.6 to 6.5, then average inventory would *decrease* from $65,000 to $56,000 ($365,000/6.5).

10.2.3 Benchmarks for Turns

We now know three ways to measure average inventory: in dollars (e.g., $65,000), in days-of-supply (e.g., 65 days), and in turns (e.g., 5.62 per year). But we still don't have a sense of whether this is a lot or a little. Table 10.1 should help us calibrate. The table provides average inventory turns and days-of-supply for several different types (or segments) of retailers. The slowest segment is Jewelry. A typical jewelry store has inventory that turns over only 1.68 times per year. That means that an average item spends $1/1.68 = 0.595$ years in the store, or 0.595 years $\times$ 365 days per year $= 217$ days. In contrast, the fastest turning segment is food. In this case, the average item in a food store spends only 34 days in the store.

Although 34 days is the shortest period in Table 10.1, it is still long for some food items—nobody wants to buy milk that has been in the store for 34 days. Remember, 34 days is an average. Some items in the food store, like canned soup, spend much longer than 34 days, whereas other items, like milk, soda, and snacks, spend far less time. For example, it is possible that the average salty snack item turns more than 100 times per year! With 100 turns, the average item spends only $365/100 = 3.65$ days in the store. Roughly speaking, if an item moves that quickly, when you walk into a store, the inventory you see lasts only half a week (given that half a week is 3.5 days). As a rule of thumb, items that are perishable turn faster (or have lower days-of-supply) than durable goods. In addition, most items turn less often than 100 times per year, and turns higher than 100 can be considered to be extremely fast moving.

From Table 10.2 we can see that there is considerable variation in the turns across different retail segments. There is also considerable variation in turns across different companies in the same segment, as shown in Table 10.2. Again, we see in Table 10.2 that groceries tend to turn the fastest, ranging from 12 to 20, whereas apparel and hardware turn much more slowly, in the range of 3 to 8. Finally, just as there is variation in turns across segments and companies, a single company's turns can vary over time. Connections: U.S. Inventory shows how much inventory is in the United States and how it has varied in recent years.

TABLE 10.1   Inventory Turns for Selected Retail Segments

Retail Segment	Examples	Annual Inventory Turns	Days-of-Supply
Jewelry	Tiffany	1.68	217
Hobby, toy/game stores	Toys R Us	2.99	122
Department store	Sears, JCPenney	3.87	94
Radio, TV, consumer electronics	Best Buy	4.10	89
Variety stores	Kohl's, Target	4.45	82
Apparel and accessory	Ann Taylor, Gap	4.57	80
Drug and proprietary stores	Rite Aid, CVS	5.26	69
Home furniture/equipment	Bed Bath & Beyond	5.44	67
Catalog, mail-order	Spiegel, Lands' End	8.60	42
Food stores	Albertson's, Safeway, Walmart	10.78	34

TABLE 10.2 Inventory Turns for Selected Retailers

Company	Categories	Annual Inventory Turns	Days-of-Supply
Macy's	Apparel, cosmetics, home furnishings	3.1	117
Kohl's	Apparel, footwear, soft home products	3.3	111
Lowe's	Hardware, home improvement	3.9	95
Sears	Hardware, apparel, home furnishings, appliances	3.9	94
Home Depot	Hardware, home improvement	4.6	80
Ace Hardware	Hardware	6.0	60
Target	Apparel, grocery, home furnishings, electronics	6.4	57
Walmart	Apparel, grocery, home furnishings, electronics	8.2	44
Costco	Apparel, grocery, home furnishings, electronics	12.2	30
Kroger	Grocery	12.3	30
Safeway	Grocery	12.7	29
SuperValu	Grocery	17.3	21
Whole Foods	Grocery	20.2	18

CONNECTIONS: U.S. Inventory

A company is a rather large "process." For example, Walmart sells more than $1 billion of goods every day. But there is no reason why we have to stop at the company level. Consider the United States as an entire process where goods come "in" and "out." How much inventory is in the United States and how much time does it spend in process? The Census Bureau provides data to answer these questions. See Figure 10.2.

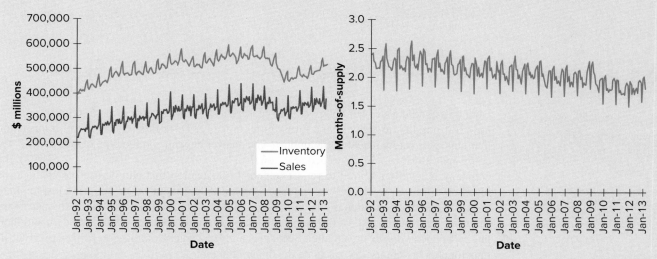

Figure 10.2 Inventory and sales (left) and months-of-supply (right) in the United States. Sales are measured in cost $s; that is, it is the cost of the items sold rather than the revenue from the items sold.

The left graph shows inventory and monthly sales since 1992 for retailers in the United States. Both series are adjusted for inflation (but not adjusted for seasonality). A couple of observations are immediately apparent from the sales curve: (1) sales have generally been growing in the United States; (2) sales follow a seasonal pattern with a peak at the end of the year due

Continued

to holiday shopping; and (3) the financial crisis in 2008 rapidly "slammed the brakes" on sales, causing a noticeable and dramatic reduction in economic activity from which the country had not fully recovered four years later. At the start of 2013, U.S. retailers held about $518 billion in inventory, which works out to about $1640 for every man, woman, and child in the country. This is enough inventory to cover about 1.8 months of demand, which is equivalent to $12/1.8 = 6.7$ turns per year. Interestingly, over the last 30 years, retailers have made steady progress in reducing the amount of inventory they carry relative to their sales. The right graph in Figure 10.2 shows the trend in months-of-supply. In the early 1990s, goods sat on retail shelves for about 2.25 months, whereas now goods last only 1.75 months in the store. In the "good old days," the stuff that you bought was indeed older.

Check Your Understanding 10.2

Question: Zaggos sells shoes and currently has 1,500,000 shoes in its inventory. It sells 10,000 shoes per day. What is Zaggos' days-of-supply of shoes?

Answer:

$$\text{Days-of-supply} = T = \frac{I}{R} = \frac{1{,}500{,}000 \text{ shoes}}{10{,}000 \text{ shoes/day}} = 150 \text{ days}$$

Question: Fresh Organic sells organic groceries online. Its annual sales are now $10,000,000 and it has, on average, $50,000 in inventory. What are its annual inventory turns?

Answer:

$$\text{Annual turns} = \frac{1}{T} = \frac{R}{I} = \frac{\$10{,}000{,}000}{\$50{,}000} = 200 \text{ turns}$$

10.3 Evaluate Inventory Turns and Days-of-Supply from Financial Reports

LO10-3 Evaluate turns and days-of-supply from financial reports.

Both turns and days-of-supply give us a measure of how long items remain in inventory. But how is it possible to evaluate the turns for a company? Does this require secret information that managers rarely reveal to the public? The answer depends on the type of company. If the company's stock is publicly traded (e.g., on the New York Stock Exchange or NASDAQ), the company is legally required to report financial information that can be used to evaluate its inventory turns. However, if the company's stock is held privately (i.e., you can't just log in to **E-Trade** and click to purchase the company's stock), then it tends to withhold the necessary financial information. All of the companies listed in Table 10.2 are publicly traded, and their public financial disclosures (called Securities and Exchange Commission filings, or SEC filings for short) were used to evaluate the data in the table.

Let's look at the fastest-turning company in Table 10.2, **Whole Foods,** an upscale grocer that emphasizes organic and fresh food. To analyze the Whole Foods process, we need a flow unit. Because they sell many different items, it is natural to use a dollar as the flow unit. In the Whole Foods 2012 balance sheet, under the "Assets" category, in the line labeled "Merchandise inventories," it reports that it had $374M in inventory, where "M" stands for "million." We can't be sure about what its average inventory was throughout the year, but we can take this snapshot of its inventory as an estimate for its average inventory. So for Whole Foods in 2012, $I = \$374M$. To evaluate turns, we are still missing R or T.

Check Your Understanding **10.3**

Question: Widner Industries reports annual sales of $160 million, cost of goods sold of $120 million, inventory of $20 million, and net income of $5 million.

   a. What are its annual inventory turns?

Answer: The flow rate is $R = \$120$ million per year and Inventory = $20 million. Turns = $R/I =$ $120M/$20M = 6 turns per year.

   b. What is its "months-of-supply" of inventory?

Answer: The flow rate is $R = \$120$ million per year = $10 million per month. Months-of-supply = $I/R = \$20M/\$10M = 2$ months-of-supply.

. . . .

In their 2012 income statement, Whole Foods reported that it collected $11,698M in revenue from its customers. (This line is usually called "revenue" or "sales.") It also reported that its "cost of goods sold" was $7543M. This means that it bought from its suppliers about $7.5 billion in goods and sold those goods to customers for about $11.7 billion. Hence, an estimate for the flow rate of goods through Whole Foods is $7.5 billion per year in "cost dollars" and $11.7 billion per year in "sales dollars."

So now we have two estimates for the flow rate through Whole Foods. Which one should we use? Remember one of the rules in choosing a flow unit—all activities must be described in the same flow unit. Inventory is reported in "cost dollars"—the total inventory is the total amount Whole Foods spent to buy the goods, not the total amount at which Whole Foods sells the inventory to customers. So if inventory is reported in "cost dollars," we should choose "cost dollars" for the flow rate. Hence, the daily flow rate is $R = \$7543M/365 = \$20.7M$. This means that each day, on average, Whole Foods sells to customers goods that it purchased for $20.7M.

Applying Little's Law to Whole Foods,

$$I = R \times T$$

$$\$374M = \$20.7M \text{ per day} \times T$$

$$T = \frac{\$374M}{\$20.7M \text{ per day}} = 18.1 \text{ days}$$

So using the information Whole Foods reports on its income statement and balance sheet, we can obtain an estimate for the time an average cost $ spends in the Whole Foods process.

To complete our analysis, annual turns for Whole Foods is

$$\text{Turns} = \frac{R}{I}$$

$$= \frac{\$7543M \text{ per year}}{\$374M}$$

$$= 20.17 \text{ per year}$$

Just to confirm again that turns and days-of-supply are essentially two views for the same thing, notice that (365 days per year)/(20.17 per year) = 18.1 days. This gives us a sense of how efficient Whole Foods is with its inventory management. At any given moment, the inventory in Whole Foods would last 18.1 days if it did not replenish any of its inventory and demand continued at the same pace.

10.4 Inventory Stockout and Holding Costs

The previous sections discussed the reasons for inventory (e.g., seasonality) and explain how to measure inventory (e.g., days-of-supply and turns). Now we need to become more precise regarding the various costs associated with either not having inventory or holding inventory.

10.4.1 Inventory Stockout Cost

If a customer wants a product and it is not available, then this situation is called a **stockout**. Simply put, a stockout is costly to a firm because it irritates customers. But not all stockouts lead to equally irritated consumers, which means that the cost of not having inventory can vary considerably. To explain, Table 10.3 divides the possible reactions of a customer to a stockout into four buckets that differ in the severity of the consequences of the stockout.

You might assume that if a retailer doesn't have a product, then the worst thing that could happen is that the customer leaves the store without buying the item, thereby denying the retailer the opportunity to make some profit on that sale. That is the second response listed in Table 10.3 and it is indeed costly to the retailer. But it is not as bad as it could be. As described in the first response listed in Table 10.3, not only might the retailer lose the opportunity to make this sale, the customer may be sufficiently irate that she switches her future business to a competitor. Now that would be super costly!

But it isn't all doom and gloom in Table 10.3. In the third response, the retailer loses the sale of the item but gains the sale of a similar item that the customer is willing to substitute. If the other item is equally profitable, then this might not be costly at all to the firm. In fact, if the customer switches to a more profitable item, then the firm might even gain in the short term! There even is a tactic to exploit this—it is called **bait and switch.** Auto dealers are known for trying to bait and switch their customers. They advertise a car that is offered with a great price, but somehow they never have that car in stock when you arrive to buy it. Instead, they have a similar car that has more features and, big surprise, a higher price. While this tactic works in the short term, it is a dangerous one to implement in the long term—customers may eventually catch wind of the slimy business practice and decide to buy their vehicles elsewhere. (There are also legal restrictions on the tactic.)

The last response in Table 10.3 causes the least pain for the firm. Sometimes customers are willing to wait for the product to arrive. This is likely to be the case when the product is specialized or customized to the customer's needs. For example, new business jets are rarely (if ever) purchased "as is" from inventory. There is a considerable amount of customization

Stockout A stockout occurs when a customer demands an item that is not available in inventory.

TABLE 10.3 Different Consequences of a Stockout in Which a Customer Wants a Product but Inventory Is Not Available

Customer Response to a Stockout	How Costly Is the Stockout?	Example
Lose the sale and lose the customer	Very high: loss of future profit from the customer	A grocery store is out of bananas yet again, so the customer decides to shop at another grocery store in the future.
Lose the sale	High: loss of profit from the sale of the item	A grocery store is out of bananas, so the customer doesn't buy bananas or any other fruit on this shopping trip but returns to the store in the future.
Lose the sale of one item, but the customer purchases another item	Moderate: loss of profit from one item is replaced, maybe in part or in full, by the profit of another item	A grocery store is out of bananas, so the customer decides to buy some apples instead.
Customer waits for the item to become available	Low: total profit doesn't change much, as long as the delay isn't too long	A grocery store is out of bananas, so the customer returns the next day when she is told they will have more.

with this product, so the buyers are patient enough to wait to get exactly what they want (or so we are told). A similar situation occurs with custom homes—some people purchase homes "as is" from inventory, but others wait to have their dream home built. On a less-expensive scale, customers are sometimes willing to wait for custom sofas or for specialized electronics (e.g., a personal computer designed for gaming).

A firm needs to know where it is on the "stockout cost spectrum" described in Table 10.3. If stockouts are very costly (the firm risks losing the customer), then the firm needs to make sure it has inventory available most of the time, if not nearly all of the time. On the other hand, if customers are willing to wait for the firm's product, then carrying inventory is clearly less important.

10.4.2 Inventory Holding Cost

Just as there are different reasons why it is costly to not have inventory, there are different reasons why it is costly to hold inventory, and all of them are linked to the amount of time a flow unit spends in inventory.

- **Opportunity cost of capital**. The opportunity cost of capital is the income not earned on the amount invested in inventory. To explain, money used to buy inventory is money that is not invested in other activities. For example, suppose we own an appliance retailer and we purchase a refrigerator for $350 on January 1. We sell the refrigerator at the end of the year and we receive the cash from that sale on December 31. Thus, for the entire year we didn't have access to the $350 we used to purchase the refrigerator. If we didn't purchase the refrigerator, we could have invested that $350 in something else. A bank might be willing to pay us 2 percent interest. So if we had put the money in the bank instead of the refrigerator, we could have ended the year with $350 × 1.02 = $357. The gain, $7, might not seem like much, but it is something— and it represents one potential opportunity cost of tying up our money in the refrigerator. Alternatively, we might have been able to invest in another business or other products that may have yielded a higher return (i.e., more than a gain of $7). The point is that when we spend $350 on the refrigerator, the cash is locked into the refrigerator until it is sold and, therefore, we incur an opportunity cost for the time when those dollars aren't being used for other activities.

- **Inventory storage cost**. This is the cost incurred to properly store, maintain, and insure inventory. If we want to sell the refrigerator as "brand new," then we must store it and maintain it in a reasonably nice place. For example, good retail space can cost $20 per square foot per year to rent and a refrigerator might use more than 10 square feet. In that case, if the refrigerator occupied those 10 square feet for the entire year, we would incur a total storage cost of $200 (10 square feet × $20 per square foot).

- **Obsolescence cost**. This is the cost associated with losing value over time because of either technological change or shifts in fashion. Even if the refrigerator is in brand new condition at the end of the year, it might not be as desirable to consumers simply because it is no longer the "latest and greatest." This can happen with relatively mundane products like a refrigerator—one year refrigerators just keep your food cold, the next they deliver ice and cold water on demand, and then they become remotely controllable from your mobile phone. Obsolescence due to "new features" or "new capabilities" is a fact of life in nearly all technology products. But obsolescence can also occur if the product doesn't lose any functionality—a ski parka might keep you as warm next winter as it does this winter, but next winter it might not be "in style." Many companies face brutal obsolescence due to changes in fashion. For example, if the parka could be sold for $250 at the start of the year, but only fetches $100 at the end of the year because it is no longer in style, then it incurred an obsolescence cost of $150.

- **Spoilage and shrinkage costs**. These are costs associated with product deterioration over time or theft. If the refrigerator is stored in a dry, clean environment, it will probably work no worse one year after being made. But the same cannot be said for all

Opportunity cost of capital The income not earned on the amount invested in inventory.

Inventory storage cost The cost incurred to properly store, maintain, and insure inventory.

Obsolescence cost The cost associated with losing value over time because of either technological change or shifts in fashion.

Spoilage and shrinkage costs Costs associated with theft or product deterioration over time.

products: fresh food spoils even if well maintained, and be careful of the pills in your medicine cabinet that expired five years ago. While spoilage is a feature of the product, shrinkage is a result of humans—"shrinkage" is a euphemism for "theft." Whether the product isn't as good as it was (spoilage) or is missing from your store (shrinkage), over time you run the risk of not being able to sell the product to a customer, thereby incurring a cost.

The combination of these various costs defines the cost to hold inventory. While each component is usually relevant at least to some degree with all products, products vary as to which of these components is of the greatest concern. For example, the opportunity cost of capital is the dominant component for a product that has little risk of technological obsolescence, doesn't deteriorate, is easy to store, and is hard to steal, whereas a new product that uses the latest technology might face primarily obsolescence risk because even the latest technology can quickly become old technology.

10.4.3 Inventory Holding Cost Percentage

LO10-4 Evaluate the holding cost of an item held in inventory using an annual holding cost percentage and days-of-supply or turns.

It can be a burden to add up the various factors that contribute to inventory holding costs. As a result, most companies use a shortcut. They usually assume a **holding cost percentage**, which is the ratio of the cost to hold an item in inventory during a designated time period relative to the cost to purchase the item. For example, an appliance retailer may assign an annual holding cost to a refrigerator equal to 20 percent of the cost to buy the refrigerator. This means that a refrigerator that cost \$350 incurs for the retailer a holding cost of $0.20 \times \$350 = \$70$ per year—if the retailer holds the refrigerator for one year, then the retailer incurs a cost of \$70.

Although it is common to define an annual holding cost percentage, it can be defined for any time period. For example, the retailer may assign a 0.5 percent weekly holding cost for a dishwasher that costs the retailer \$200. In that case, the dishwasher would cost $0.005 \times \$200 = \$1$ per week to hold in inventory and \$52 per year to hold in inventory (assuming 52 weeks per year).

While the holding cost percentage may be defined for a particular time period, there is absolutely no requirement that the item actually be held for exactly that amount of time. If the \$350 refrigerator is indeed held in inventory for one year, then it would cost the retailer \$70. But if the refrigerator is held in inventory for three months (one-fourth of a year), then it would cost $1/4 \times \$70 = \$17.5$. Similarly, if it should be held for two years, then it costs $2 \times \$70 = \$140$ to hold. Clearly, no matter what the holding cost percentage is, the longer it is held in inventory, the higher the cost.

What is a reasonable holding cost percentage? It depends on the nature of the product and the company. A well-established company that isn't growing rapidly has a lower opportunity cost of capital than a fast-growing company—the growing company has more investment opportunities for its capital that generate a higher profit. The holding cost on a durable product that doesn't suffer from the whims of fashion or technological obsolescence is lower, maybe even much lower, than a perishable product. Overall, annual holding cost percentages are generally in the 20–30 percent range, but they can be higher, say 50–100 percent or more, for technology products, high-fashion products, or highly perishable products.

10.4.4 Inventory Holding Cost per Unit

The (annual) holding cost percentage tells us how much it costs to hold an item in inventory for one year. But most items aren't held for exactly one year in inventory. The actual amount of time is given to us by turns or days-of-supply. Hence, we can combine these pieces of information to evaluate the holding cost incurred by each unit in our inventory.

Say Whole Foods' annual holding cost percentage is 30 percent—it is a growing company but doesn't face technological obsolescence or issues with changing fashion. For Whole Foods, how much inventory cost does it incur for a box of organic cereal that it buys from a supplier for \$5?

From Table 10.2 we see that the box of cereal spends, on average, 18 days in Whole Foods, which is 18 days/365 days per year = 0.049 year. To hold the \$5 box for one year would cost

Holding cost percentage The ratio of the cost to hold an item in inventory during a designated time period relative to the cost to purchase the item.

Check Your Understanding **10.4**

Question: Kohl's sells jeans for $40 a pair that it purchases for $20 a pair. Its annual holding cost percentage is 25 percent and these jeans turn 10 times per year. What holding cost does it incur for each pair of jeans?

Answer: The cost to hold the jeans for one year in inventory would be $20 × 25% = $5. The jeans actually spend one-tenth of a year in inventory (because they have 10 turns), so each pair of jeans incurs $5/10 = $0.50 in holding cost.

Whole Foods 0.3 × $5 = $1.50, but to hold it for 0.049 year costs 0.049 × $5 = $0.245. As Whole Foods might sell that box for $8, it makes a profit on the sale (total cost is $5 + $0.245 = $5.245, but sales revenue is $8).

In addition to evaluating the inventory cost for a single item, we can evaluate Whole Foods' entire annual inventory cost. If Whole Foods holds on average $374 million in inventory throughout the year, then each year it incurs 0.30 × $374 million = $112 million in inventory costs. Though $112 million is a lot of money to most people, is it a lot to Whole Foods? Another way to express this is as a percentage of the total cost of buying goods. Whole Foods' cost of goods sold (the amount it paid to buy all of the stuff it sold during the year) is $7543 million. So the inventory cost is $112 million/$7543 million = 1.5 percent. In fact, there is an easier way to get to that number:

$$\text{Inventory holding costs as a \% of COGS} = \frac{\text{Annual holding cost percentage}}{\text{Annual turns}}$$

$$= \frac{30\%}{20.17}$$

$$= 1.5\%$$

For most retailers, their final profit is generally 2–5 percent of their cost of goods sold. Hence, good inventory control is critical for retailers to turn a profit.

Conclusion

Inventory is found at all stages of processes: raw material inventory before the process, work-in-process inventory inside the process, and finished goods inventory at the end of the process. Managing inventory is critical for the success of the organization and it involves a number of challenges (e.g., forecasting), requires a number of skills (e.g., data tracking and analysis), and generally mandates significant investment (e.g., buildings, conveyors, forklifts).

There are a number of reasons why, no matter how skilled an organization is, inventory always exists in a process. First, there is simple physics. Products need to be moved from one point (e.g., a factory) to another (e.g., a store), and that movement requires some flow time. According to Little's Law, when there is flow time, there must be inventory. But there are other reasons for inventory as well. For example, variability is a big reason for inventory. Variability comes in two forms: predictable variability (also known as seasonality) and unpredictable (or stochastic) variability. With predictable variability, a firm might accumulate inventory in advance of the high-demand season; otherwise, it would not be able to satisfy demand with its regular capacity. Unpredictable variability requires the firm to build in buffer or safety stocks.

Inventory can be measured in several ways, such as merely the number of flow units (e.g., 100 cans of paint) or the amount invested to purchase the inventory (e.g., $20,000 of paint). Usually, it is more useful to measure inventory relative to time, such as days-of-supply or turns.

Not having inventory is costly because it annoys customers, which can have varying degrees of consequences, from losing the customer to a competitor forever to merely making the customer wait for additional inventory to become available. There are also costs to hold inventory. In particular, there is the opportunity cost of the capital tied up in inventory and the costs associated with storage, among others.

Most companies assess their inventory holding costs as a percentage of the cost to purchase an item. For example, if an item costs $50 and the firm assigns a holding cost percentage of 30 percent, then it costs the firm $0.3 \times \$50 = \$15$ to hold that item in inventory for an entire year. The actual inventory holding costs incurred by the item depend on how long it actually spends in inventory.

Summary of Learning Objectives

LO10-1 Explain the different types of inventory, the challenges of inventory management, and the reasons for the existence of inventory

Inventory can be divided into three types. Raw material inventory is the inventory at the beginning of a process that has not yet been transformed or "worked on" by the process. Work-in-process inventory is inventory that is inside the process—the process has started to transform or work on it. Finally, once a process is complete, the result is finished goods inventory. Finished goods inventory does not require additional processing.

The challenges of inventory management include (i) forecasting (e.g., how well can future demand be predicted), (ii) data tracking (e.g., does the organization know how many units of product it actually has), (iii) analytical skills (e.g., employee talent to operate inventory management systems), and (iv) product handling and transportation assets (e.g., distribution centers, robotic pickers, etc.).

Inventory exists for a number of reasons, and in any situation there may be multiple reasons present: (i) flow time (it takes time to move something from one place to another), (ii) seasonality (predictable periods of high or low demand), (iii) batching (fixed ordering costs), (iv) buffers (to deal with variability within a process), (v) uncertain demand (unpredictable variations in demand), and (vi) pricing (quantity discounts).

LO10-2 Evaluate inventory turns and days-of-supply for different time periods (annual, monthly, weekly, and daily)

Inventory turns and days-of-supply are ways to measure the amount of inventory in a process relative to some period of time. Inventory turns equals Flow rate/Inventory. For example, if a distribution center ships $200M per year and holds, on average, $10M in inventory, then its annual inventory turns are 20 ($200M/$10M = 20). Days-of-supply is the number of days a flow unit spends, on average, in inventory. Days-of-supply equals Inventory/Flow rate. For example, if a convenience store has 600 bottles in the store, on average, and sells 150 bottles of soda per day, then it holds four days-of-supply of soda (600/150 = 4).

LO10-3 Evaluate turns and days-of-supply from financial reports

Publicly reported financial information can be used to evaluate a company's annual inventory turns and days-of-supply. For example, suppose a company reports revenue of $56M, cost of goods sold of $32M, and inventory of $8M. Use cost of goods sold for the company's flow rate because cost of goods is reported in "cost dollars," just as inventory is reported in "cost dollars." Hence, the company turns its inventory four times per year ($32M/$8M = 4) and has 89 days-of-supply (365/4 = 89).

LO10-4 Evaluate the holding cost of an item held in inventory using an annual holding cost percentage and days-of-supply or turns

The annual holding cost percentage is the cost to hold $1 in inventory for one year. For example, a 20 percent annual holding cost percentage means that to hold $1 in inventory for one year costs $0.20. The actual cost to hold an item depends on how long the item spends in inventory. For example, if an item has four annual turns, then it spends one-fourth of a year in inventory. If the annual holding percentage is 20 percent, then the cost to hold that item in inventory is 5 percent of the cost of the item ($1/4 \times 20\% = 5\%$).

Key Terms

10.1 Inventory Management

Inventory The number of flow units within the process.

Inventory management The practice of regulating the quantity, location, and type of inventory in a process.

Raw material inventory Inventory that is used as the inputs to a process and has not undergone any transformation in the process.

Work-in-process inventory (WIP) The material and components used within the process to complete a product.

Finished goods inventory Flow units that have completed processing.

Radio-frequency identification (RFID) tag A small electronic device that transmits a unique radio signal to identify the object to which it is attached.

Seasonality A significant demand change that constitutes a repetitive fluctuation over time.

Production smoothing strategy A strategy for scheduling production such that the rate of output remains relatively stable over time even though demand varies predictably over the same period.

Stochastic demand Unpredictable variations in demand.

Safety inventory Inventory needed to buffer against demand uncertainty. Also called safety stock.

Safety stock Inventory needed to buffer against demand uncertainty. Also called safety inventory.

10.2 How to Measure Inventory: Days-of-Supply and Turns

Days-of-supply The average amount of time (in days) it takes for a unit to flow through the system.

Inventory turns The number of times the average inventory flows through a process in a designated interval of time.

10.4 Inventory Stockout and Holding Costs

Stockout A stockout occurs when a customer demands an item that is not available in inventory.

Opportunity cost of capital The income not earned on the amount invested in inventory.

Inventory storage cost The cost incurred to properly store, maintain, and insure inventory.

Obsolescence cost The cost associated with losing value over time because of either technological change or shifts in fashion.

Spoilage and shrinkage costs Costs associated with theft or product deterioration over time.

Holding cost percentage The ratio of the cost to hold an item in inventory during a designated time period relative to the cost to purchase the item.

Case Linking Turns to Gross Margin

Gross margin The difference between revenue and cost of goods.

Key Formulas

LO10-2 Evaluate inventory turns and days-of-supply for different time periods (annual, monthly, weekly and daily)

$$\text{Days-of-supply} = T = \text{Flow time}$$

$$\text{Turns} = R/I = \text{Flow rate/Inventory}$$

$$\text{Annual turns} = \text{Annual cost of goods sold/Inventory}$$

$$\text{Days-of-supply} = 365 \times \text{Inventory/Annual cost of goods sold}$$

LO10-4 Evaluate the holding cost of an item held in inventory using an annual holding cost percentage and days-of-supply or turns

$$\text{Inventory holding costs as a \% of COGS} = \text{Annual holding cost percentage/Annual turns}$$

Conceptual Questions

LO10-1

1. It is costly to hold inventory, but inventory can also be useful in a process because:
   a. adding inventory to a process will shorten the average time a unit spends in a process.
   b. adding inventory to a process can help reduce situations in which sales are lost due to uncertain demand.
   c. adding inventory to a process is likely to increase quality.
   d. adding inventory to a process will increase the profit margin of the item.

2. A delivery truck from a food wholesaler has just delivered fresh meat and produce to a local restaurant. This meat and produce would be categorized as which type of inventory by the restaurant?
   a. Raw materials inventory
   b. Work-in-process inventory
   c. Finished goods inventory
   d. Seasonal inventory

3. Tablets and laptops would be categorized as which type of inventory by an electronics retailer?
   a. Raw materials inventory
   b. Work-in-process inventory
   c. Finished goods inventory
   d. Seasonal inventory

4. Which reason for holding inventory enables a firm to reduce the impact of large fixed costs that the firm incurs whenever it places an order to a supplier?
   a. Seasonality
   b. Uncertain demand
   c. Buffers
   d. Batching

5. Which reason for holding inventory guards against a reduction in the flow rate when one assembly station is disrupted in a production line?
   a. Seasonality
   b. Uncertain demand
   c. Buffers
   d. Batching

LO10-2

6. If two firms have the same annual inventory turns, they also have the same days-of-supply. True or false?
   a. True
   b. False

LO10-3

7. Firms in the same industry will have the same inventory turns. True or false?
   a. True
   b. False

8. Which of the following figures from a firm's financial statements should be used as its flow rate when computing its inventory turns?
   a. Sales revenue
   b. Cost of goods sold
   c. Inventory
   d. Net income

LO10-4

9. All else being equal, a larger item is likely to have a higher annual holding cost percentage than a smaller item. True or false?
   a. True
   b. False

10. Which of the following possible responses by a customer who is faced with a stockout is the most costly to the firm?
    a. Lose the sale and lose the customer
    b. Lose the sale
    c. Lose the sale of one item, but the customer purchases another item
    d. Customer waits for the item to become available

11. Computers lose value as they are stored in inventory. This is an example of which component of a firm's inventory holding cost?
    a. Opportunity cost of capital
    b. Storage cost
    c. Spoilage cost
    d. Obsolescence cost

Solved Example Problems

LO10-2

1. A retailer has $500,000 in inventory and sells $15,000 per day (in cost $). What is its days-of-supply?

   Answer: Days-of-supply $= T = I/R = \$500,000/\$15,000 = 33.3$ days

2. A town reports that it has 20 weeks-of-supply of road salt. What is its months-of-supply? (Assume 4.33 weeks per month.)

   Answer: 20 weeks-of-supply/4.33 weeks per month $= 4.62$ months-of-supply

3. An automobile manufacturer sells its cars through a network of dedicated dealers. These dealers report that they have 65 days-of-supply of inventory. On average, how many days does a car remain on the dealer's lot before being sold?

   Answer: Days-of-supply is also the average time a unit spends in inventory. So the answer is simply 65 days.

4. A hospital reports that it has 10 days-of-supply of blood. What are its annual turns?

   Answer: First, convert the 10 days-of-supply to years-of-supply: Flow time is $T = 10$ days $= 10$ days/365 days per year $= 0.0274$ year. Turns $= 1/T = 1/0.0274$ year $= 36.5$ per year.

5. A wholesaler reports that a distribution center turns its inventory 5.6 times per year. What is its months-of-supply?

   Answer: Annual turns $= 1/T$, where T is the flow time in years. So $T = 1/\text{Annual turns} = 1/5.6$ per year $= 0.179$ year. There are 12 months per year, so the months-of-supply is 12 months per year $\times 0.179$ year $= 2.15$ months.

LO10-3

6. Table 10.4 provides financial information for a supermarket. Given the information in the table, what are the supermarket's inventory turns?

TABLE 10.4   Financial Information from a Supermarket (in million $s)

Sales	95,751
Cost of goods sold	76,858
Inventory	6,244

Answer: Inventory is $I = \$6244$. The flow rate is $R = \$76,858$ per year. (Use cost of goods sold because inventory is measured in cost $.) Turns $= R/I = \$76,858/\$6244 = 12.3$ per year.

7. Table 10.5 provides financial information for a hardware retailer. What are the retailer's days-of-supply?

TABLE 10.5   Financial Information from a Hardware Retailer (in million $s)

Sales	50,521
Cost of goods sold	33,194
Inventory	8,600

Answer: Inventory is $I = \$8600$. The flow rate is $R = \$33,194$ per year. (Use cost of goods sold because inventory is measured in cost $.) Years-of-supply $= T = I/R = \$8600/\$33,194 = 0.259$ year. Days-of-supply $= 365$ days per year $\times$ Years-of-supply $= 365 \times 0.259 = 94.5$ days.

LO10-4

8. The holding cost of inventory at a retailer is 35 percent per year. The retailer's annual turns are 3. How much does it cost the retailer to hold a dress that it purchased for $50?

Answer: To hold the dress for one year would cost the retailer $35\% \times \$50 = \$17.50$, but it won't hold the dress for an entire year. Years-of-supply $= T = 1/$Annual turns $= 1/3$ turns per year. So it holds the dress, on average, for one-third of a year. Hence, the cost to hold the dress is $\$17.5 \times (1/3) = \$5.83$.

9. A home-improvement retailer's annual holding cost percentage is 30 percent. Table 10.6 provides financial information for the retailer. What is the retailer's annual cost to hold inventory?

TABLE 10.6   Financial Information from a Home Improvement Retailer (in million $s)

Sales	74,754
Cost of goods sold	48,912
Inventory	10,710

Answer: Average inventory is $10,710M. The cost to hold $1 for one year is $0.30. So its annual holding costs are $10,710M \times 0.3 = \$3,213M$, or $3.2 billion.

Problems and Applications

1. Suppose a retailer turns its inventory of soda 50 times per year. On average, it has 400 bottles of soda on its shelves. What is the retailer's average daily sales rate? (Assume 365 days per year.)

2. Suppose a retailer's annual inventory turns are 7.5. What are its days-of-supply of inventory? (Assume 365 days per year.)

3. Apple's days-of-supply of inventory are 10.5. What are its annual inventory turns? (Assume 365 days per year.)

4. An electronics manufacturer has 25 days-of-supply of inventory for a particular cell phone model. Assuming 365 days per year, what are the annual inventory turns of this cell phone model?

5. A grocery chain recently reported annual sales of $89 billion, inventory of $5.8 billion, and annual cost of goods sold of $64 billion. What are the firm's annual inventory turns?

6. A manufacturer of farm equipment has annual turns of four, and its cost of goods sold (COGS) is $44 billion. What is the average inventory it holds?

7. A mining company reported annual sales revenue of $75 billion, annual cost of goods sold of $50 billion, and inventory of $15 billion. What are the firm's annual inventory turns?

8. A manufacturing company producing medical devices reported $60 million in sales over the last year. At the end of the same year, the company had $20 million worth of inventory of ready-to-ship devices. Assuming that units in inventory are valued (based on cost of goods sold) at $1000 per unit and are sold for $2000 per unit, what is the company's annual inventory turnover?

9. An online shoe retailer's annual cost of holding inventory is 35 percent. The firm operates with a days-of-supply of 20 days, and assume there are 365 days per year. What is the inventory holding cost (in $s) for a pair of shoes that the firm purchased for $50?

10. A company's holding cost is 16 percent per year. Its annual inventory turns are 10. The company buys an item for $40. What is the average cost (in $s) to hold each unit of this item in inventory?

11. A computer company's yearly inventory cost is 40 percent (which accounts for the cost of capital for financing the inventory, warehouse space, and the cost of obsolescence). Last year, the company had $400 million in inventory and cost of goods sold of $26 billion. What is the company's total inventory cost for the year (in $ million)?

12. An integrated circuit manufacturer's annual cost of holding inventory is 48 percent. What inventory holding cost (in $) does it incur for an item that costs $300 and has a one-month supply of inventory on average?

13. A restaurant has annual sales of $420,000, an average inventory of $6000, and an annual cost of goods sold of $264,000. What is the restaurant's monthly inventory turns?

14. A restaurant has annual sales of $420,000, an average inventory of $6000, and an annual cost of goods sold of $264,000. What are the restaurant's days-of-supply of inventory? (Assume 365 days per year.)

LO10-2

15. Suppose that a movie theater snack bar turns over its inventory of candy 3.2 times per month. If the snack bar has an average of 350 boxes of candy in inventory, what is its average daily sales rate for candy? (Assume that there are 30 days per month.)

16. Suppose that a local hardware store turns over its inventory of power tools 7.3 times per year. If the hardware store has an average inventory of 130 power tools, what is its average daily sales rate for power tools? (Assume that there are 365 days per year.)

LO10-3

17. A retailer has annual sales of $500,000 and an average finished-goods inventory of $15,000. If the retailer sells each unit for an average of $25 and purchases the units for $15, what is its annual inventory turnover?

LO10-4

18. A local bookstore turns over its inventory once every three months. The bookstore's annual cost of holding inventory is 36 percent. What is the inventory holding cost (in $) for a book that the bookstore purchases for $10 and sells for $18?

19. A bicycle manufacturer purchases bicycle seats from an outside supplier for $22 each. The manufacturer's inventory of seats turns over 1.2 times per month, and the manufacturer has an annual inventory holding cost of 32 percent. What is the inventory holding cost (in $) for a bicycle seat?

CASE   LINKING TURNS TO GROSS MARGIN

A firm's **gross margin** is the difference between revenue and cost of goods. For example, if Whole Foods sells a box of cereal for $8 and it cost Whole Foods $5 to purchase the cereal, then the gross margin on that item is $8 − $5 = $3. To be able to compare gross margins across products and companies, the gross margin is often expressed as a percentage of the sales price. In the case of the cereal box, it's **gross margin percentage** is ($8 − $5)/$8 = 37.5 percent. Figure 10.3 displays the gross margins (as percentages) and annual turns for the retailers in Table 10.2.

Gross margin The difference between revenue and cost of goods.

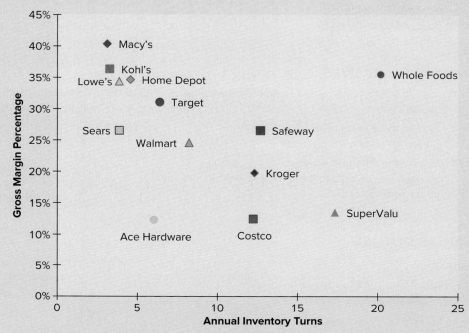

Figure 10.3   The annual inventory turns and gross margins of several retailers

1. Do you see a pattern between gross margin percentage and inventory turns in Figure 10.3?

2. Why might there be a pattern between gross margin percentage and inventory turns in Figure 10.3?

3. Ace Hardware is in the lower-left corner, meaning that it has lower gross margins than others (which isn't good) and low turns (which also is not good). How can a firm in that position be profitable?

4. What might explain why Whole Foods is in the upper-right corner?

Supply Chain Management

11

LEARNING OBJECTIVES

LO11-1 Explain the roles and value of each layer within a supply chain

LO11-2 Explain the metrics used to evaluate the performance of a supply chain

LO11-3 Explain the differences between tactical and strategic decisions and the main trade-offs in making strategic decisions

LO11-4 Explain the sources of variability within a supply chain and some approaches for mitigating variability

LO11-5 Explain and evaluate different supply chain strategies for improving performance and enhancing competitiveness

CHAPTER OUTLINE

Introduction

What do Phil Knight, Amancio Ortega, Michael Dell, and Jeff Bezos have in common? Aside from being men, they all started successful businesses, all of which you know or should know: Phil Knight began Nike in 1964 selling shoes in Oregon from the trunk of his car; Amancio Ortega opened Zara in 1975 with one clothing store in La Coruña, Spain; Michael Dell founded Dell in 1984, using his dorm room at the University of Texas to produce his personal computers (PCs); and Jeff Bezos created Amazon.com in 1994, promising the "greatest store on Earth." And due to their successes, each achieved a personal wealth in the multibillion-dollar stratosphere. But more interesting is why they all succeeded: In all four cases they created a company that introduced a new type of supply chain to the market, thereby enabling them to lower costs while providing higher value to consumers. Phil Knight discovered the advantages of not making your own shoes and moving that production overseas. In contrast, Amancio Ortega created a vertically integrated supply chain from design to retail with much of its production in "high-cost" Europe. That approach allows Zara to sell the latest fashions only weeks after their debut on the runway, an approach dubbed "cheap chic" or "fast fashion." With Dell, customers had to wait for their computer to be assembled and shipped, but they received the PC that was configured to their own preferences. And Jeff Bezos avoided traditional physical, "brick-and-mortar" stores, thereby allowing Amazon to provide an enormous assortment of products. So, in sum, you can say that the important common thread among them is their distinction as supply chain innovators.

In this chapter, we explore operations across locations and firm boundaries; that is, operations along the supply chain from raw materials, to manufacturing, to distribution, to retail, and finally to the consumer. We start with the basics: (i) what the role is that each layer plays to generate value along the supply chain and (ii) what various metrics are used to measure and track the performance of a supply chain. Next, we turn to the types of decisions that are made to manage the supply chain. At a high level, the essence of supply chain management is to balance the trade-off between costs and flexibility—fast and nimble is great for customer service, but customers also don't like to pay too much. Flexibility is particularly important for mitigating all of the bad things that come with variability. So to understand the value of flexibility, it is important to understand the sources of variability within the supply chain. Finally, we illustrate several strategies that have been effectively used by the four entrepreneurs mentioned here (and others) to not only improve supply chain performance, but to make the supply chain a key component of a firm's competitive advantage in the marketplace.

11.1 Supply Chain Structure and Roles

The supply chain for goods and services consists of a network of firms and locations that begins with raw materials and ends with final users. A supply chain can be relatively short, with only a few stages, as in strawberries grown 30 kilometers from where they are eaten. Or a supply chain can span the globe, as in bauxite mined in Australia, smelted into aluminum in New Zealand, stamped into sheet metal in Japan, and installed in an airplane in Spain.

Roughly speaking, a supply chain can be divided into five different levels, as displayed in Figure 11.1 and described in Table 11.1: tier 2 suppliers, tier 1 suppliers, manufacturers, distributors, and retailers.

11.1.1 Tier 2 Suppliers, Tier 1 Suppliers, and Manufacturers

Products start with tier 2 suppliers as individual components. Tier 2 suppliers provide their components to tier 1 suppliers, who make more complex components. For example, a tier 2 supplier might provide the electric harnesses for an aircraft wing to a tier 1 supplier that assembles the complete wing. (In some settings, another layer is identified, called tier 3, which is the set of suppliers to tier 2.)

Tier 1 suppliers are the primary suppliers to manufacturers, where products are designed and assembled into their final form for consumption. Manufacturers can be large and well-known. For example, Apple Inc. is a well-known manufacturer of computer devices and phones (e.g., iPhone, iPad, iMac, etc.). In fact, at the start of 2015, Apple Inc. was one of the world's most recognized brands and the world's most valuable company, as measured by market capitalization (i.e., the total value of its stock).

> **LO11-1** Explain the roles and value of each layer within a supply chain.

Figure 11.1
The flow of product through different levels of supply chains

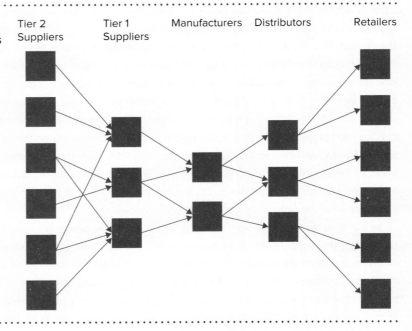

In contrast to manufacturers, most people are not as familiar with tier 1 and tier 2 suppliers. This is especially true of tier 2 suppliers because they tend to be smaller than their tier 1 customers, even if "smaller" might mean a very large company to most of us (e.g., annual sales of hundreds of millions of dollars or more). However, there are exceptions. For example, Intel Inc. is a tier 1 supplier of microprocessors to computer manufacturers. Due to its "Intel inside" marketing effort, consumers are aware of which company makes their microprocessor. Similarly, if you are an avid cyclist, you know that Shimano is a tier 1 supplier of bike components to bike manufacturers like Trek. And Alcoa, a very large producer of aluminum, could be considered a tier 2 supplier to beverage manufacturers like Coca Cola and Budweiser because it supplies the metal to the tier 1 suppliers who make the cans for the drinks.

TABLE 11.1   Different Levels of a Supply Chain and Their Function

Supply Chain Level	Role in the Supply Chain	Example
Tier II supplier	Design and manufacturing of specialized components	B&H Tool Works—metal stamping
Tier I supplier	Design and assembly of component systems	Mitsubishi Heavy Industries—aircraft wings Robert Bosch—automobile brake systems Foxconn—computers Intel—microprocessors Shimano—bike components
Original equipment manufacturer (OEM)	Design and assembly of final products	Boeing—aircraft Toyota—automobiles Apple—computers Dell—computers Trek—bicycles
Distributor	Inventory storage, break-bulk, transportation	Sysco—food McKesson—medical supplies
Retailer	Product assortment, consumer support and services	Walmart—general merchandize Home Depot—hardware Kroger—groceries

11.1.2 Distributors and Retailers

After producing a product, a manufacturer must distribute its products to final consumers. This involves two layers of the supply chain: distributors and retailers. Retailers are probably the most familiar level of the supply chain to you. Retailers generally don't make things. Instead, they provide an assortment of products and, in some cases, they assist consumers with their purchasing decisions. Traditional retailers operate physical stores close to where consumers live. They are called **brick-and-mortar retailers**, in reference to their tangible buildings. However, not all retailers need a store made of bricks (or cinder blocks, or metal framing): **mail-order retailers** (or **catalog retailers**) started in the early 1900s in the United States and **online retailers** (or **e-commerce** or **e-tailers**) like Amazon.com transferred the idea of a paper catalog onto web pages.

Distributors are the one step between manufacturers and retailers. This level is a bit "invisible" to most people, unless you happen to work in the industry that they serve. For example, McKesson is one of the largest distributors of medical supplies to hospitals—somebody needs to supply hospitals with bandages, syringes, saline solution, and myriad other things they need to treat patients.

The role of distributors is probably least understood among the various levels of the supply chain. Have you heard the cry "cut out the middleman"? That admonition suggests you can get a better deal if you deal directly with the manufacturer, bypassing the distributor. But, in fact, distributors play an important role within the supply chain. Indeed, if they didn't provide value, market forces would ensure that they would disappear!

Three of the important sources of value that distributors provide are cost-effective storage of inventory, faster delivery lead times, and smaller order quantities.

Cost-Effective Storage of Inventory While it might cost a retailer $200 to $300 each year to rent each square meter in its stores, a distributor might pay only one-fourth of that for its facilities, which are called **distribution centers (DCs)** or **fulfillment centers**. (In the old days, they were called "warehouses," but that term is no longer in vogue.) Furthermore, because a DC doesn't have to look nice for customers, a distributor can store more items per square meter in a DC than a retailer can in one of its stores. For example, a DC can stack items higher and can use deeper shelving. The combination of (i) a lower price per square meter for storage space and (ii) less space needed for the same amount of product yields a substantially lower cost to store inventory at a distributor than at a retail store.

Faster Delivery Lead Times A product is generally manufactured in a limited number of places. That means that customers are usually located far away from the manufacturer, which means it takes a considerable amount of time to receive an order from a manufacturer. The time to receive an order is called the **lead time**. And, as shown later in this chapter and in the other chapters on inventory management, the longer the lead time, the more inventory is needed to ensure that enough inventory is available for customers. Hence, because distributors are located closer to consumers than is the manufacturer, they can help their customers (usually retailers) keep less inventory, which saves them from having to purchase more costly space to house the inventory.

Smaller Order Quantities Distributors can purchase in large quantities from manufacturers but then allow their customers to purchase in smaller quantities. This service is called **breaking bulk.** For example, a distributor might purchase 200 cases on a **pallet** from a manufacturer and then allow its retail customers to purchase in case multiples smaller than a pallet, such as 50 cases. (A pallet is the wooden platform used as the base for a stack of inventory that can be moved around with a forklift.) This service allows the retailer to substantially lower its inventory.

To illustrate the value of small order quantities, consider the following example depicted in Figure 11.2. There are four suppliers, called A, B, C, and D, that need to deliver their product to four retail stores, called 1, 2, 3, and 4. There are two ways to do this. The first has a distributor between the suppliers and the retailers. In the second, there is no distributor, so the suppliers deliver directly to each retailer.

Brick-and-mortar retailer A retailer with physical stores in which consumers are able to immediately purchase goods.

Mail-order retailers Retailers that merchandise their goods via a print catalog and sell to consumers by shipping them goods via a third-party carrier like the U.S. Postal Service, UPS, FedEx, or DHL. Also called catalog retailers.

Catalog retailers Retailers that merchandise their goods via a print catalog and sell to consumers by shipping them goods via a third-party carrier like the U.S. Postal Service, UPS, FedEx, or DHL. Also called mail-order retailers.

Online retailers Retailers that merchandise their goods via an online website (or app) and sell to consumers by shipping them goods via a third-party carrier like the U.S. Postal Service, UPS, FedEx, or DHL. Also called e-commerce or e-tailers.

E-commerce Retailers that merchandise their goods via an online website (or app) and sell to consumers by shipping them goods via a third-party carrier like the U.S. Postal Service, UPS, FedEx, or DHL. Also called online retailers or e-tailers.

E-tailers Retailers that merchandise their goods via an online website (or app) and sell to consumers by shipping them goods via a third-party carrier like the U.S. Postal Service, UPS, FedEx, or DHL. Also called online retailers or e-commerce.

Distribution center (DC) A building used to receive products from suppliers and then redistribute them to retail stores or send packages to consumers. Also called a fulfillment center.

Fulfillment center A building used to receive products from suppliers and then redistribute them to retail stores or send packages to consumers. Also called a distribution center.

Lead time The time to receive an order.

Figure 11.2

Two supply chains, one with and one without a distributor

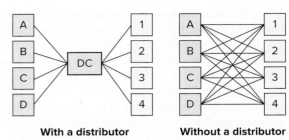

With a distributor   **Without a distributor**

Every week each retailer sells 100 units of each supplier's product for a total of 400 units per week. So each supplier sells 400 units every week—100 through each retailer. Products are delivered between stages via trucks, and each truck carries 400 units.

When there is a distributor in the supply chain, each supplier sends one truck with 400 units each week to the DC. The distributor, in turn, sends one truck each week to each retailer with 400 units of product. While the trucks going between the supplier and the DC carry product only from one supplier, the trucks going between the DC and the retailers carry a mixture of product from all four suppliers. In particular, the DC-to-retailer trucks carry 100 units from each supplier.

In the direct delivery supply chain, each week each supplier sends one truck filled with 400 units to one of the retailers. Hence, each retailer receives one delivery each week, and each week the delivery comes from a different supplier.

Although in either supply chain each supplier ships one truck each week and each retailer receives one truck each week, the inventory held by the retailers is not the same across the two supply chains. Figure 11.3 displays the pattern of inventory of supplier A's product at retailer 1 with each supply chain model. (The inventory patterns for the other three products would look identical to product A's pattern.) When there is a distributor, retailer 1 receives one truck each week with 100 units from supplier A (and 100 units from each of the other three suppliers for a total delivery of 400 units). Thus, the inventory of supplier A's product peaks at 100 units (when the truck arrives) and then declines throughout the week as units are sold. In contrast, with the direct delivery supply chain, retailer 1 receives one truck from supplier A every four weeks. The truck has 400 units of supplier A's product, so now inventory peaks at 400 and declines toward 0, when the next delivery is received.

From Figure 11.3 we can clearly see that the amount of inventory retailer 1 carries depends considerably on which supply chain is used. When there is a distributor, the retailer has 50 units, on average, whereas with direct deliveries the retailer has, on average, 200 units. Thus, removing the distributor would increase retail inventory by four times, even though the same number of trucks are used and the same number of deliveries are made! Four times more inventory requires four times more retail space, which is costly.

Breaking bulk A service in which a distributor purchases in large quantities from manufacturers but then allows customers to purchase in smaller quantities.

Pallet Either (1) a platform, often wooden, used as a base to store inventory and to facilitate moving that inventory via a forklift or (2) the quantity of inventory that is stacked on the platform.

Figure 11.3

Inventory pattern of supplier A's product at retailer 1 with the two supply chain models. The inventory for the other products and other retailers follows the same pattern.

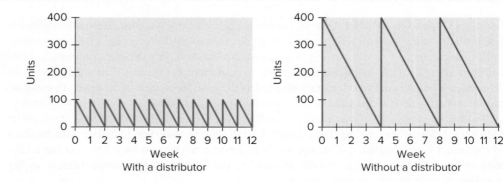

TABLE 11.2 Summary of Advantages and Disadvantages of Each Supply Chain Model

	With a Distributor	Without a Distributor
Average inventory of each product	50 units	200 units
Distance traveled	Longer because product is routed through the DC	As short as possible
Product handling	More—extra unloading and loading at the DC	Minimal—load at source, unload at store

Check Your Understanding 11.1

Question: **Although distributors do not sell products to consumers directly and they do not actually make things, they provide value to the supply chain by:**

  a. reducing the distance products travel through the supply chain.
  b. reducing the amount of labor needed to handle products.
  c. reducing the amount of storage space a retailer needs for inventory.

Answer: The addition of a distributor to a supply chain increases the distance products travel and the amount of handling. But it also allows retailers to purchase in smaller quantities, which allows them to reduce the amount of space they need for inventory storage. Therefore, the answer is C, reducing the amount of storage space a retailer needs for inventory.

Although adding a distributor to the supply chain is terrific for reducing the amount of retail space needed, it does have downsides. First, the total distance traveled is always minimized when you travel directly from one point to another. Hence, the supply chain without the distributor minimizes travel distance, and adding a distributor increases distances—units have to take a detour to the DC before they arrive at their final destination. Furthermore, the DC adds more handling to the product—somebody must unload the inbound shipments and load the outbound shipments at the DC. These trade-offs are summarized in Table 11.2. Whether it makes sense to add a DC to the supply chain depends on the costs. If retail space is very costly relative to transportation costs and product-handling costs, then the DC adds value to the supply chain (i.e., lowers net costs across the supply chain). Given that we frequently see DCs in supply chains, it must be that the DC indeed often adds value.

11.2 Metrics of Supply Chain Performance

Given the complexity of supply chains, it is important to know how to evaluate the performance of a supply chain with a few key metrics. These metrics can be divided into two categories: cost metrics and service metrics.

11.2.1 Cost Metrics

There are four key costs associated with a supply chain: procurement, labor, inventory, and transportation.

Procurement Procurement is the cost of goods purchased from suppliers. Usually, this is the largest cost associated with making physical goods. This is why most companies have procurement groups that are exclusively dedicated to buying things from suppliers. A key requirement of their job is to ensure that they negotiate good prices from their suppliers. But

LO11-2 Explain the metrics used to evaluate the performance of a supply chain.

these groups are also responsible for ensuring that they select qualified and competent suppliers. For example, does the supply deliver quickly enough, does the supplier deliver only good-quality components, and is the supplier responsive enough to adjust production volumes as needed?

Labor   Labor is the wages and salaries of the individuals in various supply chain functions. Supply chains need people to assemble things, move inventory, and manage transportation, among other tasks. As a result, labor is another large cost within a supply chain. This is true even if a company also uses a substantial amount of automation. For example, labor is a critical cost of operating a fulfillment center at Amazon.com even though in many of their facilities items are moved around on top of small orange robots (see Figure 11.4).

Inventory   If your primary responsibility at a company includes the words "supply chain," then inventory is unquestionably one of the metrics you worry about the most. The supply chain manager wants to know two things about inventory: How much do we have and where is it? For example, do you have enough toys to meet holiday demand in the fourth quarter and, if you do, is that inventory where you need it to be, as in not stuck in an overseas port in October?

There are numerous costs associated with holding inventory. Briefly, a firm needs to store the inventory (e.g., rent a building), maintain the inventory (e.g., refrigeration), and incur the opportunity cost associated with locking the cash in the inventory. For example, instead of spending $1 million to purchase additional inventory, a firm could use that $1 million to develop new products, build new stores, or do whatever it does that generates a profit. Hence, one of the costs of putting that $1 million into inventory is the loss in profit that isn't earned from whatever other use you might have for $1 million.

The opportunity cost of capital doesn't appear directly on a balance sheet or income statement (i.e., the standard documents accountants use to report on the financial health of a company). There is another critical cost associated with inventory that does not appear in those statements either—the risk of obsolescence. The longer an item remains in inventory, the more it risks becoming less valuable merely because its technology can become obsolete. You might not remember this, but at one time phones, even mobile phones, were used only to make voice calls to other people. Once the "smart" phone was introduced, all of those "dumb" phones immediately became less valuable. And this happens with all technology—the minute a new device is introduced with more memory, a faster processor, more pixels, or more "what-have-you," all the older versions of that product still in inventory suddenly are less desirable. While it makes sense that better technology is more valuable, obsolescence even happens with things that are replaced with items that are functionally no different—new clothing styles are just as warm or as soft as the old styles, but the old styles just don't have the "look" anymore.

Figure 11.4

Robots used to move portable storage units around a fulfillment center

© Stephen Brashear/Getty Images News/Getty Images/RF

Transportation Transportation costs obviously should matter in the context of supply chain management. The basic trade-off in transportation is simple: The faster you want to move something from point A to point B, the more you have to pay. Ocean/water transport is the slowest but also the most affordable (assuming you are moving large quantities). Railroad is also a low-cost transportation means, as measured in terms of $ per ton of cargo per kilometer traveled. But rail clearly only applies across land and it too can be relatively slow. Next up in terms of speed is trucking. Trucking can move cargo to many more destinations than rail, but it is more expensive. Finally, the fastest way to move product is to fly it from its origin to its destination. But air transport is very expensive, especially for heavy products—whereas ocean transport is usually priced based on the volume shipped (e.g., one container), air transport is priced based on the weight of the delivery.

11.2.2 Service Metrics

While the supply chain manager needs to carefully watch costs, the manager also needs to deliver good service to customers. In the context of supply chain management, good service is usually measured in two ways: lead time and inventory availability.

As already mentioned, the **lead time** is the time between when an order is received and when it is delivered. Online retailers carefully track their lead time to customers—customers always prefer to receive the item they ordered as soon as possible. But firms higher up in the supply chain also care about the lead time. If you are a tier 2 supplier and you want to renew your contract with your tier 1 customer, then you better deliver in the lead time that is expected of you.

Several factors influence the realized lead time for an order. Obviously, the chosen mode of transportation matters and, within a mode of transportation, the amount paid for priority service—e.g., express mail versus standard mail. Second, the lead time is influenced by the operational capabilities of the sender. For example, how long does a fulfillment center take to pick an item from inventory, place it in a box, and then prepare the box for shipping? Finally, the lead time depends on the availability of inventory: If the fulfillment center doesn't have the item in stock, it can only be shipped when more inventory is received, which extends the time a customer must wait to receive it.

There are several ways to measure the availability of inventory. A common measure is called the **in-stock probability**—the probability that all demand is served within an interval of time. For example, suppose a DC carries 10,000 items and during a particular week its customers (i.e., the retail stores it resupplies) ordered some inventory of 2400 different items. Say the DC was only able to satisfy all of the demand for 2000 items—that is, demand exceeded available inventory for 400 items. So out of the 10,000 products, the DC was able to satisfy the demand for 9600 items—note, if an item is not demanded, then it is trivial to satisfy "all" of its demand. Hence, the DC's in-stock probability for that week is 9600/10,000 = 0.96.

The **stockout probability** is closely related to the in-stock probability—it is the probability that demand for an item exceeds its inventory during a period of time. Back to the example with the DC: the stockout probability is 400/10,000 = 0.04. Because an item either satisfies all of its demand (in stock) or does not satisfy all of its demand (stockout), the in-stock and stockout probabilities always sum to 1. Hence, if you know one of those probabilities, you can quickly evaluate the other:

In-stock probability = 1 − Stockout probability

Stockout probability = 1 − In-stock probability

While the in-stock probability is a useful measure of the availability of inventory, it is not the only potential measure. An alternative is the **fill rate**, which is the fraction of demand satisfied. Both the in-stock probability and the fill rate increase when more inventory is added, but they are not identical measures. Go back to the DC example in which the in-stock probability is 0.96. Say, for simplicity, that among the 400 items in which demand exceeded supply, inventory equaled 90 percent of demand; that is, for those products, inventory was sufficient to fill only 90 percent of demand. The average fill rate across all items is then

In-stock probability The probability that all demand is served within an interval of time.

Stockout probability The probability that demand for an item exceeds its inventory during a period of time.

Fill rate The fraction of demand satisfied.

Check Your Understanding 11.2

Question: A retailer carries 10,000 items in its store. During the week, there is some demand for 6000 of the items. Among those, there are 100 products for which all of the demand was not satisfied and 400 products for which only some of demand was satisfied.

     a. What is their in-stock probability for this week?

Answer: They satisfy all demand for 10,000 − 100 − 400 = 9500 items, so their in-stock probability is 9500/10,000 = 0.95 = 95 percent.

     b. What is their stockout probability for this week?

Answer: 500 items out of 10,000 did not satisfy all demand, so the stockout probability is 500/10,000 = 0.05 = 5 percent.

. . . .

$(400/10{,}000 \times 0.90) + (9{,}600/10{,}000 \times 1.00) = 0.9960$. Hence, even though the DC was in stock with 96 percent of items, it satisfied 99.60 percent of demand.

A complication with the fill-rate measure is that to evaluate it you need to know what demand was even if the item stocked out. This is feasible if customers announce their demand before they see the inventory that is available. But in a retail store, customers usually just walk out if they don't find the item they want (or they switch to another item). Because it can be difficult to measure true demand in those situations, it can be challenging to accurately measure the fill rate. In contrast, it is generally easier to measure whether all demand was satisfied or not, which is the in-stock probability.

11.3 Supply Chain Decisions

LO11-3 Explain the differences between tactical and strategic decisions and the main trade-offs in making strategic decisions.

Because supply chains can occur over considerable distances and span the boundaries across several firms, it is clear that managing a supply chain involves a broad set of complex decisions. However, it is possible to provide some characterization of these decisions into several categories.

A useful way to distinguish supply chain decisions is along the spectrum of tactical to strategic. **Tactical decisions** are decisions that impact short-term performance, whereas **strategic decisions** have long-term implications.

11.3.1 Tactical Decisions

Tactical decisions include decisions such as:

- What do I load onto a truck today?
- How many bars of soap should I order for my grocery store?
- How many car seats should I order from my supplier?
- Should I run overtime today in my factory?
- Should I expedite a shipment from overseas?

. . . and many others. These decisions usually involve individual products or resources, and any one of these decisions influences the firm's performance in the next few days or weeks or maybe the next few months, but usually never for a year or more.

Although any one tactical decision has short-term consequences, it is still very important for a firm to make good tactical decisions. If a firm consistently makes bad tactical decisions, then its performance in the long run will suffer. For example, if a retailer consistently does not order enough of an item, then consumers might learn that the retailer is often out of stock and therefore decide to shop elsewhere.

Tactical decisions Decisions that impact short-term performance.

Strategic decisions Decisions that have long-term implications.

11.3.2 Strategic Decisions

Strategic decisions have long-run implications in the sense that they can influence performance over several quarters or years and are usually hard to alter after they are made. Consequently, it is important to make good strategic decisions because they are not made often, and making a bad strategic decision can have long-lasting negative consequences.

In the context of supply chain management, there are a number of different kinds of strategic decisions. To begin, a firm needs to decide the number and location of its facilities. For example, should a manufacturer locate production domestically or overseas, and should a retailer build a few large stores or many small stores?

A firm must decide which tasks it will do and which it will let other firms do within the supply chain. For example, does a manufacturer sell its products through its own stores or through independent retailers? Should a manufacturer assemble its products or outsource assembly to another firm? And if the decision is to let another firm do a task, then which firm should do the task?

Given the wide variety of strategic decisions, it is useful to think in terms of an overarching framework for how these decisions should be made.[1] In particular, at a high level, supply chain decisions are about variability and flexibility. As discussed in the next section in greater detail, variability comes in many forms. For example, demand can be variable in several ways: in total demand or in demand for individual products or locations. Suppliers can vary in how well they perform, and severe weather can create disruptions. In all cases, variability is destructive: it is hard to imagine a form of variability that is actually beneficial to a supply chain.

To counteract variability, a supply chain needs flexibility; for example, the flexibility to produce more of a desirable product or the flexibility to move inventory from where it isn't needed to where it is needed.

Because supply chains differ in the amount of variability they face and because flexibility is generally costly, it is important for a supply chain manager to select the right level of flexibility for its supply chain. Figure 11.5 illustrates this decision in a simplified form.

Roughly speaking, products come in two types: functional and innovative. **Functional products** are relatively "safe" products in the sense that they do not experience a considerable amount of variability. For example, past sales data can be used to forecast demand with reasonable accuracy because these products do not become obsolete quickly (e.g., black socks never go out of style). Functional products tend to have numerous competitors (or other products that are good substitutes), so it is not possible to make a large profit on each unit sold. To be specific, a product's **gross margin** is the difference between the price at which it is sold and the cost to purchase the item, expressed as a percentage of the selling price of the item. For instance, if a firm sells a product for $50 that cost $40 to make (or buy), then the gross

Functional products In the context of strategic supply chain decisions, these are products that are relatively "safe" in the sense that they do not experience a considerable amount of variability.

Gross margin The difference between the price at which a product is sold and the cost to purchase the item, expressed as a percentage of the selling price of the item.

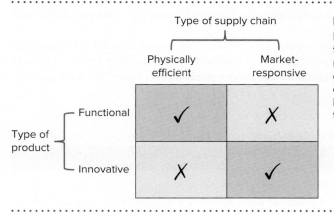

Figure 11.5

Matching the type of supply chain to the type of product. An "x" marks a mismatch between the type of supply chain and the type of product. A check mark indicates a good match between the type of supply chain and the type of product.

[1]This section is based on Marshall Fisher, "What Is the Right Supply Chain for Your Product," *Harvard Business Review* (March–April 1997).

TABLE 11.3 Summary of Characteristics of Functional and Innovative Products

	Functional	Innovative
Demand forecast uncertainty	Low	High
Risk of obsolescence	Low	High
Gross margin	Low (5–20%)	High (20–60%)
Frequency of markdowns	Low	High

margin is 20 percent: ($50 − $40)/$50 = 0.2. Functional products tend to have gross margins in the 5–20 percent range. Finally, because functional products are long lasting, discounts are rarely needed to sell inventory left over at the end of a season.

Innovative products are relatively "risky" in the sense that they can experience substantial variability. For example, there might not exist reliable past sales data to forecast future sales of a new product. These products are subject to the whims of fashion—hot one moment, cold the next. However, because innovative products are new or enjoy something distinctive, they tend to have higher gross margins, as in the 20–60 percent range. But whereas each sale can be profitable, innovative products often suffer from leftover inventory that needs to be discounted considerably to sell. Table 11.3 summarizes the characteristics of functional and innovative products

Just as products come in different types, so do supply chains. **Physically efficient** supply chains are designed to minimize costs. For example, they use the cheapest form of transportation, inventory is kept low, factories are operated with high utilization, and suppliers are selected primarily based on who delivers the lowest price per unit. In contrast, **market-responsive** supply chains emphasize flexibility over cost. Hence, these supply chains use faster, and therefore more costly, transportation. When customers demand quick service, these supply chains carry enough inventory to avoid being out of stock. Idle capacity is tolerated at factories (i.e., lower utilization) because the spare capacity could be used in case demand surges. Finally, supplier selection does depend on the per-unit prices offered, but it also depends on a supplier's ability to adjust its production volumes as needed and its ability to deliver with a short lead time. Table 11.4 summarizes the characteristics of the two types of supply chains.

The main idea in Figure 11.5 is that the type of supply chain should match the type of product that moves through it. If a product is functional, then a physically efficient supply chain should be used (upper left-hand corner of Figure 11.5). If a product is innovative, then a market-responsive supply chain should be used (lower right-hand corner of Figure 11.5). As long as the product matches the supply chain, the firms in that supply chain should be okay (i.e., competitive and profitable).

Figure 11.5 also illustrates how a supply chain manager can make a mistake. If the manager designs a physically efficient supply chain for an innovative product (lower left-hand corner) or a market-responsive supply chain for a functional production (upper right-hand corner),

Innovative products In the context of strategic supply chain decisions, these are products that are relatively "risky" in the sense that they can experience substantial variability.

Physically efficient In the context of strategic supply chain decisions, these are supply chains that are designed to minimize costs.

Market-responsive In the context of strategic supply chain decisions, these are supply chains that are designed to emphasize flexibility over cost.

TABLE 11.4 Summary of Characteristics of Physically Efficient and Market-Responsive Supply Chains

	Physically Efficient	Market-Responsive
Transportation mode	Slow and cheap	Fast and expensive
Spare capacity	Little (i.e., high factory utilization)	Some (i.e., lower factory utilization)
Supplier selection	Based only on low per-unit price	Low per-unit price is important but so is the ability to adjust production quantities and a fast lead time

Check Your Understanding 11.3

Question: Characterize the following decisions as either tactical or strategic:

a. The number of employees to assign to an afternoon shift on a particular Friday.

Answer: This decision has short-term implications for just one day, so it is tactical.

b. The number of full-time employees to have.

Answer: It takes time to adjust the number of full-time employees, so this is more of a strategic decision than a tactical one.

. . . .

then the supply chain won't correctly match the product characteristics. In these cases, either the manager is spending too much on flexibility when flexibility isn't needed (upper right-hand corner) or the manager is spending too little on flexibility when the product needs flexibility (lower left-hand corner). Either mistake deteriorates the firm's competitiveness.

Although two errors are displayed in Figure 11.5, managers are much more prone to make the mistake in the lower left-hand corner than in the upper right—managers too often underinvest in flexibility (they design a physically efficient supply chain) when their products are innovative. This occurs when a manager thinks of its product as functional, when in fact it is innovative. Furthermore, because it can be hard for a manager to quantify the benefits of faster transportation, spare capacity, or a more flexible supplier, yet it is easy to quantify the costs, managers tend to be averse to spending money on the uncertain benefits of flexibility. Unfortunately, this mistake leads to a supply chain that is not capable of effectively coping with the variability thrown upon it.

11.4 Sources of Variability in a Supply Chain

Variability comes in many forms within a supply chain. Understanding the causes of supply chain variability allows a manager to design the supply chain to better cope with that variability. We begin with an obvious source of variability: variability in consumer demand. But from the point of view of managing a supply chain, it is useful to divide demand variability into three components: level, variety, and location. Next, we explore the variability in demand within the supply chain; that is, not between consumers and a retailer but rather between different firms upstream in the supply chain. Due to the phenomenon of the bullwhip effect, variability in demand within the supply chain can be substantially greater than consumer demand variability. We conclude this section with two types of variability that are not demand-related, but rather, are due to our own capabilities or to forces outside of our immediate control.

11.4.1 Variability Due to Demand: Level, Variety, and Location

Suppose you operate a bakery and you sell vanilla éclairs. In fact, vanilla is the only flavor of éclair that you sell. With this simple assortment, each day you face only one type of uncertainty: How many customers will come to your shop with an interest in buying éclairs. Some days you might have demand for 50; other days demand is only 20. This is variability due to the level of demand; that is, uncertainty in the total amount of demand.

> **LO11-4** Explain the sources of variability within a supply chain and some approaches for mitigating variability.

Unfortunately, it takes time to make éclairs, so at the start of the day you have to decide how many éclairs to make because you won't have the opportunity to make more the rest of the day. Suppose you decide to make 40 of them. On days with high demand, you sell all of your éclairs! That might seem like a great outcome, but you might be left wondering how much more you could have sold had you made more than 40. And, of course, on days with low demand, you are left with unsold éclairs at the end of the day. You could treat yourself to the leftover éclairs, but you worry about the consequences of personally consuming so many pastries. So those éclairs might end up in the trash.

© Patricia Brabant/Cole Group/Getty Images/RF

Deciding how many vanilla éclairs to make is challenging due to the variability in the level of demand. Make too many and you waste effort and ingredients. Make too few and you disappoint some customers while also losing out on the opportunity to earn a larger profit for the day.

The "how many éclairs to make" decision becomes more challenging if you decide to introduce a new flavor, say chocolate éclairs. Now, in addition to the uncertainty over how many customers want to purchase éclairs, you face the uncertainty of which type of éclair they prefer. Even if, on average, half of your customers select chocolate and half select vanilla, there will be days in which more than half of the demand is for chocolate and other days in which more than half of the demand is for vanilla. For example, on some days in which 50 customers want to purchase an éclair, you might have 30 who want chocolate and 20 who want vanilla. But on other days, the pattern might be reversed—20 want chocolate and 30 want vanilla.

So if you offer two flavors, how many of each type should you make at the start of the day? Say you make 25 of chocolate and 25 of vanilla. On some days with 50 customers, you might not have enough chocolate and too many vanilla éclairs. On other days with 50 customers you might have the other problem—too many chocolate éclairs and not enough vanilla. With either of those days, had you made 50 éclairs of all one flavor (instead of 25 of each flavor) and 50 customers wanted to purchase an éclair (of any flavor), then you would have neither disappointed customers (i.e., stocked out) nor leftover inventory. In short, adding the additional flavor made the "how many éclairs to make" decision harder because of variability due to product variety.

Now say your bakery is doing well and you decide to open up a new store on the other side of the same city. This creates yet another source of variability. There might be 50 customers in the city that want to buy an éclair today. When you had one shop, they all went to the single shop. But now they have a choice. Maybe 28 go to the original store and 22 go to the new store. Or maybe it is the other way around. In other words, adding locations to the supply chain creates another form of demand variability, and this variability creates yet another hassle for your éclair production decision: You must decide how many éclairs to make, how to allocate that quantity across the flavors you offer, and then how to allocate for each flavor the number to have in each location.

In sum, supply chains must cope with three types of variability associated with demand:

1. Variability in the level of demand. That is, the total demand across the supply chain. For example, how many éclairs in total will be demanded?

2. Variability due to product variety. That is, how does the total demand get allocated across the various flavors, types, or versions of the offered product?

3. Variability due to location. That is, how does the total demand get allocated across the locations in the supply chain?

These forms of demand variability clearly apply to consumer demand at the bottom of the supply chain. They also apply at higher levels within the supply chain. For example, if a distributor adds a new distribution center, then it has expanded the number of locations at which demand can occur, which increases variability. If a mobile phone manufacturer adds another phone to its assortment, then it has increased the variability it faces due to product variety.

The preceding discussion is not meant to suggest that a firm should never add variety or never operate out of multiple locations. Either of those actions might bring new demand to the firm, which can be beneficial. However, there comes a point at which adding variety or adding locations only increases variability without the benefit of increased demand. For example, if you currently sell 10 flavors of éclairs, do you think total demand for éclairs would increase if you added an 11th flavor?

11.4.2 Variability Due to the Bullwhip Effect

Procter & Gamble (P&G) is a leading manufacturer of disposable baby diapers. At one point it noticed an odd feature of the demand received by its factories: demand was quite volatile. For any other product, it might have just assumed that demand was indeed volatile and just dealt with it. But intuitively, demand for diapers shouldn't be volatile: the final consumer of diapers—that is, babies—use diapers at a steady rate and, for the most part, babies are "produced" at a steady rate as well. So if demand at the downstream level of the supply chain is consistent, why was demand at the upstream level jumping up and down?

We now have a name for P&G's ailment—it is called the bullwhip effect. The **bullwhip effect** is the tendency for demand to become more volatile at higher levels of the supply chain, just like the swing in a whip can get more dramatic from handle to tip. Figure 11.6 illustrates the bullwhip effect in an example of a simple, simulated supply. Demand starts with consumers who buy the product from a retailer. The retailer orders the product from the distributor (i.e., the distributor's demand is the retailer's orders), and the manufacturer receives demand from the distributor. Each week, consumers demand from the retailer about 100 units with just a little bit of volatility. The retailer orders, on average, 100 units each week from the distributor, but that demand goes up and down a bit. Finally, the distributor also orders, on average, 100 units each week from the manufacturer, but the distributor's orders vary widely—in some weeks, it is more than 40 percent greater than the average, while in other weeks it is less than 40 percent lower than the average!

There are a couple of things to note from Figure 11.6. First, the average amount demanded at each level of the supply chain is the same: Consumers demand, on average, 100 units per week; the retailer demands, on average, 100 units per week from the distributor; and the distributor demands, on average, 100 units per week from the manufacturer. This must be true simply because of the conservation of matter: If the long-run averages don't match across the supply chain, then either inventory at some point builds and builds without limit (if one level demands more from its supplier than its customers demand from it) or inventory dwindles down to nothing (if one level demands less from its supplier than its customers demand from it). But while the average demands must be consistent across the supply chain in the long run, they clearly do not have to be consistent in the short run: During some weeks, consumers demand about 100 units, while the distributor demands as much as 181 units or as few as 6. In other words, demand volatility does not need to be consistent across the supply chain. In fact, according to the bullwhip effect, demand volatility at the higher levels of the supply chain can be substantially greater than at the lower levels!

Bullwhip effect The tendency for demand to become more volatile at higher levels of the supply chain.

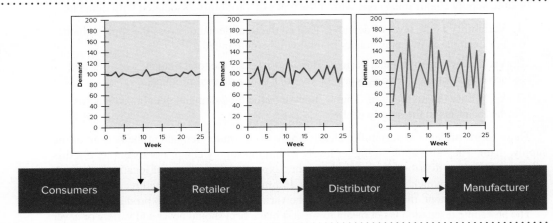

Figure 11.6

The bullwhip effect in a supply chain—the volatility of demand increases at higher levels of the supply chain

The second thing to note from Figure 11.6 is that the demand seen by a firm at the higher level of the supply chain may bear little resemblance to the demand seen by a firm at the lower level of the supply chain. In Figure 11.6, the manufacturer might assume that consumer demand is jumping up and down like crazy because its demand is doing just that. But that need not be true, and, in the presence of the bullwhip effect, it is unlikely to be true.

Third, related to the previous point, consumer demand is not the only source of volatility in the supply chain and it might not even be the major source of volatility. Put another way, demand volatility can be created within the supply chain: It might not be the fickleness of consumers that is causing the manufacturer's demand volatility headaches, but, rather, those headaches might be primarily due to the behavior of the other members of the supply chain.

If a company is able to look at demand data from different levels of the supply chain, then it can clearly see if the bullwhip effect is present—just plot the different demands side-by-side (as in Figure 11.6) or on top of each other with the same time axis. But what causes the bullwhip effect? Several reasons have been identified. We next discuss three of them: overreactive ordering, batching, and price promotions.

Overreactive Ordering Each level of the supply chain watches the demand it receives from its customers before deciding how much to order from its supplier. As a result, it is possible to overreact to changes in demand. For example, suppose you are the retailer in Figure 11.6. Consumers demanded 98 units last week and demand 104 units this week. How much should you order? One option is to just order 104 units this week. But that ignores the trend in demand—this week's demand is six units more than last week's demand. Maybe that means that future demand will be higher. So instead of ordering 104 units, you might order 112 units, adding an additional eight units just in case future demand is indeed greater.

In the following week, consumers demand 94 units. How do you respond? Again, your order could match the demand of 94 units, but now demand looks like it has dropped down again. And you ordered eight more units than you really needed last week. So you might "hit the brakes" a bit and only order 78 units.

Now consider what happens to the distributor. Last week, you ordered 112 units from the distributor, but this week you only order 78. If the distributor reacts to this sharp downtrend, like you responded to the trends you saw, then it might only order something like 24 units. To summarize, a 10-unit swing in consumer demand (from 104 to 94) results in a 34-unit swing in retailer demand (from 112 to 78), which probably causes an even bigger swing in the distributor's orders.

While it doesn't seem too damaging to order something different than your demand, the constant "accelerating" and "braking" amplify the demand volatility, especially if each level is merely reacting to the information it sees from its immediate neighbor in the supply chain. The result is the demand pattern observed in Figure 11.6: Each level of the supply chain thinks it is doing something reasonable, but the collective effect is to produce damaging volatility throughout the supply chain.

There are two solutions to overreactive ordering: (1) share information along the supply chain so that everyone is responding to actual consumer demand rather than to the orders it receives from the next level of the supply chain and (2) avoid the temptation to overreact too much to shifts in demand. For example, one option to implement the second solution is merely to order from your supplier the same amount that your customers ordered from you. In that case, the variability of your orders would exactly match the variability of your customers' orders.

Batching One way to avoid the bullwhip effect is for each level of the supply chain to order from its supplier the exact same amount that was demanded from it by its customers. However, that isn't always economically feasible. For example, as discussed earlier, one source of value for a distributor is to allow its customers to order in smaller quantities than the quantity the distributor orders from its supplier. To illustrate why this can cause the bullwhip effect, consider a simple example in which a retailer orders 10 cases every week, but the distributor must order at least 100 cases at a time from its supplier. As shown in Figure 11.7, the distributor receives a steady stream of demand from the retailer (10 cases every week). In contrast, the distributor's orders are highly variable because the distributor must order 100 cases at a time. Hence, the distributor usually orders 0 units from the supplier, but every 10 weeks the distributor orders 100 cases. With both the retailer and the distributor, they order, on average, 10 cases per week, but clearly the distributor's order pattern is much more volatile. Because the distributor's orders are its supplier's demand, the supplier experiences much more volatile demand than the distributor does.

In general, the bullwhip effect emerges whenever batching is imposed on the ordering process, thereby preventing a firm from ordering a quantity that exactly matches its demand. For example, requiring your customer to order in case quantities (when its demand is in units), pallet quantities (when its demand is in cases or smaller units), or full truckloads (when its demand is in pallets or smaller units) will lead to demand amplification in the supply chain; that is, the bullwhip effect.

The solution to batching as a cause of the bullwhip effect is to reduce the minimum batch quantities for orders. For instance, if a supplier switches from requiring orders that equal a full truckload to orders that can be as small as one-half of a truckload, then it will reduce the volatility of demand it experiences from its customers. However, smaller minimum batch quantities do lead to more frequent ordering. For example, if a retailer needs, on average, one truckload every 18 days, then it would order one-half a truckload, on average, every nine days or one-third of a truckload, on average, every six days. It is precisely this more frequent ordering that reduces variability: Large and infrequent orders create more variability than small, more frequent orders.

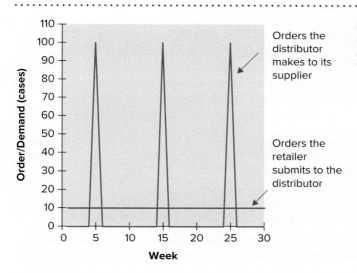

Figure 11.7

Orders a retailer submits to a distributor (a constant 10 cases per week) and the orders the distributor submits to its supplier (100 cases every 10 weeks)

Price Promotions   If you go to the grocery store and see that it is having a "buy 1, get 1 free" promotion on cans of chicken noodle soup, you might decide to buy a few more cans than you normally would. You are willing to buy more than you need for the short term because you know that the cans will last and the discount might not be available the next time you go to the store.

Consumers are not the only ones willing to "stock up" when they see an item on sale. If a supplier offers a distributor a discount for buying more than it usually buys, then the distributor might very well decide to "stock up." By doing so, the distributor lowers the average cost of the items it purchases, which helps to increase its profits on the sale of those items to retailers. In fact, even a small discount might induce a retailer or distributor to order a considerable amount—retailers have been known to buy a large enough quantity to satisfy its demand for the next six months (i.e., a six-month supply) merely to take advantage of an 8 percent discount. For such a paltry discount, most people would not want to fill their pantry with enough cans to meet their soup needs for six months. But it may be economically justifiable for a retailer to do so.

Price promotions lead to the bullwhip effect precisely the same way that batching causes the bullwhip effect: Due to the promotion, downstream customers order during the promotion larger quantities than they need. In the long run, the average amount ordered must equal the average amount sold, so if a retailer orders much more than it needs during the promotion, then it must order much less than it needs at some other time. For example, if it does order a six-month supply, then it will not place another order for another six months. Hence, the retailer's ordering pattern is much more volatile than its demand pattern, which is precisely the bullwhip effect.

The solution to the bullwhip effect caused by price promotions is to simply eliminate the price promotions. Without a promotion, customers have no incentive to "stock up" and so their demand does not become more volatile than it needs to be. Although this solution is obvious, it is not easy for everyone to implement. Suppliers and distributors offer promotions because they want their customers to purchase large quantities. They feel that shipping a large quantity of product downstream induces the downstream firm to exert more effort toward selling the product. This may be true, but the cost of a promotion strategy is increased demand volatility within the supply chain (i.e., the bullwhip effect).

Check Your Understanding 11.4

Question: A bike manufacturer sells, on average, 1000 units per week. There is one seat per bike. How many seats does the manufacturer order from its supplier, on average, each week?

    a. Fewer than 1000 so as to try to keep inventory low.
    b. Exactly 1000 per week, on average, to match the sales rate.
    c. More than 1000 per week, on average, to take advantage of quantity discounts.
    d. More information is needed to determine the manufacturer's average order quantity.

Answer: The average outflow of seats (1000 per week) must match the average inflow of seats (1000 per week). Therefore, the answer is B, exactly 1000 per week, on average, to match the sales rate.

Question: A retailer currently places orders with its suppliers on a weekly basis. It is considering a switch to a routine in which it places orders on a daily basis. No change is expected in the retailer's demand. This change will have what effect on the volatility of its orders?

    a. It will decrease because its orders will better match its demand.
    b. It will stay the same because the retailer's demand remains the same.
    c. It will increase because the more frequent orders will lead to more fickle decisions.

Answer: More frequent orders lead to smaller batches, which will lead to less volatile orders. Therefore, the answer is A, It will decrease because its orders will better match its demand.

11.4.3 Variability Due to Supply Chain Partner Performance

It can be nerve-racking to be responsible for your firm's supply chain. Usually, this means you have direct control over only one level of the supply chain, which is complicated enough to manage well. But you must also rely on the performance of your supply chain partners either to supply the parts you need or to deliver your product to consumers. Therein lies another source of variability with the supply chain: variability due to the performance of your supply chain partners.

Supply chain partners can increase the variability in the supply chain in a number of ways: failure to deliver the quantity needed, failure to deliver the quality needed, failure in finances, and failure to operate in an acceptable manner.

Failure in Quantity Say you have invented a new electronic gadget and now you want to bring your product to market. You need to make a specialized microprocessor, but you don't have the resources needed to build your own foundry to make your chip. So you hire a supplier with a foundry to make the part for you. You believe you will need 10,000 chips in your first year, but there is considerable uncertainty in this forecast: maybe you will actually need more; maybe you will actually need less.

Through your negotiations with the supplier, you agree that the supplier will be able to deliver up to 12,000 chips in the first year—you settled on 12,000 because maybe you will get lucky and your product will turn out to be a bigger success than expected. What can go wrong with your arrangement? In short, the supplier might not be able to deliver the quantity you actually need.

If you agree that the supplier should be able to produce up to 12,000 units, then why might the supplier not deliver what you eventually need? One reason is that the supplier might not be willing to invest in enough capacity to make 12,000 chips given that you are unlikely to demand as many as 12,000 chips—capacity is not cheap and so the supplier does not want to purchase capacity that ends up not being well utilized. A second reason is that the supplier might not believe your demand forecast. The supplier knows that you have an incentive to be a bit optimistic with your forecast because you are not directly paying for capacity. Consequently, the supplier might believe that demand is more likely to be 7000 chips even though you said 10,000 chips. If the supplier adopts this more conservative forecast, then the supplier will be even more reluctant to build a substantial amount of capacity.

There are a number of strategies that firms can implement to help mitigate the challenge of variable supplier output. For example, it is essential that both parties agree on a credible forecast for demand. This can be achieved through building trust over a long-run relationship: It is okay if the buyer's forecast is too high some of the time, but it cannot be too high all of the time. Sharing information with the supplier regarding customers and demand can also help convince the supplier that the forecast is credible. You can also make your forecast more believable if you are willing to "back it up" by helping to pay for the supplier's capacity. This can be done by guaranteeing a minimum order quantity or by helping fund the purchase of raw materials or equipment.

The "failure in quantity" problem is particularly acute if the supplier's capacity can only be used to make your chip and you are the only potential demand for that chip. In that case, the supplier has good reason to worry about the demand for this component. But let's say you can make your gadget with an off-the-shelf chip, meaning that you can use a standard chip that is also used by other companies in their products. Now the supplier doesn't have to worry so much about your demand forecast because the supplier's capacity can be used to serve other customers as well. And you don't have to worry so much about your supplier's capacity because there are likely to be other suppliers that can supply the standard chip if needed. Hence, designing a product with standard components helps to mitigate this source of variability within the supply chain.

Failure in Quality In 2014, there were 60 million vehicles recalled in the United States to correct quality problems. To put that figure in perspective, 60 million vehicles represents about one in every five vehicles on the road in 2014. For example, General Motors recalled

2.2 million vehicles because a small pin in the ignition key was a bit too small. Nevertheless, due to that design flaw, which has been linked to 42 deaths, a vehicle could be "turned off" while traveling, thereby disabling the power to the vehicle for steering, braking, and air bag deployment.

Even larger than the GM recall, Honda was forced to recall over 6 million vehicles due to problems with its air bags. Those airbags were produced by Honda's tier 1 supplier, Takata. When functioning properly, the small explosive included in the airbag is used to quickly inflate the bag to prevent injury to the passengers. However, the airbags were actually acting somewhat like a grenade: When they deployed, parts of the metal canister housing the airbag shattered, sending metal fragments shooting through the passenger compartment.

Starting as early as 2001, Takata engineers tried to find the possible cause of the airbag explosions. At first, they attributed the problem to mishandling of the explosives in their Mexican facility. Unfortunately, the problems continued even after that issue had been addressed. Next, they concluded that the defect was due to flawed machinery in a factory in Wisconsin or due to improper worker operation of those machines. In the end, in addition to the Honda vehicles, over 14 million vehicles were recalled due to Takata airbags.

The auto industry recalls of 2014 illustrate that a supplier's quality can create uncertainty within the supply chain. In most cases, such quality failures are usually caught either by the supplier or by its customer before they have such dramatic consequences. However, even when a quality failure is detected, it creates additional costs (e.g., wasted labor and materials) as the failure is corrected or remediated.

Failure in Finances When a supplier sends product to a retailer, the retailer is usually given some time to pay (e.g., 30 days is typical). Usually the retailer does pay the supplier, but that might not happen if the retailer begins to experience financial difficulty. The retailer could delay paying the supplier (e.g., hoping to get cash from customers before sending a portion of that revenue to the supplier) or, in the worst-case scenario, the retailer could declare bankruptcy. When a bankruptcy occurs, the supplier may eventually get a portion of what it is owed, but rarely the full amount. And the variability associated with financial problems can work in the other direction within the supply chain: A manufacturer might find itself without a critical component if a key supplier declares bankruptcy.

Due to this source of variability, most firms require that their supply chain partners are "financially sound" before they approve working with them. Such due diligence helps to avoid working with unscrupulous or financially weak firms, but clearly this source of variability cannot be completely eliminated.

Failure in Operating Practice Even if a supplier delivers the quantity expected and the quality expected, there can still be consequences for how the supplier conducts its business. For example, in 2013 the Rana Plaza, an eight-story commercial building located in Bangladesh, collapsed, killing over 1100 people. Many of the dead were garment workers who were producing clothing items for well-known clothing companies selling in Europe and North America. Outrage over this incident grew as it was discovered that the workers were told to continue sewing in the building even though cracks had been discovered several days before the disaster.

The Rana tragedy is just one of many examples in which the actions of a supplier have implications throughout the supply chain. For example, Nike for many years has tried to calm protests about the practices of its suppliers, including allegations of the use of child labor, excessive work hours, and unsafe environmental conditions, among other concerns. Foxconn, a supplier for Apple, has been accused of maintaining a work environment that contributed to a high suicide rate among its employees. In addition to having a basic responsibility for human rights, managers that do business with these suppliers need to be concerned with the potential damage these actions can have on their own product's brand image with consumers.

It can be a daunting challenge to ensure that only acceptable practices are used within the supply chain. There may be thousands of suppliers that produce some portion of a company's product. For example, if you make soccer balls, then you will have suppliers that make leather, suppliers that dye the leather, and suppliers that stitch the balls together. There can be many small firms doing each of those tasks and they can be located in numerous countries and in remote locations. Furthermore, these suppliers probably produce products for other companies as well.

One approach to mitigate this source of uncertainty is to adopt industrywide standards. For example, your company is less likely to be put at a cost disadvantage if all of the firms in your industry agree to prohibit the use of child labor, to pay fair wages, to not use old-growth lumber, and so on. Second, inspections of your suppliers and your suppliers' suppliers and potentially even your suppliers' suppliers' suppliers are needed to ensure compliance. Third, many large companies have agreed to work with NGOs (nongovernment organizations)—instead of fighting the public protests of NGOs, companies have discovered that working with them can lead to positive change.

11.4.4 Variability Due to Disruptions

Because supply chains can span the globe and contain numerous layers, it is not surprising that they can be disrupted due to either natural or economic/political events.

Natural Disruptions The massive 9.0 Tōhoku earthquake hit Japan in March 2013. Although the direct consequences of the earthquake were substantial, the worst damage came from the subsequent tsunami, which significantly damaged the Fukushima nuclear plant, causing the worse release of radiation since the Chernobyl disaster in 1986. Not only did Japan lose the electricity produced from this plant, concern over nuclear safety led them to shut down the nuclear plants throughout the country, removing almost immediately about one-quarter of Japan's capacity to produce electricity.

As a car might have 15,000 different components, the Tōhoko earthquake had the potential to influence the world's auto supply chain in ways that were not fully anticipated. For example, the entire world's supply of Xirallic pigment, used to make car paint "shinier," was produced in a single plant near the Fukushima nuclear plant by Merck Chemicals, a German company. Because the plant could not operate for many months after the disaster, consumers were told throughout the world that their preferred color was not available.

Earthquakes are not the only environmental source of disruptions to a supply chain. For example, the Eyjafjallajökull volcano in Iceland erupted in 2010, shutting down air travel in Northern Europe for six days. Many of the world's regions are vulnerable to hurricanes and typhoons. Floods in 2011 in Thailand affected up to 25 percent of the world's capacity for computer hard drives. And fires (e.g., due to lightning strikes) can render a factory inoperable for days, weeks, or even months.

There isn't much a company can do to prevent disruptions caused by natural events, but this doesn't mean they should ignore these possibilities. For example, a company could identify all of its suppliers and catalog potential risks associated with their locations. For example, is the facility in an area prone to flooding or earthquakes, and how likely are those events based on past data? Through this process, a company may discover that it is very vulnerable to a disruption in a small set of components. In those cases, the company may want to find alternative suppliers to reduce this risk.

Cataloging potential risks cannot eliminate all of them or prevent disruptions. This is why it is important for a firm to put in place contingency plans that can be implemented soon after a disruption.

Political/Economic Disruptions Supply chains can be disrupted due to wars, conflicts, or other humanitarian crises that may emerge rapidly. As with natural disruptions, a firm should consider avoiding regions of political unrest and have contingency plans in place in case it nevertheless faces such a situation.

Supply chains are also vulnerable to the variability of currency exchange rates. For example, from April 2014 to March 2015, the euro lost about 23 percent of its value relative to the U.S. dollar. This is great if you are a German supplier of medical equipment to a U.S. hospital. To explain, say the German supplier sold its product for 100 euros. In April 2014, the U.S.

Check Your Understanding 11.5

Question: The Japanese yen increases in value relative to the dollar, moving from 120 yen to 110 yen to each U.S. dollar. From the perspective of a U.S. firm that produces in the United States and exports its product to sell in Japan:

  a. This is bad news.
  b. It doesn't matter.
  c. This is good news.

Answer: Now each sale in Japan is worth more in U.S. dollars, which allows the U.S. firm to earn a higher profit in terms of U.S. dollars from its sale in Japan, or it can lower its price in Japan and earn the same profit in terms of U.S. dollars. Therefore, the answer is C, this is good news.

hospital needed about $137 to buy the unit, but one year later the same unit only required about $105, making the German supplier's product more attractive in the U.S. market. In contrast, this swing in currency value is a big headache for a U.S.-based firm trying to sell to a European company. For instance, a French company in April 2014 needed about 0.73 euro to purchase each U.S. dollar, but in March 2014 the same company needed about 0.95 euro to purchase a U.S. dollar. From the point of view of the French company, buying materials in the United States became about 30 percent more expensive over the course of just one year, even if the U.S. suppliers didn't change their prices one bit!

One effective strategy to mitigate the risk of currency fluctuations is to locate production in the country where you are selling your product. For example, BMW, a German automaker, has decided to manufacture in the United States. BMW sells its cars in the United States in U.S. dollars, but it also pays its U.S. suppliers and workers in U.S. dollars as well. Thus, if there is a shift in the exchange rate between the euro and the U.S. dollar, then at least there is a shift in both the revenue BMW receives and the costs it incurs per vehicle. If BMW sells a vehicle in the United States that is manufactured in Germany, then a shift in the euro-to-U.S.-dollar exchange rate only influences the revenue it receives for each vehicle (because the car is priced in U.S. dollars) without influencing its costs (because it pays its German workers and suppliers in euros). As already mentioned, this is great for BMW if the euro weakens (because then each U.S. dollar is exchanged for more euros, meaning its profit per vehicle, measured in euros, increases), but terrible for BMW if the euro strengthens (because then each U.S. dollar is exchanged for fewer euros, meaning its profit per vehicle, measured in euros, decreases).

11.5 Supply Chain Strategies

In general, supply chain strategies attempt to reduce variability (e.g., mitigate the bullwhip effect, make-to-order, online retailing), increase flexibility (e.g., use faster transportation), and reduce costs (e.g., overseas sourcing). No one strategy applies in all cases, but companies have successfully used each of the following to gain additional market share and profit.

11.5.1 Mode of Transportation

LO11-5 Explain and evaluate different supply chain strategies for improving performance and enhancing competitiveness.

A sure-fire way to reduce inventory in a supply chain is to use faster transportation. But faster transportation is also expensive, so there is a trade-off between speed and inventory. This trade-off can be analyzed to evaluate the best option. To see how, the example illustrated in this section uses a streamlined version of the model described in greater detail in Chapter 14, Inventory Management with Frequent Orders.

Suppose you work for a manufacturer and you manage its inventory of a single component at one of its production facilities. To replenish your inventory, you place orders with a single supplier. Figure 11.8 depicts this supply chain.

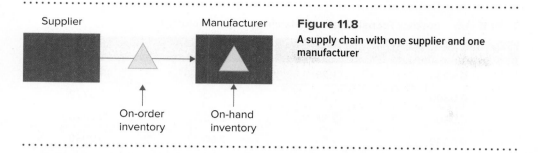

Supplier

Manufacturer

On-order
inventory

On-hand
inventory

Figure 11.8

A supply chain with one supplier and one
manufacturer

You can place an order with the supplier at regular intervals. The time between orders is called a **period**. For example, if you can place orders once a week, then the period is one week. If you can place orders once a day, then the period is a day. Let's assume your period is one week.

The **lead time** for an order is the number of periods between when the order is made and when it arrives. For example, say orders take 10 weeks to arrive, which means that the lead time is 10 weeks. If we let the variable L represent the lead time, then $L = 10$ weeks.

There is a cost, h, for each period a unit spends in inventory. For example, if we suppose it costs \$2 to hold an item in inventory for each week, then $h = 2$. There are a number of factors that contribute to the inventory holding cost h. In short, this cost accounts for the opportunity cost of the capital tied up in inventory, the cost to maintain inventory, and a cost for obsolescence risk associated with the inventory.

You are concerned with two types of inventory. **On-order inventory** is inventory that the supplier has shipped to you but you haven't received. It is also called in-transit inventory or pipeline inventory. **On-hand inventory** is inventory that is in your possession, ready to be used to serve your customer demand. Let I_o represent on-order inventory and I_h represent on-hand inventory. In Figure 11.8, the on-order inventory is depicted by the triangle between the supplier and the manufacturer, while the on-hand inventory is the triangle inside the manufacturer.

Unfortunately, demand is variable. Another way of saying this is that demand is uncertain, random, or stochastic. Although we cannot predict with certainty what demand will be in any one period, we are able to characterize the demand to some degree. In particular, we know the mean and the standard deviation of demand each period—let MEAN be the mean of demand and let STDEV.S be the standard deviation of demand in each period. In your case, for each week, MEAN = 1000 units and STDEV.S = 500.

Now we are ready to evaluate the amount of inventory in our supply chain:

$$I_o = L \times \text{MEAN}$$

$$I_h = \sqrt{L + 1} \times \text{STDEV.S} \times z$$

The first equation tells us that the amount of inventory on order, I_o, is proportional to the length of the lead time, L. The second equation tells us that the amount of inventory on hand, I_h, depends on three factors: the length of the lead time, L; the amount of demand variability, which is measured with the standard deviation of demand, STDEV.S; and z, which is the **safety factor**. The safety factor determines the probability that we are in-stock (i.e., the probability that all demand is satisfied in a period). To offer better service to our customers (in the sense of being more likely to satisfy their demand immediately), we need to choose a higher in-stock probability, which means selecting a higher safety factor. Similarly, the higher the selected safety factor, the better will be our service. Table 11.5 displays several commonly used in-stock probabilities and safety factors, z. The left-side table provides the safety factor given an in-stock probability. The right-side table gives the in-stock probability that results from a particular safety factor, z.

To continue our analysis, let's say we want an in-stock probability of 0.99. From Table 11.5, this means that we need to select a safety factor of 2.33. With the information we have collected, we can evaluate the two inventories in our supply chain:

$$I_o = L \times \text{MEAN} = 10 \times 1000 = 10,000$$

$$I_h = \sqrt{L + 1} \times \text{STDEV.S} \times z = \sqrt{10 + 1} \times 500 \times 2.33 = 3864$$

Period In the context of managing inventory, this is the time between when orders can be placed. For example, if the period is a day, then orders can be placed daily.

On-order inventory The inventory that the supplier has shipped but that has not been received.

On-hand inventory The inventory that is ready to be used to serve customer demand.

Safety factor A parameter that determines the in-stock probability. The higher the safety factor, the higher the in-stock probability as well as average on-hand inventory.

TABLE 11.5 In-Stock Probabilities and Matching Safety Factors, z

In-Stock Probability	Safety Factor, z	Safety Factor, z	In-Stock Probability
0.9000	1.28	1.25	0.8944
0.9800	2.05	2.00	0.9773
0.9900	2.33	2.25	0.9878
0.9950	2.58	2.50	0.9938
0.9999	3.72	3.00	0.9987

This means that, on average, there are 10,000 units on order and 3864 units on hand. Our total inventory in the supply chain is therefore $10,000 + 3864 = 13,864$ units.

Because our holding cost per unit per week is $h = \$2$, our total cost for holding inventory each week is

$$h \times (I_o + I_h) = \$2 \times (10,000 + 3864) = \$27,728$$

Each week we sell, on average, MEAN = 1000 units. So we can allocate the \$27,728 weekly inventory holding cost to the 1000 units that we sell each week, on average, to determine the holding cost we incur for each unit we sell:

$$\text{Holding cost per unit} = \frac{h \times (I_o + I_h)}{\text{MEAN}} = \frac{\$27,728}{1000} = \$27.73$$

In other words, in our supply chain with a 10-week lead time and a safety factor of 2.33, each unit incurs \$27.73 in inventory holding costs.

It is apparent from the equations for I_o and I_h that if we were to use faster transportation to reduce our lead time, we would need to hold less inventory while still providing the same level of service to our customers. Suppose, in fact, that there exists an opportunity to reduce the lead time to one week (e.g., via air cargo). How much would we be willing to pay per unit more for that faster lead time?

Table 11.6 summarizes the calculations for the inventory holding cost per unit when the lead time is 10 weeks, \$27.73. When those calculations are repeated for a one-week lead time, we discover that that inventory holding cost per unit drops to \$5.30. The faster lead time

TABLE 11.6 Summary of Calculations for the Inventory Holding Cost per Unit with Different Lead Times

Lead time	L	10	1
Average weekly demand	MEAN	1000	1000
Standard deviation of weekly demand	STDEV.S	500	500
Holding cost per unit	H	\$2	\$2
Safety factor	z	2.33	2.33
Average on-order inventory	$I_o = L \times \text{MEAN}$	10,000	1000
Average on-hand inventory	$I_h = \sqrt{L + 1} \times \text{STDEV.S} \times z$	3864	1648
Average total inventory	$I_o + I_h$	13,864	2648
Inventory holding cost per week	$h \times (I_o + I_h)$	\$27,728	\$5296
Inventory holding costs per unit	$\dfrac{h \times (I_o + I_h)}{\text{MEAN}}$	\$27.73	\$5.30

Check Your Understanding 11.6

Question: A firm orders on a daily basis and has a three-day lead time. Average demand each day is 20 units with a standard deviation of 10 units. The holding cost per unit is $0.01 per day and it desires an in-stock probability of 0.9773.

  a. How many units are on order on average?

Answer: On-order inventory = Lead time × Average demand = 3 × 20 = 60.

  b. How many units are on hand on average?

Answer: To achieve an in-stock probability of 0.9773 requires a safety factor of 2.0. On-hand inventory = $\sqrt{3+1}$ × 10 × 2 = 40.

  c. What is the holding cost it incurs per unit?

Answer: Average holding cost per unit = Holding cost per unit per unit of time × Total inventory/ Average demand per unit of time = $0.01 × (60 + 40)/20 = $0.05.

· ·

indeed reduces our inventory by a large amount (from 13,864 units, on average, to 2648 units, on average), which in turn dramatically reduces our inventory holding costs per unit.

So based on the figures in Table 11.6, we should be willing to pay as much as $22.43 = $27.73 − $5.30 more per unit in shipping to get the faster lead time. Put another way, if the shipping cost per unit with a one-week lead time is no more than $22.43 greater than the shipping cost per unit with our current 10-week lead time, then we are better off switching to the faster shipping. On the other hand, if the weight of these units is like bricks—meaning that shipping them by air to obtain the one-week lead time costs us more than $22.43 per unit— then we should stick with our slower and cheaper form of transportation.

11.5.2 Overseas Sourcing

Should a firm keep manufacturing within its own country or move its manufacturing to another country, potentially far away? The growth of the world economy is closely associated with more and more firms answering that question with "let's source from overseas." This has certainly helped to increase wealth in export-oriented regions, but it has also been controversial in countries that have lost jobs as a result of this shift in supply chain strategy.

Figure 11.9 helps explain why the tug of overseas sourcing can be so strong. In 2009, the average total hourly compensation cost in manufacturing in the United States was $34.19. That cost includes wages, but it also includes required social insurance expenditures (e.g., Social Security, health care) and other costs a firm may incur associated with hourly employment. In other words, workers in the United States didn't get paid $34.19 per hour, on average, but it cost their employer $34.19 per hour to employ them.

The variance in hourly compensation displayed in Figure 11.9 is stark: Norway tops the list with hourly costs that are 56 percent greater than in the United States (at $53.39 per hour), while hourly costs in China are only about one-twentieth the cost in the United States (at $1.74 per hour). Eastern Europe (e.g., Slovakia = $11.24 per hour) is indeed less expensive than northern Europe (e.g., Germany = $45.76 per hour) but is still more costly than the low-cost countries in Asia (e.g., Philippines = $1.71 per hour). But not all of Asia is low cost. The Republic of Korea has seen tremendous growth in its manufacturing compensation, and costs in Japan are comparable to those in the United States. And while some in the United States advocate for the low costs in "nearby" countries such as Mexico and Brazil, their costs are considerably higher than in China or India.

Although Figure 11.9 reveals the large differences in compensation across countries, the differences across countries have shifted considerably over time. For example, Figure 11.10 shows that hourly compensation in China grew 256 percent in the six years from 2003 to 2009! Try to imagine what would happen in the United States if compensation increased by

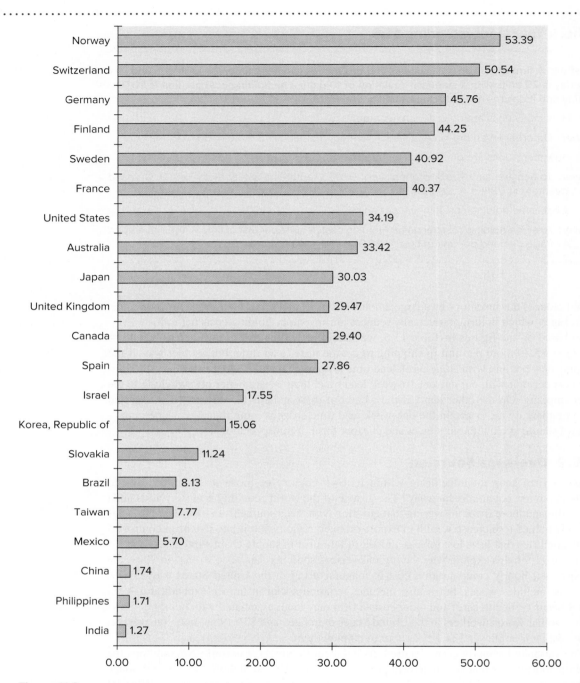

Figure 11.9

Hourly compensation costs (in U.S. dollars) for manufacturing, in 2009 in different countries
(Source: U.S. Bureau of Labor Statistics, http://www.bls.gov/fls/)

more than 2.5 times in just six years! While China remains among the low-cost countries in Figure 11.9, it will not remain that way for long if the trend in Figure 11.10 continues.

Although overseas production can reduce hourly compensation costs, a firm should not necessarily extend its supply chain to another country. Doing so usually increases the lead time to replenish inventory (because the product must be transported a far distance). Hence, a firm may face a trade-off between labor costs and inventory: the overseas location may reduce labor costs, but due to the longer lead time, it will increase the cost of holding inventory.

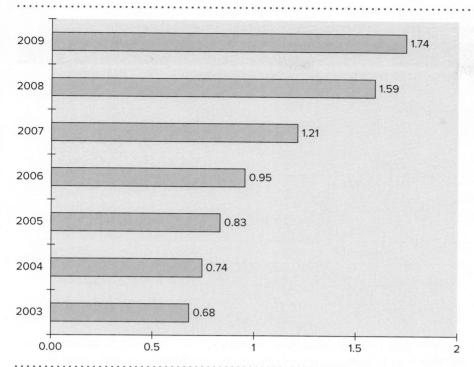

Figure 11.10

Hourly compensation costs (in U.S. dollars) for manufacturing in China (Source: U.S. Bureau of Labor Statistics, http://www.bls.gov/ilc/china.htm)

We can use the model in the previous subsection to compare supply chain options that differ in labor costs and lead times. For example, let's say we are deciding on manufacturing a shoe in China or the United States. The labor cost per shoe in China is $2.75, whereas it is $18 in the United States. The U.S. labor cost is "only" about 6.5 times greater than that in China because wages for shoe manufacturing in the United States are lower than the average manufacturing wage in the United States.

We plan to sell 3500 pairs per week with a standard deviation of 2500 pairs. The lead time from China is 12 weeks, whereas it is only 1 week with production in the United States. The holding cost per shoe per week with production in China is $0.14, while it is $0.25 with production in the United States. The difference in holding costs reflects the fact that the shoe's cost in the United States is higher, and, therefore, the opportunity cost of capital tied up in inventory is higher.

The safety factor is 2.33 no matter where production is located—we need to provide good availability to our customers!

It costs $1 per shoe to ship it from China to the United States, whereas transportation with U.S. production is only $0.25 per shoe—even with U.S. production, the shoes must be shipped from the factory to distributors and retailers.

Table 11.7 summarizes the calculations for the inventory holding cost per shoe for the two options. Although the holding cost per shoe per week is higher in the United States, sourcing in China results in much more inventory in the supply chain: 63,002 pairs of shoes, on average, versus 11,738 pairs. Consequently, inventory holding costs per pair of shoes manufactured in the United States is only one-third the cost for China: $0.84 versus $2.52.

Table 11.8 summarizes all of the costs with either option. Sourcing from China increases transportation and inventory holding costs per unit. But due to the wage differential between the two countries, the labor cost per unit is much higher in the United States. In the end, manufacturing the shoe in China results in $6.27 per shoe, whereas it is a whopping $19.09 per shoe in the United States. This difference of $12.82 per shoe is substantial. To illustrate, the manufacturer sells to the retailer at a price that equals twice its costs and the retailer sells to consumers at a price that is twice its costs because they both have other costs that they must cover (e.g., non-manufacturing employee salaries, advertising, rent, etc.). Hence, the $12.82

TABLE 11.7   Inventory Holding Cost Calculations for a Shoe Manufactured Either in China or the United States

		China	United States
Average weekly demand	MEAN	3,500	3,500
Standard deviation of weekly demand	STDEV.S	2,500	2,500
Lead time	L	12	1
Holding cost per unit per week	h	$0.14	$0.25
Safety factor	z	2.33	2.33
Average on-order inventory	$I_o = L \times \text{MEAN}$	42,000	3,500
Average on-hand inventory	$I_h = \sqrt{L + 1} \times \text{STDEV.S} \times z$	21,002	8,238
Average total inventory	$I_o + I_h$	63,002	11,738
Inventory holding cost per week	$h \times (I_o + I_h)$	$8,820	$2,935
Inventory holding costs per unit	$\dfrac{h \times (I_o + I_h)}{\text{MEAN}}$	$2.52	$0.84

difference in manufacturing cost could translate into a $12.82 × 4 = $51.28 difference in the retail price. That is a substantial increase in the cost per pair of shoes to "buy American."

The results in Table 11.8 are typical of apparel and footwear products. This is why the manufacturing of most of the items in those industries has moved to Asia—see Figure 11.11 and Connections: Nike. However, the analysis in Table 11.8 does not apply to all products. If the product is heavy or large, then it will have a high cost for transportation over long distances. If the product's labor content (the number of hours needed to make the product) is low relative to the final value of the product, then its inventory cost per unit will be high relative to the labor cost per unit. With that combination (costly to transport, low labor content, high product value), it can be better to produce locally rather than overseas even if labor is cheaper overseas. A good example of this is an automobile: Cars are heavy and large and labor isn't a large component of the product's cost. (With a car, the majority of the cost is in materials, such as metal, plastic, cloth, and electronics.) As a result, it can make good sense to manufacture cars in the country where they are sold (in addition to the benefits of protecting against exchange rate risks, as mentioned in the previous section). This is why many of the vehicles sold in the United States by "foreign" brands are actually assembled in the United States.

Local production can also make sense when it is risky to hold inventory due to obsolescence risk. For example, fashion is highly unpredictable in apparel. While most companies use overseas production to reduce their manufacturing costs, Zara takes the completely opposite strategy: They produce close to where they sell because they want to be able to bring new styles quickly to the market. See the Connections: Zara box for how they make this work.

TABLE 11.8   Comparison of Costs to Manufacture an Item in China or the United States

	China	United States
Labor cost per unit	$2.75	$18.00
Transportation cost per unit	$1.00	$ 0.25
Inventory holding costs per unit	$2.52	$ 0.84
Total cost per unit	$6.27	$19.09

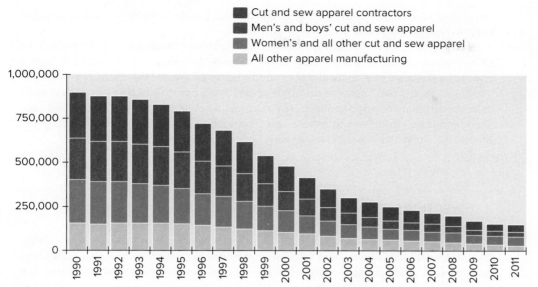

Cut and sew apparel contractors
Men's and boys' cut and sew apparel
Women's and all other cut and sew apparel
All other apparel manufacturing

Figure 11.11
Employment in apparel manufacturing and component industries, 1990–2011 (Source: U.S. Bureau of Labor Statistics)

Check Your Understanding 11.7

Question: A firm orders on a weekly basis with an eight-week lead time. Average demand each week is 100 units with a standard deviation of 50 units. The holding cost per unit is $0.10 per week and it desires an in-stock probability of 0.9773.

  a. How many units are on order on average?

Answer: On-order inventory = Lead time × Average demand = 8 × 100 = 800

  b. How many units are on hand on average?

Answer: To achieve an in-stock probability of 0.9773 requires a safety factor of 2.0. On hand inventory = $\sqrt{8+1} \times 50 \times 2 = 300$

  c. What is the holding cost it incurs per unit?

Answer: Average holding cost per unit = Holding cost per unit per unit of time × Total inventory/ Average demand per unit of time = $0.10 × (800 + 300)/100 = $1.10

CONNECTIONS: Nike

The emergence of Nike in the 1960s foreshadowed the growth of international trade. Before Phil Knight starting selling shoes in Oregon, running shoes were made locally and were primarily functional. Nike's success came from a realization that it could design shoes, but it didn't need to make the shoes. Consequently, shoes could be made overseas to take advantage of lower labor costs. The savings in manufacturing costs could then be used to finance endorsements from athletes, such as Michael Jordan, transforming the athletic shoe into a branded item desired for more than its functional use.

Although Nike's strategy brought it much success, it did have an Achilles' heel: Some of Nike's supplier's engaged in undesirable practices that threatened Nike's goodwill with its customers. Concerns included the use of child labor, forced overtime, wages below local

(continued)

requirements, coercion to prevent labor unions, and unsafe working conditions (e.g., fire risk, hazardous chemicals).

Nike's initial reaction to this issue was to claim that it was not responsible for the actions of its suppliers because it didn't own them. However, *Life* magazine published in 1996 a photo of a Pakistani boy stitching a Nike soccer ball in an article titled "Six Cents an Hour." The "ignorance is bliss" defense no longer seemed appropriate and Nike began to change its approach to managing suppliers. Nike now has a set of standards of conduct for suppliers and uses inspections to ensure compliance. With a network of over 700 suppliers around the world, this is a substantial task.

CONNECTIONS: Zara

It is not surprising that if overseas sourcing worked for sports apparel, then it could work for fashion apparel. Many companies followed that model, but not all. Zara was an outlier. Like many other companies, Zara designed its own clothes and sold them in its own stores. But unlike other companies, it didn't have its clothes manufactured overseas. Instead, it did its own manufacturing in the region where it started, in northern Spain.

Zara could have lowered its labor cost by moving production to countries like China, Sri Lanka, or Indonesia. But while manufacturing in Spain increased labor costs, it provided other advantages. For example, Zara's designers could imitate the latest designs coming out of Paris, Milan, or wherever, and have a similar-looking garment in its own stores within several weeks. Competitors simply could not match this capability—they didn't have control of the manufacturing process and, even if they did, the lead times from Asia were too long for such a quick response. With the ability to produce so quickly, Zara constantly changed the assortment of styles available in its stores. And because it produced only styles that it knew were popular at the moment, it rarely had excess inventory that needed to be marked down. Customers soon learned that if you liked an item at Zara, you should buy it because (i) you know it must be in style and (ii) the absence of markdowns and sales meant that the price will not be lower in several weeks. For Zara, the advantages of "fast fashion" (as it became known) outweighed the high cost of production in Europe. In fact, by 2014, Zara (along with several other brands that were later created by the parent company, Inditex) had become the world's largest fashion apparel company.

11.5.3 Make-to-Order

Many supply chains operate on a **make-to-stock** basis, meaning that production of an item occurs before the demand for that item has been identified. For example, a farmer grows a potato before she knows (or anyone else knows) who will actually eat the potato. Medtronic manufactures a device to keep a patient's heart working properly before it knows which patient will receive the device. And when a teenager purchases a Sony Xbox game console, the teenager is willing to take any new Xbox in the store.

With make-to-stock operations, a product is made and then it must wait for a customer to purchase it. This is done because customers can be impatient: Once they have identified their need, they want their need satisfied quickly. For example, imagine you need diapers for your baby, but you have to wait for the diapers to be made and delivered to the grocery store. I doubt many parents would actually wait, or, at a minimum, they would be super-irritated to do so. Consequently, diapers are made in anticipation of demand; that is, they operate with make-to-stock production.

Although people are generally impatient, sometimes they are willing to wait for their need to be satisfied. In that case, the final production of an item only occurs after the customer

Make-to-stock A mode of operations in which the production of an item occurs before the demand for that item has been identified.

announces the need. For example, most nice restaurants complete your meal only after you actually order it. This allows the restaurant to present a fresh meal and even allows it to customize the dish to your taste, as in how much you would like the meat to be cooked or whether it needs to ensure that a dish is vegetarian. In this case, the restaurant is said to operate on a **make-to-order** basis, meaning that the completion of products only occurs after customers announce their demand.

From the perspective of the supply chain, the distinction between make-to-stock and make-to-order can make a substantial difference. To explain, consider an example in which you are the paint manager for a hardware store. Suppose each week there are precisely 10 customers who each wish to purchase one gallon of paint from your store; that is, there is no uncertainty with respect to the level of demand. But customers have different preferences for color; in other words, there is uncertainty with respect to variety. For now, let's say you sell 10 different colors of paint and customers are equally likely to prefer any one of them.

Each can of paint costs you $20 to purchase from your supplier and you incur $0.25 in inventory holding cost per can per week it is in your store. It is not immediately obvious how many cans of each color should be kept in the store. It is possible that all 10 customers in a week might want the same color, but that would be highly unusual given that the colors are equally popular. In fact, there is only about a 1 in 500 chance that demand for any one color would be five or more in a week. Hence, you decide to keep four cans of each color in the store at all times. In total, the store keeps 40 cans of paint—four cans for each color and 10 colors.

According to Little's Law,

$$\text{Inventory} = \text{Flow rate} \times \text{Flow time}$$

which can be rewritten as

$$\text{Flow time} = \frac{\text{Inventory}}{\text{Flow rate}}$$

Our paint inventory is 40 cans and the flow rate is 10 cans per week, so the flow time is

$$\text{Flow time} = \frac{40 \text{ cans}}{10 \text{ cans per week}} = 4 \text{ weeks}$$

Thus, on average, a can of paint spends four weeks in inventory, incurring a total inventory holding cost of $1 = 4$ weeks $\times$ $0.25 per week. That isn't too bad—in total, our purchasing and holding cost per can is $21 = $20 + $1. If you sell each can for $30, then that leaves you with $9 to pay your employees, managers, rent, and other expenses. Hopefully, you are left with some profit after all of the expenses are added up. Let's say you would earn a profit of $1.50 per can (i.e., other expenses total to $7.50 per can).

While you might be able to get away with selling only 10 colors, it is unlikely that your customers will be happy with that sparse selection. People can be picky about colors and insist on just the right shade to match the rest of their décor. But let's see what happens if you offer 100 colors. Now there is only a 3 out of 500 chance that demand for any one color in any one week equals two or more cans. Hence, you really only need to stock one can per color. But in total that adds up to 100 cans of inventory (1 for each of the 100 colors). Even though you offer more variety, let's say you still only sell at the rate of 10 cans per week. So the flow time for each can of paint in this case is

$$\text{Flow time} = \frac{100 \text{ cans}}{10 \text{ cans per week}} = 10 \text{ weeks}$$

Now each can spends, on average, 10 weeks in inventory, incurring a total of $2.50 in holding costs (10 weeks at $0.25 per week). That is a $1.50 increase over the holding cost with 10 paint colors, enough to potentially eliminate your profit!

The analysis becomes even scarier if we realize that you actually need more than 100 colors. When colors vary from Apple Blossom pink to Battleship grey to Athenian blue, you realize that maybe you actually need at least 1000 colors to satisfy your customers. But with one can

Make-to-order A mode of operations in which the final production of an item occurs after the demand for that item has been identified.

per color, that means 1000 cans in inventory, but you are still selling only 10 cans per week. It follows that

$$\text{Flow time} = \frac{1000 \text{ cans}}{10 \text{ cans per week}} = 100 \text{ weeks}$$

which implies a holding cost per can equal to a whopping $25 (100 weeks × $0.25 per week). This means you would have to sell each can for at least $45 ($20 to purchase, $25 to keep in inventory) before you have any hope of making some profit. And that doesn't cover all of your other expenses. In short, you simply cannot offer that much variety in a make-to-stock fashion and sell the paint at a price that customers are willing to pay.

The solution to the paint problem has been known for a long time—don't stock cans of paint with color already added. Instead, keep 10 cans of "blank" paint in inventory; that is, cans that have everything except the color pigment. When a customer chooses a color, add the pigment to the can, shake well, and, voilà, you have produced in a make-to-order process the customer's desired product. The customer does have to wait for you to mix the can, but this can be achieved in about 10 minutes, which is probably not an excessive burden to your customers—who needs to start painting their walls within the next 10 minutes?! Make-to-order paint does require you to stock color pigments in inventory in addition to the cans of blank paint. But if you passed kindergarten class, you know that a few pigment colors can be combined in precise ways to make essentially any possible color. Finally, this make-to-order approach requires a machine to accurately add the correct amount of each pigment to the can, but that machine isn't too costly, especially if it is used to make many cans of paint over many years.

In the end, by switching to make-to-order production (i.e., start the final production of the paint only after learning the customer's demand), you are able to keep 10 cans of blank paint in inventory and offer thousands of colors. The flow time for each can is only

$$\text{Flow time} = \frac{10 \text{ cans}}{10 \text{ cans per week}} = 1 \text{ week}$$

which means the total inventory holding cost is only $0.25 per can. Table 11.9 summarizes the differences between make-to-stock and make-to-order.

In general, make-to-order is a viable strategy when (i) customers desire a broad selection of products, (ii) customers are willing to wait to receive their product, (iii) final assembly of the product can be done relatively quickly and cheaply, (iv) holding inventory is expensive, and (v) transporting the product to consumers is not too expensive relative to the product's value.

Retail paint is a market that is ideal for make-to-order. Customers indeed have a strong preference for variety (i.e., they are picky about color), and, as a result, they are willing to wait the 10 minutes needed for their paint to be mixed in the store. Their waiting time is minimal because the final assembly of the paint is relatively simple—all that needs to be done is to drop the right amount of each of the color pigments into the blank can. Consequently, only a few cans of blank paint are needed, saving on inventory holding costs. And because customers wait for their can in the store, there is no expense to ship the product to them.

TABLE 11.9   Summary of Inventory Differences between Make-to-Stock Operations and Make-to-Order Operations for a Paint Retailer

	Make-to-Stock			Make-to-Order
Number of colors offered	10	100	1000	1000+
Inventory (cans)	40	100	1000	10
Flow time (weeks)	4	10	100	1
Holding cost per can	$1	$2.50	$25.00	$0.25

Check Your Understanding **11.8**

Question: Company A sells four different mobile phones, while Company B wants to sell 40 different mobile phones. Which company is more likely to benefit from make-to-order production relative to make-to-stock production?

Answer: Company B has substantially more product variety, so it would benefit more from waiting for each customer to announce which product type he or she wants. Therefore, the correct answer is Company B.

· ·

CONNECTIONS: Dell

© Keith Eng/RF

The retail paint market is well-suited for make-to-order. The personal computer market from the mid 1980s to the mid 2000s was another setting that was particularly well-suited for make-to-order operations. Before Michael Dell started his company, all of the large firms in the industry operated make-to-stock and they struggled with the same problems of all make-to-stock operations: either too much or too little inventory.

To understand Dell's advantage, it is important to realize that during that time period, the prices of components continued to fall rapidly, in part from what has become known as Moore's Law: The number of transistors per square inch on integrated circuits doubled every two years. Due to this phenomenon, the cost of computing power fell continuously at a sharp rate. For example, a microprocessor that cost $1000 at the start of the year might fall at the rate of $8 per week, ending the year costing only $584.

Hewlett-Packard (HP), Compaq, and IBM were some of Dell's competitors. They all operated in a make-to-stock fashion and had up to 10 weeks of inventory in their supply chain. Consequently, when HP sold a computer in March, it probably contained a microprocessor that was purchased for $1000 about 10 weeks earlier. In contrast, Dell's make-to-order supply chain only had about 2 weeks of inventory. So on the same day HP sold its computer,

Continued

Dell could sell a computer with the same microprocessor, but Dell purchased that microprocessor only two weeks earlier, for around $936. Dell spent less on the microprocessor because it was about eight weeks "younger" than HP's. Hence, due to its lean inventory, Dell enjoyed a considerable cost advantage over its rivals. This allowed Dell to sell computers for less than its competitors, thereby enabling Dell to gain a greater share of the market, while at the same time earning a higher profit on each computer.

Unfortunately for Dell, their party didn't last forever. The world eventually moved away from personal computers to mobile devices and the needs in that market are different: mobile emphasizes design; consumers don't demand as much variety; and the pace of change is not as fast (e.g., Apple would introduce a new phone once a year rather than every couple of months).

Make-to-order can be an effective strategy for the supply chain because it delays the point at which a considerable amount of variety is added to the product. For example, with a make-to-stock paint process, color variety is created at the factory, upstream in the supply chain from the retailer. As discussed earlier, this is not effective. With make-to-order, the color variety is created downstream in the supply chain, at the retail store. In fact, some refer to the make-to-order strategy by the term **delayed differentiation**, meaning a supply chain in which product differentiation is delayed as late as possible in the process.

Delaying the creation of variety is useful because it eliminates one source of variability in the supply chain. In the paint example, there is no uncertainty with respect to the level of demand (it is always 10 cans per week), but there is considerable uncertainty with respect to the variety of demand, especially when many colors are offered. Make-to-order gives the flexibility needed to respond to that variety uncertainty after it is revealed. Consequently, with make-to-order, the retailer does not have to guess as to which color the customer wants, as with make-to-stock. Instead, the retailer merely waits for the customer to announce her color preference, thereby eliminating that uncertainty. See the Connections: Dell box for how Michael Dell used the make-to-order strategy so effectively in the personal computer industry.

11.5.4 Online Retailing

This may surprise you, but in the "old days," most people purchased books by going to a bookstore. They would browse the books on the shelves and possibly enjoy a cup of coffee or a conversation with another customer (imagine that). While actual physical bookstores still exist, online book retailers (of physical hard and soft cover) have clearly become a successful alternative.

All manner of things are now sold through online retailers. Compared to traditional brick-and-mortar retailers with physical stores, online retailers hold inventory in far fewer locations. And because there are fewer locations, on average they are farther from their customers. Consequently, online retailers must generally ship products to customers (which incurs a cost) and customers need to wait for their product to arrive. However, online retailers spend less than traditional retailers on the space to store their inventory, so it cannot be said that one type of retailing is always better than the other.

Let's use a very simple example to illustrate the pros and cons of online retailing as compared to traditional retailing. Figure 11.12 illustrates the two approaches to retailing. In either case, demand occurs in two distinct markets. The traditional retailer has a store in each market, so customers always visit the store nearest to them. The online retailer has a single fulfillment center, located somewhat distant from either market but nevertheless close enough so that products can be shipped to either market to arrive within several days.

Suppose that both retailers sell books and they sell the same book, *The Great Tramps of New Zealand*. In case you are wondering why anyone would write a book about tramps, or want to read about them, a "tramp" in New Zealand is a hike, and New Zealand has many spectacular trails to walk. That said, there are only so many people who are interested in a

Delayed differentiation A strategy in which product differentiation is delayed as late as possible in the supply chain.

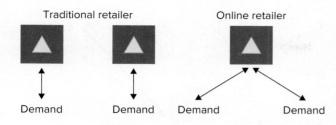

Traditional retailer   Online retailer

Demand   Demand   Demand   Demand

Figure 11.12

Two types of retailing. The traditional retailer serves two markets with one store located in each of the two markets. The online retailer serves the two markets with a single fulfillment center located some distance away from either market (so the product must be shipped to customers).

book focused on such a specific topic. So let's say that in any given month there is a four out of five chance that there is absolutely no customer interested in the book. However, there is a 0.2 probability that precisely one customer wants to purchase the book. Unfortunately, there does not exist a month in which two or more customers are willing to buy this book. Finally, if there is one unit of demand in a month, then it is equally likely to be in either market.

The traditional retailer stocks one copy of this book in each of its two stores. The online retailer only carries a single copy—no need to carry two given that demand is at most one unit. The traditional retailer incurs $1 in holding cost for each month a book spends in its inventory. The online retailer incurs only $0.20 in holding cost because it isn't paying for a store in a prime location. However, it costs the online retailer $3 to ship the book to a customer. Either retailer earns a gross margin of $10 on each sale (i.e., the selling price is $10 greater than the cost to purchase the book from the publisher). Table 11.10 summarizes the data in these two cases.

Both retailers face uncertainty in the level of demand: Demand can be either 0 units (with 0.8 probability) or 1 unit (with 0.2 probability). However, the traditional retailer also faces demand location uncertainty: If there is a unit of demand, then it can materialize in either of the two markets. In contrast, the online retailer does not face demand location uncertainty: No matter which market the demand materializes in, the customer is served from the same location. In effect, the online retailer supply chain avoids a source of demand variability with which the traditional retailer supply chain must cope. Put another way, a unit of inventory at the online retailer has the flexibility to serve demand in either market, but a book at one of the traditional retailer's stores can only serve demand in one market.

The traditional retailer incurs higher holding costs because, as already mentioned, it pays for nicer real estate, but also because it must stock two units (one in each market) rather than a single unit, which is all the online retailer needs. But the online retailer needs to pay for shipping, whereas the traditional retailer doesn't.

So what is the profit that either retailer can expect to make? For the traditional retailer, the expected profit each month is

$$\text{Profit} = (0.2 \times \$10) - \$2 = \$0$$

that is, there is a 0.2 probability a book is sold, earning a profit of $10, but $1 is incurred for each of the 2 books in inventory. Hence, the traditional retailer merely breaks even.

TABLE 11.10 Data for Each Type of Retailer

	Traditional Retailer	Online Retailer
Probability of one unit of demand	0.2	0.2
Gross margin on each unit	$10	$10
Holding cost	$1	$0.20
Shipping cost	$0	$3

Figure 11.13

The expected profit of a traditional retailer with two stores and the expected profit of an online retailer as a function of the probability that a customer arrives in a given month to purchase a unit

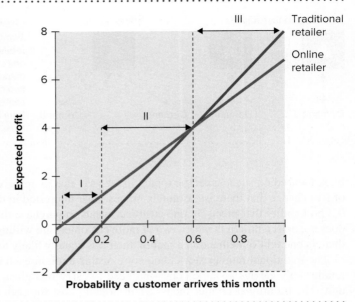

For the online retailer, the expected profit is

$$\text{Profit} = 0.2 \times (\$10 - \$3) - \$0.2 = \$1.2$$

that is, there is a 0.2 probability a book is sold, earning a profit of $7 = \$10 - \$3$ (accounting for the shipping cost), but $0.20 is incurred to hold inventory.

So if there is a one in five chance of selling a unit (i.e., a 0.2 probability), then the online retailer earns a positive profit, but the traditional retailer does not. But you shouldn't assume this is always true.

Figure 11.13 displays the expected profit of the two types of retailing for different values for the probability of demand. A couple of insights emerge from Figure 11.13. First, if there is a sufficiently small chance that somebody will want the book, then neither form of retailing makes a positive profit—it is hard to make money selling a book that very few people want to buy. But if enough demand occurs, the online retailing model makes a higher profit than the traditional retailer. This is the case if the probability of demand is between about 0.03 and 0.6, as indicated by regions I and II in Figure 11.13. In these cases, the online model is better because it is too costly to store inventory in multiple, high-priced locations when demand is uncertain to materialize.

In region I, the online retailer can make a positive profit, but the traditional retailer cannot. In region II, they both make a profit, but the online retailer earns more. In region III, they both make a profit, but the traditional retailer earns more. Table 11.10 summarizes cost and profit parameters.

All is not lost for the traditional retailer. According to Figure 11.13, if the probability of demand is sufficiently high (i.e., higher than 0.60), then it is better to sell through a physical store and avoid costly shipping (i.e., region III). Put another way, the online retailer must pay for shipping no matter how fast the product sells, but the holding cost depends on the demand rate, so when demand is sufficiently high, it is better to stock the item in a store for a short period of time and avoid the costly shipping.

The conclusion from our simple model is that if demand for a product in the area that could be served by a physical store is too small, then the traditional store cannot make a profit selling that item because it will spend too much time incurring costs on the store's shelves before it is sold (i.e., inventory holding costs are too high). However, because a retailer's fulfillment center can serve a much larger geographic region, it may be able to sell that slower-selling item profitably. This is why a traditional store almost always carries fewer than 100,000 different items, and often fewer than 50,000 different items—adding more products would mean

Check Your Understanding **11.9**

Question: Which product is more amenable to online retailing: regular dog food or a particular type of bird seed used only by customers who are avid about bird feeding?

Answer. Regular dog food probably has high demand in any market and would be costly to transport because it is heavy. Bird seed is probably lighter (relative to the value of the product) and a specialty bird seed is likely to have sparse demand in any one market. Thus, the correct answer is the bird seed.

....

including products with too little demand to be sold profitably. In contrast, an online store can offer millions of different items. Not only can the online store carry the most popular items (those with a high probability that demand materializes), it can make a profit on items that sell more slowly. This is the secret to Amazon.com's success—see the Connections: Amazon box for more.

   You may have noticed a similarity between online retailing and make-to-order production. Both of those strategies enable a firm to dramatically increase the variety of products offered to consumers while also keeping costs under control. In fact, these two approaches work in essentially the same way: They both increase flexibility and reduce variability associated with product variety.

CONNECTIONS: Amazon

© Gregor Schuster/Photographer's Choice RF/Getty Images/RF

When Jeff Bezos started his company in 1994, he wanted to create the world's largest bookstore in terms of selection. So he named it Amazon.com after the world's largest river system. His initial business model was simple. He would have a single warehouse in Seattle, near a large book distributor. The tech climate of Seattle allowed him to hire the coders he needed, and the time difference with the rest of the country allowed him a few extra hours to package books for shipment to the East Coast. His plan was to offer at least a million titles, substantially more than the typical bookstore with 40,000 or fewer titles. But he didn't want to hold much inventory, in part because, as a startup, he didn't have the cash. Instead, when he received an order, he would request the book from the nearby distributor and only then ship the book to the customer.

Continued

The Amazon.com model worked great for books and it worked great for plenty of other things as well. Amazon.com really was on its way to becoming the worlds biggest retailer—Figure 11.14 shows the near meteoric rise of sales revenue at Amazon.

While Amazon was able to maintain torrid growth for its first 20 years, its business model did not exactly stay the same. Now Amazon needs to operate many fulfillment centers for two reasons: (i) no single fulfillment center can efficiently handle Amazon's current sales volume and (ii) Amazon recognizes that customers want fast delivery, which can only be achieved if the inventory is moved closer to where they live. In fact, Amazon is dreaming of delivery times measured in hours rather than in days—and possibly delivering products with its own drones! As a result of its desire to provide quick service to customers, Amazon now actually holds more inventory than Walmart relative to its sales rate (i.e., Amazon's average unit of inventory spends more time in its system than a unit of inventory spends in Walmart's system). This completely contradicts the initial premise that online retailers do not have to carry inventory. But what remains true is that Amazon's selection of products is indeed the world's largest.

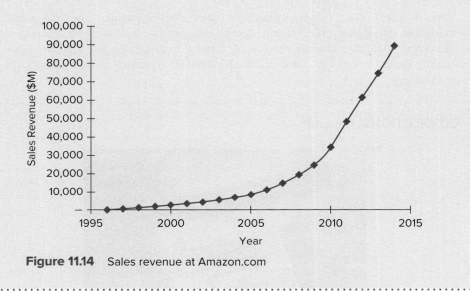

Figure 11.14   Sales revenue at Amazon.com

To explain the connection between online retailing and make-to-order production, note that with online retailing a product can be considered a bundle of two things: a physical good and a location. For example, you may want to purchase a package of rooibos tea and you live in Wappingers Falls, New York. The package of tea is held in a fulfillment center and only after you reveal that you live in Wappingers Falls is the tea sent to you. Because customers live in many different places, the beauty of online retailing is that the firm does not need to try to guess which locations will want rooibos tea. The same avoidance of variability in variety occurs with make-to-order. Now a product is a bundle of a physical good and some differentiating attribute. For example, a can of Athenian blue paint is made up of a can of blank paint and some blue pigment to give it its differentiating color. Instead of stocking Athenian blue paint, the retailer only stocks the blank paint and waits for the customer to reveal his or her preference for color. With an online retailer, the differentiating component is the customer's location, whereas with make-to-order paint, the differentiating component is color. Put another way, online retailing eliminates the considerable uncertainty associated with customer location, while make-to-order eliminates the considerable uncertainty associated with customer preferences for a product attribute. In each case, by avoiding the uncertainty (through a more flexible process), more options can be offered to the customer.

Conclusion

All modern firms are part of some supply chain. Therefore, supply chain management is as critical to the success of a firm as strong and capable internal processes.

At the highest level, supply chain management is about making a trade-off between cost and flexibility. Flexible supply chains are better able to cope with variability but are also more expensive to operate. Unfortunately, managers all too often underinvest in flexibility because the value of flexibility can be hard to quantity, but the cost of flexibility is readily apparent. That said, analytical tools are available to assist a manager in choosing between fast or slow transportation or to select a production location among several options that differ in their labor costs.

Many firms have become successful by innovating in the design and operations of their supply chain. For example, firms have used overseas sourcing to dramatically reduce their costs, or they have used domestic sourcing to ensure fast responsiveness to changes in the marketplace. To greatly expand the variety offered to customers, a firm can switch from make-to-stock production to make-to-order production. A retailer can expand the variety of products available to its customers by moving away from physical stores and instead selling through an online website or app. Although customers with make-to-order and online retailing have access to a greater breadth of options, they also must wait longer for their product to be delivered. Nevertheless, there are many markets in which consumers don't mind the delay.

Summary of Learning Objectives

LO11-1 Explain the roles and value of each layer within a supply chain

Supply chains consist of many different firms and locations. Although each supply chain has its own distinct structure, most supply chains consist of five layers, with each having its own role for creating value: tier 2 suppliers, tier 1 suppliers, manufacturers, distributors, and retailers. The supply chain starts with a firm making a raw material or specific component (tier 2 suppliers), then progresses to firms that create integrated, more complex components (tier 1 suppliers). Manufacturers design and assemble complete products. Distributors facilitate the efficient delivery of products to the market and retailers offer a product assortment to consumers and the convenience of either being in a consumer's local market or providing services to ship the product to the consumer quickly.

LO11-2 Explain the metrics used to evaluate the performance of a supply chain

Supply chains are evaluated on both cost and service metrics. The key cost metrics are procurement, labor, inventory, and transportation. Procurement is the cost of purchasing materials and labor is the cost of workers throughout the supply chain. Inventory is the cost of holding inventory, including the opportunity cost of capital tied up in inventory, the cost of storage and maintenance, and the cost of depreciation or obsolescence. Transportation is the cost of moving product within the supply chain and to consumers. The key service metric is the in-stock probability—the probability that all demand is satisfied within an interval of time.

LO11-3 Explain the differences between tactical and strategic decisions and the main trade-offs in making strategic decisions

Supply chains must make both tactical and strategic decisions and they must do both well. Tactical decisions are ones that have short-term implications, like how many boxes of a particular product should be ordered today for delivery next week. Any one tactical decision impacts the firm in the next several days or weeks. Strategic decisions have long-term implications, such as decisions that impact performance in the next year, several years, or even decade. Strategic decisions include where to locate facilities, which suppliers or distributors/retailers to work with, and what mode of transportation to use throughout the supply chain.

LO11-4 Explain the sources of variability within a supply chain and some approaches for mitigating variability

Supply chains face variability in many forms. Demand can be variable in its level (the total amount of demand), in variety (which products are demanded), and in location (where demand materializes). Although consumer demand variability can be considerable, the supply chain can generate variability within itself. This phenomenon, known as the bullwhip effect, tends to amplify demand as it moves to higher levels of the supply chain (away from retailers and toward suppliers). Aside from demand, a supply chain faces variability from the performance of the supply chain members: For example, do they deliver the quantity or quality needed, do they remain financially sound, and do they conduct their business in an acceptable manner? Finally, supply chains are subject to the variability of uncertain natural (e.g., floods, earthquakes) and political/economic (war, exchange rate fluctuations) events.

LO11-5 Explain and evaluate different supply chain strategies for improving performance and enhancing competitiveness

Supply chain strategies generally involve making a trade-off between cost and flexibility. For example, air transportation is more expensive than sea transportation, but it also allows a firm to respond more quickly to demand (i.e., it reduces the lead time). Overseas production may reduce labor costs, but it also increases the amount needed for inventory due to the longer lead times. Make-to-order production requires a firm to be able to respond quickly to consumer demand (because consumers don't want to wait too long), but it also gives the firm the ability to offer a broad selection of products without incurring substantial inventory costs. Online retailing is similar to make-to-order production in the sense that the online retailer commits to where it will sell a product only after a consumer announces his or her need. Consequently, online retailers generally offer a much broader selection of products than local, traditional retailers.

Key Terms

11.1 Supply Chain Structure and Roles

Brick-and-mortar retailer A retailer with physical stores in which consumers are able to immediately purchase goods.

Mail-order retailers Retailers that merchandize their goods via a print catalog and sell to consumers by shipping them goods via a third-party carrier like the U.S. Postal Service, UPS, FedEx, or DHL. Also called catalog retailers.

Catalog retailers Retailers that merchandize their goods via a print catalog and sell to consumers by shipping them goods via a third-party carrier like the U.S. Postal Service, UPS, FedEx, or DHL. Also called mail-order retailers.

Online retailers Retailers that merchandize their goods via an online website (or app) and sell to consumers by shipping them goods via a third-party carrier like the U.S. Postal Service, UPS, FedEx, or DHL. Also called e-commerce or e-tailers.

E-commerce Retailers that merchandize their goods via an online website (or app) and sell to consumers by shipping them goods via a third-party carrier like the U.S. Postal Service, UPS, FedEx, or DHL. Also called online retailers or e-tailers.

E-tailers Retailers that merchandize their goods via an online website (or app) and sell to consumers by shipping them goods via a third-party carrier like the U.S. Postal Service, UPS, FedEx, or DHL. Also called online retailers or e-commerce.

Distribution center (DC) A building used to receive products from suppliers and then redistribute them to retail stores or send packages to consumers. Also called a fulfillment center.

Fulfillment center A building used to receive products from suppliers and then redistribute them to retail stores or send packages to consumers. Also called a distribution center.

Lead time The time to receive an order.

Breaking bulk A service in which a distributor purchases in large quantities from manufacturers but then allows customers to purchase in smaller quantities.

Pallet Either (1) a platform, often wooden, used as a base to store inventory and to facilitate moving that inventory via a forklift or (2) the quantity of inventory that is stacked on the platform.

11.2 Metrics of Supply Chain Performance

In-stock probability The probability that all demand is served within an interval of time.

Stockout probability The probability that demand for an item exceeds its inventory during a period of time.

Fill rate The fraction of demand satisfied.

11.3 Supply Chain Decisions

Tactical decisions Decisions that impact short-term performance.

Strategic decisions Decisions that have long-term implications.

Functional products In the context of strategic supply chain decisions, these are products that are relatively "safe" in the sense that they do not experience a considerable amount of variability.

Gross margin The difference between the price at which a product is sold and the cost to purchase the item, expressed as a percentage of the selling price of the item.

Innovative products In the context of strategic supply chain decisions, these are products that are relatively "risky" in the sense that they can experience substantial variability.

Physically efficient In the context of strategic supply chain decisions, these are supply chains that are designed to minimize costs.

Market-responsive In the context of strategic supply chain decisions, these are supply chains that are designed to emphasize flexibility over cost.

11.4 Sources of Variability in a Supply Chain

Bullwhip effect The tendency for demand to become more volatile at higher levels of the supply chain.

11.5 Supply Chain Strategies

Period In the context of managing inventory, this is the time between when orders can be placed. For example, if the period is a day, then orders can be placed daily.

On-order inventory The inventory that the supplier has shipped but that has not been received.

On-hand inventory The inventory that is ready to be used to serve customer demand.

Safety factor A parameter that determines the in-stock probability. The higher the safety factor, the higher the in-stock probability as well as average on-hand inventory.

Make-to-stock A mode of operations in which the production of an item occurs before the demand for that item has been identified.

Make-to-order A mode of operations in which the final production of an item occurs after the demand for that item has been identified.

Delayed differentiation A strategy in which product differentiation is delayed as late as possible in the supply chain.

Key Formulas

LO11-2 Explain the metrics used to evaluate the performance of a supply chain

$$\text{In-stock probability} = 1 - \text{Stockout probability}$$

LO11-5 **Explain and evaluate different supply chain strategies for improving performance and enhancing competitiveness**

L = Lead time

Mean = Average demand in a unit of time (e.g., one week)

STDEV.S = Standard deviation of demand in a unit of time (e.g., one week)

z = Safety factor

h = Holding cost per unit in a unit of time (e.g., one week)

$$I_o = \text{Average on-hand inventory} = L \times \text{Mean}$$

$$I_h = \text{Average on-hand inventory} = \sqrt{L+1} \times \text{STDEV.S} \times z$$

$$\text{Holding cost per unit} = \frac{h \times (I_o + I_h)}{\text{MEAN}}$$

$$\text{Flow time} = \frac{\text{Inventory}}{\text{Flow rate}}$$

In-Stock Probability	Safety Factor, z	Safety Factor, z	In-Stock Probability
0.9000	1.28	1.25	0.8944
0.9800	2.05	2.00	0.9773
0.9900	2.33	2.25	0.9878
0.9950	2.58	2.50	0.9938
0.9999	3.72	3.00	0.9987

Conceptual Questions

LO11-1

1. Firm A manufactures brake pads, a component of a braking system, and sells them to firm B, who sells braking systems used in vehicles. Firm A is best described as a:
   a. Tier 2 supplier.
   b. Tier 1 supplier.
   c. manufacturer.
   d. distributor.
   e. retailer.

2. Which of the following statements best explains why distributors tend to spend less on storage space per square meter per year than retailers?
   a. Distributors provide break bulk service.
   b. Distributors don't actually make products.
   c. Distributors can store more items per square meter and require space that is less aesthetically pleasing.
   d. Distributors enjoy higher gross margins than retailers.

3. Which of the following best explains why distributors help to reduce the space retailers need to store inventory?
   a. Distributors allow retailers to receive truckload shipments more frequently.
   b. Distributors decrease the total distance products travel in the supply chain.
   c. Distributors allow retailers to receive smaller quantities of each supplier's product.
   d. Distributors increase the time that inventory spends in the supply chain.

LO11-2

4. What is the relationship between the average inventory and the in-stock probability?
   a. The more the inventory, the lower the in-stock probability.
   b. There isn't a definitive relationship—more inventory could mean a lower or a higher in-stock probability.
   c. The more the inventory, the higher the in-stock probability.

5. What is the relationship between a location's in-stock probability and the lead time that location delivers on shipments to its customers?
   a. The higher the in-stock probability, the smaller the lead time.
   b. There isn't a definitive relationship—a higher in-stock probability could mean a smaller or a greater lead time.
   c. The higher the in-stock probability, the greater the lead time.

LO11-3

6. Characterize the following decision as either tactical or strategic: Which tier 1 supplier should be used for a particular component system?
   a. Tactical   b. Strategic

7. Characterize the following decision as either tactical or strategic: To operate make-to-stock or make-to-order.
   a. Tactical   b. Strategic

8. Characterize the following decision as either tactical or strategic: The discounts to offer on inventory available for an end-of-season sale.
   a. Tactical   b. Strategic

LO11-4

9. Which of the following is the best reason to add a second supplier for a critical component?
   a. The primary supplier is located in a flood-prone region, while the second supplier's location is not subject to flooding.
   b. The second supplier is able to offer the same lead time as the first supplier.
   c. Adding a second supplier helps reduce the bullwhip effect.
   d. Adding a second supplier will increase the firm's purchasing power for the component.

10. Sorlini Pasta sells pasta throughout Italy. Which of the following is the strongest evidence that Sorlini Pasta is suffering from the bullwhip effect?
    a. They hold a considerable amount of inventory, enough to satisfy their average demand for the next four weeks.
    b. Just before a snowstorm in the northern part of the country, sales of pasta increased considerably.
    c. Sorlini sells both fresh and dry pasta products through different types of retailers.
    d. Most retailers only carry a subset of all of the pastas Sorlini offers.
    e. The volatility of the orders Sorlini receives from its distributors is greater than the volatility of pasta demand at retailers.
    f. Pasta consumption per capita in southern Italy is higher than in northern Italy.

11. Retailers order in full truckload quantities from a distributor. Suppose, due to a slowdown in the economy, there is an industrywide decline in demand (i.e., each retailer experiences a reduction in its sales). If retailers continue to order in full truckload quantities, what will happen to the frequency of their orders?
    a. It will decrease.
    b. It will not change.
    c. It will increase.
    d. We cannot determine how it will change from the given information.

12. Which of the following are likely to be symptoms of the bullwhip effect in a supply chain comprised of consumers, a retailer, a wholesaler, and a factory?
    I. Variability of orders from the retailer to the wholesaler is higher than variability of orders from the wholesaler to the factory.
    II. Variability of orders from the wholesaler to the factory is lower than the variability in consumer demand to the retailer.
    III. Variability in consumer demand is lower than the variability of orders from the retailer to the wholesaler.
    a. I only   e. I and III but not II
    b. II only   f. II and III but not I
    c. III only   g. I, II, and III
    d. I and II but not III

LO11-5

13. A company is deciding whether to produce a new gadget at a plant located in a country close to consumers at a higher labor cost and shorter lead time or to outsource it to a country with a low labor cost but a longer lead time. All else being equal, which of the following considerations would provide the most support to produce in the high-cost location?
    a. The holding costs per unit are low.
    b. Transportation costs per unit per km are low.
    c. The in-stock probability requirement for the product is high.
    d. Customers are willing to wait for delivery.

14. Over time, consumers have less of a need for a broad product offering. How does this shift in preferences alter the desirability of make-to-stock production relative to make-to-order production?
    a. It increases it; that is, make-to-stock becomes more desirable.
    b. It has no impact.
    c. It decreases it; that is, make-to-stock becomes less desirable.
    d. We cannot determine from the given information.

Solved Example Problems

LO 11-2

1. An online retailer carries 50,000 items. During a particular week, the retailer sold some units from 15,000 different items. There were 1000 items for which some demand was not satisfied. What was the retailer's stockout probability?

    Answer: 2 percent. The percentage of items that did not satisfy all demand = 1000/50,000 = 2 percent.

2. Adirondack Sports (AS) sells high-end climbing and hiking equipment. The following table provides data from the previous quarter for their Outback trekking poles (that differ in length):

	Outback 90 cm	Outback 100 cm	Outback 110 cm	Outback 120 cm	Outback 130 cm
Starting inventory	400	500	600	500	300
Ending inventory	50	100	75	10	0

They did not receive any inventory replenishments during the quarter. What was their in-stock probability for Outback poles?

    Answer: 80 percent. Four out of five products had inventory at the end of the quarter, so they must have satisfied all demand. The longest size ran out of inventory, so we can assume that some demand for that size was not satisfied.

LO 11-5

3. A local health clinic requires, on average, 100 hypodermic syringes each day, with a standard deviation of 30 units. Inventories are reviewed and orders are placed daily. There is a one-day lead time for orders. The holding cost per syringe per day is $0.05. The clinic wishes to operate with a 0.9987 in-stock probability.

   (a) On average, how many syringes does it have on order?

    Answer: 100. $I_o = L \times \text{MEAN} = 1 \times 100 = 100$

   (b) On average, how many syringes does it have on hand?

    Answer: 127.3. Using Table 11.5, we see that a safety factor of $z = 3$ is needed for an in-stock probability of 0.9987. Thus,

$$I_h = \sqrt{L+1} \times \text{STDEV.S} \times z = \sqrt{1+1} \times 30 \times 3 = 127.3$$

(c) If its average inventory was 250 units, what would be its average holding cost per day?

> **Answer:** $12.50. Holding cost per day = Inventory × Holding cost per day per unit = 250 × $0.05 = $12.50

(d) If its average inventory was 300 units, what would be its average holding cost per unit?

> **Answer:** $0.15. Holding cost per unit = Holding cost per unit per day × Total inventory/Average demand per day = $0.05 × 300/100 = $0.15

4. Albrech's is an upscale garden center that sells a clay orchid pot. Inventory is reviewed weekly and there is a one-week lead time to receive orders. Average weekly demand is 20 units with a standard deviation of 10. On average, they have 36.5 pots on hand in the store. What in-stock probability do they offer to their customers?

> **Answer:** 0.9950. $I_h = \sqrt{(L+1)} \times$ STDEV.S $\times z = 36.5$. The lead time is 1 and the standard deviation is 10, so the on-hand inventory equation can be written as $\sqrt{1+1} \times 10 \times z = 36.5$.
>
> We can solve for z, obtaining $z = 2.58$. From Table 11.5, a safety factor of 2.58 yields an in-stock probability of 0.9950.

5. Peron Appliances is a Spanish company that is considering moving its manufacturing of dishwashers from Spain to Mexico. It requires three hours of labor to make a dishwasher. In Spain, the cost of each hour of labor is 25 euros. In Mexico, the cost of each hour would be 5 euros. The holding cost per dishwasher per week in Spain is 2 euros, while in Mexico it is 1.5 euros. In Spain, it places orders with the factory weekly and there is a three-week lead time. If production moves to Mexico, the lead time would be 15 weeks. Weekly demand is 500 dishwashers with a standard deviation of 100 dishwashers. It operates with a safety factor of 3.

(a) If it keeps production in Spain, on average how many units of inventory will it have on order and on hand?

> **Answer:** 2100. Given a three-week lead time, its on-order inventory = 3 × 500 = 1500. Its on-hand inventory = $\sqrt{3+1} \times 100 \times 3 = 600$. Total inventory = 1500 + 600 = 2100

(b) If it moves production to Mexico, on average how many units of inventory will it have on order and on hand?

> **Answer:** 8700. Given a 15-week lead time, their on-order inventory = 15 × 500 = 7500. Their on-hand inventory = $\sqrt{15+1} \times 100 \times 3 = 1200$. Total inventory = 7500 + 1200 = 8700

(c) If it keeps production in Spain, what is its holding cost per dishwasher (in euros)?

> **Answer:** 8.4 euros. Holding cost per unit = Holding cost per unit per week × Total inventory/Mean demand = 2 × 2100/500 = 8.4

(d) If it moves production to Mexico, what is its holding cost per dishwasher (in euros)?

> **Answer:** 26.1 euros. Holding cost per unit = Holding cost per unit per week × Total inventory/Mean demand = 1.5 × 8700/500 = 26.1

(e) What would be the change in the cost per dishwasher (holding cost and labor cost) if it moves production to Mexico?

> **Answer:** 42.3 euros. The labor cost in Spain is 3 hours × 25 euros per hour = 75 euros. In Mexico, it is 3 hours × 5 euros per hour = 15 euros. So if production is moved to Mexico, then the difference in cost per dishwasher is (75 + 8.4) − (15 + 26.1) = 42.3.

Problems and Applications

LO11-2

1. For 10 percent of the products in a category, a firm fails to satisfy all demand during the month. What is its in-stock probability?

LO11-5

2. Anvils Works' requires, on average, 2800 tons of aluminum each week, with a standard deviation of 1000 tons. The lead time to receive its orders is 10 weeks. The holding cost for one ton of aluminum for one week is $11. It operates with a 0.98 in-stock probability.
   a. On average, how many tons does it have on order?
   b. On average, how many tons does it have on hand?
   c. If its average inventory was 5000 tons, what would be its average holding cost per week?
   d. If its average inventory was 10,000 tons, what would be its average holding cost per ton of aluminum?
   e. Suppose its on-hand inventory is 4975 tons, on average. What in-stock probability does it offer to its customers?

3. A laptop manufacturer wants to compare the total cost of assembling its laptops in the United States versus Taiwan. All of the laptops will be sold in the United States. To evaluate inventory, it uses a safety factor of 2.25. The holding cost per laptop is $4 per week in the United States and $3.50 per week in Taiwan. The lead time with U.S. production is one week, whereas it is eight weeks with production in Taiwan. In addition, it costs $2 to ship laptops to the United States from Taiwan. Weekly demand is 1000 laptops, with a standard deviation of 800.
   a. What is the per unit holding cost of a laptop with U.S. production?
   b. What is the per unit holding cost of a laptop with production in Taiwan?
   c. A laptop requires 40 minutes of labor to assemble in the United States or in Taiwan. The total cost of labor in the United States is $40 per hour, while in Taiwan it is $10. What is the change in cost per laptop if it switches production to Taiwan?

CASE   TIMBUK2

Rob Honeycutt created Timbuk2 to offer consumers the ability to make their own, custom, three-panel messenger bags. And instead of following the standard strategy of manufacturing in Asia, Rob set up Timbuk2 in San Francisco with its own facility. But is this the best strategy? Should it consider moving production to China?

The image on the right displays a screenshot from Timbuk2's online retailing website that allows customers to customize their messenger bag to their own particular tastes. A customer can select one color for each of the three panels and a separate color, if they want, for the Timbuk2 "swirl" logo. The color options change over time, to keep things "fresh," but at any one time Timbuk2 generally offers at least 16 options for each panel and the logo.

Once customized, Timbuk2 manufactures the bag in San Francisco and then ships the bag to the customer within two to three days.

www.timbuk2.com. Courtesy of TIMBUK2

Timbuk2 sells bags though its online store for about $100 per bag. Although it would love to sell bags only through its website and to sell many more of them, the market for custom bags at this price point is only so big. So Timbuk2 sells bags through other channels as well. For example, retailers such as REI purchase a limited selection of bags to sell in their stores. While Timbuk2 appreciates sales through this wholesale channel, they don't generate the same revenue per bag as the online channel—more like

$35 per bag. Even though the wholesale bags generally do not involve nearly the same level of customization as the online bags (i.e., retailers tend to select more conservative color combinations), those bags are made on the same production line as the online bags. However, the promised lead time to wholesale customers is longer, more like two to three weeks.

The decision as to whether to send production to China involves a number of issues. Table 11.11 provides a cost comparison between production in San Francisco and in China. There is clearly a dramatic difference in labor costs on a per-hour basis, but the workers in San Francisco are slightly more productive (they require 49 minutes per bag instead of 63 minutes). Material costs do not differ between the two options, because in both cases materials are procured in China. It costs $1 per bag to send it from China via ocean carrier, but the lead time is probably eight weeks when all of the steps are accounted for (e.g., production, movement to the port, and actual shipping). To get a faster lead time would require air shipments, but that is much more expensive: $15 per bag.

Of course, Table 11.11 doesn't tell the entire story. There would be costs associated with finding a good supplier and monitoring that supplier. And it isn't clear how Timbuk2's customers would react to the move—from its start, Timbuk2 emphasized with pride that it was made in San Francisco. Does moving production to China eliminate part of the brand's cache with customers?

1. What is the total cost of making a bag in San Francisco? What is the total cost of making a bag in China, including the transportation cost of shipping the bag from China to the United States?

2. Suppose Timbuk2 does move production of wholesale bags to China. Let's say it can place orders with its Chinese supplier every four weeks; that is, one period equals four weeks. Its lead time is two periods; that is, $L = 2$. Average demand for one type of wholesale bag is 200 bags per period (i.e., they sell, on average, 200 bags every four weeks), with a standard deviation of 100 bags. The holding cost for each bag each period is $1, and it would operate with a 2.5 safety factor. How much inventory, on average, would it have on order and on hand? What would be the inventory holding cost per bag?

3. Should it move production of custom bags to China? Should it move production of wholesale bags to China?

TABLE 11.11 Production and Shipment Costs per Bag by Production Location

	San Francisco	China	Comments
Hourly wage	$12.50	$1.25	Includes benefits
Labor content	49 minutes	63 minutes	
Materials	$13	$13	
Other manufacturing expenses	$1.50	$0.75	Includes items such as insurance, equipment maintenance, and warranty expenses
Shipment to San Francisco	$0	$1	By ocean carrier. Air freight is $15 per bag.
Shipment from San Francisco to customers	$3	$3	

12

Inventory Management with Steady Demand

LEARNING OBJECTIVES

LO12-1 Evaluate optimal order quantities and performance measures with the EOQ model

LO12-2 Recognize the presence of economies of scale in inventory management and understand the impact of product variety on inventory costs

LO12-3 Evaluate optimal order quantities when there are quantity constraints or quantity discounts are offered

© Ingram Publishing/SuperStock/RF

Introduction

Imagine (i) you are standing in the aisle of a grocery store, (ii) you are staring at the packages of ramen noodles, and (iii) you actually like to eat ramen noodles—they are tasty, convenient, and relatively cheap (What's not to like?). You probably would grab a few packages, maybe even more than a handful, without much thought. But let's think about what the "optimal" quantity to buy could be. You eat these noodles at a consistent pace. So you know that you will go through the packages pretty quickly. It is a hassle to go to the grocery store and to worry about remembering to buy noodles, so maybe you should stock up. That way you don't have to deal with buying them for quite some time. On the other hand, you are a bit tight on cash at the moment and you dread explaining to your roommate why you are filling up one entire cabinet in your kitchen with just noodles. Hence, if you buy only a few packages, you are likely to find yourself buying noodles frequently, while if you buy a cartful, you will find yourself storing them in odd places in your apartment. Given all of this, what is the "optimal" number of packages to buy? And to make your decision even more complicated, if the ramen noodles happen to be on sale—buy four, get one free—how many would you buy?

This chapter focuses on two reasons why inventory exists: batching due to fixed costs and price discounts. We begin with an inventory management model to rigorously analyze questions like "How many packages of ramen noodles should I buy?" (section 12.1). While it might be silly for you to take this data-driven and hyperanalytical approach with your grocery store purchases, firms do not have the luxury of being so casual with their inventory decisions. This is especially true given that firms incur substantial costs for holding inventory and generally must manage thousands of different products in each of their locations. In particular, we'll analyze Walmart's inventory purchasing decision for one analgesic, Extra Strength Tylenol caplets (24 count), manufactured by Johnson & Johnson.

Beyond making specific decisions, our inventory model provides some managerial guidance with respect to the set of products offered to customers—what are the inventory consequences of adding or subtracting products from this set? As is so common in operations, we'll see that there are economies of scale in inventory management (section 12.2).

Finally, we deal with the issue of quantity constraints and quantity discounts. Quantity constraints restrict order quantities to some multiple of a standard size, such as a case. Quantity discounts give us the opportunity to order a large quantity to get a discount off the purchase price. Our inventory model allows us to precisely evaluate whether the quantity discount is a good deal or not (section 12.3).

12.1 The Economic Order Quantity

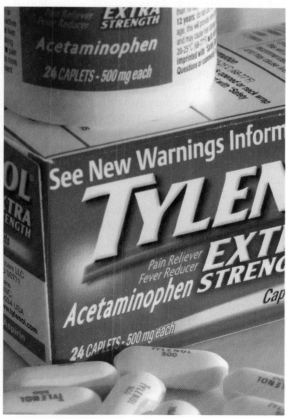

© Jill Braaten RF/Jill Braaten/RF

Walmart is the world's largest retailer. One reason it became so big is because it is very good at managing its inventory. To help us get a handle on its capability, let's focus on one of the many, many inventory decisions it must make. This decision takes place in one of its retail stores, a supercenter, in the United States. If you haven't been to a supercenter, then you should know that these are big stores—a typical supercenter encompasses about 180,000 square feet (not including the parking lot), which is bigger than the combined area of three American football fields, or four acres of land. Given its size, a supercenter stocks tens of thousands of different products. But let's pick just one product—Extra Strength Tylenol (Tylenol) caplets (24 count), an analgesic made by Johnson & Johnson. (Actually, Tylenol is made by the McNeil Consumer Healthcare division of McNeil Inc., but McNeil is owned by Johnson & Johnson.)

Walmart buys each bottle of Tylenol for $3.00. Walmart sells 624 bottles through this store every year and demand is relatively constant throughout the year. Walmart can place orders for more Tylenol whenever it wants. However, each order costs Walmart a fixed $6 no matter the quantity ordered. This $6 represents the costs related to the processing of the order and stocking the product on the shelf (which do not depend on the amount actually stocked). The other relevant cost is the holding cost of inventory. Walmart believes that it incurs a 25 percent inventory holding cost. This means that it incurs $0.25 in cost to hold a dollar of inventory for one year. For example, if a bottle of Tylenol spends one year in the supercenter (which it is unlikely to actually do, but let's say it does), then Walmart would incur a cost of $3 \times 0.25 = $0.75.[1]

12.1.1 The Economic Order Quantity Model

Walmart can use the **economic order quantity (EOQ) model** for the management of its Tylenol inventory. The model is built on the following assumptions.

- **Demand occurs at a constant rate R.** For Tylenol, $R = 624$ bottles per year, or 12 bottles per week (624/52). See Connections: Consumption for a discussion of this assumption.

- **There is a fixed order cost K per order.** The order cost per order is independent of the amount ordered. For Tylenol, it is $K = $6 per order.

- **There is a holding cost per unit per unit of time, h.** This holding cost represents all of the costs associated with keeping a unit of inventory for a period of time. For example, it includes the opportunity cost of capital—if Walmart has $10B invested in inventory, then it cannot use that $10B to earn a rate of return with other investments (such as building new stores, investing in other companies, or expanding its e-commerce site, etc.). It also includes the cost to rent and maintain the building space that stores the inventory, among other costs. For a bottle of Tylenol, the holding cost is 25 percent of its value per year, which is $h = 25\% \times $3.00 = $0.75 per year. Note that the holding cost per unit, $0.75, is the product of the holding cost percentage (e.g., 25 percent) and the *purchase cost per unit,* not the selling price per unit. This is because the opportunity cost of capital is based on the cost to buy the unit (i.e., the amount of cash "locked up" in inventory for a period of time) rather than the amount eventually earned on the unit (which is received after the unit is no longer in inventory).

- **All demand is satisfied from inventory.** We do not want to run out of inventory because doing so risks losing some sales, which is viewed as too costly.

- **Inventory never spoils, degrades, or is lost.** This assumption means that everything purchased is eventually sold. In other words, no matter how long an item remains in inventory, it is considered to be in "as good as new" condition. While it is true that there is an expiration date on medicines, it is safe to assume that Walmart sells all of its inventory well before any of it approaches its expiration date.

Economic order quantity (EOQ) model A model used to select an order quantity that minimizes the sum of ordering and inventory holding costs per unit of time.

Order cost, K The fixed cost incurred per order, which is independent of the amount ordered.

Holding cost per unit, h The cost to hold one item in inventory for one unit of time.

---

[1]These data are only representative to protect confidential information.

- **Orders are delivered with a reliable lead time.** The **lead time** for an order is the time between when an order is placed with the supplier and when the order is received by the customer. The EOQ model assumes the supplier reliably delivers orders, which means that there is a constant delay between when the order is placed and when it is received. As a result, we can time orders to arrive at our facility so that we do not run out of inventory—that is, orders arrive just before inventory is about to run out. Walmart is its own supplier for its supercenters—it receives deliveries from one of Walmart's distribution centers. Therefore, it is safe to assume that deliveries to the supercenter are indeed reliable.

- **There is a purchase price per unit that is independent of the quantity purchased.** In short, there are no quantity discounts. For example, Walmart pays J&J $3.00 per bottle whether Walmart purchases 1 bottle or 1000 bottles. In the last section of this chapter, we explore how to include quantity discounts in this decision.

Table 12.1 summarizes the relevant parameters of the EOQ model applied to the Tylenol order quantity decision. It is critical that the various parameters use the same units. For example, the model gives the same answer whether demand and the holding cost per unit are expressed in terms of one year, one week, or one hour. However, it is critical that they are both defined for the same time period—the model gives an incorrect answer if the demand rate is expressed in units per year while the holding cost per unit is in dollars per week. Similarly, don't measure the order cost in euros while holding cost per unit is measured in dollars. And if demand is expressed in bottles per year, then the holding cost per unit should be for one bottle held for one year, not one case of bottles or one pill.

The goal of the EOQ model is to minimize the sum of ordering and holding costs per unit of time, which is referred to as the EOQ cost per unit of time:

- **Ordering cost per unit of time.** This is the sum of all order costs in a period of time. For example, if Walmart places 12 orders per year, then its ordering cost per year is $72 ($6 per order × 12 orders per year).

- **Holding cost per unit of time.** This is the total cost to hold inventory for a period of time. For example, if Walmart holds 100 bottles, on average, in inventory throughout the year, then its holding cost for the year is $75 (100 bottles × $0.75 per bottle per year).

- **EOQ cost per unit of time.** This is the sum of ordering and holding costs per unit of time.

Be careful to note the difference between the order cost per order (e.g., $K = \$6$) and the ordering cost per unit of time (e.g., $72 per year if 12 orders are made each year). The first one is an input to the model and is not influenced by the decision—Walmart incurs an order cost of $6 per order whether it orders frequently or not. The second one is a result of the decision—the ordering cost per year depends on the order quantity decision. A similar distinction applies between the holding cost per unit (e.g., $h = \$0.75$) and the holding cost per unit of time (e.g., $75 if 100 bottles are held in inventory, on average, throughout the year). The holding cost per unit does not depend on the order quantity decision, whereas the holding cost per year does depend on that decision (and therefore is not constant).

Lead time The time between when an order is placed and when it is received. Process lead time is frequently used as an alternative term for flow time.

Ordering cost per unit of time The sum of all fixed order costs in a period of time.

Holding cost per unit of time The total cost to hold inventory for a period of time.

EOQ cost per unit of time The sum of ordering and holding costs per unit of time.

TABLE 12.1 EOQ Model Parameters and Values for the Tylenol Product Sold through One of Walmart's Distribution Centers

EOQ Model Parameter	Variable	Walmart/Tylenol Value
Demand rate (units per year)	R	624
Order cost ($ per order)	K	$6
Holding cost per unit ($ per unit per year)	h	$0.75
Order quantity (units)	Q	To be determined

Besides ordering and holding costs, it is also useful to define the purchasing cost per unit of time:

- **Purchasing cost.** This is the cost to purchase inventory in a period of time, such as $1872 per year ($3 per bottle × 624 bottles per year).

Given that Walmart spends a sizable amount to buy Tylenol for this one supercenter each year ($1872), you might be surprised that the EOQ model does not include the purchasing cost in its objective. The reason is simple: Walmart's annual purchasing cost does not depend on the quantity it purchases with each order. If Walmart orders 12 bottles per order, then Walmart makes 52 orders per year (624 bottles per year/12 bottles per order). If Walmart orders 48 bottles per order, then Walmart makes 13 orders per year (624 bottles per year/48 bottles per order). So the number of orders made in a year depends on the order quantity, but not the total quantity actually ordered. The total quantity ordered per year should match the demand per year because Walmart does not run out of stock and everything purchased is eventually sold. Hence, the order quantity decision does not actually influence Walmart's annual purchasing cost for Tylenol.

It is reasonable to ignore purchasing cost when deciding on an order quantity when there are no quantity discounts. However, if there are quantity discounts, like "5 percent off for a full truck order," then purchasing cost does become relevant for the order quantity decision. That case is handled in section 12.3.2 on quantity discounts.

Purchasing cost The cost to purchase inventory in a period of time.

Check Your Understanding 12.1

Question: A retailer purchases a snowblower for $400 and sells it for $600. The retailer incurs a 25 percent annual inventory holding cost. What is the holding cost per unit per year, h?

Answer: 25% × $400 = $100

. . . .

CONNECTIONS: Consumption

One of the assumptions of the EOQ model is that the demand rate does not depend on the amount actually ordered. But there are several reasons to believe that this might not always be the case.

Say you open your refrigerator and you see a pile of yogurt containers. Are you as likely to eat a yogurt in this case as compared to the time when you open the refrigerator and you see only a couple of yogurts? It turns out that most people don't treat these two cases the same: When they see a stockpile of inventory, they are more likely to consume relative to when inventory is limited. And as you might expect, marketers have devised a strategy to take advantage of this behavior—temporary price promotions! In particular, one of the motivations of a price promotion strategy is to encourage consumers to "stock up" with the hope that doing so gets them to consume more.

Inventory might influence your demand even if it isn't in your refrigerator. Say you want to purchase a midsized sedan. You visit a local dealer, call it "Full," and you see that it has 20 versions of its midsized sedan. Next, you visit another dealer, call it "Lean," from a different car company and it has only one of its mid-size sedans on its lot. Do these inventory numbers influence your preference? They could. You might conclude that Full has so many cars because the car is popular, and it would only be popular if it were a well-designed and reliable vehicle. Or you might prefer the car from Lean because you infer that the car must be so popular that it cannot keep the car on its lot. In the context of cars, evidence suggests that Lean would be more likely to get your sale, which is called the "scarcity effect": Limited inventory can increase demand because it is scarce. However, there are settings in which the opposite occurs. When you go to a grocery store, do you prefer the last package of hamburger? Chances are "no"—if it is the last package, then it must be old. However, if the grocery store fills up an entire shelf with the same flavor of coffee, you are more likely to grab that version, probably because the large inventory "catches your eye," thereby drawing your attention.

Sources: Ailawadi, Kusum L., and Scott A. Neslin. "The Effect of Promotion on Consumption: Buying More and Consuming It Faster." *Journal of Marketing Research* 35, no. 3 (August 1998), pp. 390–98.

Cachon, Gerard; Santiago Gallino; and Marcelo Olivares. *Does Adding Inventory Increase Sales? Evidence of a Scarcity Effect in U.S. Automobile Dealerships* (June 28, 2013). Available at SSRN: http://ssrn.com/abstract=2286800 or http://dx.doi.org/10.2139/ssrn.2286800

12.1.2 EOQ Cost Function

Let's begin to understand the trade-offs associated with the order quantity decision. Figure 12.1 displays how inventory at the DC changes over time for two different order quantities. In the top panel, the order quantity is 50 bottles per order, while in the bottom panel it is 150 bottles per order.

We can see from Figure 12.1 that inventory follows a "saw-toothed" pattern: When an order arrives, inventory immediately spikes to a higher level, and then it begins to fall at a constant rate. The inventory jumps equal the order quantity Q, and inventory falls at the rate of demand R; that is, R equals the slope of each triangle in the sawtooth.

The inventory pattern in Figure 12.1 indicates that new orders arrive just as inventory falls to zero. This ensures that customers can always find inventory but also keeps inventory as low

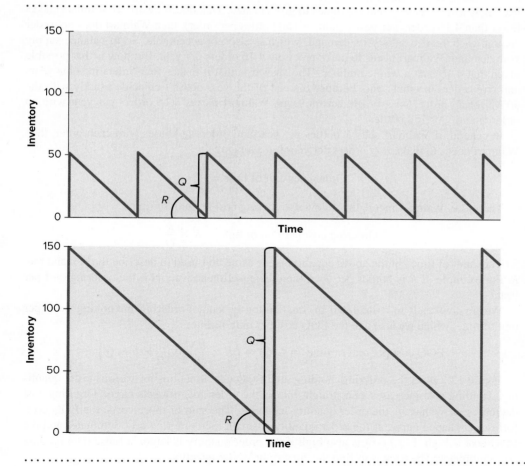

Figure 12.1

Pattern of inventory (in bottles) if Walmart purchases 50 bottles with each order (top panel) or 150 bottles with each order (bottom panel)

as possible. It is possible to time the arrival of orders "just so" because we assume the supplier delivers orders reliably on time.

In addition to the saw-toothed pattern, we see from Figure 12.1 that there seems to be more inventory with the larger order quantity but more orders with the smaller order quantity. This identifies the key trade-off in the model: Large order quantities add to holding cost, but small quantities suffer from high ordering cost.

So what exactly is the average amount of inventory for a given order quantity? Looking at the triangles in the upper panel of Figure 12.1, we see that inventory peaks at 50 bottles and then steadily falls to 0 over the course of a little over four weeks (50 bottles/12 bottles per week = 4.17 weeks). The average inventory over that time is just one-half of the peak inventory, or 25 bottles. In general,

$$\text{Average inventory} = \frac{\text{Order quantity}}{2} = \frac{Q}{2}$$

Once we know the average inventory, we can evaluate the holding cost per unit of time:

$$\text{Holding cost per unit of time} = \frac{1}{2} \times h \times Q$$

For example, if Walmart orders 50 bottles with each order, then Walmart has 25 bottles, on average, in its supercenter. It costs Walmart $0.75 per bottle per year to hold inventory. So Walmart's holding cost per year for Tylenol in its supercenter would be 25 bottles × $0.75 per bottle per year = $18.75 per year.

We also have to worry about ordering cost. For now, let's assume Walmart orders 150 bottles at a time. We also know that Walmart sells 624 bottles per year. So Walmart needs to make 4.16 orders per year (624 bottles per year/150 bottles per order). If Walmart makes more orders per year (at 150 bottles each), then it purchases more each year than it can sell, leaving it with inventory that continues to grow in size. That doesn't work. If Walmart makes fewer than 4.16 orders per year (again, at 150 bottles per order), then Walmart does not order enough each year to satisfy its demand, which is also not acceptable. So to balance supply with demand, Walmart needs to make precisely 4.16 orders per year. But how is that possible given that 4.16 isn't a whole number? The answer is that it makes four orders in some years and five orders in other years because the end of the year doesn't coincide exactly with the arrival of an order. On average, across years, Walmart makes 4.16 orders per year with an order quantity of 150 bottles.

In general, if Walmart sells R bottles per year and orders Q bottles with each order, then Walmart needs to make R/Q orders per year (on average):

$$\text{Orders per unit of time} = \frac{R}{Q}$$

Therefore, Walmart incurs the following ordering cost per unit of time:

$$\text{Ordering cost per unit of time} = K \times \frac{R}{Q}$$

The "unit of time" in the above equation is the same unit used to describe the demand rate R. For example, if R is bottles per year, then the equation above yields the ordering cost per year.

We are now ready to write down an equation for the sum of ordering and holding costs per unit of time, which we also call the EOQ cost per unit of time:

$$\text{EOQ cost per unit of time } = C(Q) = \left(K \times \frac{R}{Q} \right) + \left(\frac{1}{2} \times h \times Q \right)$$

Figure 12.2 plots the ordering, holding, and EOQ cost functions for various order quantities. Holding cost increases as a straight line as the order quantity gets larger. Ordering cost decreases as a curve as the order quantity increases. The sum of those costs, the EOQ cost, forms a U-shaped curve. If the order quantity is small, then ordering cost dominates and the EOQ cost is high. EOQ cost is also high if the order quantity is large, because then holding cost dominates. The trick is to find the "just right" order quantity.

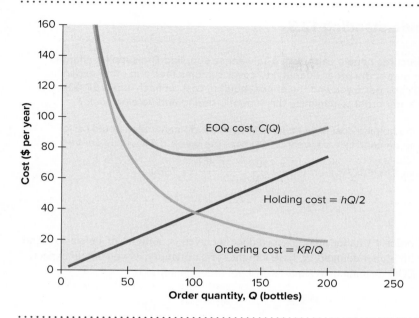

Figure 12.2
Ordering, holding, and EOQ costs per unit of time (per year) as a function of the order quantity

Check Your Understanding 12.2

Question: A drill in a hardware store incurs a holding cost per unit of $10 per year. The store sells one of these drills per week all year long. Each time the store orders more drills, it orders a case that contains 12 drills. What is the average inventory of drills at this hardware store?

Answer: The order quantity is $Q = 12$ and average inventory is $Q/2 = 12/2 = 6$.

Question: What holding cost does the hardware store incur per year to stock this drill?

Answer: Holding cost per unit of time $= 0.5 \times h \times Q = 0.5 \times \$10$ per year per drill $\times 12$ drills $= \$60$.

Question: The hardware store incurs a $6 cost with each order. What ordering cost does the hardware store incur per year?

Answer: The order cost per order is $K = \$6$. The flow rate is $R = 52$ drills per year. The ordering cost per year $= K \times R/Q = \$6 \times 52$ drills$/12$ drills $= \$26$.

© Ron Chapple Stock/FotoSearch/Glow Images/RF

12.1.3 Optimal Order Quantity

Figure 12.2 suggests that the optimal order quantity is about 100 bottles. But we should be more precise. If you have taken a calculus class, then you might remember how to derive the formula for the minimum of a function (take the first derivative, set it equal to 0, and solve for Q). But if you didn't take calculus or don't remember the procedure, don't worry; you can just use the following equation for the order quantity Q^* that minimizes the sum of ordering and holding costs per unit of time (i.e., minimizes $C(Q)$):

$$Q^* = \sqrt{\frac{2 \times K \times R}{h}}$$

This quantity Q^* is called the economic order quantity (which gives the model its name). Looking at the equation we can confirm that Q^* increases if the order cost, K, increases; in that case, it makes sense to order a larger quantity to reduce the number of orders placed per unit of time. Similarly, Q^* decreases if the holding cost per unit, h, increases: If it costs more

Check Your Understanding 12.3

Question: Xootr procures handle caps from a Taiwanese supplier. The supplier charges $300 per order (no matter the order quantity) to cover customs fees and other expenses. Xootr requires 700 caps per week and the annual holding cost on each cap is $0.40. How many caps should Xootr order to minimize the sum of ordering and holding costs?

Answer: Because the holding cost is given for one year, the demand rate should be for one year as well. The demand rate per year is 700 caps per week × 52 weeks per year = 36,400 caps per year. The EOQ is then $\sqrt{\dfrac{2 \times \$300 \times 36,400}{\$0.40}} = 7389.$

to hold inventory, order a smaller quantity to reduce the average amount of inventory. And, finally, products with higher demand, *R*, have a higher order quantity, as you would expect.

Let's apply the EOQ formula to Walmart's Tylenol order quantity:

$$Q^* = \sqrt{\frac{2 \times K \times R}{h}} = \sqrt{\frac{2 \times \$6 \times 624}{\$0.75}} = 100$$

Thus, to minimize the sum of ordering and holding costs, Walmart should order about 100 Tylenol bottles per order. This is consistent with the graph in Figure 12.2, but now we have an equation to find the optimal quantity.

Looking further at Figure 12.2 you may notice that it appears that the holding cost curve and the ordering cost curve cross right about at the point that minimizes total cost, 100 bottles. This is actually not a coincidence. In the EOQ model, the quantity Q^* that minimizes total cost is also the quantity at which the holding cost per unit of time equals the ordering cost per unit of time.

12.1.4 EOQ Cost and Cost per Unit

We now know that the EOQ, Q^*, minimizes the sum of the ordering and holding costs per unit of time; that is, the EOQ cost. So what is that minimum EOQ cost? We can calculate it by plugging the order quantity, Q^*, into the EOQ cost equation, $C(Q)$:

$$C(Q^*) = \left(K \times \frac{R}{Q^*}\right) + \left(\frac{1}{2} \times h \times Q^*\right) = \left(\$6 \times \frac{624}{100}\right) + \left(\frac{1}{2} \times \$0.75 \times 100\right) = \$74.94$$

Hence, if each of Walmart's orders for Tylenol contains 100 bottles, then Walmart incurs an EOQ cost of $74.94 per year. (We know that this cost is "per year" because we evaluated the cost function using the demand rate for one year and the holding cost per unit for one year.)

Is $74.94 per year a lot? To answer that question, it is helpful to measure the $74.94 relative to something else. One approach is to measure it against the purchase cost per unit of time. Each year Walmart purchases $1872 of Tylenol ($3 per bottle × 624 bottles per year) for this super-center. Hence, $74.94 is 4.0 percent ($74.94/$1872) of the purchase cost. Another approach is to allocate the cost to each unit sold: $74.94 per year/624 bottles per year = $0.12 per bottle. Hence, Walmart incurs about a total of 12 cents in ordering and holding costs per bottle. It shouldn't come as a surprise that $0.12 per bottle is 4.0 percent ($0.12/$3) of the cost of the bottle: If the sum of the ordering and holding costs of 624 bottles is 4.0 percent of the purchase cost, then the sum of the ordering and holding costs for one of those 624 bottles is also 4.0 percent of its purchase cost.

Is 4.0 percent a lot? At first glance it doesn't seem like much. But remember that a retailer's final profit is often only about 1 percent to 3 percent of its sales revenue. So 4 percent is the same order of magnitude as the firm's profit. Hence, it is important to do inventory management well. For instance, if inventory costs were to double, to 8 percent, then this could turn this product from a profitable one to an unprofitable one.

Check Your Understanding 12.4

Question: Xootr procures wheels from a Chinese supplier. The supplier charges $200 per order (no matter the order quantity) to cover customs fees and other expenses at $3 per wheel. Xootr requires 80,000 wheels per year and its annual holding cost percentage is 40 percent. Suppose Xootr orders 8000 wheels with each order. What is the sum of its ordering and inventory holding costs per year?

Answer: The holding cost per unit per year is $3 × 0.4 = $1.20. The sum of the ordering and inventory holding costs per year is then

$$C(Q) = \left(K \times \frac{R}{Q}\right) + \left(\frac{1}{2} \times h \times Q\right) = \left(\$200 \times \frac{80{,}000}{8000}\right) + \left(\frac{1}{2} \times \$1.20 \times 8000\right) = \$6800$$

Question: If Xootr orders 5000 wheels per order, then the sum of its ordering and holding costs per year is $6200. What would be the ordering and holding cost per wheel?

Answer: The ordering and holding cost per wheel is $6200 per year/80,000 wheels per year = $0.078.

. . . .

12.2 Economies of Scale and Product Variety

The fixed ordering cost feels somewhat like the fixed setup time discussed in Chapter 7, Process Interruptions. Recall that a setup time is a fixed amount of time for a process to get ready for production. No production occurs during the setup time and the setup time is the same duration no matter how many units are produced in the batch after the setup. When the setup time is substantial, it is intuitive that it makes sense to produce in large batches. In that way, the setup time is in some sense divided among the many units in the batch and the capacity of the process increases as the batch size gets larger. As a result, processes with setup times are said to exhibit **economies of scale**: They become more efficient when larger quantities are produced.

The EOQ model does not have a setup time, but it does have a fixed order cost. Walmart incurs a cost of $6 per order no matter if it orders one bottle or 1000 bottles. So it is best to order in sufficiently large quantities. However, the order quantity also cannot be completely unaligned with demand. Ordering 1000 bottles at a time is potentially okay if Walmart is selling thousands of bottles per year. But if it is only selling a couple hundred bottles per year, then an order quantity of 1000 bottles is likely to incur a crazy high inventory holding cost.

To illustrate the economies of scale created by the fixed order cost, let's apply the EOQ model to the Tylenol ordering decision for different demand rates. Table 12.2 evaluates the total of ordering and holding costs for five different scenarios. The middle one, scenario III, is the base case that we have already analyzed. It has an annual demand rate of 624 bottles, an EOQ of 100 bottles, and an annual EOQ cost that is 4 percent of the annual purchase cost. The other four scenarios either ramp up or ramp down demand by some multiple. In particular, annual demand in scenarios I and II is only one-fourth or one-half, respectively, of the base, while in scenarios IV and V demand is either twice or four times as large as the base scenario.

Let's first focus on how the demand rate influences the EOQ. As we would expect, as demand increases, the optimal order quantity increases. But it doesn't increase at the same rate of demand. For example, if the demand rate increases from 156 bottles per year (scenario I) to 624 bottles per year (scenario III), demand has increased by a factor of four (624/156 = 4), but the EOQ only doubles, from 50 to 100 bottles. Similarly, scenario V has 16 times more demand than scenario I (2496 versus 156 bottles per year), yet the EOQ in scenario V is only four times greater.

The annual EOQ cost also increases as demand increases. But like the EOQ, it doesn't increase at the same rate as demand. As a result, the annual EOQ cost becomes a smaller and

Economies of scale Describes a relationship between operational efficiency and demand in which greater demand leads to a more efficient process.

. . . .

TABLE 12.2   How Changes in Demand Influence Costs

	Scenario	I	II	III	IV	V
	Demand rate, R (bottles per year)	156	312	624	1248	2496
	Demand multiple	1/4	1/2	1	2	4
	EOQ, Q* (bottles)	50	71	100	141	200
(a)	Annual EOQ cost, C(Q*) ($)	$37.50	$53.00	$74.90	$106.00	$149.90
(b)	Annual purchase cost ($3 × R)	$468	$936	$1872	$3744	$7488
(c = a/b)	Annual EOQ cost as % of annual purchase cost	8.0%	5.7%	4.0%	2.8%	2.0%

Note: "Demand multiple" is the ratio of the flow rate in that scenario to the base scenario (III).

. . . .

smaller percentage of the annual purchase cost. For example, in scenario I, when the demand rate is only 156 bottles per year, the annual EOQ cost is 8.0 percent of the annual purchase cost. That percentage drops to 4.0 percent as demand increases to the base scenario III, which has a demand rate of 624 bottles per year, and further drops to 2.0 percent when the demand rate is 2496 bottles per year (scenario V). This illustrates the economies of scale that are present in the EOQ model: As the demand rate increases, as long as the order quantity is chosen to minimize EOQ costs (the sum of ordering and holding costs), that cost becomes a smaller percentage of the purchase cost.

At this point, you may have picked up on a pattern in the results presented in Table 12.2: Every time demand doubles (i.e., increases by 100 percent), the EOQ and the annual EOQ cost only increase by a factor of 1.41 (i.e., 41 percent), which happens to be the square root of 2. You also may have noticed another pattern: Each time demand doubles, the annual EOQ cost as a percentage of the annual purchase cost decreases, but at a decreasing rate. For example, doubling demand from 156 to 312 bottles per year lowers the annual EOQ cost from 8.0 percent to 5.7 percent of the annual purchase cost, which is a nice reduction. But then the next doubling of demand, from 312 bottles to 624 bottles, lowers that percentage by a smaller amount, from 5.7 percent to 4.0 percent. In fact, doubling demand from 1248 to 2496 bottles per year (from scenario IV to scenario V) only reduces the EOQ total cost percentage from 2.8 percent to 2.0 percent. This observation suggests that low demand can be very expensive, but once an adequate volume of demand is achieved, further reductions in costs require very large increases in demand. As a rule of thumb, to cut in half the EOQ cost as a percentage of purchase cost (as in moving from scenario I to III or scenario III to V) requires that demand quadruple.

So we have determined that the EOQ exhibits economies of scale. This means that it is important to operate with a sufficient demand rate: If demand is low, then ordering and holding costs are a substantial portion of the purchase cost. But how can a manager ensure that demand is sufficiently high? The first answer is rather obvious: Choose products to include in the offered assortment that are sufficiently popular. If a product is not sufficiently popular (its demand rate is too low), then ordering and holding costs may be too high to earn a profit on the product. In that case, it should not be offered at all.

The second answer is not quite as obvious. To ensure that demand is sufficiently high for each product in the assortment of offered products, be careful to avoid offering too many different products. For example, we have focused on Extra Strength Tylenol with 24 caplets in a bottle, but Walmart could also choose to sell Extra Strength Tylenol with 50 caplets, or 100 caplets, or 225 caplets, or 500 caplets—or in small pouches each containing only

2 caplets. By adding different versions to its assortment, Walmart is giving customers more variety, and therefore it should be able to attract a greater amount of total demand. That sounds great, but that greater total demand is divided across more products. If adding a product to an assortment increases the total demand across the assortment by only a little bit, then the existing products in the assortment may actually see a decline in their demand.

Imagine Walmart can sell 624 bottles per year of Extra Strength Tylenol with 24 caplets when that is the only option it offers customers. This is pretty good, but somebody at the company then suggests that it might be losing some customers who want to buy 225 caplets at a time. This may indeed be true. If it were to add the 225-caplet option, it might sell 150 of those bottles per year. But what would happen to demand of the 24-caplet version? It would almost surely decrease! Why? Because when only the 24-caplet version is offered, some customers buy it even though they prefer the 225-caplet option. In marketing this is called **product substitution:** People may be willing to purchase (i.e., substitute) a less-preferred version if their most-preferred version is not available. So while adding the 225-caplet option might increase total sales revenue for Extra Strength Tylenol, it would decrease the demand rate of the 24-caplet version. And we now know that a decrease in the demand rate makes inventory management less efficient. Thus, expanding variety can be a good thing if it increases the overall demand rate by enough to compensate for the fact that each of the initial products is likely to then operate at a less efficient scale.

When is expanding product variety not likely to be a good idea; that is, when does the decrease in operating efficiency tend to dominate the benefit of higher overall demand? This occurs when adding variety doesn't increase total demand by very much. And that tends to happen when adding variety doesn't really increase consumer value by much. For example, it might make sense to offer a 24-caplet, 100-caplet, and 500-caplet version of Extra Strength Tylenol. But would it then make sense to add a 225-caplet version? Some customers might prefer the 225-caplet version over the 100- or 500-caplet versions, but do you think overall demand will increase all that much? If it doesn't, then the same total demand will be divided among four products (24-, 100-, 225-, and 500-caplet versions) instead of three products (24-, 100-, and 500-caplet versions). This could reduce overall profitability.

This discussion is biased toward the perspective of the operating manager. The marketing manager may respond with additional reasons why the company must carry a broader assortment of products (i.e., why the company must offer more products in its assortment). Some of those reasons may indeed be legitimate. Nevertheless, it is worth pointing out to the marketing manager that a broader assortment doesn't come without additional operating costs.

Check Your Understanding 12.5

Question: A retailer owns two stores that sell arts and crafts. In each store, it sells canvases for painting. Store A sells 10 different sizes and store B sells 15 sizes. The two stores have about the same level of total sales for canvases and this total is roughly divided equally among the offered sizes. They incur holding costs for inventory and a fixed order cost for each canvas size. Which of the two stores is likely to have a higher ordering and holding cost for canvases expressed as a percentage of purchase cost?

   a. Store A because it has higher sales per offered size.
   b. Store B because it has lower sales per offered size.
   c. They will have about the same ordering and holding cost as a percentage of purchase cost because they have about the same total sales for canvases.

© Stockbyte/Exactostock/SuperStock/RF

Answer: Given that both stores sell the same total amount of canvases, store B's sales per canvas must be lower than store A's because store B sells more sizes. Hence, each item in store B has a lower scale than the items in store A, meaning that store B has higher ordering and inventory costs. Choice B is the best.

CONNECTIONS: Girl Scout Cookies

The Girl Scouts of the USA have been selling Girl Scout cookies since 1917 to raise funds. Maybe they have been doing it for so long because they are very good at it: Each year they sell about 200 million boxes and take in about $714 million in cookie sales. If you are one of their many customers (or if you have sold Girl Scout cookies at some point in your business career), then you know that Girl Scout cookies come in a number of flavors. Thin Mints are the most popular, making up about 25 percent of their sales. Rounding out the top five flavors are Samoas, Peanut Butter Patties, Peanut Butter Sandwiches, and Shortbread. Together, the top six flavors account for about three-fourths of their sales.

Each year, the Girl Scouts need to decide which flavors to include in their assortment. Perennial favorites, such as Thin Mints, would be hard to not include—people love them, both for their flavor and their nostalgia. But how many is too many? In 2011, the Girl Scouts decided that "more than six" might be too many. Why only six? Well, it surely isn't because they could satisfy all human cookie taste preferences with just six flavors of cookies— although flavors like Thank U Berry Much did not generate "top six" sales, there were still a substantial number of customers who purchased and enjoyed them. Instead, they decided to experiment with a more limited assortment because of operational concerns related to excessive product variety.

Adding a cookie flavor does two things to demand. First, it allows the Girl Scouts to sell to some customers who would only purchase that particular flavor; for example, those people who say, "Thank U Berry Much or nothing at all!" But it also steals some demand from the other flavors: Some people would buy one box of Thin Mints, but they prefer Thank U Berry Much, so they purchase one box whether Thank U Berry Much is available or not. Hence, the Girl Scouts recognize that they face a trade-off: The first few flavors clearly bring in incremental sales, but, eventually, adding flavors increases total sales by a small amount relative to the sales stolen from other flavors. If there are order costs (or fixed setup costs) associated with cookie production and distribution (which there likely are), then too much variety can make them worse off.

Source: Shelly Banjo, "Cookie Cutters: Girl Scouts Trim Their Lineup for Lean Times," *The Wall Street Journal*, January 27, 2011.

12.3 Quantity Constraints and Discounts

In section 12.1, we determined that Walmart's order quantity should be 100 bottles. Sometimes it is possible to indeed order the amount recommended by the EOQ model—and sometimes there are constraints imposed on the order quantity that prevent the firm from following the EOQ recommendation. Quantity discounts present another possible complication. The EOQ model ignores purchasing costs because it assumes that the cost to purchase each unit does not depend on the number of units purchased. But that is not the case when a supplier offers a quantity discount. In this section, we deal with both of these complications (quantity constraints and quantity discounts).

12.3.1 Quantity Constraints

To avoid excessive handling costs, products are generally moved around from a supplier's factory to retail stores in batches of various sizes. A common batch size is called a **pallet**—a pallet of product is the quantity that sits on top of a platform that allows the stack of product to be moved all at once by a forklift. These platforms, which are also called *pallets,* are generally wood, but they can be made of other materials as well (such as plastic or metal). (See Photo 12.1.) The amount of product that can be placed on a pallet depends on the weight of the product (more units of a lighter product can be added to a pallet) and the "stackability" of the product (how high the product can be stacked without causing damage to the lower layers).

Pallet Either (i) a platform which is used to stack inventory to facilitate moving the inventory, or (ii) the quantity of inventory that is stacked on the platform.

© Stockbyte/Getty Images/RF

© Image Source/Getty Images/RF

PHOTO 12.1A AND B A wood pallet (left) and a forklift (right) moving a pallet of goods

Pallets vary in dimension across the world, but in North America they are typically 40" × 48" (or about 1 by 1.2 meters) and are generally stacked 3 to 4 feet high. If you visualize a pallet, you can see that it can contain a large amount of product. For example, a single pallet of Tylenol contains 10,080 bottles of Tylenol—that is, 241,920 pills—enough to cure the headaches of a small city for a year or more. The key advantage of a pallet is that it allows a single worker driving a forklift to be able to move a large quantity of product quickly and safely.

The disadvantage of a pallet is that it is a large quantity of product—so much product that in some locations it takes too long to sell the entire quantity. Furthermore, there is no hope that a person can move a pallet without specialized equipment like a forklift. It is too bulky and almost always too heavy for a normal person. Consequently, it is desirable to have a smaller quantity that still enables moving the product but is small enough to be handled by a single worker, like a **case.** For Tylenol, each case contains 72 bottles and each pallet has 140 cases.

So when Walmart orders Tylenol for its supercenter, it orders an integer multiple of a case. For example, it can order 72 bottles (one case), or 144 bottles (two cases), but it cannot order 100 bottles. While an order of 100 bottles is ideal if the focus is exclusively on ordering and holding costs, Walmart also needs to be concerned with handling costs, which are not explicitly considered in the EOQ model. If it receives Tylenol in cases of 72 bottles, then sending precisely 100 bottles to a supercenter requires it to break up a case, count out precisely 100 bottles, and then repackage the 100 bottles into a new container before shipping the set of bottles to the supercenter. All of that requires extra labor, and therefore extra cost.

Given that Walmart is constrained to order an integer number of cases, what should it do? The first step in deciding on an order quantity is to evaluate the EOQ, which we already have done. Recall that the EOQ is 100 bottles. Next, find the two quantities that can be ordered that are close to the EOQ; that is, the closest case quantity smaller than the EOQ and the closest quantity larger than the EOQ. For example, looking at Figure 12.2, we see that the closest case quantities to 100 are either 72 bottles (one case) or 144 bottles (two cases). Finally, evaluate the total ordering and inventory cost with the two quantities and then choose the quantity with the lower cost.

Table 12.3 displays the cost results for the two different case quantities and the EOQ. As expected, the EOQ delivers lower costs, but not by a huge amount. Ordering one case at a time yields an annual ordering and holding cost of $79.00, whereas the EOQ incurs a cost of $74.94. The former is 4.2 percent of annual purchase costs, while the EOQ's cost is 4.0 percent. Even though one case (72 bottles) has a lower cost than two cases (144 bottles), the difference is not huge: Ordering two cases at a time increases cost relative to ordering one case at a time by only $1 (from $79 to $80).

We can conclude from the results in Table 12.3 that if we cannot order the EOQ (100 bottles), then we should order one case at a time (72 bottles).

TABLE 12.3 Ordering and Inventory Costs for Order Quantities Equal to the EOQ; also One Case (72 Bottles) and Two Cases (144 Bottles)

	One Case	EOQ	Two Cases
Q (bottles)	72	100	144
Holding cost per year	$27.00	$37.50	$54.00
Ordering cost per year	$52.00	$37.40	$26.00
Annual EOQ (ordering and holding cost, $C(Q)$)	$79.00	$74.90	$80.00
Annual purchasing cost	$1872	$1872	$1872
EOQ cost as % of purchase cost	4.2%	4.0%	4.3%

Check Your Understanding 12.6

Question: A firm incurs $30 in fixed order costs per order and a holding cost per unit of $1 per year. Annual demand is 10,000 units. The firm is required to order an integer multiple of 500 units. What order quantity should the firm use to minimize ordering and holding costs?

Answer: Evaluate the EOQ:

$$Q^* = \sqrt{\frac{2 \times 30 \times 10,000}{1}} = 775$$

The firm cannot order 775 units, but it can order either 500 units or 1000 units. Evaluate ordering and holding costs for each of those two quantities:

$$C\,(Q = 500) = \left(K \times \frac{R}{Q} \right) + \left(\frac{1}{2} \times h \times Q \right) = \left(\$30 \times \frac{10,000}{500} \right) + \left(\frac{1}{2} \times \$1 \times 500 \right) = \$850$$

$$C\,(Q = 1000) = \left(K \times \frac{R}{Q} \right) + \left(\frac{1}{2} \times h \times Q \right) = \left(\$30 \times \frac{10,000}{1000} \right) + \left(\frac{1}{2} \times \$1 \times 1000 \right) = \$800$$

Hence, the order quantity 1000 units has a lower cost.

Because there is a bit of calculating involved to derive the results in Table 12.3, you might wonder if there is a simpler approach. For example, why not choose the feasible quantity that is closest to the EOQ and save yourself the hassle of the extra math. In this situation, that heuristic works: 72 is indeed closer to 100 than is 144, and it has the lower cost. But that heuristic doesn't always work. For example, an order quantity of 130 bottles yields a lower cost than 72 bottles even though 130 bottles is "further" from the EOQ of 100 bottles.

Table 12.3 also suggests that while it is beneficial to be able to order approximately the EOQ, it is not necessary to be very close to the EOQ. Consequently, order quantity restrictions do not increase costs as much as you might suppose. This is very good news. It means that the organization can choose batch sizes (e.g., cases, pallets, etc.) so as to be sure that the product can be handled efficiently, and then choose the best feasible quantity to minimize ordering and holding costs.

12.3.2 Quantity Discounts

As consumers, we often experience quantity discounts like "buy three, get one free." Businesses also are offered quantity discounts. For example, a supplier might offer a retailer "8 percent off for a full truckload" or "5 percent off for a pallet." In this section, we explore how to incorporate the added twist of a quantity discount into the EOQ analysis to yield an optimal order quantity. To do this, we turn our attention to another part of Walmart's supply chain.

Walmart's supercenters receive product from one of their distribution centers. The role of a **distribution center (DC)** is to receive product from suppliers, store inventory, and ship products to its retail stores (like its supercenters). As big as a Walmart supercenter is, the DC that serves it is even bigger: Each DC is about 1 million square feet (92,903 square meters), which is greater than 17 football fields (or about the base area of the two largest pyramids in Giza, Egypt). In the United States alone, Walmart has about 40 DCs (in 2014) and each DC serves about 100 retail stores.

Annual demand for Extra Strength Tylenol caplets (24 count) in one of their DCs is 65,000 bottles. Let's assume that this demand is consistent throughout the year. As in the decision for the supercenter, Walmart must decide on a quantity for each order. Walmart's supplier, Johnson & Johnson (J&J), requires that Walmart order an integer multiple of a **tier**; that is, ordering one, two, or three tiers is fine, but ordering 1.5 tiers is not. A tier is one layer of a pallet, and with Tylenol this amounts to 20 cases. There are seven tiers in each pallet of Tylenol, so a pallet contains 140 cases (as already mentioned). J&J charges $3.00 per bottle for orders that are less than one pallet but offers a 4 percent discount if Walmart orders an integer number of pallets. J&J may offer this discount because it saves on labor costs when it ships in pallet quantities rather than in tier quantities. To complete the relevant information for this decision, Walmart believes its annual holding cost percentage for inventory in the DC is 20 percent and it incurs an $8 fixed cost per order. The holding cost percentage is a bit lower than the cost for the supercenter because storage and maintenance costs for a DC are lower than for a retail store. The fixed ordering cost is a bit higher than for the supercenter because these orders involve coordination with another firm and the DC is a larger building than a supercenter (thus requiring more distance to travel to load and unload items).

Table 12.4 summarizes the data needed for deciding on an order quantity.

To evaluate a quantity discount opportunity, we begin with the EOQ that minimizes ordering and holding costs, ignoring purchasing costs. If that quantity is larger than the threshold needed to obtain the discount, then we know we will order enough to get the discount. However, if the EOQ is less than what is needed to qualify for the discount, then we have the option of ordering that quantity or increasing our order to get the discount. In that case, we compare costs between the two options to decide which one to choose. Exhibit 12.1 provides the detailed process for making the order quantity decision in the presence of a quantity discount.

Distribution center (DC) A facility designed to receive product from suppliers, store inventory, and ship products to retail stores.

Tier The quantity of product in one layer of a pallet.

TABLE 12.4 Relevant Data for Walmart's DC Order Quantity Decision

	Walmart/Tylenol Value
Demand rate, R (bottles per year)	65,000
Order cost, K ($ per order)	$8
Regular price per bottle	$3
Order quantity multiple	One tier = 20 cases = 1440 bottles
Minimum order quantity for discount	One pallet = 140 cases = 10,080 bottles
Discount	4%
Annual holding cost percentage	20%
Holding cost per unit ($ per unit per year), h	Depends on Q
Order quantity (units), Q	To be determined

EXHIBIT 12.1

The Decision Steps for How Much to Order When Offered a Quantity Discount If at Least Q_d Is Ordered

1. Evaluate the EOQ given the regular price (or the best quantity if there are quantity restrictions). Call this quantity $\mathbf{Q}^*$.

2. If the EOQ given the regular price, Q^*, is greater than the threshold needed for the quantity discount, Q_d, evaluate the EOQ given the discount price. Call that quantity Q^{**} and order Q^{**}. (Note: Q^{**} is greater than Q^* because the discount price yields a lower holding cost per unit than the regular price.)

3. If the EOQ given the regular price, Q^*, is less than the threshold needed for the quantity discount, Q_d, then:
   a. Evaluate the sum of ordering and holding costs with the EOQ quantity given the regular price, $C(Q^*)$. Add the purchase cost to obtain a total cost with the regular discount. Call that cost C^*.
   b. Evaluate the sum of the ordering and holding costs assuming the minimum threshold to obtain the quantity discount is ordered, $C(Q_d)$. Add the purchase cost (which includes the discount) to obtain a total cost. Call that cost C^d.
   c. If the total cost evaluated in step 3a, C^*, is lower than the total cost evaluated in step 3b, C^d, order the EOQ quantity given the regular price, Q^*. Otherwise, order the minimum threshold quantity to obtain the quantity discount, Q_d.

Let's follow the process outlined in Exhibit 12.1. In step 1, we evaluate the EOQ quantity given the regular purchase price. The purchase price is $3 per bottle and the annual holding cost per bottle is $3 × 20% = $0.60. Therefore, the EOQ is

$$Q^* = \sqrt{\frac{2 \times \$8 \times 65{,}000}{\$0.60}} = 1317$$

Although 1317 bottles minimizes ordering and holding costs, Walmart cannot order exactly 1317 bottles. It is restricted to ordering an integer number of a tier, which is 1440 bottles. Thus, they can order one tier (1440 bottles), two tiers (2880 bottles), three tiers (4320 bottles), and so on. Given that the desired quantity, 1317 bottles, is very close to one tier (and, in fact, less than one tier), Walmart orders one tier at a time.

One tier is not enough for the quantity discount, which is one pallet. So step 2 in Exhibit 12.1 does not apply. Which means we move to step 3.

For step 3a, if Walmart orders one tier at a time, the annual sum of ordering and holding costs is

$$C(Q) = \left(K \times \frac{R}{Q}\right) + \left(\frac{1}{2} \times h \times Q\right) = \left(\$8 \times \frac{65{,}000}{1440}\right) + \left(\frac{1}{2} \times \$0.60 \times 1440\right) = \$793$$

Its annual purchasing cost for the DC is $195,000 (65,000 bottles per year × $3 per bottle). So its total annual cost of purchasing, ordering, and holding is $195,793. Note that we are now combining all three costs because the quantity discount can influence the annual purchasing cost.

For step 3b, assuming Walmart orders one pallet to get the 4 percent discount, Walmart pays $3 per bottle minus the 4 percent discount, or $2.88 per bottle ($3 × 0.96). Therefore, the annual holding cost per bottle is $0.576 = $2.88 × 20%—not only does the discount save on purchasing cost, it reduces the holding cost per unit because each unit requires less capital.

Now that we know the holding cost per bottle, we can evaluate the sum of ordering and holding costs per year:

$$C(Q) = \left(K \times \frac{R}{Q}\right) + \left(\frac{1}{2} \times h \times Q\right) = \left(\$8 \times \frac{65{,}000}{10{,}080}\right) + \left(\frac{1}{2} \times \$0.576 \times 10{,}080\right) = \$2955$$

That is indeed a sizeable jump in those costs, from $790 to $2955, primarily because the higher order quantity leads to a greater average inventory, which means a higher inventory

holding cost. But now the annual purchasing cost is $187,200 = 65,000 bottles per year ×
$2.88 per bottle. So if Walmart takes advantage of the quantity discount, its total annual cost of
purchasing, ordering, and holding is $190,155 ($187,200 + $2955), which completes step 3b.

In step 3c, we simply compare the cost of ordering the "small" EOQ or the "large" quantity needed for the discount. From our calculations, Walmart's total annual cost drops from
$195,790 to $190,155, which is a reduction of 2.9 percent. The clear conclusion is that
Walmart should order one pallet at a time rather than one tier at a time so it can get the
4 percent discount.

It is worthwhile to step back and put these quantities into perspective. One tier is
1440 bottles, and this is about one week's worth of demand at the DC. To be precise, the DC
ships 1250 bottles each week to the stores it serves (65,000/52), so 1440 bottles is 1.15 weeks
of demand, or about eight days of demand. This means that if Walmart orders one tier at a
time, it would receive a delivery from J&J about every eight days. However, the one-pallet
quantity, 10,080 bottles, is a sevenfold increase in the order quantity. So jumping from one
tier to one pallet means the average inventory increases by a factor of seven and deliveries
are received about every 56 days! And Walmart is willing to do that for a 4 percent discount!
Imagine you were to go to a Walmart supercenter and you see that they have a 4 percent
discount if you purchase seven bottles of Tylenol. Would you be excited enough by a 4 percent discount to buy seven bottles? If you are, then you probably expect to suffer from a lot
of headaches in the future or you really believe in always getting the lowest price. But most
people, fortunately, would not be that excited about a 4 percent discount. And this leads to
an interesting observation: When firms are contemplating quantity discounts, they tend to be
willing to increase their purchase quantity by much more than consumers. Put another way,
firms are more sensitive to price changes than consumers—a small discount (like 4 percent)
gets a firm more excited, sometimes much more excited, than a typical consumer.

To push the previous point a bit further, Table 12.5 summarizes the results for several order
quantities. The first two columns give the results that we have already evaluated for the one-
tier and one-pallet order quantities. The final two columns evaluate total costs with even larger
quantities: two pallets or three pallets. We see that Walmart would lower its total costs even if
it were required to purchase two pallets to receive the 4 percent discount. In that case, the net
savings is only 1.4 percent, which means that 3.6 percent of the discount is lost to higher EOQ
costs (ordering plus holding), but it is still a net savings and would not be ignored.

Only when the order quantity reaches three pallets does the increase in EOQ cost swamp
the purchasing cost savings. But three pallets is a huge quantity—even Walmart takes more
than 24 weeks to sell 30,240 bottles of Tylenol through one of its DCs. So we again can conclude that when it comes to quantity discounts, while it isn't optimal to order an unlimited
quantity to obtain a discount, it may still be optimal to order a large quantity.

TABLE 12.5 Cost Calculations for Different Order Quantities at the Walmart DC

	1 Tier	1 Pallet	2 Pallets	3 Pallets
Q (bottles)	1440	10,080	20,160	30,240
Order cost, K ($)	$8	$8	$8	$8
Annual holding cost %	20%	20%	20%	20%
Discount	0%	4%	4%	4%
Holding cost per unit ($ per year), h	$0.60	$0.576	$0.576	$0.576
Holding cost ($ per year) = 1/2 hQ	$432	$2903	$5806	$8709
Ordering cost ($ per year) = KR/Q	$361	$52	$26	$17
Annual purchasing cost ($)	$195,000	$187,200	$187,200	$187,200
Total annual cost (purchasing + ordering + holding) $	$195,793	$190,155	$193,032	$195,926
Annual cost savings relative to the one-tier order quantity		−2.9%	−1.4%	0.1%

Check Your Understanding 12.7

Question: A firm incurs a fixed order cost of $10 per order and 20 percent annual holding costs. It purchases an item for $2.50 and sells 1000 units per year. It is offered a 5 percent discount if it purchases 800 units or more. How much does it save each year (including purchasing, ordering, and holding costs) if it purchases enough units to get the discount?

Answer: If it does not get the discount, then the holding cost per unit per year is $2.50 × 0.2 = $0.50. In that case, the EOQ is

$$Q^* = \sqrt{\frac{2 \times 10 \times 1000}{0.5}} = 200$$

The ordering and holding costs are then

$$C(Q = 200) = \left(K \times \frac{R}{Q}\right) + \left(\frac{1}{2} \times h \times Q\right) = \left(\$10 \times \frac{1000}{200}\right) + \left(\frac{1}{2} \times \$0.5 \times 200\right) = \$100$$

Purchasing cost is $2500 per year = $2.50 per unit × 1000 units per year. So total cost is $100 + $2500 = $2600.

If the discount is received, the per-unit cost is $2.50 × 0.95 = $2.375. The holding cost per unit per year, h, is then $2.375 × 0.2 = $0.475. The ordering and holding costs for an order of 800 units is

$$C(Q = 800) = \left(K \times \frac{R}{Q}\right) + \left(\frac{1}{2} \times h \times Q\right) = \left(\$10 \times \frac{1000}{800}\right) + \left(\frac{1}{2} \times \$0.475 \times 800\right) = \$202.50$$

Purchasing cost is $2375 per year = $2.375 per unit × 1000 units per year. So total cost is $202.50 + $2375 = $2577.50. Annual savings are $2600 − $2577.50 = $22.50. Thus, the answer is $22.50.

Conclusion

This chapter focuses on two reasons why inventory exists: batching due to fixed costs and price discounts. When there is a fixed cost to place an order, the economic order quantity (EOQ) model can be used to choose an order quantity that minimizes the sum of ordering and inventory holding costs per unit of time. The EOQ model reveals that there are economies of scale in managing inventory when there are fixed order costs: As the demand rate increases, the sum of ordering and holding costs as a percentage of purchase cost decreases. As a result of these economies of scale, it can be costly to expand the number of different products offered in an assortment. If adding an additional product reduces the demand of the existing products, then each of those products becomes less efficient and may even become unprofitable.

Besides fixed ordering costs, price discounts can have a powerful effect on the optimal order quantity. While the order quantity needed to obtain the discount may be much larger than the EOQ, and therefore that quantity increases the sum of ordering and holding costs, the price discount can be justified because it reduces the purchase cost. Interestingly, it can be optimal for a firm to increase its order quantity by a large amount, say two to three times more than the EOQ, even for a small discount like 4 percent off. Consequently, firms are much more responsive to small price changes than are typical consumers.

Summary of Learning Objectives

LO12-1   Evaluate optimal order quantities and performance measures with the EOQ model

The economic order quantity (EOQ) is the order quantity that minimizes the sum of ordering and holding costs per unit of time. It depends on the fixed ordering cost and the cost to hold a unit of inventory per unit of time.

LO12-2   Recognize the presence of economies of scale in inventory management and understand the impact of product variety on inventory costs

It is possible to evaluate the sum of ordering and holding costs per period for a given order quantity. Assuming the EOQ is chosen, this cost increases as the flow rate (demand) increases. However, it increases at a slower rate than demand. This means that the sum of ordering and holding costs becomes a smaller percentage of the purchase cost as the demand rate increases. In other words, when there is larger demand, the system is more efficient and this is why the EOQ model exhibits economies of scale.

A consequence of the economies of scale is that it can be costly to add a product to an assortment. This is especially true if adding the product reduces the demand of the existing products because then the existing products lose scale and become less efficient.

LO12-3   Evaluate optimal order quantities when there are quantity constraints or quantity discounts are offered

A quantity discount can motivate a firm to order in larger quantities than it would otherwise choose. The larger quantity increases the sum of ordering and holding costs (above the minimum cost) but also reduces the purchasing cost. Remarkably, a very large quantity may be optimal even if the discount appears to be rather small (like 4 percent). Because of this, firms are said to be more price sensitive than consumers (i.e., they change their behavior in greater proportion to a price discount than consumers do).

Key Terms

12.1   The Economic Order Quantity

Economic order quantity (EOQ) model   A model used to select an order quantity that minimizes the sum of ordering and inventory holding costs per unit of time.

Order cost, K   The fixed cost incurred per order, which is independent of the amount ordered.

Holding cost per unit, h   The cost to hold one item in inventory for one unit of time.

Lead time   The time between when an order is placed and when it is received. Process lead time is frequently used as an alternative term for flow time.

Ordering cost per unit of time   The sum of all fixed order costs in a period of time.

Holding cost per unit of time   The total cost to hold inventory for a period of time.

EOQ cost per unit of time   The sum of ordering and holding costs per unit of time.

Purchasing cost   The cost to purchase inventory in a period of time

12.2   Economies of Scale and Product Variety

Economies of scale   Describes a relationship between operational efficiency and demand in which greater demand leads to a more efficient process.

12.3   Quantity Constraints and Discounts

Pallet   Either (i) a platform which is used to stack inventory to facilitate moving the inventory, or (ii) the quantity of inventory that is stacked on the platform.

Distribution center (DC)   A facility designed to receive product from suppliers, store inventory, and ship products to retail stores.

Tier   The quantity of product in one layer of a pallet.

Key Formulas

LO12-1 Evaluate optimal order quantities and performance measures with the EOQ model

Q = Order quantity

h = Cost to holding one unit for one unit of time

R = Flow rate

K = Fixed cost per order

$$\text{Average inventory during the unit of time} = \frac{Q}{2}$$

$$\text{Holding cost per unit of time} = \frac{1}{2} \times h \times Q$$

$$\text{Number of orders per unit of time} = \frac{R}{Q}$$

$$\text{Ordering cost per unit of time} = K \times \frac{R}{Q}$$

$$\text{Total ordering and holding costs per unit of time} = C(Q) = \left(K \times \frac{R}{Q}\right) + \left(\frac{1}{2} \times h \times Q\right)$$

$$\text{Economic order quantity} = Q^* = \sqrt{\frac{2 \times K \times R}{h}}$$

Conceptual Questions

LO12-1

1. Which of the following is NOT an assumption of the EOQ model?
   a. It is possible to receive a purchase discount if the order quantity is sufficiently large.
   b. There is a fixed cost to submit each order that is independent of the amount ordered.
   c. Demand occurs at a constant rate per unit of time.
   d. There is a cost to hold each unit of inventory per unit of time.

2. The EOQ minimizes the sum of the ordering cost and which of the following costs?
   a. Stockout cost   c. Purchasing cost
   b. Holding cost   d. Quality cost

3. If the order quantity doubles, what happens to the frequency of orders (i.e., the number of orders submitted per unit of time)?
   a. Decreases by more than 50 percent   d. Increases by 100 percent or doubles
   b. Decreases by 50 percent   e. Increases by more than 50 percent
   c. Remains unchanged

LO12-2

4. If the order quantity doubles but the flow rate remains constant, what happens to the average amount of time a unit spends in inventory?
   a. Decreases by more than 50 percent   d. Increases by 50 percent
   b. Decreases by 50 percent   e. Increases by more than 50 percent
   c. Remains unchanged

LO12-1

5. A firm evaluates its EOQ quantity to equal 180 cases, but it chooses an order quantity of 200 cases. Relative to the order quantity of 180 cases, the order quantity of 200 cases has:
   a. higher ordering cost and higher holding cost.
   b. higher ordering cost and lower holding cost.
   c. lower ordering cost and higher holding cost.
   d. lower ordering cost and lower holding cost.

LO12-2

6. If the order quantity doubles but the flow rate remains constant, what happens to the sum of ordering and holding costs?
   a. Decreases by 50 percent
   b. Decreases by less than 50 percent
   c. Remains unchanged
   d. Increases by less than 50 percent
   e. Increases by 50 percent

7. If a firm wanted to reduce the annual EOQ cost as a percentage of the annual purchase cost by 50 percent, how would the demand rate have to change?
   a. Decrease by 50 percent
   b. Remain unchanged
   c. Increase by 50 percent
   d. Double
   e. Quadruple

LO12-3

8. Vetox sells industrial chemicals. One of their inputs can be purchased in either jugs or barrels. A jug contains one gallon, while a barrel contains 55 gallons. The price per gallon is the same with either container. Vetox is charged a fixed amount per order whether it purchases jugs or barrels. The inventory holding cost per gallon per month is the same with either jugs or barrels. Vetox chooses an order quantity to minimize ordering and holding costs per year. Would Vetox purchase a greater number of gallons with each order if it purchased with jugs or with barrels?
   a. They would order a greater number of gallons with barrels.
   b. They would order the same number of gallons with either container.
   c. They would order a greater number of gallons with jugs.
   d. They might order a greater number of gallons with jugs or with barrels, depending on various factors like the demand rate, ordering cost, and holding cost.

9. Sarah is a buyer for a department store. A supplier offers her a 5 percent discount if she triples her usual order quantity. Which of the following best explains why Sarah should take the deal?
   a. Even though the increase in the operating costs is likely to exceed the benefit of the 5 percent discount, Sarah feels that her customers expect the lowest possible price.
   b. Sarah hopes that customers are likely to purchase more if they see an increase in the inventory in the store.
   c. Sarah knows that even though she may triple her order quantity, this would increase her operating costs by far less than a factor of three.
   d. Sarah knows that the sum of operating costs is probably less than 5 percent of the purchase cost, so an increase in the operating costs is unlikely to be a concern.

Solved Example Problems

LO 12-1

1. A firm's demand rate is 1000 units per year. If the firm orders 400 units per order, how many orders does the firm make per year on average?
   a. 0.4
   b. 1.0
   c. 2.0
   d. 2.5
   e. 3.0

   Answer: d. The firm makes 1000/400 = 2.5 orders per year.

LO12-1, 12-2, 12-3

2. Powered by Koffee (PBK) is a new campus coffee store. PBK uses 50 bags of whole bean coffee every month, and demand is steady throughout the year. PBK has signed

a contract to purchase its coffee from a local supplier, Phish Roasters, for a price of $25 per bag and an $85 fixed cost for every delivery independent of the order size. PBK incurs an inventory holding cost of 24% per year.

a. If PBK orders 125 bags at a time, how many orders will it place per year?

Answer: 4.8. The annual flow rate, R, is 50 bags per month × 12 months per year = 600 bags per year. If its order quantity is 125 bags, then it orders R/Q = 600 bags per year/125 bags per order = 4.8 orders per year.

b. What is PBK's annual inventory holding cost per bag?

Answer: 6. Annual inventory holding cost per bag, h, is $25 per bag × 24% per year = $6 per bag per year.

c. If PBK orders 200 bags at a time, what is its inventory holding cost per year?

Answer: $600. With Q = 200 and h = $6 (from part B), the inventory holding cost per year is 0.5 × h × Q = 0.5 × $6 per year per bag × 200 bags = $600.

d. What order quantity minimizes PBK's ordering and holding costs per year?

Answer: 130. K = $85. From part B, h = $6. R = 600 bags per year = 50 bags per month × 12 months per year.

$$\sqrt{\frac{2 \times K \times R}{h}} = \sqrt{\frac{2 \times \$85 \times 600}{\$6}} = 130 \text{ bags}$$

e. If PBK chooses an order quantity to minimize ordering and holding costs, what is its ordering and holding costs per year expressed as a percentage of its annual purchase cost?

Answer: 5.21 percent. $C(Q) = (K \times R/Q) + (1/2 \times h \times Q)$ = ($85 × 600 bags per year/130 bags) + (1/2 × $6 × 130 bags) = $782. It orders 600 bags per year at a price of $25 each, which is a total annual purchase cost of 600 × $25 = $15,000. The ordering and holding costs expressed as a percentage of the annual total cost are $782/$15,000 = 5.21 percent.

f. A South American import/export company has offered PBK a deal. PBK can buy a year's worth of coffee directly from South America for $20 per bag and a fixed cost for delivery of $1000. If PBK took this deal, what would be the sum of its purchasing, ordering, and holding costs per year?

Answer: $14,440. The order quantity would be Q = 600 bags. The holding cost per bag is h = $20 × 0.24 = $4.80. The fixed ordering cost is K = $1000. Ordering and holding costs are therefore $C(Q) = (K \times R/Q) + (0.5 \times h \times Q)$ = ($1000 × 600 bags/600 bags) + (0.5 × $4.80 per bag × 600 bags) = $2440. Purchasing cost = $20 per bag × 600 bags = $12,000. The total of purchasing, ordering, and holding costs is $12,000 + $2440 = $14,440.

LO12-1, 12-3

3. Cat Lovers Inc. (CLI) is the distributor of a very popular blend of cat food that it sells for $1.25 per can. CLI sells 500 cans per week. It orders the cans of cat food from Nutritious & Delicious Co. (N&D). N&D sells cans to CLI at $0.50 per can and charges a flat fee of $20 per order for shipping and handling. CLI's annual inventory holding cost percentage is 25 percent.

a. How many cans of cat food should CLI order at a time?

Answer: 2884. K = $20. h = 25% × $0.50 = $0.125. R = 500 cans per week × 52 weeks per year = 26,000 cans per year.

$$Q^* = \sqrt{\frac{2 \times K \times R}{h}} = \sqrt{\frac{2 \times \$20 \times 26,000}{\$0.125}} = 2884 \text{ cans}$$

b. If CLI orders 1000 cans with each order, what is the sum of CLI's ordering and holding costs per year?

Answer: $582.50. $C(Q) = (K \times R/Q) + (0.5 \times h \times Q) = (\$20 \times 26{,}000 \, \text{cans}/1000 \, \text{cans}) + (0.5 \times \$0.125 \times 1000) = \$582.50$

c. If CLI orders 6000 cans with each order, what is CLI's inventory holding cost incurred per can?

Answer: $0.014. The annual holding cost is $0.5 \times h \times Q = 0.5 \times \$0.125$ per can $\times \, 6000 \, \text{cans} = \$375$. Annual demand is 26,000 cans. So the holding cost per can is $375/26{,}000 = \$0.014$.

d. If CLI is restricted to ordering in tier quantities, a tier has 20 cases, and a case contains 96 cans, what should CLI's order quantity be (in tiers)?

Answer: 2. A tier contains $20 \times 96 = 1920$ cans. The EOQ is 2884 cans. So it should order one tier (1920 cans) or two tiers (3840 cans). Evaluate ordering and holding costs for each order quantity. $C(Q = 1920) = (K \times R/1920) + (0.5 \times h \times 1920) = \$391$ and $C(Q = 3840) = (K \times R/3840) + (0.5 \times h \times 3840) = \$375$. Thus, order two tiers.

e. N&D offers a 4 percent discount if CLI orders at least one pallet (7680 cans). If CLI decides to order one pallet, what would be its annual ordering cost?

Answer: $67.70. $R = 26{,}000$ cans. So if $Q = 7680$ cans, then annual ordering costs are $K \times R/Q = \$20 \times 26{,}000/7680 = \$67.71$.

f. N&D offers a 4 percent discount if CLI orders at least one pallet (7680 cans). If CLI decides to order one pallet, what would be its annual holding cost?

Answer: $460.80. The holding cost per unit per year is $h = 0.25 \times \$0.5 \times 0.96 = \$0.12$. Annual holding cost is $0.5 \times h \times Q = \$460.80$.

Problems and Applications

LO12-1, 12-3

1. Millennium Liquors is a wholesaler of sparkling wines. Its most popular product is the French Bete Noire, which is shipped directly from France. Weekly demand is 45 cases. Millennium purchases each case for $120, there is a $300 fixed cost for each order (independent of the quantity ordered), and its annual holding cost is 25 percent.
   a. What order quantity minimizes Millennium's annual ordering and holding costs?
   b. If Millennium chooses to order 300 cases each time, what is the sum of its annual ordering and holding costs?
   c. If Millennium chooses to order 100 cases each time, what is the sum of the ordering and holding costs incurred by each case sold?
   d. If Millennium is restricted to ordering in multiples of 50 cases (e.g., 50, 100, 150, etc.), how many cases should it order to minimize its annual ordering and holding costs?
   e. Millennium is offered a 5 percent discount if it purchases at least 1000 cases. If it decides to take advantage of this discount, what is the sum of its annual ordering and holding costs?

2. Sarah's Organic Soap Company makes organic liquid soap. One of the raw materials for her soaps is organic palm oil. She needs 1000 kg of palm oil per day, on average. The supplier charges a $60 delivery fee per order (which is independent of the order size) and $4.75 per kg. Sarah's annual holding cost is 25 percent. Assume she operates and sells five days per week, 52 weeks per year.
   a. If Sarah wants to minimize her annual ordering and inventory holding costs, how much palm oil should she purchase with each order (in kg)?
   b. If Sarah orders 4000 kg with each order, what would be the annual sum of the ordering and holding costs?

c. If Sarah orders 8000 kg with each order, what would be the sum of the ordering and holding costs per kg sold?

d. Sarah's supplier is willing to sell her palm oil at a 5 percent discount if she purchases 15,000 kg at a time. If she were to purchase 15,000 kg per order, what would be her annual sum of the ordering and holding costs?

LO12-1, 12-2, 12-3

3. Joe Birra needs to purchase malt for his microbrewery production. His supplier charges $35 per delivery (no matter how much is delivered) and $1.20 per gallon. Joe's annual holding cost per unit is 35 percent of the price per gallon. Joe uses 250 gallons of malt per week.

   a. Suppose Joe orders 1000 gallons each time. What is his average inventory (in gal)?

   b. Suppose Joe orders 1500 gallons each time. How many orders does he place with his supplier each year?

   c. How many gallons should Joe order from his supplier with each order to minimize the sum of the ordering and holding costs?

   d. Suppose Joe orders 2500 gallons each time he places an order with the supplier. What is the sum of the ordering and holding costs per gallon?

   e. Suppose Joe orders the quantity from part (C) that minimizes the sum of the ordering and holding costs each time he places an order with the supplier. What is the annual cost of the EOQ expressed as a percentage of the annual purchase cost?

   f. If Joe's supplier only accepts orders that are an integer multiple of 1000 gallons, how much should Joe order to minimize ordering and holding costs per gallon?

   g. Joe's supplier offers a 3 percent discount if Joe is willing to purchase 8000 gallons or more. What would Joe's total annual cost (purchasing, ordering, and holding) be if he were to take advantage of the discount?

LO12-1, 12-3

4. Bruno Fruscalzo decided to start a small production facility in Sydney to sell gelato to the local restaurants. His local milk supplier charges $0.50 per kg of milk plus a $20 delivery fee (the $20 fee is independent of the amount ordered). Bruno's holding cost is $0.03 per kg per month. He needs 9000 kg of milk per month.

   a. Suppose Bruno orders 9000 kg each time. What is his average inventory (in kg)?

   b. Suppose Bruno orders 7000 kg each time. How many orders does he place with his supplier each year?

   c. How many kg should Bruno order from his supplier with each order to minimize the sum of the ordering and holding costs?

   d. If Bruno's storage vessel can hold only 3000 kg of milk, what would be Bruno's annual ordering and holding costs?

   e. If Bruno's storage vessel can hold only 6000 kg of milk, what would be Bruno's annual ordering and holding costs?

   f. Bruno's supplier's truck can carry 20,000 kg of milk. The supplier does not want to deliver to more than three customers with each truck. Thus, the supplier requires a minimum order quantity of 6500 kg. If Bruno orders the minimum amount, what would be the sum of his annual ordering and holding costs? Assume he has a storage vessel large enough to hold 6500 kg.

   g. Bruno's supplier offers a 5 percent discount when a customer orders a full truck, which is 20,000 kg. Assume Bruno can store that quantity and the product will not spoil. If Bruno orders a full truck, what would be the inventory holding and ordering cost incurred per kg of milk?

LO12-1, 12-2, 12-3

5. BZoom sells toy bricks that can be used to construct a wide range of machines, animals, buildings, and so on. It purchases a red dye powder to include in the resin it uses to make the bricks. The powder is purchased from a supplier for $1.30 per kg. At one production facility, BZoom requires 400 kg of this red dye powder each week. BZoom's annual holding costs are 30 percent and the fixed cost associated with each order to the supplier is $50.

a. How many kg should BZoom order from its supplier with each order to minimize the sum of the ordering and holding costs?

b. If BZoom orders 4000 kg at a time, what would be the sum of the annual ordering and holding costs?

c. If BZoom orders 2000 kg at a time, what would be the sum of the ordering and holding costs per kg of dye?

d. If BZoom orders the quantity from part (A) that minimizes the sum of the ordering and holding costs, what is the annual cost of the EOQ expressed as a percentage of the annual purchase cost?

e. BZoom's purchasing manager negotiated with its supplier to get a 2.5 percent discount on orders of 10,000 kg or greater? What would be the change in BZoom's annual total cost (purchasing, ordering, and holding) if it took advantage of this deal instead of ordering smaller quantities at the full price?

   i. It would decrease by more than $1000.

   ii. It would decrease by less than $1000.

   iii. It would increase by less than $1000.

   iv. It would increase by more than $1000.

CASE   J&J AND WALMART[2]

Michelle Sayer is Johnson & Johnson's Walmart account manager, meaning that she oversees all operational interactions between Walmart and Johnson & Johnson. The Walmart account is so important to J&J that Michelle actually lives in Bentonville, Arkansas, which is where Walmart's corporate headquarters is located.

    Rafael Ellwood works for Walmart and is Michelle's main contact person. Rafael was concerned that Walmart was not purchasing as efficiently from J&J as it could, so he arranged for a meeting with Michelle to discuss their strategy.

    To focus the conversation, Rafael suggested they look at one product, Listerine Cool Mint 250 ml. Table 12.6 reports

© John Flournoy/McGraw-Hill Education

TABLE 12.6   Weekly Sales of Listerine Cool Mint 250 ml at One Walmart Supercenter

Week	Sales	Week	Sales	Week	Sales
1	18	11	9	21	11
2	16	12	10	22	10
3	19	13	9	23	12
4	15	14	5	24	13
5	12	15	6	25	19
6	15	16	7	26	14
7	17	17	11	27	13
8	13	18	10	28	18
9	8	19	10	29	18
10	9	20	7	30	15

---

[2]Names and data have been disguised to maintain confidentiality.

Continued

sales data for that product in one of Walmart's stores over a 30-week period, while Figure 12.3 displays the data in a graph. Table 12.7 provides data on demand, ordering costs, and holding costs for this product.

1. Rafael turns to Michelle and asks, "What order quantity do you recommend we use for this product? Remember, we only ship in case quantities."

2. Michelle reminds Rafael that the two companies are looking for ways to streamline the flow of product through the supply chain. One way to do so would be to ship only in tier quantities. If each order to the store was for a single tier, then the tier could be created in J&J's warehouse. The tier would then be shipped to Walmart's distribution center and immediately sent on from the distribution center to the supercenter. Rafael agrees that a tier quantity might help the rest of the supply chain, but he fears that it would be costly to order one tier at a time for this supercenter. Are Rafael's concerns justified?

3. Putting aside the issue of ordering a single tier (which requires some more information to come to a resolution), Rafael wanted to raise another issue with Michelle. Looking at Figure 12.3, he points out that there are periods of time when demand looks like it is 50 percent higher than the average, and other times when demand is as much as 50 percent lower than the average. Given this variation in demand, he wonders if choosing a single order quantity (in cases) is a reasonable strategy. Or should it adjust its order quantity throughout the year? Making adjustments to the order quantity would be a hassle, especially given the number of products it manages and the number of stores it has, but if it needs to do that to save on costs, it will.

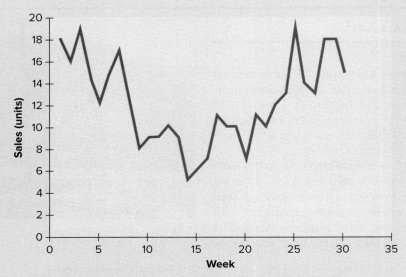

Figure 12.3   Weekly sales of Listerine Cool Mint 250 ml at one Walmart supercenter

TABLE 12.7   Information Regarding Demand, Ordering Costs, and Holding Costs for Listerine Cool Mint 250 ml

Purchase price per unit	$2.50
Annual holding cost percentage	25%
Fixed ordering cost	$6
Average weekly sales (units)	12.3
Units per case	12
Cases per tier	24
Tiers per pallet	5

Inventory Management with Perishable Demand

13

Introduction

O'Neill Inc. is a designer and manufacturer of apparel, wet suits, and accessories for water sports such as surfing, diving, water-skiing, wake boarding, triathlons, and wind surfing. It divides the year into two selling seasons: spring and fall. With each season, it faces a challenging decision: How many units of each product should it order from its Asian supplier? It has a sense of what demand could be during the season, but it never knows for sure—some products turn out to be more popular than expected, while others fail to gain traction. To complicate matters, it must make this decision well before the season actually starts (because its supplier needs time to make the product) and it is only allowed to submit a single order for each item (no second chances). The combination of the single order and uncertain demand means that it never ever seems to "get it right"—either it orders too many units or too few. The "too many" error is clearly painful, forcing inventory at the end of the season to be sold off at a deep discount. But the "too

few" error is also painful: While it might seem great that it sold everything it had ordered, this means it could have sold even more and earned a higher profit. In short, due to the inhibitors of variability (i.e., uncertain demand) and inflexibility (i.e., a single ordering opportunity), it is difficult for O'Neill to match its supply with its demand.

The "too much versus too few" challenge applies to O'Neill's ordering decisions, and applies to a great deal more than just that—this challenge occurs whenever a single decision is made before some uncertain event. Companies like O'Neill deal with this in a variety of settings. For instance, a pharmaceutical company may need to decide the capacity for a new production facility: Build too much capacity and the extra capacity is wasted (in the form of idle time and poor utilization), but build too little capacity and suffer the opportunity cost of sales that cannot be satisfied. Or the manager of a distribution center must decide the staffing level for the next month. Too many workers leaves them relatively idle and unproductive, while too few workers creates the need for expensive overtime. And this challenge even applies to everyday decisions. For example, say you invite a group of friends over for a barbeque party on Saturday. You plan to keep it simple—you will only grill hamburgers. So how many buns should you buy? The problem is that you don't really know how many friends will show up or how hungry they will be. Buy too many buns and they are likely to be thrown out as they get moldy on your counter next week. Buy too few and your friends will look at you like you are too cheap to buy enough buns.

Or think about the process of getting to the airport to catch a flight. Between traffic and airport security, you are not exactly sure how long it will take to get to your gate. Leave too early for the airport and you will spend a relatively unproductive and boring time at the airport waiting for your flight. But leave too late and you miss your flight.

In this chapter, we develop a tool, called the newsvendor model, to help O'Neill (and others) decide its order quantities for each product and each season. Although it is true that no matter what quantity it chooses it is likely to have ordered either too much or too little, we will learn that there is still a single order quantity that maximizes the company's expected profit (section 13.1). In addition to the optimal order quantity, we want to understand how to evaluate various performance measures for any chosen quantity, such as expected sales, inventory, and profit (section 13.2). These performance measures allow us to decide if we want to choose something other than the order quantity that maximizes expected profit (section 13.3). For example, we might want to order enough to ensure that there is a small chance that some customers experience a stockout (i.e., reduce the chance that we run out of inventory). In general, we also want to understand under which settings the "too much versus too little" challenge is most challenging: There are some situations in which profits suffer tremendously even if we get the decision right, and other situations in which the consequences are minor even if we make a poor decision (section 13.4). Finally, as with all operations, it is important to make changes that improve the performance of the system. We conclude with a discussion of several options for bettering the newsvendor situation (section 13.5).

13.1 The Newsvendor Model

In this section, we begin with more details regarding O'Neill's ordering decision (section 13.1.1). Then we use the newsvendor model to make an actual decision. But before we continue, let's answer one question that you might already have: How does selling newspapers help us decide how many wet suits to order? Clearly, selling newspapers is a very different business than selling wet suits. For one thing, some people still value wet suits, whereas physical newspapers will never regain their prominence as a source of information. But think about the choices a newsvendor makes. Each morning the newsvendor needs to decide how many newspapers to bring to his or her stand on the street corner. Demand during the day is uncertain. If the newsvendor purchased too many papers, then they are thrown out—nobody wants to read yesterday's news. If the newsvendor purchases too few papers, then some sales (and therefore profit) are lost (because there is no opportunity to obtain additional inventory during the day). Thus, while few people need to know how to manage newspaper inventory, many people do face decisions that are just like the newsvendor's. Hence, while the name of the model is somewhat anachronistic, it does provide a memorable metaphor for a very important type of decision in operations management.

13.1.1 O'Neill's Order Quantity Decision

As mentioned in the introduction, O'Neill sells clothing for water sports. Some of its products are not considered fashionable (i.e., they have little cosmetic variety and they sell from year to year); for example, standard neoprene black booties. With product names like "Animal," "Epic," "Hammer," "Inferno," and "Zen," O'Neill clearly also has products that are subject to the whims of fashion. For example, color patterns on surf suits often change from season to season to adjust to the tastes of their users, who are generally young and athletically fit.

O'Neill operates its own manufacturing facility in Mexico, but it does not produce all of its products there. Some items are produced by the TEC Group, O'Neill's supplier in Asia. While TEC provides many benefits to O'Neill (low cost, sourcing expertise, flexible capacity, etc.), it does require a three-month lead time on all orders. For example, if O'Neill orders an item on November 1, then O'Neill can expect to have that item at its distribution center in San Diego, California, ready for shipment to customers only on January 31.

To better understand O'Neill's production challenge, let's consider a particular wet suit used by surfers and newly redesigned for the upcoming spring season, the Hammer 3/2. (The "3/2" signifies the thickness of the neoprene on the suit: 3mm thick on the chest and 2mm everywhere else.) Photo 13.1 displays the Hammer 3/2 and O'Neill's logo. O'Neill has decided to let TEC manufacture the Hammer 3/2. Due to TEC's three-month lead time, O'Neill needs to submit an order to TEC in November before the start of the spring season. Figure 13.1 summarizes the timeline of events for the Hammer 3/2.

As shown in Table 13.1, the economics of the Hammer are pretty good. O'Neill sells the Hammer to retailers for $190 while it pays TEC $100 per suit. If O'Neill has inventory at the end of the season, it is O'Neill's experience that it is able to sell that inventory through various channels for $70 per wet suit, which is called the **salvage value**—the value that can be obtained per unit for inventory at the end of the selling season.

> **LO13-1** Use the newsvendor model to decide how much product to order when demand is perishable and uncertain.

> **Salvage value** The value that can be obtained per unit for inventory left over at the end of the selling season.

PHOTO 13.1 O'Neill's Hammer 3/2 wet suit and logo for the surf market

Figure 13.1

Timeline of events and economics for O'Neill's Hammer 3/2 wet suit

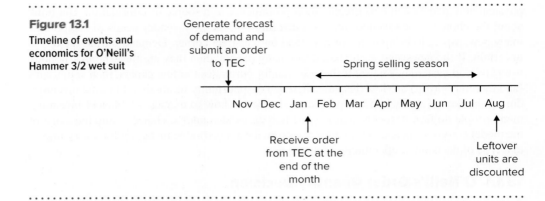

TABLE 13.1 Economics of the Hammer 3/2 Wet Suit

Selling price	$190
Purchase price from TEC	$100
Discount price at end of season (the salvage value)	$ 70

A crucial input to this decision is the forecast for demand. Using past sales data for similar products and the judgment of its designers and sales representatives, O'Neill believes that demand for the Hammer 3/2 during the spring season (at the regular price of $190) can be represented by a normal distribution with a mean (i.e., average) of 3000 and a standard deviation of 1000. (All normal distributions are defined by just two parameters: the mean and the standard deviation.)

The plot of the density function for a normal distribution has a bell shape—see Figure 13.2. Recall that the **density function** returns the probability that a given outcome occurs. The peak of the normal distribution's bell is at the mean of the distribution. In this case, the peak is at 3000 units—the most likely outcome is that demand is for 3000 units. But there is considerable variation about that average. The amount of variation is determined by the standard deviation. If the standard deviation is small relative to the mean, then the bell is tall and thin, meaning that the likely outcomes are clustered about the mean (left panel in Figure 13.2). However, if the standard deviation is large relative to the mean, then the bell is wide and short, meaning that outcomes far from the average are somewhat likely (right panel in Figure 13.2). The middle panel in Figure 13.2 plots the density function for the normal distribution that

Density function A function that returns the probability a given outcome occurs for a particular statistical distribution.

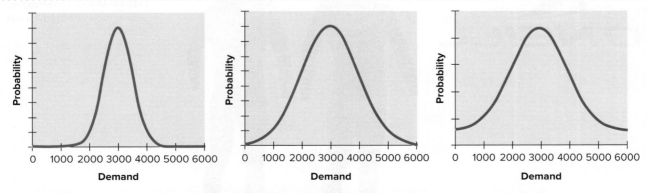

Figure 13.2 Density functions for three normal distributions with mean of 3000 and standard deviation of either 500 (left), 1000 (middle), or 1500 (right)

represents demand for the Hammer 3/2. We can see that while it is not highly likely that demand is either below 1000 units or above 5000 units, both of those outcomes are possible.

Although the density function is probably what people think about when they are thinking about a statistical distribution (to the extent that they think in terms of statistical distributions at all), for the implementation of the newsvendor model it is actually more convenient to work with the **distribution function** of the normal distribution—the distribution function provides the probability that the uncertain outcome is a certain level or lower. For example, say $F(Q)$ is the distribution function of the normal distribution with mean 3000 and standard deviation 1000. Then, $F(Q)$ is the probability that demand is Q or lower. That distribution function is plotted in Figure 13.3. Like all distribution functions, (i) $F(Q)$ is between 0 and 1 (because it is reporting a probability) and (ii) it starts low (usually around 0) and increases toward 1 (usually with an S shape). Notice that $F(3000) = .5$, which means that there is a .5 probability that demand is the mean or lower. That is true with all normal distributions because the normal distribution is symmetric about its mean—half of the probability is below the mean and half above the mean.

Figure 13.3 provides a visual of the distribution function, but it is also useful to work with a table of the distribution function, like Table 13.2. Each row in Table 13.2 corresponds to a demand quantity Q; the second column lists the probability demand is that quantity or lower. For example, demand is 1500 or fewer with only a .0668 probability, while demand is 5000 or fewer with a .9772 probability. Note, Table 13.2 only displays quantities in multiples of 100 units. This is done for convenience—it requires a large table to list the probabilities for all possible demand outcomes. The third column in Table 13.2 is also useful for the newsvendor analysis, but we will discuss it in section 13.2.

The uncertainty in the forecast displayed in Figure 13.2 and Table 13.2 pose an obvious question: Why is there so much uncertainty? Unfortunately, uncertainty in forecasts is a fact of life even if care and attention are placed in the development of the forecast. For example, it is O'Neill's experience that, for about 50 percent of its products, actual demand deviates from its initial forecast by more than 25 percent of the forecast. In other words, only 50 percent of the time is the actual demand between 75 percent and 125 percent of its forecast. This is roughly true for the Hammer 3/2. To explain, the range from 2300 to 3700 corresponds to 77 percent and 123 percent of the mean (i.e., approximately 75 percent to 125 percent of the 3000–wet suit forecast). From Table 13.2, $F(2300) = .2420$ and $F(3700) = .7580$, which means that there is a .2420 probability that demand is 2300 or fewer and a .7580 probability it is 3700 or fewer. Thus, there is a .5160 ($= .7580 - .2420$) probability that demand is between 2300 and 3700 wet suits, or about a 52 percent probability that demand for the Hammer 3/2 is between 77 percent and 123 percent of its mean forecast.

> **Distribution function** A function that returns the probability the outcome of a random event is a certain level or lower. For example, if $F(Q)$ is the distribution function of demand, then $F(Q)$ is the probability that demand is Q or lower.

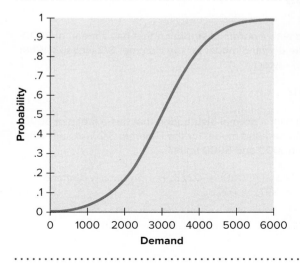

Figure 13.3

The distribution function F(Q) of a normal distribution with mean 3000 and standard deviation 1000

TABLE 13.2   The Distribution, *F(Q)*, and Expected Inventory, *I(Q)*, Functions for a Normal Distribution with Mean 3000 and Standard Deviation 1000

Q	F(Q)	I(Q)	Q	F(Q)	I(Q)	Q	F(Q)	I(Q)
0	.0013	0	2100	.1841	100	4100	.8643	1169
100	.0019	1	2200	.2119	120	4200	.8849	1256
200	.0026	1	2300	.2420	143	4300	.9032	1346
300	.0035	1	2400	.2743	169	4400	.9192	1437
400	.0047	1	2500	.3085	198	4500	.9332	1529
500	.0062	2	2600	.3446	230	4600	.9452	1623
600	.0082	3	2700	.3821	267	4700	.9554	1718
700	.0107	4	2800	.4207	307	4800	.9641	1814
800	.0139	5	2900	.4602	351	4900	.9713	1911
900	.0179	6	3000	.5000	399	5000	.9772	2008
1000	.0228	8	3100	.5398	451	5100	.9821	2106
1100	.0287	11	3200	.5793	507	5200	.9861	2205
1200	.0359	14	3300	.6179	567	5300	.9893	2304
1300	.0446	18	3400	.6554	630	5400	.9918	2403
1400	.0548	23	3500	.6915	698	5500	.9938	2502
1500	.0668	29	3600	.7257	769	5600	.9953	2601
1600	.0808	37	3700	.7580	843	5700	.9965	2701
1700	.0968	46	3800	.7881	920	5800	.9974	2801
1800	.1151	56	3900	.8159	1000	5900	.9981	2901
1900	.1357	69	4000	.8413	1083	6000	.9987	3000
2000	.1587	83						

Check Your Understanding 13.1

Question: Suppose demand is modeled with a normal distribution that has a mean of 3000 and a standard deviation of 1000, like the demand model for the Hammer 3/2 wet suit. What is the probability that demand is 4000 or fewer?

Answer: From Table 13.2, $F(4000) = .8413$.

Question: Suppose demand is modeled with a normal distribution that has a mean of 3000 and a standard deviation of 1000, like the demand model for the Hammer 3/2 wet suit. What is the probability that demand is between 1000 and 5000 units?

Answer: From Table 13.2, $F(5000) = .9772$ and $F(1000) = .0228$. The probability demand between those two values is then .9544 (= .9772 − .0228).

So how many units should O'Neill order from TEC? You might argue that O'Neill should order the forecast for total demand, 3000, because it is the most likely outcome. However, you might feel this is too aggressive because with that order quantity there is too high a chance at the end of the season that some inventory will need to be discounted for a loss. A contrasting view suggests ordering more than 3000 because you make $90 on each sold wet suit but lose only $30 on each wet suit that needs to be discounted. So which is it? The newsvendor model tells us.

13.1.2 The Objective of and Inputs to the Newsvendor Model

The newsvendor model represents a situation in which a decision maker must make a single bet (e.g., an order quantity) before some random event occurs (e.g., demand). There are costs if the bet turns out to be too high (e.g., inventory that is salvaged for a loss on each unit). There are costs if the bet turns out to be too low (e.g., the opportunity cost of lost sales). The newsvendor model's objective is to bet an amount that correctly balances those opposing forces. In many situations, the objective of the newsvendor model can be described as "maximize expected profit," as in the case of O'Neill's decision. However, in some cases the objective is better described as "minimize expected costs," like the hamburger bun example mentioned earlier. Either way, the same process is used to decide upon an order quantity.

There are three key inputs to the newsvendor model: a cost of ordering too little, a cost of ordering too much, and a demand forecast.

The cost of ordering too few is called the **underage cost** and it is represented with the variable C_u. Specifically, the underage cost is the cost of ordering *one* unit too few; that is, the cost of underordering by one unit. For example, say O'Neill orders 3000 wet suits, but demand turns out to be 3001 wet suits. It ordered one unit too few—had it known that demand would be 3001 wet suits, it would have ordered one more unit, paid $100 for it, sold it for $190, and earned a higher profit of $90 (= $190 − $100). Thus, the underage cost for O'Neill is $C_u =$ $90. Note, the underage cost is *not* $190. Yes, had it known that it could sell one more wet suit than it had purchased, it would have earned an additional $190 in revenue. But that is not the change in its profit; it would also have had to spend $100 to buy the wet suit. So its incremental profit is only $90, and that is the underage cost.

The cost of ordering too many is called the **overage cost** and it is represented with the variable C_o. The overage cost is the cost of ordering *one* unit too many; that is, the cost of overordering by one unit. For example, say O'Neill orders 3000 wet suits, but demand turns out to be 2999 wet suits. It ordered one unit too many—had it known that demand would be 2999 wet suits, it would have ordered one fewer wet suit. Because it would have avoided ordering that last unit, it would have saved itself the $100 purchase cost. However, it also would not have collected the $70 in salvage value from that unit. So the cost of overordering by one unit is not the full $100 but, rather, just the loss on that unit. Hence, for O'Neill, $C_o =$ $30 (= $100 − $70). Put another way, overordering by one unit decreases O'Neill's profit by $30, which is why the overage cost is $30 instead of $100.

Table 13.3 summarizes the overage and underage cost calculations for O'Neill and the two examples mentioned earlier.

The third key input is the demand forecast. The essential feature of the demand forecast is that it must give a probability for all of the possible outcomes of demand, and not just the most likely demand. The easiest way to express the probability for all of those outcomes is to use a statistical distribution function. A commonly used distribution function from statistics is the normal distribution, and that is what O'Neill is using for its forecast of the Hammer 3/2 wet suit—demand is forecasted to be normally distributed with a mean of 3000 and a standard deviation of 1000. Figure 13.3 provides this forecast in graphical form and Table 13.2 provides it in tabular form.

Underage cost The cost of ordering *one* unit too few; that is, the cost of underordering by one unit. It is represented with the variable C_u.

Overage cost The cost of ordering *one* unit too many; that is, the cost of overordering by one unit. It is represented with the variable C_o.

TABLE 13.3   Three Newsvendor Examples and Their Overage and Underage Costs

Example	Decision	Data	Overage Cost, C_o	Underage Cost, C_u
O'Neill Hammer 3/2	Number of wet suits to order	Selling price = $190 Purchase cost = $100 Salvage value = $70	Ordering one too many means incurring the loss on that unit, which is $30 (= $100 − $70)	Ordering one too few means not earning the profit on that sale, which is $90 (= $190 − $100)
Pharmaceutical capacity	Number of doses to be able to produce per year	Revenue per dose = $5000 Cost of capacity for one dose = $1000 Salvage value of capacity = $0	Building capacity to make one more dose than needed means losing the cost of that capacity without earning any salvage revenue, so C_o = $1000	Not building the capacity needed to make one more dose that could be sold means losing the profit on that dose, which is $4000 (= $5000 − $1000)
Distribution center staffing	Number of hours to staff in a month	Cost of one hour of regular time = $12 Cost of one hour of overtime = $18 Value of idle labor = $1	Staffing one more hour than needed incurs a cost of $11 (= $12 − $1)—had it known that the hour would not be needed, it would not have staffed it, saving $12, but it would not have earned the $1 of incidental value from the hour	Staffing one hour too few means overtime, which has an incremental cost of $6 per hour—had it known it would need the extra hour, it would have staffed it at the regular-time pay of $12 instead of using overtime, which costs $18, so it would have saved $6

Check Your Understanding 13.2

© Don Farrall/Getty Images/RF

Question: A retailer has one opportunity to purchase a holiday gift basket. The retailer buys each basket for $10 and sells each basket for $25. Baskets left at the end of the season are sold to a discounter for $1. What is the underage cost?

Answer: If it underorders by one unit, then it could have purchased the basket for $10, sold it for $25, and earned an additional $15 (= $25 − $10) in profit. Thus, the answer is $15.

Question: A retailer has one opportunity to purchase a holiday gift basket. The retailer buys each basket for $10 and sells each basket for $25. Baskets left at the end of the season are sold to a discounter for $1. What is the overage cost?

Answer: If it overorders by one unit, then it would have not purchased the unit, saving the $10 in purchase cost. But it would also not have collected $1 in salvage revenue. So the consequence of ordering one too many units is $1 (= $10 − $9) in lost profit. Thus, the answer is $9.

13.1.3 The Critical Ratio

Before stating how to find the order quantity that maximizes expected profit, let's build some intuition. Suppose we start with an order quantity of zero units. Should we stick with our current order (zero wet suits) or should we order one more wet suit? Given our demand forecast, it is highly likely that it will sell during the season for $190. So we can pretty much expect to earn a profit of $90 on that unit. Hence, we should definitely order it; that is, we should increase our order quantity from zero to one.

Now let's say we have decided to order 6000 wet suits and we are contemplating ordering the 6001st wet suit. Chances are the 6001st unit will not sell during the regular season because it will only sell if demand is much higher than the mean forecast. Instead, there is a very good chance it will be left in inventory and we will then lose $30 on that unit (we bought it for $100 but can only salvage it for $70). Hence, we should stick with our current order of 6000 (i.e., not order the 6001st unit).

We can apply this logic to all order quantities. Say we have already decided to order Q units and we are contemplating whether we should order one more unit (the $(Q+1)$th unit). If we order that unit, according to our demand forecast, there is a $F(Q)$ chance it will be left in inventory. (Recall, $F(Q)$ is the probability that demand is Q or lower.) If it is left in inventory, we incur the overage cost C_o. So the expected cost of ordering one more unit is $F(Q) \times C_o$ (i.e., the expected cost is the probability it happens, F(Q), times the cost if it happens, C_o). However, there is also a benefit of ordering one more unit: By ordering one more unit, we can avoid the underage cost C_u. We avoid the underage cost if demand is greater than Q units, and that happens with probability $(1 - F(Q))$. Hence, the expected benefit of ordering one more unit is $(1 - F(Q)) \times C_u$.

Figure 13.4 displays how the expected gain and loss change throughout the range of reasonable order quantities. The expected-gain curve starts at the high point of C_u ($90) with the zero order quantity because the next unit ordered will almost surely sell. The expected gain curve then declines as we reach higher order quantities because there is a smaller and smaller chance that the last unit in the order sells as we order more. In contrast, the expected loss starts at a low point of $0 because the first unit we order has a very small chance of remaining in inventory at the end of the season—it is highly unlikely that it doesn't even sell one unit. But as we order more units, the last unit ordered has a higher and higher chance of being left in inventory, so the expected loss on the last unit increases to a high point of C_o ($30).

We can see in Figure 13.4 that the gap between the expected gain and the expected loss gets smaller as we order more and more units. By about the 3700th unit, it appears that the expected gain from ordering an additional unit is about equal to the expected loss, which means that there really isn't much of a net gain from ordering more. The same applies for all higher order quantities—with all of those quantities, the expected gain from ordering an additional unit is less than the expected loss. Thus, we should only order additional units up to the point where the expected gain from ordering more is less than the expected loss. Let's now determine how to find that point more precisely.

Let Q^* be the quantity that maximizes expected profit. Based on our reasoning, the expected gain at Q^* should equal the expected loss, or

$$(1 - F(Q^*)) \times C_u = F(Q^*) \times C_o$$

We can rearrange the above equation to express it in the following, more convenient, form and we will call it Equation 13.1:

$$F(Q^*) = \frac{C_u}{C_o + C_u}$$

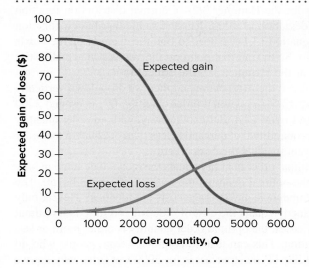

Figure 13.4

The expected gain and loss from ordering the Qth Hammer 3/2 wet suit

---

Check Your Understanding 13.3

Question: A newsvendor determines that the underage cost is $100 and the overage cost is $25. What is the newsvendor's critical ratio?

Answer: The critical ratio is determined by dividing the underage cost, $100, by the sum of the overage and the underage cost, $125. Thus, critical ratio is .80.

· ·

Equation 13.1 says that with the order quantity that maximizes expected profit, $Q*$, $C_u/(C_o + C_u)$ is the probability that demand is less than or equal to $Q*$. That is a bit of a mouthful, so let's parse it. The right-hand side of Equation 13.1 is a ratio of the underage cost to the sum of the underage and overage costs. That ratio is given a special name: the **critical ratio**. The critical ratio balances the costs of ordering too much (C_o) against the cost of ordering too little (C_u). For the Hammer 3/2, the overage cost is $C_o = \$30$ and the underage cost is $C_u = \$90$, so the critical ratio is $\$90/(\$30 + \$90) = .75$. This means that at the optimal order quantity for the Hammer 3/2, there is a 75 percent chance demand is less than or equal to that quantity and a 25 percent chance it is greater than the quantity. Thus, it is more likely that with the optimal order quantity O'Neill has leftover inventory (demand is less than the order quantity) than lost sales (demand is greater than the order quantity).

The left-hand side of Equation 13.1 contains the demand forecast in the form of the distribution function. So Equation 13.1 allows us to combine our demand forecast (the left-hand side) with the economics of the product (the right-hand side) to obtain a quantity that maximizes expected profit.

13.1.4 How to Determine the Optimal Order Quantity

Now we need to learn how to use Equation 13.1 to actually determine the order quantity that maximizes expected profit. Three methods for doing this are described: (i) using a graph, (ii) using a statistical table, and (iii) using a computer program like Excel. The graphical method provides the best intuition, but it is the least convenient to use, and so it is not used in practice. The statistical table is the best method if you don't have access to a computer, but as you might expect, using a computer is the fastest method. Exhibit 13.1 summarizes the process for finding the order quantity that maximizes expected profit.

Optimal Order Quantity—Graph Method Figure 13.5 displays the demand distribution that represents O'Neill's forecast for the Hammer 3/2—a normal distribution function with a mean of 3000 and a standard deviation of 1000. It is the same distribution function shown in Figure 13.3. According to Equation 13.1, we need to find the quantity on the x-axis that sets $F(Q)$ equal to the critical ratio. So to find that point on the x-axis, we actually start with the critical ratio on the y-axis. For the Hammer 3/2, the critical ratio is .75. From that point on the y-axis we move horizontally to the $F(Q)$ curve and then we drop down vertically to the x-axis to reveal $Q*$. From Figure 13.5, the optimal order quantity, $Q*$, is around 3700 units, which matches our analysis from Figure 13.4. Put another way, with an order quantity of 3700 wet suits, there is about a .75 probability that demand is less than or equal to the order quantity, which is the probability we want to equal the critical ratio.

From Figure 13.5 we see that the optimal order quantity equals the mean of demand in only one special case. For the mean to be the optimal quantity, the critical ratio must be .50. The critical ratio equals .50 only when the underage and overage costs are identical. Hence, only when the cost of ordering too much exactly equals the cost of ordering too little is it optimal to order expected demand. In all other cases, the optimal order quantity is either more or less than the mean of the demand distribution. This can lead to comments from people who do not understand the newsvendor model like "If our forecast is for 3000 wet suits, why are we

Critical ratio The ratio of the underage cost, C_u, to the sum of the overage cost and the underage cost, $C_u + C_o$.

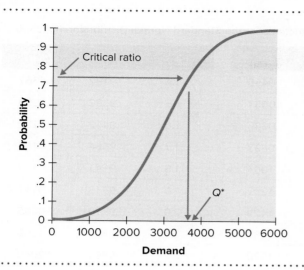

Figure 13.5
How the Hammer 3/2's critical ratio leads to an optimal order quantity given the demand distribution function

ordering more than that?" The answer is that it can be more costly to run out of inventory than to have inventory left over at the end of the season, so balancing the risk of ordering too few against the risk of ordering too many requires an order quantity that is different than the forecast. In particular, the larger the critical ratio, the larger the optimal order quantity. For example, when the critical ratio is large (e.g., close to 1), the optimal order quantity can be much greater than the mean. That happens when the cost of ordering too little (the underage cost C_u) is much larger than the cost of ordering too much (the overage cost C_o). In contrast, when the cost of inventory is much greater than the cost of lost sales, then the critical ratio is small (e.g., close to 0) and the optimal order quantity is small (less than the mean).

Optimal Order Quantity—Statistical Table Method The graph method for finding an optimal order quantity is cumbersome, so an alternative is needed, such as using a statistical table.

Table 13.2 provides the distribution function for O'Neill's demand model. We can use Table 13.2 to find the order quantity Q such that $F(Q)$, the probability that demand is Q or lower, equals the critical ratio, which is .75 for the Hammer 3/2. Looking down the second column in the table, which has the $F(Q)$ values, we find $F(3600) = .7257$ and $F(3700) = .7580$. Thus, the critical ratio falls between two entries in the table. Neither of them is exactly the critical ratio: .7257 is smaller than the critical ratio and .7580 is greater. In cases like this, we should follow the **round-up rule**: When looking up a probability in a statistical table and the probability falls between two entries, choose the one with the larger probability. Hence, based on the round-up rule, O'Neill should choose $F(3700) = .7580$—ordering 3700 Hammer 3/2 wet suits maximizes expected profit. This is consistent with our observation from Figure 13.5, as it should be (i.e., the statistical table method provides a different path to the same answer).

If O'Neill knows the critical ratio for its product and has Table 13.2 handy, then it is possible to quickly determine the order quantity that maximizes expected profit. But what if an order quantity is needed for hundreds or thousands of products and they all have different demand? It would be burdensome to have to create one version of Table 13.2 for each one of them. Fortunately, for all products with normally distributed demand, we can find an order quantity using a single table.

There is an infinite number of normal distributions, each with a unique mean and standard deviation. Despite the tremendous variety within this family, they are all related to the **standard normal distribution**, which is a normal distribution with mean 0 and standard deviation 1. The standard normal is like the master lock to the family of normal distributions. Hence, instead of needing a table for every possible normal distribution, we only need one table, the table for the standard normal distribution—Table 13.4.

Round-up rule If the probability you look up in a statistical table falls between two entries, choose the one with the larger probability.

Standard normal distribution A normal distribution with mean 0 and standard deviation 1.

TABLE 13.4   The Distribution, $F(Q)$, and Expected Inventory, $I(Q)$, Functions for the Standard Normal Distribution Function

z	F(z)	I(z)	z	F(z)	I(z)	z	F(z)	I(z)
−4.0	.0000	.0000	−1.3	.0968	.0455	1.4	.9192	1.4367
−3.9	.0000	.0000	−1.2	.1151	.0561	1.5	.9332	1.5293
−3.8	.0001	.0000	−1.1	.1357	.0686	1.6	.9452	1.6232
−3.7	.0001	.0000	−1.0	.1587	.0833	1.7	.9554	1.7183
−3.6	.0002	.0000	−0.9	.1841	.1004	1.8	.9641	1.8143
−3.5	.0002	.0001	−0.8	.2119	.1202	1.9	.9713	1.9111
−3.4	.0003	.0001	−0.7	.2420	.1429	2.0	.9772	2.0085
−3.3	.0005	.0001	−0.6	.2743	.1687	2.1	.9821	2.1065
−3.2	.0007	.0002	−0.5	.3085	.1978	2.2	.9861	2.2049
−3.1	.0010	.0003	−0.4	.3446	.2304	2.3	.9893	2.3037
−3.0	.0013	.0004	−0.3	.3821	.2668	2.4	.9918	2.4027
−2.9	.0019	.0005	−0.2	.4207	.3069	2.5	.9938	2.5020
−2.8	.0026	.0008	−0.1	.4602	.3509	2.6	.9953	2.6015
−2.7	.0035	.0011	.0	.5000	.3989	2.7	.9965	2.7011
−2.6	.0047	.0015	.1	.5398	.4509	2.8	.9974	2.8008
−2.5	.0062	.0020	.2	.5793	.5069	2.9	.9981	2.9005
−2.4	.0082	.0027	.3	.6179	.5668	3.0	.9987	3.0004
−2.3	.0107	.0037	.4	.6554	.6304	3.1	.9990	3.1003
−2.2	.0139	.0049	.5	.6915	.6978	3.2	.9993	3.2002
−2.1	.0179	.0065	.6	.7257	.7687	3.3	.9995	3.3001
−2.0	.0228	.0085	.7	.7580	.8429	3.4	.9997	3.4001
−1.9	.0287	.0111	.8	.7881	.9202	3.5	.9998	3.5001
−1.8	.0359	.0143	.9	.8159	1.0004	3.6	.9998	3.6000
−1.7	.0446	.0183	1.0	.8413	1.0833	3.7	.9999	3.7000
−1.6	.0548	.0232	1.1	.8643	1.1686	3.8	.9999	3.8000
−1.5	.0668	.0293	1.2	.8849	1.2561	3.9	1.0000	3.9000
−1.4	.0808	.0367	1.3	.9032	1.3455	4.0	1.0000	4.0000

To use the standard normal to find an order quantity, we first find the order quantity that maximizes expected profit, assuming demand followed the standard normal distribution. Demand never follows a standard normal, so that order quantity is meaningless in practice. But we can convert it into one that maximizes expected profit for the actual demand distribution, which is the order quantity we want.

Let's begin the process of using Table 13.4 to find the order quantity that maximizes O'Neill's expected profit for the Hammer 3/2. First note that Table 13.4 uses the variable z to represent quantities. This helps to distinguish a quantity z that applies if demand is standard normal from the quantity Q that applies for the actual demand distribution. Next, you might notice that half of the z values in Table 13.4 are negative. Don't be alarmed. As we will see later, this doesn't make us order negative quantities (which would make no sense).

The second column in Table 13.4 is the distribution function $F(z)$ for the standard normal distribution. Just like any distribution function, this provides the probability that the outcome of the standard normal distribution is z or lower. For example, $F(z = 1) = .8413$, which means that there is an 84.13 percent chance that the outcome of a standard normal is 1 or lower. Similarly, $F(z = -1) = .1587$, meaning that the standard normal returns an outcome that is -1 or lower only 15.87 percent of the time.

We are now ready to find the z that maximizes expected profit (if demand were represented by a standard normal distribution). Looking down the second column in Table 13.4 for the critical ratio, we find $F(0.6) = .7257$ and $F(0.7) = .7580$. As with Table 13.2, the critical ratio that we want, .75, falls between two probabilities in the table, so we apply the round-up rule and select the row with the larger probability, .7580. Hence, if the standard normal distribution were the appropriate model for demand, then the order quantity that maximizes expected profit would be $z = 0.7$. But, of course, our demand is not standard normal. So now what?

Any quantity in a standard normal distribution can be converted to a corresponding quantity in another normal distribution. To make this conversion, use the following Equation 13.2:

$$Q = \mu + (z \times \sigma)$$

where

   z = the quantity in the standard normal distribution

   μ = the mean of the true demand distribution

   σ = the standard deviation of the true demand distribution

   Q = the order quantity for the true demand distribution

The two Greek letters, μ and σ, are commonly used to represent the mean and standard deviation of a distribution. For the Hammer 3/2, $\mu = 3000$ and $\sigma = 1000$. Thus, the order quantity that maximizes expected profit for the Hammer 3/2 is

$$Q = 3000 + (0.7 \times 1000) = 3700$$

which matches the answer found using Table 13.2. However, unlike Table 13.2, which is useful for only one specific normal distribution (mean 3000 and standard deviation 1000), we can use Table 13.4 to find the optimal order quantity for any normal distribution. See Exhibit 13.1 for a summary of the process to find an optimal order quantity.

Check Your Understanding 13.4

Question: The critical ratio is .90. Using Table 13.4, what z value is selected in the process to find the quantity that maximizes expected profit?

Answer: In Table 13.4, $F(1.2) = .8849$ and $F(1.3) = .9032$, so choose the z that corresponds to the larger probability. The answer is thus 1.3.

Question: Demand is normally distributed with a mean of 1000 and a standard deviation of 300. Given the critical ratio, $z = 1.3$ is selected. What order quantity maximizes expected profit?

Answer: $Q = \mu + (z \times \sigma) = 1000 + (1.3 \times 300) = 1390$

Optimal Order Quantity—Computer Method   The computer method for finding the optimal order quantity essentially replicates the statistical table method, but the computer can do this process faster than people. Assuming demand is normally distributed, first find the z value that corresponds to the optimal order quantity. We do this with the following function in Excel:

$$z = \text{NORM.S.INV(Critical ratio)}$$

Excel returns that NORM.S.INV(.75) = 0.674, meaning that when $z = 0.674$, there is a .75 probability the outcome of the standard normal is that value or lower. This z value is slightly different than the one we evaluated with Table 13.4 because Excel uses a table that has many more entries and is therefore more precise.

Now we convert our z value into a Q^* value that is an actual order quantity:

$$Q = \mu + (z \times \sigma) = 3000 + (0.674 \times 1000) = 3674$$

This value is probably more accurate than the answer we obtained with Table 13.4 (3700 wet suits). Nevertheless, the quantity from Table 13.4 is acceptable.

Check Your Understanding 13.5

Question: Using Excel, what z would be chosen if the critical ratio is .95?

Answer: In Excel, use the function NORM.S.INV(.95). The answer is 1.64.

EXHIBIT 13.1

How to Find the Order Quantity that Maximizes Expected Profit in the Newsvendor Model

Step 1: Evaluate the critical ratio,

$$\frac{C_u}{C_o + C_u}$$

For the Hammer 3/2, given that the selling price is $190 per unit, the purchase cost is $100 per unit, and the salvage value is $70 per unit, $C_u = \$190 - \$100 = \$90$ and $C_o = \$100 - \$70 = \$30$. So the critical ratio is

$$\frac{C_u}{C_o + C_u} = \frac{90}{30 + 90} = .75$$

Step 2: Use a statistical table or Excel.

   a.   If a table is available that provides the distribution function of demand, find the critical ratio in the $F(Q)$ column of probabilities. If the critical ratio falls between two rows in the table, according to the round-up rule, choose the quantity in the row with the larger probability. That quantity maximizes expected profit. You are done; step 3 is not needed.

   b.   If demand is normally distributed, you can use Table 13.4. With Table 13.4, find the critical ratio in the $F(z)$ column. If the critical ratio falls between two rows in the table, according to the round-up rule, choose the z value in the row with the larger probability.

   c.   If demand is normally distributed, you can use Excel:

$$z = \text{NORM.S.INV(Critical ratio)}$$

For the Hammer 3/2, using Table 13.2, the critical ratio, .75, falls between two entries: $F(3600) = .7257$ and $F(3700) = .7580$, so choose $Q = 3700$. With Table 13.4, the critical ratio falls between two entries: $F(0.6) = .7257$ and $F(0.7) = .7580$, so choose $z = 0.7$. With Excel, $z = \text{NORM.S.INV}(.75) = 0.674$.

Step 3: Convert the z found in the previous step to an order quantity with the equation

$$Q = \mu + (z \times \sigma)$$

where μ is the mean of the demand distribution and σ is the standard deviation of the demand distribution.

For the Hammer 3/2, the z value from Table 13.4 in step 2 yields

$$Q = \mu + (z \times \sigma) = 3000 + (0.7 \times 1000) = 3700$$

and the z value obtained with Excel yields

$$Q = \mu + (z \times \sigma) = 3000 + (0.674 \times 1000) = 3674$$

CONNECTIONS: Flexible Spending Accounts

Everyone knows that health care costs are high. From 2009 to 2013, the United States spent about 18 percent of its gross domestic product on health care (Worldbank.org). It is also known that people tend to spend less on health care if they spend their own money, which motivated the creation of flexible spending accounts (FSAs). Roughly speaking, an FSA works as follows: (i) at the start of the year, an employee decides how much she will contribute to her FSA; (ii) the contribution is taken from pre-tax dollars, which means the employee does not have to pay payroll taxes on the contribution; (iii) the employee uses her contribution in the FSA to pay for qualified medical expenses during the year, such as eyeglasses and dental work; (iv) any money left in the FSA at the end of the year is lost.

If you know that you will spend $500 on glasses during the year, it makes total sense to contribute $500 to your FSA. Because of the contribution, you pay $500 for the glasses and avoid paying payroll taxes on the same $500. The amount you save in taxes depends on your income. Say you are fortunate enough to be a high-income earner, which means that your marginal tax rate is around 40 percent—for every additional dollar you earn, you pay $0.40 in payroll taxes. In that case, if you pay for the glasses through an FSA, your total cost is just the $500 for the glasses. But if you don't make contributions to your FSA, then you have to pay $500 for the glasses and $200 = 500 × .40 in taxes! Clearly, it can make good sense to use the FSA.

But there is a catch. You have to decide on your contribution amount at the start of the year before you really know all of your expenses, and if you over contribute, you lose the

Continued

excess amount! The government probably didn't realize this when they created FSAs, but by doing so they have imposed a newsvendor decision problem on millions of Americans.

So what are the underage and overage costs in the FSA newsvendor problem if you have a 40 percent marginal tax rate? If you contribute $1 too few to your FSA, then you end up spending $1 outside your FSA on health care. Had you contributed the $1 to your FSA, you would have reduced your tax bill by $0.40 = .4 × $1. Thus, $C_u = \$0.40$. If you contribute $1 too much to your FSA, then you lose the $1 at the end of the year. Had you known that you would not use the $1, you would not have contributed it to the FSA and you would still have the $1 at the end of the year. However, you also would have to pay $0.40 in additional taxes (because the $1 was not contributed to the FSA), so you are really only $0.60 = $1 – $0.40 better off. Thus, $C_o = \$0.60$. The critical ratio is then

$$\frac{C_u}{C_u + C_u} = \frac{\$0.40}{\$0.60 + \$0.40} = .40$$

Hence, you should contribute an amount to your FSA such that there is a .40 probability your expenses will be less than your contribution and a .60 probability your expenses will be more than your contribution. In other words, it is slightly more expensive to overcontribute than to undercontribute, so the optimal contribution amount is somewhat conservative (but not so conservative that you don't contribute).

You can also confirm that if your marginal tax rate is lower than 40 percent, then your optimal contribution to an FSA is more conservative. This is related to one of the critiques of these accounts: People with higher income (and in a higher tax bracket) enjoy a greater benefit than people with lower income.

13.2 Newsvendor Performance Measures

No matter the order quantity O'Neill chooses for the Hammer 3/2, it is useful to be able to evaluate several performance measures that could be of interest to a manager. We focus on five of them:

- **Expected inventory**: the expected number of units not sold at the end of the season that therefore must be salvaged.
- **Expected sales**: the expected number of units sold during the season at the regular price.
- **Expected profit**: the expected profit earned from the product, including the consequences of inventory that needs to be salvaged.
- **In-stock probability**: the probability that enough inventory is available to satisfy all demand.
- **Stockout probability**: the probability that some demand was not able to purchase a unit; that is, that demand experiences a stockout.

Expected inventory The expected number of units not sold at the end of the season that therefore must be salvaged.

Expected sales The expected number of units sold during the season at the regular price.

Expected profit The expected profit earned from the product, including the consequences of leftover inventory.

In-stock probability The probability that all demand was able to purchase a unit.

Stockout probability The probability that some demand was not able to purchase a unit; that is, that demand experiences a stockout.

13.2.1 Expected Inventory

For any possible order quantity, there is some chance that some wet suits will be left in inventory at the end of the season and need to be salvaged. For example, suppose O'Neill orders 4000 wet suits—it is not immediately apparent why they would order that quantity, but just say they do. How many of those 4000 wet suits should they expect to be left over at the end of the season to be sold off at $70 per wet suit? The actual amount of inventory depends on what happens with demand. If they are lucky and demand is greater than 4000 units, then there will be zero units of inventory. But demand could also be 500 units, in which case they will be strapped with 3500 (= 4000 – 500) wet suits at the end of the season. Hopefully demand is better than 500 units, but as long as demand is less than 4000, there will be some units left over.

To evaluate the expected inventory, we return to the statistical table. Our task is simple if we happen to have a table with a column for the expected inventory, like Table 13.2. For example, say O'Neill orders 4000 wet suits. According to the third column in Table 13.2, $I(4000) = 1083$. Hence, with an order quantity of 4000 wet suits, O'Neill can expect to have 1083 wet suits remaining in inventory at the end of the season.

It is important to emphasize that 1083 is the *expected* number of wet suits left over at the end of the season, meaning that it is an expectation over many possible outcomes. Given that 4000 wet suits are ordered, there could be anywhere from 0 to 4000 in inventory. If we were to take the expectation over all of those outcomes, the answer would be 1083, but the actual number of wet suits left over can be more or less than 1083.

A glance through Table 13.2 reveals that expected inventory changes as a function of the order quantity. The same data are displayed visually in Figure 13.6. As you might expect, if the order quantity is relatively low (say 1000 or lower), then expected inventory is almost zero. However, as the order quantity increases, so does the expected inventory. For example, if O'Neill were to order 6000 wet suits, then it could expect to have about 3000 wet suits left over.

As with the process to find the expected order quantity, Table 13.2 is only useful for one particular normal distribution, a normal with a mean of 3000 and a standard deviation of 1000. And again, it is possible to use the standard normal to find expected inventory for any normal distribution. We do this with a three-step process: (i) convert an order quantity Q into its corresponding z value, (ii) look up the expected inventory for the standard normal, and then (iii) convert that expected inventory into the expected inventory that would occur for the actual demand distribution.

Step one is to convert an order quantity Q into a z value with the following equation, which is equivalent to Equation 13.2, just written in a different form:

$$z = \frac{Q - \mu}{\sigma}$$

Say we order 4000 wet suits. The z that corresponds to that order quantity is

$$z = \frac{4000 - 3000}{1000} = 1$$

Next, we look up the expected inventory $I(z)$ for $z = 1$. From the third column of Table 13.4, $I(1) = 1.0833$.

Finally, the third step is to convert $I(z)$ into the expected inventory for the actual demand. We do that with the next equation, Equation 13.3,

$$\text{Expected inventory} = \sigma \times I(z)$$

Figure 13.6

Expected sales and expected inventory of the Hammer 3/2 wet suit as a function of the order quantity

In this case, we get

$$\text{Expected inventory} = 1000 \times 1.0833 = 1083$$

As you would hope, the answer we obtain using the standard normal distribution matches the answer from Table 13.2. The key difference is that the single standard normal table can be used with any normal distribution.

As with the order quantity, it is possible to use Excel to evaluate the expected inventory. The formula in Excel for $I(z)$ is

$$I(z) = \text{NORM.DIST}(z, 0, 1, 0) + (z \times \text{NORM.S.DIST}(z))$$

The first part, NORM.S.DIST(z,0,1,0), is the probability that the standard normal exactly equals z (i.e., that is the density function of the standard normal). The second part, NORM.S.DIST(z), is the distribution function of the standard normal; that is, it is $F(z)$. Once $I(z)$ is evaluated in Excel, according to Equation 13.3, it merely remains to multiply $I(z)$ by the standard deviation.

See Exhibit 13.2 for a summary of the steps to evaluate expected inventory.

EXHIBIT 13.2

How to Evaluate Expected Inventory in the Newsvendor Model Given an Order Quantity Q

If a table is available with the distribution function $F(Q)$ and the expected inventory function $I(Q)$, then follow Method I; otherwise, follow the steps in Method II.

Method I

Look up expected inventory in the table, $I(Q)$.

If O'Neill orders 4000 wet suits, then (from the third column of Table 13.2) expected inventory is $I(4000) = 1083$.

Method II (For normally distributed demand)

Step 1: Find the z that corresponds to the order quantity Q:

$$z = \frac{Q - \mu}{\sigma}$$

where μ is the mean of the demand distribution and σ is the standard deviation.

For the Hammer 3/2 and an order quantity of 4000 wet suits:

$$z = \frac{Q - \mu}{\sigma} = \frac{4000 - 3000}{1000} = 1$$

Step 2: Look up in Table 13.4 or use Excel to evaluate the expected inventory with the standard normal distribution.

     a. With Table 13.4, expected inventory, $I(z)$, is the entry in the third column in the row corresponding to the z value found in step 1.

     b. With Excel:

$$I(z) = \text{NORM.DIST}(z,0,1,0) + (z \times \text{NORM.S.DIST}(z))$$

For the Hammer 3/2, using Table 13.4, $I(z=1) = 1.0833$. The same value is obtained for $I(z)$ using Excel.

Step 3: Convert the expected inventory for the standard normal into the expected inventory for the actual demand distribution:

$$\text{Expected inventory} = \sigma \times I(z)$$

For the Hammer 3/2, expected inventory $= 1000 \times 1.0833 = 1083$.

Check Your Understanding 13.6

Question: A newsvendor orders 12,000 units. Demand is normally distributed with a mean of 10,000 and a standard deviation of 4000. What is the expected inventory?

Answer: Find the z value that corresponds to the order quantity of 12,000 units: $z = (12{,}000 - 10{,}000)/4000 = 0.5$. From Table 13.4, $I(z=0.5) = 0.6978$. Convert this to expected inventory: $\sigma \times I(z) = 4000 \times 0.6978 = 2791$.

13.2.2 Expected Sales

Every unit that is ordered is either sold or left in inventory at the end of the season. For example, if O'Neill orders 4000 wet suits and demand equals 2500 wet suits, then it sells 2500 wet suits and 1500 wet suits are left in inventory. Similarly, if demand is 4500 wet suits, then it sells all 4000 wet suits and there are no wet suits left in inventory. Thus, no matter what the demand is, the following is true:

$$\text{Sales} + \text{Inventory} = Q$$

It then is also true that

$$\text{Expected sales} + \text{Expected inventory} = Q$$

and therefore Equation 13.4 can be written as

$$\text{Expected sales} = Q - \text{Expected inventory}$$

Thus, once expected inventory is evaluated, it is relatively simple to evaluate expected sales. For example, in the previous section we determined that with an order quantity of 4000 units, the expected inventory is 1083. It follows that with an order quantity of 4000 units,

$$\text{Expected sales} = 4000 - 1083 = 2917$$

As with expected inventory, expected sales are only an expectation. Actual sales can vary from as low as 0 to as high as the order quantity. Taking an expectation over all possible outcomes yields the expected sales of 2917 units when 4000 units are ordered.

Figure 13.6 plots the expected sales curve as a function of the order quantity. If O'Neill doesn't order any wet suits, expected sales are zero. As more wet suits are ordered, expected sales grow quickly because, with low order quantities, most of the units ordered are sold. However, once the order quantity becomes large (above the mean in this case), increasing the order quantity does continue to increase sales, but at a slower and slower rate. Eventually, the expected sales curve flattens out because sales cannot exceed demand. So when the order quantity is 6000, expected sales nearly equal expected demand. In fact, expected sales can never be more than expected demand—O'Neill can, at most, EXPECT to sell to every potential customer. (Note: actual sales can exceed expected demand, and often does, but expected sales cannot.)

See Exhibit 13.3 for a summary of the steps to evaluate expected sales.

How to Evaluate Expected Sales and/or Expected Profit in the Newsvendor Model Given an Order Quantity Q

EXHIBIT 13.3

Step 1: Evaluate expected inventory using a method in Exhibit 13.2.

Step 2: Use the expected inventory found in step 1 and the following equations to evaluate expected sales and expected profit

$$\text{Expected sales} = Q - \text{Expected inventory}$$

$$\text{Expected profit} = (\text{Price} \times \text{Expected sales}) + (\text{Salvage value} \times \text{Expected inventory}) - (\text{Cost per unit} \times Q)$$

For the Hammer 3/2 with $Q = 4000$

$$\text{Expected sales} = Q - \text{Expected inventory} = 4000 - 1083 = 2917$$

$$\text{Expected profit} = (\$190 \times 2917) + (\$70 \times 1083) - (\$100 \times 4000) = \$230{,}040$$

Check Your Understanding 13.7

Question: A newsvendor orders 25,000 units and expected inventory is 4000 units. What are expected sales?

Answer: Expected sales = Q – Expected inventory = 25,000 – 4000 = 21,000

. . . .

13.2.3 Expected Profit

One reason to evaluate expected inventory and expected sales is so that expected profit can be evaluated:

$$\text{Expected profit} = (\text{Price} \times \text{Expected sales}) + (\text{Salvage value} \times \text{Expected inventory}) \\ - (\text{Cost per unit} \times Q)$$

The first term above, Price × Expected sales, is the revenue earned from sales during the season. The second term, Salvage value × Expected inventory, is the revenue earned from salvaging the units that don't sell during the season. The final term, Cost per unit × Q, is the amount spent to purchase the units at the start of the season.

Let's evaluate O'Neill's profit if they happen to order 4000 wet suits. Recall that, with that order quantity, Expected sales = 2917 wet suits and Expected inventory = 1083 wet suits. Thus,

$$\text{Expected profit} = (\$190 \times 2917) + (\$70 \times 1083) - (\$100 \times 4000) = \$230{,}040$$

Although $230,040 sounds great, the optimal order quantity, 3700 wet suits, yields a higher profit: $231,840.

Figure 13.7 displays how expected profit changes with the order quantity. O'Neill could clearly suffer if it orders too few or too many wet suits. Interestingly, while ordering the expected demand of 3000 wet suits is not a disaster, it does lower profits by a noticeable amount—ordering expected demand yields a profit of $222,120, which is $9720 lower than the optimal profit. To put that in perspective, $9720 is 1.9 percent of expected revenue when the order quantity is 3000 units. Hence, ordering expected demand rather than the profit-maximizing order quantity could reduce profits by about 1.9 percent of revenue. Given that the profit for companies like O'Neill rarely exceeds 2–3 percent of revenue, failing to order the optimal order quantity could significantly hurt the company's overall profitability.

. . . .

Figure 13.7

Expected profit for the Hammer 3/2 wet suit as a function of the order quantity

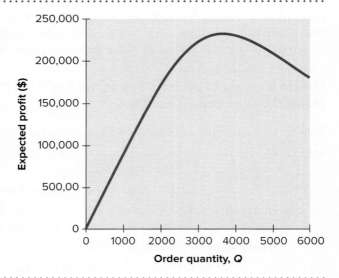

. . . .

Check Your Understanding 13.8

Question: A newsvendor purchases units for $10 and sells each one for $18. Inventory is salvaged for $6. He orders 45,000 units and expected sales are 35,000. What is his expected profit?

Answer: Expected inventory = Q − Expected sales = 45,000 − 35,000 = 10,000. Profit is ($18 × 35,000) + ($6 × 10,000) − ($10 × 45,000) = $240,000.

. . . .

13.2.4 In-Stock and Stockout Probabilities

Expected profit measures how much the company earns, but it doesn't directly measure how well the company serves customers. A common measure of service to customers is the in-stock probability. The **in-stock probability** is the probability the firm satisfies all (regular price) demand during the season; that is, it is the probability the firm has stock available for every customer. That occurs if demand is less than or equal to the order quantity. Hence, we have Equation 13.5:

$$\text{In-stock probability} = F(Q)$$

Let's measure the in-stock probability if O'Neill orders 4000 wet suits. If we have the distribution function table for demand, like Table 13.2, then the in-stock probability is $F(4000) = .8413$.

If we don't have the distribution function table for demand, but demand is normally distributed, then we can use the standard normal distribution function table, Table 13.4. First, convert the order quantity, $Q = 4000$ wet suits, into its corresponding z value:

$$z = \frac{Q - \mu}{\sigma} = \frac{4000 - 3000}{1000} = 1$$

Next, look up $F(z)$ in Table 13.4 and find that $F(1) = .8413$. Hence, if O'Neill orders 4000 wet suits, it will satisfy all demand with a .8413 probability, which matches the answer from Table 13.2.

What would be the in-stock probability if O'Neill orders the quantity that maximizes expected profit? With the expected profit-maximizing quantity, Q^*, according to Equation 13.1, $F(Q^*)$ equals the critical ratio. But according to Equation 13.5, $F(Q^*)$ also equals the in-stock probability. That means that when the expected profit-maximizing quantity is chosen, the in-stock probability is the critical ratio. For the Hammer 3/2, the critical ratio is .75. Hence, if O'Neill maximizes expected profit, then it will satisfy all of its demand with a .75 probability. (Actually, because it may not be possible to choose a Q such that $F(Q)$ exactly equals the critical ratio, the in-stock probability with the chosen order quantity may not precisely equal the critical ratio. Nevertheless, when choosing an order quantity to maximize expected profit, the resulting in-stock probability will be very close to the critical ratio. For example, with an order quantity of 3700 wet suits, the in-stock probability is .7580.)

The flip side to the in-stock probability is the **stockout probability**—the probability that at least some demand is not satisfied during the season; that is, that some customer wants to purchase a product but finds that the firm no longer has inventory. When that happens, we say the firm experiences a **stockout**. Because the firm either satisfies all demand (it is in stock) or the firm experiences a stockout, it follows that

$$\text{Stockout probability} = 1 - \text{In-stock probability}$$

So if O'Neill orders 3700 wet suits, then it has a .2420 stockout probability (1 − .7580).

See Exhibit 13.4 for a summary of the steps to evaluate the in-stock and stockout probabilities.

In-stock probability The probability that all demand was able to purchase a unit.

Stockout probability The probability that demand for an item exceeds its inventory during a period of time.

Stockout A stockout occurs when a customer demands an item that is not available in inventory.

EXHIBIT 13.4

How to Evaluate the In-Stock Probability or Stockout Probability in the Newsvendor Model Given an Order Quantity Q

If a table is available with the distribution function $F(Q)$, then follow Method I; otherwise, follow the steps in Method II.

Method I

Look up $F(Q)$ in the distribution function table, which is the in-stock probability. The stock-out probability is $1 - F(Q)$.

If O'Neill orders 4000 wet suits, then from the second column of Table 13.2, $F(Q) = .8413$, which is the in-stock probability. The stockout probability is $1 - .8413 = .1587$.

Method II (For normally distributed demand)

Step 1: Find the z that corresponds to the order quantity Q:

$$z = \frac{Q - \mu}{\sigma}$$

where μ is the mean of the demand distribution and σ is the standard deviation.

For the Hammer 3/2 and an order quantity of 4000 wet suits:

$$z = \frac{Q - \mu}{\sigma} = \frac{4000 - 3000}{1000} = 1$$

Step 2: Look up in Table 13.4 or use Excel to evaluate $F(z)$, the probability that demand is z or lower.

  a. With Table 13.4, $F(z)$ is the entry in the second column in the row corresponding to the z value found in step 1.

  b. With Excel:

$$F(z) = \text{NORM.S.DIST}(z)$$

$F(z)$ is the in-stock probability. For the stockout probability, proceed to step 3.

For the Hammer 3/2, using Table 13.4, $F(z=1) = .8413$. The same value is obtained for $F(z)$ using Excel.

Step 3: The stockout probability is

$$\text{Stockout probability} = 1 - \text{In-stock probability}$$

For the Hammer 3/2 and an order quantity of 4000 units:

$$\text{Stockout probability} = 1 - .8413 = .1587$$

A manager at O'Neill probably likes the idea of maximizing expected profit but may be uncomfortable with the corresponding in-stock (.7580) and stockout (.2420) probabilities. The manager may be concerned that customers will be irritated if the product they want is not available and the manager might not like that it will happen about 24 percent of the time. If this is indeed a concern, the manager could order more than the expected profit-maximizing quantity. Doing so would lower expected profit but increase the in-stock probability (and decrease the stockout probability). Thus, the manager faces a trade-off between profit and service. That trade-off is displayed in Figure 13.8. Note that the trade-off curve is relatively flat at the top. This means that the initial increase in the in-stock probability is possible without a steep decline in expected profit. However, in this case the expected profit starts to drop quickly once enough is ordered to raise the in-stock probability to 85–90 percent. And a large chunk of expected profit is sacrificed to achieve an in-stock probability beyond 95 percent, mostly because O'Neill would need to increase its order quantity substantially to achieve that level of service, as is discussed in the next section.

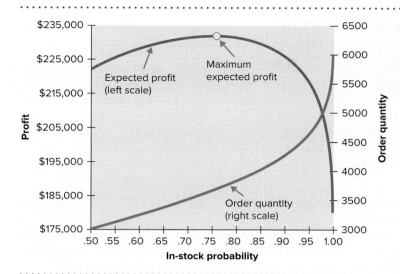

Figure 13.8

The trade-off between the in-stock probability and expected profit for the Hammer 3/2. The circle indicates the outcome if the expected profit-maximizing quantity is ordered, 3700 wet suits. The order quantity that corresponds to each in-stock probability is displayed with the right axis

---

Check Your Understanding 13.9

Question: A newsvendor orders 14,000 units. Demand is normally distributed with a mean of 11,000 and a standard deviation of 1500. What is the in-stock probability?

Answer: The z value that corresponds to the order quantity is $z = (14{,}000 - 11{,}000)/1500 = 2$. From Table 13.4, $F(z=2) = 0.9772$.

Question: A newsvendor orders 8000 units. Demand is normally distributed with a mean of 9000 and a standard deviation of 2000. What is the stockout probability?

Answer: The z value that corresponds to the order quantity is $z = (8000 - 9000)/2000 = -0.5$. From Table 13.4, $F(z=-0.5) = .3085$, which is the in-stock probability. The stockout probability is $1 - .3085 = 0.6915$.

13.3 Order Quantity to Achieve a Service Level

Figure 13.8 illustrates that O'Neill can choose its in-stock probability by adjusting its order quantity. This section details a process for finding the order quantity that achieves a particular in-stock probability.

Suppose O'Neill is very concerned with customer service. So it decides that it wants to be in stock with a .99 probability! How many Hammer 3/2 wet suits does it need to order to achieve that objective? If we have the distribution function table available, like Table 13.2, we can scan down the $F(z)$ column of probabilities until we find the desired in-stock probability. For example, in Table 13.2, $F(5300) = .9893$ and $F(5400) = .9918$. Hence, an order quantity of 5300 units does not quite achieve the desired in-stock probability, while the order quantity 5400 yields a slightly better in-stock probability than the .99 target. Given a choice between these two options, firms usually opt for the choice that provides at least the target rather than falling just short. Hence, for a .99 in-stock probability, O'Neill should order 5400 Hammer 3/2 wet suits.

As discussed in the previous sections, if demand is normally distributed, but you don't have the distribution function table for the particular normal that represents demand, then you can use the standard normal distribution function table. With the standard normal distribution, the

Check Your Understanding 13.10

Question: A newsvendor wants to achieve a 0.975 in-stock probability. Demand is normally distributed with a mean of 15,000 and a standard deviation of 5000. How many units should be ordered?

Answer: From Table 13.4 we see that $F(z = 1.9) = 0.9713$ and $F(z = 2.0) = 0.9772$. The target in-stock probability falls between those two values, so choose the larger z to ensure that service is at least as good as the target. Convert to an order quantity: $Q = \mu + (z \times \sigma)$ = $15,000 + (2.0 \times 5000) = 25,000$.

in-stock probability is $F(z)$, which is the probability that demand is z or lower. O'Neill wants $F(z) = .99$. Scanning down Table 13.4, we find that $F(2.3) = .9893$ and $F(2.4) = .9918$. Let's choose $z = 2.4$ because it achieves even a little bit better service than the in-stock target. It remains to convert the z that is appropriate for the standard normal distribution into an order quantity for the actual demand distribution. This is done, as before, with Equation 13.2:

$$Q = \mu + (z \times \sigma) = 3000 + (2.4 \times 1000) = 5400$$

So, as expected, we get the same answer using the standard normal distribution: O'Neill needs to order 5400 wet suits to achieve a .99 in-stock probability. This is a considerable increase from 3700 wet suits, the quantity that maximizes expected profit and yields only a .758 in-stock probability. From Figure 13.8 we can also see that the order quantity of 5400 wet suits lowers expected profit considerably. So to offer such high service quality comes with a substantial cost in the form of lower expected profit!

13.4 Mismatch Costs in the Newsvendor Model

The poor newsvendor can't get it quite right. Either the chosen supply is greater than demand, in which case some units need to be salvaged, or supply is less than demand, in which case some customers are not happy. In short, there is no way around demand–supply mismatch costs. In this section, we define what those costs are and determine when they are most significant.

Let's continue with O'Neill's Hammer 3/2. We can use the process described in section 13.2 to determine that if O'Neill orders 3700 units (the newsvendor quantity that maximizes expected profit), then its expected profit is $231,840. How good is this? As usual, we need to measure it relative to some benchmark.

One benchmark to which we can compare the newsvendor's profit is the **maximum profit**—the highest possible expected profit. To evaluate the maximum profit, assume expected demand for the Hammer 3/2 remains 3000 units and O'Neill still earns $90 in profit per wet suit sold during the season. The only change to the newsvendor model is that now O'Neill can place its order at the end of the season *after* observing demand and receive the inventory in time to satisfy all demand. For example, suppose demand turns out (unfortunately) to be 1278 units. O'Neill would then only order precisely 1278 units and would not be left with any unsold inventory at the end of the season. But say demand is terrific, like 5200 units. In that case, O'Neill orders 5200 units and sells all of them for a profit of $90 per wet suit! Being able to order after seeing demand is ideal for O'Neill because it can always avoid having left-over inventory or stockouts. That is why it achieves the maximum expected profit.

Given that O'Neill can now decide its order quantity after observing demand, at the start of the season it can expect to satisfy all demand and earn $90 per unit of demand. Hence, O'Neill's maximum profit is

Maximum profit = Expected demand × Profit per unit sold

Maximum profit The highest possible expected profit. This occurs when inventory is available for all customers.

Thus, for the Hammer 3/2, the maximum profit is $270,000 = 3000 units × $90 per unit.

It is important to recognize that the maximum profit is the best the newsvendor can *expect* to earn, meaning that this is the highest profit the newsvendor can expect to earn before it actually observes demand even though it knows it is able to choose a production quantity after observing demand. It is clearly not the highest possible profit. For instance, say demand turns out to be super high, like 6000 units. Then O'Neill produces 6000 units and earns a whopping $540,000 (= 6000 × $90) in profit. While that is awesome for O'Neill, it is not very likely. It is also possible that demand turns out to be only 500 units, in which case O'Neill earns a paltry $45,000 in profit. The maximum profit is the average profit resulting from all possible demand outcomes, including the good and the bad ones.

So O'Neill's maximum profit depends on only two factors: the expected demand and the profit per unit sold. Both of those factors are also relevant for the newsvendor's expected profit, but the newsvendor's expected profit should intuitively depend on the amount of demand uncertainty, which is measured by the standard deviation. The newsvendor's "too much/too little" challenge is clearly harder as demand uncertainty increases. This is illustrated in Figure 13.9: As the standard deviation of demand increases, the expected profit in the newsvendor model decreases. The gap between the maximum profit and the expected profit is due to the consequences of demand uncertainty. In particular, the maximum profit does not suffer from the two types of **mismatch costs** that create headaches for the newsvendor: (i) the cost of inventory (i.e., too much supply) and (ii) the opportunity cost of stockouts (i.e., too little supply). Thus, the difference between the maximum profit and the newsvendor expected profit equals the sum of mismatch costs:

LO13-4 Understand the conditions in which mismatches between supply and demand are most costly.

$$\text{Expected profit} = \text{Maximum profit} - \text{Mismatch costs}$$

Given that the maximum profit is the best we can do, we can use it as the benchmark to measure expected profit. A natural way to do this is simply to measure expected profit as a percentage of the maximum profit because we know that expected profit cannot be greater than 100 percent of the maximum profit. For example, if the order quantity is 3700 wet suits, expected profit is $231,840, which is 86 percent of the maximum profit ($231,840/$270,000).

Now we are ready to return to the main question for this section: When is expected profit relatively close to the maximum profit? Or, equivalently, when are mismatch costs small relative to the maximum profit? The answer is that it depends on only two factors, one that is related to demand uncertainty and the other to the economics of the product.

The first factor that influences mismatch costs is the **coefficient of variation**, which is the ratio of the standard deviation of demand to the expected demand. For the Hammer 3/2, the coefficient of variation is 1000/3000 = 0.33. The coefficient of variation measures the amount of demand uncertainty (i.e., standard deviation) relative to expected demand (i.e., the mean).

Mismatch costs Costs related to a mismatch between demand and supply. These usually include the cost of leftover inventory and the opportunity cost of stockouts.

Coefficient of variation The ratio of the standard deviation to the mean.

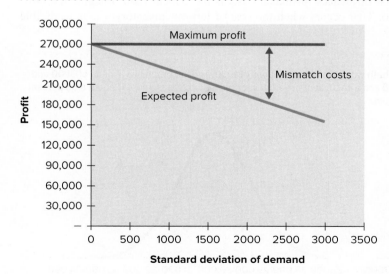

Figure 13.9

The expected profit of the Hammer 3/2 wet suit as a function of the standard deviation of demand. Also shown are the maximum profit and mismatch costs, which are calculated as the difference between maximum profit and expected profit.

The coefficient of variation is the ratio of the standard deviation to the mean (and not just equal to the standard deviation), because the standard deviation is only an absolute measure of uncertainty. To explain, Figure 13.10 displays the density function of two normal distributions with standard deviations of 1000. Thus, from the point of view of the standard deviation, these two normal distributions have the same amount of uncertainty. In fact, in both cases, there is about a .68 probability that the outcome will be within one standard deviation of the mean. (In general, there is about a two-thirds chance that a random outcome will be within one standard deviation of the mean.) However, it is more consequential to be 1000 units away from 3000 than it is to be 1000 units away from 30,000. While the two functions in the graphs appear similar, the *x*-axes are very different. When the mean is 3000 (left side), demand can plausibly be anywhere from 100 percent less (0) to 100 percent more (6000) than the mean. But when the mean is 30,000 (right side), the same absolute range extends from 10 percent below the mean (27,000) to 10 percent above the mean (33,000). In that sense, the two demand distributions do not have the same amount of uncertainty relative to their mean.

The coefficient of variation captures that difference in uncertainty: with a mean of 3000, the coefficient of variation is 0.33; while with a mean of 30,000, the coefficient of variation is 0.03, even though they have the same standard deviation. The coefficient of variation of a demand forecast can vary considerably. Table 13.5 describes several possible ranges for the coefficient of variation. In the low range, there is a high probability that demand is within 25 percent of the mean and the density function has a narrow bell shape. In the medium range, the density function retains the bell shape, but it spreads out beyond the mean—it is possible that demand can be considerably lower or higher than the mean. The Hammer 3/2 falls within this category. In the third range, "high," there is a considerable degree of demand uncertainty. The density function starts to look less like a bell, and the most likely outcome (the peak of the bell) is less than the mean. With these products, there is a chance that demand can be very high, but it is more likely that demand is lower than the mean. Given that the normal distribution always has a bell shape, the normal distribution is generally suitable to model demand in the first two categories; that is, when the coefficient of variation is no greater than 0.4. The last category, with a coefficient of variation above 1.0, has an "extreme" amount of variability. Now the density function has completely lost the "bell shape." Instead, most of the probability is associated with very small demands and the most likely demand could be 0. Nevertheless, in the "extreme" category there is a small chance that a high demand is realized.

In most newsvendor settings, the coefficient of variation falls within the "low" to "medium" range in Table 13.5, with some products occasionally in the "high" range. Higher coefficients of variation are unlikely to occur because in those cases demand is too uncertain to gamble on any level of production (as we later discuss).

The second factor that influences mismatch costs is the critical ratio. Imagine the critical ratio were nearly 1.0. That occurs when the cost of leftover inventory, C_o, is negligible

Figure 13.10 The density function for two normal distributions, both with standard deviations of 1000. The left graph has a mean of 3000 and a coefficient of variation of 1. The right graph has a mean of 30,000 and a coefficient of variation of 0.1. In both cases, there is about a 68 percent probability that demand is within one standard deviation of the mean.

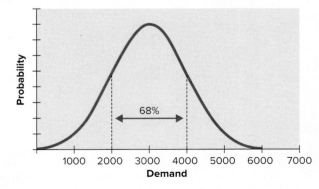
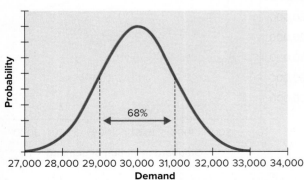

TABLE 13.5 Ranges and Examples for the Coefficient of Variation of Demand Forecasts

Coefficient of Variation	Range	Example	Probability Demand Is within 25% of the Mean	Sample Density Function
0–0.2	Low	A product with little year-to-year change in style or technology (e.g., black booties), so good past demand data are available	.80–1.00	
0.2–0.4	Medium	A new product that is similar to previously sold products but has some fashion or technology change (e.g., wet suit with new color patterns)	.47–.80	
0.4–1.0	High	A completely new type of product in terms of fashion, technology, and/or function (e.g., a wet suit for a new type of water sport using a different type of fabric)	.18–.47	
1.0–2.0	Extreme	A product for a specialized/niche market (e.g., wet suits for free divers to go beyond 100 meters deep)	.07–.18	

compared to the underage cost. For example, say the overage cost for the Hammer 3/2 were only $0.01, while the underage cost remains $90. This means that O'Neill makes $90 on each unit it sells, but it loses one penny on leftover inventory. In that case, the critical ratio is .9999 (= $90/($0.01 + $90)). Intuition suggests that O'Neill can order a very large quantity to prevent stockouts and even though it would have plenty of inventory left over, the cost of that inventory would be trivial. For example, say it ordered 7000 wet suits. It will almost surely have no stockouts, so it will sell to every possible customer. Hence, expected sales will equal expected demand, which is 3000. It will profit $90 on each of those sales, or $270,000. However, it will probably have about 4000 wet suits left over. Although that is a lot of inventory to salvage, the cost of salvaging is only $40 (= 4000 × $0.01), which leads to a minuscule reduction in its profit (from $270,000 to $269,960). So this intuition suggests that with a high critical ratio, a newsvendor should be able to earn a high percentage of the maximum profit.

Now imagine that the overage cost is large compared to the underage cost. If the overage cost is very large, the newsvendor must order a conservative amount, probably less than expected demand. For example, say C_o is so large relative to C_u that the critical ratio is .25. In that case, the newsvendor orders much less than average demand to maximize expected profit. Even if demand turns out to be strong, the total profit is constrained by the amount ordered, leaving the newsvendor with a small fraction of maximum profit. To illustrate, with a critical ratio of .25, the optimal order quantity is 2400 wet suits. In the best outcome for O'Neill, it sells all 2400 wet suits, but even in that case it still only earns $216,000, which is 20 percent lower than the maximum profit.

Figure 13.11 illustrates how the coefficient of variation and the critical ratio interact to influence the newsvendor's expected profit. It displays on the y-axis the newsvendor's expected profit as a percentage of maximum profit. On the x-axis, it varies the coefficient of variation of demand and shows five curves with different critical ratios. In all cases, the curves meet at 100 percent when there is no demand uncertainty (the coefficient of variation is 0). When there is no demand uncertainty, no matter the critical ratio, the newsvendor is able to earn 100 percent of the maximum profit. The story is different, however, if there is uncertainty. No matter the critical ratio, expected profit decreases as the coefficient of variation increases—uncertainty in the demand forecast always reduces profit. However, the negative effects of uncertainty are much higher for lower critical ratios. In fact, it is a deadly combination to have high demand uncertainty and a low critical ratio.

To summarize, the newsvendor suffers from two types of mismatch costs: the cost of inventory (too much supply) and the opportunity cost of stockouts (too little supply). The relative consequence of those mismatch costs is small if there is little demand uncertainty or if the critical ratio is high. However, for products with a moderate to low critical ratio (say .75 and lower), an increase in the coefficient of variation (which is how demand uncertainty is measured) lowers profits substantially. In other words, you don't want to be a newsvendor if you are highly unsure about demand and it is costly to have inventory left over relative to the profit you earn on each sale (i.e., C_o is high relative to C_u).

Figure 13.11

Expected profit as a percentage of maximum profit and as a function of the coefficient of variation of demand and five different critical ratios: .25, .5, .75, .90, and .98

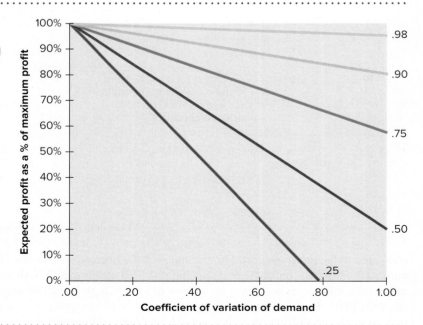

Check Your Understanding 13.11

Question: Among the four products described in Table 13.6, which is most likely to have the highest mismatch costs expressed as a percentage of maximum profit?

TABLE 13.6   **Four Products with Different Demand Forecasts and Critical Ratios**

Product	Demand		Critical Ratio
	Mean Demand	Standard Deviation of Demand	
A	100	40	.5
B	100	20	.6
C	200	50	.7
D	200	60	.8

Answer: Product A has the highest coefficient of variation, which is the ratio of the standard deviation to the mean (0.4), and the lowest critical ratio. The answer is A.

13.5 Strategies to Manage the Newsvendor Environment: Product Pooling, Quick Response, and Make-to-Order

Say you are trying to sell a product that is likely to have substantial mismatch costs. The product has high demand uncertainty (a large coefficient of variation) and a low to medium critical ratio (e.g., .75 or lower). What options do you have to manage this situation? There are several to choose from: (i) don't sell the product, (ii) increase the profit margin (increase C_u) relative to the cost of leftover inventory (C_o), thus increasing the critical ratio, (iii) reduce demand uncertainty, (iv) develop the capability to order or produce additional supply before the end of the season, or (v) only make a customer's product after the customer orders it. In this section, we discuss each of those options, with an emphasis on the final three.

The first choice is the "throw in the towel" option; that is, don't try to sell the product. In some cases, that might be the reasonable choice—not every product that could be made can be made profitably. If demand uncertainty is too high and/or the critical ratio is too low, then even if a conservative amount is ordered, the expected profit may not justify the time and effort to sell the product. Although it can be prudent to not sell a product, you clearly do not want to use this option with all products—you need to sell something!

The second option to help the newsvendor is to increase the profit margin relative to the cost of leftover inventory. Either one, or better yet both, of those changes increases the critical ratio, thereby reducing mismatch costs (as discussed in section 13.4). There are several levers to pull in this case. The firm could raise its price. For example, if O'Neill raises the price of its Hammer 3/2 wet suit from $190 to $220, then it increases its critical ratio from .75 to .80. But the problem with increasing price is that it also, naturally, reduces demand, which isn't great for profit. Another approach is to reduce the purchase cost. O'Neill currently buys wet suits for $100, but say it could find another supplier that would be willing to sell the wet suit for $95. Then the underage cost increases by $5 to $95, the overage cost decreases by $5 to $25, and the critical ratio increases to .79. Again, there are limits to this strategy. Even suppliers need to earn a profit and a cheap supplier might have lower quality or less-reliable delivery.

> **LO13-5** Understand several strategies to increase profit and to reduce the costs associated with mismatches between supply and demand.

13.5.1 Product Pooling

The third option for the newsvendor is to reduce demand uncertainty. One way to do this is to improve the quality of the forecast. This can be achieved by implementing rigorous, data-driven forecasting techniques, like those described in Chapter 15, Forecasting. While it definitely makes sense to try to obtain more accurate forecasts, this strategy does have its limits: Even with the best data and forecasting methods, the world can be an uncertain place. A firm should not assume that it can eliminate all uncertainty through the use of better forecasting—some uncertainty may inevitably remain.

A second approach to reduce demand uncertainty is to change which products are available so that each faces less demand uncertainty. This can be done via **product pooling**—reducing the variety offered to customers by combining, or pooling, similar products. To understand this strategy, it is important to first be clear as to how demand uncertainty should be measured. As section 13.4 reveals, the key measure of demand uncertainty is the coefficient of variation. Reduce the coefficient of variation and you reduce mismatch costs. And one way to reduce the coefficient of variation is to combine, or pool, the demands across products. This works, roughly speaking, because the forecast for the total demand across a set of products is more accurate than the forecast for each individual product. We can make this statement more precise with an example from O'Neill.

The Hammer 3/2 wet suit displayed in Photo 13.1 is sold to surf shops as a wet suit for surfing. O'Neill also sells a version of the Hammer 3/2 to dive shops as a wet suit for recreational scuba diving. The only difference between the surf Hammer and the dive Hammer is the logo silk screened on the chest. The dive Hammer has the logo displayed in Figure 13.12, rather than the "wave" logo on the surf suit. As the logo is the only difference, the surf and dive Hammer wet suits provide identical fit and thermal protection. In addition, the two suits have the same economics: They both (i) sell for $190, (ii) are purchased for $100, and (iii) are salvaged for $70. Consequently, the surf and dive wet suits have the same underage cost ($90), same overage cost ($30), and the same critical ratio (.75). For the purpose of this illustration, let's also assume they have identical demand, which is normally distributed with a mean of 3000 and a standard deviation of 1000.

We have already evaluated the optimal order quantity and expected profit for the surf Hammer: Order 3700 units and the expected profit is $231,840. Because the dive Hammer is identical to the surf Hammer, it has the same optimal order quantity and expected profit. Therefore, the total profit from both Hammer wet suits is $463,680 (= 2 × $231,840).

Instead of selling two wet suits that are nearly identical, let's consider what happens if O'Neill were to sell a single Hammer 3/2 wet suit with a single logo. Let's refer to it as the "one Hammer 3/2," as opposed to the "dive Hammer" or the "surf Hammer." Because the economics of the surf and dive Hammers are identical, it is natural to assume that the one Hammer inherits those economics: It is sold for $190, purchased for $100, and salvaged for $70. However, we need to determine the demand model for the one Hammer.

If we are willing to assume that every customer willing to purchase a surf or dive Hammer is also willing to purchase the one Hammer, then expected demand for the one Hammer is just the sum of the expected demands for the other two, which would then be 6000 units (= 2 × 3000).

We also need the standard deviation of demand for the one Hammer. To obtain the standard deviation, we need to make an assumption about how the two demands tend to interact.

Product pooling The strategy to reduce the variety offered to customers by combining, or pooling, similar products.

Figure 13.12
O'Neill's logo for the dive Hammer 3/2 wet suit

Statisticians use the term **correlation** to measure the interaction between two uncertain events. The correlation between two events can range from as low as –1 to as high as 1. If the correlation between two events is positive (i.e., they are **positively correlated**), then that means the two events tend to be similar, in the sense that if the outcome of one event is "high," then the outcome of the other event tends to be "high" as well. If two events are **negatively correlated** (i.e., their correlation is negative), then they tend to be dissimilar, in the sense that if the outcome of one event is "high," then the outcome of the other event tends to be "low." Finally, two events are said to be **independent** if their correlation is zero. In that case, the outcome of one event provides no information about the outcome of the other event. For example, say we flip a coin and it lands "heads." This tells us nothing about whether the flip of a second coin will be "heads" or "tails"—the outcomes from the flips of different coins are independent.

Demand for the surf and dive Hammers could be positively correlated if they both tend to respond in the same way to some underlying uncertainty. For example, they might both experience strong sales in a growing economy but weak sales in a depressed economy. Or they could both gain sales if the popularity of water sports increases or both lose sales if there is a reason to avoid both activities (e.g., a massive oil spill). Alternatively, it is possible that demand for the two suits is somewhat negatively correlated. For example, say there are a stable number of people who dive and surf, but they have limited time to do these activities. If they surf more, they must dive less, and if they surf less, they dive more. In that case, the popularity of one type might detract from the popularity of the other. Finally, it is possible that the demands for these two wet suits are independent. They are sold in different distribution channels (surf shops don't sell dive equipment and vice versa), they are popular in different geographic regions (surf is mainly in California and Hawaii, whereas divers prefer the warmer waters of the Caribbean), and they have different customer demographics (surfers are generally younger than divers because it is less expensive and requires more physical skill).

Figure 13.13 illustrates how the demands of two products can interact depending on their correlation. The graphs display 100 randomly simulated demand outcomes from two products, each with normally distributed demand with a mean of 10 and a standard deviation of 3.

Correlation A measure of the interaction between two uncertain events. Correlation ranges from –1 to 1.

Positively correlated Two events are positively correlated (i.e., have a positive correlation) when the outcomes tend to have similar magnitudes. If the outcome of one event is "high," then the outcome of the other event tends to be "high" as well.

Negatively correlated Two events are negatively correlated (i.e., their correlation is negative) when the outcomes tend to have dissimilar magnitudes. If the outcome of one event is "high," then the outcome of the other event tends to be "low."

Independent Two events are independent (i.e., their correlation is 0) when the outcome of one event has no relationship to the outcome of the other event.

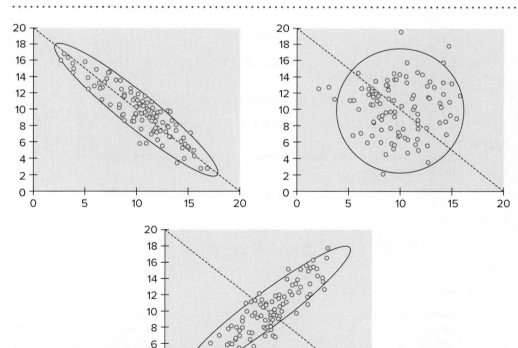

Figure 13.13

Random demand for two products. In the graphs, the x-axis is demand for product 1 and the y-axis is demand for product 2. Dots are the outcomes of 100 random simulations in which, for each product, demand is normally distributed with a mean of 10 and a standard deviation of 3. In the upper-left graph, the correlation between the two products is –0.90. In the upper-right graph, the correlation is 0 (i.e., they are independent). In the lower graph, the correlation between the two products is 0.90.

For example, if the random demands of the two products are five and seven, respectively, then a point is plotted at {5,7}. In the upper-left graph, the products have a correlation of –0.90, so when one product has a low outcome (say 5), the other product tends to have a high outcome (say 15). As a result, the outcomes tend to cluster along a negatively sloped 45-degree line in which the total demand of the two products is approximately 20 units, which is displayed as a dashed line. In contrast, the lower graph displays a situation with 0.90 correlation. Now the two products tend to behave similarly: When one has a low outcome (say 5), the other tends to have a low outcome as well (say 5). Consequently, the outcomes cluster along a positively sloped 45-degree line. In addition, there is considerable variation in the total demand: total demand is around 30 units in the upper-right portion of the cluster, but more like 10 units in the lower-left portion of the cluster. Finally, the upper-right graph in Figure 13.13 displays what can happen when the two products have 0 correlation; that is, they are independent. Now the outcomes cluster more like a circular cloud because the outcome of one product, low or high, doesn't reveal information about the outcome for the other product.

We are now ready to fully characterize the demand for the one Hammer. Let μ and σ be the mean and standard deviation of demand for either the surf or dive Hammer; that is, $\mu = 3000$ and $\sigma = 1000$. The mean and standard deviation of the one Hammer is then

$$\text{Expected pooled demand} = 2 \times \mu$$
$$\text{Standard deviation of pooled demand} = \sqrt{2 \times (1 + \text{Correlation})} \times \sigma$$

If we assume the surf and dive Hammer demands are independent (i.e., their correlation is 0), then for the one Hammer:

$$\text{Expected demand for the one Hammer} = 2 \times 3000 = 6000$$
$$\text{Standard deviation of demand for the one Hammer} = \sqrt{2 \times (1 + 0)} \times 1000 = 1414$$

Now we have all the information we need to evaluate the performance of the one Hammer. The one Hammer's overage cost is $C_o = \$30$ and the underage cost is $C_u = \$90$. Thus, the critical ratio is

$$\frac{C_u}{C_o + C_u} = \frac{\$90}{\$30 + \$90} = .75$$

From Table 13.4, we select $z = 0.70$ because $F(0.6) = .7257$ and $F(0.7) = .7580$. Converting to an order quantity yields

$$Q = \mu + (z \times \sigma) = 6000 + (0.7 \times 1414) = 6990$$

Thus, if O'Neill only sells the one Hammer 3/2, then it should order 6990 units to maximize expected profit.

To complete the analysis of the one Hammer 3/2, let's evaluate its performance measures. From Table 13.4, $I(z=0.7) = 0.8429$, so

$$\text{Expected inventory} = \sigma \times I(z) = 1414 \times 0.8429 = 1192$$

It follows that

$$\text{Expected sales} = Q - \text{Expected inventory} = 6990 - 1192 = 5798$$

and

$$\text{Expected profit} = (\$190 \times 5798) + (\$70 \times 1192) - (\$100 \times 6990) = \$486,060$$

The combined profit with two wet suits is \$463,680. Hence, the one Hammer can increase expected profit by \$22,380 (= \$486,060 – \$463,680), which is an increase of 4.8 percent (= \$22,380/\$463,680). And note, this increase in profit is achieved even though the total number of wet suits ordered is lower: 7400 dive and surf wet suits versus 6990 one Hammers.

Selling one type of Hammer 3/2 instead of two increases profit without changing total demand or the economics (e.g., price, cost, or salvage value). So why did profit increase? From section 13.4, there are two factors that influence profit: the critical ratio and the coefficient of variation. The one Hammer has the same critical ratio as the surf and dive Hammers, so the answer must be that combining the demands from the two wet suits reduces the coefficient of variation of demand. For the surf and dive Hammers, the coefficient of variation is 0.33 (= 1000/3000). But for the one Hammer, the coefficient of variation is 0.24 (= 1414/6000)— there is less uncertainty in the combined demand for the wet suits than in the demand for each individual type of wet suit.

Product pooling is an example of **statistical economies of scale**—pooled demand is better than separate demand from the perspective of operations because the larger scale of pooled demand leads to a reduction in uncertainty, as measured by the coefficient of variation.

Our analysis so far assumes that the demands for the surf and the dive Hammers are independent (i.e., zero correlation). Figure 13.14 illustrates how the one Hammer's profit varies with the correlation between the two wet suits: the smaller the correlation, the higher the expected profit of the one Hammer 3/2. For example, while we evaluated that there is a nice increase in profit if the dive and surf wet suits are independent (zero correlation), the profit increase from pooling them is even higher if their demands are negatively correlated. Correlation has a strong impact on expected profit because it directly affects the coefficient of variation of pooled demand. As seen in Figure 13.14, the coefficient of variation decreases as the correlation becomes smaller.

The reduction in the coefficient of variation can also be seen in Figures 13.13. When there is a –0.90 correlation (upper-left graph), there is some variation in the total demand of the two products (which would be the demand of the combined product), but most of the dots in the graph are close to the 45-degree line that represents a total demand of 20 units—each product's demand varies considerably in the range from 0 to 20, but the total varies very little about the expected value of 20. In contrast, when the correlation is 0.90 (lower graph), the outcomes for each product vary across the range 0 to 20 and the total varies considerably as well, from low values around 10 in the lower-left part of the cluster to high values around 30 in the upper-right part of the cluster.

The lesson from Figures 13.13 and 13.14 is that pooling demands can increase expected profit because the demand uncertainty of the combined product is less than the demand uncertainty of each individual product. Furthermore, pooling is most effective the lower the correlation between the products—pooling provides some benefit for positively correlated products, but it provides a much larger benefit for negatively correlated products.

Statistical economies of scale
The property in which aggregating demand into a large scale tends to reduce uncertainty, as measured by the coefficient of variation.

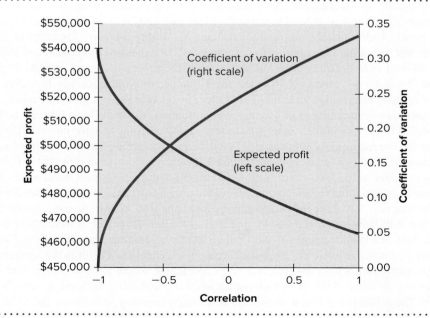

Figure 13.14

The expected profit and coefficient of variation of the one Hammer 3/2

13.5.2 Quick Response

O'Neill's selling season is six months long, but it only gets to submit one order to its supplier. This inflexibility in its supply process, combined with demand uncertainty, leads to mismatch costs (inventory or stockouts). If O'Neill could increase the flexibility of its supply process, it should be able to reduce some of those mismatch costs.

Imagine O'Neill could place a second order for at least some wet suits after the first month of the season and receive those wet suits within one to two months. How useful is this small increase in supply flexibility? The short answer is "a good amount, more than you probably would guess." To explain, the first few weeks of a selling season reveal a considerable amount of information about which styles are selling well and which are not. (For a somewhat related example, compare who the favorite teams are before a sports tournament or season with those after a few matches—actual results provide much more accurate assessments of the teams' strengths.) Using the information O'Neill learns from sales in the early part of the season, O'Neill could order additional inventory of the styles that are selling above expectation, thereby preventing some lost sales.

The ability to place a second order helps O'Neill prevent the mismatch cost of stockouts, but it also helps reduce the mismatch cost of leftover inventory. Because O'Neill knows that the second order can allow it to replenish styles that are selling well, O'Neill can be more conservative with its initial order quantity. By lowering the first order quantity, O'Neill faces less risk from leftover inventory, while the second order protects O'Neill from the risk of stockouts. Thus, with just one additional opportunity to order inventory, O'Neill can increase expected profit by reducing both types of mismatch costs. This capability to respond to updated demand information is called **quick response**. The capacity used in the second order is sometimes called **reactive capacity**—it is the capacity that allows the firm to react to changes in its demand forecast.

To illustrate the advantages of a second ordering opportunity with quick response, say O'Neill has convinced its supplier to provide that supply flexibility. In addition to the regular first order, shortly after the season begins, O'Neill can place a second order for the Hammer 3/2 wet suit. The second order of wet suits will be delivered in several weeks, quick enough to satisfy O'Neill's demand in the later part of the season. The advantage of the second order is that O'Neill can use sales information from the early part of the season to update its prediction of total demand before it submits the second order. Let's assume that its updated demand forecast is perfectly accurate; that is, it knows with certainty what demand will be during the season when it places its second order. This is a reasonable approximation because it has been shown that early season sales are highly correlated (i.e., informative) with total season sales—"hit" products for the season tend to start off selling well and "dog" products tend to start off selling poorly. Unfortunately, this additional supply flexibility is costly: The supplier charges $120 per wet suit in the second order to cover the costs of expedited production and shipping.

The second order quantity decision is simple. If the updated demand forecast is greater than the first order quantity, O'Neill orders the difference to avoid stockouts. However, if the updated demand forecast is less than the first order quantity, it doesn't order any more.

To determine the best first order quantity, we can continue to use the logic from the newsvendor model. If O'Neill overorders in the first order quantity decision, then the unit is left in inventory and must be salvaged for $70, costing O'Neill $30 in lost profit because it was purchased for $100. Hence, as in the original newsvendor model, the overage cost remains the same: $C_o = \$30$.

Now consider the underage cost for the first order quantity. If O'Neill underorders by one unit, then it can order the wet suit in the second order quantity to avoid the stockout. So it pays $120 for that unit in the second order quantity and sells it for $190, earning a profit of $70 on the wet suit. However, had it known that it would sell that wet suit, it would have ordered it in the first ordering decision and paid only $100 for it, earning a profit of $90. Thus, the underage cost is the reduction in its profit because it ordered the wet suit in the second ordering opportunity rather than the first ordering opportunity, which is $C_u = \$20 = \$90 - \$70$. Another way to think of this is that no matter when the wet suit is ordered, it earns $190 in revenue. The difference is that it costs $100 in the early ordering opportunity but $120 in the second. So if O'Neill knows that it will sell the unit, it saves $20 (= $120 - $100) in the purchase cost by ordering it in the first opportunity.

Quick response A strategy that increases supply flexibility to allow a response to updated information about demand. For example, with quick response, a firm can obtain additional supply for products that are selling above expectation, thereby reducing the number of stockouts.

Reactive capacity Capacity that allows a firm to react to changes in its demand forecast.

We now can evaluate the critical ratio:

$$\frac{C_u}{C_o + C_u} = \frac{\$20}{\$30 + \$20} = .40$$

From Table 13.4, we select $z = -0.20$ because $F(-0.30) = .3821$ and $F(-0.20) = .4207$. Converting to an order quantity yields,

$$Q = \mu + (z \times \sigma) = 3000 - (0.2 \times 1000) = 2800$$

Thus, if O'Neill has a second opportunity to purchase inventory at $120 per unit, it should order 2800 wet suits in the first ordering opportunity. O'Neill still orders a decent amount in the first ordering opportunity because wet suits purchased at that time are much cheaper. Nevertheless, the second ordering opportunity makes O'Neill more conservative with its initial buy. The order quantity drops from 3700, when there is only one ordering opportunity, to 2800 when there are two.

Now let's evaluate O'Neill's expected profit. From Table 13.4, $I(z=-0.2) = 0.3069$, so the expected inventory from the first order is

$$\text{Expected inventory} = \sigma \times I(z) = 1000 \times 0.3069 = 307$$

Expected sales from the inventory in the first order is

$$\text{Expected sales from 1st order} = Q - \text{Expected inventory} = 2800 - 307 = 2493$$

The second order complicates the evaluation of expected profit. In particular, how many units should O'Neill expect to order in the second opportunity? Every unit of demand is satisfied with a wet suit from either the first ordering opportunity or the second opportunity. Thus,

$$\text{Expected sales from 1st order} + \text{Expected sales from 2nd order} = \mu$$

which can be rewritten as

$$
\begin{aligned}
\text{Expected sales from 2nd order} &= \mu - \text{Expected sales from 1st order} \\
&= 3000 - 2493 \\
&= 507
\end{aligned}
$$

Hence, if O'Neill orders 2800 wet suits initially, it can expect to order 507 wet suits in the second order to satisfy the additional demand beyond the initial 2800. As with all expectations, this is just the expected amount—the actual second order quantity could be as low as 0 (if demand is 2800 or fewer) or much higher (e.g., if demand turns out to be 5000 units, then the second order is $5000 - 2800 = 2200$).

We can now evaluate expected profit:

$$
\begin{aligned}
\text{Expected profit} = &(\text{Price} \times \text{Expected sales from 1st order}) + (\text{Salvage value} \\
&\times \text{Expected inventory}) - (\text{Cost per unit} \times \text{1st order quantity}) \\
&+ (\text{Profit on units in the 2nd order} \times \text{Expected sales from 2nd order})
\end{aligned}
$$

The first three terms evaluate the expected profit if there is only one ordering opportunity. That is the classic newsvendor profit. The last term includes the impact of the second ordering opportunity. For O'Neill, it earns $70 (= $190 - $120) on each unit in the second order. Multiply that by the expected sales from the second order and you get the expected profit from the second ordering opportunity. So,

$$\text{Expected profit} = (\$190 \times 2493) + (\$70 \times 307) - (\$100 \times 2800) + (\$70 \times 507) = \$250,650$$

With just one ordering opportunity, O'Neill orders 3700 wet suits and earns $231,840. Given a second ordering opportunity to purchase wet suits at $120, O'Neill reduces its first order quantity to 2800 units but increases its profit to $250,650. Thus, the second ordering opportunity increases profits by 8 percent (= ($250,650/$231,840) − 1). It also dramatically reduces mismatch costs. When there is only one ordering opportunity, mismatch costs equal $36,160 (= $270,000 − $231,840). With the second ordering opportunity, mismatch costs are reduced to $19,350 (= $270,000 − $250,650). That is a 49 percent reduction in mismatch costs (1 − ($19,350/$36,160))!

We can conclude from this example that adding some additional flexibility to the supply process can significantly reduce mismatch costs, even if it is just one additional well-timed ordering opportunity and that second source of supply is costly (e.g., per-unit costs increase 20 percent from $100 to $120).

13.5.3 Make-to-Order

The newsvendor setting is an example of one extreme form of production, called make-to-stock. In a **make-to-stock** system, the production of each item begins before the item's eventual owner is known. For example, O'Neill makes each Hammer 3/2 wet suit before knowing who will eventually buy it. The problem, as we have discussed, with make-to-stock is that it leads to mismatch costs: either too many units are produced, resulting in leftover inventory, or too few are produced, which creates stockouts.

Make-to-order is the opposite of make-to-stock. With a **make-to-order** system, the production of a unit only begins once a customer commits to purchase it. Make-to-order systems don't have leftover inventory that needs to be salvaged—if inventory isn't made before its demand has been identified, there should be no "orphaned" units waiting for customers. Make-to-order systems also help to reduce stockouts. In the newsvendor model, all demand in excess of the order quantity is lost even if some of those customers are willing to wait to receive their order. In a make-to-order system, customers wait to receive their units and all of the customers are eventually served (assuming they are willing to wait long enough). Thus, with an ideal make-to-order system, production of each unit can begin after demand is observed, which means that such a system could, in theory, yield the maximum profit. This is most advantageous—relative to make-to-stock production, as discussed in section 13.4— when the critical ratio is low (it is expensive to have leftover inventory relative to the profit earned on each unit sold) and the coefficient of variation of demand is high.

But all is not perfect with make-to-order. Make-to-order acts like the queuing systems discussed in our service systems chapters (Chapters 16 and 17). The challenge with a queuing system is to prevent customers from waiting beyond the point that causes them to walk away without buying an item. And they might "walk away" even before joining the firm's queue because of the firm's reputation for slow delivery. Recall that the time a customer waits to complete service is primarily determined by the utilization of the servers, the variability of the arrival and service processes, and the processing time. Furthermore, the waiting time in a queue grows exponentially as the utilization increases. Thus, to avoid excessively long waits for customers, a make-to-order system cannot allow its utilization to be too high. Unfortunately, it is costly to have a "low" utilization—idle equipment and labor generate costs even if they are not producing.

So time is the Achilles heel of make-to-order. There are some settings in which customers are not willing to wait as long as a make-to-order system would need to deliver their product. For example, people generally want a grocery store to have inventory available for immediate purchase. The same can even be true for expensive items: Most cars in the United States (though not in Europe) are purchased immediately from a dealer's inventory on its lot. In those cases, the retailer needs to incur the mismatch costs because customers are too impatient.

Although we all prefer "now" to "later," for some products customers are willing to wait. This is particularly true with products that are customized. For example, some homes are sold on a make-to-stock basis (the home is built before the buyer is known), but many homes are also built on a make-to-order basis to accommodate the unique preferences of the customer (e.g., color of the walls, type of flooring, etc.). Related to real estate, a good amount of furniture is sold make-to-order: If you want a particular fabric on a sofa, you will need to wait for that sofa to be made. Because there are so many different types of fabrics, it simply would not be possible for a firm to sell that much variety on a make-to-stock basis. To illustrate, suppose the company sells 10,000 sofas per year (roughly 30 per day) but offers 100,000 different fabrics. To sell that much variety on a make-to-stock basis would require at least one sofa of each type, or 100,000 sofas. But it takes 10 years to sell that many sofas at 10,000 per year! Hence, make-to-stock is simply not economically feasible for that product (i.e., the accumulated holding costs over 10 years would exceed the profit earned on the sofa at the price people are willing to pay).

Make-to-stock A production system in which an item's production begins before the customer for the item is known. In a make-to-stock system, units are generally placed in inventory to await customer demand.

Make-to-order A production system in which an item's production begins after the customer for the item is known. In a make-to-order system, units are generally delivered to a customer immediately after production is completed, thereby not spending time in inventory.

To summarize, make-to-order systems are most effective in environments with the following characteristics:

- *Customers are sufficiently patient.* How long people are willing to wait depends in part on the context: They will not wait for milk in a grocery store, but they will wait for a custom sofa.

- *Customers have a strong preference for variety.* Variety creates variability. When hundreds or thousands of different versions of a product need to be offered (because customers truly want the variety), the coefficients of variation on each one may be very high, which would create mismatch costs that are too high to make the product profitable with make-to-stock production. In its extreme form, a make-to-order system might make a unique product for every customer. In that case, the system is often called **mass customization**: With mass customization, each customer can receive a unique product. For example, several companies have experimented with mass customized clothing—a client's body is scanned and clothing is made to his or her precise dimensions.

- *Leftover inventory is expensive.* If leftover inventory is expensive (e.g., changes in fashion, concerns with perishability, or the risk of technological obsolescence), then the critical ratio will be low, meaning that make-to-stock incurs high mismatch costs and only make-to-order may be viable. However, if inventory is relatively cheap to hold, then it is probably better to operate make-to-stock to reduce customer waiting time.

- *Production is reasonably quick.* Part of the time a customer must wait in make-to-order is simply the processing time. If that time is much longer than the customer is willing to wait, then make-to-order cannot work. To facilitate fast production, it helps to use modular components so that they can be assembled quickly once the customer places an order. Modular components are ones that have standardized interfaces to the other components so that the particular version selected of one component has no influence on the use of the other components. For example, the galley kitchen on an aircraft could be made modular, meaning that different versions of the kitchen can be installed in precisely the same way no matter the other design choices made on the plane. Make-to-order systems that use modular components are often called **assemble-to-order** systems because at the time an order is received, all that remains to complete the product is to assemble it from a set of modular components.

To conclude, there are some settings in which make-to-stock is better and others where make-to-order is better. But don't forget, these are two extreme strategies. Sometimes, an even better approach is to blend a bit of both of them. For example, in a quick response system, some units are ordered before demand is known (make-to-stock style) and others are ordered after demand is observed (make-to-order style). That hybrid approach attempts to gain the benefits from both approaches while avoiding their major limitations.

Mass customization A make-to-order system in which each customer's order is unique, customized to his or her exact preferences.

Assemble-to-order A make-to-order system in which a product is assembled from a set of standardized modular components after an order is received.

Check Your Understanding 13.12

Question: Which of the following is an operational advantage of make-to-order relative to make-to-stock?

- A. Make-to-order provides faster delivery to customers than make-to-stock.
- B. Make-to-order can always have higher utilization of resources than make-to-stock.
- C. Make-to-order allows a firm to focus on producing a more limited variety of products.
- D. Make-to-order is less likely to have leftover inventory that needs to be salvaged.

Answer: Make-to-order generally increases delivery times (this rules out A), requires lower resource utilization so that delivery times are not too long (this rules out B), and allows for more (not less) variety (this rules out C). Make-to-order indeed avoids leftover inventory. Thus, the answer is D.

CONNECTIONS: Make-to-Order—Dell to Amazon

© Siri Stafford/Getty Images/RF

From the early 1980s to the mid 2000s, the dominant electronic device for individuals was the personal computer (PC). And early on in that period the dominant firms were "old-guard" computer firms like IBM and Hewlett-Packard. But Dell, a company started by Michael Dell from his University of Texas dorm room, grew rapidly to eventually become the largest and most feared in the industry. Dell's key to success was its operations strategy. The other firms made PCs like they made other products: They would create a line of different types of PCs, forecast demand for each type of PC, produce to their forecast, and then hope that their production quantity was reasonably accurate. Unfortunately, more often than not, they had too many of some types of PCs and not enough of others. In short, these companies found it difficult to implement their make-to-stock style of production in a market character-ized by rapid growth, tremendous variety, and substantial uncertainty.

Dell's solution to the forecasting challenge was to avoid trying to predict demand for each possible type of PC. Instead, it would assemble its PCs from orders and only start the assembly of a PC once it knew it had a customer—it brought make-to-order production to the PC industry. Customers would have to wait to receive their order, but they were willing to do so because they received exactly the PC they wanted, quickly and efficiently assem-bled from a set of modular components.

Although Dell implemented precisely the right operations strategy during that period, industries change. In particular, the dominance of the desktop PC faded as preferences switched to more mobile devices such as laptops, phones, tablets, and phablets. And along with those new devices, consumers needed less variety, thereby reducing the effectiveness of the make-to-order model. But this hardly means that the make-to-order model is no longer viable. Instead, it appears in other places.

While Dell was at its prime, a new type of retailer started in Seattle, called Amazon. com. Amazon's innovation was to eliminate thousands of physical "brick-and-mortar" stores. Instead, it ships books to customers only when it received their orders. In effect, while traditional bookstores operate make-to-stock, Amazon operates more like make-to-order. To explain, think of a book as having two features: One is the physical book and the other is its location. The traditional bookstore decides a book's location before customers reveal their demand. Amazon doesn't decide the final location for a book until a customer places the order. Hence, with respect to location, Amazon operates make-to-order. As a result, Amazon only needs to forecast the total number of books it needs for the U.S. market, whereas a traditional retailer needs to decide the number of books for each store. Thus, Amazon has a much easier forecasting task. Consequently, Amazon can sell books that cannot be sold in local stores, thereby allowing Amazon to offer much more selection than its traditional make-to-stock competitors. However, like all make-to-order systems, buying from Amazon means waiting for Amazon to deliver. Many customers seem to think that the wait is worth it.

Conclusion

The newsvendor model represents one of the canonical challenges faced in operations—the combination of uncertain demand with inflexible supply. In this situation, the newsvendor invariably chooses an order quantity that either fails to satisfy all demand or leaves some units left over at the end of the season to salvage. Nevertheless, the newsvendor can make smart trade-offs between the cost of ordering too much (the overage cost) and the cost of ordering too little (the underage cost). The critical ratio, which balances those two types of costs, determines the quantity that maximizes expected profit. That quantity is rarely the mean of the demand distribution—more is ordered when the underage cost exceeds the overage cost, and less is ordered when the overage cost dominates.

Although it is reasonable to order a quantity that maximizes expected profit, the newsvendor may also be interested in the service provided to customers. Service is often measured with the in-stock probability—the probability that there is enough inventory to satisfy all demand during the season. The order quantity that maximizes expected profit yields an in-stock probability that equals the critical ratio. A higher in-stock probability can be achieved if the order quantity is increased further, but this lowers expected profit.

There are several strategies for improving operations in a newsvendor setting. These strategies change the economics (e.g., increasing the critical ratio), reduce the uncertainty faced by the newsvendor (e.g., product pooling, make-to-order production), or increase the flexibility of the supply process (e.g., quick response).

Summary of Learning Objectives

LO13-1 Use the news vendor model to decide how much product to order when demand is perishable and uncertain

The newsvendor model can be used when demand is uncertain and there is a single opportunity to order inventory. There is a cost if too much is ordered (leftover inventory must be salvaged) and a cost if too little is ordered (the opportunity cost of lost profit). The critical ratio balances these costs to determine an order quantity that maximizes expected profit. In general, that quantity does not equal expected demand.

LO13-2 Use the news vendor model to evaluate important performance measures like the expected profit and the probability that all demand is served

For any order quantity, it is possible to evaluate several performance measures that are of interest to management. As the order quantity increases, so do expected sales and expected inventory. However, expected sales are never greater than expected demand. The in-stock and stockout probabilities are measures of customer service. At the quantity that maximizes expected profit, the in-stock probability equals the critical ratio. It is possible to increase the in-stock probability beyond that point by ordering a larger quantity, but this lowers expected profit.

LO13-3 Evaluate the order quantity needed to ensure a desired level of service

It is possible to find an order quantity that achieves any in-stock probability.

LO13-4 Understand the conditions in which mismatches between supply and demand are most costly

A product cannot earn more than the maximum profit in expectation. The difference between the maximum profit and the newsvendor expected profit is the total of mismatch costs—the costs of leftover inventory and stockouts. There are two factors that determine how much lower (as a percentage) expected profit is relative to the maximum profit: the critical ratio and the coefficient of variation of demand. Expected profit decreases as the coefficient of variation increases or as the critical ratio decreases. Expected profit is particularly low (again, relative to maximum profit) when the critical ratio is low and the coefficient of variation of demand is high.

LO13-5 Understand several strategies to increase profit and to reduce the costs associated with mismatches between supply and demand

There are several strategies a newsvendor can implement to improve operations: (i) don't sell the product, (ii) increase the profit margin relative to the cost of leftover inventory, (iii) reduce demand uncertainty through better forecasting or product pooling, (iv) increase supply flexibility with quick response, and (v) switch to make-to-order production. Product pooling can be effective because it exploits statistical economies of scale—as demand is aggregated, the coefficient of variation tends to decrease, thereby reducing mismatch costs. Quick response is effective because it allows the firm to be more conservative with its initial order quantity, thereby reducing the risk of leftover inventory, while the second source of supply reduces the cost of stockouts. Make-to-order avoids the cost of leftover inventory but does make customers wait for the product.

Key Terms

13.1 The Newsvendor Model

Salvage value The value that can be obtained per unit for inventory left over at the end of the selling season.

Density function A function that returns the probability a given outcome occurs for a particular statistical distribution.

Distribution function A function that returns the probability the outcome of a random event is a certain level or lower. For example, if $F(Q)$ is the distribution function of demand, then $F(Q)$ is the probability that demand is Q or lower.

Underage cost The cost of ordering *one* unit too few; that is, the cost of underordering by one unit. It is represented with the variable C_u.

Overage cost The cost of ordering *one* unit too many; that is, the cost of overordering by one unit. It is represented with the variable C_o.

Critical ratio The ratio of the underage cost, C_u, to the sum of the overage cost and the underage cost, $C_u + C_o$.

Round-up rule If the probability you look up in a statistical table falls between two entries, choose the one with the larger probability.

Standard normal distribution A normal distribution with mean 0 and standard deviation 1.

13.2 Newsvendor Performance Measures

Expected inventory The expected number of units not sold at the end of the season and that therefore must be salvaged.

Expected sales The expected number of units sold during the season at the regular price.

Expected profit The expected profit earned from the product, including the consequences of leftover inventory.

In-stock probability The probability that all demand was able to purchase a unit.

Stockout probability The probability that some demand was not able to purchase a unit; that is, that demand experiences a stockout.

Stockout The event in which one or more customers are unable to purchase a unit because inventory is not available.

13.4 Mismatch Costs in the Newsvendor Model

Maximum profit The highest possible expected profit. This occurs when inventory is available for all customers.

Mismatch costs Costs related to a mismatch between demand and supply. These usually include the cost of leftover inventory and the opportunity cost of stockouts.

Coefficient of variation The ratio of the standard deviation to the mean.

13.5 Strategies to Manage the Newsvendor Environment: Product Pooling, Quick Response, and Make-to-Order

Product pooling The strategy to reduce the variety offered to customers by combining, or pooling, similar products.

Correlation A measure of the interaction between two uncertain events. Correlation ranges from –1 to 1.

Positively correlated Two events are positively correlated (i.e., have a positive correlation) when the outcomes tend to have similar magnitudes. If the outcome of one event is "high," then the outcome of the other event tends to be "high" as well.

Negatively correlated Two events are negatively correlated (i.e., their correlation is negative) when the outcomes tend to have dissimilar magnitudes. If the outcome of one event is "high," then the outcome of the other event tends to be "low."

Independent Two events are independent (i.e., their correlation is 0) when the outcome of one event has no relationship to the outcome of the other event.

Statistical economies of scale The property in which aggregating demand into a large scale tends to reduce uncertainty, as measured by the coefficient of variation.

Quick response A strategy that increases supply flexibility to allow a response to updated information about demand. For example, with quick response, a firm can obtain additional supply for products that are selling above expectation, thereby reducing the number of stockouts.

Reactive capacity Capacity that allows a firm to react to changes in its demand forecast.

Make-to-stock A production system in which an item's production begins before the customer for the item is known. In a make-to-stock system, units are generally placed in inventory to await customer demand.

Make-to-order A production system in which an item's production begins after the customer for the item is known. In a make-to-order system, units are generally delivered to a customer immediately after production is completed, thereby not spending time in inventory.

Mass customization A make-to-order system in which each customer's order is unique, customized to his or her exact preferences.

Assemble-to-order A make-to-order system in which a product is assembled from a set of standardized modular components after an order is received.

Key Formulas

C_u = underage cost

C_o = overage cost

μ = the mean of demand

σ = the standard deviation of demand

z = the quantity in the standard normal distribution

LO13-1 **Use the news vendor model to decide how much product to order when demand is perishable and uncertain**

$$F(Q^*) = \frac{C_u}{C_o + C_u} \quad \text{[Equation 13.1]}$$

$$Q = \mu + (z \times \sigma) \quad \text{[Equation 13.2]}$$

$$z = \text{NORM.S.INV(Critical ratio)}$$

LO13-2 **Use the news vendor model to evaluate important performance measures like the expected profit and the probability that all demand is served**

$$z = \frac{Q - \mu}{\sigma}$$

Expected inventory $= \sigma \times I(z)$ \quad [Equation 13.3]

$$I(z) = \text{NORM.DIST}(z, 0, 1, 0) + (z \times \text{NORM.S.DIST}(z))$$

Expected sales $= Q -$ Expected inventory \quad [Equation 13.4]

Expected profit $=$ (Price $\times$ Expected sales) $+$ (Salvage value $\times$ Expected inventory) $-$ (Cost per unit $\times Q$)

In-stock probability $= F(Q)$ \quad [Equation 13.5]

Stockout probability $= 1 -$ In-stock probability

LO13-4 **Understand the conditions in which mismatches between supply and demand are most costly**

Maximum profit $=$ Expected demand $\times$ Profit per unit sold

LO13-5 **Understand several strategies to increase profit and to reduce the costs associated with mismatches between supply and demand**

Expected sales from 2nd order $= \mu -$ Expected sales from 1st order

Conceptual Questions

LO13-1

1. Which of the following is NOT true about the distribution function for a normal distribution?
   a. It ranges from 0 to 1.
   b. It increases as the quantity increases.
   c. It generally has a bell shape when graphed.
   d. It returns the probability that the outcome from the normal distribution is a certain quantity or lower.

2. A newsvendor orders the quantity that maximizes expected profit for two products, X and Y. The critical ratio for both products is .8. The demand forecast for both products is 9000 units and both are normally distributed. Product X has more uncertain demand in the sense that it has the larger standard deviation. Of which of the two products does the newsvendor order more?

a. Product X because it has less certain demand.

b. Product Y because it has more certain demand.

c. The order quantities are the same because they have the same critical ratio.

d. More information is needed to determine which has the higher order quantity.

3. Consider two products, X and Y, that have identical cost, retail price, and demand parameters and the same short selling season (the summer months from May through August). The newsvendor model is used to manage inventory for both products. Product X is to be discontinued at the end of the season this year and the leftover inventory will be salvaged at 75 percent of the cost. Product Y will be reoffered next summer, so any leftovers this year can be carried over to the next year while incurring a holding cost on each unit left over equal to 20 percent of the product's cost. The quantity of each product is selected to maximize expected profit. How do those quantities compare?

a. The quantity of product X is higher.

b. The quantity of product Y is higher.

c. The quantities are equal.

d. The answer cannot be determined from the data provided.

LO13-2

4. Suppose the newsvendor model describes a firm's operations decision. Is it possible to have positive stockout probability and positive expected leftover inventory? Choose the best answer.

a. No. If there is leftover inventory, then a stockout doesn't occur.

b. No. If the stockout probability is positive, then expected inventory must be negative.

c. No. Actual demand can differ from sales.

d. Yes. A firm does not stock out and have leftover inventory at the same time, but the stockout probability can be positive even though there is positive expected leftover inventory.

e. Yes, as long as the underage cost is greater than the overage cost.

5. A newsvendor faces normally distributed demand and the critical ratio is .8. If the profit-maximizing quantity is ordered, which of the following statements is true?

a. Expected sales are less than expected demand.

b. Expected sales are greater than expected demand.

c. Expected sales are exactly equal to expected demand.

d. Expected sales could be less than, equal to, or greater than expected demand.

6. A company uses the newsvendor model to manage its inventories and faces normally distributed demand with a coefficient of variation of 0.75. The company decides to order a quantity that exactly equals the mean of its demand forecast. Which of the following is true regarding this company's performance measures?

a. There is a .50 probability that there is enough inventory to serve all demand.

b. Expected inventory equals 50 percent of the mean of the demand forecast.

c. The stockout probability is .25.

d. Expected inventory is 0.

7. A retailer has two merchandizers, Sue and Bob, who are responsible for setting order quantities for the products they manage. For all of their products, the critical ratio is .7 and the coefficient of variation of their demand forecasts is 0.35. At the end of the season, Sue is proud to report that she has sold the entire inventory she purchased. Bob, on the other hand, sold only about a third of his products. Who is more likely to be choosing quantities that maximize expected profit?

a. Sue because she doesn't incur the cost of salvaging inventory.

b. Sue because she must have sold more units than Bob.

c. Bob because even leftover inventory generates some additional revenue.

d. Bob because he is probably ordering more than the mean of the demand forecast.

8. Suppose the newsvendor model is used to manage inventory. Which of the following can happen when the order quantity is increased by one unit?

a. Expected sales increases by more than one unit.

b. Expected leftover inventory increases by more than one unit.

c. Expected sales decrease by less than one unit.

d. Expected leftover inventory increases by less than one unit.

LO13-3

9. Which of the following changes in the in-stock probability increases the order quantity the most?
   a. An increase in the in-stock probability from 70 percent to 80 percent.
   b. An increase in the in-stock probability from 70 percent to 85 percent.
   c. An increase in the in-stock probability from 80 percent to 90 percent.
   d. An increase in the in-stock probability from 80 percent to 95 percent.

LO13-4

10. A change in which of the following does not result in a change in the mismatch costs incurred by a newsvendor?
    a. The quantity ordered
    b. The revenue received from salvaging inventory
    c. The regular selling price of the product
    d. The coefficient of variation of the demand forecast
    e. The quality of the product

11. A change in which of the following results in a change in the maximum profit in a news-vendor setting?
    a. The revenue received from salvaging inventory
    b. The regular selling price of the product
    c. The standard deviation of the demand forecast
    d. The coefficient of variation of the demand forecast

12. For which of the following products is there the highest probability that demand is within 50 percent of the mean of the demand forecast?
    a. Mean = 1000, standard deviation = 200
    b. Mean = 1000, standard deviation = 300
    c. Mean = 2000, standard deviation = 300
    d. Mean = 2000, standard deviation = 500
    e. Mean = 4000, standard deviation = 1600
    f. Mean = 4000, standard deviation = 2000

LO13-5

13. Product X's demand is normally distributed with mean 150 and standard deviation 50. Product Y's demand is also normally distributed with a mean of 150 and a standard deviation of 50. The sum of demand for these two products is normally distributed with a mean of 300 and a standard deviation of 50. Which of the following results is most likely?
    a. Demands for these products are negatively correlated.
    b. Demands for these products are positively correlated.
    c. Demands for these products are independent.
    d. It is not possible to determine with this information the correlation of these products.

14. Each day, QBlitz, a Seattle-based startup, offers a single product through its website. The product is available for order only on one day, and no other products are available during that day. To add to this odd selling strategy, QBlitz does not post prices for its products. Instead, for each product there is a reserve price. On the day a product is avail-able, customers can submit bids. All of the bids that exceed the reserve price are told at the end of the day that they "won" the product and they pay the price they bid. QBlitz then adds up all of the winning bids and submits an order to a supplier for the needed quantity. If the supplier delivers that quantity, then QBlitz ships the product to the win-ners once the product is received. However, if the supplier delivers only a portion of the ordered quantity, then QBlitz ships the product to the highest bidders that it can satisfy and notifies the others that they will receive a refund because they will not in fact receive the product. The QBlitz system is best described as:
    a. make-to-stock.
    b. make-to-order.
    c. assemble-to-order.
    d. mass customization.

Solved Example Problems

LO13-1, 13-2, 13-3, 13-4

1. The National Football Association (NFA) has granted Tike an exclusive license to sell NFA replica jerseys. Tike outsources the jersey cutting and sewing operations to an off-shore manufacturer. The jerseys are then delivered to Tike's distribution center (DC). Because of the long production and shipment lead times, Tike must decide in advance how much inventory to hold at the DC in anticipation of retailers' orders for the coming season. Table 13.7 displays Tike's demand forecasts for four of the players on the Philadelphia Talons for the upcoming season, assuming independent normal demand distributions.

TABLE 13.7 Demand Forecast for the Replica Jerseys for Four Players on the Philadelphia Talons

Product Description	Mean	Standard Deviation
Nick Goles	35,000	10,000
LeSean McBoy	30,000	10,000
Jeremy Macman	25,000	10,000
Zach Hurts	20,000	10,000

Tike sells the NFA jerseys to retailers at a wholesale price of $24 per jersey. Tike buys each jersey from the offshore manufacturer for $11. Tike does not have the opportunity to make a midseason replenishment. At the end of the season, Tike sells its unsold jerseys at a discount price of $7 per jersey.

(a) What is the probability that demand for the Nick Goles jersey is fewer than 25,000?

Answer: .1587. Convert $Q = 25,000$ to its corresponding z value: $z = (Q - \mu)/\sigma = (25,000 - 35,000)/10,000 = -1$. Look up the distribution function in Table 13.4: $F(z=-1) = .1587$.

(b) What is the probability that demand for the Nick Goles jersey is between 25,000 and 45,000?

Answer: .6826. Convert $Q = 45,000$ to its corresponding z value: $z = (Q - \mu)/\sigma = (45,000 - 35,000)/10,000 = 1$. Look up the distribution function in Table 13.4: $F(z=1) = .8413$. The same calculations for $Q = 25,000$ reveal $F(z=-1) = .1587$. The probability demand is between 25,000 and 45,000, so the difference between those two probabilities is $.8413 - .1587 = .6826$.

(c) What is the overage cost for the Nick Goles jersey?

Answer: $4. The overage cost is the cost of ordering one jersey too many. The jersey is purchased for $11 and salvaged for $7, so the loss on one jersey that is purchased but not sold at the regular price is $11 - $7 = $4.

(d) What is the underage cost for the Nick Goles jersey?

Answer: $13. The underage cost is the cost of ordering one jersey too few. The jersey is purchased for $11 and sold for $24, so the loss on not having a jersey to sell at the regular price is $24 - $11 = $13.

(e) What is the critical ratio for the Nick Goles jerseys?

Answer: .7647. The critical ratio is $C_u/(C_o + C_u) = \$13/(\$4 + \$13) = .7647$.

(f) How many Nick Goles jerseys should Tike order to maximize expected profit?

Answer: 43,000. The critical ratio is .7647. From Table 13.4, $F(z=0.70) = .7580$ and $F(z=0.8) = .7881$. According to the round-up rule, select the row with the higher probability, which means $z = 0.8$. Convert that z value into a Q: $Q = \mu + (z \times \sigma) = 35,000 + (0.8 \times 10,000) = 43,000$.

(g) If Tike orders 38,000 LeSean McBoy jerseys, how many of these jerseys can Tike expect to sell at the discount price of $7?

> **Answer:** 9202. Convert $Q = 38,000$ into $z = (Q - \mu)/\sigma = (38,000 - 30,000)/10,000 = 0.8$. Look up the expected leftover inventory in Table 13.4: $I(z=0.8) = 0.9202$. Convert to the expected leftover inventory for the actual demand distribution: Expected leftover inventory $= \sigma \times I(z) = 10,000 \times 0.9202 = 9202$.

(h) If Tike orders 38,000 LeSean McBoy jerseys, how many of these jerseys can Tike expect to sell at the regular wholesale price of $24?

> **Answer:** 28,798. Expected sales $= Q -$ Expected leftover inventory $= 38,000 - 9202 = 28,798$.

(i) If Tike orders 38,000 LeSean McBoy jerseys, what is its expected profit from selling this jersey?

> **Answer:** $337,566. Expected profit $=$ (Price $\times$ Expected sales) $+$ (Salvage value $\times$ Leftover inventory) $-$ (Cost $\times$ Q) $= (\$24 \times 28,798) + (\$7 \times 9202) - (\$11 \times 38,000) = \$337,566$.

(j) If Tike orders 30,000 Jeremy Macman jerseys, what is the probability that it has enough inventory to satisfy all regular-priced demand?

> **Answer:** .6915. Convert $Q = 30,000$ to its corresponding z value: $z = (Q - \mu)/\sigma = (30,000 - 25,000)/10,000 = 0.5$. Look up the distribution function in Table 13.4: $F(z=0.5) = .6915$.

(k) If Tike orders 37,000 Jeremy Macman jerseys, what is the probability that Tike does not satisfy all demand for this jersey?

> **Answer:** .1151. Convert $Q = 37,000$ to its corresponding z value: $z = (Q - \mu)/\sigma = (37,000 - 25,000)/10,000 = 1.2$. Look up the distribution function in Table 13.4: $F(z=1.2) = .8849$. The probability that it fails to satisfy all demand is $1 - F(z=1.2) = .1151$.

(l) If Tike wants to ensure that there is a 90 percent in-stock probability for the Jeremy Macman jersey, then how many units should it order?

> **Answer:** 38,000. Look up the target in-stock probability in Table 13.4: $F(z=1.2) = .8849$ and $F(z=1.3) = .9032$, so choose $z = 1.3$. Convert to the order quantity for the actual demand distribution: $Q = \mu + (z \times \sigma) = 25,000 + (1.3 \times 10,000) = 38,000$.

(m) What is the maximum profit for the Zach Hurts jersey?

> **Answer:** $260,000. Maximum profit $=$ Expected demand $\times$ (Price $-$ Cost) $= 20,000 \times (\$24 - \$11) = \$260,000$.

2. Pony Express Creations (PEC) is a manufacturer of party hats, primarily for the Halloween season. Eighty percent of its yearly sales occur over a six-week period. One of its popular products is the Elvis wig, complete with sideburns and metallic glasses. The Elvis wig is produced in China, so PEC must make a single order well in advance of the upcoming season. Ryan, the owner of PEC, expects demand to be 25,000; Table 13.8 provides his entire demand forecast.

TABLE 13.8 The Distribution Function, $F(Q)$, and Expected Leftover Inventory, $I(Q)$, for PEC's Demand Forecast

Q	F(Q)	I(Q)	Q	F(Q)	I(Q)
5000	.0181	0	45,000	.9787	20,168
10,000	.0914	91	50,000	.9919	25,061
15,000	.2381	548	55,000	.9972	30,021
20,000	.4335	1738	60,000	.9991	35,007
25,000	.6289	3906	65,000	.9997	40,002
30,000	.7852	7050	70,000	.9999	45,001
35,000	.8894	10,976	75,000	1.0000	50,000
40,000	.9489	15,423			

PEC sells the Elvis wig for $25 and its production cost is $6. Leftover inventory can be sold to discounters for $2.50.

(a) What is the probability that demand is more than 40,000 units.

Answer: .0511. Demand 40,000 units or fewer with probability $F(40,000) = .9489$. Demand is greater than 40,000 with probability $1 - F(40,000) = .0511$.

(b) Suppose PEC orders 40,000 Elvis wigs. What is the chance it has to liquidate 10,000 or more wigs with a discounter?

Answer: .7852. If it orders 40,000 wigs, it will need to discount 10,000 or more of them if demand is 30,000 or fewer. The probability that demand is 30,000 or fewer is $F(30,000)$, which is .7852.

(c) What order quantity maximizes PEC's expected profit?

Answer: 35,000. The overage cost is $C_o = \$6 - \$2.50 = \$3.50$. The underage cost is $C_u = \$25 - \$6 = \$19$. The critical ratio is $C_u/(C_o + C_u) = \$19/(\$3.50 + \$19) = .8444$. From Table 13.8, $F(30,000) = .7852$ and $F(35,000) = .8894$. According to the round-up rule, select the larger quantity, which is 35,000.

(d) If PEC orders 25,000 wigs, what is its expected inventory?

Answer: 3906. From Table 13.8, $I(25,000) = 3906$.

(e) If PEC orders 55,000 wigs, what are its expected sales?

Answer: 24,979. From Table 13.8, $I(55,000) = 30,021$. Expected sales $= Q - I(Q) = 55,000 - 30,021 = 24,979$.

(f) If PEC orders 40,000 wigs, what is its expected profit?

Answer: $412,983. From Table 13.8, $I(40,000) = 15,423$. Expected sales $= Q - I(Q) = 40,000 - 15,423 = 24,577$. Profit $= (\$25 \times 24,577) + (\$2.50 \times 15,423) - (\$6 \times 40,000) = \$412,983$.

(g) What is the maximum profit for PEC?

Answer: $475,000. Maximum profit $=$ (Price $-$ Cost) $\times$ Expected demand $= (25 - 6) \times 25,000 = \$475,000$.

(h) If PEC wants to achieve at least a 98 percent in-stock probability, what quantity should it order?

Answer: 50,000. From Table 13.8, $F(45,000) = .9787$ and $F(50,000) = .9919$. Choose the larger quantity to ensure at least a 98 percent in-stock probability.

(i) If PEC orders 30,000 wigs, what is its total mismatch cost?

> **Answer:** $63,625. First evaluate expected profit. From Table 13.8, $I(30,000) = 7050$. Expected sales $= Q - I(Q) = 30,000 - 7050 = 22,950$. Profit $= (\$25 \times 22,950) + (\$2.50 \times 7050) - (\$6 \times 30,000) = \$411,375$. Maximum profit is (Price $-$ Cost) $\times$ Expected demand $= (\$25 - \$6) \times 25,000 = \$475,000$. Total mismatch cost is the difference between maximum profit and expected profit: $\$475,000 - \$411,375 = \$63,625$.

Problems and Applications

LO13-1, 13-2

1. Dan McClure owns a thriving independent bookstore in artsy New Hope, Pennsylvania. He must decide how many copies to order of a new book, *Power and Self-Destruction,* an exposé on a famous politician's lurid affairs. Interest in the book will be intense at first and then fizzle quickly as attention turns to other celebrities. The book's retail price is $20, and the wholesale price is $12. The publisher will buy back the retailer's leftover copies at a full refund, but McClure Books incurs $4 in shipping and handling costs for each book returned to the publisher. Dan believes his demand forecast can be represented by a normal distribution with a mean of 200 and a standard deviation of 80.
   a. Dan will consider this book to be a blockbuster for him if it sells more than 400 units. What is the probability that *Power and Self-Destruction* will be a blockbuster?
   b. Dan considers a book a "dog" if it sells less than 50 percent of his mean forecast. What is the probability this exposé is a "dog"?
   c. What is the probability that demand for this book will be within 20 percent of the mean forecast?
   d. What order quantity maximizes Dan's expected profit?
   e. If Dan orders the quantity needed to achieve a 95 percent in-stock probability, what is the probability that some customer won't be able to purchase a copy of the book?
   f. Suppose Dan orders 300 copies of the book. What is Dan's expected leftover inventory?
   g. Suppose Dan orders 300 copies of the book. What are Dan's expected sales?
   h. Suppose Dan orders 300 copies of the book. What is Dan's expected profit?
   i. How many books should Dan order if he wants to achieve a 95 percent in-stock probability?

2. Flextrola, Inc., an electronics systems integrator, is planning to design a key component for its next-generation product with Solectrics. Flextrola will integrate the component with some software and then sell it to consumers. Given the short life cycles of such products and the long lead times quoted by Solectrics, Flextrola only has one opportunity to place an order with Solectrics prior to the beginning of its selling season. Flextrola's demand during the season is normally distributed with a mean of 1000 and a standard deviation of 600. Solectrics' production cost for the component is $52 per unit, and it plans to sell the component for $72 per unit to Flextrola. Flextrola incurs essentially no cost associated with the software integration and handling of each unit. Flextrola sells these units to consumers for $121 each. Flextrola can sell unsold inventory at the end of the season in a secondary electronics market for $50 each. The existing contract specifies that once Flextrola places the order, no changes are allowed to it. Also, Solectrics does not accept any returns of unsold inventory, so Flextrola must dispose of excess inventory in the secondary market.
   a. What is the probability that Flextrola's demand will be within 25 percent of its forecast?
   b. What is the probability that Flextrola's demand will be more than 40 percent greater than Flextrola's forecast?
   c. Under this contract, how many units should Flextrola order to maximize its expected profit?

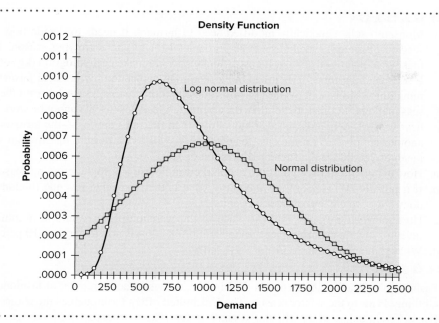

Figure 13.15

The density functions for a log normal and a normal distribution with mean 1000 and standard deviation 600

d. If Flextrola orders 1200 units, how many units of inventory can Flextrola expect to sell in the secondary electronics market?

e. If Flextrola orders 1200 units, what are expected sales?

f. If Flextrola orders 1200 units, what is expected profit?

g. A sharp manager at Flextrola noticed the demand forecast and became wary of assuming that demand is normally distributed. She plotted a histogram of demands from previous seasons for similar products and concluded that demand is better represented by the log normal distribution. Figure 13.15 plots the density function for both the log normal and the normal distributions, each with mean = 1000 and standard deviation = 600; Figure 13.16 plots the corresponding distribution functions. Using the more accurate forecast (i.e., the log normal distribution), approximately how many units should Flextrola order to maximize its expected profit?

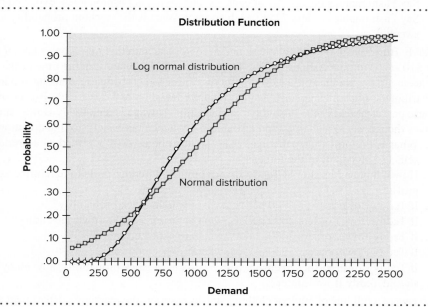

Figure 13.16

The distribution functions for a log normal and a normal distribution with mean 1000 and standard deviation 600

LO13-1, 13-2, 13-3, 13-4

3. Monsanto sells genetically modified seed to farmers. It needs to decide how much seed to put into a warehouse to serve demand for the next growing season. It will make one quantity decision. It costs Montanso $8 to make each kilogram (kg) of seed. It sells each kg for $45. If it has more seed than demanded by the local farmers, the remaining seed is sent overseas. Unfortunately, it only earns $3 per kg from the overseas market (but this is better than destroying the seed because it cannot be stored until next year). If demand exceeds its quantity, then the sales are lost—the farmers go to another supplier. As a forecast for demand, it will use a normal distribution with a mean of 300,000 and a standard deviation of 100,000.
   a. How many kilograms should it place in the warehouse before the growing season?
   b. If it puts 400,000 kg in the warehouse, what is their expected revenue (include both domestic revenue and overseas revenue)?
   c. How many kilograms should it place in the warehouse if it wants to minimize its inventory while ensuring that the stockout probability is no greater than 10 percent?
   d. What is the maximum profit for this seed?

LO13-1, 13-2, 13-3

4. Fashionables is a franchisee of The UnLimited, the well-known retailer of fashionable clothing. Prior to the winter season, The UnLimited offers Fashionables the choice of five different colors of a particular sweater design. The sweaters are knit overseas by hand; because of the lead times involved, Fashionables will need to order its assortment in advance of the selling season. As per the contracting terms offered by The UnLimited, Fashionables will also not be able to cancel, modify, or reorder sweaters during the selling season. Demand for each color during the season is normally distributed with a mean of 500 and a standard deviation of 200. Further, you may assume that the demands for each sweater are independent of those for a different color.

The UnLimited offers the sweaters to Fashionables at the wholesale price of $40 per sweater, and Fashionables plans to sell each sweater at the retail price of $70 per unit. The UnLimited does not accept any returns of unsold inventory. However, Fashionables can sell all of the unsold sweaters at the end of the season at the fire-sale price of $20 each.
   a. How many units of each sweater type should Fashionables order to maximize its expected profit?
   b. If Fashionables wishes to ensure a 97.5 percent in-stock probability, what should its order quantity be for each type of sweater?
   c. Say Fashionables orders 725 of each sweater. What is Fashionables' expected profit?
   d. Say Fashionables orders 725 of each sweater. What is the stockout probability for each sweater?

5. Teddy Bower is an outdoor clothing and accessories chain that purchases a line of parkas at $10 each from its Asian supplier, TeddySports. Unfortunately, at the time of the order placement, demand is still uncertain: Teddy Bower forecasts that its demand is normally distributed with a mean of 2100 and a standard deviation of 1200. Teddy Bower sells these parkas at $22 each. Unsold parkas have little salvage value; Teddy Bower simply gives them away to a charity (and also doesn't collect a tax benefit for the donation).
   a. What is the probability this parka turns out to be a "dog," defined as a product that sells less than half of the forecast?
   b. How many parkas should Teddy Bower buy from TeddySports to maximize expected profit?
   c. If Teddy Bower orders 3000 parkas, what is the in-stock probability?
   d. If Teddy Bower orders 3000 parkas, what is the expected leftover inventory?
   e. If Teddy Bower orders 3000 parkas, what are expected sales?
   f. If Teddy Bower orders 3000 parkas, what is expected profit?
   g. If Teddy Bower wishes to ensure a 98.5 percent in-stock probability, how many parkas should Teddy Bower order?

6. To ensure a full line of outdoor clothing and accessories, the marketing department at Teddy Bower insists that it also sell waterproof hunting boots. Unfortunately, Teddy Bower

does not have expertise in manufacturing those kinds of boots. Hence, Teddy Bower contacted several Taiwanese suppliers to request quotes. Due to competition, Teddy Bower knows that it cannot sell these boots for more than $54. However, $40 per boot was the best quote from the suppliers. In addition, Teddy Bower anticipates excess inventory will need to be sold off at a 50 percent discount at the end of the season. Given the $54 price, Teddy Bower's demand forecast is for 400 boots, with a standard deviation of 300.

    a. If Teddy Bower decides to include these boots in its assortment, how many boots should Teddy Bower order from the supplier?

    b. Suppose Teddy Bower orders 380 boots. What is Teddy Bower's expected profit?

    c. The marketing department insists that its in-stock probability be at least 98 percent. Given this mandate, how many boots does it need to order?

    d. John Briggs, a buyer in the procurement department, overheard at lunch a discussion of the "boot problem." He suggested that Teddy Bower ask for a quantity discount from the supplier. After following up on his suggestion, the supplier responded that Teddy Bower could get a 10 percent discount if it were willing to order at least 800 boots. If the objective is to maximize expected profit, how many boots should Teddy Bower order given this new offer?

7. Goop Inc. needs to order a raw material to make a special polymer. The demand for the polymer is forecasted to be normally distributed with a mean of 250 gallons and a standard deviation of 100 gallons. Goop sells the polymer for $25 per gallon. Goop purchases raw material for $10 per gallon and must spend $5 per gallon to dispose of all unused raw material due to government regulations. (One gallon of raw material yields one gallon of polymer.) If demand is more than Goop can make, then Goop sells only what it has made and the rest of the demand is lost.

    a. How many gallons should Goop purchase to maximize its expected profit?

    b. Suppose Goop purchases 150 gallons of raw material. What is the probability that it will run out of raw material?

    c. Suppose Goop purchases 300 gallons of raw material. What are the expected sales (in gallons)?

    d. Suppose Goop purchases 400 gallons of raw material. How much should it expect to spend on disposal costs (in dollars)?

    e. Suppose Goop wants to ensure that there is a 92 percent probability that it will be able to satisfy its customers' entire demand. How many gallons of the raw material should it purchase?

LO13-1, 13-2

8. Geoff Gullo owns a small firm that manufactures "Gullo Sunglasses." He has the opportunity to sell a particular seasonal model to Land's Start, a catalog retailer. Geoff offers Land's Start two purchasing options.

    • Option 1: Geoff offers to set his price at $65 and agrees to credit Land's Start $53 for each unit Land's Start returns to Geoff at the end of the season (because those units did not sell). Because styles change each year, there is essentially no value in the returned merchandise.

    • Option 2: Geoff offers a price of $55 for each unit, but returns are no longer accepted. In this case, Land's Start throws out unsold units at the end of the season.

This season's demand for this model will be normally distributed with a mean of 200 and a standard deviation of 125. Land's Start will sell those sunglasses for $100 each. Geoff's unit production cost is $25.

    a. How much would Land's Start buy if it chose option 1?

    b. How much would Land's Start buy if it chose option 2?

    c. Which option will Land's Start choose?

    d. Suppose Land's Start chooses option 1 and orders 275 units. What is Geoff Gullo's expected profit?

LO13-1, 13-2, 13-3

9. CPG Bagels starts the day with a large production run of bagels. Throughout the morning, additional bagels are produced as needed. The last bake is completed at 3 p.m. and

the store closes at 8 p.m. It costs approximately $0.20 in materials and labor to make a bagel. The price of a fresh bagel is $0.60. Bagels not sold by the end of the previous day are sold the next day as "day old" bagels in bags of six for $0.99 a bag. About two-thirds of the day-old bagels are sold; the remainder are just thrown away. There are many bagel flavors, but for simplicity, concentrate just on the plain bagels. The store manager predicts that demand for plain bagels from 3 p.m. until closing is normally distributed with a mean of 54 and a standard deviation of 21.

a. How many bagels should the store have at 3 p.m. to maximize the store's expected profit (from sales between 3 p.m. and closing)? (*Hint:* Assume day-old bagels are sold for $0.99/6 = $0.165 each; that is, don't worry about the fact that day-old bagels are sold in bags of six.)

b. Suppose the store manager has 101 bagels at 3 p.m. How many bagels should the store manager expect to have at the end of the day?

c. Suppose the manager would like to have a .95 in-stock probability on demand that occurs after 3 p.m. How many bagels should the store have at 3 p.m. to ensure that level of service?

10. The Kiosk sells spicy black bean burritos during the weekday lunch hour. It charges $4.00 for each burrito and all burritos are made before the lunch crowd arrives. Virtually all burrito customers also buy a soda, which is sold for 60¢. The burritos cost the Kiosk $2.00, while sodas cost the Kiosk 5¢. Kiosk management is very sensitive about the quality of food it serves. Thus, it maintains a strict "no old burrito" policy, so any burritos left at the end of the day are disposed of. Table 13.9 gives the distribution function of demand for the burrito.

. . . .

TABLE 13.9 The Distribution Function, *F(Q)*, and Expected Leftover Inventory, *I(Q)*, for Burrito Demand

Q	F(Q)	I(Q)
0	.0000	0.00
1	.0000	0.00
2	.0000	0.00
3	.0000	0.00
4	.0001	0.00
5	.0003	0.00
6	.0010	0.00
7	.0029	0.00
8	.0071	0.00
9	.0154	0.01
10	.0304	0.03
11	.0549	0.06
12	.0917	0.11
13	.1426	0.20
14	.2081	0.35
15	.2867	0.55
16	.3751	0.84
17	.4686	1.22
18	.5622	1.68
19	.6509	2.25
20	.7307	2.90

TABLE 13.9 (concluded)

Q	F(Q)	I(Q)
21	.7991	3.63
22	.8551	4.43
23	.8989	5.28
24	.9317	6.18
25	.9554	7.11
26	.9718	8.07
27	.9827	9.04
28	.9897	10.02
29	.9941	11.01
30	.9967	12.01
31	.9982	13.00
32	.9990	14.00
33	.9995	15.00
34	.9998	16.00
35	.9999	17.00
36	.9999	18.00
37	1.0000	19.00
38	1.0000	20.00
39	1.0000	21.00

  a. Suppose burrito customers buy their snack somewhere else if the Kiosk is out of stock. How many burritos should the Kiosk make for the lunch crowd?

  b. Suppose the Kiosk makes 24 burritos. How many burritos should it expect to discard at the end of the day?

  c. Suppose the Kiosk makes 24 burritos. How many burritos should it expect to sell?

  d. Suppose the Kiosk makes 24 burritos. What is the Kiosk's expected profit, including the profit from the sale of sodas?

  e. Suppose the Kiosk makes 30 burritos. What is the probability that some customer is unable to purchase a burrito?

  f. If the Kiosk wants to be sure it has inventory for its customers with at least a .985 probability, how many burritos should it make?

  g. Suppose that any customer unable to purchase a burrito settles for a lunch of Pop-Tarts and a soda. Pop-Tarts sell for 75¢ and cost the Kiosk 25¢. (As Pop-Tarts and soda are easily stored, the Kiosk never runs out of these essentials.) Assuming that the Kiosk management is interested in maximizing profits, how many burritos should it make?

11. Share&Care is a nonprofit car-share company that rents cars. When customers make a reservation, they specify their pickup time and the number of time slots they will hold the vehicle, where each time slot equals 15 minutes. For example, if the pickup time is 1 p.m., then possible drop-off times are 1:15 (one slot), 1:30 (two slots), and so on. Share&Care charges $1.50 for each time slot in the reservation. To discourage customers from returning the rented cars beyond their drop-off time, it charges $20 per time slot used beyond the drop-off time. For example, if a customer's drop-off time is 2:30 and he returns the vehicle at 2:47, then he is charged $40 for the two time slots he used beyond his reservation (and, of course, $1.50 per slot that he reserved). Larry runs a small business that makes deliveries on Fridays. To ensure availability of a car, he books his car two days in advance. However, he doesn't know his exact needs when he books. Table 13.10 provides information regarding Larry's demand (in terms of slots). For example, if he needs five slots but booked four slots, then he uses the car for five slots,

for a total charge of $(4 \times \$1.50) + \$20 = \$26$. If he ends up booking the car for more time than he needs, the extra time on the car has no value to him.

. . . .

TABLE 13.10 **The Distribution Function, *F(Q)*, and Expected Leftover Inventory, *I(Q)*, for the Number of Slots Larry Needs**

Q	F(Q)	I(Q)
0	.0183	0.00
1	.0916	0.02
2	.2381	0.11
3	.4335	0.35
4	.6288	0.78
5	.7851	1.41
6	.8893	2.20
7	.9489	3.08
8	.9786	4.03
9	.9919	5.01
10	.9972	6.00
11	.9991	7.00
12	.9997	8.00
13	.9999	9.00
14	1.0000	10.00

. . . .

a. Suppose Larry books the car for two time slots. How likely is he to pay $40 or more in late fees?
b. To minimize his rental costs, how many time slots should Larry reserve?
c. Suppose Larry books the car for five time slots. How many time slots can he expect to waste (i.e., they end up being of no use to him)?
d. Larry hates paying any late penalty fee. Suppose he wants to be 99.9 percent sure that he will not have to pay a late fee. How many slots should he book?

CASE LE CLUB FRANÇAIS DU VIN

Stéphane Zanella is the directeur général (general manager) of Le Club Français du Vin (The French Wine Club). Founded in 1973, Le Club is a large catalog retailer offering an exciting collection of French wines to consumers in France, Switzerland, and Germany. The mission of Le Club is to offer wines of good to very good quality to its members, who receive interesting wines delivered directly to their homes. Because most consumers in France purchase wine through their supermarkets (some with outstanding selections) and local specialty stores, Le Club capitalizes on a niche market. Le Club employs several wine experts and specializes in identifying small and midsize growers typically below the radar screen of the big French hypermarkets such as Carrefour and Champion.

Zanella's current task is to decide Le Club's order for the wines in an upcoming catalog. Ordering occurs several months before publishing the catalog and at a point when little information beyond the wine experts' personal opinions is available. Upon receiving the order, the grower decorates the bottles with a label unique to Le Club and sends the order to Le Club's warehouse in Dijon (some 300 km south of Paris). Le Club's exclusive label prevents consumers from comparing prices with supermarket offerings and allows Le Club to enjoy comfortable gross margins of about 50 percent (i.e., Le Club sets its price to consumers at twice the price it pays to buy wine from growers). In addition to the cost of purchasing each bottle, Le Club incurs a €1.25 shipping and handling cost per bottle on its outbound shipments to customers (€ is the symbol for the euro). For example, for a bottle with a €10 retail price, Le Club pays about €5 in procurement costs and €1.25 to ship the bottle to the customer. Customers do not pay for shipping, but the growers pay for inbound shipping to the Dijon warehouse.

Zanella knows that if he buys too many bottles for a catalog season, then the excess bottles are stored in the

© lynx/iconotec.com/Glow Images/RF

warehouse and are discounted in a future catalog. As a rule of thumb, Zanella assumes that an overbought wine needs to be discounted by 35 percent off its retail price (i.e., a €10 bottle would be sold for €6.5) to liquidate the inventory. Each bottle sold through a discount page still incurs a €1.25 cost to ship the bottle to the customer. Furthermore, due to the extra time spent in the warehouse each discounted bottle incurs a €1.1 storage cost and an opportunity cost of capital equal to 15 percent of the purchase price. For example, a bottle Le Club purchases for €5 and sold through a discount page incurs a storage cost of €1.1 and an additional €0.75 for the opportunity cost of capital (15 percent of €5).

While it is costly to overbuy, Zanella knows that it can also be costly to be too conservative—given the long lead times in wine production, Le Club is generally unable to later place additional orders for wine. Thus, while Zanella knows he shouldn't complain about selling out a wine, he also worries about the sales Le Club could have made had it ordered more.

(continued)

Although each catalog usually offers a selection of around 30 wines, including whites, reds, and rosés from different regions of France, Zanella decided to think carefully about the sample of eight red wines displayed in Table 13.11 for an upcoming catalog. Each wine occupies a different price point and the forecasts vary considerably, depending on the quality of the wine, where it will be included in the catalog (e.g., cover, back page, middle, etc.), and how much space it will be given in the catalog (e.g., full page, quarter page, etc.). Zanella would love its forecasts to be more accurate, but he also recognizes that tastes in wine are fickle. Still, sipping from a glass of the Pessac Leognan from Chateau Haut Nouchet, he wonders how a wine that tastes that good could possibly sell poorly.

1. To maximize LeClub's expected profit, how much of each of the wines in Table 13.11 should Zanella order?
2. If Zanella orders the quantity that maximizes expected profit, for each wine what is the probability that it will have inventory left over that must be discounted?
3. From the wines listed in Table 13.11, which are the most profitable and which are the least profitable? Why?
4. If Zanella decides that it must have at least a .75 in-stock probability with each wine, how much of each wine would it order? Do you recommend that it order those quantities?
5. How could Zanella improve his business?

TABLE 13.11 A Sample of Red Wines to Be Sold in One of Le Clubs Upcoming Catalogs

Appellation	Designation	Retail Price (€ per bottle)	Demand Forecast (bottles) Mean	Demand Forecast (bottles) Standard Deviation
VDP des Côteaux de L'Ardèche	La Réserve Rouge du Club	3.25	3500	1280
Bordeaux	Réserve du Club	4.50	2900	1080
Minervois	Domaine des Arcades—FID	5.21	4000	1430
Côtes du Ventoux	Gabriel Meffre (6)	5.60	1200	480
Côtes de Bourg	Ch. Florimond	7.20	1300	510
Madiran	Folie de Roi	9.00	12,000	3000
Givry	La Buxynoise	12.90	900	360
Pessac Leognan	Ch. Haut Nouchet	18.90	1300	510

Appendix 13A

TABLE 13A.1 The Distribution, *F(Q)*, and Expected Inventory, *I(Q)*, Functions for the standard normal distribution function

z	F(z)	I(z)	z	F(z)	I(z)	z	F(z)	I(z)
−4.0	.0000	.0000	−1.3	.0968	.0455	1.4	.9192	1.4367
−3.9	.0000	.0000	−1.2	.1151	.0561	1.5	.9332	1.5293
−3.8	.0001	.0000	−1.1	.1357	.0686	1.6	.9452	1.6232
−3.7	.0001	.0000	−1.0	.1587	.0833	1.7	.9554	1.7183
−3.6	.0002	.0000	−0.9	.1841	.1004	1.8	.9641	1.8143
−3.5	.0002	.0001	−0.8	.2119	.1202	1.9	.9713	1.9111
−3.4	.0003	.0001	−0.7	.2420	.1429	2.0	.9772	2.0085
−3.3	.0005	.0001	−0.6	.2743	.1687	2.1	.9821	2.1065
−3.2	.0007	.0002	−0.5	.3085	.1978	2.2	.9861	2.2049
−3.1	.0010	.0003	−0.4	.3446	.2304	2.3	.9893	2.3037
−3.0	.0013	.0004	−0.3	.3821	.2668	2.4	.9918	2.4027
−2.9	.0019	.0005	−0.2	.4207	.3069	2.5	.9938	2.5020
−2.8	.0026	.0008	−0.1	.4602	.3509	2.6	.9953	2.6015
−2.7	.0035	.0011	.0	.5000	.3989	2.7	.9965	2.7011
−2.6	.0047	.0015	.1	.5398	.4509	2.8	.9974	2.8008
−2.5	.0062	.0020	.2	.5793	.5069	2.9	.9981	2.9005
−2.4	.0082	.0027	.3	.6179	.5668	3.0	.9987	3.0004
−2.3	.0107	.0037	.4	.6554	.6304	3.1	.9990	3.1003
−2.2	.0139	.0049	.5	.6915	.6978	3.2	.9993	3.2002
−2.1	.0179	.0065	.6	.7257	.7687	3.3	.9995	3.3001
−2.0	.0228	.0085	.7	.7580	.8429	3.4	.9997	3.4001
−1.9	.0287	.0111	.8	.7881	.9202	3.5	.9998	3.5001
−1.8	.0359	.0143	.9	.8159	1.0004	3.6	.9998	3.6000
−1.7	.0446	.0183	1.0	.8413	1.0833	3.7	.9999	3.7000
−1.6	.0548	.0232	1.1	.8643	1.1686	3.8	.9999	3.8000
−1.5	.0668	.0293	1.2	.8849	1.2561	3.9	1.0000	3.9000
−1.4	.0808	.0367	1.3	.9032	1.3455	4.0	1.0000	4.0000

Inventory Management with Frequent Orders

14

LEARNING OBJECTIVES

LO14-1 Explain the operation of the order-up-to model and develop an order-up-to model for a given situation

LO14-2 Evaluate several performance measures for the order-up-to model

LO14-3 Evaluate the appropriate order-up-to level to achieve a desired service target and understand what determines an appropriate service target

LO14-4 Explain the factors that determine the required amount of inventory

LO14-5 Explain several strategies to restructure a supply chain to increase profit and reduce the costs of mismatches between supply and demand

CHAPTER OUTLINE

Introduction

Many products are sold over a long time horizon with numerous replenishment opportunities. To draw upon a well-known example, consider the Campbell Soup Company's flagship product, chicken noodle soup. It has a long shelf life and future demand is assured. Hence, if in a particular month Campbell Soup has more chicken noodle soup than it needs, it does not have to dispose of its excess inventory. Instead, Campbell need only wait for its pile of inventory to draw down to a reasonable level. And if Campbell Soup finds itself with less inventory than it desires, its soup factory cooks up another batch. Because obsolescence is not a major concern and Campbell is not limited to a single production run, the newsvendor model is not the right inventory tool for this setting. The right tool for this job is the order-up-to model.

© Fancy Collection/SuperStock RF

Although multiple replenishments are feasible, the order-up-to model still faces the "too little/too much" challenge associated with matching supply and demand. Because soup production takes time, Campbell cannot wait until its inventory draws down to zero to begin production—you would never let your vehicle's fuel tank go empty before you begin driving to a refueling station! Hence, production of a batch should begin while there is a sufficient amount of inventory to buffer against uncertain demand while we wait for the batch to finish. Because buffer inventory is not free, the objective with the order-up-to model is to strike a balance between running too lean (which can lead to running out of inventory) and running too fat (which leads to inventory holding costs).

Instead of soup, this chapter applies the order-up-to model to the inventory management of a technologically more sophisticated product, a device made by Medtronic Inc. to help cardiac patients. We begin with a description of Medtronic's supply chain for these devices and then detail the order-up-to model. Next, we consider how to use the model to achieve a desired service level and we discuss what service level is appropriate. We conclude with how the order-up-to model can be used to make supply chains more effective.

14.1 Medtronic's Supply Chain

Medtronic is a designer and manufacturer of medical technology. It is well known for its line of cardiac rhythm products, but its product line extends into numerous other areas: products for the treatment of cardiovascular diseases and surgery, diabetes, neurological diseases, spinal surgery, and ear/nose/throat diseases.

Inventory in Medtronic's supply chain is held at three levels: manufacturing facilities, distribution centers (DCs), and field locations. The manufacturing facilities are located throughout the world, and they hold little finished goods inventory. In the United States, there is a single DC, located in Mounds View, Minnesota, responsible for the distribution of cardiac rhythm products. That DC ships to approximately 500 sales representatives, each with his or her own defined territory. All of the Medtronic DCs are responsible for providing very high availability of inventory to the sales representatives they serve in the field, where availability is measured with the in-stock probability.

Sales representatives hold the majority of finished goods inventory. They store some of the inventory at their customers' facilities, such as closets in hospitals. They also keep inventory on their person or in the trunk of their vehicle.

Let's now focus on a particular DC, a particular sales representative, and a particular product. The DC is the one located in Mounds View, Minnesota. The sales representative is Susan Magnotto, whose territory includes some of the major medical facilities in Madison, Wisconsin. Finally, the product is the InSync implantable cardioverter-defibrillator (ICD) device, Model 7272, which is displayed in Photo 14.1. An ICD device is like a pacemaker in that it can facilitate keeping the heart in a proper rhythm. But it is also more than a pacemaker because it is capable of dynamically responding to a patient's changing conditions and applying appropriate interventional actions (e.g., a shock to restart the heart).

An ICD is demanded when it is implanted into a patient via surgery. Even though a surgeon can anticipate the need for an ICD for a particular patient, a surgeon may not know the appropriate model for a patient until the actual surgery. For this reason, and for the need to maintain a good relationship with each physician, Susan attends each surgery and always carries the various models that might be needed. She can replenish her inventory after an implant by calling an order into Medtronic's customer service, which then sends the request to the Mounds View DC. If the model she requests is available in inventory at the DC, it is sent to her via an overnight carrier. The time between when Susan orders a unit and when she receives the unit is generally one day, and rarely more than two days.

PHOTO 14.1 Medtronic's InSync implantable cardioverter-defibrillator (ICD) device

© Carolina K. Smith, M.D./Shutterstock, RF

The Mounds View DC orders replenishments from the production facilities on a weekly basis, and the DC receives an order three weeks after it is submitted.

For the InSync device at the Mounds View DC, Figure 14.1 provides one year of data on monthly shipments out of the DC to the field representatives, as well as end-of-month inventory. Figure 14.2 provides data on monthly implants (i.e., demand) and inventory for the InSync device in Susan's territory over the same year. As can be seen from the figures, there is a considerable amount of variation in the number of units demanded at the DC, and in particular in Susan's territory. Interestingly, it appears that there is more demand in the summer months in Susan's territory, but the aggregate shipments through the DC do not indicate the same pattern. Therefore, it is reasonable to conclude that the "pattern" observed in Susan's demand data is not real: Just like a splotch of ink might look like something on a piece of paper, random events sometimes appear to form a pattern.

If the decision on inventory investment were left up to Susan, she would err on the side of extra inventory. There are a number of reasons why she would like to hold a considerable amount of inventory:

- Due to the sales incentive system, Susan never wants to miss a sale due to a lack of inventory: Because patients and surgeons do not tolerate waiting for backordered inventory, if Susan does not have the right product available, then the sale is almost surely lost to a competitor.

- Medtronic's products are generally quite small, so it is possible to hold a considerable amount of inventory in a relatively small space (e.g., the trunk of a vehicle).

- Medtronic's products have a relatively long shelf life, so spoilage is not a major concern.

- While Susan knows that her supply can be replenished relatively quickly from the DC (assuming the DC has inventory available), she is not always able to find the time to place an order immediately after an implant. An inventory buffer thereby allows her some flexibility with timing her replenishment requests.

- Although the production facilities are supposed to ensure that the DCs never stock out of product, sometimes a product can become unavailable for several weeks, if not several months. For example, the production yield might not be as high as initially planned, or a supplier of a key component might be capacity-constrained. Whatever the cause, having a few extra units of inventory helps protect Susan against these shortages.

An issue for Medtronic is whether its supply chain is supporting its aggressive growth objectives. In particular, does it have the right amount of inventory both at the DC and in the field to ensure great service to its customers while also not incurring excessive inventory holding costs? We next use the order-up-to model to help answer that question.

Figure 14.1

Monthly shipments to field representatives (columns) and end-of-month inventory (line) for the InSync device at the Mounds View distribution center

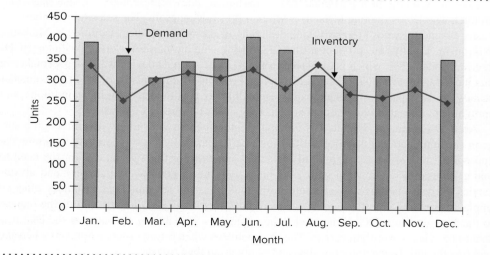

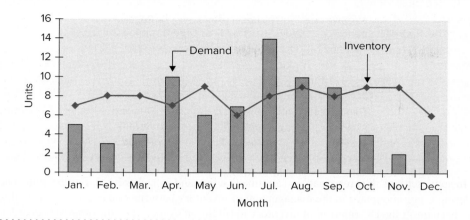

Figure 14.2

Monthly demand (columns) and end-of-month inventory (line) for the InSync device in Susan's territory

14.2 The Order-up-to Model

The order-up-to model is designed to manage inventory for a product that can be replenished many times over a long time horizon. In this section, we detail how the order-up-to model is calibrated and functions in a particular setting.

14.2.1 Design of the Order-up-to Model

Opportunities to order replenishment inventory occur at regular intervals. The time between two ordering opportunities is called a **period**, and all of the periods are of the same duration. While one day seems like a natural period length for the InSync in the field (e.g., in Susan's territory), one week is a more natural period length for the Mounds View DC. In other settings, the appropriate period length could be an hour, a month, or any other interval.

Three events occur during a period. First, there is an opportunity to submit an order for additional inventory to the supplier—the DC's supplier is Medtronic's factory and Susan's supplier is the DC. Second, orders are received from the supplier. Third, random demand occurs; that is, customers request inventory. Figure 14.3 illustrates the sequence of events across time.

Replenishment orders are received after a fixed amount of time called the **lead time**, which is represented with the variable L. The lead time is measured in periods; if one day is a period, then the lead time to receive an order should be measured in days. For example, Susan's lead time is one day (e.g., orders submitted Monday morning are received Tuesday morning), whereas the DC's lead time is three weeks (e.g., orders submitted at the start of the first week of the month are received at the beginning of the fourth week).

There is no limit to the quantity that can be ordered within a period, and no matter the order quantity, the order is always received in the lead-time number of periods. Hence, supply in this model is not capacity-constrained, but delivery of an order does take some time.

Random demand occurs during each period, and the model assumes the same demand distribution represents demand in every period. This does not mean that actual demand is the same in every period; it just means that each period's demand is represented by the same distribution function.

Within each period, demand can be either greater or less than the inventory available in that period. If demand is less than available inventory, all demand is satisfied and the inventory left over at the end of the period simply carries over to the next period—in the order-up-to model, inventory does not spoil or deteriorate or become obsolete in any way. However, if demand exceeds the available inventory, then the entire inventory is used to satisfy as much demand as possible and the remaining demand is *backordered*. Backordered demand waits for inventory to become available, and once the inventory is available, the backordered demand is satisfied. Hence, in the order-up-to model, all demand is eventually served.

Period In the context of managing inventory, this is the time between when orders can be placed. For example, if the period is a day, then orders can be placed daily.

Lead time The time between when an order is placed and when it is received. Process lead time is frequently used as an alternative term for flow time.

Figure 14.3

Sample sequence of events in the order-up-to model with a one-period lead time, $L = 1$, to receive orders

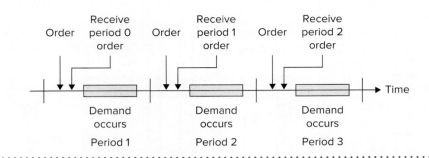

In some settings, it is reasonable to assume that demand is backordered. For example, backordering is commonplace in the management of inventory between two organizations within a supply chain: If the DC runs out of inventory to fill Susan's order, then the order is backordered and Susan receives the inventory as soon as it becomes available. However, as with the InSync in the field, when end consumers generate demand (instead of a firm), the backorder assumption is probably violated (at least to some extent). Nevertheless, if enough inventory is held so that backorders are rare, then the order-up-to model is a reasonable approximation. Hence, we use it for the InSync to manage both the DC inventory as well as Susan's field inventory.

14.2.2 The Order-up-to Level and Ordering Decisions

In the order-up-to model, it is necessary to keep track of several metrics related to inventory and demand.

On-order inventory is the number of units we ordered in previous periods that we have not yet received but will eventually receive. On-order inventory is not available to serve demand at the moment.

On-hand inventory is the number of units of inventory we have on hand, available to serve demand.

The **backorder** is the number of units backordered; that is, the total amount of demand that has occurred but has not been satisfied. For example, say there are six units in inventory before demand occurs and then demand is eight units in the period. In that case, six units of demand are satisfied and two units are backordered. Hence, at the end of the period, on-hand inventory is zero units and the backorder is two units. Note that the backorder is recorded as a positive number. Finally, the two units of demand on backorder will be satisfied as soon as two more units of inventory arrive.

The last metric, the **inventory position**, combines the three measures just mentioned:

$$\text{Inventory position} = \text{On-order inventory} + \text{On-hand inventory} - \text{Backorder}$$

The inventory position is needed to decide how much to order in each period. To explain, in the order-up-to model, the critical decision is the choice of the order-up-to level, which is denoted by the variable S. The **order-up-to level** is the desired inventory position after an order is submitted, which means that, in each period, we order the difference between S and the inventory position:

$$\text{Each period's order quantity} = S - \text{Inventory position}$$

To see how this works, say Susan implements the order-up-to model and she chooses her order-up-to level to be four units; that is, $S = 4$. At the start of each period, she compares her inventory position to her order-up-to level. If her inventory position is lower than the order-up-to level, she orders enough units to raise her inventory position to the order-up-to level. For example, if she finds that her inventory position is one at the start of some day, then she orders three units because her order-up-to level is $S = 4$ (i.e., $4 - 1 = 3$). This order increases her inventory position because it increases the on-order inventory and on-order inventory is part of the inventory position. If her inventory position happens to be higher than the order-up-to level, she does nothing but wait for demand to reduce her inventory position—demand

On-order inventory The inventory that the supplier has shipped but that has not been received.

On-hand inventory The inventory that is ready to be used to serve customer demand.

Backorder The total amount of demand that is waiting for inventory to arrive before it can be satisfied.

Inventory position On-order inventory plus on-hand inventory minus the backorder.

Order-up-to level The desired inventory position after an order is submitted.

reduces the inventory position by reducing on-hand inventory and possibly increasing the backorder.

Notice that the inventory position drops below S only when demand occurs. Let's continue with our example in which $S = 4$ and the inventory position equals one at the start of the period. If we followed our order-up-to policy in the previous period, then we must have had an inventory position of four after our order in the previous period. The only way that we could then observe an inventory position of one in this period is if three units of demand occurred in the previous period. As a result, we order three units in this period to raise our inventory position back to $S = 4$. In general,

> In the **order-up-to inventory model**, *the order quantity in each period equals the demand in the previous period.*

The order-up-to model is an example of a system that operates on the pull principle of production/inventory control—the key feature of a **pull system** is that production or replenishment of a unit is only initiated when a demand of another unit occurs. Hence, inventory is pulled through a pull system only by the occurrence of demand. In contrast, a **push system** initiates production or orders more inventory in anticipation of demand. The newsvendor model is a push system, while a bucket brigade is an example of a pull system. (A literal bucket brigade is a line of people who pass buckets of water to each other in unison to move water from a source, such as a lake, to its destination, such as a burning building.) A kanban system, which is a critical component of any just-in-time system, is also a pull system. Pull systems impose discipline on the ordering process to prevent the excessive buildup of inventory, but they are not good about anticipating shifts in future demand. Hence, pull systems are most effective when demand is represented by the same distribution function in every period, as is assumed in the order-up-to model and is reasonable for the InSync device.

14.2.3 Demand Forecast

The final piece needed for the order-up-to model, like any model to manage inventory, is a demand forecast. Actually, because the order-up-to model occurs over multiple periods, several demand forecasts are needed that differ by the length of time to which they apply. Let's start with the demand forecast for the DC and then consider the demand forecast for Susan's territory.

Figure 14.1 displayed the monthly demand for the DC, but we need weekly demand for the order-up-to model because that is the period length that applies for the DC. Employing the same data used to construct Figure 14.1, we can evaluate the average and standard deviation of weekly demand. Say we discover that average weekly demand for the InSync device at the DC is 81 and the standard deviation is 20. We can therefore use a normal distribution with a mean of 81 and a standard deviation of 20 for the distribution function that represents our forecast for demand for one week.

As we later learn, in the order-up-to model, it is necessary to have a demand forecast for different intervals of time. One crucial interval is the lead time plus one period; that is, $(L + 1)$ periods. For example, the lead time for the DC is three weeks. Hence, we will need a demand forecast for demand over $3 + 1 = 4$ weeks.

Order-up-to inventory model An inventory model that is appropriate when inventory can be periodically ordered, there is a lead time to receive orders, and inventory is not perishable.

Pull system The resource furthest downstream (i.e., closest to the market) is paced by market demand. In addition to its own production, it also relays the demand information to the next station upstream, thus ensuring that the upstream resource also is paced by demand. That is, it is an operating system in which the production or replenishment of a unit is only initiated when a demand occurs.

Push system An operating system in which the production or replenishment of a unit is initiated in anticipation of demand.

Check Your Understanding 14.1

Question: At the start of a period, a firm has five units on hand, three units are on order and will be received in one period, and seven units are on order and will be received in three periods. There are no other units on order. The order-up-to level is 22. How many units will be ordered in this period?

Answer: The inventory position is 15, the sum of on-hand and on-order inventory. (There is no backorder.) The order quantity is the difference between the order-up-to level, 22, and the inventory position, 15. So $7 = 22 - 15$ units will be ordered.

. . . .

Say we have a demand forecast for one period, but we want a demand forecast for n consecutive periods. When you combine means, you simply add them together. Thus, the mean demand over n identical periods is just n times the mean in a single period:

$$\text{Expected demand over } n \text{ periods} = n \times \text{Expected demand in 1 period}$$

For example, mean demand over four periods for the DC is $4 \times 81 = 324$.

Combining standard deviations across multiple periods is not quite as straightforward as combining means. If we are willing to assume that the demands across periods are independent, then the standard deviation of demand over n periods is

$$\text{Standard deviation of demand over } n \text{ periods} = \sqrt{n} \times \text{Standard deviation of demand in 1 period}$$

For the DC, the standard deviation of demand over four periods is $\sqrt{4} \times 20 = 40$. The assumption of independent demand across periods is valid in many cases. For example, the number of implants Susan has on Monday might have no influence on the number she has on Tuesday (i.e., they are independent of each other).

Now let's turn to the demand forecast for Susan's territory. Based on the data in Figure 14.2, Susan sells 78 InSync devices per year, or 0.30 device per day (assuming 52 weeks per year and 5 days over a week) with a standard deviation of about 0.55. With these data, we could choose to use a normal distribution with a mean of 0.30 and a standard deviation of 0.55 to model Susan's daily demand. However, that would be a poor choice.

Figure 14.4 displays the density function of a normal distribution with mean 0.30 and standard deviation 0.55. Like all normal distributions, the density function has a symmetric bell shape that peaks at the mean, 0.30. The first problem with the normal distribution is that because the mean is close to 0, it assigns a substantial amount of probability to negative outcomes—notice that there is a decent amount of area under the curve in Figure 14.4 in the negative demand range. Demand is clearly never negative. The second problem with the normal distribution is that it assigns a positive probability to noninteger outcomes. For example, there is a .28 probability that the outcome of a normal distribution with mean 0.30 and standard deviation 0.55 is between 0.1 and 0.5. Susan never sells between 0.1 and 0.5 InSync device—no patient wants only 0.5 of a device!

Figure 14.4

The density function of a normal distribution with a mean of 0.30 and standard deviation of 0.55.

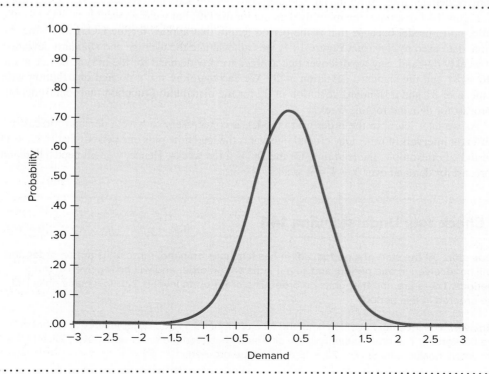

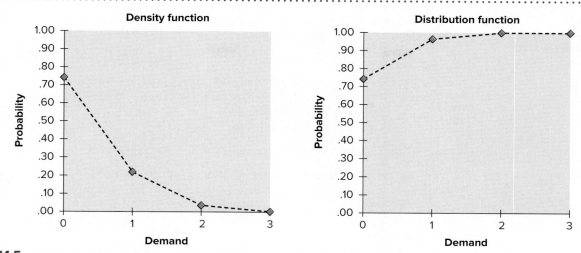

Figure 14.5

The density function (left) and the distribution function (right) of a Poisson distribution with mean 0.30. Diamonds represent values for the function, which are defined only for integer values of demand—the dashed lines are only for visualization.

In this setting with "low" demand (i.e., mean demand close to 0), the normal distribution just cannot be a good representation for actual demand. The statistical distribution for this job is the **Poisson distribution**. Figure 14.5 displays both the density function and the distribution function of the Poisson distribution.

There are two features of the Poisson that make it desirable for this setting. First, the Poisson distribution never assigns a positive probability to a negative outcome: demand can be zero with the Poisson, but it is never negative. Second, the Poisson only assigns a probability to integer outcomes (e.g., 0, 1, 2, ...)—with the Poisson, demand can never be 0.5 unit. Consequently, the dashed lines in Figure 14.5 are only for visualization—the density and distribution functions are valid only at the diamonds that correspond to integer demand values.

Another difference between the Poisson and the normal is that the Poisson is defined by only one parameter, its mean. The Poisson has a standard deviation, but you don't get to choose its standard deviation. The standard deviation of a Poisson distribution equals the square root of its mean. For Susan's territory, with a mean of 0.3 unit per day, the standard deviation is $\sqrt{0.3} = 0.55$.

Given that the Poisson distribution is better than the normal distribution when demand is "low," the natural next question is "How low is 'low?'" Figure 14.6 provides some guidance. Displayed in the figure is the density function from six Poisson distributions with different means. The density function of the Poisson distribution does not at all resemble a bell when the mean is less than 1, as in the 0.5 mean example in Figure 14.6. However, starting with a mean of around 2, the density function starts to resemble a bell shape. When the mean is 20, the density function of the Poisson distribution clearly resembles a symmetric bell, just like a normal distribution. In other words, as the mean of the Poisson distribution increases, it begins to look more and more like a normal distribution. In sum, if the mean is less than 20, the Poisson is likely to provide a better representation of demand than the normal; otherwise, the normal is likely to be better. And if demand is lower than two units per period, then there is little doubt that the Poisson distribution is the better choice.

Now that we have selected the Poisson distribution to represent Susan's daily demand, it remains to determine Susan's demand over a longer interval of time. Say demand in one period is Poisson. Demand over an interval of n periods is also represented with a Poisson distribution, with a mean that is just n times the mean of a single period:

$$\text{Poisson mean over } n \text{ periods} = n \times \text{Poisson mean over 1 period}$$

For example, Susan's demand over four periods can be modeled with a Poisson distribution that has a mean of $4 \times 0.3 = 1.2$.

Poisson distribution A statistical distribution that is suitable for modeling demand with a low mean (e.g., 20 or lower).

Figure 14.6

The density functions of six Poisson distributions with means 0.5, 2, 5, 10, 15, and 20

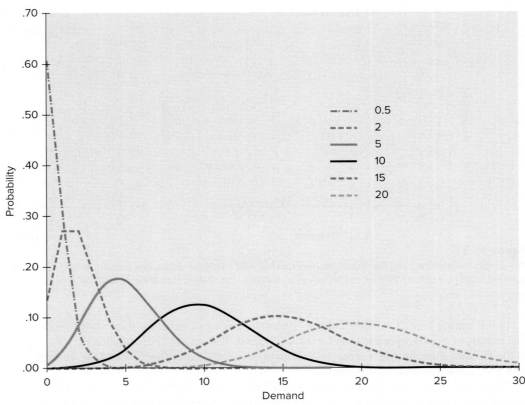

Check Your Understanding 14.2

Question: Demand in each period is normally distributed with a mean of 100 and a standard deviation of 50. What is the mean of the normal distribution that describes demand over 4 periods?

Answer: The mean demand over an interval is the sum of the means for demand in each period of the interval. Thus, the answer is 400.

Question: Demand in each period is normally distributed with a mean of 100 and a standard deviation of 50. Assuming demands across periods are independent, what is the standard deviation of the normal distribution that describes demand over 4 periods?

Answer: The standard deviation of demand over an interval is the square root of the number of periods in the interval times the standard deviation of demand in one period; that is, the standard deviation for 4 periods $= \sqrt{4} \times 50 = 100$.

Question: Demand in each period is Poisson with a mean of 0.5. What mean should be used for the Poisson distribution to describe demand over 3 periods?

Answer: The mean of a combination of Poisson distributions is the sum of the means of the Poisson distributions that are combined. In this case, we are combining three Poisson distributions, each with a mean of 0.5, so the combination is Poisson with mean $3 \times 0.5 = 1.5$.

CONNECTIONS: Poisson

The Poisson distribution is named after the French mathematician Simeon Denis Poisson, who introduced it in 1837. Although "poisson" means "fish" in French, there is nothing fishy about the Poisson distribution—it is one of the most useful statistical distributions available for modeling demand.

An early application of the Poisson was done by Ladislaus Bortkiewicz, who in 1898 analyzed data on the number of soldiers killed by horse kicks in 14 calvary corps over a 20-year period in the Prussian Army. On average, 0.7 soldiers were killed each year in each corps. Figure 14.7 displays the actual frequencies. For example, fortunately, each corps had no deaths in about 51 percent of the years. However, the corps also had four deaths in about 1 percent of the observed years. Figure 14.7 also plots the probabilities associated with the Poisson distribution with a mean of 0.7. As is evident in the figure, the Poisson distribution provides a great fit.

Most people don't have to worry about being killed by a horse kick, but the Poisson distribution applies much more broadly—when we need to count the number of events that occur during an interval of time, and those events happen independent of each other, then the Poisson is likely to be the distribution that best describes the likelihood of each possible outcome. For example, there are many potential callers who could call a help desk. The actual number who call during a given hour is often well described by a Poisson distribution. Or say you sell bed linens in several sizes and in many different types of fabrics and patterns. The demand for one particular store in one particular week for one particular size, shape, and style is likely to be at most a couple of units. In that case, the Poisson is again the correct distribution for the job.

It is also worth noting that the Poisson is actually closely related to the exponential distribution. The exponential distribution describes the time between events; for example, the time between sales of a particular bedspread. If the time between events is exponentially distributed, then the number of events occurring in an interval (say a week) is Poisson distributed.

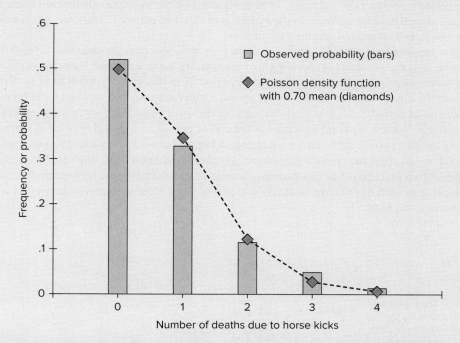

Figure 14.7 Observed frequency (bars) of the number of cavalry soldiers killed in one year in one of the 14 Prussian corps between 1875 and 1894. Average deaths are 0.70 per year per corps. The density function of a Poisson distribution with mean 0.70 is also shown (diamonds).

Sources: http://en.wikipedia.org/wiki/Poisson_distribution
http://www.math.uah.edu/stat/data/HorseKicks.html

14.3 Performance Measures

In this section, we evaluate several performance measures given a chosen order-up-to level S. In the subsequent section, we decide on what order-up-to level to choose.

14.3.1 Expected On-Hand Inventory

A critical performance measure with the order-up-to model is **expected on-hand inventory**—the average amount of inventory on hand at the end of each period. As with all inventory, the more inventory held, the higher the inventory holding costs will be.

Figure 14.8 illustrates an example that helps to determine the relationship between the order-up-to level and expected inventory. In the example, the order-up-to level is $S = 5$ and the lead time is two periods. In this particular case, at the start of period 1, there are two units of inventory on hand and three units on order, with triangles to represent these five units. The inventory position at the start of period 1 is five units, which matches the order-up-to level as you would expect—orders are submitted at the start of each period to raise the inventory position to the order-up-to level.

Given the setting displayed in Figure 14.8, what will be on-hand inventory at the end of period 3? As you would expect, it depends on the amount of demand in periods 1, 2, and 3: The more demand in that interval, the lower the on-hand inventory will be at the end of period 3. Less obvious, but just as important, the amount of on-hand inventory at the end of period 3 does not depend on how much is ordered in periods 2 and 3—those orders arrive after period 3 and therefore have no influence on the inventory at the end of period 3. Thus, we can focus on the inventory that is in the system (either on hand or on order) at the beginning of period 1 and total demand across the three periods.

Suppose total demand across the three periods is more than the order-up-to level. In that case, we surely end period 3 with zero units on hand. For example, say the demands across the three periods are two, two, and three. Total demand across the three periods is seven units, but we have only five units available in the system at the start of period 1. Thus, we end period 3 with two units backordered and no units on hand.

Now suppose total demand across the three periods is less than the order-up-to level. For example, say the demands across the three periods are zero, zero, and three, respectively. How much inventory is on hand at the end of period 3? In this case, by the start of period 3, there are five units on hand. At the end of period 3, there are only two units on hand because of demand in period 3. Now say demands across the three periods are three, zero, and zero, respectively. What is on-hand inventory at the end of period 3? It is still two! Let's see why. During the first period, three units are demanded, but we have only two units. So two units of demand are satisfied and one unit of demand is backordered. Inventory comes to the rescue in period 2: Two units arrive in that period, allowing us to satisfy the one backordered demand and leaving us with one unit on hand. Then in period 3 one more unit arrives, leaving us with the two units on hand.

Expected on-hand inventory The average amount of inventory available at the end of each period to serve demand.

Figure 14.8

A set of three periods in the order-up-to model. The lead time is two periods, the order-up-to level is $S = 5$, and at the start of period 1 there are two units on hand (triangles) and three units on order (triangles on "trucks"). Of the three units on order at the start of period 1, two units arrive in period 2 and one unit arrives in period 3. Uncertain demand occurs within each period (rectangles).

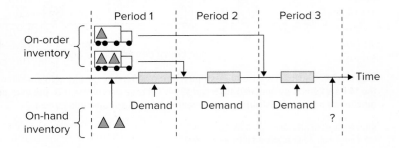

Although these examples do not provide a formal proof, in general the following is true:

On-hand inventory at the end of a period equals the order-up-to level, S, minus demand over (L + 1) periods, or zero, whichever is greater.

The important insight from the above statement is that the on-hand inventory only depends on the order-up-to level and does not depend on where inventory is in the system (either on order or on hand). For example, say the example in Figure 14.8 were changed so that there were five units on order at the start of period 1 and no units on hand. The inventory position remains five, which it should because the order-up-to level is still five. And if total demand over the three periods is three units, the on-hand inventory even in this case is two units at the end of period 3.

In sum, in the order-up-to model, the order-up-to level, S, is like an order quantity in the newsvendor model—it determines the amount of inventory that is available in the system before demand occurs. The available inventory is then reduced by demand, leaving the firm potentially with some inventory. In the newsvendor model, the inventory after demand is called "leftover inventory." In the order-up-to model, it is called on-hand inventory. The only difference is that in the newsvendor model the leftover inventory must be salvaged for a loss, whereas in the order-up-to model the on-hand inventory carries over to the next period.

Fortunately, the method used in the newsvendor model to evaluate expected inventory works just as well to evaluate expected on-hand inventory in the order-up-to model. Let's do this for both the DC and Susan's territory.

Suppose the DC sets its order-up-to level to $S = 404$. Recall that demand over $(L + 1)$ periods is normally distributed with mean 324 and standard deviation 40. In this case, the evaluation of expected on-hand inventory in the order-up-to model is identical to the process of evaluating the expected inventory in the newsvendor model with an order quantity of 404 and demand that has a mean of 324 and a standard deviation of 40.

In the newsvendor model, we convert the order quantity Q to a z value, find the expected inventory for that z value, and then convert that value into the actual expected inventory. We do the same in the order-up-to model. In particular, the z value that corresponds to the chosen order-up-to level is

$$z = \frac{S - \mu}{\sigma} = \frac{404 - 324}{40} = 2$$

Now use the standard normal table, Table 14.1, to look up expected inventory: $I(z=2) = 2.0085$. Finally, convert that expected inventory to the expected on-hand inventory for the DC:

$$\text{Expected on-hand inventory} = \sigma \times I(z) = 40 \times 2.0085 = 80$$

Thus, if the DC operates with an order-up-to level of $S = 404$, then, on average, the DC will have 80 units of inventory on hand at the end of each period. Sometimes the on-hand inventory at the end of a period is greater than 80 units, sometimes it is less than 80 units, but on average it is 80 units.

Now let's turn to Susan's territory and let's say she operates with an order-up-to level equal to $S = 2$. Expected demand in one period is 0.30 unit and her lead time is $L = 1$ period. The demand in her territory over $(L + 1)$ periods is a Poisson distribution with mean 0.6 (= 0.3 × 2). Table 14.2 gives the distribution function, $F(S)$, and the expected inventory, $I(S)$, for that Poisson distribution. Appendix 14A provides a broader set of Poisson tables.

From Table 14.2, if Susan operates with an order-up-to level equal to $S = 2$, then her expected on-hand inventory is $I(S) = 1.43$ units—once you have identified the correct Poisson table, determining the expected on-hand inventory is no more difficult than reading $I(S)$ from the table for the chosen order-up-to level S.

For the Poisson distribution, there is no "standard Poisson" like there is a standard normal for the normal distribution. Hence, when working with the Poisson distribution, it is necessary to have a table like Table 14.2 for the particular Poisson that represents demand. While it is cumbersome to need a table for every possible Poisson, once a table is available, as already mentioned, it immediately provides the expected on-hand inventory.

TABLE 14.1 The Distribution Function, *F(z)*, and the Inventory Function, *I(z)*, for the Standard Normal Distribution Function

z	F(z)	I(z)	z	F(z)	I(z)
−4.0	.0000	0.0000	0.1	.5398	0.4509
−3.9	.0000	0.0000	0.2	.5793	0.5069
−3.8	.0001	0.0000	0.3	.6179	0.5668
−3.7	.0001	0.0000	0.4	.6554	0.6304
−3.6	.0002	0.0000	0.5	.6915	0.6978
−3.5	.0002	0.0001	0.6	.7257	0.7687
−3.4	.0003	0.0001	0.7	.7580	0.8429
−3.3	.0005	0.0001	0.8	.7881	0.9202
−3.2	.0007	0.0002	0.9	.8159	1.0004
−3.1	.0010	0.0003	1.0	.8413	1.0833
−3.0	.0013	0.0004	1.1	.8643	1.1686
−2.9	.0019	0.0005	1.2	.8849	1.2561
−2.8	.0026	0.0008	1.3	.9032	1.3455
−2.7	.0035	0.0011	1.4	.9192	1.4367
−2.6	.0047	0.0015	1.5	.9332	1.5293
−2.5	.0062	0.0020	1.6	.9452	1.6232
−2.4	.0082	0.0027	1.7	.9554	1.7183
−2.3	.0107	0.0037	1.8	.9641	1.8143
−2.2	.0139	0.0049	1.9	.9713	1.9111
−2.1	.0179	0.0065	2.0	.9772	2.0085
−2.0	.0228	0.0085	2.1	.9821	2.1065
−1.9	.0287	0.0111	2.2	.9861	2.2049
−1.8	.0359	0.0143	2.3	.9893	2.3037
−1.7	.0446	0.0183	2.4	.9918	2.4027
−1.6	.0548	0.0232	2.5	.9938	2.5020
−1.5	.0668	0.0293	2.6	.9953	2.6015
−1.4	.0808	0.0367	2.7	.9965	2.7011
−1.3	.0968	0.0455	2.8	.9974	2.8008
−1.2	.1151	0.0561	2.9	.9981	2.9005
−1.1	.1357	0.0686	3.0	.9987	3.0004
−1.0	.1587	0.0833	3.1	.9990	3.1003
−0.9	.1841	0.1004	3.2	.9993	3.2002
−0.8	.2119	0.1202	3.3	.9995	3.3001
−0.7	.2420	0.1429	3.4	.9997	3.4001
−0.6	.2743	0.1687	3.5	.9998	3.5001
−0.5	.3085	0.1978	3.6	.9998	3.6000
−0.4	.3446	0.2304	3.7	.9999	3.7000
−0.3	.3821	0.2668	3.8	.9999	3.8000
−0.2	.4207	0.3069	3.9	1.0000	3.9000
−0.1	.4602	0.3509	4.0	1.0000	4.0000
0.0	.5000	0.3989			

TABLE 14.2 The Distribution Function, $F(S)$, and the Expected Inventory, $I(S)$, for a Poisson with Mean 0.60

S	F(S)	I(S)
0	.5488	0.00
1	.8781	0.55
2	.9769	1.43
3	.9966	2.40
4	.9996	3.40
5	1.0000	4.40
6	1.0000	5.40
7	1.0000	6.40

Check Your Understanding 14.3

Question: A product's demand over $(L + 1)$ periods follows a normal distribution with mean 1000 and standard deviation 400. The order-up-to level is 1600. What is the expected on-hand inventory?

Answer: Convert the order-up-to level to $z = \frac{1600 - 1000}{400} = 1.5$. From Table 14.1, $I(1.5) = 1.5293$. Convert that inventory to the actual inventory, $400 \times 1.5293 = 612$.

Question: A product's demand over $(L + 1)$ periods follows a Poisson distribution with mean 3. The order-up-to level is 5. What is the expected on-hand inventory? The Poisson distribution table can be found in Appendix 14A.

Answer: From the Poisson distribution table with mean 3, $I(S = 5) = 2.13$.

14.3.2 In-Stock and Stockout Probability

As in the newsvendor model, the in-stock probability is the probability that all demand is satisfied. Let's again refer to Figure 14.8. Demand in period 3 is satisfied if the period does not end with a backorder. It doesn't end with a backorder if total demand in periods 1, 2, and 3 is less than five units. In other words,

In-stock probability = Probability demand over $(L + 1)$ periods is S or lower

which is identical to the in-stock probability in the newsvendor problem.

In the newsvendor problem, we use the distribution function to find the in-stock probability; the same is done in the order-up-to model. Let's again consider the DC with an order-up-to level of $S = 404$ and demand over $(L + 1)$ periods that is normally distributed with mean 324 and standard deviation 40. As we did before, we first convert the order-up-to level S to a z value:

$$z = \frac{S - \mu}{\sigma} = \frac{404 - 324}{40} = 2$$

Now use Table 14.1 to find the distribution function: $F(z = 2) = .9772$. Thus, the DC's in-stock probability is .9772.

For Susan, say she uses an order-up-to level of $S = 2$. Her demand over $(L + 1)$ periods is Poisson with mean 0.6. From Table 14.2, $F(S = 2) = .9769$. Hence, with that order-up-to level, Susan's in-stock probability is .9769.

Check Your Understanding 14.4

Question: A product's demand over $(L + 1)$ periods follows a normal distribution with mean 1000 and standard deviation 400. The order-up-to level is 1600. What is the in-stock probability?

Answer: Convert the order-up-to level to $z = \frac{1600 - 1000}{400} = 1.5$. From Table 14.1, $F(1.5) = .9332$.

Question: A product's demand over $(L + 1)$ periods follows a Poisson distribution with mean 3. The order-up-to level is 5. What is the in-stock probability? The Poisson distribution table can be found in Appendix 14A.

Answer: From the Poisson distribution table with mean 3, $F(S = 5) = .9161$.

. . . .

Either all demand is satisfied (you are in stock) or not (you stock out); thus, as with the newsvendor model,

$$\text{Stockout probability} = 1 - \text{In-stock probability}$$

Hence, for the DC the stockout probability is $1 - .9772 = .0228$ and for Susan the stockout probability is $1 - .9769 = .0231$.

14.3.3 Expected On-Order Inventory

The **expected on-order inventory** is the average amount of inventory on order at any given time. It is also sometimes referred to as the **pipeline inventory** because it is the average amount of inventory in the "pipeline" in the supply chain on its way to the location where it can be used to serve demand.

Medtronic cares about the expected on-order inventory because it owns the inventory between its factory and the Mounds View DC center and between the Mounds View DC and Susan Magnotto's territory. Hence, it incurs holding costs for that inventory, such as the opportunity cost of capital, storage costs, and costs related to obsolescence.

To evaluate expected on-order inventory, we refer back to Little's Law:

$$\text{Inventory} = \text{Flow rate} \times \text{Flow time}$$

In the context of the order-up-to model, the flow time in the pipeline is, by definition, the lead time because the lead time is the time each and every unit spends on order. The flow rate is the rate of demand (i.e., the average demand per period) because that is the rate at which units are flowing through the system. Therefore,

$$\text{Expected on-order inventory} = \text{Expected demand in one period} \times \text{Lead time}$$

For the InSync device, the expected on-order inventory between the DC and Susan is 0.30 unit ($= 0.30$ units per day $\times$ 1 day). Between the factory and the Mounds View DC, the pipeline inventory is 243 units ($= 81$ units per week $\times$ 3 weeks).

The expected on-order inventory is based on demand during just the lead time, l. The expected on-hand inventory depends on demand over $(L + 1)$ periods. To explain the difference, note that inventory is on order only for one period, which is why the flow time on order is one period. In particular, inventory is ordered at the start of a period and it arrives at the start of a period. In contrast, on-hand inventory is measured at the end of a period, so there are $(L + 1)$ periods of demand between the time the inventory is ordered and when it is measured as on-hand inventory.

There is another important difference between expected on-order inventory and expected on-hand inventory. Expected on-order inventory only depends on average demand over one period—it does not matter whether demand over one period is variable or not. Consequently, reducing or increasing the variability of demand has absolutely no impact on the average amount of inventory on order. However, expected on-hand inventory does depend on the variability of demand.

Expected on-order inventory The average amount of inventory on order at any given time.

Pipeline inventory Another term to describe expected on-order inventory.

Check Your Understanding 14.5

Question: A product's demand in each period follows a normal distribution with mean 400 and standard deviation 100. The order-up-to level is 1200 and the lead time is two periods. What is the expected on-order inventory?

Answer: Expected on-order inventory equals the mean demand per period times the number of periods in the lead time: $400 \times 2 = 800$.

Question: A product's demand per period is Poisson with mean 0.25. The lead time is 4 periods and the order-up-to level is 3. What is the expected on-order inventory? The Poisson distribution table can be found in Appendix 14A.

Answer: Expected on-order inventory equals the mean demand per period times the number of periods in the lead time: $0.25 \times 4 = 1$.

. . . .

14.4 Choosing an Order-up-to Level

The previous section provides Medtronic with methods for evaluating the performance of any order-up-to policy it chooses. This section tackles the question of how to find the order-up-to level that achieves a desired performance target.

Surgeons are not tolerant of stockouts (rightfully so). And losing a sale is costly to Medtronic—they earn a large profit on each sale. Hence, Medtronic wants to ensure that it rarely (if ever) runs out of inventory. A secondary, but still relevant, concern is to minimize inventory to avoid excessive holding costs. Given these objectives, say Medtronic decides that it wants a .9999 in-stock probability—this is almost as close as one can realistically get to being guaranteed that something is in stock (which would be a 1.0 in-stock probability). Table 14.3 helps put that in-stock probability into perspective. If it indeed achieves a .9999 in-stock probability, then the first period with a stockout is, on average, the 10,000th period. Even if we assume that Susan works 260 days per year (five days per week, 52 weeks per year), then 10,000 periods is equivalent to 38.5 years ($= 10,000/260$). This model of InSync device will probably be in production for three to five years before a more sophisticated model replaces it. Hence, a .9999 in-stock probability for the sales representatives should be sufficient to ensure that inventory is nearly always available to serve demand.

For the distribution center, the in-stock probability should be high, but it probably doesn't need to be as high as the one selected for the sales representatives. We don't have to be as aggressive with the DC because a stockout at the DC does not automatically lead to a stockout for a sales representative. The sales representatives have a good buffer of inventory to protect Medtronic from the occasional stockout at the DC. Hence, for the DC we can choose a .999 in-stock probability. According to Table 14.3, with a .999 in-stock probability, the expected time to the first stockout is 1000 days, which is somewhere between three and four years. That should be sufficient for the DC.

Now that we have our target in-stock probabilities, .9999 for Susan and .999 for the DC, we need to find the order-up-to levels, S, that achieve them. As discussed in section 14.3.2, the relevant demand distribution is the one that describes demand over $(L + 1)$ periods. For Susan, that is a Poisson distribution with mean 0.60; for the DC, it is a normal distribution with mean 324 and standard deviation 40.

Table 14.2 provides the distribution function, $F(S)$, for demand in Susan's territory over $(L + 1)$ periods. The distribution function is also the in-stock probability. For example, if Susan chooses $S = 3$, then her in-stock probability is $F(S = 3) = .9966$. That isn't quite enough. But even $S = 4$ isn't good enough: $F(S = 4) = .9996$, which is just short of the target, .9999. Hence, for Susan to be able to achieve at least a .9999 in-stock probability, she should choose the order-up-to level $S = 5$.

With the Mounds View DC, we must work with the normal distribution. We first find the order-up-to level that meets our in-stock probability service requirement with the standard

LO14-3 Evaluate the appropriate order-up-to level to achieve a desired service target and understand what determines an appropriate service target

TABLE 14.3   For Various In-Stock Probabilities, the Expected Number of Periods before the First Period with a Stockout. If p is the In-Stock Probability, Then the Expected Number of Periods before the First Period with a Stockout Is $1/(1 - p)$.

In-stock Probability	Expected Number of Periods to the First Period with a Stockout
0.80	5
0.90	10
0.95	20
0.96	25
0.98	50
0.99	100
0.9950	200
0.9990	1000
0.9995	2000
0.9999	10000
0.99995	20000
0.99999	100000

normal distribution and then convert that standard normal order-up-to level to the order-up-to level that corresponds to the actual demand distribution. In Table 14.1, we see that $F(z=3.0)$ = .9987, which isn't quite high enough. To achieve a .999 in-stock probability then, we need to choose $z = 3.1$ because $F(z=3.1) = .9990$. So an order-up-to level of 3.1 would generate our desired in-stock probability if demand over $(L + 1)$ periods followed a standard normal distribution. It remains to convert that z into an order-up-to level:

$$S = \mu + (z \times \sigma)$$

Remember, the mean and standard deviation should be from the normal distribution of demand over $(L + 1)$ periods. Hence,

$$S = 324 + (3.1 \times 40) = 448$$

See Exhibit 14.1 for a summary of the process to choose an order-up-to level to achieve a target in-stock probability.

EXHIBIT 14.1

How to Choose an Order-Up-to Level to Achieve a Target In-Stock Probability

If demand over $(L + 1)$ periods is a normal distribution with mean μ and standard deviation σ, then follow steps 1 and 2:

Step 1: Use Table 14.1 to find the probability that corresponds to the target in-stock probability. Then find the z that corresponds to that probability. If the target in-stock probability falls between two entries in the table, choose the entry with the larger z. In Excel, the appropriate z can be found with the following equation: $z = $ NORM.S.INV (Target in-stock probability).

Step 2: Convert the z chosen in step 1 to an order-up-to level:

$$S = \mu + (z \times \sigma)$$

If demand over $(L + 1)$ periods is not a normal distribution, then you need the distribution function table that corresponds to demand over that interval of time. Find the S in that table such that $F(S)$ equals the target in-stock probability. If the target in-stock probability falls between two entries in the table, choose the larger S.

Check Your Understanding 14.6

Question: A product's demand over $(L + 1)$ periods follows a normal distribution with mean 1000 and standard deviation 400. What order-up-to level minimizes inventory while achieving at least a .98 in-stock probability?

Answer: From Table 14.1, $F(z = 2.0) = .9772$ and $F(z = 2.1) = .9821$. Select $z = 2.1$. Convert into an order quantity: $1000 + (2.1 \times 400) = 1840$.

Question: A product's demand over $(L + 1)$ periods follows a Poisson distribution with mean 3. What order-up-to level minimizes inventory while achieving at least a .98 in-stock probability? The Poisson distribution table can be found in Appendix 14A.

Answer: From the Poisson distribution table with mean 3, $F(S = 6) = .9665$ and $F(S = 7) = .9881$. To achieve a .98 in-stock probability, it is necessary to choose $S = 7$.

. . . .

14.5 Inventory and Service in the Order-up-to Level Model

The goal of this section is to answer one question: What are the factors that determine the amount of inventory in the order-up-to model?

We begin with Figure 14.9, which displays expected on-hand inventory as a function of the chosen in-stock probability. Six cases are considered. In each one, demand over $(L + 1)$ periods is a normal distribution with mean 100. They differ in the standard deviation of demand over $(L + 1)$ periods: 10, 20, 30, 40, 50, and 60. It follows that these cases differ in their coefficient of variation (the ratio of the standard deviation to the mean), ranging from a low of 0.1 to a high of 0.6.

Three general insights emerge from Figure 14.9:

1. *As the in-stock probability increases, on-hand inventory always increases.* Put another way, to give customers better service requires increasing the expected on-hand inventory. It is costly to hold inventory, and more costly to hold more inventory. Thus, better customer service creates additional inventory holding costs.

2. *The higher the coefficient of demand, the greater the needed inventory for any in-stock probability.* In Figure 14.9, choose any in-stock probability and look at what happens to the required amount of inventory as the coefficient of variation of demand changes. In all cases, as the standard deviation (and thus the coefficient of demand) increases, more inventory is needed. This is yet another manifestation of the central tenet in operations management that "variability is a system inhibitor"—if demand variability increases, then more inventory is needed to achieve the same level of service.

3. *The required amount of on-hand inventory increases at an increasing rate as the target in-stock probability approaches 1.0.* In Figure 14.9, each curve becomes steeper and steeper as the desired in-stock probability gets larger. This means that to raise the in-stock probability from .90 to .91 requires some additional inventory, while increasing the in-stock probability from .95 to .96 requires adding even more inventory. This implies that as the desired in-stock probability approaches 1.0, each incremental increase in the in-stock probability requires a greater and greater increase in the on-hand inventory.

The curves in Figure 14.9 are similar to the curves that describe the relationship between server utilization and expected waiting time in a queuing system (see Chapter 16). In a queuing model, either the server waits for customers or customers wait for the server. When servers wait for customers, the utilization of the servers is low, but customers do not have a long wait. However, as the utilization of the servers increases, the servers spend less time waiting for customers (i.e., less idle time) and customers spend more and more time waiting for servers.

Figure 14.9

The trade-off between expected on-hand inventory and in-stock probability. In all cases, demand over ($L + 1$) periods is a normal distribution with mean 100. The curves differ in the standard deviation of demand over ($L + 1$) periods: 10, 20, 30, 40, 50, and 60.

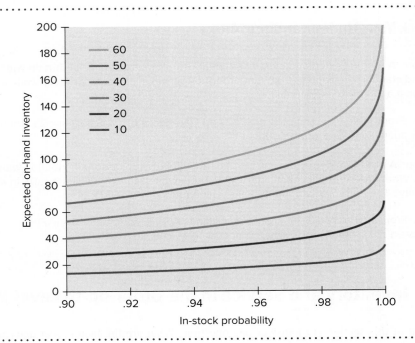

As the servers' utilization approaches 100 percent, the waiting time for customers explodes. Essentially the same phenomenon happens in the order-up-to model. As the in-stock probability approaches 1.0, the amount of inventory in the system increases dramatically: To avoid having customers wait for inventory (i.e., to have a high in-stock probability), it is necessary to make inventory wait for customers, which means having plenty of on-hand inventory.

Figure 14.9 holds lead time constant in all cases. In contrast, Figures 14.10 and 14.11 illustrate the impact of changing the lead time. Three additional insights emerge:

1. *The longer the lead time, the more inventory is needed to achieve an in-stock probability.* Figure 14.10 demonstrates this result for on-hand inventory: In all cases, as the lead time gets longer, more inventory is needed to achieve an in-stock probability. Figure 14.11 shows this result for on-order inventory. As both on-hand and on-order inventory increase as the lead time gets longer, so the total inventory in the system increases as well.

2. *The higher the in-stock probability, the more sensitive inventory is to the lead time.* In Figure 14.10, look at the top curve, which corresponds to a .9999 in-stock probability,

Figure 14.10

Expected on-hand inventory as a function of the lead time. Demand in one period in all cases is a normal distribution with mean 100 and standard deviation 60. The four curves differ in the target in-stock probability: .95, .99, .999, and .9999.

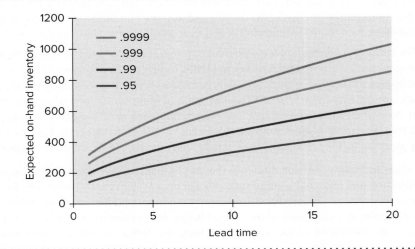

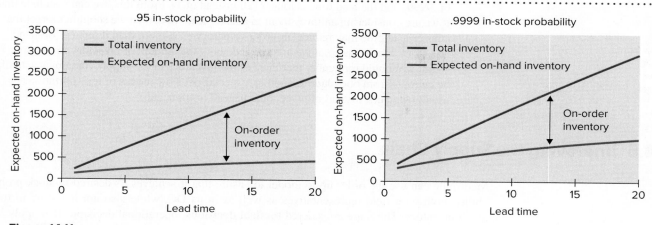

Figure 14.11

Expected on-hand inventory and total inventory (i.e., the sum of on-hand and on-order inventory) as a function of the lead time when demand in one period is a normal distribution with mean 100 and standard deviation 60 and the in-stock probability is either .95 (left panel) or .9999 (right panel).

and the bottom curve, which is for a .95 in-stock probability. Now look at how those two curves change as the lead time is increased from 1 period to 20 periods. Both curves show an increase in inventory, but the higher in-stock probability curve increases much more. For example, the .95 in-stock probability curve increases from 141 units to 458, an increase of 317 units, while the .9999 in-stock probability curve increases from 316 to 1023, an increase of 707 units. An important implication of this observation is that if a firm is considering an investment to reduce its lead time (e.g., pay for air shipment rather than ground shipment), then that investment is more beneficial (in the sense of generating a larger inventory reduction) for high in-stock probabilities.

3. *Most of the inventory in the supply chain may be on order rather than on hand, especially with long lead times.* Figure 14.11 displays total inventory in the system, the sum of on-hand and on-order inventory. It is natural to focus on on-hand inventory because that is the inventory that is visible, filling up the store or the distribution center. But most of the inventory in the supply chain may actually be on order, loaded into a truck, plane, train, or boat. This is especially true when the in-stock probability is not very high (so on-hand inventory isn't very high) and the lead time is long. If you compare the two graphs in Figure 14.11, you will notice that on-order inventory is indeed a greater proportion of total inventory when the in-stock probability is lower (.95 instead

Check Your Understanding 14.7

Question: Which of the following performance measures change when demand variability increases?

a. On-hand inventory and on-order inventory

b. On-hand inventory but not on-order inventory

c. On-order inventory but not on-hand inventory

d. Neither on-order nor on-hand inventory

Answer: Demand variability does not change on-order inventory because on-order inventory only depends on mean demand per period and the length of the lead time. Answer is B.

of .9999) and the lead time is longer (20 instead of 1). From this, we can conclude that if we are considering an investment in a faster lead time, then we shouldn't forget that a faster lead time may reduce on-order inventory even more than it reduces on-hand inventory. Furthermore, if we are worried about the amount of inventory in a supply chain, we should remember that most of the inventory in the supply chain may actually be en route from one place to another, especially if slow modes of transportation are used (e.g., truck instead of plane, boat instead of train, etc.).

14.6 Improving the Supply Chain

Medtronic can use the order-up-to model to ensure that it achieves its desired in-stock probability, both with field representatives as well as in its DC, while also not investing in too much inventory. These are considered **tactical decisions**, operational decisions that apply in the short term (e.g., day to day, or possibly up to a month or a quarter). Making good tactical decisions is critical for the success of the firm. But a firm must also make **strategic decisions**, decisions about how the firm operates in the long term (e.g., decisions that can be changed only over a long period of time, such as a quarter or year). For instance, the number of InSync devices to send to Susan in the third week of the year is a tactical decision. Whether or not Susan should even hold her own inventory is a strategic decision.

In this section, we discuss how the order-up-to model can inform us to make better strategic decisions. We consider three possible modifications to the supply chain: (1) should we change where we hold inventory to serve customer demand; (2) should we hold inventory in an intermediate step in the supply process, such as a distribution center; and (3) should we change where variety is added to a product?

14.6.1 Location Pooling

LO14-5 Explain several strategies to restructure a supply chain to increase profit and reduce the costs of mismatches between supply and demand

An important strategic decision in a supply chain is where to hold inventory that is used to serve customer demand. For example, instead of Medtronic's current system in which each sales representative manages his or her own inventory, maybe the representatives in adjacent territories could share inventory. To make this work, Medtronic could rent a small space in a centrally located and easily accessible location (e.g., a back room in a strip mall off the interchange of two major highways) and two to five representatives could pool their inventory at that location. Sharing inventory means that each representative would only carry inventory needed for immediate use. Ordering decisions for the pooled inventory could be determined by a computer system that uses the order-up-to model and a forecast of demand in the pooled region. What impact would this new strategy have on inventory performance? Let's use the order-up-to model to find out.

The average daily demand for Medtronic's InSync device in Susan Magnotto's Madison, Wisconsin, territory is represented with a Poisson distribution with mean 0.30 unit per day. Let's suppose there are several other territories adjacent to Susan's, each with a single sales representative and each with average daily demand of 0.30 unit for the InSync device. Instead of each representative holding his or her own inventory, now they share a common pool of inventory. We refer to the strategy of combining the inventory from multiple territories/locations into a single location as **location pooling**. We have already evaluated the expected inventory with the current system in which representatives have their own inventory. So now we need to evaluate the performance of the system with pooled territories; that is, determine the impact of location pooling.

The order-up-to model is used to manage the inventory at the pooled territory. The same aggressive target in-stock probability is used for the pooled territory as is used at the individual territories, .9999. Furthermore, the lead time to replenish the pooled territory is also one day. (There is no reason to believe the lead time to the pooled territory should be different than to the individual territories.)

We know that daily demand in each territory is Poisson with mean 0.3. The demand in multiple, pooled territories is then also Poisson, with a mean that equals the sum of the mean

Tactical decisions Decisions that impact short-term performance.

Strategic decisions Decisions that have long-term implications.

Location pooling A strategy of combining the inventory from multiple territories/locations into a single location.

TABLE 14.4 Inventory Needed to Achieve a .9999 In-Stock Probability across Different-Sized Territories with a One-Period Lead Time. Daily Demand in Each Territory Is Poisson with Mean 0.3. Days of Supply Is the Ratio of Inventory in the Territory to Mean Demand in the Territory.

Number of Territories Pooled	Mean Demand Over $L + 1$ Periods in Pooled Territories	Inventory (units)			Days of Supply		Coefficient of Variation of Daily Demand
		S	On-Hand, $I(S)$	On-Order	On-Hand Inventory	On-Order Inventory	
1	0.6	5	4.4	0.3	14.7	1.0	1.83
2	1.2	7	5.8	0.6	9.7	1.0	1.29
3	1.8	8	6.2	0.9	6.9	1.0	1.05
4	2.4	10	7.6	1.2	6.3	1.0	0.91
5	3.0	11	8.0	1.5	5.3	1.0	0.82
6	3.6	12	8.4	1.8	4.7	1.0	0.75
7	4.2	13	8.8	2.1	4.2	1.0	0.69
8	4.8	14	9.2	2.4	3.8	1.0	0.65

demand from the individual territories. For example, suppose Susan shares inventory with two nearby sales representatives and they all have mean demand for the InSync device equal to 0.3 unit per day. Then, total demand across the three territories is Poisson with mean 0.9 ($= 3 \times 0.30$ unit per day). We can then apply the order-up-to model to that pooled territory, assuming a lead time of one day and a mean daily demand of 0.90 unit.

Table 14.4 presents data on the impact of pooling the sales representatives' territories. To achieve the .9999 in-stock probability in just one territory requires an order-up-to level of $S = 5$, which results in 4.4 units of on-hand inventory. If two territories are combined, then the mean daily demand is 0.6 unit, demand over ($L + 1$) periods is 1.2 units (because $L = 1$), and now 5.8 units of on-hand inventory are needed.

We can see from Table 14.4 that as territories are combined, more on-hand and on-order inventory are needed to achieve the in-stock probability. However, because combining territories increases the demand in the newly pooled territory, you would expect that more inventory is needed. In other words, we are not making an "apples to apples" comparison if we merely read down the on-hand and on-order inventory columns. One way to compare across the different levels of pooling is to evaluate the days of supply. Recall that days of supply is the ratio of inventory to mean daily demand. For example, with just one territory (i.e., no pooling), on-hand inventory is 4.4, mean daily demand is 0.3, so days of supply is 14.7 ($= 4.4/0.3$). In other words, if Susan holds 4.4 units of inventory on average, then that inventory is equivalent to 14.7 days' worth of average demand.

Table 14.4 reveals that combining territories dramatically reduces the required days of supply! For example, if each representative holds his or her own inventory, then each needs to hold 14.7 days' worth of inventory, but if eight territories are pooled together, then that larger territory only needs 3.8 days' worth of inventory even though it achieves exactly the same level of customer service!

There is another way to look at the data in Table 14.4. If eight different representatives operate independently, then each needs 4.4 units of on-hand inventory, which totals to 35.2 units. However, if they are pooled into a single territory, then only 9.2 units of on-hand inventory are needed. That is a 74 percent ($= 1 - 9.2/35.2$) reduction in inventory. Wow!

The data in Table 14.4 clearly indicate that location pooling can reduce on-hand inventory. But why does it reduce the required on-hand inventory even though it achieves the same in-stock probability? The answer, like many answers in operations, is that location pooling changes the variability in demand. Recall that the coefficient of variation (the ratio of the standard deviation to the mean) is the key measure of demand variability. The standard deviation of a Poisson distribution equals the square root of its mean. Thus, for the Poisson distribution,

$$\text{Coefficient of variation} = \frac{1}{\sqrt{\text{Mean}}}$$

Table 14.4 also evaluates the coefficient of variation for each level of pooling. Notice that the days of supply of on-hand inventory decreases along with the coefficient of variation of demand. Pooling locations reduces variability because it simply is easier to predict the total number of devices needed across eight territories than it is to predict the number of devices needed in each territory. This reduction in demand variability (as measured with the coefficient of variation) reduces the amount of on-hand inventory needed to achieve any in-stock probability.

Although location pooling is wonderful for reducing on-hand inventory, according to Table 14.4, it doesn't do anything for on-order inventory. Look at the days of supply of on-order inventory across the different levels of pooling—they are all one day! Location pooling does nothing for on-order inventory because on-order inventory only depends on the length of the lead time and average demand. Due to Little's Law, on-order inventory does not depend at all on the variability of demand. So reducing demand variability through location pooling has absolutely no effect on on-order inventory.

Although we have so far emphasized that location pooling can reduce on-hand inventory, this is not the only improvement that location pooling enables. As was illustrated in Figure 14.9, there is a trade-off between the in-stock probability and on-hand inventory. Location pooling essentially takes that trade-off curve and shifts it down and to the right, as shown in Figure 14.12. Say we are initially located at the circle on the higher trade-off curve in Figure 14.12. Once we implement location pooling, it reduces variability and our trade-off curve shifts in a favorable direction. This creates several options. We can hold the in-stock probability constant and exclusively reduce on-hand inventory—the down arrow in Figure 14.12. That is the approach taken in Table 14.4. However, we could also keep our inventory investment constant and choose to increase the in-stock probability—the horizontal arrow in Figure 14.12. Given that Medtronic already is starting with a very high in-stock probability, this option

Figure 14.12

The shift in the trade-off curve between in-stock probability and on-hand inventory due to location pooling. If a firm is positioned on the upper curve (circle), then after location pooling it can either (i) reduce inventory while keeping the in-stock probability the same (downward arrow), (ii) increase the in-stock probability while keeping on-hand inventory the same (horizontal arrow), or (iii) increase the in-stock probability and decrease on-hand inventory at the same time (diagonal arrow).

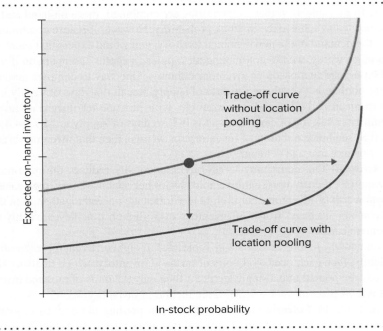

Trade-off curve without location pooling

Trade-off curve with location pooling

Expected on-hand inventory

In-stock probability

isn't very attractive—they really don't need an in-stock probability higher than .9999. But sometimes that option is attractive, especially with a lower initial in-stock probability. Finally, the third option is to both improve the in-stock probability and reduce on-hand inventory—the diagonal arrow in Figure 14.12. This is like "having your cake and eating it too"! Normally, we cannot both improve customer service and reduce inventory. But we can if we reduce demand variability through location pooling.

Given the wonders of location pooling, why does Medtronic let the sales representatives hold their own inventory? The answer is that location pooling also changes something that we have not yet discussed. Pooling inventory from multiple sales representatives requires that the inventory be kept in a central place. That central place is surely further away, on average, from each representative than where the inventory is currently held, mostly in the hospitals or in the sales representatives' cars. Hence, while location pooling allows for less inventory, it also makes the inventory less convenient for the final consumers because it moves the inventory farther away from them.

The pros and cons of location pooling are crucial for understanding the effectiveness and limitations of electronic commerce. An e-retailer usually holds inventory in far fewer locations than traditional **brick-and-mortar retailer** stores (i.e., a retailer with physical stores that consumers can enter to purchase inventory). Fewer locations means less demand variability, which means less inventory is needed to serve demand. In fact, some products could not be profitably sold in a traditional retailer because they sell too slowly and their demand is too variable. But these products can be profitable if pooled into a limited number of locations, thereby making their demand less variable. However, the more location pooling is done, the further the inventory moves away from customers. And moving inventory away from customers means that somebody must pay to ship stuff to them and they have to wait for their stuff to arrive. For many products, the extra shipping cost and delay are acceptable to customers, but not for all products.

14.6.2 Lead-Time Pooling

We just learned that locating inventory near customers can require a substantial amount of inventory to achieve a target level of service. Inventory is needed due to two types of uncertainty. The first uncertainty is the total number of units demanded. For example, how many InSync devices are demanded in the United States on a given day or in a given week. The second uncertainty is how many units are demanded in each location. For example, say we know that on a particular day 20 devices are demanded across the United States. That piece of information eliminates the aggregate demand uncertainty, but unfortunately we still face the uncertainty of not knowing where those 20 devices are demanded.

Location pooling helps to reduce the second risk: If we hold inventory in fewer locations, there is less uncertainty with respect to demand in each location. Unfortunately, location pooling also moves inventory away from customers, thereby preventing customers from physically seeing a product before purchase, increasing the time a customer must wait to receive a product, and generally increasing the delivery cost. When the limitations of location pooling are substantial, it is desirable to find another strategy. One option, as we discuss in this section, is lead-time pooling.

The **lead-time pooling strategy** reduces the demand uncertainty faced in a supply chain, while still keeping inventory reasonably close to customers, by adding an intermediate decision-making point to delay when a commitment is made to a particular product feature that contributes to demand uncertainty. That definition is a mouthful, so an example would be useful. In fact, we can use Medtronic as the example because they are already implementing lead-time pooling.

Figure 14.13 displays two supply chain strategies for Medtronic. The upper panel displays their current strategy: Product is produced in the factory and shipped to the distribution center (DC) and then sales representatives order replenishments from the DC. The lower panel displays an alternative strategy that doesn't use a distribution center: Sales representatives order replenishments directly from the factory. The first strategy (upper panel) uses lead-time risk

Brick-and-mortar retailer A retailer with physical stores in which consumers are able to immediately purchase goods.

Lead-time pooling strategy A strategy that reduces the demand uncertainty faced in a supply chain, while still keeping inventory reasonably close to customers, by adding an intermediate decision-making point to delay when a commitment is made to a particular product feature that contributes to demand uncertainty.

Figure 14.13

Two supply chain strategies for Medtronic. In the upper panel, product flows from the factory to a distribution center (DC) with a three-week lead time, and sales representatives order from the DC with a one-day lead time. In the lower panel, sales representatives order directly from the factory with a three-week lead time.

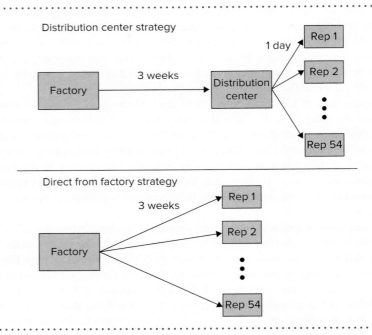

pooling because it adds an intermediate decision point (the DC) between the factory and the sales representatives. The second strategy (lower panel) does not use lead-time risk pooling because there is no intermediate decision point between the two ends of the supply chain.

At first glance the "direct from factory" strategy in Figure 14.13 seems better than adding a DC to implement lead-time risk pooling: adding a DC increases the total lead time from factory to sales representatives (from three weeks to three weeks and one day), and the DC adds another location in the supply chain holding inventory. However, there is a subtle but very important difference between the two approaches. In the upper panel of Figure 14.13, there is only one location that faces a three-week lead time, the DC. In the lower panel, all of the sales representatives face a three-week lead time. Thus, adding a DC dramatically reduces the number of locations that must cope with a long lead time. This is why that strategy is called "lead-time pooling"—by adding the intermediate decision point (the DC), the long lead times faced by many locations are pooled into a single lead time faced by one location. A less precise way of saying this is that the many long arrows in the lower panel of Figure 14.13 are combined (or pooled) into a single long arrow in the upper panel.

So which strategy in Figure 14.13 is better? Let's use the order-up-to model to help us decide. Let's say there are 54 sales representatives who sell the InSync device across the country—Medtronic has hundreds of representatives, but not all of them work with surgeons that use the device or have been convinced to use the device. Furthermore, for simplicity, let's say they all have mean demand of 0.30 unit per day and their demands can be represented with the Poisson distribution. Finally, weekly demand at the DC, if there is a DC in the supply chain, is modeled with a normal distribution with mean 81 and standard deviation 20 (as in section 14.2.3).

We have already done most of the calculations for the "with DC" supply chain. Each representative has 4.4 units of on-hand inventory, so collectively they hold 237.6 units ($= 54 \times 4.4$). Each representative also has 0.3 unit on-order on average, so collectively they have 16.2 units ($= 54 \times 0.3$). The distribution center holds 124 units ($40 \times L(3.1)$) on hand to achieve its target .999 in-stock probability and due to the three-week lead time, it has 243 ($= 81 \times 3$) units on-order.

Now let's evaluate the inventory needed for the without DC supply chain. Each sales representative has a 15-day lead time ($= 3$ weeks $\times 5$ days per week) and can place orders daily. Hence, $(L + 1)$ periods equal 16 days. If mean demand for one day is 0.3 unit, then mean demand over 16 days is 4.8 units ($= 0.3$ unit per day $\times 16$ days). From Table 14.5, each

TABLE 14.5   Distribution Function and Expected Inventory for a Poisson Distribution with Mean 4.8

S	F(S)	I(S)
0	.0082	0.00
1	.0477	0.01
2	.1425	0.06
3	.2942	0.20
4	.4763	0.49
5	.6510	0.97
6	.7908	1.62
7	.8867	2.41
8	.9442	3.30
9	.9749	4.24
10	.9896	5.22
11	.9960	6.21
12	.9986	7.20
13	.9995	8.20
14	.9999	9.20
15	1.0000	10.20
16	1.0000	11.20
17	1.0000	12.20

representative needs an order-up-to level equal to 14 to achieve the desired in-stock probability (because $F(S=14) = .9999$). From the same table, expected on-hand inventory is then $I(S=14) = 9.2$ units for each representative. Across the 54 representatives, they need to hold 496.8 units (= 54 × 9.2). These representatives also have three weeks' worth of on-order inventory, which is 4.5 units per representative (= 15 days × 0.3 unit per day) and 243 units in total across all representatives (= 4.5 × 54).

Table 14.6 provides the summary of the results. In short, adding the DC to the supply chain reduces the total amount of inventory in the supply chain even though it doesn't change the number of locations in which demand is served or the in-stock probability customers experience. Hence, customers cannot see the difference between the two strategies—either way, they get reliable service with inventory that is held close to them to ensure that their demands are satisfied quickly. The difference is that adding the DC allows Medtronic to reduce the inventory it needs to hold, which lowers Medtronic's costs.

As with location pooling, lead-time pooling works by reducing the uncertainty within the supply chain. As already mentioned, adding the DC to the supply chain reduces the number of locations that face a long lead time: Without the DC there are 54 representatives that have a three-week lead time, but with the DC there is a single location with that long lead time. Over that long lead time, it is easier to predict the number of units needed in total (because they are all going to a single location) than it is to predict the needed number of units across 54 different locations. Due to this reduction in demand uncertainty, the entire system can generate the same quality of service to customers while also holding less inventory.

14.6.3 Delayed Differentiation

Medtronic uses a distribution center to create the intermediate point in the supply chain that pools lead times. This isn't the only way to create an intermediate point in a supply chain. To explain, consider selling paint through a hardware store. When it comes to paint, we can't just

TABLE 14.6 A Comparison of Two Supply Chain Strategies, One with a Distribution Center (DC) and One Without, as Shown in Figure 14.13

	With DC	Without DC
On-hand inventory		
Sales representatives	237.6	496.8
DC	124.0	0.0
Total	361.6	496.8
On-order inventory		
Sales representatives	16.2	243.0
DC	243.0	0.0
Total	259.2	243.0
All Inventory	620.8	739.8

sell one color—people like variety in paint color, so we probably have to sell at least several hundred different colors. Unfortunately, paint takes up a considerable amount of room in the store (i.e., inventory holding costs are substantial) and there is a long lead time to receive paint from the factory (at least several weeks, if not longer).

There are two strategies for selling paint. One way is to order different colors of paint from the factory and to hold inventory of paint in various colors in the store. That strategy is represented by the bottom panel in Figure 14.14. A second strategy is to send paint from the factory without any color, which we call "generic paint." The store only carries inventory of this generic paint and no customer wants the generic paint. However, when a customer requests a particular color, the store adds the necessary pigments to a can of the generic paint, shakes the can until the color is fully mixed throughout, and then sells the can with the desired color to the customer.

Which strategy is better? To help answer that question, compare Figures 14.14 and 14.13. Do you notice that they are essentially the same figures, just with different labels? The generic paint strategy is like adding a distribution center between the factory and Medtronic's sales

Figure 14.14

Two strategies for selling paint to customers. In the top panel, generic paint is shipped to the store and color is added in the store to serve demand. In the bottom panel, color is added in the factory before shipping to the store, where no further processing occurs.

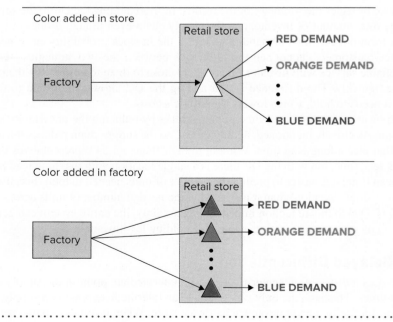

Check Your Understanding 14.8

Question: Which of the following best explains why location pooling, lead-time pooling, and delayed differentiation all can reduce the amount of inventory in the supply chain?

   a. All three strategies reduce the in-stock probability.

   b. All three strategies make customers wait longer to receive their product.

   c. All three strategies reduce the total lead time from the supply source (e.g., a factory) to the end consumer.

   d. All three strategies reduce the variability of demand within the supply chain.

   Answer: Those three strategies work by reducing demand variability. Answer is D.

---

representatives—it creates an intermediate point in the supply chain from factory to customers that allows us to delay making a commitment regarding paint color. With the other approach, the bottom panel in Figure 14.14, we are forced to decide the paint color for each can before it leaves the factory. It is much harder to decide the quantities to ship from the factory for every possible paint color than it is to merely decide how many cans of generic paint to send to the store. Thus, the generic paint strategy faces less demand uncertainty even though it offers the same set of products to customers. And based on our analysis of Medtronic's supply chain, we can conclude that the generic paint strategy requires less inventory for the same level of customer service.

The strategy in the top panel of Figure 14.14 is called **delayed differentiation**—the delayed-differentiation strategy attempts to add variety to a product as late in the supply process as possible. For example, instead of adding color at the factory, with delayed differentiation color is added at the store. This delay in creating variety allows us to reduce inventory for all the same reasons that adding a distribution center in Medtronic's supply chain allows them to reduce inventory.

There is no question that delayed differentiation is a great strategy for selling paint. In general, delayed differentiation is effective when:

- Customers have a strong preference for many different versions of the product.

- Variety can be added quickly and cheaply late in the supply process.

- The components needed to create variety are inexpensive relative to the generic component (i.e., the main body of the product).

Each of the above applies to paint: (i) customers are very picky about the particular paint color they want; (ii) the equipment to add pigment to paint is not too expensive or difficult to operate in a store, and a can of paint can be mixed in a reasonable amount of time; (iii) only a limited set of pigments are needed to make a wide variety of colors and these pigments do not take up a considerable amount of space in the store. Furthermore, there are many other markets for which the delayed-differentiation strategy is effective.

> **Delayed differentiation** A strategy in which product differentiation is delayed as late as possible in the supply chain.

Conclusion

The order-up-to model is appropriate for managing the inventory of a product that has many replenishment opportunities because it does not become obsolete or deteriorate in the short term. Medtronic's InSync device is a good example—the product can be ordered on a daily or weekly basis and is expected to last several years.

The critical performance measures in the order-up-to model are expected on-hand inventory, on-order inventory, and the in-stock probability. Because perishability is not a concern, the target in-stock probability is generally reasonably high (e.g., .95 or higher). Nevertheless, there remains a trade-off between the desired in-stock probability and on-hand inventory:

Each incremental increase in the in-stock probability causes a larger and larger increase in on-hand inventory.

The order-up-to model illustrates two of the three inhibitors of operations management: variability and inflexibility. The more variable demand is, the more on-hand inventory is needed to achieve a desired in-stock probability. Inflexibility comes in the form of the lead time. An inflexible lead time (i.e., a long lead time) contributes to an increase in both on-hand inventory and on-order inventory. In fact, on-order inventory is only linked to the length of the lead time.

Several strategies exist to reduce variability and inflexibility in the supply chain. Location pooling combines locations to reduce the number of places in which inventory is held, which reduces demand variability. Adding an intermediate decision point in the supply chain, such as through a distribution center or delayed differentiation, also reduces variability, and therefore the needed inventory to achieve a desired service level. Finally, while faster modes of transportation are more expensive (e.g., ground versus air), the reduction in the lead time reduces the needed inventory.

Summary of Learning Objectives

LO14-1 Explain the operation of the order-up-to model and develop an order-up-to model for a given situation

The order-up-to model can be used to manage the inventory of a product that has a lead time to receive orders and for which many orders are feasible over the lifetime of the product. With the order-up-to model, the order quantity in each period equals the difference between the chosen order-up-to level and the inventory position. The order quantity is generally equal to demand in the previous period.

LO14-2 Evaluate several performance measures for the order-up-to model

There are three key performance measures in the order-up-to model: on-hand inventory, on-order inventory, and in-stock probability. On-hand inventory is the average inventory on hand at the end of a period, available to serve customer demand. On-order inventory is inventory that has been ordered but has not been received yet and so is not available to satisfy demand. The in-stock probability is a measure of customer service.

LO14-3 Evaluate the appropriate order-up-to level to achieve a desired service target and understand what determines an appropriate service target

The target in-stock probability is generally high (greater than .95) because inventory does not become obsolete or deteriorate in any way. For any target in-stock probability, it is possible to evaluate an order-up-to level that achieves the in-stock probability with the minimum inventory.

LO14-4 Explain the factors that determine the required amount of inventory

On-hand inventory depends on three factors: the in-stock probability, the coefficient of variation of demand, and the length of the lead time. In all cases, an increase in the factor results in higher on-hand inventory. In particular, each incremental increase in the in-stock probability increases on-hand inventory by a larger and larger amount.

LO14-5 Explain several strategies to restructure a supply chain to increase profit and reduce the costs of mismatches between supply and demand

It is possible to change the structure of the supply chain to reduce the needed investment in inventory. Location pooling combines inventory locations so that there are fewer locations at which inventory is held. This reduces demand uncertainty (as measured by the coefficient of variation) and therefore reduces inventory. However, it also moves inventory away from consumers. Alternatively, with lead-time pooling, a decision point is introduced at some intermediate point in the supply chain. This can be done with a distribution center or by moving final assembly to a point lower in the supply chain, as with delayed differentiation. These strategies reduce inventory without altering where inventory is sold to customers.

Key Terms

14.2 The Order-up-to Model

Period In the context of managing inventory, this is the time between when orders can be placed. For example, if the period is a day, then orders can be placed daily.

Lead time The time between when an order is placed and when it is received. Process lead time is frequently used as an alternative term for flow time.

On-order inventory The inventory that the supplier has shipped but that has not been received.

On-hand inventory The inventory that is ready to be used to serve customer demand.

Backorder The total amount of demand that is waiting for inventory to arrive before it can be satisfied.

Inventory position On-order inventory plus on-hand inventory minus the backorder.

Order-up-to level The desired inventory position after an order is submitted.

Order-up-to inventory model An inventory model that is appropriate when inventory can be periodically ordered, there is a lead time to receive orders, and inventory is not perishable.

Pull system The resource furthest downstream (i.e., closest to the market) is paced by market demand. In addition to its own production, it also relays the demand information to the next station upstream, thus ensuring that the upstream resource also is paced by demand. That is, it is an operating system in which the production or replenishment of a unit is only initiated when a demand occurs.

Push system An operating system in which the production or replenishment of a unit is initiated in anticipation of demand.

Poisson distribution A statistical distribution that is suitable for modeling demand with a low mean (e.g., 20 or lower).

14.3 Performance Measures

Expected on-hand inventory The average amount of inventory on hand available at the end of each period to serve demand.

Expected on-order inventory The average amount of inventory on order at any given time.

Pipeline inventory Another term to describe expected on-order inventory.

14.6 Improving the Supply Chain

Tactical decisions Decisions that impact short-term performance.

Strategic decisions Decisions that have long-term implications.

Location pooling A strategy of combining the inventory from multiple territories/locations into a single location.

Brick-and-mortar retailer A retailer with physical stores in which consumers are able to immediately purchase goods.

Lead-time pooling strategy A strategy that reduces the demand uncertainty faced in a supply chain, while keeping inventory reasonably close to customers. This is achieved by adding an intermediate decision-making point to delay when the end retailer must commit to a particular product feature, thus decreasing demand uncertainty.

Delayed differentiation A strategy in which product differentiation is delayed as late as possible in the supply chain.

Key Formulas

LO14-1 **Explain the operation of the order-up-to model and develop an order-up-to model for a given situation**

Inventory position = On-order inventory + On-hand inventory − Backorder

Each period's order quantity = S − Inventory position

Expected demand over n periods = $n \times$ Expected demand in 1 period

Standard deviation of demand over n periods $= \sqrt{n} \times$ Standard deviation of demand in 1 period

Poisson mean over n periods $= n \times$ Poisson mean over 1 period

LO14-2 Evaluate several performance measures for the order-up-to model

If demand is normally distributed:

Expected on-hand inventory $= \sigma \times I(z)$

In-stock probability $=$ Probability demand over $(L + 1)$ periods is S or lower

Stockout probability $= 1 -$ In-stock probability

Expected on-order inventory $=$ Expected demand in one period $\times$ Lead time

Conceptual Questions

LO 14-1

1. Demand in each period follows the same normal distribution (i.e., there is one demand distribution that represents demand in any single period). Assuming demand is independent across periods, which of the following statements about mean demand over five periods is true?
   a. It equals the mean of demand over one period.
   b. It is greater than the mean of demand over one period but less than five times the mean of demand over one period.
   c. It equals five times the mean of demand over one period.
   d. It is even more than five times the mean of demand over one period.

2. Demand in each period follows the same normal distribution (i.e., there is one demand distribution that represents demand in any single period). Assuming demand is independent across periods, which of the following statements about the standard deviation of demand over five periods is true?
   a. It equals the standard deviation of demand over one period.
   b. It is greater than the standard deviation of demand over one period but less than five times the standard deviation of demand over one period.
   c. It equals five times the standard deviation of demand over one period.
   d. It is even more than five times the standard deviation of demand over one period.

3. For products with slow-moving demand—for example, one unit per week—the Poisson distribution is likely to be a better model for demand than the normal distribution because: (choose the best answer)
   a. the Poisson's standard deviation is equal to the square root of its mean.
   b. the normal distribution does not allow the freedom to choose any standard deviation for any given mean.
   c. the Poisson distribution is a continuous distribution.
   d. only the standard normal distribution would apply in this setting.
   e. the Poisson distribution does not assign any probability to negative outcomes.

4. A firm manages its inventory with an order-up-to model. Each period is one day, the lead time is two days, the order-up-to level is 10, and its inventory position at the start of a day (before it submits an order for that day) is –4. Which of the following statements is definitely true?
   a. Demand was four units yesterday.
   b. Demand was 10 units yesterday.
   c. There are at least four units backordered.
   d. There are 14 units on order before it orders today.
   e. After today's order, there will be 14 units on order.
   f. It will receive more inventory today.

5. In the order-up-to model, the standard deviation of the order quantities:
   a. is higher than the standard deviation of demand in one period.
   b. is lower than the standard deviation of demand in one period.
   c. is equal to the standard deviation of demand in one period.
   d. cannot be compared to the standard deviation of demand in one period.

LO 14-2

6. Suppose the order-up-to model is used. The probability that you end any given period with no on-hand inventory equals:
   a. the in-stock probability.
   b. the critical ratio.
   c. the gross margin.
   d. the ratio of inventory turns to days of supply.
   e. the stockout probability.

7. A retailer is considering two possible definitions of "in stock":
   I. A product is in stock if it has at least one unit on hand at the end of the day.
   II. A product is in stock if it has satisfied all demand during a day.

   For a fixed order-up-to level, which definition yields the higher in-stock probability?
   a. Definition I because if one unit is on hand, then all demand must have been satisfied.
   b. Definition II because the firm is more likely to satisfy all demand than to end the day with one unit on hand.
   c. Definition II because if all demand is satisfied, then there must be some inventory left over.
   d. Either one is possible because it will depend on the particular order-up-to policy chosen, the distribution function of demand, and the lead time.

8. Suppose inventory is managed using the order-up-to model. The inventory position is 20 and demand in the last period was 10. What is the target in-stock probability?
   a. 95 percent
   b. 96 percent
   c. 97 percent
   d. 98 percent
   e. 99 percent
   f. Could be any of the above a–e
   g. Cannot be any of the above a–e

LO 14-3

9. If the target in-stock probability increases, then the expected time between stockouts:
   a. increases.
   b. remains the same.
   c. decreases.
   d. could increase or decrease.

10. Demand each period is normally distributed and an order-up-to model is used to decide order quantities. Which of the following influences the chosen order-up-to level (i.e., a change in which of the following would change the chosen order-up-to level)?
    I. The mean of demand in one period
    II. The standard deviation of demand over $(L + 1)$ periods
    III. The target in-stock probability
    a. Only I
    b. Only II
    c. Only III
    d. I and II
    e. I and III
    f. II and III
    g. I, II, and III

11. Suppose in the order-up-to model the target in-stock probability is .95 and demand across periods is independent and normally distributed. If the lead time is doubled but the target in-stock probability remains .95, what happens to the order-up-to level?
    a. It more than doubles (increases by more than a factor of two).
    b. It doubles (increases exactly by a factor of two).
    c. It increases but by less than a factor of two.
    d. It decreases.
    e. The answer cannot be determined with the given information.

LO 14-4

12. A firm uses the order-up-to model to manage its inventory. It wants to increase its in-stock probability while decreasing its holding costs (i.e., reducing its average inventory). Which of the following actions will help to achieve this goal? (Consider each action independently.)
    I. Decrease the lead time.
    II. Increase the order-up-to level.
    III. Increase the average quantity on order.
    a. Only I
    b. Only II
    c. Only III
    d. I and II
    e. I and III
    f. II and III
    g. Any of them will help (that is I, II, or III).
    h. None of them will help.

13. In the order-up-to model, assume that the mean of demand in a period remains the same and the target in-stock probability is kept at a constant level. If the demand uncertainty (the standard deviation of demand in each period) increases, then:
    a. expected on-hand inventory increases.
    b. expected on-hand inventory decreases.
    c. expected on-hand inventory remains the same.
    d. expected on-hand inventory may increase or decrease, depending on the demand distribution and other parameters.

14. Suppose the order-up-to model is used to manage inventories. The firm is planning changes that will reduce the lead time to receive replenishments because the firm anticipates that the coefficient of variation of demand will increase even though mean demand per period remains the same. What can be said about the likely change in the firm's on-order inventory?
    a. It will surely decrease.
    b. It will remain the same.
    c. It will surely increase.
    d. More information is needed to determine the impact of these changes.

15. Suppose inventory is managed using the order-up-to model. Which of the following actions will certainly lead to a higher order-up-to level? In all cases, assume the characteristics of the demand process do not change.
    I. Increase in the target in-stock probability (for the same lead time)
    II. Increase in the lead time (for the same in-stock probability)
    a. I only
    b. II only
    c. I and II
    d. None of the above

16. Anna Litic, a new supply chain manager at High Precision Inc. (HP), decides to check some data on the supply chains she manages. She discovers that HP's in-transit inventory of electronic components from its Tacoma, Washington, factory to its Asian distribution center (DC) has increased from two quarters ago. However, the distribution of demand at the Asian DC has not changed over this period of time. Anna knows that the Asian DC manager is controlling inventory to achieve a fixed in-stock probability target, so she is happy to see that indeed the in-stock inventory at the Asian DC has also not deviated off the target. Anna wonders what has happened to the Asian DC's average inventory. What is she likely to discover regarding the Asian DC's on-hand inventory?
    a. On-hand inventory has not changed because the in-stock probability has not changed at the Asian DC.
    b. On-hand inventory has increased because the lead time from Tacoma, Washington, to the Asian DC must have increased.
    c. On-hand inventory has not changed because average demand has not changed at the Asian DC.
    d. On-hand inventory has decreased because the variability of demand must have decreased.
    e. It is not possible to predict what Anna is likely to observe with respect to the change in on-hand inventory; that is, it could be lower, higher, or unchanged.

LO 14-5

17. Which of the following is a strategic decision for a grocery retailer?
    a. The number of boxes of cereal to order in the first week of a month
    b. Whether to open new stores that have twice the square footage of current stores
    c. Whether or not to hire Bob for a store manager position
    d. Which items to place on the end of an aisle for this week's promotion

18. Location pooling is most effective at generating which of the following changes to performance objectives?
    a. Increasing the gross margin
    b. Increasing the target in-stock probability
    c. Decreasing on-order inventory
    d. Decreasing days of supply of on-hand inventory

19. A firm sells a product whose demand over the next couple of years will be stable (so the order-up-to model is used to manage its inventory). When the demand uncertainty is small (for example, the weekly demand has a mean of 100 and a standard deviation of 5), the main benefit of reducing the lead time is:
    a. to do more lead-time pooling.
    b. to reduce the expected on-hand inventory at the end of every period.
    c. to increase the stockout probability.
    d. to reduce the on-order inventory.

Solved Example Problems

LO 14-1

1. The order-up-to model is used to manage inventory. The order-up-to level is 50, the lead time is 5 periods, there are 25 units on order, and there are 10 units on hand. How many units will be ordered this period?

   Answer: 15. The inventory position is $25 + 10 = 35$. To raise the inventory position to 50 requires an order of $50 - 35 = 15$ units.

2. A Poisson distribution with mean 1.5 represents demand in a single period. A Poisson distribution with what mean should be used to represent demand over three periods?

   Answer: 4.5. The mean demand across several periods is the sum of the mean demand in each period.

LO14-1, 14-2, 14-3

3. Quick Print Inc. uses plain paper for copying needs. Weekly demand for that paper follows a normal distribution with mean 100 and standard deviation 50 (measured in reams). Each week, a replenishment order is placed with its supplier and the order arrives one week later. All copying orders that cannot be satisfied immediately due to the lack of paper are backordered.
   a. Suppose that Quick Print decides to establish an order-up-to level of 300 for plain paper. At the start of this week, there are 200 boxes in inventory and 60 boxes on order. How much will Quick Print order this week?

      Answer: 40. The inventory position is on-order inventory plus on-hand inventory minus the backorder. There are no units backordered, so the inventory position is $60 + 200 = 260$. The order quantity is the difference between the order-up-to level, 300, and the inventory position, 260, which is 40 boxes.
   b. What is the standard deviation of demand over two weeks? Assume demands are independent across weeks.

      Answer: 70.7. The standard deviation over two weeks is $\sqrt{2} \times 50 = 70.7$.
   c. Suppose it uses 306 boxes as its order-up-to level. What is its expected on-hand inventory?

      Answer: 108. The mean of demand over $(L + 1)$ periods is 200 (2×100) and the standard deviation is 70.7 (from part B). $z = \frac{306 - 200}{70.7} = 1.5$. From the normal distribution table, $I(z = 1.5) = 1.53$. Convert this to on-hand inventory by multiplying by the standard deviation of demand over $(L + 1)$ periods: $70.7 \times 1.53 = 108$.

d. Suppose it uses 306 boxes as its order-up-to level. What is its expected on-order inventory?

Answer: 100. On-order inventory equals demand over l periods, which in this case is demand over one period.

e. Suppose it uses 278 boxes as its order-up-to level. What is its in-stock probability?

Answer: .8643. The mean of demand over $(L + 1)$ periods is 200 and the standard deviation is 70.7 (from part B). $z = \frac{278 - 200}{70.7} = 1.1$. From the normal distribution table, $F(z = 1.1) = .8643$.

f. Suppose it uses 334 boxes as its order-up-to level. What is its stockout probability?

Answer: .0287. The mean of demand over $(L + 1)$ periods is 200 and the standard deviation is 70.7 (from part B). $z = \frac{334 - 200}{70.7} = 1.9$. From the normal distribution table, $F(z = 1.9) = 0.9713$, which is the in-stock probability. The stockout probability is $1 - .9713 = .0287$.

g. Suppose it wants to have an in-stock probability of at least .998. What order-up-to level should it use?

Answer: 405. The mean of demand over $(L + 1)$ periods is 200 and the standard deviation is 70.7 (from part B). From the normal distribution table, $F(z = 2.8) = .9974$ and $F(z = 2.9) = .9981$, so $z = 2.9$ delivers the needed in-stock probability. Convert to an order quantity: $S = 200 + (2.9 \times 70.7) = 405$.

4. Main Line Auto Distributor is an auto parts supplier to local garage shops. None of its customers have the space or capital to store all of the possible parts they might need so they order parts from Main Line several times a day. To provide fast service, Main Line uses three pickup trucks to make its own deliveries. Each day Main Line orders additional inventory from its supplier, who delivers three days later. Consider part A153QR, or part A for short. Average daily demand for this part follows a Poisson distribution with mean 0.5 unit. The distribution and inventory functions for the Poisson distribution can be found in Appendix 14A.

a. Suppose at the start of a day, just before placing an order, Main Line currently has a backorder of part A. In particular, one unit is backordered, it has no on-hand units, and it has four units on order. Say it uses an order-up-to level equal to six parts. How many parts will it order today?

Answer: 3. The inventory position is $4 + 0 - 1 = 3$, so to raise the inventory position to 6, it must order 3 units.

b. Suppose it uses an order-up-to level of five units. What is its average on-hand inventory?

Answer: 3.02. Demand over $(L + 1)$ periods is Poisson with a mean of $(3 + 1) \times 0.5 = 2$. From the Poisson distribution table in Appendix 14A, with a mean of 2, average on-hand inventory is $I(5) = 3.02$.

c. Suppose it uses an order-up-to level of five units. What is its average on-order inventory?

Answer: 1.5. On-order inventory equals expected demand over l periods, which in this case is $3 \times 0.5 = 1.5$.

d. Suppose it uses an order-up-to level of six units. What is its in-stock probability?

Answer: .9955. Demand over $(L + 1)$ periods is Poisson with a mean of $(3 + 1) \times 0.5 = 2$. From the Poisson distribution table in Appendix 14A, with a mean of 2, $F(S=6) = .9955$.

e. Suppose it uses an order-up-to level of four units. What is its stockout probability?

Answer: .0527. Demand over $(L + 1)$ periods is Poisson with a mean of $(3 + 1) \times 0.5 = 2$. From the Poisson distribution table in Appendix 14A, with a mean of 2, $F(S=4) = .9473$. The stockout probability is $1 - .9473 = .0527$.

f. Main Line wants to minimize its inventory but also deliver at least a .97 in-stock probability. What order-up-to level should it use?

Answer: 5. Demand over $(L + 1)$ periods is Poisson with a mean of $(3 + 1) \times 0.5 = 2$. From the Poisson distribution table in Appendix 14A, with a mean of 2, $F(S = 4) = .9473$ and $F(S=5) = .9834$. To achieve at least a .97 in-stock probability, it should choose $S = 5$.

Problems and Applications

LO 14-1

1. A firm implements the order-up-to model with weekly ordering. In week 11, it observes that demand is much lower than expected demand. At the start of week 12 (before it orders), it decides to change its forecast of demand per week and consequently it lowers its order-up-to level. Its order in week 12 will:
   a. be less than the demand it observed in week 11.
   b. equal the demand it observed in week 11.
   c. be greater than the demand it observed in week 11.
   d. equal the change in the order-up-to level from week 11 to week 12.

2. Assume a firm implements an order-up-to inventory model with an order-up-to level of 10. The lead time is two periods and demand is normally distributed. Which of the following is definitely *not* true?
   a. The last order was 12.
   b. The backorder in the previous period was 14.
   c. There are 11 units in on-hand inventory.
   d. Demand in the previous period was 13.
   e. There are 12 units on order and 2 units are backordered.
   f. There are 2 units on order and 8 units on hand.

3. A retailer uses the order-up-to model to manage inventory of an item in a store. The lead time for replenishments is four weeks and it can place orders weekly. Weekly demand is Poisson with mean 0.10 unit. Its order-up-to level is five and unfilled demand is backordered. What is the coefficient of variation of its orders?

LO14-2, 14-3

4. You are the owner of Hotspices.com, an online retailer of hip, exotic, and hard-to-find spices. Consider your inventory of saffron, a spice (generally) worth more by weight than gold. You order saffron from an overseas supplier with a shipping lead time of four weeks and you order weekly. Average weekly demand is normally distributed with a mean of 40 ounces and a standard deviation of 30 ounces.
   a. Suppose it uses an order-up-to level of 301 ounces. What is its expected on-hand inventory?
   b. Suppose it uses an order-up-to level of 250 ounces. What is its expected on-order inventory?
   c. Suppose it uses an order-up-to level of 368 ounces. What is its in-stock probability?
   d. Suppose it wants a .96 in-stock probability. What should its order-up-to level be?

5. ACold Inc. is a frozen-food distributor with 10 warehouses across the country. Ivan Tory, one of the warehouse managers, wants to make sure that the inventory policies used by the warehouse are minimizing inventory while still maintaining quick delivery to ACold's customers. Because the warehouse carries hundreds of different products, Ivan decided to study one. He picked Caruso's Frozen Pizza (CFP). Demand for CFPs averages 400 per day with a standard deviation of 152. Because ACold orders at least one truck from its supplier each day, ACold can essentially order any quantity of CFP it wants each day. In fact, ACold's computer system is designed to implement an order-up-to policy for each product. Ivan notes that any order for CFPs arrives four days after the order.
   a. Suppose it uses an order-up-to level of 2410. What is its expected on-hand inventory?
   b. Suppose it uses an order-up-to level of 2500. What is its expected on-order inventory?
   c. Suppose it uses an order-up-to level of 2000. What is its in-stock probability?
   d. Suppose it wants a .90 in-stock probability. What should its order-up-to level be?

LO14-1, 14-2, 14-3

6. Cyber Chemicals uses liquid nitrogen on a regular basis. Average daily demand is normally distributed with a mean of 178 gallons and a standard deviation of 45. Cyber operates six days a week and orders from its supplier once each week. The supplier takes one week to deliver Cyber's order.
   a. Suppose it uses an order-up-to level of 2200. What is its average order quantity?
   b. Suppose it uses an order-up-to level of 2480. What is its expected on-hand inventory?
   c. Suppose it uses an order-up-to level of 2600. What is its expected on-order inventory?

   d. Suppose it uses an order-up-to level of 2697. What is its in-stock probability?
   e. Suppose it uses an order-up-to level of 2400. What is its stockout probability?
   f. Suppose it wants a .945 in-stock probability. What should its order-up-to level be?
7. EShack sells an ergonomic keyboard in one of its stores. Average weekly demand for this keyboard follows a Poisson distribution with mean 0.8 unit. It submits orders to the supplier weekly and the supplier delivers with a two-week lead time.
   a. Suppose it uses an order-up-to level of five. What is its average order quantity?
   b. Suppose it uses an order-up-to level of nine. What is its expected on-hand inventory?
   c. Suppose it uses an order-up-to level of six. What is its expected on-order inventory?
   d. Suppose it uses an order-up-to level of seven. What is its in-stock probability?
   e. Suppose it uses an order-up-to level of four. What is its stockout probability?
   f. Suppose it wants a .97 in-stock probability. What should its order-up-to level be?

LO14-1,14-2

8. Shelf space in the grocery business is a valuable asset. Every good supermarket spends a significant amount of effort attempting to determine the optimal shelf-space allocation across products. Many factors are relevant to this decision: the profitability of each product, the size of each product, the demand characteristics of each product, and so forth. Southern Fresh sells Jalapeño Spicy Hot Bull corn chips, a local favorite. Average daily demand for this product in one of its stores is 3.5 bags and demand can be represented with a Poisson distribution. Replenishment orders are made daily and are received one day later.
   a. Suppose it uses an order-up-to level of 11. What is its expected on-hand inventory?
   b. Suppose it uses an order-up-to level of 12. What is its expected on-order inventory?
   c. Suppose it uses an order-up-to level of 13. What is its in-stock probability?
   d. Suppose it uses an order-up-to level of 14. What is its stockout probability?
   e. Southern Fresh has decided to make a policy that every product will receive enough shelf space to ensure a .98 in-stock probability. What should its order-up-to level be?
   f. What is the probability that on any particular day it doesn't submit an order?
   g. What is the probability that on any particular day it orders four or fewer bags?
   h. What is the probability that on any particular day it orders five or more bags?

CASE   WARKWORTH FURNITURE[1]

Warkworth Furniture specializes in environmentally friendly and sustainable furniture. One of its products, the TePaki desk, uses bamboo for the surface and recycled aluminum for the supports. The desk is made in its factory in Vietnam and shipped to all of its 30 stores throughout the United States, primarily in the large urban areas on either coast. Karen Williamson, the owner of Warkworth Furniture, is struggling with how it should organize its supply chain.

Currently, it ships the desks from Vietnam to the United States via ocean carrier. Once they arrive in the United States, they are shipped via a third-party carrier to each store. It usually takes 10 weeks between when an order is placed with the factory and when the product is received in a store.

The TePaki desk may be eco-friendly, but it isn't wallet friendly: Each desk costs Warkworth $325 to make and it sells the desk for $850. Nevertheless, Warkworth has been able to identify a market segment of customers that value the look of the desk and what it represents. Across its stores, it sells six desks per week, or 0.2 desk per week per store.

© Thomas Barwick/Photographer's Choice RF/Getty Images/RF

Given the upscale nature of its business, Warkworth's stores are located in nice areas that unfortunately have high rents. Consequently, between the opportunity cost of capital and the cost of physical space, Karen estimates that it costs Warkworth $150 to hold each TePaki desk in one of its stores for one year. It would be a financial disaster if each desk actually spent the entire year in inventory in a store, but the $150 does represent the true cost of holding a desk in a store for that period of time.

Shipping a TePaki desk from Vietnam to a store costs Warkworth $80 per desk, about $40 for the ocean portion of the journey and $40 for the land portion within the United States.

Andy Philpot, Warkworth's director of operations, has been arguing for some time that Warkworth should set up a distribution center in southern California to receive products from Asia, and from there distribute them to its various stores. Warehouse space is much cheaper than prime retail space. Hence, the holding cost per TePaki desk per year in a warehouse would only be $60. The only problem with this approach, according to Andy, is that the total shipping cost from factory to store could increase by $8 per desk due to the extra handling and shipping distance once all of the desks are routed through a distribution center.

Karen understands why the distribution center approach could make sense, but she worries about getting all of the execution done right. Instead, she suggests that it ship all of the desks directly to the stores as it currently does, but then ship product between stores as needed. The only problem with that approach is that it probably will cost it about $40 per desk to ship from one store to another.

[1] This case describes a fictitious company and product.

To add to the discussion, Kathy White, Warkworth's marketing director, is concerned with how these ideas will affect the desks' in-store availability. She proudly reminds everyone that Warkworth currently has a .99 in-stock probability for the TePaki desk. Andy, a typical ops guy, quips that it could save a ton if it were willing to make its customers wait a week or so to get their desk delivered to the store from a distribution center.

1. How much does Warkworth incur in holding costs each year with its current system of delivering directly from the factory to its stores?

2. Say Warkworth opens a distribution center in southern California. How much would it incur in holding costs each year with that strategy?

3. Say Warkworth opens a distribution center in southern California. How much does it incur in holding costs per desk?

4. Would you recommend that it consider Karen's idea of holding all inventory at the stores but shipping between stores as needed?

5. Say Warkworth listened to Andy and didn't hold inventory at the stores. Instead, inventory would be held in a distribution center and shipped to the stores as needed. How much would it save in inventory holding costs with this strategy?

Appendix 14A

TABLE 14A.1   The Distribution Function, $F(z)$, and the Inventory Function, $I(z)$, for the Standard Normal Distribution Function

z	F(z)	I(z)	z	F(z)	I(z)
−4.0	.0000	0.0000	0.1	.5398	0.4509
−3.9	.0000	0.0000	0.2	.5793	0.5069
−3.8	.0001	0.0000	0.3	.6179	0.5668
−3.7	.0001	0.0000	0.4	.6554	0.6304
−3.6	.0002	0.0000	0.5	.6915	0.6978
−3.5	.0002	0.0001	0.6	.7257	0.7687
−3.4	.0003	0.0001	0.7	.7580	0.8429
−3.3	.0005	0.0001	0.8	.7881	0.9202
−3.2	.0007	0.0002	0.9	.8159	1.0004
−3.1	.0010	0.0003	1.0	.8413	1.0833
−3.0	.0013	0.0004	1.1	.8643	1.1686
−2.9	.0019	0.0005	1.2	.8849	1.2561
−2.8	.0026	0.0008	1.3	.9032	1.3455
−2.7	.0035	0.0011	1.4	.9192	1.4367
−2.6	.0047	0.0015	1.5	.9332	1.5293
−2.5	.0062	0.0020	1.6	.9452	1.6232
−2.4	.0082	0.0027	1.7	.9554	1.7183
−2.3	.0107	0.0037	1.8	.9641	1.8143
−2.2	.0139	0.0049	1.9	.9713	1.9111
−2.1	.0179	0.0065	2.0	.9772	2.0085
−2.0	.0228	0.0085	2.1	.9821	2.1065
−1.9	.0287	0.0111	2.2	.9861	2.2049
−1.8	.0359	0.0143	2.3	.9893	2.3037
−1.7	.0446	0.0183	2.4	.9918	2.4027
−1.6	.0548	0.0232	2.5	.9938	2.5020
−1.5	.0668	0.0293	2.6	.9953	2.6015
−1.4	.0808	0.0367	2.7	.9965	2.7011
−1.3	.0968	0.0455	2.8	.9974	2.8008
−1.2	.1151	0.0561	2.9	.9981	2.9005
−1.1	.1357	0.0686	3.0	.9987	3.0004
−1.0	.1587	0.0833	3.1	.9990	3.1003
−0.9	.1841	0.1004	3.2	.9993	3.2002
−0.8	.2119	0.1202	3.3	.9995	3.3001
−0.7	.2420	0.1429	3.4	.9997	3.4001
−0.6	.2743	0.1687	3.5	.9998	3.5001
−0.5	.3085	0.1978	3.6	.9998	3.6000
−0.4	.3446	0.2304	3.7	.9999	3.7000
−0.3	.3821	0.2668	3.8	.9999	3.8000
−0.2	.4207	0.3069	3.9	1.0000	3.9000
−0.1	.4602	0.3509	4.0	1.0000	4.0000
0.0	.5000	0.3989			

TABLE 14A.2 Poisson Tables

$F(S)$ is the distribution function—the probability the outcome of a Poisson is S or lower. $I(S)$ is the expected inventory function—given an initial quantity, S, $I(S)$ is the expected amount of inventory remaining after demand.

	Mean									
	0.1		0.2		0.3		0.4		0.5	
S	F(S)	I(S)	F(S)	I(S)	F(S)	I(S)	F(S)	I(S)	F(S)	I(S)
0	0.9048	0.00	0.8187	0.00	0.7408	0.00	0.6703	0.00	0.6065	0.00
1	0.9953	0.90	0.9825	0.82	0.9631	0.74	0.9384	0.67	0.9098	0.61
2	0.9998	1.90	0.9989	1.80	0.9964	1.70	0.9921	1.61	0.9856	1.52
3	1.0000	2.90	0.9999	2.80	0.9997	2.70	0.9992	2.60	0.9982	2.50
4	1.0000	3.90	1.0000	3.80	1.0000	3.70	0.9999	3.60	0.9998	3.50
5	1.0000	4.90	1.0000	4.80	1.0000	4.70	1.0000	4.60	1.0000	4.50

	Mean									
	0.6		0.7		0.8		0.9		1.0	
S	F(S)	I(S)	F(S)	I(S)	F(S)	I(S)	F(S)	I(S)	F(S)	I(S)
0	0.5488	0.00	0.4966	0.00	0.4493	0.00	0.4066	0.00	0.3679	0.00
1	0.8781	0.55	0.8442	0.50	0.8088	0.45	0.7725	0.41	0.7358	0.37
2	0.9769	1.43	0.9659	1.34	0.9526	1.26	0.9371	1.18	0.9197	1.10
3	0.9966	2.40	0.9942	2.31	0.9909	2.21	0.9865	2.12	0.9810	2.02
4	0.9996	3.40	0.9992	3.30	0.9986	3.20	0.9977	3.10	0.9963	3.00
5	1.0000	4.40	0.9999	4.30	0.9998	4.20	0.9997	4.10	0.9994	4.00
6	1.0000	5.40	1.0000	5.30	1.0000	5.20	1.0000	5.10	0.9999	5.00
7	1.0000	6.40	1.0000	6.30	1.0000	6.20	1.0000	6.10	1.0000	6.00

	Mean									
	1.2		1.4		1.6		1.8		2.0	
S	F(S)	I(S)	F(S)	I(S)	F(S)	I(S)	F(S)	I(S)	F(S)	I(S)
0	0.3012	0.00	0.2466	0.00	0.2019	0.00	0.1653	0.00	0.1353	0.00
1	0.6626	0.30	0.5918	0.25	0.5249	0.20	0.4628	0.17	0.4060	0.14
2	0.8795	0.96	0.8335	0.84	0.7834	0.73	0.7306	0.63	0.6767	0.54
3	0.9662	1.84	0.9463	1.67	0.9212	1.51	0.8913	1.36	0.8571	1.22
4	0.9923	2.81	0.9857	2.62	0.9763	2.43	0.9636	2.25	0.9473	2.08
5	0.9985	3.80	0.9968	3.60	0.9940	3.41	0.9896	3.21	0.9834	3.02
6	0.9997	4.80	0.9994	4.60	0.9987	4.40	0.9974	4.20	0.9955	4.01
7	1.0000	5.80	0.9999	5.60	0.9997	5.40	0.9994	5.20	0.9989	5.00
8	1.0000	6.80	1.0000	6.60	1.0000	6.40	0.9999	6.20	0.9998	6.00
9	1.0000	7.80	1.0000	7.60	1.0000	7.40	1.0000	7.20	1.0000	7.00

Continued

	Mean									
	2.2		2.4		2.6		2.8		3.0	
S	F(S)	I(S)	F(S)	I(S)	F(S)	I(S)	F(S)	I(S)	F(S)	I(S)
0	0.1108	0.00	0.0907	0.00	0.0743	0.00	0.0608	0.00	0.0498	0.00
1	0.3546	0.11	0.3084	0.09	0.2674	0.07	0.2311	0.06	0.1991	0.05
2	0.6227	0.47	0.5697	0.40	0.5184	0.34	0.4695	0.29	0.4232	0.25
3	0.8194	1.09	0.7787	0.97	0.7360	0.86	0.6919	0.76	0.6472	0.67
4	0.9275	1.91	0.9041	1.75	0.8774	1.60	0.8477	1.45	0.8153	1.32
5	0.9751	2.83	0.9643	2.65	0.9510	2.47	0.9349	2.30	0.9161	2.13
6	0.9925	3.81	0.9884	3.62	0.9828	3.42	0.9756	3.24	0.9665	3.05
7	0.9980	4.80	0.9967	4.60	0.9947	4.41	0.9919	4.21	0.9881	4.02
8	0.9995	5.80	0.9991	5.60	0.9985	5.40	0.9976	5.20	0.9962	5.01
9	0.9999	6.80	0.9998	6.60	0.9996	6.40	0.9993	6.20	0.9989	6.00
10	1.0000	7.80	1.0000	7.60	0.9999	7.40	0.9998	7.20	0.9997	7.00
11	1.0000	8.80	1.0000	8.60	1.0000	8.40	1.0000	8.20	0.9999	8.00
12	1.0000	9.80	1.0000	9.60	1.0000	9.40	1.0000	9.20	1.0000	9.00

	Mean									
	3.2		3.4		3.6		3.8		4.0	
S	F(S)	I(S)	F(S)	I(S)	F(S)	I(S)	F(S)	I(S)	F(S)	I(S)
0	0.0408	0.00	0.0334	0.00	0.0273	0.00	0.0224	0.00	0.0183	0.00
1	0.1712	0.04	0.1468	0.03	0.1257	0.03	0.1074	0.02	0.0916	0.02
2	0.3799	0.21	0.3397	0.18	0.3027	0.15	0.2689	0.13	0.2381	0.11
3	0.6025	0.59	0.5584	0.52	0.5152	0.46	0.4735	0.40	0.4335	0.35
4	0.7806	1.19	0.7442	1.08	0.7064	0.97	0.6678	0.87	0.6288	0.78
5	0.8946	1.97	0.8705	1.82	0.8441	1.68	0.8156	1.54	0.7851	1.41
6	0.9554	2.87	0.9421	2.69	0.9267	2.52	0.9091	2.36	0.8893	2.20
7	0.9832	3.82	0.9769	3.64	0.9692	3.45	0.9599	3.26	0.9489	3.08
8	0.9943	4.81	0.9917	4.61	0.9883	4.42	0.9840	4.22	0.9786	4.03
9	0.9982	5.80	0.9973	5.60	0.9960	5.41	0.9942	5.21	0.9919	5.01
10	0.9995	6.80	0.9992	6.60	0.9987	6.40	0.9981	6.20	0.9972	6.00
11	0.9999	7.80	0.9998	7.60	0.9996	7.40	0.9994	7.20	0.9991	7.00
12	1.0000	8.80	0.9999	8.60	0.9999	8.40	0.9998	8.20	0.9997	8.00
13	1.0000	9.80	1.0000	9.60	1.0000	9.40	1.0000	9.20	0.9999	9.00
14	1.0000	10.80	1.0000	10.60	1.0000	10.40	1.0000	10.20	1.0000	10.00

Forecasting

15

LEARNING OBJECTIVES

CHAPTER OUTLINE

Introduction

Imagine you had a crystal ball—a crystal ball that would show you the future. What type of things would you look for in the crystal ball? Next week's winning lottery numbers? The stock market data for next year? Being able to foresee the future is an ancient dream of mankind. And being able to predict the future and to forecast what will happen would come with substantial economic advantages.

This chapter is about forecasting future events. In particular, we want to forecast the future demand for the products or services we supply. And we should break the bad news right at the beginning of the chapter: We cannot offer you a crystal ball. To the best of our knowledge (and we are pretty confident on this one), there exists no such thing. But the absence of crystal balls does not mean we cannot make good forecasts. We might not be able to make perfect forecasts, but, as we will see, a little bit of intelligence goes a long way.

© Adam Gault/OJO Images/
Age Fotostock/RF

Forecasting how much customers like our products or services in the future is hard. In fact, it is very hard, as the following two examples from history illustrate:

- Thomas Watson, legendary CEO of IBM, forecasted the demand for computers. He predicted that the world market demand for computers would be—five. Yes, you read correctly, not 5 million—5 computers. In his defense, he made this forecast in the 1950s—we weren't even born back then.
- In the 1960s, the managers at Decca Recording were offered the opportunity to publish the music of a Liverpool guitar band. Decca's forecast for sales of this band was pessimistic—"guitar groups are on the way out" was the management consensus. Unfortunately for Decca, the band that they rejected was the Beatles, a band that subsequently went on to become one of the most successful music bands in history.

In defense of Watson and the folks at Decca Recording, forecasting something radically new, something for which no prior history existed, is particularly challenging. Such forecasting problems are typical in business when it comes to predicting the sales of a new product or service before launch. The focus of this chapter is about forecasting in business settings for which we already have some data from past transactions.

Consider the following situation. Every year, millions of Americans are impacted by the flu. You might have had that experience yourself and so you know this is no fun. Especially as far as infants, the elderly, and other vulnerable population groups are concerned, the flu can be a matter of life or death. During flu season, patients with the flu flood the emergency departments of hospitals and demand medical services. Patients suffering from the flu also come to pharmacies and demand pharmaceutical products such as TamiFlu (a drug that helps to ease flu-related symptoms). So, forecasting the number of patients with the flu is critical.

Figure 15.1 shows the data for the number of patients visiting hospitals with the flu over the time period from 2009 to 2014. Imagine you were in charge of forecasting the number of flu cases, be it for a hospital or a pharmaceutical company. Can you perfectly predict the number of flu patients in 2015? Perfect forecasts are typically impossible. Each year is different and, short

Figure 15.1

Flu data from 2009 to 2014 (Source: CDC)

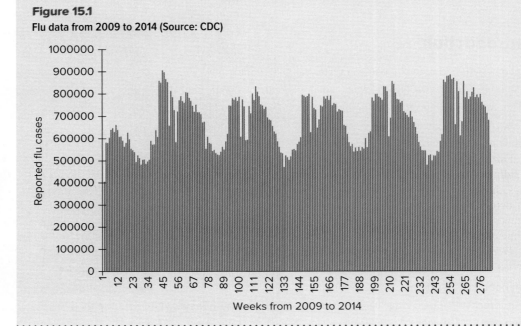

of crystal balls, every forecast will be wrong. But just "eyeballing" the data, you have some idea about the future. And this is the intuition you need for this chapter.

This chapter helps you forecast future demand. We proceed using the following steps:

- We first outline a framework for forecasting. We introduce some terminology, describe different forecasting methods (not including the acquisition of a crystal ball), and overview forecasting problems in business.
- We then discuss what makes a forecast a good forecast, defining a number of quality metrics that can be used when comparing forecasts with reality.
- Next, we introduce a simple set of forecasting methods, including naïve forecasts, moving average, and exponential smoothing.
- The next two sections then introduce more advanced forecasts that allow you to deal with seasonality and trends.
- The final section discusses the use of expert panels and points to some organizational challenges when dealing with subjective forecasts.

15.1 Forecasting Framework

© *Gérard Cachon*

Forecasting is the process of creating statements about outcomes of variables that presently are uncertain and will only be realized in the future. **Demand forecasting** is thus the process of creating statements about future realizations of demand.

During the FIFA soccer world cup 2010, zookeepers in a German zoo made international headlines because they were able to forecast the outcomes of all matches of the German team, including Germany's loss in the semifinals against Spain. How did they do this? The zoo had an octopus by the name of Paul. Before each match of the German national team, the zookeepers offered Paul food in two boxes that were colored with the flags of the opposing teams. Depending on which box Paul would go to first, the zookeepers made their forecast.

Does watching an octopus having lunch qualify as forecasting? We argue it does. Let's revisit our definition. Forecasting is the process of creating statements about outcomes of variables that are presently uncertain and will only be realized in the future:

- The zookeepers clearly had a process in place because they had marked the food boxes and had agreed on how to interpret Paul's behavior.

Forecasting The process of creating statements about outcomes of variables that presently are uncertain and will only be realized in the future.

Demand forecasting The process of creating statements about future realizations of demand.

- The outcomes of the matches were uncertain at the time of Paul's food choice.

- The outcomes of the matches were realized in the future.

So, all considered, watching Paul pick the box with a Spanish flag on it and declaring that Spain would win against Germany squarely qualifies as forecasting.

We find it helpful to formalize the process of demand forecasting a little further. Let y_t be the demand in period t, where a period can be a day, a week, or a month, or any other unit of time. We want to forecast the demand in the next period and potentially beyond. So we want to say something about y_{t+1} before being able to observe it. It is common to use a "^" symbol as a sign that a value for a variable is a forecast, as opposed to being its true realized value. So, y_{t+1} is the demand for period $t + 1$, while $\hat{y}_{t+1}$ is the forecasted value (pronounced y $t + 1$ hat) for period $t + 1$ before y_{t+1} itself is known.

So, when we forecast, we want to say something about $\hat{y}_{t+1}$, while we are still at time t or before. By definition, at time t, we only have data about demand and about any other variable from period t and before. Consider Figure 15.2, which provides a high-level framework for the forecasting process. The output of the process, as already mentioned, is the demand forecast for period $t + 1$, $\hat{y}_{t+1}$.

The inputs to this process can be broken up into three groups: old realizations of demand, old realizations of other variables, and subjective opinions about the future. Consider old realizations of demand first. When we forecast demand for period $t + 1$, we know the demand for previous periods. We define **time series analysis** as the process of analyzing the old (demand) data $y_1 \ldots y_t$. A **time series–based forecast** is a forecast that is obtained based on nothing but old demand data. We can think of time series–based forecasting as a form of **extrapolation**; that is, of estimating a value beyond the range of the original observations assuming that some patterns in the data observed so far will also prevail in the future. Here are some examples for time series–based forecasting:

- *Soccer:* If you forecast a team's victory on nothing but the outcomes of past matches ("Brazil will win because they have won the last 10 matches"), you are extrapolating a time series.

- *Flu season:* The data in Figure 15.1 show that there are many more flu-related patients in January than in July. If you forecast the number of January 2015 patients by taking the average of the number of patients for January 2009, 2010, 2011, 2012, 2013, and 2014, you are creating a time series–based forecast.

- *Stock market:* Many people (not including the authors) believe that they can forecast the stock market's movement by looking for patterns in old stock market data, such as trends, cycles, and other formations. Whether they are foolish to believe so or not

Time series analysis Analysis of old demand data.

Time series–based forecast An approach to forecasting that uses nothing but old demand data.

Extrapolation Estimation of values beyond the range of the original observations by assuming that some patterns in the values present within the range will also prevail outside the range.

Figure 15.2

Forecasting framework

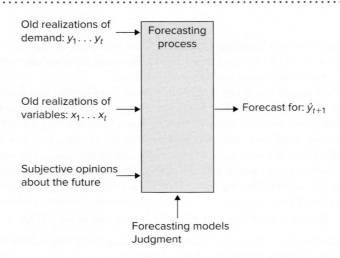

Old realizations of demand: $y_1 \ldots y_t$

Old realizations of variables: $x_1 \ldots x_t$

Subjective opinions about the future

Forecasting process

Forecast for: $\hat{y}_{t+1}$

Forecasting models
Judgment

is worth a discussion at another time. What matters now is that this is a form of time series analysis.

- *Weather:* When you predict that August is a bad month to come to Philadelphia, because temperatures are likely to be in the 100s, you most likely will do so based on looking at previous years of temperature data; again, a case of time series–based forecasting.

In addition to just looking at the past realizations of the variable we try to forecast (old y_t data in our case), we might look at other data to forecast $\hat{y}_{t+1}$. We define **regression analysis** as the statistical process of estimating the relationship of one variable with multiple variables that influence this one variable. In regression analysis, we call the one variable that we try to understand the **dependent variable** (also called the *outcome variable*) and the other variables influencing the dependent variable the **independent variables**. So, in the context of forecasting, we can look at many other independent variables influencing our forecast for the dependent variable. Again, looking at examples helps:

- *Soccer:* Chances are that when you predict the outcome of your favorite team's next match, you would not just look at how often the team has won recently, you would also look at who the opponent is and how they have recently been scoring. You might also factor in that the top player is injured or that the next game is a home game. In other words, you are looking at many other variables. And, yes, looking at the movements of an octopus having lunch also corresponds to considering an additional variable.

- *Flu season:* When forecasting the number of flu patients, it is informative to not just look at the number of patients in past months, but to also consider other data. These include the amount of vaccination and flu data from other countries. Researchers forecasting flu outbreaks have also analyzed to what extent the number of times "flu" is entered into Google is a good predictor of how many patients will seek medical help for flu-related symptoms (the evidence for the predictive power in this case is mixed).

- *Stock market:* In addition to the stock market values from the past, economists consider variables such as growth rates, recent monetary policy decisions, earnings announcements, and many more.

- *Weather:* You might think that August is hot in Philadelphia, but when you see the wind change and a cold front moving in, you might want to update your forecast.

Determining the effects of playing a home game on winning, of Google search terms on flu patients, of unemployment data on stock market prices, or of cold fronts on future temperatures—all of this is the domain of regression analysis.

An implicit risk in forecasting based on old data, be it in the form of time series–based forecasting or regression analysis, is that these techniques assume that the future will behave according to the past. In contrast, an informed expert might have a "gut feel" that something will happen that cannot be explained by past data. Whether or not we should trust such experts is a topic for discussion further on in this chapter. For now, what matters is that such subjective opinions can also be considered when determining a forecast. So, the third set of variables determining a forecast in Figure 15.2 is subjective.

In the remainder of this chapter, we mostly focus on time series–based forecasts. In the last section, we discuss how to deal with subjective opinions. However, this chapter does not cover regression analysis. Not that we don't feel regression analysis is important, we simply think it deserves the proper treatment in a statistics book, as opposed to being covered in passing in an operations book.

The three different types of input variables discussed in conjunction with Figure 15.2 also point to different methods and organizational processes of generating forecasts. We find it helpful to distinguish between:

- **Automated forecasting**: When weather.com makes a prediction for the temperature in Manhattan tomorrow at 9 a.m., it cannot convene an expert panel of meteorologists. Most forecasts in business need to be made millions of times, so they have to be done

Regression analysis A statistical process of estimating the relationship of one variable with multiple variables that influence this one variable.

Dependent variable The variable that we try to explain in a regression analysis.

Independent variables The variables influencing the dependent variable.

Automated forecasting Forecasts that are created by computers, typically with no human intervention.

> ## CONNECTIONS: Predicting the Future?
>
> Is it possible to correctly predict the future? This has been the subject of centuries of debate by scientists and philosophers. Though opinions are divided on this question, we found that the following quotes nicely summarize some of the main challenges related to forecasting.
>
> "Those who have knowledge, don't predict. Those who predict, don't have knowledge." (Lao Tzu, 6th-century B.C. Chinese poet)
>
> "The best qualification of a prophet is to have a good memory." (Marquis of Halifax)
>
> "Prediction is very difficult, especially if it's about the future." (Niels Bohr, Nobel laureate in Physics)
>
> "An unsophisticated forecaster uses statistics as a drunken man uses lampposts—for support rather than for illumination." (Andrew Lang)
>
> "An economist is an expert who will know tomorrow why the things he predicted yesterday didn't happen today." (Evan Esar)
>
> *Source:* http://www1.secam.ex.ac.uk/famous-forecasting-quotes.dhtml

cheaply, which typically means without human involvement. How many cheeseburgers will customers order in an hour at a particular McDonald's? How many rental cars will be needed on a particular day at a particular airport? Forecasts of these types are created by computers, typically with no human intervention. You might have heard buzzwords such as machine learning and Big Data; both of these stand for sophisticated versions of regression analysis in which computers find out what variables best help make a good prediction.

- **Expert panel forecasting**: When McDonald's needs to make a forecast for corporate sales, however, there is so much at stake that the costs of generating the forecast simply matter less. So, for forecasts where there is a lot at stake, automated forecasting is typically augmented by expert panels. On such panels, a group of managers share their subjective opinions and try to reach a consensus about a demand forecast.

After discussing how to generate a forecast, consider the question of what to do with the forecast after it has been generated. We find it helpful to distinguish between three types of forecasting applications in business. These three types can be categorized based on the time horizons that they consider:

- **Short-term forecasts** are used to support decisions that are made for short time periods ranging from the daily level to the monthly level. In extreme cases, forecasts might even be made at the hourly level. These forecasts are used to help decisions related to staffing (restaurants have more servers at lunch than in the afternoon) and short-term pricing. They can also be used to predict waiting times and help with scheduling decisions. In the flu example, this corresponds to making a forecast for tomorrow or the next week so that an appropriate number of nurses can be scheduled.

- **Mid-term forecasts** are forecasts that are made from the monthly level to the yearly level. They drive capacity-related decisions (recruiting, acquisition of machinery), but also are used for financial planning. In the flu example, this corresponds to making a forecast for the entire flu season so that the right number of nurses can be recruited or the right number of flu vaccines/medications can be produced.

- **Long-term forecasts** are forecasts that are made over multiple years. These forecasts help with strategic decisions such as entering new markets, launching new products or services, expanding capacity by investing in new facilities, or closing facilities. In the flu example, we might think of the decision of drug store giant CVS to launch its MinuteClinic (a walk-in medical service) as one that was made after forecasting many years of data.

Expert panel forecasting Forecasts generated using the subjective opinions of management.

Short-term forecasts Forecasts used to support tactical decision making with typical time ranges from hours to weeks.

Mid-term forecasts Forecasts used to support capacity planning and financial accounting with typical time ranges from weeks to a year.

Long-term forecasts Forecasts used to support strategic decisions with typical time ranges of multiple years.

We find this distinction between the three horizons helpful, though we admit it is not always possible to draw clear lines between these three categories. One reason this distinction is nevertheless useful relates to the forecasting methodology. Short-term forecasts tend to be automated forecasts, relying primarily on extrapolation of old data and regression analysis. Long-term forecasts, in contrast, tend to be based on a combination of old realizations of demand data, independent variables, and expert opinions. They thus are typically created by expert panels.

15.2 Evaluating the Quality of a Forecast

Imagine you work for an emergency department that wants to get ready for the flu season. You are asked to forecast the number of flu cases showing up to the emergency department over the course of the next four weeks. Before you start looking at any old data, you decide to seek advice from some experts, so you go to four doctors, who give you their forecasts for the next four weeks (Table 15.1).

Which forecast should you use? Which forecast is the best one? Clearly, this cannot be answered BEFORE we have seen the true demand; that is, the number of flu-related patients who actually show up to the ED over these four weeks. But, as we will now show, determining the best forecast is even difficult AFTER we have seen the true demand.

Table 15.2 repeats the four forecasts of our docs, but it also shows the true number of patients who came to the ED. To determine which forecast is best, we must first define what we mean by best. As is apparent from the preceding text, none of the four forecasts is right every single time, and so all of them are wrong to some extent. We thus have to define the extent to which a forecast is wrong. This can be done in multiple ways.

We define the **forecast error** for period t as the difference between the forecast for period t and the actual value for period t:

$$\text{Forecast error in } t = \text{Forecast for } t - \text{Actual value for } t$$

Forecast error The difference between a forecasted value and the realized value.

....

TABLE 15.1 Four Forecasts for the Number of Flu-Related Patients Coming to the ED in the Next Four Weeks

	Doc 1	Doc 2	Doc 3	Doc 4
Week 1	70	50	29	43
Week 2	55	32	52	44
Week 3	40	48	62	54
Week 4	80	60	47	49

....

TABLE 15.2 Four Forecasts for the Number of Flu-Related Patients Coming to the ED in the Next Four Weeks and the True Demand Data

	Doc 1	Doc 2	Doc 3	Doc 4	True Demand
Week 1	70	50	29	43	38
Week 2	55	32	52	44	49
Week 3	40	48	62	54	59
Week 2	80	60	47	49	44

....

TABLE 15.3   Comparison of Doctor 1 and Doctor 2

	Forecast Doc 1	Forecast Doc 2	True Demand	FE Doc 1	FE Doc 2
Week 1	70	50	38	32	12
Week 2	55	32	49	6	−17
Week 3	40	48	59	−19	−11
Week 4	80	60	44	36	16
Average	61.25	47.5	47.5	13.75	0

For doctor 1, we compute the forecast errors, oftentimes abbreviated FE, for the four periods as

Forecast error in week 1 = Forecast for week 1 − Actual value for week 1 = 70 − 38 = 32

Forecast error in week 2 = Forecast for week 2 − Actual value for week 2 = 55 − 49 = 6

Forecast error in week 3 = Forecast for week 3 − Actual value for week 3 = 40 − 59 = −19

Forecast error in week 4 = Forecast for week 4 − Actual value for week 4 = 80 − 44 = 36

So, the forecast errors for doctor 1 are $FE_1 = 32$, $FE_2 = 16$, $FE_3 = -19$, and $FE_4 = 36$. But how do we interpret these forecast errors? Consider the information displayed by Table 15.3. The table shows the forecast errors for doctor 1 and for doctor 2 over the four weeks, along with their initial forecasts and the true number of patients who showed up. Which of the two doctors does a better job at forecasting?

A first way to measure the quality of a forecast is to see if it is right, on average. We define a forecast as an **unbiased forecast** if the forecast is, on average, correct. This is equivalent to having the average forecast error be zero. Doctor 2 is sometimes forecasting on the high side, sometimes on the low side, but, on average, she is right. So, her forecast is unbiased. This is consistent with the average of her forecast errors being equal to zero. Doctor 1, in contrast, seems to be mostly forecasting on the high side. His average forecast error is 13.75. We don't know why: Maybe the doctor feels stressed out and overworked and so always believes that there are many patients out there. But always forecasting too much is not a good thing. We define a forecast that is wrong, on average, as a **biased forecast**.

Next, compare doctor 2 with doctor 3. As we can see in Table 15.4, both of them are giving us an unbiased forecast. They are both right, on average. Does this mean that they are equally good at forecasting?

Though both of the doctors have a forecast that is correct, on average, most of us would agree that doctor 3 is doing a better job forecasting. This points to an important principle of forecasting. In forecasting, it is not the average alone that determines the quality of a forecast. Yes, being wrong, on average, is a bad thing. But if you forecast too much for today and too

Unbiased forecast A forecast that is correct on average, thus an average forecast error equal to zero.

Biased forecast A forecast that is wrong on average, thus an average forecast error different from zero.

TABLE 15.4   Comparison of Doctor 2 and Doctor 3

	Forecast Doc 2	Forecast Doc 3	True Demand	FE Doc 2	FE Doc 3
Week 1	50	29	38	12	−9
Week 2	32	52	49	−17	3
Week 3	48	62	59	−11	3
Week 4	60	47	44	16	3
Average	47.5	47.5	47.5	0	0

little for tomorrow, that does not make you a good forecaster. Imagine the weather forecaster who announces a snowstorm with freezing temperatures today and a heat wave tomorrow, when in reality both days are mild. Being right, on average, can still create a bad forecast.

To capture this intuition, we need to create another measure of forecast quality that goes beyond simply averaging out the forecast errors. A commonly used metric is the **mean squared error (MSE)**, which simply takes the average of the squared forecast errors:

$$\text{MSE} = \frac{\sum_{t=1}^{N} \text{FE}_t^2}{N}$$

Instead of adding up the forecast errors, FE, and then averaging them, the idea behind the mean squared errors is to first square the errors and then average them. Why would one want to do this? Because by squaring the numbers, a negative forecast error is turned into a positive number. And, thus, a negative forecast error and a positive forecast error combined will no longer cancel each other out. This is shown in Table 15.5. Observe that doctor 2 has a much higher mean squared error than doctor 3, confirming our intuition that doctor 3 does a better job at forecasting.

Now, you might say that squaring the forecast errors is a really complicated way of turning a negative number into a positive number. Why would one not simply take the absolute values of the forecast errors and average those out. You are right, you can do this. We define the **mean absolute error (MAE)** as the average of the absolute values of the forecast errors. Often, this is also referred to as the mean absolute deviation (MAD). This is shown in the last two columns of Table 15.5.

$$\text{MAE} = \frac{\sum_{t=1}^{N} \left| \text{FE}_t \right|}{N}$$

This new measure also confirms our intuition. The forecasts of doctor 3 are better than the forecasts of doctor 2, no matter if we look at the MSE or the MAE.

One other way in which we can aggregate forecast errors is called the mean absolute percentage error (MAPE). This measure does not look at the forecast errors in absolute terms, but in relative terms. This is achieved by dividing the forecast errors by the actual demand y_t. So we get

$$\text{MAPE} = \frac{\sum_{t=1}^{N} \left| \frac{\text{FE}_t}{y_t} \right|}{N}$$

So, what constitutes a good forecast? The answer to this question is more complicated than we would like. In general, we like the forecast to have the following properties:

- The forecast should be unbiased; that is, be correct on average.
- The forecast should come close to the real outcomes as measured by the mean squared error (MSE) or the mean absolute error (MAE).

Mean squared error (MSE) A measure evaluating the quality of a forecast by looking at the average squared forecast error.

Mean absolute error (MAE) A measure evaluating the quality of a forecast by looking at the average absolute value of the forecast error.

TABLE 15.5 Comparison of Doctor 2 and Doctor 3

	Forecast Doc 2	Forecast Doc 3	True Demand	FE Doc 2	FE Doc 3	FE_t^2 Doc 2	FE_t^2 Doc 3	$|FE_t|$ Doc 2	$|FE_t|$ Doc 3
Week 1	50	29	38	12	−9	144	81	12	9
Week 2	32	52	49	−17	3	289	9	17	3
Week 3	48	62	59	−11	3	121	9	11	3
Week 4	60	47	44	16	3	256	9	16	3
Average	47.5	47.5	47.5	0	0	202.5	27	14	4.5

TABLE 15.6　Comparison of Doctor 3 and Doctor 4

	Forecast Doc 3	Forecast Doc 4	True Demand	FE Doc 3	FE Doc 4	FE_t^2 Doc 3	FE_t^2 Doc 4	$|FE_t|$ Doc 3	$|FE_t|$ Doc 4
Week 1	29	43	38	−9	5	81	25	9	5
Week 2	52	44	49	3	−5	9	25	3	5
Week 3	62	54	59	3	−5	9	25	3	5
Week 4	47	49	44	3	5	9	25	3	5
Average	47.5	47.5	47.5	0	0	27	25	4.5	5

Sometimes, these two properties are in conflict with each other. We might prefer a forecast with a small bias if that comes with a dramatically lower value of MSE or MAE. Note further that MSE and MAE do not always agree on which forecast is better. Consider the data displayed by Table 15.6. Note that doctor 4 has the lower mean squared error while doctor 3 has the lower mean absolute error.

Which forecast is better? That really depends on what you are looking for. When evaluating the mean squared errors, we notice that this score can be heavily influenced by one single mistake. Take the case of doctor 3. The reason why doctor 3 did so poorly on the MSE score is that for week 1, her forecast error was −9. Now, squaring (−9) leads to a big number (81, to be exact), which is so large that the next three very good forecasts are not compensating for this mistake. So, the MSE value penalizes a forecaster for one large mistake, while the MAE views each deviation as equally bad.

Which measure of forecast quality you use is really up to you. The key, however, is that you use a metric and assess the quality of old forecasts. This first and foremost requires that you keep data from your old forecasts. Many companies have a hard time doing so, because those who came up with the forecasts don't want to be reminded how wrong they were. Yet, keeping old forecasting data is extremely informative in detecting systematic deviations between forecasts and reality. So, keeping old forecasts and then analyzing these data, no matter which forecast quality measure you use, already gets you 90 percent of the way.

© Onoky/SuperStock/RF

Check Your Understanding 15.1

Question: Two students predict the attendance for their seminar. Joe predicts the attendance to be 12 for day 1, 15 for day 2, 14 for day 3, and 11 for day 4. Mary predicts 14, 11, 12, and 16 for the four respective days. The actual attendance turns out to be 13, 12, 11, and 14. Who has the bigger forecast bias? What are the MSE and the MAE for Joe and Mary?

Answer: The calculations in Table 15.7 show that Joe has an average forecast error of 0.5, while Mary has one of 0.75. So, both of their forecasts are biased. Joe has an MSE of 7 and an MAE of 2.5. Mary has an MSE of 1.75 and an MAE of 1.25.

TABLE 15.7

Day	Joe	Mary	Actual	Joe: FE	Joe: FE_t^2	Joe: $|FE_t|$	Mary: FE	Mary: FE_t^2	Mary: $|FE_t|$
1	12	14	13	−1	1	1	1	1	1
2	15	11	12	3	9	3	−1	1	1
3	14	12	11	3	9	3	1	1	1
4	11	16	14	−3	9	3	2	4	2
			Average	0.5	7	2.5	0.75	1.75	1.25

15.3 Eliminating Noise from Old Data

Now that we know how to evaluate the quality of a forecaster by comparing some old forecasts with the true outcomes of the forecasted variables, we can turn to the question of how to create a forecast. As mentioned earlier, we restrict our discussion in this chapter to time series–based forecasting. In other words, we will try to obtain a forecast, $\hat{y}_{t+1}$, by looking at old data $y_1 \ldots y_t$. We now introduce three simple methods that accomplish this: the naïve forecasting model, moving averages, and exponential smoothing. We illustrate all three methods using the flu-related data shown in Figure 15.3. The figure shows the number of flu-related patients in the first 10 weeks for the year 2014 for the average U.S. hospital. Our goal is, using this information, to forecast the number of cases in week 11.

15.3.1 Naïve Model

Because our focus is on time series–based forecasting, we look at old data (number of flu cases from previous weeks) to predict new data (number of flu cases for next week). So, the simplest way of forecasting the demand for the next period is to assume that it is the same as in the last period. More formally, we define

$$\hat{y}_{t+1} = y_t$$

Applied to our flu example, this implies that we predict demand for week 11 to be 404 because

$$\hat{y}_{11} = y_{10} = 404$$

We call this method of creating a forecast for the next period by just using the last realized value the **naïve forecasting method**, as shown in Table 15.8. This method is extremely simple to use. Its main downside is that it ignores all other old data. As a result, the forecast is subject to a lot of **statistical noise**. We define the statistical noise in the demand for a process as the amount of demand that is purely a result of randomness (good or bad luck) and that could not have been forecasted even with the best forecasting methods.

Naïve forecasting method A forecasting method that predicts that the next value will be like the last realized value.

Statistical noise Variables influencing the outcomes of a process in unpredictable ways.

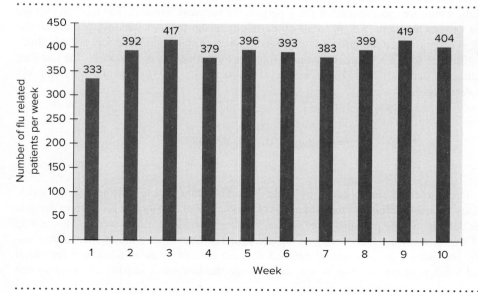

Figure 15.3
Number of flu-related patients in the first 10 weeks of 2014

....

TABLE 15.8   The Naïve Forecasting Method

Week	Patients per Week	Forecast for Next Week
1	333	333
2	392	392
3	417	417
4	379	379
5	396	396
6	393	393
7	383	383
8	399	399
9	419	419
10	404	404

....

Check Your Understanding 15.2

Question: A pizza chain has had sales for take-out food over the last four evenings—Monday, Tuesday, Wednesday, and Thursday—of 29, 25, 35, and 30 pizzas, respectively. What would be their forecast for Friday using a naïve forecasting approach?

Answer: The naïve forecast would be 30, because this corresponds to the last observed demand.

....

15.3.2 Moving Averages

The best way to take care of statistical noise in data is by taking averages. Maybe last week was special. So, how about we look at the average of the last three weeks? Or the last six weeks? We define the **moving average forecast** as the forecast that is based on the average of the last T periods, where we call the time of the T periods the **forecast window.** The moving average forecast assigns the same weight to all observations in the forecast window. Moreover, the moving average forecast assigns zero weight to all observations outside the forecast window.

Consider the four-week moving average forecast for period 11. At period 11, the last four realizations of demand are 404 (this week), 419 (last week), 399 (two weeks ago), and 383 (three weeks ago). So we get

$$\hat{y}_{t+1} = \text{Average}(y_t, y_{t-1}, y_{t-2}, y_{t-3})$$
$$= \text{Average}(404, 419, 399, 383)$$
$$= 401.25$$

Consider the calculations shown in Table 15.9. The table shows, starting with period 5, how many patients we forecast for the next week. In each week, we look at the current demand and the demand for the previous three weeks, creating a window of four weeks. This is why we call this forecast the four-week moving average. The four-week window then moves forward by one week. The new period demand data are entered in the window and the oldest demand window drops out. Just as we can compute the four-week moving average, we can

Moving average forecasting method A forecasting method that predicts that the next value will be the average of the last realized values.

TABLE 15.9   The Moving Average Forecasting Method

Week	Patients per Hospital	1 Week Ago	2 Weeks Ago	3 Weeks Ago	Forecast for Next Week
1	333				
2	392	333			
3	417	392	333		
4	379	417	392	333	380.25
5	396	379	417	392	396
6	393	396	379	417	396.25
7	383	393	396	379	387.75
8	399	383	393	396	392.75
9	419	399	383	393	398.5
10	404	419	399	383	401.25

Check Your Understanding 15.3

Question: A pizza chain has had sales for take-out food over the last four evenings—Monday, Tuesday, Wednesday, and Thursday—of 29, 25, 35, and 30 pizzas, respectively. What would be their forecast for Friday using a three-day moving average forecasting approach?

Answer: With a three-day moving average, we would forecast the demand for Friday as the average of the demand of Tuesday, Wednesday, and Thursday. That would be

$$\text{Forecast for Friday} = \text{Average}(25, 35, 30) = 30$$

compute the two-week, three-week, five-week, six-week, and so on, moving averages. Note that the one-week moving average forecast corresponds to the naïve forecast, because it would just take the average over one (the last) week.

By taking the moving averages, we reduce the effect of the statistical noise. The bigger the window over which we compute the moving averages, the stronger the effect of noise reduction. This begs the question of why not take the average over a large—a really large—window. Can we take a 30-week moving average? The answer to this question is a simple YES, we can. But do we want to?

Recall from our definition of the moving average forecasting method that each week in the forecasting window has an equal weight assigned to it. So, the question this boils down to is: Do we really believe that the demand from 30 weeks ago has as much information in it about the next week as the demand from last week? If the answer to this question is YES, we indeed should use the 30-week moving average. More likely, however, you might argue that the older a demand (the longer ago it happened), the less of an impact it should have on the forecast for the next week. This is exactly the intuition behind our next forecasting method.

15.3.3 Exponential Smoothing Method

The moving average forecasting method implicitly assigns an equal weight to each time period in the window. In contrast, every period outside the window is entirely ignored. For example, when we took the four-week moving average, the current (period t), last ($t-1$), last but one

($t-2$), and last but two ($t-3$) periods all have the same influence on our forecast. In contrast, all periods prior to this have absolutely no influence. Put differently, an old demand value is either in the forecast window or it is out.

The idea of **exponential smoothing** is to put more weight on recent data and less weight on older data. We simply take a weighted average between the current demand and the old demand forecast.

The method works as follows:

$$\begin{array}{c}\text{Next period}\\\text{demand forecast}\end{array} = \left[\alpha \times \begin{array}{c}\text{Current}\\\text{demand}\end{array}\right] + \left[\left(1-\alpha\right) \times \begin{array}{c}\text{Last period}\\\text{demand forecast}\end{array}\right]$$

Or, put more formally:

$$\hat{y}_{t+1} = (\alpha \times y_t) + (1-\alpha) \times \hat{y}_t$$

where α is called the **smoothing parameter**, which is a number between zero and one. If α is small (say 0.1), we put little weight on the current demand and thus a lot of weight on old data. In contrast, if α is large (say 0.9), we put a lot of weight on the current demand and thus only a little weight on the old demand. In the extreme case of $\alpha = 1$, we are back to the naïve forecast.

Consider how we would forecast the number of flu cases for week 11. Let's assume a smoothing parameter of $\alpha = 0.1$ and let's assume that the forecast for week 10 was 370. We can compute the new forecast for week 11 as

$$\hat{y}_{t+1} = (\alpha \times y_t) + (1-\alpha) \times \hat{y}_t$$
$$\hat{y}_{t+1} = (0.1 \times 404) + [(1 - 0.1) \times 370]$$
$$= 373.4$$

Exponential smoothing forecasting method A forecasting method that predicts that the next value will be a weighted average between the last realized value and the old forecast.

Smoothing parameter The parameter that determines the weight new realized data have in creating the next forecast with exponential smoothing.

Note that this forecast for week 11 is much lower than what we had computed with the naïve forecasting method and the four-week moving average. The reason for this is simply that with $\alpha = 0.1$, we put a lot of weight on the old data. And, as you could see in Figure 15.3, the first-week demand was only 333 patients. This one single period has a very strong influence if we have such a small smoothing parameter. Table 15.10 (left) shows the application of the exponential smoothing for $\alpha = 0.1$. Table 15.10 (right) shows the same calculations, this time with a smoothing parameter of $\alpha = 0.4$.

TABLE 15.10   The Exponential Smoothing Method with $\alpha = 0.1$ (left) and $\alpha = 0.4$ (right)

	$\alpha = 0.1$				$\alpha = 0.4$		
Week	Patients per Week	Old Forecast	New Forecast	Week	Patients per Week	Old Forecast	New Forecast
1	333	333	333	1	333	333	333
2	392	333	338.9	2	392	333	356.6
3	417	338.9	346.71	3	417	356.6	380.76
4	379	346.71	349.939	4	379	380.76	380.056
5	396	349.939	354.545	5	396	380.056	386.434
6	393	354.545	358.391	6	393	386.434	389.060
7	383	358.391	360.852	7	383	389.060	386.636
8	399	360.852	364.666	8	399	386.636	391.582
9	419	364.666	370.100	9	419	391.582	402.549
10	404	370.100	373.490	10	404	402.549	403.129

In this case, as we forecast demand for week 11, we have an old forecast of 402.55 and a realized demand for week 10 of 404. The forecast for week 11 is thus computed as

$$\hat{y}_{t+1} = (\alpha \times y_t) + (1 - \alpha) \times \hat{y}_t$$
$$\hat{y}_{t+1} = (0.4 \times 404) + [(1 - 0.4) \times 402.549]$$
$$= 403.129$$

There exists no general theory for finding the optimal smoothing parameter, but we encourage you to consider the following observations when choosing α:

- *Fit with historical data:* In the previous section, we explained how to evaluate the quality of a forecast and/or a forecaster. You can think of each possible value of α as its own set of forecasts. We can then use historical data and compare the mean squared errors or the mean absolute errors for different values of α.

- *Importance of new information:* Note that the higher smoothing parameter puts a much larger weight on the more recent data. In a fast-changing world, this favors higher values of α, corresponding to a range of $0.2 < \alpha < 0.4$. If one wants to be more conservative and thus assign a larger weight to old data, one ought to choose smaller values of α, such that $0.05 < \alpha < 0.2$.

Figure 15.4 shows the effect of using two different smoothing parameters. Observe that the line for the lower value of α (with $\alpha = 0.1$) is much "smoother"; that is, it does not change as much from one period to the next as the line with $\alpha = 0.4$.

Another practical question is how to get started with the exponential smoothing method. After all, the method assumes that you have had an exponentially smoothed forecast in the last period. To come up with the first (initial forecast), we suggest you use the naïve forecasting method; that is, simply use the last available demand data. Note that the longer ago the initial period is, the lower the importance of the initial forecast. Especially for larger values of α, the old data matter less and less as time progresses.

Exhibit 15.1 summarizes the previously discussed approach of exponential smoothing.

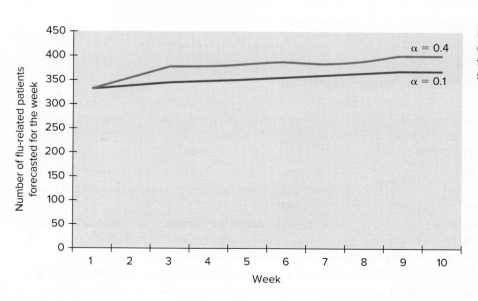

Figure 15.4

Comparison of two exponential smoothing forecasts, using different values of the smoothing parameter α

EXHIBIT 15.1

Summary of Forecasting with the Exponential Smoothing Method

Step 1: Set $t = 1$ (or to whatever first period you want to use).

Step 2: Obtain a forecast for the first period $\hat{y}_t$; use the naïve forecasting method for this.

Step 3: Compute the forecast for the next period as $\hat{y}_{t+1} = (\alpha \times y_t) + (1 - \alpha) \times \hat{y}_t$

Step 4: Increase t to $t + 1$.

Step 5: Go back to step 3 until you have reached the current period.

Check Your Understanding 15.4

Question: A pizza chain has had sales for take-out food over the last four evenings—Monday, Tuesday, Wednesday, and Thursday—of 29, 25, 35, and 30 pizzas, respectively. What would be their forecast for Friday using an exponential smoothing forecasting approach? Use $\alpha = 0.2$ and a forecast for Monday of 28.

Answer: With the exponential smoothing method, we cannot just forecast for Friday. Instead, we have to start at the beginning and first forecast for Tuesday. We can then, day by day, update our forecast for the next day.

Day	Demand (Actual)	Forecast for Tommorow ($\alpha = 0.2$)
		28
Monday	29	28.2
Tuesday	25	27.56
Wednesday	35	29.048
Thursday	30	29.2384

So the forecast for Friday is 29.2384 pizzas.

15.3.4 Comparison of Methods

So far, we have introduced three methods of forecasting based on time series analysis: the naïve method, moving averages, and exponential smoothing. Before we turn to more sophisticated methods, let's pause for a moment and reflect upon the strengths and weaknesses of these approaches:

- The naïve method is very vulnerable to noise. One period of exceptionally high (or low) demand data will likely make the next period forecast highly incorrect. We see no reason to use this method in practice.

- Moving averages take care of statistical noise by averaging it out. One has to choose the length of the window over which the average is taken. All periods in the forecast window are weighted equally when computing the new forecast.

- Exponential smoothing puts more weight on the recent demand data. This makes it more responsive to changes in demand. Note that to compute the new forecast, all data needed are the latest demand data and the last forecast. However, in a world of spreadsheets, we argue that this computational simplicity should not be seen as too big of an advantage.

- All three methods are data-driven. As simple (and maybe even simplistic, see the previous point) as they might be, they help establish a managerial discipline of collecting data, and they also support a statistical analysis of old forecast errors.

All three methods fail to detect systemic variation in the data. Patterns such as long-term trends (for example, the demand rate going up over time) or seasonal variation (more patients suffering from the flu in January than in June) are not captured in any of these methods. More advanced methods are needed, as we will explore in the next two sections.

15.4 Time Series Analysis—Trends

© Jacek Lasa/Alamy/RF

Given the way they are constructed, all of the three previously introduced forecasting methods (naïve method, moving averages, and exponential smoothing) are backward looking. The next period's demand is forecasted by taking old demand realizations and then somehow finding a "compromise" between these values. As a result, none of these methods is able to create a forecast that is higher than any of the previously realized demand values or that is lower than any of the previously realized demand values.

Many demand rates in practice, however, are characterized by long-term trends. In these cases, it oftentimes is entirely plausible to expect the next period demand to exceed (or fall short of) any realization of past demand. Consider the following three examples captured in Figure 15.5:

- The social network site Facebook had only a couple of million users in 2006. However, by 2013, the number of users had reached 1 billion.

- From 2006 to 2013, demand for motor vehicles in China was growing by over 10 percent each year, making each new year a record in sales.

- Trends don't only go up. Consider the circulation of newspapers in the UK. Year after year, the number has been shrinking,

Facebook users, vehicle demand in China, or newspapers—all three examples have in common that there seems to exist a long-term trend. We define a **trend** as a continuing increase or decrease in a variable that is consistent over a long period of time. When you have to forecast the number of Facebook users in 2010 for 2011, would you really want to take an average over the last three years? Or would it make more sense to extrapolate the trend going forward?

Trend A continuing increase or decrease in a variable that is consistent over a long period of time.

Figure 15.5

Examples of demand trajectories including a long-term trend (Sources: http://en.wikipedia.org/wiki/Facebook, http://www.shanghaijungle.com/news/China-Auto-Sales-Rise-9, http://blogs.spectator.co.uk/coffeehouse/2013/06/david-dinsmore-is-the-new-editor-of-the-sun)

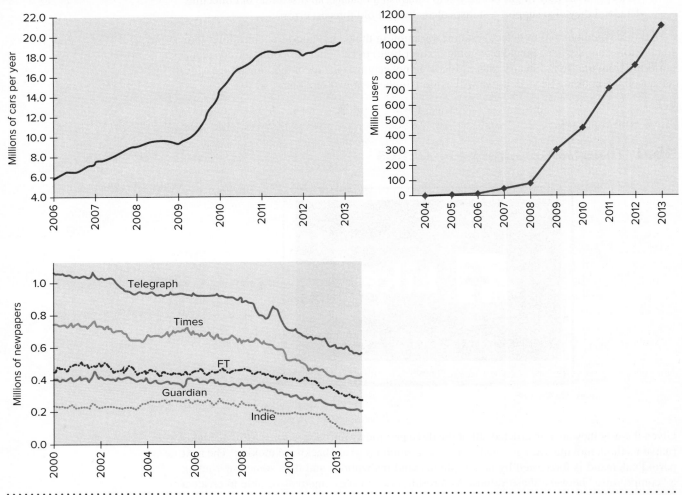

We now introduce a method that extends our previous forecasting methods to business settings characterized by a long-term trend. We should preface this extension with two remarks:

- Trends are statistically observed patterns in old data. The fact that a trend has been present for the last couple of years should be considered when making a new forecast. But trends are not a guarantee for the future. In the late 1990s, the number of AOL users (an Internet service and content provider) showed a similar pattern to what we saw with Facebook a couple of years later. But, then, in 2001, the increasing trend turned into a decreasing trend and the number of subscribers plummeted from over 25 million to less than 10 million.

- Considering the effects of a trend that occurred in the past still fits our framework of time series–based forecasting and extrapolating past data. The difference relative to the naïve forecast, the moving averages, and the exponential smoothing, however, is that we don't just look at the realized values of the past, but we also look at the trend that the data displayed in the past. So, we assume that it is not just the realized values that will be similar to the past, but that the underlying pattern will continue. Trend-based forecasts are often called **momentum-based forecasts**, to reflect the fact that there exists an underlying process that has some momentum and hence will continue into the future.

To create a momentum-based forecast, we have to disentangle the trend from the other variation in demand rate. Assuming we are able to do this, we can then forecast the demand rate for the next period, $\hat{y}_{t+1}$, including the trend, as follows:

Forecast for $t + 1$ considering trend = Forecast for $(t + 1)$ + Forecast for trend in $(t + 1)$

Thus, to forecast demand for $t + 1$ given a trend, we forecast demand without the trend for $t + 1$ and then add our forecast for the trend. How do we forecast for $t + 1$ and how do we forecast the trend for $t + 1$? Any of the previously introduced forecasting methods (naïve, moving averages, exponential smoothing) will do the job. Given the previously discussed advantages of the exponential smoothing method, we use it to forecast both the demand rate for $t + 1$ (without the trend) as well as to forecast the trend.

Because we are doing two exponential smoothing methods at the same time, the following method is often referred to as the **double exponential smoothing** method. Consider the forecasting without the trend first. We again have to assume a smoothing parameter, α, that will dictate how much weight our model puts on old data. And, again, we need to have an initial forecast for the first period. We assume that the smoothing parameter $\alpha = 0.2$ and that the forecast for the first period was 360.

In the same way, we have to determine the parameters for the trend forecasting. Let beta (β) be the smoothing parameter and assume $\beta = 0.4$. And let T_t be the forecast for the trend in period t. Let's assume that this forecast for the first week is $T_1 = 5$. We will comment on these assumptions toward the end of the section, but, for now, let's just get started.

We start with our old exponential smoothing equation:

Next period demand forecast = $(\alpha \times$ Current demand$)$ + $[(1 - \alpha) \times$ Last period demand forecast$]$

Given the presence of a trend, we modify this equation slightly. Our forecast for the current period (made in the last period) used to be the demand forecast. But with a trend, the forecast now really ought to be the forecast plus the forecast of the trend. Thus, we write:

$$\underset{\text{demand forecast}}{\text{Next period}} = \underbrace{(\alpha \times \text{Current demand}) + \left[(1-\alpha) \times \underset{\text{demand forecast}}{\text{Last period}}\right]}_{\text{Smoothed demand forecast}} + \underbrace{\underset{\text{for trend}}{\text{Forecast}}}_{\text{Added trend}}$$

And, to keep an up-to-date forecast of the trend, we forecast the trend using the exponential smoothing method:

Trend forecast = $(\beta \times$ Current trend$)$ + $[(1 - \beta) \times$ Old trend forecast$]$

The current realization of the trend is the difference between the old and the new demand forecasts. We can rewrite this to

Trend forecast = $[\beta \times$ (New demand forecast − Old demand forecast)$]$
+ $[(1 - \beta) \times$ Old trend forecast$]$

So, as we obtain new data for period t, we create a new forecast for period $t+1$ by:

- Exponentially smoothing the demand forecast and then forecasting the next period demand as the smoothed demand rate plus our forecast for the trend.

- Exponentially smoothing the trend forecast and then updating our trend forecast for the next period.

This is why we called this method the double exponential smoothing method.

Momentum-based forecasting
An approach to forecasting that assumes that the trend in the future will be similar to the trend in the past.

Double exponential smoothing A way of forecasting a demand process with a trend that estimates both the demand and the trend using exponential smoothing. The resulting forecast is the sum of these two estimates. This is a type of momentum-based forecasting.

More formally, define the following:

y_t: realized demand in period t

$\hat{y}_{t+1}$: forecasted demand for period $t+1$ obtained via exponential smoothing using smoothing parameter α

$\hat{T}_t$: forecasted trend for period $t+1$ obtained via exponential smoothing using smoothing parameter β

With this notation, we write the demand rate exponential smoothing as

$$\hat{y}_{t+1} = (\alpha \times y_t) + [(1-\alpha) \times \hat{y}_t] + \hat{T}_t$$

and the exponentially smoothed trend as

$$\hat{T}_{t+1} = [\beta \times (\hat{y}_{t+1} - \hat{y}_t)] + (1-\beta)\,\hat{T}_t$$

where $(\hat{y}_{t+1} - \hat{y}_t)$ can be thought of as our latest estimate of our trend.

Let's illustrate this method with some more flu data, specifically the data shown in Table 15.11. It is week 1 and we want to make a forecast for week 2. Recall that we assumed a smoothing parameter $\alpha = 0.2$, a forecast for the first period of 360, a trend smoothing parameter $\beta = 0.4$, and an initial trend forecast of $\hat{T} = 5$.

With this information, we can compute the smoothed demand forecast:

$$\begin{aligned}
\hat{y}_{t+1} &= (\alpha \times y_t) + [(1-\alpha) \times \hat{y}_t] + \hat{T}_t \\
&= (0.2 \times 377) + [(1-0.2) \times 360] + 5 \\
&= 368.4
\end{aligned}$$

and the exponentially smoothed trend as:

$$\begin{aligned}
\hat{T}_{t+1} &= [\beta \times (\hat{y}_{t+1} - \hat{y}_t)] + (1-\beta) \times \hat{T}_t \\
&= [(0.4 \times (368.4 - 360)] + [(1-0.4) \times 5] \\
&= 6.36
\end{aligned}$$

Table 15.12 shows all calculations for the next periods.

Figure 15.6 compares the realized value of the demand with the forecasted demand. Unlike the realized demand data, the forecasted data do not show the many ups and downs—instead, it is steadily increasing over time. This is a result of smoothing. The first smoothing reduces any ups and downs. The second smoothing makes sure that the trend is relatively steady, creating almost a constant increase from one period to the next.

Exhibit 15.2 summarizes the previously discussed approach dealing with trends in forecasting. A couple of comments are in order about the double exponential smoothing method:

- The double exponential smoothing method is an additive method. Every period, we add the forecasted (smoothed) trend to our demand forecast. Often, however, trends are

TABLE 15.11   Number of Flu Patients at the Beginning of the 2013 Flu Season

Week	Patients
1	377
2	402
3	409
4	413
5	428
6	409
7	446
8	458
9	462

TABLE 15.12   Trend Forecast with the Double Exponential Smoothing Method

Week	Patients	Forecast for Next Period ($\alpha = 0.2$)	Trend Forecast ($\beta = 0.4$)
		360.000	5.000
1	377	368.400	6.360
2	402	381.480	9.048
3	409	396.032	11.250
4	413	410.675	12.607
5	428	426.747	13.993
6	409	437.191	12.573
7	446	451.526	13.278
8	458	466.099	13.796
9	462	479.075	13.468

not additive, but multiplicative in nature. Facebook did not add 1 million users every year. Instead, it grew its users exponentially every year. In such cases of rapid growth, the double exponential smoothing method will underestimate the demand for the next period. One way of handling demand data with exponential growth is to not forecast demand y_t, but the logarithm of demand $\log(y_t)$. If demand grows exponentially, the logarithm of demand grows linearly.

- As with the simple exponential smoothing method, we need to pick a value for the smoothing parameter. The only difference, this time, is that we have to pick values for two smoothing parameters. The smoothing parameters need to be numbers between zero and one. Larger values put more weight on recent observations. Again, looking at old data and seeing which values of α and β fit the data best is a good starting point.

- There exist other, more mathematically sophisticated methods of estimating trends, including the previously mentioned regression analysis. However, we find that this increased sophistication often comes at the expense of transparency. The more math

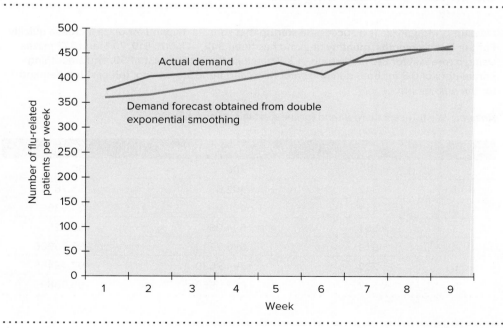

Figure 15.6

Trend forecast with the double exponential smoothing method

EXHIBIT 15.2

Summary of Forecasting Adjusting for Trends: The Double Exponential Smoothing Method

Step 1: Set $t = 1$ (or to whatever first period you want to use).

Step 2: Obtain a forecast for the first period $\hat{y}_t$ and a forecast for the first trend $\hat{T}_t$. Use the naïve forecast in the first period.

Step 3: Compute the smoothed forecast for the next period as

$$\hat{y}_{t+1} = (\alpha \times y_t) + [(1 - \alpha) \times \hat{y}_t] + \hat{T}_t$$

Step 4: Compute the smoothed forecast for the trend as

$$\hat{T}_{t+1} = [\beta \times (\hat{y}_{t+1} - \hat{y}_t)] + (1 - \beta) \times \hat{T}_t$$

Step 5: Increase t to $t + 1$.

Step 6: Go back to step 3 until you have reached the current period.

we use, the harder it becomes to know what really goes on "under the hood" of a forecasting method. In our view, the double exponential smoothing method is a good compromise between transparency and ease of use on the one side and mathematical sophistication on the other side.

- There exist no big shortcomings of the double exponential smoothing method as long as the data follow a long-term trend with some variation around this trend. In fact, the method also is perfectly applicable in the case of no trend. However, to the extent that there exists some form of seasonality pattern, the method does not work well, especially if low values of β are chosen. In such cases, it is much better to either pick a very high value of β, or, better still, use the method described in the next section.

© BananaStock/PunchStock/RF

Check Your Understanding 15.5

Question: MegaPizza is a successful startup that sees its demand for pizza increase quickly. For the last six months, monthly demand has been 342, 411, 501, 619, 702, and 777 pizzas. Using a forecast for the first month of 300, an initial trend forecast of 90, and smoothing parameters of 0.3 for both demand smoothing and trend smoothing, forecast the demand for the next month.

Answer: We forecast the demand for the next month as follows:

t	D_t	Forecast for Next Period	Trend
		300	90
1	342	402.6	93.78
2	411	498.9	94.536
3	501	594.066	94.725
4	619	696.2712	96.96906
5	702	794.9589	97.48465
6	777	887.0559	95.86835

15.5 Time Series Analysis—Seasonality

Trends are one type of pattern that we can observe in our past demand data. Our logic in the previous section can be summarized as "if it rose in the past, it will rise in the future." Another commonly observed pattern in demand data relates to seasonality. We define **seasonality** as a significant demand change that constitutes a repetitive fluctuation over time. This fluctuation can happen at any frequency, including an hourly, daily, weekly, monthly, or yearly recurrence of the season. Seasonality stands in contrast to the previously introduced concept of statistical noise. The key difference is that the repetitiveness of the pattern in the old data in the case of seasonality makes us confident to predict that this pattern will continue into the future. In the case of statistical noise, however, we would not be willing to extrapolate the data.

Figure 15.7 shows an illustration of seasonality in water consumption. It is a little odd for an example, but we believe that will make you more likely to remember it. The blue line shows the water consumption for the city of Edmonton, Canada, on February 28, 2010. February 28, 2010 was a special day for the Canadians because their hockey team was playing for Olympic gold. Half of Canada was glued to their TV screens watching the live broadcast of the game—except, of course, during the breaks between quarters. We can only speculate what Canadians were drinking and what exactly they did during the breaks, but they certainly needed a lot of water (and, we argue, it is unlikely that they took a shower between the quarters).

The pattern in Figure 15.7 is an example of seasonality. The spikes in water consumption are not the outcome of randomness; they reflect significant demand changes causing a repetitive fluctuation of water demand.

Seasonality is by no means limited to bathroom breaks during hockey games. Instead, it is a common pattern in the practice of operations, as the following examples help illustrate:

- *Amazon:* Amazon faces dramatic increases in their demand in the months of November and December. People order gifts for the holidays. These increases oftentimes require a doubling or tripling of capacity. So, predicting them ahead of time is important. And because these demand increases are clearly a result of seasonality (as opposed to resulting from variability), there exists no reason why the company should not be able to plan for it.

- *Flu data:* As you saw in the beginning of the chapter (Figure 15.1), demand for medical services and pharmaceutical products related to the flu is not entirely a result of randomness. True, each flu season might differ in terms of severity and the exact start date, but strong seasonal patterns can be observed.

Seasonality A significant demand change that constitutes a repetitive fluctuation over time.

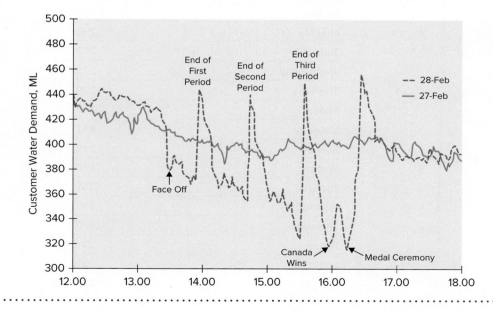

Figure 15.7

Water consumption in Edmonton (Canada) during the Olympic Gold medal hockey game (Source: http://www.smartplanet.com/ blog/smart-takes/infographic-water-consumption-in-edmonton-canada-during-olympic-gold-medal-hockey-game/)

- *Rush hour traffic:* If you are commuting to school or work during rush hour, you know the effect. Demand for toll booth capacity and road space is much higher from 7–9 a.m. and from 4–6 p.m. The exact seasonal pattern varies by metropolitan area (cities with manufacturing labor tend to work earlier in the day, while bankers show up to work later), but it is certainly predictable.

We now introduce a forecasting method that allows us to handle seasonality. We will again use data from the emergency room, with Table 15.13 showing the last three weeks of arrival data, and Figure 15.8, the distribution of daily arrivals over the seven days in a week (so each day of the week in Figure 15.8 corresponds to three data points in Table 15.13).

The first step of our forecasting method incorporating seasonality is to determine the seasonality pattern. Are we facing a season within a day, within a week, within a year, or another recurring fluctuation? For the purpose of this chapter, we find it sufficient to simply "eyeball" past data and apply some basic knowledge about the operations that we face. Patients are most likely to go to the ED on Mondays—the weekends tend to be calmer (see Figure 15.8). More formal statistical tests can be used to confirm such patterns. We thus decide on a seasonality at the level of the day of the week.

In the second step, we try to quantify the effect of seasonality. We will illustrate this with a weekly seasonality, in which the seasonality pattern recurs every seven days (periods). The method easily extends to 24 hours a day, 12 months a year, or any other seasonality you might think of.

We compute the average demand per time period as

$$\text{Average demand} = \text{Average}(y_t,\ t = 1\ \ldots\ N)$$

TABLE 15.13 Number of Patients Showing Up in the Emergency Department

Week	Day of Week	ER Visits
1	Monday	265
	Tuesday	260
	Wednesday	255
	Thursday	261
	Friday	264
	Saturday	220
	Sunday	255
2	Monday	290
	Tuesday	250
	Wednesday	222
	Thursday	230
	Friday	282
	Saturday	211
	Sunday	215
3	Monday	280
	Tuesday	261
	Wednesday	230
	Thursday	240
	Friday	271
	Saturday	223
	Sunday	228

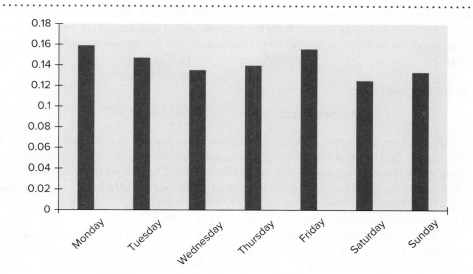

Figure 15.8
Day of the week seasonality

We then compute the average demand for Mondays as

$$\text{Average Monday demand} = \text{Average } (y_t,\ t = 1 \ldots N,\ t = \text{Monday})$$

In the same way, we can define the average demand for Tuesdays, Wednesdays, and all other days of the week. Of course, if seasonality is not a weekly pattern, but a monthly pattern, we would do this for each of the 12 months in the year. Or we could do this for the 24 hours in the day or the four quarters in the year. This is entirely a question of what time periods constitute the seasonality. Equipped with the average demand across all periods and average demand for each day in the week, we can then compute the **seasonality index (SI)** for each day of the week:

$$\text{Seasonality index Monday} = \text{SI}_{\text{Monday}} = \frac{\text{Average Monday demand}}{\text{Average total demand}}$$

Table 15.14 shows this for our ED example. We see that the seasonality index for Monday is greater than one, reflecting that more patients go to the ED on Monday. A seasonality index of 1.12 can be interpreted as Monday demand being 12 percent greater than the average demand. Similarly, we interpret the seasonality index for Saturday, which is 0.88, as indicating that Saturday has about 12 percent less demand than the average day of the week.

Equipped with the seasonality indices, we now turn back to our raw data in Table 15.3. For each of the old time periods (in our case, days), we **deseasonalize** the old demand. To deseasonalize (a word that is not in the dictionary) means to remove the seasonal effect from

Seasonality index (SI) The estimated multiplicative adjustment factor that allows us to move from the average overall demand to the average demand for a particular season.

Deseasonalize To remove the seasonal effect from past data.

TABLE 15.14 Average Number of Patients Showing Up in the Emergency Department by Day of the Week

	Average across all x-days	Seasonality Index
Monday	278.33	1.12
Tuesday	257.00	1.04
Wednesday	235.67	0.95
Thursday	243.67	0.98
Friday	272.33	1.10
Saturday	218.00	0.88
Sunday	232.67	0.94

past data. When we observed a demand of 290 patients on the Monday in week 2, we have to separate between this being a really busy day because of bad luck and this being a really busy day because it was a Monday. We define the deseasonalized demand for period t as

$$\text{Deasonalized demand in } t = \frac{\text{Demand in } t}{\text{Seasonality index}}$$

In our case, we have

$$\text{Deseasonalized demand in } t = \frac{290}{1.12} = 258.64$$

These calculations are shown in Table 15.15. Note the effect of deseasonalizing the data by comparing the Sunday of week 1 (255 patients) with the Monday of week 2 (290 patients). Looking at the demand data alone, one might think of the 290 patients being a much greater demand rate. However, if one adjusts for the effect that Sundays tend to be 6 percent less busy ($SI_{Sunday} = 0.94$) and Mondays tend to be 12 percent more busy ($SI_{Monday} = 1.12$), we actually find that the Sunday of week 1 was the bigger surprise to the ED.

Once we have removed the seasonality from the old demand data by deseasonalizing them, we can proceed as we did before. Each time period still includes a fair bit of noise (see our discussion from the Sunday in week 1 compared to the Monday in week 2). Now that the effect of seasonality is removed, all variation that is left is a result of statistical noise. Some days have more patients and some have less. And we know how to deal with statistical noise—we can rely on either moving averages or exponential smoothing.

Using a smoothing parameter of $\alpha = 0.25$ and an initial forecast for the first Monday of 240, Table 15.6 shows this smoothing process. Each day, we obtain a smoothed forecast,

TABLE 15.15   Number of Patients Showing Up in the Emergency Department Adjusted for Seasonality Effects

Week	Day of Week	ER Visits	Seasonality Index (SI)	Deasonalized (ER Visits/SI)
1	Monday	265	1.12	236.35
	Tuesday	260	1.04	251.14
	Wednesday	255	0.95	268.60
	Thursday	261	0.98	265.90
	Friday	264	1.10	240.64
	Saturday	220	0.88	250.52
	Sunday	255	0.94	272.07
2	Monday	290	1.12	258.64
	Tuesday	250	1.04	241.48
	Wednesday	222	0.95	233.84
	Thursday	230	0.98	234.32
	Friday	282	1.10	257.05
	Saturday	211	0.88	240.27
	Sunday	215	0.94	229.39
3	Monday	280	1.12	249.72
	Tuesday	261	1.04	252.10
	Wednesday	230	0.95	242.27
	Thursday	240	0.98	244.50
	Friday	271	1.10	247.02
	Saturday	223	0.88	253.93
	Sunday	228	0.94	243.26

TABLE 15.16 Smoothed Number of Patients Showing Up in the Emergency Department after Adjusting for Seasonality

Week	Day of Week	ER Visits	Seasonality Index (SI)	Deasonalized (ER Visits/SI)	Smoothed Forecast (alpha = 0.25, Week 1 Monday forecast 240)
1	Monday	265	1.12	236.35	239.09
	Tuesday	260	1.04	251.14	242.10
	Wednesday	255	0.95	268.60	248.72
	Thursday	261	0.98	265.90	253.02
	Friday	264	1.10	240.64	249.92
	Saturday	220	0.88	250.52	250.07
	Sunday	255	0.94	272.07	255.57
2	Monday	290	1.12	258.64	256.34
	Tuesday	250	1.04	241.48	252.62
	Wednesday	222	0.95	233.84	247.93
	Thursday	230	0.98	234.32	244.52
	Friday	282	1.10	257.05	247.66
	Saturday	211	0.88	240.27	245.81
	Sunday	215	0.94	229.39	241.70
3	Monday	280	1.12	249.72	243.71
	Tuesday	261	1.04	252.10	245.81
	Wednesday	230	0.95	242.27	244.92
	Thursday	240	0.98	244.50	244.82
	Friday	271	1.10	247.02	245.37
	Saturday	223	0.88	253.93	247.51
	Sunday	228	0.94	243.26	246.45

combining the latest data with the old forecast as discussed earlier. As the old data come to an end, we have a last smoothed forecast of 246.45 patients for the next day.

How do we interpret this amount of 246.45 patients? Recall that we are looking at data that have been both deseasonalized and smoothed. Thus, our forecast for an average day in the next week would be 246.45 patients. However, the first day we have to forecast for is a Monday and we know that Monday is not an average day of the week. So, at this last step, in the seasonality-adjusted forecasting method, we have to **reseasonalize** the data. Again, we are not sure if reseasonalizing is an actual verb, but it captures what we mean: We have to bring back the effect of seasonality that we previously took out of the data. This is done simply by computing the forecasts as the product of the smoothed forecast for an average day and the appropriate seasonality index:

Forecast for next Monday = Smoothed forecast for an average day $\times$ SI_{Monday}

Table 15.17 shows these data. We have extrapolated the past demand data by imposing the previously observed seasonality pattern. Simple and elegant!

A couple of further comments on forecasting with seasonality are in order:

- An important building block in the previously introduced method was the estimation of the seasonality indices, SI. We estimated the SI's by simply averaging over old data; for example, by computing the SI_{Monday} by averaging across all Mondays. Instead of averaging these values, we could also have applied an exponential smoothing method. In that case, we would have a smoothing parameter for the seasonality index that would get updated in the way we updated the trend forecast in the double exponential smoothing method.

Reseasonalize To reintroduce the seasonal effect to the forecasted data.

TABLE 15.17 Forecasted Number of Patients Showing Up in the Emergency Department after Reseasonalizing the Data

Week	Day of Week	Base	SI	Forecast (Base × SI)
4	Monday	246.45	1.12	276.33
	Tuesday	246.45	1.04	255.15
	Wednesday	246.45	0.95	233.97
	Thursday	246.45	0.98	241.91
	Friday	246.45	1.10	270.37
	Saturday	246.45	0.88	216.43
	Sunday	246.45	0.94	230.99

- We assumed the effect of seasonality to be a multiplicative effect. We deseasonalized by dividing by the appropriate SI and we reseasonalized by multiplying by it. Note that when we handled trends in the previous section, we assumed the trend was additive, as we estimated the new demand and then added the adjustment for the trend. Whether to use an additive or multiplicative model for trends or seasonality really is best answered by trying out the methods on past data.

- There are lots of bells and whistles that could be added to this model. However, we feel that this model is pretty good and gets you as far as you can get without using regression analysis. More sophisticated regression models allow you to combine the effects of trends, seasonality, and other explanatory variables into one single, integrated model. But that really is a story for another day.

Exhibit 15.3 summarizes this forecasting method.

EXHIBIT 15.3

Summary of Forecasting When Adjusting for Seasonality

Step 1: Determine the seasonality pattern.

Step 2: Compute the seasonality index for all seasons:

$$\text{SI}_{\text{Season}} = \frac{\text{Average season demand}}{\text{Average total demand}}$$

Step 3: For all time periods t, deseasonalize the data:

$$\text{Deseasonalized demand in } t = \frac{\text{Demand in } t}{\text{SI}(t)}$$

Step 4: For all time periods t, apply exponential smoothing to deseasonalized demand.

Step 5: Compute the average forecast as the smoothed value for the last period.

Step 6: Reseasonalize the data: Forecast for $s > t =$ Smoothed forecast for last period $\times \text{SI}_s$

Check Your Understanding 15.6

Question: SummerPizza is a restaurant at the beach that sees most of its demand during the warm weather period of the year. For the last three years, the demand was as shown in Table 15.18:

TABLE 15.18 SummerPizza

Year	Quarter	Demand
2012	1	7122
	2	12345
	3	11022
	4	8019
2013	1	7507
	2	11088
	3	10733
	4	9431
2014	1	8456
	2	11777
	3	12111
	4	7992

Using a smoothing parameter of 0.3 and an initial forecast of 9500, forecast demand for the first four quarters in 2015.

Answer: We forecast the demand for the next year as follows in Table 15.19.

TABLE 15.19 SummerPizza

Quarter	Season Average	SI	Deseasonalized Demand	Smoothed Demand	Forecast	
1	7695	0.785	9070.49	9371.15	2015Q1	7772.521
2	11736.67	1.198	10308.22	9652.27	2015Q2	11854.9
3	11288.67	1.152	9568.74	9627.21	2015Q3	11402.39
4	8480.667	0.865	9266.75	9519.07	2015Q4	8566.103
Overall	9800.25		9560.82	9531.60		
			9258.61	9449.70		
alpha	0.3		9317.85	9410.14		
			10898.45	9856.64		
			10769.45	10130.48		
			9833.93	10041.51		
			10514.16	10183.31		
			9235.55	9898.98		

15.6 Expert Panels and Subjective Forecasting

The approaches discussed in the previous sections share two advantages. First, forecasting methods that follow a mathematical algorithm are efficient and thus can be automated. This is especially important in operational settings where we need to make daily or even hourly forecasts across many locations. Second, these methods are based on hard data—there is no wiggle room for feelings, opinions, and other soft stuff.

However, no matter the sophistication of the analytical forecasting methods, all of them have in common that they assume that the future will be like the past. Some patterns will be extrapolated—but there is no room for human intelligence. The forecast is produced by a method, not a human being.

Sometimes, you want to allow for human input into the forecasting method. In such case, we speak about creating a **subjective forecast.** There are many ways in which you can take the opinion(s) of one or multiple persons as an input and then turn out a forecast as an output. Depending on who gets involved in the process and how the individual opinions are synthesized, we find it helpful to distinguish between three types of subjective forecasting methods.

- **Forecast combination**: Each forecaster will use different mental models to make a forecast. Most likely, each of the forecasters will be wrong at least occasionally, creating some forecast errors. The idea of forecast combination is to average the forecasts of multiple forecasters in the hope that the forecast errors will at least partially average themselves out. John is an optimist, Mary a pessimist, but if we average their forecasts, the hope is that the laws of statistics will kick in and the resulting forecast will be a better one. There exists a fair bit of research supporting this claim. Many ways to combine the forecasts have been presented, but the simplest one is to just take the average across the forecasts done by each forecaster individually.

- **Forecast with consensus building**: Instead of just collecting the forecasts of several experts and then averaging them, we can also ask each expert to explain how she arrived at her forecast. This has the potential to facilitate information sharing: Mary might know that the Chinese market is growing, while John has some insights into the U.S. market. Having Mary and John exchange that knowledge before they forecast is thus a good idea that will make both of their forecasts a better one. A common problem in such meetings is a phenomenon called **groupthink**—where all the experts agree, although the outcome is fundamentally wrong and unlikely. Groupthink can be a result of all experts using the same information (in which case, the idea of forecast errors being averaged out simply does not make sense). Oftentimes, groupthink also reflects fears of disagreement with more senior managers. To counter this problem, we suggest the following: (a) Have participating members first individually and independently create their own forecasts. These data are then a starting point for discussion. During the discussion, special attention should be given to the highest and lowest values of the individual forecasts with the request to the associated forecasters to explain the logic behind their forecasts. (b) Any discussion should start with the most junior experts in the group. A senior executive is more likely to voice her own opinion. A more junior manager is at bigger risk of feeling the pressure to conform. So, by having the senior expert speak last, we get the true beliefs of everybody.

- **Prediction markets**: Imagine you and your classmates go to a horse race but have no knowledge about any of the participating horses. At the race you get asked, "Who is going to win?" You could just ask each of your classmates to make a prediction about the horses' performance and then take some form of an average. This is the idea of the forecast combination. But why not take a look at the betting odds published by the horse track? If, at the betting office, they offer you $25 for a $1 bet for a victory by horse A and only $3 for a victory by horse B, wouldn't you think that horse B is a faster horse? So, instead of relying on yourself and your classmates, unknowledgeable (and potentially even unmotivated) as you are, why not rely on the people who have put their money on this? The idea of prediction markets is that prices can help to aggregate information. For example, if we promise to pay you $1 if our new product sells at least 1 million units, and you are willing to pay us $0.10 for that promise, that means you believe that the likelihood of selling 1 million is low (10 percent to be exact). If somebody feels that he has better information than the current market price, he can trade on that information, thereby moving the future price. If somebody feels that she has better information but would not be willing to trade on this information, we should probably not put too much weight on her opinion either.

Forecast combination Combining multiple forecasts that have been generated by different forecasters into one single value.

Forecast with consensus building An iterative discussion among experts about their forecasts and opinions that leads to a single forecast.

Prediction markets A betting game in which forecasters can place financial bets on their forecasts.

Unlike the automated methods of time series extrapolation, subjective forecasts have the potential to be forward looking. They use management intuition and human intelligence to either replace or augment the forecasts done by our models. That is the biggest strength of subjective forecasting. However, as we will discuss in the next section, this is also its biggest weakness.

15.6.1 Sources of Forecasting Biases

We previously defined a biased forecast as a forecast that not only is wrong, but it is wrong on average. In other words, forecasts display a consistent pattern between the outcomes predicted in the forecasts and the actually realized outcomes. Biases exist in all types of human decision making, though they are particularly prevalent in the world of forecasting. The reason for this is that when we forecast, by definition we don't know yet if we are right or wrong. So, "talk is cheap" and the outcome is in a distant future. In forecasting and beyond, the most common biases to be aware of are:

- **Overconfidence:** One of the strongest results in the literature on human decision making is that we all overestimate how smart we are. As a result, we are overly confident in succeeding and we are overly confident in being right in terms of our forecast for the future. On the other hand, we underestimate the role of luck (risk) and the effect of others. As a result, we forecast our sales higher and we are more optimistic with respect to the success of our new product launches.

- **Anchoring:** As human decision makers, we oftentimes pick a piece of information and then have this piece dictate how we handle new information. That initial piece of information sets a reference point. Consider a new student venture that is forecasting demand for the future. If the student team uses Facebook's growth as a reference point, it simply will bias the team toward an unrealistic demand trajectory.

- **Incentive alignment:** In the previous two biases, decision makers were caught in their own cognitive decision-making process. They tried their best, but they were subjected to overconfidence and anchoring without realizing it. In forecasting, another bias often results from incentives and personal objectives that the forecasters might have. When asked for their forecast, forecasters know that the forecast is used to make a decision. That decision will most likely impact their work. So, it is only rational for these forecasters to start with the preferred outcome of that decision and then work backward to the forecast that is likely to trigger that decision. For example, a salesperson wants to make sure there is enough inventory in the supply chain so he can fulfill all customer demand. He also knows that the higher the demand he forecasts, the more units the factory will produce and put into the supply chain. For a salesperson who is paid a commission on sales, it is hence only rational to forecast a demand that is much greater than what he truly believes. This behavior of not truthfully sharing one's forecast with the intent of achieving a certain outcome is called **forecast gaming** or **forecast inflation** (because, typically, the resulting forecast is higher than the actual).

The best way to deal with bias is feedback. Those who forecast should always be confronted with the forecasts they made in the past. Forecast errors should be measured and analyzed for the presence of biases. That way, the forecasting process can be improved over time, just as we like to improve any other operational process in our business.

Conclusion

Forecasting demand has a substantial impact on many operational decisions we take and thus on the future of the overall business. So, forecasting well is critical. In the absence of a crystal ball, good forecasting means to carefully choose the forecasting method. As we saw, each of the quantitative methods had its strengths and weaknesses. No one best method exists.

Beyond the mathematical modeling, the process of forecasting is embedded into an organizational context. Understanding this context is important.

Overconfidence bias The fact that human decision makers are overly confident in their ability to shape a positive outcome.

Anchoring bias The fact that human decision makers are selective in their acquisition of new information, looking for what confirms their initially held beliefs.

Forecast gaming A purposeful manipulation of a forecast to obtain a certain decision outcome for a decision that is based on the forecast.

When implementing a forecasting process in practice, we suggest the following five-step approach:

1. Collect data, including old demand forecasts (subjective data) and the actual demand outcomes.
2. Establish the forecasting method: Decide on the balance between subjective and objective data and look for trends and seasonality.
3. Forecast future demand using a forecasting method.
4. Make decisions based on step 3.
5. Measure the forecast error; look for biases and improve the process.

Summary of Learning Objectives

LO15-1   Understand the types of demand forecasts and the different forecasting methods

Forecasting is the process of creating statements about outcomes of variables that presently are uncertain and will only be realized in the future. Forecasting can be done based on a statistical analysis of old data, attempting to extrapolate past patterns into the future. Forecasting can also be done based on an aggregation of subjective opinions. Statistical methods can be automated and thus used for short-term forecasting, creating thousands of forecasts in a business. For high-stake decisions with a long-term impact on the forecasts, statistical methods are typically combined with subjective opinions.

LO15-2   Determine if a forecast is a good forecast using multiple metrics

The quality of a forecast can only be assessed once the real outcomes have been observed. With the realized outcomes in hand, we would like the forecast to be (a) unbiased—that is, correct on average—and (b) close to the real outcomes as measured by either the mean squared error (MSE) or the mean absolute error (MAE).

LO15-3   Create forecasts using naïve forecasts, moving averages, and exponential smoothing

The naïve forecasting method predicts that the next value will be like the last realized value. This is vulnerable to statistical noise. To reduce the effect of noise, we can take averages. The moving average forecasting method predicts that the next value will be the average of the last realized values. This method assigns an equal weight to all realized values in the forecast window. In contrast, the exponential smoothing forecasting method predicts that the next value will be a weighted average between the last realized value and the old forecast, which implicitly assigns a higher weight to more recent data.

LO15-4   Measure long-term trends in a time series and create forecasts adjusting for them

Oftentimes, demand data exhibit a long-term increase or decrease, which we call a trend. The idea of momentum-based forecasting is to continue that trend into the future. One way to do this is by using the double exponential smoothing method. This method estimates the trend using exponential smoothing and then also uses exponential smoothing to estimate the demand rate net of the trend.

LO15-5   Measure seasonality in a time series and create forecasts in adjusting for it

A common pattern in demand rates is called seasonality, a significant demand change that constitutes a repetitive fluctuation over time. To forecast demand in the presence of seasonality, we have to separate the effect of the season from the effects of statistical noise. We compute the seasonality index as the multiplicative adjustment factor that allows us to move from the average overall demand to the average demand for a particular season. We then can look at realized demand data and deseasonalize them by dividing each demand by the appropriate seasonality index. This removes the seasonal effect from past data. We can then smooth and extrapolate these data. Finally, when making the forecast for a particular period in the future, we reseasonalize them by multiplying by the seasonality index, which reintroduces the seasonal effect to the forecasted data.

LO15-6 Use expert panels to forecast and be aware of problems related to subjective forecasts

There exist multiple ways to create a subjective forecast. We can either combine the forecasts of a number of forecasters using a simple formula (for example, take the average) or we can allow for a less-structured discussion among the forecasters, hoping that this leads to information exchange and ultimately a consensus forecast. The problem with subjective forecasts is that they are subject to biases common in human decision making and to forecast gaming.

Key Terms

15.1 Forecasting Framework

Forecasting The process of creating statements about outcomes of variables that presently are uncertain and will only be realized in the future.

Demand forecasting The process of creating statements about future realizations of demand.

Time series analysis Analysis of old demand data.

Time series–based forecast An approach to forecasting that uses nothing but old demand data.

Extrapolation Estimation of values beyond the range of the original observations by assuming that some patterns in the values present within the range will also prevail outside the range.

Regression analysis A statistical process of estimating the relationship of one variable with multiple variables that influence this one variable.

Dependent variable The variable that we try to explain in a regression analysis.

Independent variables The variables influencing the dependent variable.

Automated forecasting Forecasts that are created by computers, typically with no human intervention.

Expert panel forecasting Forecasts generated using the subjective opinions of management.

Short-term forecasts Forecasts used to support tactical decision making with typical time ranges from hours to weeks.

Mid-term forecasts Forecasts used to support capacity planning and financial accounting with typical time ranges from weeks to a year.

Long-term forecasts Forecasts used to support strategic decisions with typical time ranges of multiple years.

15.2 Evaluating the Quality of a Forecast

Forecast error The difference between a forecasted value and the realized value.

Unbiased forecast A forecast that is correct on average, thus an average forecast error equal to zero.

Biased forecast A forecast that is wrong on average, thus an average forecast error different from zero.

Mean squared error (MSE) A measure evaluating the quality of a forecast by looking at the average squared forecast error.

Mean absolute error (MAE) A measure evaluating the quality of a forecast by looking at the average absolute value of the forecast error.

15.3 Eliminating Noise from Old Data

Naïve forecasting method A forecasting method that predicts that the next value will be like the last realized value.

Statistical noise Variables influencing the outcomes of a process in unpredictable ways.

Moving average forecasting method A forecasting method that predicts that the next value will be the average of the last realized values.

Exponential smoothing forecasting method a forecasting method that predicts that the next value will be a weighted average between the last realized value and the old forecast

Smoothing parameter The parameter that determines the weight new realized data have in creating the next forecast with exponential smoothing.

15.4 Time Series Analysis—Trends

Trend A continuing increase or decrease in a variable that is consistent over a long period of time.

Momentum-based forecasting An approach to forecasting that assumes that the trend in the future will be similar to the trend in the past.

Double exponential smoothing A way of forecasting a demand process with a trend that estimates the trend using exponential smoothing and then also uses exponential smoothing to estimate the demand rate net of the trend.

15.5 Time Series Analysis—Seasonality

Seasonality A significant demand change that constitutes a repetitive fluctuation over time.

Seasonality index (SI) The estimated multiplicative adjustment factor that allows us to move from the average overall demand to the average demand for a particular season.

Deseasonalize To remove the seasonal effect from past data.

Reseasonalize To reintroduce the seasonal effect to the forecasted data.

15.6 Expert Panels and Subjective Forecasting

Forecast combination Combining multiple forecasts that have been generated by different forecasters into one single value.

Forecast with consensus building An iterative discussion among experts about their forecasts and opinions that leads to a single forecast.

Prediction markets A betting game in which forecasters can place financial bets on their forecasts.

Overconfidence bias The fact that human decision makers are overly confident in their ability to shape a positive outcome.

Anchoring bias The fact that human decision makers are selective in their acquisition of new information, looking for what confirms their initially held believes.

Forecast gaming A purposeful manipulation of a forecast to obtain a certain decision outcome for a decision that is based on the forecast.

Key Formulas

15.2 Determine if a forecast is a good forecast using multiple metrics

Forecast error in $t = \text{FE}_t = $ Forecast for $t -$ Actual value for t

$$\text{MSE} = \frac{\sum_{t=1}^{N} \text{FE}_t^2}{N}$$

$$\text{MAE} = \frac{\sum_{t=1}^{N} |\text{FE}_t|}{N}$$

$$\text{MAPE} = \frac{\sum_{t=1}^{N} \left|\frac{\text{FE}_t}{Y_t}\right|}{N}$$

15.3 Create forecasts using naïve forecasts, moving averages, and exponential smoothing

Naïve forecast: $\hat{y}_{t+1} = y_t$

Moving average (in this case, four period) forecast:

$\hat{y}_{t+1} = \text{Average}(y_t, y_{t-1}, y_{t-2}, y_{t-3})$

Exponential smoothing: $\hat{y}_{t+1} = (\alpha \times y_t) + (1 - \alpha) \times \hat{y}_t$

15.4 Measure long-term trends in a time series and create forecasts adjusting for them

Double exponential smoothing:

$$\hat{y}_{t+1} = (\alpha \times y_t) + [(1 - \alpha) \times \hat{y}_t] + \hat{T}_t$$

$$\hat{T}_{t+1} = [\beta \times (\hat{y}_{t+1} - \hat{y}_t)] + (1 - \beta)\,\hat{T}_t$$

15.5 Measure seasonality in a time series and create forecasts adjusting for it

$$\text{Seasonality index for season } x = \text{SI}_{\text{Season}\,x} = \frac{\text{Average season } x \text{ demand}}{\text{Average total demand}}$$

$$\text{Deasonalized demand in } t = \frac{\text{Demand in } t}{\text{Seasonality index}}$$

Forecast for next season x = Smoothed forecast for an average day (use the last value in the deseasonalized smoothed exponential forecast) $\times$ SI$_{\text{Season}\,x}$

Conceptual Questions

LO15-1

1. When creating a time series–based forecast for the amount of soda to be sold in the cafeteria next week, which data sources can you include in your forecasting process?
   a. The opinion of the principal
   b. Old demand data
   c. Data about upcoming sports events
   d. The age of the cafeteria worker

2. A company wants to use regression analysis to forecast the demand for the next quarter. In such a regression model, demand would be the independent variable. True or false?
   a. True
   b. False

3. A pizza chain wants to forecast the demand rate for each store for each hour in the day. What type of forecasting method is it most likely to deploy?
   a. Automated forecasting
   b. Expert panel forecasting
   c. Weather forecasting
   d. Macroeconomic forecasting

LO15-2

4. What is the definition of a forecast error?
   a. The average difference between the forecast and the actual outcome
   b. The maximum difference between the forecast and the actual outcome
   c. The difference between the forecast and the actual outcome
   d. The percentage difference between the forecast and the actual outcome

5. A company has an unbiased forecast for its demand. What does that mean?
   a. All forecast errors are equal to zero.
   b. All forecast errors are less than 1 percent.
   c. The average of all forecast errors is zero.
   d. The standard deviation of forecast errors is zero.

6. The intuition behind the MSE metric to evaluate old forecasts is:
   a. to sum up the forecast errors.
   b. to sum up the squared forecast errors.
   c. to sum up the absolute values of the forecast errors.
   d. to average the squared forecast errors.
   e. to average the absolute values of the forecast errors.

7. The intuition behind the MAE metric to evaluate old forecasts is:
   a. to sum up the forecast errors.
   b. to sum up the squared forecast errors.
   c. to sum up the absolute values of the forecast errors.
   d. to average the squared forecast errors.
   e. to average the absolute values of the forecast errors.

LO15-3

8. How big is the effect of statistical noise on the naïve forecast?
   a. Large
   b. Medium
   c. Small

9. Using the moving average forecast, is it possible to forecast a demand that is bigger than any previously observed demand?
   a. Yes
   b. No

10. Using the exponential smoothing forecast, is it possible to forecast a demand that is bigger than any previously observed demand?
    a. Yes
    b. No

LO15-4

11. Using the double exponential smoothing forecast, is it possible to forecast a demand that is bigger than any previously observed demand?
    a. Yes
    b. No

12. A startup has a demand that goes up by 50 percent each year. This demand increase is multiplicative. True or false?
    a. True
    b. False

LO15-5

13. The seasonality index is based on demand fluctuations that are additive. True or false?
    a. True
    b. False

14. Deseasonalizing old demand data is the process of reintroducing the seasonal effect to forecasted data. True or false?
    a. True
    b. False

LO15-6

15. A sales organization creates a new sales forecast by simply taking the average of demand forecasts that each sales manager generated individually. What type of subjective forecasting approach best describes this?
    a. Forecast combination
    b. Forecast with consensus building
    c. Prediction market
    d. Time-series forecasting

Solved Example Problems

LO15-2

1. Jim and John run a barber shop. Every night, both of them predict how many guests will come on the next day. Over the last four days, they have collected some data about their predictions and the actual outcome. Jim predicts the number of guests to be 56 for day 1, 50 for day 2, 45 for day 3, and 59 for day 4. John predicts 47, 49, 51, and 51 for the four

respective days. The actual numbers of guests turn out to be 45, 51, 41, and 61. Who has the bigger forecast bias? What are the MSE and the MAE for Jim and John?

Answer: The calculations in the following table show that Jim has an average forecast error of 3, while John has one of 0. So Jim is biased, while John is not. Jim has an MSE of 35.5 and an MAE of 4.5. John has an MSE of 52 and an MAE of 6.

Day	Jim	John	Actual	Jim:FE	Jim:FExFE	Jim:Abs(FE)	John:FE	John:FExFE	John:Abs(FE)
1	56	47	45	11	121	11	2	4	2
2	50	49	51	−1	1	1	−2	4	2
3	45	51	41	4	16	4	10	100	10
4	59	51	61	−2	4	2	−10	100	10
			Average	3	35.5	4.5	0	52	6

LO15-3

2. Tom's Towing LLC operates a fleet of tow trucks that it sends to help drivers in need on the nearby highway. The numbers of calls requesting a tow truck for Monday, Tuesday, Wednesday, and Thursday were 27, 18, 21, and 15, respectively. What would be its forecast for Friday using a naïve forecasting approach?

Answer: The naïve forecast would be 15, because this corresponds to the last observed demand.

3. Tom's Towing LLC operates a fleet of tow trucks that it sends to help drivers in need on the nearby highway. The numbers of calls requesting a tow truck for Monday, Tuesday, Wednesday, and Thursday were 27, 18, 21, and 15, respectively. What would be its forecast for Friday using a four-day moving average approach?

Answer: With a four-day moving average, we would forecast the demand for Friday as the average of the demands of Monday through Thursday. That would be

$$\text{Forecast for Friday} = \text{Average}(27, 18, 21, 15) = 20.25$$

4. Tom's Towing LLC operates a fleet of tow trucks that it sends to help drivers in need on the nearby highway. The numbers of calls requesting a tow truck for Monday, Tuesday, Wednesday, and Thursday were 27, 18, 21, and 15, respectively. What would be its forecast for Friday using an exponential smoothing forecasting approach? Use $\alpha = 0.4$ and a forecast for Monday of 18.

Answer: With the exponential smoothing method, we cannot just forecast for Friday. Instead, we have to start at the beginning and first forecast for Tuesday. We can then, day by day, update our forecast for the next day. This gives us a forecast for Friday of 18.30.

Day	Demand	Forecast for Tomorrow ($\alpha = 0.4$)
		18
Monday	27	21.6
Tuesday	18	20.16
Wednesday	21	20.496
Thursday	15	18.2976

LO15-4

5. Online-MBA is an online university that allows students to get credit for various online courses they have taken, as long as they come to campus for a six-week intense boot camp. Demand for this program is quickly increasing. For the last six months, monthly applications were 345, 412, 480, 577, 640, and 711. Using a forecast for the first month

of 250, an initial trend forecast of 50, and smoothing parameters of 0.2 for the demand smoothing and 0.5 for the trend smoothing, forecast the demand for the next year using double exponential smoothing.

Answer: We forecast the demand for the next year as follows:

t	D_t	Forecast for Next Period	Trend
		250	50
1	345	319	59.5
2	412	397.1	68.8
3	480	482.48	77.09
4	577	578.474	86.542
5	640	677.3212	92.6946
6	711	776.75156	96.06248

So, the forecast for the next period is 776.8.

LO15-5

6. GoPro is a training company that helps athletes applying for college improve their sports. Most colleges have their application deadline at the end of December, so the third and fourth quarters tend to be the busiest for the company. Based on the last three years, management has collected a set of old demand data for the various quarters:

Year	Quarter	Demand
2012	1	111
	2	120
	3	350
	4	333
2013	1	130
	2	109
	3	299
	4	305
2014	1	143
	2	122
	3	401
	4	307

Using a smoothing parameter of 0.2 and an initial forecast for the deseasonalized demand of 130, forecast demand for the first four quarters in 2015.

Answer: We forecast the demand for the next year as follows:

Quarter	Deseasonalized Demand	Smoothed Demand
1	197.29	143.46
2	233.33	161.43
3	227.50	174.65
4	240.50	187.82
1	231.05	196.46
2	211.94	199.56
3	194.35	198.52
4	220.28	202.87
1	254.16	213.13
2	237.22	217.95
3	260.65	226.49
4	221.72	225.53

(b)

Quarter	Season Average	SI
1	128	0.563
2	117	0.514
3	350	1.538
4	315	1.385
Overall	227.5	

(a)

Forecast	
2015Q1	126.8941
2015Q2	115.9892
2015Q3	346.9762
2015Q4	312.2785

(c)

LO15-6

7. Four partners in a big consulting firm try to estimate the number of new recruits needed for the next year. Their forecasts are 32, 44, 21, and 51, respectively. What would be the result of a simple forecast combination?

   Answer: The forecast combination is simply the average of the four forecasts. In this case, it would be 37.

Problems and Applications

LO15–2

1. Two servers in a restaurant predict how many guests will come for dinner in the next four days. The first server predicts the number of guests to be 23 for day 1, 35 for day 2, 30 for day 3, and 28 for day 4. The second server predicts 26, 27, 28, and 29 for the four respective days. The actual attendance turns out to be 30, 22, 31, and 25. Who has the bigger forecast bias? What are the MSE and the MAE for the two servers?

LO15-3

2. A police station had to deploy police officers for emergencies multiple times the last four evenings. The numbers of emergencies for Monday, Tuesday, Wednesday, and Thursday were 7, 4, 8, and 11, respectively. What would be the station's forecast for Friday using a naïve forecasting approach?

3. A police station had to deploy police officers for emergencies multiple times the last four evenings. The numbers of emergencies for Monday, Tuesday, Wednesday, and Thursday were 7, 4, 8, and 11, respectively. What would be the station's forecast for the emergencies on Friday using a two-day moving average approach?

4. A police station had to deploy police officers for emergencies multiple times the last four evenings. The numbers of emergencies for Monday, Tuesday, Wednesday, and Thursday were 7, 4, 8, and 11, respectively. What would be the station's forecast for Friday using an exponential smoothing forecasting approach? Use $\alpha = 0.3$ and a forecast for Monday of 9.

LO15-4

5. MyApp is a small but growing startup that sees demand for several of its apps increase quickly. For the last six months, monthly downloads were 235,000, 290,000, 336,000, 390,000, 435,000, and 498,000. Using a forecast for the first month of 220,000, an initial trend forecast of 40,000, and smoothing parameters of 0.25 for both demand smoothing and trend smoothing, forecast the demand for the next month using double exponential smoothing.

6. La Villa is a ski resort in the Italian Alps. Many guests visit the town; however, most of them come in the winter season because of the phenomenal skiing. A group of hotels has analyzed their demand for the last three years (see the table below):

Year	Quarter	Demand
2012	1	22100
	2	14900
	3	13700
	4	19000
2013	1	20100
	2	17000
	3	16500
	4	18700
2014	1	23400
	2	12100
	3	13200
	4	19700

Using a smoothing parameter of 0.25 and an initial forecast of 17,000, forecast demand for the first four quarters in 2015.

LO15-6

7. Mary, Susan, and Sarah are running a beach boutique on the boardwalk of Ocean City. Their favorite product is a red lifeguard hoodie. Mary believes it will sell 340 times next season. Susan forecasts sales of 522 and Sarah forecasts 200. What would be the result of a simple forecast combination?

CASE   International Arrivals

The U.S. Department of Transportation publishes the number of international passengers that come through U.S. airports. The busiest airports for international travel are in New York (JFK), Miami (MIA), Los Angeles (LAX), Newark (EWR), and Chicago (ORD). The most popular destinations are London (LHR), Toronto (YYZ), Tokyo (NR), Frankfurt (FRA), and Paris (CDG).

Consider the data in the following table and answer these questions:

1. How would you estimate the passenger volume for the coming year?
2. What is the role of trends and seasonality?
3. What other variables do you expect to influence the number of international travelers?

© Rodrigo Alberto Torres/Glow Images/RF

JFK Airport in New York, the airport with the most international travelers in the United States					
Year	Month	Passengers	Year	Month	Passengers
2012	January	13,441,718	2013	January	13,970,077
2012	February	11,942,221	2013	February	12,230,963
2012	March	14,670,996	2013	March	15,447,435
2012	April	14,286,844	2013	April	14,507,038
2012	May	14,537,314	2013	May	15,516,063
2012	June	15,906,101	2013	June	16,487,702
2012	July	17,362,586	2013	July	17,954,910
2012	August	16,969,528	2013	August	17,786,357
2012	September	14,010,920	2013	September	14,408,817
2012	October	13,599,030	2013	October	14,374,254
2012	November	12,919,746	2013	November	13,258,104
2012	December	14,289,105	2013	December	15,182,616

Source: http://www.dot.gov

Literature / Further Reading

http://blogs.spectator.co.uk/coffeehouse/2013/06/david-dinsmore-is-the-new-editor-of-the-sun/
http://en.wikipedia.org/wiki/Facebook
http://www.shanghaijungle.com/news/China-Auto-Sales-Rise-9

16 Service Systems with Patient Customers

LEARNING OBJECTIVES

LO16-1 For a queue with a constant demand rate that exceeds the service rate, evaluate several performance measures related to the length of the queue, the average wait, and the time to serve customers

LO16-2 For a queue with variable interarrival and processing times and one server, evaluate several performance measures and understand the factors that influence those measures

LO16-3 For a queue with variable interarrival and processing times and multiple servers, evaluate several performance measures and understand the factors that influence those measures

LO16-4 Understand why there are economies of scale in queuing systems, and understand the pros and cons of pooling

CHAPTER OUTLINE

Introduction

For consumers, one of the most visible—and probably annoying—forms of supply–demand mismatches is waiting in queues. We seem to spend a significant portion of our life waiting in line, be it physical lines (e.g., supermarkets, check-in at airports) or "virtual" lines (listening to music in a call center or waiting for a response e-mail). What we don't generally see as a consumer is that the people or resources serving us can also spend a considerable amount of their time idle, waiting around for something to do or a person to help. The manager of the process sees both problems: customers dissatisfied with waiting and underutilized employees (or resources). Thus, the manager of a process needs to understand why queues form and how to better manage them to improve service or lower cost, or both.

In this chapter, we explore two different situations in which queues occur. In the first, demand exceeds the capacity of a process in a sustained manner. For example, at the end of a sporting match, a long queue of cars forms trying to leave the parking lot. In the second, capacity exceeds demand, on average, but due to variability, there can be times in which a queue forms. For example, due to random chance, several clients may want to speak to their financial advisor at nearly the same time, leaving some of them waiting for the advisor to become available. Once we explore why queues occur, we evaluate several measures related to performance of a system that experiences queues. For example, we examine how long customers wait (on average) and how many people are expected to be in the system. Finally, we discuss how to better manage a system that has queues.

16.1 Queues When Demand Exceeds Supply

Ski Butternut is a small ski resort in the Berkshire Mountains of eastern Massachusetts. Like most ski resorts, it has a shop that allows skiers to rent ski and snowboard equipment.

Figure 16.1 displays a simple process flow diagram of the rental shop at Butternut. The triangle represents the inventory of customers waiting to be served, which is essentially a queue. The process of filling out forms, fitting boots, and adjusting equipment is done in the rental shop, which is the square in the diagram.

As you would expect, most of its customers like to arrive in the morning, and they often experience queues at the rental shop. In particular, let's say customers begin arriving at 8 a.m., and for the next two hours they arrive at a constant rate of 1.5 customers per minute. Thus, during the first two hours of the morning, demand equals 1.5 customers per minute. Even though nobody likes to wait, they all do given that they took the time to travel to Butternut to enjoy a day on the slopes.

The people in the rental shop are experienced and work quickly, but they still can only manage to fully process 1.25 customers per minute—for the rental shop, capacity equals 1.25 customers per minute. These data are displayed in Table 16.1.

If you are responsible for the rental shop, you want to know, during the morning rush, (1) what is the length of the queue, (2) how long does a customer have to wait to be served,

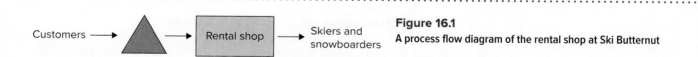

Figure 16.1

A process flow diagram of the rental shop at Ski Butternut

Customers → (triangle) → Rental shop → Skiers and snowboarders

TABLE 16.1 Parameters to Describe Demand and Capacity during the First Two Hours of Operation in the Morning

Rental Shop Parameters	Customers per Minute
Demand rate	1.50
Capacity	1.25

Figure 16.2

Number of customers who have not yet received their equipment as a function of the number of minutes after the shop opens

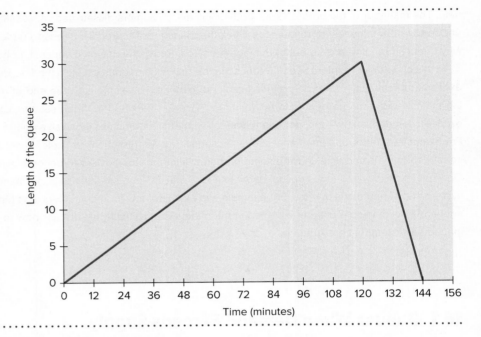

and (3) what is the average time customers wait to rent equipment? And, of course, beyond knowing how you are currently performing, you want to know what you could do to improve performance.

Let's begin our analysis with some intuition. As you would expect, a queue forms as customers begin to arrive and then the queue eventually dissipates when demand tapers off. Figure 16.2 displays this pattern of growth and decline. We now proceed to better understand this queue with some formal analysis.

16.1.1 Length of the Queue

LO16-1 For a queue with a constant demand rate that exceeds the service rate, evaluate several performance measures related to the length of the queue, the average wait, and the time to serve customers

With 1.5 customers arriving each minute, and the rental shop only able to process 1.25 customers per minute, it is intuitive that a queue of customers begins to form. Think of this like water filling a bathtub—if water flows into a bathtub faster than it drains, water starts to accumulate in the tub. In fact, over any interval of time in which demand exceeds capacity, the queue grows. As we are assuming that capacity is constant throughout the morning and the demand rate remains 1.5 customers per minute from 8 a.m. to 10 a.m., the queue for renting equipment grows during this entire time. In particular,

$$\text{Queue growth rate } = \text{ Demand} - \text{Capacity}$$

For the rental shop, the queue grows at the rate of $1.5 - 1.25 = 0.25$ customer per minute. In Figure 16.2, the inventory line from 8 a.m. to 10 a.m. has a positive slope of 0.25 customer per minute.

After T units of time, the length of the queue is

$$\text{Length of queue at time } T = T \times \text{Queue growth rate}$$
$$= T \times (\text{Demand} - \text{Capacity})$$

Thus, at 10 a.m., which is 120 minutes after customers had started arriving, the queue at the rental shop is 120 minutes $\times$ 0.25 customer per minute = 30 customers. This matches our observation in Figure 16.2.

Check Your Understanding 16.1

Question: During the three hours of the morning rush from 6 a.m. to 9 a.m., 10,000 cars per hour arrive at the toll plaza of a bridge. However, only 8000 cars can be processed per hour. At what rate does the queue of cars at the plaza grow during this time?

Answer: The queue grows at a rate equal to the difference between demand and capacity: 10,000 cars per hour − 8000 cars per hour = 2000 cars per hour.

. . . .

16.1.2 Time to Serve Customers

Suppose customers stop arriving at 10 a.m. Hence, the customer arriving at 10 a.m. is the last one to receive her equipment and, unfortunately, she must wait the longest. How long does she wait? Before she can get on the slopes, the system must process Q people and it does so at a rate equal to its capacity. So the time to serve the Qth person in the queue is

$$\text{Time to serve the } Q\text{th person in the queue} = \frac{Q}{\text{Capacity}}$$

The last person to be served arrives at 10 a.m. and she is the 30th person in the system. Thus, she receives her equipment only after 30 customers/1.25 customers per minute = 24 minutes. In Figure 16.2, we can see that the last customer arrives 120 minutes into the process and is served 24 minutes later, at minute 144 into the process. (We know the last customer is served at minute 144 because she is the last customer in the queue and the queue is emptied at minute 144.)

Combining the equation for the length of the queue at time T with the equation for the time to serve the Qth person in the queue, we can write an equation for the time to serve the person arriving at time T:

$$\text{Time to serve the person arriving at time } T = T \times \left(\frac{\text{Demand}}{\text{Capacity}} - 1\right)$$

Let's confirm that this equation gives the same answer. The last person arrives at time $T = 120$ minutes and, according to the equation, requires

$$120 \text{ minutes} \times \left(\frac{1.5 \text{ customers per minute}}{1.25 \text{ customers per minute}} - 1\right) = 24 \text{ minutes, which matches our previous}$$

calculation (as it should).

Check Your Understanding 16.2

Question: During the three hours of the morning rush from 6 a.m. to 9 a.m., 10,000 cars per hour arrive at the toll plaza of a bridge. However, only 8000 cars can be processed per hour. How long does the car arriving at 9 a.m. have to wait to get through the toll plaza?

Answer: The car arriving at 9 a.m. arrives three hours from the time the queue starts to build. So,

$$\text{Time to serve the car arriving at 9 a.m.} = 3 \text{ hours} \times \left(\frac{10,000 \text{ cars per hour}}{8000 \text{ cars per hour}} - 1\right)$$

$$= 0.75 \text{ hour}$$

. . . .

16.1.3 Average Waiting Time

We have determined that the longest wait at the rental shop is 24 minutes, but what is the average amount of time its customers wait? We could evaluate the time to serve each customer and then take an average over all of those values. But 180 customers arrive in the morning rush, so that is a tedious calculation. Fortunately, there is a relatively straightforward way to evaluate this average:

$$\text{Average time to serve a unit} = \frac{1}{2} \times T \times \left(\frac{\text{Demand}}{\text{Capacity}} - 1 \right)$$

Thus, during the 120-minute rush in the morning to rent equipment, a person must wait, on average, $\frac{1}{2} \times 120 \text{ minutes} \times \left(\frac{1.5 \text{ customers per minute}}{1.25 \text{ customers per minute}} - 1 \right) = 12 \text{ minutes}$. This is exactly one-half the wait of the last person to arrive during the morning rush!

Looking at the equation for the average time to serve a unit, we see that there are two things that determine the average wait. The first is the ratio of demand to capacity,

$$\frac{\text{Demand}}{\text{Capacity}}$$

which is the implied utilization! The higher the implied utilization, the longer customers need to wait to be served. The greater the implied utilization, the greater demand exceeds supply, which leads to a longer queue. The second is the duration of the busy period, T. The queue grows as long as the demand rate exceeds capacity. So if demand exceeds capacity for a longer period of time, then the queue grows longer and the average time to be served increases.

While queues consistently grow when the arrival rate exceeds capacity, we know that queues do not grow forever. There are several reasons for this. First, the period in which demand exceeds capacity generally does not last forever. Customers stop arriving (in substantial numbers) to the ski resort by late morning, the rush to get into a stadium does not last much beyond the start of the match, and the surge on a highway to get through a toll plaza does not last into the wee hours of the morning. Eventually, demand tends to calm down to a point that allows the queue to shrink. Put another way, demand is predictably variable with known periods in which demand exceeds capacity. These periods can last for a considerable amount of time (e.g., most of the day in the case of a toll booth during a holiday weekend), but they don't last forever. Second, while Butternut offers an enjoyable day on the slopes, there is often a limit to the patience of customers. If the wait gets too long, customers simply walk away. If customers walk away, then demand is effectively reduced.

Check Your Understanding 16.3

Question: During the three hours of the morning rush from 6 a.m. to 9 a.m., 10,000 cars per hour arrive at the toll plaza of a bridge. However, only 8000 cars can be processed per hour. On average, how long does a car arriving during this three-hour period wait to get through the toll plaza?

Answer:

$$\text{Average time to serve a unit} = \frac{1}{2} \times 3 \text{ hours} \times \left(\frac{10,000 \text{ cars per hour}}{8000 \text{ cars per hour}} - 1 \right) = \frac{3}{8} \text{ hour}$$

16.1.4 Managing Peak Demand

Now that we know a queue forms when demand is consistently above capacity (assuming patient customers), what can be done to improve the situation? Well, there really are only two options: reduce demand or increase capacity. Let's explore both.

Reducing demand during peak times is surely one way to reduce the queue. The trick is to reduce demand without also reducing revenue, at least by not too much. One technique is to do **peak-load pricing**, which is also called *congestion pricing*—charging more during the times that you know are busiest. (See Connections: Traffic and Congestion Pricing.) Some customers will choose not to pay the higher price, lowering demand and therefore the time to serve the customers that do arrive. Hopefully, the higher price paid by the customers who do arrive offsets or nearly offsets the loss in revenue from the customers who no longer desire the service. Alternatively, the firm could try an **off-peak discount**—offering a discount during the nonbusy period in the hope that some customers will arrive during those times rather than the peak time. With this approach, the service tries to retain as many customers as possible but hopes they do not all arrive at the same time.

Of course, off-peak discounts and peak-load pricing are two ways to describe essentially the same thing. For example, Butternut could have a regular price of $40 to rent equipment for the day but offer a $10 discount if you rent after 10 a.m. Alternatively, it could have a regular price of $30 but charge $10 extra if you rent between 8 a.m. and 10 a.m. The first approach is an off-peak discount and the second implements peak-load pricing, but with either approach a customer pays the same amount. Even though the amount paid is the same, customers tend to prefer the off-peak discount approach—it seems better to get a discount than to have to pay a penalty.

The flip side of adjusting demand is to adjust capacity. For example, Butternut could try to hire workers in the rental shop during the peak time in the morning. Or it could try moving employees, who normally do other tasks, to the rental shop in the morning. A more sophisticated approach is to increase the capacity of the rental shop while using the same staffing. For example, this may be possible with better line balancing of tasks within the rental shop. Alternatively, Butternut could try a **pre-processing strategy**—reducing the amount of work needed to process a customer during the peak time period by moving some of the work to an off-peak time. For instance, if it provided forms online, customers could complete the forms before they arrived, thereby reducing the amount of time needed to process them when they do arrive. In other words, if you cannot move demand outside of the peak time, try to move some of the work outside the peak time, thereby minimizing the amount of work that needs to be done during the peak time. If each customer requires less work during the peak time, the process's capacity to serve customers during that time is increased.

Peak-load pricing Charging more during the time period with the highest demand.

Off-peak discount Offering a discount during a time period with low demand.

Pre-processing strategy Reducing the amount of work needed to process a customer during the peak time period by moving some of the work to an off-peak time.

CONNECTIONS: Traffic and Congestion Pricing

Most major cities suffer from the problem of traffic jams during the morning and late afternoon "rush hours." People need to get to work at about the same time in the morning and they also tend to want to return home at about the same time. The problem is that roads and bridges have a limited capacity, which often is less than peak demand. Consequently, queues form.

It might not be obvious to a driver on a road, but they are "consuming" some of the limited capacity on the road. Yes, they are only using a small portion of that capacity, but the cumulative effect of thousands of drivers is readily apparent in the bumper-to-bumper traffic.

One remedy is to build more capacity in the form of more bridges and highways. Unfortunately, this type of construction is not cheap and cities may not have the space to accommodate the expansion. Furthermore, there is evidence that in the context of traffic, "capacity generates its own demand": If a road is expanded, people in the long run make decisions

Continued

© Charles Smith/Digital Stock/Corbis/RF

that actually increase the demand on the road, mitigating the benefit of the extra capacity. For example, they might use their car more relative to public transportation or they might choose to live outside of the city. A more sophisticated remedy is to get more capacity from the same set of resources. For example, the capacity of a road is primarily a function of the number of cars that travel on the road. If it is possible to increase the occupancy of each car (e.g., carpooling), then the capacity of the road, measured in "persons per hour," increases. Alas, people don't like to carpool.

An alternative remedy is *congestion pricing:* charge vehicles more during the congestion period to reduce demand during that period and to either encourage the use of public transportation (which is assumed to not have a congestion issue) or motivate drivers to use the roads during off-peak times. The theory behind congestion pricing is simple: If you use a resource, like road capacity, then you should pay for it. But not everyone is a fan of this theory. When New York City attempted to use congestion pricing in 2008 to alleviate traffic in Manhattan, the plan encountered stiff resistance. Concerns included that the fee was a regressive tax (i.e., it hits the poor proportionally harder than the rich), it would encourage people to park just outside of Manhattan (causing problems in those neighborhoods), and it would reduce demand for businesses in Manhattan (because fewer people would travel to the island). Although not adopted in New York, the idea has been successfully implemented in many other cities in the world, including Singapore and London.

16.2 Queues When Demand and Service Rates Are Variable—One Server

An-ser Services is a small call center operation in Wisconsin. It specializes in providing answering services for financial services, insurance companies, and medical practices. The call volume is light from 1 a.m. to 2 a.m., so it has only one employee answering calls. In particular, during that hour, 12 calls arrive on average and, based on prior observations, each call only takes, on average, four minutes to complete. Hence, the demand rate is 12 calls per hour and the capacity of the one employee is 15 calls per hour (= 60 minutes per hour/4 minutes per call). The process flow diagram for this system is displayed in Figure 16.3. The agent is able to serve one caller at a time and completes serving a customer before moving to the

© Digital Vision/Getty Images/RF

next available customer. If the agent is busy, callers wait on hold (listening to that wonderful music that tells you that your call is "important to us"). In the diagram, callers on hold wait in a queue, represented by the inventory triangle. The combination of the queue and the agent is referred to as "the system."

Given that capacity exceeds demand, one might assume that a queue would not form (i.e., the triangle in Figure 16.3 would always be empty). And that assumption would be correct if calls arrived *precisely* every five minutes and calls took *precisely* four minutes. In that case, the following rhythmic sequence of events occurs: (i) a call arrives, (ii) the caller spends four minutes with the agent, (iii) the caller leaves and the agent waits one minute for the next caller to arrive. This is beautiful from an operational perspective because there is never a queue of waiting customers! But the world does not usually work that way. Unfortunately, there can be variability in both how customers arrive and how long it takes to serve them, either of which (or both) can lead to queues, as we will see next.

Table 16.2 displays data from 12 calls that arrive between 1 a.m. and 2 a.m. Although the number of callers matches the historical average (12 callers per hour), the table reveals that the callers do not arrive precisely every five minutes. The time between arrivals can be as small as one minute and as long as 13 minutes. However, on average, the time between calls is indeed five minutes. Customers simply do not arrive in a consistent pattern with evenly spaced intervals.

There is also variation in the amount of time the agent spends with a caller. On average, the calls displayed in Table 16.2 last four minutes, but five of the calls are quick, lasting only one minute. One of the calls lasts 13 minutes! This variation can be caused by a number of factors. People might be calling for different reasons, and those reasons influence the time needed to complete the call. For example, some might only need to check a balance on an account, whereas others might need an explanation for why there are additional charges that they didn't expect. Even with the same type of call, there can be variation due to the behavior of the caller or agent. For example, when doing a "change of address," one agent might ask about the caller's new neighborhood while another agent might be "all business" (i.e., to the point).

Figure 16.3

Process flow diagram for the An-ser call center from 1 a.m. to 2 a.m.

Callers → △ → [An-ser Agent] → Completed calls

Callers waiting on hold in the queue | Up to one caller being served by the agent

TABLE 16.2 From 1 a.m. to 2 a.m., the Arrival Time of 12 Callers and the Time Each Caller Spends with the An-ser Agent

Caller	Arrival Time	Time with Agent (Minutes)
1	1:01	4
2	1:04	10
3	1:06	1
4	1:07	5
5	1:11	1
6	1:28	13
7	1:40	2
8	1:41	1
9	1:46	1
10	1:53	7
11	1:59	1
12	2:00	2

The consequence of variation in arrivals and call times is displayed in Figure 16.4, which uses the data from Table 16.2 to plot the number of callers over the hour either talking to the agent or waiting to talk to the agent. As we can see in the figure, sometimes there are as many as four callers in the system. In those cases, there must be one caller talking to the agent and three who are waiting to talk to the agent. In other words, there is a queue whenever there is more than one customer in the system.

Why did a queue form at An-ser when the capacity to serve customers (15 per hour) exceeds the demand from customers (12 per hour)? In short, because of variability. Even though, on average, there is enough capacity to serve all of the customers, because of variability in either

Figure 16.4

The number of customers either talking to an agent or waiting to talk to an agent over the one hour interval from 1 a.m. to 2 a.m.

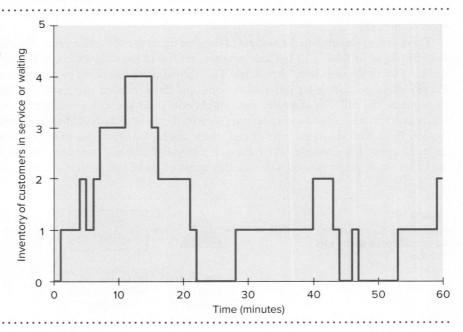

the arrival of customers or the time to serve them, there are periods of time in which demand exceeds capacity. During those bursts of demand, or slowdowns in capacity, a queue forms. For example, four callers arrive in the first 10 minutes, which is an arrival rate of 24 per hour, much greater than the average capacity of 15 callers per hour. Similarly, the agent spends 20 minutes to serve the first four callers, which is five minutes per caller. That is equivalent to about 12 callers per hour (= 60 minutes per hour/5 minutes per caller), which is lower than the average capacity of 15 callers per hour. Hence, it was unlucky in the first 10 minutes that the arrival rate of callers exceeded the average and the capacity to serve them was lower than the average. Consequently, a queue formed. Of course, An-ser cannot be unlucky forever—at some point, averages prevail and capacity indeed exceeds demand, allowing An-ser to eliminate the queue. For example, in the second 10 minutes, only one customer arrives and that customer's call only takes one minute. Hence, the demand rate is only six customers per hour, while the capacity is 60 customers per hour! In sum, when there is variability in either the arrival rate of customers or the rate to serve them (or both), queues can form even if, on average, capacity exceeds demand.

16.2.1 The Arrival and Service Processes

Our discussion of the An-ser call center indicates that, in order to understand queues, we need to understand both the process by which customers arrive to the system and how they are served by the system. The first one is called the **arrival process**—the flow of customers arriving to the system. The second one is called the **service process**—the flow of customers when they are being served.

A key feature of the arrival process is the **interarrival time**, which is the time between customer arrivals to the system. From Table 16.2, the interarrival time between the first and second callers is three minutes, and between the second and third callers is two minutes.

A key feature of the service process is the **processing time**, which is the time a customer spends with a server. From Table 16.2, the processing times are given in the third column: 4 minutes for the first caller, 10 minutes for the second, and so forth. Note that the processing time is the time between when a customer enters service (i.e., is no longer waiting) and when the service is completed. It does not include the time the customer waits.

Clearly, both interarrival times and processing times can vary, but before we discuss how they vary, let's define their average value:

a = Average interarrival time

p = Average processing time

For An-ser in the 1 a.m. to 2 a.m. hour, the average interarrival time is $a = 5$ minutes and the average processing time is $p = 4$ minutes. These are important measures, but we also need a measure of how variable each process is.

It is not immediately obvious how to measure variability. To illustrate, Figure 16.5 displays 25 observations from two different arrival processes. The average interarrival time for one is 10 seconds (red squares) and for the other it is 100 seconds (blue diamonds). Which one is more variable? The quick process (squares), with relatively short interarrival times, ranges roughly from 0 to 40 seconds, about 10 seconds below the average to about 30 seconds above the average. The slow process (diamonds), with relatively long interarrival times, ranges roughly from 90 to 130 seconds, also about 10 seconds below the average to 30 seconds above the average. Given that they both have a range of about 40 seconds, you might argue that they are equally variable. That notion of variability, which measures the absolute amount each observation deviates from the mean, is measured by the standard deviation. In fact, the standard deviation of both processes is about 10. So according to this measure of variability, they are equally variable.

But does the absolute difference between an observation and the average value really capture the important notion of variability? Consider two observations, one that is 8 seconds away from an average of 10 seconds and the other that is 8 seconds away from an average of 100. The first observation, which is 80 percent away from its average, seems to be a bigger deviation from "normal" than the second observation, which is only 8 percent away from its average: losing 8 points on a 10-point quiz seems to hurt more than losing 8 points on a

LO12-2 For a queue with variable interarrival and processing times and one server, evaluate several performance measures and understand the factors that influence those measures

---

Arrival process The flow of customers arriving to the system.

Service process The flow of customers when they are being served.

Interarrival time The time between customer arrivals to a system.

Processing time The time a customer spends with a server.

Figure 16.5

Twenty-five observations of interarrival times from two different processes. The quick process (red squares) has an average interarrival time of 10 seconds and the slow process (blue diamonds) has an average interarrival time of 100 seconds.

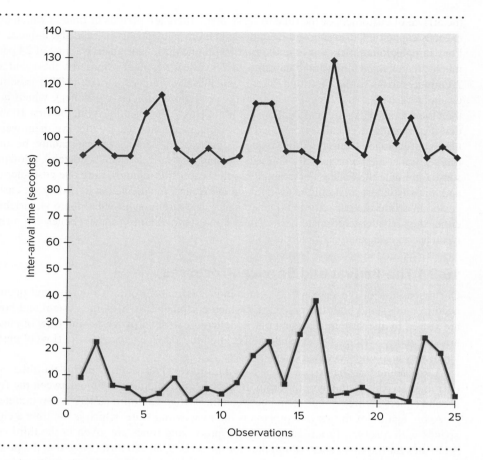

100-point test. In other words, another way to gauge variability is to track deviations relative to the average. This is done in Figure 16.6, which shows the same set of data as in Figure 16.5, but now each observation is drawn relative to its average. For example, all of the observations in the fast process (squares) are divided by 10 seconds and all of the observations of the slow process (diamonds) are divided by 100 seconds. Now which process is more variable? Seems obvious, doesn't it?

From Figure 16.6 we see that, for the slow process (diamonds), the observations never exceed more than 140 percent of their average, but with the quick process (squares), the observations can be as much as 400 percent larger than their average. Hence, we need a measure that captures this notion of variability. That measure is called the **coefficient of variation**, which is the ratio of the standard deviation to the average. The average interarrival time for the quick process (squares) displayed in Figure 16.5 is 10 seconds and its standard deviation is 10 seconds. Thus, its coefficient of variation is 1 (= 10/10). For the slower process (diamonds), the coefficient of variation is 0.1 (= 10/100). Thus, even though the two processes have the same standard deviation, they have very different coefficients of variation—one is 10 times more variable than the other, according to their coefficients of variation, which reflects the differences we visually observe in Figure 16.6. That is why the coefficient of variation is the better way to measure variability.

In general, the coefficient of variation of the arrival process is defined as

$$CV_a = \frac{\text{Standard deviation of arrival process}}{a}$$

and the coefficient of variation of the service process is defined as

Coefficient of variation The ratio of the standard deviation to the average.

$$CV_p = \frac{\text{Standard deviation of service process}}{p}$$

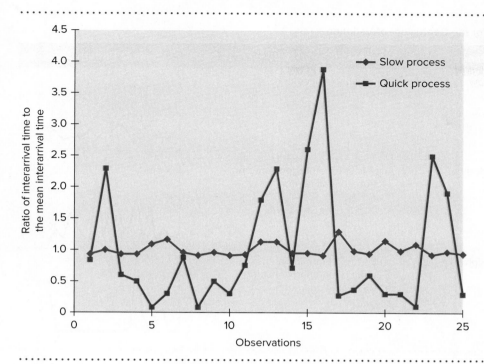

Figure 16.6
Twenty-five observations from two arrival processes, plotted as the ratio of the observations to their averages.

Returning to the data from the An-ser call center, recall that in the 1 a.m. to 2 a.m. hour, $a = 5$ and $p = 4$. The standard deviations are 5 and 4, respectively. Thus, during that time period, the coefficients of variations are:

$$CV_a = \frac{5}{5} = 1$$

$$CV_p = \frac{4}{4} = 1$$

In this case, the arrival process and the service process have about the same amount of variability relative to their average.

Are the coefficients of variation for An-ser's arrival and service processes unusual? Actually, it is common to observe a coefficient of variation close to one. With an arrival process, this occurs when arrivals are independent of each other. For example, the population of people who could call An-ser at any given moment is probably very large. There is a very small chance that any one person in this set will decide to call it at 1:05 a.m., but the chance isn't zero because sometimes a person does call at 1:05 a.m. Furthermore, the chance that Jack decides to call is probably completely unrelated to whether Juanita decides to call. This is what is meant by independent events: The fact that Jack calls or doesn't call has no influence on whether Juanita calls. When there is a relatively large population of potential callers, and their decisions to call at any one moment are roughly independent, then the coefficient of variation of the resulting arrival process tends to be close to one. Other examples where this tends to occur include (among many possible examples) arrivals to an emergency room at a hospital (my decision to break my arm is probably independent of your decision to get the flu) and arrivals to a store (my decision to purchase a TV is probably independent of your decision to shop for a new mobile phone).

The coefficient of variation of a service process can be close to one, but it often is less than one or greater than one. A coefficient of variation less than one suggests some consistency in the process. This could occur if there is little variety in the types of transactions the server needs to do or if the server is trained to be consistent in his or her work. However, it is also possible that the coefficient of variation is greater than one because the server must handle a

TABLE 16.3 Ranges and Examples for the Coefficient of Variation

Coefficient of Variation	Range	Example	Sample Pattern
0–0.5	Low	Only routine call center transactions	
0.5–1.5	Medium	Arrivals to an emergency room, store, or call center	
1.5–2.5	High	Arrivals occurring in batches or service requiring considerable variation in effort	

Check Your Understanding 16.4

Question: The average time to process a request at a web server is 10 milliseconds. The standard deviation of the processing times is 15 milliseconds. What is the coefficient of variation of the processing times?

Answer:

$$\text{Coefficient of variation} = \frac{\text{Standard deviation}}{\text{Average}} = \frac{15}{10} = 1.5$$

---

broad scope of work or if the work is inherently uncertain. For example, an emergency room that is designed to only handle twisted ankles has less variability in its processing times than a normal emergency room that handles everything from asthma to broken bones to severe traumas. Table 16.3 gives a sense of what is a "low," "medium," or "high" coefficient of variation.

16.2.2 A Queuing Model with a Single Server

Now that we have characterized the arrival and service processes, how can we estimate the average time a customer must wait in the call center and the total time they spend in the call center? One way is to collect data from actual observations. Table 16.4 expands the data in Table 16.2 to include the departure times for each caller (i.e., when they finish their service) and the resulting time they wait to speak to the agent. The average waiting time is 2.8 minutes. This is a measure of the waiting time at this call center for one particular day and one particular hour. But we don't know if this is an accurate measure of the expected waiting time— maybe the waiting time was somewhat long or somewhat short just by chance. And it does not provide us with a sense of why the waiting time is what it is. Thus, for this call center, it could be useful to build a **queuing model**, an abstract representation of the queue that enables us to predict waiting times and other performance measures.

Queuing model An abstract representation of the queue that enables us to predict waiting times and other performance measures.

TABLE 16.4   Departure and Waiting Times for Each Caller Who Called the An-ser Call Center between 1 a.m. and 2 a.m.

Caller	Arrival Time	Time with Agent (minutes)	Departure Time	Time Waiting (minutes)
1	1:01	4	1:05	0
2	1:04	10	1:15	1
3	1:06	1	1:16	9
4	1:07	5	1:21	9
5	1:11	1	1:22	10
6	1:28	13	1:41	0
7	1:40	2	1:43	1
8	1:41	1	1:44	2
9	1:46	1	1:47	0
10	1:53	7	2:00	0
11	1:59	1	2:01	1
12	2:00	2	2:03	1

There are many different queuing models. Some are simple and some are complex. In this case, a relatively simple model is reasonable for the An-ser call center from 1 a.m. to 2 a.m.; it is displayed in Figure 16.7. With all queuing models, there is a list of assumptions and parameters that determine how the model works. For this model, the list includes the following:

- There is one server.
- There is a single queue.
- Once a customer arrives to the system, the customer waits until service is completed.
- p = The server's processing time.
- a = The average interarrival time of customers.
- CV_a and CV_p are the coefficients of variation of the interarrival times and the processing times, respectively.
- The average interarrival time is greater than the average processing time: $p < a$.

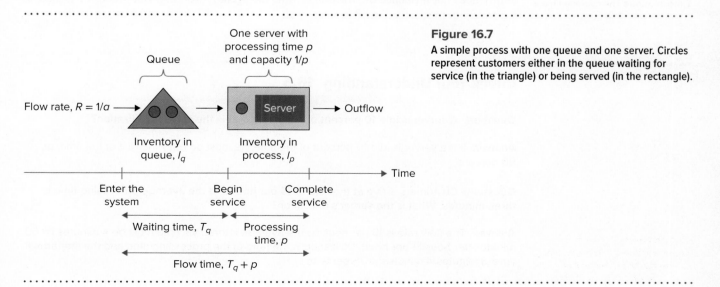

Figure 16.7

A simple process with one queue and one server. Circles represent customers either in the queue waiting for service (in the triangle) or being served (in the rectangle).

With this model, the key inputs are the average interarrival time (a), the average processing time (p), and the coefficients of variation of the interarrival times and processing times (CV_a, CV_p). We use these inputs to immediately evaluate the capacity of the server, $1/p$, and the flow rate of customers, $R = 1/a$. The performance measures for the system that are of interest include

- T_q = Average time a customer waits in the queue; also called **time in queue**, for short
- I_q = Average number of customers waiting in the queue
- I_p = Average number of customers in service (being processed)
- T = Flow time; that is, the average time a customer spends in the system (waiting and in service): $T = T_p + p$

16.2.3 Utilization

Using the inputs to the model, our first calculation is the utilization of the server:

$$\text{Utilization} = \frac{\text{Flow rate}}{\text{Capacity}} = \frac{1/a}{1/p} = \frac{p}{a}$$

Note that $p < a$ is assumed in the model. This means that the time to process a customer is shorter than the time between customer arrivals. It also means that the capacity of the server, $1/p$, is greater than the demand rate. In other words, because $p < a$, we have a system in which, on average, there is more capacity than demand (i.e., the flow rate). This is a critical assumption. If it does not hold, then the queue behaves quite differently than this model predicts. In particular, if $p > a$, then the queue tends to continue to grow and grow as long as $p > a$. In those cases, a different type of queuing model is needed, like the one for the Ski Butternut rental shop.

For the one agent working 1 a.m. to 2 a.m. at An-ser, recall that $p = 4$ and $a = 5$; that is, the agent can process a customer on average in four minutes and one customer arrives, on average, every five minutes. Given these numbers, the agent's utilization is $4/5 = 0.8$, or 80 percent.

The utilization of the server is the fraction of time the server is working. Thus, the server for An-ser works 80 percent of the time. If the agent is not working, then the agent is idle, so the agent must be idle 20 percent of the time (= $100\% - 80\%$).

Although we have emphasized the importance of variability for generating queues, variability has no influence whatsoever on the server's utilization. The An-ser agent would also be busy 80 percent of the time if calls arrived precisely every five minutes ($CP_a = 0$) and calls took precisely four minutes to serve ($CV_p = 0$). The same would be true if calls arrived with considerable variability ($CP_a = 2$) and service was equally variable ($CV_p = 2$). Hence, variability does not influence the fraction of time the agent is working. But it does influence, as we are about to see, the time customers wait.

Time in queue The average time a customer waits in a queue.

Check Your Understanding 16.5

Question: A server is idle 10 percent of his time. What is the server's utilization?

Answer: If the server is idle 10 percent of the time, he must be busy the rest of the time, or 90 percent.

Question: Customers arrive at the rate of 15 per hour and the average processing time is three minutes. What is the server's utilization?

Answer: The flow rate is 15 per hour, so the average interarrival time must be 4 minutes (= 60 minutes per hour/15 per hour). Utilization is the ratio of the processing time and the interarrival time: 3 minutes/4 minutes = 75 percent.

16.2.4 Predicting Time in Queue, T_q; Time in Service; and Total Time in the System

Given the queuing model displayed in Figure 16.7, the average time a customer waits in the queue is

$$T_q = p \times \left(\frac{\text{Utilization}}{1 - \text{Utilization}} \right) \times \left(\frac{CV_a^2 + CV_p^2}{2} \right)$$

Let's use the above equation to estimate the average wait for customers at the An-ser call center in the hour between 1 a.m. and 2 a.m.:

$$T_q = 4 \text{ minutes} \times \left(\frac{0.8}{1 - 0.8} \right) \times \left(\frac{1^2 + 1^2}{2} \right) = 16 \text{ minutes}$$

Recall that we observed for one particular day that the average waiting time for customers was only 2.8 minutes. Hence, they were lucky on that day. On other days, the average waiting time could be longer than 16 minutes. On average, the waiting time is 16 minutes, which is very long for a call center.

Besides the time waiting, customers also spend time with the agent receiving service. Hence, their total time in the system, from start to finish, is $T_q + p$. In the case of the An-ser call center, the total average time to resolve your issue in the early morning hour is 20 minutes ($= 16 + 4$). However, it is the time-in-queue portion of the total time that probably is the most frustrating to customers. (See Connections: The Psychology of Waiting.)

16.2.5 Predicting the Number of Customers Waiting and in Service

In addition to the average time customers wait, we may also want to know how many customers are waiting or in service. From Figure 16.7, I_q is the average number of customers waiting and I_p is the average number of customers in service. As these are "inventories," we can apply Little's Law to evaluate them:

$$I_q = R \times T_q = \frac{T_q}{a}$$

and

$$I_p = R \times p = \frac{p}{a}$$

As you might expect, if the time waiting in the queue, T_q, increases, then the number of people in the queue increases as well. Interestingly, the average number of people in service, I_p, is the same as the utilization of the server: If the server is busy 80 percent of the time, then 80 percent of the time there is one person in service!

Check Your Understanding 16.6

Question: A server operates with 75 percent utilization. The average processing time is two minutes and the standard deviation of processing time is one minute. The coefficient of variation of the arrival process is one. What is the average time in the queue for customers?

Answer: The coefficient of variation of the service process is 1/2.

$$T_q = 2 \text{ minutes} \times \left(\frac{0.75}{1 - 0.75} \right) \times \left(\frac{1^2 + (1/2)^2}{2} \right) = \frac{15}{4} \text{ minutes} = 3.75 \text{ minutes}$$

Check Your Understanding 16.7

Question: On average, a customer waits 10 minutes in a queue and customers arrive at the rate of two per minute. How many customers are waiting in the queue on average?

Answer: Time in queue is 10 minutes. The arrival rate is 2 per minute; that is, $1/a = 2$ per minute. Hence, the average interarrival time is 1/2 minute. The inventory of waiting customers is then 2 per minute. Hence, the average interarrival time is 1/2 minute. The inventory of waiting customers is then

$$I_q = \frac{T_q}{a} = \frac{10 \text{ minutes}}{1/2 \text{ minute per customer}} = 20 \text{ customers}$$

16.2.6 The Key Drivers of Waiting Time

Let's use the equation for T_q to better understand the key drivers of waiting time. Looking at the equation, you can observe three parts. The first part of the equation is p, the processing time. This is called the "capacity" factor because the capacity of the server, $1/p$, is determined by the processing time. It is intuitive that when there is less capacity (p is larger), the average waiting time for customers increases. Hence, if capacity increases (i.e., the processing time decreases), the average wait for service decreases.

The second part of the T_q equation is the "utilization factor":

$$\frac{\text{Utilization}}{1 - \text{Utilization}}$$

Recall that the utilization is always less than one because $p < a$. Hence, the utilization factor is never negative. Not only is the utilization factor not negative, it can be very large. Figure 16.8 displays the utilization factor for a range of utilizations. First, notice that the utilization factor always increases as the utilization increases. This means that as the agent becomes busier a greater fraction of the time, the average wait in the queue increases. Put another way, a busy agent means that customers spend more time waiting.

The next readily apparent feature of the curve in Figure 16.8 is that it becomes steeper and steeper as the utilization increases: Each incremental increase in utilization causes the utilization factor to increase by a larger amount. For example, increasing the utilization from 50 percent to 60 percent increases the utilization factor by 0.5 (from 1 to 1.5), but a 10 percent increase in utilization from 80 percent to 90 percent increases the utilization factor by five (from 4 to 9). In fact, once the utilization is greater than 90 percent, the utilization factor is large and the utilization factor is extremely sensitive to changes in utilization—a small increase in the utilization can have a dramatic increase in the time in queue for customers.

Given that the An-ser agent is paid whether she is idle or not, the owner of An-ser might prefer that she works with a high utilization—why pay an employee to be idle? But if the agent is rarely idle (i.e., her utilization is high), then customers will wait a substantial amount of time in the queue. Thus, the manager faces a clear trade-off: Either the agent is idle and customers spend little (to no) time waiting, or the agent is busy and customers spend a considerable amount of time waiting.

The third factor in the T_q equation is the "variability" factor:

$$\frac{CV_a^2 + CV_p^2}{2}$$

This factor contains the squares of the coefficients of variation. Here, we clearly see the impact of variability on the system. If there were no variability in either the arrival process, $CV_a = 0$, or the service process, $CV_p = 0$, then the variability factor would equal zero and customers would spend absolutely no time in queue: $T_q = 0$! However, any amount of variability, in either

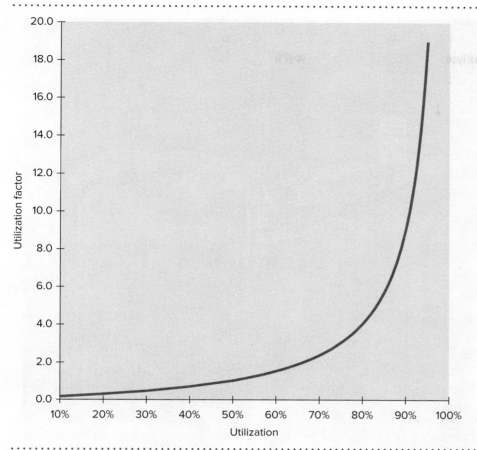

Figure 16.8
The utilization factor in the time-in-queue equation as a function of the utilization of the server

the arrival process or the service process, and a queue forms at least some of the time. Furthermore, the more variability in either process, the longer the customers must wait in the queue.

In sum, there are three drivers of waiting time in a queue: capacity, utilization, and variability. To reduce the amount of time customers wait, a manager has three levers to work with: increase capacity, decrease utilization, or decrease variability.

CONNECTIONS: The Psychology of Waiting

We hate to wait. It follows that a three-minute wait should be less painful than a four-minute wait. That would always be true if we only cared about the actual time we wait. But, in fact, the actual time we wait is only one factor that determines how onerous we perceive our wait to be. And it might not even be the dominant factor. Imagine calling bank A: While you waited, not only were you not told how long it would take a representative to answer your call, you were forced to "listen" to dead silence until a customer service representative said "hello" after three minutes. Now imagine calling bank B: You were immediately told that your wait would be four minutes; while you waited, you listened to several tips about how best to manage your money; and, in fact, after four minutes, a customer service representative joined your call. Even though you waited one minute less with the silent bank A, you might rate your experience with bank B more positively. In short, the actual time waiting is important, but not the only important factor that determines how satisfied we are. This is a key finding in a body of research that investigates the psychology of waiting with the goal to better understand what influences our perception of how long we wait and how

Continued

unpleasant the wait is. From this research, we learn that the pain of waiting often depends on how "occupied" you feel during a wait. You are not making good use of your time while listening to silly music while waiting to talk to somebody or watching an entertainment "news" show on TV in an emergency room lobby while you wait for a doctor, but at least you are not completely idle, staring into space or twiddling your thumbs.

From the research we also learn that the perceived cost of waiting grows as we wait longer. You probably can imagine that, as you wait, your anger and frustration accumulate at a faster and faster pace: The first minute of waiting is "no problem," but after waiting 50 minutes, you feel like screaming at somebody if you have to wait "one minute more." Because of this, most people prefer to wait five minutes for sure rather than accept a 10 percent chance of a 50-minute wait and a 90 percent chance of zero wait. The average wait in those two cases is the same (five minutes), but the second option clearly has more variability in the waiting time.

Even worse than known variability is unknown variability. For example, imagine you think a wait shouldn't be more than five minutes. You start your wait and five minutes go by. Then you wait another 10 minutes and now you have no idea how long your wait will be. The uncertainty is killing you. In the end, you wait a total of 16 minutes. Compare that to a situation in which you were told at the very beginning that you would wait 16 minutes. You might not be happy about the news, but at least you know what to expect. This is why it can be prudent to let customers know how long you think they will have to wait, especially if their wait will be longer than usual.

16.3 Queues When Demand and Service Rates Are Variable—Multiple Servers

In the early morning hours, the volume of calls to An-ser is light. But demand doesn't stay light once the regular workday starts. From 8 a.m. to 10 a.m., the call center operates at an entirely different pace. Based on historical data, during those two hours, it receives 288 calls, on average, or one every 25 seconds. Fortunately, these calls can be processed more quickly than in the early morning hour. Figure 16.9 displays a histogram of the processing times for a sample of calls during this period. On average, a call requires 120 seconds to process, but as can be seen in Figure 16.9, there remains considerable variation. Some calls are over within 30 seconds, but others take nearly 10 minutes.

From 8 a.m. to 10 a.m., An-ser does not operate with a single agent. The data on call arrivals and processing times immediately reveal why: If a call arrives every 25 seconds and an agent takes 120 seconds, on average, to process a call, then one agent simply cannot keep up with the call volume. On average, four to five customers arrive during the time an agent is processing a single customer's request. Hence, a queuing model with a single server does not work for this situation. We need a queuing model that allows for multiple servers. Such a model is displayed in Figure 16.10. It resembles the model in Figure 16.7, with the key difference being that now there are multiple agents able to process customers. For completeness, the assumptions for this model are the following:

- There are m servers.
- There is a single queue.
- Once a customer arrives to the system, the customer waits until service is completed.
- Each customer is served by only one agent.
- p = The servers' average processing time.
- a = The average interarrival time of customers.
- CV_a and CV_p are the coefficients of variation of the interarrival times and the processing times, respectively.
- The capacity of the system, m/p, is greater than the flow rate, $1/a$, that is, $m/p > 1/a$, which can also be written as $p/m < a$.

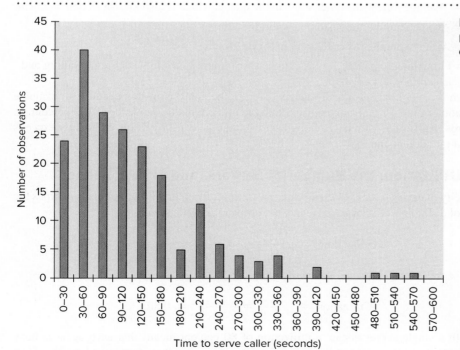

Figure 16.9

Histogram of processing times at An-ser's call center from 8 a.m. to 10 a.m.

Figure 16.10

A queuing model with *m* servers. Circles represent customers either in the queue waiting for service (in the triangle) or being served (in the rectangle).

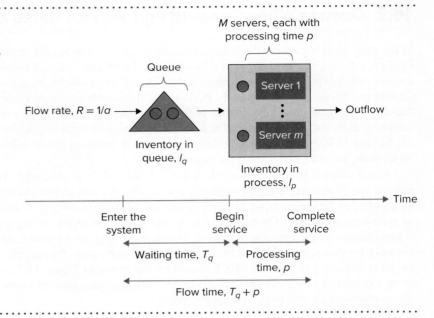

Based on An-ser's data, for the 8 a.m. to 10 a.m. period, $a = 25$ seconds and $p = 120$ seconds. Furthermore, based on the standard deviations of the interarrival and processing times, the coefficients of variation are $CV_a = 1$ and $CV_p = 0.75$. Hence, arrivals are as variable at 8 a.m. as they are at 1 a.m., but processing times are somewhat less variable (0.75 versus 1). This could be due to better-trained agents (who are able to better handle even unusual calls) or because the calls that arrive in the morning have more consistency (as in fewer "out of the blue" request types). Nevertheless, as Figure 16.9 shows, there is still variability in the processing times.

The same performance measures are relevant for this queuing model as the single-agent model:

- T_q = Average time a customer waits in the queue, which is also known as *time in queue*
- I_q = Average number of customers waiting in the queue
- I_p = Average number of customers in service (being processed)
- T = Flow time; that is, the average time a customer spends in the system (waiting and in service): $T = T_p + p$

As with the single-agent model, the first step in the analysis of this queue is to evaluate the utilization of the servers and to ensure that the utilization does not exceed 100 percent. In other words, An-ser needs to have enough servers that the capacity of the call center exceeds the arrival rate of demand.

16.3.1 Utilization, the Number of Servers, and Stable Queues

The capacity of each server is $1/p$. The capacity of the call center with *m* servers is *m* times the capacity of a single server, or m/p. Hence, the utilization of the servers is

$$\text{Utilization} = \frac{\text{Flow rate}}{\text{Capacity}} = \frac{1/a}{m/p} = \frac{p}{a \times m}$$

If An-ser has six agents, then their utilization is

$$\text{Utilization} = \frac{p}{a \times m} = \frac{120}{25 \times 6} = 0.80$$

As with a single-server queue, a utilization of 80 percent means that each agent is busy serving customers 80 percent of his or her time. It also means that at any one time there is a

.80 probability that any randomly selected server is busy. Furthermore, it means that, on average, 80 percent of the agents are serving customers and 20 percent of them are idle, waiting for customers.

It is critically important that demand (1/a) be less than capacity (m/p). If demand exceeds capacity, then there is not enough capacity to satisfy the demand. In those situations, like at the Ski Butternut rental shop, the queue continues to grow and grow during the time that demand exceeds capacity.

Using the equation for utilization, we can evaluate the minimum number of servers to ensure that demand is less than capacity:

$$\text{Minimum number of servers} > \frac{p}{a}$$

In this case, the minimum number of servers must be greater than 120 seconds/25 seconds = 4.8. Because we cannot have 4.8 servers, we must round up to five to get the realistic number of servers. Thus, if An-ser has five or more servers, their utilization is less than 100 percent and capacity exceeds demand. If An-ser has four or fewer servers, the capacity is insufficient to meet demand. In that case, the last assumption in our list of assumptions for the model is not satisfied.

To illustrate why it is so important that An-ser have sufficient staffing to handle the call volume, Figure 16.11 displays what can happen to the number of customers in the system when there are only four servers. The total inventory of customers sometimes decreases, but the overall trend is unmistakable: On average, the queue continues to grow during the entire two-hour period. By the end of the two hours, there are about 60 customers in the system (54 of them are waiting) and clearly they need to wait a considerable amount of time to complete their service. Figure 16.11 displays only one possible outcome from the queue (after all, arrivals and processing times are random), but the pattern displayed in the figure is representative of what would happen.

In stark contrast, Figure 16.12 displays the total number of customers in the system when there are six servers. Now there is enough capacity to serve demand. Instead of a queue that grows steadily, seemingly without a limit, with six servers the queue exhibits a pattern of growth and decline. While the queue can be long, it never gets out of control.

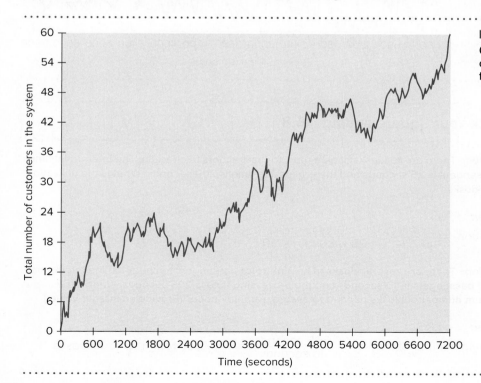

Figure 16.11

One possible outcome for the total number of customers in the system when there are only four servers

The queue displayed in Figure 16.11 is referred to as an **unstable queue**, whereas the queue displayed in Figure 16.12 is referred to as a **stable queue**. An unstable queue is one in which demand ($1/a$) exceeds capacity (m/p). If in that case we were to use the equation for utilization, we would get a value that is greater than 100 percent, which is not possible—utilization cannot be greater than 100 percent. (Recall that implied utilization is the ratio of demand to capacity, so when demand exceeds capacity, the implied utilization is greater than 100 percent.) A stable queue has more capacity than demand. When we use the utilization equation with a stable queue, we get a value that is less than 100 percent. The methods applied for the Ski Butternut rental shop are best used for queues that are not stable. For the model described in Figure 16.10, it is assumed that the queue is stable; that is, demand is less than capacity and the utilization is less than 100 percent.

Unstable queue A queuing system in which the demand rate exceeds capacity.

Stable queue A queuing system in which the demand rate is less than capacity.

Figure 16.12

One possible outcome for the total number of customers in the system when there are six servers

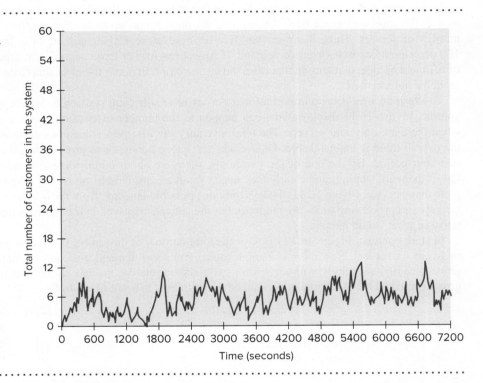

Check Your Understanding 16.8

Question: There are 10 kiosks at an airport for passengers to check in. The interarrival time of passengers is 25 seconds and the processing time is 200 seconds. What is the utilization of the kiosks?

Answer:

$$\text{Utilization} = \frac{p}{a \times m} = \frac{200 \text{ seconds}}{25 \text{ seconds} \times 10} = 80\%$$

Question: There are several kiosks at an airport for passengers to check in. The interarrival time of passengers is 10 seconds and the processing time is 205 seconds. What is the minimum number of kiosks needed to ensure a stable queue? (Provide an integer value.)

Answer:

$$\text{Minimum number of kiosks} > \frac{205 \text{ seconds}}{10 \text{ seconds}} = 20.5, \text{ so round up to 21 kiosks}$$

16.3.2 Predicting Waiting Time in Queue, T_q; Waiting Time in Service; and Total Time in the System

The equation for the average waiting time in queue is similar to the analogous equation in the queuing model with a single server:

$$T_q = \left(\frac{p}{m}\right) \times \left(\frac{\text{Utilization}^{\sqrt{2(m+1)}-1}}{1 - \text{Utilization}}\right) \times \left(\frac{CV_a^2 + CV_p^2}{2}\right)$$

The differences between the equations are that (i) the processing time must be divided by the number of servers, m, and (ii) there is a new exponent on the utilization term. Although the above equation is at first intimidating, it merely requires careful calculation to lead to an answer. In particular, notice that in the exponent $(\sqrt{2(m+1)} - 1)$, the "-1" is outside of the square root.

If there is only one server—that is, $m = 1$—then the above time-in-queue formula is exactly the same as the one in the single-server model. Thus, we can think of the above formula as the more general equation: It applies both when there is a single agent as well as when there are multiple agents.

Applying the time-in-queue formula to the An-ser call center in the two hours between 8 a.m. and 10 a.m. (assuming six agents are working) yields:

$$T_q = \left(\frac{120}{6}\right) \times \left(\frac{0.8^{\sqrt{2(6+1)}-1}}{1 - 0.8}\right) \times \left(\frac{1^2 + 0.75^2}{2}\right) = (20)(2.712)(0.7813) = 42.4 \text{ seconds}$$

On average customers wait about 42 seconds before they start talking to an agent. Then they spend, on average, 120 seconds with the agent, for a total average time in the system of $T = 162$ seconds. Of course, this is just an average and the actual time a customer spends can vary.

16.3.3 Predicting the Number of Customers Waiting and in Service

Once we have an estimate for the average time a customer spends waiting, we can use Little's Law to evaluate the number of customers, on average, that are waiting,

$$I_q = R \times T_q = \frac{T_q}{a}$$

and the number of customers in service,

$$I_p = R \times p = \frac{p}{a}$$

These formulas are identical to the ones used for the single-server queue.

Check Your Understanding 16.9

Question: There are 10 kiosks at an airport for passengers to check in. The interarrival time of passengers is 25 seconds and the processing time is 200 seconds. The coefficients of variation for the arrival process and the service process are both one. What is the average time in queue?

Answer: Utilization is $200/(25 \times 10) = 0.8$. Average time in queue is then

$$T_q = \left(\frac{200}{10}\right) \times \left(\frac{0.8^{\sqrt{2(10+1)}-1}}{1 - 0.8}\right) \times \left(\frac{1^1 + 1^1}{2}\right) = 43.9 \text{ seconds}$$

The number of agents surely influences the time in queue: If we add agents, then the utilization falls, the capacity of the system increases, and the average time in queue naturally decreases. If customers spend less time in the queue, there naturally will be fewer people in the queue (I_q decreases). But oddly enough, the number of agents has *no* influence on the number of people in service. For example, if the number of agents were doubled from 6 to 12, the average number of customers in service would remain 120/25 = 4.8. Why? Little's Law tells us that the number of customers in service depends on the flow rate and the time they spend in service. The number of servers neither alters the flow rate of customers nor the average time a customer spends in service because each customer is served by only one agent and that agent takes, on average, 120 seconds to serve the customer (no matter the number of other agents available). Thus, while your intuition might be that with more agents there would be, on average, more customers talking to agents, this actually is not true in this queuing model. (See Connections: Self-Service Queues for a discussion of what happens when the customers are their own servers.)

Check Your Understanding 16.10

Question: There are 10 kiosks at an airport for passengers to check in. The interarrival time of passengers is 25 seconds and the processing time is 200 seconds. On average, how many people are using the kiosks?

Answer: The number of customers in service is

$$I_p = R \times p = \frac{p}{a} = \frac{200}{25} = 8$$

CONNECTIONS: Self-Service Queues

© John Tlumacki/Boston Globe/Getty Images

You have probably encountered a self-service lane in a grocery store. (They are also used in airports to check in for a flight.) Do they actually help you get through the checkout process more quickly? The queuing formulas can help us answer that question.

Let's begin with the obvious: You are slower at checking out your groceries than a store employee. It is not that the store hires people who are innately talented at grocery checkout. You probably have the ability as well. What you don't have is experience. And in this case, "practice surely makes perfect." In the language of queuing, your processing time, p, is longer than the processing time of a store employee. This does not bode well for the system. If we increase the average processing time and hold everything else equal, then (i) utilization increases, (ii) the capacity factor in the time-in-queue equation increases, and (iii) the utilization factor in the time-in-queue equation increases. There will be more people waiting to check out, more people will be in the checkout process, and the total time it takes to check out increases (waiting plus service time). The store might save on the cost of checkout employees, but none of this is good from the point of view of the customer.

So how can you make self-service lanes more attractive to customers? Have more of them than you would have employees! Again, using the language of queuing, you would increase the number of servers, m. Suppose customers are twice as slow as employees (their p is twice as large as an employee's p), but twice as many customers can be in the checkout process than the number of employees. The last point means that the number of servers with self-checkout is twice as large as with employee checkout: m doubles. What does that do to the system? First, utilization remains the same: If you double p and m, utilization doesn't change. Next, notice that the capacity factor in the time-in-queue equation also doesn't change. Let's also say that the coefficients of variation don't change. Although several things don't change, notice that the utilization factor in the time-in-queue equation becomes smaller because the exponent in the numerator becomes larger. Hence, even if customers are twice as slow as an employee, if you can have twice as many customers checking themselves out, you can reduce the time they spend waiting.

We just observed that if self-service increases the number of servers, it can reduce the time in queue even if the servers are slower. However, the total time in the grocery store depends on how much you wait and the processing time. So even if self-service reduces waiting time, it increases processing time, which means that total time in the system (the sum of those two) could increase. Is this necessarily a problem? Maybe not. As described in Connections: The Psychology of Waiting, people perceive time to slow down if they are busy. Five minutes checking out your groceries on your own might seem like much less time than watching an employee spend five minutes doing the task. Hence, even if self-service increases the total time to pay for your groceries, you might perceive that time to be shorter than the time with the traditional way using a store employee. Throw in the fact that the store doesn't have to pay an employee, and everyone could be better off.

16.4 Queuing System Design—Economies of Scale and Pooling

What are the key drivers of time in queue in the multiple-server queue? There are three key factors and they are essentially the same three as in the single-server queue. The first is the capacity factor, p/m. If each agent spends less time with customers (p decreases) or there are more agents (m increases), then the system has more capacity and customers spend less time waiting. The second is the utilization factor:

$$\frac{\text{Utilization}^{\sqrt{2(m+1)}-1}}{1-\text{Utilization}}$$

As is displayed in Figure 16.8, the higher the utilization, the longer customers wait on average, especially as the utilization approaches 100 percent. The third is the variability factor:

$$\frac{CV_a^2 + CV_p^2}{2}$$

Again, variability in either the arrival process or the service process, or both, leads to a queue.

Beyond the three factors, the time-in-queue formula reveals an important managerial insight. Figure 16.13 plots the average time in queue for three different staffing levels: the upper curve is for a call center with six agents (like An-ser), the middle curve is for a call center with 12 agents, and the bottom curve is for a call center with 60 agents. All three cases have the same processing time (120 seconds) and coefficients of variation. In all three cases, the time in queue increases with the utilization of the agents. But what is substantially different is how these three call centers respond to changes in utilization. In short, as the call centers get bigger—in the sense of having more agents—they become far less sensitive to utilization. With only six agents (the top curve), the time in queue is rapidly increasing even when the system has utilization less than 85 percent. With 12 agents, the time in queue starts its rapid ascent at higher utilizations. And with 60 agents, the trade-off between utilization and time in queue almost does not exist below 90 percent utilization.

The relative "flatness" of the trade-off curve between utilization and time in queue gives large call centers a substantial advantage. As a call center becomes bigger, the manager of the center has three options:

1. Keep the utilization of the servers constant but lower the average waiting time for customers.

2. Keep the average waiting time of customers constant but increase the utilization of the servers.

3. Do a blend of the first two options: increase the utilization of the servers *and* reduce the waiting time for customers.

Figure 16.13

Time in queue for An-ser with three staffing levels. The top curve is with six agents, the middle curve is with 12 agents, and the bottom curve is with 60 agents.

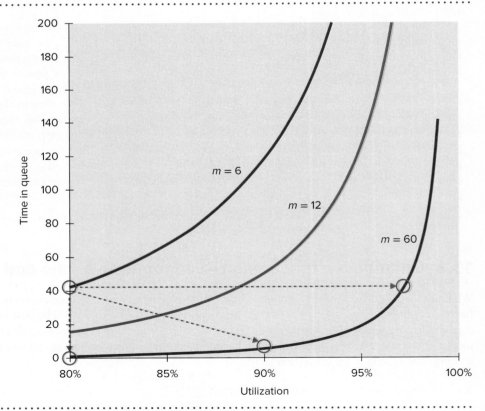

Figure 16.13 illustrates these options. Begin where the An-ser call center is now, at the red circle on the curve for six agents and 80 percent utilization. The waiting time is about 42 seconds. But if it could keep 80 percent utilization while growing its staff to 60 agents, it would be able to drop the waiting time to practically nothing (less than one second)! This moves it to the first red circle on the 60-server curve. In this case, its agents are no more or less busy than before, but its customers are much happier.

The second option is to keep customers waiting the same amount of time but to increase the utilization of the agents. This is a move from the red circle on the six-server curve to the far-right red circle on the 60-agent curve. Customers continue to experience the same quality of service (they wait 42 seconds), but now the agents have a utilization of 97 percent. This means that instead of being idle 20 percent of the time, they are idle only 3 percent of the time. Less idle time means a lower cost of labor per served customer!

The third option is to adopt a blend of the two extreme strategies. For example, the manager could move from the red circle on the six-agent curve to the middle circle on the 60-agent curve. Customers are happier because their average waiting time decreases from 42 seconds to 5.4 seconds. The manager focused on labor costs is happier too because the utilization of the agents increases from 80 percent to 90 percent.

In sum, the important managerial insight from the time in queue formula is that there are **economies of scale** in the operations of a system with queues. When a process has economies of scale, it means that it becomes more efficient as it becomes larger. We see here that a larger call center is able to have lower labor costs per served customer (i.e., higher utilization of agents) while also providing better service to customers (lower waiting times). Simply put, bigger queuing systems work better.

So if there are economies of scale in a queuing system, why doesn't everyone operate very large systems? Because there is a catch. To operate a call center with many employees at a high utilization requires that you have enough demand to utilize those employees. To have an 80 percent utilization with 60 servers (and a processing time of 120 seconds) requires an average interarrival time of 2.5 seconds, which yields a demand rate that is 10 times larger than the demand rate with six employees. To have a 97 percent utilization with 60 servers requires a demand rate of 1746 callers per hour (again, assuming a processing time of 120 seconds), which is more than 12 times An-ser's current demand rate. If it can get the extra demand, then An-ser would have several desirable options. The challenge is to get the demand.

LO16-4 Understand why there are economies of scale in queuing systems, and the pros and cons of pooling

16.4.1 The Power of Pooling

There are economies of scale in queuing systems: Queues with more demand and more servers work better. So it is better to operate a system with more demand. But what if that is not possible? Given a fixed amount of demand, is there something a manager can do to ensure the best operational performance? Yes, there is, as is illustrated next via an example.

Economies of scale A property of an operating system in which the efficiency of the system increases as the system gets larger.

Check Your Understanding 16.11

Question: If the arrival rate doubles and the number of servers doubles, what is the change in the system's utilization, assuming there are no other changes (e.g., the processing time and the coefficients of variation remain the same)?

A. Utilization increases.
B. Utilization remains the same.
C. Utilization decreases.
D. It is not possible to determine how those changes will influence utilization.

Answer: If the arrival rate doubles, then the interarrival time is cut in half. Utilization is $p/(a \times m)$. If a is cut in half and m doubles, utilization stays the same. So, the correct answer is B.

Consider system 1 (on the left) displayed in Figure 16.14. There are four servers and a single queue. A single queue means that when a customer arrives, the customer waits in the queue for the first available agent. Thus, any one of the four agents can serve a customer, and the customer doesn't know when she arrives to the system which agent will eventually serve her. Customers arrive with an interarrival time of 25 seconds and each server has a processing time of 90 seconds. Finally, the coefficients of variation (CV_a, CV_p) both equal one. This is the same type of system as displayed in Figure 16.10. This is called a **pooled-queue** system because all demand is shared, or pooled, across the four servers.

In many respects, system 2, displayed on the right side of Figure 16.14, is similar to system 1. There are four servers, each still has a processing time of 90 seconds, and the coefficients of variations also equal one. In addition, one customer arrives to the system every 25 seconds, just as in system 1. However, when a customer arrives, she is immediately placed into one of four separate queues, one for each server. For example, if she is placed in the second queue, she waits until the second server is available and is surely served by the second server. Each queue in system 2 is assigned one-fourth of the demand (i.e., the servers share the demand equally). Consequently, the interarrival time to each queue is 100 seconds: If one customer arrives every 25 seconds and a queue receives one out of four customers, then it receives a customer every 100 seconds (= 25 × 4). System 2 operates like four separate queues, each with a single server, as in Figure 16.7. This is called a **separate-queue** system because demand is immediately divided among the servers and a customer is only served by her designated agent. A doctor's office might work like system 2: Each patient is assigned to one doctor (a server) and the patient always sees the same doctor. Hence, each doctor is assigned one-fourth of the patients. In contrast, if the office operates like system 1, then patients see whichever doctor is available.

Let's now analyze the waiting time in these two systems. We first evaluate the utilization of the servers. In the system with a single pooled queue, the processing time is 90 seconds, the interarrival time is 25 seconds, and there are four servers. So utilization is 0.9 (= 90/(25 × 4)). In the second system, there are four separate queues. Each one has a processing time of 90 seconds, an interarrival time of 100 seconds, and one server. Each server's utilization is still 0.9 (= 90/(100 × 1)). Thus, both systems have four servers in total, the same capacity, the same demand rate, the same variability in processing and arrivals, and the servers are equally busy (they work 90 percent of the time in either system). With all of this similarity, it might come as a bit of a surprise to see the difference in the waiting times displayed in Table 16.5: Customers wait 179 seconds in the pooled-queue system, but they have to wait 810 seconds, on average, in the separate-queue system. That means that even though the separate-queue system has the same capacity and the same demand, and its servers are no busier nor idle than

Pooled queue A queuing system in which all demand is shared across all servers. Hence, each customer is served by the first available server and each customer can be served by any agent.

Separate queue A queuing system in which demand is initially divided among different servers, and customers are eventually served only by their designated agent.

Figure 16.14

Two queuing systems, one with one pooled queue (left) and the other with four separate queues (right)

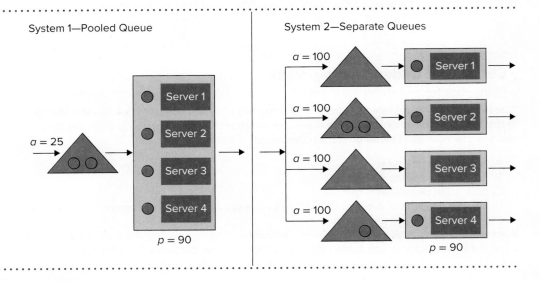

in the pooled-queue system, customers in the separate-queue system have to wait 4.5 times longer! That is a huge difference in performance; to emphasize the point further, these systems have exactly the same set of resources (four agents, equally skilled at serving customers). The time a customer waits does not just depend on the amount of resources available. It also depends on how we manage those resources, as in whether we operate with a pooled queue or separate queues.

Why is a pooled system able to operate much more effectively than a system with separate queues with exactly the same resources? One answer is "economies of scale." A single pooled system that combines all of our demand and all of our servers delivers shorter waiting times than four separate systems, each with one-fourth of our demand and one-fourth of our servers. However, it is possible to dive even further into why there are economies of scale. Figure 16.14 shows that there are six customers in each system. In the pooled system, there are four customers being served and two waiting for service. In the separate-queue system, there are three in service and three waiting. Most importantly, in the separate-queue system, there are customers waiting at the same time that there is an idle server: Customers are waiting for servers 2 and 4 even though server 3 is idle and could potentially help one of them. This is the problem with separate queues: With separate queues, there can be waiting customers and idle servers at the same time. That is clearly inefficient.

It is worth emphasizing that the superior performance of the pooled system is not achieved by making the servers work more or faster. In both systems, the servers are busy 90 percent of the time and they have a processing time of 90 seconds. So if the servers are equally busy in both systems, how can it be that waiting times in the pooled system are so much lower? The reason is that in a pooled system, the workers tend to be busy at the same time, and, in particular, they are busy when there are many customers in the system. Whenever there are four or more customers in the pooled system shown in Figure 16.14, all of the servers are busy. But we see that this is not necessarily the case in the separate-queue system. There can be six customers in the separate queue system and yet only three out of the four servers are busy.

We see via the example in Table 16.5 that pooling is capable of creating economies of scale that lead to substantially lower waiting times with exactly the same resources. So why don't all systems operate with a single, pooled queue? For example, why are people assigned to specific doctors, or why does the Transportation Safety Administration have a "regular" screening lane at airports and a "priority" screening lane for airline employees and customers who paid for a first-class seat? In the case of doctors, patients value seeing the same physician on each visit—who wants to describe his or her medical history to every physician in the practice? Put in terms of the language of operations, an ongoing relationship between a patient and a doctor can lower the processing time of each visit, and a faster processing time helps reduce the time in queue. Furthermore, it simply generates more perceived value for the customer.

TABLE 16.5 Average Waiting Time Calculations for System 1 (Pooled Queue) and System 2 (Separate Queues)

	System 1—Pooled Queue	System 2—Separate Queues
a (seconds)	25	100
p (seconds)	90	90
CV_a	1	1
CV_p	1	1
m	4	1
Utilization $= p/(a \times m)$	0.9	0.9
T_q (seconds)	179	810

In the case of "priority" security screening lanes at an airport, it is true that the average time to screen passengers would be reduced if all screening lanes (servers) were available to everyone. But making everyone better off, on average, does not mean that everyone is better off. The "regular" passengers are better off because they would have access to the priority lane when there are no priority customers—pooled servers avoid situations in which there are waiting customers and idle servers at the same time. But the "priority" passengers could be worse off in a pooled queue system—rather than get priority service, now they get average service. If it is costlier to have priority customers wait than regular customers, then it might make sense to have the priority customers get better service. This could apply to the airline employees—if crews are delayed through screening, then the entire flight might be delayed. Alternatively, the lane for the priority customers could be justified if they generate more revenue, as in the example of customers who pay for first-class tickets.

Although pooling is not perfect, it is a very powerful tool for reducing waiting times in a queuing system—the benefits of reduced waiting time via pooling are often too great to ignore. (See Connections: The Fast-Food Drive-Through for an application of pooling to fast-food restaurants.)

Check Your Understanding 16.12

© Yellow Dog Productions/Lifesize/Getty Images/RF

Question: A school has three student advisors who are assigned students based on their last name. For example, the first advisor handles students with names that start with the letters A–G. Each advisor is assigned the same number of students. However, for the next academic year, the school will no longer assign students to advisors. Instead, students will see the first available advisor in the office. All else remains the same. How will this change influence the time a student waits to see an advisor?

A. Time in queue increases.
B. Time in queue remains the same.
C. Time in queue decreases.
D. It is not possible to determine how those changes will influence time in queue.

Answer: The utilization of the advisors remains the same, but time in queue decreases because the school is switching from a system with three separate queues to a system with a single queue. Thus, the correct answer is C.

CONNECTIONS: The Fast-Food Drive-Through

Most people refer to establishments like McDonald's, Burger King, and Wendy's as "fast-food," but these chains prefer to refer to themselves as "quick-service restaurants." While quick-service restaurants might sound fancier, the emphasis is still on being fast and cheap. This is particularly important in the drive-through lane—if a customer doesn't want to take the time to leave his or her vehicle and is willing to eat the food while driving, then the customer wants to be in and out in a jiffy.

You might assume that the person saying, "May I take your order" through the speaker at the drive-through is an employee in the restaurant, but you might be wrong. In fact, that person might be hundreds of miles away in a call center. Why would that make any sense?

To answer that question, consider two ways of running a drive-through. The traditional way is to have an employee in each restaurant take orders. You need one employee per restaurant—an employee at the Walnut Street location cannot help a customer at the Maple Street location in another city. Hence, with the traditional system, there is a separate queue

© Photodisc/Getty Images/RF

for each restaurant. Now consider the "call center" way in which order-takers are in a call center and can handle orders from any of the restaurants. This is a pooled system. The utilization of the order-takers doesn't change, but the call center approach gives the restaurant some options. If it maintains the same staffing level, it can reduce the time in queue substantially. This is important for sales: If customers see a queue of cars at the drive-through, or expect to have slow service, they are likely to go to a competitor. Alternatively, the restaurant could reduce staffing substantially while maintaining the same time in queue. This allows it to lower costs, which is also important for competitiveness. Finally, it could combine lower staffing with faster service. This is like "having your cake and eating it, too"— meaning that pooling could allow it to offer better service at a lower price. What's not to like about that?

Conclusion

A queue forms when customers are patient enough to wait for service and for a period of time when the demand arriving to a process exceeds its capacity to serve customers. Demand can exceed capacity in a sustained manner. Think of this as predicable variability. For example, just before the start of a sporting event, we can predict that there is a rush to arrive before the game starts and that a queue forms at the entrance to the stadium. Demand can also exceed capacity because of random variability in either the arrival of customers or the time to serve them, or both. For example, even though most of the time it may be sufficient to have one pharmacist at a drugstore to answer questions and fill prescriptions, occasionally the pharmacist might find herself with a queue of waiting customers. We know that those busy periods for the pharmacist will occur, but we don't know exactly when they will occur—they happen by chance, as in random variability.

A queuing model allows a manager to predict average waiting times and the average number of customers at different stages of the system (e.g., waiting or in service). The key factors that influence these performance measures include (i) the amount of capacity in the system, (ii) the utilization of the servers, and (iii) the coefficients of variation of the arrival and service processes. An important feature of all queuing systems is that the average time in queue is sensitive to the utilization of the servers: as utilization increases, time in queue increases and it increases at a faster and faster rate. It is tempting to operate with a high utilization because it is costly to pay employees who are idle, but while high-utilization systems rarely have idle employees, they have idle customers who are forced to wait for service.

The presence of a queue reveals direct evidence for two of the system inhibitors of operations management: variability and inflexibility. If there were no variability in demand or service, or if we were able to adjust capacity as flexibly as needed, there would not be a queue. Thus, to improve performance in a queuing setting requires either reducing variability or increasing flexibility.

For example, although all queuing systems are sensitive to the utilization of the servers, queuing systems with many servers are less sensitive. Consequently, systems with many servers are able to operate with relatively high utilizations and offer a reasonably short time in queue for customers. This is an example of economies of scale: Large systems operate more efficiently than small systems.

Beyond increasing the total demand in a system, managers can employ many strategies to increase efficiency. All else being equal, a pooled-queuing system, in which customers could be served by any server, are much more efficient than a separate-queuing system, in which each customer is served by a designated server. Pooling effectively increases the flexibility of the supply process: In a pooled system, each server can serve any customer, whereas without pooling a server can only serve a subset of the customers. While there are some drawbacks to a pooled-queuing system, the operational benefits are substantial and are important to consider in the design of the service system.

Summary of Learning Objectives

LO16-1 **For a queue with a constant demand rate that exceeds the service rate, evaluate several performance measures related to the length of the queue, the average wait, and the time to serve customers**

When the demand rate exceeds the capacity of the process over a sustained period of time, a queue will grow. The maximum length for the queue depends on how much and for how long demand exceeds capacity. The average time in queue equals half of the maximum time in queue. Techniques to better manage these situations include to (i) move some demand outside of the peak period and/or (ii) obtain more capacity during the peak period.

LO16-2 **For a queue with variable interarrival and processing times and one server, evaluate several performance measures and understand the factors that influence those measures**

Three factors determine the time in queue: (i) a capacity factor, (ii) a utilization factor, and (iii) the variability factor. As expected, if the system has more capacity, customers spend less time waiting on average. If the utilization of the servers increases, the time in queue increases, and it increases at a faster and faster rate: If a system has high utilization, then it will also have a long queue. Finally, queues increase when there is more variability in the arrival process or the service process.

LO16-3 **For a queue with variable interarrival and processing times and multiple servers, evaluate several performance measures and understand the factors that influence those measures**

A service system with multiple servers behaves in a similar manner to a system with a single server: Queues increase if there is less capacity, higher utilization, or more variability. When capacity exceeds demand, the system is said to be stable, meaning that queues come and go, but they do not consistently grow.

LO16-4 **Understand why there are economies of scale in queuing systems, and the pros and cons of pooling**

Queuing systems exhibit economies of scale, meaning that larger systems (with more servers) are more efficient than smaller systems. In particular, larger systems are less sensitive to utilization: A large system can have high utilization of servers without as much of a penalty in terms of time in queue. In addition to large systems, pooled-queue systems perform better than separate-queue systems: In a pooled-queue system, a customer can be served by any server, whereas in a separate-queue system, a customer is served by a designated server.

Key Terms

16.1 Queues When Demand Exceeds Supply

Peak-load pricing Charging more during the time period with the highest demand.

Off-peak discount Offering a discount during a time period with low demand.

Pre-processing strategy Reducing the amount of work needed to process a customer during the peak time period by moving some of the work to an off-peak time.

16.2 Queues When Demand and Service Rates Are Variable—One Server

Arrival process The flow of customers arriving to the system.

Service process The flow of customers when they are being served.

Interarrival time The time between customer arrivals to a system.

Processing time The time a customer spends with a server.

Coefficient of variation The ratio of the standard deviation to the average.

Queuing model An abstract representation of the queue that enables us to predict waiting times and other performance measures.

Time in queue The average time a customer waits in a queue.

16.3 Queues When Demand and Service Rates Are Variable—Multiple Servers

Unstable queue A queuing system in which the demand rate exceeds capacity.

Stable queue A queuing system in which the demand rate is less than capacity.

16.4 Queuing System Design—Economies of Scale and Pooling

Economies of scale A property of an operating system in which the efficiency of the system increases as the system gets larger.

Pooled queue A queuing system in which all demand is shared across all servers. Hence, each customer is served by the first available server and each customer can be served by any agent.

Separate queue A queuing system in which demand is initially divided among different servers, and customers are eventually served only by their designated agent.

Key Formulas

LO16-1 For a queue with a constant demand rate that exceeds the service rate, evaluate several performance measures related to the length of the queue, the average wait, and the time to serve customers

Queue growth rate $=$ Demand $-$ Capacity

Length of queue at time $T = T \times$ (Demand $-$ Capacity)

Time to serve the Qth person in the queue $= \dfrac{Q}{\text{Capacity}}$

$$\text{Time to serve the person arriving at time } T = T \times \left(\frac{\text{Demand}}{\text{Capacity}} - 1 \right)$$

$$\text{Average time to serve a unit} = \frac{1}{2} \times T \times \left(\frac{\text{Demand}}{\text{Capacity}} - 1 \right)$$

LO16-2 For a queue with variable interarrival and processing times and one server, evaluate several performance measures and understand the factors that influence those measures

a = Average interarrival time

p = Average processing time

$$CV_a = \frac{\text{Standard deviation of arrival process}}{a}$$

$$CV_p = \frac{\text{Standard deviation of service process}}{p}$$

$$\text{Utilization} = \frac{p}{a}$$

$$T_q = p \times \left(\frac{\text{Utilization}}{1 - \text{Utilization}} \right) \times \left(\frac{CV_a^2 + CV_p^2}{2} \right)$$

$$I_q = \frac{T_q}{a}$$

$$I_p = \frac{p}{a}$$

LO16.3 For a queue with variable interarrival and processing times and multiple servers, evaluate several performance measures and understand the factors that influence those measures

m = Number of servers

$$\text{Utilization} = \frac{p}{a \times m}$$

$$\text{Minimum number of servers} = \frac{p}{a}$$

$$T_q = \left(\frac{p}{m} \right) \times \left(\frac{\text{Utilization}^{\sqrt{2(m+1)} - 1}}{1 - \text{Utilization}} \right) \times \left(\frac{CV_a^2 + CV_p^2}{2} \right)$$

$$I_q = R \times T_q = \frac{T_q}{a}$$

$$I_p = R \times p = \frac{p}{a}$$

Conceptual Questions

LO16-1

1. A summer camp that offers one-week programs faces the challenges of long queues as parents try to check in their children each Saturday morning. If they were to add more staff to assist with the check-in process, then which of the following will occur?
   i. The average time parents wait decreases.
   ii. The maximum time the parents wait decreases.
   iii. The average number of parents waiting to check in their child decreases.
   a. Just I
   b. Just II
   c. Just III
   d. I and II
   e. I and III
   f. II and III
   g. I, II, and III

LO16-2

2. Queuing system A has a utilization of 80 percent, and queuing system B has a utilization of 90 percent. Both have a single server. Say the utilization of both systems increases by 5 percent; that is, A increases from 80 percent to 85 percent while B increases from 90 percent to 95 percent. Which system is likely to experience the bigger change in the average time in queue?
   a. System A
   b. System B
   c. Time in queue for each system will increase by the same amount.
   d. More information is needed to determine which has a bigger change in average time in queue.

LO16-3

3. The following four graphs (Figure 16.15A, B, C, and D) display the number of customers in a queuing system (y-axis) over a long period of time (x-axis). Which of the following is most likely a stable system?
   a. A
   b. B
   c. C
   d. D

Figure 16.15

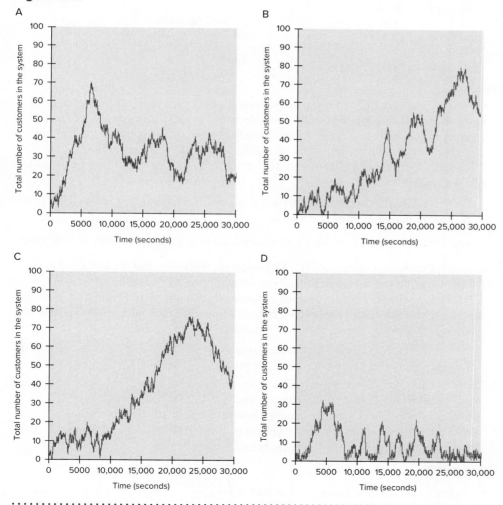

LO16-4

4. Which of the following best reflects pooling capacity to reduce restroom queue lengths?
   a. Add more toilets to increase capacity.
   b. Install a flexible partition that can alter the size of the women's and the men's restrooms.
   c. Convert the separate men's and women's rooms into a single unisex restroom (that both men and women can use).
   d. Remove mirrors in the restroom to decrease the time users spend in the restroom.
   e. Add automatic flush capability to each toilet to decrease processing times.

5. YourNurse (YN) Inc. uses certified nurses to answer medical queries from customers over the phone. When patients call into YN, they are first asked to provide their zip code, which then allows YN to route their call to the call center nearest to the patient (it operates 10 across the country). Which single suggestion in the following list (and explanation) is most likely to reduce the average time callers wait before speaking with a nurse?
   a. Run an advertising campaign to increase demand and to better utilize its nurses.
   b. Train its nurses so that they spend more time answering the patients' questions.
   c. Instead of using callers' zip codes, route calls to the call center with the fewest callers to help prevent situations in which there are idle nurses at the same time that there are callers on hold.
   d. Play a recording of useful medical information while callers are on hold so as to decrease their perception of how long they are waiting.
   e. None of the above

Solved Example Problems

LO16-1

1. Cranston Cranberry Cooperative (CCC) processes cranberries that are harvested in the local area. Barrels of cranberries arrive on trucks to CCC's facility at a rate of 150 barrels per hour and are processed continuously at a rate of 100 barrels per hour.

   Trucks arrive at a uniform rate over eight hours, from 6:00 a.m. until 2:00 p.m. What is the maximum number of barrels of cranberries that are waiting on the trucks at any given time?

   Answer: The longest queue occurs at 2 p.m., eight hours into the process. Hence, the number of barrels waiting at 2 p.m. is

   $$\text{Length of queue at time } T = 8 \text{ hrs} \times (150 \text{ barrels per hr} - 100 \text{ barrels per hr}) = 400 \text{ barrels}$$

2. Cranston Cranberry Cooperative (CCC) processes cranberries that are harvested in the local area. Barrels of cranberries arrive on trucks to CCC's facility at a rate of 150 barrels per hour and are processed continuously at a rate of 100 barrels per hour. Trucks arrive at a uniform rate over eight hours, from 6:00 a.m. until 2:00 p.m. How long does the last truck wait before it is processed?

   Answer: At 2 p.m., there are 400 barrels in the queue. It takes CCC 400 barrels/100 barrels per hour = 4 hours to completely process the last truck.

3. Cranston Cranberry Cooperative (CCC) processes cranberries that are harvested in the local area. Barrels of cranberries arrive on trucks to CCC's facility at a rate of 150 barrels per hour and are processed continuously at a rate of 100 barrels per hour. Trucks arrive at a uniform rate over eight hours, from 6:00 a.m. until 2:00 p.m. How long does a truck wait, on average, before it is processed?

   Answer:

   $$\text{Average time to serve a unit} = \frac{1}{2} \times 8 \text{ hr} \times \left(\frac{150 \text{ barrels per hr}}{100 \text{ barrels per hr}} - 1 \right) = 2 \text{ hours}$$

LO16-2

4. GottaGo rents portable toilets for small outdoor events. The El Paso softball league championship game is expected to draw several hundred participants, and the plan is to rent one portable toilet from GottaGo. During the event, one person will need to use the toilet every five minutes, with a standard deviation of five minutes. On average, a person uses the GottaGo toilet for two minutes, with a standard deviation of three minutes. What fraction of time (as a percent) is the GottaGo toilet occupied?

   Answer: The processing time is two minutes and the interarrival time is five minutes. Utilization is $p/a = 2/5 = 40$ percent.

5. GottaGo rents portable toilets for small outdoor events. The El Paso softball league championship is expected to draw several hundred participants, and the plan is to rent one portable toilet from GottaGo. During the event, one person will need to use the toilet every five minutes, with a standard deviation of five minutes. On average, a person uses the GottaGo toilet for two minutes, with a standard deviation of three minutes. How long does a person have to wait, on average, before he or she can use the GottaGo toilet?

   Answer: $p = 2$ minutes and $a = 5$ minutes, so Utilization $= p/a = 2/5 = 0.4$. $CV_a = 1$ and $CV_p = 1.5$. Therefore,

   $$T_q = \frac{2}{1} \times \left(\frac{0.4}{1 - 0.4}\right) \times \frac{1^2 + 1.5^2}{2} = 2.2 \text{ minutes.}$$

LO16-3

6. UP Fitness will install four new "trapezoidal gel-resistance toners" ("trappies" for short), their latest exercise gadget, which is specifically designed to contour upper back muscles. Clients who want to use these machines arrive at the rate of 90 per hour. If all four machines are busy, UP Fitness clients use other pieces of equipment, waiting for one of the trappies to become available. The trappy experience is intense: 120 seconds of explosive exercise intensity. What is the utilization of the trappies?

   Answer: Utilization $= p/(a \times m)$. The arrival rate of 90 per hour translates into $a = 3600$ seconds per hour/90 customers per hour $= 40$ seconds per customer. Hence, utilization is 120 seconds/(40 seconds $\times$ 4) $= 75$ percent.

7. Using the information in the preceding question regarding the trappies, the coefficient of variation of the interarrival times is one. If all four trappies are busy, UP Fitness clients use other pieces of equipment, waiting for one of the trappies to become available. The standard deviation of the usage times (measured in seconds) is small—only 60 seconds. On average, how long do clients wait to use a trappy?

   Answer: Utilization is 75 percent and the coefficient of the service process is $60/120 = 0.5$.

   $$T_q = \left(\frac{120}{4}\right) \times \left(\frac{0.75^{\sqrt{2(4+1)} - 1}}{1 - 0.75}\right) \times \left(\frac{1^2 + 0.5^2}{2}\right) = 40.3 \text{ seconds}$$

8. Again, using the information from question 6, on average, how many clients are using a trappy?

   Answer: Inventory in process $= p/a = 120/40 = 3$.

LO16-4

9. A university has two offices for processing student identification cards and other records. The first has an interarrival time of 15 minutes and the second has an interarrival time of 20 minutes. The university plans to open a single office for the entire campus. This new office's demand will equal the sum of the demand received by the original two offices. What is the interarrival time for the new office (in minutes)?

   Answer: The first office has an arrival rate of four students per hour. The second office receives three students per hour. The combined rate is thus seven students per hour, which implies an interarrival time of $60/7 = 8.6$ minutes.

Problems and Applications

LO16-1

1. The Shady Farm Milk Company can process milk at a fixed rate of 7500 gallons/hour. The company's clients request 100,000 gallons of milk over the course of one day. This demand is spread out uniformly from 8 a.m. to 6 p.m. The company starts producing at 8 a.m. and continues to work until all of the demand has been satisfied. At noon, how many gallons of milk are in the queue to be processed?

2. Using the previous question, change the fixed rate that milk is processed to 6000 gallons/hour; all the other factors remain the same. How long does the client requesting milk at 6 p.m. have to wait to have its demand satisfied (in hours)?

3. Using question 1, change the fixed rate that milk is processed to 5000 gallons/hour; all the other factors remain the same. On average, how long does a client wait (in hours) to receive its product?

LO16-2

4. Which of the following lines in the graphs in Figure 16.16 best depicts the relationship between utilization and waiting time in a queuing system? (Assume the utilizations depicted are less than 100 percent.)

Figure 16.16

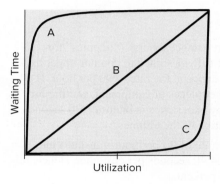 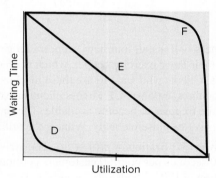

a. A
b. B
c. C
d. D
e. E
f. F

5. Huduko Inc. offers a number of computer services. One server handles its own web page. It receives requests for web pages at the rate of 90 per second. The standard deviation of these interarrival times is 0.02 second. What is the coefficient of variation of the interarrival times for this server?

6. Max Stamp approves study abroad documents for the university. Students must wait in line with their forms outside Max's office. One student at a time is allowed in his office and Max takes precisely 15 minutes to evaluate each student's set of documents. On average, two students per hour go to his office and they spend, on average, 160 minutes trying to get their forms approved (time waiting in queue plus time in Max's office having him evaluate their documents). On average, how many students are waiting outside of Max's office?

7. CPU-on-Demand (CPUD) offers real-time high-performance computing services. CPUD owns one supercomputer that can be accessed through the Internet. Its customers send jobs that arrive, on average, every five hours. The standard deviation of the interarrival times is five hours. Executing each job takes, on average, three hours on the supercomputer and the standard deviation of the processing time is 4.5 hours. What is the utilization (as a percent) of CPUD's supercomputer?

8. Using the information in the previous question, how long does a customer have to wait to have a job completed?

LO16-3

9. The graph in Figure 16.17 plots the number of customers in a queuing system with two servers. The average processing time of each server is 400 seconds, with a standard deviation of 400 seconds. Customers wait in a single queue. Which of the following average interarrival times, a (in seconds), is consistent with the data observed in the graph?

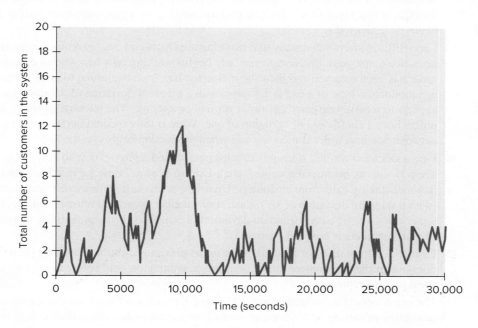

Figure 16.17

   a. $a = 50$
   b. $a = 100$
   c. $a = 150$
   d. $a = 200$
   e. $a = 250$
   f. All of the above average interarrival times are consistent with the graph.
   g. None of the above average interarrival times are consistent with the graph.
   h. It is not possible to determine which interarrival times are consistent with the graph.

10. Go Fly (GF), a startup airline, installed five self-serve kiosks to check in passengers at its Denver gate. In comparison to the five employees that were previously responsible for checking in passengers, the average processing time per customer is higher with the kiosks. In addition, customers are still trying to learn the menus in the kiosk, and some passengers just don't quite get it: The coefficient of variation of the processing time is higher with the kiosks than with the employees. In terms of demand, the interarrival time of customers has decreased, but the coefficient of variation of interarrival times has not changed. Which of the following will happen regarding the average number of passengers waiting in line to check in with the kiosks relative to the average number when the employees did this task?
   a. It will decrease.
   b. It will stay the same.
   c. It will increase.
   d. It may decrease or increase.

11. Camile owns Crunch Code, a company that provides quick programming solutions. Clients send Crunch projects via its web page and Crunch bangs out the needed code

as quickly as possible. Camile has five programmers who do all of the coding. On average, a project arrives once every 4.8 hours. Each project is assigned to one programmer and that programmer takes, on average, 19.2 hours to complete each project. Camile wants to know what fraction of the time (as a percent) each of her programmers is busy coding?

12. In the previous question, a project arrives at Crunch once every 4.8 hours, with a standard deviation of 6.00 hours. Again, each project is assigned to one programmer and that programmer takes, on average, 19.2 hours to complete each project, with a standard deviation of 19.2 hours. How many uncompleted projects does Crunch Code have, on average, at any given time? (Include projects waiting for a programmer as well as those being programmed.)

13. Larry Ellison starts a company that manufactures high-end custom leather bags. He hires two employees. Each employee only begins working on a bag when a customer order has been received and then she makes the bag from beginning to end. The average production time of a bag is 1.8 days, with a standard deviation of 2.7 days. Larry expects to receive one customer order per day on average. The interarrival times of orders have a coefficient of variation of one. What is the expected duration, in days, between when an order is received and when production begins on the bag?

14. Find a Doctor is a small startup that helps people find a physician who best meets their needs (location, insurance accepted, etc.). During a "slow" time for it, it has seven staff members taking calls from customers. On average, one call arrives every six minutes (with a standard deviation of six). Each staff member spends 20 minutes with each customer (on average, with a standard deviation of 30). What is the probability that one of its staff members is busy (as a percent)?

15. Using the information for Find a Doctor in the previous question, how long (in minutes) does one of their customers spend, on average, waiting on hold before he or she can start speaking to a representative?

16. The organizers of a conference in the Houston Convention Center are evaluating the possibility of setting up a computer area where attendees can check their e-mail on computers provided by the organization. There will be one common queue for all computers and only one person uses a computer at a time. On average, there are 15 attendee arrivals per hour and the average time a person spends on the computer is 10 minutes. To ensure that waiting times are not too long, the organizers want to ensure that the utilization of the computers doesn't exceed 90 percent. At least how many computers do they need to have?

17. A small call center normally has five employees answering calls while open. On average, five calls arrive every four minutes. Under normal operating conditions, each employee on average handles each call in 3.5 minutes. But today, one employee has the flu, so the center needs to operate with four employees during this time. The manager is nervous that it may be supply-constrained and so she directs her employees to hurry up their processing of calls today. What is the maximum average processing time (in minutes) for each call that they need to achieve today so that they have a stable queue?

18. Experience the Tour de France (ETF) is a specialty travel agent. It arranges vacations for amateur cyclists who want to experience the Tour de France by riding through one or more stages in the race. It has four people who take calls from clients. Each call lasts 30 minutes, on average, with a standard deviation of 60 minutes. A call arrives, on average, every 20 minutes, with a standard deviation of 20. On average, how many minutes does a caller wait before talking to an agent?

19. CloudRack provides web hosting services on its five servers. When a person requests a page from one of its hosted websites, the server must find the page and send it to the person's browser. These requests arrive at the rate of 400 per second. The coefficient of variation of the interarrival times is two. The processing time for a server is 0.01 second

with a coefficient of variation of one. On average, how much time (in seconds) does a request take to be filled (i.e., include time waiting for a server and the actual processing by the server)?

20. Huduko operates with a utilization of 30 percent. The interarrival time of jobs is 8 milliseconds (0.008 second) with a coefficient of variation of 1.5. On average, there are 20 jobs waiting in the queue to be served and 60 jobs in process (i.e., being processed by a server rather than waiting to be sent to a server for processing). How many servers does it have in this system?

LO16-4

21. A pediatric practice has five physicians. Historically, patients were assigned to one physician and these patients always were treated by the same physician. For example, Alice's patients always visited her (for "well visits" and "sick visits") and never interacted with the other physicians. However, the practice has decided to change how it sees patients. Now patients will be seen by whoever is available (i.e., not treating patients). Based on our discussion of queuing theory, which of the following three outcomes is/are likely to occur due to this change?
   i. The coefficient of variation of patient interarrival times will increase.
   ii. The utilization of the physicians will increase.
   iii. The average number of patients actually with a physician (that is, "inventory in process") will increase.
   a. I only
   b. II only
   c. III only
   d. I and II only
   e. I and III only
   f. II and III only
   g. All of them (I, II, and III)
   h. None of them (neither I, II, nor III)

CASE POTTY PARITY

Here is a question you might not have thought about much, unless you are a woman: "What is the right number of toilets to have in a bathroom?" We all must use toilets every day, and we often need to use public toilets. So somebody in charge of building codes needs to determine if there should be a standard for restroom construction in public buildings.

Before 2005, New York City architectural codes stipulated that there should be an equal amount of space given to the men's and women's rooms. For example, if the women's room has 25 square meters, then the men's room should have 25 square meters. Sounds fair, right? Not so fast. Women's rooms only have toilets, whereas men's rooms can have toilets and urinals. Urinals take less space than a toilet, so it is possible that a men's room with the same area as a women's room actually has more "flushing capacity." For example, with equal space dedicated to the two restrooms, a building might have five toilets in the

women's room and three toilets and three urinals in the men's room.

In 2005, New York City changed the requirements. In what has been come to be called "potty parity," New York City stipulated that there should be at least a 2:1 ratio of flushing units between the women's room and the men's room.

The issue of potty parity is not just for New Yorkers. In China, petitions have been filed with the Ministry of Housing and Urban-Rural Development and other departments to account for the extra time women need on each bathroom visit—89 seconds instead of 39 seconds for men. Maybe as a result of their efforts, the World Expo in Shanghai in 2010 used a ratio of 2.5 to one with its new bathrooms.

1. To what extent does the equation for the waiting time in a queue help explain why queues for the women's room might be longer than queues for the men's room before 2005 in New York City?

© Jeffery Coolidge/Photodisc/Getty Images/RF

© Jeffery Coolidge/Photodisc/Getty Images/RF

2. Say women on average take twice as long in the restroom (not including waiting time) than men. Is the 2:1 ratio for flushing capacity the right ratio?

3. Besides adding flushing capacity, what can be done to reduce waiting times for restrooms?

SOURCES:

http://www.nytimes.com/2009/04/13/sports/baseball/13potty.html?pagewanted=all

http://sinosphere.blogs.nytimes.com/2014/11/19/demanding-toilet-justice-for-the-women-of-china/

Service Systems with Impatient Customers

17

LEARNING OBJECTIVES

LO17-1 Use the Erlang loss model to understand and evaluate performance measures in services with impatient customers

LO17-2 Use the Erlang loss model to understand the value of economies of scale, pooling and buffers in services with impatient customers

LO17-3 Understand how variability can reduce capacity and how to restore capacity via standardized work, buffers, or elimination of sequential work

CHAPTER OUTLINE

Introduction

As we know, people hate to wait for service. And sometimes they won't or can't wait. For example, patients with severe injuries cannot wait for a trauma bay to become available in the emergency department of a hospital. They need service right away and must go to the hospital that can deliver it immediately. Alternatively, a customer might need to confirm that a financial transaction has been completed and intends to wait for as long as needed. However, if the system does not have enough phone lines to keep the customer on hold, then the customer simply can't wait. Combine impatient customers with the system inhibitors of inflexibility (e.g., lack of space in the queue) and variability (e.g., arrival times and customer needs) and you have a recipe for a system that struggles to match supply with demand. In particular, the system might lose demand in the form of customers who are unwilling or literally unable to wait for service.

© *Ocean/Corbis/RF*

Even if customers are somewhat patient and are able to wait, inflexibility and variability can create another problem—they can actually destroy capacity. The more capacity is lost, the more the problem of long waits is aggravated. Fortunately, there are steps that can be taken to combat this issue.

In this chapter, we first develop a queuing model that applies to the emergency department of a hospital. From this model, we analyze several performance measures, explore the extent to which this model exhibits economies of scale, and evaluate the benefits from pooling. Next, we investigate a simple process that consists of two back-to-back queues. In that setting, we observe that inflexibility and variability can reduce the capacity of the process. We then discuss how to maximize the capacity of the process even in the presence of those inhibitors.

17.1 Lost Demand in Queues with No Buffers

Trauma centers in hospitals handle patients with severe injuries. These patients generally arrive at the hospital via an ambulance or helicopter. While en route, a triage system evaluates the patients and directs the less severe cases to the emergency room, while the patients with substantial injuries are sent to the trauma center.

Consider the following situation of a trauma center in the northeastern United States. It has three trauma bays, each used by at most one patient. The hospital has enough staffing to enable it to use all three trauma bays at the same time. On average, patients spend two hours in the trauma bay. During that time, the patients are diagnosed and—if possible—stabilized. The most severe cases, which are difficult or impossible to stabilize, spend very little time in a trauma bay and are moved directly to an operating room.

Given the severe conditions of patients coming into the trauma center, any delay of care can have fatal consequences for the patient. Thus, having patients wait for service is not an option in this setting. If, as a result of either frequent arrivals or long service times, all three trauma bays are utilized, the trauma center declares that it is on **diversion** status. Diversion status means that the hospital is accepting no more patients and any patient needing care must be sent to another hospital (that is not on diversion). The announcement of diversion status is sent to the regional emergency services (e.g., police and ambulances) so those services know that they should not transport patients to the hospital. Diversion is a clear indication of the inflexibility of the process—diversion would not be needed if the process were flexible enough to adjust the number of trauma bays. See Connections: Ambulance Diversion for more information about diversion of ambulances in the United States.

Figure 17.1 displays a process flow diagram for this trauma center. It shows that there are three trauma bays, each of which acts as a server in this system. There is intentionally no

Diversion The practice of sending demand away from a system when it cannot be served by the system in a sufficiently timely manner. For example, a hospital may divert patients to another hospital when it is unable to care for more patients.

Figure 17.1

Process flow diagram of a trauma center with three trauma bays and diversion when the trauma center is full

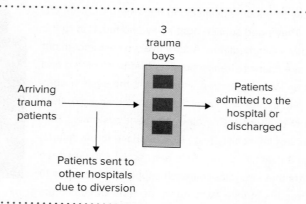

triangle in front of the servers to represent a queue of waiting customers because customers cannot wait in this system. As usual, demand "arrives" from the left side of the diagram. Here, "arrives" means that a person becomes in need of trauma services that the hospital could potentially serve. If one of the trauma bays is idle, then that patient goes immediately into service with that server. If all three trauma bays are occupied at the time that a patient arrives, then the patient is diverted to another hospital and is not served by this hospital. Patients diverted to another hospital are considered **lost demand**—potential demand that the system is unable to serve. For simplicity, we do not include in the diagram the time and process of transporting the patient to the hospital.

This particular trauma center handles about 2000 cases per year. For our analysis, we focus on the late evening hours, during which, on average, a new patient arrives every three hours. The late evening hours are among the busiest for the trauma center, as many of the incoming patients are there because they were involved in a vehicle accident (alcohol-induced car accidents tend to happen in the evening) or are the victims of violence (especially in the summer months).

There are two critical parameters for understanding the performance of this system. The first is the average interarrival time, a, which is the average time between the arrival of two successive patients. For this trauma center, $a = 3$ hours. Note, a is the time between arrival of potential patients and not between patients who enter service into the trauma center. In other words, a is the time between patient arrivals if all potential patients could be served.

The second critical parameter is p, which is the average processing time. For this trauma center, $p = 2$ hours. As with the average interarrival time, a, the average processing time, p, is just an average: There can be considerable variation in the interarrival and processing times. In fact, if there were no variation in the interarrival and processing times (and assuming the capacity of the trauma center exceeds the demand rate), the system would operate without ever needing to divert a patient to another hospital. We measure the amount of variability in a process with the coefficient of variation, which is the ratio of the standard deviation to the average. In this case, the coefficient of variation of the interarrival times is 1, which means

Lost demand Potential demand that a system is unable to serve. This demand does not count toward a process's flow rate.

CONNECTIONS: Ambulance Diversion

© Paul Burns/Blend Images/RF

Emergency departments (EDs) in the United States experience considerable demand: In 2010, there were about 130 million visits to EDs and approximately one person in five visits an ED each year. Under U.S. federal law, all hospitals that participate in Medicare are required to screen—and if an emergency condition is present, stabilize—any patient who comes to the ED regardless of the individual's ability to pay. Consequently, only about 35 percent of ED patients have private insurance, and 16 percent have no insurance.

In response to increasing cost pressures, many hospitals have downsized important resources that are part of the emergency care process. This has led to a decrease in the number of hours hospitals are "open" for emergency patients arriving by helicopter or ambulance. It is therefore not surprising that 29 percent of hospitals report diverting ambulances at least once per year. It should also be noted that the frequency of diversion is not uniform across the country. Large hospitals located in metropolitan areas are more likely to divert ambulances than smaller or rural hospitals—38 percent of metropolitan hospitals experience diversion each year.

Sources: http://www.cdc.gov/nchs/data/ahcd/NHAMCS_2011_ed_factsheet.pdf. Accessed May 31, 2014. http://www.cdc.gov/nchs/data/ahcd/nhamcs_emergency/2010_ed_web_tables.pdf. Accessed May 31, 2014.

that both the standard deviation of interarrival times and the average of the interarrival times equal *a*. In this particular setting, the coefficient of variation of processing times does not matter—the amount of variability in processing times does not influence the performance measures we are interested in.

17.1.1 The Erlang Loss Model

LO17-1 Use the Erlang loss model to understand and evaluate performance measures in services with impatient customers

The process flow diagram displayed in Figure 17.1 is an example of a queuing model called the **Erlang loss model**. It is named after Agner Krarup Erlang, a Danish engineer who defined and analyzed many of the most commonly used queuing models. (See Connections: Agner Krarup Erlang for more information on him.) The following list summarizes the assumptions in the Erlang loss model:

- There are *m* servers.
- Customers are processed by a single server.
- The average interarrival time is *a*.
- The average processing time is *p*.
- The coefficient of variation of the interarrival times is one.
- Customers do not wait, so there are at most *m* customers in the system.

It is the last assumption (there are no waiting customers) that really distinguishes the Erlang loss model from the one discussed in Chapter 16. As a result of this assumption, the rate of potential customers can be (and usually is) greater than the rate of served customers—not every customer is served because some are lost due to the inability to wait.

We should also comment on the second-to-last assumption: The coefficient of variation of the interarrival times is one. This might seem somewhat limiting: The results of the model need to change if the interarrival times are either more or less variable than a coefficient of variation of one. However, fortunately, a coefficient of variation of one is common for interarrival times—as discussed in Chapter 16, it occurs when there are many potential customers, each has a small chance of becoming demand (e.g., there are many people in a city and few visit the trauma center on any given day), and each independently decides whether to become demand.

The preceding list also seems to be missing an assumption—there isn't any mention of processing times. Curiously, the results from the Erlang loss model are correct no matter how variable or not variable the processing times are. All that matters is the average processing time, *p*.

Erlang loss model A queuing model in which the total number of flow units in the system cannot exceed the number of servers. If a flow unit arrives to the system when it is full, the flow unit is not served by the system and becomes lost demand.

CONNECTIONS: Agner Krarup Erlang

Agner Erlang lived from 1878 to 1929. In 1908, he was employed by the Copenhagen Telephone Company, where he worked on the question of how much capacity the company needed to serve its customers. To understand this question, he considered a simple example: There are two equal-sized villages and people want to call from one village to the other. The telephone lines between the villages are called trunk lines. Each trunk line can handle one call at a time. Erlang understood that the company faced a trade-off. Install only one line and then only one call can occur at a time. This is the cheapest solution, but it makes customers wait to make a call and the wait would probably be unacceptable even with small villages. Alternatively, the company could install one trunk line for each telephone in each village. This is beautiful from the customer's point of view but not very cost-effective for the company—most of the lines would be idle most of the time. Trunk lines are expensive, so the company wants to minimize the number of trunk lines while still maintaining an acceptable level of service to its customers, meaning that they don't have to wait too long.

The company could take a trial-and-error approach to decide how many trunk lines to install. But with that approach, it could take several iterations to get close to a good solution. It is expensive each time a trunk line is added or deleted from the network. Erlang's approach to this challenge was to collect data and then build rigorous queuing models like the ones described in this chapter and the previous chapter. This scientific approach allowed the company to be more precise when it made capacity decisions, resulting in better service for customers and lower costs for the company.

Although the technology related to communication networks has changed tremendously since Erlang's days at the Copenhagen Telephone Company, remarkably, the work Erlang did in the early 1900s is still the basis for capacity decisions in all modern telephone and data networks.

Now that we have defined how our process works, we first evaluate the capacity and implied utilization of the system. Next, we identify a set of performance measures that could interest a manager. Finally, we consider the staffing problem: If we can choose the number of servers, how many servers should we have to ensure that the percentage of lost demand does not exceed a target threshold. For example, how many trauma bays does the hospital need to ensure that it is on diversion status no more than 1 percent of its operating time?

17.1.2 Capacity and Implied Utilization

Let's begin our analysis of the Erlang loss model by evaluating the capacity of the system:

$$\text{Capacity} = \frac{\text{Number of resources}}{\text{Processing time}} = \frac{m}{p} = \frac{3}{2 \text{ hours per patient}} = 1.5 \text{ patients per hour}$$

Next, evaluate the implied utilization, u, of the system:

$$\text{Implied utilization} = \frac{\text{Demand}}{\text{Capacity}} = \frac{1/a}{m/p} = \frac{p}{a \times m} = \frac{2 \text{ hours per patient}}{3 \text{ hours per patient} \times 3} = \frac{2}{9} = 0.222$$

For this trauma center, the implied utilization is less than 100 percent. However, in other systems, the implied utilization could be greater than 100 percent, in which case demand exceeds capacity. But remember, even though demand can be greater than capacity, there is never a queue—whenever all servers are busy and there is an arrival, the arrival does not wait in a queue, but, rather, the arrival is lost (or diverted in the case of the trauma center). Hence, when the implied utilization is greater than 100 percent, there is a considerable amount of lost demand. But even with this trauma center's relatively low implied utilization, of about 22 percent, there can be some diversion due to variability. While on average the implied utilization is 22 percent, variability in the arrival rate or processing times can contribute to a situation in which all trauma bays are occupied and an additional patient arrives who then needs to be diverted.

17.1.3 Performance Measures

The following is a list of performance measures that could interest a manager:

- What percent of the time is the system unable to serve demand (e.g., percent of time on diversion)? This is also the probability that a customer is denied service (i.e., must be diverted to another hospital).
- How many flow units of demand are lost (e.g., number of diverted patients)?

Check Your Understanding 17.1

Question: A trauma center in a West Coast hospital has two trauma bays. The interarrival time of potential demand is 2.5 hours and the processing time is 2 hours.

a. What is the capacity of this trauma center (in patients per hour)?

Answer:

$$\text{Capacity} = \frac{m}{p} = \frac{2}{2 \text{ hours per patient}} = 1 \text{ patient per hour}$$

Thus, the answer is 1 patient per hour.

b. What is the implied utilization of this trauma center?

Answer:

$$\text{Implied utilization} = \frac{p}{a \times m} = \frac{2 \text{ hours per patient}}{2.5 \text{ hours per patient} \times 2} = 0.4$$

Thus, the answer is 0.4.

- What is the flow rate (e.g., patients per hour) through the system?
- What is the average utilization of the resources in the system?
- On average, how many resources (e.g., trauma bays) are busy serving a customer?

The first performance measure, the percentage of time on diversion, provides us with some indication of how well the hospital is serving the community—diversion is something to be avoided because it cannot be helpful for health outcomes. Intuitively, the more a hospital is on diversion, the more patients are diverted, which is the second performance measure. And the second measure is directly important to us because it is related to the third measure: The more patients are diverted, the fewer patients the process actually serves. Furthermore, the flow rate of patients is directly related to the last two measures: the utilization of the trauma center and the average number of occupied trauma bays. While the flow rate is directly related to revenue (each served patient generates revenue for the hospital), the last two measures are related to costs. The hospital pays for the equipment in the trauma center and probably most of the employees, whether they are being used or not. They are fixed costs because the hospital incurs those costs whether the hospital serves many patients or very few. Hence, when those costs are allocated across the patients, the more patients the hospital serves, the lower the fixed cost per served patient.

17.1.4 Percentage of Time All Servers Are Busy and the Denial of Service Probability

While it is relatively straightforward to evaluate the capacity and implied utilization in the Erlang loss model, the trickiest aspect of this system is the fact that some patients are diverted. If there were no diversion, then the flow rate of served patients would equal the flow rate of all possible patients (in this case, one-third patient per hour). But we can't count on that ideal case—the trauma center is sometimes fully occupied and that can lead to some diversion. Thus, we need to figure out the percent of time the trauma center is fully occupied; that is, all servers are busy. For example, suppose we collect data over a sufficiently long period of time and we observe that 10 percent of the time the trauma center is fully occupied. That would mean that if we randomly selected a moment in time, there would be a 0.1 probability that the trauma center is fully occupied. It also means that a randomly selected potential patient has a 10 percent chance of being diverted: Each patient "selects" a random time to arrive (we don't tend to schedule car accidents) and so her chance of being diverted equals the fraction of time the trauma center is fully occupied. The **denial of service probability** is the probability that a flow unit becomes part of lost demand—that is, is not served by the system.

Denial of service probability The probability that a flow unit in the Erlang loss model is not served; that is, it becomes part of lost demand.

It is one thing to know what you need (the percentage of time the trauma center is fully occupied); it is another to know how to evaluate it. Fortunately, we can use results from the Erlang loss model to estimate it. From that model, P_m is defined as the probability that all m servers are occupied. As already discussed, P_m is also the fraction of time that the system is on diversion (or losing demand) and the denial of service probability. Although we can write down an equation for P_m, it looks nasty and is cumbersome to evaluate. See the Appendix 17A for the actual equation. Instead, we use a table to evaluate P_m, like the one shown in Table 17.1. The appendix also has expanded versions: Tables 17A.1 and 17A.2.

To use Table 17.1, find the column that corresponds to the number of servers in the system. In this case, $m = 3$, and so we are looking in the third column. Next, evaluate the ratio of the average processing time, p, to the average interarrival time, a, which is

$$r = \frac{p}{a}$$

For the trauma center, $r = 2/3$. This ratio is called the **offered load**—the ratio of demand, $1/a$, to the capacity of one server, $1/p$. It is a measure of how much demand is loaded onto the system relative to the capacity of one server. For example, if the offered load is 5, then the demand rate is five times the capacity of a single server, while if the offered load is 1/2, then the demand rate is only half of the capacity of a single server. Think of the offered load as the demand "load" put on, or "offered," to the system. It is said that the demand is "offered" to the system because the system only "accepts" a portion of the demand, with the remainder becoming lost demand, or, in the case of the trauma center, diverted demand.

P_m Probability that all servers are occupied in an Erlang loss model.

Offered load The ratio of demand, $1/a$, to the capacity of one server, $1/p$.

TABLE 17.1 An Erlang Loss Table for the Probability P_m that All m Servers in the System Are Occupied, Which Is Also the Denial of Service Probability

	m					
$r = p/a$	1	2	3	4	5	6
0.10	.0909	.0045	.0002	.0000	.0000	.0000
0.20	.1667	.0164	.0011	.0001	.0000	.0000
0.25	.2000	.0244	.0020	.0001	.0000	.0000
0.30	.2308	.0335	.0033	.0003	.0000	.0000
0.33	.2500	.0400	.0044	.0004	.0000	.0000
0.40	.2857	.0541	.0072	.0007	.0001	.0000
0.50	.3333	.0769	.0127	.0016	.0002	.0000
0.60	.3750	.1011	.0198	.0030	.0004	.0000
0.67	.4000	.1176	.0255	.0042	.0006	.0001
0.70	.4118	.1260	.0286	.0050	.0007	.0001
0.75	.4286	.1385	.0335	.0062	.0009	.0001
0.80	.4444	.1509	.0387	.0077	.0012	.0002
0.90	.4737	.1757	.0501	.0111	.0020	.0003
1.00	.5000	.2000	.0625	.0154	.0031	.0005
1.10	.5238	.2237	.0758	.0204	.0045	.0008
1.20	.5455	.2466	.0898	.0262	.0063	.0012
1.25	.5556	.2577	.0970	.0294	.0073	.0015
1.33	.5714	.2759	.1092	.0351	.0093	.0021
1.40	.5833	.2899	.1192	.0400	.0111	.0026
1.50	.6000	.3103	.1343	.0480	.0142	.0035

Check Your Understanding 17.2

Question: A trauma center in a West Coast hospital has two trauma bays. The interarrival time of potential demand is 2.5 hours and the processing time is 2 hours.

   a. What is the offered load?

Answer: The offered load, r, is p/a = (2 hours per patient)/(2.5 hours per patient) = 0.8. Thus, the offered load is 0.8.

   b. What is the probability that all servers are busy?

Answer: From Table 17.1, given an offered load of 0.8 and two servers, the probability all servers is busy is .1509. Thus, the probability is .1509.

. . . .

You might be tempted to think that the offered load is the same thing as the implied utilization—they both give a sense of the amount of demand relative to the capacity of the system. However, the offered load doesn't include the actual number of servers in the system—it is always a measure of demand relative to the capacity of a *single* server. In contrast, implied utilization does account for the actual number of servers. Once the actual number of servers, m, is known, it is possible to relate the offered load to the implied utilization:

$$r = \text{Implied utilization} \times m$$

or

$$\text{Implied utilization} = \frac{r}{m}$$

Returning to Table 17.1, find the row that corresponds to the ratio r. The intersection of this row with the column for the number of servers gives us P_m. For the trauma center ($r = 0.67$, $m = 3$), we see that $P_m = .0255$. This means that there is a .0255 probability that all three servers are busy and they are all busy 2.55 percent of the time. It also means that there is a .0255 probability a patient is denied service (i.e., diverted). Converting those numbers into actual hours, being on diversion 2.55 percent of the time corresponds to about 0.6 hour per day and about 18 hours per month.

Based on Table 17.1, we can see that there are two things that determine the percentage of time the trauma center is on diversion. The first is the offered load, r. Choose any column and see how the percentage of diversion time increases as the offered load increases—the higher the ratio r, the greater the demand relative to one server's capacity and, thus, the greater the time spent on diversion. Notice that neither the interarrival time, a, nor the processing time, p, matters directly regarding the probability that the system is fully loaded. For example, if the interarrival time were to be cut in half from 3 hours to 1.5 hours, while at the same time the processing time were also cut in half from 2 hours to 1 hour, then the probability the system is fully loaded stays absolutely the same, .0255, because the offered load, r, would not change. What matters for the probability that the system is full is only the *ratio* of the processing time to the interarrival time.

The number of servers, m, is the second parameter that influences the probability the system is full. In Table 17.1, within any row, the value P_m declines as m increases—with more servers, there is a smaller chance they are all busy.

17.1.5 Amount of Lost Demand, the Flow Rate, Utilization, and Occupied Resources

How many patients are diverted to another hospital? Patients arrive at rate $1/a = 1/3$ per hour. Among those patients, 2.55 percent of them arrive when the trauma center is on diversion. Hence,

$$\text{Rate of lost demand} = \frac{1}{a} \times P_m = \frac{1}{3} \times .0255 = 0.0085 \text{ per hour}$$

Over the course of a month, this amounts to about six patients of lost demand. This might not seem like much, but if you are one of the those six patients, you might not be too happy—if the closest hospital is on diversion, then the patient needs to travel a bit further before receiving care, and that delay could have serious consequences.

The flip side of lost demand is the demand that is actually served by the trauma center. If 2.55 percent of patients experience the trauma center on diversion, then 97.45 percent ($= 1 - .0255$) find the trauma center with at least one server available. Hence,

$$\text{Flow rate} = \frac{1}{a} \times (1 - P_m) = \frac{1}{3} \times (1 - .0255) = 0.3248 \text{ per hour}$$

Thus, one-third patient arrives per hour in need of trauma care, but because of variability in the arrival process, only 0.3248 patient per hour actually receives care from this trauma center. The remaining 0.0085 patient per hour is diverted to another hospital.

Once we have evaluated the flow rate of the process, we are able to evaluate the utilization of the servers:

$$\text{Utilization} = \frac{\text{Flow rate}}{\text{Capacity}} = \frac{\text{Flow rate}}{m/p} = \frac{p}{m} \times \text{Flow rate}$$

For the trauma center:

$$\text{Utilization} = \frac{2 \text{ hours per patient}}{3} \times 0.3248 \text{ patient per hour} = 0.217$$

Hence, the servers at the trauma center are busy 21.7 percent of the time. As always, utilization is never greater than 100 percent, even if the demand rate is very high relative to the capacity of the system (i.e., if the offered load, r, is greater than 1). No matter how high demand is, the servers can never be utilized more than 100 percent. If demand is indeed very high, the servers' utilization will be high, but so is lost demand. Also, even though implied utilization is less than 100 percent, it does not equal the utilization. The gap between the implied utilization (the ratio of potential demand to capacity) and utilization (the ratio of the flow rate of served customers to capacity) is due to the fact that some demand is lost even if the implied utilization is less than 100 percent.

Once we know the utilization of the servers, 21.7 percent, it is simple to evaluate the average number of occupied servers:

$$\text{Average number of occupied servers} = m \times \text{Utilization} = 3 \times 0.217 = 0.651$$

Hence, on average, less than one trauma bay is serving a patient. It follows that, on average, $3 - 0.651 = 2.349$ trauma bays are idle on average.

Check Your Understanding 17.3

Question: A trauma center in a West Coast hospital has two trauma bays. The interarrival time of potential demand is 2.5 hours and the processing time is 2 hours.

a. At what rate is demand lost per hour?

Answer: Given an offered load of 0.8, from Table 17.1, the probability that all servers are busy, P_m, is .1509. Thus, the rate that demand is lost per hour is .1509/2.5 hours per customer = 0.0604 customer per hour.

b. What is the flow rate of the process?

Answer: Flow rate = $(1 - P_m)/a$ = (1 − .1509)/2.5 hours per customer = 0.34 customer per hour

c. What is the utilization of the process?

Answer: Utilization = $(p/m) \times$ Flow rate = (2 hours per customer/2) × 0.34 customer per hour = 0.34

17.1.6 Staffing

The approach we have taken so far in the analysis of the trauma center is to start with a given capacity and then to evaluate several performance measures. For example, we determined that with three trauma bays there is about a .026 probability that the trauma center is on diversion. However, there is another approach that a manager could take. Instead of asking, "How well are we doing given our current capacity?" the manager could ask, "How much capacity should we have to achieve to provide a desired level of service to our customers?" The second question is more long term—a trauma bay cannot be added or removed overnight—but is clearly relevant to the well-being of the organization.

In the context of the Erlang loss model, "service to our customers" refers to the probability that a customer is denied service—that is, diverted to another hospital. A hospital would love to avoid all diversion, but doing so probably requires too many trauma bays to be cost-effective—the hospital also needs to cover its costs. Closing the hospital due to a lack of funds does not serve the community in the long run. So instead of declaring a goal of "no diversion," a more realistic approach is to decide on a threshold level of diversion. For example, the hospital could say that it wants to be on diversion no more than 1 percent of its operating time (i.e., a diversion probability no more than .01). How many trauma bays does it need to achieve that objective?

In the language of the Erlang loss model, we need to determine the minimum number of servers, m, such that the service denial probability, P_m, is less than the target threshold, which in this case is .01. To find the answer to this question, begin with the offered load, $r = p/a$. Recall that the offered load does not depend on the number of servers, so we don't need the answer to our question (the number of servers) to evaluate the offered load. For our trauma center, $r = 2/3 = 0.67$.

With the offered load in hand, look at the Erlang loss table, such as the one shown in Table 17.1. If the offered load is 0.67, then we can see from the table that, with one server, the denial of service probability is .4, or 40 percent. That is way beyond our acceptable limit of .01! So we need to consider more servers (i.e., trauma bays). With two trauma bays, according to the table, the denial of service probability drops to .1176, which is still too high. With three trauma bays, like it currently has, the probability is .0255. That is still too high. However, with four trauma bays, the denial of service probability drops to .0042, comfortably below our desired threshold of .01. So to achieve no more than a .01 denial of service probability, the hospital must have at least four trauma bays.

In general, to find the minimum number of servers to achieve a threshold denial of service probability, follow these steps: (i) evaluate the offered load, $r = p/a$; (ii) find the row in the Erlang loss table that corresponds to the offered load of the system; and (iii) read across until you reach a value that is below the desired threshold probability; (iv) the number of servers at the head of that column is the number of servers that are required to achieve a denial of service that does not exceed the target threshold.

You might have noticed that the denial of service probabilities in Table 17.1 do not decline "smoothly"—adding one more server can make the denial of service probability jump down by a considerable amount. Consequently, it is likely that you will "overshoot" your threshold. For example, our threshold for the trauma center is .01, but with four servers the denial of service probability is only .0042. That is better service than we wanted, but we cannot achieve exactly the service threshold of .01: If we take away one trauma bay, the denial of service probability jumps to .0255, which is over our acceptable target.

So three trauma bays provide slightly worse service than our desired threshold, and four trauma bays provide better service. Which should we choose? Do we absolutely and positively have to have no more than a .01 denial of service probability? Maybe. For example, there could be an industry standard that is widely reported that requires us to achieve a certain service level. Or there could be substantial penalties imposed by a regulatory agency (e.g., a government) for failing to achieve a threshold. But those are somewhat extreme cases. In most settings, some managerial judgment is needed. For example, if our threshold were instead .0250, would we really invest in a fourth trauma bay because three trauma bays deliver

Question: The interarrival time for a trauma center in a southwestern hospital is two hours. The average processing time is three hours. How many trauma bays (i.e., servers) does this hospital need to ensure a denial of service probability that is no greater than .02?

Answer: The offered load is $r = p/a = 3/2 = 1.5$. From Table 17.1, the probability of a full system (which is the same as the denial of service proability) is .048 with $m = 4$, and .0142 with $m = 5$. So, five trauma bays are needed to ensure a denial of service probability that is no greater than .02.

a denial of service probability that is .0005 too high (.0255)? Probably not. But given the threshold of .01, we might want to invest in a fourth trauma bay. One thing that is clear from the analysis is that having one or two trauma bays won't be acceptable from the point of view of service, and having five or more trauma bays is a waste of money.

17.2 Managing a Queue with Impatient Customers: Economies of Scale, Pooling, and Buffers

LO17-2 Use the Erlang loss model to understand the value of economies of scale, pooling and buffers in services with impatient customers

The case of the trauma center provides another example of why sufficient capacity is needed to accommodate variability. Because trauma centers have high fixed costs, the chief financial officer of a hospital might cringe at the thought of only 21.7 percent utilization—the trauma center is full of very expensive equipment and the staff in the center are very well paid, so why should they be utilized only 21.7 percent of the time? However, even the chief financial officer knows that the mission of the trauma center is not to maximize utilization but rather to help people in need and ultimately save lives. Still, does utilization have to be so low? Is there something that a manager can do to improve systems like this?

17.2.1 Economies of Scale

One advantage of using the Erlang loss model is that we can quickly evaluate how changes in the process impact diversion. For example, we can compute the probability of diversion that would result from an increased utilization. Such a calculation would be important, both to predict diversion frequencies, as well as to predict the flow rate (e.g., number of patients served per month).

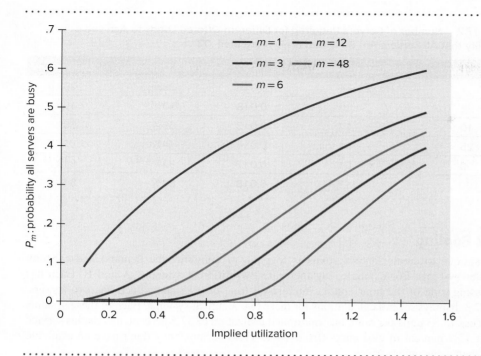

Figure 17.2

The relationship between implied utilization and the probability that all servers are busy for different system sizes (m = the number of servers in the system)

Consider, for example, an implied utilization of 50 percent. Such a case could result from a substantial increase in the arrival rate (e.g., consider the case that a major trauma center in the area closes because of the financial problems of its hospital).

Based on the increased implied utilization to 0.5 and the same number of trauma bays, $m = 3$, we compute the offered load to be r = Implied utilization $\times$ $m = 1.5$. We then use the Erlang loss formula table to look up the probability, P_m, that all m servers are utilized: $P_m = .1343$. Thus, this scenario of increased implied utilization would lead to ambulance diversion more than 13 percent of the time, corresponding to close to 100 hours of diversion every month.

Figure 17.2 shows the relationship between the level of implied utilization and the probability that the process cannot accept any further incoming arrivals. The figure demonstrates that, like waiting-time problems, there exist significant scale economies in an Erlang loss system—systems with more servers and proportionally the same amount of demand perform better than systems with few servers. To explain, note that while a 60 percent implied utilization leads to a diversion probability of .38 with one server ($m = 1$), it only leads to a .18 diversion probability with three servers and less than .02 for 12 servers. In all cases, demand is 60 percent of capacity—the larger systems have more capacity but also more demand. Nevertheless, the larger system with 12 servers is able to cope with its demand much better than the smaller system with one server.

Table 17.2 provides another perspective on economies of scale. Each row of the table corresponds to a different offered load. For example, in the first row, the arrival rate equals the capacity of a single server, while in the last row the arrival rate is 100 times the capacity of a single server. Clearly more servers are needed as demand increases relative to the capacity of one server. However, holding the quality of service approximately constant (only a .02 probability of being denied service in Table 17.2), the number of servers does not increase as fast as the demand rate. For example, when the offered load is only one, the system needs four servers to ensure that 98 percent of customers are served. If demand increases by 100-fold, so the offered load becomes 100, the system now needs 113 servers to ensure roughly the same level of service. Hence, although demand increases by a factor of 100, the capacity needed only increases by a factor of about 28 (= 113/4). Consequently, the servers are utilized only 25 percent of the time when the offered load is one, but they are utilized 87 percent of the time when the offered load is 100. This is a remarkable difference.

TABLE 17.2 Number of Servers Required for Different Offered Loads to Achieve a Probability that All Servers Are Busy that Is No More than .02

Offered Load, r	Number of Servers, m	P_m	Implied Utilization	Utilization
1	4	0.015	25%	25%
5	10	0.018	50%	49%
10	17	0.013	59%	58%
25	34	0.016	74%	72%
50	61	0.017	82%	81%
100	113	0.018	88%	87%

17.2.2 Pooling

One technique to create large systems is to pool, or combine, the demand and capacity of smaller systems. For example, say there are two different systems, A and B. Each has a processing time of 0.2 hour and an interarrival time of 0.15 hour. Each has two servers. Table 17.3 displays several calculations for these two identical systems. Each of these systems can process 13.33 units per hour, has an implied utilization of 37.5 percent, and denies service to about 13.9 percent of customers (from Table 17.1) because they don't have an available server when a customer arrives.

The combined system, C, is assumed to have the same processing time, 0.15 hour, and the same total number of servers, four. A bit of care must be taken to evaluate the interarrival time for the combined system. You cannot simply add or average the interarrival times to derive the interarrival time of the combined system. To make that calculation, the best approach is first to evaluate each system's demand and then to add those demands together to obtain the demand for the pooled system. For example, the demand for each of the smaller systems is 5 (= 1/0.2) customers per hour. Therefore, the combined demand is 10 customers per hour (= 5 + 5). Next, convert the demand of the pooled system into an interarrival time. For example, if demand is 10 customers per hour, then the interarrival time is 0.1 hour per customer = 1/10 customer per hour.

The offered load for the separate systems is 0.75. The offered load of the pooled system increases to 1.5 because the pooled system has twice the demand. However, the pooled system also has two times the number of servers, so the implied utilization stays the same, 37.5 percent.

TABLE 17.3 The Performance of Two Separate Erlang Loss Systems, A and B, Compared to the Performance of the Pooled System that Combines the Two Together

	A	B	A + B = C
a	0.20	0.20	0.10
p	0.15	0.15	0.15
m	2	2	4
Demand rate = $1/a$	5	5	10
Capacity = m/p	13.33	13.33	26.67
Implied utilization = $p/(a \times m)$	37.5%	37.5%	37.5%
Offered load, $r = p/a$	0.75	0.75	1.5
P_m	0.1385	0.1385	0.0480
Flow rate = $(1 - P_m)/a$	4.31	4.31	9.52
Utilization = (Flow rate)/Capacity	32%	32%	36%

From Table 17.1, the pooled system denies service to only 4.8 percent of customers. Therefore, with the same total demand and the same total capacity, the system is able to reduce the denial of service probability by a whopping 65 percent! (The pooled denial of service probability is .0480, which is about 35 percent of the original, .1385, so the rate is reduced by 65 percent = 100 percent − 35 percent.)

So if pooling exploits the benefits of economies of scale, why not always pool? The start of an answer is provided in Table 17.4. That table studies the impact of different levels of pooling. In the first column, there is no pooling—there are 16 independent systems, each just like system A or B in Table 17.3. The second column combines pairs to create eight independent systems. Each one of those systems is like system C in Table 17.3. The next three columns continue the process of combining systems. In the last column, all 16 of the original systems have been combined into one single system with 16 times the demand and capacity of each of the original systems.

Looking at Table 17.4, we see that the denial of service probability drops from 13.85 percent to 4.8 percent from the first level of pooling. As already mentioned, this is a considerable improvement in the performance of the system with exactly the same set of resources. Let's see what happens if we continue to combine systems. According to the third column of Table 17.4, when four of the original systems are combined, the denial of service probability drops to .0081. The first combination reduced denial of service from .1385 to .048, and the second combination reduced denial of service from .048 to .0081. The second improvement is still substantial, but not as substantial as the first. In fact, while the next combination of systems continues to reduce the denial of service probability, now it only drops from .0081 to .0003. That drop might not be noticeable—the utilization of the system increases only from 37.2 percent to 37.5 percent. And the final combination makes an even smaller improvement. The general principle revealed by Table 17.4 is that there are **declining marginal returns** to pooling, meaning that the incremental benefit of pooling decreases as you do more pooling. Put another way, a little bit of pooling can provide a tremendous benefit, but a lot of pooling may not be much more beneficial.

Even though there are declining marginal returns to pooling, pooling always reduces the denial of service probability and increases utilization. So why stop at a little bit of pooling?

Declining marginal returns When the incremental benefit of an activity decreases as the amount of the activity increases. For example, if the return from one hour of training declines as the worker receives more hours of training, then the training exhibits declining marginal returns.

TABLE 17.4 The Performance of Different Levels of Pooling

	Number of Independent Systems				
	16	8	4	2	1
a	0.2000	0.1000	0.0500	0.0250	0.0125
p	0.15	0.15	0.15	0.15	0.15
m	2	4	8	16	32
Demand rate = $1/a$	5	10	20	40	80
Capacity = m/p	13.33	26.67	53.33	106.67	213.33
Implied utilization = $p/(a \times m)$	37.5%	37.5%	37.5%	37.5%	37.5%
Offered load, $r = p/a$	0.75	1.5	3	6	12
P_m	0.1385	0.0480	0.0081	0.0003	0.0000
Flow rate = $(1 - P_m)/a$	4.31	9.52	19.84	39.99	80.00
Utilization = (Flow rate)/ Capacity	32.3%	35.7%	37.2%	37.5%	37.5%

Note: The column header is the number of independent systems. For example, the first column has 16 independent systems, while the second column describes pooling pairs of systems to create eight independent systems. The third column takes the 16 original systems and creates four independent systems, each with the demand and capacity from the combination of four of the original systems.

Question: Consider two separate systems. One has an interarrival time of two hours and the other an interarrival time of four hours. If the two systems are combined such that the combined system's demand is the sum of the demands from the two original systems, what is the interarrival time for the combined system?

Answer: The demand of the first system is 1/2 customer per hour and the demand of the second system is 1/4 customer per hour. The demand of the combined system is $1/2 + 1/4 = 3/4$ customer per hour. The interarrival time is then 4/3 hours or 1.33.

The reason is because there are some costs to pooling that we have not included in the analysis. In particular, in the case of trauma centers, pooling capacity means having capacity in fewer locations, and fewer locations means that customers have to travel further to get to a trauma center. Say a city starts off with four trauma centers spread throughout the city but then somebody suggests that they should have a single trauma center in the middle of the city that combines all of the resources of the original four. This is a wonderful suggestion if you happen to have an accident right next to the new center. But if you have the accident on the outskirts of the city, then your ambulance ride to the new mega trauma center might be considerably longer than the drive to one of the original four centers. This is not good for health outcomes. The primary reason the trauma centers have low utilization is so that patients can be served quickly. Quick service at the trauma center is not useful if it takes too long to get to the trauma center. Hence, there is a trade-off here: Pooling trauma centers makes the trauma centers more efficient, but this also tends to increase the distance customers must travel to get to a center. A manager must choose how to balance these competing objectives: neither a single trauma center for a large region (due to travel distances) nor a trauma center on every city block (due to poor utilization of resources) is acceptable.

17.2.3 Buffers

In the trauma center, patients are diverted not because there is a lack of space to let them wait, but rather because letting them wait is too risky for their health. However, in other settings, customers may be willing to wait but simply cannot. For instance, a customer on hold in a telephone communication network is still using a connection to the system even if the customer is not talking to anyone. If the system runs out of connections, then the customer cannot wait. As some customers might be willing to wait at least for some amount of time, it is intuitive that the performance of the Erlang loss model could be improved if the system were allowed to have a limited number of customers wait.

Inventory within a process is often called a **buffer** because inventory helps a process mitigate (i.e., buffer) the negative consequences of variability. The inventory can literally be physical items or parts waiting, or it can be people, as in a service setting. In the context of a trauma center, a buffer would be patients waiting to be served by a specialized team. In a call center, callers on hold represent the buffer.

To see how buffers help a process, let's add a buffer to the Erlang loss model, as shown in Figure 17.3. Recall that with the Erlang loss model, customers are lost if all servers are occupied when they arrive. If a buffer with K spots is added to the Erlang loss model, then up to K customers can wait while the servers are busy. In Figure 17.3, there are three spots for waiting customers, so $K = 3$. Thus, when a customer arrives, if one of the servers is idle, the customer immediately enters service, just as in the original Erlang loss model. But if all of the servers are occupied and there are fewer than K customers waiting, then the customer enters the buffer to wait for a server to become available. Thus, with a buffer, demand is lost only if all servers are occupied and there are K customers waiting. In short, the buffer provides the

Buffer Inventory within a process that helps to mitigate the consequences of variability.

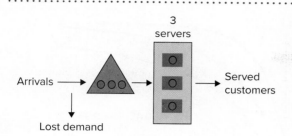

3 servers

Arrivals →

Served customers

Lost demand

Figure 17.3

A queuing model with a limited buffer. Each circle represents a space that can be occupied by a customer: Each server can accommodate one customer and the buffer can accommodate three customers. If demand arrives and all spaces are occupied, then the demand is lost.

system with some protection against variability. If the buffer has an unlimited number of spots (or at least is very large), then the queuing model depicted in Figure 17.3 becomes equivalent to the queuing model discussed in Chapter 16, Service Systems with Patient Customers.

Figure 17.4 illustrates what happens to the system if a buffer is added. Three different implied utilizations are shown (45, 75, and 95 percent) and in each case there is a single server. The left graph shows the probability of a full system. When the system is full, additional arrival of demand is lost, so the lower the probability of a full system, the less demand is lost. That effect is shown in the right graph: As the buffer increases, the percentage of demand actually served increases (and the percentage of demand lost decreases).

From Figure 17.4, we see that if there is no buffer ($K = 0$), which is the original Erlang loss model, the probability of a full system is high—almost 49 percent when implied utilization is 95 percent. Adding a buffer immediately and dramatically reduces the probability of a full system. When the implied utilization is 95 percent, the first unit of a buffer reduces the probability of a full system from .49 to .32! Each additional increase in the size of the buffer continues to reduce the probability of a full system, but Figure 17.4 illustrates that there are decreasing marginal returns: Each increase in the buffer has a smaller and smaller benefit in terms of either reducing the probability of a full system or increasing the percentage of demand served.

Although there are declining marginal returns to buffer space, the addition of a small buffer can have a dramatic impact on the performance of the system. For example, starting from 95 percent implied utilization, adding one buffer space increases the percentage of demand served from 51 percent to 68 percent. This same improvement could also be achieved by reducing the implied utilization of the server. For example, say the server is a computer system and with the speed of the current system the server achieves 95 percent implied utilization. However, there also exists a faster, but more expensive computer system. In fact, the faster computer's capacity is more than twice the capacity of the slower computer, resulting in an implied utilization of 45 percent. (Specifically, the ratio of the faster computer's capacity to the slower computer's capacity is 0.95/0.45 = 2.1.) Looking at the right graph of Figure 17.4, we see that the faster computer with no buffer serves about the same percentage of demand (69 percent) as the slower computer with one buffer (68 percent). So, to serve about 68 percent of demand, a manager could choose a slow computer with one buffer or a much faster computer with no buffer. A computer with twice the capacity is likely to be much more expensive. A single buffer may not be very expensive at all. We can conclude that some use of a buffer, even a buffer of a limited size, may be the most economical means to improve a system.

We have already extensively discussed one limitation of buffers—some customers may not be able to wait (as in trauma patients). But there are two other limitations to the "add buffers" strategy. First, even if the buffer size is sufficiently large to let customers wait, they may choose not to wait. This behavior is called **balking**—a customer balks from a queue when he or she arrives at the queue and immediately chooses not to enter it. For example, say we invest in our system and now we have a buffer that can accommodate up to 10 customers. A customer arrives and sees nine customers already waiting. There is one more spot to wait, so the customer could wait, but the customer nevertheless chooses not to wait, probably because he

Balking The practice of not joining a queue. Customers generally balk when they believe the total time needed to receive service exceeds the amount of time they are willing to wait.

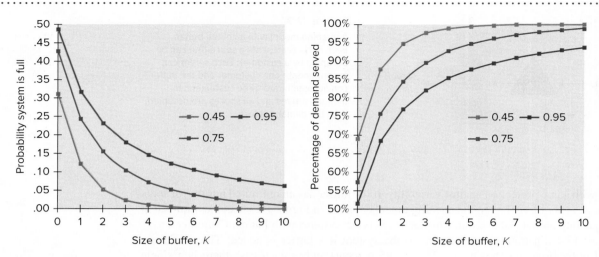

Figure 17.4

With one server, the impact of increasing the buffer of waiting customers is shown on the probability of a full system (left) and the percentage of demand served (right). In each case, there is one server and implied utilization (and offered load) is either 45, 75, or 95 percent.

or she infers from the size of the queue that the wait will be too long. An immediate implication of balking is that a buffer does not prevent as much lost demand when customers choose to balk. In the right graph of Figure 17.4, if some customers balk, then each "percentage of demand served" curve shifts down—any given buffer size captures a smaller percentage of demand when balking is possible.

The second limitation of buffers is **reneging**, which is also called **abandoning**—customers renege from or abandon a queue when they leave a queue that they have already joined. Reneging is terrible for the system. From the point of view of the manager of the service, reneging is the same as lost demand, which effectively means lost revenue and a lost opportunity to serve a customer. From the point of view of the customer, reneging means incurring the cost of waiting without even getting the satisfaction of service. Nobody benefits from reneging.

Reneging is an interesting behavior. Why would a customer join a queue and later renege? Clearly, if a customer knew that she was going to renege, she would be better off to balk from the queue before joining it. But reneging can occur for several reasons. For one, customers might not be sure about how long their wait will be when they first join. They might expect their wait will be short, but with the passage of time discover (or infer) that the wait will be longer, possibly too long to remain in the queue. They could be uncertain about the duration of the wait because they don't know how many customers are in front of them—in a call center queue, you generally do not "see" how many other customers are waiting to talk to an agent. Alternatively, a customer might not know how long it will take the system to process each customer—you might think it will take only a minute or two to process each customer in front of you but then learn that each customer is taking much more time to process than you expected.

Figure 17.5 provides some data on reneging at a call center. Only about 8 percent of customers renege if they wait 30 seconds, but about 35 percent of customers renege if they wait 150 seconds. Consequently, reneging limits the effectiveness of buffers: While you might hope that a buffer allows a process to capture a high fraction of demand, some demand may be lost due to reneging.

Even though balking and reneging might limit the effectiveness of a buffer, they become most problematic with large buffers. Small buffers still retain the ability to reduce lost demand, and so should be an effective option for a manager to consider.

Reneging The practice of leaving a queue after joining it. Also known as abandoning.

Abandoning The practice of leaving a queue after joining it. Also known as reneging.

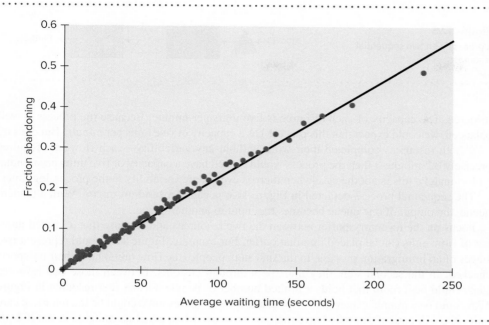

Figure 17.5
Fraction of customers who renege as a function of their time waiting. (Source: Gans, Koole, and Mandelbaum (2003))

Check Your Understanding 17.6

Question: Annick and Lela walk to the Cynwyd Ice Cream shop. When they arrive, they are surprised to see 10 people in line, but they decide to wait. The first two customers in line get their ice cream in a reasonable amount of time, but the next group of customers takes what seems like forever to decide what to order. Because they promised their parents they would be home within 20 minutes, Annick and Lela reluctantly leave the shop without any ice cream. Their action is best described as which of the following?

a. Joining
b. Balking
c. Reneging
d. Strategizing

Answer: They joined the queue but left the queue before being served, which is known as reneging or abandoning. Therefore, the correct answer is C.

17.3 Lost Capacity Due to Variability

Variability in demand or service can create queues of waiting customers, or, worse, can cause a process to lose demand when combined with inflexible capacity. But those are not the only negative consequences of variability. Variability can actually also cause a process to lose capacity. And if a process loses capacity, the other problems (waiting and/or lost demand) only become worse. In this section, we explore why variability can destroy capacity and what a manager can do to alleviate this problem.

Consider the rather simple process displayed in Figure 17.6. There are two resources and flow units are first processed by the first resource before they are completed by the second

LO17-3 Understand how variability can reduce capacity and how to restore capacity via standardized work, buffers, or elimination of sequential work

Figure 17.6

A process with two sequential resources

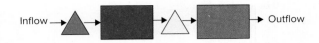

resource. The capacity of each resource is five units per minute. Because the process is well balanced, we could expect that this process has a capacity of five units per minute. But does it?

If both resources completed their work without any variability—each flow unit requires precisely 0.2 minute—then the process would indeed have a capacity of five units per minute. Unfortunately, this is not the case when there is even some variability in the processing times.

The sequential process depicted in Figure 17.6 is called a **tandem queue**. With a tandem queue, the output of one queue becomes the input to another queue.

Focus on the inventory buffer between the two resources and suppose that a limited number of flow units can be placed into that buffer. For example, Figure 17.6 could represent two stages of an immigration process. In the first step, people (the flow units) have their passports checked. In the second step, they must pass through customs. Between those two resource steps could be a room that holds a limited number of people. Or the first resource in Figure 17.6 could be a trauma center in a hospital and the second resource could be the intensive care unit (ICU). A patient can only leave the trauma center when a bed is available in the ICU. If there are no available beds in the ICU, the patient remains in the trauma center.

The limited size of the inventory between the two resources would not be a problem if there were no variability in processing times. Every 0.2 minute, a unit would leave the first resource and immediately pass on to the second resource. No inventory builds between them because the two resources are synchronized to complete their units at exactly the same time. However, if processing times vary due to randomness, then that perfect synchronization between the two resources is not possible.

Two problems arise when there is variability in processing times and resources are organized sequentially, as in a tandem queue. The first is **blocking**. A resource is blocked when it is unable to complete the processing of one unit and begin the processing of another unit. The second is **starving**. A resource is starved when it would like to begin working on a unit, but there is no unit available to work on. Both of these problems are depicted in Figure 17.7.

The first queue in Figure 17.7 depicts blocking. The inventory buffer between the two resources can hold up to three flow units, and in the first queue, at this moment, all three spots in that inventory are filled. Hence, even if the first resource has completed the processing of its unit, it cannot begin the process for a new unit because it has no place to put the completed unit. In effect, it is blocked from working. The second queue in Figure 17.7 depicts starving. The second resource is ready and able to work, but there are no units in the inventory behind it. Hence, it is starved from the opportunity to work.

Tandem queue A process that has a sequence of queues in which the output of one queue can be the input to the next queue.

Blocking The event in which a resource completes a flow unit but is prevented from working on a new flow unit because there is no place to store the completed unit.

Starving The event in which a resource is capable of working on a flow unit but there is no flow unit available to work on.

Figure 17.7

Blocking and starving in a tandem queue in which at most three units can be held in each inventory

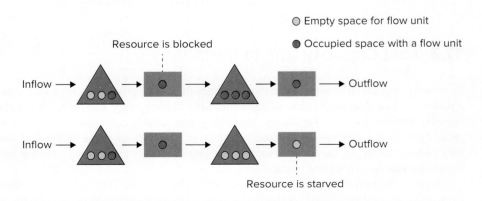

Both blocking and starving destroy capacity. In either case, a resource is prevented from working. The resource is forced to be idle even though there may be a considerable amount of work to do in the system. Consequently, the flow rate of output from the process is not as high as it could be. And the negative effects of blocking and starving can be substantial, as we soon will see.

Unlike queues in which a flow unit is processed by a single server, there are no simple mathematical equations to predict the performance of a tandem queue. These systems, even if they have only two resources, are too complex to be boiled down to a neat equation (or even a messy equation). But they can readily be analyzed via **discrete event simulation**. A discrete event simulator is a software program that carefully tracks flow units through a process and simulates the random time flow units require to be processed at each resource. For example if a customer required either one, two, three, four, five, or six minutes to be processed at a resource, all equally likely, we could simulate a customer's processing time by rolling a six-sided die. Think of a discrete event simulator as computer code that virtually rolls many different dice and uses the outcomes of those rolls to carefully track flow units through a process.

Figure 17.8 displays the results of a discrete event simulator of the process in Figure 17.6. The capacity (or flow rate) is expressed as a percentage of the maximum capacity, which in this case is five units per minute. Thus, 60 percent of the maximum capacity would be three units per minute ($0.6 \times 5 = 3$). In fact, according to Figure 17.8, that is about the flow rate of the process when the inventory between the two resources is limited to one unit and the coefficient of variation of the processing times is two (very high).

Figure 17.8 reveals several patterns. First, in all cases, the more variability in processing times, the lower the process's capacity—all of the curves "drop down" as the coefficient of variation in processing time increases. In effect, variability in processing times is destroying capacity—each resource can produce, on average, five units per minute, but in many cases the process comes nowhere near that flow rate because of blocking and starving. Second, in all cases, the capacity of the process increases as the buffer size increases. Yes, there are some ups and downs with each curve, but those are merely due to the fact that a simulation provides the results from a set of random events (as in a set of dice rolls). The overall trend in each curve is unquestionably increasing.

Given the behavior we see in our simulation, there are three strategies that a manager can implement to help improve this process: reduce variability in processing times, increase the size of the buffer, and avoid sequential processes.

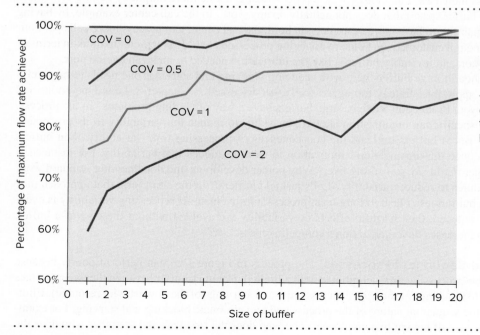

Figure 17.8

The flow rate of a two-resource tandem queue, expressed as a percent of the flow rate (assuming there is no variability in processing times). Different levels of variability in processing times (COV) are displayed on different lines. In all cases, the coefficient of variation of the arrival process is one.

Reduce the Variability of Processing Times Variability is not your friend! Take a look at the extreme case in which the buffer size is one unit. When the processing time has a coefficient of variation of 0.5, the process's flow rate is nearly 90 percent of the maximum—the process is only losing 10 percent of capacity due to blocking and starving. However, when the coefficient of variation increases to one, lost capacity increases to 24 percent. And a whopping 40 percent of capacity is lost when the coefficient of variation is at a high level, such as two.

How can variability in processing times be reduced? A good place to start is with **standard working procedures**—a set of guidelines and instructions that detail how a task is to be completed. In the context of a call center, standard working procedures may specify how an agent should greet a client and how the agent should end the call. In a health care setting, a standard working procedure could detail the steps to prepare a patient for surgery: which step is done first, which is done second, how long each step takes, and so forth.

Standard working procedures are particularly useful for training new employees. Instead of letting each new employee figure out on his or her own the best way to do a task, which can only lead to variable processing times, the organization should immediately train new employees using the standard working procedures so that they can "march down" their learning curve as quickly as possible.

Increase the Size of the Inventory Buffer: Buffer or Suffer After as much processing variability is eliminated as possible, a manager can improve the performance of the process by expanding the size of the inventory buffer between resources. This is the idea behind the principle called **buffer or suffer**: If a process is not sufficiently buffered, it suffers the loss of capacity.

Return to Figure 17.8. An inventory buffer size of 10 practically eliminates all blocking and starving when the coefficient of variation is 0.5. When processing time variability is higher, a larger buffer is needed, but it still may be a reasonable size. For example, when the coefficient of variation is one, a buffer of 20 units seems to do the trick in this model.

The "expand the buffer" strategy can be particularly effective because in many situations it is much cheaper to add buffer space than it is to add additional capacity. For example, in a call center it can be cheaper to add more phone lines (to allow more people to be on hold) than it is to hire and train employees. In fact, this strategy seems to work magically. The manager expands an inventory buffer, which offers no capacity whatsoever, and yet the capacity of the process increases! Put another way, a process can generate more output by adding something (more buffer space) that does not actually do any work. In the call center example, by having the capability to have more customers on hold, the call center can process more calls per hour even though customers on hold are not being processed at all! If you prefer to think in terms of metaphors, an inventory buffer is like the lubrication needed to make an engine purr.

Although large buffers help with reducing blocking and starving, one needs to be careful not to apply this strategy too aggressively. As discussed in Chapter 8, Lean Operations and the Toyota Production System, large buffers have a way of "hiding problems" in the process. To be specific, an organization should always try to reduce the variability in its processing times. But if buffers mitigate the consequences of processing time variability, then buffers also reduce the organization's motivation to work to reduce that variability. For instance, a manager might say something like, "Why bother developing and documenting standard work procedures to reduce variability? Let's just add buffers." In the short term that approach may work, but it doesn't lead to long-term process improvement. If processing variability is eventually reduced, then harmful effects of variability are avoided without the cost of a buffer, which increases the organization's competitiveness.

Standard working procedures A set of guidelines and instructions that detail how a task is to be completed.

Buffer or suffer A principle that states that a system's capacity decreases if sufficiently large buffers are not included in the system.

Avoid Sequential Processes The process in Figure 17.6 can perform poorly because variable processing times combined with a limited inventory buffer between the two resources leads to blocking (of the upstream resource) and starving (of the downstream resource). Eliminate the sequential nature of the process and you eliminate blocking and starving. For example, instead of having two employees, one who does the first task and the other who does the second task, have each employee do both tasks.

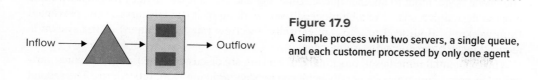

Figure 17.9

A simple process with two servers, a single queue, and each customer processed by only one agent

---

Check Your Understanding 17.7

Question: A biologics production process uses a series of vats to make pharmaceutical products. Each vat contains a mixture of compounds and live organisms (e.g., bacteria) and must be strictly controlled in terms of temperature, acidity, and other factors. Storage tanks are used between production steps. If a storage tank is full, the upstream batch is held in a steady state before it can be transferred to the storage tank. This is an example of which of the following?

 a. Balking
 b. Blocking
 c. Reneging
 d. Starving

Answer: The upstream resource is blocked from continuing its production. Thus, the correct answer is b.

There is no blocking and starving when a worker takes a customer through a process from start to finish—an employee cannot block or starve herself! Even with processing time variability, if the process in Figure 17.6 were configured as in Figure 17.9, the average capacity of the process could equal the maximum possible flow rate of five flow units per minute as long as each worker can do both tasks as effectively as a single worker who specializes in that task. For example, if the processing time of each worker is 0.4 minute, then the capacity of the process is 2 workers/0.4 minute per worker per unit = 5 units per minute, just as in the tandem queue process in Figure 17.6. Even if there is some productivity loss by not having the workers specialize in tasks, it is possible that the downside to this approach (longer processing times) could be outweighed by the benefits of eliminating sequential processing (no blocking and starving).

Conclusion

This chapter is about the impact of variability and inflexibility on process performance. Two consequences of these system inhibitors are discussed: loss of demand and loss of capacity.

We use the Erlang loss model to understand the consequences of variability in demand. When customers are impatient or unable to wait, some demand might be lost (i.e., not served by the system) because, due to variability and inflexible supply, there can be times when all of the servers are occupied and none are able to immediately serve additional customers. This is generally neither good for the system (e.g., revenue is rarely earned from a customer who is not served) nor good for the customer (e.g., searching for service is irritating and can be costly).

The capability of a system to serve customers depends on two key parameters: the offered load and the number of servers. As the offered load increases (the ratio of demand to the capacity of a single server), holding the number of servers fixed, more and more demand is lost and customers experience a greater likelihood that they are denied service. In contrast, holding the offered load fixed, increasing the number of servers reduces the amount of lost demand, increases the flow rate, and decreases the likelihood that service is denied. While adding more servers improves service to customers, additional servers are not free.

Lost capacity is another consequence of variability and inflexibility. Flow units are often served by a series of resources. This structure is called a tandem queue because the output of one queue is the input to another queue. Blocking and starving are major problems with this process design: a resource can be blocked from working or it can be starved (i.e., prevented from working). Both lead to a loss in capacity: the flow rate (i.e., output) of the system is reduced when blocking and starving occur.

Three potential remedies to blocking and starving are discussed. The first is to reduce variability in processing times, generally achieved by standardizing work procedures. The second is to add buffer space between the resources—"buffer" the process so that you don't "suffer" the loss of capacity. The third is to remove the sequential flow to the process. For example, let workers process flow units from start to finish. While this strategy eliminates blocking and starving, it reduces the ability of workers to specialize in their tasks.

Summary of Learning Objectives

LO17-1 Use the Erlang loss model to understand and evaluate performance measures in services with impatient customers

In the Erlang loss model, customers cannot wait—when a customer arrives, either he enters service immediately with one of the available servers or, if there are no idle servers, he leaves the system. The Erlang loss model applies when either customers are impatient (e.g., they are injured and need the service of a trauma center as soon as possible) or there is no ability for them to wait (e.g., there are no additional telephone lines to keep them "on hold"). Using the Erlang loss model, it is possible to evaluate the percentage of time all servers are busy, the rate of lost demand, and the utilization of the server.

LO17-2 Use the Erlang loss model to understand the value of economies of scale, pooling and buffers in services with impatient customers

The probability that all servers are busy is greatly influenced by the implied utilization of the system: The higher the implied utilization, the more frequent the system has all of its servers occupied. However, the sensitivity of the system to the implied utilization depends significantly on the number of servers in the system. For the same implied utilization, a system with more servers has all of its servers occupied less often than a system with fewer servers. Even though larger systems are less likely to have all of their servers occupied, servers in large systems are busier, on average—they have a higher utilization because there is less lost demand.

LO17-3 Understand how variability can reduce capacity and how to restore capacity via standardized work, buffers, or elimination of sequential work

A tandem queue is a system with two or more sequential resources. Due to variability in processing times, a resource can be blocked from working if the downstream inventory buffer is full. Alternatively, a resource can be starved, meaning that its upstream source of flow units is empty. Blocking and starving reduce a system's capacity. To combat this problem, a manager can (i) try to standardize work in an effort to reduce the variability of processing times, (ii) expand the size of the inventory buffers between the resources, and/or (iii) eliminate the sequential nature of the process flow. The second strategy is based on the principle of "buffer or suffer": If a process does not have sufficient inventory buffers, then it suffers a loss in capacity.

Key Terms

17.1 Lost Demand in Queues with No Buffers

Diversion The practice of sending demand away from a system when it cannot be served by the system in a sufficiently timely manner. For example, a hospital may divert patients to another hospital when it is unable to care for more patients.

Lost demand Potential demand that a system is unable to serve. This demand does not count toward a process's flow rate.

Erlang loss model A queuing model in which the total number of flow units in the system cannot exceed the number of servers. If a flow unit arrives to the system when it is full, the flow unit is not served by the system and becomes lost demand.

Denial of service probability The probability that a flow unit in the Erlang loss model is not served; that is, it becomes part of lost demand.

P_m Probability that all servers are occupied in an Erlang loss model.

Offered load The ratio of demand, $1/a$, to the capacity of one server, $1/p$.

17.2 Managing a Queue with Impatient Customers: Economies of Scale, Pooling, and Buffers

Declining marginal returns When the incremental benefit of an activity decreases as the amount of the activity increases. For example, if the return from one hour of training declines as the worker receives more hours of training, then the training exhibits declining marginal returns.

Buffer Inventory within a process that helps to mitigate the consequences of variability.

Balking The practice of not joining a queue. Customers generally balk when they believe the total time needed to receive service exceeds the amount of time they are willing to wait.

Reneging The practice of leaving a queue after joining it. Also known as abandoning.

Abandoning The practice of leaving a queue after joining it. Also known as reneging.

17.3 Lost Capacity Due to Variability

Tandem queue A process that has a sequence of queues in which the output of one queue can be the input to the next queue.

Blocking The event in which a resource completes a flow unit but is prevented from working on a new flow unit because there is no place to store the completed unit.

Starving The event in which a resource is capable of working on a flow unit but there is no flow unit available to work on.

Standard working procedures A set of guidelines and instructions that detail how a task is to be completed.

Buffer or suffer A principle that states that a system's capacity decreases if sufficiently large buffers are not included in the system.

Key Formulas

LO17-1 Use the Erlang loss model to understand and evaluate performance measures in services with impatient customers

$$\text{Capacity} = \frac{\text{Number of resources}}{\text{Processing time}} = \frac{m}{p}$$

$a = \text{interarrival time}$

$$\text{Implied utilization} = \frac{\text{Demand}}{\text{Capacity}} = \frac{1/a}{m/p} = \frac{p}{a \times m}$$

$$\text{Offered load} = r = \frac{p}{a} = \text{Implied utilization} \times m$$

$P_m = \text{the probability that all } m \text{ servers are occupied}$

$$\text{Rate of lost demand} = \frac{1}{a} \times P_m$$

$$\text{Flow rate} = \frac{1}{a} \times (1 - P_m)$$

$$\text{Utilization} = \frac{\text{Flow rate}}{\text{Capacity}} = \frac{\text{Flow rate}}{m/p} = \frac{p}{m} \times \text{Flow rate}$$

Conceptual Questions

LO17-1

1. If capacity exceeds demand, then all flow units are served. True or false?
   a. True
   b. False

2. The denial of service probability decreases if more servers are added and nothing else changes. True or false?
   a. True
   b. False

3. In the Erlang loss model, which of the following most likely increases lost demand?
   a. An increase in the average interarrival time
   b. An increase in the average processing time
   c. An increase in the number of servers
   d. A decrease in implied utilization

4. In the Erlang loss model, which best describes the relationship between implied utilization and utilization?
   a. Implied utilization is always greater than utilization.
   b. Implied utilization is only greater than utilization when implied utilization is greater than 100 percent.
   c. Implied utilization, like utilization, does not exceed 100 percent.
   d. Implied utilization is the same as utilization.

5. In the Erlang loss model, which of the following is a benefit of reducing the variability of processing times?
   a. The denial of service probability decreases.
   b. The flow rate increases.
   c. Implied utilization increases.
   d. Utilization increases.
   e. All of the above.
   f. None of the above.

LO17-2

6. In the Erlang loss model, system A has 5 servers and an implied utilization of 125 percent, while system B has 15 servers and an implied utilization of 125 percent. Which of the following statements is true?
   a. System A has the higher utilization because it has fewer servers relative to the potential demand.
   b. The two systems have the same utilization because they have the same implied utilization.
   c. System B has a higher utilization because the fraction of lost demand is lower in that system.
   d. More information is needed to determine which system has the higher utilization.

7. In the Erlang loss model, pooling is an effective strategy because it always increases implied utilization. True or false?
   a. True
   b. False

LO17-3

8. Which of the following most directly expresses the motivation behind the expression "buffer or suffer"?
   a. Adding inventory to a process is likely to increase the flow time.
   b. To increase capacity, it is important to pool queues.
   c. If you want to increase the capacity of a process, add capacity first to the bottleneck.
   d. If there is variability in the arrival process or in processing times, make sure there is sufficient inventory between stages; otherwise, capacity will be reduced.
   e. Variability in the service process reduces capacity more than variability in the arrival process.

9. At the Millbrook High School cafeteria, students proceed along a series of stations in a single line: (1) get tray and utensils, (2) choose food, (3) select beverage, (4) pay. The school is concerned that students are taking too long to get their meal. The school has analyzed the capacities of each of the four steps in isolation and found there exists sufficient capacity at each resource in isolation. Which of the following is most likely to be causing the congestion?

a. The bottleneck is probably at the last station because capacity is reduced the most when the bottleneck is at the end of the process.

b. The implied utilization of the bottleneck is too low.

c. Due to variability in processing times, both blocking and starving could be occurring.

d. The process must be demand-constrained.

e. The stations have similar utilizations.

Solved Example Problems

LO17-1

1. A private home security service guarantees to either dispatch one of its four guards immediately if a customer sets off an alarm or, if all of its guards are responding to other calls, divert the alarm to the local police. The company receives 1.25 alarms per hour. It takes a guard, on average, 84 minutes to respond to an alarm.

a. What is the interarrival time of alarms (in minutes)?

Answer: 48 minutes. The interarrival time is the reciprocal of the arrival rate. Hence, the interarrival time is 1/1.25 hours per alarm = 0.8 hour per alarm. Convert to minutes: 0.8 hour per alarm × 60 minutes per hour = 48 minutes per alarm.

b. What is the offered load?

Answer: 1.75. The offered load is $r = p/a$. From the problem, $p = 84$ minutes. From part A, $a = 48$ minutes. Hence, $r = 84/48 = 1.75$.

c. What is the implied utilization?

Answer: 0.4375. Implied utilization = $p/(a \times m) = 84$ minutes per alarm per agent/ (48 minutes per alarm × 4 agents) = 0.4375.

d. What is the rate of lost demand per hour (i.e., alarms directed to the police)?

Answer: 0.088. From the Erlang loss table with the offered load of 1.75 and four servers, $P_m = .0702$. Hence, 7.0 percent of the alarms are directed to the police. It receives 1.25 alarms per hour, so 1.25 × .0702 = 0.088 alarm per hour is diverted to the police.

e. What is the flow rate of alarms per hour through this system?

Answer: 1.16. From part D, the rate of lost demand is 0.088 alarm per hour. Hence, 1.25 − 0.088 = 1.16 alarms per hour is the flow rate.

f. On average, how many guards are responding to alarms?

Answer: 0.406. Utilization = Flow rate/Capacity. From part E, the flow rate is 1.16 alarms per hour. Capacity = $m/p = 4/84 = 0.0476$ alarm per minute or 60 × 0.0476 = 2.86 alarms per hour. So Utilization = 1.16/2.86 = 0.406.

g. How many guards does it need to hire to ensure that it serves at least 99 percent of calls (i.e., it diverts 1 percent or fewer calls to the police)?

Answer: 2. With an offered load of 1.75 and five servers, the denial of service probability is 2.4 percent, which is higher than the target of 1 percent. With six servers, the denial of service probability is 0.69 percent, which is acceptable. It has four guards, so it needs to hire two more.

2. A hardware store rents its one wood chipper. A request for the chipper arrives every four days with a standard deviation of four days. On average, clients rent the chipper for one day. If a request arrives and the chipper is not available, customers rent from another company.

   a. What is the offered load?

   Answer: 0.25. The processing time is one day and the interarrival time is four days, so the offered load is $r = 1/4 = 0.25$.

   b. What fraction of demand is not served?

   Answer: .2. From the Erlang loss table, with $r = 0.25$ and $m = 1$, $P_m = .2$.

   c. What fraction of demand is served?

   Answer: .8. From part B, the fraction of demand that is not served is .2. The fraction that is served is then $1 - .2 = .8$.

   d. What is the utilization of the chipper?

   Answer: 0.2. Flow rate $= (1 - P_m)/a = (1 - 0.2)/4 = 0.2$ chipper per day. Capacity $= p/m = 1/1 = 1$ chipper per day. Utilization $=$ Flow rate/Capacity $= 0.2$ chipper per day/1 chipper per day $= 0.2$.

   e. What fraction of time is the chipper rented?

   Answer: 0.2. The fraction of time the chipper is rented is the utilization, which, from part D, is 0.2.

   f. A new manager insists that it be able to satisfy 99.99 percent of all demand (i.e., the denial of service probability cannot be greater than 0.01 percent). How many chippers does it need to have to ensure that level of service?

   Answer: 4. From the Erlang loss table, with an offered load of 0.25, three servers achieves a denial of service probability of 0.2 percent, which is too high. With four servers, the denial of service probability is 0.01 percent, which meets the target threshold.

LO17-2

3. Computer server A receives requests at the rate of 100 per second. Computer server B receives requests at the rate of 50 per second. If the two computers are decommissioned and replaced by server C, what is server C's interarrival time (in seconds)? Assume server C's demand equals the sum of the demands from the two previous servers.

   Answer: 0.0067. Server C's arrival rate is $100 + 50 = 150$ per second. Server C's interarrival time is then 1/150 second $= 0.0067$ second.

4. Quick Clinic (QC) operates clinics throughout the country that are staffed by nurse practitioners and physician assistants. They provide primarily family health services (e.g., screening for strep throat, joint sprains, etc.). QC currently operates two clinics in a town. The clinics receive patients with an interarrival time of 15 minutes and 10 minutes, respectively. QC plans to close one of the clinics; it hopes that total demand from the town remains the same even though it will have only one remaining clinic. If this occurs, what is the interarrival time (in minutes) for the remaining clinic?

   Answer: 6. Convert the interarrival times to demand rates: If $a = 15$ minutes, then demand equals 1/15 patient per minute, which equals $60 \times 1/15 = 4$ patients per hour. If $a = 10$ minutes, then demand equals 1/10 patient per minute, which equals $60 \times 1/10 = 6$ patients per hour. Therefore, total demand is $4 + 6 = 10$ patients per hour. The interarrival time is therefore 1/10 hour, which is $60 \times 1/10 = 6$ minutes.

Problems and Applications

· ·

LO17-1

1. Mr. Cherry owns a gas station on a highway in Vermont. In the afternoon hours, there are, on average, 30 cars per hour passing by the gas station that would like to refuel. However, because there are several other gas stations with similar prices on the highway, potential customers are not willing to wait—if they see that all of the pumps are occupied, they continue on down the road.

   The gas station has three pumps that can be used for fueling vehicles, and cars spend four minutes, on average, parked at a pump (filling up their tank, paying, etc.).
   a. What is the offered load?
   b. What is the implied utilization?
   c. What is the capacity of the gas station (cars per hour)?
   d. What is the probability that all three pumps are being used by vehicles?
   e. How many customers are served every hour?
   f. What is the utilization of the pumps?
   g. How many pumps should it have to ensure that it captures at least 98 percent of the demand that drives by the station?

2. Jiffy Service is a call center with several business units. One of its business units staffs four operators who provide support for an industrial plumbing supply company. Calls arrive during business hours every three minutes, with a standard deviation of interarrival times equal to three minutes as well. If all four operators are busy when a call arrives, it is rerouted to another business unit instead of being put on hold. The processing time for calls is five minutes on average.
   a. What is the offered load?
   b. What is the implied utilization?
   c. What is the capacity of this call center (calls per hour)?
   d. What is the probability that all four operators are talking to customers?
   e. How many customers are served every hour?
   f. What is the utilization of the operators?
   g. How many operators should it have to ensure that it serves at least 97 percent of demand?

3. Los Angeles Reporters Associated (LARA) is a newsgroup that specializes in making videos and photos of Hollywood celebrities. LARA has a large network of people who report viewings of celebrities via text messages to LARA's headquarters. LARA has a set of five reporters. Upon the arrival of a text message indicating a viewing, a reporter jumps into his or her car and drives to the reported viewing location. On average, it takes three hours for a reporter to complete the process of each viewing (driving there and collecting material), with a standard deviation of two hours. Once they start an assignment, reporters always complete it without interruption. If no reporter is immediately available when a text message arrives, then the opportunity is lost—no reporter is deployed for this potential viewing.

   Text messages come in at a rate of two per hour (i.e., the interarrival times are, on average, 30 minutes between viewings) and the standard deviation of the interarrival times is 30 minutes.
   a. What is the offered load?
   b. What is the implied utilization of LARA's reporters?
   c. What is their capacity to complete assignments (in assignments per hour)?
   d. What is the probability that an incoming text message reporting a viewing cannot be pursued?
   e. What is the flow rate of completed assignments (assignments per hour)?
   f. What is the utilization of LARA's reporters?
   g. How many reporters does LARA need to have on its staff to ensure that it takes advantage of at least 85 percent of the text messages that it receives?

4. RideShare offers short-term rentals of vehicles that are kept in small lots in urban neighborhoods with plenty of potential customers. With one lot, it has eight cars. The interarrival time of potential demand for this lot from its base of customers is 40 minutes. The average rental period is five hours. If a customer checks availability of vehicles in this lot online and finds that they are all rented for the desired time, the customer skips renting and finds alternative arrangements. However, because customers pay a monthly fee to subscribe to this service, RideShare does not want customers to be disappointed too often.
   a. What is the offered load?
   b. What is the implied utilization?
   c. What is the capacity of the process (rentals per hour)?
   d. What is the probability that all eight cars are rented at the same time?
   e. How many customers are served every hour?
   f. What is the utilization of the cars?
   g. How many cars should it have in this lot to ensure that it serves at least 90 percent of demand?

LO17-2

5. The Los Angeles Reporters Associated (LARA) is considering a merger with its competitors Fast Paparazzi of America (FPA). LARA receives two viewings per hour. FPA obtains one viewing per hour. What is the interarrival time (in minutes) for the combined firm, LARA-FPA?

6. RideShare is considering combining two lots. One receives a rental request every 45 minutes, while the other receives a rental request every 90 minutes. What would be the interarrival time (in minutes) of the combined lot? (Assume total demand does not change.)

References

Gans, N., G. Koole, and A. Mandelbaum. "Telephone Call Centers: Tutorial, Review and Research Prospects." *Manufacturing & Service Operations Management* 5, no. 2 (2003), pp. 79–141. http://dx.doi.org/10.1287/msom.5.2.79.16071

CASE   BIKE SHARING

Bike-sharing programs are now common in many of the world's large cities, including London, Paris, Singapore, and New York, along with many smaller cities. These programs are meant to provide an environmentally friendly alternative mode of transportation. But they are also viewed as a bit of a status symbol—the Bloomberg administration in New York City (which established New York's program) describes bike sharing as a hallmark of a world-class city. While there is a strong "feel good" nature to bike sharing, to ultimately have an impact, a bike-sharing program needs to work, meaning it needs to provide a service that customers value at a price they are willing to pay. And that requires that a bike-sharing program gets its operations right.

When it started in 2013, the New York City Citi Bike sharing program had about 6000 bikes and 330 stations. Each station consists of a series of docks (generally in the range of 10 to 40). Each dock can hold a single bike. To use the program, a rider first purchases an access pass (e.g., an annual pass, a daily pass, etc.) and then uses that pass to unlock a bike at a station. Next, the individual rides wherever he or she wants and then returns the bike to another dock at another station.

From the point of view of the rider, there are a few potential inconveniences. For one, there might not be a station close to where the rider is (work or home) or where the rider wants to go. However, Figure 17.10 shows that in many cases there is a bike station every couple of blocks. Another issue is the availability of bikes—a rider might walk to a station only to discover that all of the bikes are in use.

© Aaron Roeth Photography/RF

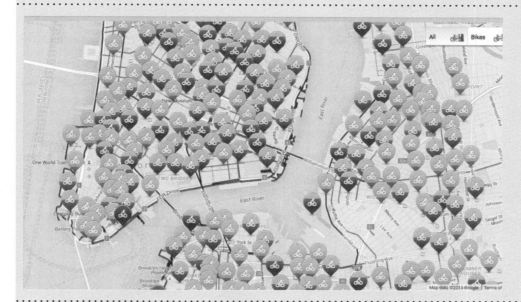

Figure 17.10

Locations of Citi Bike stations in lower Manhattan

(continued)

Figure 17.11

Daily trips in New York's
bike-sharing program

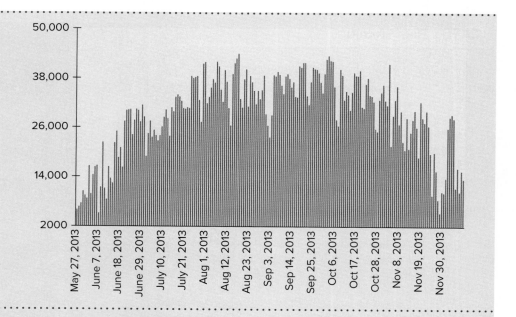

Figure 17.11

Daily trips in New York's
bike-sharing program

Finally, there is the availability of docks—a rider might ride to a station, hoping to return a bike, but find all of the docks at that station occupied with another bike. There are apps available to help riders predict where bikes and docks are available, but those apps cannot eliminate this issue.

For a program to be successful, it must ensure that the earlier mentioned inconveniences of "no bikes" or "no docks" are not too problematic; otherwise, people won't use the system. But there are several obstacles that make it challenging to achieve that service goal, while also keeping investment in the program at a reasonable level. For instance, demand for bike sharing varies throughout the year. As Figure 17.11 reveals, and as you would expect, riding a bike is more pleasant when the weather is nice—not too hot, not too cold, and definitely not too rainy. The day of the week also matters for the number of desired rides—weekend versus workday. Finally, there is a predictable ebb and flow of bikes throughout the day in the city.

Figure 17.12 shows the location of bikes at two different times of day. At 11:14 a.m., many of the bikes are in the financial district—people ride bikes to work and then leave the bikes near where they work. At 3:29 a.m., most people are

Figure 17.12

Location and number of available bikes (measured by the width of the circle) at two different times on June 21, 2013. The left panel is 11:14 a.m. and the right panel is 3:29 a.m.

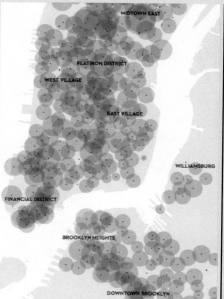

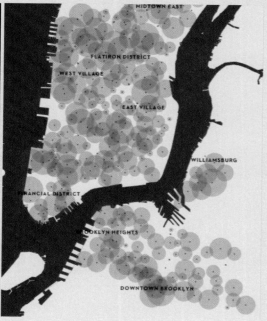

at home, which is why at that time there are more bikes in the East and West Village. As a result of this pattern, if you take a bike to the financial district late in the morning, you might not be able to find a dock at your preferred station. Similarly, if you leave your apartment in the East Village late in the morning, you might not find a bike.

1. What are some examples of system inhibitors—variability, waste, and inflexibility—present in a bike-sharing program?

2. Is there evidence of blocking and starving in the bike-sharing program?

3. What are some of the options to improve the quality of the service? What are the pros and cons of each option from various perspectives (e.g., the cost of the program, the quality of the service provided, etc.)?

Sources:
http://nyti.ms/1lL5aZ9. Accessed December 14, 2014.
https://sites.google.com/site/citibikestats/. Accessed December 14, 2014.
https://www.citibikenyc.com/stations#. Accessed December 14, 2014.
http://www.newyorker.com/news/news-desk/interactive-a-month-of-citi-bike. Accessed December 14, 2014.
http://www.nytimes.com/2013/08/15/nyregion/the-balancing-act-that-bike-share-riders-just-watch.html?smid=pl-share. Accessed December 14, 2014.

Appendix 17A: Erlang Loss Tables

The probability all servers are occupied in the Erlang loss model is P_m. P_m can be evaluated with the following cumbersome equation:

$$P_m = \frac{\dfrac{r^m}{m!}}{1 + \dfrac{r^1}{1!} + \dfrac{r^2}{2!} + \ldots + \dfrac{r^m}{m!}}$$

The exclamation mark (!) in the equation refers to the factorial of an integer number. To compute the factorial of an integer number x, write down all numbers from 1 to x and then multiply them by each other. For example, $4! = 1 \times 2 \times 3 \times 4 = 24$. In Excel, this calculation can be done with the FACT(x) function: FACT(4) = 24.

TABLE 17A.1   Erlang Loss Table

r = p/a	1	2	3	4	5	6	7	8	9	10
0.10	.0909	.0045	.0002	.0000	.0000	.0000	.0000	.0000	.0000	.0000
0.20	.1667	.0164	.0011	.0001	.0000	.0000	.0000	.0000	.0000	.0000
0.25	.2000	.0244	.0020	.0001	.0000	.0000	.0000	.0000	.0000	.0000
0.30	.2308	.0335	.0033	.0003	.0000	.0000	.0000	.0000	.0000	.0000
0.33	.2481	.0393	.0043	.0004	.0000	.0000	.0000	.0000	.0000	.0000
0.40	.2857	.0541	.0072	.0007	.0001	.0000	.0000	.0000	.0000	.0000
0.50	.3333	.0769	.0127	.0016	.0002	.0000	.0000	.0000	.0000	.0000
0.60	.3750	.1011	.0198	.0030	.0004	.0000	.0000	.0000	.0000	.0000
0.67	.4012	.1185	.0258	.0043	.0006	.0001	.0000	.0000	.0000	.0000
0.70	.4118	.1260	.0286	.0050	.0007	.0001	.0000	.0000	.0000	.0000
0.75	.4286	.1385	.0335	.0062	.0009	.0001	.0000	.0000	.0000	.0000
0.80	.4444	.1509	.0387	.0077	.0012	.0002	.0000	.0000	.0000	.0000
0.90	.4737	.1757	.0501	.0111	.0020	.0003	.0000	.0000	.0000	.0000
1.00	.5000	.2000	.0625	.0154	.0031	.0005	.0001	.0000	.0000	.0000
1.10	.5238	.2237	.0758	.0204	.0045	.0008	.0001	.0000	.0000	.0000
1.20	.5455	.2466	.0898	.0262	.0063	.0012	.0002	.0000	.0000	.0000
1.25	.5556	.2577	.0970	.0294	.0073	.0015	.0003	.0000	.0000	.0000
1.30	.5652	.2687	.1043	.0328	.0085	.0018	.0003	.0001	.0000	.0000
1.33	.5708	.2751	.1087	.0349	.0092	.0020	.0004	.0001	.0000	.0000
1.40	.5833	.2899	.1192	.0400	.0111	.0026	.0005	.0001	.0000	.0000
1.50	.6000	.3103	.1343	.0480	.0142	.0035	.0008	.0001	.0000	.0000
1.60	.6154	.3299	.1496	.0565	.0177	.0047	.0011	.0002	.0000	.0000
1.67	.6255	.3431	.1604	.0627	.0205	.0057	.0014	.0003	.0001	.0000
1.70	.6296	.3486	.1650	.0655	.0218	.0061	.0015	.0003	.0001	.0000
1.75	.6364	.3577	.1726	.0702	.0240	.0069	.0017	.0004	.0001	.0000
1.80	.6429	.3665	.1803	.0750	.0263	.0078	.0020	.0005	.0001	.0000
1.90	.6552	.3836	.1955	.0850	.0313	.0098	.0027	.0006	.0001	.0000
2.00	.6667	.4000	.2105	.0952	.0367	.0121	.0034	.0009	.0002	.0000
2.10	.6774	.4156	.2254	.1058	.0425	.0147	.0044	.0011	.0003	.0001
2.20	.6875	.4306	.2400	.1166	.0488	.0176	.0055	.0015	.0004	.0001
2.25	.6923	.4378	.2472	.1221	.0521	.0192	.0061	.0017	.0004	.0001
2.30	.6970	.4449	.2543	.1276	.0554	.0208	.0068	.0019	.0005	.0001
2.33	.6997	.4491	.2586	.1309	.0575	.0218	.0072	.0021	.0005	.0001
2.40	.7059	.4586	.2684	.1387	.0624	.0244	.0083	.0025	.0007	.0002
2.50	.7143	.4717	.2822	.1499	.0697	.0282	.0100	.0031	.0009	.0002
2.60	.7222	.4842	.2956	.1612	.0773	.0324	.0119	.0039	.0011	.0003
2.67	.7275	.4927	.3048	.1691	.0828	.0355	.0134	.0044	.0013	.0004
2.70	.7297	.4963	.3087	.1725	.0852	.0369	.0140	.0047	.0014	.0004
2.75	.7333	.5021	.3152	.1781	.0892	.0393	.0152	.0052	.0016	.0004

Continued

					m					
r = p/a	1	2	3	4	5	6	7	8	9	10
2.80	.7368	.5078	.3215	.1837	.0933	.0417	.0164	.0057	.0018	.0005
2.90	.7436	.5188	.3340	.1949	.1016	.0468	.0190	.0068	.0022	.0006
3.00	.7500	.5294	.3462	.2061	.1101	.0522	.0219	.0081	.0027	.0008
3.10	.7561	.5396	.3580	.2172	.1187	.0578	.0249	.0096	.0033	.0010
3.20	.7619	.5494	.3695	.2281	.1274	.0636	.0283	.0112	.0040	.0013
3.25	.7647	.5541	.3751	.2336	.1318	.0666	.0300	.0120	.0043	.0014
3.30	.7674	.5587	.3807	.2390	.1362	.0697	.0318	.0130	.0047	.0016
3.33	.7691	.5615	.3840	.2422	.1389	.0716	.0329	.0135	.0050	.0017
3.40	.7727	.5678	.3915	.2497	.1452	.0760	.0356	.0149	.0056	.0019
3.50	.7778	.5765	.4021	.2603	.1541	.0825	.0396	.0170	.0066	.0023
3.60	.7826	.5848	.4124	.2707	.1631	.0891	.0438	.0193	.0077	.0028
3.67	.7859	.5905	.4194	.2779	.1694	.0939	.0469	.0211	.0085	.0031
3.70	.7872	.5929	.4224	.2809	.1721	.0960	.0483	.0218	.0089	.0033
3.75	.7895	.5968	.4273	.2860	.1766	.0994	.0506	.0232	.0096	.0036
3.80	.7917	.6007	.4321	.2910	.1811	.1029	.0529	.0245	.0102	.0039
3.90	.7959	.6082	.4415	.3009	.1901	.1100	.0577	.0274	.0117	.0046
4.00	.8000	.6154	.4507	.3107	.1991	.1172	.0627	.0304	.0133	.0053

TABLE 17A.2 Erlang Loss Table

					m					
r = p/a	1	2	3	4	5	6	7	8	9	10
1.00	.5000	.2000	.0625	.0154	.0031	.0005	.0001	.0000	.0000	.0000
1.50	.6000	.3103	.1343	.0480	.0142	.0035	.0008	.0001	.0000	.0000
2.00	.6667	.4000	.2105	.0952	.0367	.0121	.0034	.0009	.0002	.0000
2.50	.7143	.4717	.2822	.1499	.0697	.0282	.0100	.0031	.0009	.0002
3.00	.7500	.5294	.3462	.2061	.1101	.0522	.0219	.0081	.0027	.0008
3.50	.7778	.5765	.4021	.2603	.1541	.0825	.0396	.0170	.0066	.0023
4.00	.8000	.6154	.4507	.3107	.1991	.1172	.0627	.0304	.0133	.0053
4.50	.8182	.6480	.4929	.3567	.2430	.1542	.0902	.0483	.0236	.0105
5.00	.8333	.6757	.5297	.3983	.2849	.1918	.1205	.0700	.0375	.0184
5.50	.8462	.6994	.5618	.4358	.3241	.2290	.1525	.0949	.0548	.0293
6.00	.8571	.7200	.5902	.4696	.3604	.2649	.1851	.1219	.0751	.0431
6.50	.8667	.7380	.6152	.4999	.3939	.2991	.2174	.1501	.0978	.0598
7.00	.8750	.7538	.6375	.5273	.4247	.3313	.2489	.1788	.1221	.0787
7.50	.8824	.7679	.6575	.5521	.4530	.3615	.2792	.2075	.1474	.0995
8.00	.8889	.7805	.6755	.5746	.4790	.3898	.3082	.2356	.1731	.1217
8.50	.8947	.7918	.6917	.5951	.5029	.4160	.3356	.2629	.1989	.1446
9.00	.9000	.8020	.7064	.6138	.5249	.4405	.3616	.2892	.2243	.1680

Continued

$r = p/a$	m									
	1	2	3	4	5	6	7	8	9	10
9.50	.9048	.8112	.7198	.6309	.5452	.4633	.3860	.3143	.2491	.1914
10.00	.9091	.8197	.7321	.6467	.5640	.4845	.4090	.3383	.2732	.2146
10.50	.9130	.8274	.7433	.6612	.5813	.5043	.4307	.3611	.2964	.2374
11.00	.9167	.8345	.7537	.6745	.5974	.5227	.4510	.3828	.3187	.2596
11.50	.9200	.8410	.7633	.6869	.6124	.5400	.4701	.4033	.3400	.2811
12.00	.9231	.8471	.7721	.6985	.6264	.5561	.4880	.4227	.3604	.3019
12.50	.9259	.8527	.7804	.7092	.6394	.5712	.5049	.4410	.3799	.3220
13.00	.9286	.8579	.7880	.7192	.6516	.5854	.5209	.4584	.3984	.3412
13.50	.9310	.8627	.7952	.7285	.6630	.5987	.5359	.4749	.4160	.3596
14.00	.9333	.8673	.8019	.7373	.6737	.6112	.5500	.4905	.4328	.3773
14.50	.9355	.8715	.8081	.7455	.6837	.6230	.5634	.5052	.4487	.3942
15.00	.9375	.8755	.8140	.7532	.6932	.6341	.5761	.5193	.4639	.4103
15.50	.9394	.8792	.8196	.7605	.7022	.6446	.5880	.5326	.4784	.4258
16.00	.9412	.8828	.8248	.7674	.7106	.6546	.5994	.5452	.4922	.4406
16.50	.9429	.8861	.8297	.7739	.7186	.6640	.6102	.5572	.5053	.4547
17.00	.9444	.8892	.8344	.7800	.7262	.6729	.6204	.5687	.5179	.4682
17.50	.9459	.8922	.8388	.7859	.7334	.6814	.6301	.5795	.5298	.4811
18.00	.9474	.8950	.8430	.7914	.7402	.6895	.6394	.5899	.5413	.4935
18.50	.9487	.8977	.8470	.7966	.7467	.6972	.6482	.5998	.5522	.5053
19.00	.9500	.9002	.8508	.8016	.7529	.7045	.6566	.6093	.5626	.5167
19.50	.9512	.9027	.8544	.8064	.7587	.7115	.6647	.6183	.5726	.5275
20.00	.9524	.9050	.8578	.8109	.7644	.7181	.6723	.6270	.5822	.5380
20.50	.9535	.9072	.8611	.8153	.7697	.7245	.6797	.6353	.5913	.5480
21.00	.9545	.9093	.8642	.8194	.7749	.7306	.6867	.6432	.6001	.5576
21.50	.9556	.9113	.8672	.8234	.7798	.7364	.6934	.6508	.6086	.5668
22.00	.9565	.9132	.8701	.8272	.7845	.7420	.6999	.6581	.6167	.5757
22.50	.9574	.9150	.8728	.8308	.7890	.7474	.7061	.6651	.6244	.5842
23.00	.9583	.9168	.8754	.8343	.7933	.7525	.7120	.6718	.6319	.5924
23.50	.9592	.9185	.8780	.8376	.7974	.7575	.7177	.6783	.6391	.6003
24.00	.9600	.9201	.8804	.8408	.8014	.7622	.7232	.6845	.6461	.6079
24.50	.9608	.9217	.8827	.8439	.8053	.7668	.7285	.6905	.6527	.6153
25.00	.9615	.9232	.8850	.8469	.8090	.7712	.7336	.6963	.6592	.6224
25.50	.9623	.9246	.8871	.8497	.8125	.7754	.7385	.7019	.6654	.6292
26.00	.9630	.9260	.8892	.8525	.8159	.7795	.7433	.7072	.6714	.6358
26.50	.9636	.9274	.8912	.8552	.8192	.7835	.7479	.7124	.6772	.6422
27.00	.9643	.9287	.8931	.8577	.8224	.7873	.7523	.7174	.6828	.6483
27.50	.9649	.9299	.8950	.8602	.8255	.7910	.7565	.7223	.6882	.6543
28.00	.9655	.9311	.8968	.8626	.8285	.7945	.7607	.7269	.6934	.6600
28.50	.9661	.9323	.8985	.8649	.8314	.7979	.7646	.7315	.6985	.6656

Scheduling to Prioritize Demand

18

LEARNING OBJECTIVES

LO18-1 Understand the diversity of scheduling applications

LO18-2 Understand and evaluate the shortest-processing-time scheduling rule

LO18-3 Understand and evaluate the weighted-shortest-processing-time scheduling rule

LO18-4 Understand and evaluate the earliest-due-date scheduling rule

LO18-5 Understand the motivation behind the theory of constraints

LO18-6 Understand the design choices and the pros and cons of an appointment system for scheduling

CHAPTER OUTLINE

Introduction

Introduction

If you need a surgical operation and you live in England, you can rest assured that the British government sets targets for how long patients should wait for various procedures. For example, a hospital might be required to schedule 90 percent of its patients within 18 weeks. While that seems like a reasonable goal, it still gives hospitals considerable latitude with respect to how they actually schedule surgeries. Naturally, some surgeries need to be done without much delay: If Uncle Bruce is having a heart attack, he needs stents inserted into his arteries immediately. But there is much more flexibility with other surgeries, such as a knee replacement: Although Aunt Janet would prefer to have her knee fixed this week, she can get about with some care and her cane.

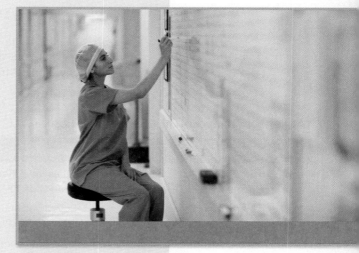
© ERproductions Ltd/Blend Images LLC/RF

Scheduling The process of deciding what work to assign to which resources and when to assign the work.

In this chapter, we explore the practice of **scheduling**, the process of deciding what work to assign to which resources and when to assign the work. For example, the work could be "a knee replacement," the resource could be "an orthopedist" or an "operating room," and the when could be "May 19 at 8:00 a.m."

We begin by exploring the breadth of situations in which scheduling is required. Clearly, scheduling is relevant in health care, but it is relevant even more broadly. In fact, some form of scheduling probably applies in all operations. Next, we study how to schedule work in the simplest of situations with just one resource. For example, say you are an underwriter of mortgages and you must decide which of the 10 mortgage applications on your desk you should work on next. You could use the intuitive "first-come-first-served" rule (FCFS)—just line up the applications as they arrive and process them in that order. But as we will discover, there can be reasons to do something other than FCFS.

Sticking with a single resource, we then complicate our scheduling task in four different ways. First, how should you schedule when different types of work have different priorities in terms of their need to be completed quickly. Second, we consider scheduling work that has due dates. Third, we consider how to schedule in complex processes with many types of jobs and servers. Fourth, we investigate scheduling via a reservation or appointment system. You might assume that not much thought is needed to design an appointment system—just determine the time slots and then let customers select which one they want. While you could do that, we will learn that an effective appointment system must carefully balance several important trade-offs.

18.1 Scheduling Timeline and Applications

LO18-1 Understand the diversity of scheduling applications

Though it has already been mentioned, it bears repeating, a common thread in all scheduling applications is the matching of demand to resources: When will a particular resource be used to process a particular demand? Given the emphasis it puts on time, scheduling can occur over substantially different time horizons, from immediate decisions to decisions spanning a decade, as described in Table 18.1.

Not only does scheduling occur over a large span of different time horizons, it is not surprising that scheduling is implemented in a wide spectrum of operations. A few are mentioned below.

Project management. Large, one-time projects require a vast array of activities and resources that must be coordinated; that is, scheduled. For example, the development of healthcare.gov for the Affordable Health Care Act required extensive integration of numerous

TABLE 18.1   Different Time Horizons for Scheduling

Time Period	Examples
Long: 1 year or more	An airline schedules the delivery of new aircraft over the next decade. A sports league schedules next year's matches between teams.
Medium: 1 month to 1 year	Scheduled shutdowns of a nuclear power plant for maintenance. The number of temporary workers to hire for the fourth quarter.
Short: 1 minute to 1 month	Which patient to treat next in the emergency room. Which caller to respond to in a call center. Workforce scheduling for next week.

different databases and software systems managed by both private enterprises and government agencies. The Channel Tunnel was a huge public infrastructure project that cost about $7 billion (in 1985 prices) and required six years to build. Scheduling is critical for the success of projects, which is why we devote an entire chapter to it.

Manufacturing. An automobile assembly line usually produces different versions of the same model. Every fourth car coming down the line might be a hatchback (rather than a sedan) and every tenth car might have a sunroof. Scheduling the manufacturing sequence of vehicles influences how well the line is balanced, as well as the variability of requests from suppliers for parts. Speaking of which, most manufacturing operations require a **materials requirement planning (MRP)** system. An MRP system contains a **bill of materials** database, which is a listing of all of the parts of every product made—the bill of materials for a car would include thousands of different components. Using the bill of materials and the production schedule, the MRP system evaluates how many of each part are needed and when they are needed. It then schedules deliveries of those parts to ensure that they arrive early enough for assembly, but not so early that too much inventory accumulates.

Service scheduling. If you reserve a mid-sized vehicle from a car rental agency, the company needs to decide (schedule) the particular car in its fleet that it will use to serve you. And if you call a small bed and breakfast (B&B) to request a room for Saturday night, it must decide if it is willing to offer you a room for that evening—if it gives you the room for just Saturday, it might not be able to sell a reservation to someone else who wants a room for Friday and Saturday. Scheduling decisions like these are often grouped under the heading of **revenue management**: the practice of trying to maximize the revenue generated from a set of fixed assets (like cars in a rental fleet, rooms in a hotel, or tables in a restaurant).

Transportation scheduling. As a customer, you probably look at posted schedules whenever you fly, take a train, or ride a bus. Somebody had to develop those schedules—and he or she had to make many more decisions than you might see. For example, an airline not only decides when it will offer a flight between two cities, it also must decide which plane will fly that route and which gate the plane will use at the airport. The flight controller needs to decide when the plane is cleared for landing or takeoff and on which runway.

Patient scheduling. Patients with chronic conditions often need to make regular visits to a health care facility for treatment. For example, radiotherapy for oncology patients is often performed over multiple sessions over a long duration of time. Because this equipment is very expensive, the hospital wants to ensure that it is highly utilized. At the same time, however, each patient requires a regimen of procedures that need to be performed at precise intervals—not too close to each other, but also not too far apart. The challenge for a scheduling system is to balance the desire for high utilization with the goal to maximize the effectiveness of treatment.

Materials requirement planning (MRP) A system that plans the delivery of components required for a manufacturing process so that components are available when needed but not so early as to create excess inventory.

Bill of material The list of components needed for the assembly of an item.

Revenue management The practice of maximizing the revenue generated from a set of fixed assets (like cars in a rental fleet, rooms in a hotel, or tables in a restaurant).

Workforce scheduling. Some people are fortunate enough to have a job with regular hours. But many jobs involve irregular hours that can change from week to week as needs change. This is relatively common in retail, but nurses and airline crews are often scheduled on a week-to-week basis as well.

Tournament scheduling. Scheduling a season for a professional sports league is a huge challenge, primarily because there are many constraints and objectives that need to be satisfied. For example, leagues want teams to play both home and away games throughout the season—a schedule is unacceptable if one team plays at home for the first half of the season and then away for the second half. Leagues also want to minimize travel, both for cost and for the well-being of the players: Imagine playing a game on the East Coast of the United States on Thursday, then a West Coast game on Friday, and then back to the East Coast for a game on Saturday.

The preceding examples reveal several common themes. For one, scheduling can be immensely complex primarily because of the staggering number of possible combinations for many real-life problems. Second, although scheduling applies in diverse settings, the objectives across the systems are similar: to ensure that resources are highly utilized and demand is served in a timely manner.

18.2 Resource Scheduling—Shortest Processing Time

In Chapter 5, Process Analysis with Multiple Flow Units, we discuss a loan underwriting process at Capital One. Recall that the underwriters are responsible for deciding which loans to fund and which to deny. Capital One has eight underwriters in one of its offices and each underwriter takes, on average, 40 minutes to process a loan. In Chapter 5, we assume that there is no variation in the processing times (they all take exactly 40 minutes) and we ignore the sequence in which loans are processed. In this chapter, we change both of those assumptions.

While an underwriter takes 40 minutes, on average, to process a loan, there naturally is some variation in the processing times. In addition, it is also likely that an underwriter can quickly ascertain the needed time for a loan when he or she first looks at the loan. Say one of the underwriters, Annick Gallino, currently has five loans on her desk, which we label A, B, C, D, and E, but she hasn't started to process any of them. In the language of scheduling, each loan is called a **job**—a job is a flow unit that requires processing from one or more resources. Table 18.2 lists the jobs and Annick's estimates for each job's processing time. Annick quickly determines each job's processing time by looking at a few key pieces of information in the application. Let's assume (i) Annick has enough experience that her estimates are accurate, (ii) each of the jobs has equal priority (they are all equally valuable to complete quickly), and (iii) there are no due dates (ideally each job is finished as soon as possible). We'll later discuss how to handle situations in which those three assumptions do not apply.

Job A flow unit that requires processing from one or more resources.

First-come-first-served (FCFS) A rule that sequences jobs to be processed on a resource in the order in which they arrived.

The average processing time across the five jobs on Annick's desk is indeed 40 minutes. However, not all of the jobs are the same. Loan B looks relatively simple, requiring only 20 minutes of time to process. In contrast, loan C is more involved because it requires 65 minutes.

With 200 minutes of work on her desk, Annick should get busy processing some loans. But in which order should she work on these loans? **First-come-first-served (FCFS)** is an intuitive sequence. With FCFS, the resource (Annick) works on jobs in the sequence in which they arrive, which in this case is in alphabetical order (i.e., A arrived first, E arrived last). But is

TABLE 18.2 **Processing Time for Five Loans, Which Arrived in Alphabetical Sequence (i.e., A arrived first, E arrived last)**

Job	A	B	C	D	E
Processing time (minutes)	45	20	65	30	40

this the best way to sequence the jobs? To answer that question, we need to decide on how to measure "best"; that is, we need some performance measures.

18.2.1 Performance Measures

Chapter 2, our Introduction to Processes chapter, highlights three key process performance metrics: inventory, flow rate, and flow time. To refresh your memory:

- *Inventory, I,* is the average number of flow units in the system over an interval of time.
- *Flow rate, R,* is the average rate at which flow units enter or exit the system.
- *Flow time, T,* is the average time a flow unit (i.e., a job) spends in the system.

All three are relevant in a scheduling application, but according to Little's Law (see Chapter 2), we only need to track two of them—once you know two of the metrics, you can evaluate the third using the following equivalent equations:

$$I = R \times T$$
$$R = \frac{I}{T}$$
$$T = \frac{I}{R}$$

In the case of Annick, we know that she has 200 minutes of work ahead of her no matter how she sequences the various jobs. Thus, after 200 minutes she will have completed five jobs. This means that her flow rate over the next 200 minutes, R, is 5 jobs/200 min = 0.025 job per min. While the flow rate is independent of the sequence, we will soon see that the flow time does depend on the chosen schedule for processing the jobs. Given that R is fixed and T depends on the chosen schedule, I also depends on the chosen schedule.

The measures of inventory, flow rate, and flow time are all based on averages. There is no doubt that average performance is relevant and important. But a manager may also be interested in outlier performance. Take the example from the beginning of the chapter: In England, hospitals are required to schedule 90 percent of surgeries within 18 weeks. That performance measure focuses on ensuring that bad outcomes (patients who have to wait more than 18 weeks) are infrequent (less than 10 percent of surgeries). Although a target like "X percent of jobs are completed in T units of time" is intuitively reasonable, it also suffers from a potential limitation: It gives the scheduler an incentive to strategically manipulate the schedule. For example, if a patient's surgery cannot be scheduled within 18 weeks, then the scheduler no longer has an incentive to schedule the surgery "as soon as possible"—from the perspective of the target, a surgery scheduled for week 19 is not any worse than the same surgery scheduled for week 30 in the sense that neither situation contributes toward the goal of 90 percent of surgeries within 18 weeks. However, from the perspective of an average waiting time, 19 weeks is still 11 weeks less of a delay than 30 weeks. Put another way, average performance measures always have an incentive to reduce the time a job is in the system, no matter how long it has been in the system. Thus, doing well, on average, also tends to avoid bad outlier outcomes. For that reason, we focus on average performance measures.

18.2.2 First-Come-First-Served vs. Shortest Processing Time

First-come-first served is the natural way to sequence jobs. It doesn't require much thinking on the part of the resource (just do the jobs in the order they arrive) and it seems fair (more on that later). But it isn't the only way to sequence the jobs. Let's focus on one particular alternative, the **shortest-processing-time (SPT)** rule—with SPT, jobs are sequenced in increasing order of processing times. For example, from the data in Table 18.2, Annick would process job B first (it has the shortest processing time, 20 minutes), then D, E, A, and finally C (it has the longest processing time, 65 minutes). If additional jobs were to arrive before these five are completed, then the new jobs would be placed in their proper place in the "to be completed" queue so that processing times are always sequenced in increasing order.

LO18-2 Understand and evaluate the shortest-processing-time scheduling rule

Shortest processing time (SPT)
A rule that sequences jobs to be processed on a resource in ascending order of their processing times.

So which is better, FCFS (A, B, C, D, E) or SPT (B, D, E, A, C)? As already mentioned, no matter what the sequence, Annick takes 200 minutes to complete all five jobs. (This assumes that no other job arrives in the next 200 minutes with a processing time that is less than 65 minutes, which we assume for simplicity.) Given that the two sequences require the same total amount of time, you might assume that the sequence doesn't matter all that much for the various performance measures. While you are correct with respect to the flow rate, you are wrong with respect to the flow time and inventory.

Figure 18.1 illustrates Gantt charts for FCFS and SPT sequencing. Time is shown on the horizontal axis and each job is displayed in the time interval it is processed. It is customary to show each job on a different row, which helps to highlight the time each job waits and when it is completed.

Let's now evaluate the flow times for each job with each sequencing rule. With FCFS, job A goes first and has a flow time equal to its processing time, 45 minutes, because it doesn't wait. Job B is next, with a flow time of 65 minutes: job B waits 45 minutes for A to be completed and then is processed in 20 minutes. The other flow times are 130 minutes for job C (65 minutes waiting, 65 minutes processing), 160 minutes for job D (130 minutes waiting, 30 minutes processing), and finally 200 minutes for job E (160 minutes waiting, 40 minutes processing). The average flow time among these jobs is

$$\frac{45 + 65 + 130 + 160 + 200}{5} = 120 \text{ minutes}$$

With SPT, the flow times are 20, 50, 90, 135, and 200 (see Figure 18.1). The average flow time is

$$\frac{20 + 50 + 90 + 135 + 200}{5} = 99 \text{ minutes}$$

Although the flow time of the last job is the same with either sequencing (200 minutes), the average flow times are indeed different. Even though SPT does exactly the same amount of work as FCFS and it works at the same speed (the processing times are not different), each job, on average, spends 21 minutes fewer in the system with SPT relative to FCFS $(120 - 99 = 21)$!

To understand why SPT is more effective than FCFS (in terms of flow), note that the early jobs all impose waiting times on the jobs that come afterward. For example, job A is first with FCFS and it requires 45 minutes to process. This means that if A were to go first, then

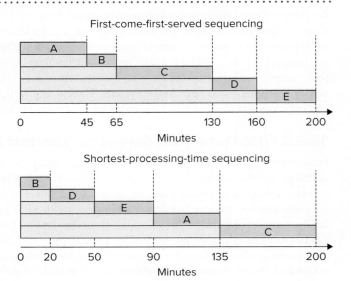

Figure 18.1

Two different approaches to sequencing five jobs (A, B, C, D, E): first-come-first-served (top) and shortest processing time (bottom)

45 minutes is added to the flow time of each of the four other jobs. In contrast, with SPT, the first job, B, only requires 20 minutes to process. So job B only adds 20 minutes to the flow time of the other four jobs. Clearly, the choice of the first job to process makes a big difference because it causes a delay in all of the other jobs. In contrast, the last job processed doesn't add flow time to any of the other jobs. So you want the shortest-processing-time job to go first (because it imposes the least cost on the other jobs) and the longest-processing-time job to go last (because it doesn't make any other job wait). That is precisely what SPT does!

Jobs spend less time in the system with SPT than with FCFS, but that doesn't mean the system has more capacity with SPT. Jobs flow at the same rate with either system—the flow rate, R, is 0.025 job per minute with SPT and FCFS. This is initially confusing: How is it that jobs spend less time in the system with SPT, but they flow at the same rate? The answer is that the average inventory in the system, I, is less with SPT than with FCFS. To be specific, with FCFS the average number of jobs in the system is

$$I = R \times T = 0.025 \text{ job per min} \times 120 \text{ min} = 3 \text{ jobs}$$

whereas with SPT the average number of jobs in the system is

$$I = R \times T = 0.025 \text{ job per min} \times 99 \text{ min} = 2.5 \text{ jobs}$$

Check Your Understanding 18.1

Say a resource needs to process the three jobs displayed in Table 18.3 and no other job arrives in the next 12 minutes.

TABLE 18.3 Processing Times for Three Jobs, Where A Arrived First, Then B, and Then C

Job	A	B	C
Processing time (minutes)	5	3	4

Question: In what order would the jobs be processed if the SPT rule were used?

a. A, B, C
b. A, C, B
c. B, A, C
d. B, C, A
e. C, A, B
f. C, B, A

Answer: Sort the jobs in ascending order of their processing time. The answer is D.

Question: What is the average flow rate of jobs in this system (jobs per minute)?

Answer: Three jobs are completed in 5 + 3 + 4 = 12 minutes. Three jobs in 12 minutes yields an average flow rate of 3/12 = 0.25. The average flow rate is 0.25 jobs/minute.

Question: If the jobs are processed in SPT order, what is the average flow time?

Answer: SPT order is B, C, A. The flow times are then 3, 3 + 4 = 7, and 3 + 4 + 5 = 12, for a total flow time of 22 minutes. The average flow time is then 22/3 = 7.3.

Question: If the jobs are processed in SPT order, what is the average inventory?

Answer: Inventory = Flow rate × Flow time = 3/12 × 22/3 = 11/6 = 1.83

SPT looks great relative to FCFS in this particular instance, when Annick has these five jobs on her desk. But is this just a special case? It isn't. No matter how many jobs need to be processed or what their processing times are, SPT always beats FCFS in terms of average flow time. Because the flow rate is constant, SPT also always beats FCFS in terms of average inventory.

Although our example illustrates how SPT can do better than FCFS, it is also possible that SPT can do much better than FCFS. To explain, suppose the jobs arrive in the following order: C, A, E, D, B. In other words, the jobs arrive in descending order of processing time: The longest job arrives first and the shortest job arrives last. That sequence is the complete opposite of SPT and is sometimes called the **longest-processing-time (LPT)** rule. If we draw a Gantt chart (as in Figure 18.1) for the LPT sequence and then evaluate the average flow time, we get

$$\frac{65 + 110 + 150 + 180 + 200}{5} = 141 \text{ minutes}$$

Wow! FCFS could actually generate an average flow time that is 42 minutes $(141 - 99)$ longer than SPT—that is a 42 percent increase in average flow time across all of the jobs (not just one of the jobs). Again, this gap occurs without changing the total amount of work done or the flow rate of jobs.

FCFS can be pretty bad, but in fairness to FCFS, it is really bad only in the special case in which the jobs arrive (by chance) in descending order of processing time. To understand SPT's real advantage, we should consider all possible arrival sequences and see how much better SPT is on average. To do that, we can use a discrete event simulator.

The simulation is done in four steps:

1. Generate a bunch of different processing times. For this simulation there are 25,000 processing times. A histogram of those processing times is displayed in Figure 18.2. To help visualize this process, imagine we create a bag containing 25,000 balls, each with a processing time written on it.

Longest processing time (LPT)
A rule that sequences jobs to be processed on a resource in descending order of their processing times.

Figure 18.2

Histogram of 25,000 processing times. The average processing time is 40 minutes and the standard deviation is 15 minutes.

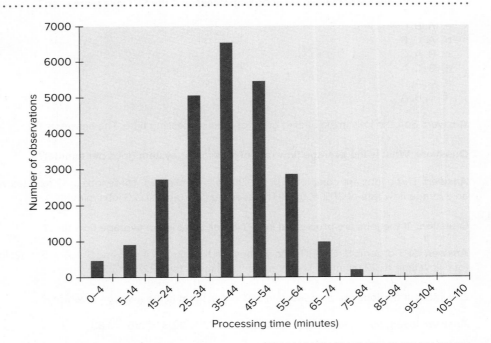

2. Randomly choose a sequence of processing times from the sample to simulate the jobs that are on an underwriter's desk ready to be processed. This is like reaching into our "bag" and grabbing five balls, one at a time, to construct a sequence of jobs like that displayed in the top panel of Figure 18.1.

3. Evaluate the average flow time using the FCFS rule, as well as the SPT rule. As in Figure 18.1, the average flow times are likely to be different.

4. Repeat steps 2 and 3 many times and then average the flow times obtained with those iterations. In this case, we did 2500 iterations. Note: All of the 25,000 processing times are used only when there are 10 jobs waiting to be processed—2500 iterations × 10 jobs = 25,000 processing times.

Figure 18.3 displays the results from the discrete event simulation for different values for the number of jobs waiting to be processed. In the example displayed in Figure 18.1, there are five jobs waiting to be processed. In that particular example, the average flow times are 99 and 120 minutes for SPT and FCFS, respectively. According to Figure 18.3, across a large sample of different sequences with five jobs, the average flow times are 103 minutes for SPT and 120 minutes for FCFS. Thus, the example shown in Figure 18.1 is reasonably representative of the difference one might expect in performance between SPT and FCFS with five jobs.

Figure 18.3 reveals one additional important finding. The gap between FCFS and SPT grows as the number of jobs in the queue grows. If there are only two jobs in the queue, then, by a 50/50 chance, FCFS might sequence the jobs exactly the same way as SPT. Hence, FCFS does okay when there are only two jobs in the queue—the flow times are 55 and 59 minutes for SPT and FCFS, respectively. However, when there are 10 jobs in the queue, the average flow time for SPT is 182 minutes, but the average flow time for FCFS is 37 minutes higher (219 minutes)! We can conclude that it is most important to use SPT instead of FCFS when it is

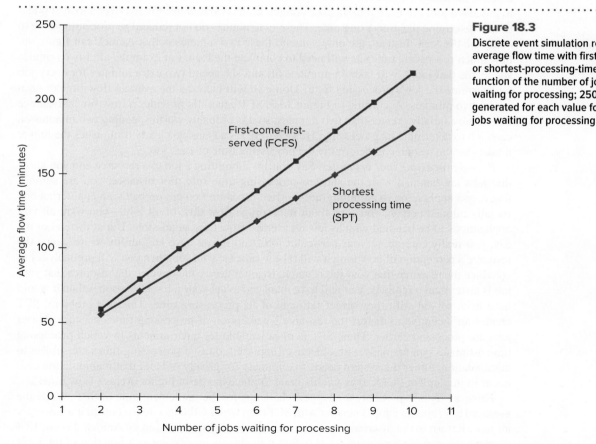

Figure 18.3

Discrete event simulation results for the average flow time with first-come-first-served or shortest-processing-time sequencing as a function of the number of jobs in the queue waiting for processing; 2500 samples are generated for each value for the number of jobs waiting for processing

likely that there will be many jobs in the system. And when is that likely? The system is likely to have more jobs when the system's utilization is very high. When demand is close to capacity, using SPT instead of FCFS can make a big difference in terms of flow time and inventory.

So SPT always gives a lower flow time than FCFS and the gap between the two is largest when there are many jobs waiting for service. This makes SPT look very good. And, in fact, it has been proven to be the very best sequencing rule: If you want to minimize the average flow time (and in turn the average inventory of jobs in the system), you cannot do any better than SPT!

18.2.3 Limitations of Shortest Processing Time

With so much going for it, why wouldn't a manager always use SPT? There are three reasons why you might choose FCFS rather than SPT: (i) it takes too long to determine the processing time of the jobs; (ii) the estimates of the processing times may be biased; and/or (iii) SPT raises concerns of fairness—it does not treat all jobs equally. Let's discuss each reason.

Delay to determine processing times. In one extreme, when a job arrives, it is possible to immediately determine its processing time with high accuracy and nearly no cost. For example, if a data packet arrives to a telecommunications server, the time to process the packet might be a function of the amount of data in the packet, which might be trivial to observe. Or a translator might know how long it will take to translate a document merely by the number of pages in the document. These situations are ideal for SPT because SPT doesn't lose any time in determining the best sequence. In the other extreme, it is also possible that the only way to know the processing time for a job is to actually do the job. In those situations, SPT provides no benefit relative to FCFS: If you have to complete the job to know how long it will take to do the job, then you cannot do any better than FCFS sequencing. As with all extremes, there are plenty of cases in the middle, situations in which it takes some time merely to learn how long it will take to process a job. For example, suppose Annick needs two minutes to look over a loan application to determine the processing time. These two minutes do not reduce the processing time to complete the loan. Instead, the only value to these two minutes is that Annick can figure out how much processing time she will need to complete the loan. For example, after two minutes she learns that job A will take 45 minutes. Should she spend two extra minutes for every job to determine the job's processing time? Doing so will increase the average flow time of each job by two minutes. According to Figure 18.3, SPT generally provides a flow time advantage that is substantially greater than two minutes, so it is probably worth spending two minutes on each job to determine its processing. However, SPT's advantage clearly diminishes the longer it takes for the resource to determine the processing time of each job.

Biased processing time estimates. Say you are submitting a job to a resource and you know that jobs are handled with the shortest-processing-time rule. For instance, you are submitting a visa application to an immigration office. Because you are probably an egalitarian and socially minded person, you care about the average flow time of all jobs—you want all visa applications to be handled with as low an average flow time as possible. But at the end of the day, you really care about your particular job. And if you have any ability to influence the resource's perception of how long it will take to process your job, then you will probably try to convince the resource that your job is quick. If you indeed can convince the resource that your job is faster than it really is, you will have managed to get your job served sooner than it would have been served with the correct estimate of its processing time. This is a problem: SPT creates an incentive to distort the resource's perception of processing times because shorter jobs are processed earlier. Thus, SPT is most suitable for environments in which processing time estimates can be made with objective (unbiased) data. If processing times are subject to manipulation, either the system needs to eliminate (or greatly reduce) that manipulation or it needs to implement FCFS to avoid this issue (at the expense of higher average flow times).

Fairness. This is probably the biggest challenge for the implementation of SPT. While the average flow time for a job is smaller with SPT than with FCFS, this doesn't mean it is lower for all jobs. Return to the discrete event simulator for the loans processed by Annick. Figure 18.4 displays the average time a job waits before it begins its processing as a function of the job's

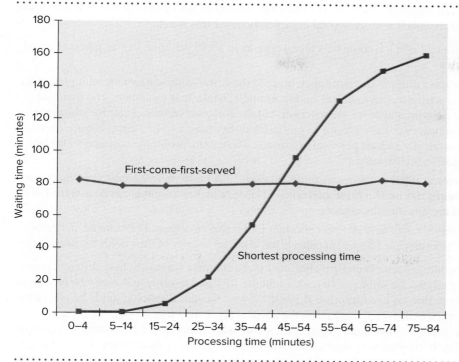

Figure 18.4
Average time a job waits before beginning to be processed as a function of a job's processing time when there are five jobs to be processed. The average processing time is 40 minutes.

processing time when there are five jobs to be processed (as in our earlier example). With FCFS, every job basically waits 80 minutes before it begins processing, no matter if it is a small job (10 minutes) or a large job (80 minutes). (The flow times of these jobs are different because the flow time includes the processing time, and the processing time for a small job is different than for a large job.) The same is clearly not true with SPT. SPT puts small jobs at the front of the queue and large jobs at the back of the queue. Hence, small jobs wait less time to begin processing, while a large job might spend a considerable amount of time waiting. For example, a 10-minute job is likely to be the smallest job, so it spends essentially no time waiting before it begins processing. However, an 80-minute job is likely to be the last of five jobs, so its flow time is essentially 160 minutes—it must wait for four jobs to be completed, which takes, on average, 4 × 40 minutes = 160 minutes. Thus, if it is important to treat all jobs equally, FCFS is the better approach. This is most likely an issue when people are able to observe the flow times of the other jobs. However, equality definitely comes at a cost: To treat all jobs equally means that, on average, a job spends more time in the system.

One reason to not avoid using SPT is uncertainty in the processing time estimates. For example, say job X might take between 20 and 50 minutes, while job Y might take between 40 and 70 minutes. It is possible that job X takes longer than job Y, but it is more likely that job X will take less time to process. Hence, job X should be processed first to minimize average flow time. In general, if there is some uncertainty in the processing time estimates, SPT is still effective and it works merely by sorting the jobs in increasing order by their expected processing times.

18.3 Resource Scheduling with Priorities—Weighted Shortest Processing Time

If you want to minimize the average flow time across all jobs, use the shortest processing time to schedule resources. But is that still true if it costs more to have some jobs wait than others? As you might expect, it isn't. But neither do we have to completely throw away SPT.

Consider the situation displayed in Table 18.4. There are five jobs to process on a single resource. They vary in processing times, from 6 hours to 24 hours. They also vary in terms of the cost they incur for each unit of time they remain in the system, which is listed as the "weight" of the job. There are several interpretations for this weight:

- The weight of a job could be a literal cost, as in $0.10 per hour, like an inventory holding cost.

- Customers differ in the profit they bring to the firm—some customers are highly profitable, whereas others are less so. For example, banks love customers who maintain large deposits and never use tellers or call the customer service center for assistance. In contrast, customers are not so profitable if they have a low balance, bounce checks, and frequently request personal assistance. Thus, more profitable customers may be assigned a higher weight.

- Customers differ in their sensitivity to delays. It is costly to lose a customer, but some customers are more patient than others. Hence, a higher weight could be assigned to the more impatient customers.

- The server might have different priorities for serving customers. For example, in health care, priorities are assigned to patients based on the severity of their needs for fast service.

The scheduling decision certainly becomes more complex when jobs have different priorities. If they all had the same priority, we could use SPT and job B would surely be processed first. But now that isn't so clear. Job B has the lowest weight. So should job B be one of the later jobs processed, even though it has the shortest processing time?

To help make this decision, Figure 18.5 shows what happens if SPT is used to schedule the jobs. The horizontal axis shows time, while the vertical axis shows costs. Each rectangle represents a job: The rectangle's width is the time the job remains in the system and its height is its weight. For example, job C remains in the system for 73 hours and incurs six units of cost per hour during that entire time. The total cost of job C is then $73 \times 6 = 438$, which is the area of the C rectangle.

TABLE 18.4   **Processing Time for Five Loans**

Job	A	B	C	D	E
Processing time (hours)	10	6	24	15	18
Weight/priority (cost per unit of time)	2	1	6	5	2

Figure 18.5

Costs and times to process five jobs in SPT order

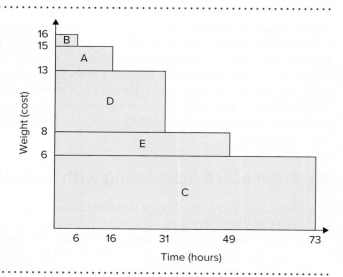

From Figure 18.5 we can see that what we want to do is minimize the total shaded area—the sum of the areas of the rectangles—because that is the total cost. And the problem with SPT is clearly apparent: SPT processes job C last, but job C has a lot of weight (i.e., a tall rectangle), so leaving it in the system for a long time is costly.

Fortunately, the solution we need is a relatively simple tweak on SPT. The ideal job to put first has a high priority (so we get it out of the system quickly) and a low processing time (so it doesn't make the other jobs wait too long). Hence, to minimize total cost, we should use the **weighted-shortest-processing-time (WSPT)** rule: For each job, evaluate the ratio of its weight to its processing time and then sequence the jobs in decreasing order of this ratio. For example, job D's weight is 5 and its processing time is 15, so the ratio of weight to processing time is 1/3.

Table 18.5 displays the jobs in decreasing order of their weighted processing times. According to WSPT, job C should be one of the earlier jobs—the second job to be precise. And job B, despite having the shortest processing time, is processed second to last because it has the lowest weight.

Figure 18.6 displays the five jobs in WSPT order. Comparing Figure 18.5 to Figure 18.6, you probably can notice that the total shaded area has indeed decreased by using WSPT. In fact, the total cost decreases from 729 with SPT to 608 with WSPT—a 17 percent reduction in cost! (In case you are curious, FCFS yields a total cost of 697, which is less than with SPT—by chance, FCFS does a better job of accounting for the job's priorities than SPT.)

So WSPT minimizes the total weight cost of processing the jobs, which is great. But WSPT is a bit cumbersome to implement. It requires calculating the weight-to-processing-time ratios and then sorting those ratios across all of the jobs. However, there are two cases in which WSPT is easier to use. The first case is when all jobs have the same weights. In such instances, WSPT sequences jobs the same as SPT. The second case is when there are only a few weights

Weighted shortest processing time (WSPT) A rule that sequences jobs to be processed on a resource in descending order of the ratio of their weight to their processing time. Jobs with high weights and low processing times tend to be sequenced early.

TABLE 18.5 Jobs Sequenced by Weighted Shortest Processing Time

Job	D	C	A	B	E
Processing time (hours)	15	24	10	6	18
Weight/priority (cost per unit of time)	5	6	2	1	2
Ratio of weight to processing time	1/3	1/4	1/5	1/6	1/9

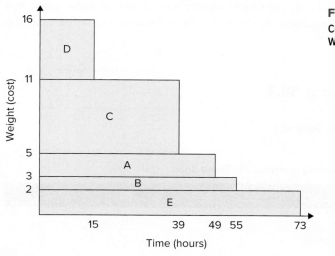

Figure 18.6

Costs and time to process five jobs in WSPT order

TABLE 18.6   Six Jobs that Differ in Processing Times and Priority

Job	A	B	C	D	E	F
Processing time (hours)	1	1.5	0.75	5	4	4.5
Weight/priority (cost per unit of time)	1	1	1	100	100	100
Ratio of weight to processing time	1	2/3	4/3	20	25	16.7

and the weights are very different from each other. For example, look at the sample of jobs in Table 18.6. Three of the jobs have a relatively short processing time of about one hour. Three of the jobs have a long processing time of about 4.5 hours. Nevertheless, the long-processing-time jobs have a much higher priority, 100 times higher to be precise. Hence, we clearly should process the higher-priority jobs first, no matter their particular processing time.

Emergency rooms tend to operate with a strict priority scheme. Patients are first assigned an **Emergency Severity Index (ESI)** score between 1 and 5: 1—resuscitation, 2—emergent, 3—urgent, 4—less urgent, and 5—nonurgent. A patient's ESI score influences the type of care received. For example, ESI 1 and 2 patients are immediately sent into treatment, whereas ESI 3, 4, and 5 patients can safely wait. The emergency room is one service provider where you really don't want to be the one with the highest priority.

Like SPT, WSPT can be implemented if uncertainty remains in the processing time estimates—just use the expected processing time to implement the rule. Also like SPT, there are some situations that make WSPT less attractive, such as the following:

Delay to determine priority or processing time. WSPT is less attractive if it takes a long time to determine the flow unit's priority or processing time. However, if jobs can have a wide range of priorities (as in an emergency room), then the time to do this activity might be needed even if it is longer than desirable.

Biased priority or processing time estimates. With SPT, the user can only bias the perception of the processing time. But with WSPT, the user can also get better service than he or she deserves if the user can convince the resource that his or her priority is higher than it really should be. For example, imagine there is a line to use the restroom and you are next, but somebody comes up to you and asks to go ahead of you because she "really needs to go." If she really does need to go, you probably would be okay with letting her cut in front of you. But how do you know she isn't just pretending? You probably would not want to do what is needed to actually confirm her need!

Fairness. As with SPT, not all jobs are treated equally with WSPT. In some cases, this might not be desirable. See Connections: Net Neutrality for a discussion of fairness and the operations of the Internet.

Emergency Severity Index (ESI)
A scoring rule used by Emergency Rooms to rank the severity of a patient's injuries and then to prioritize their care.

Check Your Understanding 18.2

Consider the three jobs shown in Table 18.7.

TABLE 18.7   Processing Times and Priorities for Three Jobs

Job	A	B	C
Processing time (hours)	6	10	20
Weight/priority (cost per unit of time)	1	2	5

Question: In what order would the jobs be processed if the WSPT rule were used?

a. A, B, C
b. A, C, B
c. B, A, C
d. B, C, A
e. C, A, B
f. C, B, A

Answer: The ratios of weights to processing times are 1/6, 1/5, and 1/4. Sequence the jobs in descending order of those ratios. Thus, F is the correct answer.

. . . .

CONNECTIONS: Net Neutrality

© Ingram Publishing/RF

Although first-come-first-served is often implemented, there are situations in which we tolerate deviations. For example, nobody can (justly) complain if a car accident victim gets more priority in the emergency room than somebody with a twisted ankle from a softball game. And we seem to tolerate giving first-class ticket holders priority when boarding airplanes. But we expect the queue to be FCFS in the grocery store and at the Department of Motor Vehicles.

For now, we also operate the Internet on a FCFS basis in the United States. You probably pay some Internet service provider (ISP) company each month to have Internet access to your apartment or mobile device. Large ISPs in the United States include Verizon and AT&T. Think of the ISP as the provider of the Internet "pipe" that delivers content to you. See Figure 18.7 for a diagram of this structure. On the other end of the pipe are content providers such as Google (search), Netflix (movies), and Amazon (goods). Those content providers pay the ISPs as well to use their pipes.

Continued

Net neutrality The principle that Internet service providers must treat all data that traverses their network equally in the sense that priority can be given to some data over other types of data, even if the provider of the data (e.g., Google) pays for better service.

At this point, you might be asking why you should care about the details of the network structure. The Internet seems to work, so why worry about the details? And why is this topic in a chapter on scheduling? Net neutrality is the reason you should care and it is why it has been included here. **Net neutrality** is a principle that states that an ISP must treat all data that traverse its network equally. In other words, the ISP is not allowed to treat one packet of data differently than another packet just because it came from a particular content provider. This implies that an ISP is not allowed to charge one online retailer (e.g., Amazon) more so that its data reaches the ISP's users faster than another online retailer that didn't pay for the faster service. In the language of scheduling, the ISP is not allowed to use something like weighted shortest processing time, where the weights would depend on how much the content provider paid for priority.

Any discussion of net neutrality can easily slip into technical jargon. At a high level, ISPs are arguing that they should be able to provide a "fast lane" through their pipe and charge companies like Google to use it. Content providers, like Google, are opposed to this, arguing that (i) the status quo, net neutrality, should remain because it fosters more innovation and (ii) departing from net neutrality will reduce the overall quality of the Internet (especially for those who don't pay for faster service). The ISPs counter that (i) congestion is inevitable in the network, so priority lanes should be offered for a fee, and (ii) if they collect revenue from content provides, they can then reduce the fees they charge users. So you see, how jobs (data packets) are scheduled on a resource (the ISP "pipe") has some substantial public policy implications.

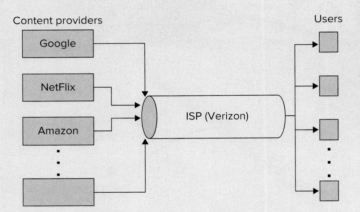

Figure 18.7   The structure of the Internet in which Internet service providers (ISPs) provide the network connection between content providers and end users

18.4 Resource Scheduling with Due Dates—Earliest Due Date

In some settings, we want to get all jobs done as soon as possible. But that is not always the case. In some situations, jobs arrive over time and they have due dates associated with them. For example, you might start a semester knowing that in three of your five classes you must write a paper. These three papers are due in 6, 9, and 10 weeks. Surely these due dates might influence which paper you work on first. So how should you schedule your work on those papers?

To explore how to deal with due dates, consider the example in Table 18.8. There are five jobs that vary in processing times and due dates. In particular, they are arranged in increasing order of processing time and decreasing order of due dates. This special (i.e., contrived) structure helps us illustrate why due dates present a challenge for scheduling.

TABLE 18.8 Five Projects with Due Dates

Job	A	B	C	D	E
Processing time (days)	2	4	6	8	10
Due date (days from today)	20	18	16	14	12

Before we actually start sequencing jobs, let's think about the performance measures we could use. In the example with no due dates, it is reasonable to measure the average flow time of jobs and the average number of jobs in the system (the inventory). But other metrics may come to mind, such as the following:

- **Percent on time**. This is the fraction of jobs that are completed on or before their due date.
- **Lateness**. The lateness of a job is the difference between its completion time and its due date. For example, if a job is due on day 10 and it is completed on day 12, then it is late $12 - 10 = 2$ days. Lateness can also be negative. For example, if the job is due on day 10, but it is completed on day 7, then it is -3 days "late," which means it is three days early. It might seem odd to have a negative lateness, which means the job is early, but this is a relatively common definition of lateness, so we'll stick with it.
- **Tardiness**. If a job is completed after its due date, then the tardiness of a job is the difference between its completion time and its due date. If the job is completed before its due date (i.e., it is early), then its tardiness is 0. In some sense, the tardiness measure makes more sense than lateness because a job never has negative tardiness.

Related to the percent on time, if you prefer, we could measure the percent of tardy jobs (i.e., the fraction of jobs completed beyond the due date). Lateness and tardiness are measures that apply to individual jobs. It is useful to aggregate these measures over many jobs by taking their average (e.g., the average lateness) or evaluating their maximum value (e.g., the maximum tardiness).

Now return to the set of jobs listed in Table 18.8. We could use shortest processing time to schedule the jobs, but that rule completely ignores the due dates. For example, if we use SPT on the jobs in Table 18.8, then the first job we do has the latest due date and the last job we do has the earliest due date. That is a rather odd way of dealing with due dates.

Because SPT ignores due dates, maybe we should develop a sequencing rule that explicitly accounts for them. You probably can quickly develop several ways to handle due dates, and maybe you would even consider the simple **earliest-due-date (EDD)** rule: Process the jobs in increasing order of due dates. In the special case of the projects in Table 18.8, the EDD rule sequences the jobs in exactly the opposite order of SPT! Note, while SPT ignores due dates, EDD ignores processing times! So which does better? The answer is "it depends." To see why, let's evaluate several performance measures for both SPT and EDD.

Table 18.9 shows the flow times for each of the jobs in Table 18.8 using the SPT rule. For example, job A is completed within two days and then job B is completed on day six: The flow time for a job is the sum of its processing time and the processing times of the jobs completed before it. With SPT, the average lateness is -2, meaning that, on average, jobs are completed two days before their due date. But the maximum lateness is 18 days. In terms of on-time performance, three of the jobs, or 60 percent, are not tardy.

Table 18.10 shows the results for EDD. In many ways, EDD does worse that SPT. We know that the average flow time with EDD is higher (22 days versus 14 days) because SPT minimizes average flow time. What is somewhat surprising is that EDD does worse than SPT even on some of the measures that focus on due dates, such as the average lateness (6 days versus -2 days), average tardiness (6.4 days versus 4.8 days), or the percent on time (20 percent versus 60 percent). The one metric that EDD does well with is the maximum tardiness (10 days versus 18 days).

Percent on time The fraction of jobs that are completed on or before their due date.

Lateness The difference between the completion time of a job and its due date. Lateness is negative when the job is completed before the due date (i.e., it is early).

Tardiness If a job is completed after its due date, then tardiness is the difference between the completion time of a job and its due date. If the job is completed before its due date, then tardiness is 0. Tardiness is always positive.

LO18-4 Understand and evaluate the earliest-due-date scheduling rule

Earliest due date (EDD) A rule that sequences jobs to be processed on a resource in ascending order of their due dates.

TABLE 18.9 Performance Measures for Shortest Processing Time

Job	Processing Time (days)	Due Date (days)	Flow Time	Lateness	Tardiness	Tardy
A	2	20	2	−18	0	0
B	4	18	6	−12	0	0
C	6	16	12	−4	0	0
D	8	14	20	6	6	1
E	10	12	30	18	18	1
Average			14	−2	4.8	0.4
Maximum				18	18	1

TABLE 18.10 Performance Measures for Earliest Due Date

Job	Processing Time (days)	Due Date (days)	Flow Time	Lateness	Tardiness	Tardy
E	10	12	10	−2	0	0
D	8	14	18	4	4	1
C	6	16	24	8	8	1
B	4	18	28	10	10	1
A	2	20	30	10	10	1
Average			22	6	6.4	0.8
Maximum				10	10	1

TABLE 18.11 Performance Measure Comparison between Shortest Processing Time (SPT) and Earliest Due Date (EDD)

Performance Measure	Recommendation
Average flow time, average lateness	SPT minimizes both.
Maximum lateness or tardiness	EDD minimizes both.
Average tardiness	SPT is often better, but not always better than EDD.
Percent on time	SPT is often better, but not always better than EDD.

Check Your Understanding 18.3

Consider the three jobs shown in Table 18.12.

TABLE 18.12 Processing Times and Priorities for Three Jobs

Job	A	B	C
Processing time (hours)	10	25	20
Due time (hours)	25	30	45

Question: In what order would the jobs be processed if the EDD rule were used?

a. A, B, C
b. A, C, B
c. B, A, C
d. B, C, A
e. C, A, B
f. C, B, A

Answer: Earliest due date sequences the jobs in ascending order of due date. Thus, answer A is correct.

Question: If EDD is used to sequence the jobs, what is the lateness of job A?

Answer: Job A is done first and its lateness is 10 − 25. Thus, the answer is −15.

Question: If EDD is used to sequence the jobs, what is the tardiness of job C?

Answer: Job C is completed at time 10 + 25 + 20 = 55 and it is due at time 45, so its tardiness is 55 − 45. Thus, the answer is 10.

. . . .

The results in Tables 18.9 and 18.10 provide one snapshot of the comparison between SPT and EDD. Nevertheless, the results are consistent with findings from detailed studies that compare the two approaches, which are summarized in Table 18.11.

In sum, it is actually pretty hard to beat SPT even if due dates are important and even though SPT ignores them. The main advantage of SPT is that it keeps the average flow time as low as possible, which is valuable whether or not there are due dates. However, if there is a strong preference for avoiding very late jobs, then EDD might be the best approach because it minimizes the maximum lateness/tardiness among the jobs. But this is a conservative approach: By avoiding very late jobs, EDD might make all jobs, on average, a bit later than SPT.

18.5 Theory of Constraints

Scheduling jobs on a single resource is complex, but scheduling jobs across multiple resources can be mind-boggling. Take, for instance, a semiconductor manufacturing process. Roughly speaking, making a semiconductor starts with a wafer of silicon, which then goes through a series of steps, as shown in Figure 18.8, that can include (i) deposition, (ii) lithography, (iii) etching, and (iv) testing. Each step usually includes a number of machines, wafers frequently recirculate through steps (e.g., a single wafer can pass through lithography and etching several times), different types of wafers have different processing times at the various steps, and many of the steps include setup times that depend on the particular type of semiconductor being made. A typical semiconductor manufacturing facility has hundreds, if not thousands, of jobs in process, all with different due date requirements and revenue potential. Finally, each piece of equipment can cost several million dollars and the total cost of a modern semiconductor facility can be more than $1 billion, sometimes more than several billion. With such a large capital investment, it is of utmost importance to maximize flow rate, which generally means ensuring high utilization.

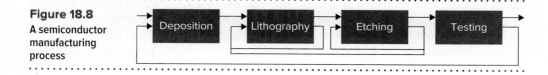

Figure 18.8
A semiconductor manufacturing process

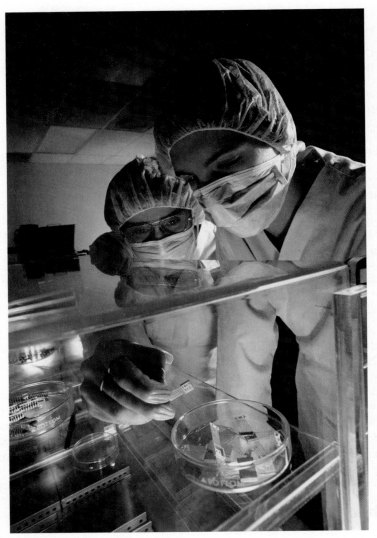

© *Digital Stock/Corbis*

LO18-5 Understand the motivation behind the theory of constraints

theory of constraints An operation guideline that recommends managerial attention be focused on the bottleneck of a process.

Even in processes that are simpler than semiconductor manufacturing, there can be essentially a limitless number of different schedules for moving flow units through the process. So how is a manager to choose among them if it might not even be possible to count all of them? One effective approach is to "see through" the complexity by simplifying the analysis. This is the idea behind the **theory of constraints**. The theory of constraints states that the flow rate of a process is primarily dictated by the flow rate through the bottleneck resource, so all managerial attention should be placed on the bottleneck. In other words, the main constraint on a system is the bottleneck. Consequently, all a manager needs to do to maximize the flow rate through the process is to ensure that the flow rate through the bottleneck is as high as it can be. In particular, a manager should not pay much attention to nonbottleneck resources because idle time on those resources does not constrain the overall flow through the process, and therefore should not be a concern.

The first step in the application of the theory of constraints is to identify the bottleneck. The bottleneck is the resource with the highest implied utilization (the ratio of demand to capacity). Next, care should be taken to ensure that the flow rate through the bottleneck is maximized, which also maximizes the utilization of the bottleneck. For example, if the bottleneck involves setups, then batch sizes should be sufficiently large to avoid adding too much unproductive time. Finally, it is critical to schedule work through the process so that the bottleneck is never blocked or starved. Hence, jobs should be scheduled on nonbottleneck steps to ensure that there is always a buffer of work in front of the bottleneck (to prevent starving) and sufficient space after the bottleneck (to prevent blocking). Interestingly, this might require a combination of sequencing rules. In general, the jobs in the buffers before the bottleneck and after the bottleneck should be scheduled with SPT to minimize the average inventory in those buffers. But there are times in which the scheduling rule should actually switch to longest processing time (LPT)! For example, suppose the buffer after the bottleneck is starting to get full. In that case, the bottleneck is at risk of getting blocked. If the bottleneck switches to LPT, then it reduces the chance that it will be blocked because LPT temporarily slows down the inflow of jobs into the buffer after the bottleneck. Alternatively, suppose the buffer before the bottleneck is nearly empty. An empty buffer in front of the bottleneck risks starving the bottleneck. Hence, the bottleneck should switch to LPT to give the upstream resources an opportunity to increase the jobs in front of the bottleneck.

At a higher level, the theory of constraints recognizes that limited managerial time is another constraint on a system. Consequently, that time should best be used by focusing it on the part of the process that has the greatest influence over its overall performance (i.e., the bottleneck).

18.6 Reservations and Appointments

LO18-6 Understand the design choices and the pros and cons of an appointment system for scheduling

No discussion of scheduling is complete without including reservations and appointments. The intent behind an appointment system is clear: Rather than have people arrive as they want, which can create long queues or idle servers, use appointments to add predictability and smoothness to the arrival process. Consider the process flow for a physician, as shown in Figure 18.9. Unlike most process flow diagrams, Figure 18.9 shows two places for "inventory" next to each other: Patients can wait for the doctor either at home or at the doctor's office. All else being equal, patients obviously prefer waiting at home than at the doctor's office.

Before proceeding further, let's be clear that using an appointment system does not actually increase the capacity of the system. If the flow rate of patients wanting to see a doctor is larger than the doctor's capacity, then the number of patients waiting grows very large, whether an appointment system is used or not. This can indeed be a source of irritation: Patients might call their doctor only to learn that the next available appointment is months away. The primary solution for that problem is to add capacity to the system.

So an appointment system deals with matching supply with demand when there is sufficient capacity. Each person (or job) is scheduled to arrive just as the previous person finishes service. This way, in theory, the server is never idle and jobs never wait. However, there are several complications that challenge an appointment system: (1) processing times are not perfectly predictable, so it is not clear when the next person should arrive for her appointment, and (2) people don't always arrive for their appointment—that is, demand, even scheduled demand, is not perfectly predictable.

To explore the design challenges of an appointment system, let's make the example of the doctor's office concrete. Suppose we are scheduling appointments for a primary care physician. Each patient requires, on average, 20 minutes of the doctor's time, but the actual time for each patient varies uniformly between 10 minutes and 30 minutes. For simplicity, let's say the doctor only sees patients—she doesn't eat lunch, have other paperwork to attend to, or even need a bathroom break. Finally, the doctor starts seeing patients at 8:00 a.m. and wants to treat 20 patients during the day. How should we set the appointment times?

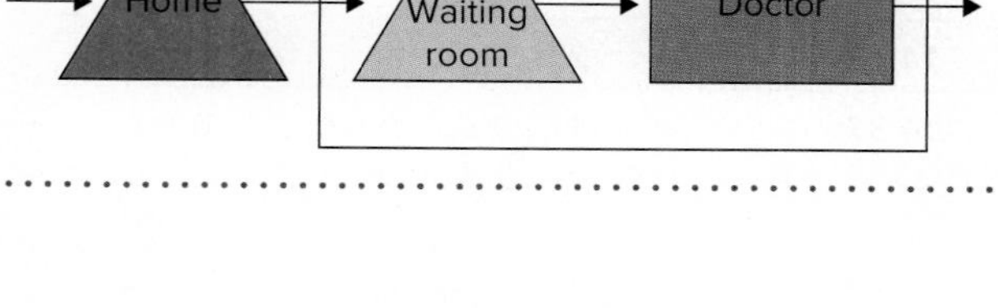

Figure 18.9
Process flow diagram for a doctor

As usual, before making appointment decisions, we need to be clear about the performance measures we care about:

- Utilization of the resource (the physician).
- Average flow time for each flow unit (the patients).

Utilization measures how well we are using our resource's time. Given a fixed physician salary, a more highly utilized physician either works fewer hours to treat the same number of patients or treats more patients per hour worked. The average flow time measures how well we are using our flow units' time. It might not be possible to put a credible cost on patient time, but they will be happier with the service they receive if they spend less time in the doctor's office. Clearly, we want utilization to be as high as possible and flow time to be as low as possible.

18.6.1 Scheduling Appointments with Uncertain Processing Times

Let's choose an appointment schedule for the physician, assuming her patients are very responsible—they always arrive at their set appointment time. One natural choice is to schedule patients to arrive every 20 minutes because that is how long the doctor sees each patient, on average. Table 18.13 shows the results for one possible day—the processing times are randomly generated, assuming each processing time between 10 and 30 minutes is equally likely. (This is another discrete event simulator.) For example, the first patient spends 18 minutes

TABLE 18.13   Simulation Results for One Day Treating 20 Patients with 20-Minute Intervals between Appointments

Patient	Scheduled	Processing Time (min)	Start Time	End Time	Patient Flow Time (min)	Physician Idle Time (min)
1	8:00	18	8:00	8:18	18	0
2	8:20	11	8:20	8:31	11	2
3	8:40	18	8:40	8:58	18	9
4	9:00	20	9:00	9:20	20	2
5	9:20	10	9:20	9:30	10	0
6	9:40	29	9:40	10:09	29	10
7	10:00	29	10:09	10:38	38	0
8	10:20	18	10:38	10:56	36	0
9	10:40	16	10:56	11:12	32	0
10	11:00	21	11:12	11:33	33	0
11	11:20	15	11:33	11:48	28	0
12	11:40	18	11:48	12:06	26	0
13	12:00	18	12:06	12:24	24	0
14	12:20	13	12:24	12:37	17	0
15	12:40	16	12:40	12:56	16	3
16	13:00	30	13:00	13:30	30	4
17	13:20	16	13:30	13:46	26	0
18	13:40	18	13:46	14:04	24	0
19	14:00	19	14:04	14:23	23	0
20	14:20	14	14:23	14:37	17	0

with the physician, while the second patient spends 11 minutes. Because the first patient is finished before the second patient arrives, the physician has two minutes of idle time before treating the second patient and then nine minutes of idle time before treating the third patient. Unfortunately, patient six requires 29 minutes, which means patient seven must wait nine minutes before seeing the doctor, leading to a total flow time of 38 minutes (9 minutes waiting and 29 minutes seeing the doctor).

The fourth column of Table 18.14 summarizes the results from the data in Table 18.13. The average flow time is the average of the times in the Patient Flow Time column in Table 18.13. The average processing time is also the average of the actual processing times shown in Table 18.13. Notice that the average processing time is slightly less than the expected value, 18.35 versus 20 minutes. This is just by chance.

To evaluate the total work time for the physician, note that the physician starts at 8:00 and finishes with the last patient at 14:37, which is 397 minutes or 6.62 hours. The total time to process a set of jobs (in this case, 20 patients) is also called the **makespan**. The makespan can never be smaller than the sum of the processing times, but it can be larger if the resource has some idle time.

Makespan The total time to process a set of jobs.

With an average processing time of 18.35 minutes, a physician's capacity is 1/Processing time, which is 0.0545 patient per minute or 3.27 patients per hour. The flow rate is the number of patients served (20) divided by the time to serve them (6.62 hours), or 3.02 patients per hour. Finally, utilization is the flow rate divided by capacity, which is 92 percent.

A 92 percent utilization for the physician and only 5.45 minutes of waiting, on average, for patients (23.80 − 18.35) seems reasonable. But Table 18.14 also reveals what happens with a shorter (15-minute) or longer (25-minute) interval between appointments.

Patients get great service when there are 25 minutes between appointments! In that case, they wait, on average, a grand total of 0.9 minute to see the physician. However, this great service comes at a price. The poor physician's utilization has dropped to 75 percent and instead of working 6.62 hours to treat 20 patients, she must spend 8.15 hours. That means that moving from 20-minute intervals to 25-minute intervals saved 20 patients a total of 91 minutes waiting (= 20 × (5.45 − 0.90)), but the physician has about 1.5 hours added on to her day (= 8.15 − 6.62). This is a reasonable trade-off if physician time is cheap relative to patient waiting time, but a terrible trade-off if physician time is expensive relative to patient waiting time.

The other extreme displayed in Table 18.14 is a 15-minute interval. Now patients are arriving faster than the physician can treat them, on average. As you might expect, this keeps the physician occupied—her utilization is now 100 percent—but patients must wait a considerable amount of time—the average waiting time is 32.75 minutes. Waiting about one-half hour

TABLE 18.14 Performance Measure Results with Appointments Spaced Out at Different Intervals

Calculation	Measure	Interval between Appointments (min)		
		15	20	25
a	Average flow time (min)	51.1	23.80	19.25
b	Average processing time (min)	18.35	18.35	18.35
c	Number of patients	20	20	20
d	Makespan (hr)	6.13	6.62	8.15
e = 60/b	Capacity (patients/hr)	3.27	3.27	3.27
f = c/d	Flow rate (patients/hr)	3.26	3.02	2.45
g = f/e	Utilization	1.00	0.92	0.75
h = a − b	Average waiting time (min)	32.75	5.45	0.90

Figure 18.10

Wait time for each of the 20 patients when the appointment interval is 15 minutes

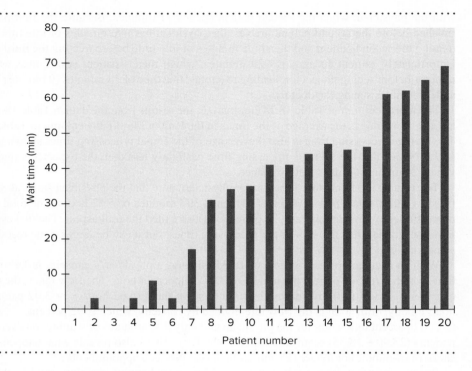

might not seem like a disaster, but remember that that is an average. Some patients have to wait much longer. Figure 18.10 displays the waiting time for each of the 20 patients. The last four patients scheduled have to wait more than an hour each, which is about twice the average wait. This is one reason why you want to grab an early morning appointment rather than one in the afternoon.

A scheduling system that schedules more flow units (patients) than can be handled by the resource (physician) in a period of time is said to be **overbooking**—deliberately scheduling more work than can be handled to try to maintain a high utilization for the resource. See Connections: Overbooking for a description of how overbooking is done with other services.

Overbooking The practice of intentionally assigning more work to a resource than the resource can process so as to maintain a high utilization for the resource. Overbooking is meant to mitigate the consequences of no-show demand.

18.6.2 No-Shows

Looking at the results in Table 18.14, it seems like the 20-minute interval might be a good compromise between making patients wait for the doctor (a short appointment interval) or making the doctor wait for patients (a long interval). But there is one key assumption that needs to be revisited: Patients don't always arrive for their appointments. In fact, the rate of **no-shows**, patients who do not arrive for their appointment, can be as high as 20 to 30 percent in many physician offices.

No-show A customer who does not arrive for his or her appointment or reservation.

To see the impact of no-shows, let's assume that about 20 percent of the patients do not arrive for their scheduled appointment. Nevertheless, the physician still wants to treat 20 patients during the day. Consequently, let's say the physician schedules 25 appointments with the hope of having 20 patients treated. Table 18.15 displays one possible outcome. Notice that the processing times in Table 18.15 are identical to the processing times in Table 18.13. The only difference between the results in the two tables is that 20 percent of the patients in Table 18.15 are no-shows.

Table 18.16 evaluates the performance measures when there are 20 percent no-shows. Comparing Table 18.14 to Table 18.16, we can see that no-shows are not good for the efficient use of the physician's time. For each of the appointment intervals, the physician's utilization decreases when no-shows are possible. However, no-shows seem to help reduce average waiting times: If some patients don't show up for their appointment, then the patients that do show up don't have to wait as long. Thus, it is not immediately obvious that no-shows are bad.

TABLE 18.15   Simulation Results for One Day Treating 20 Patients with 20-Minute Intervals between Appointments and Five No-Show Patients

Patient	Scheduled	Status	Processing Time (min)	Start Time	End Time	Patient Flow Time (min)	Physician Idle Time (min)
1	8:00		18	8:00	8:18	18	0
2	8:15	No-show					
3	8:30		18	8:40	8:58	18	22
4	8:45		20	9:00	9:20	20	2
5	9:00		10	9:20	9:30	10	0
6	9:15		29	9:40	10:09	29	10
7	9:30		29	10:09	10:38	38	0
8	9:45		18	10:38	10:56	36	0
9	10:00		16	10:56	11:12	32	0
10	10:15		21	11:12	11:33	33	0
11	10:30		15	11:33	11:48	28	0
12	10:45		18	11:48	12:06	26	0
13	11:00		18	12:06	12:24	24	0
14	11:15	No-show					
15	11:30		16	12:40	12:56	16	16
16	11:45		30	13:00	13:30	30	4
17	12:00		16	13:30	13:46	26	0
18	12:15	No-show					
19	12:30	No-show					
20	12:45		14	14:20	14:34	14	34
21	13:00	No-show					
22	13:15		11	15:00	15:11	11	26
23	13:30		13	15:20	15:33	13	9
24	13:45		18	15:40	15:58	18	7
25	14:00		19	16:00	16:19	19	2

Figure 18.11 makes it clear that no-shows are positively and unambiguously not helpful. The figure plots the trade-off between utilization and average waiting time. Each observation in each curve corresponds to a particular appointment interval. For example, a 24-minute appointment interval with 20 percent no-shows has a utilization of about 62 percent and an average waiting time of 1.25 minutes, whereas with an 18-minute appointment interval and all patients arriving (0 percent no-shows), the utilization is 97 percent and the waiting time is 14 minutes. The key finding from the figure is that the trade-off curve moves up and to the left as patients become more likely to not show up for their appointment. This is simply not good. For example, suppose the office wants to keep the average patient waiting time to under five minutes. If all patients show up for their appointment, then the physician's utilization can be above 90 percent (the 0 percent no-shows curve crosses the horizontal five-minute waiting line at about 91 percent utilization). But if 20 percent of patients are no-shows, then the

TABLE 18.16 Performance Measure Results with Appointments Spaced Out at Different Intervals and 20 Percent of Patients Do Not Arrive for Their Appointment

Calculation	Measure	Interval between Appointments (min) 15	20	25
a	Average flow time (min)	38.10	22.95	19.25
b	Average processing time (min)	18.35	18.35	18.35
c	Number of patients	20	20	20
d	Total work time (hr)	6.37	8.22	10.32
$e = 60/b$	Capacity (patients/hr)	3.27	3.27	3.27
$f = c/d$	Flow rate (patients/hr)	3.14	2.43	1.94
$g = f/e$	Utilization	0.96	0.74	0.59
$h = a - b$	Average waiting time (min)	19.75	4.60	0.90

Figure 18.11

The trade-off between utilization and average waiting time in two cases: (i) all customers arrive for their appointments (red square markers) and (ii) 20 percent of customers are no-shows (blue diamond markers). Numbers next to markers indicate the interval length between appointments (in minutes).

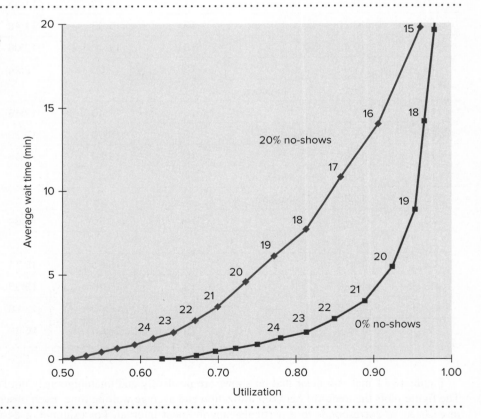

physician's utilization is likely to drop to around 75 percent (the 20 percent no-shows curve crosses the horizontal five-minute waiting line at about 75 percent utilization). Holding the physician's salary fixed, a drop in utilization translates into a higher cost to serve each patient.

If Figure 18.11 looks familiar, then you have probably read Chapter 16, Service Systems with Patient Customers. In Chapter 16, Figures 16.8 and 16.13 show the trade-off between utilization and time in queue in a system with random processing times, random interarrival times, and no appointments. Even though those systems are not exactly the same as the doctor's office with appointments, the fundamental trade-off between utilization and flow time continues to be true.

CONNECTIONS: **Overbooking**

© Ingram Publishing/SuperStock/RF

Say you purchased a seat on a flight from New York to San Francisco, you reserved a compact car in San Francisco to drive to a hotel room that you booked in the Mission District, and you reserved a table for 7 p.m. at the best new Thai restaurant in town for that same

Continued

evening. In each of these cases, you expect that your reservation will be honored when you show up on time—you will have a seat on the plane, your car will be ready for you at the airport, the hotel will have a room for you, and the restaurant will seat you promptly at 7 p.m. It doesn't always work out that way.

Sometimes the service provider cannot honor your reservation because of unforeseen events (the sprinkler system accidentally flooded 15 rooms in the hotel) or because of bad luck (the Thai restaurant didn't expect the previous diners would linger so long). But sometimes they cannot honor your reservation because they overbooked their capacity—they sold more reservations than they could honor if everyone with a reservation shows up.

While overbooking might seem like a "breach of contract" and a slimy business practice, there is a logic behind why companies overbook. Clearly, the airline or the other companies have no desire to deal with irate customers when they get "caught" overbooking—the customer might not return for future business or, in the case of the airline, there are government regulations that stipulate the minimum compensation that must be provided to a passenger who is denied boarding. So they don't want to overbook too much. But if they don't overbook at all, then they face another problem: some customers make a reservation and don't show up.

For example, if you unfortunately get hit with the flu on the day of your trip, you might not show up for any of those reservations. No-shows mean unused resources and an unused resource is costly. Hence, these companies attempt to balance the cost of overbooking too much (irate customers) with the cost of overbooking too little (idle resources). Put another way, overbooking is just another way that companies try to do a better job of matching supply with demand.

So we see that appointment systems are not the perfect panacea for all operational ills. Variable processing times create uncertainty. Appointment no-shows create uncertainty. Managing this uncertainty requires a trade-off between physician utilization and patient waiting. Either the physician waits for patients (long intervals between appointments) or patients wait for the physician (short intervals between appointments). This trade-off cannot be avoided and it certainly becomes worse as more uncertainty is added to the system.

Beyond choosing the appropriate point on the trade-off curve, is there something that can be done to improve the situation? As with most cases in operations, the obvious solution is to reduce the variability that is causing the problem!

The first issue to tackle is the variability in processing times. This can be addressed by adopting standardized procedures, better and quicker training of new staff, and an effort by physicians to avoid cases taking longer than necessary (e.g., learn how to politely move on when dealing with a chatty patient).

The second issue to tackle is no-shows. Several techniques have been adopted. For example, the physician's office could contact the patient the day before his or her appointment to remind the patient. A more heavy-handed approach is to actually charge the patient if he or she does not arrive for the scheduled appointment. In some cases, this may be difficult to do and it surely risks creating ill will with the patient. Furthermore, even though it removes some of the sting from the physician's office because it collects some revenue, the absence of a patient still can create some physician idle time, which is not ideal. Finally, it has been noticed that the likelihood a patient doesn't arrive for an appointment depends heavily on how long ago the patient made the appointment. If the patient called two months ago to make the appointment, then he or she might be more likely to forget about the appointment. This insight has led some physician practices to move to an **open-access appointment system**. With an open-access system, appointments are only available one day in advance and are filled on a first-come-first-served basis. It has been found that open-access scheduling can dramatically reduce the rate of no-shows, while at the same time increasing physician utilization.

Open-access appointment system An appointment system in which appointments are only available one day in advance and are filled on a first-come-first-served basis.

Conclusion

Scheduling involves assigning when resources should work on which demand. Although first-come-first-served is the intuitive way to sequence work, it is generally not the best approach from the point of view of operational performance measures unless there is a strong concern for equity across flow units. Shortest processing time (SPT) is generally a better approach, or its cousin, weighted shortest processing time (WSPT), can be when jobs differ in their priorities. When there are due dates, then the earliest-due-date (EDD) rule minimizes the maximum lateness or tardiness, but it might not do as well as SPT on average performance or the percent of on-time jobs.

When scheduling work in a complex system, the theory of constraints suggests the focus should be on maximizing the flow rate through the bottleneck resource—to ensure there is a buffer of flow units in front of the resource (to avoid starving) and ample space after the resource (to avoid blocking)—and if the resource has setup times, to make sure batches are sufficiently large to avoid needlessly low utilization.

Reservations and appointments are viewed as one solution to scheduling, but even those systems have challenges. In particular, when processing times are uncertain or arrivals are uncertain (as in no-shows), then an appointment system must balance the utilization of the resource against the flow time of the flow units.

In each example discussed in this chapter, we see the ill effects of the three system inhibitors: variability, waste, and inflexibility. Variability comes in the form of arrival time uncertainty and processing time uncertainty. Waste manifests itself in ways that contribute to longer processing times, such as poorly trained service providers. And the lack of flexibility to increase and decrease staffing on a moment's notice is a key reason why scheduling is needed.

Summary of Learning Objectives

LO18-1 Understand the diversity of scheduling applications

Scheduling is the process of assigning when resources will work on demand. The key objectives of scheduling are to provide timely service to demand and high utilization of resources. Given its importance, scheduling applies in essentially all operations.

LO18-2 Understand and evaluate the shortest-processing-time scheduling rule

If it is possible to determine the processing time for jobs awaiting service from a resource, then the shortest-processing-time (SPT) rule minimizes the average flow time and therefore also minimizes the average number of jobs in the system.

LO18-3 Understand and evaluate the weighted-shortest-processing-time scheduling rule

Jobs can vary in terms of their processing times and importance, or weight. The weighted-shortest-processing-time (WSPT) rule minimizes the weighted average flow time of the jobs in the system. If all jobs have equal weights, then WSPT yields the same results as SPT. If there are different types of jobs and their weights are vastly different, then WSPT becomes a simple priority rule in which the resource works on the highest-priority job before switching to lower-priority jobs.

LO18-4 Understand and evaluate the earliest-due-date scheduling rule

Additional performance measures become relevant when jobs have due dates. In particular, lateness is the difference between the completion time and the due date, and tardiness is the amount by which a job is completed past its due date. The earliest-due-date (EDD) rule minimizes the maximum lateness and tardiness, but it does not guarantee the minimum average tardiness. While SPT cannot be guaranteed to perform well on all performance measures, it generally performs quite well even though it ignores due dates.

LO18-5 Understand the motivation behind the theory of constraints

Scheduling work can become daunting when there are hundreds or thousands of jobs, many resources, and many paths through the resources. The theory of constraints provides a guideline to managers to simplify their task yet also make good choices—managers should focus on maximizing the flow rate through the bottleneck.

LO18-6 Understand the design choices and the pros and cons of an appointment system for scheduling

Appointment systems can alleviate waiting for resources. A key design choice with an appointment system is the interval between appointments. If the interval is long, flow units are unlikely to have to wait for the resource, but the resource is likely to be poorly utilized. If the interval is short, then a buffer of flow units is likely to develop, causing inventory and waiting, but the resource is likely to be well utilized. Appointment systems are most effective when flow units always arrive for their appointment.

Key Terms

Introduction

Scheduling The process of deciding what work to assign to which resources and when to assign the work.

18.1 Scheduling Timeline and Applications

Materials requirement planning (MRP) A system that plans the delivery of components required for a manufacturing process so that components are available when needed but not so early as to create excess inventory.

Bill of materials The list of components that are needed for the assembly of an item.

Revenue management The practice of maximizing the revenue generated from a set of fixed assets (like cars in a rental fleet, rooms in a hotel, or tables in a restaurant).

18.2 Resource Scheduling—Shortest Processing Time

Job A flow unit that requires processing from one or more resources.

First-come-first-served (FCFS) A rule that sequences jobs to be processed on a resource in the order in which they arrived.

Shortest processing time (SPT) A rule that sequences jobs to be processed on a resource in ascending order of their processing times.

Longest processing time (LPT) A rule that sequences jobs to be processed on a resource in descending order of their processing times.

18.3 Resource Scheduling with Priorities—Weighted Shortest Processing Time

Weighted shortest processing time (WSPT) A rule that sequences jobs to be processed on a resource in descending order of the ratio of their weight to their processing time. Jobs with high weights and low processing times tend to be sequenced early.

Emergency Severity Index (ESI) A scoring rule used by Emergency Rooms to rank the severity of a patient's injuries and then to prioritize their care.

Net neutrality The principle that Internet service providers must treat all data that traverses their network equally in the sense that no priority cannot be given to some data over other types of data, even if the provider of the data (e.g., Google) pays for better service.

18.4 Resource Scheduling with Due Dates—Earliest Due Date

Percent on time The fraction of jobs that are completed on or before their due date.

Lateness The difference between the completion time of a job and its due date. Lateness is negative when the job is completed before the due date (i.e., it is early).

Tardiness If a job is completed after its due date, then tardiness is the difference between the completion time of a job and its due date. If the job is completed before its due date, then tardiness is 0. Tardiness is always positive.

Earliest due date (EDD) A rule that sequences jobs to be processed on a resource in ascending order of their due dates.

18.5 Theory of Constraints

Theory of constraints An operation guideline that recommends managerial attention be focused on the bottleneck of a process.

18.6 Reservations and Appointments

Makespan The total time to process a set of jobs.

Overbooking The practice of intentionally assigning more work to a resource than the resource can process so as to maintain a high utilization for the resource. Overbooking is meant to mitigate the consequences of no-show demand.

No-show A customer who does not arrive for his or her appointment or reservation.

Open-access appointment system An appointment system in which appointments are only available one day in advance and are filled on a first-come-first-served basis.

Key Formulas

LO18-2 Understand and evaluate the shortest-processing-time scheduling rule

$$\text{Inventory} = \text{Flow Rate} \times \text{Flow Time, or } I = R \times T$$

Conceptual Questions

LO18-2

1. Which of the following performance measures depend(s) on how work is sequenced at a resource?
   a. Only inventory
   b. Only flow rate
   c. Only flow time
   d. Inventory and flow rate
   e. Inventory and flow time
   f. Flow rate and flow time

2. Suppose there is a set of jobs to be processed at a resource. Shortest processing time always sequences the jobs in a different order than first-come-first-served. True or false?
   a. True
   b. False

3. Shortest processing time minimizes the flow time of jobs at a resource because it reduces the processing times of the jobs. True or false?
   a. True
   b. False

4. Depending on how jobs arrive to a resource, it is possible that the average flow time of the jobs with first-come-first-served is lower than that with shortest processing time. True or false?
   a. True
   b. False

5. The flow time of every job is lower with shortest processing time than with first-come-first-served. True or false?
   a. True
   b. False

6. The difference in the average flow time between shortest processing time and first-come-first-served is greatest when:
   a. all of the jobs have the same processing times.
   b. the utilization of the resource is low.
   c. there are many jobs waiting to be processed at the resource.
   d. jobs arrive in increasing order of their processing times.

LO18-3

7. With weighted shortest processing time, jobs are scheduled at a resource in what order?
   a. In increasing order of their processing times
   b. In the order they arrived
   c. In decreasing order of their priority/weight
   d. In decreasing order of the ratio of weight to processing time

8. Which of the following statements best explains why an organization would use weighted shortest processing time instead of shortest processing time?
   a. Jobs differ in how important it is for them to be completed quickly.
   b. It wants to minimize the average flow time across all jobs.
   c. WSPT is a simple rule to implement because jobs are processed in the order in which they arrive.
   d. It wants to minimize the average number of jobs in the system waiting to be processed.

LO18-4

9. Jobs have different processing times and due dates. If a job is finished earlier than its due date but one day sooner than expected, how does this change the job's lateness?
   a. Lateness decreases by one day.
   b. Lateness does not change.
   c. Lateness increases by one day.
   d. It is not possible to determine the impact on lateness of the job with the given information.

10. Jobs have different processing times and due dates. If a job is finished earlier than its due date but one day sooner than expected, how does this change the job's tardiness?
    a. Tardiness decreases by one day.
    b. Tardiness does not change.
    c. Tardiness increases by one day.
    d. It is not possible to determine the impact on the tardiness of the job with the given information.

11. The earliest-due-date rule always minimizes the average lateness across jobs. True or false?
    a. True
    b. False

12. The earliest-due-date rule always minimizes the maximum tardiness across jobs. True or false?
    a. True
    b. False

LO18-5

13. Why does the theory of constraints advocate that a manager's attention be directed to the bottleneck of a process?
    a. It is useful to lower the utilization of the bottleneck.
    b. The bottleneck has considerable influence on the average flow rate of a process.
    c. It is important to minimize the buffer inventory in front of the bottleneck.
    d. First-come-first-served scheduling of jobs at the bottleneck ensures that all jobs have the same expected waiting time before they are processed at the bottleneck.

14. The theory of constraints is most applicable in which of the following processes?
    a. An auto repair shop with one mechanic

b. A chemical processing plant with numerous pieces of equipment with significant setup times and a large number of products, each requiring different sequences of resources to be completed

c. A well-balanced assembly line that makes lawnmowers

LO18-6

15. If an appointment system evenly spaces out appointments throughout the day, then patients arriving during the second half of the day can expect to wait the same amount of time as patients arriving during the first half of the day. True or false?

a. True

b. False

16. Which of the following is a benefit of overbooking a resource?

a. It helps to reduce the average number of jobs waiting to be processed on the resource.

b. It helps to reduce the average flow time of jobs through a resource.

c. It helps to increase the utilization of the resource.

d. It helps to reduce the processing times of jobs at a resource.

Solved Example Problems

LO18-2

1. There are 10 jobs waiting to be processed at a resource. The total processing time across those jobs is 200 minutes. During the period of time in which those jobs are processed, what is the flow rate through the resource (jobs per hour)?

   Answer: 3. 10 jobs in 200 minutes yields a flow rate of 10 jobs/200 min = 0.05 job per minute, which is 60 min per hr × 0.05 job per min = 3 jobs per hour.

TABLE 18.17 Processing Time for Six Jobs

Job	A	B	C	D	E	F
Processing time (minutes)	5	11	8	2	1	9

2. Given the jobs displayed in Table 18.17, if SPT is used to sequence the jobs, which job would be the fourth to be processed?

a. A

b. B

c. C

d. D

e. E

f. F

   Answer: Sequence the jobs in ascending order of their processing times (E, D, A, C, F, B). Thus, the correct answer is C.

3. Given the jobs displayed in Table 18.17, if SPT is used to sequence the jobs, what is the flow time of job F (in minutes)?

   Answer: 25. F is the fifth job processed because it has the fifth largest processing time. Its flow time is then the sum of the five smallest processing times: $1 + 2 + 5 + 8 + 9 = 25$.

4. Given the jobs displayed in Table 18.17, if SPT is used to sequence the jobs, what is the flow rate of jobs (jobs per minute)?

   Answer: 1/6. Six jobs are completed in a total of 36 minutes, so the flow rate is 6/36 = 1/6 job per minute.

5. Given the jobs displayed in Table 18.17, if SPT is used to sequence the jobs, what is the average flow time of jobs in the system?

> **Answer:** 14.8. The flow times of the six jobs are 1, 1 + 2 = 3, 1 + 2 + 5 = 8, 1 + 2 + 5 + 8 = 16, 1 + 2 + 5 + 8 + 9 = 25, and 1 + 2 + 5 + 8 + 9 + 11 = 36. The average flow time is then (1 + 3 + 8 + 16 + 25 + 36)/6 = 89/6 = 14.8 minutes.

6. Given the jobs displayed in Table 18.17, if SPT is used to sequence the jobs, what is the average inventory of jobs in the system?

> **Answer:** 2.47. To evaluate inventory, we need the flow rate and flow time, which we evaluated in the previous questions. Hence, Inventory = Flow rate × Flow time = 1/6 job per min × 14.8 minutes = 2.47 jobs.

TABLE 18.18   Processing Times and Weights for Four Jobs

Job	A	B	C	D
Processing time (minutes)	15	5	25	30
Weight	5	10	1	15

LO18-3

7. Assume the jobs displayed in Table 18.18 need to be processed on a single resource and are sequenced with the WSPT rule. Which job would be processed third?
   a. A
   b. B
   c. C
   d. D

> **Answer:** A. The ratios of weights to processing times for jobs A–D are 5/15 = 1/3, 10/5 = 2, 1/25, and 15/30 = 1/2, respectively. The third largest ratio is 1/3, from job A.

TABLE 18.19   Number of Passengers on Five Planes Ready for Departure

Plane	A	B	C	D	E
Passengers	150	50	400	200	250

8. There are five planes ready for departure at an airport. The number of passengers on each plane is displayed in Table 18.19. Each plane requires 10 minutes to taxi to the runway and 2 minutes to take off (i.e., there needs to be two minutes between departures). If the air traffic controller wants to minimize the weighted average number of passengers waiting for departure (i.e., weighted by the number of passengers on the plane), in what sequence should the planes take off?
   a. A, B, C, D, E
   b. B, A, D, E, C
   c. C, B, E, A, D
   d. C, E, D, A, B
   e. It doesn't matter what sequence they depart in because they have equal processing times.

> **Answer:** d. They should use weighted shortest processing time. Because they all have the same processing time, they should depart in decreasing order of the number of passengers on the plane.

TABLE 18.20   Processing Times and Due Dates for Five Jobs

Job	A	B	C	D	E
Processing time (days)	10	25	40	5	20
Due date (days)	100	40	75	55	30

LO18-4

9. If the jobs displayed in Table 18.20 are processed using the earliest-due-date rule, what would be the lateness of job C?

   Answer: 15. Using EDD, job C is processed fourth because it has the fourth due date (the order is E, B, D, C, A). Thus, it is completed at time $20 + 25 + 5 + 40 = 90$. It is due on day 75, so its lateness is $90 - 75 = 15$.

10. If the jobs displayed in Table 18.20 are processed using the earliest-due-date rule, what would be the lateness of job E?

    Answer: −10. Using EDD, job E is processed first because it has the earliest due date. Thus, it is completed at time 20, but it is due at time 30, meaning that its lateness is $20 - 30 = -10$.

11. If the jobs displayed in Table 18.20 are processed using the earliest-due-date rule, what would be the tardiness of job D?

    Answer: 0. Using EDD, job D is processed third because it has the third due date. It is completed at time $20 + 25 + 5 = 50$. It is due at time 55, so it is completed before its due date. Hence, its tardiness is zero.

12. If the jobs displayed in Table 18.20 are processed using the earliest-due-date rule, what is the maximum tardiness?

    Answer: 15. Given EDD, the jobs are processed in the following sequence: E, B, D, C, A. The jobs are completed at times 20, $20 + 25 = 45$, $20 + 25 + 5 = 50$, $20 + 25 + 5 + 40 = 90$, $20 + 25 + 5 + 40 + 10 = 100$. The corresponding due dates are 30, 40, 55, 75, and 100. Thus, only jobs B and C are tardy. Job B is tardy by five days and job C is tardy by 15 days, so the maximum tardiness is 15.

Problems and Applications

LO18-2

1. An architect has five projects to complete. She estimates that three of the projects will require one week to complete and the other two will require three weeks and four weeks. During the time these projects are completed (and assuming no other projects are worked on during this time), what is the architect's flow rate (projects per week)?

TABLE 18.21   Processing Time for Eight Projects, Displayed in the Sequence They Arrived

Project	P1	P2	P3	P4	P5	P6	P7	P8
Processing time (hours)	4	1	2	3	6	5	1	0.5

2. Given the projects displayed in Table 18.21, if FCFS is used to sequence the jobs, what is the average flow rate of the projects (in projects per hour)?

3. Given the projects displayed in Table 18.21, if FCFS is used to sequence the jobs, what is the average flow time of the projects (in hours)?

4. Given the projects displayed in Table 18.21, if FCFS is used to sequence the jobs, what is the average inventory of the projects (in projects)?
5. Given the projects displayed in Table 18.21, if SPT is used to sequence the jobs, what is the average flow rate of the projects (in projects per hour)?
6. Given the projects displayed in Table 18.21, if SPT is used to sequence the jobs, what is the average flow time of the projects (in hours)?
7. Given the projects displayed in Table 18.21, if SPT is used to sequence the jobs, what is the average inventory of the projects (in projects)?

TABLE 18.22   Processing Times and Weights for Five Jobs

Job	A	B	C	D	E
Processing time (minutes)	1	4	2	3	5
Weight	1.5	1	1.25	0.5	2

LO18-3

8. Assume the jobs displayed in Table 18.22 need to be processed on a single resource and are sequenced with the WSPT rule. Which job would be processed second?
   a. A
   b. B
   c. C
   d. D
   e. E
9. Assume the jobs displayed in Table 18.22 need to be processed on a single resource and are sequenced with the WSPT rule. What is the average flow rate of the jobs (in jobs per minute)?
10. Assume the jobs displayed in Table 18.22 need to be processed on a single resource and are sequenced with the WSPT rule. What is the average flow time of the jobs (in minutes)?
11. Assume the jobs displayed in Table 18.22 need to be processed on a single resource and are sequenced with the WSPT rule. What is the average inventory of the jobs?

TABLE 18.23   Processing Times and Due Dates for Five Jobs

Job	A	B	C	D	E
Processing time (weeks)	2	0.5	1	3	1.5
Due date (weeks)	3	6	4	5	2

LO18-4

12. If the jobs displayed in Table 18.23 are processed using the earliest-due-date rule, what would be the lateness of job B?
13. If the jobs displayed in Table 18.23 are processed using the earliest-due-date rule, what would be the tardiness of job E?
14. If the jobs displayed in Table 18.23 are processed using the earliest-due-date rule, what is the maximum tardiness?
15. If the jobs displayed in Table 18.23 are processed using the earliest-due-date rule, what is the average flow time?

References

Cox, Jeff, and Eliyahu M. Goldratt. *The Goal: A Process of Ongoing Improvement.* Great Barrington, MA: North River Press, 1986.

Goldratt, Eliyahu M. *Essays on the Theory of Constraints.* Great Barrington, MA: North River Press, 1990.

Pinedo, Michael. *Planning and Scheduling in Manufacturing and Services.* New York: Springer-Verlag, 2009.

CASE DISNEY FASTPASS

Disney operates theme parks throughout the world, and in each park it wants to ensure that its guests have a magical experience. Waiting in line for the attractions is surely not part of the memory that Disney wants guests to keep. Disney could avoid lines by letting fewer people into the park, but it would either lose revenue (not good) or have to charge more (which risks ill will). So lines are a fact of life and the question then turns to how to better manage them.

In the old days, Disney would have guests queue up in first-come-first-served order for each attraction. The most popular attractions could have lines that lasted more than an hour during busy times of the year. To make lines more enjoyable, or at least less irritating, Disney tried to provide some entertainment while guests waited, such as showing Disney programs on televisions. But there is only so much you can do to distract a four-year-old child who is cranky because he or she is not actually inside the Pirates of the Caribbean.

But why do the guests actually have to stand in the line? That insight led to the development of Disney's Fastpass system in 1999. With the Fastpass system, a guest doesn't physically enter the line for an attraction but, rather, receives a reservation for an interval of time to enter the attraction later on, say 1.5 hours later. If the guest returns at that time, he or she can enter a short line dedicated to Fastpass users that puts the guest on the attraction within a few minutes. More recent versions of this idea, such as Fastpass+, allow users to reserve their arrival window as much as 60 days in advance.

© Ilene MacDonald/Alamy/RF

The actual implementation of Fastpass requires Disney to make some important and complicated decisions. For example, say an "experience" (i.e., ride, attraction, or show) can serve 20 guests per minute, which is 1200 guests per hour. Guests can arrive at the experience and wait in a first-come-first-served queue. Alternatively, some guests are given a Fastpass arrival time window. For example, a family might hold an arrival time of 10:10 a.m. to 11:10 a.m. for the Pirates of the Caribbean. If they indeed arrive during that interval, they wait in the Fastpass queue, which gives them priority for entering the experience—they might still need to wait a bit, but they would wait only if a bunch of other Fastpass-using guests arrive at nearly the same time during that window.

1. Keeping the number of guests in the park constant, by adding Fastpass, does the average number of guests served per attraction change? For which types of attractions does it change the most (e.g., the busiest or the least busy ones)?

2. Disney needs to decide how many Fastpass tickets to issue for each time window. What are some of the trade-offs associated with this decision? For example, what are good and bad issues about increasing the number of tickets available?

3. Is Fastpass fair?

4. Should Disney charge for Fastpass?

Project Management

Introduction

Processes are all about repetition—we don't perform an operation once; we perform it over and over again. This process management view fits many, if not most, operations problems well. Mining and production plants, back offices of insurance companies or banks, hospitals, or call centers are all about repetition and many flow units journey through the corresponding processes on a daily basis.

There are, however, a number of operations for which the repetition-based approach of process management is less appropriate. Consider, for example, a major construction project, the development of a new product, or the planning of a wedding party. In these

UAV offered by Boeing (http://en.wikipedia.org/wiki/Dragonfly_(UAV))

© Tech. Sgt. Sabrina Johnson/ U.S. Air Force

situations, your primary concern is about planning the completion of one flow unit and, typically, you would like to see this completion happen sooner rather than later.

Whether you care about the completion of one or many flow units often depends on which role you play in an operation. While most of us think about one wedding (at a time) and thus should think of a wedding event as a project, a wedding planner organizes numerous weddings and thus should think of weddings as flow units in a process. Similarly, a developer working on the launch of a new product or the construction worker building a new office complex is likely to think about his or her work as a **project**, while many echelons up in the organization, the vice president of product development or the owner of a real estate development company thinks about these projects as flow units in a big process.

We define a project as a temporary (and thus nonrepetitive) operation. Projects have a limited time frame, one or more specific objectives, and a temporary organizational structure, and thus often are operated in a more ad-hoc, improvised management style.

Consider the following example of a project—the development of an unmanned aerial vehicle (UAV). UAVs are aircraft that are flown without a human being on board. They either are controlled remotely or have built-in navigation intelligence to determine their direction. Most of their applications lie in the military space, but UAVs can also be used for scientific exploration or search-and-rescue operations.

In this chapter, we use the example of the development of a UAV to illustrate several tools and techniques of project management. In particular, we look at the decision situation of a developer that has just completed a prototype UAV and now is putting together a more detailed proposal for commercial development.[1]

The team that puts together the proposal needs to complete a number of activities. Time is critical. Yet, unlike in the case of process management, concepts such as "capacity" and "bottleneck" appear less relevant. For this team, the question of how many UAV proposals can be processed per month (capacity) is less of an issue compared to the question of how this one specific proposal can be completed as quickly as possible.

In this chapter, you will learn the basics of project management, including:

- How to map out the various activities that need to be completed as part of the project in the form of an activity network.
- How to determine the completion time of the project and how to create a project plan showing the timing of all activities of the project.
- How to accelerate the project to achieve an earlier completion time.
- How to manage the objectives and the organization of the project.

> **Project** A temporary (and thus nonrepetitive) operation. Projects have a limited time frame, one or more specific objectives, and a temporary organizational structure, and thus often are operated in a more ad-hoc, improvised management style.

[1]The description of the UAV case is based on a case study by Kavadias, Loch, and DeMeyer. We are grateful to the authors for allowing us to use this example. See the reference for further details.

19.1 Creating a Dependency Matrix for the Project

Table 19.1 lists the activities that need to be done to complete the proposal for the UAV. Note that this entirely captures the work required for the proposal, not the actual development itself. We see that, in total, 10 activities are required, and activities range in activity times from 3 days to 21 days. We define the **activity time** of an activity as the amount of time it takes a resource to complete the activity once it has started to work on it. The concept of an activity time is the same as the processing time in a process analysis.

A quick (and rather naïve) view of Table 19.1 suggests that the total time to complete the proposal will be $9 + 3 + 11 + 7 + 8 + 6 + 21 + 10 + 15 + 5 = 95$ days. That is simply the

> **Activity time** The amount of time it takes a resource to complete the activity once it has started to work on it. The concept of an activity time is the same as the processing time in a process analysis.

TABLE 19.1   Activities for the UAV Proposal Development

Activity	Description	Activity Times (days)
A_1	Prepare preliminary functional and operability requirements and create preliminary design configuration	9
A_2	Prepare and discuss surface models	3
A_3	Perform aerodynamics analysis and evaluation	11
A_4	Create initial structural geometry and prepare notes for finite element structural simulation	7
A_5	Develop structural design conditions	8
A_6	Perform weights and inertia analyses	6
A_7	Perform structure and compatibility analyses and evaluation	21
A_8	Develop balanced freebody diagrams and external applied loads	10
A_9	Establish internal load distributions and evaluate structural strength stiffness: preliminary manufacturing planning and analysis	15
A_{10}	Prepare proposal	5

Precedence relationship The dependency of activities on each other.

Dependency matrix In the dependency matrix, each column represents an activity that provides information and each row indicates an activity that receives information. An entry in column *i* and row *j* suggests that the activity in the *i*th column (A_i) provides information to the activity in the *j*th row (A_j).

Predecessor activity A_i is the predecessor activity of A_j if A_i needs to be completed before starting A_j.

Sequentially dependent A form of dependence in which a successor depends on a predecessor.

Successor activity A_j is the successor activity of A_i if A_j needs to be completed before starting A_i.

Independent Two events are independent (i.e., their correlation is 0) when the outcome of one event has no relationship to the outcome of the other event.

Interdependent A form of dependence in which two activities require input from each other.

Coordination Information exchange among activities.

sum of all activity times. Alternatively, one might (equally naïvely) claim the proposal development should take 21 days, the longest activity time of the 10 activities.

Both of these views omit an important aspect of the nature of project management. Some, but not all, of the activities are dependent on each other. For example, activity A_3 (aerodynamics analysis) requires the completion of activity A_2 (prepare and discuss surface models). Such dependencies are also referred to as **precedence relationships**. They can be summarized in a **dependency matrix**, as shown in Table 19.2. In the dependency matrix, each column represents an activity that provides information and each row indicates an activity that receives information. An entry in column i and row j suggests that the activity in the *i*th column (A_i) provides information to the activity in the *j*th row (A_j).

We also say that A_i is the **predecessor activity** of A_j or that A_j is **sequentially dependent** of A_i. Sequentially dependent activities require information or physical outputs from the predecessor activities. The activities that are on the receiving side of such **precedence relationships** are also called the **successor activities**. The dependency matrix implicitly suggests a sequencing of the activities and thus dictates the flow of the project. The project will start with activity A_1 because it does not have any predecessor activities. It will end with activity A_{10}. Similar to process flow terminology, people often refer to a predecessor activity as "upstream" and the successor activity as "downstream." If there exists no predecessor relationship between two activities, we say the two activities are **independent** of each other.

Table 19.2 has a very remarkable pattern. All dependencies are below the diagonal line. This means that there exists some sequence of activities as we move through the project, starting with the first activity and ending with the last. Every time that we start a new activity, we can be comfortable that all predecessor activities have been completed. In this case, we say that there exists a linear flow through the project.

This does not always have to be the case. Consider a project with two activities, A_1 and A_2, in which A_1 depends on A_2 and A_2 depends on A_1. The dependency matrix for this case would look like what is shown in Table 19.3. For example, we can think of the development of a video game title. A game designer and a programmer are both involved in the work. The game designer crafts the characters for the game (e.g., the soccer players in FIFA or the cars in Need for Speed). The programmer implements these ideas by coding the properties of these characters. In this work, the game designer needs to see what the programmer does. Yet, the programmer needs to get the input from the game designer to know what to program.

In cases like this, we say the two activities are **interdependent**. When executing a project with interdependent activities, we have to carefully **coordinate** the activities. Such coordination can take two forms:

TABLE 19.2 Dependency Matrix for the UAV

UAV dependency matrix		Predecessor activity (upstream)									
		A_1	A_2	A_3	A_4	A_5	A_6	A_7	A_8	A_9	A_{10}
Successor activity (downstream)	A_1	■									
	A_2	x	■								
	A_3		x	■							
	A_4		x		■						
	A_5				x	■					
	A_6				x		■				
	A_7			x			x	■			
	A_8			x		x	x		■		
	A_9								x	■	
	A_{10}							x		x	■

TABLE 19.3 Dependency Matrix for a Video Game

Video game dependency matrix		Predecessor activity	
		A_1	A_2
Successor activity	A_1	■	x
	A_2	x	■

- **Static coordination**: Oftentimes, the coordination between two interdependent activities can be accomplished by just getting the team members in charge of the interdependent activities together and engaging them in a dialogue. Instead of one team member completing her activity and then just "throwing it over the wall" to the other team member, static coordination is an attempt to understand the objectives and constraints of other activities when executing your own activity. For example, in the design of a new house, the architect of the house should consult with the builder in charge of the construction. This way, the architect knows about what it will cost to build the house and if there exist any specific challenges in the construction process. Engaging the builder early is thus a form of static coordination.

- **Dynamic coordination**: Sometimes, however, the interdependence is so strong that it cannot be addressed by static coordination alone. It simply is not possible for one activity to already provide all information to the other activity without actually engaging in some work. As a result, it is necessary for the projects to iterate between the two interdependent activities. An **iteration** means that we go forth and back from one activity to the other. The two activities are carried out simultaneously, with both activities providing information to each other. In product development projects, this practice is often referred to as **concurrent engineering**. Instead of designers designing a car and then worrying about production later on, designers and production engineers work together in cross-functional teams.

For now, we focus on projects that have a dependency matrix that can be arranged so that all dependencies are to the lower left of the diagonal (see Figure 19.1).

Static coordination The consultation with team members who are in charge of project activities that happen further downstream in the project.

Dynamic coordination Iterative execution of interdependent activities where both activities provide input to each other.

Concurrent engineering The (partially) simultaneous execution of multiple development activities with a strong emphasis on coordination.

Figure 19.1

Possible relationships between activities

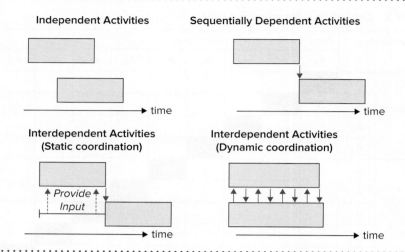

Independent Activities

Sequentially Dependent Activities

Interdependent Activities (Static coordination)

Interdependent Activities (Dynamic coordination)

Check Your Understanding 19.1

Question: Consider the following two projects. Project 1 is the construction of a tree house. Activity 1 looks for sites and seeks permission to use the one (or multiple) trees the tree house will be based on. Activity 2 chooses a tree house design from a catalog of tree houses, with designs varying depending on the number of trees used to support the house.

Project 2 is the production of a movie based on an existing novel. Activity 1 casts the actors. Activity 2 shoots the actual video footage.

Create a dependency matrix for both projects.

Answer: Consider the tree house first. To find the right site, we need to know what type of tree house we would like to build, a design that uses a single tree or a design that uses multiple trees. To choose the right design, we need to know the site. The two activities are interdependent and one should probably iterate between the two.

The movie, in contrast, is more of a dependence with the casting preceding the video footage. We clearly cannot shoot the video footage without the cast. However, in the process of casting, we really don't need much input from the production crew.

The two dependency matrices are shown in Table 19.4.

TABLE 19.4   Dependency Matrices for the Tree House and Movie Production

Tree house dependency matrix		Predecessor activity	
		A_1	A_2
Successor activity	A_1	■	x
	A_2	x	■

Movie production dependency matrix		Predecessor activity	
		A_1	A_2
Successor activity	A_1	■	
	A_2	x	■

19.2 The Activity Network

The dependency matrix is a very concise way of documenting the relationships among activities. But it is also hard to grasp and so it would be helpful to visualize the same information in a way that is easier to understand. We now introduce a way to use a graph to visualize dependencies. In general, we define a **graph** as a collection of objects or nodes that are connected by links. Figure 19.2 shows an example of a graph. Note that this is a different type of graph compared to what you might have seen in an algebra course.

There exist multiple approaches to use graphs as ways to represent dependencies in project management. In the **activity-on-node (AON) graph**, nodes correspond to project activities and arrows correspond to precedence relationships (with an arrow going from the predecessor activity to the successor activity). In this chapter, we focus on AON graphs because they are similar to the process flow diagrams we discussed in other chapters of this book. To sound less academic, we will also refer to the AON graph as an **activity network**.

To create an AON graph of a project, we start with the activity that requires no input; that is, the activity without any predecessor activity. In our case of the UAV, that is activity A_1. Next, we seek to find all activities that are successors of this first activity. We ask ourselves the question, "Now that A_1 is complete, what activities could start?" In the UAV project, this would identify activity A_2.

We then work our way through the dependency matrix mimicking the evolution of the project:

1. We create a node in the form of a box for the activity, including its name as well as its expected activity time.
2. After creating the node for the activity, we consider the activity as done. Thus, all information provided by the activity to its successor activities is now available. We can draw a line through the corresponding column, and draw an arrow out of the activity for each dependency (for each "X").
3. Next, we look for any other activity in the dependency matrix that has all its predecessor activities completed and go back to step 1.
4. We continue steps 1–3 until we have worked ourselves to the last activity.

If we repeatedly execute these three steps, we obtain the graph shown in Figure 19.3. This graph provides a practical and visual way to illustrate the evolution of the project. It resembles the process flow diagram used in process management.

Note the linear flow visible in Figure 19.3. We start with activity 1. There exist multiple paths through the graph, but no matter what path we take, as long as we only follow the arrows, we end up at activity 10. There are no loops in the graph, which reflects our earlier observation of sequential dependencies and the dependency matrix only having entries below

Graph A collection of objects or nodes that are connected by links.

Activity-on-node (AON) graph A graph capturing the project activities and its dependencies in which nodes correspond to project activities and arrows correspond to precedence relationships (with an arrow going from the predecessor activity to the successor activity). Also called activity network.

Activity network A graph capturing the project activities and its dependencies in which nodes correspond to project activities and arrows correspond to precedence relationships (with an arrow going from the predecessor activity to the successor activity). Also called an activity-on-node (AON) graph.

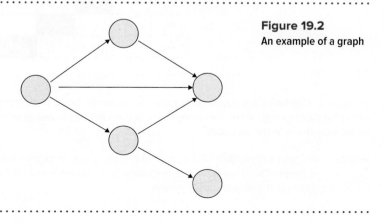

Figure 19.2
An example of a graph

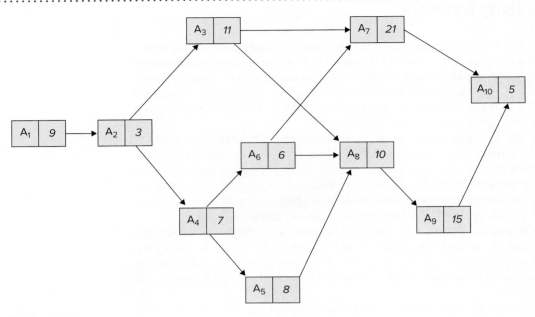

Figure 19.3

Activity-on-node (AON) graph of the UAV project. Left part of the box is the activity name; right part is the activity time

the diagonal. If we had had interdependencies (recall the example of the video game development), our graph for the activity network would contain loops. These loops would correspond to the previously discussed iterations. Again, in our UAV project, we do not need to iterate, though we briefly discuss iterative projects toward the end of this chapter.

Check Your Understanding 19.2

TABLE 19.5   Dependency Matrix for project X

Project X		Predecessor activity (upstream)			
		A_1	A_2	A_3	A_4
Successor activity (downstream)	A_1	■			
	A_2	x	■		
	A_3	x		■	
	A_4		x	x	■

Question: **Consider the dependency matrix shown in Table 19.5. Build an activity network using an AON graph. Note: Because there are no activity times provided, you do not need to include them in the network.**

Answer: We start with activity A_1 because it has no predecessor activity. This will be the first node in our graph. Once we have put the node for A_1 down in our AON graph, we cross off the first column in the dependency matrix.

(continued)

Now, we see that activities A_2 and A_3 have no predecessor activity left (their corresponding rows, now that the first column is deleted, are empty). So, we show A_2 and A_3 as successor activities to A_1. We can also cross out the columns for A_2 and A_3.

Finally, we see that A_4, now that the first three columns have been crossed out, has no predecessor activity left. We put A_4 down in the AON graph and draw links from A_2 to A_4 and from A_3 to A_4, capturing the dependencies in the last row of the dependency matrix, as shown in Figure 19.4.

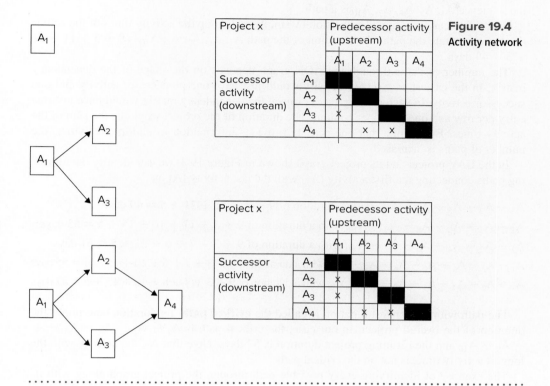

Figure 19.4

Activity network

Project x		Predecessor activity (upstream)			
		A_1	A_2	A_3	A_4
Successor activity (downstream)	A_1	■			
	A_2	x	■		
	A_3	x		■	
	A_4			x	x	■

Project x		Predecessor activity (upstream)			
		A_1	A_2	A_3	A_4
Successor activity (downstream)	A_1	■			
	A_2	x	■		
	A_3	x		■	
	A_4			x	x	■

19.3 The Critical Path Method

Despite the similarity between the process flow diagram and the AON graph, we should remember the fundamental difference between process management and project management. In process management, we directed our attention to the resource that had the lowest capacity, the bottleneck. If each activity in the process flow diagram was staffed by one worker (or machine), the bottleneck was the activity with the longest processing time.

What matters for the completion time of the project, however, are not the individual activity times but the completion time of the last activity. This completion time requires ALL activities to be completed. In fact, we will see that in the UAV project, the activity with the longest activity time (A_7) will not constrain the duration of the overall project.

So, how long will the project in Figure 19.3 take to complete? This turns out to be a tricky question. It is intuitive that the project can be carried out in less than $9 + 3 + 11 + 7 + 8 + 6 + 21 + 10 + 15 + 5 = 95$ days (the sum of the activity times). Some activities can be carried out in parallel and so the 10 activities do not create a 10-person relay race. On the other hand, the degree to which we can execute the activities in parallel is limited by the dependency matrix. For example, activity A_3 requires the completion of activity A_2, which, in turn, requires the completion of activity A_1. Things get even more convoluted as we consider activity A_7. For it to be complete, A_3 and A_6 have to be complete. A_3, in turn, requires completion of A_2 and A_1, while A_6 requires completion of A_4, which, once again, requires completion of A_2 and A_1. What a mess . . .

To correctly compute the completion time of the project, a more structured approach is needed. This approach is based on considering all possible paths through the network in Figure 19.3. A **path** is a sequence of nodes (activities) and (directional) arrows. For example, the sequence A_1, A_2, A_3, A_7, A_{10} is a path.

Every path can be assigned a duration by simply adding up the activity times of the activities that constitute the path. The duration of the path A_1, A_2, A_3, A_7, A_{10} is $9 + 3 + 11 + 21 + 5 = 49$ days.

The number of paths through the AON graph depends on the shape of the dependency matrix. In the easiest case, every activity would just have one predecessor activity and one successor activity. In such a (relay race) project, the dependency matrix would have just one entry per row and one entry per column. The duration of the project would be the sum of the activity times. Every time that one activity provides information to multiple activities, the number of paths is increased.

In the UAV project and its project graph shown in Figure 19.3, we can identify the following paths connecting the first activity (A_1) with the last activity (A_{10}):

$A_1 - A_2 - A_3 - A_7 - A_{10}$, with a duration of $9 + 3 + 11 + 21 + 5 = 49$ days

$A_1 - A_2 - A_3 - A_8 - A_9 - A_{10}$, with a duration of $9 + 3 + 11 + 10 + 15 + 5 = 53$ days

$A_1 - A_2 - A_4 - A_6 - A_7 - A_{10}$, with a duration of $9 + 3 + 7 + 6 + 21 + 5 = 51$ days

$A_1 - A_2 - A_4 - A_6 - A_8 - A_9 - A_{10}$, with a duration of $9 + 3 + 7 + 6 + 10 + 15 + 5 = 55$ days

$A_1 - A_2 - A_4 - A_5 - A_8 - A_9 - A_{10}$, with a duration of $9 + 3 + 7 + 8 + 10 + 15 + 5 = 57$ days

The path with the longest duration is called the **critical path**. Its duration determines the duration of the overall project. In our case, the critical path is $A_1 - A_2 - A_4 - A_5 - A_8 - A_9 - A_{10}$ and the resulting project duration is 57 days. Note that A_7, the activity with the longest activity time, is not on the critical path.

The exercise of identifying every possible path through the project graph along with its duration is a rather tedious one. The more activities and the more dependency relationships we have, the greater the number of paths we have to evaluate before we find the one we truly care about, the critical path.

Fortunately, there is a simpler way to compute the project duration. The idea behind this simpler way is to compute the earliest possible start time for each activity. For each activity, we can find the **earliest start time (EST)** by looking at the earliest time all predecessor activities have been completed. The earliest start time of the first activity is time zero. The **earliest completion time (ECT)** of an activity is the earliest start time plus the activity time. We then work our way through the activity network, activity by activity, starting from the first activity and going all the way to the last.

More formally, we can define the following method to compute the ECT of the project. The approach is similar to our method of coming up with the AON graph:

1. Start with the activity that has no information-providing activity and label that activity as the start. The earliest start time of that activity is defined as 0. The earliest completion time is the activity time of this activity.

2. Identify all activities that can be initiated at this point (i.e., have all information-providing activities complete). For a given such activity i, compute the earliest start time as $EST(A_i) = Max\{ECT(A_j)\}$ where A_j are all activities providing input to A_i

3. Compute the earliest completion time of A_i as $ECT(A_i) = EST(A_i) + $ Activity time(A_i)

4. Consider activity i as completed and identify any further activities that now can be initiated. Go back to step 2.

Path A sequence of nodes (activities) and (directional) arrows.

Critical path The path with the longest duration.

Earliest start time (EST) The earliest time an activity can begin, which is given by the earliest time all predecessor activities have been completed.

Earliest completion time (ECT) The earliest time an activity can be completed, which is given by the earliest time all predecessor activities have been completed plus the activity time.

TABLE 19.6 Computing the Completion Time of a Project; Table Is Created Row by Row, Starting with the First Activity

Activity	Earliest Start Time (EST)	Activity Time (days)	Earliest Completion Time (ECT)
A_1	0	9	9
A_2	$ECT(A_1) = 9$	3	12
A_3	$ECT(A_2) = 12$	11	23
A_4	$ECT(A_2) = 12$	7	19
A_5	$ECT(A_4) = 19$	8	27
A_6	$ECT(A_4) = 19$	6	25
A_7	$Max\{ECT(A_3),ECT(A_6)\} = Max\{23,25\} = 25$	21	46
A_8	$Max\{ECT(A_3),ECT(A_5),ECT(A_6)\}$ $= Max\{23,27,25\} = 27$	10	37
A_9	$ECT(A_8) = 37$	15	52
A_{10}	$ECT(A_9) = Max\{ECT(A_7),ECT(A_9)\}$ $= Max\{46,52\} = 52$	5	57

This method applied to the UAV is illustrated in Table 19.6. The table is created from the top to the bottom, one activity at a time. As you construct a given row i, you have to ask yourself, "What activities provide information to i? What activities does i depend on?" You can see this by reading row i in the dependency matrix or you can see this in the activity network.

Check Your Understanding 19.3

Question: Consider again the project with four activities. The activity network is shown in Figure 19.5.

Activity A_1 takes three weeks, A_2 takes five weeks, A_3 takes four weeks, and A_4 takes one week. Compute the earliest completion time of the project.

Answer: We start the project with A_1, because it has no predecessor activity. A_1 will take three weeks, so the ECT for A_1 is 3. Once A_1 is complete, we can start on A_2 and A_3. Both of them thus have an EST of 3. A_2 takes five weeks and hence has an ECT of 8. A_3 only takes four weeks and thus has an ECT of 7.

In order to start A_4, we must have A_2 and A_3 complete. This can happen in week 8 (8 is the maximum between the ECT for A_2 and the ECT of A_3). If we start A_4 in week 8, we are done in week 9. The corresponding calculations are shown in Table 19.7.

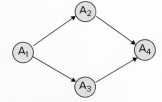

Figure 19.5

TABLE 19.7 Computing the Completion Time of a Project

Activity	Earliest Start Time (EST)	Expected Activity Time (weeks)	Earliest Completion Time (ECT)
A_1	0	3	3
A_2	$ECT(A_1) = 3$	5	8
A_3	$ECT(A_1) = 3$	4	7
A_4	$Max\{ECT(A_2),ECT(A_3)\} = Max\{8,7\} = 8$	1	9

19.4 Slack Time

It lies in the nature of the critical path that any delay in activities on the critical path will immediately cause a delay in the overall project. For example, a one-day delay in activity A_9 will automatically delay the overall project by one day. However, this is not true for activities that are not part of the critical path. We can delay activity A_7 even by several days (six to be exact) without impacting the overall completion of the project. In other words, activity A_7 has some built-in "wiggle room." The technical term for this wiggle room is **slack time**. It is the amount of time an activity can be delayed without affecting the overall completion time of the project.

The slack time of an activity is determined based on an additional set of calculations known as the **late start schedule**. So far, we have computed the earliest start time (EST) and earliest completion time (ECT) of each activity by going through the project from beginning to end. We now compute the **latest start time (LST)** and **latest completion time (LCT)** for each activity such that the project still completes on time. We do this by beginning with the last activity and working our way backward through the project until we reach the beginning. Thus, we start with the last activity (A_{10}) and end with the first activity (A_1).

So, let's start with the last activity. Assuming we want to complete the project as early as possible, we define the latest completion time, LCT, of the last activity as being the same as its earliest completion time, ECT:

$$\text{LCT(Last activity)} = \text{ECT(Last activity)}$$
$$\text{LCT}(A_{10}) = \text{ECT}(A_{10}) = 57$$

There exist some cases in which an early completion is not desired; for instance, there may be a **target date** for when the project should be complete. In this case, we can define the LCT of the last activity as the target date.

The latest start time of the last activity is simply the latest completion time minus the activity time of the last activity:

$$\text{LST(Last activity)} = \text{LCT(Last activity)} - \text{Activity time(Last activity)}$$
$$\text{LST}(A_{10}) = \text{LCT}(A_{10}) - 5 = 57 - 5 = 52$$

So, the latest A_{10} can start without delaying the overall project is on day 52. Note that this is also the same day as the earliest the activity can start (see our computations earlier), so there is really no wiggle room for this activity.

More generally, we define the LCT for any activity A_i as the smallest (earliest) LST of all activities that succeed the activity:

$$\text{LCT}(A_i) = \text{Min}\{\text{LST}(A_j) \text{ for which } A_j \text{ is a successor of } A_i\}$$

and we define the LST as the LCT minus the activity time:

$$\text{LST}(A_i) = \text{LCT}(A_i) - \text{Activity time}(A_i)$$

Let's try this definition out on the other activities. Consider activity A_9 next. A_9 only has A_{10} as a successor activity. Thus, we can define

$$\text{LCT}(A_9) = \text{Min}\{\text{LST}(A_j) \text{ for which } A_j \text{ is a successor of } A_9\} = \text{Min}\{\text{LST}(A_{10})\} = 52$$

And we compute the latest start time of A_9 as

$$\text{LST}(A_9) = \text{LCT}(A_9) - \text{Activity time}(A_9) = 52 - 15 = 37$$

Next, we tackle activity A_8. A_8 only has A_9 as a successor activity. Thus, we can define

$$\text{LCT}(A_8) = \text{Min}\{\text{LST}(A_j) \text{ for which } A_j \text{ is a successor of } A_8\} = \text{Min}\{\text{LST}(A_9)\} = \text{LST}(A_9) = 37$$

Slack time The amount of time an activity can be delayed without affecting the overall completion time of the project.

Late start schedule The latest possible timing of all activities that still allows for an on-time completion of the overall project.

Latest start time (LST) The latest possible start time of an activity that still allows for an on-time completion of the overall project.

Latest completion time (LCT) The latest possible completion time of an activity that still allows for an on-time completion of the overall project.

and we compute the latest start time for A_8 as

$$LST(A_8) = LCT(A_8) - \text{Activity time}(A_8) = 37 - 10 = 27$$

You may start noticing the pattern. If an activity only has one successor, this is easy. We just take the latest start time for that succeeding activity. Activity A_7 also only has one successor (namely, A_{10}) and so we calculate

$$LCT(A_7) = LST(A_{10}) = 52$$
$$LST(A_7) = LCT(A_7) - \text{Activity time}(A_7) = 52 - 21 = 31$$

Note the difference between the earliest start time of A_7, which we previously computed to be 25, and the latest start time of A_7, which we just found to be 31. In other words, we can delay the start of A_7 by six days without impacting the overall completion time of the project.

Based on this observation, we define the slack of an activity as

$$\text{Slack time} = \text{Latest start time} - \text{Earliest start time}$$

which is equivalent to

$$\text{Slack time} = \text{Latest completion time} - \text{Earliest completion time}$$

Okay, on we go to activity A_6. A_6, for a change, is a little trickier because it has two succeeding activities, namely A_7 and A_8. So, this time we get

$$\begin{aligned}
LCT(A_6) &= \text{Min}\{LST(A_j) \text{ for which } A_j \text{ is a successor of } A_6\} \\
&= \text{Min}\{LST(A_7), LST(A_8)\} \\
&= \text{Min}\{31, 27\} = 27
\end{aligned}$$

In the same way, we can compute the other information of the late schedule. This information is shown in Table 19.8. Note that the columns LST and LCT are computed by going backward through the project graph. We start with the rows at the bottom of the table and work our way up. Note that the slack time of all activities on the critical path is zero.

TABLE 19.8 Computation of Slack Time

Activity	EST	Activity Time	ECT	LCT	LST = LCT − Activity Time	Slack = LST − EST = LCT − ECT
A_1	0	9	9	$LST(A_2) = 9$	$9 - 9 = 0$	0
A_2	9	3	12	Min$\{LST(A_3),LST(A_4)\}$ = Min$\{16,12\}$ = 12	$12 - 3 = 9$	0
A_3	12	11	23	Min$\{LST(A_7),LST(A_8)\}$ = Min$\{31,27\}$ = 27	$27 - 11 = 16$	$27 - 23 = 4$
A_4	12	7	19	Min$\{LST(A_5),LST(A_6)\}$ = Min$\{19,21\}$ = 19	$19 - 7 = 12$	0
A_5	19	8	27	$LST(A_8) = 27$	$27 - 8 = 19$	0
A_6	19	6	25	Min$\{LST(A_7),LST(A_8)\}$ = Min$\{31,27\}$ = 27	$27 - 6 = 21$	$27 - 25 = 2$
A_7	25	21	46	$LST(A_{10}) = 52$	$52 - 21 = 31$	$52 - 46 = 6$
A_8	27	10	37	$LST(A_9) = 37$	$37 - 10 = 27$	0
A_9	37	15	52	$LST(A_{10}) = 52$	$52 - 15 = 37$	0
A_{10}	52	5	57	57	$57 - 5 = 52$	0

What is the benefit of knowing how much slack time is associated with an activity? The main benefit from knowing the slack time information is as follows:

- *Potentially delay the start of the activity:* To the extent that we can delay the start of an activity without delaying the overall project, we might prefer a later start over an earlier start. Starting an activity is often associated with spending some money (hiring somebody, renting equipment). All else being equal, we prefer to pay other people later rather than sooner.

- *Accommodate the availability of resources:* Internal or external resources might not always be available when we need them. Slack time provides us with a way to adjust our schedule without compromising the completion time of the overall project.

- *Insights and understanding about the project dynamics:* Knowing which activities have little slack will help us direct our attention when the project is executed.

Figure 19.6 summarizes the steps to plan the time line of a project and identify the critical path as well as the slack times of the activities. Based on this information, we can augment the initial project graph and present all information we computed for each activity in a graphical format, similar to what is shown in Figure 19.4. This graph is the output of many commercial software packages dealing with project management, as well as a set of consulting tools.

Figure 19.6

Augmented project graph. The top row includes the earliest start time, the activity time, and the earliest completion time. The middle row is the activity name. The bottom row is the latest start time, the slack, and the latest completion time.

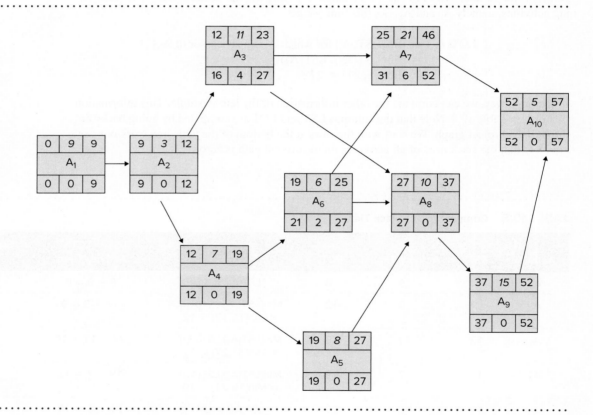

Check Your Understanding 19.4

Question: Consider again the project with four activities for which we previously found the activity network and the earliest completion times, as well as the latest completion times. What are the slack times for the four activities?

(continued)

Answer: To find the slack times, we start with the last activity A_4. For the last activity, we set the latest completion time equal to the earliest completion time. So the LCT for A_4 is 9. We find the latest start time using the equation

$$LST(A_i) = LCT(A_i) - \text{Activity time}(A_i) = 9 - 1 = 8$$

Next, we look at activities A_2 and A_3. Note that both of them only have one successor activity (namely A_4) and so we get

$$LCT(A_2) = \text{Min}\{LST(A_j) \text{ for which } A_j \text{ is a successor of } A_2\} = \text{Min}\{LST(A_4)\} = 8$$

$$LCT(A_3) = \text{Min}\{LST(A_j) \text{ for which } A_j \text{ is a successor of } A_3\} = \text{Min}\{LST(A_4)\} = 8$$

Because the activity time of A_3 is 4 weeks, we get

$$LST(A_3) = LCT(A_3) - 4 = 8 - 4 = 4$$

Similarly, for A_2 with an activity time of 5 weeks, we get

$$LST(A_2) = LCT(A_2) - 5 = 8 - 5 = 3$$

Things get interesting for activity A_1, because this activity has two successor activities, A_2 and A_3. So, we write

$$LCT(A_1) = \text{Min}\{LST(A_j) \text{ for which } A_j \text{ is a successor of } A_1\} = \text{Min}\{LST(A_2), LST(A_3)\} = \text{Min}\{3, 4\} = 3$$

and compute the latest start time for A_1, which has an activity time of 3, as

$$LST(A_1) = LCT(A_1) - 3 = 3 - 3 = 0$$

These calculations are shown in Table 19.9. Once we have all the values for the LCTs, we can compute the slack time as

$$\text{Slack} = LCT - ECT$$

We see that only activity A_3 has some slack in it.

TABLE 19.9 Computation of Slack Time

Activity	EST	Activity Time	ECT	LCT	LST = LCT − Activity Time	Slack = LCT − ECT
A_1	0	3	3	Min$\{LST(A_2),LST(A_3)\}$ = Min$\{3,4\}$ = 3	$3 - 3 = 0$	0
A_2	3	5	8	8	$8 - 5 = 3$	0
A_3	3	4	7	8	$8 - 4 = 4$	$8 - 7 = 1$
A_4	8	1	9	9	$9 - 1 = 8$	0

19.5 The Gantt Chart

When working on a project, you want some form of a time line that depicts what activities are going on at each moment in time. For the case of our UAV project, such a timeline based on the earliest start times and earliest completion times is shown in Figure 19.7. The **Gantt chart** is basically a time line with the activities included as horizontal bars. Gantt diagrams are named after the 19th-century industrialist **Henry Gantt**.

Gantt chart A time line with the activities included as bars.

Henry Gantt A 19th-century industrialist.

Figure 19.7
Gantt chart for the UAV project

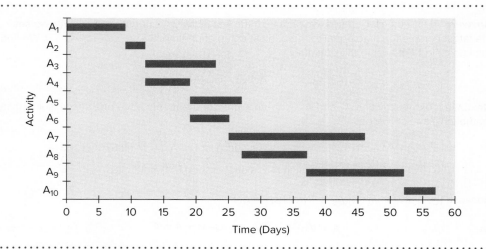

Gantt charts are probably the most commonly used visualization for project time lines. Note that unlike the AON graph, the Gantt chart itself does not capture the dependencies of the activities. Based on the previously explained computations of the earliest start and completion times, we have already ensured that activities only get initiated when all required information is available.

It is possible to provide additional information to what is shown in Figure 19.7. For example, it is common to include the following:

- *The critical path:* We can simply choose a different color to highlight the critical path in the project.

- *Important dependencies:* Unlike in the activity network, the Gantt chart does not have to include the dependencies among the activities. However, we can nevertheless

Check Your Understanding 19.5

Question: Consider the project with four activities discussed earlier. The earliest start times for the four activities are 0, 3, 3, and 8, respectively, and the earliest completion times are 3, 8, 7, and 9. Draw a Gantt chart based on this information.

Answer: The Gantt chart is shown in Figure 19.8. Note that it also includes the slack time we previously computed for activity A_3.

Figure 19.8
A Gantt chart for the project

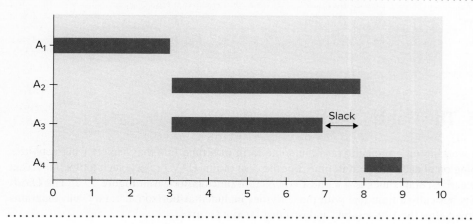

include them by drawing an arrow from the end of an activity to the beginning of its successor activity

- *Slack time:* We can extend the bars capturing the activity times in a different color to capture potential slack time.

Gantt charts are typically created using software packages such as Microsoft Project. Note that all of the computations we have made so far in this chapter assume that there exists no uncertainty in the activity times.

Exhibit 19.1 provides a summary of the steps required for using the critical path method.

EXHIBIT 19.1

Summary of Calculations for a Critical Path Analysis

Step 1: Identify all activities that constitute the project.

Step 2: Determine the dependencies among the activities by creating either a dependency matrix or the project graph. Make sure no circularity exists in the dependencies (i.e., the dependency matrix only has entries to the lower left of the diagonal and the project graph does not contain any loops).

Step 3: Compute the earliest start time (EST) and the earliest completion time (ECT) by working forward through the project graph (from start to end).

$$EST(A_i) = Max\{ECT(A_j)\} \text{ where } A_j \text{ are all activities providing input to } A_i$$

$$ECT(A_i) = EST(A_i) + Activity\ time(A_i)$$

Step 4: Compute the latest start time (LST) and the latest completion time (LCT) by working backward through the project graph (from end to start).

$$LCT(A_i) = Min\{LST(A_j) \text{ where } A_j \text{ are all activities receiving input from } A_i\}$$

$$LST(A_i) = LCT(A_i) - Activity\ time(A_i)$$

Step 5: Compute the slack of an activity as

$$Slack(A_i) = LCT(A_i) - ECT(A_i)$$

Step 6: Create the critical path by highlighting all activities with zero slack.

Step 7: Create a Gantt chart outlining a schedule for the project.

19.6 Uncertainty in Activity Times and Iteration

Given our definition of projects as a temporary operation that is dealing with nonroutine work, projects often face a significant amount of uncertainty at their outset. Incorporating this uncertainty into the project plan is thus a central concern of project management.

19.6.1 Random Activity Times

So far, we have behaved as if all activity times in the project were deterministic; that is, one would be able to accurately predict the duration of an activity on the first day of the project. However, it lies in the nature of many project activities that their duration can vary considerably from the initial prediction, typically not in the desired direction (i.e., it takes longer than expected). In such cases, we are dealing with **random activity times**.

To illustrate the concept of random activity times, Figure 19.9 shows the activity times for a sample of cardiac surgeries in the operating room of a large hospital. We observe that there exists a considerable amount of procedure variation. Moreover, we observe that the distribution is not symmetric: Activity times that are more than double the mean time can happen—the distribution has a "long tail."

Random activity time The fact that the time of an activity is not known with certainty but subject to some statistical variation.

Figure 19.9

Figure 19.9

Procedure times in the OR for open heart surgery (data taken from Olivares, Terwiesch, and Cassorla)

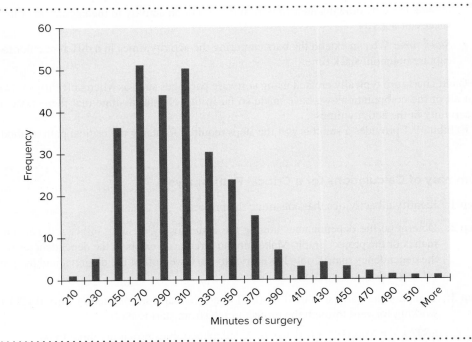

When facing uncertainty in the form of random activity times, it is important to understand that such uncertainty is a bad thing. The reason for this is that it will, on average, lead to a later completion time of the project. It is a misconception that uncertainties in activity times will cancel each other out, or, in other terms, the randomness will average itself out over a large number of activities. However, as the following example shows, variation in activity time will not average itself out. When some activities are completed early and others are completed late, the project will be delayed.

To see this, consider the simple activity network displayed in Figure 19.10. On the left side of the figure, we have a project with deterministic activity times. Given the activity times of five days for A_1, four days for A_2, and six days for A_3, as well as the dependency structure shown by the activity network, the critical path of this project is $A_1 - A_3$ and the earliest completion time is 11 days.

Now, consider the activity times on the right side of the figure. A_1 now has a completion time of three days with a 50 percent probability and seven days with a 50 percent probability, while A_2 has a completion time of two days with a 50 percent probability and six days with a 50 percent probability. Note that in expectation (on average) the completion times of A_1 and A_2 have not changed. A_1, on average, will still take five days and A_2 will take, on average, four days. But the expected completion time of the project will change.

How is it possible that the activity times will stay, on average, the same, but the completion time will get longer? To see this, consider the calculations displayed in Table 19.10. The table shows four scenarios, each scenario being a combination of the outcome of the time for A_1 (early versus late; 50:50 probability) and the outcome of the time for A_2 (early versus late; again, 50:50 probability).

Figure 19.10

A simple example of a project with uncertainty in the activity time

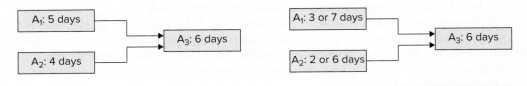

TABLE 19.10 Example Calculations for a Small Project with Three Activities (based on Figure 19.10)

Scenario	Probability	Explanation	Start of A_3	Completion
A_1 late and A_2 late	0.25	A_1 would take 7 days (during which time the 6 days of A_2 will also be completed)	7	13
A_1 early, A_2 late	0.25	A_2 would take 6 days (during which time the 3 days of A_1 would also be completed)	6	12
A_1 late, A_2 early	0.25	A_1 would take 7 days (during which time the 2 days of A_2 would also be completed)	7	13
A_1 early and A_2 early	0.25	A_1 would take 3 days (during which time the 2 days of A_2 would also be completed)	3	9

The worst-case scenario is that both A_1 and A_2 run late. In this case, A_1 will take six days and A_2 will take seven days, so that A_3 can be initiated after seven days, leading to a completion time of 13 days. Things cannot get any slower than this worst case. Notice, however, the scenarios in which one activity is done early and the other activity is late. In that case, the completion time of the project barely is any faster than in the worst-case scenario. Only in the very best case, if both A_1 and A_2 are completed early, do we see a significant reduction in the project completion time.

Because each of the four scenarios is equally likely, each one occurs with a probability of $0.5 \times 0.5 = 0.25$. With this, we can compute the expected completion time as

$$(0.25 \times 13 \text{ days}) + (0.25 \times 12 \text{ days}) + (0.25 \times 13 \text{ days}) + (0.25 \times 9 \text{ days}) = 11.75 \text{ days}$$

almost one day (0.75 day, to be exact) longer than in the case with the same average activity times but no randomness. When we get lucky and one activity is completed early, we don't benefit because chances are that the other activity is running late (it really takes a 1:4 chance that both activities are completed early to get lucky and be done early). But if we get unlucky and one activity (or both) runs late, we get a later project completion time. Thus, we are not just exposed to the risk of the project running later than in the deterministic case, but we will be running later on average.

Note, that even this disappointing outcome still relies on a rather optimistic assumption. It assumes that in the case that both activities are completed early, A_3 has the flexibility of starting earlier than planned. If we cannot benefit from the early completion of activities, the overall penalty we incur from uncertainty would be even higher.

The reason for the project taking longer than we initially predicted based on simply taking the average activity times is that the critical path of the project can potentially **shift**:

- In the case without randomness (Figure 19.10, left), the critical path was $A_1 - A_3$. The time of A_2 did not matter.

- However, this is different with random activity times (Figure 19.10, right). If the time of A_1 turns out to be three days and the time for A_2 is six days, the critical path is $A_2 - A_3$. Otherwise, it is $A_1 - A_3$.

In a world with random activity times, correctly estimating the time of the activity is a challenge. Estimates of activity times are often inflated, especially when working with internal resources: Because nobody on the team wants to be blamed for potential schedule overruns, it is common to quote excessively long estimates of activity times (the estimates are "**padded**"). This is especially common if there exist no threats of substitution for a resource, as is common with resources internal to the organization (e.g., the IT department). Resources

Shifted critical path A change in the activities making up the critical path triggered by some unexpectedly long activity time on a noncritical path activity.

Padded activity time Forecasted activity time that is longer than the actual amount of time required.

simply declare that it takes 10 days to complete the activity, even if their true forecast for the completion is five days. After all, what would be the incentive for the resource to commit to an aggressive schedule? Once the project gets on its way, the schedule looks very tight. However, if one truly observes the execution of the project, most activities make little progress and the corresponding resources are either idle or working on other projects, even if they are associated with the critical path. Obtaining honest (unbiased) activity times is thus essential.

At other times, estimates of activity times can be underestimated, especially when working with external resources: If contractors for a project are asked to submit a time estimate, they have a substantial incentive to underestimate the project completion time because this increases their likelihood of being selected for the project. Once on the job, however, they know they cannot be easily kicked off the project should their activity run late.

19.6.2 Iteration and Rework

The previously introduced dependency matrix had an important property: All dependencies were on the lower left of the diagonal. In other words, there existed a one-way path from the beginning of the project to the end.

In practice, however, when project activities are interdependent, oftentimes iterations are required. In fact, the previously discussed UAV project commonly (in about 3 out of 10 cases) iterates between activities A_4 and A_9. Such iterations are typical for product development and innovation projects where problem solving can be a more organic, iterative process. It is often referred to as **rework**.

In general, such rework loops are more likely to happen in high uncertainty environments. In environments with lower degrees of uncertainty, interdependence can be addressed based on static coordination—the expertise and input from one activity guides the execution of the other activity. In contrast, static coordination is harder to achieve in rapidly changing environments and so iteration is oftentimes needed. For example, a development team for an Internet platform might want to adjust its business plan after having launched a beta prototype, creating a rework loop. In contrast, we hope that the architect in charge of a major construction project does not want to revisit her drawings after the first tenants have moved into the building. Consequently, project planning tools such as Gantt charts and the critical path method are more valuable for low-uncertainty projects and can provide a false sense of planning accuracy when applied in high-uncertainty environments.

Several tools exist for modeling and analyzing projects with iteration. We restrict ourselves to the main insight from this line of research. The presence of iteration loops typically dominates the effect of uncertain activity time. In other words, when faced with the potential of some activities taking longer than expected and an unexpected iteration requiring reworking one or multiple previously completed activities, a project manager should focus on the threat of the iteration because it has a stronger effect on the overall completion time.

19.6.3 Unknown Unknowns (Unk-unks)

When Christopher Columbus set out to find a new way to sail to India, he (most likely) did not set up a project plan. Even for modern-day explorers, be it in sailing or in business, there exist situations where the amount of uncertainty we face is simply too large to make any careful planning process meaningful. In such settings, we face so much uncertainty that we don't even know what we don't know. We face unknown unknowns, also referred to as **unk-unks**.

It lies in the nature of many high-uncertainty projects that they will not be completed. In that sense, a timely abandonment often is the goal because it avoids an escalation in costs. Often, a useful exercise is simply to list all variables in the project that are currently not known and look for activities that would help resolve these unknowns. At any moment in time, the project manager should then attempt to spend as little as possible to learn enough to decide whether or not to move forward with the project. This technique, also referred to as **discovery-driven planning**, will help resolve some uncertainties and potentially identify new ones.

Rework The repetition of activities or an extra set of activities that have to be completed by a defective flow unit in order to be restored to a good flow unit.

Unk-unks Unknown unknowns, which describes uncertainties in a project that the project management is not yet aware of.

Discovery-driven planning An approach to project management that emphasizes iteration and dynamic adjustment.

COLUMBUS EXPLAINING HIS DISCOVERY OF AMERICA TO KING FERDINAND AND QUEEN ISABELLA.—Drawn by John Gilbert.—[See next Page.]

Courtesy of John Gilbert (1817–1897)/Library of Congress, Prints and Photographs Division (LC-USZ62-3035)

Check Your Understanding 19.6

Question: A construction project needs to complete three activities before the construction can begin. Activity A_1 takes 8 weeks, activity A_2 takes 9 weeks, and activity A_3 takes 10 weeks. However, the activity times are somewhat uncertain—sometimes they happen up to four weeks faster, while at other times they take four weeks longer. The project manager suggests starting A_1 two weeks late because the activity is not on the critical path, and so this delay will not impact the project completion time. What is your reaction to this suggestion?

Answer: Because the activity times vary substantially, A_1 can very well end up on the critical path. In the extreme case, A_1 runs four weeks over (it takes 12 weeks), and A_2 and A_3 are completed four weeks early (they take 5 and 6 weeks, respectively). With this in mind, one would need very strong reasons to delay A_1.

© Paul Bradbury/OJO Images/ Getty Images/RF

19.7 Project Management Objectives

So far, our emphasis has primarily been on the objective of completing the project on time. However, that should not be the only objective of the project. Project managers typically pursue a combination of two additional objectives:

- *Project cost:* Just as a project needs to plan how it spends its time, it needs to plan how it spends its money. The **project budget** outlines the main expenses associated with the project. In most cases, these expenses are related to the resources required to carry out the activities that constitute the project. This mostly relates to personnel expenses to pay for the staff but could also include expenses for any needed equipment, travel expenses, rents, or other costs. The project budget is a simple list of these expenses, which are added up to create the total budget.

- *Project scope:* The **project scope** determines what must be accomplished in order for the project to be complete. This could be the completion of a building or the completion of a product development project. Beyond simply completing the project, of course, we want to complete the project well. So the project scope should state a set of quality specifications that the project needs to achieve. For example, in a product development project, the scope should include the features of the new product, as well as the costs of making the product.

Typically, the objectives of project completion time, project budget, and project scope are in conflict with another. Consider the development of the UAV discussed earlier. Most likely, more time would allow the developers to put together an even more convincing proposal. Similarly, if the budget is not a constraint, it might be possible to outsource at least some work, which, if it shortens the duration of a critical path activity, would lead to an earlier project completion time.

This conflict between these three objectives is sometimes referred to as the **project management triangle** (see Figure 19.11). Every project manager should carefully track a project's progress on these three dimensions, and so the project management triangle is a useful framework to be aware of.

However, the project management triangle is also misleading. When a project falls behind schedule, the project management triangle (and our intuition) suggests to simply add more manpower (which sacrifices some budget) to get it back on time. Unfortunately, that rarely works in practice. In a famous study of software development projects, **Fred Brooks** of IBM observed that adding manpower to a late software project makes it later. The reason for this, Brooks argues, is that projects simply cannot perfectly be subdivided into smaller and smaller activities. Further, as you increase the number of people working on a project, you dramatically increase the need for communication. Between two people, there is only one possible communication path. Between three people, there are already three paths; we are up to six paths among four people and 10 paths among five.

Another reason why the trade-off between project time and project budget can be a misperception relates to the project cost structure. As mentioned earlier, project personnel tend to be one of the biggest expenses in a project budget. But what happens to these expenses if the project goes on longer? Exactly! You have to pay for these resources longer. So, longer

Project budget Outline of the main expenses associated with the project.

Project scope Description of what must be accomplished in order for the project to be complete.

Project management triangle The tension between the three objectives of a project: time, budget, and scope.

Figure 19.11
The project management triangle

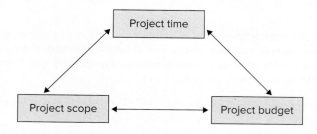

project completion time is often correlated with significant schedule overruns, as the following examples help illustrate:

- *Berlin airport:* Since becoming the new German capital, the city of Berlin has been planning a new airport (Hauptstadtflughafen, which stands for the airport of the capital; only Germans can come up with such lovely long names). Initial cost estimates were just above $1.5 billion with an opening date of 2012. Subsequently, the opening has been delayed to 2013, 2014, and then all the way to 2017. What happened to costs? The 2017 launch date came with a cost projection of well over $10 billion.

- *Boeing 787:* Staying with the theme of air travel, consider the development of the Boeing 787. Because of numerous technical glitches, the project ended up being three years behind schedule and causing an increase in development costs of multiple billions of U.S. dollars. In the defense of Boeing, we observe that their rival, EADS, maker of the Airbus, experienced similar cost and budget overruns in their development of the Airbus 380.

19.8 Reducing a Project's Completion Time

Beyond trading off completion time with either scope or budget, we can also try to "break the trade-off" and just be smarter about how we manage the project. The following provides a set of inexpensive actions a project manager can take to accelerate the completion time of the project without necessarily sacrificing the quality of the accomplished work or the project budget:

- *Start the project early:* The last day before the project due date is typically a day of stress and busyness. In contrast, the first day of the project is typically characterized by little action. This effect is similar to the "term paper syndrome" well familiar to most students. It reflects human optimism and overconfidence in the ability to complete work in the future. At the risk of stating the obvious—a day at the beginning of the project is equally as long as a day at the end of the project—so why do little or no work on the former and jam all the work into the latter?

- *Manage the project scope:* One of the most common causes of delay in projects is that the amount of work that is part of the project changes over the course of the project. Features are added and engineering change orders requested. If such changes occur late in the project, they often cause significant project delays and budget overruns for relatively little increased quality. For this reason, it is advisable to finalize the scope of the project early on.

- *Crash activities:* Often, an increase in spending allows for a faster completion time of a project. Contractors are willing to work overtime for a premium, and expensive equipment might help further shorten activity time. As we discussed earlier, however, the concept of **crashing** is a difficult one because spending more money is not a guarantee of making things move faster.

- *Overlap critical path activities:* A central assumption underlying the dependency matrix discussed earlier has been that an activity that is dependent on an information-providing activity needs to wait until that activity is completed. However, it is often possible to allow the dependent activity to start early—to **overlap dependent activities**—relying on preliminary information from the information-providing activity. For example, it seems plausible that the activity "Building design" should be completed before starting the activity "Building construction." However, does this imply that all of the design has to be completed? Or, maybe, it would be possible to begin digging the foundation of the building while the designers are still finalizing the shape of the windows? By identifying the exact dependencies between activities, it is often possible to provide the dependent activity with a head start.

Crashing An increase in spending that allows for a faster completion time of a project.

Overlapping dependent activities The simultaneous execution of dependent activities to facilitate information exchange and shorten project completion time.

All of these actions only work if applied to the critical path. Crashing an activity off the critical path or trying to overlap non–critical path activities will not reduce the project completion time.

19.9 Organizing a Project

Imagine you are put in charge of managing a project. This might be a small project at college such as the preparation of an event (planning a graduation party, getting your team ready for a major athletic competition) or it might be a bigger project in your professional life, such as the opening of a new store or developing a new product or service. Either way, you are in charge and you now have to decide what to do. As the project manager in charge of the project, we want you to think about three pieces of work that you will have to tackle: defining the project, planning the project, and controlling the project, as encapsulated in Table 19.11.

Defining the project includes defining and negotiating the three variables making up the project triangle: project time, project budget, and project scope. You then should think about the activities that are necessary to accomplish the project scope. You take the scope and break it up into pieces of work. This is often referred to as the **work breakdown structure**. The scope defines WHAT the project needs to accomplish, and the work breakdown structure defines HOW these accomplishments will be achieved. Finally, you need to understand what resources you have at your disposition. Who will help you to get the job done? And will these folks spend five hours on this project every other week or is this project the main part of their job? Finally, we find it helpful to document a set of assumptions about the project, including how much time the resources will be available, technical feasibilities, and environmental conditions such as weather, the competitive landscape, or macroeconomic variables.

Planning the project starts once you have defined the project—it is time to think about the execution of the work. This is when you apply the tools outlined at the beginning of the chapter: You create a dependency matrix, draw the activity network, find the critical path, and ultimately create the Gantt chart. For each activity you need to identify a person who is in charge of the activity (which might be you) and confirm that the Gantt chart is feasible (the resources needed are available at the time).

While the first two pieces of work happen before the project gets underway, the important work of a project manager happens during the actual execution of the project. We refer to this as **controlling the project**. As the project unfolds, your job is to track its progress. This includes carefully tracking the Gantt chart to see that all activities take place as planned. This also includes managing the interdependencies among the project activities. For example, in the case of static coordination of interdependent activities, it is critical to involve the activity owners of both activities early on so that one activity can provide early input to the other instead of simply completing its work and then "throwing its output over the wall" to the other activity.

A common pattern during project execution is that everything looks fine on the surface until halfway through the project, sometimes even later. Then, bad news accumulates rapidly. To avoid this, it is important to define a set of milestones that provide a realistic picture of the progress of the project. At these milestones, the project should be carefully reviewed and the progress should be carefully evaluated relative to scope, budget, and time. This includes the following:

- Revisiting the assumptions of the project and evaluating whether something fundamental has changed. For example, the project might be facing delays because of bad weather or a competitor has entered the market, requiring us to change course. Other

Defining the project Defining and negotiating the three variables making up the project triangle: project time, project budget, and project scope.

Work breakdown structure The translation of the project scope into specific activities.

Planning the project Preparation of the execution of the project.

Controlling the project Tracking the progress of the project as it unfolds.

TABLE 19.11 **Project Management Responsibilities**

Define the Project	Plan the Project	Control the Project
• Project triangle • Project scope • Work breakdown structure defining the activities • Project resources • Planning assumptions	• Dependency matrix • Activity network • Critical path • Gantt chart • Activity owners	• Ensure early communication for dependent activities • Define milestones • Hold regular reviews

things might have come up (unk-unks) and the longer a project continues, the less likely it is that the project environment at the completion of the project is the same as it was at the outset.

- Tracking the project scope is important because projects have a tendency to try to accomplish more than what was initially agreed on.

- Putting together a task list of all unresolved issues and assigning a team member to be responsible for resolving this issue. Can you imagine that the previously mentioned delay in the opening of Berlin's airport was a result of 66,500 unresolved issues, of which over 5,000 were deemed critical to opening (including fire safety and elevator functionality)?

A common point of contention in the planning of projects, as well as during the controlling of the project, relates to the availability of time from team members. We define a **dedicated project team** as a project team in which the team members spend 100 percent of their work time on the project. The benefit of the dedicated team is that team members are not distracted by their regular work. Dedicating team members to a project tends to also reduce coordination needs. You get the same hours out of two full-time employees that you get out of four half-time employees, but the communication requirements are drastically lower.

But such dedication to the work of the project is not always possible. As we defined previously, a project is a temporary operation. Especially in corporate settings, this temporary organization is embedded in a larger organization. And these organizations tend to have organizational structures and hierarchies. The **organizational chart** (also known as **org chart**) of the organization is a visual representation of the reporting relationships in the organization. To use a military term, the org chart shows the chain of command, with the general at the top of the org chart and the foot soldier at the bottom.

What is special about project management organization is that the organizational chart might not neatly map out the organizational hierarchy that the project is embedded in. Oftentimes, projects bring together members of a diverse set of organizational functions to form a cross-functional team; for example, to develop a new product, to open a new factory, or to manage the acquisition of another business. So it is common that members of a project team report to their "regular" boss (based on their usual position in the org chart) and to the project manager. Such multiple reporting lines create what is called a **matrix organization**.

Figure 19.12 shows a simplified org chart for a large automotive company. The company has various functions, such as manufacturing, sales, development, finance, human resources, and so on.

Each function has a senior executive in charge (say the Vice President of Marketing). The project team consists of a project manager and some dedicated staff who report to the project

Dedicated project team A project team in which the team members spend 100 percent of their work time on the project.

Organizational chart (org chart) A visual graph of the reporting relationships in the organization. Shows the chain of command, with the general at the top of the org chart and the foot soldier at the bottom.

Matrix organization An organization with multiple lines of reporting relationships.

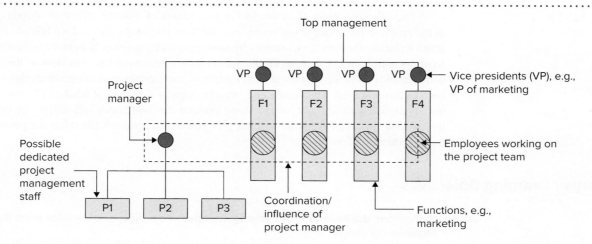

Figure 19.12 Simplified org chart for a large automotive company

manager. However, most of the employees working on the project team report to their corresponding vice president. You can imagine the type of conflicts that arise in the matrix organization:

- *Conflicts related to scope:* Who on the automotive development project will have the final say on the sales and marketing plan? The project manager or the Vice President of Marketing?

- *Conflicts related to resources:* The project might be at a critical juncture in its execution, but the Vice President of Engineering needs to take five engineers off the project to support another project in the company. Who on the project can decide what the team members work on?

Heavyweight project manager A project manager who has a strong influence on the scope and the resources of the project.

Increasingly, companies have moved toward providing the project manager with more authority. In cases in which the project manager has a strong influence on the scope and the resources of the project, we speak of a **heavyweight project manager**.

Conclusion

Managing a project is different from managing a process. Instead of doing things over and over again, and thereby having plenty of opportunities to take corrective actions in the case of problems, projects are a one-shot deal. Instead of monitoring the ongoing flow of the process as we do with process analysis, in project management we define a project, we plan it, and we control it. But then it is done.

This distinction between project management and process management is helpful because it reminds us to use different tools in our analysis. At the heart of process management is the concept of the bottleneck. In contrast, at the heart of project management is the concept of the critical path.

Though this distinction between project management and process management is academically concise, the lines between these two can sometimes be a bit blurry in practice. Consider the following examples:

- Opening a new restaurant will certainly benefit from the project management tools outlined in this chapter. For the one in charge of that opening, this corresponds to managing a project. However, large restaurant chains have 1000s of outlets. From the perspective of McDonald's, opening up new stores is a process. They have the capacity to open multiple outlets in a week. So whether work is a project or a process really depends on the perspective.

- Project management principles even apply in highly repetitive operations. Let's stay with the theme of restaurants. In our introduction to processes chapter (Chapter 2), we defined the flow time of a customer as the amount of time the customer spends in the process. We talked about increasing the flow rate (capacity) and we talked about reducing the flow time, mostly by managing waiting times (Chapter 16: Service Systems with Patient Customers). But we can also think about the flow time as the completion time of a project. For each customer, there exists a set of activities that need to be computed. The dependency matrix helps us think about what can be carried out in parallel. This will not increase the flow rate (the bottleneck still will be the bottleneck and working in parallel will not give you more capacity), but it has the potential to reduce the flow time.

Summary of Learning Objectives

LO19-1 Understand the dependencies among activities in a project and visualize them in a dependency matrix

To complete a project, a set of activities needs to be completed. Typically, not all of these activities can be started at once, because some activities have to be completed before other activities can start. This creates a dependency among activities. The dependency matrix captures these relationships between activities.

LO19-2 Translate a dependency matrix into an activity network

The activity network is a graph in which the nodes correspond to the activities of the project and the links correspond to the precedence relationship among activities. Such a network can be created directly based on the dependency matrix by starting with the graph with the activity that has no predecessors. Next, one looks for the activities that only have this one activity as a predecessor and includes these in the graph. This way, step by step, the graph is created mimicking the sequence in which the activities will later be carried out in the project.

LO19-3 Determine the earliest project completion time with the critical path method

An activity can only start once all predecessor activities are completed. By working through the activity network, one activity at a time, for each activity, we can look at the earliest possible starting time and (by adding the activity time) at the earliest possible completion time. The earliest completion time of the last activity determines the earliest completion time of the entire project. The critical path is then found as the longest path through the activity network.

LO19-4 Compute the slack time in the critical path method

In addition to looking for the earliest start time for each activity, we can also look for the latest start time that still allows for an on-time completion of the overall project. The difference between the earliest start time and the latest start time determines the slack time. It tells us how much "wiggle room" we have in the execution of the activity without delaying the overall project.

LO19-5 Create a Gantt chart for a project

Once we know the earliest start and earliest completion times for each project, we can visualize this information in a time line. We draw a line showing the time over which the project is carried out. Each activity corresponds to a bar, with the beginning of the bar being the earliest start time and the end of the bar being the earliest completion time.

LO19-6 Understand the impact of uncertain activity time and iteration on the critical path and on project completion time

Projects are oftentimes facing some level of uncertainty. Thus, the activity times are subject to some statistical fluctuation and cannot be predicted exactly. Such variation in activity time can lead to a shift in the critical path and delay the actual and the expected completion times of the project.

LO19-7 Understand the key objectives of a project

Project managers typically face three objectives: the timing of the project, its budget, and its scope. Oftentimes, trade-offs among these dimensions are required.

LO19-8 Know the ways in which a project can be accelerated

Projects can be accelerated in a number of ways, including an early/on-time start, a careful management of the project scope, the crashing of activities, and an overlapping of sequentially dependent activities.

LO19-9 Understand the various responsibilities of a project manager in organizing a project

Projects are typically temporal and thus often occur embedded in a bigger organizational context. In a dedicated project team, team members are working on the project 100 percent of their time. However, projects typically involve people who are working on the project only part time. This can lead to multiple lines of authority in the organization, as can be seen in a matrix organization. Heavyweight project managers are project managers who have direct authority over budgets, scopes, and time lines instead of simply acting as coordinators.

Key Terms

19.1 Creating a Dependency Matrix for the Project

Activity time The amount of time it takes a resource to complete the activity once it has started to work on it. The concept of an activity time is the same as the processing time in a process analysis.

Precedence relationship The dependency of activities on each other.

Dependency matrix In the dependency matrix, each column represents an activity that provides information and each row indicates an activity that receives information. An entry in column i and row j suggests that the activity in the ith column (A_i) provides information to the activity in the jth row (A_j).

Predecessor activity A_i is the predecessor activity of A_j if A_i needs to be completed before starting A_j.

Sequentially dependent A form of dependence in which a successor depends on a predecessor.

Successor activity A_i is the successor activity of A_j if A_j needs to be completed before starting A_i.

Independent Two events are independent (i.e., their correlation is 0) when the outcome of one event has no relationship to the outcome of the other event.

Interdependent A form of dependence in which two activities require input from each other.

Coordination Information exchange among activities.

Static coordination The consultation with team members who are in charge of project activities that happen further downstream in the project.

Dynamic coordination Iterative execution of interdependent activities where both activities provide input to each other.

Concurrent engineering The (partially) simultaneous execution of multiple development activities with a strong emphasis on coordination.

19.2 The Activity Network

Graph A collection of objects or nodes that are connected by links.

Activity-on-node (AON) graph A graph capturing the project activities and its dependencies in which nodes correspond to project activities and arrows correspond to precedence relationships (with an arrow going from the predecessor activity to the successor activity). Also called activity network.

Activity network A graph capturing the project activities and its dependencies in which nodes correspond to project activities and arrows correspond to precedence relationships (with an arrow going from the predecessor activity to the successor activity). Also called an activity-on-node (AON) graph.

19.3 The Critical Path Method

Path A sequence of nodes (activities) and (directional) arrows.

Critical path The path with the longest duration.

Earliest start time (EST) The earliest time an activity can begin, which is given by the earliest time all predecessor activities have been completed.

Earliest completion time (ECT) The earliest time an activity can be completed, which is given by the earliest time all predecessor activities have been completed plus the activity time.

19.4 Slack Time

Slack time The amount of time an activity can be delayed without affecting the overall completion time of the project.

Late start schedule The latest possible timing of all activities that still allows for an on-time completion of the overall project.

Latest start time (LST) The latest possible start time of an activity that still allows for an on-time completion of the overall project.

Latest completion time (LCT) The latest possible completion time of an activity that still allows for an on-time completion of the overall project.

19.5 The Gantt Chart

Gantt chart A time line with the activities included as bars.

Henry Gantt A 19th-century industrialist.

19.6 Uncertainty in Activity Times and Iteration

Random activity time The fact that the time of an activity is not known with certainty but subject to some statistical variation.

Shifted critical path A change in the activities making up the critical path triggered by some unexpectedly long activity time on a non–critical path activity.

Padded activity time Forecasted activity time that is longer than the actual amount of time required.

Rework The repetition of activities or an extra set of activities that have to be completed by a defective flow unit in order to be restored to a good flow unit.

Unk-unks Unknown unknowns, which describes uncertainties in a project that the project management is not yet aware of.

Discovery-driven planning An approach to project management that emphasizes iteration and dynamic adjustment.

19.7 Project Management Objectives

Project budget Outline of the main expenses associated with the project.

Project scope Description of what must be accomplished in order for the project to be complete.

Project management triangle The tension between the three objectives of a project: time, budget, and scope.

19.8 Reducing a Project's Completion Time

Crashing An increase in spending that allows for a faster completion time of a project.

Overlapping dependent activities The simultaneous execution of dependent activities to facilitate information exchange and shorten project completion time.

19.9 Organizing a Project

Defining the project Defining and negotiating the three variables making up the project triangle: project time, project budget, and project scope.

Work breakdown structure The translation of the project scope into specific activities.

Planning the project Preparation of the execution of the project.

Controlling the project Tracking the progress of the project as it unfolds.

Dedicated project team A project team in which the team members spend 100 percent of their work time on the project.

Organizational chart (org chart) A visual graph of the reporting relationships in the organization. Shows the chain of command, with the general at the top of the org chart and the foot soldier at the bottom.

Matrix organization An organization with multiple lines of reporting relationships.

Heavyweight project manager A project manager who has a strong influence on the scope and the resources of the project.

Key Formulas

LO19-3 Determine the earliest project completion time with the critical path method

$EST(A_i) = Max\{ECT(A_j)\}$ where A_j are all activities providing input to A_i

$ECT(A_i) = EST(A_i) + Activity\ time(A_i)$

LO19-4 Compute the slack time in the critical path method

$LCT(A_i) = Min\{LST(A_j)$ for which A_j is a successor of $A_i\}$

$LST(A_i) = LCT(A_i) - Activity\ time(A_i)$

$Slack\ time(A_i) = LST(A_i) - EST(A_i) = LCT(A_i) - ECT(A_i)$

Conceptual Questions

1. A project has four activities that take 4, 3, 6, and 7 days, respectively. What is the total completion time for the project?
   a. 3 days, because this is the minimum time
   b. 7 days, because this is the maximum time
   c. 20 days, because this is the sum of the times
   d. It is not possible to determine the total completion time from the given information.

2. Consider the simple dependency matrix shown in Table 19.12.

TABLE 19.12   Simple Dependency Matrix

Simple dependency matrix		Predecessor activity	
		A_1	A_2
Successor activity	A_1	■	
	A_2	x	■

Which of the following statements is correct?
   a. The two activities are independent of each other and the project can carry out both of them immediately.
   b. A_1 is a predecessor activity to A_2.
   c. A_2 is a predecessor activity to A_1.
   d. None of these statements is correct.

3. Consider a project with two activities that are interdependent. Which of the following statements is correct?
   a. Both activities can be carried out in parallel without coordination.
   b. Static coordination of the two activities implies that the two activities are carried out in an iterative manner.
   c. Dynamic coordination of the two activities implies that the two activities are carried out in an iterative manner.
   d. None of these statements is correct.

4. Which of the following statements is correct with respect to an AON graph of a project?
   a. In an AON graph, the activities are on the edges of a graph.
   b. In an AON graph, the activities are on the nodes of a graph.
   c. AON stands for the American Operations Norm.
   d. None of these statements is correct.

5. In an AON graph of a project, there only exists one path from the first to the last activity. True or false?
   a. True
   b. False

6. The critical path in a project is the sequence of activities that:
   a. has the shortest time.
   b. has the smallest number of activities.
   c. has the shortest budget.
   d. None of these statements is correct.

7. What is the relationship between the earliest start time (EST) of an activity and the earliest completion time (ECT) of the activity?
   a. EST + Activity time = ECT
   b. EST × Activity time = ECT

   c. EST = ECT

   d. None of these statements is correct.

LO19-4

8. Which of the following statements is correct with respect to slack time?

   a. The slack time of an activity is the latest completion time of the activity minus the earliest completion time.

   b. The slack time of an activity is the latest start time of the activity minus the earliest start time.

   c. The slack time of an activity determines how long an activity can be delayed without impacting the overall completion of the project.

   d. All of these statements are correct.

9. What is the late start schedule for a project?

   a. It is the latest start and the latest completion times of the project activities so that the overall project is still completed on time.

   b. It is a schedule that measures the amount of time an ongoing project is late.

   c. It is an accelerated schedule in order to get a project with a late start still completed on time.

   d. None of these statements is correct.

LO19-5

10. Which of the following statements is correct with respect to a Gantt chart?

   a. The x-axis of a Gantt chart shows a time line.

   b. The y-axis shows the activities of a project.

   c. The Gantt chart itself does not show all dependencies among activities.

   d. The Gantt chart is named after 19th-century industrialist Henry Gantt.

   e. All of these statements are correct.

LO19-6

11. Consider two projects that have the same activities and the same dependencies. In the first project, the activity times are expected outcomes. The actual times will vary. In the second project, the activity times are always as expected. Assuming the expected activity times are identical across the two projects, which project will be completed first?

   a. The first

   b. The second

   c. Cannot be determined

12. A project manager is concerned about rework, specifically about having to iterate on two activities that are on the critical path. A consultant tells the project manager not to worry, because the effect of uncertain activity times is likely to dominate the effect of iteration. The project manager disagrees. Who is right?

   a. The project manager

   b. The consultant

LO19-7

13. They key objectives of a project can be summarized in the form of a:

   a. line.

   b. triangle.

   c. square.

   d. hexagon.

14. The key objectives of a project are given by:

   a. time, scope, and budget.

   b. cost, quality, and location.

   c. customers, suppliers, and employees.

   d. efficiency, effectiveness, and success.

LO19-8

15. What is the effect of overlapping activities that are not on the critical path?

   a. An earlier project completion time

   b. A later project completion time

   c. No effect

LO19-9

16. Which of the following descriptions best captures the project manager's responsibilities?
    a. Define the project, plan the project, control the project.
    b. List all activities, determine the critical path, compute slack time.
    c. Raise money, determine a budget, and keep costs under control.
    d. None of these descriptions is correct.

Solved Example Problems

LO19-1

1. Consider the following project. A team of students contemplates launching a new venture instead of doing a summer internship. With the help of their college, they have reached out to a successful entrepreneur who encourages the team to come up with an idea and explain that idea in the form of a storyboard.

   To get to the storyboard, the following eight activities are required. The students first list 20 business opportunities in which they have an interest (A_1, 4 days). Once they have completed this, they should pick their favorite idea based on the feedback of the entrepreneur and his friends (A_2, 2 days). Upon completion of A_2, they should then:

   - Conduct detailed observations of 10 potential customers (A_3, 10 days).
   - Run focus groups with 20 customers (A_4, 4 days).
   - Look at 10 products sold related to that opportunity (A_5, 2 days).

   When A_3 and A_4 are complete, the team can start A_6, the preparation of a detailed user-needs analysis (3 days). Following the completion of A_5 and A_6, the team can spend 5 days brainstorming various solution concepts that meet the customer needs (A_7). And then, finally, they can create the storyboard (A_8, 2 days).

   How many dependencies will there be in the dependency matrix?

   Answer: 9.

   The dependency matrix looks as shown in Figure 19.13.

TABLE 19.13   Dependency matrix for a new venture

Student venture		Predecessor							
		A_1	A_2	A_3	A_4	A_5	A_6	A_7	A_8
Successor	A_1	■							
	A_2	x	■						
	A_3		x	■					
	A_4		x		■				
	A_5		x			■			
	A_6			x	x		■		
	A_7					x	x	■	
	A_8							x	■

LO19-2

2. Consider the dependency matrix shown in Figure 19.13. Build an activity network using an AON graph.

   Answer: We start with activity A_1 because it has no predecessor activity. This will be the first node in our graph. Once we have put the node for A_1 down in our AON graph, we cross off the first column in the dependency matrix.

   Now, we see that activity A_2 no longer has a predecessor activity (its corresponding row, now that the first column is deleted, is empty). So, we show A_2 as the successor activity to A_1. We can also cross out the column for A_2.

Next, note that activities A_3, A_4, and A_5 are ready to go. So, we show A_3, A_4, and A_5 as successor activities to A_2. We can also cross out the columns for A_3, A_4, and A_5.

We continue this process until we get the activity network shown in Figure 19.14.

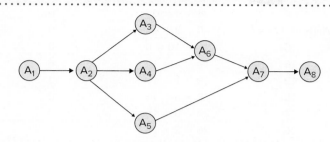

Figure 19.14

Activity-on-node graph for student project

LO19-3

3. Consider again the project with the activity network shown in Figure 19.14.

   Activity A_1 takes 4 days; A_2, 2 days; A_3, 10 days; A_4, 4 days; A_5, 2 days; A_6, 3 days; A_7, 5 days; and A_8, 2 days. Compute the earliest completion time of the project.

   Answer: 26 days.

   We start the project with A_1 because it has no predecessor activity. A_1 will take 4 days, so the ECT for A_1 is 4. Once A_1 is complete, we can start on A_2. A_2 thus has an EST of 4. A_2 takes 2 days and hence has an ECT of 6.

   Following the completion of A_2, we can initiate A_3, A_4, and A_5. These activities thus can all have an EST of 6. We continue this process as shown in Table 19.13 and find that the earliest completion time is 26 days.

TABLE 19.13 Computing the Earliest Completion Time of a Project

Activity	Earliest Start Time (EST)	Expected Time (days)	Earliest Completion Time (ECT)
A_1	0	4	4
A_2	ECT(A_1) = 4	2	4 + 2 = 6
A_3	ECT(A_2) = 6	10	6 + 10 = 16
A_4	ECT(A_2) = 6	4	6 + 4 = 10
A_5	ECT(A_2) = 6	2	6 + 2 = 8
A_6	Max{16,10} = 16	3	16 + 3 = 19
A_7	Max{8,19} = 19	5	19 + 5 = 24
A_8	ECT(A_7) = 24	2	24 + 2 = 26

LO19-4

4. Consider again the project with eight activities, for which we previously found the activity network and the earliest completion times, as well as the latest completion times. What is the largest slack time of the eight activities? Consider again the project with eight activities, for which we previously found the activity network and the earliest completion times, as well as the latest completion times. What is the largest slack time of the eight activities?

   Answer: 11 days.

   To find the slack times, we start with the last activity, A_8. For the last activity, we set the latest completion time equal to the earliest completion time. So the LCT for A_8 is 26. We then work backward through the table, as shown in Table 19.14.

TABLE 19.14   Computation of Slack Time

Activity	EST	Time	ECT	LCT	LST = LCT − Activity Time	Slack = LCT − ECT
A_1	0	4	4	4	$4 - 4 = 0$	0
A_2	$ECT(A_1) = 4$	2	$4 + 2 = 6$	$Min\{6, 12, 17\} = 6$	$6 - 2 = 4$	0
A_3	$ECT(A_2) = 6$	10	$6 + 10 = 16$	16	$16 - 10 = 6$	0
A_4	$ECT(A_2) = 6$	4	$6 + 4 = 10$	16	$16 - 4 = 12$	6
A_5	$ECT(A_2) = 6$	2	$6 + 2 = 8$	19	$19 - 2 = 17$	11
A_6	$Max\{16, 10\} = 16$	3	$16 + 3 = 19$	19	$19 - 3 = 16$	0
A_7	$Max\{8, 19\} = 19$	5	$19 + 5 = 24$	24	$24 - 5 = 19$	0
A_8	$ECT(A_7) = 24$	2	$24 + 2 = 26$	26	$26 - 2 = 24$	0

LO19-5

5. Consider the project with eight activities discussed above. Draw a Gantt chart for this project.

    Answer: The Gantt chart is shown in Figure 19.15. Note that it also includes the slack time we previously computed for activities A_4 and A_5.

Figure 19.15

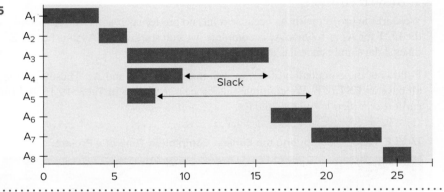

LO19-6

6. Consider a project with four activities. Activities A_1, A_2, and A_3 all can start immediately. However, A_4 requires the completion of A_1, A_2, and A_3. A_1 can take any time between 4 and 8 days. A_2 can take any time between 2 and 6 days. A_3 always takes 5 days. In addition to A_4, which activity (or activities) has the potential to be on the critical path?
    a. A_1
    b. A_1 and A_2
    c. A_2 and A_3
    d. A_1, A_2, and A_3
    e. None of these options is correct.
       Answer: d.

    A_1, A_2, and A_3 can all be on the critical path. If A_1 takes 8 days while A_2 takes 6 days, it is on the critical path. However, if A_1 takes 4 days while A_2 takes 6 days, A_2 is on the critical path. And if A_1 takes 4 days and A_2 takes 2 days, A_3 is on the critical path.

LO19-7

7. What are the main objectives of a project?
    a. The main objectives are to complete the project on time and on budget while fulfilling the scope of the project.
    b. The main objectives are to complete the project on time and in the right location.
    c. The main objectives are to complete the project spending less money than in the budget and with an emphasis on employee satisfaction.
    d. None of these statements is correct.
       Answer: a.

8. Consider the Gantt chart shown in Figure 19.16. A_2 is dependent on A_1, and A_3 is dependent on A_2. In what way does this project attempt to accelerate its project completion time?
   a. Crashing activities
   b. Early start
   c. Overlapping activities on the critical path
   d. None of these options is correct.

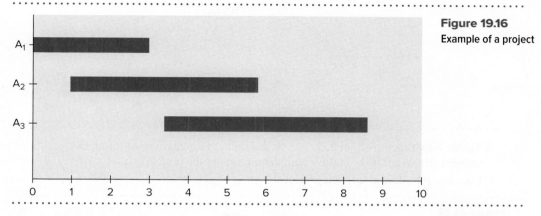

Figure 19.16
Example of a project

   Answer: c.

   This project is overlapping activities despite their dependencies.

9. Which of the following is/are not part of the three main responsibilities of a project manager?
   a. Defining the project
   b. Raising a sufficient project budget
   c. Planning the project
   d. Determining a strategic vision
   e. Controlling the project
   f. b and d
   g. a, c, and e

   Answer: f.

Problems and Applications

1. Which of the following statements is correct with respect to a dependency matrix?
   a. An activity can have multiple predecessor activities.
   b. An activity can have multiple successor activities.
   c. If an activity is a predecessor and a successor activity to another activity, the two activities are interdependent.
   d. All of these statements are correct.

2. Consider the AON graph of a project shown in Figure 19.17.
   Which of the following statements is correct?

Figure 19.17

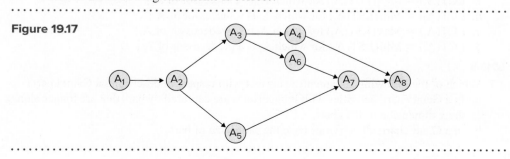

a. A_1 is a predecessor activity to A_2.
b. A_2 is a successor activity of A_1.
c. A_3 and A_5 can be carried out in parallel.
d. All of these statements are correct.

LO19-3

3. Consider the AON graph of a project shown in Figure 19.18.

Figure 19.18

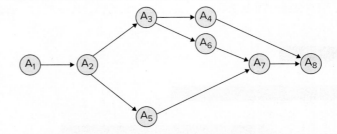

The activity times are 3, 4, 2, 5, 7, 2, 2, and 3 days for activities A_1 through A_8, respectively. What is the earliest completion time of the project?

4. Consider the AON graph of a project shown in Figure 19.19.

Figure 19.19

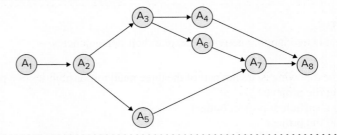

The activity times are 3, 4, 2, 5, 7, 2, 2, and 3 days for activities A_1 through A_8, respectively. What is the critical path?
a. A_1, A_2, A_3, A_4, A_8
b. A_1, A_2, A_3, A_6, A_7, A_8
c. A_1, A_2, A_5, A_7, A_8
d. None of these options is the critical path.

LO19-4

5. A project activity has an earliest completion time of 5, an activity time of 3, and a latest completion time of 6. What is the slack time for the activity?
a. 1
b. 2
c. 3
d. 4
e. 5
f. 6

6. What is the definition of the latest completion time (LCT) of a project activity?
a. $LCT(A_i) = Max\{LST(A_j)$ for which A_j is a successor of $A_i\}$
b. $LCT(A_i) = Min\{LST(A_j)$ for which A_j is a successor of $A_i\}$
c. $LCT(A_i) = Max\{LST(A_j)$ for which A_j is a predecessor of $A_i\}$
d. $LCT(A_i) = Min\{LST(A_j)$ for which A_j is a predecessor of $A_i\}$

LO19-5

7. Which of the following statements is correct with respect to describing a Gantt chart?
a. In a Gantt chart, activities with longer times are captured by bars that are longer along the x-dimension of the chart.
b. In a Gantt chart, all activities have the same size of bars.

c. In a Gantt chart, activities with longer times are captured by bars that are longer along the *y*-dimension of the chart.

d. None of these statements is correct.

LO19-6

8. A project consists of three tasks: A, B, and C. Task A is known to take five days for sure. Tasks B and C are each dependent on A. B takes five days. C takes seven days with a probability of 0.5 and three days with a probability of 0.5. What is the expected completion time of the project?

a. 8 days

b. 10 days

c. 11 days

d. 12 days

LO19-7

9. Which of the following statements best defines the scope of a project?

a. What must be accomplished in order for the project to be completed

b. What budget is required to complete the project

c. What authority the project manager has over the project team

d. None of these statements is correct.

10. What happens as you increase the number of people working on a project from three to six?

a. The project will get done twice as quickly.

b. The communication requirements for the project double.

c. The project might or might not be accelerated.

d. The communication requirements for the project increase by far more than 2x.

e. The project will get done twice as quickly and the communication requirements for the project double.

f. The project might or might not be accelerated and the communication requirements for the project increase by far more than 2x.

LO19-8

11. You manage a project with 10 activities. Activities A_1, A_3, A_5, and A_9 form the critical path. Because you have a large budget for the project, you consider crashing activity A_2, which has the potential to shorten the time of A_2 by three days. What do you think about this opportunity?

a. It is a good idea because it will reduce the project duration by three days.

b. It is a bad idea because A_2 is not on the critical path.

LO19-9

12. Which of the following activities is not part of defining a project?

a. The project triangle

b. The project resources

c. The work breakdown structure

d. The critical path

13. You have been asked by the CEO of your company to manage a really important project. The CEO suggested five employees to be on your project team. You now think about the right organizational structure. Under what project management structure would these five employees face the least trade-offs with their current responsibilities?

a. A dedicated project team

b. A heavyweight project manager

c. An advisory team

d. A matrix organization

CASE   BUILDING A HOUSE IN THREE HOURS

Habitat for Humanity International is a nonprofit organization dedicated to eliminating poverty housing worldwide. The organization was founded in 1976 and since then has built hundreds of thousands of homes that are sold to those in need at no profit through no-interest loans. Houses built by Habitat for Humanity are decent and affordable.

How long does it take to build a house from scratch? Most residential construction projects take between three months and a full year. Habitat for Humanity can do so much faster. In fact, they can do this much, much faster, as they demonstrated in the construction of Bonnie Lilly's new home near Birmingham, Alabama. Bonnie, together with her two children, moved into a home that has officially been labeled the world's fastest house by Habitat for Humanity International. The house has three bedrooms and two bathrooms. It was built—yes, you are reading correctly—in three hours and twenty-six minutes.

If you enter "fastest house ever built" into YouTube, you can watch a short movie that shows the construction. The construction was started using a previously installed foundation. It was completed when the entire house met all township codes and requirements.

Almost 200 carpenters, electricians, plumbers, roofers, and painters collaborated on this project. They followed a carefully laid-out project plan. Each task was executed in the allotted time. Whenever a task was complete, the successor tasks were immediately started because workers were standing next to the construction site eagerly awaiting the authorization to start their work.

The project was planned and managed by project manager Chad Calhoun of Brice Construction Company.

© *Ariel Skelley/Blend Images LLC/RF*

Chad and his team practiced for the build at an old schoolhouse. He coordinated the work, defined a project plan, and created a detailed schedule just as he does on his other construction projects.

1. How is it possible to build a house so quickly? Or, asked differently, why are other residential construction projects taking 100 times longer?

2. What lessons can be learned from this record-time construction for other projects, such as the construction of new airports, ocean liners, or campus buildings?

Source:
http://www.bizjournals.com/birmingham/stories/2002/12/23/editorial1.html?page=all

http://www.shelbycountyreporter.com/2002/12/23/worlds-fastest-house-built-in-montevallo/

References

Kavadias, S., C. H. Loch, and A. DeMeyer. "DragonFly: Developing a Proposal for an Uninhabited Aerial Vehicle (UAV)." Insead case 600-003-1.

Loch, C. H., A. DeMeyer, and M. T. Pich. *Managing the Unknown: A New Approach to Managing High Uncertainty and Risk in Projects.* New York: John Wiley & Sons, 2006.

Olivares, Marcelo; Christian Terwiesch; and Lydia Cassorla. "Structural Estimation of the Newsvendor Model: An Application to Reserving Operating Room Time." Management Science 54, no. 1 (2008), pp. 45–55.

Terwiesch, Christian, and Karl T. Ulrich. Innovation Tournaments: Creating and Selecting Exceptional Opportunities. Cambridge, MA: Harvard Business School Press, 2009.

Ulrich, K. T., and S. Eppinger. *Product Design and Development.* 5th ed. New York: McGraw-Hill/Irwin, 2011.

Literature/Further Reading

Loch et al. (2006) provides a comprehensive framework for managing projects with uncertainty. The authors use many illustrative examples and target experienced project managers as their audience. Terwiesch and Ulrich (2009) deals with far horizon innovation projects as well as multiple challenges associated with financial evaluations of innovation projects. Ulrich and Eppinger (2011) is the classic textbook for product development and includes an easy-to-follow introductory chapter on project management and project organization.

New Product Development

20

LEARNING OBJECTIVES

LO20-1 Explain different types of innovation

LO20-2 Identify the activities in a product development process

LO20-3 Explain the Kano model and be able to create an organized user-needs hierarchy

LO20-4 Generate product concepts by decomposing a product or service based on its attributes or its user interaction

LO20-5 Identify rapid validation methods for a concept

LO20-6 Forecast sales based on a purchase intent survey

© Sarah Hadley/Alamy/RF

Introduction

Segway introduced its personal transporter with great fanfare in 2000. The product was designed and developed by entrepreneur Dean Kamen, who planned for his company to make 40,000 units per month by the end of the company's first full year of production. At prices exceeding $5000 per unit, this would amount to annual sales of more than $2.5 billion. Dreams of this kind of fortune enticed a prominent venture capitalist, John Doerr of Kleiner Perkins Caufield & Byers, to lead an investment syndicate that bet $80 million on Kamen's company. Segway was a promising new product for Kamen and his investors, representing the application of a new technology to an emerging market for light-duty, battery-powered personal transportation devices.

From the perspective of matching supply with demand, the Segway can be thought of as a new form of supply. But is there demand for it? It is the role of product development, the subject of this chapter, to ensure that the new products or services supplied by organizations match the market demand of those who are supposedly buying them. Unfortunately, that was not the case for Segway. In fact, after *five years,* Segway had sold 23,000 units—about two weeks' worth of the demand that Kamen had originally forecasted. We can only imagine the underutilization of the corresponding production process.

The Segway example points to the first and foremost goal of successful product development processes—to create products and services that match the needs of the potential customers. For most of this book, we take the product or service as given and look at what organizations can do to "make it right." But what good is a product or service that is available, well produced, delivered on time, but not needed by anyone? In other words, we can think of the first goal of product development as making the right "it," while the rest of operations is concerned about making "it" right.

Another reason why product development is a part of this book is that it relates to the cost of supply. Throughout this book, we look for ways to increase the efficiency of the operation. We cut waste, be it in the form of idle time, inventory, quality problems, or other forms. But there is only so much you can change in the production or service delivery process. Consider again the example of the Segway.

When you add up the costs of the electronics components in a Segway, you don't have to be an expert to figure out that this product is not cheap. So even if you optimize the assembly and source the module just-in-time so that you avoid unnecessary inventory costs, the mere procurement costs of the electronics will determine most of the costs of supply. In other words, once a product is developed, there exist only so many cost savings we can obtain from cost reductions in operations. For the Segway, at the time of launch, most of the product costs at that time were written in stone.

The observation that product development has a huge impact on cost is shown in the cost build-up curve (see Figure 20.1). Estimates vary concerning the exact magnitudes, but the basic message is consistent across all studies we are aware of. The vast majority of costs are determined by the time production starts. About half of these costs are determined during product development, with the other half being a result of strategic planning and defining the market segment to be served.

The purpose of this chapter is to introduce the topic of product development. Entire books have been written on this topic,[1] so we clearly can only scratch the surface here. After reading this chapter, you should know:

- How to distinguish between different types of innovations.
- What the process of product development looks like.
- How to discover and codify customer needs.
- How to turn these needs into product concepts.
- How to validate these concepts in order to ensure that they indeed meet the needs of the customers.
- How to predict the demand for the new product.

© Ksenia Usata/Shutterstock.com/RF

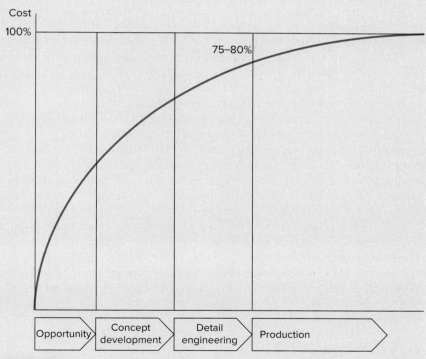

Figure 20.1
The cost build-up curve (Source: Ullman 2009)

---

[1]We recommend the book by Ulrich and Eppinger (2011) as a great introduction to the topic. Much of this chapter is based on this source. We are grateful to Karl Ulrich for sharing his knowledge on this topic.

20.1 Types of Innovations

We define an **innovation** as a novel match between customer needs (the foundation of demand) and solutions in the form of physical goods or services (the supply). Consider the following examples:

- Most of us would say that the Internet service Twitter was an innovation when it launched in May 2006. Before the arrival of Twitter, most of us did not feel the need to tweet at all times, so one might argue that the innovation in Twitter was the identification of an unmet user need.

- While Twitter innovated by identifying a novel and previously unaddressed need, many innovations happen by companies providing new solutions to existing needs. For example, the makers of medical devices, such as Minnesota-based medical device company Medtronic, innovate by creating new products in response to well-established needs. For example, when Medtronic launched a product for neuromodulation, it addressed a longstanding need for pain management. The novelty in Medtronic's solution has been an implantable drug delivery system.

In addition to being a novel match between a solution and a need, we want to impose an additional condition on our definition of an innovation. An innovation has to create value. We want to be somewhat vague in how we measure value, be it in the form of financials, healthier patient lives, or clearer water. If we focus on a financial metric of value, a new product or service generates value if it costs the innovating organization less to supply the new product or service than the customers are willing to pay for it.

How does a company create a new product or service? Where did innovations such as the iPhone, movies such as *Pirates of the Caribbean,* or American Express's latest reward card come from? Most organizations have a process of **opportunity identification**. This process oftentimes is located in specific organizational units with names such as business development or R&D. Sometimes, however, opportunities can also come out of other parts of the organization, including marketing or operations.

An **opportunity** is an idea—it is a new product or service at the embryonic state. The role of product development is to translate the opportunity into a new product or service that the organization then supplies and its customers demand. Only then does the opportunity create value and hence moves from being an opportunity to being an innovation.

As we saw in this chapter's Introduction, the novelty associated with an innovation can come either from the customer need (demand side) or from the solution (supply side). Depending on the novelty associated with the customer side and with the solution side of the innovation, we can categorize an innovation into different horizons, as is explained in Figure 20.2. Each **innovation horizon** corresponds to a comparable degree of novelty, with horizon 1 consisting of mostly **incremental innovation** and horizon 3 consisting of very **radical innovations**. In horizon 1, innovations tend to be refinements of existing technologies and solutions that we serve to our existing customers.

As we move toward the upper left of this figure, we increase the novelty in the customer needs. The upper left represents an attempt to use our existing solutions to reach new customers by entering new markets, either in the form of new geographic markets or in the form of new market segments. In the extreme case, the markets are entirely new, which means that customers in these markets are presently not served at all and thus might not even think of themselves as potential customers.

As we move toward the bottom right of this figure, we increase the novelty of the solution approach. We move from technologies and solutions that we currently master to inventing new solutions. This might involve solutions that currently exist outside our organization (e.g., when smartphones were equipped with navigation capability, navigation functionality was new to smartphone makers but not entirely new to the world). In the extreme case of novelty, these solutions don't exist yet, and it is up to us to invent them. So, one way to distinguish between different innovations is to measure their novelty using the framework outlined in Figure 20.2.

LO20-1 Explain different types of innovation

Innovation A novel match between customer needs (the foundation of demand) and solutions in the form of physical goods or services (the supply) that create value.

Opportunity identification The process of generating opportunities.

Opportunity An idea—it is a new product or service at the embryonic state.

Innovation horizon A measure of the novelty of an innovation, with horizon 1 being less novel than horizon 2, which in turn is less novel than horizon 3.

Incremental innovation A horizon 1 innovation; uses existing technology and serves existing customers.

Radical innovation A horizon 3 innovation; oftentimes serves new markets and/or employs new technology.

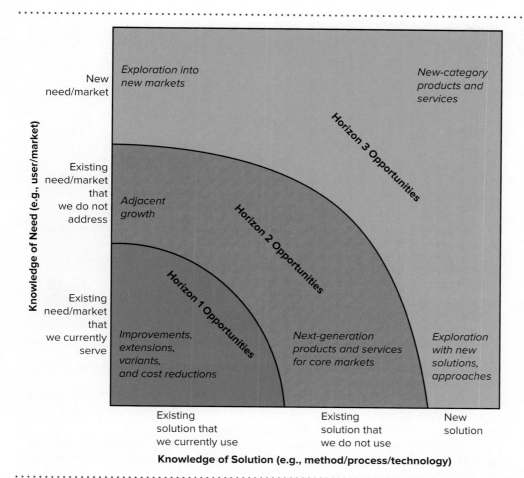

Figure 20.2

The three horizons of growth (Source: Terwiesch and Ulrich, 2009)

Firms can innovate beyond creating new products and services. Firms can come up with new production processes, new service delivery models, or new distribution systems, or they can innovate in many other ways. We encourage you to think of all the chapters in this book providing ideas for which a company can innovate in its operations. Common to all of them is the desire to match solutions to the needs of the customers. For the remainder for this chapter, however, we focus on the process of generating new products and services.

CONNECTIONS: Innovation at Apple

One of the most successful innovators is Apple. Apple has had a continuous flow of new products, including devices such as the iPhone, the iPad, and the iPod, alongside a portfolio of laptop computers and desktop computers.

But Apple did not just innovate by creating devices. In 2001, Apple launched its digital music offering iTunes. By now, iTunes has grown to be a digital retailer for content, providing a significant part of Apple's revenue streams while also further enhancing the desirability of its main products.

Beyond this, Apple launched a direct-to-consumer online retailing service that allows consumers to buy Apple products directly from Apple. This is not a new product, not a new service offering, but a new distribution channel and thus an innovation.

This online channel is complemented by over 400 Apple stores throughout the world where Apple uses traditional, brick-and-mortar retail outlets to sell its products. Stores selling computers have been around long before Apple, but, for Apple, these stores were an

Continued

© John Flournoy/McGraw-Hill Education

innovation. Moreover, the fancy design and the shopping experience certainly required many additional innovations.

Finally, Apple also innovated by creating a large supply chain operation. This includes a network of contract manufacturers, most notably the Chinese company FoxConn, but, more recently, also includes its own manufacturing facilities.

So, innovations come in various forms. The focus in this chapter is on new products and services. However, the other chapters in this book ought to provide you with ideas to innovate in the operations such as stores or supply chains.

Check Your Understanding 20.1

Question: A cancer center in a large academic medical center considers a set of innovations:

- The first proton beam in the region, which is a device that targets cancer cells without hurting other tissues in patients with prostate cancer who were previously treated with other forms of radiation therapy.
- An exploration into a new form of gene therapy to treat leukemia by manipulating the patients' blood cells in ways no one has ever tried before.
- A new computer system that allows patients to see their latest lab tests online, something that previously only the doctors could have access to.

In which of the three horizons of innovation does each of these innovations fall?

Answer: The proton beam seems to be a new technology to the region and thus to the hospital. It is used to treat an existing type of patient (those with prostate cancer). It thus falls into horizon 2.

The new form of gene therapy is a horizon 3 innovation. It involves experiments with blood cell manipulations never done before.

The new computer system is a horizon 1 innovation. It caters to the existing customers and uses technology that the hospital is already actively using internally.

Question: Beyond the offerings of new services, what other innovations might the cancer center consider?

Answer: There are many ways in which the cancer center might innovate. Possible innovations include:

- A more pleasant waiting room design.
- An online scheduling system.
- Outsourcing of the pharmacy operation.
- A new bed management system to reduce the time an admitted patient has to wait for a bed.

These innovations have in common that they are not new products or services by themselves. Instead, they support the existing service of the center.

. . . .

20.2 The Product Development Process

Throughout this book, we have looked at operations through the lens of process analysis. We analyzed manufacturing processes, distribution processes, and the processes of delivering services to our customer. So it should not surprise you that the perspective we take when looking at the innovation of new products and services is, once again, process-based. So, we now define a **product development process** and, more broadly, a process for innovation. A product development process takes an opportunity as its input and translates this into a new product or service.

At first, the notion of an *innovation process* presents an apparent contradiction. After all, innovation is fundamentally concerned with creating new things, while a process does the same things repeatedly. This contradiction is resolved by viewing the process at the right level of abstraction. For the remainder of this chapter, we will focus on new product development (NPD) projects as the unit of analysis. The NPD project is our flow unit. Each project is managed according to its unique characteristics using the tools of project management discussed in Chapter 19, Project Management. Yet, as we will explain, each project will follow a similar path.

As discussed earlier, the seed of an innovation is the business opportunity. In this chapter, we take this opportunity as given. Our focus is on the product development process that includes the following activities:

- The identification and documentation of user needs.
- The generation of multiple concepts that are responsive to these needs and the selection of the most promising concepts.
- An empirical validation of the quality of the most promising concepts and a subsequent refinement.
- The forecasting of sales as a confirmation of the viability of the product concept as a starting point for planning the required operations.

Figure 20.3 summarizes this product development process. Upstream from the product development process is the process of opportunity identification.[2] Downstream of the product development process is the actual productions, sales, and distribution of the product or service developed. Though the figure suggests a linear, sequential process, product development oftentimes is an **iterative process**. This is indicated by the arrows looping back from the activities in the figure. An iterative process is a process in which one or several of the activities are repeated one or multiple times. From a process analysis perspective, one might call such iterations "rework."

Product development process A process that takes an opportunity as its input and translates this into a new product or service. The process includes needs identification, the generation of product concepts, an empirical validation of the concepts, and a business analysis, involving a sales forecast.

Iterative process A process in which one or several of the activities are repeated one or multiple times.

---

[2]See Terwiesch and Ulrich 2009.

Figure 20.3 A generic product development process based on Ulrich and Eppinger

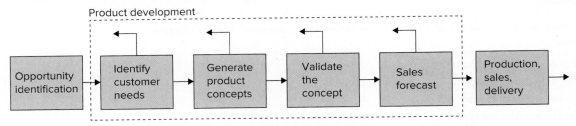

20.3 Understanding User Needs

Just like the operations of a restaurant (including its choice of capacity and location) ought to be driven by customer demand, the design of the product or service we develop ought to be responsive to the needs and desires of our customers. In the introductory chapter, we articulated a number of dimensions of customer needs that, taken together, determine customer utility. We distinguished between the utility of consumption (including performance, fit, and conformance as its key drivers), the utility of convenience (location and timing), and the customer's desire for affordability. A consumer's utility function determines to what extent a consumer desires a product or service. Utility functions have many input variables, which we refer to as **user needs**.

For example, we can write the utility function of a consumer as

$$\text{Utility} = U(\text{Consumption utility, price, convenience})$$

As we try to measure or even predict the desire for a product or service of a consumer based on utility, we face two challenges: the functional form of the utility function and the dimensionality of the user needs.

20.3.1 Attributes and the Kano Model

Consider the dimensionality of the user needs first. Price is a variable that we feel we can easily measure and quantify. As consumers, we are used to thinking about the affordability need associated with a product or service. In contrast, consumption utility and convenience might appear as somewhat more opaque. The reason for that is that these dimensions of the utility function are themselves functions of other, more granular user needs. In other words, the utility function has subdimensions.

Imagine you want to purchase a new smartphone. Your utility of the phone would be driven by the consumption utility, the price of the product and associated calling and data plans, as well as the convenience of obtaining the phone. Now, as we discussed in the introductory chapter, consumption utility consists of the three subdimensions: performance, conformance, and fit. For example, the performance quality of the phone will be driven by its product features. The conformance quality captures whether the phone works as well as the manufacturer promises it will. And the fit of your phone is affected by your personal preferences (you might like the phone in a white case and with a four-inch screen).

Now, the performance quality again has its subdimensions. For example, we can think of durability, battery life, screen resolution, memory space, and processor speed as the subdimensions of performance quality. And, to make things even more complicated, we can break up durability into shock resistance, watertightness, temperature tolerance, and so on. In short, there exists a **hierarchy of needs** associated with a product or service starting with a few high-level needs (e.g., performance quality), which in turn consist of many low-level needs (e.g., watertightness). We refer to the needs at the top of this needs hierarchy as **primary needs** and the needs at the lower levels as **secondary needs** and **tertiary needs**. Note, however, that this does not mean that primary needs are the most important needs—they are simply more aggregated.

User needs The drivers of customer utilities.

Hierarchy of needs The organization of user needs into primary needs, secondary needs, and tertiary needs.

Primary needs Needs that are at the top of the needs hierarchy. Note that this implies that they are more aggregated. This says nothing about importance.

Secondary needs Needs that are in the middle of the needs hierarchy. Note that this implies that they are less aggregated than the primary needs. This says nothing about importance.

Tertiary needs Needs that are at the bottom of the needs hierarchy. Note that this says nothing about their importance.

Next, consider the role of the functional form. We know that, everything else held constant, consumers prefer products or services with higher consumption utility, lower price, and better convenience. So, mathematically speaking, the utility function is increasing in these variables. But how quickly? And with what functional form? Is a price increase from $1 to $2 as big of a disutility as a price increase from $100 to $101? And is an increase in customer waiting time (as a measure of convenience) from one minute to two minutes as annoying to a consumer as an increase from 1 hour to 1:01 hour?

Now, don't worry; we will not bombard you with calculus and functional forms in this chapter. From a practical perspective, it is useful to distinguish between three functional forms of the utility function along a given user need (or sub-need). These forms are illustrated in Figure 20.4:

- **Performance needs** are those needs that will lead to customer satisfaction when fulfilled and dissatisfaction when not fulfilled. Utility grows more or less linearly in the extent to which the customer needs are met, which is why we also refer to these needs as **linear satisfiers**. For example, when purchasing a smartphone, a consumer might think about battery life as a linear satisfier—one day is good, two days are better, and five days would be a lot better still.

- **Delighters** are those needs that will lead to customer satisfaction when fulfilled but will not lead to dissatisfaction when not fulfilled. For example, some hotels offer their guests a free chocolate cookie at the time of check-in. When you would ask hotel guests what they want from a good check-in, most of them might not think of a cookie and so they would not be dissatisfied should there be none. However, once you provide them with the (unexpected) cookie, the customer is delighted (at least as long as they are not on a diet).

- **Must-haves** are those needs that will not really drive customer satisfaction upward when fulfilled, but could drive customer satisfaction substantially downward when not fulfilled. No phone company selling smartphones would advertise that its product actually can be connected to e-mail servers. Consumers simply assume this and (almost) all existing offerings fulfill that need. So a customer will express no delight when being able to connect to his or her e-mail server, but the customer would be severely frustrated if this would not work.

Performance needs Needs that will lead to customer satisfaction when fulfilled and dissatisfaction when not fulfilled. Utility grows more or less linearly in the extent to which customer needs are met. Also called linear satisfiers.

Linear satisfiers Needs that will lead to customer satisfaction when fulfilled and dissatisfaction when not fulfilled. Utility grows more or less linearly in the extent to which customer needs are met. Also called performance needs.

Delighters Needs that will lead to customer satisfaction when fulfilled but will not lead to dissatisfaction when not fulfilled. Frequently associated with latent needs.

Must-haves Needs that will not really drive customer satisfaction upward when fulfilled but could drive customer satisfaction substantially downward when not fulfilled.

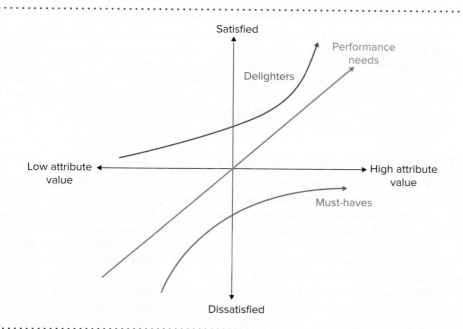

Figure 20.4
The Kano model

Check Your Understanding 20.2

Question: Think about the preparation for the SAT or another form of standardized testing. Many students seek help from professional tutoring companies. These students report the following user needs with respect to the tutoring service:

1. The tutoring service offers practice tests using old tests.
2. The tutoring service increases test performance.
3. The tutoring service offers sessions in a nearby location.
4. The staff of the tutoring service is courteous and professional.
5. The tutoring service provides a wake-up call on the day of the test.
6. The tutoring service has flexible hours.

Classify these needs using the Kano model. Which of these needs would you expect to be latent?

Answer: We suggest that needs 1 and 4 are must-haves; needs 2, 3, and 6 are performance needs; and need 5 is a delighter. Most likely, need 5 is also a latent need.

- -

LO20-3 Explain the Kano model and be able to create an organized user-needs hierarchy

These three types of needs were first described by the Japanese design professor **Noriaki Kano** and, for this reason, this way of thinking about customer needs is often referred to as the **Kano model**. Some comments about the Kano model are in order:

- **Latent needs**: Oftentimes, when asked about their needs and preferences, customers might not be aware of their need. Before Toyota introduced power sliding doors to their minivan model Sienna, most consumers, we argue, did not have the desire for doors automatically opening in response to a click of a button. But once they saw it, they loved it (and other car manufacturers soon followed). We refer to such needs as latent. Latent needs are typically categorized as delighters in the Kano model.

- *Kano model:* The Kano model is not meant to be an exact mathematical science; it rather is a conceptual framework. For example, you might argue that the user need *battery life,* which we classified as a performance need, really should be seen as a must-have; after all, what good is a phone if it has zero minutes of battery life? In practice, it is rare to find user needs that have exact linear functions over all possible outcomes. However, as we will capture and codify needs later on in this chapter, it is always helpful to have the Kano model and its three types of needs in mind.

- *Time drift:* If you would have introduced a smartphone with a Twitter link in 2006, you would likely have gathered a few "wows" among consumers. However, just a year or two later, that "wow" would have turned into a yawn. Innovations diffuse and what once was a delight is soon taken for granted (and thus becomes a must-have). Take the example of the hotel check-in. The first time you visit the hotel, you will be surprised and delighted by that cookie at check-in. However, it only takes a couple of visits and you show up at check-in with the attitude, "Hey, where is my cookie?"

20.3.2 Identifying Customer Needs

Imagine that a group of students launch a startup called HealthyFood@Work with the goal of providing a healthy lunch to hungry office workers. We don't know how they came up with this business opportunity. Recall our discussion of Figure 20.3; they must have used some opportunity identification process to get to this point in the venture. Now the team is ready for the next step.

Noriaki Kano A 20th-century Japanese design professor.

Kano model A framework that distinguishes between three types of needs: performance needs, delighters, and must-haves.

Latent needs Needs that customers are not aware that they have.

According to the idea, customers would place an order and the food would be delivered to them right to their desk in the office. The team wants to collect information about the customer needs of this new service. But where to start?

If we truly want to understand customer needs, we need to move beyond stating the obvious. Yes, our customers most likely want good and healthy food, freshly made, with little wait time, and delivered right to their desk at a low price. But to truly gain an edge over our competitors and truly delight our customers, we have to do more work—much more. We have to make sure that we find all needs, not just the obvious; even better, we want to get to know our customers with such an intimacy that we can understand their latent needs, even before they understand these themselves. This is why good product development always starts with a careful assessment of customer needs.

In order to get to know our customers well, we have to get close to them. It is not enough to send them a link to an online survey; instead, we suggest three methods of gathering customer needs:

- **Interviews**: In interviews, one or multiple team members discuss user needs with one customer at a time. Interviews tend to last for 30 minutes to 1 hour, though longer interviews are possible. They should be audio recorded and/or transcribed.
- **Contextual observation**: As the term *contextual research* suggests, these methods take place in the context in which the customer would be most likely to use the new product or service. The emphasis is on observation and discussion with the user and can take multiple hours, during which time the developer takes notes and photos. This technique can also be combined with interviews.
- **Focus groups**: A focus group is a moderated group discussion of four to eight customers that typically lasts for about two hours. Customers answer questions and the answers are discussed and reflected on as a group.

There exist many more techniques to elicit the needs of the customer, though we feel that these three are the most relevant for an introductory chapter on product development.

For our startup HealthyFood@Work, this means that the first thing our team should do is immerse itself in the environment of their customers. This most likely implies visiting a number of office buildings at lunch time and then starting a discussion with the potential customers. During these visits, the team should dig for information and ask interview questions, such as the following:

- Walk us through the process with which you usually get your lunch.
- Can you show us what you are eating today?
- What do you like about this way of getting your lunch? What do you dislike?
- What other options for lunch in the office have you tried in the past?

The emphasis of the interview is on "show and tell"—it is the interviewee who is talking while the developers take notes and provide occasional prompts or broad questions. The main benefit of interviewing the user in the context of the product use (at the office eating lunch) is that the developers can learn more than just verbal information—they can observe the actual behavior and get visual clues about delights and frustrations.

Depending on the product or service to develop and the resources of the team, we suggest that the developers do some 10 to 20 such interviews. With each interview, the team learns something new. However, after a while, the stories are likely to repeat themselves and, on average, each interview yields less information than the previous one. At some point, the newly gained learning is no longer worth the extra effort.

These marginally diminishing returns for interviews are shown in Figure 20.5. The figure shows on the x-axis the number of interviews conducted. It shows on the y-axis the percentage of user needs that are typically identified given the number of interviews. The figure also compares the percentage of needs identified from interviews relative to the percentage of needs uncovered from focus groups. Note that to identify, for example, 80 percent of the needs, we need about four focus groups or seven interviews. Note further that focus groups tend to be much more expensive (typically by a factor of 10 and more) than interviews, and so for each dollar invested, interviews tend to provide you with more information.

20.3.3 Coding Customer Needs

Once our team has concluded the interviews, it compiles all the user needs it has identified at this point. The needs should be categorized hierarchically, reflecting the multiple levels of the customer needs given by the primary needs, the secondary needs, and the tertiary needs. So, a primary need consists of multiple secondary needs, which in turn depend on tertiary needs, creating a tree-like hierarchy.

Interviews In interviews, one or multiple team members discuss user needs with one customer at a time.

Contextual observation Observing the user in the context in which he or she would be most likely to use the new product or service. The emphasis is on observation and discussion with the user and can take multiple hours, during which time the developer takes notes and photos.

Focus group A moderated group discussion of four to eight customers that typically lasts for about two hours.

Figure 20.5

Number of interviews (focus groups) and percentage of user needs uncovered (Griffin and Hauser 1993, in Ulrich and Eppinger, 2011)

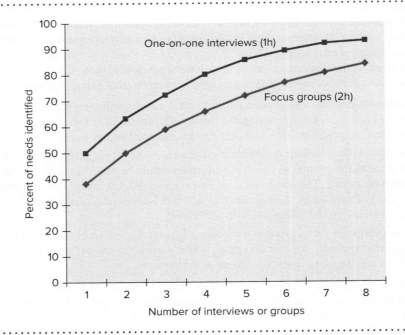

Figure 20.6   List of user needs

HealthyFood@Work...

© *Monkey Business Images/Cutcaster/RF*

Gets me healthy food ***

- provides fresh food
- uses ingredients that are known to be healthy

Gets me food that I like ***

- allows me to customize the food to my preferences
- makes suggestions of new food that I might like (!)
- allows me to ban ingredients that I don't like or I am allergic to

Is compatible with my busy work schedule **

- takes little or no time to order
- adjusts to changes in my work schedule

- requires minimal time to get
- comes when I want it

Is affordable **

- is inexpensive in its daily use

Sometimes surprises me *

- encourages trying out new food (!)
- makes eating fun

Is delivered in a private and discrete manner *

- is brought to me by a professional delivery person
- is packaged in a way that does not let the smell come out of the package during delivery

Supports healthy consumption of food ***

- allows me to store leftover food in case I am not hungry
- encourages me to eat slowly (!)

Supports a healthy diet ***

- is compatible with popular diets
- counts calories and food groups (e.g., proteins) (!)
- can be connected to apps that track calories
- adjusts portion sizes based on my workout diary (!)

Has an easy payment system **

- requires little time to pay for the meal

Makes eating a social experience *

- supports user rating and peer recommendation
- delivers to co-workers at the same time

Figure 20.6 shows an example of what the HealthyFood@Work team might have come up with. Note that in addition to organizing the needs hierarchically, we see that asterisks (*) are used to quantify the importance of the needs and exclamation marks (!) are used to capture latent needs the team has identified. Many of these needs, such as affordability, we could have identified without even leaving our desk. But would you really have thought about the need to encourage the customer to eat more slowly?

20.4 Concept Generation

In the previous section, our focus was on the user needs—we asked, WHAT is it that the consumer needs? Now, we shift from the WHAT to the HOW. We now ask, HOW might we address user needs in the form of a new product or service? This is the part of product development known as **concept generation**. In concept generation, a product development team generates a large and diverse set of product concepts in the hope that one or several of these concepts will be the foundation for our new product or service.

LO20-4 Generate product concepts by decomposing a product or service based on its attributes or its user interaction

We define a **product concept** as a preliminary articulation of a solution for a given set of user needs. Product concepts typically should address two questions:

- WHAT are the needs that this particular concept fulfills really well (e.g., a lunch service that provides food to your desk and simultaneously updates your health profile with the calories and nutrients of this meal)?

- HOW are we going to fulfill these needs (e.g., the lunch is prepared by a third-party vendor based on recipes that have nutritional characteristics stored in a database; we deliver the lunch to the desk of the customer and update the customer's dietary profile with the nutritional characteristics of the meal)?

Product concepts can take many different forms. They can be textual descriptions, sketches drawn on a napkin or a Post-it note, or computer renderings. A key element of our definition of a product concept is the word *preliminary*. Product concepts are in idea format, they are half-baked, they are incomplete, and they need further refinement.

20.4.1 Prototypes and Fidelity

We refer to a **prototype** as a representation of the final product or service that allows the product development team to predict how well a particular product concept might fulfill the customer needs. The word *prototype* comes from the Greek word *prototypon,* which can be translated as "a primitive form." Prototypes are primitive because they can only approximate the fulfillment of the needs of real customers. This is similar to the use of process flow diagrams earlier on in this book, which were helpful representations of the underlying business processes, but only approximate representations. Our definition of prototypes is arguably very broad and we consider product sketches, computer models, physical mock-ups, and the output of pilot production all as prototypes.

Depending on how well a prototype approximates the actual user experience, we distinguish between several levels of **fidelity** in a prototype:

- Low-fidelity prototypes are really rough representations of the final solution. Their roughness makes them an imperfect and noisy predictor of how well the customer need will be fulfilled. However, they have one critical advantage: They are fast and cheap to make.

- High-fidelity prototypes provide almost perfect representations and therefore give us a very accurate prediction about real customer response. This accuracy comes at a price—high-fidelity prototypes are very expensive to make and so we typically cannot afford to create a high-fidelity prototype for every concept we consider.

As the product development process unfolds, the fidelity of prototypes tends to increase. Early on in the product development process, when we are in concept generation, we want to search broadly and hence will use many low-fidelity prototypes. As we narrow our search, we will reduce the number of prototypes but increase their fidelity. Over the course of a product development project, the number of concepts explored in parallel decreases while the fidelity of the prototypes used increases.

Concept generation In concept generation, a product development team generates a large and diverse set of product concepts in the hope that one or several of these concepts will be the foundation for our new product or service.

Product concept A preliminary articulation of a solution for a given set of user needs.

Prototype A representation of the final product or service that allows the product development team to predict how well a particular product concept might fulfill the customer needs.

Fidelity The extent to which a prototype approximates the actual user experience.

CONNECTIONS: Crashing Cars

© Caspar Benson/Getty Images/RF

An important user need in the development of the car is passenger safety during accidents. As the development team considers many different vehicle designs, varying with respect to weight and geometry, it needs to predict the safety of a design long before the start of mass production.

Prototypes are used to predict how well a given design will perform in a crash. Many different crash scenarios are considered, including frontal collision with another vehicle, sideways collisions, or the car heading straight into an obstacle.

One way to prototype a crash is to build a prototype car, put one or multiple test dummies into the car, and then just head right into a crash while simultaneously measuring various impact forces to the vehicle and the test dummies. This approach has a high fidelity but is very costly. Every test crashes a car. That would already be expensive if you value a car at its retail price (say $30k). However, because this happens during the development of the vehicle, these prototypes are made on a much smaller scale and cost several $100k's per unit.

Over the last 20 years, engineers have been able to simulate car crashes using computer models. Though initially these models had a relatively low fidelity, advances in computing have made the underlying models more and more accurate and so their fidelity is now almost as good as for a real crash while being much less expensive. This now allows development teams to carry out many more crash tests and do this much earlier in the development process, while considering a wide range of different vehicle designs.

20.4.2 Generating Product Concepts Using Attribute-Based Decomposition

Decomposition Breaking up a problem into smaller, manageable subproblems and solving these subproblems first. Decomposition is based on the idea of divide and conquer.

Coming up with many different product concepts seems at first to be a daunting task. The key idea behind successfully generating product concepts is **decomposition**. Decomposing a problem means breaking it up into smaller, manageable subproblems and solving these subproblems first. Decomposition is based on the idea of divide and conquer.

You can decompose a concept development problem for a new product or service in one of two ways: You can decompose the product into its product attributes or you can decompose it based on the interaction of the user with the product. We will call the former approach **attribute-based decomposition** and the latter approach **user interaction–based decomposition**.

Consider the attribute-based decomposition first. In an attribute-based decomposition, we focus on a subset of attributes of a new product or service and try to generate a concept that performs well on these attributes, even at the risk of performing poorly on others.

We define the customer **value curve** as a graphic depiction of a new product's relative performance across the key attributes, comparing it with existing offerings in the market. Figure 20.7 compares the value curve of two fast-food restaurants that currently are active in serving a large office campus. The restaurants compete against each other and have similar performance with respect to most attributes, such as the courtesy of the service and the ease of access from the office. Restaurant A allows a little more customization and has slightly higher-quality food (better tasting food and fresher food). Restaurant B has a slightly lower price and a shorter response time.

Looking at the customer value curve, we can find new product concepts by reflecting upon the following questions (the value curve concept and its usage for concept generation is based on the work by Kim and Mauborgne):

- How might we go about dramatically improving the performance of the new offering along one particular attribute, even if that means sacrificing other attributes?

- How might we introduce new attributes that presently are not addressed in existing product offerings?

For example, we might focus on the user needs related to convenience, which would be waiting time and access to the food. We then could look for a product concept that would excel on these dimensions, ignoring what this would do to the other dimensions. We can look for inspirations from other industries that we feel do a particularly good job with a given need. For example, we can think about how high-end airlines prepare meals for their first-class passengers. This way, we would come up with concepts such as "have a chef come to the customer's desk and make the food right in front of the customer" or "have lunch carts with prepared food-boxes sufficiently close to the customer so that customers can just grab the food when they feel like it."

We also can think about introducing new attributes to the value curve; for example, electronic integration with dietary apps. To do so, we might think about the work of a nutrition counselor, not worrying about any other user need (including affordability). This might get us to ideas such as "customize the food and adjust the portion size to the dietary goals of the customer," "have bigger portion sizes if the customer has been active before the meal," or

Attribute-based decomposition In an attribute-based decomposition, we focus on a subset of attributes of a new product or service and try to generate a concept that performs well on these attributes, even at the risk of performing poorly on others.

User action–based decomposition Decomposition of a product or service into the activities the user goes through when using the product.

Value curve A graphic depiction of a new product's relative performance across the key attributes, comparing it with existing offerings in the market.

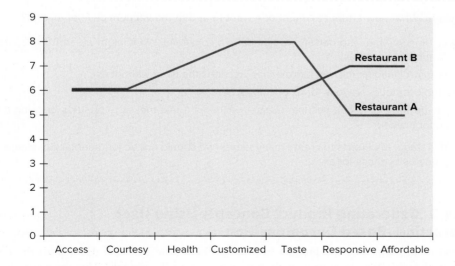

Figure 20.7
The value curve

"automatically upload the customer's diet data based on the food we provide to him or her." You don't like these ideas and already have some that are better? Great—that is exactly the point of concept generation.

Check Your Understanding 20.3

© Digital Vision/Punchstock/RF

Question: Consider two vacuum cleaners, A and B, with the following attributes. Each attribute is scored on a scale from 1 to 10, with 10 being the best value:

- Affordability: A, 8; B, 3
- Weight: A, 6; B, 4
- Durability: A, 4; B,10
- Noise: A, 4; B, 8
- Suction power: A, 3; B, 9

Create a value curve comparing these two products.

Answer: We draw the value curve as shown in Figure 20.8.

Figure 20.8

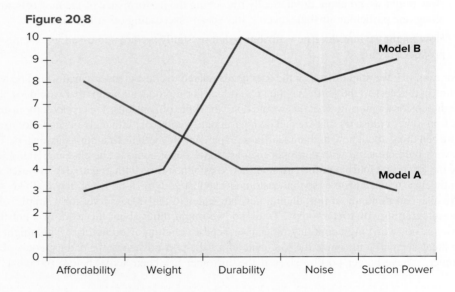

Question: What new attributes might one want to add to the vacuum cleaner market?

Answer: Imagine that affordability would not be a constraint. What might we add? We could think of attributes such as:

- User effort (imagine the vacuum cleaner just does the work without us).
- Design/aesthetics (various forms of color schemes).
- Clean-up reminders (the vacuum cleaner sends us a text message or starts beeping if not used for a week).

At this stage, the idea is to create many ideas—we should not be judgmental. So, please, don't judge us by these ideas. . . .

• •

20.4.3 Generating Product Concepts Using User Interaction–Based Decomposition

Instead of decomposing the product into its attributes, we can also decompose the product into the activities the user goes through when using the product. This approach should come naturally to you after studying the earlier chapters in this book with their emphasis on activities and process flows. In the context of our lunch example, we can think of the key steps as being:

- Choose the food.
- Pay for the food.
- Get the food.
- Eat the food.
- Dispose of the food and the container.

A user interaction–based decomposition would then pick one of these steps and generate concepts by asking, for example, "How might we go about the activity 'pay for the food'?" We can then look for inspiration from other industries where many more forms of payment have been used, as we typically see in most food courts. This might lead to ideas such as subscription plans, automatic withdrawals, tokens, and many more.

One form of user interaction–based decomposition that we find particularly useful, particularly in the service setting, is a tool known as **service blueprints**.[3] This tool breaks up the flow of activities required to serve the customer in a diagram very similar to our process flow diagram (see, e.g., Chapter 3). The service blueprint also distinguishes which activities are done by the customer alone, which activities are carried out "on stage" (which means during the interaction of us with the customer), and which activities we do without the involvement of the customer. Figure 20.9 provides a service blueprint for the lunch example.

Service blueprint A user interaction–based decomposition that breaks up the flow of activities required to serve the customer. The service blueprint also distinguishes which activities are done by the customer alone, which activities are carried out "on stage" (which means during the interaction of us with the customer), and which activities we do without the involvement of the customer.

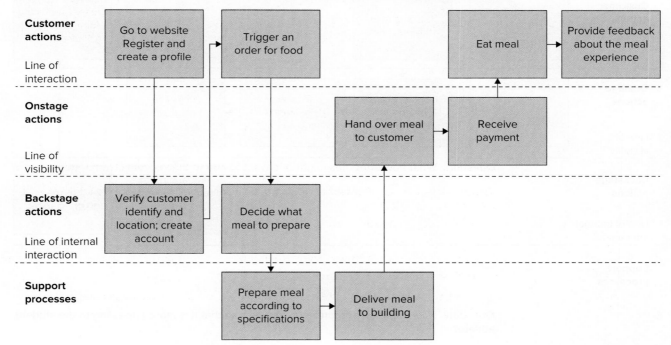

Figure 20.9 Service blueprint. The service blueprint is based on work of Osterwalder, Pigneur, and Smith

---

[3]Osterwalder, Pigneur, Bernarda, and Smith 2014.

Service blueprints help us come up with new ideas. Some questions to wrestle with as part of the concept generation process are:

1. How might we move work from onstage to backstage (e.g., process payments independent of meal handover)?
2. How might we eliminate steps (e.g., automatic withdrawals for payments)?

© Terry Vine/Blend Images/RF

Check Your Understanding 20.4

Question: The practice of a sports physician receives a large number of requests from high school athletes for a physical examination, which is required by their school so that the student athlete can engage in varsity sports activities.

The process works as follows. The student makes an appointment with the office. At the time of the appointment, the student comes to the practice. In the waiting room, the student fills out a set of medical forms inquiring about any preexisting conditions. The student also deals with insurance issues and provides the co-pay. The doctor then examines the student. Based on some notes the doctor leaves on a voice recorder, a staff member later prepares a report that is sent to the student. The student takes that report and hands it to the athletic director at the school.

Create a service blueprint for this process, similar to Figure 20.9.

Answer: The service blueprint might look like that in Figure 20.10:

Figure 20.10

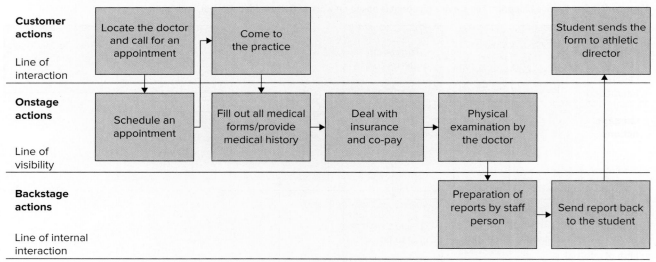

Question: How might one organize the process so that it is more appealing to the student athlete?

Answer: Observe the large number of "onstage" actions. Would it be possible to deal with insurance and medical history from home? Could the making of the appointment be taken offstage by using an online interface to make the appointment? Or could the practice mail the form directly to the athletic director?

In response to these questions, we might generate new concepts for the subproblem (the activity) "pay for the food" that we could use in our lunch example. For example we could have:

- Credit card on record (no onstage work).
- Monthly subscription (no onstage work).
- PayPal submission (requires effort when ordering).
- Cash on delivery (requires effort when handing over the meal).
- Credit card on delivery (requires effort when handing over the meal).
- Tokens on delivery (requires getting tokens before).
- Direct bank withdrawal (no onstage work).
- Weekly bill sent as an invoice (no onstage work but some extra customer work).
- Electronic micropayment using apps (onstage work but really fast).

The two previously discussed decomposition techniques are meant to facilitate the generation of concepts. They are there to help and support a systematic and careful exploration of the large space of possible product concepts. At the end of both product decomposition techniques, you have to shift gears and move from looking at subproblems (attributes or activities) and go back to consider the product concept in its entirety. You also have to start eliminating many, and probably even most, of the ideas you have considered so far. This is when you move from generated product concepts to selecting product concepts.

20.4.4 Concept Selection

During concept generation, the product development team should create a broad set of ideas. Many of these ideas are not fully elaborate product concepts, they might just be fragments and might still require a lot more work (they are low fidelity). At the end of concept development, the team needs to combine the best aspects of these ideas and create a number of higher-fidelity product concepts. The team also needs to eliminate many (in fact, most) concepts and focus on the most promising concepts generated so far. This prioritization of the concepts is called **concept selection**. As the team picks a concept, it should consider three questions:

- *Need fulfillment:* Does the product concept meet the user needs?
- *Feasibility:* Is the product concept feasible and can we execute on it? This includes the question: Does it cost less to deliver the product concept to the customer than what the customer is willing to pay for it?
- *Wow factor:* Does the product concept have a certain "wow factor"; that is, does it surprise our (potential) customer and ultimately delight her? Oftentimes, such a delight is a result of addressing some previously latent needs.

To help with the concept selection, the team should compare the most promising concepts along the three dimensions of need fulfillment, feasibility, and wow factor using a **selection matrix**. The rows in the selection matrix are the concepts, with the columns being the three dimensions of comparison. This allows for a targeted discussion of the relative merits of each concept and for further improvement. The final vote as to which concept to move forward with at this time should be based on a group vote. Table 20.1 shows the selection matrix for the lunch problem, comparing four possible product concepts:

- *Pandora for food:* Tell us your preferences and we bring you great food; learns over time what you like.
- *Health advisor:* Tell us your health goals (build muscle, lose weight) and we do the rest.
- *WholeFoods on demand:* Tell us what you want to eat and we get it for you; no hassle, no wait.
- *Business-class meal:* Know before you choose; we come to you and let you choose from a menu of options we can prepare right in front of you.

Concept selection Prioritization of the concepts generated so far in the development.

Selection matrix A table that compares product concepts. The rows in the selection matrix are the concepts, with the columns being the three dimensions of comparison: need fulfillment, feasibility, and wow factor.

TABLE 20.1 Concept Selection Matrix

Concept	Need Fulfillment	Feasibility	Wow Factor
Pandora for food	***	**	**
Health advisor	***	*	***
WholeFoods on demand	**	***	*
Business-class meal	***	*	***

20.5 Rapid Validation/Experimentation

LO20-5 Identify rapid validation methods for a concept

No matter how carefully you studied the customer needs and no matter how creatively you generated product concepts, chances are that your favorite concept will work less than perfectly. In fact, chances are that it will not work at all. Product development almost always is an iterative process, especially if we are dealing with more radical innovations in horizons 2 and 3.

Failure is part of the process; knowledge is created when teams learn from failure and this knowledge allows the team to come up with better new products or services. Given that teams will fail initially with almost certainty, the team should not focus on avoiding failure. Instead, the team should attempt to fail as quickly and cheaply as possible. Iterating on a new product concept when it is still an inexpensive prototype is easy; iterating when the production plant is ready and the marketing campaign rolled out is not. So the mantra of innovation is "Fail quickly and fail cheaply," or, as IDEO, one of the world's leading design firms, stipulates, "Fail early to succeed sooner."

Recall the cost buildup curve from the beginning of this chapter. When the Segway team first asked consumers to vote on the product concept with their wallets, it had already committed to the final design (including the previously mentioned electronics components and the associated procurement costs) and had prepared for large-scale production. At this point, any form of iteration becomes prohibitively expensive.

Product development teams use prototypes to overcome the uncertainties associated with the novelty of the innovation. This includes the market uncertainty ("Will they buy it?") and the technical uncertainty ("Will we be able to deliver?").

Given the complexity and rapid evolution of consumer preferences, most firms struggle, particularly with the market uncertainty. In response to this, the last couple of years have witnessed a trend favoring a product development process that rapidly iterates with real customers using very simple and inexpensive prototypes. This technique is often referred to as **lean startup** or **pretotyping** (our discussion of the lean start-up framework and pretotyping is based on the work by Ries and by Savoia). Instead of relying too much on marketing to document customer preferences, development teams evaluate the attractiveness of product concepts based on true purchase decisions that customers make. Oftentimes, this involves the product team selling the product or service pretending that it is ready for use, while, in reality, the product still requires several months more of development.

The key concept of rapid validation and the lean startup methodology is the concept of a **minimum viable product**. The minimum viable product is a prototype of a new product or service that allows the team to collect the maximum amount of learning about customer preferences with the least amount of effort. The most common forms of the minimum viable product are[4]:

Lean startup A product development process that rapidly iterates with real customers using very simple and inexpensive prototypes. Also known as pretotyping.

Pretotyping A product development process that rapidly iterates with real customers using very simple and inexpensive prototypes. Also known as lean startup.

Minimum viable product A prototype of a new product or service that allows the team to collect the maximum amount of learning about customer preferences with the least amount of effort.

- *The fake door:* When the founders of Zappos wanted to launch their venture selling shoes online, they wrestled with a major assumption underlying their business idea. Would customers be willing to buy shoes online, which means without trying them on? Building a shoe distribution system only to find out that customers are not

---

[4]We are grateful to Roy Rosin of Penn Medicine for this classification.

willing to buy online would have been very expensive. Their solution to resolve that uncertainty was to build a minimum viable product using a fake door. The entrepreneurs went to local shoe stores and took pictures of the inventory. They then created a website and waited for "buy" clicks. With no clicks, they knew their idea was not ready for prime time. With clicks, they had to politely tell the customers that things were still under development—but the team then knew that they were onto something big[5]. So the fake door corresponds to offering something you don't yet have.

- *The fake back-end:* Instead of telling the customer who clicked on the Buy button, "Sorry, we actually don't do business yet," we could do something else. Imagine that, once we have the customer order in our hands, we would ourselves order a pair of shoes from an existing retailer. Vis-à-vis the customer, we then pretend that the shoes came right from our warehouse. Unlike in the case of the fake door, with the fake back-end, the customer will not even notice. This might not be cost-effective at scale, but it is a fast way to learn.

- *The impersonator:* Usually, impersonators tend to be entertainers imitating celebrities. But in the context of a minimum viable product, an impersonator is a prototype that is created using mostly parts or system elements from an existing product or service. If you are selling a new energy drink flavor but are not sure if this flavor is attractive to consumers, why not just take the bottle and the logo from Gatorade and pretend this is a new Gatorade flavor. Allowing reuse of elements of existing products or services reduces the costs of making the prototype and allows you to isolate the thing you are testing—in our case, the flavor of the drink as opposed to its packaging.

- *The one-night stand* (sorry, it really is called this): As the name might suggest, the idea behind this type of minimum viable product is to test something for a very limited time only. Imagine you want to try out a new restaurant concept, such as a pancake café or a yogurt bar. Setting up a restaurant, equipping it, hiring employees, and so on—all these things are very expensive. How about you set up a tent or a kiosk and build a very temporary service first. If it works, you can expand; if not, you learned about the limitations of your idea much faster and at a lower cost.

Consider, once again, the example of HealthyFood@Work. How might we go about finding out if customers are as excited about our favorite product concepts as we are? Here are some examples of how a development team might go about gauging customer interest without (yet) committing the resources for the actual implementation of the process:

- The team could claim that the ordering interface would automatically optimize the food in response to the dietary needs of the user. In reality, however, it could use a (human) nutritionist who makes these decisions "manually." This corresponds to a fake back-end.

- The team could take orders from customers, say for custom-made sandwiches, and then itself place orders for these sandwiches at local restaurants. It could then deliver these sandwiches to the office, maybe using a different package. This corresponds to an impersonator, because the team is taking credit for making food it just bought from somewhere else (this also has the flavor of a fake back-end, but the lines here are arguably somewhat blurry).

- The team could launch the website or app associated with the service, including a button to place the order. However, when customers actually place an order, they would receive a message that the service is still under development. This is an example of a fake door.

- The team could go to a large office building and, once there, make the tour with a mobile kitchen cart (as on an airplane) offering to prepare salads or sandwiches on demand. This would be a one-night stand approach.

---

[5]Ries 2011.

Experiments of this type—testing product concepts with real customers—generate objective data about which product concepts will succeed in the marketplace. Instead of relying on individual opinions, the team can thus follow a more scientific method to validate its ideas.

CONNECTIONS: The Fake Back-end and the Story of the First Voice Recognition Software

Early in the days of the personal computer (think about the 1980s), a large computer manufacturer contemplated the following business opportunity. Computers were the future and one day, the development team argued, every office worker would have a computer on his or her desk. However, in the 1980s only a few office workers could type at a decent speed. With this user inability in mind, the team envisioned a new product concept—data entry through a microphone. The early market research was extremely promising. When asked what they thought of the idea, most people said they would purchase such a microphone.

But the team was clever enough to not rush into a massive rollout based on these data. Creating good voice recognition software at that time, building a product, and running a marketing campaign would have taken years of development and tens of millions of dollars.

Instead, the development team built a prototype. They created a computer with a microphone next to it. They invited customers to try out the user experience. However, what the users did not know was that the microphone was not even connected to the computer. Instead, a typist sat in the room next door, listened to the user, and typed what the user had to say. For the user, this was exactly the same as modern voice recognition software. For the computer manufacturer, this took a couple of hours of work for the same amount of information that would have been gained from a "real" prototype.

The lesson the team learned? Though it looked like a good idea and the need was certainly a real one, this simply was not the right solution. After trying it out, only very few customers were satisfied. The sooner you can find out that your idea is not as good as you think it is, the sooner you can start looking for a better idea. . . .

Source: Savoia, 2012.

© Christopher Robbins/Image Source/RF

Check Your Understanding 20.5

Question: A startup is contemplating launching a service, TestMeNow, to high school students. TestMeNow allows students to predict their SAT, ACT, and TOEFL (Test of English as a Foreign Language) score in a 20-minute diagnosis using a website or an app. The team wants to use the minimum viable product idea to validate its concept. What would be some ways to rapidly validate the idea of TestMeNow?

Answer: Some rapid validations would be

- *Fake door:* Create a Facebook or other web presence that announces the service and look at the number of "Likes" as a proxy for user interest.
- *Fake back-end:* Have a couple of test questions and then use the judgment of an experienced test tutor to make a subjective prediction on how the student will do on the test.
- *Impersonator:* Take a number of test questions from an existing SAT test prep and put them into a simple web interface.
- *One-night stand:* Set up a table at the school's cafeteria and offer a paper (survey)–based version of the service.

20.6 Forecasting Sales

LO20-6 Forecast sales based on a purchase intent survey

At some point, the product development team will have found a product concept that gains some traction with customers. But how much will it sell? 1000 units per year? 10,000 units per year? Or even more? From an operations management perspective, we would like to be able to predict the demand for our new product or service so we can either pre-produce the appropriate amount of inventory before the launch or put the necessary service capacity in place at the launch. Such a demand prediction for a new product or service is called a **sales forecast**.

When making forecasts for new product sales, development teams typically rely on surveys asking customers to express their purchase intent. A **purchase intent survey** communicates the product concept with the customer in the form of either a description, a photo, a video, or a physical mock-up.

When doing a survey, teams first identify customers in the market segment relevant to their innovation. Then, the team asks customers to respond to questions such as "If HealthyFood@ Work would be offered in your building for $10 per meal, how likely are you to purchase a subscription to this service?" Customers are asked to express their purchase intent using a scale such as:

- Definitely would buy
- Probably would buy
- Might or might not buy
- Probably would not buy
- Definitely would not buy

Based on the responses to this survey, the team then computes a **purchase probability**. A naïve calculation of a purchase probability would simply measure the percentage of customers who respond positively to the survey question. However, experience shows that the actual probability of purchase is dramatically lower than the purchase probability customers express on surveys. For this reason, it is important to discount the purchase probability.

Research in marketing has looked at the relationship between the customer response on a purchase intent survey and the actual likelihood of purchase. While the exact numbers vary across settings, it has been demonstrated repeatedly that customers purchase goods and services far less often than they say they would on a purchase intent survey.

With this in mind, we have to discount the purchase probability using two calibration constants. The first constant, $C_{definite}$, determines by how much we discount the purchase intent of those who respond "definitely will buy." Typically, this constant is set to a value such that $0.1 < C_{definite} < 0.5$. For the purpose of our analysis, we assume $C_{definite} = 0.4$. This means we assume that 40 percent of those who say they definitely will buy actually end up buying.

Similarly, we define a second constant, $C_{probably}$, which determines by how much we discount the purchase intent of those who respond "probably would buy." This constant should be set so that $0 < C_{probably} < C_{definite} < 0.25$. For the purpose of our analysis, we assume $C_{probably} = 0.2$. Moreover, for simplicity, we assume that the likelihood of purchase is zero for customers who answered the purchase intent survey with "definitely would not buy," "probably would not buy," or "might or might not buy."

So, we can write the purchase probability as:

$$\text{Purchase probability} = (C_{definite} \times \text{Fraction "definitely buy"})$$
$$+ (C_{probably} \times \text{Fraction "probably buy"})$$
$$= (0.4 \times \text{Fraction "definitely buy"})$$
$$+ (0.2 \times \text{Fraction "probably buy"})$$

Once we have the purchase probability, we can move along to predict sales. For that, we have to keep in mind that before customers will be able to purchase a new product or service,

Sales forecast Demand prediction for a new product or service.

Purchase intent survey A survey that communicates the product concept with the customer and then asks the customer how likely he or she is to purchase the product.

Purchase probability A prediction on the likelihood with which a given consumer would purchase the product or service.

they will have to become aware of it. What good is a high purchase probability if few customers are aware of the innovation? Firms use advertising to improve **product awareness**, but this is a costly and slow process, especially for small entrepreneurial ventures. The product awareness is defined by the fraction of the relevant population that is aware of the new product or service.

We compute our sales forecast as

Sales forecast = (Market size) × (Awareness probability) × (Purchase Probability)

where **market size** measures the number of customers who are in the market that we aim to serve. Imagine that out of a survey population of 200, 10 customers answered the survey of HealthyFood@Work with a "will definitely buy" and 22 customers answered us with "will likely buy" (see Figure 20.11). We first compute the purchase probability as described earlier to be

$$\text{Purchase probability} = 0.4 \times \frac{10}{200} + 0.2 \times \frac{22}{200} = 0.042$$

Assuming there are 10,000 customers in the office environment whom we will target and that we can reach a 10 percent product awareness for our new service, we can compute a sales forecast of

$$\text{Sales forecast} = 10{,}000 \times 0.042 \times 0.1 = 42$$

Contrast this sales forecast of 42 with a more naïve forecasting process. If one ignores the effects of awareness and discounting to acknowledge that consumers don't always follow the purchase intent they put into a survey, one would have predicted sales as (Market size) × (Purchase probability). Because the purchase probability (again, using a naïve analysis) would be $(10 + 22)/200 = 0.16$, we would get a forecast of $10{,}000 \times 0.16 = 1600$, which is almost 40 times bigger than the professional forecast that adjusts for product awareness and discounts the expressed purchase probability.

Product awareness The fraction of the relevant population that is aware of the new product or service.

Market size The number of customers who are in the market that we aim to serve.

Figure 20.11   Analysis of a purchase intent survey

Healthy Food@ Work is an online service that provides office workers with healthy meals right to their desk. Customers place an order and within 30 minutes the service delivers a meal that is prepared to meet the dietary goals of the customer. Calories and nutrients are saved and are routinely analyzed by our nutritional experts with personalized suggestions.

If HealthyFood@Work is offered in your building for $10 per meal, how likely are you to purchase a subscription to this service?

Survey to Customers	Definitely would buy	Probably would buy	Might or might not buy	Probably would not buy	Definitely would not buy

Internal Analysis of Results					
Results	10	22	48	59	61
Proportion	$\frac{10}{200}$	$\frac{22}{200}$	$\frac{48}{200}$	$\frac{59}{200}$	$\frac{61}{200}$
Purchase probability	$0.4 \times \frac{10}{200} + 0.2 \times \frac{22}{200} = 0.042$				

Check Your Understanding 20.6

Question: You are given the answers to a purchase intent survey for a new airport shuttle service between your college and the local airport. The customer responses were as follows:

- Definitely would buy: 20
- Probably would buy: 33
- Might or might not buy: 48
- Probably would not buy: 54
- Definitely would not buy: 77

Out of a target market of 12,000 potential customers, how many do you expect to adopt the service, assuming that you can reach a 20 percent awareness in the population? Assume $C_{probably} = 0.2$ and $C_{definite} = 0.4$.

Answer: We add up all the responses and see that we have data from 232 customers. We next translate these data into relative percentages (by dividing the number of answers in each of the five categories by 232). We then take the "definitely would buy" category and discount that proportion by 0.4 (an airport shuttle service is a nondurable product) and the "probably would buy" category by 0.2.

This analysis is shown below:

	Count	Percentage	Adjustment	Overall
Definitely yes	20	0.086	0.4	0.062931
Probably yes	33	0.142	0.2	
Maybe	48	0.207		
Probably no	54	0.233		
Definitely no	77	0.332		
Total	232			

We get an overall purchase probability of 0.062931. We multiply this probability by the size of the target market and the product awareness:

$$\text{Estimated number of adopters} = (\text{Population size}) \times (\text{Awareness and availability})$$
$$\times (\text{Purchase probability})$$
$$= 12{,}000 \times 0.2 \times 0.062931$$
$$= 151.0345$$

Conclusion

Innovations don't just happen. They are the outcome of a process—a process that organizations, small and big alike, need to deliberately manage. Once an organization has identified an opportunity, it goes through a sequence of activities that together make up its product development process. This includes the identification of customer needs, the generation of product concepts, the validation of the concepts, and a prediction of the level of adoption.

Over the last couple of years, the term **design thinking** has gained a fair bit of traction and has been widely recognized as a best practice to follow in the product development process. Figure 20.12 shows a representation of the design thinking framework. This visualization of

Design thinking An approach to product development consisting of contextual observation, problem definition, concept generation, and rapid validation.

Figure 20.12 A slightly different representation of the product development process (Source: Asch, Rosin, and Terwiesch, 2013. Also based on www.designcouncil.org.uk.)

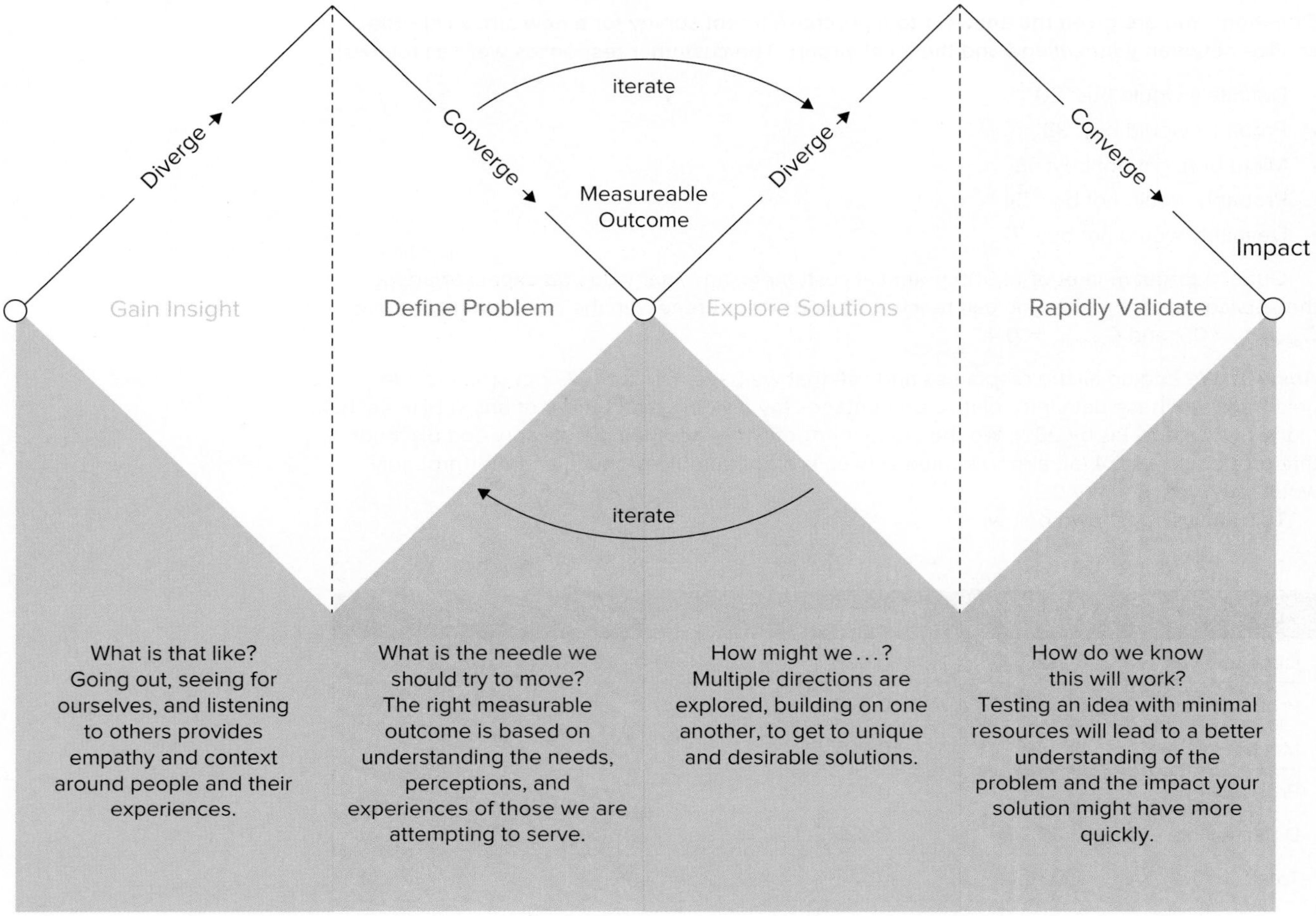
iterate
Diverge
Converge
Measureable Outcome
Diverge
Converge
Impact
Gain Insight
Define Problem
Explore Solutions
Rapidly Validate
iterate
What is that like? Going out, seeing for ourselves, and listening to others provides empathy and context around people and their experiences.
What is the needle we should try to move? The right measurable outcome is based on understanding the needs, perceptions, and experiences of those we are attempting to serve.
How might we . . . ? Multiple directions are explored, building on one another, to get to unique and desirable solutions.
How do we know this will work? Testing an idea with minimal resources will lead to a better understanding of the problem and the impact your solution might have more quickly.

the process is oftentimes referred to as the **double diamond** (reflecting the shape of the two adjacent squares).

Note the similarity between the steps in the design thinking process and our product development process outlined at the beginning of the chapter. As we go from left to right in Figure 20.12, we see steps such as gain insights (similar to our identification of user needs), define the problem (similar to our two forms of decomposition), explore solutions (similar to our search for many and diverse solution concepts), and then finally rapidly validate.

In addition to representing this flow from left to right in the figure (including potential iterations), Figure 20.12 also has a vertical direction:

- During the first phase, when the goal is to gain insights about the customer needs, we want to understand the customer broadly. We explore customer behavior open-mindedly, not yet knowing what exact information will be useful later on in the process. Figure 20.12 captures this in the shape of the "diverge" in the left diamond.
- Before we can solve a problem, we have to define what the problem is. At some point, we have to converge on a specific piece of the user experience we want to improve. We have to answer the question "What is the needle we are trying to move?" Our two forms of product decomposition—one based on user attributes and one based on the activities that shape the user interaction—help us articulate where we want to focus. Defining such an outcome variable (making it easier to pay for the lunch, making the eating experience social) is critical because this constitutes the yardstick we use in the

Double diamond A metaphor describing the design thinking approach.

rapid validation phase. Only if we have an outcome variable can we judge if a concept is successful in changing this outcome variable.

- Once we have zoomed in on one particular outcome variable, we set our sights on a particular subproblem of the broader opportunity that we develop. This could be either a specific activity or a specific customer attribute. Whatever that outcome variable may be, we should consider many and very different solution approaches when generating product concepts. This is the "diverge" in the right diamond.

- Finally, we want to measure whether we have had an impact—did our best concept move the needle or not? For this, we have to narrow down ("converge") the set of product concepts. Some of this can be done with concept selection using a simple concept selection table as discussed in Table 20.1. Beyond this, the best product concepts should not be evaluated in a conference room but, instead, should be validated with real customers.

Summary of Learning Objectives

LO20-1 Explain different types of innovation

An innovation is a novel match between a solution and a need that creates value. Innovations vary in their extent of novelty on the need and the solution sides. The novelty of the solution ranges from existing solutions to new technology development. The novelty of the needs ranges from serving our existing markets to developing new markets for which the need still is unfulfilled. Depending on the amount of novelty, we can classify an innovation into horizons 1 (incremental, little novelty), 2, and 3 (radical, a lot of novelty).

LO20-2 Identify the activities in a product development process

A product development process consists of a set of activities. These include the identification of the customer needs, generation of product concepts, concept validation, and sales forecasting. These activities are typically carried out in this sequence, though some iteration can be required.

LO20-3 Explain the Kano model and be able to create an organized user-needs hierarchy

The utility a customer derives from a product or service is a result of how the product or service fulfills a number of customer needs. Customer needs can be organized hierarchically, defining a set of product attributes. According to the Kano model, these attributes can be categorized into three classes. Attributes for performance needs (linear satisfiers) linearly increase utility—the more the better. Attributes for delighter needs will lead to utility if present, but they will not lead to dissatisfaction if not present. They often are associated with latent needs. Attributes for must-have needs, in contrast, will lead to dissatisfaction if not present, but not to a big increase in utility if present.

LO20-4 Generate product concepts by decomposing a product or service based on its attributes or its user interaction

A product concept is a preliminary articulation of a solution for a given set of needs. During the product development process, many such concepts ought to be developed. This is facilitated by decomposing the products based either on the product attributes or on the user interaction with the product. Following the generation of concepts, concepts should be evaluated on the dimensions of need fulfillment, feasibility, and the concept's wow factor.

LO20-5 Identify rapid validation methods for a concept

Product development is an inherently uncertain process; it is almost always difficult to determine which concepts resonate best with the customer. Rather than spending a long time engineering and planning, the idea of rapid validation is to take prototypes representing a concept and get customer feedback as early as possible. This is oftentimes referred to as pretotyping or lean startup. The minimum viable product is a special case of such a prototype. It allows the developer to get customer feedback not by merely surveying the customer, but by assessing to what extent the customer is willing to take on an action such as pre-ordering the product or endorsing it on Facebook.

LO20-6 Forecast sales based on a purchase intent survey

To prepare for the production and distribution of a new product or service, a developer has to plan a supply process. Such planning requires a forecast of how many units will be demanded by the customer. A purchase intent survey asks customers about their willingness to purchase a new product or service. When interpreting the data of such a purchase intent process, it is important to factor in that customers first have to become aware of the new product and typically are less likely to buy a new product or service compared to what they say in a survey.

Key Terms

20.1 Types of Innovations

Innovation A novel match between customer needs (the foundation of demand) and solutions in the form of physical goods or services (the supply) that create value.

Opportunity identification The process of generating opportunities.

Opportunity An idea—it is a new product or service at the embryonic state.

Innovation horizon A measure of the novelty of an innovation, with horizon 1 being less novel than horizon 2, which in turn is less novel than horizon 3.

Incremental innovation A horizon 1 innovation; uses existing technology and serves existing customers.

Radical innovation A horizon 3 innovation; oftentimes serves new markets and/or employs new technology.

20.2 The Product Development Process

Product development process A process that takes an opportunity as its input and translates this into a new product or service. The process includes needs identification, the generation of product concepts, an empirical validation of the concepts, and a business analysis, involving a sales forecast.

Iterative process A process in which one or several of the activities are repeated one or multiple times.

20.3 Understanding User Needs

User needs The drivers of customer utilities.

Hierarchy of needs The organization of user needs into primary needs, secondary needs, and tertiary needs.

Primary needs Needs that are at the top of the needs hierarchy. Note that this implies that they are more aggregated. This says nothing about importance.

Secondary needs Needs that are at in the middle of the needs hierarchy. Note that this implies that they are less aggregated than the primary needs. This says nothing about importance.

Tertiary needs Needs that are at the bottom of the needs hierarchy. Note that this says nothing about their importance.

Performance needs Needs that will lead to customer satisfaction when fulfilled and dissatisfaction when not fulfilled. Utility grows more or less linearly in the extent to which customer needs are met. Also called linear satisfiers.

Linear satisfiers Needs that will lead to customer satisfaction when fulfilled and dissatisfaction when not fulfilled. Utility grows more or less linearly in the extent to which customer needs are met. Also called performance needs.

Delighters Needs that will lead to customer satisfaction when fulfilled but will not lead to dissatisfaction when not fulfilled. Frequently associated with latent needs.

Must-haves Needs that will not really drive customer satisfaction upward when fulfilled but could drive customer satisfaction substantially downward when not fulfilled.

Noriaki Kano A 20th-century Japanese design professor.

Kano model A framework that distinguishes between three types of needs: performance needs, delighters, and must-haves.

Latent needs Needs that customers are not aware that they have.

Interviews In interviews, one or multiple team members discuss user needs with one customer at a time.

Contextual observation Observing the user in the context in which he or she would be most likely to use the new product or service. The emphasis is on observation and discussion with the user and can take multiple hours, during which time the developer takes notes and photos.

Focus groups A moderated group discussion of four to eight customers that typically lasts for about two hours.

20.4 Concept Generation

Concept generation In concept generation, a product development team generates a large and diverse set of product concepts in the hope that one or several of these concepts will be the foundation for our new product or service.

Product concept A preliminary articulation of a solution for a given set of user needs.

Prototype A representation of the final product or service that allows the product development team to predict how well a particular product concept might fulfill the customer needs.

Fidelity The extent to which a prototype approximates the actual user experience.

Decomposition Breaking up a problem into smaller, manageable subproblems and solving these subproblems first. Decomposition is based on the idea of divide and conquer.

Attribute-based decomposition In an attribute-based decomposition, we focus on a subset of attributes of a new product or service and try to generate a concept that performs well on these attributes, even at the risk of performing poorly on others.

User interaction–based decomposition Decomposition of a product or service into the activities the user goes through when using the product.

Value curve A graphic depiction of a new product's relative performance across the key attributes, comparing it with existing offerings in the market.

Service blueprint A user interaction–based decomposition that breaks up the flow of activities required to serve the customer. The service blueprint also distinguishes which activities are done by the customer alone, which activities are carried out "on stage" (which means during the interaction of us with the customer), and which activities we do without the involvement of the customer.

Concept selection Prioritization of the concepts generated so far in the development.

Selection matrix A table that compares product concepts. The rows in the selection matrix are the concepts, with the columns being the three dimensions of comparison: need fulfillment, feasibility, and wow factor.

20.5 Rapid Validation/Experimentation

Lean startup A product development process that rapidly iterates with real customers using very simple and inexpensive prototypes. Also known as pretotyping.

Pretotyping A product development process that rapidly iterates with real customers using very simple and inexpensive prototypes. Also known as lean startup.

Minimum viable product A prototype of a new product or service that allows the team to collect the maximum amount of learning about customer preferences with the least amount of effort.

20.6 Forecasting Sales

Sales forecast Demand prediction for a new product or service.

Purchase intent survey A survey that communicates the product concept with the customer and then asks the customer how likely he or she is to purchase the product.

> **Purchase probability** A prediction on the likelihood with which a given consumer would purchase the product or service.
>
> **Product awareness** The fraction of the relevant population that is aware of the new product or service.
>
> **Market size** The number of customers who are in the market that we aim to serve.

Conclusion

> **Design thinking** An approach to product development consisting of contextual observation, problem definition, concept generation, and rapid validation.
>
> **Double diamond** A metaphor describing the design thinking approach.

Key Formulas

LO20-6 Forecast sales based on a purchase intent survey

$$\text{Purchase probability} = (C_{\text{definite}} \times \text{Fraction ``definitely buy''})$$
$$+ (C_{\text{probably}} \times \text{Fraction ``probably buy''})$$
$$\text{Sales forecast} = (\text{Market size}) \times (\text{Awareness probability}) \times (\text{Purchase probability})$$

Conceptual Questions

LO20-1

1. Your friend Tony has many ideas. Five times a week, he calls you and explains to you a new device he invented. However, few of these devices address a user need. Are these ideas innovation?
   a. Yes, because they are novel.
   b. Yes, because he invented them.
   c. No, because they don't address a user need.
   d. No, at best they are opportunities, because without user need and value, they are still at the embryonic stage.
   e. c and d
   f. a and b

2. BMW launches a new 3-series model every four to six years. Such launches are which type of innovation?
   a. Horizon 1 innovations
   b. Horizon 2 innovations
   c. Horizon 3 innovations
   d. Cannot determine from the given information

3. Walter is vice president of product development at a big computer maker. At a strategic planning retreat, he talks with the vice president of purchasing and the vice president of production. The computer maker spends about 80 percent of its cost on purchasing, 10 percent on production, and only 2 percent on product development. Which of the following statements is correct?
   a. Product development only corresponds to 2 percent of total cost and hence it is not an important source for future cost reductions.
   b. The costs for production and purchasing are mostly determined during product development and that is why, to reduce costs, product development is critical.
   c. Product development has to do more with marketing, not with costs.
   d. None of these statements is correct.

LO20-2

4. Which of the following activities is not part of the product development process?
   a. Strategic planning
   b. Identification of customer needs

   c. Generation of product concepts

   d. Empirical validation of the concepts

   e. Forecasting of sales for a new product

5. A manager of a product development project reviews the results of the concept validation performed by the team. By showing some concepts to consumers, the team discovered an additional need and now wants to add it to the needs document. However, the manager argues that the identification of customer needs is long over and thus should not be changed. Which statement is correct?

   a. Once the customer needs are documented, they should not be revisited.

   b. Product development is an iterative process, and it is common that activities are repeated.

   c. Neither of these statements is correct.

LO20-3

6. The Kano model classifies needs into three categories. Which of the following is not a category in the Kano model?

   a. Performance needs

   b. Delighters

   c. Must-haves

   d. Important needs

7. Latent needs are typically associated with which category in the Kano model?

   a. Performance needs

   b. Delighters

   c. Must-haves

   d. None of these options is correct.

8. Which of the following statements about contextual observation is correct?

   a. Contextual observation can be combined with interviews.

   b. Contextual observation takes place in the context of the usage of the new product or service.

   c. Oftentimes, photos are taken during the contextual observation.

   d. All of these statements are correct.

   e. None of these statements is correct.

9. What is the difference between primary needs and secondary needs?

   a. Primary needs are more important than secondary needs.

   b. Primary needs consist of multiple secondary needs.

   c. Primary needs are the needs that the product development team discovers first.

LO20-4

10. The product concept is concerned with:

   a. the solution approach.

   b. the consumer needs.

   c. both the consumer needs and the solution approach.

   d. None of these options is correct.

11. Consider two prototypes of a new race car. One is a two-dimensional sketch; the other one is a physical model that almost looks like the new race car, except it has no engine inside. Which of the two is a higher-fidelity prototype?

   a. The two-dimensional sketch

   b. The physical model

   c. The word *fidelity* only applies to processes, not to prototypes.

12. Which of the following techniques is not a form of decomposing a product for the sake of generating product concepts?

   a. Attribute-based decomposition

   b. User interaction–based decomposition

   c. Expert-based decomposition

   d. None of these options is correct.

13. A value curve shows what type of information for a product concept?

   a. The value of the product over time

   b. The degree to which various needs are fulfilled with the product concept

    c. The dollar value for each user need that is part of the product concept

    d. None of these options is correct.

14. Which of the following statements is correct as far as the definition of a service blueprint is concerned?

    a. A service blueprint is a special form of a user-interaction decomposition.

    b. A service blueprint distinguishes between customer actions, onstage actions, backstage actions, and support processes.

    c. Both of these statements are correct.

    d. None of these statements is correct.

LO20-5

15. A minimum viable product is:

    a. a prototype of a new product or service that allows the team to collect the maximum amount of learning with the least amount of effort.

    b. a product that is financially viable at minimum scale.

    c. a part of the lean startup framework.

    d. a and b

    e. a and c

16. What is the purpose of building a minimum viable product?

    a. To test the technical feasibility of the product

    b. To test whether or not the product can be produced economically at scale

    c. To test if consumers want to buy the product

    d. None of these options is correct.

LO20-6

17. The purchase probability is the percentage of customers on the purchase intent survey who indicated they would want to buy the product. True or false?

    a. True

    b. False

18. To get to the sales forecast, we just multiply the market size by the purchase probability. True or false?

    a. True

    b. False

19. Consider two products, A and B, both of which have the same purchase probability. Product A has a population size of 1000 and a 50 percent awareness probability. Product B has a population size of 10,000 and a 5 percent awareness probability. Which product do you expect to sell more?

    a. Product A

    b. Product B

    c. They are expected to sell the same amount.

Solved Example Problems

LO20-1

1. In 2013, technology giant Google had, among many other projects, the following three innovations in its business development pipeline. Which of these innovations is a horizon 1 innovation?

    a. The driverless car, which allows a vehicle to be operated without human intervention

    b. An upgrade to the cloud-based word processing software in Google Docs

    c. Google glasses—a technology that lets users wear a mini computer screen integrated into their eyeglasses.

    Answer: b.

LO20-2

2. Which of the following activities is typically the first activity in the product development process?

   a. Generation of product concepts

   b. Validation of product concepts

   c. Sales forecasting

   d. Identification of customer needs

   e. Pricing

   Answer: d.

LO20-3

3. ErgoCrutch is a startup that designs more ergonomic crutches for athletes recovering from ankle and knee injuries. The key innovation is a more ergonomic grip that significantly reduces the fatigue in the hands/lower arms. The team has done some market research and has listed a set of user needs. Some of these needs are listed below:

   a. The crutches are light.

   b. The crutches are resistant to corrosion.

   c. The crutches have a built-in pedometer that counts the number of steps.

   d. The crutches can be adjusted to different body heights.

   e. The crutches are affordable.

   Which of these needs would you expect to be latent?

   Answer: c.

4. A team thinks about user needs related to a wearable pocket for a smartphone that could be used while running or biking. They create a detailed list of user needs and order them by primary, secondary, and tertiary needs. Latent needs are flagged by an exclamation mark (!). The number of asterisks (*) indicates the strength of the need.

The smartphone pocket we develop. . .

is able to contain a smartphone ***
- fully encloses the smartphone
- the smartphone does not fall out while running

allows the user to access the device while it is still in the pocket **
- allows access to the volume adjustment and other controls located on the rim of the phone
- allows access to the touchscreen

protects the phone from the elements **
- is waterproof relative to water coming in from the outside/rain
- is waterproof relative to sweat developing on the skin

is affordable **
- is inexpensive in its acquisition

is durable **
- can be used many times without wear and tear on its component

provides extra storage space ** (!)
- allows the user to store an ID or a credit card
- allows the user to store cash

is comfortable to wear ***
- can be put on easily
- adjusts to the arm size of the user
- stays snug to the arm instead of bouncing around
- does not restrict the blood flow through the arm

Which of the following statements is/are correct?

a. "Provides extra storage space" is a latent need.

b. "Is affordable" is the most important need.

c. "Is comfortable to wear" is a primary need.

d. a and b

e. a and c

Answer: e.

LO20-4

5. Consider two commuter bicycles, A and B, with the following attributes. Each attribute is scored on a scale from 1 to 10, with 10 being the best value:
   - Affordability (1: expensive, 10: affordable)
   - Available gears (1: few, 10: many)
   - Weight (1: heavy, 10: light)
   - Durability (1: not durable, 10: durable)
   - Handling (1: poor handling, 10: good handling)
   - Rolling resistance (1: high, 10: low)

   Shown below is a value curve comparing these two products.

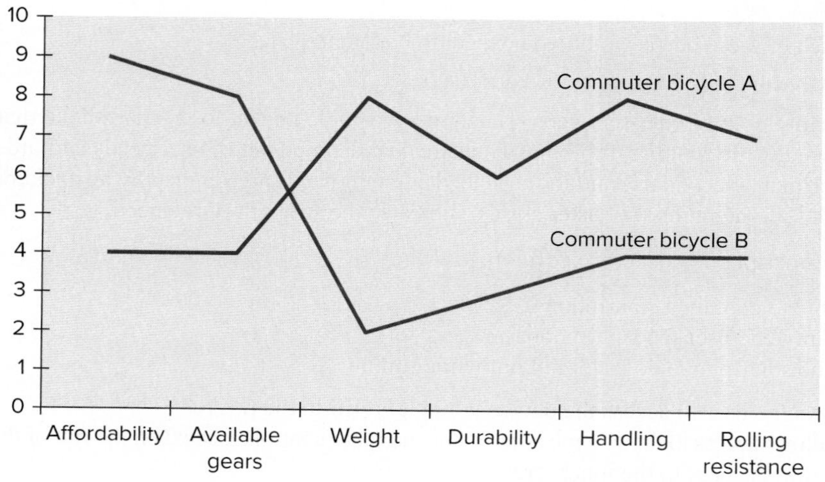

Which of the following statements can be made based on this information?

a. Product B is more expensive.

b. Product A has better durability.

c. Product A is heavier.

d. All of the above are correct.

e. None of the above is correct.

Answer: b.

6. A national restaurant chain is trying to change the traditional way that guests pay for their food. In the current process, like in most restaurants with sit-down service, guests order from the menu by interacting with a waiter. Once ready to leave, the guests call the waiter, who brings them the bill. The guests then get out a credit card and the waiter runs back to the cash register to run the card.

   They create a service blueprint for this process, which is shown in Figure 20.13.

Figure 20.13

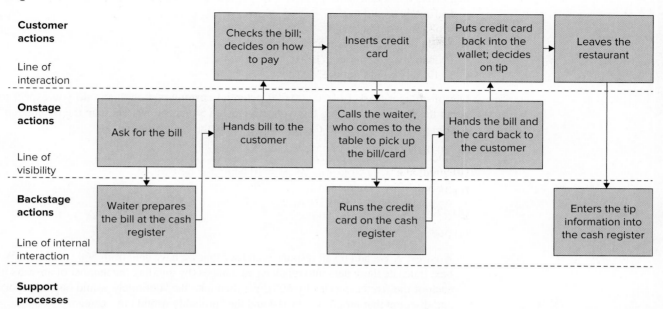

What statements are consistent with this service blueprint?

a. The waiter prepares the bill together with the customer.

b. The payment process can be completed without any back and forth between waiter and guest.

c. A and B

d. None of the above is correct.

   Answer: d.

LO20-5

7. A large medical equipment maker wants to move forward with the following concept for a new device that would be sold to patients at around $200 plus a monthly subscription fee of $15. The smart pill bottle is a technology that reminds patients to take their medicine. The cap of the pill bottle includes a motion sensor. If the motion sensor has not been activated for 24 hours, it sends an electronic message to a base station that is plugged into a nearby power outlet. The base station uses a proprietary data network to send a message to the patient's phone. Initial discussions with doctors and patients have been very positive and so the company considers moving forward by building the data network. However, a new member on the development team suggests that before moving forward, the team should engage in some rapid validation.

Which of these following approaches would you consider a rapid validation?

a. Build a functional prototype and demonstrate the technical feasibility at a large-scale trial.

b. Offer this device to patients at the suggested price (without having it available yet). See what percentage of patients would take the offer in order to overcome market uncertainty.

c. Advertise at nursing homes.

d. Test the reliability of the motion sensor.

   Answer: b.

8. You are given the following customer responses to a purchase intent survey for a service that offers quick dermatology advice on pictures sent to a patient portal:
   - Definitely would use: 37
   - Probably would use: 63
   - Might or might not use: 55
   - Probably would not use: 192
   - Definitely would not use: 221

   Out of a target market of 20,000,000 potential customers, how many do you expect to adopt the service, assuming that you can reach a 5 percent awareness in the population? Assume $C_{probably} = 0.2$ and $C_{definite} = 0.4$. Select the closest option.

   (a) 20,000,000

   (b) 960,000

   (c) 48,000

   (d) 4700

   (e) 568

   Answer: c. We add up all responses and see that we have data from 568 customers. We next translate these data into relative percentages (by dividing the number of answers in each of the five categories by 568). We then take the "definitely would buy" category and discount that proportion by 0.4 and the "probably would buy" category by 0.2.

   This analysis is shown in Table 20.2.

TABLE 20.2

	Count	Percentage	Adjustment	Overall
Definitely yes	37	0.065	0.4	0.048239
Probably yes	63	0.111	0.2	
Maybe	55	0.097		
Probably no	192	0.338		
Definitely no	221	0.389		
Total	568	1		

   We get an overall purchase probability of 0.048239. We multiply this probability by the size of the target market and the product awareness:

   Estimated number of adopters = (Population size) × (Awareness and availability)

   × (Purchase probability)

   = 20,000,000 × 0.05 × 0.048239

   = 48,239.44

Problems and Applications

LO20-2

1. Which of the following activities is not part of the product development process?
   a. Generation of product concepts
   b. Validation of product concepts
   c. Sales forecasting
   d. Identification of customer needs
   e. New product strategy

LO20-3

2. Dishwasher 2020 is a new product under development at a large appliance company looking to develop the next generation of products in the dishwasher market. The team has done some market research and has listed a set of user needs. Water conservation/reducing energy consumption emerges as a need expressed by many consumers. The team debates how that need fits into the Kano model. In your opinion, which type of need is captured by the conservation of water?
   a. Linear satisfier—the more water saved, the better
   b. Must-have—as long as it consumes less water than the last model, nobody cares
   c. Delighter

3. A need related to a product triggers the following reaction by consumers. Consumers are happy if the need is fulfilled but not really dissatisfied if the need is not fulfilled. What type of need in the Kano model fits this description?
   a. Linear satisfier—the more water saved, the better
   b. Must-have—as long as it consumes less water than the last model, nobody cares.
   c. Delighter

LO20-4

4. Which of the following statements is correct as far as a service blueprint is concerned?
   a. A service blueprint helps in identifying the bottleneck.
   b. A service blueprint distinguishes between customer actions, onstage actions, backstage actions, and support processes.
   c. A service blueprint distinguishes between customer defects, onstage defects, backstage defects, and process capability.
   d. None of these statements is correct.

LO20-5

5. Which of the following statements correctly captures the idea of a minimum viable product?
   a. A minimum viable product is a product that is financially viable at minimum scale.
   b. A minimum viable product works great for new product offerings, but it is impossible to apply the idea to a new service.
   c. A product development team should at most build one minimum viable product during the development process.
   d. None of these statements is correct.

6. Which of the following statements best describes the idea of a minimum viable product?
   a. A prototype of a new product or service that tests the technical feasibility of the product.
   b. A prototype of the new production facility or service delivery organization that determines if the product or service can be produced economically at scale.
   c. A prototype of a new product or service that allows the team to collect the maximum amount of learning with the least amount of effort.
   d. None of these statements is correct.

LO20-6

7. You are given the following customer responses to a purchase intent survey for a new electric bicycle that has all its batteries built into the frame and hence almost looks exactly like a regular bike:
   - Definitely would use: 12
   - Probably would use: 22
   - Might or might not use: 31
   - Probably would not use: 111
   - Definitely would not use: 201

   Out of a target market of 1,500,000 potential customers, how many do you expect to adopt the product, assuming you can reach a 5 percent awareness in the population? Assume $C_{probably} = 0.2$ and $C_{definite} = 0.4$. Select the closest option.
   a. 150
   b. 243
   c. 1830
   d. 24,290
   e. 1,500,000

CASE   INNOVATION AT TOYOTA

© Hannu Liivaar/Alamy

In the early 1990s, Toyota's chairman Eiji Toyoda was concerned about the future of his company. He asked his board, "Should we continue building cars as we have been doing? Can we survive in the 21st century with the type of R&D we are doing? There is no way that this booming situation will last much longer."

In response to this challenge, Yoshiro Kimbara, then executive vice president of R&D, initiated the G21 project. The project goal was to develop a fuel-efficient car, exactly the opposite of the gas-guzzling SUVs that were selling well at the time.[5] The G21 launched in 1997 and became the Toyota Prius.

Sales for the Prius started out slow. In the first few years, only a couple of thousand vehicles were sold, all of them in Japan. By 2010, however, 500,000 Prius vehicles had been purchased each year, comprising more than half of all hybrid vehicle sales.

For 2015, Toyota announced the launch of the FCV for the California market. The FCV operates based on hydrogen, which makes water the car's only emission.

1. In your opinion, are the Prius and the FCV horizon 1, 2, or 3 innovations?

2. From the perspective of today, what would a horizon 3 innovation in the automotive industry look like?

3. Would you as an executive in the automotive industry invest in a project like this?

[5] Jeffrey K. Liker, *The Toyota Way* (Tata McGraw-Hill, 2004).

References

Asch, David A., Christian Terwiesch, Kevin B. Mahoney, and Roy Rosin. "Insourcing Health Care Innovation." *New England Journal of Medicine* 370, no. 19 (May 8, 2014), pp. 1775–77.

Griffin, Abbie, and John Hauser, "The Voice of the Customer," *Marketing Science,* vol. 12, no. 1 (1993), p. 1–27.

Kim, W. Chan, and Renee Mauborgne. *Blue Ocean Strategy: How to Create Uncontested Market Space and Make the Competition Irrelevant.* Boston: Harvard Business School Publishing, 2005.

Osterwalder, Alexander; Yves Pigneur; Gregory Bernarda; and Alan Smith. V*alue Proposition Design: How to Create Products and Services Customers Want.* Hoboken, New Jersey: John Wiley & Sons, 2014.

Ries, Eric. *The Lean Startup: How Today's Entrepreneurs Use Continuous Innovation to Create Radically Successful Businesses.* New York, Crown Business, 2011.

Savoia, Alberto. *Pretotype It: Make Sure You Are Building the Right* It *before You Build* It *Right.* 3rd ed. Amazon Digital Services, 2012.

Terwiesch, Christian, and Karl T. Ulrich. *Innovation Tournaments: Creating and Selecting Exceptional Opportunities.* Cambridge, MA: Harvard Business Review Press, 2009.

Ullman, David. *The Mechanical Design Process.* 4th ed. New York: McGraw-Hill, 2009.

Ulrich, Karl T., and Steven D. Eppinger. *Product Design and Development.* 5th ed. New York: McGraw-Hill Education, 2011.

http://www.managementexchange.com/hack/pretotype-it-make-sure-you%E2%80%99re-building-right-%E2%80%9Cit%E2%80%9D-you-build-it-right

4Ps of Toyota   Business principles embraced by Toyota that include philosophy, processes, people, and problem solving.

Abandoning   The practice of leaving a queue after joining it. Also known as reneging.

Abnormal   A variation is abnormal if it is not behaving in line with past data; this allows us to conclude that we are dealing with an assignable cause variation and are not just facing randomness in the form of common cause variation.

Activity network   A graph capturing the project activities and its dependencies in which nodes correspond to project activities and arrows correspond to precedence relationships (with an arrow going from the predecessor activity to the successor activity). Also called an activity-on-node (AON) graph.

Activity time   The amount of time it takes a resource to complete the activity once it has started to work on it. The concept of an activity time is the same as the processing time in a process analysis.

Activity-on-node (AON) graph   A graph capturing the project activities and its dependencies in which nodes correspond to project activities and arrows correspond to precedence relationships (with an arrow going from the predecessor activity to the successor activity). Also called activity network.

Anchoring bias   The fact that human decision makers are selective in their acquisition of new information, looking for what confirms their initially held beliefs.

Andon   A system consisting of a visible board and a cord running adjacent to the assembly line. An employee who detects a problem can pull the cord to stop the line. This will be indicated on the board.

Arrival process   The flow of customers arriving to the system.

Assemble-to-order   A make-to-order system in which a product is assembled from a set of standardized modular components after an order is received.

Assignable cause variation   Variation that occurs because of a specific change in input or in environmental variables.

Attribute-based control chart   A special control chart used for dealing with binary outcomes. It has all the features of the X-bar chart, yet does not require a continuous outcome variable. However, attribute-based charts require larger sample sizes, especially if defects occur rarely. Also known as p-charts.

Attribute-based decomposition   In an attribute-based decomposition, we focus on a subset of attributes of a new product or service and try to generate a concept that performs well on these attributes, even at the risk of performing poorly on others.

Attrition loss   In a process with attrition losses, all flow units start at the same resource but then drop out of the process (or are actively removed from the process) at different points.

Automated forecasting   Forecasts that are created by computers, typically with no human intervention.

Autonomation   Automation with a human touch; use machines, but combine them with the intelligence of the workers.

Autonomous learning   Improvements due to on-the-job learning of employees.

Average labor utilization   The average utilization across resources.

Average tenure   The average time an employee has spent on his or her job. Average tenure = $1/(2 \times$ Employee turnover).

Backorder   The total amount of demand that is waiting for inventory to arrive before it can be satisfied.

Balancing for a fixed sequence of activities   Balancing a line in which the activities have to be completed in a predefined order.

Balancing for activities with no fixed sequence   Balancing a line in which the activities do not have to be completed in a predefined order, which typically leads to higher utilization levels.

Balking   The practice of not joining a queue. Customers generally balk when they believe the total time needed to receive service exceeds the amount of time they are willing to wait.

Batch   A collection of units.

Batch process   A type of production in which units are produced in batches.

Baton passing zone   Instead of having fixed allocations of activities to workers, the idea of a baton passing zone is that the process can absorb variations in speed and starting time.

Biased forecast   A forecast that is wrong on average, thus an average forecast error different from zero.

Bill of materials   The list of components needed for the assembly of an item.

Blocking   The event in which a resource completes a flow unit but is prevented from working on a new flow unit because there is no place to store the completed unit.

Bottleneck   Resource with the lowest capacity in a process.

Breaking bulk   A service in which a distributor purchases in large quantities from manufacturers but then allows customers to purchase in smaller quantities.

Brick-and-mortar retailer   A retailer with physical stores in which consumers are able to immediately purchase goods.

Buffer   Inventory within a process that helps to mitigate the consequences of variability.

Buffer or suffer   A principle that states that a system's capacity decreases if sufficiently large buffers are not included in the system.

Bullwhip effect   The tendency for demand to become more volatile at higher levels of the supply chain.

Capabilities   The dimensions of the customer's utility function a firm is able to satisfy.

Capacity   The maximum number of flow units that can flow through that resource per unit of time.

Capacity-constrained   The case in which demand exceeds supply and the flow rate is equal to process capacity.

Catalog retailers   Retailers that merchandize their goods via a print catalog and sell to consumers by shipping them goods via a third-party carrier like the U.S. Postal Service, UPS, FedEx, or DHL. Also called mail-order retailers.

Cause-effect diagram   A structured way to brainstorm about the potential root causes that have led to a change in an outcome variable. This is done by mapping out all input and environmental variables. Also known as a fishbone diagram or Ishikawa diagram.

Changeover time   A setup time to change production from one type of product to another.

Coefficient of variation   The ratio of the standard deviation to the mean.

Common cause variation   Variation that occurs in a process as a result of pure randomness (also known as natural variation).

Concept generation   In concept generation, a product development team generates a large and diverse set of product concepts in the hope that one or several of these concepts will be the foundation for our new product or service.

Concept selection   Prioritization of the concepts generated so far in the development.

Concurrent engineering   The (partially) simultaneous execution of multiple development activities with a strong emphasis on coordination.

Consumption utility   A measure of how much you like a product or service, ignoring the effects of price and of the inconvenience of obtaining the product or service.

Contextual observation   Observing the user in the context in which he or she would be most likely to use the new product or service. The emphasis is on observation and discussion with the user and can take multiple hours, during which time the developer takes notes and photos.

Control charts   A control chart is a visual representation of variation in the process. It has time on its x-axis and an outcome variable on the y-axis. In each time period, we collect a sample of outcomes, which we plot in the control chart. The control chart also shows a long-run center line (called X-bar-bar), which is the average across all points. It also shows an upper and a lower control limit, which are computed based on past data.

Controlling the project   Tracking the progress of the project as it unfolds.

Coordination   Information exchange among activities.

Correlation   A measure of the interaction between two uncertain events. Correlation ranges from -1 to 1.

Costs of direct labor   The labor cost associated with serving one customer, which is the total wages paid per unit of time divided by the flow rate.

Crashing   An increase in spending that allows for a faster completion time of a project.

Critical path   The path with the longest duration.

Critical ratio   The ratio of the underage cost, C_u, to the sum of the overage cost and the underage cost, $C_u + C_o$.

Cumulative learning curve coefficient   The cost of producing x units in a process that has an initial cost of $c(1) = 1$ and a learning rate of LR.

Cycle time   The time between completing two consecutive flow units.

Days-of-supply   The average amount of time (in days) it takes for a unit to flow through the system.

Declining marginal returns   When the incremental benefit of an activity decreases as the amount of the activity increases. For example, if the return from one hour of training declines as the worker receives more hours of training, then the training exhibits declining marginal returns.

Decomposition   Breaking up a problem into smaller, manageable subproblems and solving these subproblems first. Decomposition is based on the idea of divide and conquer.

Dedicated project team   A project team in which the team members spend 100 percent of their work time on the project.

Defect probability   The statistical probability with which a randomly chosen flow unit does not meet specifications.

Defective   Not corresponding to the specifications of the process.

Defining the project   Defining and negotiating the three variables making up the project triangle: project time, project budget, and project scope.

Delayed differentiation   A strategy in which product differentiation is delayed as late as possible in the supply chain.

Delighters   Needs that will lead to customer satisfaction when fulfilled but will not lead to dissatisfaction when not fulfilled. Frequently associated with latent needs.

Demand   The set of customers for whom a specific product or service is the best choice (also called the utility maximizing choice).

Demand-constrained   The case in which process capacity exceeds demand and thus the flow rate is equal to the demand rate.

Demand forecasting   The process of creating statements about future realizations of demand.

Demand leveling   A way to sequence flow units so that the workflow causes a stable workload for all workers involved in the process.

Demand matrix   Determines how many flow units of each type are flowing through each resource. For resource i, $D(i,j)$ is the number of flow units of type j that need to be processed.

Demand rate   The number of flow units that customers want per unit of time.

Deming cycle   Synonym for PDCA cycle.

Denial of service probability   The probability that a flow unit in the Erlang loss model is not served; that is, it becomes part of lost demand.

Density function   A function that returns the probability a given outcome occurs for a particular statistical distribution.

Dependency matrix   In the dependency matrix, each column represents an activity that provides information and each row indicates an activity that receives information. An entry in column i and row j suggests that the activity in the ith column (A_i) provides information to the activity in the jth row (A_j).

Dependent variable   The variable that we try to explain in a regression analysis.

Deseasonalize   To remove the seasonal effect from past data.

Design thinking   An approach to product development consisting of contextual observation, problem definition, concept generation, and rapid validation.

Detect-stop-alert   The philosophy of halting production when a quality problem is discovered.

Diminishing returns   A performance trajectory in which the improvement rate decreases over time or experience.

Discovery-driven planning   An approach to project management that emphasizes iteration and dynamic adjustment.

Distribution center (DC)   A building used to receive products from suppliers and then redistribute them to retail stores or send packages to consumers. Also called a fulfillment center.

Distribution function   A function that returns the probability the outcome of a random event is a certain level or lower. For example, if $F(Q)$ is the distribution function of demand, then $F(Q)$ is the probability that demand is Q or lower.

Diversion   The practice of sending demand away from a system when it cannot be served by the system in a sufficiently timely manner. For example, a hospital may divert patients to another hospital when it is unable to care for more patients.

Double diamond   A metaphor describing the design thinking approach.

Double exponential smoothing   A way of forecasting a demand process with a trend that estimates both the demand and the trend using exponential smoothing. The resulting forecast is the sum of these two estimates. This is a type of momentum-based forecasting.

Downstream   The parts of the process that are at the end of the process flow.

Dynamic coordination   Iterative execution of interdependent activities where both activities provide input to each other.

E-commerce   Retailers that merchandise their goods via an online website (or app) and sell to consumers by shipping them goods via a third-party carrier like the U.S. Postal

Service, UPS, FedEx, or DHL. Also called online retailers or e-tailers.

E-tailers   Retailers that merchandize their goods via an online website (or app) and sell to consumers by shipping them goods via a third-party carrier like the U.S. Postal Service, UPS, FedEx, or DHL. Also called online retailers or e-commerce.

Earliest completion time (ECT)   The earliest time an activity can be completed, which is given by the earliest time all predecessor activities have been completed plus the activity time.

Earliest due date (EDD)   A rule that sequences jobs to be processed on a resource in ascending order of their due dates.

Earliest start time (EST)   The earliest time an activity can begin, which is given by the earliest time all predecessor activities have been completed.

Economic order quantity (EOQ) model   A model used to select an order quantity that minimizes the sum of ordering and inventory holding costs per unit of time.

Economies of scale   Describes a relationship between operational efficiency and demand in which greater demand leads to a more efficient process.

Efficiency   A process is efficient if it is able to achieve a high flow rate with few resources.

Efficient frontier   The set of firms that are not Pareto dominated.

Emergency Severity Index (ESI)   A scoring rule used by Emergency Rooms to rank the severity of a patient's injuries and then to prioritize their care.

Employee turnover   Employee turnover = (Number of new employees recruited per year)/(Average number of employees). The higher the employee turnover, the less experience the average employee will have with his or her job.

Environmental variables   Variables in a process that are not under the control of management but nevertheless might impact the outcome of the process.

EOQ cost per unit of time   The sum of ordering and holding costs per unit of time.

Equipment replication   The need to provide extra equipment to nonspecialized labor at resources often leads to a low level of equipment utilization.

Erlang loss model   A queuing model in which the total number of flow units in the system cannot exceed the number of servers. If a flow unit arrives to the system when it is full, the flow unit is not served by the system and becomes lost demand.

Estimated standard deviation of all parts   The standard deviation that is computed across all parts.

Estimated standard deviation for X-bar   The standard deviation of a particular sample mean, x-bar.

Event tree   Visual representation of binary outcome variables. It supports the defect probability calculations by connecting the defects in the process to an overall outcome measure.

Expected inventory   The expected number of units not sold at the end of the season that therefore must be salvaged.

Expected on-hand inventory   The average amount of inventory available at the end of each period to serve demand.

Expected on-order inventory   The average amount of inventory on order at any given time.

Expected profit   The expected profit earned from the product, including the consequences of leftover inventory.

Expected sales   The expected number of units sold during the season at the regular price.

Experience curve   Synonym for learning curve; the term *experience* emphasizes that learning is driven by experience.

Expert panel forecasting   Forecasts generated using the subjective opinions of management.

Exponential growth   An improvement trajectory in which the rate of improvement increases over time or experience.

Exponential smoothing forecasting method   A forecasting method that predicts that the next value will be a weighted average between the last realized value and the old forecast.

External setups   Activities that can be done while production continues to occur.

Extrapolation   Estimation of values beyond the range of the original observations by assuming that some patterns in the values present within the range will also prevail outside the range.

Fidelity   The extent to which a prototype approximates the actual user experience.

Fill rate   The fraction of demand satisfied.

Finished goods inventory   Flow units that have completed processing.

First-come-first-served (FCFS)   A rule that sequences jobs to be processed on a resource in the order in which they arrived.

Fishbone diagram   A structured way to brainstorm about the potential root causes that have led to a change in an outcome variable. This is done by mapping out all input and environmental variables. Also known as a cause-effect diagram or Ishikawa diagram.

Fit   A subcomponent of the consumption utility that captures how well the product or service matches with the unique characteristics of a given consumer.

Five Whys   A brainstorming technique that helps employees to find the root cause of a problem. In order to avoid stopping too early and not having found the real root cause, employees are encouraged to ask, "Why did this happen?" at least five times.

Fixed costs   Those costs that a firm has to pay anyway, independent of how much it produces and sells.

Flow rate   The rate at which flow units travel through a process.

Flow time   The time a flow unit spends in a process, from start to finish.

Flow unit   The unit of analysis that we consider in a process analysis; for example, patients in a hospital, scooters in a kick-scooter plant, and calls in a call center.

Flow unit–dependent processing times   The fact that the processing times can vary across flow unit types.

Focus group   A moderated group discussion of four to eight customers that typically lasts for about two hours.

Forecast combination   Combining multiple forecasts that have been generated by different forecasters into one single value.

Forecast error   The difference between a forecasted value and the realized value.

Forecast gaming   A purposeful manipulation of a forecast to obtain a certain decision outcome for a decision that is based on the forecast.

Forecast with consensus building   An iterative discussion among experts about their forecasts and opinions that leads to a single forecast.

Forecasting   The process of creating statements about outcomes of variables that presently are uncertain and will only be realized in the future.

Frederick Winslow Taylor   An engineer who pioneered the concept of scientific management at the end of the 19th century.

Fulfillment center   A building used to receive products from suppliers and then redistribute them to retail stores or send packages to consumers. Also called a distribution center.

Functional products   In the context of strategic supply chain decisions, these are products that are relatively "safe" in the sense that they do not experience a considerable amount of variability.

Gantt chart   A time line with the activities included as bars.

Genchi genbutsu   Gather firsthand information from the situation by going and observing the situation yourself, collecting data, and analyzing the data.

Graph   A collection of objects or nodes that are connected by links.

Gross margin   The difference between the price at which a product is sold and the cost to purchase the item, expressed as a percentage of the selling price of the item.

Heavyweight project manager   A project manager who has a strong influence on the scope and the resources of the project.

Heijunka   Leveling production by reducing variation in the work schedule that arises from either demand variation or the desire to run production or transports in large batches. This is a principle of the Toyota Production System that strives to have production match the true rate of demand.

Henry Gantt   A 19th-century industrialist.

Herbie   A fictitious character in Eli Goldratt's book *The Goal*. Herbie is the slowest hiker in a troop of Boy Scouts. He thus holds up the troop in the same way a bottleneck holds up a process.

Heterogeneous preferences   The fact that not all consumers have the same utility function.

Hierarchy of needs   The organization of user needs into primary needs, secondary needs, and tertiary needs.

Holding cost per unit, h   The cost to hold one item in inventory for one unit of time.

Holding cost per unit of time   The total cost to hold inventory for a period of time.

Holding cost percentage   The ratio of the cost to hold an item in inventory during a designated time period relative to the cost to purchase the item.

Idle time   The amount of time per flow unit for which a resource is paid but is not actually working.

Implied utilization   The ratio of demand to capacity: Implied utilization = Demand at the resource / Capacity at the resource. The implied utilization captures the mismatch between demand and capacity.

In-stock probability   The probability that all demand is served within an interval of time.

Inconvenience   The reduction in utility that results from the effort of obtaining the product or service.

Incremental innovation   A horizon 1 innovation; uses existing technology and serves existing customers.

Independent   Two events are independent (i.e., their correlation is 0) when the outcome of one event has no relationship to the outcome of the other event.

Independent variables   The variables influencing the dependent variable.

Induced learning   A deliberate action and an investment in resources, be it in the form of time or material.

Inefficiency   The gap between a firm and the efficient frontier.

Inflexibility   The inability to adjust to either changes in the supply process or changes in customer demand.

Information turnaround time (ITAT)   The time between creating a defect and receiving the feedback about the defect.

Innovation   A novel match between customer needs (the foundation of demand) and solutions in the form of physical goods or services (the supply) that create value.

Innovation horizon   A measure of the novelty of an innovation, with horizon 1 being less novel than horizon 2, which in turn is less novel than horizon 3.

Innovative products   In the context of strategic supply chain decisions, these are products that are relatively "risky" in the sense that they can experience substantial variability.

Input variables   The variables in a process that are under the control of management.

Interarrival time   The time between customer arrivals to a system.

Interdependent   A form of dependence in which two activities require input from each other.

Internal setups   Activities that can only be done during the actual setup, for example, when the machine is not producing.

Interviews   In interviews, one or multiple team members discuss user needs with one customer at a time.

Inventory   The number of flow units within the process.

Inventory management   The practice of regulating the quantity, location, and type of inventory in a process.

Inventory position   On-order inventory plus on-hand inventory minus the backorder.

Inventory storage cost   The cost incurred to properly store, maintain, and insure inventory.

Inventory turns   The number of times the average inventory flows through a process in a designated interval of time.

Ishikawa diagram   A structured way to brainstorm about the potential root causes that have led to a change in an outcome variable. This is done by mapping out all input and environmental variables. Also known as a fishbone diagram or cause-effect diagram.

Iterative process   A process in which one or several of the activities are repeated one or multiple times.

James Womack   An MIT professor who founded the International Motor Vehicle Program and later the Lean Enterprise Institute.

Jidoka   Upon detection of a problem, shutting down the machine to force a human intervention, which in turn triggers process improvement.

Job   A flow unit that requires processing from one or more resources.

Just-in-time (JIT) production   Supplying a unit of demand when and where it is needed, thus avoiding unnecessary inventory.

Kaizen   The process of making small changes to the process with the goal of eliminating waste.

Kanban   Production and inventory control system in which production instructions and parts delivery instructions are triggered by the consumption of parts downstream.

Kano model   A framework that distinguishes between three types of needs: performance needs, delighters, and must-haves.

Labor content   The amount of work that goes into serving one customer (or, more generally, one flow unit), which is the sum of the processing times involving labor.

Late start schedule   The latest possible timing of all activities that still allows for an on-time completion of the overall project.

Lateness   The difference between the completion time of a job and its due date. Lateness is negative when the job is completed before the due date (i.e., it is early)

Latent needs   Needs that customers are not aware that they have.

Latest completion time (LCT)   The latest possible completion time of an activity that still allows for an on-time completion of the overall project.

Latest start time (LST)   The latest possible start time of an activity that still allows for an on-time completion of the overall project.

Lead time   The time between when an order is placed and when it is filled. Process lead time is frequently used as an alternative term for flow time.

Lead time   The time to receive an order.

Lead-time pooling strategy   A strategy that reduces the demand uncertainty faced in a supply chain, while still keeping inventory reasonably close to customers, by adding an intermediate decision-making point to delay when a commitment is made to a particular product feature that contributes to demand uncertainty.

Lean startup   A product development process that rapidly iterates with real customers using very simple and inexpensive prototypes. Also known as pretotyping.

Learning curve A function that captures the relationship between a performance metric of an operation and the experience as measured in the number of repetitions with which the operation has been performed.

Learning curve coefficient The cost of producing one unit in a process that has an initial cost of $c(1) = 1$, a cumulative output of x, and a learning rate of LR.

Learning rate The amount by which the process performance is multiplied every time the cumulative experience doubles. The learning rate (LR) is a number between 0 and 1. Higher numbers correspond to slower learning. 1-LR is the percent improvement associated with a doubling of cumulative experience.

Leveling demand Setting an expected demand rate for a given period of time so that one can look for an appropriate staffing plan for that time period.

Line balancing The act of allocating the activities that need to be carried out in the process across the process resources as evenly as possible so that all resources have a comparable utilization level.

Linear satisfiers Needs that will lead to customer satisfaction when fulfilled and dissatisfaction when not fulfilled. Utility grows more or less linearly in the extent to which customer needs are met. Also called performance needs.

Little's Law The law that describes the relationship between three key process metrics: inventory, flow rate, and flow time.

Location The place where a consumer can obtain a product or service

Location pooling A strategy of combining the inventory from multiple territories/locations into a single location.

Log-log plot A graphical representation in which we plot the logarithmic value of both the x and y variables.

Long-term forecasts Forecasts used to support strategic decisions with typical time ranges of multiple years.

Longest processing time (LPT) A rule that sequences jobs to be processed on a resource in descending order of their processing times.

Lost demand Potential demand that a system is unable to serve. This demand does not count toward a process's flow rate.

Lower control limit (LCL) A line in a control chart that provides the smallest value that is still acceptable without being labeled an abnormal variation.

Lower-skilled labor Labor that is not able to master multiple activities and thus can only work as a resource with very short processing times.

Lower specification limit (LSL) The smallest outcome value that does not trigger a defective unit.

Machine-paced A process in which all steps are connected through a conveyor belt and all of the steps must work at the same rate even if some of them have more capacity than others.

Mail-order retailers Retailers that merchandize their goods via a print catalog and sell to consumers by shipping them goods via a third-party carrier like the U.S. Postal Service, UPS, FedEx, or DHL. Also called catalog retailers.

Make-to-order Making the activation of resources in a process contingent on receiving a specific order.

Make-to-stock A mode of operations in which the production of an item occurs before the demand for that item has been identified.

Makespan The total time to process a set of jobs.

Market segment A set of customers who have similar utility functions.

Market size The number of customers who are in the market that we aim to serve.

Market-responsive In the context of strategic supply chain decisions, these are supply chains that are designed to emphasize flexibility over cost.

Marketing The academic discipline that is about understanding and influencing how customers derive utility from products or services.

Mass customization A make-to-order system in which each customer's order is unique, customized to his or her exact preferences.

Materials requirement planning (MRP) A system that plans the delivery of components required for a manufacturing process so that components are available when needed but not so early as to create excess inventory.

Matrix organization An organization with multiple lines of reporting relationships.

Maximum profit The highest possible expected profit. This occurs when inventory is available for all customers.

Mean absolute error (MAE) A measure evaluating the quality of a forecast by looking at the average absolute value of the forecast error.

Mean squared error (MSE) A measure evaluating the quality of a forecast by looking at the average squared forecast error.

Mid-term forecasts Forecasts used to support capacity planning and financial accounting with typical time ranges from weeks to a year.

Minimum viable product A prototype of a new product or service that allows the team to collect the maximum amount of learning about customer preferences with the least amount of effort.

Mismatch costs   Costs related to a mismatch between demand and supply. These usually include the cost of leftover inventory and the opportunity cost of stockouts.

Mixed-model assembly   An assembly process in which production resembles the true rate of demand, even over a short time horizon. Also known as heijunka.

Momentum-based forecasts   An approach to forecasting that assumes that the trend in the future will be similar to the trend in the past.

Moving average forecasting method   A forecasting method that predicts that the next value will be the average of the last realized values.

Muda   Waste.

Multitask job assignment   A technique to reduce idle time by avoiding a worker watching a machine do work.

Mura   Unevenness in flow.

Muri   An unreasonable amount of work, overburdening a machine or operator.

Must-haves   Needs that will not really drive customer satisfaction upward when fulfilled but could drive customer satisfaction substantially downward when not fulfilled.

Naïve forecasting method   A forecasting method that predicts that the next value will be like the last realized value.

Natural variation   Variation that occurs in a process as a result of pure randomness (also known as common cause variation).

Negatively correlated   Two events are negatively correlated (i.e., their correlation is negative) when the outcomes tend to have dissimilar magnitudes. If the outcome of one event is "high," then the outcome of the other event tends to be "low."

Net neutrality   The principle that Internet service providers must treat all data that traverses their network equally in the sense that priority cannot be given to some data over other types of data, even if the provider of the data (e.g., Google) pays for better service.

No-show   A customer who does not arrive for his or her appointment or reservation.

Non-value-added work   Those operations that do not add value in the eyes of the customer but must be done under the current conditions of the process in order to complete a unit.

Noriaki Kano   A 20th-century Japanese design professor.

Number of units started to get Q good units   Number of units started to get Q good units = Q/Process yield

Obsolescence cost   The cost associated with losing value over time because of either technological change or shifts in fashion.

Off-peak discount   Offering a discount during a time period with low demand.

Offered load   The ratio of demand, $1/a$, to the capacity of one server, $1/p$.

On-hand inventory   The inventory that is ready to be used to serve customer demand.

On-order inventory   The inventory that the supplier has shipped but that has not been received.

Online retailers   Retailers that merchandize their goods via an online website (or app) and sell to consumers by shipping them goods via a third-party carrier like the U.S. Postal Service, UPS, FedEx, or DHL. Also called e-commerce or e-tailers.

Open-access appointment system   An appointment system in which appointments are only available one day in advance and are filled on a first-come-first-served basis.

Opportunity   An idea—it is a new product or service at the embryonic state.

Opportunity cost of capital   The income not earned on the amount invested in inventory.

Opportunity identification   The process of generating opportunities.

Order cost, K   The fixed cost incurred per order, which is independent of the amount ordered.

Order-up-to inventory model   An inventory model that is appropriate when inventory can be periodically ordered, there is a lead time to receive orders, and inventory is not perishable.

Order-up-to level   The desired inventory position after an order is submitted.

Ordering cost per unit of time   The sum of all fixed order costs in a period of time.

Organizational chart (org chart)   A visual graph of the reporting relationships in the organization. Shows the chain of command, with the general at the top of the org chart and the foot soldier at the bottom.

Outcome variables   Measures describing the quality of the output of the process.

Overage cost   The cost of ordering *one* unit too many; that is, the cost of overordering by one unit. It is represented with the variable C_o.

Overall equipment effectiveness (OEE)   The percentage of total available time that is used in a way that adds value to the customer.

Overbooking The practice of intentionally assigning more work to a resource than the resource can process so as to maintain a high utilization for the resource. Overbooking is meant to mitigate the consequences of no-show demand.

Overconfidence bias The fact that human decision makers are overly confident in their ability to shape a positive outcome.

Overlapping dependent activities The simultaneous execution of dependent activities to facilitate information exchange and shorten project completion time.

p-**chart** A special control chart used for dealing with binary outcomes. It has all the features of the *X*-bar chart, yet does not require a continuous outcome variable. However, *p*-charts require larger sample sizes, especially if defects occur rarely. Also known as attribute-based control charts.

Padded activity time Forecasted activity time that is longer than the actual amount of time required.

Pallet Either (1) a platform, often wooden, used as a base to store inventory and to facilitate moving that inventory via a forklift, or (2) the quantity of inventory that is stacked on the platform.

Pareto diagram A graphical way to identify the most important causes of process defects. To create a Pareto diagram, we need to collect data on the number of defect occurrences as well as the associated defect types. We can then plot simple bars with heights indicating the relative occurrences of the defect types. It is also common to plot the cumulative contribution of the defect types.

Pareto dominated Pareto dominated means that a firm's product or service is inferior to one or multiple competitors on all dimensions of the customer utility function.

Parts per million The expected number of defective parts in a random sample of one million.

Path A sequence of nodes (activities) and (directional) arrows.

PDCA cycle Plan-do-check-act cycle; a sequence of steps an organization needs to take to improve the process.

Peak-load pricing Charging more during the time period with the highest demand.

Percent on time The fraction of jobs that are completed on or before their due date.

Performance A subcomponent of the consumption utility that captures how much an average consumer desires a product or service.

Performance gap The difference between the current process performance and some target or optimal value.

Performance needs Needs that will lead to customer satisfaction when fulfilled and dissatisfaction when not fulfilled. Utility grows more or less linearly in the extent to which customer needs are met. Also called linear satisfiers.

Period In the context of managing inventory, this is the time between when orders can be placed. For example, if the period is a day, then orders can be placed daily.

Physically efficient In the context of strategic supply chain decisions, these are supply chains that are designed to minimize costs.

Pipeline inventory Another term to describe expected on-order inventory.

Planning the project Preparation of the execution of the project.

P_m Probability that all servers are occupied in an Erlang loss model.

Poisson distribution A statistical distribution that is suitable for modeling demand with a low mean (e.g., 20 or lower).

Poka-yoke Foolproofing an operation to avoid the recurrence of defects.

Pooled queue A queuing system in which all demand is shared across all servers. Hence, each customer is served by the first available server and each customer can be served by any agent.

Positively correlated Two events are positively correlated (i.e., have a positive correlation) when the outcomes tend to have similar magnitudes. If the outcome of one event is "high," then the outcome of the other event tends to be "high" as well.

Pre-processing strategy Reducing the amount of work needed to process a customer during the peak time period by moving some of the work to an off-peak time.

Precedence relationship The dependency of activities on each other.

Predecessor activity A_i is the predecessor activity of A_j if A_i needs to be completed before starting A_j.

Prediction markets A betting game in which forecasters can place financial bets on their forecasts.

Pretotyping A product development process that rapidly iterates with real customers using very simple and inexpensive prototypes. Also known as lean startup.

Price The total cost of owning the product or receiving the service.

Primary needs Needs that are at the top of the needs hierarchy. Note that this implies that they are more aggregated. This says nothing about importance.

Process   A set of activities that take a collection of inputs, perform some work or activities with those inputs, and then yield a set of outputs.

Process analysis   A rigorous framework for understanding the detailed operations of a business. Among other things, the process analysis determines how many flow units can be processed per unit of time (the process capacity) and how busy the resources of the process are (utilization).

Process capability index   The ratio between the width of the specification interval of the outcome variable and the variation in the outcome variable (measured by six times its estimated standard deviation). It tells us how many standard deviations we can move away from the statistical mean before causing a defect.

Process capacity   The maximum flow rate a process can provide per unit of time. This determines the maximum supply of the process. The process capacity is the smallest capacity of all resources in the process.

Process flow diagram   A graphical way to describe the process. It uses boxes to depict resources, arrows to depict flows, and triangles to depict inventory location.

Process layout   The spatial location of resources in a process that drives the needs for transportation.

Process metric   A scale or measure of process performance and capability.

Process scope   The set of activities and processes included in the process.

Process standardization   A careful documentation so that the operation does not permanently have to "reinvent the wheel." Standardization can take the form of a standard work sheet.

Processing time   The time it takes a resource to complete one flow unit.

Product awareness   The fraction of the relevant population that is aware of the new product or service.

Product concept   A preliminary articulation of a solution for a given set of user needs.

Product development process   A process that takes an opportunity as its input and translates this into a new product or service. The process includes needs identification, the generation of product concepts, an empirical validation of the concepts, and a business analysis, involving a sales forecast.

Product mix   A combination of different flow unit types moving through a process.

Product pooling   The strategy to reduce the variety offered to customers by combining, or pooling, similar products.

Production cycle   A repeating sequence of produced units that can include setup time, production time, and idle time.

Production smoothing strategy   A strategy for scheduling production such that the rate of output remains relatively stable over time even though demand varies predictably over the same period.

Profit maximization   The objective of an enterprise—to maximize the difference between revenue and costs.

Project   A temporary (and thus nonrepetitive) operation. Projects have a limited time frame, one or more specific objectives, and a temporary organizational structure, and thus often are operated in a more ad-hoc, improvised management style.

Project budget   Outline of the main expenses associated with the project.

Project management triangle   The tension between the three objectives of a project: time, budget, and scope.

Project scope   Description of what must be accomplished in order for the project to be complete.

Prototype   A representation of the final product or service that allows the product development team to predict how well a particular product concept might fulfill the customer needs.

Pull system   An operating system in which the production or replenishment of a unit is only initiated when a demand occurs.

Purchase intent survey   A survey that communicates the product concept with the customer and then asks the customer how likely he or she is to purchase the product.

Purchase probability   A prediction on the likelihood with which a given consumer would purchase the product or service.

Purchasing cost   The cost to purchase inventory in a period of time.

Push system   An operating system in which the production or replenishment of a unit is initiated in anticipation of demand.

Queuing model   An abstract representation of the queue that enables us to predict waiting times and other performance measures.

Quick response   A strategy that increases supply flexibility to allow a response to updated information about demand. For example, with quick response, a firm can obtain additional supply for products that are selling above expectation, thereby reducing the number of stockouts.

Radical innovation   A horizon 3 innovation; oftentimes serves new markets and/or employs new technology.

Radio-frequency identification (RFID) tag   A small electronic device that transmits a unique radio signal to identify the object to which it is attached.

Random activity time   The fact that the time of an activity is not known with certainty but subject to some statistical variation.

Raw material inventory Inventory that is used as the inputs to a process and has not undergone any transformation in the process.

Reactive capacity Capacity that allows a firm to react to changes in its demand forecast.

Reduction in processing times due to elimination of setups The fact that specialization increases efficiency by eliminating setups.

Reduction in processing times due to learning The fact that specialization increases efficiency by providing more practice to the operator in the execution of a particular activity.

Regression analysis A statistical process of estimating the relationship of one variable with multiple variables that influence this one variable.

Reneging The practice of leaving a queue after joining it. Also known as abandoning.

Reseasonalize To reintroduce the seasonal effect to the forecasted data.

Resource The entity of a process that the flow unit has to visit as part of its transformation from input to output

Revenue management The practice of maximizing the revenue generated from a set of fixed assets (like cars in a rental fleet, rooms in a hotel, or tables in a restaurant).

Rework The repetition of activities or an extra set of activities that have to be completed by a defective flow unit in order to be restored to a good flow unit.

Robust The ability of a process to tolerate changes in input and environmental variables without causing the outcomes to be defective.

Robust process A process that is robust can tolerate variation in input variables and environmental variables without leading to a defect.

Root cause A root cause for a defect is a change in an input or an environmental variable that initiated a defect.

Round-up rule If the probability you look up in a statistical table falls between two entries, choose the one with the larger probability.

Run like the tortoise, not the hare An ancient fable used by Ohno to illustrate that steady work, even when slow, is better than bursts of speed followed by periods of no movement.

Safety factor A parameter that determines the in-stock probability. The higher the safety factor, the higher the in-stock probability as well as average on-hand inventory.

Safety inventory Inventory needed to buffer against demand uncertainty. Also called safety stock.

Safety stock Inventory needed to buffer against demand uncertainty. Also called safety inventory.

Sales forecast Demand prediction for a new product or service.

Salvage value The value that can be obtained per unit for inventory left over at the end of the selling season.

Scheduling The process of deciding what work to assign to which resources and when to assign the work.

Scientific management A management framework created by Frederick Winslow Taylor that emphasizes efficiency and optimization.

Scrap Defective flow units that are eliminated from the process.

Seasonality A significant demand change that constitutes a repetitive fluctuation over time.

Seasonality index (SI) The estimated multiplicative adjustment factor that allows us to move from the average overall demand to the average demand for a particular season.

Secondary needs Needs that are at in the middle of the needs hierarchy. Note that this implies that they are less aggregated than the primary needs. This says nothing about importance.

Selection matrix A table that compares product concepts. The rows in the selection matrix are the concepts, with the columns being the three dimensions of comparison: need fulfillment, feasibility, and wow factor.

Separate queue A queuing system in which demand is initially divided among different servers, and customers are eventually served only by their designated agent.

Sequentially dependent A form of dependence in which a successor depends on a predecessor.

Service blueprint A user interaction–based decomposition that breaks up the flow of activities required to serve the customer. The service blueprint also distinguishes which activities are done by the customer alone, which activities are carried out "on stage" (which means during the interaction of us with the customer), and which activities we do without the involvement of the customer.

Service process The flow of customers when they are being served.

Set of specifications A set of rules that determine if the outcome variable of a unit is defective or not.

Setup A set of activities (i) that are required to produce units but (ii) for which the time to complete these activities does not depend directly on the number of units produced.

Seven sources of production waste Seven ways in which, in the eyes of Ohno, a resource can waste its capacity: waiting (idle time), overproduction, inventory, transport, overprocessing, rework, and unnecessary motions.

Shifted critical path A change in the activities making up the critical path triggered by some unexpectedly long activity time on a non–critical path activity.

Short-term forecasts   Forecasts used to support tactical decision making with typical time ranges from hours to weeks.

Shortest processing time (SPT)   A rule that sequences jobs to be processed on a resource in ascending order of their processing times.

Signal-to-noise ratio   The relationship between the size of an effect and the statistical noise in the process. A large signal-to-noise ratio is required so that an effect in the process can be identified.

Single-Minute Exchange of Die (SMED)   A goal to reduce the setup time to a single-digit number of minutes (i.e., nine or fewer).

Single-unit flow   Operate at a flow of one unit at a time from one resource to the next instead of operating based on transfer batches.

Six-sigma program   A process that has 6 standard deviations on either side of the mean and the specification limit.

Slack time   The amount of time an activity can be delayed without affecting the overall completion time of the project.

Smoothing parameter   The parameter that determines the weight new realized data have in creating the next forecast with exponential smoothing.

Spoilage and shrinkage costs   Costs associated with theft or product deterioration over time.

Stable queue   A queuing system in which the demand rate is less than capacity.

Standard normal distribution   A normal distribution with mean 0 and standard deviation 1.

Standard work sheet   A form of standardization compiling the processing time for an activity, the work sequence of all steps comprising the activity, and the standard amount of inventory at the resource.

Standard working procedures   A set of guidelines and instructions that detail how a task is to be completed.

Starving   The event in which a resource is capable of working on a flow unit but there is no flow unit available to work on.

Static coordination   The consultation with team members who are in charge of project activities that happen further downstream in the project.

Statistical economies of scale   The property in which aggregating demand into a large scale tends to reduce uncertainty, as measured by the coefficient of variation.

Statistical noise   Variables influencing the outcomes of a process in unpredictable ways.

Statistical process control (SPC)   A framework in operations management built around the empirical measurement and the statistical analysis of input, environmental, and outcome variables.

Stochastic demand   Unpredictable variations in demand.

Stockout   A stockout occurs when a customer demands an item that is not available in inventory.

Stockout probability   The probability that demand for an item exceeds its inventory during a period of time.

Strategic decisions   Decisions that have long-term implications.

Successor activity A_i is the successor activity of A_j if A_j needs to be completed before starting A_i.

Supply   Products or services a business offers to its customers.

Switchover time   See changeover time.

Tactical decisions   Decisions that impact short-term performance.

Taiichi Ohno   An engineer who pioneered the Toyota Production System, built around the principles of waste reduction.

Takt time   The ratio between the time available and the quantity that has to be produced to serve demand.

Tandem queue   A process that has a sequence of queues in which the output of one queue can be the input to the next queue.

Tardiness   If a job is completed after its due date, then tardiness is the difference between the completion time of a job and its due date. If the job is completed before its due date, then tardiness is 0. Tardiness is always positive.

Target manpower   The ratio between the labor content and the takt time determines the minimum number of resources required to meet demand. Note that this minimum does not have to be an integer number and that it assumes all resources are perfectly utilized.

Target variation   The largest amount of variation in a process that does not exceed a given defect probability.

Tertiary needs   Needs that are at the bottom of the needs hierarchy. Note that this says nothing about their importance.

Theory of constraints   An operation guideline that recommends managerial attention be focused on the bottleneck of a process.

Throughput   A synonym for flow rate, the number of flow units flowing through the process per unit of time.

Tier   The quantity of product in one layer of a pallet.

Time in queue   The average time a customer waits in a queue.

Time required to produce a given quantity X starting with an empty system   The time it takes a process with no inventory to produce a given quantity.

Time series analysis   Analysis of old demand data.

Time series–based forecast   An approach to forecasting that uses nothing but old demand data.

Time through the empty system   The time it takes the first flow unit to flow through an empty process; that is, a process that has no inventory.

Timing   The amount of time that passes between the consumer ordering a product or service and the consumer obtaining the product or service.

Total available time   The amount of time a resource has available to fulfill demand.

Total demand rate   The total demand rate for resource i tells us how many flow units need to be processed at resource i across all different flow units.

Total idle time   The amount of idle time per flow unit added up across all resources.

Toyota Production System (TPS)   A framework used to run operations with the goal of reducing both the waste of capacity and the waste of flow time, thereby making sure supply and demand are matched just in time.

TPS house   A representation of the Toyota Production System in the shape of a house with the roof capturing the main goal of the TPS, which is waste reduction; the pillars being just-in-time flow and built-in-quality; and the foundation being process improvement.

Trade-offs   The need to sacrifice one capability in order to increase another one.

Transaction costs   Another term for the inconvenience of obtaining a product or service.

Trend   A continuing increase or decrease in a variable that is consistent over a long period of time.

U-shaped line   Locating resources in a way that they create a "U," which increases the flexibility of workers to perform multiple tasks.

Unbiased forecast   A forecast that is correct on average, thus an average forecast error equal to zero.

Underage cost   The cost of ordering *one* unit too few; that is, the cost of underordering by one unit. It is represented with the variable C_u.

Unk-unks   Unknown unknowns, which describes uncertainties in a project that the project management is not yet aware of.

Unstable queue   A queuing system in which the demand rate exceeds capacity.

Upper control limit (UCL)   A line in a control chart that provides the largest value that is still acceptable without being labeled an abnormal variation.

Upper specification limit (USL)   The largest outcome value that does not trigger a defective unit.

Upstream   The parts of the process that are at the beginning of the process flow.

User action–based decomposition   Decomposition of a product or service into the activities the user goes through when using the product.

User needs   The drivers of customer utilities.

Utility   A measure of the strength of customer preferences for a given product or service. Customers buy the product or service that maximizes their utility.

Utilization   The ratio between the flow rate (how fast the process is currently operating) and the process capacity (capturing how fast the process could be operating if there was sufficient demand). Note that utilization can be defined at the level of an individual resource or at the level of the entire process.

Value curve   A graphic depiction of a new product's relative performance across the key attributes, comparing it with existing offerings in the market.

Value-added percentage   The percentage of flow time used for value-added work.

Value-added work   Those operations valued by the customer because they are absolutely required to transform the flow unit from its inputs to being the output the customer wants.

Variability   Predictable or unpredictable changes in the demand or the supply process.

Variable costs   Those costs that grow in proportion to the amount a firm produces and sells.

Waste   The consumption of inputs and resources that do not add value to the customer.

Waste of time at a resource   The waste of time from the perspective of a resource, which reduces the capacity of the resource.

Waste of time of a flow unit   The waste of time from the perspective of a flow unit, which makes the flow time of that flow unit longer than what is needed in the eyes of the customer.

Weighted shortest processing time (WSPT)   A rule that sequences jobs to be processed on a resource in descending order of the ratio of their weight to their processing time. Jobs with high weights and low processing times tend to be sequenced early.

William Edwards Deming   A 20th-century statistician who pioneered many of the methods of modern quality control.

Work breakdown structure   The translation of the project scope into specific activities.

Work cells   An organization of work where small teams of employees perform a job (complete a flow unit) from beginning to end.

Worker-paced   A process line in which each resource is free to work at its own pace: if the first resource finishes before the next one is ready to accept the flow unit, then the first resource puts the completed flow unit in the inventory between the two resources.

Work-in-process inventory (WIP)   The material and components used within the process to complete a product.

Workload matrix   For each resource i and for each flow unit type j, $WL(i, j)$ = Number of flow units of type i that need to be processed by resource j × Processing time that resource j takes for customer type i.

X-bar   The average of a sample.

X-bar charts   A special control chart in which we track the mean of a sample (also known as X-bar).

X-double-bar   The average of a set of sample averages.

Yield   The yield of a resource measures the percentage of good units that are processed at this resource.

Index